HYPNOSIS:
Developments in Research and New Perspectives

New and Revised
Second Edition

EDITED BY

Erika Fromm
University of Chicago

Ronald E. Shor
University of New Hampshire

ALDINE PUBLISHING COMPANY   New York

Library of Congress Cataloging in Publication Data

Fromm, Erika.
    Hypnosis: developments in research and new perspectives.

    Bibliography: p.
    Includes indexes.
    1. Hypnotism--Addresses, essays, lectures.
I. Shor, Ronald E.   II. Title. [DNLM: 1. Hypnosis.
2. Research. WM415.3 H998]
BF1141.F93 1979   154.7   79-89279
ISBN 0-202-26085-2

THE EDITORS

Professor Erika Fromm, of the University of Chicago (Departments of Behavioral Sciences and Social Service Administration), is the Clinical Editor of the *International Journal of Clinical and Experimental Hypnosis.* She has been President of the Society for Clinical and Experimental Hypnosis (1975-1977), President of the American Psychological Association's Division of Psychological Hypnosis (1972-1973), and President of the American Board of Psychological Hypnosis (1971-1974).

Ronald E. Shor is Professor and Chairman of the Department of Psychology at the University of New Hampshire; he is Past President of the Division of Psychological Hypnosis of the American Psychological Asssociation (1976-1977).

First published 1972
Second edition 1979 by
Aldine Publishing Company
200 Saw Mill River Road
Hawthorne, New York 10532

ISBN: 0-202-26085-2
Library of Congress Catalog Number 79-89279

Printed in the United States of America

10 9 8 7 6 5 4 3 2 1

to the memory
of our friend
ARTHUR SHAPIRO

Contents

Preface
to First
Edition

There are times when it is good to pause for a moment and ask ourselves: Whence have we come? Where do we stand now? Where are we going? This book attempts to answer these questions for the field of hypnosis research. The book was conceived when its senior editor, as program chairman for the Twentieth Annual Convention of the Society for Clinical and Experimental Hypnosis, organized a symposium on research in experimental hypnosis. Later, in order to secure representation for all the major experimental viewpoints in hypnosis research, other scholars were also invited to prepare chapters.

Describing the status of the field involves three tasks: earmarking the obstacles that have stood in the way of the study of hypnosis as a science, presenting the current state of knowledge concerning hypnosis, and pointing the way toward future study.

The first two chapters of the book set the stage. Chapter One establishes the theoretical base, and Chapter Two sketches the historical background. The final chapter surveys predicted future trends. The other seventeen chapters focus directly on key aspects of present-day hypnosis research.

We sought contributions of three types:

1. Surveys of broad topic areas.
2. Descriptions in depth of individual investigator's programmatic lines of research.
3. Reports on research within specific areas, especially those representing new viewpoints and promise for programmatic developments.

We solicited a number of papers in the third category in order to capture the excitement investigators experience as they get new ideas and eagerly pursue them. As the chapters developed and were revised, the lines of demarcation between the three types of papers became blurred, but in the main the basic structure held.

The majority of currently active investigators in experimental hypnosis are contributors to this volume. Inevitably there is overlapping when the same material is reviewed from divergent perspectives. Where we felt the overlap was simply redundant we worked to reduce it; where it provided an opportunity to see divergent viewpoints we retained it. Brief biographies of the contributors preface each chapter.

None of the chapters have been published elsewhere. Where authors reviewed their own previously published work, they updated and substantially expanded their materials.

All of the chapters have been written so that experimental researchers, clinicians, and students can read them with profit. Obviously readers with extensive backgrounds in the field will see wider implications and appreciate challenging subtleties.

As editors we sought to encourage diversity, and so the chapters vary considerably in length. We discussed length with authors in terms of scope and function, not pages. Each contributor was instructed to use no more space than was necessary to make his material challenging to new investigators and helpful to his colleagues. Given this mission some chapters became long, others short. One contributor whose viewpoint differs substantially from the rest felt that he needed a long chapter to present his dissent. So also the paper on hypnotic amnesia, for example, had to be long in order to help the new investigator who wishes to do research in this area avoid spending most of his time falling into old pitfalls.

This volume is devoted mainly to experimental research, but also addresses itself to clinicians. For clinicians can be good clinicians only if they keep abreast of research developments and modify their techniques in accordance with unfolding relevant research findings. The editors hope that bringing together these papers on current research efforts will stimulate young laboratory and clinical researchers to search out and examine facts about hypnosis so far ignored, to ask questions not yet posed, and to test ideas as yet untested.

The editors wish to express their appreciation to the contributors for their splendid cooperation in bringing this collaborative volume into being.

Doris Gruenewald, Louis Gottschalk, and Randolph Easton read chapters of this book; we thank them for their helpful comments. We also wish to thank Joseph Litchman and Kay Levensky Shanks for compiling the index.

E.F.
R.E.S.

Preface
to Second
Edition

The field of hypnosis research is expanding fast. More than 1,000 scientific publications on hypnosis have appeared since the first edition of this book was published in 1972. Accordingly, a revision seemed appropriate.

The most exciting changes in the field have been made in the areas of theory and method. Ernest R. Hilgard discovered the "hidden observer" in the hypnotized subject and produced his Neo-Dissociation Theory. Erika Fromm brought hypnosis researchers together with scientific investigators of other altered states of consciousness (see October 1977 Special Issue of the *International Journal of Clinical and Experimental Hypnosis*); and developed a multifactor psychoanalytic theory to help clarify the nature of the various altered states—including hypnosis—as well as distinguish the similarities and differences between them. Ronald E. Shor has been working on a new, phenomenological method that will serve to measure hypnotizability and other variables of great importance for the understanding of the essence of hypnosis.

Accordingly, a whole new section—*Section II: New Theories*—has been added, consisting of chapters by Ernest R. Hilgard, Erika Fromm, and Ronald E. Shor, written in 1977-78 especially for the second edition of this book.

Thirteen of the twenty chapters in the first edition were updated by their authors, half of them being reworked so extensively that in the second edition these chapters (Chapters 10, 11, 13, 15, 21 and 22) essentially amount to new chapters, as is indicated in most instances by a change of title, and in the two co-authored chapters by a change in the order of authors.

Chapter Eight has been shortened; and Chapter Seventeen of the first edition has been replaced by the new Chapter Three.

Four chapters (Chapters 16, 17, 18 and 20) remain unchanged. Their authors felt that no real progress had been made in the last six years in the fields they cover. A minor correction was made in Chapter Two.

Adding a chapter on child hypnosis to the second edition was considered. However, G. Gail Gardner, an authority in this subspecialty, convinced us that while substantial progress in hypnotherapy with children has been made, not enough experimental work in child hypnosis has been done yet to warrant a chapter on this topic in a book devoted to experimental hypnosis.

Three hundred forty-two new bibliographical references have been added.

The editors warmly thank all the contributors for their splendid collaboration in making this second and revised edition possible; and also want to express deep appreciation to Joseph Litchman for compiling the index again, to Andrew M. Boxer for checking the new bibliographical references for accuracy, and to Susan K.B. Urbas for secretarial assistance.

Erika Fromm

February 28, 1978

Acknowledgments

We are grateful to the following for permission to reproduce material: *International Journal of Clinical and Experimental Hypnosis* for quotes, tables and figures from the April, 1970 and October, 1977 issues, copyrighted by the Society for Clinical and Experimental Hypnosis, 1970 and 1977; *Journal of Transpersonal Psychology* for a figure from Vol. 2, No. 1, 1970; copyright by *Journal of Transpersonal Psychology*. Reprinted by permission. Andre M. Weitzenhoffer and Ernest R. Hilgard, *Stanford Hypnotic Susceptibility Scale, Form C*. Palo Alto: Consulting Psychologists Press, 1962, © 1962 by the Board of Trustees of the Leland Stanford Junior University. Calvin S. Hall and Robert L. Van de Castle, *The Content Analysis of Dreams*, New York: Appleton-Century-Crofts, 1966. Copyright 1966 by Meredith Publishing Company. University of Chicago Press for tables and figures from *Personality and Hypnosis: A Study of Imaginative Involvement* by Josephine R. Hilgard, © 1970 by the University of Chicago. *Behavioral Science* for tables from Vol. 13, 1968 issue. *The Psychological Record* for tables from Vol. 14, 1964. *Psychological Reports* for tables from Barber, T.X., Measuring "hypnotic like" suggestibility with and without "hypnotic induction." *Psychological Reports*, 1965, *16*, 809-844, Tables 3 and 5. *Psychosomatic Medicine* for table data from Vol. 25, 1963. *Psychological Bulletin* for table data from Vol. 63, 1965. *Journal of Consulting Psychology* for table data from Vol. 25, 1961. University Microfilms, Inc. for table and figure from Plapp, J.M., Hypnosis, conditioning, and physiological responses, 1967. *Journal of Abnormal Psychology* for figure from Vol. 70, 1965. *American Journal of Clinical Hypnosis* for figures from Vol. 11, 1968; copyright 1968 by the American Society of Clinical Hypnosis. *Journal of Nervous and Mental Disease* for tables from Vol. 148, 1969; © 1969 by the Williams & Wilkins Co., Baltimore, Md. 21202, U.S.A.

I

Theoretical and Historical Perspectives

1

Underlying Theoretical Issues:
An Introduction

ERIKA FROMM AND RONALD E. SHOR

Scientific research on hypnosis began two centuries ago with Mesmer's first "magnetic" treatments in 1774. Hypnosis had been known and practiced for thousands of years, but Mesmer was the first to seek a scientific explanation for the powerful psychological forces he had learned to control. In the two centuries since then, research on hypnosis has been vigorous. While cycles of greater or lesser activity have occured, research has gone on more or less continually. Often researchers have drawn unwarranted conclusions; often their work has seemed to be demolished by the polemics of their critics. Nonetheless, the fabric of interest was never torn for long. For hypnosis was a phenomenon that would not go away, even though it was sometimes roundly misconceptualized and often encountered resourceful enemies.

Hypnosis was an area of psychological research long before the phenomenon was recognized as primarily psychological, and more than a century before the emergence of psychology as a separate discipline after the founding of Wundt's laboratory in 1879. In fact, research in hypnosis was a major influence on the development of the psychologies of motivation, the unconscious, and social influence. A number of historically important persons, known primarily for their work in other areas, have made significant contributions to the study of hypnosis: Jean Charcot, Wilhelm Wundt, Sigmund Freud, Alfred Binet, Charles Féré, Ivan Pavlov, Vladimir Bechterev, Pierre Janet, Henri Bergson, Auguste Forel, Richard von Krafft-Ebing,

3

Frederick Myers, Théodule Ribot, Charles Richet, Morton Prince, Sandor Ferenczi, William James, Eugen Bleuler, William McDougall, Vittorrio Benussi, Paul Schilder, Clark Hull, and Henry Murray.

Despite such credentials, [both historical and individual,] the study of hypnosis has not yet reached an advanced stage of scientific development. In terms of clinical skill and practical application we know a great deal about hypnosis, but the art of its application is far ahead of its scientific elucidation. The situation is analogous to the scientific study of humor. Everyone has an intuitive grasp of humor, and comedians and writers of comic drama have practiced their craft for many centuries. This fund of practical know-how does not, however, help to build a psychology of humor, because that practical knowledge is not in a form amenable to direct use by the scientist. The scientist must tread his own paths and he must put his findings into his own forms.

We believe it will be useful to begin this book by summarizing and highlighting the underlying theoretical issues that have divided and united our contributors. We will not attempt to tally votes but will be content simply to sensitize the reader to important issues—scientific truth is not arrived at by poll taking. Nor do we emphasize those areas where there is general agreement; such areas might be called solved issues, or nonissues. For example, our contributors generally would agree that, at its best, hypnosis is a method of tapping potent psychological forces. Yet the day is not far behind us when this statement would have been hotly debated.

In our view, the key issues fall into the following categories:

- the role of unconscious mentation in hypnosis;
- phenomenological versus behaviorist aspects of hypnosis—with special emphasis on the confusion of metatheories with scientific methodology;
- continuity and discontinuity between waking and hypnotic states; and
- physiological changes and psychological behaviors distinguishing hypnosis from the waking state.

Altogether twelve key issues are presented. Usually two alternatives are set forth. However, presenting these alternatives is not intended to deny that some of the contributors may have taken intermediary positions, or that others may be unconcerned with certain issues.

These key items are expressed in various levels of generality. In some instances, redefinitions or elaborations of a particular item merit development through subquestions, or even the rewriting of the item in the form of an additional one.

The Role of Unconscious Mentation in Hypnosis

The first four items concern themselves with the nature of hypnosis, broadly stated.

ITEM 1

> *In any complete theory of hypnosis the concept of unconscious mental functioning (more or less in the psychoanalytic sense) will be found to be necessary and important;*

or, alternatively,

> *will be found to be unnecessary and unimportant.*

While most of the contributors feel that the concept of the unconscious is indispensable to their thinking about hypnosis, a small minority take pains not to use it in their formulations.

ITEM 2

> *In any complete theory of hypnosis the concept of usually unavailable modes of mentation will be found necessary and important;*

or, alternatively,

> *will be found to be unnecessary and unimportant.*

To investigators who use the concept of the unconscious, Item Two would seem to be almost a derivative of Item One. Those who start with the concept of the unconscious also view hypnosis as a way of tapping usually unavailable modes of mentation. Many terms are used to describe these modes of mentation: primary process, regression, primitive, dreamlike, nonrational thinking, trance logic, utilization of nonconscious resources, wellsprings of buried human potentialities, retrieval of fantasy residues, and so forth.

We decided to list Item Two separately because investigators can refer to usually unavailable mentation without necessarily subscribing to the concept of the unconscious, and some do. Thus two contributors theorize that subjects have usually unavailable experiences as a function of intensive organismic involvement in the hypnotic role, and deny the need to invoke the concept of unconscious mental functioning.

ITEM 3

> *At its best hypnosis involves a transcendence that is something more than a profoundly compelling imaginal fantasy;*

or, alternatively,

> *hypnosis is nothing but a profoundly compelling imaginal fantasy without such a transcendence.*

To our contributors Item Three may appear to be a nonissue. All of them would agree with the second alternative. Perhaps such agreement is possible today because we have reached a stage in the development of psychology where we can readily acknowlege the power of the processes of imagination. But what are the processes of imagination? That issue merits the attention it is now receiving.

ITEM 4

> *Learning to be a good hypnotic subject basically involves the development of a cognitive skill, of increasing one's capacities for cognitive control;*

or, alternatively,

> *it involves succumbing to the control of others, decreasing one's capacities for cognitive control.*

Again, this appears to be a non-issue today. All our contributors would agree that the first alternative applies to their own work. However, some clinicians would urge keeping open the possibility that an unscrupulous hypnotist might be able to use hypnosis to take advantage of his subjects (see Kline, 1970). But no one doubts that, in responsible hands, hypnosis involves learning a cognitive skill.

Phenomenological versus Behaviorist Aspects of Hypnosis: Metatheories versus the Scientific Method

The next six items (items 5—11) focus on major theoretical issues that are still unsolved and hotly debated. In our view, this lack of resolution is at least partly due to the so far neglected task of separating metatheories from systems of scientific inquiry. Item Five raises this issue.

ITEM 5

> *The ultimate issue to be explained with regard to hypnosis is the subject's inner subjective experience;*

or, alternatively,

> *the ultimate issue is the subject's outward, observable, behavior.*

This item poses the issue that is central to the classic dispute between phenomenology and behaviorism. The phenomenological position is that the subjective experience of hypnosis is the fundamental fact to be explained, and that it provides the primary defining datum of hypnosis. Phenomenologists contend that outward behavior is a meaningful index of hypnosis only to the extent that it accurately reflects the primary subjective events. The behaviorist position is that behaviors observable by an outsider are the fundamental indices, and that reports of subjective experience are simply one form of behavior—verbal behavior. The behaviorist thinks it is irrelevant to discuss whether people have subjective experiences; he flatly states that unless such experiences are translated into observable behavior they have no place within the scientific system.

Two examples help to clarify these two positions. Let us suppose that an investigator initially became interested in hypnosis because he himself had had profound subjective hypnotic experiences; no amount of rational argument could shake his conviction of the reality of these experiences. These subjective experiences have become the fundamental puzzle he wants to explain; they are the reason why he is willing to devote his professional energies to the study of hypnosis. Nothing will convince him that outward behavior is more real, or more fundamental, than his own subjective experiences. He will argue that if science is not big enough to encompass and explain these primary subjective events, then the conception of science must be broadened. If these experiences do not fit into the scientific test tube, he will insist science needs a bigger test tube.

However, a second investigator, also initially interested in hypnosis because of compelling subjective hypnotic experiences, may arrive at a radically different conception of the kind of science that should be developed to explain hypnotic experiences. He may conclude that it is folly to try to pursue subjective events in their own terms, and that the only way to build a fruitful, coherent science is on the basis of observed behavior. In his view, if science is broadened to include pure mentalisms, inevitably it will become pseudoscience. He will insist that men have no direct pipeline to mentalisms, and that the sooner they acknowledge this fact and get on with the business of building a solid behavioral science, the better off the discipline will be.

These issues have not been resolved since the battle lines were drawn by J.B. Watson in the 1920s; it is obvious that they will not be resolved in the confines of this volume.

In our judgment, allegiance to the phenomenological or to the behaviorist position is basically a matter for the philosophy of science, not science; it is a philosophic commitment, not a scientific decision. However, once such a philosophic commitment has been made one way or the other, it determines the kind of scientific system that can unfold within it.

In our view science does not begin in a vacuum. Prior to the scientific enterprise all science begins with a set of philosophic assumptions, a philosophic metatheory, a bedrock of unassailable "givens" that are axiomatically assumed to be true. While, by selected criteria, one scientific system may prove more fruitful than another, the philosophic metatheories themselves are not amenable to scientific proof or disproof within the scientific systems that arise out of them. Metaphorically speaking, these metatheories create "elbow room," the context of definition and outlook within which the scientist can set about doing his work. We believe that many of the current controversies among hypnosis researchers have their origin in a philosophic commitment to either a fundamentally phenomenological or a fundamentally behaviorist metatheory. To so assert is not to resolve the differences between the two views; but it is useful to put them on the table where they can be seen more clearly.

The controversy between these two points of view has often been phrased in terms of "inner subjective experience of the hypnotic effects" on the one hand, and "outwardly observable behavior" on the other. These phrasings carefully avoid specifying the nature of the subjective or the behavioral events—except to say that they are somehow hypnotic. A variety of scientific theories can flow from both philosophic positions. Scientific theories and philosophical commitments, however, are in different realms of discourse. We believe that it is important to try to separate scientific theoretical formulations from metatheories. This can best be done by asking two series of questions, one from the phenomenological position, and the other from the behaviorist position.

Key Questions from the Phenomenological Point of View

Eleven questions should be raised from the phenomenological point of view.

1. Do the subjective events in hypnosis involve some kind of alteration or change in the organism?
2. Assuming a Yes answer to the above question, is it meaningful to say that this change is a change in the *state* of the organism?
3. Do the subjective changes in hypnosis involve some kind of change in consciousness?
4. Do the subjective changes in hypnosis represent a fundamental discontinuum from nonhypnotic subjective events?
5. Assuming Yes answers to questions 2 and 4, do the subjective changes in hypnosis involve a fundamentally discontinuous change in the state of the organism?
6. Assuming Yes answers to questions 2, 3, and 4, do the subjective changes in hypnosis involve a fundamentally discontinuous change in the state of consciousness?
7. Are the subjective changes in hypnosis somehow responsible for (the cause, the explanation, the mediating event for) hypnotic phenomena?
8. Assuming Yes answers to questions 2 and 3, is the altered state of consciousness an intrinsic element in all hypnosis or does it occur only some of the time?
9. Assuming a Yes answer to question 7 and to the first alternative in question 8, is the altered state of consciousness somehow responsible for (the cause, the explanation, the mediating agent for) hypnotic phenomena?
10. Under what circumstances can objective behavioral responses be

trusted to be meaningful reflections of the primary subjective events?
11. Is behavioral responsiveness to test suggestions (suggestibility) an invariant defining characteristic of hypnosis or can there be hypnosis without suggestibility?

Key Questions from the Behaviorist Point of View

The second set of questions, posed from the behaviorist point of view, involves fewer issues, and they follow each other more obviously. This may be a tribute to the greater parsimony of the behaviorist position—or a sign of its limitations.

1. Do the behavioral events in hypnosis refer to the subject's observable responses (muscular and verbal) to such suggestions as, "your arm is growing heavy?"
2. Assuming a Yes answer to question 1, is there a certain basal level of responsiveness to test suggestions in nonhypnotized subjects?
3. Assuming a Yes answer to the two preceding questions, are the behavioral events that define hypnosis indexed by the *increase* in responsiveness to test suggestions beyond this basal level?
4. Assuming a Yes answer to questions 1 through 3, is it necessary to posit some kind of special hypnotic agency to account for the increased responsiveness to test suggestions? Or is such a notion merely excess conceptual baggage—superfluous, circular, misleading?
5. How and under what circumstances can reports of subjective experiences be trusted as reliable behavioral data?

These 16 questions concerning the phenomenological and behaviorist positions all could have been translated into separate items with alternative formulations; however, such treatment would have taken the spotlight away from what we see as the six major points of controversy. Five of these six points are involved in the phenomenology versus behaviorism debate; these are items 6 through 10.

ITEM 6

Altered states of consciousness are valid psychological phenomena worthy of scientific study in their own right. Whether they cause, mediate, predict, or correlate with responsiveness to test suggestions are separate issues;

or, alternatively,

altered states of consciousness can be considered valid psychological phenomena worthy of scientific study only if some kind of independent, nontautological, noncircular behavioral criterion can be found for them.

This item clearly reflects the dispute between the phenomenological and behaviorist positions in regard to the concept of an altered state of consciousness.

ITEM 7

> *In any complete theory of hypnosis the concept of an altered state of consciousness will be found necessary and important;*

or, alternatively,

> *will be found unnecessary and unimportant.*

This item must be kept separate from the preceding one because an investigator can believe that the concept of altered states is valid in its own terms yet feel that it is unnecessary or unimportant in explaining hypnosis.

ITEM 8

> *In any complete theory of hypnosis all of the concepts used to explain hypnosis will be part of the fabric of psychology in general;*

or, alternatively,

> *at least one aspect of the explanation must be special and unique to hypnosis.*

On first glance this appears to be a non-issue. All of our contributors would say that they want to integrate the study of hypnosis into the framework of general psychology. Indeed, they would assert that if hypnosis were only a unique and circumscribed phenomenon—a foreign body standing apart from other psychological processes—they would lose interest in it and turn their attention to more important matters. Dissenters would argue, however, that those investigators who adhere to the traditional hypnotic trance state viewpoint have in fact selected the second alternative, whether they realize it or not. The heart of the matter is expressed in the next item.

ITEM 9

> *In any complete theory of hypnosis the concept of a special mediating agent unique to hypnosis will be found to be necessary and important;*

or, alternatively,

> *will be found unnecessary and unimportant.*

Interpretation of this issue depends on what precisely is meant by "special mediating agent" and "unique to hypnosis." While these are subtle matters it is the stance of the dissenters that they can explain hypnosis without having to invoke a concept of a unique mediating agency but that those who hold to the traditional hypnotic trance state position have no choice but to do so.

ITEM 10

> *Suggestibility (responsiveness to test suggestions) is an invariant, irreducible, defining feature of hypnosis;*

or, alternatively,

> *suggestibility is nonintrinsic to hypnosis.*

This issue is mentioned explicitly only in one paper in regard to expectancies arising historically from Puységur's observations, but it arises implicitly wherever hypnosis is somehow equated to, or explained by, suggestibility, or where hypnotic depth is measured by amount of responsiveness to test suggestions.

Continuity versus Discontinuity Between Hypnosis and Waking State

Item 11 involves the sixth key issue in the behaviorism versus phenomenology controversy. It has been set off from the preceding five key points in order to emphasize its importance in the struggle of metatheoretical stances. This item is concerned with the issue of continuity versus discontinuity between hypnosis and waking states. Three questions (4, 5, and 6) in the section on the phenomenological point of view also deal with this issue.

ITEM 11

> *There is a quantitative continuity between the usual waking state of everyday life and deep hypnosis;*

or, alternatively,

> *there is a fundamental qualitative discontinuity between them.*

Item 11 would seem a non-issue. All of the contributors hold that hypnotic depth is a quantitative continuum along one or more dimensions of depth. However, at least one contributor insists that it is still an issue. The assertion is that a fundamental, qualitative discontinuity between hypnosis and the usual waking state is implicit in the traditional hypnotic trance state paradigm.

In the hope of helping to clarify the problem, let us draw the following analogy: the dissent expressed is that, according to the traditional paradigm, being in hypnosis is something like the issue of whether or not a woman is pregnant. To be pregnant is fundamentally, qualitatively different from not being pregnant. A woman cannot be a little bit pregnant. Whether in early or late pregnancy, she is totally pregnant. In regard to hypnosis the dissenting view is that the traditional hypnotic trance state paradigm implies that a special altered state causes or mediates increased responsiveness to suggestion. In this context, depth of hypnosis refers to the extensiveness of the altered state. The altered state, like pregnancy, is defined as fundamentally discontinuous from the usual waking state regardless of its extent. The dissenter usually comes across to readers as if he vigorously were demonstrating and believing that there is no such thing as hypnosis—which de facto is not his position at all.

Physiological Changes and Psychological Behaviors Distinguishing Hypnosis from the Waking State

Another significant group of issues centers on the extent to which changes in physiological and psychological behavior in hypnosis differ from those that can be produced in the waking state. These are the issues of transcendence of normal volitional capacities.

ITEM 12

> *There is convincing evidence that deeply hypnotized subjects can produce certain observable behaviors and physiological changes that even highly motivated nonhypnotized subjects in the usual waking state are unwilling or unable to produce or unable to mimic;*

or, alternatively,

> *there is no such convincing evidence.*

This item focuses on the issue of transcendence of normal volitional capacities and it should be reiterated that it refers to outward behaviors and physiological changes only, not to subjective events. Most of our contributors have been concerned with this issue in one form or another; several have developed specialized methodologies for dealing with it. The item encompasses the issues of sensitivity to subtle demand characteristics, discernment of experimental deception, ability to fool the experimenter, antisocial and self-destructive behavior, and the ability to figure out what a deeply hypnotized person would do.

Most of the contributors would agree with the second alternative: there is at present no *convincing* evidence. The hard fact is that in the last two decades of research in hypnosis all claims made for the unique behavioral and physiological effects of hypnosis have proved unconvincing when subjected to careful experimental scrutiny. Two of our contributors, however, believe that they have discovered several typical psychological hypnotic behaviors that simulators are not able to figure out.

Doubtless this list of key issues is incomplete. But posing it may help to alert the reader to a number of underlying themes reflected throughout the volume in a variety of ways.

Prologue 1979

The chasm between those who conceive of hypnosis as a trait or nonstate and those who see it as an altered state of consciousness will probably be narrowed now by E.R. Hilgard's Neo-Dissociation Theory of hypnosis (Chapter 3, this volume). This theory allows for degrees of dissociative experiences ranging from superficial responses to direct suggestion (accompanied by some shifts between voluntary and involuntary control systems but lacking essential modification of consciousness) to deep alterations of consciousness experienced *as such* by the individual.

Ronald E. Shor *is Professor and Chairman, Department of Psychology, University of New Hampshire. He received his Ph.D. from Brandeis University in 1960, and joined the staff of the Studies in Hypnosis Project at the Massachusetts Mental Health Center and Harvard Medical School, becoming Associate Director in 1963. He continued in that role when the laboratory became the Unit for Experimental Psychiatry at the University of Pennsylvania. Shifting to a greater commitment in teaching, he joined the staff of La Salle College in 1966, and moved to the University of New Hampshire the following year. He has co-edited* The Nature of Hypnosis: Selected Basic Readings *with Martin Orne. He is Past President of the Division of Psychological Hypnosis of the American Psychological Association. His major interests are a cognitive approach to the study of alterations in conscious experiencing, concept identification, skill in symbol use, and social action.*

Shor *argues that there are two intertwined—and fundamental—dangers in hypnosis reasearch: not maintaining the disciplined skepticism of the scientist, and not maintaining the confident persuasiveness of the hypnotist. The more the scientist-hypnotist tries to avoid one of these two dangers, the more likely it is that he will succumb to the other. In the first part of his chapter Shor surveys the major events in the history of hypnosis. He shows how the fundamental problem has been manifested at different times in ways that differ only superficially. In the second part he presents an exposition of this fundamental problem as it has emerged from its historic background.*

2

The Fundamental Problem
in Hypnosis Research
as Viewed
from Historic Perspectives

RONALD E. SHOR

On one side of the narrow strait lay Scylla, a treacherous rock; on the other side lay an equal danger, Charybdis, a dreadful whirlpool. The only safe passage was to sail the narrow course in between. Sailing to either one side or the other brought unfailing disaster. The only method for avoiding either of these two dangers was therefore to take the terrible risk of succumbing to its counterpart danger. The more leeway the navigator allowed himself in avoiding the danger to port meant just that much less leeway in avoiding the reciprocal danger to starboard. These two entirely distinct and separate dangers of rock and whirlpool were thus so situated that unavoidably they had to be faced together, as if one single, unitary problem.

The Straits of Messina

The fundamental problem in hypnosis research is that it is faced with two dangers, which like the rock and whirlpool of Scylla and Charybdis, are so situated that they must be encountered together, as if they were one. The two inextricable dangers are the danger of not providing sufficient disciplined skepticism, and the danger of not providing sufficient positive catalyst. The investigator of hypnosis is always faced with the extremely difficult task of maintaining both caution and conviction at one and the same time, that is, maintaining both the disciplined skepticism of the scientist and the confident persuasiveness of the hypnotist. Fulfilling the two roles of scientist and hypnotist simultaneously is a slippery task, beset with many subtle difficulties. The more the scientist-hypnotist tries to avoid one of the two dangers, the more likely it becomes that he will succumb to the other.

The fundamental problem has emerged repeatedly throughout the two centuries since Mesmer's first "magnetic" treatments. The specific forms it has taken have been as superficially different in every era as is the antelope from the whale, but with proper background the underlying uniformity can be discerned.

I. Survey of Major Historic Events

From time immemorial men in the most diverse cultures have discovered how to use hypnotic and suggestive phenomena with immense pragmatic effectiveness for faith healing and for magico-religious and other purposes. But it was during the ultrarational Age of Enlightment in the late eighteenth century, as belief in fundamentalist religion was waning and the physical sciences were gaining prominence, that a physician-faith healer, Franz Anton Mesmer, devoted his life to the development of a scientific understanding of the powerful therapeutic forces which he had learned to control. Mesmer's theories have been proved untenable, but the insights they contained initiated and provoked continuing scientific study. (See Figure 2.1)

The history of hypnotism from Mesmer to the present day may conveniently be divided into four periods, representing stages of scientific sophistication. These four stages are: Presomnambulistic Mesmerism, Somnambulistic Mesmerism (later renamed Hypnotism), the Early Psychological Period, and the Later Psychological or Modern Period. In the first stage mesmeric-hypnotic phenomena were brought within the general boundaries of science; in the second stage attention was recentered on artificial somnambulism as the pivotal event; in the third stage many inaccurate, prepsychological interpretations were eliminated in favor of more accurate, psychological interpretations; in the present, fourth stage the insights of psychodynamics and precise quantitive methods have been and are being incorporated. The chief events in this development have been summarized in Table 2.1. The four stages are, of course, interpretive classifications rather than entities or events. Once stated, however, they are assumed valid and will be referred to throughout as guideposts to the historic development. (For further reading the following secondary sources are recommended: Ackerknecht, 1948; Boring, 1950; Bromberg, 1959; Conn, 1957; Ellenberger, 1970; Galdston, 1948a; Marks, 1947; Murphy, 1949; Pattie, 1967;

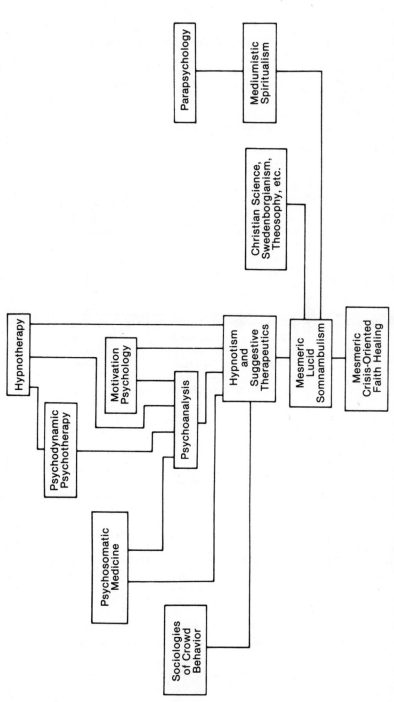

FIGURE 2.1. *Mesmer's intellectual progeny. (Height indicates rough chronology and is not an evaluation of relative importance. Mesmerism's precursors are not indicated, nor are the other roots contributing to the development of the various offshoots.)*

TABLE 2.1 Synoptic chart of major historic events in hypnosis

Stage of Scientific Sophistication		Essential Contribution	Beginning of Period
1. Presomnambulistic Mesmerism		Insistence that the observable therapeutic successes had a scientific explanation	1774—Mesmer begins treatment of F. Oesterlin's conversion hysteria with metallic magnets
2. Somnambulistic Mesmerism		Recognition of the pivotal importance of the mesmerically-induced somnambulistic state with lucid speech, responsiveness to the mesmerist's wishes, and subsequent amnesia	1784—Puységur writes letter outlining his discovery of artificial somnambulism
3. Early Psychological Period		Merged recognition of both (a) that mesmeric-hypnotic phenomena were in some sense genuine and important, and (b) that such phenomena were essentially psychological in nature	1814—Faria comes to Paris from Goa and expounds teachings
	T H E O R Y	Discovery of the unconscious mind and its psychodynamic processes	1893—Original chapters of Breuer and Freud's Studien über Hysterie published
4. Later Psychological, or Modern Period	M E T H O D	Development of precise scientific methods, creating a tradition of continuing scientific evolution	1878—Charcot begins demonstrations of hypnotism at Salpêtrière hospital

Major Contributor		Entrance into History of Hypnosis	
Name	Life Span	Year	Event
Mesmer, F.A.	1734-1815		
Puységur, A. Marquis de	1751-1825		
Elliotson, J.	1791-1868	1837	Begins magnetic experiments at University Hospital
Braid, J. (early)	1795-1860	1843	Publishes *Neurypnology*
Charcot, J. M. (theory)	1825-1893	1882	Gives nosological description to Academy of Sciences
Faria, J. C. di	1756-1819		
Bertrand, A. J. F.	1795(?)-1831	1823	Publishes *Traité du somnambulisme...*
Braid, J. (later)	(above)	1847	Advances psychological view
Liébeault, A. A.	1823-1904	1866	Publishes *Du sommeil...*
Bernheim, H. M.	1837-1919	1884	Publishes *De la suggestion...*
Freud, S.	1856-1939		
Erickson, M. H.	1901-	1923	Gives graduate seminar on hypnosis
Charcot, J. M. (method)	(above)		
Hull, C. L.	1884-1952	1933	Publishes *Hypnosis and Suggestibility*

Podmore, 1909; Rosen, 1948, 1963; Sarbin, 1962; Shor, 1968; Tinterow, 1970; Watson, 1971; Williams, 1952; Zilboorg & Henry, 1941; Zweig, 1922).

PRESOMNAMBULISTIC MESMERISM

There was little if any historic novelty in Mesmer's therapeutic successes nor in the theoretical pseudology he derived to account for them. His contribution lay not in originality but in his insistence that the observable therapeutic effects had a scientific explanation.

Mesmer's therapy and theory were minor variants of the teachings of many other faith healers throughout history. His therapy was a combination of the ancient procedure of laying on of hands with a disguised version of medieval demonic exorcism. His theory was a combination of ancient astrological concepts, medieval mysticism, and seventeenth-century vitalism. But Mesmer viewed himself as a thoroughgoing mechanist, and thus garbed his teachings in the terminology of eighteenth-century physical science, particularly of magnetism and electricity.

Health to Mesmer was the harmonious distribution in mind and body of an impalpable, ethereal fluid that permeated the universe; disease was fluidic imbalance. To some extent the cosmic fluid could be controlled by the human will, and even stored in inanimate objects. Mesmer's clinical investigations soon led him to observe extreme agitation, convulsive seizure, and other temporarily deteriorated behaviors in his patients after therapeutic manipulations.[1] From these observations he concluded that an indispensable first step in treatment was to cause some of his own stored cosmic fluid to flow into a receptive patient to provoke thereby an even more severe fluidic imbalance. The patient's behavior would then deteriorate into a violent convulsive seizure, meaning that the malady had reached a head or crisis, after which equilibrium would tend to become restored.

These convulsive crises became the pivotal event in Mesmer's therapeutic system. We know today that they were purely artifacts of mutually shared expectations. But Mesmer, his disciples, and his patients became convinced that the crises were indispensable preliminaries to cure. And just so long as these beliefs were firmly shared, it remained (thereby) pragmatically true that mesmerized patients did not derive therapeutic benefit without first experiencing this type of crisis. The necessity and therapeutic effectiveness of

---

1. These original agitated reactions were probably due to three factors: expectations deriving from medieval demonic exorcism rites, the dancing manias (St. Vitus's Dance, for example), and possibly epilepsy: a probable aftereffect of anxiety release after direct symptom suppression (see particularly the case of Maria Theresa von Paradis in Mesmer's *Mémoire...,*first published in 1774); a derivation of the *vapeurs,* the hysterical fainting and nervous fits fashionable among society women at that time.

the interposed crisis thus was repeatedly verified clinically, strengthening the conviction even more.

Mesmer's was an age of fanatic ultrarationalism and emotive alienation of the doctor from the folk culture, but the orthodox physicians had little to offer sufferers of functional ailments beyond impersonalized faith healing rationalized in the form of potions, bleeding, and purges. Mesmer's brand of faith healing on the other hand was a credo that enlisted enthusiastic belief and high expectancy of cure; it was emotionally comprehensible and sensitively attuned to the emotive needs of the multitudes. While untenable from the standpoint of objective scientific truth, Mesmer's powerful therapeutic theories were functionally, pragmatically true.

Mesmer did not fail to note that unless his patients were cooperative and sincerely wished to be cured they would not allow themselves to become receptive to the physician's healing influences. In other words, although his physicalistic theoretical interpretations were incorrect, as a clinical practitioner Mesmer had an astute working knowledge of the importance of a favorable doctor-patient relationship.

He also evolved highly successful methods of group treatment by using the storage condenser principle of accumulating the cosmic fluid in inamimate objects, later to supply quantities of the fluid to large numbers of persons at a time. In addition, by enlisting the credulous yearnings of the populace in mystic ceremonials, Mesmer and his disciple d'Eslon developed to a fine theoretical art the heightening of expectancy of the crisis and cure.

But these important insights were ignored in the controversy over whether the cosmic fluid, whose effect on living organisms was called animal magnetism, was a physical entity, and thus a legitimate object of scientific study, or mere imagination, and thus nothing but fraud and collusion, with overtones of danger to morality.

Mesmer, although disheartened eventually by ceaseless vitriolic rebuff from official quarters, had defenders who were both eloquent and incisive; but the French Revolution and the Napoleonic Wars soon scattered the protagonists. Presomnambulistic mesmerism, with the convulsive crisis as the pivotal event, disappeared from the center of the historic stage. (Recommended primary and secondary sources are Bailly et al., 1784a, 1785, 1784b; Barbarin, 1786; Bergasse, 1784; Bonnefoy, 1784; Darnton, 1968; Eslon, 1780, 1784; Galdston, 1948b; Goldsmith, 1934; Grimm & Diderot, 1784; Jussieu, 1784; Ludwig, 1964; Mesmer, 1774, 1785, 1814; Pattie, 1956b; Poissonnier et al., 1784; Sernan, 1784; Wydenbruck, 1947).

SOMNAMBULISTIC MESMERISM

In 1784, the same year that the Royal Commissioners disaffirmed the existence and value of animal magnetism, one of Mesmer's many layman disciples, Armand Chastenet, Marquis de Puységur, wrote a letter to a colleague outlining his discovery of artificial somnambulism. Later that same year Puységur expanded on his findings in the first edition of his *Mémoires*. To Puységur belongs the credit for the first clear recognition of the pivotal importance of mesmerically induced sleepwalking, in which strange, mystic-like events seemed to occur. With this recentering of concern on artificial somnambulism, and away from the convulsive crises, mesmerism entered its second stage of scientific sophistication.

Puységur and his followers discovered that in this special entranced, sleeplike state, the mesmerized subjects could speak lucidly, open their eyes and walk about, respond to the mesmerist's wishes and commands, and subsequently forget their experiences when aroused. They also discovered that crises were not indispensable to cure, and thus the crises slowly slipped into historic obscurity, less and less expected and thus less and less seen.

While it is true that Puységur independently discovered mesmeric somnambulism, Mesmer and others had witnessed it earlier. But as this sleeplike condition was irrelevant to the production of the convulsive crises, these earlier observers had viewed somnambulism only as an unfortunate interruption to their therapeutic process.[2]

Puységur's reorientation in outlook could come only under conditions where people were far less convinced that the crisis was the dominating event in therapy. At Puységur's provincial estate, peasants and villagers were treated who were far removed from the sophisticated Parisian gossip about what to expect during mesmeric treatments. Dispensing with somber surroundings and mystic ceremonials, Puységur adopted the less theatrical simpler methods that Mesmer had evolved earlier, such as accumulating animal magnetism in a tree, under the open sky.

Inordinate responsiveness. To the peasants and artisans of Puységur's province it was assuredly a gratifying event to have the prestigious marquis show profound concern for their welfare by mesmerizing them, and these humble folk basked in his aristocratic presence. It is hardly surprising that Puységur discovered that his somnambulists were inordinately responsive to his directions, and were trying very hard to please him.

Recall that Mesmer's initial observations on agitated reactions soon led him to conceptualize and instill firm expectations of crises, which then precipitated these crises just so long as the expectations remained shared. Perhaps similarly, an inordinate responsiveness is not intrinsic to artificial somnambulism either, but is demonstrably true so long as the shared

2. Some historians have held that Mesmer suppressed knowledge of mesmeric somnambulsim because of its unwelcome resemblence to sorcery. Also prior to Puységur's discovery, the Chevalier de Barbarin and his devotees had routinely induced somnambulism, but their zealous animistic interpretations likewise blocked clear recognition of its pivotal importance.

expectations—fabricated from Puységur's initial observations—remain to make it functionally true. Such shared expectations of increased responsiveness when entranced persist into our own day[3] (see especially Ellenberger, 1965b; Puységur, 1784a, 1784b, 1807, 1811, 1837).

The Doctrine of Will Power. The discovery of the somnambulist's inordinate responsiveness to the wishes and commands of the mesmerist initiated two concomitant theoretical developments. The first was a shift away from Mesmer's view of man as some kind of animal "magnet" who could to some extent willfully control a physical, external, impersonal cosmic fluid. The second was a concomitant shift toward the highly personalized doctrine of will power.

To Puységur and his followers the curative fluid was secreted by the mesmerist's brain and passed along his nerves to the peripheral organs in response to his will. The manufacture and transmission of the vital fluid depends on the mesmerist's exuberant faith and unaltering self-confidence in his own dominating powers. Albeit an easy vehicle for the expression of the mesmerist's egoistic fantasies, the doctrine of will power nonetheless represented an advance in translating the interpersonal aspects of the mesmeric process into psychological terms.

The discovery of this mesmerically induced trance state in which wondrous phenomena seemed to occur led to widespread and enthusiastic experimentation by Puységur and his followers. This experimentation in turn soon led to the clear recognition of just about all of the major mesmeric-hypnotic phenomena acknowledged today: the motor automatisms and catalepsies, amnesias, anaesthesias, positive and negative hallucinations, posthypnotic phenomena, and individual differences in susceptibility.

Credulous excess. But inextricably confounded with the genuine observations there grew up a tangle of wild pseudologizing and extravagent, mystic claims of paranormal powers conferred in the special state: clairvoyance, transposability of the senses, somnambulistic medical diagnosis, foretelling

3. Although theoretical interpretations differ, this same observation of inordinate responsiveness finds expression in the later concepts of remarkable docility, hypersuggestibility, increased motivation, role-taking, and increased responsiveness to test suggestions. Ellenberger (1965b) has pointed out that the kind of authoritarian relationship between the magnetizer and his somnambulist became transformed as a function of the change from an aristocratic to a bourgeoisie dominated society. In Puységur's day the type of relationship between the nobleman and his peasant was manifested as a kind of "bargaining therapy," with the personality of the somnambulist more brilliant than usual. This was replaced during the nineteenth century by forms of treatment based on hypnotic command and direct suggestion, with the subject a mere automaton in the style of the relationship between the bourgeois master and his servant. In our own day, the enormous psychological and social distance supportive of the authoritarian hypnotic relationship has faded, but the concept of suggestibility and its variant expressions remain.

of the future, spiritualistic mediumship, and so forth. These credulous ex-cesses were inevitable both because they fit the mood of nineteenth-century Romanticism and because at a nonconscious (if not also conscious) level the mesmerized somnambulist was strongly impelled to produce the phenomena that he perceived were expected of him.

Because mesmeric phenomena are initiated by enthusiasm and expec-tancy, credulous excess tens to augment the phenomena and scientific skep-ticism (doubt) tends to attenuate them. Thus investigators with cooler heads were often at a disadvantage, whereas those with wilder fantasies and blinder resolve were more readily able to produce striking effects. There was consequently a natural selection in the direction of extravagance.

Thus each mesmerist would tend to see his expected and as yet unfor-mulated speculations repeatedly proved true by the behavior of his trained somnambulists, and the more outspoken his position became, the clearer was the proof engendered. While apparently utilizing a process roughly akin to hypothetic-deductive scientific method—by hypothesis, experimental test, verification, reformulation, etc.—many of the mesmerists evolved the most extravagent, mutually contradictory pseudologies.

But the very multiplicity of the mesmerists' divergent doctrines served to undermine the plausibility of any one of them, and thus, in a negative fashion, helped prepare the advent of more sedate theories. Despite the jib-berish and nonsense, too many genuine and startling effects had been un-covered not to lead some wiser minds to recognize that there was something important in mesmerism to be explained. And once thoughtful men sought to encompass what seemed genuine in mesmerism within the conservative framework of existing physical and physiological science, a psychological interpretation became inevitable.

But even in the mid-1820s, when at least two men, José Faria and Alexan-dre Bertrand, had already arrived at the third stage of sophistication, the issues were nonetheless still being misstated at the prepsychological, second stage when the French Academy of Sciences reopened its inquiry into mesmerism. The investigators were primarily interested in whether there were psychical phenomena in somnambulism, such as clairvoyance, which were beyond the bounds of ordinary science. Since under careful scrutiny no such miracles were forthcoming, mesmerism was again officially re-jected. (Recommended sources are Bennett, 1851; Binet and Féré, 1886; Burdin & Dubois, 1841; Carlson, 1960; Colquhoun, 1844; Deleuze, 1819, 1825; Hall, 1845; Husson et al., 1833; Kerner, 1847; Lafontaine, 1860; Leger, 1846; Macchi, 1858; Poe, 1837; Reichenbach, 1850; Schneck, 1959.)

Braid's early theory. Nothing substantive prevented the formulation of conservative theories at the second stage of sophistication, however. One such second-stage theory of considerable historic importance was advanced by James Braid in his book *Neurypnology* (1843). Braid recognized that certain mesmeric phenomena were genuine but rejected all mesmeric theories of external influences. Taking as his starting point the eye fixation induction technique that he had observed in demonstrations by the mesmerist Lafontaine, Braid advanced a naturalistic physiological explanation. He theorized that staring fixedly at a bright object for a protracted period induces fatigue of the levator muscles of the eyelids, which in turn promotes a general exhaustion or derangement of the nerve centers. Or, stated more broadly, by deliberately fixing attention on a single, continuous, monotonous stimulation, a special nervous sleep or stupor results, in which the functional activity of the central nervous system is decreased. This condition Braid termed neuro-hypnotism.

A few years later, in 1847, Braid revised his thinking to give preeminence to psychological factors and somewhat minimized the physiological; thus he advanced to the third stage. At that point he regretted his general use of the term neuro-hypnotism, because the nervous sleep had become for him only a special case of the more fundamental principle of exclusively concentrated attention (monoideism, that is, single-idea-ism). But the very change from one misnomer to another, from mesmerism to hypnotism, helped to alter mesmerism's public and professional image. And because the age found that the new name had the proper antimesmeric and physiological ring to it, the phenomena could more easily be brought within the bounds of cautious, respectable science. The change in name thus helped transform the spirit of investigation from credulous excess to naturalistic science.

Charcot's neurological theory. Three decades later, in 1878, Jean Martin Charcot, the eminent clinical neurologist, began his demonstrations of hypnotism at the Salpêtrière Hospital in Paris. Charcot offered precise scientific descriptions based on the meticulous empiricist methodology of the neurological examination. In 1882, he presented his neurological theory of hypnosis to the French Academy of Sciences. In a precise nosologic classification, hypnotism was described as three distinct sequential physiological reflex stages in hysterically predisposed individuals. These three stages were induced and terminated by certain definite physical stimuli.

We know today that Charcot's theory of hypnotism was for the most part a disguised return to many of the old mesmeric errors, phrased in advanced neurological terminology. As a theorist, Charcot was deluded by procedural artifacts introduced by the very nature of the meticulous scientific methodology he adopted. These delusions were the same errors and pitfalls that the practicing clinicians of that period, Liébeault, Bernheim, and others, had so successfully learned to recognize and avoid. In other words, Charcot's theory was a blind insistence on a naive, prepsychological explanation at a time when practicing clinicians had clearly advanced to the third, more sophisticated level of understanding.

But despite the objective weakness of Charcot's theoretical views, his eminence as one of the world's leading neurologists, his rigorous methodology, and his precise nosological descriptions removed any lingering doubts in the medical profession about the scientific respectability of studying hypnotism. Although from the standpoint of theory, Charcot's rigorous approach was a hindrance that led him to repeat many of the old second-stage mistakes, his work paradoxically represents a methodological advance to the fourth stage of sophistication, if only because of what he was trying to accomplish. This paradox in the work of Charcot foreshadows a disparity in the fourth stage between theory and method, which will be discussed later in more detail (Charcot, 1882a, 1882b, 1893; Ellenberger, 1965a; Schneck, 1952, 1961a, 1961b).

EARLY PSYCHOLOGICAL PERIOD

The third stage of sophistication was marked by the concurrent recognition of two basic insights: that mesmeric-hypnotic phenomena are in some sense genuine and important, and that mesmeric-hypnotic phenomena are essentially psychological in nature. These two basic insights then fused to produce a third, derivative insight: that the psychological processes underlying mesmeric-hypnotic phenomena—imagination, expectancy, belief, enthusiasm, receptivity, attention, attitude, monoideism, ideoexpressive tendency, suggestion, hypersuggestion, motivation, etc.—are scientifically valid and important.

The validity of either the first basic insight or of the second had been recognized by every interested observer from the time of Mesmer's first cases in Vienna. But the intellectual climate was such that to accept either one seemed tantamount to rejecting the other.

The mesmerists clearly recognized the therapeutic potency and scientific importance of their procedures. But despite their astute clinical acumen in manipulating psychological variables, they had at best only a defensive inkling that the source of their influence was imagination and not a physical agency. Mesmer's detractors on the other hand had realized that the agent was primarily psychological, but for them this realization constituted more than ample proof of trickery and unworthiness.

Faria's notion of lucid sleep. Although in the early periods someone occasionally caught a fleeting glimpse of both basic insights together, the first person to do so seriously was the abbot José Custodi di Faria, who in 1814 arrived in Paris from Goa, a Portugese colony in India. Faria rejected mesmeric theories of special agencies and stressed that lucid sleep (somnambulism) was produced solely by the subject's heightened expectations and receptive attitude.

Mesmer had clearly recognized the value of heightened expectancy and the indispensable importance of the patient's receptive attitude; later workers like Puységur and Deleuze further stressed these factors. But in Mesmer's theoretical view expectant receptivity had meant only something like completing electric circuits and the willful opening or closing of hydraulic-like valves to receive or impede the flow of cosmic fluid; Puységur and Deleuze also adhered to a fluidic formulation. In a sense, Faria merely saw what is now obvious: that the elaborate mesmeric pseud-ologies had pragmatic value in helping to initiate psychological processes within the subject, but had no validity independent of that consequence.

One expression of Faria's new psychological outlook was the use in his in-duction procedure of verbal suggestion, both soothing and commanding. Mesmer's induction procedures has been based on direct physical contacts that were designed to promote the flow of cosmic fluid into the receptive pa-tient. Puységur and his followers had elaborated these procedures to in-clude waving movements of the hands without direct physical contact, in order to radiate the nervous fluid from a distance. Another second-stage elaboration was talking to the entranced somnambulist, but the induction procedure as such remained nonverbal. Only when it was recognized that the mesmeric influences lay within the subject himself did words become important elements in the process of induction.

In 1823, and again in 1826, Alexandre Bertrand, originally an orthodox mesmerist, published works vigorously expounding and developing Faria's psychological point of view (Bertrand, 1823, 1826a, 1826b; Faria, 1906).

Braid's later theory. In his theory of 1847, Braid's interest shifted away from the rather mechanical physiological changes of exhausted nervous centers, and toward events at the psychological level of analysis. The psychological concept of monoideism now became central for Braid, but he continued to maintain that it resulted in definite physiological changes in the subject.

In monoideism the mental attention becomes so engrossed in a single idea, a single train of thought, that for the time being the attention is thereby rendered insensible and indifferent to all other considerations and influences. One active train of ideation becomes extraordinarily intense and subjectively real to the subject because all of his attention is exclusively con-centrated on it, rather than diffused and distracted into a multitude of com-peting ideas and impressions. All of the various mesmerically, hypnotically, and verbally suggestive induction procedures have only one objective: to help promote this state of single-mindedness, of exclusively concentrated attention, letting other ideas pass into torpid oblivion. Because the monoide-ized attention has heightened the intensity of the one focal or dominant idea, the power of the imagination on mind and body is considerably greater that in the ordinary waking state, and thus suggestions are likely to initiate correspondingly greater influences.

Monoideism became for Braid the central unifying concept, of which neuro-hypnotism was but a subconcept, designating a special, extreme state characterized by oblivious nervous sleep with subsequent amnesia until again hypnotized. Braid said that this rare state was achieved by only about one tenth of his subjects. The majority showed no loss of consciousness. Moreover, some subjects immediately passed into an alert, active somnambulistic state with eyes open the very first time they were hypnotized, without previously passing through a condition in any way resembling the nervous sleep (Braid, 1846, 1852; Bramwell, 1896-97a, 1896-97b, 1903).

Liébeault and the Nancy Practitioner's tradition. In France, Braid's third-stage theory did not become known until it was published in a condensed version along with the first French translation of *Neurypnology* in 1883. But as early as 1859, Braid's earlier views began to be publicized by a number of French physicians.

We have already seen how, from a modern perspective, Braid's pre-psychological, second-stage theory from its earliest inception was only a hair's breadth away from the third stage. That decisive step was independently taken in France by Ambroise Auguste Liébeault, a kindly and unassuming country doctor who settled in Nancy in 1864. Liébeault's vigorously psychological viewpoint was presented in his book *Du sommeil. . .*, first published in 1866. The book was ignored for 20 years until Hippolyte Marie Bernheim, then professor of medicine at Strasbourg, "discovered" Liébeault, and championed his viewpoint. Bernheim soon succeeded in drawing worldwide attention to the importance of mental therapeutics based on verbal suggestion.

Liébeault and Bernheim were essentially clinical practitioners, interested mainly in curing and teaching how to cure. They were far less seriously concerned with developing a systematic theory of hypnosis for its own sake than had been Mesmer or Braid.

Outgrowths of Liébeault's and Bernheim's teachings revolved about the doctrine of suggestion, which became both the fundamental description and the unifying explanation of hypnosis and related events. From today's advanced orientation, it is difficult to comprehend the style of thinking in that earlier era, except as a random collection of pragmatic teachings. But the underlying internal coherence of their views must be grasped, because even now, long after the theoretical substrate of these teachings has withered from view, its product—the doctrine of suggestion—remains deeply infused in modern thinking about hypnosis in many subtle and unanalyzed ways.

The doctrine of suggestion. At that time, ideas were understood to be atomic entities swarming in the arena of the mind. By a kind of mental chemistry—by combination, permutation, closeness, and distance between ideas—was created the panoply of waking rationality, waking suggestibility, sleep, monoideism, indirect suggestion, reverie, and hypnosis. Each separate idea possessed some quantity of energy that blindly, automatically pressed toward translation into its motoric and sensory equivalents. The ideoexpressive energies of all of the ideas in the mind's arena were seen to enhance and complement one another as well as to compete and inhibit. The net effect of this complex interaction was that the blind, automatic ideo-expressive energies of each idea were held in check by the ideoexpressive energies of all of the many other ideas. Waking suggestibility was seen as the state of mind where a dominant idea became relatively stronger than competing ideas. Hypnosis was seen as an extension of suggestibility that began by having the subject focus on the idea of sleep. During the ensuing sleep the idea of the hypnotist was retained within the sleeper's awareness. Thus the sleeper was in rapport with the hypnotist. Since the critical faculties—that is, the swarm of competing ideas—were in abeyance during sleep, the result was a state of heightened suggestibility. The hypnotized subject had to obey without volition ideas implanted by the hypnotists, as would an automaton.

In sum, ordinary waking suggestibility and hypnotic heightened suggestibility were both seen to result from a temporary weakening of the usual critical faculties. But it was also possible to slip ideas past the intact critical faculties by indirection, thus circumventing rationality. This latter process was called indirect suggestion.

Theoretical deficiencies. The doctrine of suggestion provided many useful insights, but also missed and obscured other important factors. The ideoexpressive principle did provide an organized account of the continuity from ordinary waking rationality to waking suggestion and then to hypnosis, but its stress on debilitated functioning, automatism, "will-less" obedience, and exclusive rapport, overlooked the assertive, alert, active, and productive capacities of the hypnotized individual. The stress on sleep shaped the outward appearance of hypnotic behavior from that time through our own; it also obscured the fact, noted so clearly by Braid, that some subjects could enter a highly active somnambulistic state without at any time passing through a condition resembling sleep in any way, even the first time hypnotized.

The doctrine of suggestibility was especially weak in illuminating the factors of enthusiastic credence and firm expectation. The central feature of Mesmer's method of faith healing was, for example, more sensibly viewed as a matter of enlisting rational belief than of releasing ideoexpressive energies. Mesmer's main emphasis was not placed on causing the critical faculties of his patients to become temporarily suspended—that is, it was not a matter of waking or hypnotic suggestion. Nor did Mesmer stealthily try to slip ideas past his patients' intact critical faculties unbeknown to them—that is, he did not practice indirect suggestion. Instead, Mesmer tried to enlist the critical faculties of his patients in the most direct manner possible. Mesmer was himself convinced, and tried hard to convince his patients of the truth and potency of his scientific doctrines at the level of full critical rationality, and not at all in spite of it.

A second example of the importance of expectant belief is John Elliotson's observation that, as the crest of popular enthusiasm and credence in mesmerism waned in London, and was replaced more and more by widespread scorn and skepticism, mesmeric anesthesia seemed to lose its power to remove pain.

> I believe I was not wrong; I believe that in what I originally saw, mesmerism played the parts precisely that I claimed for it. It is a wicked error to suppose that I was a party to a deception, or to a whole series of deceptions, if you like; but I candidly say...that mesmerism, at the present moment, has no power to remove pain. It is a mystery; it had power, and I once saw a leg painlessly removed under its influence; but we are now in another cycle, and it seems to me that there are special periods only in which mesmeric phenomena can be induced. (Quoted in Rosen, 1948.)

The kinds of variables illustrated in these two examples are not fully expressed by the concepts of ordinary suggestion and indirect suggestion, and are only slightly embodied by the even later concept of prestige suggestion. Far richer and more accurate characterizations are terms such as enthusiastic credence, exalted confidence, intense emotive excitement, firm expectancy of influence, faith healing, and charismatic personality, which imply a good deal more than the often tacit, limited, mechanical, and perfunctory suggestion influence. Rather, they refer to emotionally highly charged beliefs giving expression to core energies of the personality.

By maintaining the generic term "suggestion," concepts such as indirect suggestion, prestige suggestion, and the other later accretions seemed to preserve the single-principle explanatory character of the doctrine of suggestibility, but in actuality psychological processes quite different in character were thereby obscured.

As a conceptual tool, the single-principle doctrine of suggestion was useful in discrediting a number of then current physical and physiological second-stage theories. The doctrine disavowed all but a parsimonious description of events at the psychological level of analysis. The doctrine found its most cogent expression in the extended polemic controversy between the clinical practitioners led by Bernheim at Nancy and the puristic scientists led by Charcot at the Salpêtrière Hospital in Paris. The eventual victory of the more accurate Nancy suggestionist viewpoint unfortunately tended to obscure the recognition that a psychological analysis is not in any sense inherently antagonistic to a concern with underlying physiology, as Braid had earlier come to recognize so clearly. (Recommended sources are Baudouin, 1922; Benussi, 1927; Bleuler, 1907; Dessior, 1888, 1890; Elliotson, 1846, 1848-49; Esdaile, 1846, 1852; Forel, 1907; Hart, 1898; Heidenhain, 1888; James & Carnochan, 1885-89; LeBon, 1895, 1911; Marmer, 1956; Moll, 1898; Rand, 1925; Richet, 1881; Rosen, 1936, 1946; Sarbin & Kroger, 1963; Schneck, 1956; Sidis, 1898; Solomons & Stein, 1896; Tarde, 1907.)

LATER PSYCHOLOGICAL OR MODERN PERIOD

Because we are presently living in the fourth stage of scientific sophistication about hypnosis, we cannot yet know where it will eventually lead. But the beginning of the fourth stage is characterized by two important intellectual contributions and their ongoing elaborations. One of these contributions relates to theory, the other to method. That relating to theory was Sigmund Freud's charting of the unconscious mind and of psychodynamic processes. The contribution relating to method was Charcot's fundamental commitment to an extremely precise and purified scientific method, which established a tradition of a continuing scientific evolution.

These two contributions have been and remain somewhat incompatible. Although some day it would seem that they must fuse into one, there is as yet no clear alternative to describing the fourth stage as two separate lines of development. Perhaps the fifth stage will emerge only after these two lines fuse, or perhaps the fifth stage will itself be their fusion.

CONTRIBUTION RELATING TO THEORY

Hypnotic therapy in the Nancy tradition consisted essentially of induction of the state of heightened suggestibility, and then verbal suggestion of general well-being and direct symptom disappearance in a tone of authority and confidence.[4] This overly mechanical approach allowed for little concern with the causal etiology of the symptoms. Pierre Janet, Morton Prince, Frederick Myers, and some others soon began to think in terms of multiple systems of consciousness where serious attention was given to underlying dynamics, but these developments were soon overshadowed by the contribution of Sigmund Freud and his psychoanalytic movement.

It was while visiting the clinic of Liébeault and Bernheim in Nancy that

---

4. Braid's therapeutic practice was substantially the same. In his theoretical view, however, suggestion always remained only a procedure and never an explanation. Unlike the lengthy induction procedures common today, Liébeault usually allotted only a couple of minutes, telling his subjects simply to close their eyes and go to sleep.

Freud made the fundamental observation that determined the direction of his life's work. Freud observed that a suggestion given during hypnosis often would not be available to recall upon awakening. The forgotten suggestion was nonetheless carried out posthypnotically, with the patient readily able to rationalize pseudoreasons for his unconsciously motivated act.

> [Visiting Nancy in 1889] I witnessed the moving spectacle of old Liébeault working among the women and children of the laboring classes. I was a spectator of Bernheim's astonishing experiments upon his hospital patients; and I received the profoundest impression of the possibility that there could be powerful mental processes that nevertheless remained hidden from the consciousness of men. (1925, 1952 trans.)

Here was Freud's first impressive inkling that beneath the conscious mind lay a hidden, seething cauldron of immense unconscious forces which were the primary determinants of human affairs.

In the meantime, Josef Breuer, an older colleague of Freud, had discovered that the root causes of hysteric symptoms were painful memories and pent-up emotions, buried below consciousness. The hysteric symptoms could be eliminated in an indirect manner by encouraging spontaneous verbalizations by patients under hypnosis, to evoke a free venting or catharsis of the bottled-up energies causing the symptoms. Freud collaborated with Breuer in pursuing this discovery. Versions of the first chapters of their *Studien über Hysterie* were published in 1893.

Breuer chose not to pursue the matter further, but for Freud the discovery of a positive etiology of hysteria was only the first step in his exploration of the unconscious mind and his learning to speak its special language.

Freud was neither the first nor the only man to discern the existence of unconscious mental processes, in the sense of a subterranean region of the mind with its own laws, contents, and dynamic forces. But he was the first to chart this region systematically, and his discoveries revolutionized man's conception of himself.

Freud's development of psychoanalysis began somewhat paradoxically with his rejection of hypnotism as his scientific and therapeutic method—but he never lost interest in developing a theoretical understanding of hypnosis. Freud turned instead to free association and the analysis of dreams as his "royal road" to the unconscious, but hypnotism is properly recognized as the treasure map that sent him forth on his journey.

Freud's abandonment of hypnosis as a therapeutic method was a wise decision if not a historic necessity, since the authority and obedience brand of hypnotism that dominated his era was too unwieldly, artifact-laden, and encrusted with transference and countertransference problems to allow the slow, painstaking, detached exploration of the hidden inner world which he needed. Hypnotism, moreover, allowed access to certain repressed contents too quickly; it suppressed symptoms too easily, yet often without per-manence; and the hypnotized individual's responses were too readily swayed by what he perceived the hypnotist wanted. Hypnotism was thus a swampy terrain that Freud as a pioneer explorer did well to avoid. Later in-vestigators, however, had far less cause for such trepidation (Breuer & Freud, 1883a, 1883b; Burchard, 1958; Chertok, 1967; Freud, 1925; Gurney, 1884; Janet, 1919; Kline, 1958; Myers, 1886-87, 1891-92; M. Prince, 1920; Schilder & Kauders, 1927; Schneck, 1954b, 1963a).

Renaissance. The revolutionary discoveries of one generation become the basic axioms of following generations. From the light of the psychodynamic insights provided by the Freudian heritage it was inevitable that therapists would evaluate the potentialities of hypnotism afresh. Thus there occurred a renaissance of interest in hypnotism, but now from a broader point of view, a fourth stage of sophistication.

Milton H. Erickson was probably the first, and certainly the boldest, most ingenious, and influential of these new fourth-stage hypnotists. In 1923, while still an undergraduate pre-medical student at the University of Wisconsin, Erickson gave, at Clark Hull's request, a graduate seminar on his intriguing informal researches on hypnotism. Not only were these events the beginnings of Erickson's productive career, but in all likelihood they helped spark Hull's contributions to hypnotism as well.

Stated concisely, Erickson's therapeutic approach emphasizes brevity and limited goals without insight. Figuratively speaking, Erickson enters the world of the patient's neurosis with him, and, with clinical artistry and in-tuitive understanding of nonrational dynamics, rearranges definitions and symptoms to make the neurosis more successfully adaptive.

In broader terms, modern hypnotherapy takes the form of a developing relationship between the therapist and his patient, who is in an altered state of responsiveness in which repressed materials are often more readily avail-able than in the usual waking state. Although hypnosis now is sometimes used as a tool in the context of long-term conventional psychotherapy and psychoanalysis, the emphasis is usually on brevity. Times of war have given special impetus to the development of brief hypnotherapies to deal with soldiers emotionally traumatized by battle conditions (Erickson, 1939b, 1941, 1960, 1964a, 1967b).

CONTRIBUTION RELATING TO METHOD

The clinical practitioner's prime objective in using hypnotic techniques is to cure the patient, if possible, here and now. The pure scientist's prime objec-tive is to accumulate and generalize from present findings succinctly and in a form that helps lay the groundwork for a continuing process of skeptical reappraisal, now and in the future. Knowledge about hypnosis in the clinical tradition is established mainly in terms of pragmatic effectiveness, clinical experience, sensitivity, skill, general plausibility, and the consensus of authoritative opinion. While a valuable wealth of knowledge has been provided by this authority-based clinical tradition of pragmatic teachings, the practitioner's knowledge has generally not taken the form most readily useful to the method-oriented pure scientist.

The end product of knowledge—the facts—are quite reasonably what matter most to the practitioner, oriented as he is toward cure. But of equal importance to the scientist are the conditions under which the facts were gathered. The conditions must be specified precisely so that procedures can be closely replicated and systematically varied in continuing research. The scientific method, in other words, requires that knowledge be formulated in terms amenable to minute scrutiny of all phases of the knowledge-generating process.

Charcot's contribution to method. Charcot's rigorous empiricism derived from an unswerving commitment to precise scientific method as his fundamental concern. This commitment created a point of departure for a continuing scientific evolution. As noted earlier, however, the very nature of Charcot's farsighted puristic methodology led him to adopt a rather inaccurate second-stage, prepsychological theory, at a time when the practitioners in the Nancy tradition had already advanced to a more accurate third-stage, psychological formulation.

The aim of the scientific method is the cautious accumulation and purification of verifiable knowledge. The merit of the scientific method is that it is a self-correcting process. All knowledge is considered tentative, a spring-board for disciplined skepticism. Even when, as with Charcot, purified methodology leads to an inaccurate theory, it nonetheless embodies the logical machinery for a perpetual reappraisal. Accuracy as such, particularly in the first stages of an inductive scientific development, is thus far less important to the working scientist than is verifiability and fruitfulness. Irrespective of its accuracy, to be scientific, knowledge must be in a form that provides the basis for further advancement. The scientist's exposition of the procedures he has used to reach his conclusions must be so explicit as to provide other scientists with the means to disprove and transcend them. It is thus no denial of Charcot's important contribution to realize that his findings were soon critically reappraised and rejected.

It would be of some cogency to argue that the first clear advancement to the fourth stage of sophistication in terms of method should be ascribed to Braid rather than to Charcot. There is no doubt that Braid, and indeed some others, went beyond discursive clinical observation to carry out painstaking experimentation, much as Charcot was later to do. But scientific method as such did not become their central allegiance as it did for Charcot.

There are several illuminating parallels between the contributions of Charcot and Mesmer. Both developed theories that were later found to be quite inaccurate and confounded with procedural artifacts. Both developed theories that were restatements of formulations advanced by earlier workers —of Mead, Paracelsus, and others in the case of Mesmer; of Du Potet and others in the case of Charcot. Both created traditions of continuing scientific development—insistent belief that his therapeutic method was subject to scientific explanation in the case of Mesmer; allegiance to rigorous scientific method in the case of Charcot. For his work, however, Mesmer frequently has been judged as a charlatan, a simpleton, and a plagiarist. For the most part, Charcot has been spared similar accusations, perhaps because of his undeniably brilliant and original contributions in other areas.

Hull's contribution to method. The next important step in the application of scientific method to the study of hypnosis was made possible when mathematicians developed the powerful Null Hypothesis statistical model that provided a procedure for dealing in a systematic and quantitative fashion with the otherwise confusing variability inherent in human responses. This Null Hypothesis model enabled the experimenter to estimate precisely the probable differences in the distributions of responses in experimental and control groups. Thus the new statistical technique made it possible to design more exact and sensitive control experiments than even the most conscientious and ingenious of the earlier experimenters had been able to attain.

The Null Hypothesis model was first used in hypnosis research by Clark L. Hull, around 1930. Hull and his students carried out a broad program of intensive research, which still stands today as a paradigm and foundation for much of the current psychological experimentation in hypnosis.

Statistical techniques were also available at this time for describing the degree of linear correlation between variables in precise quantitative terms. These correlation techniques were used by various workers in conjunction with scales of hypnotic depth to ascertain the psychometric correlates of hypnotic responsiveness, again in a more precise manner than had been achieved earlier. The observation of individual differences in mesmeric-hypnotic responsiveness had been made by everyone from Mesmer onward, but it became the object of serious theoretical attention only after it had been made the chief item of dispute in the Nancy-Salpêtrière controversy. Scientists in the Salpêtrière tradition held that hypnosis was pathological because they believed that only persons with hysterical predispositions could be hypnotized. Practitioners in the Nancy tradition held that hypnosis was a normal process because they believed that virtually everyone under appropriate circumstances would manifest some degree of suggestibility.

To codify their viewpoint, the practitioners evolved scales in which various suggestibility phenomena were arranged by observed order of difficulty, from the simplest induced relaxation to the most profound amnesias and visual hallucinations. These graded scales enabled the skilled examiner to ascertain the depth of hypnosis in any given hypnotized individual. This clinical traditional for measuring hypnotic depth has continued with minor modifications into the present day.

Around 1930, various investigators began to develop standardized objective procedures for rating hypnotic depth in terms of outwardly observable behavioral criteria that minimized the role of the examiner's diagnostic judgment. This second, or behavioral, tradition for measuring hypnotic depth has also continued, with various psychometric improvements, into the present day (Barry et al., 1931; Hull, 1929, 1930, 1931, 1933; M. White, 1930; Williams, 1953; P. Young, 1925).

II. The Fundamental Problem in Hypnosis Research

The fundamental problem in hypnosis research is the necessity of maintaining at the same time both caution and conviction. As Hull's adoption of the Null Hypothesis probability model marks the beginning of modern experimentation in hypnosis, the discussion can be introduced by stating how the fundamental problem manifested itself in Hull's contribution.

HULL'S METHODOLOGICAL CONTRIBUTION

To understand Hull's contribution to scientific method, the paradox inherent in Charcot's contribution should be recalled. Charcot advanced to the fourth stage of sophistication in terms of scientific method, but the very nature of his advanced methodology introduced unrecognized procedural artifacts that grossly distorted the hypnotic phenomena he produced. Hull's contribution manifests a similar paradox. His adoption of the Null Hypothesis probability model provided a marked increase in experimental precision, but the very nature of his laudable scientific objectivity tended subtly to destroy the hypnotic phenomena under investigation. Hull and other method-oriented academic experimentalists failed to realize that the experimenter's job is directly opposed to the hypnotist's job. The experimenter's job is to maintain an attitude of questioning skepticism; the hypnotist's job is to maintain the opposite attitude of assured optimism. Whereas the experimenter must keep himself impartial and neutral regarding the outcome of his investigation, the hypnotist must commit himself with an avowed partisanship to making his induction procedures "come true" for the subject.

Although no experimenter is ever disinterested in his experimental results, his role as scientist requires that he keep his normal enthusiasm and partisanship in abeyance, that he adopt the somewhat unnatural stance of skeptical objectivity in order to prevent prejudgments and unknown factors from confounding his results. Many investigators have succeeded so well in this laudible sterilization of procedure that they have thereby unwittingly tended to inhibit the fullest unfolding of the hypnotic processes supposedly under investigation. The posture of impartial neutrality simply does not evoke in subjects the enthusiastic expectancies and deep emotional commitments that mobilize and sustain the hypnotic processes.

PSYCHOLOGICAL CATALYST

A useful analogy can be drawn here to the well-known concept of catalysis as used in chemistry. Many chemical reactions take place rapidly and fully only in the presence of certain chemical substances, called catalysts, that are not themselves permanently altered in the chemical transformations they augment. Other chemical substances, called negative catalysts, impede the rate of certain chemical reactions.

Likewise, hypnotic processes are set into motion within the subject, strengthened, and brought to their fruition only when the positive psychological catalysts of assured confidence, expectant enthusiasm, and persuasive authority are present in notable concentrations. When these positive psychological catalysts are absent, insufficient, or offset by the negative psychological catalysts of skepticism, discouragement, and the impression of possible failure, then only diluted and incompleted versions of the hypnotic phenomena can generally be produced.

Whereas contemporary experimentalists often tend to provide insufficient positive catalyst, in earlier periods the problem was typically apparent as a contest between positive and negative factors. By way of illustration, for both John Elliotson and his critics in the 1830s the efficacy of mesmeric procedures signified either the existence of some unknown physical agency or outright fraud. With battle lines thus drawn, Elliotson explored the pragmatic usefulness of the unknown agency with little concern for its underlying nature; his critics hounded his efforts with vitriolic denunciation. This bitter and unrelenting opposition soon forced Elliotson and his band of loyal devotees to drift in the direction of cultism. Inasmuch as the mesmeric-hypnotic processes require for their fruition a marked superiority of positive catalysts, this drifting was necessary to generate the indispensable enthusiastic expectancies and deep emotional commitments from subjects. To be effective as mesmerists, Elliotson and his circle had to infuse their procedures with ever more evangelistic zeal to counteract the corrosive currents of skepticism and scorn gathering about them. But the increased fervor of their catalytic appeals itself provided more fuel for the polemics of their critics, augmenting even further the level of skepticism and scorn. By this spiral process, Elliotson's mesmeric structure was extended so far that it eventually collapsed, leaving behind the unwarranted residue of absurdity and charlatanism.[5]

THE VALIDATING TENDENCY

From an even broader perspective, however, the generic problem of relative catalyst is only one manifestation of the basic fact that hypnotized individuals tend to produce the responses that they believe are expected from them. At least since Puységur this tendency to conform to expectations has typically been described as a tenacious compulsion extending far beyond ordinary rational compliance; it is best characterized by terms such as inordinate responsiveness, remarkable docility, and hypersuggestibility. Whether these expectations stem from the verbal communications of the hypnotist while the subject is hypnotized, from cues implicit in the hypnotic situation, or from beliefs existing prior to hypnosis is irrelevant, as Braid for one so clearly noted. For example, Mesmer's nonverbal faith-healing procedures and the complex behavior they engendered were predicated in large measure on belief systems inculcated prior to induction.

This impulse to produce the expected responses obviously can not yield what is physically impossible. For example, in response to a hypnotist's directions to sprout wings and to fly, the subject, of course, will not develop a wingspan measurable by any material yardstick. But in response to such unrealizable hypnotic directions the proficient subject can secretly arrange at a nonconscious level to delude himself into believing with the fullest subjective conviction and sincerity that he has indeed grown wings and flown. In the most detailed and compelling subjective fantasy the proficient subject can spin a wondrous tale for himself and for his listeners.

Few observers would believe that a subject is flying when they see that he is not. But when a subject is given an impossible task that the hypnotist believes is possible, the subject can again secretly arrange with himself at a nonconscious level to find devious and clever methods of cheating in order to gratify the hypnotist with an outwardly convincing performance. Although in subtler guises the phenomenon of nonconscious deception is just as prevalent today, it was most blatant during the nineteenth century when the mesmerists believed that the somnambulist was endowed with clairvoyance and other paranormal powers. Before the inception of stringent controls, such as specially designed blindfolds, proficient somnambulists were able to give striking demonstrations of clairvoyance. But even when subjects were caught cheating, the allegations of fraud were sincerely

5. A similar drifting toward cultism characterized the Societies of Harmony (patterned after Freemasonry), organized by Mesmer's disciples for the promulgation of his teachings.

denied since the subject's secret arrangement with himself had been to delude his own subjective experience as well as to convince observers.

The hypnotized subject's impulsion to produce expected responses, which even incorporates his own subjective conviction, may also be described as the subject's impulsion to validate what he believes the hypnotist expects. Moreover, this tendency to validate the shared expectations is quite independent of the contents of these beliefs.

It will be recalled that it was this same tendency toward automatic validation that built the edifice of nineteenth century mesmeric extravagance. We noted earlier how each mesmerist was able to see his expectancies and as yet unformulated speculations repeatedly proved true before his eyes by his subjects' responses. The more the mesmerist's beliefs became trenchant and outspoken, the more unequivocally were they proved in the corresponding responses of his enthusiastic and committed subjects. Thus there was a natural selection in the direction of extravagance because the more reasonable and sober-minded mesmerists tended to exude weaker catalysts than investigators with wilder fantasies and blinder resolve. Thus the mesmerist was inexorably drawn down into the vortex of a conceptual whirlpool in which his expectations and unstated speculations were repeatedly validated by the responses of subjects strongly impelled to do so. This validation, of course, crystalized the shared expectations even further. Since each mesmerist tended to evolve his own variant belief system, and since each belief system—quite irrespective of its contents—would tend to be validated, it was inevitable that the whole wildly sprouting mesmeric edifice would eventually have to crumble under the weight of its own grossly unresolvable contradictions.

From a contemporary point of view, mesmerism is merely the quaint relic of a bygone era. In the more subdued tones of modern terminology, however, investigators are still being seductively lured into pseudologies by this same double-vectored process in which the hypnotist is trying his best to make the hypnotic procedures come true for his subjects, and the subjects in return are trying their best to make the hypnotist's fondest theoretical dreams come true—even if to comply sometimes requires that they secretly arrange to cheat and delude themselves. Under these mutually bewitching circumstances of trying to make shared expectations become functionally true for each other, wishes easily are made to appear as if so, and arbitrary artifices are easily made to appear as if they were natural law.

No investigator is such a paragon of scientific objectivity that he completely escapes blinding emotional commitment to his favorite hypotheses. Even the most brilliant and cautious of men have a sizable talent for intellectual self-delusion. When, however, as in the investigation of hypnosis, this penchant to self-delusion is harnessed to the hypnotized subject's validating tendency, it is extremely difficult—unless the most rigorous experimental controls are applied—for *any* investigator to avoid being drawn into the vortex of pseudology.

THE TWO GENERIC DANGERS

But as we have already seen, the moment an investigator tries to apply these necessary scientific controls he thereby leaves himself open to the danger of dashing his study against the rock of failing to give sufficient catalyst to subjects' enthusiasms and commitments. There are, to reiterate, two generic methodological dangers in hypnosis research which, like Scylla and Charybdis, are inextricable: the first is the danger of not providing sufficient disciplined skepticism, and the second is the danger of not providing sufficient positive catalyst. The more an investigator tries to avoid one of these two separate and distinct dangers, the more likely it becomes that he will succumb to the other.

In practical terms, the attitude of disciplined skepticism, so essential for building a realistic science, must not become such a blinding preoccupation that the investigator thereby becomes an inept hypnotist. But equally important, the hypnotist's exuding of confident persuasiveness, so essential for properly catalyzing the hypnotic processes, must not become such a blinding preoccupation that the investigator thereby loses his scientific objectivity. Thus, taking the "magic" out of hypnosis debilitates the phenomena but taking the "magic" too seriously deludes the investigator.

Investigators in the academic experimentalist's tradition have generally been most vulnerable to the danger of insufficient catalyst; investigators in the clinical practitioner's tradition have generally been most vulnerable to the danger of insufficient skepticism. The experimentalists have been mainly concerned with rigorous method and the practitioners mainly with improving their clinical skill and effectiveness. Attempts to understand and share each other's objectives and points of view unfortunately have frequently been hampered by clannish loyalties and polemics. This itself is another manifestation of the fundamental problem.

Postscript

In keeping with the aim of providing historic perspectives, this chapter is limited to discussing events sufficiently in the past to see their historic impact. Recent and current developments are consequently not reviewed. (See the remainder of this book and also Barber, 1969b; Brenman & Gill, 1947; Chertok, 1959, 1966; Gordon, 1967; Gormly, 1961; Hilgard, 1965b; Jenness, 1944; Kaufman, 1961; Marcuse, 1964; Pattie, 1958; R. Prince, 1968; Shor & Orne, 1965; Stukát, 1958; Szasz, 1963; Tart, 1969; Weitzenhoffer, 1953; Wolberg, 1945, 1948).

The questions that emerge from the past need to be pondered in relation to the present and future. How well have modern investigators learned to sail between Scylla and Charybdis? To what extent will modern viewpoints be seen through time as true advances—perhaps to a fifth stage of sophistication—and to what extent merely as changes to culturally more acceptable misnomers and disguised returns to old mistakes?

I shall not try to answer these questions because, regrettably, I do not know the answers. To try to speak with authority about the long-range impact of our present era would be premature. I can neither see into the future nor adopt the same degree of impartiality and objectivity toward the contemporary scene, in which I have deep personal commitments and hopes, as I can toward the more distant past. This chapter thus serves to raise questions; answers will inevitably come as the verdict of our posterity.

II

New Theories

Ernest R. Hilgard *is an Emeritus Professor of Psychology at Stanford University, still actively engaged in research and teaching. He received his Ph.D. in experimental psychology from Yale in 1930 and taught there until 1933, when he moved to Stanford where he has been ever since, except for an interruption for war service in Washington during World War II. His research activity has covered such fields as the experimental study of learning in animals and man, social influences upon level of aspiration, and problem solving. During the last two decades he has headed a Laboratory of Hypnosis Research in the Department of Psychology at Stanford. His books include* Theories of Learning, Introduction to Psychology, Hypnotic Susceptibility, Hypnosis in the Relief of Pain *(with Josephine R. Hilgard), and* Divided Consciousness. *He is Past President of the American Psychological Association, has served as President of the APA Division of Psychological Hypnosis, and as President of the International Society of Hypnosis.*

Hilgard *deals with some of the divisions of consciousness dramatically illustrated in his laboratory studies of hypnotically suggested analgesia and deafness, utilizing the "hidden observer" technique. The method has shown that the hypnotized subject, while oblivious to pain or to sounds, may, with some part of his cognitive apparatus, be processing the incoming information in a split-off or dissociated manner. The recovered information suggests that parallel processing of the information occurs, so that information is accepted and rejected simultaneously. Although these effects are limited to a small fraction of hypnotized subjects, these "pure cases" are thought to be important for their bearing on cognitive psychology.*

3

Divided Consciousness in Hypnosis: The Implications of the Hidden Observer

ERNEST R. HILGARD

A person can do more than one thing at a time, and usually does. Some things that he does are more automatic than others, and his attention is diverted to the less automatized activities. Driving a car while carrying on a conversation is a familiar example: the driver of the car, behaving automatically to a large extent, is still responsive to the road signs, the traffic signals, and the moving traffic as well, but these matters are handled with little investment of consciousness. Conversation runs smoothly until an unusual demand arises, requiring more attention be paid to the driving. Consciousness is both active and receptive, as "paying attention" implies. Hence in approaching problems of consciousness it is important to keep in mind the processes by which experience is controlled (the voluntary-involuntary distinction) as well as the receptive aspects of being aware (e.g., the conscious-subconscious distinction). These distinctions are familiar in ordinary experience, although our understanding of them is far from satisfactory.

The research upon which much of this chapter depends has been generously supported by a continuing grant from the National Institute of Mental Health (MH-03859), for which I am grateful. Many of the interpretations have been condensed from a book treating the problems at a greater length and in a nonhypnotic context as well (Hilgard, 1977a).

Other approaches to the hypnotic consciousness are possible. See for example Fromm (1977) and Chapter 4 in this volume.

Hypnosis bears on these problems because it serves both to magnify them and to dramatize their importance. In hypnosis, activities once voluntary may no longer be performed when the person desires to perform them, or they may take place involuntarily; activities usually involuntary may come under voluntary control. Things ordinarily remembered with ease may be blocked from memory 'temporarily, only to be recovered promptly at a signal. Through appropriate suggestions the hypnotized person may engage in automatic writing without knowing what his hand is doing; at the same time he may openly engage in another activity, such as reading aloud from a book. These happenings within hypnosis are largely exaggerations of things that happen normally outside hypnosis; they are readily found when they are looked for. As we understand hypnosis better we ought also come to understand consciousness and personality better, independent of hypnosis.

Executive and Monitoring Functions in Hypnosis

To describe what happens in hypnosis as an *altered state of consciousness* (ASC) may overlook the fact that an alteration in control systems is more often in evidence than any profound change in subjective experience. That is, the change from waking to hypnosis may not feel anything like the change from waking to sleep or from sobriety to alcoholic intoxication. The hypnotized person may carry on a very normal conversation and be fully aware of the surroundings, even while having a paralyzed or anesthetized arm as a consequence of the hypnotic interaction. Modification of central control systems is more familiar in hypnosis than any widespread alteration in consciousness of the self or of the environment. Lack of widespread experiences of altered consciousness occasionally cause hypnotically responsive subjects to insist that they were not hypnotized.

Alteration of the subjective experience as a whole—altered state of consciousness—is a matter of degree, and under some circumstances of deep hypnosis profound changes do take place. When profound and significant changes occur they lead to such descriptive expressions as "timelessness," "pure being," or "ecstasy." These alterations, prominent in discussions of human potential and consciousness expansion, are worthy of investigation and interpretation. In the more usual behavior of the hypnotized person, shown in responses to specific suggestions of the hypnotist, the changes in experience that occur are often very moderate ones. In this chapter, attention is directed to the more moderate changes as they are reflected in the experiments under consideration, particularly experiments on the hypnotic reduction of pain and hearing. In such instances, the changes in control and monitoring processes are more in evidence than pervasive changes in the quality of consciousness.

The acceptability of central controls, in the form of executive and monitoring functions, does not mean that all behavior and experience must be referred to them. What happens is that once an activity is under way it becomes relatively self-sustaining. Woodworth (1918) recognized this long ago in his principle that any activity once aroused may generate its own "drive," and Allport (1937) later indicated that motives may lose connections with their origins and become "functionally autonomous" in sustaining behavior.

To represent the fact that subsytems have some measure of autonomy when actuated, while at the same time subject to central control, I earlier presented the diagram of Figure 3.1. At the time I referred to the subsystems

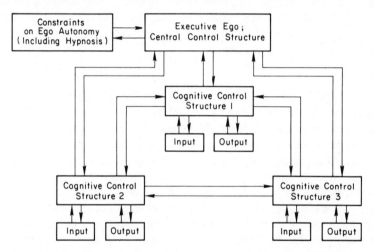

FIGURE 3.1. *Subsystems conceived as Cognitive Control Structures.* (Hilgard, 1973b, p. 405.)

as cognitive control structures, and I included both executive and monitoring functions as part of an executive ego. To indicate that the executive is not entirely a free agent, the box at the upper left indicates that there are constraints upon it. The positions of the three cognitive substructures is designed to symbolize their hierarchical nature, so that one of them may be actuated while the others are latent. The position in the hierarchy is subject to change. Each substructure is shown to have its own input and output, hence a degree of autonomy and automatization of activity in the subsystem as actuated.

Hypnosis may modify executive and monitoring functions so that the hierarchical relationships of the subsystems are changed. What was voluntary may become involuntary; what was involuntary may come under voluntary control; what was perceived may not now be perceived; something absent in perception may be hallucinated. Hence some subsystems are split off from their usual relationships and it is this split-off character that is described as dissociative.

HOW HYPNOSIS PRODUCES A READINESS FOR DISSOCIATIVE EXPERIENCE

Hypnosis typically requires an initial agreement to cooperate in the generation of the behaviors that are expected without, however, requiring a play-acting of the roles to please the hypnotist. This initial agreement to cooperate, to let happen what happens is sometimes referred to as the hypnotic contract (Hodge, 1976). The requirement of an initial agreement to cooperate in not unique to hypnosis and does not reflect on the genuineness of the subsequent hypnotic experience. Initial cooperation is needed also in a memory experiment if recall is desired that goes beyond what would be found in uninstructed incidental memory. The difference between intentional and incidental memory provides acceptable and important scientific data.

The hypnotic induction that follows the initial agreement provides a training ground for the cooperative subject to learn what it is like to experience what he can of hypnotic behavior. Again, such preliminary acquaintance is not unique to hypnosis. In reaction-time experiments, or investigations of perceptual discrimination or psychological tests—whenever the context is unfamiliar—some initial experience or training is provided before the main measurements are made. What is measured is not solely a result of learning, for the basic differences in talent that are revealed are better measured after they are stabilized through the initial experience.

Included in this initiation is a preparation for dissociative experience brought about in a number of ways. The familiar eye-closure illustrates the role of the "double-bind" (Haley, 1958) in which the suggestion to keep looking at the target conflicts with the suggestion that the eyes are tired, and soon will be closing "of themselves." The resolution is that "I" am holding my eyes open but "they" are closing involuntarily. This division of the two control systems is itself an illustration of dissociation, and provides a readiness for further dissociative experiences. Stress on muscular relaxation assists in disorientation, because one of the ways in which we keep oriented is to know where our hands and feet are. People are usually moving a little, adjusting their clothing, putting their hands to their faces, changing position in a chair. With immobility these ties to reality are weakened, and dissociations are more readily accepted.

The disruption of memory is very important in the total process. The continuity of memories is basic to self-awareness. When consciousness is interrupted by sleep or in other ways, the sense of self is restored by reorientation through memory. The hypnotist says that in the session there will be no cares, nothing will bother the subject. When the hypnotist says, "Think only of my words," the implication is that everything familiar will be set aside. When the need to plan is diminished, the memory function is weakened. With the weakening of memory, critical abilities are also lost, for reality judgments are made by bringing memory to bear on the present to decide whether the present conforms to previously experienced reality. With critical abilities reduced, imagination readily becomes hallucination.

The nature of the cognitive condition of a highly hypnotizable person when hypnotized is well characterized by the responses of a few highly hypnotized subjects when confronted with the broken watch suggestion on one of our susceptibility scales (Weitzenhoffer & Hilgard, 1967). A hypnotized person is told that when the eyes are open a broken watch will be seen, with the long minute hand operating, but the shorter hour hand missing. Ordinarily the working memory, as it has come to be called, would keep the subsequent events in order; that is, I am about to be confronted with a broken watch. This does seem to occur, for the subjects, when they open their eyes, see a defective watch, with the hour hand not perceived because it is negatively hallucinated. However, the meaning of the absent hour hand as the sign of a defective watch may be ignored because of a failure of the continuity of the working memory. When asked to tell the time, the subject may ignore the context entirely, and react as if the watch is not defective but has the hour hand concealed beneath the minute hand. Hence, although the watch may read 11:10, it is read as though the time is 2:10, the reading determined by the perceived minute hand. The subject has not lost that aspect of memory which includes the residues of earlier experience, for the information from the past that the watch was to appear defective has been retained. This information is dissociated, however, from the working memory, and the subject acts on the information given by the watch as now perceived, independent of the source of the perception. The crucial correctives against distortion that working memory ordinarily provides are missing.

EXECUTIVE FUNCTIONS IN HYPNOSIS

The central executive functions in hypnosis are typically thought to be divided between the hypnotist and the hypnotized person. Hypnotized persons retain a considerable portion of their executive functions from the normal state; they can answer questions about their past and about plans for the future; they can accept or reject invitations to move about, or to participate in particular kinds of activities. At the same time, they turn over some of their executive functions to the hypnotist, so that, within the hypnotic contract, they will do what the hypnotist suggests, experience what they are told to experience, and lose control of movements. The retained and relinquished fractions will depend upon circumstances, including the degree of hypnotic responsiveness or talent that the subject brings to hypnosis, and the depth of involvement in hypnosis as a function of what transpires between subject and hypnotist.

The central executive functions typically become sufficiently divided that the usual initiative of the executive is lost. The planning function is inhibited, and the hypnotized person does not independently undertake new lines of thought or action. The hypnotized person, asked to behave normally in the presence of other people while remaining hypnotized, may find the effort distasteful and end up by seeking out a comfortable chair in which to relax away from other people.

Self-hypnosis well illustrates how the executive functions may be divided, as one part represents the role of the hypnotist, the other part the hypnotized. Although this appears essentially irrational, it is no more irrational than heterohypnosis, in which dissociated controls are the very essence of what happens. In fact, usual heterohypnosis may be thought of as primarily "aided self-hypnosis" with an external hypnotist present; the person accepts the aid of the hypnotist in order to hypnotize himself. It has often been supposed that self-hypnosis must be a response to the posthypnotic suggestion by a subject who has "internalized" the hypnotist. This interpretation is not quite correct, for with the barest of instructions a subject can begin to engage in self-hypnosis, even if he or she has never had the experience of being hypnotized by another (Ruch, 1975). Surprising as it may seem, hypnotically responsive subjects may suggest to themselves that an arm will become stiff until they give themselves a release signal, and they may be unable to bend that arm, no matter how hard they try. When they exercise the release suggestion agreed upon by themselves, such as counting to five, the arm will become normal again. This is the essence of the split of the executive function in hypnosis. There is a retained normal part that has permitted the hypnotized part to become active and that observes what happens. There is also the hypnotized part which, in its own sphere, exerts considerable strength in conflict with the residual normal executive.

MONITORING FUNCTIONS IN HYPNOSIS

After the executive functions have "issued orders" to the monitoring functions to reduce the amount of critical scanning, to relinquish, as Shor (1970) has put it, the usual "reality orientation," the monitoring functions recede, without completely destroying the observing function. That is, the monitoring function may report, "The arm is now stiff," a correct interpretation of the phenomenal reality, without showing an understanding of the causes of the arm's stiffness. In the normal waking condition the monitoring functions are satisfactorily integrated as they perceive and account for the information that becomes available from the external world and from the body. In hypnosis, reality is distorted, more or less, according to the degree of hypnotic involvement, often with a large fraction of normal monitoring retained. A subject who is hypnotically analgesic or deaf, or amnesic for a list of words previously learned, is still able to use the unaffected senses normally, and has access to his usually available memories, except for those specifically obliterated by the suggestions. The characteritic distortion that can be used to indicate a partial fractionation of the monitoring functions is the uncritical acceptance of distorted reality as though it were undistorted, without making the usual reality tests. Examples of hypnotic distortion include hallucinations, both positive and negative. The exact relation between the monitoring and the actuated subsystem is not readily specified. For example, in age regression the subject may feel himself to be a child again on the playground of the third grade in school. The details of this actuated experience, whether it is a reliving of an actual experience or a fantasy construction, are reported accurately by the monitor. The activated subsystem—the child in age regression—does not use all the information about how the regression was suggested and produced, and the monitoring functions do not offer any correction for this omission. This lack of normal criticism was called "trance logic" by Orne (1959) who used as his illustration the ready acceptance of the hallucination of a person who was the double of one actually present. The point is that, within hypnosis, the monitoring functions have been limited until their full capacities are reactivated by terminating hypnosis.

Except for some information denied it and the lack of the criticism shown by the failure to insist on reality tests, much of the normal monitoring function is retained in hypnosis at the ordinary levels of involvement. The metaphor has long been used of a normal observer standing in the wings and watching the actuated hypnotic subsystem perform at the center of the stage. Macmillan (1977) has attributed this form of characterizing the hypnotic experience to the French philosopher and critic Hippolyte Taine (1878). Taine described this as a doubling of the self *(doublement du moi),* a position coherent with the dissociation viewpoint.

Hypnotic Concealment of Normally Conscious Experiences

Alterations in both executive and monitoring functions through hypnosis find their conscious representation most clearly in experiences that are denied conscious representation, as in the memories concealed through hypnotic amnesia and in closely related phenomena. A brief summarization is given here in order to provide a background for attempts described later to recover some of these concealed processes or events.

AMNESIA

The experience of posthypnotic amnesia, discovered in the 1700's by

Puységur, became the hallmark of hypnosis. This led to the conception of somnambulism and of the highly hypnotizable person as a somnambulist or somnambule. Hypnosis resembled sleepwalking because the person did things as though awake, but, like a sleepwalker, forgot them when aroused from hypnosis. It was thought for a time—and some still believe this to be the case—that a very highly responsive subject will be spontaneously amnesic for events within hypnosis. However, this may be a result of expectations created by the folklore of hypnosis, and in laboratory experimentation such *spontaneous* amnesia is very rare, although *suggested* posthypnotic anmesia is readily produced in about a fourth of unselected college students (Hilgard & Cooper, 1965). By tradition, amnesia is usually posthypnotic, but it is readily produced within hypnosis by direct suggestion; consequently there is no need to change the state from hypnosis to nonhypnosis in order to produce amnesia. For a fuller account see the chapter by Cooper in this book, and a summary by Kihlstrom (1977b).

In amnesia memories have not been destroyed; instead their retrieval has been inhibited, until a release signal reverses the amnesia and the memories (with minor exceptions, Kihlstrom and Evans, 1977) are available as before. Hence what we see is an alteration of a control system (one that usually permits retrieval of freshly stored memories), a system that can be manipulated through suggestion either to conceal or to reveal. Consciousness has been altered in its contents, not in its flavor.

AUTOMATIC WRITING

Another illustration of concealment is provided by automatic writing, in which a hand can carry out an intellectual task while the subject does not know that the task is being performed, even if the subject is performing another task. The method originated in the studies of psychic researchers, but was early picked up by psychotherapists and used (without the implication of spirit control) fairly widely in the late nineteenth century and early twentieth. It went out of favor, and the book by Mühl (1930) represents the last extended discussion of it.

Experiments by Messerschmidt (1927-1928), performed under Hull's supervision and thoroughly reported in his book (Hull, 1933), were directed at the proposal that the two tasks, one conscious and one subconscious, should not interfere, a conclusion derived from an extreme form of dissociation theory which implied that the two tasks should be completely isolated from each other. The conscious tasks Messerschmidt used were the oral reading of words or oral additions; the subconscious tasks were written additions. She showed that the tasks, even though one was performed subconsciously, did indeed interfere with each other.

In an extension of her work, employing a design originally used by Cass

(1942), two investigations were carried out in the Stanford laboratory. The first of these, appearing second in journal publication, was that of Stevenson (1976). The tasks he used were conscious color naming as interfering with (and interfered by) two forms of arithmetic operations carried out in automatic writing: the first, an easier counting task; the second, a more difficult task of successive additions. His results agreed with those of Messerschmidt in finding interference between the two tasks, whether the arithmetic was done consciously or subconsciously. In addition, however, he showed that some impairment was due to the effort to meet the requirement of amnesia when automatic writing was subconscious. This was apparent when the arithmetic was done alone, without interference by color naming; even then the arithmetic suffered when it was done subconsciously. Simulators, pretending to be hypnotized, did not have to maintain any true amnesia; they succeeded with the same tasks with much less interference. Stevenson's interpretation was that some attentive effort is required to divert conscious attention away from the task to sustain the amnesia, and this interferes with the subconscious performance. He found, as Messerschmidt had, that the more difficult the subconscious task, the more the interference by the conscious one.

The second of the experiments, by Knox, Crutchfield, and Hilgard (1975), was similar to that of Stevenson, but it permitted a more microscopic analysis of the strategies used in doing the two tasks at once. With both tasks conscious, several strategies could be used for overcoming the interference. Generally, the subconscious task was key-pressing a series of 3R-3L (three presses on the right key, followed by three on the left, repeatedly); the conscious task was always color-naming. What the subjects tended to do when both tasks were conscious was to "store" the next pressing sequence, announce the name of the color, then press the sequence, say 3-R, name another color, then 3-L, and so on. Other strategies were used, but each had some evident structure integrating the two tasks. These strategies broke down when the key-pressing was subconscious, as if an effort was being made, not too successfully, to carry out the two tasks independently of each other.

ANALGESIA

The denial of painful experiences, shown repeatedly in the use of hypnosis in major surgery in the early 1800's, is today one of the areas of greatest usefulness of hypnosis (Hilgard & Hilgard, 1975). The relationship between measured hypnotic responsiveness and the capacity to reduce pain in the laboratory has been demonstrated repeatedly, as indicated in Figure 3.2.

There are some puzzling issues in the reduction of pain by hypnosis. For one thing, there are claims that waking suggestion is as effective as hypnosis,

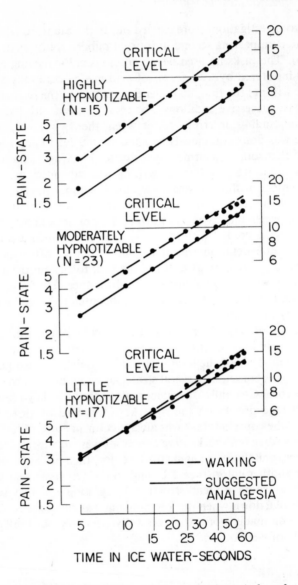

FIGURE 3.2. *Hypnotic reduction of overt pain by sub-jects classified according to levels of measured hyp-notizability. In each group the upper line represents nor-mal nonhypnotic pain, the lower, pain reduced at the overt level by hypnotic analgesia suggestions.* (Hilgard, 1967, p. 1582.)

provided analgesia suggestions are given as in Evans & Paul (1970).

However, in their study they interpreted as noninduction a 25-minute period of self-relaxation, which for a hypnotically responsive person may be equivalent to autohypnosis, and their data give no indication as to what fraction of their random groups were responsive to the pain reduction suggestions. Later studies have shown that waking suggestion, when not preceded by the equivalent of induction, is not as effective as hypnotic suggestion (Hilgard, Macdonald, Morgan, and Johnson, 1978). A second question has been raised by a study of J. Barber (1977), in which dental procedures were performed without discomfort following a specific procedure stressing relaxation and comfort, said to produce results independent of measured hypnotic susceptibility. The issues involved are discussed later in this chapter.

Another point, on which nearly all investigators agree, is that a paradox is involved in that even when pain is reduced, the physiological indicators of stress have not been reduced in hypnotic (or waking suggested) analgesia beyond what they are in the ordinary experience of pain (Barber & Hahn, 1962; Evans & Paul, 1970; Hilgard, 1967b, 1971; Shor, 1962a; Sutcliffe, 1961). The evidence on the other side is to be noted (Lenox, 1970; Sachs, 1970), but the generalization is still permissible that physiological indicators of pain commonly persist within hypnotic analgesia.

DEAFNESS

Suggested hypnotic deafness is also correlated with measured hypnotic susceptibility. This was shown earlier in the Stanford Profile Scales (Weitzenhoffer & Hilgard, 1967), but the deafness was rather crudely measured by the distance at which a ticking watch could be heard. A more careful experiment performed in the Stanford laboratory led to results similar to those with pain (Figure 3.3). The correlation between measured reduction in hearing and hypnotic responsiveness was the same for hearing as it was for pain, $r = .50$.

It is quite probable that the physiological indicators of hearing persist in hypnotic deafness, as those for pain exist in analgesia (Halliday and Mason, 1964b).

These examples of the reduction of normally conscious experiences within hypnosis suffice to show an important aspect of the hypnotic control over consciousness.

The Recovery of Concealed Experiences: The Hidden Observer Method

A chance observation in a laboratory demonstration led to a new direction in the exploration of the hypnotic consciousness in our laboratory. The details have been presented elsewhere, and need not be repeated here (Hilgard, 1973b, 1977a & b). What happened was that a hypnotically deaf

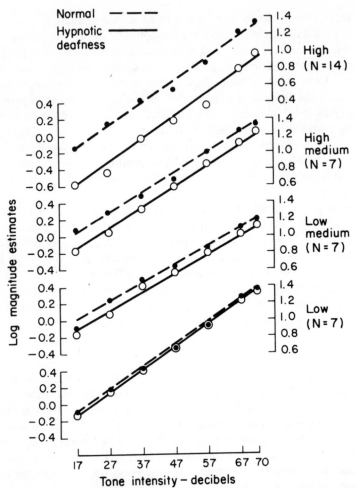

FIGURE 3.3. *Hypnotic reduction of overt hearing by subjects classified according to levels of measured hypnotizability. The dashed lines with open circles represent the level of normal hearing within hypnosis without deafness suggestions; the solid lines with solid dots represent the reported overt hearing within hypnotically suggested deafness. The upper three groups all reduced their hearing; the lowest hypnotizables reported little change in hearing.* (Crawford, Macdonald and Hilgard, in press.)

subject was asked in a quiet voice, while still deaf, to permit the index finger of his right hand to rise if "some part" of him was hearing the hypnotist's voice. The finger rose, and the subject asked to have his hearing restored because he felt the finger rise, but did not know what had been done to him. This led to an inquiry by an "automatic talking" technique, in which he was told that, when the hypnotist placed a hand on his arm, there would be contact with a concealed part of himself, unknown to the hypnotized part, that could describe what had gone on while he was deaf, but would recede again when the hypnotist's hand was lifted. The subject, under these circumstance, gave a description of what he had heard while deaf; when the hypnotist's hand was lifted, and he was questioned, he recalled something having been said about his talking, and asked: "Did I talk?" The metaphor of a "hidden observer" has since been used to describe the part of him that knew what was going on, without implying that there is a homunculus inside him responsible for such observations.

There are seldom any genuine discoveries in psychology; instead advances are made by subjecting earlier discovered phenomena to systematic study. In the early history of hypnosis, "double consciousness" was a favorite topic and many of the illustrations were of phenomena similar to those of a hidden observer (Binet, 1889-1890; Dessoir, 1890). These responses were usually confined to hysterical persons, however, and considered to be anomalies associated with that disorder. That is, the hysterical person might be unable to tell whether touched by one or two points of an esthesiometer, yet, if the subconscious part was whispered to, the patient might describe accurately what took place. William James (1889) reported a clear instance of an anesthetized arm that on subsequent inquiry by automatic writing gave a satisfactorily accurate report of the times the arm had been pricked. Later Estabrooks (1943) and Kaplan (1960) reported somewhat similar cases. These few isolated and somewhat ambiguous case reports were never followed up so that the exact circumstances leading to the phenomenon could become known. The work reported here is the first, to my knowledge, in which an initial observation of the revelation of the concealed experience led to systematic investigation. The single case of the hypnotically deaf subject reported above came at an appropriate time when our laboratory had been investigating both automatic writing and hypnotic analgesia. Hence, more extended investigation was possible with techniques already available.

THE HIDDEN OBSERVER REVEALED BY AUTOMATIC WRITING

It was soon found in pilot experiments that highly hypnotizable subjects, experienced in hypnotic pain reduction, would report pain as completely absent while one hand was immersed in circulating ice water. At the same time, while reports of zero pain were given when magnitude estimates were called for, the other hand, concealed from view, and writing automatically, would report pain with ascending magnitude the longer the hand was immersed in the water. The level of pain approached but remained somewhat below the pain normally felt in the ice water when not hypnotized.

Systematic experimentation was then undertaken with less experienced subjects. Experiments were limited to those who could reduce their pain by a third or more through suggested hypnotic analgesia. For them it turned out that the maximum pain reported in automatic writing was consistently the same as that reported by the automatic talking technique, the maximum typically lower than in the normal waking condition. The advantage in automatic writing was that covert pain could be reported simultaneously with the overt pain, and the course of pain followed at both levels of report. An illustration of the course of normal overt pain, pain reported overtly (verbally) in hypnotic analgesia, and pain reported covertly by automatic writing while anesthetized, is given for cold pressor pain (the pain of circulating ice water) in Figure 3.4.

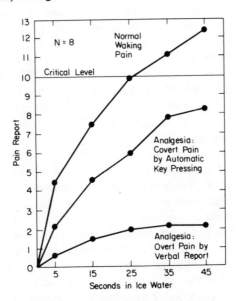

FIGURE 3.4. *Pain of ice water ("cold pressor pain"): normal waking pain; overt pain in hypnotic analgesia; covert pain in hypnotic analgesia by "hidden observer" technique, using automatic key-pressing as equivalent to automatic writing.* (Hilgard, 1977, p. 190; data from Hilgard, Morgan, and Macdonald, 1975.)

THE HIDDEN OBSERVER REVEALED BY AUTOMATIC TALKING

Analgesia. It is not quite correct to say that the automatic writing technique is necessary to obtain essentially simultaneous reports of overt and covert pain. In the form of ischemic pain that we have used (pain produced by a tourniquet to the upper arm, followed by exercise, as developed by Smith et al., 1966), there is more time for reporting because the pain mounts in minutes rather than in seconds, as it does in ice water pain. With ischemic pain it is possible to alternate reports of overt and covert pain over the course of the experiment. This is accomplished by asking for the usual verbal report of overt pain during the suggested hypnotic analgesia every two minutes. Immediately following this overt report, the hypnotist places a hand on the subject's shoulder, the signal for covert pain. The pain report now called for is a covert report from the hidden observer. When the hand is removed the previous condition is restored, so that when the next report is called for it will be a usual overt one.

In order to prepare for hidden observer reports when the experimenter's hand is placed on the subject's shoulder, the following instructions have been given in advance under hypnosis:

> When I place my hand on your shoulder, I shall be able to talk to a hidden part of you that knows things that are going on in your body, things that are unknown to the part of you to which I am now talking. The part to which I am now talking will not know what you are telling me or even that you are talking. When I remove my hand from your shoulder your memories will be just as they are now.

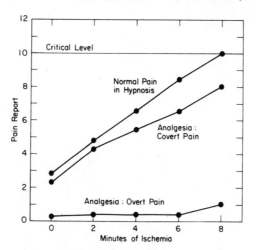

FIGURE 3.5. *Pain of tourniquet to upper arm, followed by limited exercise ("ischemic pain"): normal pain in hypnosis without analgesia; overt pain in hypnotic analgesia; covert pain reported in analgesia by intermittent "automatic talking" with hidden observer technique.* (Modified from Knox, Morgan, and Hilgard, 1974, p. 844.)

For those who are able to uncover a concealed experience of pain (about half of those who reduce their pains substantially through hypnotically suggested analgesia) this rapid alternation between overt and covert reporting causes no problems. Such rapid alternations of conditions have been used for many years in other contexts by Blum (e.g., Blum, This volume).

Results for ischemic pain, with the verbal reports alternated between the usual ones (overt) and the ones called automatic talking by analogy with automatic writing (covert) are plotted in Figure 3.5. The results are essentially alike for cold pressor pain and ischemic pain, despite the differences in arrangements and in the methods of reporting.

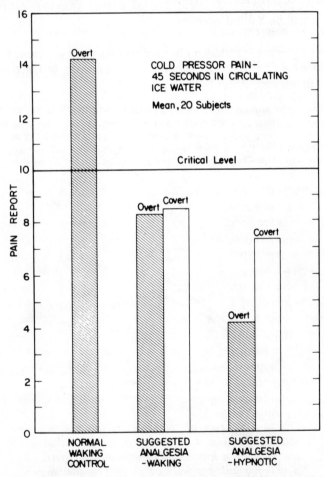

FIGURE 3.6 *Overt and covert pain with suggested analgesia in waking condition and in hypnotic condition; cold pressor pain.* (Hilgard and Hilgard, 1975, p. 171.)

We are left with two questions about each case. First: Why does the covert pain fall below the normal pain? Second: Why do some subjects report a hidden observer, and others do not?

Some data from the cold pressor experiments indicate a possible answer to the first question. We find, as Figure 3.6 shows, that for hypnotizable subjects, overt pain is less reduced by waking suggestion than by the same suggestions following induction of hypnosis. In order to obtain a report of covert pain in waking suggestion, it was necessary to hypnotize the subject after completing the waking suggestion portion of the experiment, and then to inquire by the hidden observer technique whether there had been any concealed or covert pain. When this was done, the data of Figure 3.6 provided the answer to the first question. Following a waking suggestion of analgesia, the pain reported overtly and covertly were alike, so that there was no indication of hidden or covert pain. By contrast, for these same subjects the overt pain in hypnotic analgesia, reduced below the level achieved in waking suggestion, recovered somewhat at the covert level; it recovered to the level reported in waking analgesia. It appears that the pain reduced in waking therefore persists at that reduced level in hypnotic analgesia, when tested by the hidden observer technique. A two-component interpretation of pain reduction through suggestion and hypnosis is implied. The first component, attributable to waking sugestion, is available also to less hypnotizable subjects. As is noted later on, this component may be due to relaxation and reduced anxiety, something of which nonhypnotizables are capable. The second component is available only to those more responsive to hypnosis. It is the component that can be recovered in the form of covert pain by the more hypnotizable. This recovery has so much in common with recovery from posthypnotic amnesia that the inner mechanisms are probably similar.

The answer to the second question—why the hidden observer method yields reports of covert experience for some, but not all, of those who are able to reduce pain and hearing as a result of hypnotic suggestion—is more difficult. A hidden observer has been reported in half of those subjects studied in pain experiments who were able to reduce their overt pains by at least a third in hypnotic analgesia. No obvious differences in hypnotizability or responsiveness to amnesia suggestions can be detected to separate those who do and those who do not report hidden observers but, based on interviews with subjects, two explanations may be proposed for the absence of reports of covert pain. The first is that for a limited number of those not reporting a hidden observer, access to the two experiences—overt and covert—is available to the subject without the hidden observer technique; such subjects report that the usual covert experience is forced out of attention during hypnosis but can occasionally be sampled. Hence, with the hidden observer technique, there is nothing new to report. A second possibility is that the amnesia for the experience that has never been conscious may be too profound to be recovered from some subjects by the methods used. The matter of depth of amnesia is suggested in part by comparison with recovery by automatic writing. In automatic writing the subject is assigned to do a task before the automatic writing occurs. Although he is amnesic for what he has written, or even that he has written, when the hidden observer method was used with automatic writing in an experiment with pain, twelve out of twelve highly hypnotizable subjects recovered covert experience of the automatic writing, whereas only six of the same twelve recovered covert pain by the technique. In that case it would not be any resistance to the idea of a hidden observer that impeded the report of covert pain, for the resistance was not shown in respect to automatic writing. However, more information was available about the automatic writing before the memory was recovered because the automatic writing had been suggested in the manner of a posthypnotic response. The pain that was concealed in hypnotic analgesia had not been a performance that was known to have occurred; that is, it was merely the absence of something that might have been felt. Hence, the recovery of the automatic writing performance was more like ordinary amnesia, and easier than the recovery of pain.

The question may be raised about the influence of the strong demands for compliance that are made in the hidden observer method. When the real-simulator design of Orne (this volume) was used, it was found that the demands created by the hidden observer instructions were strong enough that the low hypnotizables simulating hypnosis could predict very well the *objective* behavior of responsive high hypnotizables, and hence could imitate their objective performances when simulating hypnosis (Hilgard, Hilgard, Macdonald, Morgan, and Johnson, 1978). The differences between the reals and simulators were clear, however, in their reported *subjective* experiences. The reals insisted on the genuineness of their testimony, both as to the reduced pain in analgesia, and the increase in pain during the hidden observer condition. The simulators reported that subjectively they had been uninfluenced by any of the suggestive procedures except one: the suggestion of waking analgesia, in which their pains had been slightly reduced. While simulating, they tended to report overt pain in hypnotic analgesia below that of the reals; such overreaction is familiar in simulation experiments. In common with this tendency to overreact, the simulators accepted the idea of hidden observer more frequently than the reals. For the reals, some who in advance accepted the idea of a hidden observer failed to discover any; some who thought it a strange and implausible idea were surprised to find that they indeed had a covert experience to report.

Deafness. The hidden observer method was also used in the study of deafness. The overt reports from the study have already been described

(Figure 3.3). Because the tones to be reported were presented in fairly rapid succession, randomized in their loudness, the hidden observer reports were obtained at the end of the session, with a report of the remembered covert magnitude of the loudest of the tones. The hidden observer method is appropriate only for those who have substantially reduced their hearing under the conditions of hypnotic deafness. To determine what fraction of the subjects report covert hearing above overt hearing in hypnosis without deafness instructions, the criterion was established of including all subjects who reduced their overt hearing by a fraction equal to or greater than that of the subject with the least reduction who reported a change between the overt and covert report. The criterion adopted was a reduction of twenty percent. When this was done, there were twelve subjects who reported a modified covert report (indicating a hidden observer), and twenty-one subjects who did not (giving no evidence of a hidden observer). The reports of the two groups of subjects are shown in Figure 3.7.

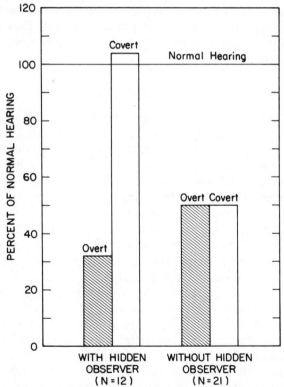

FIGURE 3.7. *Overt and covert deafness in subjects capable of hearing reduction by 20 percent or more through hypnotic suggestion: Those with and without access to "hidden observer" reports.* (Crawford, Macdonald, and Hilgard, in press.)

Although there was a slight tendency for those with the greater hearing loss following suggested deafness to be the ones most likely to report a hidden observer, the differences in these small groups did not prove statistically significant.

Analgesia and deafness compared. Records exist for seventeen subjects who participated in both the analgesia experiments (cold pressor) and the deafness experiments with interrogation by the hidden observer method. In general, subjects had more difficulty in reducing hearing than pain. All seventeen of these very highly hypnotizable subjects reduced their pain by more than thirty percent, but only twelve of them reduced their hearing by that much. Comparability was shown, however, in that there was a rank order correlation of .54 between pain and hearing reduction.

Consistency was shown also in the presence or absence of a hidden observer as indicated by covert reports in both analgesia and deafness. Of the seventeen subjects fourteen were consistent, with six reporting hidden observers in both conditions, eight in neither condition. This left three subjects inconsistent, one who reported a hidden observer only in deafness, and two only in pain.

PROBLEMS IN THE USE OF THE HIDDEN OBSERVER METHOD

The dramatic results occasionally found by the use of the hidden observer method must not be permitted to obscure the difficulties limiting its wider use. At least with performances as difficult as the reduction of intense pain and the hearing of suprathreshold tone, the method is applicable only to the very hypnotizable, perhaps not over one to five percent of an unselected student population. Hence, in selecting an appropriate sample, a great many subjects have to be screened for their hypnotic responsiveness, and even the top scorers on the widely used hypnotic responsiveness tests have to be tested with more difficult items if appropriate selection is to be made.

Despite some uncertainties about the extent to which consistently high scorers on these scales can be produced by training the initially low responders, there is no doubt that among the initially highly responsive subjects special hypnotic performances can be improved with practice. Automatic writing, for example, is strange even for the highly responsive and is better made use of in quantitative studies after there has been practice. A difficulty arises, of course, in that the practice also imposes strong demands upon the subject because the practice is aimed at producing behavior of the kind the experimenter desires (Orne, 1962b). Experimenters must exercise care to distinguish between what they have produced and what they have discovered; there are no specific methodological rules to protect investigators when they are seeking to open the paths that give access to the phenomena that may interest them. It is reassuring that many subjects do not respond to demands for compliance, so that the underlying abilities according to which subjects differ come into focus. The circumstance of selection plus training is not so different from that of a coach who is interested in producing record-breaking high jumpers. It is clear enough what he wants, but only a few can comply even if they wish to. The promising ones who are accepted are then improved by training, with the advice and help of the coach. The hypnotist-experimenter is protected from misleading results due to compliance by the honesty of the subject when questioned about subjective experience. Honesty reports, obtained in interviews following hypnotic experiences, are both revealing and convincing, especially if the questioning is done by someone other than the hypnotist-experimenter (Bowers, 1967).

A pilot study was performed before adopting the strongly demanding hidden observer instructions. The automatic writing technique was used. In one set of instructions nothing at all was said about a hidden part of the person, the assumption being that instructions to report by a hand that was doing subconscious writing would suffice. It turned out that under these circumstances most subjects simply duplicated their overt reports. It is difficult enough to retain amnesia for automatic writing, without having to engage in a more difficult task, and apparently even these highly hypnotizable subjects settled on doing what was easiest. At a second level of demand, the suggestion was made very mildly that there might or might not be some registration different from that overtly reported. This resulted in more hidden observers, but not all of those who had previously shown hidden observers by the automatic talking method gave evidence of them through automatic writing. Only when the idea of some latent part was made more positive, and that this part would be controlling the hand, did the automatic writing conform to the reports of automatic talking.

That it is necessary to strongly invite the possibility of an alternate form of experiencing is evident from the failure of subjects in earlier experiments to give any indication of concealed pain. In some 10 years of prior experimentation with pain reduction, we never had a spontaneous report of a concealed pain experience differing from the reduced pain that was reported in hypnotic analgesia. These reports emerged only when they were specifically requested after the hidden observer method had been stumbled upon.

As noted earlier, the real-simulator control demonstrated that there were strong compliance demands within the adopted hidden observer instructions, so that, in their objective reports, the simulators were quite able to fake the hidden observer results. Their subjective reports, honestly given, were convincingly different from those of the truly hypnotized.

Implications of the Hidden Observer Method for Research

Much remains to be done with respect to the findings of the hidden observer method itself, particularly to resolve the puzzle why some highly responsive hypnotizable subjects, successful in reducing pain and hearing at the overt level, are able to recover overt experiences while others are not. The possibility that two levels'of amnesia are involved needs to be carefully explored. In pilot experiments in our laboratory we have been unable to find more than one concealed level; that is, we have been unable to hypnotize at the hidden observer level, and then uncover another level below this. The concept of level may indeed be an inappropriate one. Some experienced clinicians, however, believe that there are two levels of hypnotic pain reduction below normal pain: one at which the pain can be recovered; the other at which it cannot, perhaps because it is not then experienced at all. Cheek and LeCron (1968) believe that it is only when pain has been eliminated at the subconscious level that the healing processes (in the case of organic pain) are furthered by the hypnotic pain therapy. These major claims require more research demonstration than they have received before they can be admitted as established scientific knowledge.

The method of interrogation that Cheek has used widely in his studies of recovery of memories within chemical anesthesia is, of course, closely related (e.g., Cheek, 1959, 1961, 1964, 1966). He has used a finger signaling method, in which he receives answers of "yes" and "no" to his questions. But after recovering some information in this way, he may actually talk about the recovered experience in a manner that is comparable to what we have been calling automatic talking. It may be that our collaborative study of the recovery of memories following thiopentol administration was defective in not having tried a more subtle method of inquiry (Osborn et al., 1967). In that study, recovery was attempted through the familiar methods of regression in time back to the experience and the reversal of posthypnotic amnesia. Now, with better evidence available on how to explore for covert experiences, it would be desirable for the study to be repeated.

The paradox that physiological responses are usually retained in experiments in which subjects report complete overt absence of pain as a result of hypnotic suggestion is resolved if it can be shown that they are experiencing the pain covertly, and the covert pain is being reflected in the physiological reactions. If the hypothesis of a more complete elimination of pain for those who have no covert experience is correct, they ought to show less physiological responsiveness than those, equally analgesic at the overt level, who report covert pain by the hidden observer method. An experiment to test this possibility, while feasible, has not been performed.

The physiological pertinence of the study of experience can be generalized even further. *It is only experiences that are absent at the covert level that can be expected to reflect significant physiological changes.* It may be assumed that the subjects whom Pattie studied in his investigations of hypnotic blindness and deafness would have revealed their covert experiences through appropriate techniques, even when the hypnotic experiences were genuine (Pattie, 1935, 1950). The same would apply to Sutcliffe's (1961) findings. Subjects are not necessarily deluding themselves when there is a separation between overt and covert experience: that is merely one of the ways in which conscious experiences get divided.

Some hypotheses to be tested by hypnosis require the hidden observer technique or some equivalent to it. An illustration is provided by an experiment designed to test a hypothesis about the natural morphine-like substances (endorphins) known to be present in the brain (Goldstein & Hilgard, 1975). The hypothesis to be tested was that suggestions of hypnotic anesthesia might cause the secretion of the endorphin in the midthalamic areas sensitive to morphine. To test this hypothesis, however, it was necessary to select subjects who could reduce both pain and distress through hypnotic suggestion, but *whose distress was lacking* in their covert reports. If the covert reports recovered both distress and pain, according to the principle discussed in the preceding paragraph, the physiological reduction of pain would not be expected, and testing the hypothesis would not be appropriate. Two subjects were found to be available, so that the experiment proved feasible. The idea was that if the effect of hypnosis in relieving distress altogether (including at the covert level) was due to the release of the endorphin, then the morphine antagonist naloxone might reverse the effect, as indeed it does not only for morphine and the electrical stimulation of the area, but perhaps also for acupuncture. The results were negative, but some pertinent evidence was obtained on the differences between pain and distress at a covert level (Table 3.1). For the selected subjects *both* sensory pain and distress were absent at the overt level, while both subjects experienced pain but no distress at the covert level. In this instance, and perhaps in some other settings also, only the hidden observer method can reveal the crucial evidence required by the hypothesis proposed for testing.

Without the hidden observer method it would not have been possible to support as clearly the two-component interpretation of pain reduction through hypnosis (see Figure 3.6). This interpretation becomes important because it resolves one of the areas of disagreement between the clinician and the experimenter. Hypnotic procedures are often effective with the majority of patients, so that the clinician who uses hypnosis disagrees with the experimenter who finds successes related to measured hypnotizability, and therefore may expect good results from hypnosis in a smaller fraction of patients. If the two-component interpretation is correct, pain can become much more tolerable for everyone by using suggestion techniques for the reduction of anxiety and for producing a relaxed condition in the face of threatened pain. That is all the practitioner may require in the face of minor pains, such as the physician who wishes to draw a blood sample, or the dentist who wishes to calm a frightened child before proceeding with simple dental procedures. For more severe pain, however, such as the pains of childbirth, the sensory pain itself can be further reduced if the person is hypnotizable as shown by measured hypnotic responsiveness. These conjectures bear on the success of J. Barber (1977) in reducing dental pain—a success we have been unable to repeat when using his method to reduce the pain of ice water in the laboratory. His method is no more successful than the methods we have been using right along; hence it may be particularly effective when increased relaxation and the reduction of anxiety are of greater importance than sensory pain.

TABLE 3.1.   Overt and covert pain and distress in two selected high hypnotizables. (Data from Goldstein & Hilgard, 1975)

	Pain rating			Distress rating		
	Normal	*Analgesia*			*Analgesia*	
	Waking	Overt	Covert	*Waking*	Overt	Covert
Subject 1	12	0	13	12	0	0
Subject 2	12	0	15a	4	0	0

a. The tourniquet was kept in place longer under analgesia than in waking. The covert pain continued to mount, although overt pain was absent.

A Neo-Dissociation Interpretation of Division Within Control Systems

The concept of dissociation was introduced by Janet (1889) to account for split-off parts of the personality or experience that he found in the patients that he studied. As noted elsewhere (Hilgard, 1973a), the concept flourished for a time and was then largely discarded because of the belief that it required a complete separation between the dissociated parts of the person.

DISSOCIATION, NEO-DISSOCIATION, AND STATE-NONSTATE THEORIES

Experimental tests of dissociation, such as those previously described on automatic writing, show indeed that a subjectively real dissociation might exist even though there was demonstrable interference between the simultaneous activities, one conscious, the other subconscious. In order to recognize the historical continuity between the older dissociation theory, while not being too committed to it in detail, I have preferred to describe a contemporary version of dissociation as a neo-dissociation interpretation. In this contemporary version, dissociative phenomena are recognized as widespread, and not limited to hysterical personalities, as Janet thought.

The interference between two activities, one conscious, the other sub-conscious, can be thought of as a matter of degree; it is therefore an empirical matter to be investigated, and not directly related to the reality of the partial dissociations that occur.

The concept of partial dissociation serves to soften the contrasting views of those who set a "nonstate" interpretation of hypnosis against a "state" interpretation (e.g., T. Barber, this volume; Sarbin and Coe, 1972). Even for those who are willing to use the concept of state somewhat freely as a descriptive term for the total changes that some subjects report when they are hypnotized, the concept of state need not be a central explanatory concept (Hilgard, 1973c).

The neo-dissociation interpretation mediates between the extreme positions of the nonstate and state theories by proposing that there are degrees of dissociative experiences. These may vary from limited and superficial responses to direct suggestion, in which, apart from some shifts in voluntary and involuntary control systems, there is little modification of consciousness, to the massive dissociations of very deep hypnosis or in pathological conditions such as fugues or multiple personalities. Only when dissociations become sufficiently widespread are the changes appropriately described as alterations in consciousness or as a change in state. Even then, there is no assurance that all changes of state have common properties merely because hypnotic procedures have been used to bring them about. This is a far cry from making the state the cause of the dissociations, rather than the result of them. Whether some people have a greater capacity for dissociative experiences, self-generated or hypnotically produced, is an empirical problem; the widespread individual differences in hypnotic responsiveness imply that such differences in ability exist.

EVIDENCE FROM THE HIDDEN OBSERVER STUDIES

Interviews with highly responsive hypnotic subjects, conducted by Josephine Hilgard with the subjects participating in our laboratory experiments following the interviewing method used successfully earlier (J.R. Hilgard, 1970), provide a valuable source of information about the nature of the hidden observer in relation to normal control processes (Hilgard, 1977a). Many of the subjects interviewed had experienced, at different times, the reduction of both pain and hearing, and through the hidden observer technique had uncovered covert responses to the stimuli. These hidden experiences may represent the more profound kind of dissociation limited to highly hypnotizable persons—those in the upper mode of a bimodal distribution.

Not all of those who experienced a hidden observer had initially thought the idea plausible. Here are statements by three of these:

—I thought the hidden observer was corny, because I thought it impossible. I told the hypnotist so at the time.

—I was skeptical. I didn't see how I could alter who I was. . . I was skeptical that I could really be objective about the experience I was going through while I was in the midst of imagining.

—I was somewhat confused because I thought there could be a difference, but I didn't think there really would be a difference.

Despite these negative or uncertain expectations, all subsequently experienced a hidden observer (E.R. Hilgard, 1977a).

Although the initial attitude is not controlling in all instances, there is a good reason why more of those who succeeded were favorable in advance to the idea of recovering a concealed experience. The reason is that a number of these subjects had had previous experiences, outside hypnosis, in which they acted on information that reached them when they were not aware of it, or information to which they had responded without being aware of responding.

—Mother would call me; I'd answer, but I wasn't aware I was answering.

—Yesterday, when reading *God Is an Englishman,* a friend who lives next door was talking with my roommate in her room. The walls are thin in the trailer we live in. I didn't know what they were talking about. Later, about six o'clock, I asked Mary, "When are you and Evelyn going out?". . .Suddenly I wondered: How did I know that?. . .I could not remember having heard it.

It should not be surprising that these subjects were favorably disposed to the idea of a hidden observer in advance, and that they might be the ones for whom the method was appropriate.

Perhaps because of the choice of metaphor, the hidden observer has tended to become personified by those who read the reports, either as some sort of persisting secondary personality or as a mysterious part of the subconscious mind. The evidence from the reports of our subjects is quite different. They report discovering genuinely concealed or covert experiences, but these have turned out to be objective, matter-of-fact, scientific, accurate descriptions of contemporary events. There is little evidence of any upsurge from the deeper recesses of the mind. The overt experiences of hypnosis contained more of the distortions that might be classified as "primary process" experiences than the covert experiences did.

Here are some of the comments by the subjects:

—The hidden part doesn't deal with pain, it looks at what is, and doesn't judge it. It is not a hypnotized part of the self. It knows all the parts.

—The hidden observer is watching, mature, logical, has more information.

—The hidden observer seemed like my real self when I'm out of hypnosis, only more objective. When I'm in hypnosis, I'm imagining, letting myself pretend, but somewhere the hidden observer knows what's really going on. I think this is part of the same process as the tendency in hypnosis to stand back and say: Look what's happening to you. You're slowly going under hypnosis.

One of the subjects, whom we may call Rachel, characterized very well the splits in her cognitive systems:

—The hidden observer is a portion of Me. There's Me 1, Me 2, and Me 3. Me 1 is hypnotized; Me 2 is hypnotized and observing; and Me 3 is when I'm awake. The hidden observer, a part of Me 3, is cognizant of everything that's going on; it's a little more narrow in its field of vision than Me 3, like being awake in a dream and fully aware of your action...The hidden observer sees more, he questions more, he's aware of what's going on all of the time but getting in touch is totally unnecessary.

The first time (the ice water pain) I thought maybe it was an artifact of the situation, but after the second time, with hearing, I don't think that's the case. He's like a guardian angel that guards you from doing anything that will mess you up...The hidden observer is looking through a tunnel, and sees everything in the tunnel...It's focused, doesn't pay attention to extraneous things. It's aware that the tones are coming through, aware that I was saying "zero," that the Me 1 was busy floating. Me 2 is watching all of this. Unless someone tells me to get in touch with the hidden observer, I'm not in contact. It's just there.

Rachel has described the fractionation of her cognitive functions or systems as three fractions of the "Me":

Me 3, the awake Me, of which the hidden observer is a restricted fraction, concealed until called forth.

Me 2, the observing part in the midst of hypnosis, described as hypnotized because, even if watching the hypnotized part (Me 1) it is subject to some of the distortions of perception.

Me 1, the hypnotized part, busy floating, and overtly reporting no pain or hearing.

Observations such as hers permit a formulation of the relationships as they are represented phenomenally.

As noted earlier, the temptation is strong to see the hidden part as a persistent system that may have been there all along. Many practicing hypnotists, for example, believe that they can "talk to the unconscious" by way of the finger-signalling technique. Under the conditions of our experiments, the characterization of the hidden observer that emerges from the interviews with our subjects does not correspond with these interpretations. A summary of what our subjects have told us would read more like this: *"The hidden observer is in all respects like the normal observing part as found in waking. It is objective and well oriented to reality."*

The experiments conducted with the hidden observer method have thus far explored only a limited range of experiences. They should not be generalized to cover the whole range of experiences, especially those with deep emotional commitment, where highly charged emotional or motivational conflicts may be present. The results of the reported experiments are genuine, but how far they can be generalized must await further investigation. That the covert experiences appear to be highly rational and reality-oriented may be in part a consequence of the options that are open. That is, the overt analgesia and deafness following hypnotic suggestions are distortions of reality; if there is a concealed part that "knows more," there is a high probability that it will report either pain or hearing. Realistic reporting under these circumstances must not be allowed to exclude the possibility that in some other arrangement the dissociated part, concealed by the hypnotic interactions, may be laden with affect and then will show derivatives from the deeper unconscious.

Louella, one of our subjects, threw some additional light on the hidden observer because she felt somewhat "betrayed" by it. She was shocked by the appearance of the hidden observer in the foreground, driving the usual hypnotized part into the background. "There's an unspoken agreement that the hidden observer is supposed to stay hidden and not come out. He broke his promise; he's not abiding by the rule. He's stealing something from the hypnotized part. He's stealing by taking his power." Despite this resentment of the hidden observer, she thought of the hidden observer as more mature than the rest of her, and he had more information than the hypnotized part. In fact, the hidden observer brought back all of the information: "The hidden part has all the information. . . He knows that sounds are coming into my ear and I must be hearing, that it's only due to suggestion that I'm not."

From the reports of our subjects, that part of the monitoring function revealed as the hidden observer can be further characterized as follows:

1. It is split off from the normal monitor and differs from it possibly because of more limited focus, but primarily because it is concealed behind an amnesic barrier.

2. The fractionation occurs at the time that the pain and hearing are denied conscious expression.

3. The hidden part, after it has been reintegrated with the normal monitoring function through release of amnesia, persists only as a memory for an incident connected with the hypnotic experience. It has no independent existence as part of the personality or its control systems, although it can of course be created again under appropriate circumstances.

PARALLEL OR INTERMITTENT INFORMATION PROCESSING?

The evidence from the analgesia and deafness experience showed that the overt and covert experiences differed; because this is crucial evidence for a dissociation between two information-processing systems, it has theoretical interest for cognitive psychology generally. If the two experiences take place simultaneously this is evidence for parallel processing. At a more microscopic or analytic level, however, the possibility exists that there may be alternation of the experiences. Instead of continuously experienced pain or hearing at the covert level, there may be an occasional experience of pain or hearing followed by a rapid amnesia for it, giving the impression that the covert experience had been continuous when the amnesia is ultimately reversed. This is often described as serial processing, but intermittent processing may describe it better, as shown in Figure 3.8.

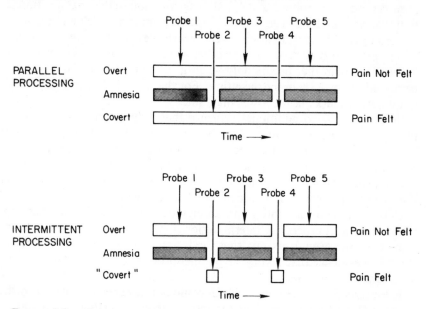

FIGURE 3.8. *Two interpretations of the relationship between overt and covert pain.* (Hilgard, 1977, p. 237.)

The diagrams of Figure 3.8 represent a parallel processing interpretation (upper diagram) and an intermittent processing interpretation (lower diagram). Because a succession of probes is shown, alternating between those searching the overt and covert levels of pain, the diagrams best represent the investigation of ischemic pain (Knox, Morgan, & Hilgard, 1974). In that study, at the end of each two minutes the subject reported the experience in hypnotic analgesia, and, with the hypnotist's hand on the subject's shoulder according to the hidden observer technique, reported any covert experience. The typical overt report was of little or no pain and the covert report of pain near to but slightly below normally felt pain.

The parallel processing interpretation (upper diagram) is that both the overt and covert experiences are continuous, hence simultaneous and in parallel. They are separated by an amnesic barrier. The typical questioning of the subject in hypnotic analgesia, yielding reports of the overt experience of no pain, are shown as Probes 1, 3, and 5. Probes 2 and 4, using the hidden observer technique, temporarily break the amnesic barrier and yield reports of the covert pain at that moment, a pain inferred to have been continuous.

The intermittent interpretation (lower diagram) is that there is no covert pain felt at the time that no overt pain is reported to Probes 1, 3, and 5; that is, when pain is not reported there is no felt pain at either level. The hidden observer inquiry, Probes 2 and 4, redirects attention to the noxious stimulation that has all along been ignored, and the pain is now felt and reported. According to this interpretation, overt experiences are the only ones in consciousness, and they succeed each other at intervals; what has been called "covert" is pain that occurs only when it is sampled; it has not been experienced at any level in the meantime. For that reason, "covert" is written in quotation marks in the lower diagram.

Before turning to additional evidence that may influence a choice between the two interpretations, it can be affirmed that the two experiences of pain and of no pain are appropriately classified as dissociated experiences regardless of which interpretation is accepted. This follows because the presence of the amnesic barrier in both instances convinces the subject that the two reports represent a pair of simultaneous experiences.

Despite some uncertainties and ambiguities, the observations that support the parallel processing interpretation appear to require fewer assumptions than the arguments favoring the intermittent processing interpretation. The evidence that favors the parallel processing interpretation can be summarized as follows:

1. Patterned series of stimuli which could not have been recovered by the occasional probing required in the intermittent processing interpretation can be recovered from memory by the hidden observer method. Experiments with a highly hypnotizable subject have been conducted in our laboratory with moderately painful electric shocks administered through electrodes attached prior to the experiment to three separated positions on the forearm. Shocks were then delivered at three discriminable intensities in six possible orders by position. Even though the subject felt nothing at all at the overt level, at the covert level by the hidden observer method he was able to recall through memory the correct order and correct intensities of the delivered shocks. It is obvious that the information required him to have paid continuous attention during its storage, hence indicating a concealed cognitive system operating in parallel to the overt anesthesia.

2. Related to this finding is the one based on a much larger population of subjects that the memory for the maximum pain felt, or the tone of

maximum loudness, agreed with the results that were obtained by probes while the experience was being produced. Plausibility for intermittent processing comes primarily from probes that are injected while the stimulation is going on, but the postexperimental inquiry through memory supports parallel processing.

3. Subjective reports have never been those of "sampled" or "intermittent" experiences of stimulation, as the hidden experiences have been reviewed after all amnesia has been eliminated. The only exceptions are reports by a few subjects who did not meet the criteria of covert reporting at all. By contrast, at the overt level within hypnotic analgesia, or hypnotic deafness, reports of occasional intrusions of the pain (or tone) are not infrequent. These show that the subject is quite capable of reporting occasional or intermittent intrusions when they occur; because these reports are not given when the covert experience is being described, the continuity of the concealed experience is supported.

The simultaneous experiences are not completely independent as our experiments on conflicting tasks and automatic writing have shown. Holding a task subconscious does not reduce the interference between it and a conscious task; on the contrary, in some instances the interference may increase. As previously pointed out, such interferences pose empirical problems for study, but they are not decisive with respect to the concept of dissociation.

If parallel processing is accepted as demonstrated in these experiments, the possibility is opened up of parallel processing in other cases of simultaneous task performances, including dichotic listening, and bears on the possibilities of subliminal perception.

Dissociation and the Unconscious

Dissociation implies the automatization of selected experiences so that their controls are not deliberate, hence to a degree, subconscious; some dissociated experiences are entirely concealed from consciousness, until such time as awareness of them is restored. Because these concepts overlap with areas covered by the more familiar concepts of unconscious processes, more needs to be said about their similarities and overlaps, and about their differences.

The most familiar conceptions of unconscious derive primarily from Freud and Jung. Both of them produced theories that evolved during their lifetimes; those who have attempted to summarize and interpret their views do not always agree with each other. Without delving thoroughly into these matters, a few observations may be made about the differences between the theories of Freud and Jung, on the one hand, and a neo-dissociation interpretation, on the other.

Freud's earlier conceptions led to the tripartite division of conscious, preconscious, and unconscious. Because these represent the total mental apparatus as divided into levels, psychoanalysts refer to this as the *topographic* analysis, as distinct from the later, and now more familiar, *structural* analysis into id, ego, and superego. The earlier topographic analysis is most usefully compared with dissociation. The conscious, or perceptual-conscious, as Freud sometimes called it, is the ordinary waking consciousness with which we are familiar as we go about our daily lives. The preconscious represents those memories and thoughts of which we are not now conscious but which are readily available and capable of becoming conscious. One way of stating this is that the threshold between the preconscious and the conscious is highly permeable, readily crossed. The unconscious, lying below a less permeable barrier, is less accessible. This deeper unconscious is known mostly through its derivatives, as in dreams, unconscious mannerisms, or pathological symptoms; these have to be interpreted, because the representation of the unconscious is ordinarily symbolic rather than direct. In Freudian theory, one does *not* talk directly to the unconscious, as some clinical hypnotists believe they do. For our purposes it is somewhat simpler to stay with the topographic analysis into conscious, preconscious, and unconscious divisions, in full recognition that this is a partial view of Freudian theory in its later forms.

By contrast with that deeper aspect of the unconscious that is known only though its derivatives, dissociated aspects of consciousness, when they enter consciousness, are fully restored, as when amnesia is cancelled and the memories are recovered. In this respect dissociated experiences are comparable to preconscious processes rather than unconscious ones. The unconscious differs also in that its materials are considered to be highly charged with affect and emotion, driven by the basic instincts of sex and aggression, and composed of memories based on wishes that are repressed because they are not acceptable to the conscious ego. In any case, the deeper unconscious is not directly accessible.

This contrast must not be carried too far because within Freudian interpretations some repressed material can become fully conscious. Examples are events in childhood, concealed from memory by childhood amnesia, and repression of traumatic experiences of more recent date, as in the war neuroses. Freud was puzzled by the repetition neuroses in which experiences, normally unconscious, are relived from time to time (Freud, 1920). This "return of the repressed" is similar to the fugue states that Janet observed and called "dissociated." Such exceptions do not deny the general principle that the deeper unconscious is ordinarily not directly accessible; some of its inaccessible material may derive from infantile wishes which, because they were preverbal, are difficult to translate into adult consciousness.

Jung's unconscious also has its more accessible and its less accessible parts: the former are assigned by him to the personal unconscious, the latter to the collective unconscious. Much of the personal unconscious is recoverable in consciousness, and hence is coherent with a dissociative interpretation. The deeper unconscious, however, has to be inferred. The archetypal figures that appear in dreams or fantasies do not represent their meanings directly, but in the symbolism of mythological characters. Jung is quite explicit about the inaccessibility of the unconscious: "It is *really* unconscious" (Jung & Evans, 1964).

One way of conceiving the difference between the accessibility of dissociated material, by contrast with the inaccessibility of deeply unconscious material, is to consider dissociation as a vertical split at the level of consciousness, while the unconscious split is a horizontal one, with the unconscious material appropriately considered to be deeper (Figure 3.9). Morton Prince (1909) spoke of the co-conscious, making the same point of a division at a common level.

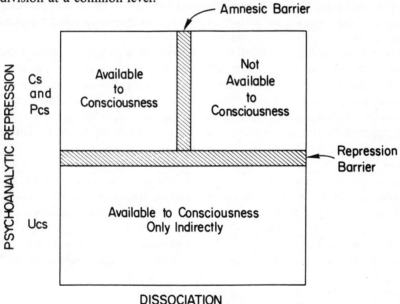

FIGURE 3.9. *A distinction between divisions of consciousness in dissociation, and some aspects of psychoanalytic interpretations.* (Hilgard, 1976, p. 143.)

The diagram of Figure 3.9 represents the alternate analysis that is made according to a dissociation interpretation; no conflict between a "depth" interpretation and a "divided consciousness" interpretation is implied. That is, there may be unconscious derivatives that affect dissociated activities; the unconscious in the diagram underlies all of consciousness above.

The interrelationship between the two approaches is well illustrated by the differences and overlaps between amnesia and repression. The amnesias found in some pathological conditions, if interpreted as repression, represent a very mild repression, with the concealed condition resembling the foreconscious much more than the deeper unconscious.

The basis for the concealment in repression, however, is emotional and motivational; the material that is repressed is somehow unacceptable or anxiety-producing. In hypnotic amnesia the material may be entirely impersonal, concealed as a result of suggestion. Hypnotic amnesia may also be influenced by personal dynamics. This was shown in the experiment of Clemes (1964), in which word-association tests were used to select words that were emotionally loaded for the learner, to compare with neutral words when lists of words were to be remembered and temporarily forgotten by posthypnotic amnesia. The experiment demonstrated that in suggested partial amnesia (half of the words remembered, half forgotten) the words with emotional loadings for the individual were disproportionately the "targets" of the amnesia. Hence, it was demonstrated that a repression process influenced the hypnotic amnesia process. Such an interplay is to be expected, but it does not *equate* amnesia with repression.

The differences as described have a bearing on therapy. In hypnoanalysis, whatever has been learned from hypnosis and from psychoanalysis may be used together, depending only on the skill and ingenuity of the therapist in combining them. In hypnotherapy, defined more narrowly, if the therapist uses the dissociation interpretation, the essence is to integrate the dissociated aspects of consciousness, and, in some instances, to manipulate dissociations for the benefit of the person. For example, in her study of phobias, Horowitz (1970) was able to use age regression to restore memories of earlier experiences that were associated with the snake phobia, while at the same time dissociating the emotional arousal from the cognitive aspects of the memory. That is, by recalling the event, without emotion in the present, the event belonged in memory where it properly should be placed, without magnifying emotional responses in the present. This method proved more therapeutic than a recall of the earlier event with experienced emotion.

Concluding Remarks

Studies of consciousness, in the mode of expanded sensitivity and awareness, have not always given due consideration to the central processes, here characterized as executive and monitoring functions. Such processes recently have received increasing recognition by both experimental and social psychologists. These issues intrude themselves necessarily within an account of hypnotic phenomena because of the dramatic changes that take place in the hypnotic interaction, and the equally dramatic restoration of function when the interaction is terminated. The evidence brought out by the hidden observer technique makes the concept of dissociation appropriate because it indicates that a concealed intellectual activity may go on in parallel with altered cognition at the overt level.

The fractionation of the monitoring function is particularly impressive, with its three major divisions: (1) the preserved normal observing function; (2) a fraction of this normal observing function concealed beneath an amnesic barrier; and (3) a distorted, uncritical function, which as a consequence of suggestion accepts distorted reality as though it were undistorted. The experiments on which these conclusions are based are of limited scope. The directions in which they point are clear, however. New findings will place the facts as they have been observed in perspective, and they may assign them a more restricted place in the totality of experience. Human psychology is too unfinished a science for any one set of demonstrations to describe human consciousness in all its richness.

The parallel processing that appears to occur in these experiments contributes to the understanding of a problem baffling in other areas, such as attention and memory. Although some of these demonstrations can be made only with the help of those in the general population who are highly responsive to hypnosis, these persons are just as "normal" as the virtuosos in other areas of skill and creative activity. The lessons learned from them are essential to a deeper understanding of human psychology.

Erika Fromm, *University of Chicago, received her Ph.D. at the age of 23 from the University of Frankfurt, Germany, working under Max Wertheimer on Gestalt laws of perception. She then became a research associate in the Department of Psychiatry at the University of Amsterdam, Holland, and established the first Psychology Laboratory in a State Hospital in that country. During that time her interests centered on psychoanalytic theory and projective techniques. She emigrated to the United States with her husband in 1938, spent several years raising her family, took more training in psychoanalytic child therapy, and became a research associate at the Chicago Institute for Psychoanalysis. Professor Fromm served on the faculties of the University of Illinois Medical School and Northwestern University Medical School. In 1961 she joined the Department of Psychology at the University of Chicago. Her research interests expanded to ego psychology, dream interpretation, psychoanalytic approaches to artistic creativity, hypnosis, and other altered states of consciousness. She is the author of* Intelligence: A Dynamic Approach *(with Lenore Hartman) and* Dream Interpretation: A New Approach *(with Thomas M. French). She has been the Clinical Editor of the* International Journal of Clinical and Experimental Hypnosis *since 1969. Dr. Fromm has been President of the American Board of Psychological Hypnosis (1971-1974), of the American Psychological Associations's Division of Psychological Hypnosis (1972-1973), and of the Society for Clinical and Experimental Hypnosis (1975-1977).*

This is a new chapter, written for the second edition. Since the first edition of this book was published, in 1972, the author has become interested in other altered states of consciousness and aware of the need for comparative research between hypnosis and the various other states of consciousness. Building on her psychoanalytic background, she has developed a new ego psychological theory that may contribute to the elucidation of the nature of hypnosis and related states.

The perceptual continua of primary process—secondary process, ego receptivity—ego activity, fantasy—reality orientation, imagery—conceptualization, free floating—focused attention, and automatization—deautomatization are discussed with regard to waking states, hypnosis, daydreaming, creativity, psychedelic states, biofeedback and four types of meditation.

4

The Nature of Hypnosis
and Other Altered States
of Consciousness:
An Ego Psychological Theory[1]

ERIKA FROMM[2]

Introduction

Many states of consciousness exist and are now being investigated scientifically. They range from hyper-alert waking states to the deepest stages of sleep and anesthesia. Based on a nineteenth century prejudice that the only normal state is the waking state, states of consciousness (*SoCs*) different from waking have come to be called altered states of consciousness (*ASCs*). Hypnosis is one of them.

A brief look at the history of the concept of consciousness might be illuminating.

Until about 1885 psychology acknowledged two states only, the waking state and sleep. Waking was defined as the state in which we operate with

1. This chapter is the full version of a shortened paper published in 1977 in the *International Journal of Clinical and Experimental Hypnosis* (Fromm, 1977a). The study was supported in part by a grant given by the Social Science Divisional Research Fund of the University of Chicago.

2. The author wishes to express her thanks to the following colleagues and friends who have read the manuscript at various stages and made valuable contributions for revisions: Drs. Doris Gruenewald, Mark Oberlander, Harry Summerfield, Francesca von Broemsben, Daniel P. Brown, and the author's daughter, Joan Greenstone.

consciousness; also, implicitly, as the "normal" state. Sleep was considered as a no-consciousness state, not worth exploring.

In the 1890s Freud began to struggle with and clarify for himself the concept of the unconscious (Freud, 1900). He identified three modes of the mind: the conscious (that which at a given time is in full awareness); the preconscious (that which is not in full awareness but can be brought into awareness simply by turning one's attention to it); and the unconscious (those mental contents, affects and memories which resist being brought into consciousness). One could say that he thought of dreams as a special *SoC* of great significance, in fact as "the royal road to the unconscious."

At about the same time, i.e., in 1902, William James wrote:

> Our normal waking consciousness...is but one special type of consciousness, whilst all about it, parted from it by the flimsiest of screens, there lie potential forms of consciousness entirely different. We may go through life without suspecting their existence; but apply the requisite stimulus, and at a touch they are all there in all their completeness, definite types of mentality which probably somewhere have their field of application and adaptation. No account of the universe in its totality can be final which leaves these other forms of consciousness quite disregarded. How to regard them is the question—for they are so discontinuous with ordinary consciousness. (James, 1935, p. 298).

From Kleitman (1939) and those who followed him in sleep laboratory research across the U.S. and Europe we have learned since that sleep has four stages, and that during those stages mentation is going on. They are: Descending Stage I, i.e., the hypnagogic state just before falling asleep; Stages II and III; and IV, the deepest stage of sleep. The Ascending Stage I is a stage characterized by rapid eye movements and dreams. In dreams, while by definition *not conscious,* we are aware of imagery.

More recently we have come to recognize that there are many states of "altered" consciousness, that is, *SoC*s that differ from the waking state. They constitute a continuum between waking awareness and the deepest forms of sleep. The important ones are:

- daydreaming and other relaxation states
- states of creativity, particularly the inspirational phase of the creative act
- the hypnagogic and the hypnopompic states
- hypnosis
- sensory deprivation states
- nocturnal dreams
- psychedelic states caused by drug use
- concentrative and mindful meditation
- states of mystical rapture and shamanistic ecstasy
- states of dissociation
- states of depersonalization

- fugue states
- psychotic states, particularly the hallucinatory ones.

The last two (fugues and psychoses) are pathological states.

To the minor *ASC*s we assign being absorbed in reading a book or watching TV, viewing a piece of art, seeing the colors change as the sun sets ondesert mountains, or being fascinated while observing the busy life of an anthill, also daydreaming, the inspirational phase of the creative act, and the beginning stages of transcendental meditation (TM). The major *ASC*s comprise medium and deep hypnosis, psychedelic states, classical Eastern meditation, and states of mystical rapture; in addition, the fugues, and the psychotic hallucinations. Dissociation can occur in either major or minor *ASC*s and is one of the specific characteristics of hypnosis (see E.R. Hilgard, this volume).

In this chapter I will confine myself to five types of *ASC*s: hypnosis, daydreaming, *ASC*s induced by psychedelic drugs, meditative states, and the inspirational phase of the creative process.

An altered state of consciousness is a cognitive state different from the waking state. While some *ASC*s occur naturally and commonly, others are induced by various psychological maneuvers or by pharmacological agents. Frequently, but by no means always, *ASC*s bring with them physiological changes that can be measured. *ASC*s can be recognized subjectively by the individual himself as different from the waking state (for experiential criteria see Tart 1975, pp. 12–13). The outside observer can sometimes also recognize objectively that the individual in an *ASC* acts differently. However, more frequently, subjectively very vivid altered states do not translate themselves into objectively measurable behavior. This poses an important problem, particularly for American psychology.

In 1919, John Watson, the father of behaviorism, argued that only that which can be observed by an outside observer—i.e., the *behavior* of a person—can be the subject of scientific research. Soon this scientific attitude deteriorated into the reductionist credo "there is no mind, only behavior." All research using introspective methods was abandoned—and to a large degree is even now viewed with suspicion by academic psychology.

In the 1960s, however, young scientists in contact with the youth culture and its psychedelic drug experimentation heard so much about the fascinating imagery and changes in awareness produced by the drugs that their scientific curiosity was awakened. They revolted against the establishment's ruling that *ASC*s could not be the topic of scientific investigation and began to do research on cognitive processes, imagery and other subjective phenomena in *ASC*s. They had learned from their elders the use of respected scientific methods and now employed them as their tools in working with these taboo mental data. Many of them first used themselves and their own experiences in *ASC*s for the purpose of developing hypotheses that could be tested on naive subjects (*Ss*). They found that the *S* experiences a change in his own mental state. This change occurs in the way of experiencing of both the outer world and one's own body, i.e. there is a change in "gating" (Melzack and Wall, 1968) of sensory stimuli. In some *ASC*s more sensory stimuli can enter awareness than in the waking state; in other *ASC*s fewer stimuli are perceived. Sensory excitement and intensity can either be enhanced or decreased. Alterations in the outflow of motor impulses are common. Once more, in some *ASC*s we find much more motor activity than in the waking state, in others much less. Time distortions may appear, or alterations in emotional responses to stimuli, or changes in the mode of attention. Frequently the imagery increases and the interaction with the environment takes on a different tone concurrent with changes in the organization and mode of cognitive structures and in the formal characteristics of thought.

In fact, most of these changes refer to reorganizations of cognitive structures, i.e. the way in which perceptions of the outer and inner world are represented in forms of consciousness differing from the waking state, changes that can occur in perception, cognition, attention, memory organization and emotions.

In order to maintain reality-oriented waking consciousness, there has to be an *optimal range of stimulation* coming from the reality of the external world. Think of the understimulated, bored child in school. He either withdraws into his own world of daydreams or he acts out in order to attract responses, as well as more stimulation, such as the laughs of his peers. Too little as well as too much stimulation can produce *ASC*s. For instance, on the one hand sensory deprivation work shows that too little stimulation leads to *ASC*s; on the other, religious ecstatic experiences during revival meetings, or in the dancing "whirling dervishes" also produce *ASC*s.

TOWARDS A PSYCHOANALYTIC THEORY
OF ALTERED STATES OF CONSCIOUSNESS

According to psychoanalytic theory (Rapaport, 1957) cognitive modes and organizations range on a continuum from the drive-dominated, prelogical, preverbal, imaginative primary process to the reality oriented, goal-directed, logically ordered, rational, concrete or abstract conceptual secondary process.

Already in 1951 Rapaport (1951) discovered a number of different parameters that can serve to distinguish one *SoC* from another. He ranged the continuum of *SoC*s alongside the continuum of organization of cognitive structures, the one in inverse order to the other. This alignment clearly indicates the nature of the changes in cognitive mode made from one state to another. For instance, in the progress from waking thought to daydreaming, hypnagogic hallucination and dreaming he found a gradual increase in visual imagery, in multiple "implicit" connotations, and in the use of the mechanisms of condensation, symbolization and displacement. At the same time verbal, rational, reality-oriented secondary process type of thinking diminishes, as does reflective awareness ("awareness of awareness") and the ability to extend effort, "to will" (Gill, 1967a, p. 394).

As a first example, let us take the case of the daydreamer. The person who daydreams usually stares at something without seeing; he is not reality oriented. He sits motionless. He may feel thoughtful, depressed or elated. His thought processes are not quite as fully linear, logical or consciously goal-directed as they are in the waking state. His ideation is more diffuse and in the form of visual imagery rather than in that of logic or language. His attention is focused on his inner imaginary processes to the extent of partial exclusion of reality. He is not actively directing his attention but passively or receptively watching the stream of consciousness, admitting into his consciousness imagery, thoughts and feelings below the threshold of awareness in the waking state. There is a decrease of voluntary control over thoughts.

A second example might be hard rock concerts before mass audiences. In hard rock there is an excessive inflow of sensory stimuli which leads to a great outflow of motor impulses. By means of the motor activity, the ego attempts to deal with the sensory overload and to prevent being overwhelmed by it, or by the high pitch of emotion which hard rock creates. Cognitive processes are pretty much abolished in favor of emotional frenzy, and normal concentration of attention is impossible.

There are certain *ASCs* in which there is an increased alertness, a heightened ability to work with preconscious and unconscious processes rather than with pure conscious logic. In these states one understands a problem by allowing more of the unconscious to float into awareness—though not necessarily into consciousness—by letting the pieces of the puzzle fall together in new ways, as if turning a kaleidoscope. This is characteristic of the inspirational phase of the creative process. As I (Fromm, 1965b) have pointed out earlier, one must differentiate between awareness and consciousness. Awareness *can* be conscious. It can also be preconscious or unconscious, as exemplified by the flash of inspiration in the creative process or by the imagery of the nocturnal dream. Wallas (1926) demonstrated that the creative process consists of four steps: preparation, relaxation, inspiration, and evaluation. The inspirational phase must be preceded by careful preparation in the waking state, and by relaxation, i.e. by stepping away from the problem for a while so that unconscious and preconscious processes may come into play. It should be followed by a state of critical evaluation. That is, the artist or creative scientist in the preparatory phase uses active, goal-directed thinking. When that does not get him to the point to which he aspires, he is wise to relax his efforts, to step back in order to be able to make larger steps forward later. This process Kris (1952) termed "regression in the service of the ego." Hartmann (1958) called it "adaptive regression." Rothenberg (1976, 1977) speaks of homospatial and Janusian thinking in creativity; the former he defines as two or more images occupying the same space and leading to a conception that articulates new identities, the latter as a thought that consists of an active and coherent assertion of simultaneous antitheses occurring in the presence of clear logic and transcending ordinary logical operations.

I would characterize the inspirational phase of creativity as a receptive state of mind in which a person can admit into awareness a good deal of preconscious and unconscious material and prelogical thinking without being overwhelmed by it. This observation leads us to the contemporary psychoanalytic concepts of ego activity, ego passivity and ego receptivity.

Ego Activity, Ego Passivity and Ego Receptivity

The psychoanalytic (ego psychological) theory of activity and passivity was initiated by Rapaport (in Gill, 1967a, 530–568) and H.H. Hart (1961), and extended by Ekstein and Caruth (1968), Schafer (1968a), Fromm (1972), and Stolar and Fromm (1974). The concept of ego receptivity was added by Deikman (1971). Rapaport differentiated *ego* activity and passivity from active and passive *behavior,* providing an exciting, important distinction that advanced psychoanalytic theory. Hart showed that the feeling of choicelessness is the central element of passivity. The ego is active or autonomous when the individual can make a choice, according to his own "free will." It is passive or lacks autonomy when the person is overwhelmed either by his instinctual drives (Rapaport, in Gill 1967a, 530–568), by demands coming from the environment (Fromm, 1972), or by the superego (Stolar & Fromm, 1974).

The issue of activity and passivity of the ego is essentially tied to the concept of coping or failing to cope, a concept brought into focus in psychoanalytic literature by Murphy (1962) and by White (1963). There are two forms of coping: creative coping and protective or defensive coping. In both the ego is active and maintains relative autonomy. In creative coping the ego actively meets the demands coming from the instincts, from reality, or from the superego, and handles them sovereignly at its own leisure and pace. In protective coping the individual defends himself against these demands but the action lacks free, smooth, and sovereign mastery.

When the ego is passive the person submits to the demand coming from the instincts, the superego or the external world and acts accordingly even though such action is ego-dystonic; he goes along against his better will. Or he may be so helpless in the face of the demand that he freezes and cannot act at all; he feels overwhelmed. The latter is a characteristic occurrence in psychoses, in catastrophic reactions, and in psychedelic "bad trips."

However, not all states in which active control and voluntarism are relinquished are states of ego passivity. Many of them are characterized by ego receptivity. In ego receptivity, critical judgment, strict adherence to reality orientation, and active goal-directed thinking are held to a minimum and the individual allows himself freely to let unconsciousness and preconscious material float into his mind. There is an openness to experiencing. William James would have characterized it as "watching the stream of consciousness flow by." Ego receptivity is the prevailing state in many of the healthy uses of *ASC*s. Examples are states of profound cognitive relaxation such as the mystical, transcendental, revelatory states attained through meditation (satori, nirvana). It also is characteristic of and occurs spontaneously in daydreaming, reverie, even free association, as well as in states of repose associated with muscular relaxation such as floating on the water or sunbathing.

In the active mode the organism is ready and able to manipulate the environment. The psychological manifestations are a relatively high level of attention and sharp perceptual boundaries, conative activity, reality orientation, effort, rationality, and logic.

With regard to outside stimuli, the *receptive mode* is organized around intake of the environment rather than its manipulation. In the receptive mode one *allows* things to happen, one does not make them happen. The EEG in the receptive mode of thinking and feeling is characterized by a preponderance of alpha waves; baseline muscle tone is decreased; attention is diffused; there is decreased boundary perception. And in the field of cognition there is dominance of the sensory over formal conceptual thought, i.e., more prelogical imagery and thought than strictly logical processes (Deikman, 1971). In this state the barriers between conscious awareness and the unconscious and preconscious are lowered. This leads to a greater availability of unconscious material.

In an earlier part of this century (1912-1945) Gestalt theory demonstrated that the perceptual as well as the cognitive contents in our waking mind are organized in specific ways, according to Gestalt laws. The creative, productive thinker must break out of the ordinary mode of perceiving a problem and recenter his approach to it in an unusual and new way (Wertheimer, 1945). Psychoanalytic research during that same period has shown that in the creative process there is an alternation between two cognitive modes: pre-logical, pre-verbal primary process and logical, verbal secondary process thinking.

In the 1960s, with increased research in *ASC*s, we were beginning to grasp *why* dream thoughts are not simply self-evident to the dreamer. Dream states, like meditation and drug-induced psychedelic states, are *ASCs*. Thoughts experienced during an *ASC* are organized according to primary process, pre-logically, pre-verbally. Which is why it is often difficult to bring them into the waking consciousness, organized as it is according to the secondary process, i.e. according to laws of logic and linear sequential order of language (French & Fromm, 1964). This is not to deny that many a time a dream can also be repressed because it contains emotionally unacceptable material. When we interpret dreams we "translate" them for the patient from the primary process logic into secondary process logic and language.

Deikman (1971) has been able to show that in many *ASCs*, alterations occur both in ego boundaries and in the visual perception of objects. Both changes are in the direction of greater fluidity, and both cause an alteration in the usual waking state subject-object differentiation. Also, deautomatization occurs characteristically in many altered states; that is, there is a regression towards unconscious processes of thinking. This kind of deautomatization permits the adult to take a new, fresh look at the world. It frees him from a stereotyped cognitive organization built up over the years; it allows adult synthetic and associative functions access to earlier, more primary materials, giving the individual a chance to create in a new way with these materials.

THE ROLE OF IMAGERY IN THE VARIOUS STATES OF CONSCIOUSNESS

During the first quarter of this century mental imagery was felt to be an important aspect of the study of human behavior. With the advent of behaviorism, it was dropped from the list of topics considered suitable for scientific inquiry because its manifestations in another person cannot be observed by an objective outsider. The researcher has to rely on the *S*'s subjective reports of the phenomena. But in the early 1960s this long neglected topic of research began to re-emerge from its rustication (Holt, 1964).

Hartmann (1958) has shown that imagery serves the purpose of "experimental action", thus saving mental and physical energy. We use it in planning for future action, and thus avoid much trial and error in the real world.

Imagery plays a major role in daydreams, nocturnal dreams, and free association. It is particularly vivid in psychedelic states, hypnosis, and the very beginning of meditation. With regard to daydreaming, Singer and Antrobus (1963, 1972) have been able to show that the imagery of daydreams falls into three categories clearly related to personality variables: (1) healthy individuals have frequent happy, vivid and constructive daydreams which serve as experimental action; (2) compulsive self-torturers and doubters with high ego ideals and restricted egos engage in daydreams of achievement, failure, and heroism; and (3) the anxiety hysterics, i.e., the distractable, anxious worriers, usually imagine themselves in all kinds of unhappy situations.

Imagery ranges from voluntarily and ego-actively produced vivid fantasy to ego-receptivity. In the case of ego activity the individual permits imagery to arise from within; in the case of ego receptivity the ego of a patient is passive and overwhelmed.

If I now in the waking state decide to vividly imagine a friend's face and the face appears in front of my inner eye, I have been ego active. I have made the choice to imagine it and done so. In meditation if I allow the stream of consciousness to flow by, I am ego receptive, allowing imagery to rise from the unconscious or preconscious into conscious awareness. In the psychotic hallucinatory states, however, the ego is passive, overwhelmed by unbidden imagery.

In dreams we see imagery in front of our eyes. The contrast between an ordinary dream and a nightmare, I feel, will help clarify the difference between ego receptivity and ego passivity. In nightmares imagery overwhelms the ego to such a degree that the ego feels passive; it has no choice; it cannot make a decision or act upon it. The ordinary nocturnal dream state may be looked upon either as an example of ego activity (it is the ego that *produces* the dream), or as a state of ego receptivity: the ego allows the barrier between the unconscious and conscious awareness to become more permeable so that unconscious contents can float into conscious awareness. It may even become passive, overwhelmed by unconscious contents, as in the nightmare.

The first study of ego controlled imagery versus imagery that is not under the subject's control was done in 1949 by Rosemary Gordon, a British psychoanalyst and researcher. For a long time hers was the lone voice in the desert, but eventually her work sparked much of the new research of the 1960s and 1970s on waking imagery. She termed "bidden" the imagery that is voluntarily produced, "unbidden" that imagery which arises without being conjured up.

I go beyond Gordon in stating that all bidden imagery is actively produced by the ego while unbidden imagery is either a sign of ego receptivity or of ego passivity. Furthermore, I postulate that "unbidden" imagery arises from the unconscious, while "bidden" imagery—as it can be produced voluntarily by an act of attention—stems from the preconscious.

Imagery in the psychedelic states plays a most important role. In most instances it just appears, most frequently not under the voluntary control of the ego. That is, as in the nocturnal dream, the ego is open and receptive to letting imagery come up and be experienced in awareness. Some of it is of the illusory and some of the hallucinatory variety.

In psychedelically induced *ASCs* the perception system becomes infused with material stemming from two other systems: that of imagery and that of memory. Imagery is perceived with such vividness that it passes for real perception, (as does the dream image of the dreamer and the hallucination of the psychotic). Why imagery in the psychedelic states is usually so highly aesthetic is not yet clear. Not enough research has been done on this aspect. The user of psychedelic drugs has the feeling that he sees and experiences a

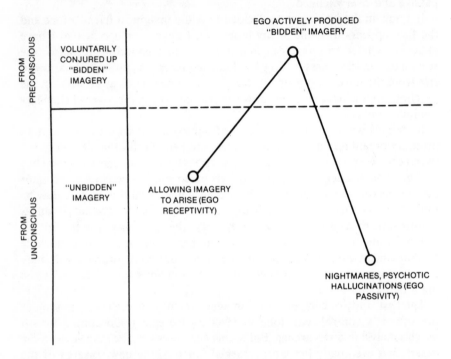

FIGURE 4.1 *The psychodynamic structure of imagery.*

new reality, a reality that lies behind the ordinary one and is more real than the "normal" day to day reality in which he lives. The experience is often described as if veil after veil was being lifted from ordinary reality, revealing what lies behind it. The individual feels he can now see a much "better," a "cosmic" reality; that is, if he has a good trip. If he has a bad trip, the imagery is frightening, overwhelming, and cannot be smoothly handled by the ego.

THE CONCEPTS OF AUTOMATIZATION AND DEAUTOMATIZATION
IN ALTERED STATES OF CONSCIOUSNESS

As a child develops into an adult, certain functions become automatic, habit-trained. While the healthy adult in a changing environment must be able to function with a good deal of flexibility, he must also be able to rely on certain learned functions which no longer require much expenditure of conscious energy and attention. We teach children the tables of multiplication so that later they need not spend time in figuring out anew how much 4 x 7 is. When we need to come to a quick stop while driving a car, our right foot—not our left foot!—automatically slams on the brake before we consciously think about the danger to be avoided. Thus, processes that no longer require conscious attention cathexis in everyday life become preconscious processes. They become automatized, making it unnecessary to constantly adapt anew to every arising occasion. In using automatization we apply channels and means already existing in our repertoire. The economy of automatized processes is the saving of conscious attention.

Habit formation, or automatization, means that with increasing practice an action's intermediate steps disappear from consciousness. This occurs in the perceptual and the cognitive field as well as the motor area. It saves energy in dealing with the outside environment.

Gill and Brenman (1959) developed the concept of de-automatization with regard to hypnosis, a concept which was expanded to other *ASC*s by Deikman (1971) and Van Nuys (1973).

De-automatization represents the undoing of automatization by reinvesting habitualized percepts, thoughts, or actions with attention (Van Nuys, 1973). For example, watch yourself walking downstairs. Pay attention to how every muscle moves. You will find you do not walk as smoothly, as well adapted to reality as you do when functioning autonomously. In fact, you are liable to stumble and fall down the stairs.

The example I just gave is one in which de-automatization is harmful because the situation is one in which it is advantageous to deal with outside reality as efficiently as possible, making use of all the structures and shortcuts one has built up. However, there are other instances, such as the creative process, in which the dissolution of cognitive and reality structures that have solidified can lead to more productive, more creative solutions. Allowing oneself from time to time to go into altered states of consciousness and to de-automatize one's solid, rigidly fixed look at life, may be one way to contribute to a fresh and creative approach to reality.

EGO ACTIVITY, EGO RECEPTIVITY, DE-AUTOMATIZATION
AND IMAGERY IN THE VARIOUS *ASC*s

In altered states, an individual opens up and allows into awareness "stream of consciousness" materials that are usually unconscious or, as in the case of hypnosis, fantasies that at least in part are suggested by another. Cognitively one moves back in the developmental hierarchy from waking, rational, reality-oriented secondary process thinking to primary process;

that is, one allows more imagery and fantasy to rise into awareness from within. In the waking state, an adult automatically thinks in a reality-oriented, rational, logical manner nearly all of the time. In *ASCs* this customary (automatic) rational thinking is de-automatized; ego receptivity to imagery, fantasy and suggestion increase markedly. Meditation techniques and certain techniques of hypnotic induction constitute types of manipulation of attention required to produce de-automatization.

As stated before, some altered, hypnotic-like states occur naturally, even daily, in the normal state of living. Others are induced by special means. Among the naturally occurring ones are the hypnagogic and hypnopompic states, i.e. the states just before falling asleep and just before waking up, states in which associations flow more freely and thinking takes on more pictorial forms.

In the hypnagogic state, lying in bed, the ego activity of the muscular as well as of the perceptual apparati is diminished. One lies quite still, with eyes closed, in a dark, quiet room, thus there are fewer perceptual stimuli and motor tasks to deal with. A shift then occurs in the cognitive apparatus. From secondary process, reality-oriented, mostly logical type of thinking, one drifts to thinking mainly in fleeting pictures; pictorial, prelogical, imaginative thinking, that is, primary process, takes over. And associations flow more freely than they do in the waking state.

The same happens in daydreaming with a minor but important difference. To some extent the daydreamer can direct his daydreams. The person in the hypnogogic state—or the nocturnal dreamer—does not consciously or voluntarily direct the flow of his imagery and associations.

Picture two children, one intently listening to a fairy tale, the other making up a story. In both there may be total absorption of attention. In the child absorbed in listening to the fairy tale, the ego allows itself to be more receptive than active in regard to imagery. In the other child, the ego is more active; he *produces* the imagery.

When there are very marked and distinct changes from reality orientation, when the subject is gently transported—or sometimes jolted—into a world of imagery and imagination, then we term the states, "altered states of consciousness." *ASCs* can be self-induced, induced by another (a hypnotist), or drug induced.

The contemporary hypnotherapist talks to his patient in the symbolic language of the primary process, deliberately employing imagery to enhance emotional learning. He also encourages the patient to use his own images. Images closely represent drives, wishes, conflicts, hopes and joys. In very deep hypnosis a good deal of the ordinary secondary process thinking is replaced by the developmentally earlier primary process thinking. Studies done in my laboratory (Fromm, Oberlander, & Gruenewald, 1970; Gruenewald, Fromm, & Oberlander, this volume) have shown that Rorschachs given to the same subjects in the waking and in deep hypnotic states contain much more primary process in the deep hypnotic than in the waking state. Many other studies have shown that in hypnosis the subject shows greater imagery and tends to think more in the pictorial mode than in verbal, logical terms (see, e.g., J.R. Hilgard, this volume, and Bowers and Bowers, this volume).

In hypnosis, ego activity in the sense of reality perception and the making of choices is diminished, but not fully abolished. There is greater sug-gestibility. What is suggestibility in ego psychological terms? I conceive of it as a form of ego receptivity. The ego in hypnosis is particularly receptive to stimuli coming from within or from without and it lets them influence im-agery, thoughts, behavioral action and feelings even if they do not conform to the laws of secondary process logic. For instance, in an age regression a subject may experience himself as a little boy or girl of five, playing in a sandbox. At the same time, some small part of his/her observing ego somehow may remain adult, observing that little boy or girl playing. However, because in hypnosis critical-judgmental and reality-oriented faculties of the ego are to a great degree temporarily excluded from func-tioning, the perceived co-existence of the adult and the child is not judged by the hypnotized subject to be absurd or illogical. The subject operates on the basis of a special logic—trance logic (Orne, 1959)—which is comparable to dream logic as described by French and Fromm (1964). No difference ex-ists for him between fantasy, imagery and actual reality. The imagery *has* reality for him, as it does for the young child in the waking state. Cognition for a hypnotized subject is organized much more along the lines of primary process, as in a young child.

In addition, the split into the child and the adult who watches the child in the age regression demonstrates another characteristic of hypnosis: the dissociation of the observing ego functions from the experiencing ego func-tions.

In the altered states of awareness induced by psychedelic drugs fast changes of overly clear imagery are projected onto unstructured outside stimuli. One major hallmark of psychedelically induced *ASC*s is that the vividness and the rate of experienced imagery is increased highly. Superim-posed upon each other in awareness and perceived simultaneously, the or-dinarily hidden unconscious, prelogical, very private world of inner drives is superimposed on the reality of the outer, objective world, and both are perceived simultaneously.

In order to begin to understand meditative states, Deikman (1963) set up a concentrative meditation experiment. In a quiet room slightly darkened so that no other sensory stimuli would intrude, he placed a beautiful small blue vase against a neutral background and asked his *S*s to stare at it for ten or fifteen minutes. They were to think of nothing but this art object. They

were told that whenever another thought occurred they were to dismiss it
and concentrate again on the object in front of them. While they stared at
it, they experienced the object as changing shape. Some Ss saw lines of light
going back and forth between them and the object. Some Ss felt as if they
and the object were merging or becoming one. It is the intense concentration on a beautiful or interesting object that enables a meditator to become
totally absorbed and to loosen his customary ties to the outside world. He
then goes into an *ASC*.

As he reaches higher and higher plateaus of meditation, the meditator
moves back in the developmental hierarchy from cognition to perception.
Cognition, a higher structure, gives way to inner perception; imagery, an
active intellectual mode, is replaced by a more receptive perceptual one.

Concentrative meditation as found in most Indian yogic and in orthodox
Buddhist systems initially requires unusually great ego activity. Attention
must strenuously be focused and held on the chosen object, and all other
stimuli must actively be prevented from entering awareness. After years of
concentration, the yogi achieves the ability to hold his mind to a single
stimulus for very long periods and to exclude any other mental content from
coming into awareness. Tibetan texts call this "one pointedness". The object to which the meditator devotes his total attention may be a visual or
acoustical stimulus in the outside world (a mantra), the breath, or an internally visualized image.

Such concentrative meditation, at least for quite a number of years, requires much ego activity. Later this attentional stance becomes automatized.

In contrast, in two other meditation systems, TM and contemporary
Eastern vipasýāna, the aim is not to concentrate. Rather, the aim is to expand awareness of the range of stimuli as far as possible. This is done by
alternating between periods of total ego-receptivity to whatever stimuli
might drift into consciousness and periods of ego-active restriction of the
range of mental events.

As I have stated before (Fromm, 1977b, p. 379–380), in certain of the
more advanced meditative states (Buddhist: samaṭṭha, Zen: beginning
satori, and the Spanish Christian observance of the mystical Prayer of the
Quiet) there is a shift away from perception of reality with its constancy and
definite structure to an obliteration of the subject/object dichotomy that
results in asymbolic, aperceptual awareness. The perceptual processes that
in effect guarantee reality have become de-automatized.

We may say that the two major elements of such meditation are either
long periods of ego activity devoted to restricting attention and motility (as
in the lotus position), or extended periods of ego receptivity to stimuli coming from within. In some forms of meditation the meditator, de facto, is instructed to alternate these two stances. The process leads to a qualitative

change in cognition, a regression from cognition to perception of imagery, or further to noncognitive, nonperceptual experience.

THE MODES OF ATTENTION IN THE WAKING STATE, DAYDREAMING, HYPNOSIS, MEDITATIVE AND OTHER ALTERED STATES OF CONSCIOUSNESS[3]

A wide variety of conflicting theories on attention in the waking state exists in the academic psychology of cognition (Broadbent, 1967; Deutsch & Deutsch, 1963; Kahneman, 1973). However, most academic researchers in the field today would subscribe to the idea that "attention" deals with that factor of selection which determines the significance of external and internal stimuli (Neisser, 1967; Silverman, 1968; Norman, 1969; Kahneman, 1973), and furthermore that it is a significant component in the hierarchy of cognitive operations to which perception, conception and memory belong. The majority of disagreements in the theories of waking attention concerns the level of stimulus-analyzing operations that attention performs. It is either assumed that the significance of the stimulus is determined largely by the nature of the stimulus itself with minimal processing, or that elaborate processing and transformation of sensory input is required (Norman, 1969, p. 34).

Certain minimal kinds of processes are agreed upon by most academic researchers concerned with attention. They may be viewed from the point of view of cognitive psychology as well as from that of ego psychology:

1) *Intensity*, i.e., the force of the stimulus necessary to reach a threshold of recognition (Silverman, 1968); in cognitive psychology this is conceived of as a stimulus property. How loud does the sound need to be to be heard? As an ego psychologist I conceive of it as the quantity of stimulation coming from an outside or inside source that will arouse the ego to become either receptively aware of it or to actively engage itself with the stimulus and deal with it.
2) *Expansiveness or Span of Attention.* This refers to the range, the spread of attention concentration: is the attention focal, restricted to a single stimulus, or is it wide, i.e. is there an expansion of awareness of the stimulus range that is attention cathected?
3) *Selectivity, field articulation and discrimination.* In ego psychological terms these cognitive processes can be described as ego activity spent in structuring the stimulus field.
4) *Activity.* Cognitive psychologists define this as the amount of effort required to engage a stimulus in attentional processing (see Kahneman;

3. Some of the materials on attention discussed on pp. 27–34, and parts of Table 4.1 have been worked out in discussion with Daniel P. Brown.

1973, Davidson & Goleman, 1977). It is the equivalent of what psychoanalysts call attention cathexis (Deikman, 1971). Attention cathexis is an ego-active process.

5) *Serial vs. Parallel Processing.* In serial processing a single stimulus, or a very few stimuli out of the total range of possible stimuli are selected and processed, one by one, i.e., serially. In parallel processing, a very large number of stimuli, òr the entire range of stimuli, or in any case those consciously as well as those unconsciously perceived, are given attention cathexis simultaneously.

Daniel P. Brown (1977), a member of my research staff who is trained both as a psychologist and as a scholar of Tibetan and Sanskrit, has reviewed and translated many of the eastern documents on meditation in an attempt to filter out culture-free variables within the eastern classification of meditation systems that could be used in western states of consciousness research. He has found that most eastern classifications of varieties of meditative practice are based on questions similar to those raised by western researchers on attention. However, the philosophic assumptions behind the questions, the methodology, the terminology, and the nature of the theories are vastly different. Buddhist psychology, abhidharma, is primarily a theory of cognition assuming a hierarchical relationship between attention and perception, attention and higher cognitive processes of conception and, most importantly, attention and affect. Elaborate classifications of specific types of meditation by attention modes and subsequent cognitive effects can be found in the Buddhist psychological texts.

Certain important points of similarity and difference between Buddhist and western research on attention need be mentioned. Most western theory and research on attention deals with attention in relation to external stimuli. Most eastern meditative analyses have an introspective bias; hence most eastern theories deal with attention in relation to internal stimuli. Furthermore, most western experimentation has been designed to study short-term, single, or multiple effects of external stimuli. Eastern meditative analyses concern long-term practice with repeated and well defined units of internal stimuli. Also, the great majority of studies of attention in western psychology has been done with subjects in the waking state, while that in eastern cultures mostly has been done with subjects in altered states of consciousness. However, there is some striking agreement at the conceptual level that makes comparison of eastern and western methodologies with regard to attention legitimate: four of the five kinds of waking state attentional operations listed above—expansiveness, selectivity, activity, and serial vs. parallel processing—not only have close counterparts in Buddhist meditation, but become major criteria by which different meditative systems are distinguished from each other. Such western researchers as Ornstein (1972) have used single attentional operations to differentiate systems of meditation, e.g. by means of restrictiveness vs. expansiveness, and by means of activity vs. passivity (Davidson & Schwartz, 1976). In Buddhist systems differentiation is more complex, requiring discrimination by several attentional operations. We have combined these data with our own research on hypnosis, and from an ego psychological point of view have worked out a new system of classifying modes of attention. With this system of attention classification, we feel we can describe and explain what happens in the waking state, in daydreaming, in hypnosis, in meditation and in many other *ASC*s.

With regard to ego modes used in the attentional process we find that very specific permutations of the interaction or alternation of the two systems—activity and receptivity—characterize daydreaming, hypnosis,

TABLE 4.1.   Typology of waking and altered states of consciousness by range of attention and ego modes

	Range of attention	Ego activity/ receptivity
1. Waking, normally alert and concentrated	N	a
2. Waking, fascinated, entranced	F	a
3. Free Association	UF	r
4. Inspirational Phase of Creativity	UF	r
5. Daydreaming	UF	r
6. Dreaming	HA	a/r
7. Hypnosis	F	r > a
8. Selfhypnosis	E	a/r
9. Biofeedback	F	a/r
10. Transcendental Meditation (TM)	F	a/r
11. Concentrative Meditation	F	a
12. Satipaṭṭhana	E	r
13. Classical Vipaśyāna	E	a
14. Psychedelic states	HA	r

N = normal average, baseline
F = focused; restriction of attention-cathected stimulus range
UF = unfocused
E = expansive; wide stimulus range attention cathected
HA = hyper-aroused

a = ego active
r = ego receptive
a/r = alternating between activity and receptivity
r < a = more receptive than active

self-hypnosis and the various meditation systems we have studied, and we will attempt to show that these permutations of attentional modes and ego activity or ego receptivity directly characterize the waking states, free association, the inspirational phase of the creative act, dreaming and daydreaming, hypnosis, psychedelic states and the meditation systems. Table 4.1 gives an overview of a variety of states of consciousness as typified by the range of attention and ego activity.

In the normal, alert, waking state the ego actively (denoted by the letter "a" on Table 4.1) cathects a certain range of stimuli, which we have here called Normal Average (N). We shall now take this normally alert and waking state as a baseline and compare it to another waking state and twelve altered states of consciousness.

When a person is awake but deeply interested in a particular thing and entranced by it, his range of attention narrows. It becomes more focussed (F) and he uses a good deal of ego activity (denoted on Table 1 by letter "a") in studying the object that has attracted his attention and fascinated him. In contrast, in the states of free association and daydreaming, attention is unfocused (UF), free floating. But is it expansive? I do not think so. While it freely and loosely goes from one object to another and alights like a butterfly one minute here and the next minute there, it does not encompass a wide range of stimuli at one and the same time. In both free association and daydreaming the mode of the ego is receptive (r): there is receptivity to imagery, thoughts, feelings and associations that arise from within. General reality orientation progressively fades into the background when we move from the waking state to free association to daydreaming to hypnosis and to dreams.

In the nocturnal dream there is no reality orientation. Attention given to promptings from within is hyper-aroused (H-A) and the ego is both active and receptive. It produces the dream and actively attempts to find solutions for the conflict expressed in the dream.[4] It also lets feelings and imagery arise from the unconscious.

In concentrative meditation, the ego makes an active effort to exclude outer and inner stimuli, to banish them, to empty mind and memory. The meditator is instructed to concentrate his attention on a particular object, an idea or a monotonous activity (such as a breathing exercise), restricting it to a very narrow focus and "emptying his mind" of all other contents. Once the mind has been actively emptied, the meditator gets absorbed in the concentrative process he initiated and after a while this process becomes autonomous, requiring little ego activity. A de-automatization of those functions of the ego apparati that ordinarily deal with structuring the

---

4. With regard to the dream as a product of the unconscious ego rather than the id and superego, and the dream's function of problem solving, see French and Fromm, 1964.

environment and cognition has set in.

De-automatization of a structure results in a structure lower in the hierarchy rather than a complete termination of the particular function involved (Brown, in preparation).

In the higher states of meditation attention is extensive and covers a wide stimulus range.

Hypnosis, self-hypnosis, biofeedback, TM and concentrative meditation are all characterized by focused attention within a restricted stimulus range. Hypnosis often is induced by the hypnotist asking the subject to stare at a particular object for a while until his eyes will want to close. The reason for this technique is, of course, that eye closure helps the subject to let general reality orientation fade into the background of his awareness. A good deal of attention cathexis is thus released and can be turned on the patient's inner life and on his interaction with the hypnotist. The patient becomes receptive to the promptings coming from his own preconscious and unconscious and to the hypnotherapist's interpretations and suggestions. At other times he may use ego activity to change suggestions the hypnosist has given to him, or change imagery which the hypnotist has vivified for him. In heterohypnosis there is more ego receptivity than ego activity. But heterohypnosis is by no means only an ego receptive state. Furthermore, in hypnosis the secondary process thinking of the waking state is replaced by earlier developed primary process thinking.

In all states of consciousness, the waking as well as the altered states, the human being functions with a balance of primary and secondary process. Primary and secondary process range along a continuum; no sharp line of distinction separates them. The primary/secondary process continuum can be pictured as a scale. Fantasy versus reality orientation is a similar continuum along which states of consciousness could be distributed.

Figure 4.2 shows the primary process versus secondary process balance for 15 states of consciousness (Fromm, 1979a). Rapaport (1951) has ordered four states of consciousness along the same continuum (waking thought, daydreaming, hypnagogic hallucination, and nocturnal dreaming). In general, the deeper or the more altered a state of consciousness is, the closer does the human being function to the primary process pole of the continuum; and vice versa, the closer to the waking state, the more secondary process is involved.

This rule seems to hold for all altered states of consciousness except for the advanced states of meditation. And perhaps it is not just chance that the advanced meditative states are generally called "higher states of meditation" rather than "deeper" states. *Advanced* states of meditation fall beyond and outside of the primary process/secondary continuum, and cannot be ranged anywhere within it.

FIGURE 4.2.   *The relationship between primary and secondary process.*

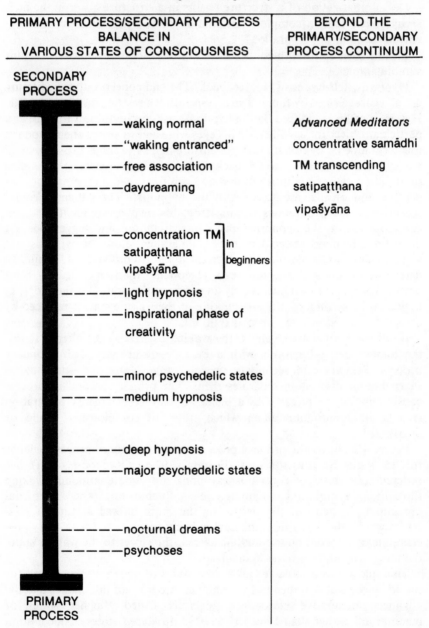

PRIMARY PROCESS/SECONDARY PROCESS BALANCE IN VARIOUS STATES OF CONSCIOUSNESS	BEYOND THE PRIMARY/SECONDARY PROCESS CONTINUUM

SECONDARY
PROCESS

—————waking normal

—————"waking entranced"

—————free association

—————daydreaming

—————concentration TM
satipaṭṭhana   } in beginners
vipaśyāna

—————light hypnosis

—————inspirational phase of
creativity

—————minor psychedelic states

—————medium hypnosis

—————deep hypnosis

—————major psychedelic states

—————nocturnal dreams

—————psychoses

PRIMARY
PROCESS

Advanced Meditators

concentrative samādhi

TM transcending

satipaṭṭhana

vipaśyāna

Reproduced by permission from the *Journal of Altered States of Consciousness,* 1978–79, *4,* 118.

ACSs and Learning

There are two types of learning: emotional learning and intellectual learning.

Intellectual learning, particularly learning about reality, requires ego activity and focused attention. The human mind is not a tabula rasa upon which reality impresses itself as on a wax tablet. Knowledge needs to be actively acquired. And attention must be paid to a *rather* narrow range of outside stimuli in order to acquire new knowledge. Therefore, I feel the acquisition of intellectual knowledge best takes place in the two waking states which we have designated on Table 4.1 as (1a) the normally alert and concentrated waking state and (1b) the waking state in which a person feels fascinated with and entranced by a piece of reality that he has newly discovered.

Some literature, as yet not quite unequivocal, indicates that hypnosis, also, aids the learning process. It, too, is a state of highly focused attention cathexis and a state in which there is ego activity as well as heightened ego receptivity (suggestibility).

One could be tempted to question how learning about reality can be improved in hypnosis, a state that is characterized by allowing oneself to let one's general reality orientation fade into the background. However, it is important to note that in hypnosis, attention cathexis is withdrawn from the normal average range of its distribution *in order* to concentrate it with full intensity on one single spot. If this spot is a piece of reality, better knowledge about it can be gained in hypnosis than in the waking state where it has to share attention cathexis with a much wider range of objects. Thus, a college student in hypnosis can be told to concentrate so well on the content of a scientific book he is reading that the material will burn itself into his memory and he will not forget it for years to come. Besides being able to concentrate on the material better in hypnosis because in this state he does not allow himself to be distracted from his book by extraneous stimuli, he is also being helped by the hypnotist's post-hypnotic suggestion, "It will burn itself into your memory so you will not forget it for years"; that is, if he accepts the suggestion, if he reacts to it with ego receptivity rather than with active resistance.

In contradistinction *emotional learning* takes place when the ego is receptive and open to promptings from without (such as the evocative interpretive comments of the psychoanalyst) and from within (unconscious and preconscious material that floats into awareness). That is why Freud invented the therapeutic method of free association, a very minor *ASC*. In (permissive) hypnosis, a more major *ASC*, the ego is much more receptive to inner and outer promptings. Therefore, the hypnoanalyst can help the patient to learn emotionally and to gain deep insight faster than in psychoanalysis. And because of the vascillation between ego activity and ego receptivity that appears to be a characteristic of permissive hypnosis, emotional learning can rather easily be integrated with intellectual learning, and deep "working through" takes place quite fast.

What holds for hypnosis with regard to intellectual and emotional learning probably also holds for TM, biofeedback, and contemporary vipaśyāna, as all of these are ASCs characterized by restriction of the range of attention cathexis to stimuli from without, and more importantly by alternations between ego activity and ego receptivity. The intellectual learning in these states takes place during phases of ego activity; the emotional learning during phases of ego receptivity.

Conclusion

There are many different altered states of consciousness—how many is as yet unknown. The states of consciousness range on a continuum from those that are very different from the waking state (as, e.g., very deep hypnosis and the highest states of eastern meditation) to those that are close to the waking state (e.g., light hypnosis and daydreaming). The range can be depicted in a two-dimensional, linear way:

$$ASCs\text{―――――――} \text{waking state}$$

In this chapter I have discussed what I consider to be the essential constituents of waking and altered states of consciousness. They are:

Ego receptivity	Ego activity
Primary process	Secondary process
Fantasy	Reality orientation
Imagery	Conceptualization
Unfocused, free-floating	Focused attention

They, too, represent continua. All are parallel to each other; each spans a particular parameter of ego functions or processes.

I suspect that ego receptivity, primary process, fantasy, imagery, and unfocused free-floating attention are produced by the right hemisphere of the brain; ego activity, secondary process, reality orientation, and conceptualization by the left hemisphere. Depending on whether it is reality oriented or not, focused attention can probably be produced either by the right hemisphere (e.g., the focused attention in hypnosis that shuts out the general reality orientation) or by the left hemisphere (e.g., the attention the construction worker pays to lowering a heavy steel girder into just exactly the right spot).

Frequently, two of the continua work in tandem in cognitive processes, as, e.g., primary process/secondary process and imagery/conceptualization. Primary process thinking is thinking in pictorial forms; secondary process is devoid of imagery—it is conceptual thinking. The way I see it at this time ego receptivity/activity is probably the guiding principle for all *ASC*s. In all *ASC*s the ego allows into awareness more unconscious and preconscious material than in the waking state.

It would be too simplistic to say that the deeper the *ASC* the more it is characterized by the categories on the left hand side of the continuum; too simplistic, because of the differences between the various *ASC*s. For instance, imagery is extremely vivid and fast-changing under psychedelic drugs and must be held on a single object in many forms or stages of meditation. It would be too simplistic also because the waking state does not always require strictly focused attention and some of the *ASC*s are characterized by *hyper*-focused attention.

In general, however, the following rule holds for all *ASC*s, with the possible exception of meditation: the deeper the *ASC* the more primary process, the more imagery, the more ego receptivity and the more free floating, or freely hovering attention.

Biographical information for Professor Shor may be found on page 14.

Ronald E. Shor *presents a method for measuring hypnotic depth based on retrospective phenomenological report that can be used to produce two types of measurement. One is a univariate measurement of overall hypnotic depth, based on the common tradition of variable difficulty level. The second is a multidimensional set of measurements of three dimensions of hypnotic depth and five other important variables. While presented as a technique of measurement, the report is also a theoretical statement about the nature of hypnosis.*

5

A Phenomonological Method for the Measurement of Variables Important to an Understanding of the Nature of Hypnosis

RONALD E. SHOR

I. Introduction

This report presents a phenomenological method for making measurements of the extent of development of variables important to an understanding of hypnosis. The measurements are made in the form of diagnostic evaluations by a skilled examiner using rating scales applied to retrospective subjective descriptions of what the experience of hypnosis was like.

The phenomenological method is designed to provide two types of measurements. One is a univariate measurement of overall hypnotic depth based on the common tradition of the successful accomplishment of hypnotic phenomena of variable difficulty levels. This will be called the traditional approach. The second type is a multidimensional set of measurements of eight dimensional variables which the writer has theorized to be psychological processes of considerable importance to understanding hypnosis. Three of these underlying processes are theorized to be dimensions of hypnotic depth, the remaining five are not. This will be called the theoretical approach.

An earlier version of this paper was presented as the Presidential Address, Division 30 (Psychological Hypnosis) at the eighty-fifth annual convention of the American Psychological Association, San Francisco, August 26-30, 1977.

105

The second section of this report presents a survey and comparison of the several methods designed to measure hypnotic depth, including the phenomenological. The third section describes the conditions under which retrospective phenomenological descriptions may be presumed to be accurate. The fourth section, the traditional approach; and the fifth, the theoretical.

The traditional and theoretical approaches yield differing operational definitions of hypnotic depth. From the perspective of the writer's theory of hypnosis, the traditional method is very largely dependent on depth along just one of the three dimensions—nonconscious involvement—somewhat dependent upon depth along a second dimension—trance—and virtually insensitive to depth along the third dimension—archaic involvement. One of the objectives behind the development of the phenomenological method is to help clarify the difference between the definitions of hypnotic depth yielded by the traditional and theoretical approaches.

In a future publication the writer will wish to argue that reliance on traditional methods of measuring hypnotic depth has led to an imbalanced view of the nature of hypnosis in many research studies. The present report is limited to describing the phenomenological method. Empirical studies will be needed to clarify the relationships among measurements derived from the two approaches.

II. Survey and Comparison of Methods

Three general methods have been developed in psychology for the measurement of hypnotic depth. These three may be briefly labled the behavioral, clinical, and subjective methods.

In the behavioral methods (see, for example, Friedlander & Sarbin, 1938; Weitzenhoffer & Hilgard, 1959; Shor & E. Orne, 1962) a set of standardized hypnotic items such as postural sway, post hypnotic suggestion, and amnesia are administered verbatim and scored in terms of precise and objective behavioral criteria. For example, a test is made as to whether a subject does or does not unclasp his fingers during an allotted test period when the suggestion is given that he will be unable to do so. The performance is scored as successfully hypnotic if the subject fails to take his hands apart. All of the items in the set are administered in a fixed order and all are scored in terms of such predetermined, overtly observable criteria of successful response. Because the items in the set are of varying difficulty, a total score based on the total number of items successfully performed serves as the measure of hypnotic depth. For example, a subject who successfully performed all twelve items in a standardized set is said to have been more deeply hypnotized than a subject who successfully performed only three of them. Defining hypnotic depth in this rigorous but rigid way has had numerous applications in research situations but has had negligible use in clinical situations.

In the clinical methods (see, for example, Bernheim, 1888; Liébeault, 1889; Davis & Husband, 1931; O'Connell, Orne, & Shor, 1966), hypnotic items are arranged in terms of presumed difficulty level and classified according to the depth of hypnosis needed to perform them successfully. The clinical methods do not rely on standardized procedures or standardized wording, however, and only a small subset of the items is typically used to make the evaluations of depth. For example, amnesia and visual hallucinations are generally taken to be indications of deep hypnosis, so the subject's convincing performance would by definition establish that the subject was deeply hypnotized, at least during the period of time of their performance. Clinical methods thus provide a way of determining depth at differing points of time in hypnotic proceedings but they are also commonly taken as providing an overall measurement of depth for the entire session. With clinical methods the measurement of depth is an interpretive diagnostic evaluation by the examiner rather than a tallying of predetermined overt behaviors. The criteria of evaluation that the examiner uses to make his diagnosis are as much a matter of how convinced the subject says he is about the subjective reality of his own hypnotic experiences as of the quality of the overt performances.

Compared with behavioral methods, the clinical provide a trade-off of greater flexibility for lesser psychometric definitiveness. There are obvious advantages in the clinical situation to defining depth in terms of the quality of responsiveness to a few or even just one selected item induced in any manner found suitable to fit the occasion. Clinical methods have also been used productively in research, although in modern times, typically in conjunction with empirical ties to behavioral measures (for example, Cobb & Shor, 1968).

In the subjective methods (see, for example, LeCron, 1953; Shor, Orne, & O'Connell, 1966; Tart, 1972) hypnotic depth is defined in terms of how the subject feels experientially rather than in terms of his hypnotic performances. To this end the subject is asked to make impressionistic experiential diagnoses of his subjective depth of hypnosis at varying points in the hypnotic procedures or as an overall evaluation. In other words, the subject is asked to rate how deeply hypnotized he feels himself to be as a purely subjective feeling. Doubtless this is not the same meaning of "depth" as provided by the behavioral and clinical methods but it is nonetheless interesting to study it.

In this paper a fourth general approach to the measurement of hypnotic depth will be presented—the phenomenological method. While the phenomenological method has some partial overlap with the other three, particularly the clinical, it is sufficiently unique in procedure and purpose to make it appropriate to consider it a separate and new method in its own right. The phenomenological method is offered as an addition to the pool of methodological techniques for the study of hypnosis and not as a competitive alternative to supplant the other methods. The relationships between measurements derived from the four different methods and the documentation of their relative usefulness for varying purposes are empirical matters which are beyond the scope of this report.

The phenomenological method is concerned with the description of consciousness, the description of the subject's conscious experiences during the time of the hypnosis. Measurements of hypnotic depth are made by the examiner in terms of rating scales applied to the subject's descriptions of his conscious experiences. The descriptive reports are gathered from the subjects retrospectively, after the hypnosis is terminated. Obviously the phenomenological method is predicated upon two assumptions: (a) that even in the deepest hypnosis the subject is conscious; and (b) that under appropriate circumstances he can retrospectively describe his hypnotic experiences accurately.

It is instructive to compare the similarities and differences among the four methods. A synopsis is presented in Table 5.1.

In the behavioral methods although subjective report is utilized in the scoring of items such as amnesia and a self-scoring system is used in the Harvard Group Scale (Shor & E. Orne, 1962), the measurements are made from the point of view of an external observer. Subjective evaluations of the quality of the experiences, while sometimes gathered, have not been made a part of the basic scoring. While the Barber Suggestibility Scale (Barber, 1965a) permits flexibility of induction or the omission of induction, the test items are standardized. It is important to reiterate that in the phenomenological method the evaluations of depth are made by the examiner and on the basis of rating scales, and not, as in the subjective method, by the subject and on the basis of unaided global feelings. Even though in the phenomenological method the objective hypnotic performances serve as a concrete referent for discussion, the examiner makes his diagnostic evaluations of depth strictly on the basis of the subject's descriptions of the quality of his phenomenological experience. Although several separate measures are provided by the Stanford Profile Scales of Hypnotic Susceptibility (Weitzenhoffer & Hilgard, 1963), these are not dimensions of hypnosis in the writer's terms. The profile scales yield "dimensions" in the factor analytic sense, not in the writer's sense of theorized underlying processes.

III. The Conditions of Presumptive Accuracy

The phenomenological method is an interview procedure to be carried out after the termination of hypnosis. Its purpose is for the examiner to make

TABLE 5.1.   Similarities and differences among the four methods

	Behavioral	Clinical	Subjective	Phenomenological
Uses standardized procedures of administering the hypnosis items	Yes	No	No	No
Employs very precise criteria of evaluation	Yes	No	No	No
Evaluations of depth based on observation of overt behaviors	Yes	Yes	No	No
Evaluations of depth based on descriptions of phenomenological experiences	No	Yes	Yes	Yes
Evaluations of depth made by the subject on impressionistic criteria	No	No	Yes	No
Provides measurements of depth for selected points in the hypnotic session as well as overall for the entire session	No	Yes	Yes	Yes
Provides a univariate measurement of hypnotic depth	Yes	Yes	Yes	Yes
Provides differential measurement of more than one dimension of hypnotic depth	No	No	No	Yes

diagnostic evaluations in regard to variables of interest based on the subject's retrospective phenomenological descriptions of what hypnosis was like experientially. The method is intended to be used only in situations explicitly defined as hypnosis; extensions of the method would be needed to use it in other situations. Throughout this report the person who induces the hypnosis will be called the hypnotist and the person who conducts the phenomenological examination will be called the examiner. Most commonly, however, one person serves both as hypnotist and examiner.

The phenomenological method is intended to be used only under conditions where it can reasonably be presumed that the subject is reporting accurately on his conscious experiences during hypnosis. There are three conditions of presumptive accuracy. It is the task of the hypnotist and examiner to try their best to establish these three conditions. Until and unless the examiner feels reasonably confident that the conditions of presumptive accuracy have been and remain established he should not use the data and/or not conduct the phenomenological interview. Whether or not in any absolute sense the retrospective descriptions are truly accurate renditions of the conscious experiences they are presumed to represent is a major metatheoretical issue not dealt with in this report.

1. *The hypnotist must lift amnesia and communicate to the subject that he wants the termination of other residual hypnotic effects.* As the phenomena of amnesia and so-called posthypnotic suggestion indicate, hypnosis has not necessarily terminated just because the hypnotist requires the subject to open his eyes and to become wide awake. Even when not explicitly requested, hypnotic influences may persist to interfere with a subject's ability to discuss his hypnotic experiences with full lucidity. It is thus important for the hypnotist to communicate that he truly wants the hypnosis to be over and that there should be no remaining encumbrances on the subject's memory and responsiveness.

2. *The hypnotist must communicate that he wants the subject to tell the examiner the truth whatever that may be.* Many theorists have pointed out that hypnotic subjects are often strongly motivated to please the hypnotist and to fulfill the role of being a good hypnotic subject. Unless neutralized, such motivations may interfere with the subject's ability to report imperfections in his hypnotic experiences, particularly if he believes that to do so would discredit his hypnotic achievements and disappoint the hypnotist. It is thus important for the hypnotist to take pains to convince the subject that the hypnotic procedure will remain meaningful only if the subject is willing to tell the examiner the complete and undistorted truth during the phenomenological interview.

A distinction needs to be drawn here between the superficial and deep levels of meaning in the communications made by hypnotists to subjects. It is common practice for a hypnotist to say that he wants one thing when the clear intent communicated to his subject is that he actually wants something quite different. For example, when the hypnotist says, "I want you to try your best to bend your arm," it is readily understood from the context that the real message is that the hypnotist wants the subject to fail to bend his arm. When the hypnotist tells the subject to "arouse" but then to carry out a posthypnotic suggestion the real communication is that the hypnotist wants the subject to maintain the hypnosis sufficiently for experiencing the so-called posthypnotic phenomenon despite acting as if hypnosis had been terminated. In practice it is typically not difficult to distinguish between the superficial words of intent spoken by the hypnotist and the fuller, actual communication. The point at issue here is that the hypnotist must try his best to communicate that he truly wants the subject to tell the examiner the truth during the phenomenological interview.

3. *The examiner must establish the subject's role as that of a*

phenomenological co-investigator in the context of an open conversational interchange. The phenomenological psychologists have argued cogently (see Lyons, 1970; Keen, 1973) that the best way to elicit phenomenological information is to adopt the method that everyone uses in everyday life— namely, to engage the other person in a conversational dialogue in which words, inflections, gestures, and emotive expressions combine to create a communications network 'of openness and immediacy. Such a conversational interchange provides an opportunity for the people to ask each other questions, agree or disagree, pursue ambiguous points, judge the adequacy of the responses, and discern other subtleties and complexities.

Other investigators have taken issue with the use of unfettered interviewing techniques in psychological research. Persuasively raising warnings about the potentially distorting effects of experimenter bias and demand characteristics, these investigators have advocated the use of control procedures such as tape recorded instructions, standardized questioning, and written responses. While valuable in many research situations, these control procedures unfortunately place sterilizing restrictions on the free conversational interchange necessary for gathering phenomenological information in its full subtlety and complexity.

The problem is how to avoid simultaneously the counterposed dangers of experimenter bias and stultified inquiry. The solution is to explain the problem to the subject, to clarify what information is being sought, why it is being sought, how it will be used, and to enlist his aid in getting it. What this means is that the examiner should strive to establish a methodological partnership with his subject in which they share equal responsibility for getting at the truth. It is not that one person in a superior social position called an examiner interrogates another person in a subordinate social position called a subject. Rather it is that two socially equal partners share in the task of helping the subject to recapitulate his hypnotic experiences.

To this end it is important that the examiner try to create an interpersonal climate in which the subject feels at ease and is motivated to get at the truth without distortion and concealment rather than to protect his self-esteem because he feels that he is being judged adversely. It is important too that the subject believe that the examiner is seriously interested in the desctiptions of inner subjective experiences he is giving. This climate of trust and active cooperation will best be fostered by the examiner being honest and genuine with his subject.

IV. The Traditional Approach

It is well established that hypnotic phenomena differ in difficulty. Some hypnotic phenomena are inherently more difficult to induce than are others. For example, an auditory hallucination is inherently more difficult to induce than a postural sway. Complete anesthesia of the entire body is more difficult to induce than a slight twitching in the fingertips. Another way to state the matter is that only a small proportion of unselected subjects will be able to achieve hypnotic anesthesia whereas a high proportion will be able to achieve a slight twitching. Among the inherently most difficult to achieve hypnotic phenomena are amnesia, complete anesthesia, and visual hallucinations with the eyes open. Among the inherently least difficult to achieve hypnotic phenomena are ideomotor movements like postural sway and minor sensory illusions such as a general feeling of bodily lightness.

The common tradition has been to define hypnotic depth in terms of difficulty level. In all the behavioral and clinical methods for measuring depth developed throughout the last century (see the review in Hilgard, 1965b), hypnotic depth has at its roots been equated with difficulty level in a direct one-to-one fashion—i.e., the more difficult the hypnotic phenomena the subject was able to experience and/or perform the deeper the hypnosis was considered to be.

The phenomenological method can be used to make diagnostic assessments of hypnotic depth as traditionally defined. The only unique features are (a) that the diagnoses are based exclusively on retrospective phenomenological descriptions of subjective experience and not at all on the quality of external performance; and (b) that the criterion of successful accomplishment is the degree of subjective convincingness of the experience to the subject at the time of the experience.

While the phenomenological method may be applied to any hypnotic phenomenon it is convenient to select a representative set of phenomena of varying difficulty to help concretize the discussion and make it explicit. Ten phenomena have been selected and are summarized in Table 5.2.

Difficulty is subdivided into five levels. The first two levels are considered nonhypnotic. The phenomena are included on the table at the level where they first become experientially convincing. Four of the ten phenomena— those dealing with forms of age regression and visual hallucination—are largely overlapping. This is intended to help highlight the important distinctions. At the end of the discussion of these ten phenomena there will be a discussion of how the difficulty level of many other phenomena can be deduced from the descriptions given. To that end descriptions of the generic categories to which the representative phenomena belong are included in the table.

The translation from difficulty level to traditional hypnotic depth is simple and direct. Easy hypnotic phenomena are taken as indicative of light hypnosis; intermediate hypnotic phenomena are taken as indicative of medium hypnosis; difficult hypnotic phenomena are taken as indicative of deep hypnosis. Diagnoses of depth may be made on the basis of phenomena singly or as an overall assessment of the entire hypnotic session. However, it

TABLE 5.2.   A representative set of phenomena of varying difficulty level

Non-hypnotic

1) None

No subjectively convincing experiences beyond the ordinary. Nothing beyond purely voluntary, consciously deliberate actions and the use of imagination as it is readily available in alert everyday life.

2) Very Easy

(a) Chevreul Pendulum Illusion. Mechanical amplification of tiny ideomotor movements with visual capture.

(b) Hands Moving Together. Sizable ideomotor movements with eyes closed to eliminate visual monitoring.

Hypnotic

3) Easy

(a) Hand Levitation. Sizable ideomotor movements with eyes open to provide visual monitoring.

(b) Inability to Stand. Apparent loss of volitional control of muscular responses.

4) Intermediate

(a) Eyes Closed Age Regression. Fantasy with eyes closed to minimize discrepant observations.

(b) Eyes Closed Visual Hallucination. Imagined perception with eyes closed to minimize discrepant observations.

5) Difficult

(a) Complete Amnesia. Prevention of memory retrieval.

(b) Eyes Open Age Regression. Fantasy with eyes open and environmental interactions that provide discrepant observations.

(c) Eyes Open Visual Hallucination. Imagined perception with eyes open and environmental interactions that provide discrepant observations.

(d) Complete Anesthesia. The complete elimination of a forceful perceptual experience from conscious experiencing.

is not felt that the method is sufficiently sensitive to make distinctions into more than five levels.

2a. The Chevreul Pendulum Illusion. This is a kinesthetic illusion (Easton & Shor, 1975, 1976, 1977) in which a small pendulum is suspended from the fingertips and the subject imaginatively concentrates on the idea that it will swing in a specified manner, for example, in a circle. The physical mechanism of the pendulum is such that it amplifies very small ideomotor muscle movements synchronous with the idea of movement so that relatively large movements of the pendulum are produced. The visually observable movements of the pendulum are so much larger than the small muscle movements producing them that it is difficult for the subject to accept the connection or even to become aware of the muscle movements. This latter point is referred to in the experimental literature as visual capture. The Chevreul Pendulum Illusion is so easy that almost everyone will experience it. The only exceptions are subjects who do not know how to go about trying or who produce synchronous contradictory muscle movements which cancel out the effect. It is so easy a phenomenon to experience with subjective conviction that it is not considered to be a hypnotic phenomenon.

2b. Hands Moving Together. In this phenomenon the hands are suspended in the air in front of the subject. The eyes are closed to eliminate visual monitoring. The subject then concentrates on the idea that the hands will be drawn together without his deliberately moving them together. The phenomenon consists of the subjectively convincing experience of the hands being drawn together without conscious voluntary action. The phenomenon is so easy that most subjects will experience it. The only exceptions are subjects who do not know how to try or who resist the effects. It is so easy a phenomenon to experience with subjective conviction that it is not considered to be a hypnotic phenomenon.

3a. Hand Levitation. In hand levitation the subject looks at his resting hand and concentrates on the idea that it will rise upward into the air a considerable distance without his deliberately lifting it. The phenomenon consists of the subjectively convincing experience of the hand rising upward against the direction of gravity without conscious voluntary action. Hand levitation is often used for hypnotic induction because it is easy to experience, is self-paced, and provides the hypnotist with many cues as to how the subject is progressing. It also provides a good opportunity for the hypnotist to encompass a number of technical aids into his induction strategy including concentrated attention (absorption), repetitive and monotonous stimulation, expectant belief that more things will happen, relaxation, and drowsiness.

3b. Inability to Stand. In this phenomenon the hypnotist tells the subject that he will be unable to stand up no matter how hard he may try to do so. The phenomenon consists of the subjectively convincing experience of two components. First, the subject must make a sincere, concerted conscious volitional effort to stand up when challenged to try to do so. The subject must experience that he really tried to stand, not just went through the motions half-heartedly without the conscious commitment to try his best. Second, the subject must experience that he really was unable to stand despite this concerted consciously governed effort. The phenomenon requires more than an awkwardness or slowing down in muscular control; it requires the experiencing of an unambiguous failure such that the subject is able to say at the end without equivocation that he knows he really tried and knows he really failed.

The phenomenon remains just as easy when it is experienced under so-called posthypnotic conditions as when it is experienced "within" hypnosis provided that it is tested soon after "awakening."

4a. Eyes Closed Age Regression. In this phenomenon the hypnotist requires that the subject spin out a fantasy for himself in which he is a younger age. The eyes are kept closed to minimize discrepant observations. Keeping the eyes closed keeps the fantasizing from the kind of interactions with the environment that occur in daily life and retains it instead in a context more akin to dreaming. The phenomenon consists of the subjectively convincing experience of the age regression as a real event.

In other words, during the time of the age regression experience the subject must believe in its reality value; he must accept the age regression as a real event as far as his conscious experience of it is concerned. If, instead, the age regression fantasy is imbedded within a conscious awareness of its unreality then it is nothing but imaginative make-believe which, although perhaps vivid and compelling, is not true age regression. It is stressed that "reality value" refers to what the experience was like to the subject during the time of the experience and not to how it appeared to him as later judged by "waking" standards of judgment. For example, the fact that the subject is spinning out a fantasy for himself is logically incongruent with his also believing in its reality. But such logical considerations may, for several reasons, not be at all relevant to the subject during the time of the experience.

It should be noted that the phenomenon is sometimes induced simultaneous with extensive drowsiness and even with the superimposition of brief periods of actual physiological sleep. The infusions of hypnagogic imagery, dreamlike ideation, and actual dreaming that may result become pertinent to the evaluation of the quality of the age regression only insofar as they contribute to the subject's belief or disbelief in the reality value of the experience during the time of the experience. Similarly, the vividness of the imagery during the fantasizing is of no pertinence to the quality of the age regression except insofar as it contributes to its subjective convincingness as a real event.

4b. Eyes Closed Visual Hallucination. In this phenomenon the hypnotist requires that the subject imagine a visual perception. The eyes are kept closed to minimize discrepant observations. Keeping the eyes closed keeps the imagining from the kinds of interactions with the environment that occur in daily life and retains it instead in a context more akin to dreaming. The phenomenon consists of the subjectively convincing experience of the imagined perception as a real event. Two types of eyes closed visual hallucinations need to be distinguished.

In the first type the subject believes in the hallucinatory experience as a real event in the sense that he is not consciously aware of its unreality during the time of the experience. The remaining statements to be made in regard to this type of hallucination are the same as the statements made in the second and third paragraphs of (4a) Eyes Closed Age Regression, with the exception that the words "imagined perception" or "visual hallucination" should be substituted for the words "age regression" or "age regression fantasy."

In the second type the subject knows that the hallucination is not a real perception during the time of the experience and may even identify it as a hallucination. He nonetheless has the subjectively convincing experience of the visual hallucination as a real event in the sense that he experiences the hallucination as a real hallucination. The key feature is that the subject experiences the hallucination as having a life of its own—i.e., as appearing to him to have an existence independent of his own deliberate creation and conscious control of it.

It needs to be stressed again here that the vividness of the imagery is not pertinent to the quality of the hallucination except insofar as it contributes to its subjective convincingness as a real event. For example, the subject may experience very vivid imagery merely as imaginative make-believe whereas he may experience very shoddy imagery as a vision having a life of its own. While it is true that better imagery may help to convince the subject in the believability of the experience the quality of the phenomenon is not indexed by the quality of the imagery.

5a. Complete Amnesia. In this phenomenon there is the systematic forgetting or dissociation from the boundaries of conscious awareness of selected memories. The phenomenon consists of the subjectively convincing experience of four components. First, the target memories must be experienced as not within the boundaries of conscious awareness. This is more than a reluctance or unwillingness by the subject to attend to memories which, though formless and unarticulated, are nonetheless experienced as within consciousness. Complete amnesia is a true inability to experience even vague glimmerings of the target memories. Second, the subject must make a sincere, concerted conscious level effort to retrieve the memories. The subject must experience that he really tried to get at the memories, not just half-heartedly went through the motions. Third, the subject must experience that he was really unable to retrieve the memories despite this effort. Complete amnesia requires more than a slowing down of the process of retrieval; it requires the experiencing of an unambiguous failure. Fourth, the target memories must be readily retrievable after a releasing signal is given.

Anything less than the subjectively convincing experience of these four components is not complete amnesia. The amnesia may be for any knowledge, not just for events within hypnosis. In this complete form the amnesia is totally impervious to any degree of breakdown even with a detailed recapitulation of events such as by showing the subject a videotape recording of the session. Under these conditions the subject recognizes that the events must have taken place but is unable to become consciously aware of his own recollections of them.

5b. Eyes Open Age Regression. The same statements as were made in the first and second paragraphs of the discussion of (4a) Eyes Closed Age Regression apply here with the exception that the subject's eyes are opened so that the hypnotist can require the subject to interact with the environment in ways that provide discrepant observations. With the subject's eyes kept closed his fantasizing is largely sealed off from reality observations. With the subject's eyes kept open the hypnotist can determine whether or not the subject can incorporate reality interactions into the fantasizing. The phenomenon consists of the subjectively convincing experience of the age regression as a real event despite these required incorporated intrusions. The phenomenon may be experienced just as readily under so-called posthypnotic conditions as when it is experienced "within" hypnosis.

5c. Eyes Open Visual Hallucination. In this phenomenon the hypnotist requires the subject to imagine seeing a visual perception. The eyes are kept open so that the hypnotist can require the subject to interact with the environment in ways that provide discrepant observations. With the subject's eyes kept closed his visual imagining is largely sealed off from reality observations. With the subject's eyes kept open the hypnotist can determine whether or not the subject can incorporate reality intrusions into the visual imagining. The phenomenon consists of the subjectively convincing experience of the visual hallucination as a real event despite these required incorporated intrusions.

The same two types of hallucinations as were discussed in (4b) Eyes Closed Visual Hallucination are again to be distinguised here. The phenomenon in either type may be experienced just as readily under so-called posthypnotic conditions as when it is experienced "within" hypnosis.

5d. Complete Anesthesia. In this phenomenon the subject must experience the complete loss of the conscious experience of pain and other sensations in designated areas of his body or his entire body in a manner subjectively equivalent to the effects of chemical anesthesia. The phenomenon consists of the subjectively convincing experience of three components. First, the subject must turn his attention to the anesthetized body area so that he will be in a position to experience clearly any sensations that are available to consciousness from that area. Second, during tests with stimuli sufficiently intense to be normally quite painful the subject must make a sincere, concerted conscious level effort to experience the sensations. Third, the subject must experience that he really was unable to experience any sensations whatsoever in the area. In other words, complete anesthesia requires an unambiguous attentive scrutiny coupled with an unambiguous failure to experience strong sensory input. The phenomenon may be experienced just as readily under so-called posthypnotic conditions as when it is experienced "within" hypnosis.

Other Phenomena. The difficulty level and thus the traditional hypnotic depth of many other phenomena can be deduced from the descriptions given. Descriptions of the generic categories to which the ten representative phenomena belong were included in the table. For example, (3b) Inability to Stand was described generically as the apparent loss of volitional control of muscular responses. This broader phrasing encompasses phenomena such as the inability to open the clasped hands, the inability to bend the rigidified arm, the inability to open one's stuck-together eyes, and the inability when tongue-tied to speak one's name. In a larger sense the generic description can be recognized to encompass apparent nonvoluntary compulsions to carry out muscular behaviors as well as the inabilities to do so.

It can be deduced that hypnotic deafness is a difficult hypnotic phenomenon and thus indicative of deep hypnosis. This is so both because concerted reality intrusions must be provided to test it and because it represents the complete elimination of a forceful perceptual experience from conscious experiencing.

The descriptions given in regard to visual hallucinations apply equally well to hallucinations in all sensory modalities. The criterion is always the same: namely, the belief in the hallucination as a real event at the time of the experience. If the subject describes the hallucination as having been phenomenologically real despite concerted reality intrusions, its achievement can be used as indicative of the highest level of difficulty; if concerted reality intrusions were not provided its achievement can be used as indicative of intermediate difficulty; if it was not really believed in as a real event, then, from the perspective of the phenomenological method, it was not a hallucination despite outward appearances. In this regard it should be understood that phenomena in less than full-fledged form are indicative of downgraded difficulty level. For example, the achievement of a sensory experience (such as floating, warmth, or tasting bitterness) that was subjectively more convincing than make-believe imaginings but not really believed in as a hallucination would be taken as indicative of a very easy to easy difficulty level depending upon whether the experience was mildly or moderately subjectively convincing.

V. The Theoretical Approach

The theoretical approach is based on the writer's theory of hypnosis (Shor, 1959, 1962b, 1970). The theoretical approach provides a different kind of operational definition and consequently a different conception of the meaning of hypnotic depth than is provided by the traditional approach. The traditional approach is concerned with denotable hypnotic phenomena graded for difficulty. The theoretical approach is not concerned at all with difficulty level; rather it is concerned exclusively with underlying psychological processes. There is no translation between the two types of measurements.

The objective of the theoretical approach is to evaluate the extent of development along the eight dimensional variables which the writer theorizes to be underlying psychological processes of considerable importance for an understanding of the nature of hypnosis. Three of these variables are theorized to be dimensions of hypnotic depth, the remaining five are not. The three dimensions of hypnotic depth are: (1) trance, (2) nonconscious involvement, and (3) archaic involvement. It is theorized that the extent of development along each of these three dimensions constitute different kinds of hypnotic influences. The five other important but nonhypnotic dimensions are: (4) drowsiness, (5) relaxation, (6) vividness of imagery, (7) absorption, and (8) access to the unconscious.

In the application of the theoretical approach the examiner's task is to make separate diagnostic ratings for each of these eight dimensional variables. It is also the examiner's task to inquire about contributory interrelationships among the variables. For example, even though drowsiness and trance are separate processes the hypnotist may have tried to induce drowsiness in order to help promote trance; consequently it becomes of interest to inquire as to whether or not there has occurred a contributory influence of drowsiness on trance.

A form for recording the diagnostic ratings is presented on the next page.

A category of "Don't Know" is also included for instances in which the examiner does not have sufficient information for making knowledgeable ratings. The examiner may select the unit of evaluation to be a single hypnotic phenomenon, a larger segment, or the entire hypnotic session. Space is provided on the record form for saying what unit is being evaluated, for comments on each of the eight ratings, and for recording other observations. It may be noted that the words "light" and "deep" may be used interchangeably for the words "slight" and "extensive" when referring to the three hypnotic dimensions but not when referring to the other five variables.

While both the traditional and theoretical approaches may be applied to

RECORD FORM

Subject: _____ Hypnotist: _____ Session _____

Evaluation of:

		1) None	2) Less than slight	3) Slight	4) Intermediate and moderate	5) Extensive	Don't know	Comments
Dimensions of hypnotic depth	1) Trance							
	2) Nonconscious involvement							
	3) Archaic involvement							
Other important dimensional variables	4) Drowsiness							
	5) Relaxation							
	6) Vividness of imagery — A							
	6) Vividness of imagery — I							
	7) Absorption							
	8) Access to the unconscious							

Observations:

the same hypnotic phenomena it should be noted that hypnotists concerned with the theoretical approach would characteristically tend to induce at least subtly different phenomena. For example, the theoretically oriented hypnotist is likely to induce phenomena to help distinguish pure trance from a mixture of trance and nonconscious involvement; this distinction would not be an issue to the traditionalist. Similarly, the difficulty level of achieved hypnotic phenomena would not be an issue to the hypnotist concerned with the theoretical approach.

The criterion is also different in the two approaches. In the traditional approach the criterion is the subject's subjective conviction in the experiential reality of the phenomenon. In the theoretical approach the criterion is the extent of occurrence of each dimensional variable as diagnosed from the subject's phenomenological descriptions. In summary: the traditional approach is concerned with hypnotic phenomena; the theoretical approach is concerned with underlying psychological processes.

For persons immersed in the traditional approach adopting the theoretical approach will require a change in perspective. One has to learn to think in terms of underlying processes rather than in terms of labelled phenomena. One has to come to think of a certain age regression, for example, as an attempt to induce trance, nonconscious involvement, and several other variables rather than as age regression as such. There is, however, no inherent antagonism between the two approaches. They are just different. A study of the literature of mesmerism and hypnotism for the past two centuries will show that both approaches to understanding hypnotic depth express perennial concerns (Shor, Chapter 2, this volume).

Theoretical descriptions of the eight variables are given below. Following that is a more concrete description of how the ratings are to be made.

It should be kept in mind that it is unlikely that there will be appreciable development along any given variable unless the hypnotist actively tries to induce it. For example, unless the hypnotist arranges conditions to promote archaic involvement it is unlikely that much if any archaic involvement will occur. Similarly, if a hypnotist actively tries to avoid permitting development along a given variable it is unlikely that much development will occur. For example, so-called "waking" hypnosis is an attempt to induce hypnosis while simultaneously avoiding drowsiness. The examiner will find that an exposition of how the hypnosis was structured will serve him as useful background information in making his ratings. He is cautioned, however, to make his ratings strictly on the basis of the subject's phenomenological descriptions of subjective effects, and not on the basis of reasonable inferences about what most likely should have taken place.

1. TRANCE

Normal everyday life is characterized by there being in the immediate background of attention a network of cognitive understandings about reality in general which serves as a context or frame of reference within which all ongoing experiences are interpreted. If such a context of generalized understandings were lacking, ongoing experiences could not have their usual wide abstract interpretative significance. This usual context of generalized understandings may be called the generalized reality orientation (GRO).

An analogy may be drawn here to context effects in perception. It is characteristic that things are perceived in terms of the perspective of their environmental context and not as stimulus qualities in and of themselves. For example, if an observer views a scene composed both of black coal in bright sunlight and white snow in deep shade, he immediately and correctly sees the coal as black and the snow as white. This is so even though a physicist can show with his instruments that the coal as a visual stimulus in and of itself is much brighter (and thus "whiter") than is the snow. The observer is not fooled by the physical brightness, however, because he takes into proper account the whole surrounding environmental context of bright sunlight, which brightens even black coal, and deep shade, which darkens even white snow.

Moreover, it is not necessary that the objects have known brightnesses as do coal and snow. Unidentified pieces of cardboard will do just as well. Coal-black cardboard in bright sunlight will look black and snow-white cardboard in deep shade will look white.

If, however, the context information is eliminated, the observer, by default, can no longer perceive the objects in terms of their true wider perspective. This can be done by placing a high fence in front of the observer with only peep holes to look through so that all he can see is the coal and snow in isolation from their true surrounding brightnesses. Under such conditions of isolation the coal wrongly looks white and the snow wrongly looks black.

In an analogous way, in normal everyday life the surrounding environmental context for ongoing experiences is an internal network of generalized ideas and understandings about the world. For example, in normal everyday life we understand the meaning of the number six because we interpret it within our generalized understandings of the entire number system; isolated from our generalized understandings of the entire number system the number six would not have wide abstract significance. In normal everyday life when we see an event in a movie we do not mistake it for a real life event because we have a larger perspective which includes knowing that it is just a movie. If, however, we were somehow to lose temporarily that background context of understandings we would by default accept what we saw for its own sake in its own terms, at least until we could regain the larger perspective.

In normal everyday life the GRO is always intact as a background context to our conscious experience, and so we take it for granted. There are times, however, when for various reasons it can be temporarily eliminated from the immediate background of consciousness, leaving the ongoing conscious experiences isolated, devoid of both perspective and wide abstract interpretative significance. The extent of such temporary elimination of the GRO from the immediate background of consciousness (temporary isolation) is called trance. Trance is considered by the writer to be one of the three dimensions of hypnotic depth.

Because in deep trance the ongoing conscious experiences are isolated from the usual interpretative framework of cognitive understandings of everyday life, the deeply entranced individual is not consciously aware of the distinction between imagination and reality; it simply could not occur to him at the time to make the distinction. It does not occur to him to doubt or to question the reality of the experience at the moment of the experience. Similarly, there is an obliviousness to abstract meanings. The subject ceases to be consciously aware of time, self, surroundings, etc. Obliviousness can take two forms. One is obliviousness to the entire world in eyes-closed hypnosis. More generally it can take the form of obliviousness to the abstract meanings of the world in which the subject opens his eyes and interacts with reality objects but perceives them in a fresh, literal, concrete, here and now way, isolated from their conventional meanings and abstract evaluative interpretations.

As trance deepens there is also a progressive temporary loss of self-reflective executive monitoring, at least within the bounds of consciousness. One of the major attributes of human mental processing is self-reflective executive monitoring. Not only do humans behave and think but they also think about their behavior and thinking and know that they are doing so. Not only do we humans consciously experience things but we also consciously experience that we are consciously experiencing. We are constantly inwardly watching, constantly reflecting on our own ongoing experiences, monitoring them, evaluating them, silently commenting to ourselves about them, critically interpreting their significance, and planning ahead. This superordinate awareness of self as a self, and this executive monitoring of self are such constant and pervasive features of normal alert everyday life that it is often taken as the mark of altered consciousness when to some notable degree they are not so—as, for example, in drowsiness and sleep, alcohol intoxication, strong emotion, etc.

Self-reflective executive monitoring is often described by hypnotized subjects as a second little disembodied "psychic self" sitting off to one side in the periphery of conscious awareness watching what is going on. Obviously a report of this sort should be diagnosed that at least at that moment in time, the trance was incomplete. This is so because evidence of self-reflective executive monitoring within consciousness would necessarily indicate a partially intact GRO within consciousness.

Implicit in discussion of this point is the question whether the GRO has truly temporarily come apart at all levels of mental functioning or is still fully intact but is being actively kept out of the boundaries of consciousness. The former condition is pure trance and the latter is a mixture of trance and nonconscious involvement (dissociation). In both cases, however, an intact GRO is not operative in the immediate background of consciousness; that is the crucial point for the definition of depth of trance.

In speaking of trance depth it would be an overstatement ever to speak of the absolutely complete elimination of the GRO. One has to maintain enough of a GRO at some level in order to maintain contact with a hypnotist, understand and use language, etc. Even in deepest sleep, enough of the GRO is intact so as not to fall out of bed at night.

2. NONCONSCIOUS INVOLVEMENT

The second dimension of hypnotic depth is the extent of nonconscious involvement. This may also be called the extent of hypnotic role-taking involvement or dissociation. (For modern clarifications of this latter term see Hilgard, 1973a, 1974.)

A hypnotized subject is not a will-less automaton. The hypnotist does not crawl inside a subject's body and take control of his brain and muscles. Motivated behaviors are carried out by the hypnotized subject only because at some level he himself is motivated to carry them out. Although the hypnotic subject may look as if he is no longer in control of his own volitional activities—for example, he may behave as if he is unable to bend his hypnotically stiffened elbow—that is only because at some deeper level than is operative within the boundaries of consciousness, he is actively, deliberately, voluntarily keeping his elbow stiff while simultaneously orchestrating for himself the illusion that he is really trying his best to bend it. In this case the volition that the subject is aware of within consciousness is subordinated to the volition that the subject is unaware of beyond consciousness. That ideas and motivational strivings may be operative beyond the bounds of conscious awareness is not a new idea in psychology.

One must learn to think in terms of two levels of volitional control. The first level refers to the ideas and motives that are within the bounds of consciousness and are thus consciously directive. The second level refers to the ideas and motives that are beyond the bounds of consciousness and are thus nonconsciously directive. The nonconscious ideas and motives are kept out of awareness by active forces of dissociation. The extent of dissociation is a matter of degree and selectivity, and not all or nothing. It should be noted that we have spoken here of nonconscious and dissociation rather than of unconscious and repression. These latter terms will be considered in the discussion of the eighth variable.

Another way to state the issue is that when a person agrees to try to become a good hypnotic subject he thereby sets up an implicit contract between himself and the hypnotist to try his best to have certain kinds of experiences and to carry out certain kinds of behaviors. In other words, the subject implicitly agrees to try his best to fulfill the role of being a good hypnotic subject as this will be continuously defined by the hypnotist and understood by the subject during the procedures. If this taking on of the hypnotic role (hypnotic role-taking) remains entirely within consciousness then it is strictly conscious level compliance, consciously voluntary, consciously deliberate, nothing out of the ordinary. Only if, and to the extent that, the set of ideas and motives to behave and experience as does a good hypnotic subject becomes dissociated beyond the bounds of conscious awareness do the hypnotic occurrences appear to take on a life of their own. In other words, it is the extent of the nonconscious involvement in the hypnotic role-taking that is the dimension of hypnotic depth and not the hypnotic role-taking as such. Depth of nonconscious involvement is defined as the extent to which the set of ideas and motives to fulfill the role of hypnotic subject are dissociated beyond the bounds of conscious awareness and are thus nonconsciously directive.

As noted earlier, the hypnotic phenomena that are included in the listings for measuring traditional hypnotic depth tend to be largely dependent upon depth of nonconscious involvement. For example, by its inherent nature a challenged arm rigidity (in the form: "You will be unable to bend your straight, stiff and rigid arm no matter how hard you may try to do so.") is largely dependent upon nonconscious involvement because the very phrasing of the phenomenon is to produce a contest between conscious and nonconscious volition. What is called amnesia would clearly better be called dissociation: the active, nonconsciously directed prevention of memory retrieval until a prearranged signal. Similarly age regression is largely dependent upon nonconscious involvement. It requires the dissociation from the bounds of consciousness of sufficient aspects of the GRO so that the person is consciously oblivious to the true state of affairs. Simultaneously the subject has to orchestrate for himself from nonconscious sources the substitution of a fantasied younger self and orientation. Thus age regression involves a mixture of nonconscious involvement and trance but the trance here is typically largely the product of nonconscious involvement and is maintained by it. In the incomplete form of age regression in which the subject feels compelled to act as if he were a younger age, despite knowing all along the true state of affairs, we see an instance of nonconscious involvement orchestrating the outward behaviors but insufficient trance to permit it to seem subjectively real.

3. ARCHAIC INVOLVEMENT

The third dimension of hypnotic depth is the extent of archaic involvement. This is the feature of hypnotic responsiveness generally stressed by psychoanalytically-oriented theorists. Depth of archaic involvement is the extent to which there occurs a temporary displacement or "transference" of core personality emotive attitudes formed early in life (most typically, in regard to parents) onto the hypnotist. In other words, depth of archaic involvement is the extent to which at any given moment in time there are archaic, primitive modes of relating to the hypnotist that echo back to the love relationships of early life. Thus, as archaic involvement deepens, (a) the subject experiences attitudes, yearnings, and modes of relating to the hypnotist as if he were an object of love and admiration; (b) profound psychodynamic meanings become infused into the interpersonal transactions of the subject to the hypnotist; (c) the central core of the subject's personality unreservedly consents to the hypnotic proceedings; (d) the central core of the subject's personality eagerly craves to please the hypnotist; and (e) the central core of the subject's personality eagerly craves to incorporate the hypnotist's wishes as his own. In sum, there takes place a perspectiveless overevaluation of the person of the hypnotist out of keeping with the objective situation. While archaic involvement may take different forms the most common consequence is that the hypnotist comes to take on an unusual importance to the subject and the subject comes to want to please the hypnotist as a labor of love. That this in some instances may be mixed with hate and other strong emotions will come as no surprise to persons who have studied the complexities and ambivalences of human personality.

As discussed earlier, it is unlikely that a hypnotist will produce much development along any given dimensional variable unless he actively tries to do so. Only the hypnotist who tries by his words and demeanor to infuse the hypnotic proceedings with the instigators of archaic involvement is likely to produce much of it. Indeed, in scientific contexts the hypnotist typically does a great deal to prevent the development of archaic involvement. Hypnotists who are scientific experimenters rarely see extensive archaic involvement for this very reason.

If because of his impersonalized scientific stance and his bias against magical mystifications the hypnotist keeps the hypnosis impersonalized; if he denies for himself the various roles of parental figure, powerful leader, all-knowing teacher, charismatic authority, therapeutic doer-of-good, lover-protector, and lover-comforter; if he fails to win belief, trust, love, admiration, loyalty, and devotion—in short, if he fails in one way or another to emotionalize the hypnotic proceedings with important interpersonal meanings which are echoes from the past—then it is unlikely that there will be much depth of archaic involvement. This is not because archaic involvement cannot occur in scientific contexts but because the scientist-hypnotist typically has not structured the interpersonal situation in keeping with its development.

Few scientist-hypnotists would feel comfortable in capitalizing on the magical wish-fantasies of their subjects for an omnipotent protector; few would agree to seductively eroticize the hypnotic proceedings; few would wish to talk to their subjects as if they were children. And yet these and similar stratagems can be powerful instigators of archaic involvement. On the other hand, the clinician-hypnotist would typically have fewer ethical qualms about elucidating dependency, symbolic sexualization, and regressive occurrences because these have been widely acknowledged to be legitimate aspects of the therapeutic process.

A distinction needs to be drawn between the motivation resulting from archaic involvement and nonconscious involvement. Motivation in nonconscious involvement is simply the subject's agreed-upon attempt to fulfill the defined hypnotic role made nonconsciously directive by active processes of dissociation. Motivation in archaic involvement is an attempt to win the love of the hypnotist and curry his favor by incorporating his wishes as if one's own. While mixtures and contributory influences may occur between these variables, their conceptual distinction is important.

4. DROWSINESS

Drowsiness also is a variable of considerable importance to an understanding of the nature of hypnosis but drowsiness is not a dimension of hypnotic depth. In other words, an increase in drowsiness does not mean that hypnosis has deepened in any sense of the term.

Drowsiness is defined as the extent to which the subject feels subjectively drowsy; it is the extent to which the subject describes having experienced at any given moment in time feelings of combined sluggishness, grogginess, sleepiness, and lulling of mental energies. The variable thus refers to the conscious experience of drowsiness and not the physiological event.

While drowsiness is commonly used as a technical aid in hypnotic induction and is a common accompaniment of hypnosis, the deepest hypnosis may be achieved with no element of drowsiness whatsoever. In so-called "waking" or "hyper-alert" hypnosis, induction techniques are used which scrupulously avoid any hint of drowsiness even during a subject's very first hypnotic session.

Further comment is needed on the relationship between drowsiness and trance. It is hard to maintain an intact GRO when its supportive energies fade. As the subject becomes progressively more drowsy, it becomes progressively more difficult to maintain an intact GRO. Hence, drowsiness is an efficient method of promoting trance depth. Since, however, the deepest trances may be induced and maintained without any drowsiness, it must be recognized that drowsiness and trance are two separate variables and so require separate measurement.

5. RELAXATION

The fifth variable is the extent of relaxation. Relaxation is the extent to which the subject feels subjectively relaxed, the extent to which the subject describes having experienced at any given moment combined feelings of the quieting down of mind and body, the decrease of muscular and mental tensions, calmness, peacefulness, being at ease, tranquility. The variable thus refers to the conscious experience of the relaxation of mind and body and not to the physiological measurement of decreased muscle tonus.

6. VIVIDNESS OF IMAGERY

The sixth variable is the vividness of mental imagery representation. Vividness of imagery is defined as the extent to which the mental imagery experienced in hypnosis varies from "none" on the one hand to the equivalent of the vividness of actual percepts on the other. This judgment is to be made in terms of fully intact "waking" standards of comparison. This latter point is a critical one. It is not the "reality value" of the imagery at the time of the experience which is at issue here—as it would be in the traditional method of measuring hypnotic depth—but rather the vividness of the imagery as it is later judged during the phenomenological interview in terms of the standards of the fully intact GRO.

Lack of clarity on this point will lead to a confusion between trance depth and vividness of imagery. When trance is sufficiently deep, a subject will accept weak and shoddy imagery as subjectively real. This is so because at the time of the experience the usual "waking" standards of judgment are so faded that by default the subject fails to doubt the reality value of the poor imagery that is present. In short, reports of such an occurrence can be taken as evidence that trance was deep but that vividness of imagery was slight at best.

This variable is a special case because it requires two types of measurement rather than just one: there is an absolute and a relative form of vividness of imagery which need to be separately recorded. In the absolute form "none" is the absolute zero of no subjectively experienced mental imagery representation—as, for example, the subject who reports having experienced no visual imagery at all during the attempted induction of a specific visual hallucination. In the relative form the visual imagery present in hypnosis is compared with the vividness of the imagery characteristically available in the usual "waking" state of normal alertness. In the relative form "none" means no increase of the vividness in hypnosis as compared with the vividness usually available. These two forms may be referred to as *absolute* vividness of imagery (A) and *increased* vividness of imagery (I).

This distinction is necessary because people differ markedly in the quality of the imagery representation characteristically available to them in everyday life. Some subjects have such excellent imagery freely available that little if any increase is possible even in the deepest hypnosis. In other subjects a notable increase in vividness in hypnosis is symptomatic of hypnotic effects particularly if the hypnotist has explicitly required increased vividness as part of the hypnotic performance. For example, if a hypnotist explicitly requires imagery subjectively indistinguishable from actual percepts as a necessary constituent of what he defines to be a good visual hallucination then the increased vividness of the imagery becomes symptomatic of hypnotic effects. Under other conditions, however, a deteriorization of hypnotic compared with waking imagery is symptomatic of hypnotic effects. This would be so where increased trance depth makes the quality of the imagery progressively less relevant. Lessened imagery might also be symptomatic of the subject being too drowsy to bother with producing better imagery.

7. ABSORPTION

Absorption is defined as the extent to which at any given moment in time the subject was attentively engrossed in the ongoing hypnotic experiences. It should be noted that extent of absorption does not necessarily covary with depth of trance. A subject may be very extensively engrossed while simultaneously possessing an intact GRO and he may have diffuse attentiveness while simultaneously possessing a markedly faded GRO.

8. ACCESS TO THE UNCONSCIOUS

Access to the unconscious is defined as the extent to which there is at any given moment in time an availability to consciousness of usually unconscious, usually repressed, primary process contents and modes of thought. A comparison is implicitly made to the thought processes of everyday life. The presumption is that many ideas and feelings are not available to consciousness in everyday life either because of an active, repressive keeping of them out of consciousness or because of a pervasive type of passive exclusion—i.e., because the ideation simply does not fit into the secondary process modes of thinking of everyday life. Note that this variable invokes the Freudian concepts of unconscious, repressed, and primary process as distinguished from the concepts of nonconscious and dissociation which were used in the description of the second variable, nonconscious involvement.

A distinction needs to be drawn between extent of access to the unconscious and depth of trance. Under conditions where the GRO is sufficiently faded it becomes easier for primary process ways of thinking to flow into the immediate background of awareness to orient experiencing in a more primitive manner. However, the fact that the GRO has considerably faded is no guarantee of its replacement. It might just more simply remain faded, leaving the ongoing conscious experiences relatively isolated from any immediate orienting context.

It should be kept in mind that it is unlikely that there will be much access to the unconscious unless the hypnotist induces hypnotic phenomena which require such ideation or which promote primitive, regressive ways of experiencing and thus create a milieu favorable for its emergence. However, access to the unconscious should not be equated with the concept of adaptive regression (regression in the service of the ego; see especially Gill and Brenman, 1959; Bowers and Bowers, 1972; Gruenewald, Fromm, and Oberlander, chapter 19 this volume). From the perspective of the writer's theory, adaptive regression is a multivariate concept encompassing a varying mixture of access to the unconscious, archaic involvement, and trance.

How to Make Ratings

To recapitulate several points made earlier, it will be recalled that the subject's role in the phenomenological interview is that of a phenomenological co-investigator who shares equal responsibility for getting at the truth. The context is that of an unfettered conversational interchange in which the examiner and subject are free to ask each other questions, agree or disagree, pursue ambiguous points, etc. It should be explained to the subject in an open and honest way what information is being sought and why. Every effort should be made to foster an interpersonal climate of trust and active cooperation in which the subject feels at ease and is motivated to want to recapitulate his hypnotic experiences fully and without distortion or concealment.

What these considerations mean for the purposes of making the theoretical approach ratings is that in the process of gathering the retrospective phenomenological report the examiner should find a way to explain clearly and in detail the meaning of the eight dimensional variables and the five category rating scale. This will permit the examiner and subject to work together to elucidate the phenomenological documentation that the examiner will need to make the diagnostic ratings with reasonable confidence for each selected unit of evaluation. It needs to be stressed that it is the examiner and not the subject who has the responsibility for making the ratings and for judging when sufficient experiential testimony has been gathered for doing so. However, if the subject's level of intellectual sophistication permits, he should play a very major role in helping to formulate the ratings; indeed, the formulation of the ratings may often take on the character of consensus negotiation rather than a one-sided decision.

In regard to the rating scale, the *None* category is to be interpreted as no experienced amount of the described variable other than what is characteristically available in normal everyday life. The one exception is the absolute form of *Vividness of Imagery* where *None* means a true absence of any experienced imagery representation in the sensory modality or modalities being considered. The category of *Less than Slight* is to be interpreted as the having experienced beginning hints of the variable but not enough to affirm its definite presence—again in the sense of not beyond what is characteristically available. *Slight* should be interpreted as having experienced as definitely present in a notable but slight amount. *Extensive* as present in quite a large amount with only minor and fleeting imperfections. The category of *Intermediate and Moderate* is to be interpreted as more than slight but not unmistakably extensive. The examiner should be conservative in his ratings; he should rate no higher than the firm evidence permits. If he cannot gather sufficient evidence for making a rating with reasonable confidence he should check the category of *Don't know*.

The examiner will need to study carefully the descriptions of the eight variables presented earlier until he understands them completely and can explain them in detail to his subjects. During the interview the examiner should obtain from the subject fairly detailed descriptions of what hypnotic phenomena were induced and other salient details of the hypnotic proceedings. These descriptions of the course of events will serve as a framework for inquiring about the concurrent subjective experiences. This background information will be especially valuable to the examiner who was not himself a witness to the hypnotic proceedings. It needs to be reemphasized, however, that the ratings should be made strictly on the basis of the reported subjective effects and not on the basis of reasonable inferences about what most likely should have taken place given the kinds of phenomena induced.

Some of the dimensional variables, such as *Trance* and *Archaic involvement,* may manifest themselves in a variety of ways; others, like *Absorption* and *Drowsiness* may manifest themselves in only one or a few ways. The basic definitions of the eight variables are repeated below along with as many of their common manifestations as it seemed useful to distinguish. The common manifestations listed are representative, not exhaustive, and are largely overlapping. They may be used to help clarify the nature of the variables to the subject or used as open-ended questions in the generic form: "To what extent and in what ways did you experience...?" When used as questions they should be varied to suit the occasion and not used mechanically. The profundity of the experience and not the number of manifestations reported is what matters. The report of the extensive enough development of even just one manifestation would be sufficient evidence for making the diagnosis of *Extensive*. Typically, however, it is the convergence of a coherent pattern of reports on an interrelated set of manifestations that would provide evidence for making a firm diagnosis.

1. Trance: The extent to which there was a temporary elimination of the GRO from the immediate background of consciousness, leaving the ongoing contents of consciousness isolated, devoid of perspective, devoid of wide abstract interpretive significance. Common manifestations are:

a. Loss of abstract frames of reference.
b. Loss of "waking" standards of judgment.
c. Non-occuring of doubting or questioning of the reality of the experience at the moment of the experience.
d. Ceasing to be consciously aware of time, self, and surroundings.
e. Loss of the distinction between imagination and reality.
f. Obliviousness to abstract meanings.
g. Loss of awareness of the true reality.
h. Loss of reality testing.
i. Failing to take the larger meaning of events into account.
j. Failing to perceive logical incongruities.
k. Loss of self-reflective executive monitoring.
l. Loss of critical thought processes.
m. Loss of self-consciousness.
n. Ceasing to reflect on his own thought and behavior.

2. Nonconscious Involvement: The extent to which the set of ideas and motives to fulfill the role of hypnotic subject were dissociated beyond the bounds of consciousness and were thus nonconsciously directive. Common manifestations are:

a. Things seeming to happen by themselves, without conscious volition and deliberation.
b. Activities seeming to take on a life of their own.
c. Loss of the feeling of doing things or of helping them along.
d. Feeling compelled to think and act in a certain way.
e. Feeling no longer in control.
f. Feeling powerless to resist.
g. Decisions and convictions seeming to well up out of nowhere.
h. Things happening despite conscious attempts to resist or rescind them.
i. Feeling a closing off of ideas and memories.
j. Inability to try to do otherwise.
k. Feeling unable to get to ideas and memories.
l. Finding oneself unable to think of the situation in any other way.
m. Finding oneself blanking when he tried to think or do otherwise.

3. Archaic Involvement: The extent to which there occurred a temporary displacement or "transference" onto the person of the hypnotist of core personality emotive attitudes originally formed early in life most typically in regard to parents, *i.e.,* the extent to which there were archaic, primitive modes of relating to the hypnotist that echo back to the love relationships of early life.

The examiner should be sensitive to the fact that some subjects may be reluctant to discuss archaic involvement because of embarrassment over the primitive and personal emotive expressions. The reticence will generally be mitigated by matter-of-fact assurances that archaic involvement is a perfectly natural process that would be expected to occur in a majority of people under appropriate psychological circumstances.

Common manifestations are:

- a. A temporary displacement on to the person of the hypnotist of strong bonds of affection properly belonging to other people—parents, special teachers, special friends, lovers, etc.
- b. Finding that pleasing the hypnotist had quite unaccountably taken on a great personal importance to him.
- c. Feeling a special personal relationship toward the hypnotist.
- d. Developing a special emotive responsiveness toward the hypnotist's every word and action.
- e. Feeling that everything the hypnotist did and said deeply mattered.
- f. Perspectiveless overevaluation of the person of the hypnotist out of keeping with the objective situation.
- g. Feeling the hypnotist was more powerful, wise, and loving than the objective situation would give a basis for believing.
- h. Feeling a special admiration and loyalty toward the hypnotist.
- i. Enjoying basking in the hypnotist's reflected power and glory.
- j. Feeling that gaining the hypnotist's approval mattered a great deal during the hypnosis.
- k. Feeling like a child in relation to his parents.
- l. Feeling like a follower in relation to a leader.
- m. Feeling like a subordinate in relation to an authority figure.
- n. Wanting the hypnotist to take care of him.
- o. Wanting the hypnotist to tell him what to do.
- p. Wanting the hypnotist to like him.
- q. Wanting the hypnotist's attention.
- r. Wanting to curry the hypnotist's favor.
- s. Wanting to please the hypnotist as a labor of love.
- t. Feeling guilty not doing what the hypnotist wanted.
- u. Worrying that the hypnotist would not like the subject.
- v. Wanting not to dissappoint the hypnotist.
- w. Wanting the hypnotist not to be angry with the subject.

4. Drowsiness. The extent to which the subject felt subjectively drowsy. Subjective drowsiness manifests itself in one consistent way; namely, as feelings of combined sluggishness, grogginess, sleepiness, and lulling of mental energies.

5. Relaxation. The extent to which the subject felt subjectively relaxed. Subjective relaxation manifests itself in one consistent way; namely, as combined feelings of the quieting down of mind and body, the decrease of muscular and mental tensions, calmness, peacefulness, being at ease, and tranquility.

6. Vividness of Imagery. The extent to which the mental imagery experienced in hypnosis was equivalent to the vividness of actual percepts as judged in terms of the judgmental standards of the fully intact GRO. Manifestations are self-evident by definition.

This variable is the special case where the two measures of absolute and increased imagery need to be taken concurrently. When the subject is unsure about the imagery he has characteristically available, the procedure is to ask him to try to produce, then and there, the same kinds of imagery as had been produced in hypnosis. The resultant product then serves as the basis of comparison.

7. Absorption. The extent to which the subject was attentively engrossed in the ongoing hypnotic experience. Manifestations take the form of affirmations by the subject that he was attentively engrossed in the moment-to-moment experiencing.

8. Access to the Unconscious. The extent to which there was an availability to consciousness of usually unconscious, usually repressed, primary process content and modes of thought.

As many people can readily produce seemingly dreamlike, bizarre, childlike, and primitive ideation using the intellective capacities of everyday life, the emergence into consciousness of such fanciful ideation is a necessary but not sufficient condition for diagnosing the breaking through of repressive barriers and/or the return of primary process mentation. Additionally, what is needed is the subject's conviction (a) that the fanciful ideation was alien to his usual imaginal capacities and (b) that it bore the stamp of long forgotten emotionally charged memories and ways of thinking.

VI. A Few Final Remarks

The phenomenological method presented in this report is a technique of measurement. But it is also a theoretical statement about the nature of hypnosis, a theoretical clarification of the two distinct meanings of hypnotic depth, and a plea for programmatic research into hypnosis as phenomenological experience. These four purposes are all aspects of a larger purpose of coming to understand hypnosis as a complex subjective event with clear continuities with everyday experience.

III

Surveys
of Broad Areas

Frederick J. Evans *is Senior Research Psychologist, Unit for Experimental Psychiatry, The Institute of Pennsylvania Hospital and an Associate Professor of Psychology in Psychiatry at the University of Pennsylvania. He was born in Australia, where he completed his formal education. He completed his Ph.D. at the University of Sydney, Australia, working with A. Gordon Hammer. As a graduate student he worked with Martin T. Orne, who visited the University of Sydney for three months in 1961. As a result, he joined the Studies in Hypnosis Project, Massachusetts Mental Health Center, and Harvard Medical School, in 1963. He remained with Martin T. Orne when the research group moved to Philadelphia in 1964. While pursuing his work on hypnosis and sleep, he is also conducting research on pain and on the placebo response. His interest in special states of consciousness and the problem of subjective experience has been responsible for a continuing concern about methodology and the social psychology of the psychological experiment. He is currently Secretary-Treasurer of the International Society of Hypnosis (1973-1979), and President of the American Psychological Association, Division 30: Psychological Hypnosis (1978-79). He has just completed editing a book with John F. Kihlstrom entitled* Functional Disorders of Memory *Hillsdale, NJ: Erlbaum, 1979).*

Evans *deals with three broad issues. The first is the extent to which there are similiarities between hypnosis and sleep. After reviewing behavioral and phenomenological similarities, he concerns himself particularly with EEG and other physiological measures. He finds that sleep and hypnosis EEGs are basically different, and that there is no convincing evidence of physiological similarities between the two states. Secondly, he asks whether hypnotic techniques can influence specific sleep characteristics such as dream content, length of sleep, and parameters of the sleep cycle. While hypnosis cannot be used as an effective substitute for sleep, Evans finds provocative pilot-study evidence of hypnotic manipulations of sleep functions. Finally, he investigates to what extent there can be cognitive and behavioral interaction between the sleeper and the external environment. Techniques for exploring cognitive activity during sleep are reviewed. He discusses investigations in which hypnosis was used as a model for studying suggestions administered and tested during sleep. In a postscript for the revised edition he summarizes advances in each of these areas, and discusses recent research indicating that hypnosis is related to sleep in terms of a broader individual-difference dimension of the voluntary control of states of consciousness.*

6

Hypnosis and Sleep: Techniques for Exploring Cognitive Activity During Sleep

FREDERICK J. EVANS

Introduction: Hypnosis and Sleep

Interest in hypnosis as a potential research tool in the study of sleep has been sparked by the compelling similarities between the two states. In this report, an attempt will be made to evaluate three broad issues. First, to what extent is there a physiological similarity between hypnosis and sleep?

The preparation of this review, as well as the substantive research conducted at the Unit for Experimental Psychiatry, was supported in part by a grant from the Institute for Experimental Psychiatry, in part by grant #AF-AFOSR-707-67 from the Air Force Office of Scientific Research (AFSC), United States Air Force, and in part by grant #MH 19156–01 from the National Institute of Mental Health, Public Health Service. Subsequent work summarized in this revision was supported by contract #DADA-17-71-C-1120 from the U.S. Army Medical Research and Development Command, and grant #MH 19156-08 from the National Institute of Mental Health, Public Health Service.

Many people have contributed substantially to the completion of this review. I would like to thank several colleagues for their valuable comments, particularly Harvey D. Cohen, Mary R. Cook, Charles Graham, A. Gordon Hammer, Emily Carota Orne, Martin T. Orne, David A. Paskewitz, and John W. Powell. Several of the reported studies completed at the Unit for Experimental Psychiatry were conducted with the active collaboration of these colleagues, and also with Jeremy Cobb, Lawrence A. Gustafson, Ulric Neisser, Donald N. O'Connell, William A. Orchard, Campbell W. Perry, and Ronald E. Shor, as well as David F. Dinges, William M. Waid and Stuart K. Wilson. I wish to thank Lillian R. Brazin, Eileen F. Grabiec, Maribeth A. Miller, Lani L. Pyles, David S. Roby, Susan Jo Russell, Deborah E. Seeley, Neal A. Shore, and Mae C. Weglarski for their invaluable assistance in such important matters as finding references, making suggestions about style and format, typing, and proofreading.

Second, to what extent could hypnotic techniques be useful in influencing the course and nature of specific sleep characteristics? Third, to what extent can hypnosis provide a useful model for studying cognitive activity that occurs during sleep and the interaction between the sleeping subject *(S)* with his external environment?

PHENOMENOLOGICAL SIMILARITIES BETWEEN HYPNOSIS AND SLEEP

If he had not witnessed the induction procedure, the casual observer might well characterize a typical hypnotized *S* as being asleep. It was this sleeplike appearance that led Braid (1852) to coin the terms "hypnosis" from the Greek *hypnos* [to sleep] and "somnambulist" from the Latin *somnus* [sleep] and *ambulae* [walk], to describe the deeply hypnotized person. According to Braid, hypnosis was an artificially induced state of somnambulism.

There are many parallels between sleep and hypnosis. The hypnotized person often appears to be asleep, and he typically describes the experience as sleeplike. When awaking from either condition, the person remembers little of what has transpired. Like the sleepwalking somnambulist, the hypnotized person may move about and talk, and he maintains contact with selected aspects of the external world. Some parallels exist in cognitive processes. Vivid dreams may occur in both states. The sleepwalker avoids obstacles; the hypnotized subject avoids colliding with a chair he is negatively hallucinating. The long historical association between hypnosis and sleep is still reflected in many of the standard induction suggestions that *S* should enter into a deep, relaxed, restful sleep.

The relationship between hypnosis and sleep has intrigued scientists throughout the history of hypnosis. The interest in the interrelationship between the two conditions reached its culmination in Pavlov's theoretical position, which is particularly influential in Eastern Europe. Sleep is considered by Pavlovian theorists as a state of cortical inhibition, while hypnosis is more or less halfway between sleeping and waking, a state of partial excitation surrounded by cortically irradiating inhibition. This viewpoint has been reviewed and evaluated recently by Edmonston (1967; see also Chapter 13 of this book).

The phenomenological similarities between sleep and hypnosis raise many interesting theoretical and methodological questions. Phenomena that appear similar may indeed have many different qualities. Hypnosis has a chameleonlike character that precludes easy determination of its essential features. The somnambulistic state studied by Braid was already quite different in appearance from animal magnetism as practised by Mesmer. For Mesmer, sleep was an aftereffect of the crises, or hysterical seizures, of his patients. Many effects that have temporarily gained vogue as invariant characteristics of hypnosis can be attributed to the influence of culturally determined factors and the expectations of the hypnotized *S*. New phenomena of hypnosis have been "invented" by subtle manipulations of *S*'s expectations. Orne's (1959) demonstration of catalepsy of the dominant hand provides a dramatic example of the "discovery" of an apparently new hypnotic phenomenon. In spite of the elusive nature of the hypnotic state and the difficulty of establishing its invariant effects, its existence as a phenomenon has been challenged by only a few modern investigators.

The relationships between sleep and hypnosis have been further obscured by the apparent interchangeability of the two states.[1] If the hypnotized *S* is left alone, or if specific suggestions are given, he may pass into a natural sleep. Similarly, in the context of hypnotic research, it appears that a sleeping *S* may sometimes awake directly into a hypnotic state rather than into a normal waking state, particularly if he has been instructed to do so before falling asleep. Whether the individual is in a sleep, hypnotic, or normal state at a given time may depend upon how he perceives what he is expected to do. The precise state in which an individual exists at any given time is extremely difficult to evaluate by objective methods. Although there are several objective behavioral and physiological characteristics that help identify *S*'s present state, *S*'s verbal description of the subjective aspects of his experiences ultimately provides the main criterion for determining his state.

CHARACTERISTICS OF THE WAKING-SLEEP CYCLE

Behaviorally, sleep is easily recognized. The behavioral evidence for sleep includes the person's general appearance, physical relaxation, lack of communication with and response to the external world, and special manifestations such as snoring. The sleeping *S* is prone and relaxed, his breathing is slow and even, and autonomic functions are depressed. Sleep can be confirmed post hoc by the person's subjective experience. The *S* reports he has not been particularly aware of anything, he usually has a poor sense of elapsed time, and he may include in his description reports of dreaming. The subjective awareness of sleep is a universal experience, and is easily described. Following the development of electronecephalographic (EEG) technology, physiological indices were developed that allowed a more stringent definition of sleep. A variety of physiological and biochemical changes during sleep have been studied extensively. The behavioral, subjective, and physiological signs of sleep are usually, although not always, in close agreement (Dittborn & O'Connell, 1967).

Sleep has commonly been considered a relatively homogeneous ex-

---

1. In this chapter the term "state" is intended primarily as a convenient descriptive term. With some possible exceptions in the last section of the paper, this usage should not affect any conclusions drawn by those who prefer not to conceptualize hypnosis as an altered state of consciousness. The author's position regarding the controversy about state and motivational or interpersonal theories of hypnosis has been made explicit elsewhere (Evans, 1968).

perience. Both subjectively and behaviorally, sleep seems to be much the same throughout a typical eight-hour night. The EEG evidence, however, shows clearly that sleep is complex, consisting of two or more separate states that occur in predictable cycles both in humans and in many species of animals. These stages are quite different physiologically, and the accompanying behavioral and cognitive activity associated with them may be different. The salient characteristics of human sleep stages (Rechtschaffen & Kales, 1968) are described below. The discussion of EEG patterns during waking and sleep (and during hypnosis) requires that special attention be paid to one particular EEG rhythm—alpha activity of 7-13 cycles per second (Hz.). Illustrative samples of occipital and frontal EEG recordings and horizontal eye movement recordings are presented in Figure 6.1.

Waking (eyes closed). The EEG will usually show alpha activity intermixed with low-voltage, mixed frequency activity. During on-line recording, alpha occurs predominantly in the occipital regions. It may occur continuously for many seconds or intermittently in "waves" or "envelopes" of a few seconds' duration. Some individuals rarely generate alpha; some do so almost continuously. Under relatively controlled, optimal conditions, the distribution of the amount of alpha (density) in a homogeneous sample is approximately normal. When alpha is present, its density within a given individual varies considerably over time, depending, in part, on what S is doing. Alpha is most likely to occur when the person is relaxed, with his eyes closed, and when he is not engaging in any particular mental activity. Complex cognitive activity may block alpha. Alpha also disappears as the person becomes drowsy. The paradox of alpha activity is that its density decreases both with drowsiness and with heightened arousal or difficult cognitive tasks. In both instances it is replaced by similar, mixed, low-voltage fast activity. The sudden appearance of alpha activity in an otherwise "flat" random record may indicate arousal if the person has been asleep, or it may indicate the onset of drowsiness if the individual has been engaged in an attentive task.

Changes in alpha density must be interpreted cautiously and only when it is known what S has been doing. If the waking EEG does not contain alpha, it is indistinguishable from the EEG during sleep stage 1 and stage REM, described below. For those individuals who show little or no alpha even under optimal waking conditions, there is no way to discriminate from the EEG alone whether the person is aroused, relaxed, drowsy, or in stage 1 or stage REM sleep. If Ss without waking alpha are not excluded from samples, critical determinations of Ss' position on the arousal (and sleep) continuum cannot be made. It has not always been reported whether samples contain some nonalpha generators.

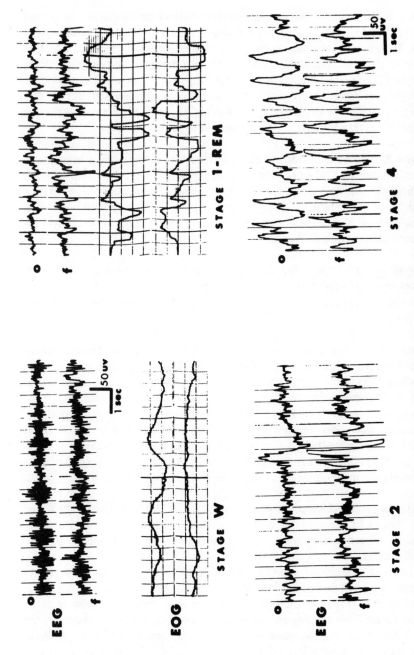

FIGURE 6.1. *Electrophysiological recordings of sleep stages. Occipital and frontal EEG and horizontal eye movements (EOG) are shown for waking and stage REM. For stages two and four, only the EEG is shown.*

Stage 1. Within the limits of his optimal waking alpha density, as *S* falls asleep alpha becomes intermittent and lower in amplitude, until it disappears. Desynchronized fast activity dominates the EEG record, which is similar to the activated waking record. Slow, rolling eye movements (SEM) are usually observed. This descending stage 1 recurs during the night whenever *S* falls back to sleep after awakening. If aroused during this descending stage, he often denies he was asleep, typically reporting that he was thinking, daydreaming, or engaging in hypnogogic reverie.

Stage 2. The stage 1 record changes into one containing a mixture of sporadic bursts of 12-14 Hz. sleep spindles (primarily in the frontal regions) with high amplitude K-complexes. These wave forms are superimposed on a background of relatively low-voltage, mixed frequency EEG activity. Although it accounts for about half of total sleep time, this stage has attracted little research attention.

Stages 3 and 4. The EEG during these stages contains high amplitude, slow wave delta activity (1-3 Hz). The stages are differentiated primarily by the density of delta. Stages 2, 3, and 4 combined are sometimes called stage NREM.

Stage REM. This stage consists of relatively low-voltage, mixed frequency EEG activity, similar to that found in stage 1 and during aroused waking periods. Alpha activity is generally absent; if present, it is sparse, and usually 1-2 Hz. slower than waking frequency. Concurrently, sporadic bursts of conjugate rapid eye movements (REM) and a relative decrease in submental electromyogram (EMG) activity occur. Paradoxically, stage REM involves activated and irregular autonomic and physiological functions (such as penile erection, and irregular breathing and heart rate) in spite of the relaxed musculature and the general appearance of *S*.

EEG diagnosis of sleep: Some limitations. For the objective diagnosis of sleep, these EEG criteria, supplemented by eye movement activity in stage REM, have been emphasized, often at the expense of other reliable physiological changes.

In practice, the simple classification of stages is complicated by a variety of irregularities observed in many sleep records. While the NREM stages (2, 3, and 4) are sometimes difficult to differentiate, they are relatively easily distinguished from waking and stage 1. Delta waves, however, may occur in awake *S*s under the influence of barbiturates, and irregularities such as these may add confusion to the interpretation of otherwise relatively straightforward studies (Beh & Barratt, 1965).

The EEG diagnosis of sleep stages is most accurate when made over intervals of several minutes. When it is necessary to evaluate on-line segments of a few seconds' duration, particularly during stage REM, the task becomes difficult and arbitrary (O'Connell, Gustafson, Evans, Orne, & Shor, 1965). The occurrence of transient alpha is particularly perplexing in this context. Short bursts of alpha are not uncommon in stage REM, particularly with Ss who generate a great amount of alpha when awake. Such intermittent alpha does not necessarily indicate transient awakening. In the absence of other evidence, however, alpha during sleep is best considered as indicating consciousness or arousal. Certainly, when S awakens fully, alpha appears in the EEG. The meaning of intermittent alpha is particularly difficult to evaluate when attempts are made to distinguish between waking and sleep (and hypnosis) using EEG criteria alone, or when attempts are made to present stimuli to sleeping individuals.

The sleep cycle. As S falls asleep, alpha activity becomes desynchronized and intermittent. After a short time in stage 1, S typically passes through stages 2, 3, and 4, sometimes alternating between them for 90 minutes to 2 hours. Then stage REM emerges for the first time. This cycle of stages is repeated several times during the night. Stage 4 occurs almost exclusively in the first part of the night. Stage REM returns about every 90 minutes and becomes progressively longer (from a few minutes to over half an hour), dominating the second half of the night. Slightly less than a quarter of an average night's sleep is spent in stage REM. However, if stage REM is prevented from occurring (because of shortened sleep, drugs, experimental awakenings, or other factors), time in stage REM will increase on subsequent nights until at least some of the lost stage REM is recovered.

Perhaps the most significant recent discovery in sleep research was reported by Aserinsky and Kleitman (1953). They observed that awakening S during a REM period almost always led to vivid reports of dreams, but waking S from NREM sleep did not usually lead to dream reports.[2] The association between stage REM and dreaming stimulated considerable interest in sleep research. Several excellent reviews of the many sleep studies completed since 1953 are available (for example, Foulkes, 1966; Kales, 1969; and Oswald, 1962).

EVALUATION OF HYPNOSIS

Several general issues in hypnosis research require some brief comments so

---

2. Frequency of dream reports from abrupt stage REM awakenings have been reported by many investigators, and is typically above 80 percent. For comparable NREM awakenings, the incidence of content reports varies in several studies, but is typically about 20 percent. Content reports from REM and NREM awakenings can be reliably discriminated by blind judges. Unfortunately, REM and NREM reports have not typically been collected "blind": the experimenter *(E)* has remained aware of the stage of sleep from which S has awakened.

that studies reviewed below can be interpreted meaningfully. These issues are concerned with the measurement of hypnosis and methodological problems arising in this kind of research.

The measurement of hypnosis. There is no single criterion that can be used to indicate reliably the presence of hypnosis or its depth. Several standardized scales of hypnotic susceptibility and hypnotic depth are available that objectively measure susceptibility to hypnosis. These scales have satisfactory psychometric properties. They include the Stanford Hypnotic Susceptibility Scale, Forms A, B, and C (SHSS:A, SHSS:B, SHSS:C) of Weitzenhoffer and Hilgard (1959, 1962) and the Harvard Group Scale of Hypnotic Susceptibility (HGSHS:A) of Shor and E. Orne (1962), a group-administered adaptation of SHSS:A. Except for the first time S is hypnotized, these scales correlate highly with each other (typically .75 and above) and with diagnostic ratings of hypnotizability made by experienced clinicians (Orne & O'Connell, 1967).

Assessments of hypnotizability based on the administration of only one such scale should be evaluated cautiously. Differences in the adequacy of establishing rapport and easing S's apprehensions arising from his expectations and misconceptions about hypnosis may affect scores. Because hypnosis is a new experience for him, S may not know what to expect nor how to behave appropriately. Striving to please E is not restricted to the good hypnotic S (Orne, 1959, 1969). The problems are particularly acute when group hypnosis evaluations are made. The correlation between an initial HGSHS:A and a subsequent SHSS:C is only about .6. This lower correlation is due in part to some Ss being influenced by the performance of neighboring Ss: for these Ss, HGSHS:A correlated only .49 with SHSS:C, while a correlation of .74 was obtained for those Ss who did not conform to their neighbors' performance.[3]

While combinations of standard scales are adequate for evaluating susceptibility to hypnosis for many purposes, these scales should be supplemented by thorough clinical evaluations (Orne & O'Connell, 1967) if the aim is to select those excellent hypnotic Ss that come from the extreme of the susceptibility distribution. The standardized scales do not always discriminate adequately in the upper ranges of hypnotic depth, and there is still no adequate substitute for diagnostic ratings when attempting to select (as is often the case) classical somnambulist Ss.

Recent evidence has shown that the phenomena traditionally associated with hypnosis can be meaningfully conceptualized in terms of relatively

3. These comments do not reflect on the value and adequacy of HGSHS:A if it is used, as originally intended, as an economical screening device in conjunction with other assessment methods, and as a first exposure to scientific hypnosis, but not as the only measure of hypnotic susceptibility used (Evans & Mitchell, unpublished manuscript).

independent clusters or dimensions, including one concerned with passive motor suggestions, one consisting of challenged motor suggestions (rigidities and inhibitions of movement), one with hallucinatory (imagery) experiences, and one, tentatively labeled "dissociation," consisting of such phenomena as posthypnotic suggestion and amnesia (Evans, 1965; Hammer, Evans, & Barlett, 1963; Hilgard, 1965b). Relationships may exist between sleeping behavior and only one of these aspects of hypnosis. Separate consideration of these hypnotic clusters may clarify the meaning of obtained relationships that might be obscured by a complex, multidetermined global hypnosis rating.

Methodological considerations. The effects of *S*'s expectations and attempts to conform to his perceptions of the hypothesis being tested are subtle, but have been amply documented (Orne, 1959, 1962b, 1969). If, for example, eye movement electrodes are applied, and it is then suggested to *S* during hypnosis that he hallucinate a visual, moving scene, then it is not too difficult for *S* to realize that eye movements are anticipated during the hallucination. It is necessary and often difficult to evaluate whether it is hypnosis or *S*'s expectation that is the causal variable. Similarly, if it is suggested hypnotically that *S* respond during sleep (by dreaming, for example), special techniques are required to determine whether *S* responds while asleep, whether he temporarily awakens (or reenters hypnosis) to respond, or even whether other techniques such as waking suggestion or a pep talk would achieve similar results. While the EEG is most helpful in this regard (and, generally, only sleep studies using EEG techniques will be considered), it is difficult to determine from the EEG alone whether *S* is awake, hypnotized, or even in stage REM sleep. It is naive to assume that if a suggestion given during hypnosis works, then it worked because of hypnosis. Because adequate control techniques such as those introduced by London and Fuhrer (1961), or the use of Orne's simulating *Ss* (1959, 1969), have not been used, many of the studies reviewed below are inconclusive.

Physiological Similarities Between Hypnosis and Sleep

If hypnosis and sleep share common mechanisms, then it should be possible to document physiological parameters that are similar under both conditions. Most studies have used the EEG; some have investigated specific variables such as the electrodermal response.

EEG PATTERNS DURING SLEEP AND HYPNOSIS

The EEG during hypnosis appears to be quite different from the basic EEG patterns of sleep stages 2, 3, and 4. Some investigators have reported that spindle and slow delta activity is occasionally found in the EEG of hypnotized Ss (Barker & Burgwin, 1949; Marenina, 1955; Schwarz, Bickford, & Rasmussen, 1955). These investigators have not been able to communicate verbally with such Ss until a waking or alpha pattern had been elicited.

Hypnotic "somnambulism" (or deep hypnosis) and sleep somnambulism appear to be different phenomena. The symptoms of sleep somnambulism —sleep-talking and sleepwalking—occur primarily in stage 4 sleep (Jacobson & Kales, 1967). Stage 4 delta waves do not occur during hypnosis, even when the induction emphasizes suggestions of sleep. The frequently assumed relationship between susceptibility to hypnosis and the incidence of sleep somnambulism has not been investigated in the sleep laboratory, although Sutcliffe (1958) reported that a questionnaire measure of the frequency of sleepwalking and sleep-talking correlated significantly with hypnotizability.

Several studies have found hints of similarities between hypnosis and specific aspects of EEG activity. These studies raise many questions that cannot be resolved, and they have been reviewed adequately by Barber (1969b), Chertok and Kramarz (1959), Domhoff (1964), Gorton (1962), Kratochvil (1970), and Tart (1965a). Similarly, several studies (reviewed by Chertok & Kramarz, 1959, and by Tart, 1965a) have indicated similarities between the EEG of hypnosis and that of "light sleep," or the descending stage 1 *transitional* sleep. Similarities between hypnosis and drowsiness, light sleep, and stage 1 sleep may be attributed to the difficulties in using the EEG as a criterion. The EEGs of aroused and relaxed waking, drowsiness, and stages 1 and REM are comprised of various mixtures of intermittent alpha and desynchronized low-voltage fast activity. The EEG is not sufficiently sensitive to discriminate between these conditions.

Even if drowsiness could be discriminated reliably from hypnosis by the EEG, paradoxical similarities between hypnosis and drowsiness could occur in the EEG of hypnotized Ss. Many investigators have used hypnotic induction techniques that include suggestions of relaxation and sleep. These inductions are often long, repetitive, and perhaps, to a very hypnotizable S, somewhat boring, particularly as he is implicitly restricted in activity. The suggestions to sleep may be taken literally and S may fall asleep briefly. In the induction procedures of the standardized scales we have observed Ss who appear to nap briefly during the relatively long, monotonous induction. These Ss may not recognize their transient napping because of the repetitiveness of the suggestions. When Ss are aware of napping, they may become confused, attributing the sleepiness to hypnosis.

When a suggestion is given, some Ss can respond even while remaining asleep (Evans, Gustafson, O'Connell, Orne, & Shor, 1969). The S may never realize he has napped if, for example, E gradually raises his voice, subtly changes his intonation, or, as part of a suggestion, unobtrusively raises *S*'s arm, thereby "reawakening" him. If *E*'s actions are carried out carefully, in a plausible hypnotic context in which the break in continuity is not apparent, *S* will not be aware that anything special has happened. The hypnotist may remain unaware of *S*'s light sleep as these "awakening" techniques are part of his natural technique during the transition between inducing hypnosis and testing its effects. Alpha desynchronizes in this transitional sleep, but it is a phenomenon of a tired *S* rather than of hypnosis. The tendency for hypnotizable *S*s to nap during hypnosis is supported by recent evidence that hypnotizable *S*s fall asleep in the laboratory more quickly than insusceptible *S*s (Evans et al., 1969; Evans, 1977a).

Most authors agree that the EEG during hypnosis is similar to waking EEG patterns consisting of desynchronized fast activity and alpha activity. The available evidence suggests that there is no similarity between hypnosis and sleep in the EEG, although without independent criteria of both hypnosis and the relevant sleep stage, any hypothesized similarity is difficult to evaluate conclusively. However, a more meaningful, related question has been investigated. What is the relationship between hypnosis and specific EEG patterns?

EEG ALPHA ACTIVITY AND HYPNOSIS

Investigations of specific EEG patterns during hypnosis have primarily involved the alpha rhythm (7–13 Hz.). Renewed interest in the alpha rhythm has been stimulated by Kamiya's (1969) claim that alpha can be operantly shaped and brought under voluntary control. The paradox of alpha activity, discussed above, is that it becomes desynchronized and disappears with both drowsiness and with heightened arousal or difficult cognitive tasks. It appears to be related to attentional processes in a U-shaped fashion. Currently, sophisticated computer techniques are being employed to investigate the EEG in ways that could not be achieved by simple on-line visual scanning and manual scoring. Most of the studies reviewed below have not employed sophisticated instrumentation, and the findings should be interpreted with reservations.

The relationship between EEG alpha activity and hypnosis may be explored in two ways: (1) Do *S*s who are highly susceptible to hypnosis have different (waking) brain wave patterns from those *S*s who are insusceptible to hypnosis? (2) Does hypnosis alter brain wave activity? Are there any changes in alpha activity after hypnosis has been induced, particularly in deeply hypnotized *S*s?

EEG alpha and susceptibility to hypnosis. London, Hart, and Leibovitz (1968) recently presented evidence that, in a sample of 125 volunteers for a "brain waves and hypnosis" study, highly susceptible *S*s generated more waking alpha than other Ss. The HGSHS:A was completed, with some imagery tests, and alpha was measured one week later. While eight Ss who scored the maximum of twelve points on HGSHS:A generated alpha for a mean of 42.3 seconds per minute during eyes-closed, awake, resting periods, twenty-five Ss who scored four or less generated alpha for only 24.0 seconds per minute ($p < .005$).

From unpublished data collected at the Unit for Experimental Psychiatry, a sample of 139 volunteer students, who had participated in hypnosis experiments and for whom resting alpha baseline measures were available, was examined. Sessions recording alpha were always presented to S as being independent of the previously completed hypnosis sessions. These Ss, who had originally volunteered for "hypnosis experiments," had been given HGSHS:A and SHSS:C. Individual clinical diagnostic ratings (Orne & O'Connell, 1967) were also available for 111 of the 139 Ss. The distribution of alpha density during two-minute rest periods for Ss classified according to their hypnotic susceptibility is presented in Table 6.1. The hypnotic susceptibility categories used by London, Hart, and Leibovitz (1968) were chosen, and the two samples are compared. In addition, Ss are reclassified according to SHSS:C scores, a more reliable estimate of hypnotic susceptibility. In Table 6.2, correlations between alpha density and HGSHS:A, SHSS:C, and diagnostic ratings, respectively, are reported. In addition, for a sample of sixty of these Ss, alpha frequency and amplitude were measured, and correlations between these measures and hypnotic susceptibility are also reported.

TABLE 6.1   Mean per cent alpha generated during two minutes rest for Ss differing in susceptibility to hypnosis

Hypnosis Score	London, Hart & Leibovitz, 1969 HGSHS:A		Evans[a] HGSHS:A		SHSS:C	
	N	X̄ percent alpha	N	X̄ percent alpha	N	X̄ percent alpha
0–4	25	37	40	65	46	46
4–7	25	56	43	40	25	39
7–11	67	42	49	45	58	46
12	8	70	3	90	10	40
Total N	125		135		139	

a. Evans (unpublished data). All Ss received both HGSHS:A and SHSS:C (four Ss who received SHSS:A instead of the group version eliminated).

Examination of the data initially appeared to confirm the exciting results of London, Hart, and Leibovitz. They reported that their eight Ss who scored twelve on HGSHS:A generated almost continuous alpha (70 percent

TABLE 6.2. Correlations between alpha activity characteristics and susceptibility to hypnosis

Hypnosis	N	Frequency	Amplitude	Density	N	Density
HGSHS:A	60	−.19	.04	.02	135	−.08
SHSS:C	60	−.01	.03	−.02	139	−.02
Diagnostic	40	−.05	−.02	.13	111	.12

NOTE: All correlations insignificant ($p > .10$).

of the two-minute period). The three Ss in our sample who scored twelve on HGSHS:A also generated continuous alpha (90 percent of two minutes). However, forty insusceptible Ss displayed considerably more alpha (for a mean of 65 percent of the rest period) than the twenty-five similarly selected insusceptible Ss (37 percent alpha during rest) reported by London, Hart, and Leibovitz. When Ss of medium susceptibility are included in both samples, no overall relationship between alpha density and hypnotic susceptibility is apparent in either sample.

Because of the earlier cautions about assessing hypnotic susceptibility by a single group measure, we examined our Ss' scores on SHSS:C. The three Ss who had scored twelve on HGSHS:A (and who had continuous alpha) subsequently scored nine, twelve, and twelve, respectively, on the individual SHSS:C. An additional eight Ss scored the maximum of 12 on SHSS:C (they had averaged 8.6 on HGSHS:A). Of these, five Ss had less than eighty percent (continuous) waking alpha and three Ss generated virtually no alpha (less than 20 percent).

The lack of relationship between hypnotic susceptibility and alpha frequency, amplitude, and density is apparent in Table 6.2. No significant correlations were found between the alpha parameters and either HGSHS:A, SHSS:C, or clinical diagnostic ratings.

Several studies involving smaller samples have reported correlations between alpha density and susceptibility to hypnosis. Galbraith et al. (1970) adminstered HGSHS:A to eighty volunteer students. Two weeks later, fifty-nine of these Ss were invited to participate in an independent "study of brain waves." The criteria for selecting the subsample are not reported. Using a complex procedure, auto- and cross-spectral frequency analyses were carried out for several EEG leads, and these results were submitted to a stepwise multiple linear regression analysis to determine the particular EEG parameters most related to hypnotic susceptibility. The density of theta activity correlated with hypnotizability, but, as theta appears in drowsiness when alpha desynchronizes, this result must be interpreted cautiously. Variables from the alpha range did not increase the predictive relationship with HGSHS:A scores. The first-order correlations between hypnosis and specific frequencies are not reported. The apparent lack of a relationship between alpha frequencies and hypnotizability is not discussed, even though it appears to be inconsistent with the previous results from the same laboratory (London, Hart, & Leibovitz, 1968).

A third study from the same laboratory was conducted by Engstrom (1970). The HGSHS:A was administered to 180 Ss, and for the two-thirds of the sample scoring seven or less (medium and low susceptible Ss) baseline alpha was subsequently recorded. From this pool, thirty Ss fulfilled the second selection criterion of less than 50 percent alpha in a four-minute baseline period. For this specially selected sample of thirty Ss with both low alpha and low hypnotic susceptibility, the correlation between alpha density and HGSHS:A was 0.56 ($p < .01$). This result is difficult to interpret. About 120 Ss met the HGSHS:A criterion of seven or less. From several sources, including the results in Table 6.1, it appears that alpha density is approximately normally distributed, with a mean and median of about 50 percent. Even if there were a zero correlation in the total sample, mathematically it would be expected that about sixty Ss should score below the dichotomy scores of seven and 50 percent (two-thirds of 180 multiplied by one-half of 180, divided by N). If alpha and hypnotizability were correlated in the total sample, the number of Ss scoring low in both alpha and hypnotizability would be correspondingly higher. However, only thirty such Ss were obtained by Engstrom. It would appear, therefore, that some unknown variable has also influenced the availability of Ss in his specially selected subsample, and that the reported correlation of .56 is only representative of a special subsample accidentally selected using unknown criteria.

The data for the Ss whose results are presented in Table 6.1 was re-examined. A subsample was selected using the same criteria as that applied by Engstrom. For the forty-eight Ss selected (forty-six would have been expected by chance), the correlation between HGSHS:A and alpha density was .26 ($p < .05$). Using the same special selection criteria, Engstrom's results are confirmed, even though the correlation between HGSHS:A and alpha in the complete sample was insignificant (−.02). It appears that there may be no inherent relationship between alpha and hypnotizability, but rather there may be special situational factors that may result in some Ss scoring low on an initial hypnosis scale, as well as producing little alpha. This possibility is further supported when the relationship between HGSHS:A and alpha density is examined for those Ss whose HGSHS:A scores are not accurate assessments of hypnotizability. For those eight Ss who decrease in hypnotizability (between HGSHS:A and SHSS:C) by at least four points, HGSHS:A and alpha correlate −.62, whereas for those fifteen Ss who increase in hypnotizability by at least four points, the correlation is .43. The two correlations differ significantly

($p = .02$).[4] In contrast, for those sixty-three Ss whose hypnotizability scores differ by no more than one point, the correlation between HGSHS:A and alpha density is -.04. It appears that the apparent relationship between alpha and hypnosis may be in part a function of the instability of a single criterion of hypnosis, and particularly of those Ss whose first hypnosis score is significantly depressed.

Engstrom then showed that for these Ss, operantly increasing alpha density, using a combination of auditory feedback and photic driving, increased scores on SHSS:B. Because of the special nature of his sample and the apparent statistical regression effects, the generality of these interesting findings requires further evaluation.

Using twenty-eight Ss selected on undefined variables, Hartnett, Nowlis, and Svorad (1969) found an insignificant correlation of -.27 between alpha density and SHSS:C. The mean SHSS:C score of 8.0 obtained by these Ss is very high. However, a rank order correlation of .69 between alpha and SHSS:C was obtained for a subsample of fourteen of the original twenty-eight Ss (mean SHSS:C, 7.9). No comments were made about how these Ss were selected. A similar rank correlation of .70 was obtained by Nowlis and Rhead (1968) between waking alpha and sum of HGSHS:A and SHSS:C scores. Again, it is not reported how the small sample of twenty-one Ss was selected. Nowlis and Rhead published a scatterplot depicting the relationship between alpha density and hypnotic susceptibility. Examination of this scatterplot clarifies the interpretation of their results. Most of their Ss were highly susceptible, as eleven of the twenty-one had combined scores of at least sixteen on the two scales. From the scales' normative data, in an unselected sample the mean and median would be about eleven out of a maximum of twenty-four points. For those susceptible Ss scoring eleven and above, the rank order correlation between alpha density and hypnotizability was calculated by this author to be .16 (insignificant). For the nine insusceptible Ss, however, the correlation between alpha density and hypnotizability was .79 ($p < .05$).

What, then, can be said about the correlation between alpha density and hypnosis? The studies reviewed are often contradictory. From one laboratory, a positive correlation (London, Hart, & Leibovitz, 1968), no apparent correlation (Galbraith et al., 1970), and a positive correlation among Ss specially selected in a manner suggesting a lack of correlation in the larger sample (Engstrom, 1970) have all been reported. Three issues are worth raising. First, in the two studies in which Ss did not know that the psychophysiological session was related to the hypnosis experiments (Galbraith et

---

4. These correlations capitalize on regression effects to some extent. The correlations between HGSHS:A and alpha for Ss who show any subsequent decrease in hypnosis is -.21 ($N = 46$), and for Ss who show any subsequent increase, is .22 ($N = 57$). Even with this less stringent criterion of instability, the two correlations differ significantly ($p < .05$, two-tailed).

al., 1970; Evans, unpublished study), no relationship was found between the two measures. In the studies finding positive relationships, Ss apparently knew that the two sets of measures were being related. This possibility suggests that problems of bias or demand characteristics (Ss' expectations) may exist in these studies. Second, it was implicit in the study by Engstrom (1970), and demonstrable in the study by Nowlis and Rhead (1968), that the positive correlation between alpha and hypnosis may hold only for Ss who are insusceptible to hypnosis.

These observations lead to a third point concerning the mechanisms underlying these findings. The inconsistencies in these results may arise in part from the tendency for both standard scale scores and baseline physiology to be affected by situational variables, even though both susceptibility to hypnosis and basal alpha production are stable characteristics of the individual. For example, earlier reports by O'Connell and Orne (1962, 1968) suggested that there were initial differences in basal skin potential (SP) level in susceptible and insusceptible Ss. Later results have shown, as was implied by O'Connell and Orne, that the apparent physiological index of hypnotic depth was an artifact of relaxation (Evans, 1970). The correlation held only if baseline SP were measured during initial physiological recording sessions. However, when insusceptible Ss were thoroughly acclimated to the laboratory over several sessions, basal SP did not differ from the lower levels of susceptible Ss. Base level continued to drop at the beginning of each session, the magnitude of the changes being positively correlated with anxiety. In addition, SP levels changed during hypnosis, but equally for susceptible and insusceptible Ss. The magnitude of change was positively correlated with the imagery-reverie-relaxation cluster of hypnotic items. This correlation is presumably determined situationally, particularly as initial differences between Ss no longer occur in later sessions.

Baseline alpha may be similarly affected by situational variables and indeed may not be as stable as it has been hitherto considered (Paskewitz & Orne, 1970). An adequate study to resolve these questions would involve repeated measures until a stable plateau is reached for both alpha and hypnosis.

I would predict that situational anxiety, adequacy of the initial session rapport, and degree of relaxation would correlate in moderator-variable fashion with several measures, including such physiological variables as SP and alpha density and conformity-prone initial group assessments of hypnotizability. Apparent correlations between single hypnosis measures and psychophysiological variables may arise because similar situational variables are operating in both conditions.

No data are available to test this prediction, but a preliminary attempt was made to test the correlation between alpha density and the hallucination-reverie cluster of hypnotic performance. The correlations between alpha density and total SHSS:C, motor suggestibility, and dissociation factors derived from SHSS:C were respectively -.02, +.01, and -.06. However, the correlation between alpha density and the imagery cluster (defined by the SHSS:C dream, taste, fly, and boxes items) was in the predicted direction of +.17, but insignificant ($N = 33$). The tetrachoric correlation was .50, indicating a more complex nonlinear relationship. In fact, Ss who had good "imagery" never had poor alpha, but predictions about alpha density could not be made if S scored low on the imagery cluster. This "imagery" factor correlates well with Ss' rated ability to relax during hypnosis (Evans, 1967), although it does *not* typically discriminate between good and poor hypnotic Ss. The imagery measure also correlates significantly with the speed of falling asleep at night, and with S's ability to respond during sleep (Evans, et al., 1969).

A poorly defined picture emerges of an anxious S, perhaps initially apprehensive about hypnosis, whose SP will change as he becomes less tense, and who does not generate a great deal of alpha initially. As he becomes less apprehensive in the experimental situation over time, he relaxes, SP decreases (lowered arousal), alpha becomes disinhibited and increases in density, he feels sufficiently comfortable to "accept" his (limited) hypnotic experiences, thereby being willing to let himself go along with the situation to have new experiences. Thus, the relationship between physiological measures and susceptibility to hypnosis may be situationally determined, and once stable baselines of both physiology and hypnotizability are determined, these apparent relationships no longer exist.

In spite of conflicting results, it is concluded that waking alpha frequency, density, and amplitude are probably not correlated with susceptibility to hypnosis.

Changes in alpha during hypnosis. Marenina (1955), and others subsequently, reported decreases in alpha amplitude and density during hypnosis. The problems inherent in determining if this is a function of hypnosis, or of Ss' napping during the hypnotic session, have been discussed. Decreases in alpha density and amplitude would be more convincingly attributed to hypnosis than to sleep if frequency did not simultaneously slow down.

Brady and Rosner (1966) reported anecdotally that some deeply hypnotized Ss showed greater alpha amplitude than they did in the waking state. We recall one S who had shown no alpha in two two-hour sessions. He was relaxed, at ease, and deeply hypnotized. No waking alpha was found. In a mildly stressful hypnotic situation, he suddenly began to show continuous large amplitude alpha for several minutes.

A definitive study would require that the relevant alpha parameter change under hypnosis from the waking level (recorded under similar conditions), and that a comparable change does *not* occur in insusceptible Ss appropriately motivated to experience hypnosis as well as they can. Two methodological techniques allow adequate exploration of these questions: the motivated insusceptible Ss paradigm of London and Fuhrer (1961), and the simulation model proposed by Orne (1959, 1969). Definitive studies do not exist, but some preliminary data are available from a study involving simulating Ss.

Table 6.3 reports mean frequency, amplitude, and density of alpha for hypnotized and simulating Ss tested by a "blind" E. Waking and hypnotic rest periods were presented identically by a tape recording, and were scored

TABLE 6.3   Mean alpha characteristics for hypnotized Ss and simulating Ss before and after induction of hypnosis

Group	Session	Frequency	Amplitude	Density (percent)
Hypnosis	Waking	10.16	7.89	27
(N = 12)	Hypnosis	10.43	7.98	17
Simulator	Waking	10.33	8.72	52
(N = 12)	"Hypnosis"	10.20	9.21	45
F: Real versus Simulator[a]		—	3.22*	13.15***
F: Waking versus Hypnosis[a]		—	1.20	8.08**

NOTE: *$p < .10$; ** $p < .01$; ***$p < .001$.
a. All interactions insignificant.

blind. Means are reported for both normal waking and deeply hypnotized (or simulating) conditions of eyes closed. Each mean is the average of three passive two-minute rest periods.

There was a tendency ($p < .10$) for simulators to have higher alpha amplitude than hypnotized Ss, both in the normal waking state and when they were simulating hypnosis. Simulating Ss generated significantly more alpha than hypnotized Ss both when awake and when simulating hypnosis (about 65 percent alpha for simulators; about 25 percent for hypnotized Ss, $p < .001$). All Ss generated less alpha during hypnosis (or while simulating hypnosis) than during waking ($p < .01$). None of the analysis of variance interactions was significant. It is surprising that the supposedly highly alert simulating Ss generated alpha so readily during "hypnosis", more readily than supposedly relaxed hypnotized Ss. These results suggest, however, that merely being in a hypnotic trance does not alter frequency, amplitude, or density of alpha.

Alpha and hypnosis: Conclusions. Alpha activity does not appear to predict hypnotizability, nor does it change during hypnosis. Reported correlations or changes are probably mediated by situationally determined factors not related to hypnosis per se. It appears that EEG alpha activity is unrelated to hypnosis.

Hypnotic Manipulation of Sleep

The apparent ease with which hypnosis has been used to control and influence behavior, the historical association between sleep and hypnosis, and concepts such as dissociated and altered states of consciousness have each contributed to the hope that hypnotic manipulations could influence special characteristics of sleep. Many studies have focused on hypnotically induced dreams. The use of hypnosis in attempts to influence dream content directly has important theoretical implications, particularly if sleep dreams and hypnotically induced dreams are similar or functionally equivalent.

HYPNOTIC DREAMS AND SLEEP DREAMS

Hypnotically induced dreams. Even Ss of only medium susceptibility to hypnosis can respond successfully to suggestions to dream during hypnosis. Hypnotically induced dreams are important for two different reasons. Any demonstration of the similarity or equivalence of hypnotic and sleep dreams would provide sophisticated evidence regarding the similarity of the two states in which the dreams are obtained. In emphasizing the importance of the interpretation of dreams, Freud (1900) stressed their symbolic meaning as a technique for evaluating unconscious mental processes. Largely on the assumption of equivalence, the hypnotic dream became, for some theorists, a method for exploring the unconscious, as it did not suffer from the effects of forgetting and time decay that plagued the collection of night dreams.

The revolution in dream research following Aserinsky and Kleitman's discovery (1953) of the relationship between rapid eye movement bursts (REM) and dream recall has been amply documented. As dreaming seems to occur throughout stage REM, about two hours are spent dreaming each night. In contrast, when dreams are collected at home or in the psychiatrist's office, recall is relatively sparse. The possibility that hypnosis could be used to increase the amount of dream material was appealing (Fisher, 1965; Jones, 1962).

Some studies have demonstrated that the content of REM awakening and home-recalled dreams are qualitatively different in several ways (Perry, 1965; Foulkes, 1966). That there are significant content differences between hypnotic and sleep dreams is not altogether surprising. Several excellent reviews of these data are available (Domhoff, 1964; Gill & Brenman, 1959; Moss, 1967; Tart, 1965a, 1966a).

Hypnotically influencing dream content. The content of sleep dreams is determined by a multiplicity of factors. Waking suggestion, direct stimulation of the sleeping *S* (in all modalities, but preferably tactile), day residues, emotional states, films of traumatic events, films of neutral travelogues, the sex of the experimenter, pictures transmitted by ESP, social isolation, spoken neutral names, spoken friends' names, details of experimental environments, drugs, as well as hypnosis, are among the experimentally manipulated variables that have allegedly become incorporated in dreams (see Tart, 1965b and Witkin, 1969, for careful reviews).

Numerous studies, both without EEG technology (such as Nachmansohn, 1925; Schroetter, 1912) and with sophisticated EEG and REM awakening techniques (Barber, 1969b; Schiff, Bunney, & Freedman, 1961; Stoyva, 1965; Tart, 1965b), have demonstrated that a posthypnotically suggested topic will appear directly or indirectly in *S*'s verbally reported dreams. These studies have been reviewed elsewhere (Barber, 1962d; Moss, 1967; Tart, 1965a). Tart concludes: "At present, then, posthypnotic suggestion seems to be the most powerful and precise method for affecting dream content, although its use is restricted to a minority of [good] subjects" (1965b, p.85). Not surprisingly, Barber (1962d, 1969b) concludes that the results depend upon how the suggestions are administered. Stoyva's study (1965), reviewed below, is the first of its kind to use objective EEG evidence of sleep and REM, and is the only one using adequate waking controls for comparison with the posthypnotic manipulation.

A word of caution is required for the researcher who would proceed to use hypnosis as a means of influencing dream content. Dream content can be affected easily by a variety of manipulations other than hypnosis. The Freudian analyst elicits psychoanalytic dreams from his patient; the Jungian analyst obtains dreams of an entirely different kind. The first year psychiatric resident may elicit higher proportions of dreams with manifest sexual content because he tends to "reinforce" the patient for such interesting, relevant material.[5] The researcher is dependent upon *S*'s verbal report (and memory) to evaluate the success of his manipulation. While subjective report is not inherently untrustworthy if it is carefully evaluated, Tart (1964) has shown, for example, that hypnotic and sleep dreams differ in quality even though *S* reports them to be similar kinds of experience. In addition, there is no objective means of knowing whether the hypnotically suggested dream actually occurs in REM sleep or whether *S* awakens, either normally or in hypnosis, and produces waking or hypnotic fantasy instead of a dream. Complicated research designs, such as simulating *S*s, will be required to control the obvious demand characteristics of this kind of procedure.

5. M.T. Orne, personal communication.

Hypnotic and sleep dreams and REM. It has already been shown that except for some special limiting cases, the EEG of the hypnotized *S* is that of a waking person rather than of a sleeping one. This is true even when it is suggested to the hypnotized *S* that he should sleep and dream. Similarly, Tart (1964) demonstrated that both basal level and nonspecific random activity of the GSR during hypnotic dreams were more similar to that of a waking than to that of a sleeping *S*. Such physiological data provide compelling evidence for the dissimilarity of sleep and hypnotic dreams. The only physiological parameter on which clear similarities between the two types of dreams have been shown is in eye movement patterns (Brady & Rosner, 1966; Schiff, Bunney, & Freedman, 1961; Tart, 1964).

Dreams are primarily visual, and when the association between REM and dreaming was discovered it was quickly hypothesized that the eye movements represented scanning of the visual scene. Like many plausible hypotheses this one has led a vigorous existence. The fortuitous early emphasis on eye movement correlates of the sleep stage, rather than any of the many concomitant physiological changes during stage REM, has been the primary stimulus, and a major hindrance, to sleep research over the past 15 years. The visual scanning hypothesis is properly losing favor with many investigators due to a lack of supporting evidence. The REMs are saccadic in nature and difficult to relate to specific content scenes. Pursuit movements normally involved in the perception of motion are rarely seen during sleep dreams, even though motion is often a characteristic of dream reports. Saccadic eye movements may occur not only in conjunction with specific visual scenes, but also often related to arousal and attention (Amadeo & Shagass, 1963; Antrobus, Antrobus & Singer, 1964) and to meditative, contemplative, and daydreaming incidents (Singer, 1966).

While the scanning role of REM is open to question, the observation by Tart (1964), the detailed case study by Schiff, Bunney, and Freedman (1961), and the careful experiments by Brady and Rosner (1966), indicate that REM may occur when deeply hypnotized *S*s are asked to dream. In each study, the investigation of REM during hypnotic dreams was the primary focus of the investigation. Eye-movement recording electrodes were applied to *S*s carefully selected for hypnotizability, and the *S*s were asked to dream. Popular magazines have widely publicized the REM-dream phenomena and the purpose of the study must have been readily apparent (even explicit) to *S*s, although no control procedures were adopted to evaluate the effects of such powerful demand characteristics.

In an unpublished study employing EEG, EOG, SP, and other physiological measures, a suggested hypnotic dream was one short, incidental, item embedded in two two-hour sessions. Testing fourteen deeply hypnotized and fourteen simulating *S*s, REM was not found in any *S* during the suggested dream. In contrast, under appropriate circumstances some *S*s can quickly learn to establish delicate control over their eye movements. Some Ss were able to produce optokinetic nystagmus voluntarily, a much more specific reflexive pattern of minute movements than that of REM saccades. Such control was not a function of either hypnosis, vivid and real hallucinations, or vividness of imagery (Evan, Reich, & Orne, 1972). The nonspecific saccades of REM would be much easier to produce when Ss are confronted with the demand characteristics of justifying one's ability as a good hypnotic S. Because of the ability of some Ss to control delicate eye movements it does not seem surprising that REM was found during dreams. Unfortunately, no quantitative analyses of the eye movements comparing sleep and hypnotic dreams were conducted. The occurrence of stage REM eye movement patterns during the hypnotic dream has not been established conclusively.

INFLUENCING SLEEP FUNCTIONS BY HYPNOTIC TECHNIQUES

Relatively few studies have used hypnotic techniques to influence and alter specific characteristics of sleep and the sleep cycle. Attempts to use hypnosis in sleep learning studies, and to explore cognitive functioning and response to suggestions during sleep, will be discussed separately in the final section.

Direct suggestions have successfully been given that Ss should awaken at a presuggested time (Tart, 1970a). It has also been suggested directly that Ss would be able to discriminate between REM and nonREM sleep (Antrobus & Antrobus, 1967). Three exploratory studies are especially important because their focus is not on the nature of hypnosis, but rather on the use of hypnosis as a special technique or tool, just as the EEG is used as a tool, to study the functions of sleep.

A study by Arkin, Hastey, and Reiser (1966) explored the use of hypnosis and posthypnotic suggestion to induce sleep-talking. One hypnotizable S who had a long history of sleep talking was studied over many nights. Following appropriate posthypnotic suggestions to talk during sleep, and during stage REM dreams, the incidence of sleep vocalization rose from one per night prehypnosis to eight and thirteen times per night respectively. However, baseline nights without hypnosis near the end of the series yielded a comparable incidence of eight episodes, similar to the posthypnotically stimulated incidence. Thus it is not clear whether hypnosis was instrumental in affecting the incidence of sleep-talking. However, sleep vocalizations were less likely to occur during REM (28 percent and 42 percent pre- and postbaselines) than were the hypnotically induced incidents (64 percent). The authors report frequent occurrence of low-voltage fast EEG activity (typically found in both waking and stage REM), alpha (indicative of awakening), and "sawtooth" waves (indicative of sleep) during vocalization. They conclude that the sleep-talking incidents contain characteristics of both sleep and the hypnotic state.

Two interesting attempts have been made to explore the function of stage REM sleep by the use of hypnosis. It has been well documented that when a person is deprived of stage REM sleep over a series of nights and is subsequently allowed to sleep normally, a greater occurrence of REM sleep is observed during the following "recovery nights." This REM-rebound effect has led investigators to postulate that dreaming involves an essential need system and that long-term REM deprivation (such as that induced by many drugs) may be deleterious to psychological health. After depriving three Ss of REM sleep for two consecutive nights, Halper, Pivik, and Dement (1969) allowed Ss, who had high scores on SHSS:A, two 2½-hour periods of hypnotic hallucinations and dreaming. If there were any functional equivalence between hypnotic and sleep hallucinations (dreams), they hypothesized that no REM rebound would occur on recovery nights: Ss had an opportunity to "make up" by hypnosis what they had lost during deprivation. This ingenious hypothesis was not confirmed—the normal REM-rebound effect occurred for these REM-deprived Ss.

Using deeply hypnotizable Ss, Stoyva (1965) gave posthypnotic suggestions, with amnesia, that Ss would dream about specified topics during sleep. He employed standard REM-awakening techniques. Although the dream reports from REM awakenings were not rated blind, Stoyva divided Ss into two groups: a "successful" group who dreamed about the suggested topic in over 70 percent (mean of 85 percent) of their average 19.4 awakenings, and an "unsuccessful" group who reported dreaming correctly on less than 60 percent of their average of 5.6 awakenings. Stoyva tested the "need to dream" hypothesis by arguing that those Ss who successfully dreamed about the suggested topic would do so during their early stage REM periods and, having quickly disposed of the "business of dreaming," would consequently have shorter REM duration than those who did not successfully dream about the topic (and implicitly did not dream well). His hypothesis was confirmed: successful dreamers had a total uninterrupted REM time of 26.6 minutes, which was 6.6 minutes less than for baseline nights and seven minutes less than the REM time of unsuccessfully stimulated Ss. It was also tentatively found that posthypnotic suggestions for more complex dreams led to a further reduction in REM time. NREM awakenings did not typically yield reports of dreams about the suggestion.

These three ingenious studies could serve as prototypes for ways in which hypnosis may be used as a technique to study characteristics and parameters of sleep. No particular conclusions are possible from these pilot studies; they should be replicated and extended. It is hoped that similar studies will be conducted more frequently.

Hypnosis as a Model for Sleep-Induced Behavior

A different set of questions has been explored recently concerning the sleeping individual's ability to interact with his environment. Hypnosis has provided both a model for studying interactions with the sleeping person and a means of exploring cognitive functioning during sleep.

Anecdotal examples support the notion that, in addition to dreaming, complex cognitive behavior can occur during sleep, particularly if an appropriate set has been established before sleep. One rarely falls out of bed, for example, even though a great deal of gross bodily activity occurs throughout the night. Loud noises that are repetitive or familiar are less likely to wake the sleeping person than softer strange noises. Mothers can sleep through conditions of high ambient noise but are easily awakened by soft familiar cries from their babies—the so-called "mother's cry" phenomenon. Some people claim they can wake regularly at a preselected time. Similar phenomena have been studied in the laboratory. For example, when appropriate waking instructions had been given, sleeping Ss woke up only when specified names of friends were spoken (Oswald, 1962). Conditioned responses and discrimination among auditory stimuli may be elicited during sleep if a waking response tendency has been established (Beh & Barratt, 1965; Granda & Hammack, 1961; McDonald, 1966; Weinberg, 1966; Williams, Morlock, & Morlock, 1966; Zung & Wilson, 1961).

Historically, it has been recognized that if a hypnotized S is given a specific suggestion, or even if he is left alone for a long period of time, he may fall asleep without passing through a natural awake state. Dittborn has been able to induce sleep by repetitive suggestion (Dittborn, Munoz, & Aristeguieta, 1963). Although the occurrence of suggested sleep was confirmed by the EEG, the ease of falling asleep following suggestions was not related to hypnotizability (Dittborn & O'Connell, 1967). Dittborn and O'Connell showed a kind of dissociation between behavioral and physiological sleep with hypnotizable Ss who, by discontinuing a repetitive response, appeared asleep behaviorally even though they were not asleep physiologically. Kratochvil (1970) has also suggested that sleep and hypnosis may be superimposed, although such combined states are difficult to demonstrate operationally.

A controversial claim has been that hypnotic-like suggestions can be given successfully during sleep (Bernheim, 1889; Bertrand, 1826b; Fresacher, 1951; Gill & Brenman, 1959; Schilder & Kauders, 1927). Barber (1956) whispered hypnotic-like suggestions to twenty-two Ss who were asleep in their rooms. Some Ss responded to the suggestions; physiological and EEG criteria were not employed to monitor sleep.

RESPONSE TO SUGGESTIONS DURING SLEEP

Our background and experience with hypnosis both provoked our interest in cognitive awareness during sleep and also provided insight into how to explore the complexity of behavior that could be induced during sleep. With the initial Ss we tested, we were tentatively exploring parallels between hypnosis and responses to suggestions we supposed might be induced successfully during sleep (Cobb et al., 1965). The general procedures were the same as in later studies and will be outlined below.

Four observations were particularly interesting: (1) Some Ss could respond, while remaining asleep, to simple hypnotic-like suggestions administered during stage REM sleep. (2) When awakened, Ss did not recall these suggestions. However, the analogy with posthypnotic amnesia was superficial, as, unlike posthypnotic amnesia, the postsleep amnesia could not be reversed. The Ss seemed to remain unaware of their sleeping activity. (3) When given the same cue after sleep that had elicited the suggested response during sleep, Ss did not respond behaviorally while awake. The sleep-induced cue was not analogous to a posthypnotic cue for S to respond to the associated suggestion. Sleep-induced behavior was at best only superficially related to hypnotic behavior. (4) The Ss' ability to respond to suggestions during sleep did appear to be related to hypnotic susceptibility. Four Ss responded to suggestions during sleep; each was a deeply hypnotizable S who had worked with E in several previous experiments. The four insusceptible Ss did not respond at all to sleep suggestions.

The implied relationship between susceptibility to hypnosis and sleep-induced response must be interpreted with caution. The susceptible and insusceptible Ss had quite diffent background experiences with hypnosis. Repeated failure by insusceptible Ss to respond to hypnotic suggestions may have changèd the interpersonal relationship between S and E. The Ss' expectations, rather than their susceptibilty to hypnosis, could have been a critical determinant of their responsivity during sleep. In addition, E administering the sleep suggestions was the same E who had evaluated S's hypnotic susceptibility; as he was quite aware of each S's susceptibility during sleep testing, the possible influence of E's biases on the predicted outcome cannot be overlooked. Nevertheless, the interrelationship between hypnosis and the sleep suggestions that were induced and tested during stage REM sleep seemed worthy of detailed exploration. A more elaborate study was designed (Evans et al., 1969, 1970). Susceptibility to hypnosis was not evaluated until after the completion of all sleep sessions, and was evaluated by hypnotists who were unaware of Ss' performance during the sleep sessions. Differences in rapport and the interpersonal factors arising in the hypnotic relationship were not present during the sleep sessions.

Procedure.[6] Nineteen male student nurses slept for two nights. Standard EEG sleep-monitoring techniques were used. During on-line visual

6. A detailed description of the procedures and results discussed below has been given elsewhere (Evans et al., 1969, 1970).

diagnosis of alpha-free stage REM sleep, suggestions were presented verbally to S. Typical suggestions were: "Whenever I say the word 'itch,' your nose will feel itchy until you scratch it"; "Whenever I say the word 'pillow,' your pillow will feel uncomfortable until you move it." The suggestion was tested by saying the cue word ("itch" or "pillow") once. An attempt was made to test each cue word on at least two separate occasions during the same stage REM period in which the suggestion was given *(immediate),* during all subsequent stage REM periods that night *(delayed),* and during stage REM periods of the second night *(carry-over).* The suggestion itself was not readministered on the second night. Suggestions were not repeated after their initial presentation. Two new suggestions were presented each night whenever possible. Suggestions were administered and cues were tested only during stage REM. At least 120 seconds of alpha-free stage REM were required between cue word presentations. It was conservatively assumed that visually-detected alpha indicated arousal (O'Connell et al., 1965). Only Ss who displayed an alpha density exceeding 40 percent of an eyes-closed waking-rest trial were included in the study.

The S's behavior was observed by E, who was in the same room. When S awakened in the morning, memory for the session was tested directly and indirectly during an interview and by administering the cue words in the context of a word association test. Any behavioral response to the critical cue word was observed. When S awakened after night two, a more detailed inquiry evaluated memory for the sleep events.

The S was not told before either session that suggestions would be given, but he was told that sleep cycles were being studied. Thus, any specific waking "set" indicating what was being tested during sleep was avoided. He was not told that he would be invited back later to participate in a hypnosis experiment.

About a month after the completion of the sleep experiment, HGSHS:A and SHSS:C were administered to these Ss by "blind" Es. Five subscores were derived from HGSHS:A and SHSS:C: waking motor suggestion, hypnotic motor suggestion, challenge suggestion, hallucinatory-reverie, and posthypnotic-dissociative.[7]

Characteristics of sleep induced behavior. A detailed parametric

7. These clusters were derived by summing scores on SHSS:C items as follows. *Hypnotic motor suggestion:* items 1 and 2, hand lowering and moving hands apart. *Challenge suggestion:* items 5 and 8, arm rigidity and arm immobilization. *Hallucinatory-reverie:* items 6 and 11, dream and negative visual hallucination. *Posthypnotic-dissociative:* item 12, posthypnotic amnesia, and item 11 from HGSHS:A, posthypnotic suggestion. The *waking motor suggestion* consisted of item 1 of HGSHS:A, head falling. These clusters do not necessarily represent the underlying dimensions adequately, particularly the hallucination and dissociative ones (Evans, 1966). Although the underlying dimensions may be unrelated, the estimated scores are moderately correlated. The highest correlation ($r = .51$) is between the hallucination and posthypnotic clusters.

description of the important characteristics of sleep-induced behavior is presented elsewhere (Evans et al., 1969, 1970) and is only summarized now. During the two nights, 416 cue words were presented during sleep, and eighty-nine correct responses were observed. On the average, the nineteen Ss responded to a mean of 21.2 per cent of all cue words: the highest response rate by a S was 48 percent.

Uninterrupted stage REM sleep continued for at least thirty seconds for seventy-one percent of all cues administered; that is, alpha activity did not occur before or while the cue word was administered. Many responses were obtained without eliciting alpha activity during the suggestion, after the cue words were administered, or before and after the response. When alpha followed a successful response, it was signficantly slower than waking alpha frequency, but it was not significantly different from the slowed frequency occurring spontaneously during unstimulated stage REM sleep.

After S awakened, he did not remember the verbally presented material, nor could he remember responding. No difference was found between the latency of word associate cue words and latency of control word associates. This lack of recall involved amnesia rather than forgetting, because the material was still available for future responding during sleep. When S returned to sleep the next night (or, in some of the cases described below, even five months later), the mere repetition of the relevant cue word (without repetition of the suggestion itself) was sufficient to elicit the appropriate response. The behavioral response appeared to be specific to sleep in spite of the intervening amnesia.

The response could not be elicited by repeating the cue word in the waking state. As in the preliminary study, behavior analogous to posthypnotic suggestion was not elicited.

A successful response tendency was mobilized slowly. The average response latency was thirty-two seconds. Latency increased as the temporal dissociation between the administration of the suggestion and the cue word increased. For example, latencies for immediate and carry-over responses were nineteen and fifty-nine seconds, respectively. In contrast, a similar suggestion given during hypnosis would be responded to immediately: even if tested posthypnotically the response latency is typically only a few seconds.

A subsequent study (Perry et al., 1978) has confirmed these characteristics, although a lower response rate and even longer response latencies were found. Three additional findings confirmed that the motor behavior during sleep was not random, but was directly elicited by the suggestions and associated cue word. (1) Correct responses could be discriminated from random body movement behavior when videotaped responses were rated by blind rater. (2) Interspersed dummy cue words not associated with any suggestion that had been administered did not elicit behavioral responses appropriate to any suggestion that had been given. (3) If a cue word was presented before the suggestion had been given, the cue word was not sufficient by itself to elicit the specific behavioral response that was to be later on associated with the suggestion.

SLEEP RESPONSE AND SUSCEPTIBILITY TO HYPNOSIS

Based on individual percentage response rates for the two nights combined, a post hoc dichotomy was made between *responsive* ($N = 9$) and *unresponsive* ($N = 10$) Ss. Mean HGSHS:A and SHSS:C scores for responsive and unresponsive Ss are presented in Table 6.4. Those Ss who repond most frequently to sleep-induced suggestions are more susceptible to hypnosis. Pearson correlations between susceptibility to hypnosis and frequencies of cue administration, response, and response rate are presented in Table 6.5. The correlations are positive and consistent for the several measures, indicating that sleep-induced response and susceptibility to hypnosis are related in some manner. The relationship is, however, complex, and several factors influence the interpretation of these correlations.

TABLE 6.4   Susceptibility to hypnosis and response to suggestion during sleep

		Hypnosis Scale			
		_HGSHS:A			SHSS:C
		X	SD	X	SD
Responsive Ss	($N = 9$)	7.6	3.5	9.5	2.1
Unresponsive Ss	($N = 10$)	5.5	2.8	5.5	2.4
Mann-Whitney U		28.5	(insig.)	8.5	($P < .01$)
t		1.41	($p < .20$)	3.93	($p < .005$)

SOURCE: Evans et al., 1969.

Response frequency. The correlations between susceptibility to hypnosis and response to sleep-induced suggestions are, then, positive and significant (see Table 6.5). However, susceptible Ss responded more often, at least in part, because they were administered more cue words. Hypnotizable Ss were found to awaken following stimulation less frequently than insusceptible Ss. Consequently they slept longer, and more cues were inadvertently tested. The correlations between response-rate percentage (which effectively controls the difference in the frequency of cue administrations) and both HGSHS:A and SHSS:C are of borderline significance (.42, $p < .10$; and .39 $p < .10$, respectively, two-tailed values).[8] However, the relationship between sleep responsivity and hypnosis depends on two factors: the delay

_____

8. The number of times S awakened during the two nights correlated $-.49$ ($p < .05$) with HGSHS:A and $-.29$ ($p > .05$) with SHSS:C.

in time between administering the suggestions and testing with the cue word: and the aspect of hypnosis (factor or cluster score) being considered.

TABLE 6.5 Correlations between sleep response and susceptibility to hypnosis

Hypnosis[a] Measure	Response Frequency	Cue Word Frequency	Per Cent Response	Delay Between Suggestion-Cue		
				immediate response	delayed response	carry-over response
HGSHS:A	.48*	.63**	.42	.23	.32	.64**
SHSS:C	.56*	.68**	.39	.38	.43	.60**
Suggestion:						
Waking	−.15	−.21	−.19	.11	−.42	.06
Passive	.32	.23	.32	.05	.40	.41
Challenge	.26	.47*	.22	.33	.08	.44
Hallucinatory-reverie	.54**	.61**	.43	.35	.42	.52**
Posthypnotic-Dissociative	.46*	.64**	.17	.23	.30	.58**

SOURCE: Evans et. al., 1969.

NOTE: * $p < .05$; **$p < .01$ (two-tailed values).

a. The clusters of hypnotic items are derived from SHSS:C. See text footnote 7.

Hypnosis and temporal dissociation of sleep response. Table 6.5 summarizes the correlations between hypnotizability and the three categories of response: immediate, delayed, and carry-over. The correlations with susceptibility to hypnosis are higher for percentage rate of delayed response than for percentage rate of immediate response. Susceptibility to hypnosis more successfully predicts ability to respond to sleep-induced suggestion when there is a temporal dissociation between the administration of the suggestion and the cue word, that is, when the response is elicited during the second night to a suggestion that has been administered only during the first night. The correlations between the carry-over response rate with HGSHS:A and SHSS:C are .64 ($p < .01$ and .60 ($p < .01$) respectively.

Sleep response and type of hypnotic performance. Correlations between the sleep-induced response and factors of hypnotic behavior are summarized in Table 6.5. These results should be interpreted with considerable caution. Neither the frequency of cues nor the frequency of responses correlates with waking suggestibility, hypnotic motor suggestibility, or challenge suggestibility. This is surprising, because the sleep behaviors suggested involved motor responses. The correlations with the hallucinatory-reverie and posthypnotic-dissociative clusters are significant for the percentage rate of carry-over (dissociative) response ($r = .52, p < .01$ and

$r = .58, p < .01$, respectively), but not for the immediate responses. These two hypnotic clusters include phemonena experienced only by the very few Ss who can be deeply hypnotized.

Sleep patterns, hypnosis, and sleep response. We were surprised to find that the more hypnotizable Ss fell asleep faster, and were less likely to be awakened during the night. This prompted us to examine Ss' subjective sleep patterns. At the beginning of their first night, a questionnaire was administered to Ss inquiring about their ability to sleep well without being disturbed. Several items from this questionnaire discriminated significantly between responding and nonresponding Ss. A combined score, including items reflecting objective measures of sleeping well during the study (Evans et al., 1969) correlated .55 ($p < .02$) with response frequency. Combining the predictive criteria, the multiple correlation between percentage response frequency and the combination of the questionnaire and SHSS:C was .48 ($p < .05$). The multiple correlations predicting the carry-over responses were .69, and .68, and .62 ($p < .01$) when the questionnaire was combined with SHSS:C, and the dissociation and hallucinatory factors, respectively.

Hypnotizability and sleep induced responsivity. Subjects who were able to remain asleep while responding to verbal suggestions administered during sleep were more susceptible to hypnosis and slept more soundly than Ss who did not respond. This joint relationship reflects the hypnotizable responder's ability to sleep well, in terms of both his verbal claims about his sleeping habits and his ability to sleep without awakening in the experimental situation. By waking more often, both spontaneously and following stimulation, the unresponsive S provided himself with less opportunity to respond because fewer cue word administrations were possible.

This result clarifies the perfect association between responding and hypnotizability observed by Cobb et al. (1965). Then, as in the present study, insusceptible Ss tended to awaken whenever there was any verbal stimulation. The interesting theoretical question is not so much the extent to which sleep suggestion is analogous to hypnotic phenomena, but rather why the hypnotizable S sleeps better than the more easily aroused insusceptible S. Ranking Ss by all available hypnosis scores, the six Ss who were least susceptible to hypnosis accounted for 48 percent of all awakenings occurring during the two experimental nights. In contrast, the six Ss who were most hypnotizable accounted for only 26 percent of the total awakenings.

The paradigm adopted for administering the suggestions during sleep was similar to that regularly used with passive motor suggestions during waking or hypnosis. The sleep response was not, however, a simple manifestation of motor or primary suggestibility as the concept is usually applied to waking and hypnotic conditions (Evans, 1967). Frequency of sleep response did not correlate with score clusters derived from the hypnosis scales measuring the various aspects of motor suggestion. Instead, sleep response frequency was related to the clusters consisting of phenomena typically obtained with somnambulistic hypnosis: hallucinations and posthypnotic effects.

The correlation between sleep-induced response to suggestion and susceptibility to hypnosis was statistically significant only when the carry-over responses (responses during night two to suggestions administered during night one) were considered. The relationship between response and hypnotic susceptibility was most apparent when there was a dissociative temporal gap between the administration of the suggestion and the related cue eliciting the response. A common mechanism may exist in both the hypnotic and sleep situations, although it takes a different form in each state. This speculative interpretation is supported by the significant correlation between the posthypnotic-dissociative cluster of items in the hypnosis scales and the frequency of carry-over or dissociated responses. In the spirit of this kind of speculation, the correlation between the hallucinatory-reverie cluster of items and sleep response is possibly consistent with data indicating that when a successful response occurs the cue word may be incorporated into ongoing dream activity (Evans et al., 1970). Some kind of facility to control imagery and ideational content seems necessary to experience convincing hypnotic hallucinations and to manipulate ongoing dream content. It is also interesting that there are some Ss who experience posthypnotic amnesia, who respond during sleep in spite of intervening waking amnesia, and who claim they do not recall dreams when they awaken.

The assumed selective attention of the hypnotized S during trance and his ability to discriminate between relevant and irrelevant stimuli have often been stressed. If this is a general characteristic of the susceptible S, then he may maintain this advantage during some stages of sleep. He is able to attend selectively and to process incoming information in a way that allows discrimination as to whether it is "neccessary" for him to arouse himself and process the information at a more integrated waking level. On some occasions this processing can be completed without arousal. Because of his lack of selective attention the insusceptible S has to awaken to process similar incoming information. From this point of view the relationship between susceptibility to hypnosis and sleep-induced response does not imply any similarity or interchangeability of trance and sleep states. Rather, the evidence seems to indicate that ability to have dissociative mental processing leading to a selective attention to external stimulation is common to both phenomena.

Alternatively, some Ss may be able to shift from one state of consciousness to another with relative ease. A fluidity, or perhaps a blurring of the boundaries between different states, occurs. There may be people who can be hypnotized readily, who can fluctuate between a variety of dissociated states, whether while awake or asleep, and who can fall asleep readily, yet be able to alert themselves quickly to process incoming stimuli, sometimes responding while remaining asleep. The common mechanism may be a fluidity or interchangeability of state boundaries rather than any specific features of any of these dissociated states.

FURTHER EXPLORATIONS OF DISSOCIATED SLEEP RESPONSES

Several important questions remained unanswered. What are the limits of the carry-over responses? Was the cue word sufficiently strong to elicit a sleep response even after several months of intervening amnesia? Was it possible to increase the response rate during sleep by appropriate sets or instructions in the waking or hypnotic conditions prior to sleep? Were there any means available, such as presleep sets or the use of hypnotic techniques after sleep, to recover memory for the sleep experiences in the waking state? While these questions have not been answered satisfactorily as yet, an attempt was made to explore some of these issues in a pilot study by making additional observations with some of the Ss already tested.

About five months after the completion of the study described above, seven of the nineteen Ss were invited to sleep another night in the laboratory. In general, the procedures already described were used. For those specific procedures, which differed from S to S, the main results are

TABLE 6.6   Relationships between hypnosis, sleep-induced response and subsequent waking recall for Ss sleeping several months after initial sessions

S	Hypnosis[a]		Use of Hypnosis on Night 3[b]	Response Percent		Recall[c]	
	level	rank		nights 1 & 2	night 3	waking	aided by hypnosis
1	High	1⎫		31	55	Nil	Nil
2	High	4⎪ No suggestion to		42	43	Some	Some
3	Med.	5⎬ respond		25	14	Poor	Nil
4	Low	7⎭		20	0	Nil	Some
5	High	2⎫ No suggestion, fell		5	9	Nil	Nil
		⎭ asleep in hypnosis					
6	High	3⎫ Suggest response,		8	39	Much	Some
7	Med.	6⎭ recall		48	63	Some	Much

a. High, medium, or low susceptibility to hypnosis based on HGSHS:A, SHSS:C, and diagnostic ratings. Rankings of hypnotizability based on all available evidence.
b. See text for description.
c. Crude rating scale of nil, poor, some, much, or complete recall of sleep suggestions and responses.

summarized in Table 6.6. The hypnotizability rankings are based both on standardized scale scores and individual diagnostic ratings that had been administered shortly after completion of the original two nights.

An attempt was made to hypnotize each S at the beginning of the sleep session. No special suggestions regarding responding or recall were given to five Ss. One of these Ss was allowed to fall asleep while hypnotized. The remaining two Ss were given strong suggestions to respond during sleep and to recall when awake. During sleep, several cue words were administered that were appropriate to the suggestions of the two nights from five months previously. New suggestions were also given. Waking recall was tested as before, but each S was hypnotized in an attempt to elicit further recall. When S was finally awakened from sleep, recall was tested as before. A variety of hypnotic techniques, including regression, was used with the more hypnotizable Ss in an attempt to reverse the amnesia for the sleep experiences.

The main results are summarized in Table 6.6. Because of the exploratory nature of these sessions conclusions are not justified. Some Ss responded much more frequently than they had during the original two nights. Under special conditions, response rates approached the initial response rates reported by Cobb et al. (1965). While the induction of hypnosis and the hypnotic experience gained since the original nights may have contributed to these increases, the evidence indicates that neither hypnotic depth nor the interpersonal variables could account for all of the increases. Specific presleep suggestions aimed at increasing sleep responsivity may have been helpful, but it cannot be judged whether the increased response rate is due to hypnosis per se or is a generalized, nonspecific response due to E's convincing S that high response rates could plausibly be expected. Certainly such influences did not merely affect new suggestions. Many responses were obtained to cue words associated with suggestions that had not been repeated, nor apparently recalled, since the first night some five to six months before.

Similar problems of interpretation recurred when attempts were made to utilize hypnosis, either before or after the sleep session, to obtain recall of the sleep events. Hypnosis helped, but again the results were not a direct function of hypnotic depth. Some hitherto unrecalled old suggestions were recalled while using hypnotic techniques. This result may indicate that the techniques originally used to probe morning recall were insufficiently sensitive. Perhaps our Ss may have deceived us. On the other hand, the possible timeless or contextless effects of hypnosis have been documented by the work on source amnesia (Evans & Thorn, 1966; Evans, 1968). The investigator working in this area may find hypnosis important, if not essential, in improving recall and response rates, but whether hypnosis per se is a causal variable requires additional sophisticated research.

SLEEP RESPONSE—THREE CASE STUDIES

Case study summaries of three *S*s who participated for three nights are presented below. These summaries will invite speculation without providing answers. They will also serve to give some insight into the dramatic quality of the sleep suggestion response that is not apparent in sterile statistical description.

Subject 1. This *S* was an exceptionally good hypnotic *S*, scoring 12 on both HGSHS:A and SHSS:C, with several 5+ diagnostic ratings (Orne & O'Connell, 1967). Before the third session he was easily and deeply hypnotized, displaying all major hypnotic phenomena.

He had responded to eleven of thirty-six cues (31 percent response rate) on the first two nights. He had recalled more than any other *S* about the two nights. He remembered the cue "itch," and said he deduced that he had been given suggestions. He felt that two other cue words ("pillow," "blanket") during the second night word association test were in some way significant. Thus, he had partial recall of three of the five suggestions that were used. In no case could details be elaborated. Of his eleven responses, seven were to the three cue words that were recalled.

This *S*'s sleep behavior during the first two nights seemed both purposeful and emotional. After he had been presented with the cue word "itch," he scratched his nose for several seconds, adjusted his "pillow" by pushing it into a new shape with both hands, pulled his "blanket" above his head, and kicked with his "leg," pausing each time between the successive movements. There was no EEG evidence of arousal. He had been given these four suggestions separately, but in this sequence, during the previous two nights. Repetition of any of the four cue words failed to elicit further response. When the next stage REM period occurred, presentation of any one of the four cue words again elicited the same sequence of responses, but no more responses could be elicited with another cue word. In the final stage REM period, the same sequence occurred again. This time *S* repeatedly thrashed his left leg with considerable violence. By responding in sequence to all suggestions, then failing to "acknowledge" further stimulation, he obtained a deceptively low response rate. (This kind of sequential "response chaining" was observed with at least two other *S*s.)

During the third night he did not respond to a new suggestion. The old cue word "leg" was administered three times. The first time he raised his left leg to almost a vertical position and held it there for several seconds. He responded again to the second repetition. On the third time, with little delay, he lifted his left leg and put it down, repeating the lifting sequence three times, each time more aggressively. This suggestion had not been given since the first night five months previously: he had responded to it then but did not recall it. He responded to two of four additional cues, the last of which involved another response chain, followed by arousal. He could not fall asleep again. He responded to five of nine cues (55 percent). He could not recall anything under some pressure while awake nor while hypnotized.

Subject 2. The *S* slept well and responded well. In all, he responded fourteen times to thirty-three cues (42 percent response rate). He responded six times on the second night to the eight testings of first night cue words. Neither recall nor dreams were elicited. He scored eleven and ten on HGSHS:A and SHSS:C respectively, and, although diagnostic ratings could not be made, he appeared to be a very susceptible *S*. On the third night he was hypnotized, displaying all standard hypnotic phenomena.

During the third night he responded to two of the seven old cues and to four of seven new cues (43 percent). Once, when the old cue word "pillow" was given, he moved his pillow and, with a significant pause each time between movements, he then scratched his nose, moved his right leg, and appeared to brush something from his chin. These were very precise, specific movements. They were appropriate responses to all of the suggestions that had been administered during the two original nights, in correct order. This response chaining occurred several times with him.

He responded twice, as he had on night two, to a verbal command to raise his left arm on the cue "arm." Unlike the suggestions, this command did not have any specific subjective experience associated with it. He continued to hold his arm up until he was told to let it drop (in one case, after about five minutes). (Maintaining responses to a command until told to stop was observed with other *S*s.) Suggestions were then given that he would dream about the experiment and that he would be able to recall the experiment, his responses, and his dreams in detail.

Upon awakening he reported one of the most vivid dreams we obtained. He was studying for an examination (not true in real life) and he was very excited, disturbed, and annoyed because he was being interrupted. During the fifteen word associates test he inappropriately moved both legs twice (to the neutral words "night" and "head"), he then correctly moved his right leg to "leg" and momentarily lifted his left arm to "arm." This was the first evidence we have obtained of a sleep state analog of a posthypnotic response.

When questioned about the night, he spontaneously recalled that he had been asked to move his leg, but could not recall any details. He was then hypnotized and, in response to suggestions of recall, he was able to elaborate upon the dream and recall the exact details of the leg suggestion and his response to it, both during sleep and during his word association response. He could recall nothing about any other suggestions used.

In general, this S did not behave very differently in this session than in his previous sessions. It is possible that the sleep and hypnotic suggestions stimulated some recall. Any differences in "rapport" variables added by the hypnotic evaluations did not result (as hypothesized by Cobb et al., 1965) in a greater response rate.

Subject 6. This S scored six and nine respectively on HGSHS:A and SHSS:C and received two clinical hypnotic ratings of five. At the beginning of the third session he had no memory for the previous suggestions. He was easily hypnotized before he slept. He was given emphatic suggestions that he would respond to any suggestions given during sleep and recall them when awake.

He had previously tended to awaken when suggestions were administered (three of seven attempts), and had been classified as a nonresponder. He responded only twice to twenty-five cues. One of these responses occurred on the second night to a first night suggestion. On the third night he responsed to seven out of eighteen cues, a change from 8 percent to 39 percent response rate following the hypnotically induced "set" to respond. These statistics, however, do not capture the quality of his performance. He was tested unsuccessfully seven times during his first stage REM period. During this time a new suggestion that "when I say the word 'blanket,' you will feel cold and pull the blanket up over you," failed to elicit a response. In the remaining stage REM periods the cue words "itch" and "leg" were given a total of three times unsuccessfully. These cue words had not elicited any response during the first two sessions either, perhaps implying a failure of stimulus registration.

The "blanket" and "pillow" suggestions were then readministered, again with no signs of arousal (alpha) in the record. The S then responded to each of the three "pillow" cues and to three of the four "blanket" cues. (Following the fourth "blanket" cue, a partial movement of the arm was made below the covers, but could not have been considered a clear response.) It is possible that S suddenly began "hearing" or "understanding" what was being said for the first time. It is not possible to tell, of course, if hypnosis was instrumental in this dramatic change in response rate from almost 0 to almost 100 percent.

Later, upon waking, S knew E had been in the room talking several times—about five times. He knew E had used the word "itch." He remembered this because one of the electrodes made him itchy. (He had not responded to this cue since his only night one response five months ago.) Gradually he recalled that he had been restless, particularly with the pillow. He then recalled that E said it was lumpy, and this is why he wanted to move it. Then he said, "Oh, another word was 'blanket.' I can recall curling into a ball under the blanket—it was rather cool. You told me I was gonna be

cool, and I would pull it up all around me." He described these things as occurring in a nonwaking state, more like sleeping than waking, but more like
hypnosis than sleep. He also recalled the word "leg," and that he had lifted
his right leg up into the air and held it there, but he thought he woke up. He
recalled that these events occurred before the "blanket" suggestion (which
had been administered early in the second stage REM period). He commented that he had been surprised to see his leg up in the air and also was
surprised to see E leaving the room. Although E had made no notes about a
response to "leg," about ninety seconds after the last cue of the first stage
REM period the technician had signaled to E that S seemed to be awakening. The E left the room immediately. The cue word at that time was "leg,"
and apparently S had responded, possibly while awakening, as E left the
room. The S also recalled the cue word "arm," and remembered that he
lifted his left arm and that this response had been suggested. In fact, this
suggestion was administered only during the first night six months previously, and he had responded to it during the second night. It was not
tested during this third night.

This S was able to recall most of what happened during the session. He
had been given a presleep hypnotic suggestion that he would be able to
remember everything that occurred during the night. Some of the memories
were of complete suggestions given *only* in the previous sessions for which
amnesia had not been successfully broken, either by direct interviewing or
by subtler word association latencies and responses. Whatever the role of
hypnosis in this session, it did not simply give S the "set" to recall only
future happenings. Rather, hypnosis may have acted in a "timeless," dissociated, or contextless way to help retrieve events that *had* transpired as well
as those which *were* to transpire.

HYPNOSIS AND SLEEP LEARNING

Since the carefully controlled EEG studies by Simon and Emmons (1956),
learning during sleep has not been seriously considered. They reported that
stimulus material presented during sleep was not recalled later when S
awakened unless alpha activity occurred simultaneously with the stimulus
material. As alpha during sleep indicates arousal, they felt that any learning
occurred in a waking state. In sleep learning studies, lack of retention upon
awakening has been considered as evidence that registration or acquisition
did not occur during sleep. However, we have shown that retention
(response to cue words) occurs during sleep, demonstrating that registration
and acquisition have occurred during sleep. Not only can S respond to
sleep-induced suggestions while remaining asleep, but he can also respond
on subsequent nights without repetition of the suggestion and without any
apparent waking memory of the suggestions or his response to them. The

problem remaining unsolved is that of the retrieval of sleep-acquired material. In this sense, the problem of retrieval of sleep-acquired material is similar to the problem of the retrieval of dreams when S awakens in the morning.

In Soviet countries hypnopaedia or sleep learning is widely practiced. Not only do individuals apparently learn languages during sleep, but it has even been claimed that whole villages have been taught languages by radio at night. These studies have been adequately reviewed (Hoskovek, 1966; Rubin, 1968). Although some studies use EEG techniques, the written and translated reports are unclear as to what the EEG shows during stimulus presentation. Nevertheless, other evidence, such as a lack of any symptoms of sleep deprivation, points to the possibility that not all Ss were really awake during stimulation. The concept of hypnopaedia implies hypnosis, and it is typically claimed that learning occurs only with "suggestible" Ss. It is not clear whether "suggestible" implies hypnotizability or whether a strong waking "set" is induced to convince the person that sleep learning is possible. Simon and Emmons (1956) did not induce such a set. The case studies summarized above support the notion that hypnosis may be implicated in the waking recall of sleep behavior.

In an unpublished study an attempt was made to maximize the possibility of sleep learning. In order to obtain waking recall of sleep-acquired material it was felt that four conditions would have to be fulfilled: (1) Subjects were chosen who could respond during sleep to sleep-administered suggestion, using the procedures already discussed. (2) Some Ss were included who were highly susceptible to hypnosis. (3) Any stimulus presented that was accompanied simultaneously by alpha was not included or scored. It was, therefore, not possible to replicate the findings by Simon and Emmons (1956); acquisition during arousal was ruled out by eliminating stimuli presented during alpha. (4) A strong waking set was established that sleep learning was possible. The sleep-induced responses were described, and Ss were told about their own sleep-induced responses during the first sleep session. Soviet hypnopaedia claims were reviewed extensively, and S was motivated both by the competitive aim to duplicate Russian studies and by his special qualifications as a likely candidate for successful sleep learning.

Procedure. Nine Ss were tested who could respond, while remaining asleep, to suggestions presented during sleep, without a presleep "set." The Ss had had no subsequent waking recall of these suggestions. An appropriate presleep "set" was then established before the sleep learning session. The Ss slept for about six hours. Several Ss were included who did not receive this "set," although E was not blind.

Material in the form of "A is for Apple," "P is for Palace," etc., was presented during sleep stages REM, two, and four, defined by standard

EEG criteria. Waking recall was tested by asking *S* to check any familiar word on a list of ten words beginning with "A," and again from ten words beginning with "P," etc. Eight stimulus words, each beginning with a different letter, were presented twice to each *S*. Where possible, at least two different letter-word pairs were presented during each stage. After awakening, *S* received the eight appropriate ten-word lists, and two similar "dummy" lists containing letter-word pairs not used during sleep. Thus, conservative probabilities of checking one correct word by guessing was .10 for each of the eight relevant lists. In addition, *S* was asked to rate on a five point scale whether he was certain or uncertain that he had heard that word or letter.

Results. The number of words correctly recognized is presented in Table 6.7. While recall was partial, it exceeded conservatively estimated chance recall (in fact none of the "dummy" lists were ever checked). Of the letter-word combinations administered during stage REM, 28 percent of the administered words were correctly checked. In addition, *S* was able to select with certainty the correct letter (without specifying a word) in an additional 17 percent of all lists. Only those letters were counted that *S* was quite certain he heard. In fact, *Ss* did not guess a letter unless they were convinced it had been spoken. Although words were rarely recalled from stages two and four, *S* could often recognize letters from these stages. The incidence of guessing, that is, incorrectly recalled words or letters, was virtually zero. No control *S* (without presleep "set") recalled any words correctly.

A secondary result is important theoretically. Although none of the words were presented simultaneously with alpha activity, whenever words presented during stage REM were subsequently recalled, transient alpha had been evoked within thirty seconds after the presentation of the stimuli during sleep. During sleep stimulation, evoked alpha for words successfully recalled was significantly ($p < .01$) slower in frequency (9.64 Hz.) than waking alpha (10.25 Hz.) and slower than alpha during sleep which was

TABLE 6.7 Waking recognition of material learned during sleep with 9 sleep-responsive *Ss* with presleep set to learn

Sleep Stage	Total Words Presented	Percentage Recall	
		correct word	addit. correct letters
1	29	28	17
2	20	10	40
4	13	0	39
All stages	62	16	29

NOTE: Words checked incorrectly: 0%; additional letters checked incorrectly: 10%.

evoked by nonrecalled stimuli. Alpha evoked by recalled stimuli was the same frequency as spontaneous alpha during sleep (9.61 Hz.). An example of the EEG during the presentation of a word that was subsequently recalled is presented in Figure 6.2. The rate of alpha following to-be-recalled stimuli is difficult to explain. Perhaps alpha activity, even of a slower frequency (lower arousal?), may be required for consolidation: perhaps an altered EEG pattern in general is required for memory consolidation.

A third important finding of this study confirms some of the Russian claims. Of the nine Ss, seven had been administered HGSHS:A and SHSS:C, and had at least two clinical diagnostic ratings of hypnotizability. The correlations between the total (all stages) recall of words and HGSHS:A, SHSS:C, and diagnostic rating were .69, .42, and .52 respectively. The respective rank correlations with stage REM recall were .41, .49, and .49. While the results of the correlational analysis on a small sample are equivocal, they are consistent with some of the case study evidence cited above, as well as with the Soviet "hypnopaedia" results.

It would seem that under optimal conditions in the laboratory, sleep learning can occur with subsequent waking recall. While the relative effects of set and susceptibility to hypnosis were not separated in this study, hypnosis would seem to play a role in further explorations of the theoretically exciting but practically limited phenomenon of sleep learning.

Summary

What use, then, does the sleep researcher have for hypnosis? It seems clear that there is no interchangeability of sleep and hypnosis. The EEG during hypnosis and sleep are basically different. For this reason, it is perhaps not surprising that hypnosis cannot be used as an effective substitute for sleep. For example, the hypnotic dream is not a functional substitute for dream activity during stage REM sleep. Visual hallucinatory activity during hypnosis cannot be substituted for sleep and REM deprivation. Hypnotic techniques will be of limited value to the sleep researcher in studying the parametric characteristics of sleep.

For the researcher interested in examining the functions of sleep and the limits of cognition during sleep, hypnosis may be an adjunct as a technical aid. It may be possible to influence and affect such things as dream content, length of sleep, and ease of falling asleep, although more evidence is required.

Hypnosis is clearly relevant to exploring the sleeping individual's interaction with his environment. Hypnotic techniques may be used to explore and facilitate sleep-induced behavior, and the subsequent recall of sleep experiences, whether they involved learned material, suggestions, commands of motor and cognitive activity, or perhaps even the recall of dreams.

FIGURE 6.2. *EEG record showing presentation of a stimulus during stage REM sleep which was learned and subsequently recalled the next morning when S was awake.*

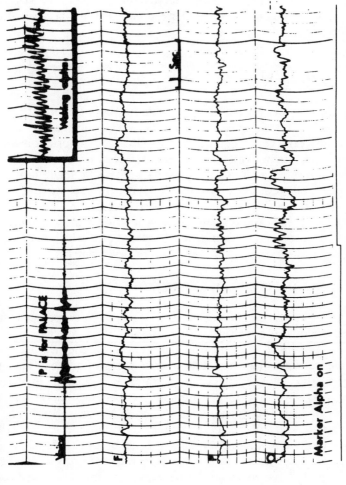

VOICE: Stimulus-activated voice-key marking administration of "P is for palace." "Palace" was successfully recognized next morning from a list of ten words beginning with P. F, P, O: Frontal, parietal, and occipital monopolar EEG recording. Compare occipital EEG during stage REM sleep and during waking (inset). MARKER: Used by technician to signal possible onset of alpha. Note typical slowed alpha elicited by a stimulus later recalled when S was awake.

Possibly because of common dissociative mechanisms, susceptibility to hypnosis may be useful for selecting Ss in studies involving sleep-induced response and learning, and even for selecting Ss who will sleep well, relatively undisturbed by distracting and arousing stimuli. While these may be the practical uses of hypnotic methods in sleep research, the provocative studies using hypnosis as a model for sleep-induced cognition, behavior, and functioning are most likely to be rewarding because of their exciting theoretical significance.

Postscript 1978
Hypnosis and the Control of Sleep Processes:

Since this chapter was written in 1972, there has been important research in each of the three main areas discussed. However, comprehensive recent reviews already exist covering much of this research. Important methodological developments in hypnosis research have been reviewed by Sheehan and Perry (1976); no additional comments need to be made bearing on specific methodological issues related to hypnosis and sleep. Developments in the three substantive areas were recently reviewed (Evans, 1977a), and it seems appropriate to present only a brief summary of these, as well as to comment on a fourth related area which may provide a basis for the integration of past and future developments.

EEG ALPHA AND THE PHYSIOLOGY OF HYPNOSIS AND SLEEP

There is no new evidence to challenge the generally accepted conclusion that the physiology of hypnosis reflects a waking state rather than a sleep state. However, this conclusion may gain added significance because of recent evidence suggesting that other altered states of consciousness may have some of the characteristics of sleep states. For example, experienced meditators may spend significant amounts of their meditation time in a state similar to stage four (delta) sleep (Albert & McNeece, 1974; Pagano, Rose, Stivers, & Warrenberg, 1976; Younger, Adriance, & Berger, 1975).

Since my critique of the early studies suggesting a possible relationship between EEG alpha activity and responsivity to hypnosis a number of controlled studies have appeared. However, conclusions are as difficult to draw now as they were several years ago. These studies have been reviewed by Paskewitz (1977) and Dumas (1977), who both come to a similar conclusion: there is no compelling evidence that EEG alpha activity and hypnotizability are correlated, and any obtained correlation is at best low.

My interpretation of the conflicting data in the early 1970's was predicated on the then widespread assumption that the relationship between alpha and arousal could be described by an inverted U-shaped function. This assumption implicitly suggests that transient situational and/or interpersonal anxieties, which could either increase arousal or decrease rapport, could temporarily reduce alpha density and/or hypnotic performance. Dumas' (1977) recent conclusion, that any correlation obtained between alpha and hypnosis is mediated by the selection of either volunteer or coerced subject samples (though his assignment of specific studies to support his hypothesis is open to some questions), implicitly invokes a similar mechanism. However, the traditional U-shaped hypothesis requires modification in view of recent evidence that alpha may increase during stress and cognitive activity in some individuals (Orne and Wilson, 1977). In addition Plotkin (1976) challenges the assumed link between alpha density (and alpha feed-back) and subjective and emotional experiences of the kind that makes a relationship between hypnosis and alpha intuitively appealing. Finally, Paskewitz (1977) cautions against an uncritical acceptance of studies purporting to show that subjects can learn to control alpha using feedback techniques. In summary, then, it is not at all clear why some studies have found relationships between hypnotic capacity and alpha parameters, but the conclusions still seem warranted that beyond situationally specific associations, there is no inherent link between hypnosis and alpha density.[9]

HYPNOTIC MANIPULATION OF SLEEP

This remains a neglected area. The evidence that hypnotic suggestion may be influential in exerting some form of control over dreaming and EEG sleep stages has received additional modest support (Albert & Boone, 1975; Jus, 1975). While hypnotic suggestions may have some influence on dreaming and REM sleep processes (Barber, Walker, & Hahn, 1973; Walker & Johnson, 1974), this effect is more likely to involve dream reports rather than the physiology of sleep-staging as such (Albert & Boone, 1975).

HYPNOSIS AND SLEEP-INDUCED BEHAVIOR

The research described above indicating that subjects can respond during sleep to verbally induced suggestions administered during sleep has been recently replicated and extended (Perry, Evans, Orne, & Orne, 1978). Perry et al. (1978) did not replicate the previous association found in two

9. A somewhat different question was addressed in an interesting study by Morgan, McDonald and Hilgard (1975). They explored the possibility that the relationship between alpha activity in the right and left brain hemispheres might be different during hypnosis compared to waking conditions.

studies between sleep-induced behavior and hypnotizability. However as both hypnotizability (Evans, 1977a) and sleep-induced behavior (Evans, 1977b) are related to the individual's control over sleep processes, a common mediating mechanism may still allow these discrepant findings to be reconciled. Our preliminary demonstration of paired-associate acquisition during sleep has been replicated (see the review by Aarons, 1976), though the mediating role of hypnotizability has not been explored further.

HYPNOTIZABILITY AND THE CONTROL OF SLEEP

The research described above on sleep-induced behavior, as well as other on-going research on napping (Evans, Cook, Cohen, Orne & Orne, 1977) and the subjective dimensions of sleep satisfaction (Evans, 1977b) lead to the hypothesis that there is an important dimension of individual differences related to the voluntary control of sleep processes, which in turn may reflect a broader ability to control states of consciousness. A factor analytic dimension obtained from subjective reports of sleep efficiency was interpreted as "the voluntary control of sleep," and was characterized by subjects who nap regularly and who claim that they can fall asleep readily at night, and easily in a variety of circumstances (Evans, 1977b). In addition to the finding that nappers score significantly higher on the control of sleep dimension, than habitual non-nappers ($p < .001$ in two samples of 92 and 190, respectively), they also claim they can fall asleep more quickly at night. In a daytime napping study, twenty-one nappers fell asleep in thirteen minutes compared to the twenty-six minutes taken by nine habitual non-nappers ($p < .05$).

Volunteer subjects who score high on HGSHS:A (8-12) also have significantly higher scores ($p < .005$, $N = 60$; $p < .05$, $N = 372$) on the control of sleep dimension than subjects with low HGSHS:A scores (0-4) in two student samples. Indeed correlations between HGSHS:A and the question about falling asleep readily at night (scored on a five-point rating scale) have ranged from .12 ($N = 469$, $p < .01$) to .51 ($N = 60$, $p < .0001$) in several samples (Evans, 1977b). Based on this and related data (reviewed by Evans, 1977a), it was hypothesized that the relationship between the capacity to enter hypnosis and the ability to control sleep processes (including sleep onset, napping, and responsivity to sleep-induced behavior) may reflect individual differences in the ability to change readily from one psychological state to another, maintaining a flexibility in changing psychological sets or controlling states of consciousness. The generality of this control mechanism and its relation to hypnosis require further exploration. However, the available data supports the hypothesis that there may well be a common underlying mechanism involved in the capacity to experience hypnosis and the ability to fall asleep easily and to maintain control of basic sleep processes. This hypothesis provides a ready explanation for several of the provocative findings relating hypnosis and sleep reported in the original review, as well as for the subsequent studies carried out in this area.

Euguene E. Levitt *is Professor of Psychology at Indiana University School of Medicine and Director of the Section of Psychology of the Department of Psychiatry at the Indiana University Medical Center since 1957. He received his Ph.D. from Columbia University in 1952, was research Assistant Professor at the Child Welfare Research Station of the University of Iowa (1952-1955), and Director of Research, Institute for Juvenile Research in Chicago (1955-1957). Of his seven books, the most relevant to hypnosis research is* The Hypnotic Induction of Anxiety: A Psycho-endocrine Investigation, *with Harold Persky and John Paul Brady. He holds diplomas in clinical psychology from the American Board of Professional Psychology, and in experimental hypnosis from the American Board of Examiners in Psychological Hypnosis.*

Rosalie Chapman, *Ph.D., is currently the Director of Psychology and Consulting Associates of San Diego, La Jolla, California. She received her Ph.D., in clinical psychology at Case Western Reserve University and has done postdoctoral work at the Department of Psychiatry, Indiana University School of Medicine.*

Levitt *and* Chapman *consider the use of hypnosis as a method for the experimental investigation of phenomena other than hypnosis itself. The authors have three main objectives: to discuss the advantages and disadvantages of using hypnosis as a research tool, to compare specific methodological strategies, and to evaluate the overall effectiveness of this research tool. Hypnosis is used as a tool whenever the researcher clearly intends to use hypnosis to induce a replica of a naturally occurring phenomenon, such as an emotion or a dream, as a way of getting useful information about the naturally occurring phenomenon. The authors conclude that hypnosis is a satisfactory method for creating usable facsimiles of a number of naturally occurring conditions, but that other claimed advantages of hypnosis as a research tool remain debatable. The chapter is intended as an evaluation of methodological issues rather than as a comprehensive review of substantive findings.*

7

Hypnosis
as a Research Method

EUGENE E. LEVITT AND
ROSALIE HENNESSY CHAPMAN

Introduction

Popular knowledge of hypnosis derives from its clinical applications, such as analgesia, hypnotherapy, and various forms of personal improvement. Most professional persons interested in the area are aware that there is also a considerable body of research into the nature of hypnosis and the hypnotic trance. The least known use of hypnosis is as a research tool, as a method for the experimental investigation of content areas other than hypnosis itself. The researcher seeks to exploit the trance state to induce in an experimental subject a replica of a naturally occurring state or phenomenon, such as an emotion or a dream, thus enabling study of that state or phenomenon.

This chapter deals with this relatively neglected use of hypnosis, but we do not propose to review substantive findings in the various content areas. A number of such reviews have already appeared (Barber, 1965b; Blum, 1967; Deckert & West, 1963; Gordon, 1967; Levitt & Brady, 1963; Reyher, 1967), and the contribution of still another is dubious. Rather, the purpose of this chapter is to discuss the advantages and disadvantages of hypnosis as a research method, to compare specific methodological strategies falling

The authors acknowledge with utmost gratitude the efforts of Kathryn N. DeWitt and Lynn Boudreaux in the preparation of this paper.

within the framework of hypnosis as a research method, and to evaluate the overall effectiveness of the technique.

Since no attempt will be made to review the literature, references will be illustrative rather than comprehensive. Even with this limitation, the selection of reports for inclusion in the chapter was no simple matter. It is often difficult to determine whether or not hypnosis has actually been used to investigate another content area. In a sense, the hypnotic state is always a research technique. Any investigation of hypnotic analgesia also has some bearing on the pain phenomenon. A study of hypnotically induced amnesia may be relevant to memory and attention. Hypnotically induced hallucinations may have something to do with the normal perceptual process. Any experimental study of the hypnotic trance may furnish data that are relevant to general methodological considerations such as demand characteristics and experimenter effects. Almost the entire literature of hypnosis could conceivably find its way into this chapter.

It appeared to us that an evaluation of hypnosis as a research method must be based on experiments in which the connection between the technique and substantive findings was unequivocal. There must be no question about the relevance of the findings to an independent content area. This can be done invariably only when the experimenter clearly intended to use hypnosis as an investigative method. Therefore, only investigations of this type are included in this chapter.

POTENTIAL ADVANTAGES OF HYPNOSIS AS A RESEARCH METHOD

Claims for administrative and technical advantages of hypnosis over other research techniques are based on allegedly unique properties of the trance state. Most of these properties have not been verified by experimentation, and remain debatable. Levitt, Persky, & Brady (1964) suggest five advantages:

1. Artificial states can be induced and terminated rapidly. In addition to being a convenience experimentally, this maximizes control over their duration.

2. Amnesia for the experience may be induced by a hypnotic suggestion to that effect. This manipulation can prove valuable for both experimental and administrative reasons.

3. By a careful formulation of the stimulus, relatively "pure" states can be induced.

4. The induced state may be prolonged, intensified, or diminished by appropriate suggestions in the course of the experiment as the experimental situation and design demand.

5. The experimental procedure can be repeated with the same subjects, making possible tests of reproducibility of the phenomenon. In addition, the effects of new experimental variables may be studied in the same

subjects by use of an own-control experimental design.

Gidro-Frank and Bull (1950) propose additional advantages: simplicity of the experimental setting, narrowing of the subjects' focus of attention, and absence of self-consciousness in the subjects.

The subject's ability to focus his attention was suggested long ago by Leuba (1941) and recently by White et al. (1968) as a unique feature of hypnosis as a research method. Despite some positive experimental findings, this phenomenon is still not clearly verified.

A reduced diffidence in the hypnotized subject is often reported by practitioners. Increased accessibility of thoughts and feelings in hypnotherapy is thought to be a consequence of this phenomenon. Shameful, embarrassing, or guilt-ridden verbalizations are more fluently emitted by the patient who believes that he is being forced to expose himself. The phenomenon was first reported in hypnosis research by Nachmansohn (Rapaport, 1951) more than forty years ago. He found that some of his subjects felt awkward when they were asked to dream in the waking state, but were more comfortable and hence more productive under hypnosis. The Nachmansohn effect can possibly be produced in an experimental sample by careful subject selection, or by exhorting instructions.

Another apparent advantage that has special relevance for the induction of states of negative affect is that the subject who has been stressed under hypnosis appears less likely to suffer any permanent effect, and rarely seems to experience postexperiment resentment toward the investigator. Debriefing the subject under hypnosis after the experiment presents no greater difficulty than inducing the artificial state. The subject is easily convinced that he is completely normal again, and that he will suffer no ill effects. He seems almost to *expect* to be deceived in some way by the hypnotist during the experiment; the severest manipulations do not prevent him from volunteering for future hypnosis studies. In contrast, a normal volunteer subject who has been convinced in the waking state by the experimenters that he has a previously undiagnosed cardiac problem (Bogdonoff et al., 1959) may never be completely debriefed.

Flexibility is yet another potential advantage. The technology of the artificial induction of natural states is chronically underdeveloped. A majority of effort has focused on two emotions that seem simplest to evoke: anxiety and hostility. Other conditions rarely have been produced in the laboratory. Hypnosis is the only technique that has a broad, general potential for artificially creating a wide range of naturally occurring conditions in the experimental subject.

POSSIBLE DEFICIENCIES OF HYPNOSIS AS A RESEARCH TECHNIQUE

The experimental use of hypnosis also has a few serious shortcomings. The most important is an unknown, but probably fairly high, possibility of sampling bias. Most investigations necessarily employ volunteer subjects. Relevant data are scanty, but a study by Lubin, Brady, & Levitt, (1962) hints at the existence of at least a few personality differences between volunteers and nonvolunteers for hypnosis experiments. The best available current estimates are that among volunteers, fewer than half will demonstrate sufficient hypnotizability to qualify for most experiments (Hilgard, 1967). A common practice is to accept only volunteers attaining scores of ten or higher on the Stanford Hypnotic Susceptibility Scale (SHSS), Forms A or B. Using this criterion, only about fifteen percent of the volunteers will qualify (Weitzenhoffer & Hilgard, 1959). It is difficult to counter the argument that the final distillate of the subject selection procedures is a sample that is unrepresentative of any large population.

The investigator may attempt to circumvent the problem of sampling bias by lowering the cutoff point. Using a score of five on the SHSS as the lower limit for qualification, for example, would permit inclusion of about fifty-five percent of the volunteers. But this introduces a fresh problem. A number of response measurements have been demonstrated to be correlated with the hypnotic capacity of the subject as determined by a standard scale (see, for examples, Hepps & Brady, 1967; Hilgard, 1967; Tart, 1966a). Responses of subjects will be determined to varying degrees by factors other than the dependent variables of the study, that is, by those that influence hypnotizability. It is conceivable, though not inevitable, that such an effect could confound experimental results.

THE POWER OF HYPNOSIS AS A RESEARCH TECHNIQUE

A relevant issue is posed by Hilgard's (1969b) postulate that "if a legitimate psychological question can be answered better by using hypnosis than by some other approach, then hypnosis should be used (p. 132)." One needs then to inquire whether hypnosis is indeed the superior method. But perhaps Hilgard has oversimplified the issue. There can be more than one fruitful approach to the investigation of a particular content area. Perhaps it is only necessary to demonstrate that the hypnotic state offers a mechanism whereby valuable information can be obtained. In most instances the use of hypnosis as a research strategy may be dictated by its methodological advantages, but in some cases, it may be complementary to other experimental avenues.

The issue raised by Hilgard is what might be called the "power" of hypnosis, its capacity to induce usable facsimiles of naturally occurring conditions of the human organism. The significance of any experiment employing the hypnotic method would seem to depend heavily on the degree of similiarity between the natural and hypnotically induced conditions. It is unlikely that the two states need to be identical, but it is obvious that some minimum degree of resemblance is required. Specifying this minimum in stimulus terms is extremely slippery. One of the perennial traps in hypnosis research is the credulous belief that the subject invariably is able to carry out the experimenter's suggestions with strict literality. It is certain, for instance, that the hypnotic suggestion, "to have a dream," does *not* guarantee the subsequent behavior of all subjects.

The problem of defining experimental stimuli pervades behavioral science research far beyond studies using the hypnotic method. Dependent variables provide the best basis for gauging the success of the experimental operations. If the aim is to stress the subject and he gives no stress responses, then the stimulus must be judged to be improperly defined. If the subject does give stress responses, then the stimulus has been successful in reproducing a natural event, for whatever reason. Thus, all experiments that seek to artificially induce naturally occurring conditions in the subject have a distinct, construct validity aspect.

In general, most laboratory methods for inducing naturally occurring conditions, especially states of arousal, are weak. Artificial methods of inducing anxiety, for example, usually fail to evoke reactions of the range and intensity found in naturally occurring situations (Levitt, 1967). We are unaware of any experiments in which the power of a hypnotic induction and a conventional laboratory technique have been compared. There are, however, a number of reports of a very particular comparison that is indigenous to the hypnosis experiment: the hypnotic subject versus the simulator control subject.

SIMULATOR VERSUS HYPNOTIC SUBJECT

Since the publication of Orne's (1959) classic study, investigators into the nature of hypnosis have been aware of the necessity for including a simulator control. Behavior that can be successfully simulated by an unhypnotized individual is evidently not of the essence of the trance state. The contrast of simulator and hypnotic subject has sometimes been misconstrued as a test of the genuineness of hypnotically induced behavior. Is the behavior *induced* by hypnotic suggestion in the classical sense that implies a force beyond the subject's control, or is it merely "requested," and the subject complies voluntarily as he might do if he were not hypnotized? The implication is that an adequate replica of the natural condition must be induced, and cannot be produced voluntarily.

This is a debatable assumption. Simulation is potentially a powerful method of bringing about temporary changes in the individual. It actually is another, though neglected, technique for artificially inducing natural states. Many individuals are capable of self-inducing, by voluntary fantasy, autonomic changes that clearly resemble the physiological concomitants of a naturally occurring emotion. This should not be surprising; emotions like anxiety and elation are often caused by anticipation or recollection, which are mental activities akin to fantasy, if not, indeed, indistinguishable from it.

Successful simulation hardly impeaches the genuineness of hypnotic behavior, any more than accurate imitations of drunkenness should be interpreted to mean that alcoholic intoxication is a myth. It does, however, question the value of hypnosis as a research strategy. Why bother to screen and train subjects if a simpler, equally effective technique is easily available? It is therefore relevant to an evaluation of hypnosis as a method to compare its effects with those of simulation.

Investigations in which hypnotized subjects and simulating controls have been compared have yielded conflicting and sometimes contradictory results. Some indicate that simulators are less convincing than, or behave differently from, hypnotic subjects (Brady & Levitt, 1964, 1966; Brady & Rosner, 1966; Dudley, Holmes, & Ripley, 1967; Evans, 1966a; Graham & Kunish, 1965; Gruenewald & Fromm, 1967; Hepps & Brady, 1967; Kehoe & Ironside, 1963; Vanderhoof & Clancy, 1962; Wiseman, 1962). Other studies suggest that simulators perform at least as credibly as hypnotized subjects, if not more so (Barber, 1965c; Barber, Chancey, & Winer, 1964; Barber & Hahn, 1964; Damaser, Shor, & Orne, 1963; Helfman, Shor, & Orne, 1960; May & Edmonston, 1966; Orzeck, 1962; Sheehan, 1969).

THE "OVERPLAY" PHENOMENON

Several comparative studies whose findings appear to suggest superior performances by simulators turn out to be, on closer analysis, peculiarly suggestive. Branca and Podolnick (1961) administered the MMPI to a group of hypnotized college students to whom an anxiety state had been directly suggested, and again in the waking state with instructions to fake anxiety. The mean MMPI subscale scores are shown in Table 7.1 along with the customary MMPI dissimulation index, F-K. Hypnotic anxiety produced modest, statistically significant increases in F, Pa, Sc, Si, and A, Welsh's anxiety index (Welsh, 1952), and a small, signficant decrease in K. The simulators, in marked contrast, produced diffuse elevation on all clinical scales except Ma. While neither profile resembles the classic 2-7 anxiety state, it is important to note that instructions to fake anxiety had a drastically different effect on MMPI scores than did hypnotically induced anxiety.

The most significant finding concerns the dissimulation index. The data in Table 7.1 bear a striking resemblance to certain F-K norms provided by Gough (1950). College students obtained a mean of -13.84, almost precisely like Branca and Podolnick's subjects in the normal state. A group of students faking psychopathology deliberately obtained an average index of $+17.19$, again practically identical with Branca and Podolnick's subjects in the faking state. The index in hypnotically induced anxiety is reasonably

TABLE 7.1 A comparison of subjects in hypnotically induced anxiety and simulating anxiety on the MMPI

	Normal State	*Hypnotic Anxiety*	*Simulated Anxiety*
F	3	6+	25*
K	58	51+	43*
F — K	-14	-7	+17
Hs	52	50	71*
D	48	56	79*
Hy	56	55	71*
Pd	54	59	81*
Mf	42	46	50
Pa	49	60+	87*
Pt	54	61	85*
Sc	55	65+	99*
Ma	61	64	72
Si	50	55+	72*
A	44	55+	73*

NOTE: F is given in raw score units, K in T-scores. The corresponding raw score K's are approximated.
A is the Welsh Anxiety Index (Welsh, 1952).
+ Significantly different from normal state.
* Significantly different from hypnotic anxiety state and the normal state.
SOURCE: Data from the study by Branca and Podolnick (1961).

close to that provided by female university hospital psychiatric patients (-8.70). In terms of the dissimulation index, one could conclude that Branca and Podolnick's subjects were normal college students on one test-taking occasion, simulating psychopathology on another, and experiencing it in some form on a third.

The data in Table 7.2 are condensed from a report by Damaser, Shor, & Orne (1963). At first glance, they appear to indicate that the simulators have had more intense physiological responses than the hypnotized subjects. This is true for heart rate and forehead muscle reaction. The hypnotized subjects manifested somewhat greater change in electrical skin potential, the most difficult of the three behaviors to control voluntarily. The muscle data for the simulators suggest an overreaction analogous to the anxiety simulators of Branca and Podolnick. Striped musculature would be, of course, the easiest system to alter voluntarily.

The heart rate data may also reflect an overreaction by the simulators, though this is not nearly so clear as in the case of the muscle reaction. As a side issue, heart rate findings of Damaser, Shor, and Orne are the opposite of those obtained by Hepps and Brady (1967).

In addition, Damaser, Shor, and Orne found that data furnished by a number of the simulators showed an interaction between the requested emotion and the state of the subject. The statistical interpretation is that some of the simulators produced higher scores in the waking state on some

TABLE 7.2   A comparison of hypnotized subjects and simulators on three physiological variables in induced states of anxiety and calmness

	Anxiety	Calmness
	Heart Rate (beats per minute)	
Hypnotized	87	77
Simulating	106	86
	Skin Potential (millivolts)	
Hypnotized	27.8	23.2
Simulating	22.3	19.9
	Muscle Reaction (No. constant voltage spikes)	
Hypnotized	18	8
Simulating	73	11

SOURCE: Data from Damaser et al. (1963).

emotions, and higher scores in the simulated hypnotic state on others. No such interactions were produced by the hypnotized subjects whose reactions were evidently more consistent across emotions and states. No substantive interpretation is apparent, but the important fact is the existence of another difference between performances of hypnotized subjects and simulators.

Reyher, (1969b) interprets the exaggerated data as evidence of the simulator's "unusual and high motivation." This cannot be a complete explanation of the overplay phenomenon. There is no sound reason why eagerness to comply with experimental instructions should impel the subject to do poorly. Theoretically, high motivation should improve, not impair, performance. An added ingredient in the explanation must be that the simulator is *unaware* of his poor performance, and actually believes that he is doing well. The simulator performs on a totally cognitive level. He plays the role as he thinks it ought to be played. There is no feedback to advise him to modify an overplayed role or to step up an underplayed one. The hypnotic subject, in contrast, is able to give a more realistic performance because he is emotionally affected, or deceived or induced, if you will, to a higher degree than is the simulator. He *feels* his role rather than develops it cognitively. The overplay phenomenon is an excellent argument in favor of the power of hypnotic suggestion.

Accuracy of the portrayal of an induced state in the trance is probably affected by many experimental factors. Several well-executed experiments (Brady & Rosner, 1966; Hilgard, 1967; Tart, 1966a) suggest that an important factor, if not the paramount one, is the subject's hypnotic capacity. Other possible influential variables are the nature of the experimental situation, the attitude and ability of the experimenter, and the relationship between experimenter and subjects.

Dudley, Holmes, & Ripley (1967) suggest that simulators will perform as well as hypnotic subjects under certain optimal conditions, but that these optimal conditions rarely occur in the laboratory. On the other hand, it is also likely there is a minimal level of experimental circumstances below which the performances of hypnotized subjects will not exceed those of simulators.

Artificial Induction of Natural States

The most frequent experimental use of hypnosis is in the artificial induction of naturally occurring conditions, primarily emotions and psychopathological symptoms. The desired state is suggested directly or indirectly to the subject. The stimulus suggestion itself may be totally concocted, or it may be "real" or "natural" in the sense that it describes an actual earlier experience of the subject, which he is directed to remember or "relive" in the trance.

Theoretically, all combinations are possible; either a contrived or a "natural" suggestion could be given directly or indirectly. In experimental practice, the bulk of the indirect approach experiments have made use of paramnesias. The stimulus in studies using direct suggestion is usually a simple description of the required state. The suggestion of an earlier experience is relatively rare, and does not warrant discussion under a separate heading. An ingenious union of early experience and indirect suggestion was pioneered by Blum (1961) and his students. Its uniqueness warrants a separate discussion along with the two major headings, direct suggestion and paramnesia.

DIRECT SUGGESTION

Suggesting the desired state directly is the most commonly used technique for inducing states, especially emotions. Direct suggestion stimuli vary greatly in length and complexity. Ikemi et al. (1959) used a simple word or term ("sadness," "resentment," "gastric disturbance"), presumably preceded by some sort of instructions that are not specified. Gidro-Frank and Bull (1950) also used single words, set in the following context:

> In a little while I shall count to five. Immediately afterward I shall say a word which denotes an emotion or state of mind. When you hear the word you will feel this emotion, experience the state of mind strongly. You will show this in your outward behavior in a natural manner. You may do anything you like, open your eyes or leave them closed, remain seated or get up, lie down on the couch or walk about—anything at all...(P. 92)

This technique or a variant of it has been used by Eichhorn and Tracktir

(1955a, 1955b) and Kehoe and Ironside (1963) in studies of the effect of emotions on gastric functioning. Levine, Grassi, & Gerson (1943) employed a variant of this method in which depression was induced by repeating three times the words "sad," "blue," and "low in spirit."

Another approach is to suggest a series of symptoms of the required state:

> You will have a pronounced feeling of sadness, discouragement, and futility. This sadness will give you a feeling of constant unpleasant tenseness. You will want to be left alone. Each new experience will cause you mental pain, and it will seem to you like you have an inability to think. You won't have any pep. It will be difficult to make decisions. Your dejection and hopelessness will be so great that you will have ideas of personal worthlessness and self-accusation. (Sweetland, 1948, p. 93)

Direct suggestion of symptoms is confounding when a verbal inventory or interview is used as a measure of the dependent variables. The fact that Sweetland's (1948) subjects obtained elevated scores on the MMPI Depression scale is an unconvincing demonstration; the experimenter, in suggesting depression, directly instructed the subjects how to respond to about a dozen D scale items.

Whitehorn et al. (1930) and Martin and Grosz (1964) used a few simple sentences as an inducing suggestion. The latter's stimulus is a condensation of the passage formulated by Levitt, den Breeijen, and Persky (1960). Damaser, Shor, and Orne (1963) introduced the subject to the experiment by describing each emotion briefly ("happiness—giddy joy, you feel wonderful"), urging the subject to "try to *feel* the emotions," and suggesting that emotions are also felt with the body. A single word such as happiness or anxiety directed the subject's behavior in the experiment proper. Another variation was used by Pattie (1954) who told his subjects that they would "feel very hostile, aggressive, and angry" toward the experimenter in the posthypnotic phase.

On purely lyrico-dramatic grounds, the most effective stimuli are passages used by Fisher and Marrow (1933-34):

> Just as soon as you are awake the most wonderful happiness will come over you that you have ever experienced. With each minute you will grow happier and happier. Everything will be sunshine and happiness. All of the most happy moments of your life will descend upon you. All your cares will be forgotten; you will know nothing but happiness, just pure unadulterated happiness. Even the saddest thing in your life will have a happy side for you. In a few moments I will awaken you; as soon as you are awake you will bubble like a mountain brook with sheer happiness. Happiness will well up within you; it will descend from all sides upon you; you will be the happiest person in the whole world; no one will be half as happy as you. As soon as you are awake you are going to experience the most undreamed of happiness. You are already beginning to grow happy. All of your worries and cares are already beginning to leave you. The wave of happiness is already descending upon you. (pp. 202-3)

Just as soon as you are awake the most terrible depression you have ever experienced will begin to descend upon you. This terrible depression will completely engulf you; sunshine will appear as shadows and shadows will become the most despairing hopelessness. All of the unhappiness of your past life will take possession of you. There will be absolutely nothing gay or happy in life for you; everything will have but one side, a dark side, and not even a glimmer of happiness will filter into your dark despondency. In a few minutes I will wake you up, and as soon as you are awake you will feel miserable and depressed. Depression and unhappiness will engulf you; darkness will pervade your soul and everything will seem utterly futile and empty. The wave of depression is already descending upon you. You are already growing despondent and everything is growing grey and devoid of joy. Unhappiness is creeping through you; you are already growing unhappy and despondent. (p. 203)

These suggestions are general and require no special knowledge of the subject. Occasionally, stimuli are derived from anamnestic examination of the subject (Erikson, 1944; True & Stephenson, 1951). The approach is apt to be discouraging because of the additional time involved in probing the subjects. The suggestion that Erikson (1944) used for his subject was a thousand-word narrative, so complex that the subject must be hard-pressed to digest and assimilate it, let alone to respond.

Comparative experimental studies of the effectiveness of different direct suggestions are lacking. On the basis of "clinical observation, logical analysis, and practical considerations," Levitt, den Breeijen, and Persky (1960) proposed that the formulation of a direct suggestion should follow these guidelines:

1. Content of the suggestion should not be based on the subject's personal experiences. An event in an individual's life may have been exceedingly anxiety producing, but it is also likely to have facets which evoke other emotional responses, or otherwise complicate the subject's reaction. Our early trial runs indicated that it is difficult to obtain a "pure" reaction when the suggestion is based on the subject's personal experience.

2. A number of synonyms should be employed in the suggestion. A single word like "fear" may evoke quite different psychophysiological reactions from different individuals depending on idiosyncratic interpretations. The use of a number of synonyms, or words with similar general meaning, maximizes the possibility that the meaning of the stimulus suggestion will have at least some common elements among the subjects.

3. The suggestion itself should not be lengthy. The hypnotized subject must understand clearly what is being suggested. His capacity to retain a suggestion will hence have some effect on his reaction. If a stimulus is, for example, several thousand words long, it is likely that the subject will not remember a considerable portion of it.

4. Key words and expressions should be repeated and paraphrased. This maximizes the probability of both comprehension and retention of the stimulus suggestion.

5. Nothing in the stimulus suggestion should lead the subject to believe that he is in an artificial situation. The transference which often exists between the

subject and the hypnotist appears to incline the former to the attitude that the latter will protect him from harm while he is hypnotized. Such a belief may vitiate the effectiveness of a suggestion intended to produce a painful emotional state. The subject's belief in the protectiveness of the hypnotist seems likely to be enhanced if he is reminded in some way that he is actually in an artificial experimental situation which is obviously under the control of the hypnotist. Of course, this is not to suggest that the subject is not at least in some way aware of this consideration in any event. None the less, it appears prudent not to emphasize the point.

A sixth adjuration could be appended. The stimulus should specify the subject's reaction as minimally as possible.

The anxiety-inducing suggestion employed by Levitt and his coworkers (1960) is reproduced below in toto. It was used in experiments by Brady, Levitt, and Lubin, (1961), Ferster et al. (1961), Levitt et al. (1961, 1963), and Levitt and Persky (1960), among others. A similar version was used in studies of Persky et al. (1959), Grosz and Levitt (1959), Levitt and Grosz (1960), and Grosz (1961).

> In a moment you will begin to experience a feeling of anxiety, of fear. (Pause, five seconds). You are now becoming afraid, very afraid. You are experiencing a strong feeling of apprehension and anxiety, as if you knew that some dreadful thing was going to happen to you. But you do not know what this awful thing is. You do not know what makes you so fearful every moment. You are becoming more and more anxious and afraid all the time, yet you have no idea what you are afraid of. You are certain that some dreadful thing is going to happen to you, perhaps something more horrible than you can possibly imagine. Your feeling of dread and fear increases with each passing second, and it will continue to increase, no matter what you try to do to stop it. You are so obsessed by this horrible fear that you cannot get if off your mind even for a moment. All that you can think of is that some dreadful thing is going to happen to you, and you are helpless to prevent it from happening. The dread is so unbearable that you cannot conceal it. No matter what you do, your feeling of fear, of anxiety, of dread, will continue to become stronger and more vivid every moment. In a very few minutes, you will find yourself on the verge of panic. (p. 209)

AN EARLY EXPERIENCE INDIRECTLY SUGGESTED

The following technique was developed by Blum (1961, 1967) and his students.[1] The procedure is essentially this: an occurrence in the subject's past that had evoked the desired state is determined, often by means of the Blacky Pictures (Blum, 1950), or by an interview. The subject is then made to "relive" this experience under hypnosis. Simple cues that can be used to evoke the desired state posthypnotically are then associated with the experience. In some studies (Benyamini, 1963; Hedegard, 1968) the subject is trained under hypnosis to respond to systematically varied cues with proportionate intensities of the desired state. For example, posthypnotic

1. Recent research by Blum and his students is presented in Chapter 14 of this book.

presentation of the numbers 0, 40, 70, and 100 evoke proportionate degrees of anxiety in the subject.

The specific contents of the subject's state-evoking experience are then dissociated by suggestion from the state itself, leaving the latter in a "free-floating" condition. Amnesia is induced for the experimental procedures to that point, and the subject is then considered to be "programmed" for the experiment proper. Theoretically, this approach could be used to produce any kind of condition. Blum's students have been guided largely by psychoanalytic theory in which anxiety holds a central place. Hence, most of their experiments have sought to induce anxiety (Benyamini, 1963; Ehrlich, 1965; Hedegard, 1968; Lohr, 1967; Mendelsohn, 1960). A study by Geiwitz (1966), in which boredom was evoked, illustrates the flexibility of the technique.

PARAMNESIA

Paramnesia is used in the specific sense of a false memory, a recollection of occurrences that did not happen, rather than in the general sense of mnemonic abnormality. The usual purpose of the paramnesia is to produce a conflict within the subject so that he will react in some desired fashion. In practice, the independent variables of the investigation are measured posthypnotically, but there is no reason why response measurements could not be made at any time after implanting the paramnesia. The technique was first used—apparently with considerable success—in the 1920s by the Russian psychologist, A.R. Luria. He describes his method as follows:

> We suggested to the person under test, while in a sufficiently deep hypnotic state, a certain situation, more often a disagreeable one, in which he was playing a role irreconcilable with his habits and contrary to his usual behavior. We made those suggestions imperatively, and forced the person under hypnotism to feel the situation suggested with sufficient painfulness; we thus obtained an actual and rather sharply expressed acute affect. After awakening the person under test and following the awakening by amnesia (a suggested one or a natural one), we had a subject who was "loaded" with certain definite affective complexes, which mostly remained unknown to himself, but which were recorded by us in almost all important details. (1932, p. 130)

A more concise, less dramatic explanation is offered by Eisenbud (1939).

> The method consists essentially in inducing a deep state of hypnosis in a suitable subject, and then introducing an artificial "complex" by causing the subject to live through a trumped-up emotional experience...the subject finally is awakened from hypnosis with a command for complete posthypnotic amnesia. (p. 377)

Some of Luria's "trumped-up" events were based on personal attributes of the subject, others on general, psychosocial considerations. The latter type, illustrated below, has been the model for later experimenters employing the technique.

You are in great need of money. You go to a friend in order to borrow from him; he is not at home. You decide to wait in his room and suddenly notice on his bureau a fat wallet with money. You open it and find many five ruble notes. You make a decision; you quickly take the wallet and conceal it on your person. You cautiously go outside and look around to see if you are detected. You have stolen money and now you are afraid that there will be a search in your home and that they will discover you. (Luria, 1932, p. 140)

In the twenty-five years following the publication of Luria's book, the paramnesia technique was used occasionally in studies of repression (Eisenbud, 1939; Bobbitt, 1958), psychosis (Brickner & Kubie, 1936), conflict (Huston, Shakow, & Erickson, 1934), psychosomatic effects (Erickson, 1943), hostility (Eisenbud, 1937; Counts & Mensh, 1950); psychotherapy (Kesner, 1954; Gordon, 1957, 1967), and in a repetition of the celebrated Bruner-Goodman (1947) study of effect of economic states on estimated sizes of coins (Ashley, Harper, & Runyon, 1951). In the Ashley study, a brief, "artificial life history," which led the subject to believe that he had been brought up either in poverty or in wealth, was implanted.

REYHER'S PARADIGM

The principal developer and exponent of the paramnestic technique in recent years has been Reyher. Unlike his predecessors, Reyher (1962) believes that is is the *only* valid hypnotic method of studying emotions and psychopathology and, presumably, other induced conditions.

According to Reyher (1967) there are five principles that should be used to formulate experiments employing hypnotic induction of emotion or psychopathology.

1. Indirect induction: Hypnotic suggestion should be used only to *induce* a process that, under certain specifiable conditions, is theoretically capable of *producing* pathogenic psychodynamics and psychopathology. This is the sine qua non of what Reyher calls his "paradigm."

2. The above process must be entirely devoid of specific cues that might suggest to the subject how the experimenter wishes him to behave in the experiment proper.

3. Some of the responses that are indirectly induced must "satisfy criteria for the identification of manifestations of psychopathology (p. 112)," especially physiological reactions because they seem to be involuntary.

4. An attempt must be made to assess the demand characteristics of the experiment by using a faking control group. Presumably, only subject behavior beyond that called forth by the demand characteristics is truly hypnotically induced.

5. The experimental subject should never be directed to carry out suggestions. He should be told, always in a "passive voice," that "he will be acted upon by something or that he is going to experience something (p. 112)."

Another indirect technique for inducing a state is to distort the subject's perception of his immediate environment. To induce anxiety, it may be suggested to him that he is teetering on the top of a tall building, or is about to face a poisonous snake, or a maniac with an ax. The suggestion of the loss of a loved one, or a severe blow of a more general sort, could be used to induce depression. Like the Luria technique, the induced misperception can be based on general, psychosocial considerations, or on a personal knowledge of the subject. Berman, Simonson, and Heron (1954) provide an example of the former type: "The subject was told that he was incarcerated in a hotel room during a fire that was destroying the building, and this situation was further elaborated" (p. 89). The perceptual distortion may also incorporate specific suggestions. For example, the suggestion that the subject was climbing an interminable hill in the teeth of a rising wind and falling snow, with the gradual development of constricting, penetrating, severe pain in the chest radiating to the left arm, was reported in the same study.

A COMPARISON OF STATE INDUCTION METHODS

The use of a paramnesia has a notable drawback when the experiment seeks to examine a single emotion or symptom in isolation. An implanted conflict does not lead invariably to the required emotion or sympton. Or, it may evoke an admixture of emotions. A notable exception has been found in the investigation of hostility. This exception illustrates the ubiquitous association that is necessary in order to use a paramnesia in the study of a single emotion. Most people, if they are led to believe that they have been wantonly mistreated, completely without cause, are likely to respond by becoming hostile. It is significant that most of the hypnosis research based on Reyher's paradigm has dealt with hostility in some form (Moore, 1964; Perkins, 1965; Pruesse, 1967; Sommerschield, 1965; Veenstra, 1969). The invention of conflicts that will consistently lead to other isolated conditions or emotional states in most individuals presents a formidable challenge to the hypnosis experimenter.

If the purpose of the investigation is to study conflict for its own sake, or to reproduce naturally occurring, gross psychopathology, such as a "miniature psychotic storm" (Brickner & Kubie, 1936) or a "miniature neurosis" (Gordon, 1967), then paramnesia is the method of choice.

Induced, posthypnotic amnesia is a fundament of any indirect method, and hence the effectiveness of the latter depends heavily on the validity of the former. It is either stated openly or is implicit that posthypnotic amnesia is an experimental analog of repression, the defense mechanism that is the cornerstone of psychoanalytic theory. Indeed, there is a marked, structural resemblance. Both have a relatively sudden onset in contrast to normal memory decay. In both, the loss of recall is actively induced, rather than simply a submerging under the weight of fresher, competing recollections. And the forgotten material is theoretically recoverable. The analogy is complete if the amnesia is applied to a stressful or unpleasant occurrence or thought.

Luria, the pioneer of the paramnestic technique, was a Pavlovian, not a Freudian. He was aware that the amnesia he induced, or which occurred spontaneously in his subjects, required an explanation, but he conceptualized in neurodynamic, not psychodynamic terms. The amnesia was a parabiosis (temporary loss of neural conductivity), rather than a defense mechanism. It remained for those more familiar with psychoanalytic theory to propose the repression analogy. "When the subject finally is awakened from hypnosis with a command for complete posthypnotic amnesia, a factor tantamount to repression has been introduced" (Eisenbud, 1939, p. 377).

This is the theoretical position adopted by several other investigators into the nature of repression as well as by Eisenbud (Bobbitt, 1958; Gordon, 1957; Imm, 1965), and in a number of psychotherapy analog studies (Gordon, 1967). Experimental support for the analogy comes from Levitt et al. (1961), Hilgard and Hommel (1961), and Clemes (1964). Reyher (1967) takes a somewhat different view.

Reyher formulated paramnesias whose intent was to create intense, hostile feelings in the subject. He carefully separated the paramnesia from the associated effect, directing the posthypnotic amnesia at the former only: "After I awaken you, you will not be able to remember anything about this session. However, anything that comes into your mind that is associated with [a class of words related to the paramnesia] will stir up overwhelming feelings of hate. If these feelings break into consciousness, you will realize that it is the person who owns these papers that you hate, and you will experience an overwhelming urge to tear them up" (1967, p. 120).

Most of the subjects failed to carry out the posthypnotic suggestion directing them to act out their hostility destructively. Reyher's view is that these failures are the consequence of repression. The conflict-inducing suggestion arouses anxiety in the subject and is hence naturally repressed. Earlier, Reyher (1961b) had theorized that in the few subjects who did tear up the paper, the hostile impulse was so strong that guilt feelings were repressed so that acting out could occur.

While the analogy between repression and induced amnesia is striking, few theorists would posit an identity. Repression, as Cooper (see Chapter 10 of this book) rightfully points out, falls short as a *complete* explanation of hypnotic amnesia. The significance of the analogy for the experimental use of hypnosis is that it points to a consideration that is relevant to evaluation of the paramnestic method—the validity of hypnotically induced amnesia itself.

The impact of an implanted paramnesia depends on the subject's lack of awareness of its existence, that is, on the dissociation of fabulated event and present state. Hypnotic amnesia must actually function tantamount to naturally occurring repression. If amnesia is a sham, what inference should be drawn from the subject's subsequent, disturbed behavior? He must know that he has not stolen any money. He must be aware that hostile feelings toward someone or other have merely been suggested to him and do not actually exist. Nothing more than the demand aspects of the experiment could be motivating him. Indirect techniques would be vulnerable to the same logical criticisms leveled at direct suggestion by Reyher (1962).

The validity of hypnotically induced amnesia is another debated issue among hypnosis researchers. The view that hypnotic amnesia is a real memory loss in some sense is represented by Hilgard (1965b, 1969b) and others. The opposing position is manned by Barber (1969b), who contends that the experimental evidence is either negative or based on equivocal tests, and that "the burden of proof is upon those who claim that suggestions of amnesia at times produce actual amnesia" (p. 216).

Cooper (see Chapter 10 of this book), after a comprehensive review, concludes that there is a flavor of genuineness to hypnotic amnesia that cannot be explained by recourse to demand characteristics, subject expectations, and similar aspects of the experimental situation. Surprisingly, no one refers to the paramnesia research as relevant evidence, not as a possible method for studying hypnotic amnesia. Most of the paramnesia research, especially Reyher's work, seems to support the validity of hypnotic amnesia, and the technique appears to be ideal for investigating the phenomenon.

No one denies that suggestions to forget, in the absence of an hypnotic induction, also produce considerable reported amnesia (see, for example, Cooper's review). This parallel is significant for the investigator who wishes to employ a paramnestic technique. Again, why bother with what may be an unnecessary step in the experimental procedure? The contention of Hilgard, Cooper, and others, that hypnotic amnesia offers something beyond requested forgetting, remains to be demonstrated.

The natural event technique and direct suggestion are both suitable for the investigation of an isolated emotion or symptom. The former would seem the more powerful of the two on the simplistic grounds that natural is usually superior to artificial. Unfortunately, there has never been an experimental comparison of the power of the two approaches, so the alleged superiority of the natural event technique remains hypothetical.

Use of the natural event technique also has certain disadvantages. There is an obvious connection between the event and the emotion that may be undesirable in the context of the experiment. If the investigator, for example, wishes to induce free-floating anxiety, additional experimental manipulations such as those used by Benyamini (1963) are necessary in order to dissociate the experimental emotional state from the natural past experience.

It is possible that a previous event that is recalled or "relived" in the hypnotic state will not lead to the emotion that it had evoked originally. In one of our studies (Levitt, 1963), natural occurrences that had been anxiety evoking brought about depression or hostility upon recall in hypnosis. Perhaps, the subject actually experiences an admixture of emotions, recalls one of them as having been prominent at the time, but experiences another when he "relives" the original experience.

People do not always respond identically to similar happenings over time. An event that may have evoked anxiety some years ago may produce a different reaction currently because of developments in personality or changes in life situation. That the experimenter can circumvent this contingency by requiring the subject to "relive" the event has not yet been demonstrated clearly.

These disadvantages of Blum's technique are merely possibilities. In a given experiment, the technique may function effectively, depending upon the particular subjects, the skill of the experimenter, and the nature of the experiment. Technical shortcomings are unlikely to appear if the purpose of the experiment requires a replica of naturally occurring psychopathology rather than an isolated symptom. Again, there is no direct comparison of the effectiveness of Blum's method and paramnesia in evoking a "miniature neurosis."

Finally, it seems logical, if not demonstrated, that the natural technique presents a greater threat to the postexperimental well-being of the volunteer subject than does direct suggestion. At one time in our research, we felt it necessary to make the subjects amnesic for the directly suggested anxiety experience. Subsequent follow-up data, however, indicated that there were no untoward reactions or other undesirable sequelae even in the occasional subject who remembered the experiment (Levitt, Persky, & Brady, 1964). Without exception, those who remembered stated that they felt perfectly comfortable after the experiment because of the realization that the anxiety had been directly suggested by the hypnotist, and thus did not represent a threat to the current adjustment. The subject seldom confuses the artificial laboratory situation with a naturally occurring situation. This may not be invariably true when the anxiety stimulus represents an actual, earlier event in the subject's life. It seems unlikely, but possible, that the fantasied event may occasionally become confused with a natural occurrence, leading to postexperimental upset.

Reyher (1962) has severely criticized the direct suggestion method, primarily on the grounds that the stimulus is not distinctly separate from the response. The subject may merely be seeking to please the hypnotist by conforming to his evident wish, that is, to the demand characteristics of the experiment. The method does not furnish evidence that the subject has been affected by the hypnotic state itself. To deny this possibility would be highly imprudent; the urge to please the experimenter appears throughout behavioral science research. But to assume that the hypnotized individual experiences nothing more than a desire to please the hypnotist would be equally incautious.

It is possible to contend also that the paramnesic subject is experiencing neither amnesia nor a distorted recollection. The posthypnotic interviewer may not at all remind the subject of the teacher he hates. The subject may clearly remember the attempt to implant this artificial conflict in the trance state. However, he may wish to please the experimenter and may be perfectly capable of discerning that he is supposed to react hostilely in the post-hypnotic interview. Sheehan's (1969) findings mildly suggest this possibility.

In laboratory research, defining an intervening condition of the subject by stimulus operations is unwise, especially when hypnosis is used. The safest approach is to lean heavily on response data. Reyher apparently agrees. He emphasizes physiological response measurement: "There is little doubt that the obtained psychopathology is genuine with many of the symptoms (such as skin disturbances, tics, tremors, sweating and changes in skin color) being objective and autonomically controlled and, therefore, outside the realm of simulation for most subjects" (1969a).

In this respect, direct suggestion has been at least as successful as the indirect techniques. Barber, a notoriously cautious appraiser, wrote in summing up a dozen experiments employing direct suggestion: "In summary, the experiments reviewed in this section indicate that suggestions designed to evoke emotional responses are at times effective in producing alterations in heart rate, skin conductance, respiration, gastric secretions, and other physiological variables" (1965b, p. 218).

The review of pre-Reyher research by Deckert and West (1963) is cited by Reyher in support of his attack on the direct suggestion method. These reviewers, according to Reyher (1967), "also have noted a general deficiency in experimental design and recognized the problem of assessing the significance and generality of the reported results" (p. 111). Deckert and West also list eleven studies as exceptions to their generally dismal appraisal of the field. Among these are such direct-suggestion experiments as Branca and Podolnick (1961), Eichhorn and Tracktir (1955a, 1955b), and Persky et al. (1959).

The intervening mechanism whereby direct suggestion evokes emotional reactions is not known, just as the essence of the hypnotic state itself is neither known nor understoood. It may be that a majority of hypnotized subjects potentiate direct suggestion by deliberately fantasying a past event in order to carry out the experimental direction. An example would be the subjects who responded to a suggestion of change in heart rate by imagining anxiety-evoking experience (Solovey & Milechnin, 1957). The mechanism has relevance for the investigator whose interest lies in the nature of hypnosis. It has scant importance for the experimenter who is employing hypnosis as a research method, whose requisite is to induce a state by whatever means.

In summary, it appears that there is no sound, consistent evidence that one method of hypnotically inducing a natural state is superior to others. The experimenter's choice should depend primarily on the intent of his investigation.

The Study of Dreams

The earliest research use of hypnosis was the investigation of the sleep dream.[2] In 1911, Schroetter attempted to verify Freud's system of symbols using hypnotically induced dreams (Rapaport, 1951). A dream study by Nachmansohn in 1925 (Rapaport, 1951) must be the first reported use of a waking control in an hypnosis investigation. The literature on the hypnotic study of dreams has been reviewed with varying degrees of comprehensiveness and criticality by Barber (1962), Tart (1964, 1965a), Moss (1967), and Stross and Shevrin (1969). A number of the early reports were collected by Rapaport (1951), and a judicious selection of twelve studies is reprinted in Moss's book (1967). There are about fifty reports in all, characterized by much variability in method and results.

The value of the data contained in these reports seems to depend on the veridicality of the parallelism of the hypnotic dream and the sleep dream. This is a highly controversial issue. It is no problem at all to obtain some sort of narrative from the hypnotized individual in response to the suggestion to have a dream. Nearly half of unexhorted subjects will give such verbalizations, but the response has one of the lowest item correlations with total scale scores on the Stanford Hypnotic Susceptibility Scale, Form C (Weitzenhoffer & Hilgard, 1962). This means that it occurs more often than other responses among those with low total scores. A verbal response by the subject following the suggestion to dream is a meager, insufficient bit of evidence linking hypnotic and sleep dreams.

SIMILARITY OF THE HYPNOTIC AND SLEEP DREAM:
SOME EXPERT OPINIONS

The controversy over the natural dream-hypnotic dream parallel is epitomized by a survey of a group of diplomates of the American Board of

2. The dream, like an emotion or symptom, is a naturally occurring phenomenon, and as such could have been discussed in the previous section. Its singular nature warrants separate treatment.

Examiners in Psychological Hypnosis, (Moss 1967) that found that fifty-six percent regarded hypnotically induced and sleep dreams similar in essential respects, while twenty-two percent disagreed with this position, and another twenty-two percent were uncertain or had no opinion.

According to Tart (1965a), ten, or twenty-eight percent, of the thirty-six articles that he reviewed, assumed or concluded that the hypnotic dream and the sleep dream were equivalent. Four, or eleven percent (including Tart, 1964), drew the contrary inference, and the remaining sixty-one percent made no assumption or conclusion at all. All but two of the studies assuming equivalence were published prior to 1960, while three of the four contrary investigations were reported in the last decade.

The trichotomy reflects differences in views among practitioners and researchers. The equivalence hypothesis is accepted by many clinicians. For example:

> My acceptance of the dream under hypnosis as *equivalent* (not necessarily identical) to the dream during natural sleep represents an equivalence in *psychological, intellectual, and emotional,* not necessarily in physiological terms (Sacerdote, 1967, p. 39).

> It is my impression that hypnotic dreams differ in certain ways from spontaneous nocturnal dreams in regard to function. . . I do feel that with allowance for comparisons of spontaneous nocturnal and hypnotic dreams derived from the same subjects and patients, that the structure of such dreams is apparently essentially similar (Schneck, 1963, p. 98).

Barber (1962) takes the opposing position that the hypnotic and natural dream differ in *every* essential respect. Most of the experimentally inclined workers in hypnosis have adopted various intermediate postures that acknowledge an essential dissimilarity but maintain that an intriguing similarity remains.

> Hypnotic dreams and spontaneous dreams are sufficiently similar in the employment of symbolism to allow crossgeneralization. (Moss, 1961, p. 109)

> Although hypnotic dreams are not night dreams, the two dream categories overlap and they undoubtedly have much in common. (Hilgard, 1965b, p. 163)

> There is a wide range of response to the hypnotic suggestion to "dream," the average production having a structure which seems intermediate between the daydream and the spontaneous night dream, in that primary processes are used more than is common in waking thought, but less than in the typical night dream. (Brenman, 1949, p. 465)

> Thought processes in hypnosis seem to follow the primary process mode of organization. In this respect, cognitive processes in hypnosis may resemble dream thinking more closely than the predominant mode of thinking that governs the waking state. (Stross & Shevrin, 1967, p. 69)

Tart represents the substantial group who are as yet uncommitted to any position in the controversy, preferring to wait for definitive data. "The general picture is that of a very large number of basic questions to which we have only a few suggestions rather than answers, largely because of important methodological shortcomings of much of the research which has been done in this area" (Tart, 1965a, p. 97).

Tart suggests that most of the relevant research has failed to consider adequately the demand characteristics of the experimental situation, has ignored idiosyncratic interpretations of instructions by experimental subjects, has naively assumed that the subject's response invariably reflected the experimenters' instructions directly, and lacks support by physiological measurement.[3]

A summary of four major criticisms leveled by Tart (1965a) at the studies he reviewed, is given in Table 7.3. Ninety percent of the studies lacked EEG monitoring, seventy-three percent inadequately described the trance level attained by the subjects, and sixty-seven percent did not clearly designate

TABLE 7.3 Methodological defects of dreams research using hypnosis

	No EEG Monitoring	Inadequate Data on Hypnotic Level of Subjects	Experimenter-Subject Relationship Unclear	Conclusions Based on Experimenters' Opinions
Number of studies	27	22	20	19
Percent of studies	90	73	67	63

SOURCE: Data from Tart (1965a). Tart's own studies and four theoretical papers are not included.

the relationship between experimenter and subjects. There was "an almost total dependence on the experimenters' opinions for the assessment of results" in sixty-three percent of the studies. The average study had three defects; no study suffered from fewer than two of the four.

SIMILARITY OF HYPNOTIC AND SLEEP DREAMS: SOME FACTS

The two types of dreams can be compared in four ways: circumstances of the occurrence, content, accompanying physiological state or reactions, and personal feeling-belief of the subject.

As Hilgard (1965b) points out, the circumstances within which the two kinds of dreams occur are evidently different. The hypnotic state is not an unconsciousness state. The time of the onset of hypnotic dreaming, and often the topic, is specified by the hypnotist, and the subject ordinarily is aware that he must report his dream.

Physiological aspects of the two kinds of dreams also differ largely,

3. In defense of hypnosis dream researchers, let us point out that Tart's charges can properly be leveled at the bulk of published reports in every area of hypnosis research.

primarily because the trance lacks the electrophysiology of actual sleep. There are, however, interesting investigations (Schiff, Bunney, & Fredman, 1961; Brady & Rosner, 1966) that suggest that the rapid eye movements (REM) that accompany natural dreaming (and do not accompany waking fantasy) may also accompany the hypnotic dream. Domhoff (1964) believes that there is as yet insufficient evidence for a definitive conclusion, but the bulk of research bearing on physiological similarity must be regarded as negative.

The experimental literature is strikingly devoid of any large-scale comparison of the content of spontaneous and hypnotic dreams. More than half of the hypnotist-psychologists surveyed by Moss (1967) apparently believe that the contents are similar. Most of the handful of serious researchers in the dream area, on the other hand, would probably agree with Barber's (1962) contention that hypnotic dreams are ordinarily considerably shorter than sleep dreams, and "appear to be prosaic products without symbolizations or distortions." D.B. Klein (1930) once reported that the duration of hypnotic dreams was 5–83 seconds with a mean of thirty-six seconds. Sleep dreams are now known to last 3–90 minutes (Kleitman, 1963).

The hypnotic dreams of Tart's (1964) subjects never exceeded four minutes, while their sleep dreams ranged 6–32 minutes wih an average length of fourteen minutes. The complexities of mental experiences lasting a few minutes, and those lasting a half-hour or more, are unlikely to be equivalent.

The early experiments with hypnotic induction of dreams usually assumed that the obtained responses literally reflected the stimulus suggestion—the report of a good hypnotic subject who is instructed to have a dream must be a dream. If the subject is asked whether he has been dreaming, he will undoubtedly respond affirmatively. Since the investigators ordinarily believed, without reservation, that they were studying, a true dream analog, the demand aspect of the inquiry is very evident.

The hard-nosed, skeptical attitude and the sophisticated inquiry in Hilgard's laboratory at Stanford surely convey a different demand. Whether that demand inclines the subject to respond objectively or critically is impossible to determine, but the Stanford data indicate that for a majority of subjects, hypnotic dreams and spontaneous dreams are dissimilar experiences. Hilgard (1965b) reports that nine of thirty-nine subjects, only twenty-three percent, considered that their hypnotic dreams were like a sleep dream. The remainder reported thinking, daydreaming, or watching a movie as responses to the suggestion to dream. Tart (1966a) found that only fifteen percent of one hundred fourteen subjects felt that they were actually "in" a dream. The others reported ideational experiences similar to those of Hilgard's subjects. Thus it seems that only a small minority of those subjects who respond positively to the suggestion to dream really believe that they are dreaming.

The weight of the experimental evidence at this time, with and without due allowance for methodological deficiences in relevant experiments, supports the view that hypnotically induced dreams and spontaneous sleep dreams are largely dissimilar and cannot be regarded as equivalents. This does not mean that the former is an area unfit for investigation. In essence, the intermediate positions taken by Hilgard, Moss, and others hold that the hypnotic dream is something more that a routine verbal response, and that it can yield meaningful experimental or clinical data even if it is not isomorphic with the sleep dream. The motor of the hypnotic dream is unclear. It may be primary process thinking[4] or an extension of the fantasy capacity for some other reason. Perhaps most people, like Nachmansohn's subjects (Rapaport, 1951), feel foolish responding to the instruction to dream in the waking state, but regard this as a very appropriate demand in the trance state, and hence perform more efficaciously.

It might be useful to clear the air of unnecessary semantic conflict. The expression, "hypnotically induced dream" implies the undemonstrated isomorphism. An expression like "hypnotically induced fantasy-dream" is more congruent with the currently available facts: a verbal production that seems to more than a daydream, but is definitely not a sleep dream. Future experimentation may be more fruitful if investigators do not need to feel that they must demonstrate that the hypnotic dream and the sleep dream are, or are not, isomorphisms.

Test Validation

Formal psychological assessment devices have sometimes been introduced to define dependent variables in hypnosis experiments. These investigations could be considered as tests of the construct validity of the instruments that were used, even though the investigator's intent had nothing whatever to do with establishing validity. In keeping with the approach of this chapter, the discussion in this section is limited to research in which it was the deliberate purpose of the investigator to examine the validity of a formal assessment device. The handful of appropriate studies constitute only a small minority of all those in which both hypnosis and formal instruments have been utilized. They illustrate three possible approaches to the problem of validity.

THE TRANCE AS A STATE OF HYPERINGENUOUSNESS

This approach is based on the conception that the hypnotized person is unable to dissemble. It is thus possible to determine whether an instrument like a verbal inventory, for example, is susceptible to such distorting

---

4. Wiseman (1962) suggests that the hypnotic dream may, in fact, be characterized by an increased amount of primary process material.

phenomena as social desirability set, malingering, deliberate faking, or other dissimulation. A study of the California Test of Personality by Mellenbruch (1962) illustrates the procedure. He found considerable differences in subtest scores between the waking and trance states, concluding that in the former, "the individual tends to make a favorable case for himself."[5]

AGE REGRESSION

Most formal diagnostic instruments should reflect differences among adults, adolescents, and children. In submitting an instrument to such a validity check, the use of hypnotic age regression circumvents the problem of sampling differences. The same subjects can be tested at each age level. The technique is obviously restricted to those procedures that are applicable, without alteration, to both children and adults. It is illustrated by a study of Rorschach responses given by a single subject regressed to eight earlier ages (Bergmann, Graham, & Leavitt, 1947).

CONTRAST OF RESPONSE IN NORMAL AND
HYNOTICALLY INDUCED STATES

The most common use of hypnosis as an approach to test validity entails a comparison of responses in the waking state and/or neutral hypnosis with those given in an hypnotically induced condition, usually an emotional state. The valid test ought to reflect the state differences.

Among those instruments that have been subjected to this approach are the Rorschach (Counts & Mensh, 1950; Lane, 1948; Levitt & Grosz, 1960; Pattie, 1954); the Hand Test (Hodge & Wagner, 1964; Wagner & Hodge, 1968); Taylor's Manifest Anxiety Scale and Barron's Ego-strength Scale (Grosz & Levitt, 1959); the Thematic Apperception Test (Levitt, Persky, & Brady, 1964); Zuckerman's Affect Adjective Check List and the IPAT Anxiety Scale (Levitt & Persky, 1962); the MMPI (Branca & Podolnick, 1961); and the polygraph (Germann, 1961; Weinstein, Abrams, & Gibbons, 1970).

Most of these investigations yielded positive results. Notable exceptions were the examinations of the lie detector. These clever experiments appear to indicate, with considerable clarity and definiteness, the relative ease with which several ordinary conditions of the subject can deceive the polygraph expert.

WHY HYPNOSIS IS SELDOM USED IN TEST VALIDATION

The use of hypnosis as a method of testing the validity of formal assessment

---

5. Mellenbruch's conclusion that the findings of his limited study "seriously undermines one's confidence in the fundamental validity of the personality inventory" is unjustifiably extreme.

devices is relatively rare. The primary reason would seem to be the fact that samples in hypnosis research are usually small and highly select. Few investigations of any kind in behavioral science research employ true random samples, but it is in the test construction area that the most attention is paid to the nature of the sample. Sophisticated test constructors must view with acute disfavor a sample of twenty hypnotic subjects which is the end product of a group of fifty intrepid or curious volunteers.

Furthermore, the belief in the hyperingenuous subject is a public misconception that has probably never been credited by hypnosis researchers, and possibly not by most experienced practitioners. Orne's (1961) conclusion that the hypnotic subject can deceive if sufficiently motivated to do so probably represents a consensus.

The perennial controversy over the validity of hypnotic age regression renders it a poor basis for inferences about test validity. In addition, there are not many formal instruments that cover a broad age range.

Reyher's (1962) claim that the contrast of normal and hypnotically induced states had been neglected by test constructors "more from the lack of criteria for determining relevance than from prejudice" is an unnecessary, and probably invalid, explanation. Interestingly enough, Reyher, in support of his position, cites a statement by Ainsworth (1954) that "hypnotic studies are open to the question of whether the hypnotically induced state is comparable enough to the 'genuine' state to provide validation evidence." Reyher implies that Ainsworth excluded hypnotic research from her review even though, in fact, she proceeded immediately to discuss six relevant investigations in a tone that clearly suggested she was not really questioning the genuineness of the hypnotically induced state.

The Study of Physiological Processes

Hypnosis has been used as a method in certain investigations of various physiological systems, primarily the cardiovascular, gastrointestinal, and sensory, but including also renal, respiratory, and endocrine systems. The general procedure is to use the trance to create an artifical state in the subject so that appropriate physiological measurements can be made.

Selecting studies is again a problem in this section. The most recent overview of psychophysiological studies involving hypnosis (Levitt & Brady, 1963) has a bibliography of more than 200 titles. The large majority are investigations of the hypnotic state, either to determine the effects of hypnosis on a physical system—for example, studying the effect of external sensory stimuli on gastric motility—or using physiological parameters to assess effects of a hypnotically induced internal feeling state. Fewer than twenty percent qualify according to the criterion for inclusion in this chapter.

Hypnotic studies of physiology can be roughly divided into three categories: investigations of physical changes as response parameters of induced states, especially emotions, studies of physical states as etiological agents in physical and emotional pathology, and studies of physiological mechanisms of normal body system changes.

When hypnosis is used to study physiological change as an emotional response parameter, it is subject to the considerations and criticisms set forth in the section on induced states, though perhaps to a lesser degree. Physiological measures are more suitable than verbal and psychological measures for laboratory research because they are more objective and less subject to voluntary control.

Direct suggestion of specific emotional states and comparison of the physical response with baseline measures is the method most commonly employed in hypnotic studies of physiological response to emotional stimuli. Examples are investigations of metabolic and endocrine responses to suggested emotions (Black & Friedman, 1968; Levitt, Persky, & Brady, 1964; Whitehorn et al., 1930); gastric motility and secretory responses (Eichhorn & Tracktir, 1955a, 1955b; Ikemi et al., 1959); cardiovascular changes (Bennet & Scott, 1949); and respiratory responses (Dudley et al., 1964). Less common are studies of physical stress reactions using hypnotic recall of a previous actual stressful experience (Kline & Linder, 1969; Vandenbergh, Sussman, & Titus, 1966), and the paramnestic method (Eisenbud, 1937) as induction techniques. Tourney (1956) suggests that paramnestic methods may be more fruitfully applied to psychosomatic research than they have been in the past, provided that more careful experimental controls are utilized.

A large group of studies concerned with physical response to induced states can be classified as psychosomatic research. The major issue in this area is the controversy over whether psychosomatic symptoms are the result of organ vulnerability (that is, genetically determined causes), or whether they can be interpreted as expressions of underlying psychodynamic phenomena and thus be precipitated by emotions or attitudes.

Attempts have been made to define psychodynamic etiology of certain physiological symptoms by investigators who measured physiological responses to hypnotically suggested "attitudes" that were hypothetically analogous to those present in clinically observed psychosomatic disorders. Examples of these include studies of Raynaud's disease (Gottlieb, Gleser, & Gottschalk, 1967; Stern et al., 1961), in which skin temperature alternations in response to induced "attitudes" were measured, and studies of autoerythrocyte sensitization (Agle, Ratnoff, & Wasman, 1967), in which the effect of suggested emotions on production of purpuric lesions was observed. Such research has offered evidence for the significance of the interaction of emotional variables with other etiological agents in psychosomatic disorders, and demonstrates that induced states can have at least some catalyzing effects on psychosomatic symptoms. The complex nature of this kind of research problem, however, is illustrated in Erickson's (1943) account of his observations of coincidental occurence of psychosomatic phenomena—for example, auditory difficulties—where in fact visual perceptual alterations had been hypnotically suggested. He points out that physical phenomena other than that which are suggested may accidentally occur and thus confound experimental results.

Studies of physical states as etiological agents in physical and emotional pathology are few, and are directly concerned with perhaps the primary consideration in this area of research, which is whether analogs of naturally occurring physiological states can be satisfactorily reproduced under hypnosis. A group of studies essentially examining this question is represented by Scantlebury and Patterson (1940), who compared effects of suggested food stimuli on gastric motility to actual responses to these stimuli, Scantlebury, Friek, and Patterson (1942), who reported a similar comparison involving natural and hypnotic dreams, and Dudley et al. (1966, 1967), who demonstrated that physical and psychological concomitants of head pain could be partially suggested in the waking state. Although identical analogs of physical states have not been produced, similarities have been found which suggest that, with better control of variables, it may be eventually possible to produce hypnotic analogs.

Methods in studies of mechanisms and theories about normal body system changes include direct suggestion of a specific physical response, or suggestion to recall a previous physical response. Representative of this area of investigation are studies by Chase (1963) and Johner and Perlman (1968) in which nystagmus was decreased by direct suggestion under hypnosis, enabling the authors to more carefully distinguish the nature of nystagmoid movements. These led to hypotheses regarding the physiological mechanisms responsible for nystagmus and the relationship of observable behavior to brain functions.

The Coercive Power of Hypnosis

The coercive power of hypnosis is a perennially intriguing and significant issue. It bears not only on alleged hypnotic causation of antisocial and supra-individual acts, but also on the efficacy of hypnotic interventions in dealing with psychopathological symptoms and unwanted behaviors.

As Orne (1972) pointed out, a number of early studies (e.g., Rowland, 1939; Wells, 1941; Young, 1952) left the issue basically unresolved. Orne contends that the coercive power of hypnosis is in principle not amenable to empirical investigation. The use of real life circumstances outside the laboratory to test the coercive power of hypnosis is contraindicated by obvious legal and moral considerations. You cannot request that the experimental subject actually rob a bank. Thus, the researcher must have recourse to the laboratory and artificiality. In the laboratory situation, the hypnotized subject responds not only to specific instructions, but also in accord with his perception of the total situation. He assumes rightfully that the experimenter will not place him in any real jeopardy. He, the subject, is being deceived when he is requested to commit an antisocial or self-injurious act. If not, the experimenter will surely protect him from the consequences of his behavior. Therefore, the experimental subject, hypnotized or not, does not hesitate to carry out even the most outrageous acts, demonstrating nothing more than his ultimate, warranted faith in the experimenter's integrity as a human being. Following Orne's persuasive argument, a true test of the coercive power of hypnosis is not possible in the laboratory.

Orne maintains further that he and his co-workers have not yet been able to devise an experimental task that all or almost all *unhypnotized* subjects will refuse to carry out if they are sufficiently motivated. A baseline for assessing trance behavior—an essential control in examining that behavior—is never available.

Some developments in research metJology in the current decade show promise of circumventing the problems cited by Orne. The designs have come from Coe's laboratory at California State University and from the work of Levitt and Overley at the Indiana University School of Medicine. The former contrived several experimental situations that appeared realistic to a number of the subjects, specifically the request to steal an important test from a department office, and to deliver a packet of heroin to an apartment off the campus (Coe, Kobayashi, & Howard, 1972, 1973). The situations were sufficiently believable so that several of Coe's subjects attempted to intervene to apprehend his collaborators instead of cooperating with the acts.

The Indiana group used disagreeable, objectionable tasks instead of antisocial or dangerous ones (Levitt, Aronoff, Morgan, Overley, Parrish, & Rubinstein, 1975). Subjects performing such acts are clearly not protected from their consequences by the experimenter. They reported a substantial degree of lack of compliance among such subjects, though the rates did not differ between hypnotized individuals and simulators.

In a recent paper, Levitt (1977) proposed some aspects of an experimental milieu that might be more realistic to subjects. He suggested that the experimental situation should take place away from the campus or hospital and that the experimenter's accomplices at least appear to be from the lower or lower middle class rather than identifiable as graduate students, junior faculty, etc. Self-injurious acts should be avoided since they are most likely to be seen by subjects as evoking protection from the experimenter.

It is possible that recent governmental regulations concerning the briefing of experimental subjects may interfere with further research in this area, since most of it depends on deception for its effectiveness. Whether these restrictions will prevent future use of the California and Indiana designs remains to be seen.

An Overview

Hypnosis has been used as a research technique in the study of content areas other than the hypnotic trance itself: emotions, psychopathology, defense mechanisms, dreams, physiological processes, and test validation, for example. Most of the proposed research advantages of hypnosis, such as the induction of "pure" states, and enhanced control of the experimental treatment, have not yet been subjected to systematic experimental test. But there seems little doubt that the hypnotic trance is a satisfactory mechanism for creating reasonable facsimiles of at least some naturally occurring conditions.

The power of hypnosis as a method of inducing states also remains to be assessed systematically. Comparisons with other artificial techniques are lacking. The available evidence, largely in the form of contrasts of hypnotically induced behavior with simulator behavior, suggests that hypnosis is at least as powerful as other laboratory techniques.

The most frequent use of hypnosis in research is in the artificial induction of emotional and psychopathological states. Three approaches have been employed: direct suggestion, a previous experience indirectly suggested, and paramnesia followed by induced amnesia.

Direct suggestion has been used most often; the length and complexity of stimulus suggestions has varied greatly. Comparisons of the relative power of the three techniques have not yet been carried out. Logical analysis suggests that each has its potential advantages and disadvantages, and that the choice of a technique for inducing a state depends largely on the experimenter's specific aim.

The use of hypnosis to study dream behavior is highly controversial. A survey of findings to date indicates that the hypnotically induced and the natural dream differ in four significant dimensions: circumstances, content, physiology, and subjective feeling. However, it is still likely that the hypnotic dream is something more than a rote verbal production, and that investigations of it may be fruitful. It is suggested that the controversial term, "hypnotically induced dream" should be replaced by "hypnotically induced fantasy-dream."

Hypnosis has potential uses in test construction and validation, but the difficulty in assembling large samples of susceptible subjects, and the high probability of sampling bias, militate against its use in this area. These drawbacks are less likely to affect findings in research on physiological processes, especially investigations of the possible role of psychological factors in physical symptoms. Yanovski (1962), for example, believes that in using hypnosis to study cardiac dysfunction, even single subjects may furnish meaningful data.

Leuba (1941) once suggested that the hypnotic trance offers impressive advantages to experimenters in all content areas. One wonders why possibilities of its use are not being explored more extensively. Experiments employing hypnosis as a method of study constitute no more than an infinitesimal fraction of the total research effort in the behavioral sciences. There are several possible reasons for this neglect. One is that hypnosis has not yet proven itself powerful enough as a method of creating state facsimiles to overbalance the time and effort it involves. A second possible reason is the unusually high probability of sampling bias. The most important reason may be its shaky status in the community of scientists, its still uncertain respectability. Until the mystical aura of the centuries has finally been dispelled, hypnosis will not be afforded a full, fair opportunity to demonstrate its value as a research method.

Theodore Xenophon Barber *is Director of Special Projects at Cushing Hospital, Framingham, Massachusetts. He received his Ph.D. in social psychology from the American University in 1956. His doctoral dissertation pertained to the relationship between light sleep and hypnosis. After his degree he became a National Institute of Mental Health Post-Doctoral Research Fellow at the Laboratory of Social Relations at Harvard University. This fellowship was sponsored by Professors William Caudill and Clyde Kluckhohn and pertained to "Cross-Cultural Aspects of Trance Behavior." In 1969 he accepted a research position at the Medfield Foundation and Medfield State Hospital where he was free to carry out full-time research in the area of hypnosis. He is author of* Hypnosis: A Scientific Approach, LSD, Marihuana, Yoga, *and* Hypnosis, Imagination, and Human Potentialities.

Barber *critically analyzes the basic underlying assumptions of the traditional hypnotic state paradigm. In its stead, he offers an alternative paradigm for conceptualizing the phenomena. The traditional paradigm postulates that responsiveness to test suggestions is increased to the extent that the subject enters into or is placed in a special state ("hypnotic trance") that is fundamentally different from and qualitatively discontinuous from the waking state of consciousness. Barber's alternative paradigm views high responsiveness to suggestions for limb rigidity, anesthesia, hallucination, age regression, amnesia, and so on as due to the following: the subject has positive attitudes, motivations, and expectancies toward the test situation and, consequently, allows himself to think with and vividly imagine those things that are suggested, while letting go of extraneous or contrary thoughts.*

8

Suggested ("Hypnotic") Behavior: The Trance Paradigm Versus an Alternative Paradigm

THEODORE XENOPHON BARBER

It has been traditionally assumed that certain types of procedures, labeled as "trance inductions," give rise to a special state of consciousness (hypnotic trance) in some individuals. It has also been assumed that as the hypnotic trance becomes deeper or more profound, the subject becomes more responsive to suggestions for age regression, analgesia, hallucinations, deafness, amnesia, and so on. In this chapter, I will critically analyze these and other assumptions that underlie the traditional (trance) paradigm and I will present an alternative paradigm for conceptualizing the experiences and behaviors that have been historically subsumed under the term "hypnotism" or "hypnosis."

Paradigms in Science

In a cogent analysis of the history of science, Kuhn (1962) has shown that scientists working in an area of inquiry usually share common basic assumptions pertaining to the nature of the phenomena they are investigating. The shared assumptions, which are often more implicit than explicit, together with a related set of criteria for asking meaningful questions and for selecting research topics, are termed a "paradigm."

Each paradigm may give rise to more than one theory that aims to explain the phenomena. Although theories deriving from any one paradigm differ in various aspects, they share the same basic assumptions, the same methodological criteria, and the same framework for asking meaningful questions. As Braginsky, Braginsky, and Ring (1969) have pointed out, "In academic psychology, for example, competing behavioristic theories of learning were for a long time able to flourish despite widespread agreement concerning how the phenomenon [of learning] should be approached—a consensus that was particularly likely to be evident when such theories were challenged by the radically different assumptions of cognitively oriented theories " (p. 30).

In the history of science, there are many important instances when the consensually shared paradigm could not easily explain new research data. In these instances, a few scientists began to question the basic assumptions underlying the traditional paradigm; a new way of viewing the phenomena (an alternative paradigm) was slowly developed; and after a period of debate, misunderstandings, and acrimony, the alternative paradigm was accepted by new generations of investigators and slowly became dominant. In astronomy, for example, the geocentric view of the planetary system was replaced by the heliocentric view; in chemistry, the phlogiston conception of combustion was replaced by the oxygen conception; in physics, theories pertaining to the ether were replaced by conceptions that did not postulate an ether; and, in psychology, introspective analysis gave way to behaviorism.

As Chaves (1968) has pointed out, it appears that a paradigm shift may be occurring at the present time in the area of inquiry historically subsumed under the term "hypnosis." In the next section, I will briefly describe the underlying assumptions of the traditional (trance) paradigm that has dominated this area of inquiry for more than a hundred years. Following this, I will formulate some of the postulates of an alternative paradigm.

The Special State (Trance) Paradigm

During the past century, terms such as "hypnotic trance state" (or "trance," "hypnosis," "hypnotic state," and "hypnotized") have been widely used by both scientists and laymen and have become part of the everyday vocabulary of children and adults. Although the implications of these terms have been slowly changing over the years, they seem to refer to some kind of fundamental change in the state of the organism.

During the nineteenth century, terms such as "hypnotic trance" or "hypnosis" typically implied that the subject resembled the sleepwalker or somnambule, that is, resembled the person who arises from his bed at night, walks around while "half asleep," and responds in a dissociated, rather automatic way to a narrow range of stimuli. Some present-day investigators also think of the "hypnotic trance" subject as resembling a sleepwalker. As Hilgard (1969a) has pointed out, "Hypnosis is commonly considered to be a 'state' perhaps resembling the state in which the sleepwalker finds himself, hence the term 'somnambulist' as applied to the deeply hypnotized person" (p. 71). Other present-day investigators who utilize the terms "hypnotic trance" or "hypnosis" do not seem to mean that the subject resembles the sleepwalker. Although, as Bowers (1966) has noted, "Most [present-day] investigators interested in hypnosis believe that there is an hypnotic state which fundamentally differs from the waking state" (p. 42), they differ among themselves as to the exact meaning to be assigned to the terms.

Bowers (1966) views hypnosis as "altered state within which suggestions have a peculiarly potent effect" (p. 50). However, Gill and Brenman (1959) use the term "hypnotic state" to refer to an "induced psychological regression, issuing, in the setting of a particular regressed relationship between two people, in a relatively stable state which includes a subsystem of the ego with various degrees of control of the ego apparatuses" (p. xxiii). Other investigators attach different connotations to the term. For instance, among the essential characteristics of the hypnotic state, Orne (1959) includes a tolerance for logical inconsistencies ("trance logic") and alterations in subjective experiences induced by suggestions. Evans (1968) views hypnosis as an altered subjective state of awareness in which dissociative mechanisms are operating, Meares (1963) sees the basic element in hypnosis as an atavistic regression to a primitive mode of mental functioning, and Shor (1962) views the hypnotic state as having three dimensions—hypnotic role-taking, trance, and archaic involvement.

Although the above and other theoretical formulations attribute somewhat different properties to the hypnotic state, they derive from a common set of basic assumptions (an underlying paradigm). Some of the underlying assumptions of the hypnosis or trance paradigm appear to include the following:

1. There exists a state of consciousness, a state of awareness, or a state of the organism that is fundamentally (qualitatively) different from other states of consciousness such as the waking state, the deep sleep state, and the state of unconsciousness. This distinct state is labeled "hypnosis," "hypnotic state," "hypnotic trance," or simply "trance."

2. The state of hypnotic trance may occasionally occur spontaneously, but it is usually induced by special types of procedures that are labeled "hypnotic inductions" or "trance inductions." Although trance induction procedures vary in content—for example, they usually include, but they need not include, fixation of the eyes, suggestions of relaxation, and suggestions of drowsiness and sleep—they all appear to have two essential features in common: they suggest to the subject that he is entering a special state (hypnotic trance) and investigators who adhere to the traditional paradigm

agree that the procedures are capable of producing hypnotic trance.

3. The hypnotic trance state is not a momentary condition that the subject enters for only a few seconds. On the contrary, when a person has been placed in a hypnotic trance, he remains in it for a period of time and he is typically brought out of it by a command from the hypnotist, such as, "Wake up!"

4. Subjects who are in a hypnotic state are responsive, both overtly and subjectively, to test suggestions for rigidity of the muscles or limbs, age regression, analgesia and anesthesia, visual and auditory hallucination, deafness, blindness, color blindness, negative hallucination, dreaming on a specified topic, heightened performance (on physical or cognitive tasks), amnesia, and posthypnotic behavior.[1]

5. As Sutcliffe (1960) pointed out, some investigators who adhere to the trance paradigm believe the suggested phenomena are "genuine" or "real," whereas others are far more skeptical. For example, some investigators who accept the trance paradigm view hypnotic deafness as indistinguishable from actual deafness, and the hypnotic dream as indistinguishable from the nocturnal dream. However, other investigators who accept the trance paradigm view the hypnotic deaf subject as a person who is able to hear but thinks that he cannot, and they perceive the hypnotic dream as differing in essential respects from the night dream. Although investigators who adhere to the trance paradigm disagree on the "reality" of the suggested phenomena, the important point to emphasize is that they all view the phenomena as associated with hypnotic trance, and they consequently label the phenomena as "hypnotic phenomena," not simply as "suggested phenomena."

6. There are levels or depths of hypnotic trance; that is, hypnotic trance can vary from light, to medium, to deep, to very deep (somnambulism).

7. As the depth of hypnotic trance increases, the subject's ability to experience suggested phenomena vividly and intensely also increases. For example, as the subject becomes more deeply hypnotized, he is more able to have a vivid and intense experience of age regression, analgesia, hallucination, or amnesia.

In brief, the dominant (trance) paradigm sees the person who responds to test suggestions as being in a fundamentally different state from the person who is unresponsive to test suggestions. The construct "hypnotic state," "trance," or "hypnosis" is used to refer to this state, which is conceived to differ, not simply quantitatively, but in some basic, qualitative way, from normal waking states and from states of sleep.

---

1. Henceforth, in this chapter, the term "response" or "responsiveness to test suggestions" will be used as a shorthand term to refer to both overt and subjective responses to each of the types of suggestions mentioned in this paragraph.

An Alternative Paradigm:
The Member of the Audience Analogy

There is another way of viewing responsiveness to test suggestions[2] that does not involve special state constructs such as "hypnosis," "hypnotized," "hypnotic state," or "trance." This alternative paradigm does not see a qualitative difference in the "state" of the person who is and the one who is not responsive to test suggestions. Although the alternative paradigm has many historical roots (discussed by Sarbin, 1962), it derives primarily from my more recent theoretical endeavors and those of Sarbin (Barber, 1964a, 1967, 1969b, 1970a; Sarbin, 1950; Sarbin & Andersen, 1967; Sarbin & Coe, 1972). An analogy to members of an audience watching a motion picture or a stage play may clarify the paradigm.

One member of an audience may be attending a performance with the purpose of having new experiences. His attitude is that it is interesting and worthwhile to feel sad, to feel happy, to empathize, and to have the other thoughts, feelings, and emotions the actors are attempting to communicate. He both desires and expects the actors to arouse in him new or interesting thoughts and emotions. Although he is aware that he is watching a contrived performance and that he is in an audience, he does not actively think about these matters. Since this member of the audience has "positive" attitudes, motivations, and expectancies toward the communications emanating from the stage, he lets himself imagine and think with the statements and actions of the actors; he laughs, weeps, empathizes and, more generally, thinks, feels, emotes, and experiences in line with the intentions of the actors.

Another member of the audience had an anxious and tiring day at the office, wanted to go to bed early in the evening, and unwillingly came to the performance in order to avoid an argument with his wife. He is not interested in having the emotions and experiences the actors are attempting to communicate. He does not especially desire and does not expect to feel empathic, happy, sad, excited, or shocked. He is continually aware that he is in an audience and that he is observing a deliberately contrived performance. Given this set of attitudes, motivations, and expectancies, this member of the audience does not let himself imagine and think with the statements and actions of the actors; he does not laugh, weep, empathize or, more generally, think, feel, emote, and experience in line with the communications from the actors.

The implications of this analogy are:

2. As stated in footnote one, in the remainder of this chapter the term "responsiveness" or "response to test suggestions" will refer to both overt and subjective responses to suggestions for limb rigidity, age regression, analgesia, hallucination, amnesia, postexperimental ("posthypnotic") behavior, and so on.

1. The experimental subject who is highly responsive to test suggestions resembles the member of the audience who experiences the thoughts, feelings, and emotions that the actors are attempting to arouse. The very suggestible subject views his responding to test suggestions as interesting and worthwhile; he desires and expects to experience those things that are suggested. Given these underlying "positive" attitudes, motivations, and expectancies, he lets himself imagine and think with the things suggested and he experiences the suggested effects.

2. The experimental subject who is very unresponsive to test suggestions resembles the member of the audience who does *not* experience the thoughts, feelings, and emotions that the actors are attempting to arouse. The very nonsuggestible subject views his responding to test suggestions as not desirable; he neither wants nor expects to experience those things that are suggested. Given these underlying "negative" attitudes, motivations, and expectancies, he does not let himself imagine and think with the things suggested and he does not experience the suggested effects.

3. It is misleading, and unparsimonious, to label the member of an audience who is thinking, feeling, and emoting in line with the communications of the actors, as being in a special state (hypnotic trance) that is fundamentally different from the waking state. In other words, it is misleading, and unparsimonious, to restrict our conceptions of normal conditions or waking conditions to such an extent that they exclude the member of the audience who is having various experiences as he listens to the communications from the stage. Furthermore, since the member of the audience, who is responding to the words of the actors, and the experimental subject, who is responding to the words (test suggestions) of the experimenter, do not differ in any important way in their attitudes, motivations, and expectations toward the communications or in the way they think along with the communications, it is also misleading and unparsimonious to label the subject who is responding to test suggestions as being in a special state (hypnotic trance).

4. Although the member of the audience who is responding to the words of the actors and the experimental subject who is responding to the test suggestions of the experimenter have similar attitudes, motivations, and expectations toward the communications and are similarly "thinking with" the communications, *they are being exposed to different types of communications.* The messages or communications from the actors are intended to elicit certain types of thoughts, feelings, and emotions—to empathize, to feel happy or sad, to laugh or to weep, to feel excited or shocked—whereas the messages or communications (test suggestions) from the experimenter are intended to elicit somewhat different types of thoughts, feelings, or emotions—to experience an arm as heavy, to experience oneself as a child, to forget preceding events, and so forth. From this viewpoint, the member

of the audience and the subject who is responding to test suggestions are having different experiences, *not because they are in different "states" but because they are receiving different communications.*

The above analogy exemplifies some of the basic assumptions underlying the alternative paradigm. These assumptions include the following:

1. It is unnecessary to postulate a fundamental difference in the "state" of the person who is and the one who is not responsive to test suggestions.

2. Both the person who is and the one who is not responsive to test suggestions have attitudes, motivations, and expectancies toward the communications they are receiving.

3. The person who is very responsive to test suggestions has "positive" attitudes, motivations, and expectancies toward the communications he is receiving. That is, he views his responding to test suggestions as interesting or worthwhile and he wants to, tries to, and expects to experience the suggested effects. Given these "positive" attitudes, motivations, and expectations, he lets himself think with and imagine those things that are suggested.

4. The person who is very unresponsive to test suggestions has "negative" attitudes, motivations, and expectations toward the communications he is receiving. That is, he views his responding to test suggestions as not interesting or worthwhile and he neither tries to nor expects to experience the suggested effects. Given these "negative" attitudes, motivations, and expectations, he does not let himself imagine or think with the suggestions; instead, he verbalizes to himself such statements as, "This is silly," or, "The suggestion won't work."

5. The three factors—attitudes, motivations, and expectations—vary on a continuum (from negative, to neutral, to positive) and they converge and interact in complex ways to determine to what extent a subject will let himself think with and imagine those things that are suggested. The extent to which the subject thinks with and vividly imagines the suggested effects, in turn determines his overt and subjective responses to test suggestions.

6. Concepts derived from abnormal psychology—such as "trance," "somnambulism," and "dissociation"—are misleading and do not explain the overt and subjective responses. Responsiveness to test suggestions is a normal psychological phenomenon that can be conceptualized in terms of constructs that are an integral part of normal psychology, especially of social psychology. Social psychology conceptualizes other social influence processes, such as persuasion and conformity, in terms of such mediating variables as attitudes, motivations, expectancies, and cognitive processes. In the same way, the mediating variables that are relevant to explaining responsiveness to test suggestions include attitudes, motivations, expectations, and cognitive-imaginative processes.

7. The phenomena associated with test suggestions are considered to be within the range of normal human capabilities. However, whether or not

the suggested phenomena are similar to or different from phenomena occurring in real life situations that bear the same name, is viewed as an open
question that needs to be answered empirically. For example, such questions as the following are open to empirical investigation: To what extent is
suggested analgesia similar to the analgesia produced by nerve section or by
anesthetic drugs? What are the similarities and differences between suggested and naturally occurring (nonsuggested) blindness, color blindness,
deafness, hallucination, dreaming, and amnesia? The empirical evidence at
present indicates that, although there are some similarities between the suggested and nonsuggested phenomena, they also differ in very important
respects. For example, suggested color blindness has only superficial resem-
blances to actual color blindness, and suggested amnesia is much more
labile or transient than actual amnesia. (Since these issues have been discussed
in detail elsewhere—Barber, 1959b, 1961b, 1962a, 1962b, 1963, 1964b,
1964c, 1965b, 1969b, 1970a—they will be discussed only peripherally here.)

   Which paradigm is more successful in explaining responsiveness to test
suggestions for limb rigidity, age-regression, analgesia, hallucination, amnesia, etc.—the traditional one that postulates a special state that is fundamentally different from the waking state, or the alternative one that focuses
on attitudes, motivations, expectancies, and thinking with and imagining
those things that are suggested? I will next summarize experimental data,
pertaining to responsiveness to test suggestions under control ("waking")
conditions, which indicate that the alternative paradigm provides a more
successful and more parsimonious explanation.

Response to Test Suggestions Without "Hypnosis"

A substantial number of subjects are highly responsive to test suggestions
when no attempt is made to place them in a "hypnotic trance state." Let us
look at a few examples.

HUMAN PLANK FEAT

The stage hypnotist suggests to a selected subject that his body is becoming
stiff and rigid. When the subject appears rigid, the stage hypnotist and an
assistant place him between two chairs, one chair beneath the subject's head
and the other beneath his ankles. The subject typically remains suspended
between the two chairs for several minutes, as if he were a human plank.
The traditional paradigm assumes that the subject is able to perform the
human plank feat because he is in a state—a hypnotic trance state—that is
qualitatively different from ordinary states of consciousness. This notion is
not supported by the empirical data.

   Collins (1961) demonstrated conclusively that, when male and female
control subjects are told directly (without any special preliminaries) to keep

their bodies rigid, practically all perform the human-plank feat, that is, they remain suspended between two chairs for several minutes, one chair beneath the head and the other beneath the ankles. In fact, Collins demonstrated that control subjects are able to perform the feat just as easily as subjects who have been exposed to a trance induction procedure and who are ostensibly in "hypnotic trance". The control ("awake") subjects and also the experimental ("hypnotized") subjects stated, at the conclusion of Collin's experiment, that they were surprised at their own performance because they did not believe initially that they could so easily perform the human plank feat.

At times, stage hypnotists ask a person to stand on the chest of the subject who is rigidly suspended between two chairs, one chair beneath his shoulders and the other beneath his calves. The traditional paradigm assumes that the suspended subject is able to support the weight of a man on his chest because he is in a special state of consciousness—a hypnotic trance state. The empirical evidence does not support this assumption. In my laboratory, six unselected male subjects were told under control conditions (without any special preliminaries) to make their body rigid and to keep it rigid. They were then suspended between two chairs, one chair beneath the shoulders and the other beneath the calves. Each subject was able to support the weight of a man on his chest. All subjects were surprised that they could so easily support the weight of a man and all disagreed vehemently with the statement that they were in a trance.

RESPONSE TO OTHER TEST SUGGESTIONS

Experimental studies that I have summarized elsewhere (Barber, 1965a) have demonstrated that a substantial proportion of individuals are responsive to various kinds of test suggestions when no attempt is made to place them in a "hypnotic trance." In these experiments, sixty-two unselected college students were assigned at random to a control condition (they were simply told that they were to receive a test of imagination). They were then assessed individually on objective and subjective responses to the eight standardized test suggestions of the Barber Suggestibility Scale: Arm Lowering (the subject's right arm is heavy and is moving down); Arm Levitation (the left arm is weightless and is moving up); Hand Lock (the clasped hands are welded together and canot be taken apart); Thirst "Hallucination" (he is becoming extremely thirsty); Verbal Inhibition (his throat and jaw muscles are rigid and he cannot speak his name); Body Immobility (his body is heavy and he cannot stand up); "Posthypnotic Like" Response (when he hears a click postexperimentally, he will cough automatically); and Selective Amnesia (when the experiment is over, he will not remember one specific test suggestion).[3]

As Table 8.1, column one, shows, about one-fourth of these control subjects, who were given the eight test suggestions immediately after they were simply told that they were to receive a test of imagination, passed the Arm Lowering, Arm Levitation, Verbal Inhibition, and Body Immobility items both objectively (manifesting the suggested overt behavior) and subjectively (testifying postexperimentally that they actually experienced the sugggested effect). In addition, nearly half of these control subjects passed the Thirst "Hallucination" item and forty percent passed the Hand Lock item (that is, they tried to unclasp their hands but had not succeeded after fifteen seconds, and they testified that they actually felt that their hands were stuck). Furthermore, about thirteen percent of these control subjects passed the "Posthypnotic Like" Response and the Selective Amnesia items.

Although a surprisingly high proportion of subjects were responsive to the test suggestions under the control condition, even more dramatic results were obtained when another group of sixty-two subjects, randomly selected from the same college population, were tested individually on the same test suggestions after receiving task-motivational instructions for forty-five seconds. These task-motivational instructions, which aimed to produce favorable motivations, attitudes, and expectancies toward the test situation and to heighten the subject's willingness to imagine and think about those things that would be suggested, were worded as follows:

> In this experiment I'm going to test your ability to imagine and to visualize. How well you do on the tests which I will give you depends entirely upon your willingness to try to imagine and to visualize the things I will ask you to imagine. Everyone passed these tests when they tried. For example, we asked people to close their eyes and to imagine that they were at a movie theater and were watching a show. Most people were able to do this very well; they were able to imagine very vividly that they were at a movie and they felt as if they were actually looking at the picture. However, a few people thought that this was an awkward or silly thing to do and did not try to imagine and failed the test. Yet when these people later realized that it wasn't hard to imagine, they were able to visualize the movie

---

3. The subject receives a maximum objective score of eight points on the Barber Suggestibility Scale (one point for each of the eight test suggestions) if: the right arm moves down four or more inches; the left arm rises four or more inches; the subject tries to but fails to unclasp his hands; he shows swallowing, moistening of lips, or marked mouth movements and states postexperimentally that he became thirsty during this test, he tries but does not succeed in saying his name; he tries but does not succeed in standing fully erect; he coughs or clears his throat when the cue is presented postexperimentally; and he does not refer to the critical item during the postexperimental interview but recalls at least four other items and then recalls the critical item when told, "Now you can remember."

In addition to the objective scores, assigned as described above, the subject also receives a maximum subjective score of eight points on the Barber Suggestibility Scale (one point for each of the eight test suggestions) if he states, during the standardized postexperimental interview, that he actually experienced each of the suggested effects and that he did not respond overtly to the test suggestion simply to follow instructions or to please the experimenter.

picture and they felt as if the imagined movie was as vivid and as real as an actual movie. What I ask is your cooperation in helping this experiment by trying to imagine vividly what I describe to you. I want you to score as high as you can because we're trying to measure the maximum ability of people to imagine. If you don't try to the best of your ability, this experiment will be worthless and I'll tend to feel silly. On the other hand, if you try to imagine to the best of your ability, you can easily imagine and do the interesting things I tell you and you will be helping this experiment and not wasting any time (Barber & Calverley, 1962, p. 366).

TABLE 8.1   Percentage of subjects passing each test suggestion both objectively and subjectively

Test Suggestion	*Percent of Subjects Passing*		
	control	*task-motivational instructions*	*trance induction procedure*
1. Arm lowering	26b	61a	72a
2. Arm levitation	24b	56a	56a
3. Hand lock	40b	81a	69a
4. Thirst hallucination	48b	76a	74a
5. Verbal inhibition	27b	69a	64a
6. Body immobility	27b	66a	63a
7. Posthypnotic like response	14b	42a	29ab
8. Selective amnesia	13b	39a	35a

SOURCE: Barber, 1965a.
NOTE: Percentages in the same row containing the same subscript letter do not differ from each other at the .05 level of confidence.

The subjects who received these task-motivational instructions showed a dramatically high level of objective and subjective responsiveness to the test suggestions (manifesting the suggested overt behaviors and testifying that they subjectively experienced the suggested effects). As Table 8.1, column two, shows, from fifty-six percent to sixty-nine percent of the subjects who received task-motivational instructions passed the Arm Lowering, Arm Levitation, Verbal Inhibition, and Body Immobility items, seventy-six percent passed the Thirst "Hallucination" item, and eighty-one percent passed the Hand Lock item. In addition, around forty percent of the subjects who received task-motivational instructions passed the Selective Amnesia and "Posthypnotic Like" Response items.

As stated above, sixty-two subjects were tested individually under the control condition and sixty-two were tested under the task-motivational condition. In addition, sixty-two subjects, randomly chosen from the same population of college students, were assessed individually on the same test suggestions after they were exposed to a standardized fifteen-minute procedure of the type traditionally labeled as a "trance induction." This trance induction procedure, which is presented verbatim elsewhere (Barber, 1969b), included the following salient features: (a) Instructions were administered to produce favorable attitudes, motivations, and expectations

(for example, "Hypnosis is nothing fearful or mysterious... Your cooperation, your interest, is what I ask for.... Nothing will be done that will in any
way cause you the least embarassment... you will be able to experience
many interesting things"). (b) The subject was asked to fixate on a light
blinking in synchrony with the sound of a metronome and was given suggestions of eye heaviness and eye closure (for example, "The strain in your eyes
is getting greater and greater.... You would like to close your eyes and relax
completely"). (c) Suggestions of relaxation, drowsiness, and sleep were administered repeatedly ("comfortable, relaxed, thinking of nothing, nothing
but what I say... drowsy... deep sound comfortable sleep... deeper and
deeper..."). (d) It was suggested to the subject that he was entering a
unique state, a deep trance, in which he would be able to have interesting
and unusual experiences.

As table 8.1, column three, shows, subjects exposed to the trance induction procedure were generally as responsive to the test suggestions as those
subjects who had received the brief task-motivational instructions under
waking conditions. Also, Table 8.1 shows that the subjects who received the
trance induction procedure as well as those who received the task-
motivational instructions were significantly more responsive to the test suggestions than the control group.

Table 8.2 shows the number of test suggestions that were passed by subjects in each of the three experimental groups. The reader will note that thirteen percent and ten percent of the subjects under the task-motivational instructions and trance induction conditions, respectively, and none of the
controls, passed all eight of the test suggestions, Also, sixteen percent, sixty
percent, and fifty-three percent of the subjects under the control, task-
motivational instructions, and trance induction condition, respectively,
were relatively highly responsive to test suggestions, passing at least five of
the eight items.

TABLE 8.2   Number of test suggestions passed (both objectively and subjectively) by
subjects in control, task-motivational instructions, and trance induction groups.

Number of Test Suggestions Passed	Percent of Subjects Passing		
	control group	task-motivational group	trance induction group
8	0 ⎫	13 ⎫	10 ⎫
7	3 ⎪ 16	16 ⎪ 60	16 ⎪ 53
6	11 ⎬	15 ⎬	16 ⎬
5	2 ⎭	16 ⎭	11 ⎭
4	11 ⎫	16 ⎫	15 ⎫
3	6 ⎬ 38	8 ⎬ 27	13 ⎬ 36
2	21 ⎭	3 ⎭	8 ⎭
1	16 ⎫ 45	10 ⎫ 13	6 ⎫ 11
0	29 ⎭	3 ⎭	5 ⎭

SOURCE: Barber, 1965a.

The data presented above indicate the following:

1. When subjects are tested on test suggestions under a control condition (immediately after they are simply told that they are to be given a test of imagination), the majority respond to some test suggestions and a small proportion manifest a rather high level of response. Under the control condition, subjects typically passed two of the eight test suggestions and sixteen percent passed at least five of the eight.

2. Although most subjects respond to some test suggestions under a control condition, a markedly higher level of response is found when subjects are given task-motivational instructions, that is, instructions designed to produce positive motivations, attitudes, and expectations toward the suggestive situation and a consequent willingness to think with and imagine those things that are suggested.

3. A trance induction procedure, which focuses on repeated suggestions of eye heaviness, relaxation, drowsiness, and sleep, also raises response to test suggestions above the control or base level.

4. Comparable high levels of response to test suggestions of arm heaviness, body immobility, inability to say one's name, selective amnesia, and so forth, are produced when task-motivational instructions are given alone (without a trance induction procedure) and when a trance induction procedure is given alone (without explicit task-motivational instructions).[4]

Why is enhanced responsiveness to test suggestions produced both by task-motivational instructions and also by a trance induction procedure? There are at least three possible interpretations:

1. From the traditional (special state) paradigm, one might hypothesize that both task-motivational instructions and a trance induction procedure give rise to a hypnotic trance state. However, with few exceptions, subjects who have received task-motivational instructions appear awake, claim they

---

4. Additional experiments, summarized elsewhere (Barber, 1969b, pp. 60—70), also found comparable high levels of response to test suggestions (suggestions for analgesia, gustatory "hallucination," enhanced cognitive proficiency, dreaming on a specified topic, time distortion, color blindness, visual-auditory "hallucination," and amnesia) in subjects exposed to task-motivational instructions alone and in those exposed to a trance induction procedure. However, several considerations noted by Hilgard and Tart (1966) and by Edmonston and Robertson (1967) led to an additional experiment (Barber & Calverley, 1968), which indicated that task-motivational instructions given alone are slightly less effective in facilitating suggestibility than task-motivational instructions given together with a trance induction procedure. Barber and Calverley (1968) hypothesized that the slightly higher level of suggestibility that was found when the task-motivational instructions were combined with the trance induction procedure was due to the fact that under this condition the situation was defined to the subjects as "hypnosis" and, vice versa, the slightly lower level of suggestibility found with task-motivational instructions alone was due to the fact that under this condition the situation was defined as a "test of imagination." This hypothesis clearly merits testing, especially since earlier experiments (Barber & Calverley, 1964e, 1965) indicated that, with everything else constant, a higher level of responsiveness to test suggestions is produced when subjects are told they are participating in a "hypnosis" experiment rather than in an "imagination" experiment.

are awake, and do not show a limp posture, passivity, a blank stare, or any other sign of trance. Are task-motivated subjects, who show no signs of being in a trance, actually in a trance? This question, which derives from the traditional paradigm, cannot be answered by any empirical method available at the present time.

2. Also, from the special state paradigm, one might hypothesize that (a) subjects who are highly responsive to test suggestions after they have received a trance induction procedure are in a hypnotic trance state whereas (b) those who are highly responsive after receiving task-motivational instructions are not in a hypnotic trance but are responsive for other reasons, for example, because they are highly motivated to respond. This interpretation also leads to an anomaly for the special state paradigm because it is now being said that the kind of high response to test suggestions that has been traditionally associated with hypnotic trance can also be produced as easily without hypnotic trance.

3. From the alternative paradigm, which does not postulate a special state, one could hypothesize that both task-motivational instructions and a trance induction procedure raise response to test suggestions above the level found under a control condition because they produce more positive attitudes, motivations, and expectancies toward the suggestive situation and a greater willingness to think with and to imagine those things that are suggested. This hypothesis can be empirically confirmed or disconfirmed by (a) assessing attitudes, motivations, expectations, and willingness to think with the suggestions prior to and also after the administration of a control, a task-motivational, and a trance induction treatment to three random groups of subjects and (b) testing responsiveness to suggestions after the second assessment (of attitudes, motivations, etc.).

A PERSONAL REPORT ON RESPONDING TO TEST SUGGESTIONS

As stated above, some individuals manifest a high level of response to test suggestions when no attempt is made to hypnotize them. I also manifest a high level of response. Let me now give a personal, phenomenological report of the factors underlying my own responsiveness to test suggestions (Barber, 1970b).

An experimenter states that he would like to assess my responsiveness to suggestions and I agree to be tested. Since I believe that it is an interesting and worthwhile learning experience to respond to the kinds of test suggestions that I expect he will give me, I have a positive attitude toward the test situation and am motivated to experience those things that will be suggested. Furthermore, I expect that suggested effects, such as arm levitation, age regression, and amnesia can be experienced. Since I have positive attitudes, motivations, and expectancies, I will not evaluate, analyze, or think contrary to those things that are suggested; for example, I will not say to myself, "This suggestion is not worded correctly," "The suggestion will not be effective," or "This is just an experiment." On the contrary, I will let myself think with, imagine, and visualize those things that the experimenter will describe.

The experimenter asks me to extend my right arm and then suggests repeatedly that it is solid, rigid, like a piece of steel. If I had a reason not to respond to the suggestion, I could prevent myself from thinking of the arm as rigid. However, since there is no reason to resist, on the contrary, since I am motivated to experience the suggested effects, I let myself think with the suggestion—I verbalize to myself that the arm is rigid and I imagine it as a piece of steel. When the experimenter then states, "Try to bend the arm, you can't," I do not say to myself, "Of course I can bend it." Instead, I continue to think of the arm as rigid, I continue to picture it as a piece of steel, and when I make an attempt to bend it, I find that I cannot.

(Thinking back to the suggestion, after the experiment is over, I realize the following: (a) when I was imagining my arm as rigid, I involuntarily contracted the muscles in the arm, (b) the involuntary muscular contractions made the arm feel rigid, (c) the actual rigidity in the arm reinforced the thought that the arm was rigid and immovable, and (d) when told to try to bend the arm, I continued to think and imagine that the arm was a piece of steel and I continued to maintain the involuntary muscular contraction. Although these considerations are clear to me retrospectively, during the experiment I was picturing the arm as a piece of steel and I was not actively thinking about these underlying mechanisms.)

The experimenter next suggests repeatedly that my left hand is dull, numb, a piece of rubber, a lump of matter without feelings or sensations. I think with the suggestions and I picture the hand as a rubbery lump of matter that is separated from the rest of my body. The experimenter then places the hand in a pain-producing apparatus that brings a heavy weight to bear upon a finger. Although this heavy weight normally produces an aching pain in the finger, I do not think of the stimulation as pain. Instead I continue to think of the hand and finger as a rubbery lump of matter "out there" and I think of the sensations produced by the heavy weight *as sensations* that have their own unique and interesting properties. Specifically, I think of the sensations as a series of separate sensations—as a sensation of pressure, a cutting sensation, a numbness, a feeling of heat, a pulsating sensation. Although under other circumstances I would label these sensations as pain, I do not let myself think of the sensations in this way; instead, I think of them as a complex of varying sensations in a dull, rubbery hand and I state honestly that although I experience a variety of unique sensations I do not experience anxiety, distress, or pain.

The experimenter then suggests that I see a cat in the corner of the room.

Since I have a positive attitude toward the suggestive situation and am motivated to experience the suggested effects, I inhibit the thought that there is no cat in the room. Instead, I let myself vividly visualize a black cat that I have often seen before and I think of it as being in the corner of the room. Since I continue to think of the cat as being "out there," and since I inhibit the thought that I am visualizing it in my mind's eye, I state that I see the cat in the corner of the room.

The experimenter next instructs me to close my eyes (presumably to remove visual distractions that might interfere with the forthcoming tasks), and then suggests that I am in Boston Symphony Hall and I hear the orchestra playing. I let myself vividly imagine that I am at the symphony and that the orchestra is playing Beethoven's Fifth Symphony. I inhibit the thought that I am really in an experimental situation, I focus on the idea that I am in Symphony Hall, and I "hear" the music, which becomes continually more vivid.

(Afterwards, thinking back to the suggestion for auditory hallucination, I realize that I was "making the music in my head." However, at the time I received the suggestion I was vividly imagining and thinking about Beethoven's symphony and I was not thinking about such matters as where the music was coming from. Although I could have stopped thinking with the suggestion, for instance, I could have said to myself that I was actually in an experimental situation, I had no reason to verbalize such contrary thoughts to myself and I continued to imagine vividly and to think of myself as being in Symphony Hall.)

The experimenter next suggests that time is going back, my body is becoming small, and I am a child of six years of age. I do not say to myself that I am an adult, that I cannot become a child, or that this suggestion won't work. On the contrary, since I have positive attitudes, motivations, and expectations toward the suggestive situation, I think with the suggestion. I let myself imagine vividly that my body is small and tiny (and I begin to feel that I am actually tiny); I think of myself as a child, and I vividly imagine myself in the first grade classroom. I then let the imaginative situation "move" by itself; the first-grade teacher talks to the students, two boys in the back of the room throw spitballs when the teacher turns her back to the class, and later the bell rings for recess. Since I focused on the idea that I was a child, since I felt myself as small and tiny, since I could "see" the events occurring in the classroom, since I did not say to myself, "I am really an adult," I testify afterwards that I actually felt that I was six years old and that I found this part of the experiment vivid and very interesting.

Later, the experimenter suggests that when the session is over I will not remember anything that occurred. Soon afterwards he states that the experiment is over and asks me what I remember. Since I have no reason to resist the suggestion for amnesia, I say to myself that I do not remember what occurred; I keep my thoughts on the present; I do not think back to the preceding events, and I state that I do not remember. The experimenter subsequently states, "Now you can remember." I now let myself think back to the preceding events and I verbalize them.

In summary, speaking personally and phenomenologically, I can experience arm rigidity, hand levitation, analgesia, visual and auditory hallucination, age regression, amnesia, and other suggested effects that have been traditionally thought to be associated with hypnotism. I do not need a "trance induction procedure" in order to experience these effects. Since I am ready at any time to adopt a positive attitude, motivation, and expectation toward the suggestive situation, I am ready at any time to think with and to imagine or visualize those things that are suggested. On the other hand, if I had a reason not to respond to the test suggestions, I could adopt a quite different set of attitudes, motivations, and expectations toward the situation, I could tell myself that I shall not respond, and I could easily prevent myself from thinking with and vividly imagining those things that are suggested.

Three additional points should be emphasized:

1. If the experimenter first suggests to me, as has happened on several occasions, that I am becoming relaxed, drowsy, sleepy, and am entering a hypnotic trance state, I can think with these suggestions and can feel relaxed, drowsy, sleepy, and passive. However, when the experimenter subsequently gives suggestions that involve effort, for example, suggestions of arm rigidity or analgesia, I no longer feel relaxed, sleepy, or passive and I may, in fact, feel very alert and aroused. The traditional "trance induction procedure" comprised of repetitive suggestions of relaxation, drowsiness, sleep, and hypnosis, appears to me to be just another set of suggestions that I can accept and it is not necessary or especially important in determining my responsiveness to test suggestions.

2. When I am experiencing suggested analgesia, age regression, amnesia, and so on, I do not feel that I am in a special state—a hypnotic state or a trance—that is discontinuous with or qualitatively different from my ordinary state of consciousness. In fact, when I am responding to test suggestions I do not feel that my "state" differs in any important way from the state I am in when I watch a motion picture or stage play. When I am in an audience, I let myself imagine and think with the communications from the stage and I empathize, laugh, feel sad, cry, and have the other emotions, feelings, and vicarious experiences, that the actors are attempting to communicate. In essentially the same way, when I am in an experimental situation and am being assessed for response to test suggestions, I let myself think with and vividly imagine those things that are suggested and I have the experiences that the experimenter is attempting to communicate.

3. If I wish, I can give myself the same suggestions that are given by the

experimenter. For instance, I can suggest to myself that time is going backwards, my body is becoming small and tiny, and I am a child of a certain age. I can then think about and vividly imagine a situation that occurred when I was a child and I can inhibit contrary thoughts. Similarly, in a dental situation I can give myself suggestions that the sensations are interesting and not uncomfortable and by thinking of each of the varying sensations (drilling, pressure, pricking, heat, and so forth) as sensations per se, I can inhibit anxiety, distress, and pain. I have also found that the same technique—focusing on the sensations as sensations—is sufficient to block the pain and distress associated with various methods used in the laboratory to produce pain, for example, pain produced by immersing a limb in ice water and pain produced by using a tourniquet to cut off the blood supply to an arm. Although these experiences have been traditionally subsumed under the term "autohypnosis," I do not feel that I am in a special state (a hypnotic trance state) fundamentally different from my ordinary state of consciousness; on the contrary, when I am having these experiences I feel as normal and as awake as when I am watching a movie, a stage play, or a television show.

Data Ostensibly Supporting the
Traditional (Special State) Paradigm

At first glance, the traditional notion that a special state underlies high responsiveness to test suggestions appears to be supported by data such as the following:

1. Stage hypnotists appear to elicit unique or special behaviors from subjects who seem to be in a special state (hypnotic trance).

2. Experimenters have reported that a variety of amazing or special effects can be elicited from subjects who are ostensibly in a hypnotic trance.

3. High response to test suggestions is associated with observable trancelike characteristics.

4. Some highly responsive subjects testify that they experienced a special state of consciousness.

5. Some highly responsive subjects do not "come out of it" immediately—they seem to remain in a trance after the experiment is over.

6. Some highly responsive subjects spontaneously forget the events and spontaneous amnesia is a critical indicant of a special state.

7. Highly responsive subjects show a special type of logic—"trance logic"—which indicates that they are in a special state.

Let us look at each of these sets of data in turn.

STAGE HYPNOSIS

The major principle of stage hypnosis is that the performer *selects* subjects who are willing and able to respond to his suggestions regardless of whether they are "awake" or in "hypnotic trance." The technique that is typically used to select cooperatively responsive subjects is as follows: before an attempt is made to induce "hypnotic trance," volunteer subjects are given preliminary test suggestions, such as arm lowering or hand lock, and only those who are highly responsive to the suggestions are used in the subsequent demonstrations. The phenomena of stage hypnosis can be explained by this principle of subject selection taken together with several additional principles such as (a) the unique social psychological characteristics of the stage setting (e.g., the "fun" aspects of participating in the show and strong expectations for unusual performance on the part of both the subjects and the audience) and (b) the utilization of "feats" (e.g., the human plank feat, the pin through the flesh, and the burning match on the hand) which seem very amazing but are actually not difficult for normal individuals to perform. Due to space limitations, these and other principles and "secrets" of stage hypnosis will not be further elaborated here (see Meeker and Barber, 1971, or the unabbreviated version of the present chapter in the first edition of the present text).

"AMAZING" EFFECTS ELICITED IN EXPERIMENTAL SITUATIONS

The traditional (special state) viewpoint seems to be supported by experimental reports that amazing or special effects were produced when suggestions were given to highly responsive subjects. These effects include the production of blisters, the cure of warts, the production of analgesia sufficient for surgery, and the production of actual age regression, hallucinations, and deafness. Let us look at the data pertaining to each of these effects.

Production of blisters. It has been claimed that blisters appear in some subjects who have been exposed to a trance induction procedure, who are highly responsive to test suggestions, and who have been given suggestions that a blister will form at a specified place on the skin. This widely publicized claim seems to lead to the conclusion that the subjects must be in a unique or special state when they manifest such a unique effect. However, a close look at the data indicates that the so-called "blister" phenomenon is far more complex than it first appears, and that there is no need to postulate a special state (hypnotic trance) in order to explain it:

1. During the past one hundred years, many researchers suggested to their hypnotic trance subjects that a blister would form on the skin. With very few exceptions, no skin changes whatsoever were observed (Barber, 1969b, Ch. 9).

2. About twelve researchers reported that suggestions for blister formation gave rise to cutaneous alterations; some of these alterations were

labeled "blisters." These reports should be viewed within a broader context by noting the following points, which have been delineated in a series or reviews (Barber, 1961b; Gorton, 1949; Pattie, 1941; Paul, 1963; Sarbin, 1956; Weitzenhoffer, 1953).

3. With very few exceptions, the positive findings were obtained between 1886 and 1927, prior to the advent of rigorous experimental controls in this area.

4. With very few exceptions, careful controls were not used to exclude the possibility that the subject may have deliberately injured his skin in attempting to comply with the suggestion for blister formation. Furthermore, one subject attempted to injure his skin by pricking it with a needle (Schrenck-Notzing, 1896), another vigorously rubbed snow on the area where the blister was supposed to form (Ullman, 1947), and another rubbed poison ivy leaves where the skin change was supposed to appear (Wolberg, 1948, p. 49).

5. With very few if any exceptions, the positive results were obtained with patients who were either suffering from various skin ailments (neurodermatitis, hysterical ecchymoses, wheals, or neurotic skin gangrene) or who were diagnosed as hysterics (hysterical blindness, hysterical aphonia, hysteroepilepsy, or hysterical hemianesthesia).

6. With one or two exceptions, it is not clear from the studies reporting positive results whether the skin alterations were blisters, wheals, or dermographism. A study that carefully considered each of these possibilities (Borelli, 1953) showed conclusively that the skin change that was produced by suggestion was dermographism, not a blister. It should be emphasized that dermographism (wheal formation in response to a single moderately strong stroking of the skin) is more common than is usually supposed. For instance, in testing eighty-four young men, T. Lewis (1927) found a clear-cut swelling of the skin as a reaction to a single firm stroke in twenty-five percent and in five percent a full wheal developed. Furthermore, as Graham and Wolf (1950) have documented, some normal individuals show wheal formation at sites of mild pressure stimulation, such as around a collar, a belt, or a wristwatch strap. These data are important in understanding the positive results obtained in the studies mentioned above because in all but one of the successful studies tactual stimulation was used to localize the place where the blister was to form, and in many of these studies the stimulus object was a small piece of metal.

7. All of the studies in this area lack a control group; suggestions for blister formation were never given to subjects who were not exposed to a trance induction procedure. It was always assumed, without apparent justification, that a hypnotic trance state is necessary in order to produce blisters by suggestions.

Further studies are needed to determine whether suggestions for blister formation are effective in producing blisters in any present day subjects under "hypnotic trance" conditions and also under "waking control" conditions. I will venture three hypnotheses: under both the hypnotic trance and the waking control conditions, fewer than one percent of the subjects will show any skin alterations, the alternations will resemble dermographism or wheals rather than blisters, and the few subjects who show a cutaneous effect when given suggestions for blister formation will normally manifest marked dermographism when appropriately stimulated on the skin.

Removal of warts. Sinclair-Gieben and Chalmers (1959) and Ullman and Dudek (1960) reported that suggestions given to hypnotic trance subjects were effective in some instances in removing warts. However, although suggestions for wart removal appear to be effective at times when they are given under "hypnotic trance" conditions, they also appear to be effective at times when they are given under "waking control" conditions. A series of investigators (Bloch, 1927; Dudek, 1967; Sulzberger & Wolf, 1934; Vollmer, 1946) found that warts at times disappear when they are simply painted with an innocuous dye and the "awake" subjects are told that the placebo-dye is a powerful wart-curing drug. Furthermore, in those instances in which suggestions for wart disappearance were effective, there is evidence that the warts may have been of the labile type, that is, of the type that would have disappeared spontaneously within a rather short period of time if no suggestions had been given (Clarke, 1965; Memmesheimer & Eisenlohr, 1931; Stankler, 1967).

Analgesia. From time to time accounts are published of hypnotic trance subjects who underwent minor or major surgery without analgesic or anesthetic drugs. These accounts imply that a unique or special state, a hypnotic trance state, is necessary in order to undergo surgery without drugs. However, the available data do not support this implication:

1. Most "hypnotic trance" subjects who undergo minor or major surgery without drugs show signs of pain. Some subjects cry, others show a "hideous expression of suppressed agony" (Barber, 1970a, p.228) and, in many instances, chemical analgesics or anesthetics have to be administered in order to complete the surgery (Anderson, 1957; Barber, 1970a, Ch. 5; Braid, 1847; Butler, 1954).

2. A few "hypnotic trance" subjects manifested very little or no pain when they underwent minor or major surgery without drugs. However, a few subjects who were not exposed to a trance induction procedure also manifested little or no pain when they underwent minor or major surgery without drugs (Chertok, 1959, pp. 3-4; Elliotson, 1843, pp. 15-17; Esdaile, 1850, pp. 214-15; Haim, 1908; Leriche, 1939, pp. 55-56; Lewis, 1942,

p. 10; Mackenzie, 1909; Mitchell, 1907; Propping, 1909; Sampimon & Woodruff, 1946; Trent, 1946).

3. The pain involved in most surgical procedures is highly overestimated. Although the skin is sensitive, most of the muscles and organs of the body are relatively insensitive to pain. More precisely, the skin is sensitive to a knife cut, but the skilled surgeon cuts through the skin smoothly and quickly and the underlying muscles and internal organs are relatively insensitive. Lewis (1942) has documented the fact that the muscles, the internal organs, and most other parts of the body (with the exception of the skin) are insensitive to incision (although they may be sensitive to other stimuli such as pulling or stretching). For instance, Lewis (1942) has noted the following:

> [The subcutaneous tissue] gives rise to little pain when injured by...incision.... [The pain in somatic muscles] is slight when elicited by...knife cut....Compact bone may be bored without pain....The articular surfaces [of joints]...are insensitive....Puncture of a vein is nearly always painless....The dura mater....pia mater and the cortex are generally regarded as insensitive...The lung and visceral pleura are insensitive...The surface of the heart is found to be insensitive...[Surgeons] have often and painlessly removed pieces of the oesophageal wall of the conscious subject for histological examination....It is common knowledge that the solid organs such as liver, spleen, and kidney, can be tightly gripped, cut, or even burnt without the subject's being conscious of it....All parts of the wall of [the stomach] may be cut, burnt, stretched or clamped without pain...cutting [the jejunum and ileum] ...is accomplished painlessly....The insensitiveness of [the colon] attracted early attention...Cutting [the great omentum] is accomplished painlessly....The body of the uterus can be cut....painlessly. (pp. 2-8)

In brief, there are rare cases of individuals who were said to be in a "hypnotic trance state" and also individuals who were said to be "awake" who underwent minor or major surgery without drugs and without manifesting much pain. These cases seem much more dramatic than they actually are because it is assumed that all parts of the body are as sensitive to pain as the skin. The truth of the matter is that although the skin is sensitive, most tissues and organs in the body are insensitive to the surgeon's scalpel. Furthermore, there is no reason to postulate a special state of consciousness in order to explain the ability to undergo noxious stimulation of the skin without manifesting distress or pain. The following points are relevent:

1. Pain is at times markedly reduced in awake subjects when placebos are administered with the implication (or the explicit statement) that they are pain-relieving drugs (Barber, 1959b; Beecher, 1959).

2. Instructions or suggestions intended to produce relaxation are at times effective with "hypnotic trance" subjects and also with "awake" subjects in reducing subjective and physiological responses to noxious stimuli (Barber & Calverley, 1969a; Jacobson, 1938, 1954; Hilgard et al., 1967).

3. Responsiveness to painful stimulation is reduced in some "hypnotic

trance" subjects and also in some "awake" subjects by instructions or suggestions intended to alleviate anxiety and anticipation or fear of pain (Hill et al., 1952a, 1952b; Kornetsky, 1954; Shor, 1967).

4. Suggestions of anesthesia or analgesia are effective in reducing subjectively reported pain in a substantial proportion of subjects who have been randomly assigned to a trance induction treatment and in an equal proportion of subjects who have been randomly assigned to a control treatment (Barber & Calverley, 1969a; Spanos, Barber, & Lang, 1969).

5. Subjectively reported pain is reduced in awake subjects when they are distracted during exposure to noxious stimulation (Kanfer & Goldfoot, 1966). Furthermore, both subjectively reported pain and physiological responses to noxious stimulation can be reduced by instructing control subjects to try to think about and to imagine vividly a pleasant situation during the stimulation (Barber & Hahn, 1962). Also, pain is reduced to an equal degree in "waking control" subjects and in "hypnotic trance" subjects when both groups of subjects are distracted during the pain-producing stimulation by having them listen to and try to remember the details of an interesting story presented on a tape recording (Barber & Calverley, 1969a). These results are consistent with the conclusion reached many years ago by Liébeault (1885) that, if and when suggestions are effective in reducing pain in "hypnotic trance" subjects, the mediating processes can be conceptualized as focusing attention on thoughts or ideas other than those concerning pain. These results are also consistent with the conclusion drawn by August (1961) from a large-scale investigation with one thousand patients, that trance induction procedures and suggestions are effective in reducing pain during childbirth to the extent that they direct "attention away from pain responses toward pleasant ideas" (p. 62).

Age regression. Several studies pertaining to hypnotic age regression seem to support the contention that subjects who are highly responsive to test suggestions are in a "special state." These studies, by Gidro-Frank and Bowersbuch (1948), Parrish, Lundy, and Leibowitz (1969), and True (1949), appeared to indicate that, when given suggestions to regress to infancy or childhood, "hypnotic trance" subjects show an amazing reinstatement of a physiological reflex which is characteristic of infancy, an amazing recall of events that occurred during childhood, and an amazing childlike performance on objective tests. A close look at these studies, however, fails to support the special state paradigm. Let us look at each of them in turn.

Gidro-Frank and Bowersbuch (1948) reported that when three selected "hypnotic trance" subjects were given suggestions to regress to four months of age, they showed a Babinski toe response, that is, stimulation of the sole of the foot produced dorsiflexion of the large toe and fanning of the other toes. Several neurology texts stated that the Babinski toe response is present in infants up to four months of age but is not present after six months of age. Consequently, it appeared that Gidro-Frank and Bowersbuch had demonstrated that suggestions to regress to early infancy, when given to "hypnotic trance" subjects, reinstate a long dormant physiological reflex that is characteristic of early infancy. However, the neurology texts were mistaken. Researchers who have actually looked at infants have consistently observed that the typical response of the four month old infant to stimulation of the sole of the foot is *not* the Babinski response, but rather sudden withdrawal of the limb with variability in response of the toes. In fact, the Babinski toe response is very rarely if ever observed in early infancy (Burr, 1921; McGraw, 1941; Wolff, 1930). Since the Babinski response is rarely if ever observed in infants, the question at issue is not how suggestions given under "hypnotic trance" revive an infantile reflex, but why these "hypnotic trance" subjects showed a Babinski toe response (not characteristic of early infancy) when they were given suggestions to regress to early infancy. There are at least two explanations of these weird results: the subjects may have realized what response the experimenters were looking for and may have voluntarily performed that response (Barber, 1962a; Sarbin, 1956); or, since the Babinski toe response is at times observed during profound relaxation, the subjects may have become very relaxed when they assumed the "sleeping posture of the infant" (Barber, 1970a, Ch. 6).

   True (1949) reported that most adult subjects who were placed in hypnotic trance, and who were given suggestions to regress to ages eleven, seven, and four, recalled the exact day of the week on which their birthday and Christmas fell in the particular year involved. Six subsequent studies failed to confirm these results (Barber, 1961a; Best & Michaels, 1954; S. Fisher, 1962; Leonard, 1963; Mesel & Ledford, 1959; Reiff & Scheerer, 1959). However, in a series of attempts I made to validate True's results, one "hypnotic trance" subject, who received suggestions to regress to *each* of her previous birthdays, correctly named the day of the week on which *each* of her previous birthdays fell. After the hypnotic trance session, the subject testified that she was able to perform this remarkable feat simply because she knew that the days of the week go backward one day each year and two on leap years and, knowing the day of the week on which her birthday fell in a recent year, she could easily and quickly (within twenty seconds) figure out the day of the week it must have fallen in an earlier year (compare Sutcliffe, 1960; Yates, 1960). In brief, although True's study seemed to support the contention that the "hypnotic trance state" gives rise to nearly miraculous feats of memory, subsequent studies strongly suggest that "hypnotic trance" is irrelevant in performing this feat and that the relevant factor is prior knowledge of the fact that the days of the week go backward one day each year and two on leap years.

   Parrish, Lundy, and Leibowitz (1969) reported that highly suggestible subjects, who were exposed to a trance induction procedure and given suggestions to regress to ages nine and five, were affected by two optical illusions (the Ponzo and Poggendorff illusions) in a similar manner as children who are actually nine and five years of age. Since there is no reason to believe that adults can figure out how children are affected by these complex illusions, the results presented by Parrish et al. could be interpreted as indicating that the highly suggestible subjects were in an unusual state (hypnotic trance) when they manifested such an unusual effect.

However, the results of the study could not be confirmed in two subsequent investigations. Ascher and Barber (1968) closely replicated the experimental procedures used by Parish et al., that is, subjects who were highly responsive to test suggestions were exposed to a trance induction procedure and were given suggestions that they were nine and five years of age. Under the regressed condition, the subjects' performance on the Ponzo and Poggendorff illusions was virtually the·same as their adult performance and not at all similar to the performance of children who are actually nine and five. Spanos and Barber (1969) also replicated the experimental procedures of Parrish, Lundy, and Leibowitz, but used only exceptionally suggestible subjects who had previously passed a large number of very difficult test suggestions. When placed in "hypnotic trance" and given suggestions to regress to ages nine and five, these exceptionally responsive subjects performed on the Ponzo and Poggendorff illusions in practically the same manner as their adult performance and their performance did not remotely resemble that of children of ages nine and five.

In brief, the traditional (special state) paradigm seemed to be supported by several studies that reported very amazing effects produced in "hypnotic trance" subjects by suggestions to regress to an earlier chronological age. However, a close look at the data fails to support the traditional paradigm. The notion of a special state is also not supported by the following considerations pertaining to suggested regression:

1. Practically all investigations in this area found that "hypnotic trance" subjects who were given suggestions to regress to a specified age performed at a level superior to the level actually found at the specified age; for example, when regressed to age six, "hypnotic trance" subjects typically performed at a nine year old level (Barber, 1969b, Ch. 11).

2. "Hypnotic trance" subjects who tend to act in a childlike way when given suggestions to regress to childhood also give an equally convincing portrayal of an older person or of a senile individual when given suggestions to progress to the age of seventy, eighty, or ninety (Kline, 1951; Rubenstein & Newman, 1954). Also, some "hypnotic trance" subjects who tend to give a childlike performance when regressed to childhood also give a convincing performance when regressed to prenatal life in the womb or to a time that preceded their present life (the "Bridey Murphy" phenomenon)

(Bernstein, 1956; Kelsey, 1953).

3. When subjects who have been randomly assigned to an "awake" group or to a "trance" group are given suggestions to go back or to regress to an earlier chronological age, the same proportion of subjects in both groups report that they imagined, felt, or believed that they had returned to the earlier age (Barber & Calverly, 1966a).

4. Although various theoretical formulations might possibly account for the foregoing data, one formulation that can parsimoniously explain the results is as follows: When it is suggested to "hypnotic trance" subjects or to "awake" subjects that they are in the past (or in the future), (a) some "hypnotic trance" subjects and also some "awake" subjects try to the best of their ability to think about continuously and to imagine vividly that they are in the past (or in the future), (b) some of the "hypnotic trance" subjects and also some of the "awake" subjects succeed in focusing imaginatively on the past (or future), and (c) when thinking about and vividly imagining themselves in an earlier time (or in a future time), some subjects in both groups feel as if they are in the past (or in the future) and tend to behave to a certain limited degree as if they are in the past (or future).

Hallucinations. Two studies (Brady & Levitt, 1966; Underwood, 1960) indicate that highly suggestible subjects, who were first exposed to a trance induction procedure and then given suggestions to hallucinate, behaved as if they actually perceived the suggested (hallucinated) object. These data were interpreted as lending support to the notion that the subjects must have been in a unique state (hypnotic trance) in order to manifest such unique behavior. However, a closer look at the data does not support the special state notion.

Brady and Levitt (1966) attempted to ascertain whether a suggested visual hallucination of an optokinetic drum (a revolving drum with alternate black and white vertical stripes) gives rise to involuntary nystagmoidlike eye movements that resemble those found when an individual actually perceives an optokinetic drum. When highly suggestible subjects were exposed to a trance induction procedure and given suggestions to hallucinate the optokinetic drum, a small percentage behaved as if they were actually perceiving the drum—manifesting nystagmoidlike eye movements. However, a subsequent study by Hahn and Barber (1966) showed that an equally small percentage of unselected subjects under a waking control condition manifested nystagmoidlike eye movements when they were simply instructed to imagine vividly the optokinetic drum. Also, Reich (1970) recently presented data indicating that some subjects are able to produce nystagmus "through conscious, voluntary effort while awake."

To ascertain whether suggested visual hallucinations produce objective consequences that resemble those produced by actual visual stimulation,

Underwood (1960) used two optical illusions in which a series of lines distorts a geometric figure. The subjects were shown the geometric figures without the distorting lines and were given suggestions to hallucinate the lines. Underwood found that when given the suggestions to hallucinate the lines, a small percentage of selected "hypnotic trance" subjects reported a few effects that tended to resemble those actually produced by the optical illusions. However, Sarbin and Andersen (1963) found that an equally small percentage of unselected waking control subjects reported the same effects when they were simply instructed to imagine the lines vividly.

In brief, suggestions to hallucinate an object, given to subjects who are said to be in hypnotic trance, at times gives rise to some objective effects that tend to resemble those found when a person actually perceives the object. However, the same objective effects are produced when waking subjects are simply asked to imagine the object vividly.

Suggested deafness. Erickson (1938a, 1938b) concluded from experimental studies that a condition indistinguishable from actual deafness can be produced by suggestions, provided that the suggestions are given to highly responsive subjects who have been exposed to a trance induction procedure. Erickson's data seemed to support the traditional notion of a special state (hypnotic trance); that is, it appeared that in order to manifest such a special or unique effect (deafness produced by suggestions), the subjects must have been in a special state. Let us look at the data presented by Erickson.

Erickson (1938a) administered suggestions of total deafness to thirty subjects who were preselected as highly suggestible and who had been exposed to a trance induction procedure. Of the thirty subjects, twenty-four (eighty percent) did not show signs of deafness. However, Erickson judged the remaining six subjects to have become deaf as indicated by such signs as "failure to show any response to deliberately embarrassing remarks," "failure to raise voice when reading aloud while an irrelevant continuous extraneous noise becomes increasingly disturbing," and failure to react to unexpected sounds. Erickson concluded from these and similar data that "there was produced a condition not distinguishable from neurological deafness by any of the ordinarily competent tests employed" (p. 149).

Erickson's conclusion is not clearly supported by his data. For instance, failure to react to unexpected sounds does not demonstrate that the sounds were not heard. In a study carried out by Dynes (1932), three selected suggestible subjects, who were judged to be in hypnotic trance and who received suggestions of deafness, did not become noticeably startled when a pistol was fired unexpectedly; however, each subject testified postexperimentally that he had heard the pistol shot. Similarly, lack of response to a disturbing noise or to embarrassing remarks does not demonstrate that the subject is deaf, since these responses can be rather easily inhibited voluntarily.

In a supplementary study, Erickson (1938b) found that two of the "hypnotic trance" subjects who appeared to be deaf did not manifest a hand-withdrawal response that had been conditioned to a sound. He interpreted this outcome as demonstrating that the subjects were "unconscious of the sound." The interpretation is not valid; many studies have demonstrated that subjects can voluntarily inhibit hand-withdrawal responses that have been conditioned to a sound (Hamel, 1919; Hilgard & Marquis, 1940, pp. 269-70).

In five more recent studies, the technique of delayed auditory feedback was used to evaluate suggested deafness produced under "hypnotic trance" (Barber & Calverley, 1964c; Kline, Guze, & Haggerty, 1954; Kramer & Tucker, 1967; Scheibe, Gray, & Keim, 1968; Sutcliffe, 1961). Each of the five experiments showed that "hypnotic trance" subjects who have received suggestions of deafness are affected by auditory stimuli in essentially the same way as any normal person who hears perfectly well; that is, when exposed to delayed auditory feedback, the "hypnotic deaf" subject and the person with normal hearing (but not the person who is actually deaf) typically stutters, mispronounces words, and speaks more loudly and more slowly. One of these studies (Barber & Calverley, 1964c) also showed that suggestions of deafness are at least as effective with "waking" control subjects as with "hypnotic trance" subjects in eliciting subjective reports of deafness; however, both the "waking" control subjects and the "hypnotic trance" subjects who accepted the suggestions of deafness responded to the delayed auditory feedback in the same way as individuals who hear normally.

Although both "hypnotic trance" subjects and "waking" control subjects who have received suggestions of deafness may be trying not to hear, they simply do not succeed in blocking out sounds. The fact that the subjects can hear is often obvious. After suggesting deafness to "hypnotic trance" subjects, the hypnotists may ask, "Can you hear me?" A few subjects reply, "No, I can't," thus admitting that they can hear. The other subjects, however, do not reply and appear to be deaf. How does the hypnotist remove the deafness? He typically states, "Now you can hear again," and since the subjects now respond normally it is obvious that they could hear all along.

OBSERVABLE TRANCELIKE CHARACTERISTICS

The special state paradigm also seems to be supported by the fact that a substantial proportion of subjects who are highly responsive to test suggestions actually appear to be in a trance. Numerous investigators (Erickson, Hershman, & Secter, 1961, pp. 55-58; Gill & Brenman, 1959, pp. 38-39; Pattie, 1956a, p. 21; Weitzenhoffer, 1957a, pp. 211-12) have pointed out that subjects who are highly responsive to test suggestions often show signs of trance such as a blank stare, a rigid facial expression, a lack of spontaneity, a limp posture, psychomotor retardation, disinclination to talk, lack of humor, and literal-mindedness. Although these observations, at first glance, seem to support the assumption that a special state (hypnotic trance) underlies high responsiveness to test suggestions, a closer look at the data fails to support the assumption:

1. When subjects who are highly responsive to test suggestions manifest trancelike characteristics, the characteristics have been explicitly or implicitly suggested. That is, the experimenter has suggested to the subject that he is becoming relaxed, drowsy, sleepy, and is entering a hypnotic trance state. These suggestions imply to subjects that they should become passive or lethargic, behave in a trancelike manner, move or respond slowly (show psychomotor retardation), and not look actively around the room (Barber & Calverley, 1969b).

2. Since the trancelike characteristics have been suggested, they can also be removed by suggestions. For instance, several years ago, I carried out the following informal study with eight suggestible subjects. The subjects were first exposed to a trance induction procedure, comprised of repeated suggestions of relaxation, drowsiness, sleep, and deep hypnosis. All subjects appeared to be in a hypnotic trance—manifesting a lack of spontaneity, psychomotor retardation, and passivity or lethargy—and also responded to test suggestions for arm heaviness, arm levitation, inability to unclasp hands, and thirst hallucination. Next, the subjects were told to become awake and alert, to stop acting as if they were in a hypnotic trance, but to continue to remain responsive to test suggestions. The subjects remained highly responsive to test suggestions for inability to say their name, body immobility, and selective amnesia, but they no longer showed signs of trance; in fact, they appeared to be just as awake as subjects who were not responsive to test suggestions.

3. Some subjects who have been exposed to a trance induction procedure manifest a high level of responsiveness to test suggestions but they do not show signs or characteristics of hypnotic trance (Erickson, 1962).

4. Some subjects who have been exposed to a trance induction procedure and who show signs of hypnotic trance are not responsive to test suggestions for analgesia, age regression, amnesia, and so on (Barber, 1957, 1963; Barber & Calverley, 1969b).

5. As pointed out previously in this chapter, some subjects who have not been exposed to a trance induction procedure manifest a high level of response to test suggestions without showing signs of hypnotic trance (Barber, 1969b; Klopp, 1961). Stated otherwise, when no attempt is made to induce a hypnotic trance, and especially when subjects are not asked to close their eyes, a substantial proportion of subjects experience such

suggested effects as limb rigidity, analgesia, age regression, hallucination, amnesia and so on, without manifesting signs of hypnotic trance such as blank stare, rigid facial expression, and passivity.

In brief, trancelike characteristics on the part of the subject appear to be artifacts that the experimenter can put into the suggestive situation and can also take out of the situation, and they certainly are not necessary (and may be extraneous) for high response to test suggestions.

SUBJECTS' TESTIMONY OF BEING IN HYPNOTIC TRANCE

At first glance, the traditional viewpoint seems to be supported by the fact that some subjects who are highly responsive to test suggestions testify that they are hypnotized or are in a hypnotic trance. A close look at subjects' testimony, however, fails to support the traditional notion that a state discontinuous with ordinary states of consciousness underlies high responsiveness to test suggestion for limb rigidity, analgesia, hallucination, and so on:

1. As stated previously in this chapter, some subjects manifest a high level of response to test suggestion when no attempt is made to hypnotize them. With few exceptions, these highly responsive subjects testify that they are *not* in a hypnotic trance. The remaining few testify that they must be hypnotized, even though they do not feel that they are hypnotized, because they actually experience those things that are suggested. These subjects are not using the term "hypnotized" to refer to a state that is basically different from ordinary states of consciousness; they are using the term "hypnotized" synonymously with the phrase "high responsiveness to suggestions."

2. A substantial proportion of subjects who are given suggestions to enter a hypnotic trance state and who are highly responsive to test suggestions state that they are not sure if they are hypnotized. The proportion of highly responsive subjects unable to state whether they are in a hypnotic trance varies from twenty-five percent to sixty-seven percent depending on the wording of the questions submitted to them in order to elicit their statements (Barber, Dalal, & Calverley, 1968; Hilgard, 1965b, p. 12).

3. As implied in the preceding paragraph, subjects' testimony pertaining to whether they think they are in hypnotic trance depends, in part, on the wording and tone of the questions that are used to elicit their testimony (Barber, Dalal, & Calverley, 1968).

4. Subjects' testimony pertaining to whether they are in hypnotic trance depends, in part, on their preconceptions of what hypnotic trance is supposed to be. Subjects differing in preconceptions give different testimony even when they are equally responsive to test suggestions. For instance, one highly responsive subject believes hypnotic trance is a state of relaxation,

whereas another highly responsive subject believes that a hypnotized person experiences spontaneous amnesia. When both of these highly responsive subjects become relaxed during the session and both fail to experience spontaneous amnesia, the former testifies that he was hypnotized or was in a hypnotic trance, whereas the latter testifies that he was not in a hypnotic trance.

5. Subjects' testimony pertaining to whether they are hypnotized is also dependent, in part, on subtle situational variables such as whether the experimenter states or implies that he believes they are hypnotized (Barber, Dalal, & Calverley, 1968).

6. Subjects who state that they are in a hypnotic trance are not necessarily saying that they are in a state that is clearly different from ordinary states of consciousness. On the contrary, they often appear to be saying no more and no less than that they are ready and willing to respond to test suggestions. Gill and Brenman (1959) have documented this important point:

> First, we would induce hypnosis in someone previously established as a "good" subject; then we would ask him how he knew he was in hypnosis. He might reply that he felt relaxed. Now we would suggest that the relaxation would disappear *but he would remain in hypnosis.* Then we would ask again how he knew he was in hypnosis. He might say because his arm "feels numb"—so again, we would suggest the disappearance of this sensation. We continued in this way until finally we obtained the reply, "I know I am in hypnosis because I *know* I will do what you tell me." This was repeated with several subjects, with the same results. (p. 36)

The subject's final assertation—"I *know* I will do what you tell me"— does *not* support the traditional paradigm, which assumes that the subject who shows high response to test suggestions is in a state fundamentally different from the waking state. However, it is in line with and can be deduced from the alternative paradigm, which views the subject who is highly responsive to test suggestions as being as awake and as normal as the member of the audience who is ready and willing to have a wide variety of experiences as he listens to the communications from the stage.

DIFFICULTY OR DELAY IN "COMING OUT OF HYPNOTIC TRANCE"

At first glance, the special state (hypnotic trance) paradigm also seems to be supported by the following two sets of interrelated data. On rare occasions, subjects who are highly responsive to test suggestions do not open their eyes immediately when told to wake up—they seem to remain in a hypnotic trance. When the experimenter leaves the room without having told the subject to wake up, subjects who are said to be in a hypnotic trance remain sitting passively with eyes closed for a longer period of time than simulating subjects who have been asked to act as if they are in a hypnotic trance. Let us look at these two sets of data in turn.

Refusing to "wake up." When told that the experiment is over, practically all subjects who have been exposed to a trance induction procedure open their eyes and converse normally (Kroger, 1970, p. 172). However, in very rare instances, subjects who have been exposed to a trance induction procedure do not open their eyes when told to wake up. They remain sitting passively with eyes closed and it appears, from the traditional special state viewpoint, that they are having difficulty making the transition from the hypnotic trance state to the waking state. The empirical evidence, however, does not support the special state viewpoint. Williams (1953) and Weitzenhoffer (1957a, pp. 226-29) have summarized data that cogently indicate that these few subjects (who do not open their eyes when told to wake up) have some special reason or motive for refusing to open their eyes; they either (a) have been given a suggestion to carry out postexperimentally that they do not want to carry out, (b) are deliberately resisting the hypnotist, (c) are testing the hypnotist's ability to control them, (d) are manifesting spite toward the hypnotist, or (e) are attempting to frighten the hypnotist by refusing to "wake up."

If a "hypnotic trance" subject does not open his eyes when told to wake up, Weitzenhoffer (1957a) recommends the following: "The simplest way of proceeding is to ask him why he does not wake up. Most subjects are quite willing to explain why. If the subject is uncooperative you may have to request an answer more forcefully. Usually the answer tells the hypnotist what to do." Weitzenhoffer adds that if the subject remains intractable, you "simply say to him, in a final tone, 'Very well then, if you will not wake up I will just have to leave you as you are.' You then ignore the subject entirely and go on to other things" (p. 228). Since the subject now cannot accomplish his purpose by remaining passive with his eyes closed, he soon opens his eyes.

Remaining in hypnotic trance when the experimenter leaves the room. Orne and Evans (1966) and Evans (1966a) contended that it is possible to test the hypnothesis that a trance induction procedure leads to a qualitative change in the organism in highly suggestible subjects. They reasoned as follows: If the highly suggestible subject actually enters a special state (a hypnotic trance) when he is exposed to a trance induction procedure, and if the hypnotist leaves the room without telling the subject to awaken, then the subject should slowly bring himself out of the special state. An active effort would be required for the subject to initiate the volitional act of arousal and, consequently, the voluntary termination of the hypnotic trance would not be immediate—it would take a period of time.

Two experiments were conducted with the aim of testing this hypothesis (Orne & Evans, 1966; Evans, 1966a). Both experiments utilized two groups of pretested subjects. Subjects in one group were highly responsive to test suggestions (suggestible subjects) and those in the other group were very unresponsive (nonsuggestible subjects). Prior to the formal experiments, the nonsuggestible subjects were told, by a person other than the experimenter, to try to simulate hypnosis—that is, they were told to try to fool the experimenter by faking or acting as if they entered a hypnotic trance. The suggestible subjects were not told to simulate and thus were categorized as real hypnotic subjects. During the experimental sessions, both the suggestible (real) and the nonsuggestible (simulating) subjects received a trance induction procedure by means of a tape recording. The suggestible (real) subjects presumably entered a hypnotic trance state and the nonsuggestible (simulating) subjects presumably did not enter a hypnotic trance state even though they acted as if they had entered such a state. In the middle of the experimental session, a switch was purposively thrown in another room, thus stopping the tape recording with a marked slur. The experimenter then left the room, ostensibly to repair the fuse that had stopped the tape recording. Both the real subjects and the simulating subjects were then observed to determine how long they would remain sitting quietly with eyes closed.

In both the first and second experiments, the real hypnotic subjects, who were presumably in a hypnotic trance state, did not open their eyes immediately; they remained sitting quietly with eyes closed for quite some time after the experimenter had left the room. In the first experiment, the simulating subjects also remained sitting quietly with eyes closed; in fact, they did not open their eyes at all until the experimenter again entered the room about one-half hour later. In the second experiment, the simulators opened their eyes soon after the experimenter left the room. The inconsistent behavior of the simulators in the first and second experiment was due to the following: In the first experiment there was a conspicuous one-way mirror in the room and the subjects knew that they were being observed. In the second experiment, the one-way mirror was completely blocked by a blackboard and the subjects believed that they were not being observed. (They were observed, however, through a peephole that they were not aware of.) Since, in both experiments, the real hypnotic subjects, who were presumably in a hypnotic trance state, did not open their eyes for quite some time after the experimenter left the room, whereas the simulators opened their eyes when they believed they were not being observed but did not open their eyes when they believed they were being observed, Evans (1966a) concluded that the experiments had demonstrated that the highly suggestible (real) subjects were actually in a special state of consciousness (hypnotic trance).

Evans's (1966a) conclusion, of course, does not clearly follow from the data he presented. The experiments are open to another interpretation, namely, that the differences between the two groups were due to the fact that subjects in one of the groups (but not the other) had been instructed to try to fool the experimenter and to make him believe that they were hyp-notized. When subjects are instructed to try to fool the experimenter into believing they are hypnotized, it can be expected that, after the ex-perimenter leaves the room, they will act as if they are hypnotized if they believe they are being observed by the experimenter or by his surrogates, and they will not act as if they are hypnotized if they believe they are not be-ing observed. The appropriate comparison is not between subjects who are asked to fool the experimenter and those who are not asked to fool the ex-perimenter. The appropriate comparison is between a group of suggestible subjects who are exposed to a trance induction procedure and who are presumably in a hypnotic trance state, and a group of control subjects who are simply told to relax. It can be hypothesized, from the viewpoint that does not postulate a special state, that control subjects who are simply told to relax will remain sitting quietly with eyes closed as long as the subjects who are presumably in a hypnotic trance. This hypothesis has been tested experimentally by Dorcus, Brintnall, and Case (1941). Let us now look at their experiment.

The experimental group was comprised of twenty subjects who had previously demonstrated that they were highly responsive to test sugges-tions. After these subjects had been exposed to a trance induction pro-cedure, an assistant came into the room and said to the experimenter, "You are wanted on the telephone about an appointment downtown." The ex-perimenter replied to the assistant that he had forgotten an appointment and that he would be gone for the remainder of the day. Both the ex-perimenter and the assistant then left the room hastily. The subject was then kept under observation through a peephole in an adjacent room. Twenty-five subjects in a control group were asked to simply close their eyes and relax and then were told that, after a few minutes of relaxation, they would be given further instructions. During the period of relaxation, the same con-versation about the appointment was carried out. After the experimenter left the room, the suggestible subjects, who had been exposed to the trance induction procedure and who were presumably in a hypnotic trance state, remained passive with eyes closed for a mean time of twenty-eight minutes. The control group, which had been simply told to relax, remained passive with eyes closed for an insignificantly shorter average period of twenty-three minutes.[5] Postexperimental interviews showed that the behavior of both the "hypnotic trance" subjects and the "relaxation control" subjects was influenced by the same factors; that is, some subjects in both groups thought they should wait for the experimenter to return, others thought the experiment was over, and others had to leave because they had previous

5. It should be noted in the Dorcus et al. experiment, both the "hypnotic trance" subjects and the "relaxation control" subjects remained passive with eyes closed about as long as the real hypnotic subjects in the Evans (1966) experiment.

appointments. Clearly, this study does not support the contention that suggestible subjects who have been exposed to a trance induction procedure have entered a special state that is qualitatively different from the ordinary state of consciousness present when people relax.

The foregoing experiments by Orne and Evans (1966), Evans (1966a), and Dorcus, Brintnall, and Case (1941) indicate that subjects who are asked to simulate hypnosis may perform differently from "hypnotic trance" subjects and also from control subjects (who are not asked to simulate), and that control subjects may behave in the same way as "hypnotic trance" subjects. These results suggest extreme caution in interpreting studies that compared simulating subjects with "real hypnotic subjects." The simulators are in a special situation—they are trying to fool the experimenter. Also, when given their original instructions, the simulators are told not to let themselves experience any of the suggested effects. Consequently, if a control group is not used, differences in performance between simulators and hypnotic subjects can be easily misinterpreted as indicating that the hypnotic subjects behaved unusually, when it was actually the simulators who behaved unusually. Other studies that found differences in the performance of simulating subjects and real hypnotic subjects, such as in the performance of posthypnotic behavior outside of the experimental setting (Orne, Sheehan, & Evans, 1968; Sheehan & Orne, 1968) and in the performance of "source amnesia" (Evans, 1968, p. 483), need to be redone with the addition of a control group that is not asked to simulate.

SPONTANEOUS AMNESIA

Individuals usually have spontaneous amnesia for the events that occurred when they were in a special state of consciousness. For instance, upon awakening, individuals usually forget the dreams and other events that occurred when they were in a special state of sleep. With these considerations in mind, the traditional (special state) paradigm seems to be supported by the fact that, after "awakening," some highly suggestible subjects state spontaneously that they have forgotten what occurred during "hypnotic trance." However, a close look at the data fails to support the special state paradigm:

1. A rather large number of subjects has been assessed on responses to test suggestions for limb rigidity, analgesia, age regression, etc., without receiving either suggestions for relaxation, drowsiness, and sleep, or suggestions to forget what occurred. To the best of my knowledge, no subject has ever manifested spontaneous amnesia under these conditions. It thus appears that all subjects, including those highly responsive to test suggestions, remember the events perfectly well if they are not exposed to a trance induction procedure and are not told to forget (Barber & Calverley, 1966b).

Stated otherwise, high responsiveness to test suggestions is not necessarily associated with spontaneous amnesia.

2. No subject has ever forgotten the events occurring during the time he was highly responsive to test suggestions (or, in the traditional terminology, was in a hypnotic trance) if told during the session that he was expected to remember the events (Barber, 1962b; Orne, 1966a; Watkins, 1966).

3. If not told explicitly to forget, almost all subjects, including those who have been exposed to repeated suggestions of relaxation, drowsiness, and sleep, remember the events perfectly well. In other words, if amnesia is not explicitly suggested, very few subjects who are highly responsive to test suggestions (or who are judged from the traditional viewpoint to be in a hypnotic trance) manifest spontaneous amnesia (Barber & Calverly, 1966b; Hilgard, 1966).

4. When a trance induction procedure is administered but subjects are not told explicitly to forget what occurred, a very small number of subjects manifest apparent spontaneous amnesia. However, this apparent spontaneous amnesia can almost always be readily removed if the experimenter suggests or insists that the subject can remember. Furthermore, there are at least three reasons (specified in the following three paragraphs) why it is seriously questionable that the apparent anmesia in these rare cases is actually spontaneous (nonsuggested).

5. These rare subjects, who seem to manifest amnesia spontaneously, have received repeated suggestions of drowsiness and sleep. Since the subjects know that people usually forget the dreams and other events that occur during sleep, the direct suggestion to sleep may include the indirect suggestion to forget the events occurring during "sleep." In other words, the apparent amnesia in these instances may not be spontaneous but may be due to implicit suggestions for amnesia conveyed by the explicit suggestions to sleep.

6. In some of these infrequent cases of apparently spontaneous amnesia, the subjects received suggestions to sleep and suggestions for amnesia in a previous session, and may have generalized or extrapolated the suggestions to apply to the present session.

7. Subjects who manifest apparently spontaneous amnesia have received suggestions to enter a "hypnotic trance state." Since subjects generally believe that a hypnotic trance state is followed by spontaneous amnesia (Dorcus, Brintnall, & Case, 1941; London, 1961), they may say that they have forgotten in order to be good subjects and to meet what they believe are the expectations of the hypnotist.

To recapitulate, several compelling considerations indicate that the rare occurrence of apparently spontaneous amnesia that follows a trance induction procedure may not be spontaneous but, instead, may have been either explicitly or implicitly suggested in the present session or in a previous one.

Even if some of these instances of apparent amnesia were actually spontaneous (nonsuggested), they would not clearly support the notion that a special state underlies high responsiveness to test suggestions because when amnesia is not suggested, almost all subjects highly responsive to test suggestions and judged by traditional investigators to be in a hypnotic trance state assert after the session that they remember everything that occurred.

"TRANCE LOGIC"

Orne (1959) presented the following data from an informally conducted study: Subjects who were highly responsive to test suggestions and who were exposed to a trance induction procedure stated that (a) they could see a suggested (hallucinated) person in a chair and, at the same time, they could see the back of the chair through the (hallucinated) person, and (b) they could see the suggested (hallucinated) coexperimenter in the chair and, at the same time, they could see the (actual) coexperimenter in another part of the room (that is, they could "see" two images of the coexperimenter). Orne also stated that nonsuggestible subjects instructed to fool the experimenter into thinking that they were hypnotized (simulators) did not give these types of reports; for instance, although the simulators reported that they could see the suggested (hallucinated) coexperimenter in the chair, they refused to see the (actual) coexperimenter in another part of the room or they claimed that they could not recognize him. Orne (1959) concluded from these informal observations that the highly suggestible subjects who were exposed to a trance induction procedure and who were presumably in a hypnotic trance state manifested a special type of logic, "trance logic," defined as the "simultaneous perception and response to both hallucinations and reality without any apparent attempts to satisfy a need for logical consistency" (p. 295). Orne also concluded that trance logic was part of the essence of hypnosis.

At first glance, it appears that Orne's data support the special state paradigm; that is, since the highly suggestible subjects who had been exposed to a trance induction procedure manifested a special type of logic, they most likely were in a special state. However, since Orne derived his data from informal observations (not from a structured experiment), the "trance logic" contention can be viewed as suggesting a hypothesis that needs to be confirmed experimentally.

Johnson, Maher, and Barber (1972) carried out two experiments to test Orne's "trance logic" hypothesis. In the first experiment, seventy subjects were pretested on their responses to test suggestions. Following the pretest, ten subjects, who had shown high response to test suggestions, were given additional "hypnotic training." They received practice in responding to a wide variety of difficult test suggestions. These ten "trained" subjects were exposed to a trance induction procedure in the experimental session. The remaining sixty subjects were subdivided into high and low responders to test suggestions, and then equal numbers of high and low responders were randomly assigned to the following three groups with twenty subjects to each group: a group that was exposed to a trance induction procedure in the experimental session, a group of simulators who were first asked to fool the experimenter by acting as if they were hypnotized and then were exposed to a trance induction procedure, and a control group that was simply asked to imagine the various suggested effects.

All subjects were tested for "trance logic" according to the two criteria specified by Orne (1959). By the first criterion, trance logic is considered to be present if the subject states that he sees the suggested (hallucinated) person in the chair and, at the same time, sees the back of the chair through the hallucinated person. By this criterion, trance logic occurred equally often among the control subjects, the trained hypnotic subjects, and the untrained hypnotic subjects. The second criterion for trance logic refers to the subjects seeing both the hallucinated coexperimenter sitting in the chair and also the actual coexperimenter in another part of the room. By this criterion trance logic was found to occur equally often among all groups (controls, simulators, trained hypnotic subjects, and untrained hypnotic subjects). Also, in each of the three groups, the high suggestible subjects did not differ from the low suggestible on either criterion of trance logic.

The second experiment included two groups of subjects. One group was selected from a large population as the most responsive to test suggestions. These very suggestible subjects were exposed to a trance induction procedure during the experimental session (real hypnotic subjects). The second group also included only very suggestible subjects; this group was first asked to simulate hypnosis and then was exposed to a trance induction procedure (simulators). Trance logic was assessed in both groups, using the criteria specified by Orne (1959). With respect to the first criterion, sixty percent of the real hypnotic subjects and fifty percent of the simulators exhibited trance logic. With respect to the second criterion, sixty percent of the real hypnotic subjects and sixty-seven percent of the simulators exhibited trance logic.

In brief, the experiments by Johnson, Maher, and Barber (1972) demonstrated that trance logic is *not* unique to subjects who are highly responsive to test suggestions and who have received a trance induction procedure. Not only is "trance logic" not a characteristic of the presumed "hypnotic trance state," but it is also not found to a greater degree in "hypnotic trance" subjects than in simulating subjects, in highly suggestible subjects than in nonsuggestible subjects, or in subjects who are "trained in hypnosis" as opposed to those who are not trained. Johnson, Maher, & Barber concluded that, "Since trance logic was not found to be a discriminating characteristic of hypnotic subjects, investigators who seek the essence of hypnosis must now search elsewhere—that is, if there is an 'essence.' "

The Search for a Physiological Index of the Presumed "Hypnotic Trance State"

Since the organism is a psychophysiological unity, special states of consciousness or special states of the organism are expected to have some physiological concomitants that distinguish them from nonspecial states. Investigators who adhere to the traditional paradigm have been trying for many years to find a physiological concomitant or index of the presumed special state that they call "hypnotic trance." Not only have they failed to find any special physiological changes associated with the presumed special state, but they have also consistently found that physiological functioning during the postulated special state varies in the same way as in nonspecial or ordinary states. The relevant data are as follows:

1. Electroencephalographic (EEG) criteria indicate that subjects who are highly responsive to test suggestions (and who are judged by traditionalists as being in a hypnotic trance) do not show any special patterns on the EEG that might distinguish them from subjects who are relatively unresponsive to test suggestions (Barber, 1961b; Chertok & Kramarz, 1959). Similarly, subjects said to be in a hypnotic trance do not show special changes on any other known physiological measure that might serve as an index of the presumed special state.

2. The EEG of the person who is responding to test suggestions varies continually with the instructions or suggestions he is given and with the activities he is asked to perform (Barber, 1961b; Chertok & Kramarz, 1959). Similarly, other physiological measures vary continually when subjects are responding to test suggestions. Subjects who are said to be in hypnotic trance show continually varying (high, medium, or low) skin conductance, basal metabolic rate, heart rate, blood pressure, respiration, peripheral blood flow, blood clotting time, oral temperature, and so forth (Barber, 1961b; Cogger & Edmonston, in press; Crasilneck & Hall, 1959; Levitt & Brady, 1963; Timney & Barber, 1969). There is no need to postulate a special state of consciousness to account for these continual variations in physiological functions that are found in subjects responding to test suggestions (or said to be in hypnotic trance). Physiological variables vary in hypnotic subjects in the same way as in normal individuals, that is, in accordance with whatever activity they are engaged in. Normal individuals tend to show a high level of skin conductance, basal metabolic rate, heart rate, blood pressure, and so forth, when they are active or aroused, and a low level when they are relaxed or passive. In the same way as any other normal individual, the subject who is highly responsive to test suggestions (and said

to be in a hypnotic trance) shows a high level of skin conductance, basal metabolic rate, heart rate, and so forth, when he is given suggestions that lead to activity or arousal, and a lower level when he is given suggestions leading to quietude or relaxation. Similarly, if a normal individual is not anxious about a painful stimulus, he will tend to show a small change in skin conductance when he is exposed to the stimulus; and, if a normal individual is anxious about a painful stimulus, he will tend to show a larger change in skin conductance. In the same way, the subject who is responsive to suggestions intended to reduce his experience of pain will show a small rise in skin conductance when he is exposed to the noxious stimulus, and the subject who is unresponsive to the suggestions for reduced pain reactivity will show a larger rise in conductance (Barber & Hahn, 1962).

"Hypnotic Trance" as a Misnomer for a Responsive Waking State

Some present day investigators who use the traditional term "hypnotic trance" (or "hypnosis" or "hypnotic state") do *not* seem to mean that the subject is in a special state basically different from ordinary waking states. On the contrary, by the term "hypnotic trance" they seem to refer to a person who is as awake and as normal as you or I and who is as ready to respond to test suggestions as I am while I write these lines and as some readers are as they read these lines. (If, as I write these lines, an experimenter entered the room and wished to assess my response to test suggestions, I would have positive attitudes, motivations, and expectations toward the test situation and I would be ready, willing, and able to respond to the test suggestions and to experience the suggested effects. Some readers of these lines would be just as ready as I am to respond to the test suggestions.) To illustrate these contentions, let us look at how the term "hypnotic trance" is used by Erickson (1967a), who has written extensively on this topic:

1. Erickson often judges subjects to be in a hypnotic trance when, from all indications, they are in the waking state. For instance, he writes: "In the well-trained subject, the [deep hypnotic trance] is that type of trance in which the subject is seemingly awake and functioning adequately, freely, and well in the total hypnotic situation, in a manner similar to that of a non-hypnotized person operating at the waking level" (1967a, p. 13).

2. Erickson notes that psychologists, psychiatrists, and experienced hypnotists often view his hypnotic trance subjects as being in the waking state. For instance, he offers the following illustrative example: "the author, as a teaching device for the audience, had a subject in a profound somnambulistic trance conduct a lecture and demonstration of hypnosis (unaided by the author) before a group of psychiatrists and psychologists. Although

many in the audience had had experience with hypnosis, none detected that she was in a trance" (1967a, p. 14).

3. Erickson's subjects disagree with his judgment. For instance, in a study with forty-eight subjects presented by Secter (1960), Erickson judged how many subjects had entered light, medium, or deep hypnotic trance and how many did not enter trance. Each of the forty-eight subjects also rated himself as having attained one of the four levels. By chance, Erickson and the subjects should agree twenty-five percent of the time. The actual percentage of agreement was twenty-nine percent, which did not significantly exceed chance expectations.

In brief, when Erickson states that a subject is in a hypnotic trance, the subject often appears to be normally awake and is often judged by other investigators as being awake. Furthermore, Erickson's subjects do not agree with his judgment that they are not in a hypnotic trance or are in a light, medium, or deep trance. It appears that when Erickson judges one of his subjects to be in a hypnotic trance, he does not mean that the subject is not awake or that the subject is in a trance in the traditional sense of the term. What then does the term "hypnotic trance" mean in Erickson's work? A close reading of his papers provides the following answer: Whenever Erickson states that a subject was in a hypnotic trance, he almost always states on the same page that the subject was highly responsive to test suggestions. In fact, it appears that quite often Erickson first observes that the subject is very responsive to test suggestions and then infers that, since he is responsive to test suggestions, he must be in a hypnotic trance. The term "hypnotic trance," as used by Erickson, appears to refer to high responsiveness to test suggestions.

When pushed to specify what he means by the term "hypnotic trance" (or "hypnosis" or "hypnotized"), Erickson states that he is referring to "a state of intensified attention and receptiveness and an increased responsiveness to an idea or to a set of ideas" (1958, p. 117) and to a person who "tends to want to understand or to receive or to respond to the stimuli which are given to him or which he can derive from his situation" (1962, p. 240). It appears that Erickson may be misusing the term to refer to the same thing I have been describing in this chapter, namely, to an awake subject who has positive attitudes, motivations, and expectations toward the situation and is ready and willing to think with and to imagine those things that are suggested.

Attitudes, Motivations, and Expectancies

A series of investigations converge on the conclusion that responsiveness to test suggestions for body immobility, hallucination, amnesia, and so forth is determined in part by the subject's attitudes, motivations, and expectations toward the test situation. These investigations have been summarized in the longer version of the present chapter that was published in the first edition of this text and also, briefly, in Barber (1969, pp. 82-89). Due to space limitations, we will not present the details of these studies here.

Thinking with the Suggestions and Imagining the Suggested Effects

If a subject has negative attitudes, motivations, and expectations toward the test situation (that is, if he views his responding to test suggestions as not worthwhile and does not want to, does not try, and does not believe that he can experience those things that are suggested) he (a) will not think with the suggestions (instead he will verbalize to himself such statements as, "This is silly" or "The suggestion won't work"), (b) will not imagine those things that are described by the experimenter, and (c) will not perform the suggested behaviors, or experience those things that are suggested.

On the other hand, if a subject has positive attitudes, motivations, and expectations toward the test situation (that is, if he views his responding to test suggestions as interesting or worthwhile and desires to, tries to, and believes that he can experience those things that are suggested), he (a) will think with (subvocally verbalize to himself) the statements of the experimenter, (b) will imagine those things that are suggested, and (c) will perform the suggested behaviors and experience the suggested effects.[6]

How does thinking with the suggestions and imagining those things described lead to the overt behaviors and the subjective experiences that have been traditionally associated with the word "hypnosis"? An important paper by Arnold (1946) provided a preliminary answer to this question.

First, Arnold pointed out that words are symbols that stand for the situation or activity to which they refer. As we hear words or speak them to ourselves, the experience to which the words refer tends to be reinstated in a fragmentary way. When a situation is described verbally, we tend to visualize ourselves or feel ourselves in the situation and to reexperience our attitudes and reactions in the situation.

Secondly, Arnold pointed out that thinking about and vividly imagining a suggested movement or activity tends to bring about that activity. Arnold referred to the experiments of E. Jacobson (1930, 1932), which showed that an imagined movement (for example, imagining bending an arm) results in

6. To simplify the discussion, I am emphasizing only the extremes of a continuum, that is, I am focusing only on the extreme negative end or positive end of a continuum of attitudes, motivations, and expectations toward the test situation. Of course, most subjects are not at the extreme ends of the continuum; most subjects have neither extremely negative nor extremely positive attitudes, motivations, and expectations, and they show neither very high nor very low response to test suggestions.

electromyographic activity in the flexor muscles of the arm. If the muscles are relaxed when the subject begins to imagine, these slight muscle contractions occur only in the limb that is imagined as being moved and do not occur in other limbs. Schultz (1932), Hull (1933), Arnold (1946), Mordey (1960), and other investigators have shown that these tiny muscular contractions that are produced when the subject imagines a movement may at times increase up to the point where they result in observable movements. In these experiments, subjects were asked to imagine that they were falling backward or forward, that an arm was moving, or that a Chevreul pendulum (which they held by two fingers of one hand) was moving to the right or left. With very few exceptions, subjects who imagined the movement tended to move either slightly or markedly in the imagined direction. In general, subjects who reported that they imagined the most vividly showed the most marked movements in the imagined direction. It is important to emphasize here that, "The experience of 'intention,' of 'willing,' is . . . absent from these imagined movements" (Arnold, 1946, p. 111).

Sarbin (1950) has pointed out that, "Common experience verifies the same notion [concerning the effects of imagining]. In imagining a former embarassing situation we can feel our ears reddening and our faces flushing; in imagining a former painful experience we may involuntarily withdraw from the direction of the imagined stimulus, or in imagining something extremely unpleasant or disgusting we may experience nausea" (p. 266). In line with these assertions is a series of experimental studies, which indicate that vividly imagining a sensation can produce physiological changes associated with the actual sensation. For example, Schultz (1926) found that relaxed subjects who imagined that a hand was exposed to heat tended to experience a sensation of warmth associated (in fifteen of eighteen subjects) with an objectively measurable rise in skin temperature (up to $2°$ C. above normal). Conversely, imagining the forehead to be cool was associated in some subjects (five of fourteen) with a fall in the temperature of the forehead, presumably produced by contraction of the superficial blood vessels.

Along similar lines, Harano, Ogawa, and Naruse (1965) instructed subjects to repeat to themselves and to concentrate on the phrase, "My arms are warm." When repeating and focusing on these words, the subjects generally showed a change in the felt warmth of the arms, an increase in the surface temperature of the arms, and an increase in the blood volume of the arms. The same investigators found that there were no significant subjective or objective changes in the temperature of the arms when the subjects tried purposively to raise the temperature of the arms without vividly imagining that the arms were warm. As Richardson (1969) reminds us, the results presented by Harano, Ogawa, and Naruse are in line with the contention of Coué (1922) that, "To make good suggestions it is absolutely necessary to do it *without effort* ... the use of the *will* ... must be entirely put aside. One must have recourse exclusively to the imagination" (Richardson, 1969, p. 10).

Menzies (1941) and Hadfield (1920) also presented data indicating that some individuals show vasodilation and a rise in skin temperature when instructed to imagine or to think of a limb as warm, and show vasoconstriction and a drop in skin temperature when thinking about or vividly imagining a limb as cold. Although other studies, summarized by Luthe (1970), pp. 50–57), failed to replicate the indicated relationship, the positive results indicate that in at least some subjects, vividly imagining heat (or cold) is associated with a measurable rise (or fall) in skin temperature.

In a series of studies (Barber, 1965a), summarized earlier in this chapter, control subjects were asked to imagine that the right arm was becoming heavy and then were given repeated suggestions that it was becoming heavy, "Imagine that your right arm is feeling heavier and heavier... It's becoming heavier and heavier." Similarly, each control subject was asked to imagine that his left arm was becoming light, his clasped hands were stuck together, he was very thirsty, his throat was rigid and he could not say his name, and he was stuck in the chair and could not get up. As Table 8.1, column one shows, more than one-fourth of the control subjects asked to imagine the suggested effects passed each of the test-suggestions both objectively and subjectively; that is, they experienced arm heaviness, arm lightness, hand lock, thirst hallucination, verbal inhibition, and body immobility.[7]

Recent studies (Spanos, 1971; Spanos & Barber, 1972) probed more intensively into the relationship between imagining or fantasying and responding to test suggestions. In the first study, Spanos worked with twenty-four female subjects, of whom approximately half were highly responsive to test suggestions. Before beginning the experimental session, Spanos told each subject individually:

> I am interested in what is going on in people's minds when they are hypnotized. I'm interested in what they are thinking, imagining, feeling, and saying to themselves during hypnosis. In this experiment I am going to hypnotize you and ask you to carry out some suggestions. After each suggestion, while you are still hypnotized, I'll ask you to tell me what was passing through your mind while you were carrying out the suggestion. In giving me your answer it's very important that you be honest and tell me everything that was passing through your mind—everything that you were thinking, imagining, feeling and saying to yourself—even if you think it silly or unimportant (p. 88).

A trance induction procedure was then administered and the subject was

---

7. In the same experiments, the control subjects were also given suggestions for "posthypnotic-like" response and selective amnesia. However, they were not given instructions to imagine these suggested effects. Instead, they were simply told that they would carry out the postexperimental response and would forget one of the preceding test suggestions.

given test suggestions (for arm levitation, limb rigidity, and selective amnesia, for example). Immediately after responding to the first test suggestion, and also immediately after responding to each of the subsequent test suggestions, the subject was asked to report what was passing through her mind during the time she was responding. In most instances, the subjects who experienced the suggested effects stated that, when they were responding to the suggestions, they were imagining in a specific way; namely, they were imagining a situation which, if it actually transpired, would result in the behavior that was suggested. Typical examples of this type of imagining, which Spanos labeled "goal-directed fantasy," were:

1. A subject who experienced suggested arm heaviness reported: "I imagined that there were all kinds of rocks tied to my arm. It felt heavy and I could feel it going down."

2. A subject who experienced suggested arm levitation reported: "I imagined that my arm was hollow, there was nothing in it, and somebody was putting air into it."

3. A subject who passed the suggestion to forget the number four (selective amnesia) stated that she first pictured the numbers in a row (one, two, three, four, five, and so on up to ten), and then she pictured taking the number four out and, finally, she pictured the numbers one, two, three, five, and so on up to ten with a blank space where the number four was formerly.

In a second experiment (Spanos & Barber), forty female subjects who had not previously participated in a hypnotic experiment were randomly assigned to four experimental groups with ten subjects to each group. All subjects were exposed to a trance induction procedure, given a test suggestion for arm levitation (worded differently for each of the four experimental groups), and then asked to report what was passing through their minds when they were responding to the test suggestions. The subjects' reports were scored for the presence or absence of goal-directed fantasy. (These judgements could be made easily and reliably by two independent raters who agreed in every instance; for example, it was clear that the following type of report should be scored as a goal-directed fantasy; "I imagined a balloon tied to my arm and the balloon was slowly rising.") The subjects who passed the test suggestion also completed a Likert-type scale that asked them to state whether they attributed the arm levitation to their own voluntary effort ("I only had the experience of causing it [the arm] to rise") or whether they considered it an involuntary occurence ("I experienced it rising completely by itself"). In those subjects who showed arm levitation, goal-directed fantasy and the experience of volition were related as follows: of those who reported a goal-directed fantasy, none stated that they experienced the arm rising as volitional; while of those who did not report a goal-directed fantasy, sixty percent stated that they experienced the arm rising as volitional. In brief, if a subject carries out a goal-directed fantasy when given a suggestion—that is, if he imagines a situation which, if it actually transpired, would result in the suggested effect—he tends to feel that his response to the suggestion is involuntary (reporting, for example, "My arm rose by itself").

Let us now summarize the data presented in this section and in the preceding one:

1. Studies that used subjects' self-ratings to assess either their attitudes, or motivations, or expectations toward the test situation generally found small but significant relations between each of these variables and response to test suggestions.

2. Studies that experimentally manipulated attitudes, motivations, and expectations in various combinations found a marked enhancement of response to test suggestions when an attempt was made to induce positive attitudes, motivations, and expectations toward the test situation, and a marked reduction in response when an attempt was made to induce negative attitudes, motivations, and expectations.

3. An underlying assumption or axiom of the alternative paradigm is that when a subject has positive atitudes, motivations, and expectations toward the test situation he thinks along with and imagines those things that are suggested.

4. A series of experimental studies indicates that thinking along with and vividly imagining those things that are suggested tends to produce both the overt response and the subjective experience that is suggested.

5. Two recent studies indicate that subjects experience suggested effects, such as arm levitation, as occurring nonvolitionally when they imagine a situation which, if it objectively transpired, would produce the suggested behavior, for example, they imagine a rising balloon tied to the arm, which is lifting the arm up.

Tangible Antecedent Variables

In this chapter, I have focused on the intervening variables (subjects' attitudes, motivations, expectations, and cognitive processes) that mediate response to test suggestions. In other papers and books (Barber, 1969a, 1969b, 1970a) I have focused primarily on denotable antecedent variables that functionally related to subjects' overt and subjective responses.

There appear to be at least three important antecedent variables that directly affect how subjects report their experiences:

1. The wording of the questions used to elicit the subjective reports (Barber, Dalal, & Calverley, 1968).

2. Whether or not honest subjective reports are demanded (K.S. Bowers, 1967; Spanos & Barber, 1968).

3. Whether the subjective reports are elicited by the experimenter or by another person (K.S. Bowers, 1967; Spanos & Barber, 1968).

Other tangible antecedent variables appear to affect subjects' overt and subjective responsiveness to test suggestions by first affecting their attitudes, motivations, and expectations, and their willingness to think with and imagine the suggested effects. These antecedent variables include the following:

1. How the situation is defined to the subject (as a test of imagination, as a test of gullibility, as "hypnosis," etc.) (Barber, 1969b).

2. Whether pre-experimental instructions that aim to alter the subjects' attitudes, motivations, and expectations toward the test situation are administered.

3. Whether the test suggestions are worded in a permissive or authoritarian manner, for example, "Try to forget" versus "You will forget," or "Try to dream on a specified topic" versus "You will dream on the topic" (Barber, 1966b).

4. Whether the test suggestions are given in a firm or lackadaisical tone of voice (Barber & Calverley, 1964a).

5. Whether the subject has been repeatedly assessed on response to the same test suggestions in previous sessions (Barber & Calverley, 1966c).

6. Whether the subject volunteered to participate in the experiment or was coerced (Boucher & Hilgard, 1962).

7. Whether the subject's performance was observed by an audience (Coe, 1966).

8. Whether the subject was provided with a clear conception of the experience that was desired and was given verbal reinforcement for each appropriate response (Giles, 1962; Sachs & Anderson, 1967).

9. If the situation is defined as hypnosis, whether an attempt was made to remove the subjects' misconceptions and fears about hypnosis (Cronin, Spanos, & Barber, 1971; Macvaugh, 1969).

The effects of these nine antecedent variables can be more satisfactorily explained by the alternative paradigm than by the traditional (trance) paradigm. For instance, it is difficult to conceive how suggestions for amnesia worded in different ways have any relevance whatsoever to whether the subject enters, remains in, or goes deeper into a state (trance) that is fundamentally different from ordinary states of consciousness. However, it is not at all difficult to see how permissive suggestions for amnesia ("Try to forget") are more effective than authoritarian suggestions ("You will forget") in motivating the subject to put the previous occurences "out of mind" (Barber & Calverley, 1966b). Similarly, it is difficult to conceive how the experimenter's tone of voice (firm or lackadaisical) in administering test suggestions for arm heaviness, inability to unclasp hands, and so forth, is relevant to whether the subject enters, remains in, or goes deeper into a special state (trance). However, since subjects who received test suggestions in a lackadaisical tone of voice tended to report that they thought the experimenter did not expect them to respond to the test suggestions, it is not difficult to conceive how the tone of voice used to administer test suggestions might affect the subjects' attitudes, motivations, or expectancies toward the test situation (Barber & Calverley, 1964a). The trance paradigm might be able to explain why subjects exposed in repeated sessions to the same test suggestions showed a continual reduction in responsiveness. However, the alternative paradigm is more consistent with the empirical data, since subjects participating in these repeated sessions testified that they became bored and lost interest, and this change in attitude was correlated with their reduced responsiveness (Barber & Calverley, 1966c). Similarly, the trance paradigm might explain the effects of some of the other antecedent variables listed above; for example, it might explain why coerced subjects are less responsive to test suggestions than volunteers (Boucher & Hilgard, 1962), why subjects are less responsive when they believe they are being observed by an audience (Coe, 1966), and why verbal reinforcement for each appropriate response enhances subsequent responses to test-suggestions (Giles, 1962; Sachs & Anderson, 1967). However, without belaboring the point and going into further details, it should be clear that these antecedent variables can be more satisfactorily conceptualized as affecting subjects' attitudes, motivations, and expectations toward the test situation and their willingness to think with and imagine the suggested effects.

The antecedent variables listed above are functionally related to the dependent variable we have labeled "response to test suggestions." A few of the above-mentioned variables also overlap with other antecedent variables to determine response on two additional dependent variables: whether and to what degree subjects (a) manifest a trancelike appearance and (b) report that they were "hypnotized."

As implied previously in this chapter, whether subjects who are highly responsive to test suggestions appear to be in "hypnosis" (that is, manifest trancelike characteristics such as a limp posture, passivity, a blank stare, rigid facial expression, and so forth) is dependent primarily on two tangible antecedent variables, namely, whether the situation was defined to the subjects as "hypnosis" and whether or not they were asked to close their eyes. If the situation is not defined as "hypnosis," but in some other way—as a "test of imagination," for example—and if the subjects are not asked to close their eyes, very few if any subjects who are highly responsive to test suggestions for limb rigidity, analgesia, age regression, amnesia, and so forth, manifest a trancelike appearance. If the situation is defined to the subjects as "hypnosis" and they are told to close their eyes, then whether and to what extent the subjects manifest a trancelike appearance is functionally related to such antecedent variables as (a) their preconceptions of what "hypnosis" is supposed to involve, (b) their pre-experimental attitudes toward whatever they conceive "hypnosis" to be, (c) their pre-experimental expectations concerning their own performance, (d) the suggestions they receive (implicit suggestions to be passive, or repeated suggestions that they are becoming relaxed, drowsy, sleepy, and are entering hypnosis), and (e) whether the experimenter, at some point, speaks to them along the following lines: "Wake up, stop acting as if you are in a trance, and continue to respond to my suggestions" (Barber, 1969b; Barber & Calverley, 1969b).

Whether subjects who are highly responsive to test suggestions report that they were in "hypnosis" is also dependent primarily on two tangible antecedent variables, namely, whether the situation was defined to the subjects as "hypnosis" and whether they were told to close their eyes. If the situation is not defined to the subjects as "hypnosis" and they are not told to close their eyes, very few if any subjects who show a high level of response to test suggestions state that they are in hypnosis. If the situation is defined as "hypnosis" and the subjects are told to close their eyes, the antecedent variables that determine whether the subjects will report that they were in "hypnosis" to some degree or were not "hypnotized" at all include (a) their preconceptions of what "hypnosis" is supposed to involve, (b) their pre-experimental expectations of their own performance, (c) whether they received repeated suggestions that they were becoming relaxed, drowsy, sleepy, and were entering a hypnotic state, (d) whether they observed that they were or were not responsive to test suggestions, (e) whether the experimenter stated or implied that he believed they were or were not hypnotized, and (f) the wording and tone of the questions used to elicit their reports (Barber, 1969a; Barber & Calverley, 1969b; Barber, Dalal, & Calverley, 1968).[8]

8. As noted above, whether a subject who is highly responsive to test suggestions manifests trancelike characteristics and whether he reports that he was "hypnotized" is dependent, in part, on whether he was told repeatedly that he was becoming relaxed, drowsy, sleepy, and was entering a hypnotic state. Repeated suggestions of this type (relaxation, drowsiness, etc.) may also affect the subjects' performance on other variables, for example, they may reduce their strength and endurance (Barber & Caverley, 1964f) and they may change their responses to projective tests, such as the Rorschach or TAT, in the direction expected when a person is relaxed or sleepy. However, whether repeated suggestions that the subject is becoming relaxed, drowsy, sleepy, and is entering hypnosis influence the subjects' responsiveness to test suggestions of analgesia, hallucination, age regression, amnesia, etc. depends primarily on how they affect subjects' attitudes, motivations, and expectations toward the test situation. I have noted (unpublished observations) that a substantial proportion of individuals, especially those who are relatively uneducated, are anxious or fearful with respect to whatever they think "hypnosis" is suppoesed to be. When these individuals receive

In brief, the dependent variables (response to test suggestions, trancelike appearance, and reports of having been hypnotized) are functionally related to the many denotable antecedent variables mentioned above and also to other tangible variables that have been discussed elsewhere (Dalal, 1966; McPeake, 1968; Nichols, 1968; Richman, 1965; Spanos, 1970; Spanos & Chaves, 1970). In fact, these behaviors and experiences appear to be as complexly determined as any behaviors and experiences that psychologists have ever attempted to study. Although the antecedent variables are many and complex, a substantial number of them can be viewed as converging on a set of mediating variables that we have called attitudes, motivations, and expectations toward the test situation and thinking with and imagining the suggested effects. These mediating variables are part and parcel of normal psychology, especially of present-day social psychology. They mediate behavior and experiences in a wide variety of situations; for instance, they mediate the experiences of the member of the audience who is listening to an orator, or who is observing a motion picture, a stage play, or a television show. It is misleading to subsume these mediating variables, which are an integral part of normal psychology, under a construct ("trance," "hypnosis," or "hypnotic trance") that derives from the psychology of the abnormal, that has been historically loaded with surplus connotations (including the connotation that the person resembles the sleepwalker), and that is used to refer to a special state basically different from ordinary states of consciousness.

Résumé and Prospects

As Kuhn (1962) pointed out, a change in scientific paradigm is preceded by a period in which research yields data that do not fit into the prevailing paradigm. Recent research has produced data incongruous with the prevalent trance paradigm. Some of the anomalous data include:

1. Some individuals are very responsive, both overtly and subjectively,

---

repeated suggestions that they are becoming relaxed, drowsy, sleepy, and are entering hypnosis, they seem to have negative attitudes, motivations, and expectations toward the test situation, and they perform less well on test suggestions than they would have if they had not received such repeated suggestions. Most college students, however, are eager to experience whatever they think "hypnosis" is supposed to be. Consequently, when given repeated suggestions of relaxation, drowsiness, sleep, and entering hypnosis, they seem to have positive attitudes, motivations, and expectations toward the test situation and they perform better on test suggestions that they would have if they had not received such repeated suggestions.

to test suggestions when they are tested under a base level (control) condition (without any special instructions). Also, when unselected subjects are simply exposed to brief instructions intended to produce positive attitudes, motivations, and expectancies toward the test situation ("task-motivational instructions"), they are about as responsive to test suggestions for body immobility, hallucination, age regression, analgesia, amnesia, etc. as unselected subjects who have been exposed to a procedure of the type traditionally termed a "trance induction" and who are, presumably, in a hypnotic trance. The trance paradigm could not have predicted these results and it requires ad hoc assumptions in order to explain them. It has to assume, after the fact, that highly responsive control subjects or task-motivated subjects who have not been exposed to a trance-induction procedure, who do not appear to be in a trance, and who do not think they are in a trance are actually in a hypnotic trance.

2. The anomaly mentioned above appeared earlier in the work of hypnotic state theorists such as Erickson. To maintain the logic of the trance paradigm, Erickson was compelled to contend that some subjects are in a deep hypnotic trance even when they do not think they are in a trance, are judged by psychologists and psychiatrists as being in a normal waking state, and are even judged by Erickson himself as being "seemingly awake and functioning...in a manner similar to that of a nonhypnotized person operating at the waking level" (Erickson, 1967a, p. 13). Why was Erickson compelled to categorize subjects as being in a deep hypnotic trance even though the subjects appeared, to objective observers and to themselves, to be normally awake? Because Erickson was certain that the subjects would respond to his suggestions. This logic led to another serious anomaly for the trance paradigm: subjects were judged to be in a hypnotic trance because they would show high response to test suggestion and, turning around circularly, the high response to test suggestions was explained as due to the presence of hypnotic trance (Barber, 1964a).

3. Since all investigators conceive of the human organism as a psychophysiological unity, special states of the organism are expected to have some physiological concomitants. For more than fifty years, investigators have been trying to find a physiological concomitant or index of the presumed special state labeled "hypnosis" or "trance." Not only have they failed to unearth any special physiological change associated with the presumed special state, but they have also consistently found that physiological functioning during the postulated special state varies in the same way as in nonspecial or ordinary states. Of course, many failures

over many years to find a physiological index does not prove that such an index does not exist or will never be found. Nevertheless, consistent findings that physiological functions during the presumed special state vary in the same way as in nonspecial states are becoming more and more anomalous for the trance paradigm as time goes on.

A traditional paradigm is not overthrown simply because some of the relevant data are incongruous with it (Kuhn, 1962). In addition to pointing out data that are anomalous for the traditional formulation, an alternative paradigm must also be able to explain all of the relevant phenomena at least as well if not better than the traditional one. The underlying contention of this chapter has been that the alternative paradigm, which has had a rather brief period of development (Barber, 1961b, 1964a, 1967, 1969b, 1970a; Barber & Calverley, 1962; Sarbin, 1950, 1956, 1962, 1964; Sarbin & Anderson, 1967; Sarbin & Coe, 1972), can explain the relevant phenomena more satisfactorily than the trance paradigm which has had more than a hundred years of development. Specifically, this chapter has shown how the alternative paradigm explains not only the "amazing" phenomena of stage hypnosis, such as, the human plank feat, stopping the pulse in the arm, and performance by the subject of weird antics such as dancing with an invisible partner, but also explains the following phenomena that can be elicited by suggestions in experimental or clinical situations: production of blisters, removal of warts, analgesia, age regression, age-progression, visual and auditory hallucinations, deafness, trancelike characteristics, difficulty or delay in coming out of trance, suggested and also spontaneous amnesia, and trance logic. These phenomena, which were explained in this chapter from the alternative paradigm, were not selected at random. On the contrary, they were selected as representing the strongholds of the trance paradigm—as representing the phenomena that had been universally accepted as explainable only by positing a special state of the organism.

Looking to the future, I will venture four predictions:

1. As more investigators adopt the alternative paradigm, the kinds of questions that are asked and the focus of research will change. Instead of asking what the most effective methods for inducing a deep hypnotic trance are or how the hypnotic state differs from the waking state, researchers will ask questions such as the following:

a. What kinds of instructions are most effective in eliciting positive attitudes, motivations, and expectations toward the test situation?

b. Are all three factors—positive attitudes, positive motivations, positive expectations—equally necessary for high response to test suggestions? How does a subject respond to test suggestions when he believes it is interesting and worthwhile to be responsive (positive attitude), when he tries to experience those things that are suggested (positive motivation), but when he does not believe that he can experience either a specific suggested effect, such as visual hallucination or amnesia, or all of those things that are suggested (negative expectations)? A rather large number of additional questions can be formulated along similar lines. For instance, how does a subject respond to test suggestions when he believes he can experience the suggested effects (positive expectation) but he has negative attitudes and motivations toward the test situation?

c. How can subjects be helped to imagine vividly those things that are suggested?

d. How can subjects be given practice in thinking with suggestions? Stated somewhat differently, how can they be given practice in covertly verbalizing the suggestions to themselves while, at the same time, inhibiting contrary thoughts such as, "This suggestion won't work," or "It's impossible to experience this suggested effect"?

2. As the alternative paradigm becomes accepted by more researchers, the kind of response to test suggestions that has been traditionally subsumed under the term "hypnosis" will no longer be viewed as closely related to abnormal phenomena such as sleepwalking and fugue states (Gill & Brenman, 1959). Instead, the processes involved in responding to test suggestions will be analyzed in a similar manner as, and will be found partially to overlap with, such social psychological influence processes as conformity, attitude change, and persuasion (Barnlund, 1968; Bettinghaus, 1968; Hartley & Hartley, 1958, pp. 15–158; McGuire, 1969; Secord & Backman, 1964, pp. 93–231). The recent formulation by Sarbin and Coe (1972), which subsumes "hypnotic" behavior under the psychology of influence communication, will be viewed as a major turning point in this area. I will also venture to predict that, in the more distant future, a unified theory of social influence processes will be used to explain not only conformity, attitude change, and persuasion but also responses to test suggestions and other types of responses that were previously thought to be associated with a qualitatively distinct state (trance).

3. Conceptions of *normal human abilities* or "human potentialities" (Otto, 1966) will be markedly broadened when the subject who is responsive to communications (test suggestions) from an experimenter is seen to be as normal and as awake as the member of the audience who is responsive to communications from the actors. Investigators will no longer think in terms of rare individuals ("somnambulists") who possess unusual capacities, who differ in some basic way from other human beings, who are able to enter a special state ("deep somnambulistic trance"), and who are able to have experiences that other human beings find it very difficult if not impossible to have. On the contrary, investigators will think in terms of a wide range of normal human abilities that can be manifested when individuals adopt positive attitudes, motivations, and expectations toward the test situation. These abilities, which will be viewed as within the normal human repertoire, will include: the ability to perform feats such as the human plank feat; the ability to control or block pain (analgesia) by thinking of other things or by thinking of the sensations as sensations; the ability to imagine and to visualize vividly (hallucination and suggested dream); the ability to imagine or fantasy events that occurred at an earlier time (age regression) or that may occur in the future (age progression); and the ability to block or stop thinking about earlier events (amnesia).

4. As Chaves (1968) has pointed out, attempts have already been made to subsume the alternative paradigm under the traditional (trance) paradigm. I expect that further attempts will be made along these lines (Kuhn, 1962). That is, adherents of the traditional paradigm may contend that hypnotic trance (or hypnosis or hypnotic state) refers to (or is) positive attitudes, motivations, and expectancies and thinking with and imagining the suggested effects. To be consistent, adherents of the traditional paradigm may also contend that all procedures instructions, and experimental manipulations that aim to produce positive attitudes, motivations, etc.-for example, task-motivational instructions (Barber & Calverley, 1962), or having the subject first observe another person who is higly responsive to test suggestions (Klinger, 1970)—are actually trance induction procedures. Also, to be consistent, they may contend that the member of the audience who is laughing, crying, empathizing, and so on, as he receives communications from the actors, is also in a hypnotic trance. These contentions will change the meaning of the term "hypnotic trance"; the term will no longer refer to a special state basically different from ordinary states of consciousness. Of course, such attempts to change the meaning of the central construct (trance) will be self-defeating for the

traditional paradigm. Since the construct "hypnotic trance" (or "hypnosis" or "hypnotic state") has always referred to some kind of basic, qualitative change in the organism and has accreted many associated connotations (including connotations of somnambulism or sleepwalking), attempts to give it a new meaning and new connotations will lead to confusion rather than clarity and, sooner or later, the construct and its many associated assumptions will be viewed as a historical curiosity by students of human behavior.

Theodore R. Sarbin *received his Ph.D. from Ohio State University in 1941. From 1938 to 1941, he served on the staff of the University of Minnesota. For several years he was in private practice and engaged in part-time teaching. In 1949, he went to the University of California at Berkeley. He was made Professor of Psychology in 1957 and Professor of Criminology in 1966. In 1969, he moved to the University of California, Santa Cruz, where he served as Professor and Chairman of the Board of Studies in Psychology and participated as a member of the graduate faculty in the History of Consciousness program. In 1976, he became Professor Emeritus of Psychology and Criminology. He continues an active program of research and writing in theoretical psychology, the social psychology of deviance, and the social psychology of counterexpectational conduct. A definitive statement of his general orientation is contained in* "Contextualism: A World View for Modern Psychology," *in* 1976 Nebraska Symposium on Motivation, *Landfield, A.W. (ed.).* His theoretical position on hypnosis is presented in detail *in* Hypnosis: The Social Psychology of Influence Communication (with W.C. Coe), New York, Holt, Rinehart, & Winston, 1972.

Robert W. Slagle *is an Associate Professor of Psychology at Sonoma State University, California. He earned his Ph.D. in 1968 from the University of California, Berkeley, while working with an interdisciplinary brain research project. Expanding his neurobiological background to the immediacy of human experience, he accepted a postdoctoral research and training fellowship at the Psychology Clinic of the University of California, where he received intensive training in psychotherapy and drug counseling. He has served as a drug consultant in a variety of postions including an Oakland high school, an experimental drop-in center sponsored by the City of Berkeley, and in private practice as a licensed psychologist and licensed marriage, family and child counselor. His interests are now centered in interdisciplinary psychology with an emphasis on integrating biological and psychological disciplines and bringing them to bear on issues of social growth and individual well-being.*

Sarbin and Slagle *survey the salient literature on physiological concomitants of hypnosis and find no evidence for a physiological process that could serve as an independent criterion of the postulated hypnotic state. They do, however, find strong evidence that symbolic stimuli and imaginings can produce impressive changes in physiological processes. They formulate their findings within a general theory of social role enactment, and conclude that the greater the intensity of organismic involvement in the enactment of the hypnotic role, the more extensive are the associated physiological concomitants.*

9

Hypnosis
and Psychophysiological Outcomes

THEODORE R. SARBIN AND ROBERT W. SLAGLE

Hundreds of reports addressed to the problem of hypnotic influence on somatic processes have been published. The motivations behind these reports appear to fall into two general categories: to use hypnotic techniques in the clinical treatment of somatic and psychological disorders, and to identify an independent criterion for the hypnotic trance. These categories are not exclusive: Some writers have referred to clinical research reports as evidence for the independent existence of the hypnotic trance. Because clinical studies in general are characterized by the absence of appropriate controls, they can only be cited as "hypothesis-finding," rather than "hypothesis-testing" studies. On the other hand, studies addressed directly to the problem of identifying an independent criterion for the hypnotic trance are usually characterized by attempts to incorporate principles of experimental design, including controls.

Not every laboratory report makes explicit that the search for a physiological indicant is to demonstrate that hypnosis is a special state of mind or an altered state of consciousness. The hypotheses are stated in such a way, however, that the reader may safely conclude that the intent is to demonstrate that the altered physiological process is a function of a hypnotic trance brought about by the hypnotic induction.

The search for a physiological indicant of the hypnotic state cannot be appreciated without placing it in the more general context of the search for a criterion that is independent of the postulated mental state. No sophisticated analysis of hypnosis can avoid recognition of the tautology contained in classical explanations of hypnosis. The tautology can be expressed simply: behaviors ordinarily subsumed under hypnosis, such as catalepsies, rigidities, paramnesias, and posthypnotic feats, are the effects of the hypnotic trance; the presence of the hypnotice trance is noted by the catalepsies, rigidities, paramnesias, and posthypnotic feats. The circularity follows from the lack of an independent criterion.

The recognition of the circularity has put pressure on exponents of the trance concept deliberately to seek independent criteria. Two types of independent criteria have been sought: "Phenomenological" tests for an altered state of consciousness, and physiological indicators.

The problems inherent in employing phenomenological criteria are discussed in detail by Sarbin and Coe (1972) in the context of the docility of reports of imaginings to role demands, to the effect of organismic involvement on stimulus inputs, to the selectivity involved in making public one's imaginings, and to the conditions that influence the assigning of credibility to imaginings. Their conclusion is that phenomenological tests of the hypnotic trance have been ineffective for breaking out of the circularity. Such ineffectiveness of phenomenological tests makes crucial the search for somatic indicators if the trance concept is to remain scientifically viable.

Experiments designed to reveal physiological indicants of the hypnotic trance are of two sorts. The first monitors somatic responses that occur consequent to the hypnotic induction procedure. In the typical experiment, a measure such as heart rate, GSR, or body temperature is assessed before, during, and after the induction procedure. If subjects are used as their own controls, the same measurements are taken under conditions where other instructions (such as imagining) are employed. If the independent group design is used, readings may be taken before, during, and after the induction for the experimental sample. In the control sample, the hypnotic induction is omitted.

The second type of experiment focuses on physiological responses to suggestions made after the induction is completed. To study hypnotically induced analgesia, for example, hypnotized subjects are given a painful stimulus; the experimenter, besides noting the subjects' verbal and expressive responses, records physiological responses, such as blood volume, that normally vary with the administration of traumatic stimuli. Experiments may be conducted with independent groups, where the subjects of the control sample are not hypnotized. Frequently, experiments are reported where the subject is his own control—hypnosis is employed at one sitting, other instructions are given at a second sitting.

After presenting a review of selected studies, we shall return to a critique of the experimental designs in studies of the physiological effects of hypnosis. Suffice it to say now that the type of experimental design selected is not without relevance to the interpretation given positive findings.

In attempting to discuss and account for physiological manifestations of hypnosis we must keep in mind not only the technical, methodological, and terminological considerations that are essential to any type of in vivo biological investigation, but also considerations concerning "hypnosis" as an independent variable. The controversial status of hypnosis both in theory and in practice should direct the investigator to scrutinize the assumptions and "givens" behind the choice of experimental designs employed in examining physiological aspects of hypnotic phenomena. Not only must we be sensitive to biological base rates but to behavioral base rates as well. We must also be sensitive to the social and cultural context in which we make our observations.

The use of the dramaturgical metaphor of "role" will permit a systematic way of defining and measuring the many contextual, historical, and imaginal accompaniments of hypnosis in the experimental situation. Some examples of the kinds of cautions that we should attend to are: What is the basis for the selection of subjects? Do the subjects in any given experiment have special characteristics such as high responsiveness to hypnotic instructions? Are they students, or patients, or otherwise representative of only a special population? Are they all men? or women? or of a particular age or socioeconomic status? If "hypnotic induction" is used, what other type of instructions are and should be administered to control groups? What indices of involvement in the hypnotic role are employed? In what way is the phenomenon termed "hypnosis" in any given experiment representative of the historical and natural observations on the presumed process under consideration as observed and reported outside the laboratory? Who are the experimenters and what subtle biases might they implicitly carry to the experimental situation? And, in general, what role demands are placed on the subjects?

With these questions as a backdrop, we now turn to a survey of the literature on physiological correlates of hypnosis with emphasis on exemplary experiments from recent publications. The review could be organized according to the type of physical measurement used; for example, bioelectrical recordings, measures of changes in pressure or volume as in the case of blood pressure or volume of tidal air, temperature, presence and concentration of chemical substances, and so forth. Or, we could group experiments according to the presumed physiological events, such as changes in muscle tone, skin resistance, heart rate, and so forth; or we could organize according to the intended effect of the induction—for example, to bring about relaxation, to call out particular emotional responses, or to cure an illness. Many different kinds of events in the body are measured by changes in electrical parameters, so the first approach has little heuristic value. We have chosen to organize our review according to the bodily

organs or processes in which changes are alleged to occur as a result of hypnotic instructions.

Survey of the Experimental Literature

The literature on physiological correlates of hypnosis has been reviewed by
several investigators: Barber (1961b), Crasilneck and Hall (1959), Gorton
(1949), Levitt and Brady (1963), Sarbin (1956), and West (1960). For this
reason, we shall not attempt a thorough survey, but rather point to selected
investigations for purposes of illustrating experimental design and interpretation of findings.

RESPIRATORY FUNCTIONS

Barber (1965b) reviewed and criticized a number of reports on the hypnotic
cure of asthma and other respiratory ailments. He pointed out that control
groups are often omitted in these reports of improved respiratory function
via hypnotic suggestions. The absence of a waking control group that
receives suggestions for improvement without hypnosis makes it particularly unparsimonious to attribute the improvement to the specific antecedent condition, namely, the "hypnotic state."

In discussing hypnotic effects on breathing, Sarbin (1956) concluded that
for subjects in "deep" hypnosis a decrease in breathing rate could be
observed. However, the pneumographic record is easily affected by the type
of suggestion given. For example, relaxation suggestions bring about
decreased respiratory rates, while the introduction of emotional stimuli
usually increases the rate.

In a study that gives particular attention to individual differences, Dudley
et al. (1964) reported systematic respiratory alterations with pain and exercise and from hypnotically suggested emotions, pain, and exercise. Experiments were carried out on ten hypnotically-naive medical students and a
tuberculosis patient with previous hypnotic experience. These men were
each interviewed to determine events in their past lives associated with
strong emotion. Hypnosis consisted of "eye fixation on a light and the
repeated suggestion of relaxation and drowsiness" (p. 47). Suggestions were
then made involving the emotion-laden interview material, and the subjects
were questioned about their feelings both during and after the hypnotic session. An independent investigator took continuous measurements of
alveolar ventilation, and tidal air concentration of CO_2 and O_2. Blood
pressure, pulse rate, and skin temperature were also monitored but not
reported. By regarding each subject as his own control, the hypnotic condition had minimal effect on respiration except for a decrease in O_2 consumption. Behavioral observations and self-reports from these subjects corroborated that they felt as if they were undergoing (experiencing) the

suggested emotions.

CARDIOVASCULAR FUNCTIONS

Heart rate. It is common to observe tachycardia during the initial period of the hypnotic induction procedure (Sarbin, 1956). This speeding up of the heartbeat can probably be attributed to the excitement and unfamiliarity of the situation. With Barber (1961b) we agree that three critical factors must be controlled in a satisfactory demonstration of hypnotic cardiac accelera- tion: level of "arousal," respiratory rate, and the capacity of a subject voluntarily to increase his heart rate without an hypnotic induction. Barber concluded that no experiments to date have met these criteria. Recent ex- periments aimed at manipulating heart rate via hypnotic instructions seem to bear out this conclusion. For example, one means of asking about possi- ble unique effects of hypnosis on cardiac function is to compare two groups of subjects who are performing the same behaviors, except that one group is told not to "slip into hypnosis" but to fake the requested performance.

Damaser, Shor, and Orne (1963) employed suggested emotional behavior to execute such an experiment. Seventeen undergraduate men and women were divided into two groups: "Real" hypnotic subjects who had had previous experience as hypnotic subjects, and "simulators" who were not susceptible to hypnosis and who were asked to fool both the experimenter and the polygraph. The experimenter was not informed which subjects were simulators. During the experiment all subjects were asked to try to *feel* the requested emotions of fear, calm, happiness, and depression. When the emotion was requested, the subject was given a description. For instance, for fear he was told, "You feel terribly frightened. You're horribly scared." Continuous recording of heart rate, muscular activity in the forehead, and electrodermal potentials were measured. No significant differences between reals and simulators were observed in the physiological variables. Both groups showed significant, comparable physiological responses to the re- quested emotions, in the direction predicted. Fear and happiness were most active while calm and depression were least active.

In an experimental design much like that of Damaser, Shor, and Orne (1963), Hepps and Brady (1967) paid twenty-five undergraduate men who were either real hypnotic or simulator subjects to undergo a fear-arousing set of taped instructions. As with the Damaser et al. study, real and simulator subjects showed a significant cardiac acceleration and higher score on the Taylor Manifest Anxiety Scale with the fear stimulus, but dif- ferences between reals and simulators were not significant. In post-session interviews, the reals reported that they felt fearful more often and to a greater intensity than did the simulators. Hepps and Brady also report that reals showed a significant positive correlation between heart rates during all aspects of the experiment, and hypnotic responsiveness as measured by standardized scales. It is appropriate to question this finding: Since the basis for selection of reals was different from that of simulators, this correlation may be the result of subject selection and experimental interaction, or of base rate phenomena in the population from which the subjects were chosen. The conclusion of Damaser et al. seems applicable to this type of research at this point in time: "the evidence does not support the view that either (1) effects in the hypnotic state are larger than in the waking state, or (2) effects in the real group are more frequent than in the simulating group" (p. 340).

Hemodynamics and vasomotor functions. Barber (1961b, 1965b) and Sarbin (1956) have reviewed numerous articles reporting local vasoconstriction and/or vasodilation with some hypnotized persons by appropriate verbal stimulation. Although these local effects can be demonstrated under hypnotic conditions, the absence of control studies makes it impossible to determine the effects of symbolic stimulation, role demands, and expectations without hypnosis. The extent to which the subjects could voluntarily control these processes without any special instructions at all is not usually assessed.

An example of a more recent report on hemodynamics during hypnosis is that of May and Edmonston (1966). They measured changes in peripheral blood volume in six male hypnotically-naive students and attempted to determine whether these men were less attentive to incidental startling stimuli when hypnotized. A six-man control group was matched on the Barber Suggestibility Scale and the Taylor Manifest Anxiety Scale. The procedure included no training sessions. During the first experimental session, all subjects were seated and blood volume was monitored with a photoelectric plethysmographic finger pickup. The experimental group listened to nineteen minutes of taped induction that paraphrased the Stanford Hypnotic Susceptibility Scale (SHSS). Control subjects listened to three taped short stories for an equivalent time. In a counterbalanced fashion, all subjects received either "anxiety" producing instructions, or an unexpected blast from an automobile horn. May and Edmonston's groups did not differ significantly for changes in blood volume in terms of base rate, or responsiveness to the horn or to the fear producing stimuli. Within the experimental group, blood volume did not change significantly during induction; however, the control group showed a significant drop in finger blood volume relative to the experimental group during the nineteen minutes of taped stories. In their discussion, these investigators point out that neither their hypothesis of differential plethysmographic changes nor differential inattentiveness to extraneous stimuli during hypnosis and nonhypnotic conditions was supported. Furthermore, the "anxiety" instructions were not rendered physiologically more effectual by virtue of the hypnotic induction.

The subjects of the May and Edmonston experiment were apparently in a "light" depth of hypnosis (the criterion was eye closure). Under these conditions, one would expect the "hypnotized" subjects to be responsive to the blast of an automobile horn. Differential thresholds to extraneous stimuli would probably not have been noticeable with such intense stimuli had they been present in the first place. Also, since subjects received tests of suggestibility *before* the experimental session, they might have expected hypnosis. Thus when the control group hears taped "stories" it is reasonable that they would interpret this to mean they are in a "control condition" and not become involved in their roles. The hypnotized subjects, however, would be expected to become more involved. Finally, the hypnotized subjects in fact responded at about the same level as control subjects to "anxiety" instructions. If hypnotized subjects are less attentive to extraneous stimuli, they would hear fewer of the anxiety instructions than would control subjects. Yet hypnotized subjects were hypothesized to be more suggestible. It follows that they would be more responsive to the smaller portion of "anxiety" stimuli that they do attend to. These opposing processes, lessened attention and enhanced responsivity, may cancel each other, making the hypnotic group comparable to controls on this measure.

Reports on hypnotic effects on anatomically proximal blood flow seem scarce; an example of this type of investigation is that of Maiolo, Porro, and Granone (1969). Five normal but deeply hypnotized subjects were compared with six normal, alert subjects in terms of cerebral blood flow, cerebrovascular resistances, and cerebral metabolic rate of oxygen consumption. No statistically significant differences between alert and hypnotized subjects were found on any of these measures, although standard deviations for the alert subjects were somewhat larger than for the hypnotized group. Maiolo and co-workers suggest that "anxiety" accounts for the greater variance among alert subjects. Hypnotic procedural details were not available in this brief report.

GENITOURINARY FUNCTIONS

As is revealed by the reviews of Dunbar (1954) and of Kroger and Freed (1943), the majority of reports on genitourinary functioning are in the form of anecdotes and clinical case histories. However, within this corpus of literature practically every type of urological, gynecological, and reproductive functions can be ablated or produced through procedures that have been termed "hypnotic." Examples of hypnotic control of menstrual cramps, frigidity, impotence, and changes in menstrual periodicity and painless childbirth are commonly reported (Sarbin, 1956).

A recent experimental report involving hypnosis and the genitourinary system is a study of immersion diuresis (urine excretion) published by McCally and Barnard (1968). Water excretion by the kidney is regulated by vasopressin, an antidiuretic hormone (ADH) secreted by the posterior lobe of the pituitary gland. Secretion of this hormone is controlled by two known mechanisms, neural cells in the hypothalamus that are sensitive to osmotic pressure, and efferent impulses from receptors in the heart, primarily in the atrial "volume" receptors, which respond to an increase in intrathoracic blood volume. When a person is immersed in water (at body temperature) up to his neck, there occurs an increase in urine flow with a concomitant change in its chemical properties. This phenomenon of immersion diuresis is presumably a result of inhibition of ADH from stimuli from the "volume" receptors of the heart.

McCally and Barnard have shown the immersion diuresis can be significantly modified through suggestion. They analyzed urine samples from seven unpaid volunteer men who had previous autohypnotic training. Experimental conditions were: rest, rest with hypnosis, rest with hypnosis plus suggestions of thirst, immersion, immersion with hypnosis, and immersion with hypnosis and thirst suggestions. These authors acknowledge that they had no measure of hypnotic depth nor suggestion-without-hypnosis condition. However, it is notable that suggestions of thirst versus no such suggestion in the immersion situation resulted in diuretic changes in the directions that might be expected: (a) urine output fell significantly ($p <$ .05), (b) urine osmolarity increased (not significant), (c) urine solute excretion decreased (not significant), (d) sodium excretion increased (not significant), (e) glomerular filtration decreased significantly ($p < $ .05), and (f) free water clearance decreased significantly. "The present study demonstrates that the hypnotic suggestion of thirst inhibits diuresis during immersion" (p. 294).

Like so many other studies, the independent variable is not fully specified. Those differences that met usual standards of statistical reliability could have been produced under "imagination" conditions. Because of the small number of subjects, mean differences could be a result of the responses of but one or two subjects.

GASTROINTESTINAL FUNCTIONS

That hunger contractions, stomach secretions, and a variety of other gastrointestinal funtions can be modified by appropriate social-psychological stimulation is evidenced by both experimental and clinical reports (Eichhorn & Tracktir, 1955c; Ikemi et al., 1959; Kehoe & Ironside, 1964; Lewis & Sarbin, 1941; and others). Which of the myriad of variables incorporated into experimental hypnotic treatments are necessary and sufficient for the respective gastrointestinal events has not been ascertained. Hall et al. (1967)

examined gastric motor and secretory function during suggested symptoms in healthy volunteers using a standard test meal under controlled conditions with and without hypnosis. Subjects (unspecified as to age or sex) were selected from university student volunteers on the basis of no history of gastrointestinal disorders, high hypnotizability, and diagnostic testing to exclude people with severe emotional problems. Measurements and feeding of a standard meal of dextrose in a phenol red solution was accomplished by nasogastric intubation. During the first and fifth of five sessions each subject heard tape-recorded Chopin nocturnes. The intervening three sessions consisted of a taped hypnotic induction plus suggestions of indigestion or constipation for experimental subjects. Control subjects received the hypnotic induction and then listened to Chopin nocturnes. After each session the subject completed a questionnaire about his sensations, then his stomach was emptied, and he was dehypnotized and interviewed in a separate room.

Hypnosis alone resulted in the greatest residual stomach volume and least passage through the pyloric sphincter; this is as compared to music alone and to indigestion and constipation sessions. The rate of emptying of the stomach during the first hypnotic session was significantly lower than during hypnosis plus suggestions of indigestion, but was also significantly lower than during the fifth session of music and no hypnosis. Considering only data for the six out of eight subjects who reported sensations of indigestion or constipation does not change the results of this experiment.

ENDOCRINE FUNCTIONS AND METABOLISM

A number of metabolic processes has been reported susceptible to hypnotic manipulation. Respiratory exchange has been cited above. Sarbin (1956) and Barber (1961b) have reviewed a number of cases reporting hypnotic modification of blood glucose levels, basal metabolic rate, and calcium metabolism. Studies of metabolism and hypnotic stimulation have added to the methodological difficulties mentioned for other types of hypnotic research, since there is extreme liability of temperature, hormone titers, activity, or in general the level of "arousal" in the human body. And since many of these reports involved patients such as diabetics the data are even further confounded.

Few endocrine functions have been studied in relation to hypnosis other than via indirect manifestations through such processes as digestion, circulation, or respiratory alterations. Some work on adrenocortical steroids and hypnosis has been published. In a very simplified way we can think of a feedback loop between the anterior pituitary and the cortex of the adrenal glands. Apparently the pituitary release of ACTH can be affected directly by emotional stimulation, chemical stimuli, or limbic system trauma via the reticular activating system. Release of ACTH from the anterior pituitary into the blood stream stimulates the adrenal cortex to release cortisol (a glucocorticoid) back into the blood stream to affect central nervous system control of ACTH release. High circulation of cortisol inhibits ACTH secretion. The circulating levels of plasma cortisol are also dependent on diurnal cycles. Detectable levels of ACTH are quite low early in the morning and around six in the evening, and reach a peak in the early afternoon.

Sachar and others have reported in replicate a drop in plasma cortisol titers to significantly low levels ninety minutes after hypnotic induction (Sachar, Fishman, & Mason, 1964; Sachar, Cobb, & Shor, 1966). Four graduate students with no previous hypnotic experience were given hypnotic training over a six-week period during which diurnal cycles, medication, and time of reading hypnotic instructions and blood sampling were controlled. At two-week intervals a ninety minute "passive trance" was induced. One hour before and one hour after this session and immediately before and after this session blood samples were taken from each subject. The samples were frozen and later analyzed.

At the end of six weeks, control blood samples were taken without hypnosis. The day before each of the three "passive trance" sessions the Stanford Hypnotic Susceptibility Scale (Form C) was administered to each subject. With the use of interviews each subject was rated on degree of "nonconscious involvement in the hypnotic role," degree of "trance," and degree of "archaic" relationship with the hypnotist. In four out of twelve post-trance assays, 17-HOCS (seventeen-hydroxycorticosteroid includes primarily cortisol and its derivations) fell below a biologically significant cutoff level (two micrograms/100cc of blood plasma). The 17-HOCS measures never reached this low level in fifty other blood samples ($p <$ .0001). These low plasma cortisol levels did not appear to be correlated with scores of hypnotic susceptibility, nor degree of "trance," nor degree of nonconscious involvement, but did for the one applicable subject seem to be related to the degree of "archaic" transference to the hypnotist. For this subject the induction sessions were exhilirating; he felt that he was becoming dependent on the hypnotist and this pleased him; he had dreams involving the hypnotist and during sessions it seemed to him that the hypnotist was doing his thinking for him. Further nonhypnotic control sessions would have been useful. Sachar and coworkers refer to the "hypnotic state," a term that arises out of his operations inducing the "passive trance." The metatheory of the investigators is revealed in that the "state" occurs at finite times and can be monitored by plasma measures from samples taken before and after the "passive trance."

Reid and Curtsinger (1968) report hypnotic effects on several metabolic-related indices including oral temperature, respiration rate, blood pressure, and pulse rate. Their conclusion is that "neutral hypnosis" is generally accompanied by increased oral and skin temperature. Seventeen men and three women, between the ages of fifteen and sixty, volunteered to participate in an experiment in hypnosis; ten of these people had been previously hypnotized. All subjects were seated in a nonhumid, draft-free room maintained at 25° C. Hypnotic inductions were not read or taped, but an attempt was made to make them invariant from subject to subject. In progressive steps the subjects were told to close their eyes, to relax their muscles, to visualize a pleasant scene, and to relax deeper and deeper while the hypnotist counted to twenty. Pulse rate, respiration rate, systolic and diastolic blood pressure, and oral temperature were measured several times before and after the "trance." Temperatures were nearly identical pre- and post-trance, that is, ten minutes before and after the entrance and exit ceremonies. During "trance" the oral temperature went up an average of 0.6° F.

In a second portion of the study, four experimental subjects received the same treatments and four controls were simply told to relax while seated as above. A rise in oral temperature comparable to the first group occurred for experimental subjects, but only a .1° F. rise occurred for controls. Pulse rate, respiration, and blood pressure dropped slightly during "trance," so the increase in oral temperature is not attributable to increases in heart rate or respiration. However, it should be noted that oral temperature is highly dependent upon how a person breathes, as well as upon the rate of respiration and what he is doing with his mouth. Independent measures of body temperature other than intraoral would be helpful to validate the findings of Reid and Curtsinger. Using infrared heat detection techniques, the distribution of temperature changes over the body surface might be monitored during hypnotic and control instructions to explore further relationships between biothermodynamics and social-psychological stimulation.

CUTANEOUS FUNCTIONS

Skin blisters and wheals. The cure, exacerbation of, and production of dermatitis has been attributed to hypnotic stimulation. Reviews of this type of research have been reported by Barber, 1961b; Pattie, 1941; Sarbin, 1956; Paul, 1963; and others. Paul (1963) reviews literature from 1886 to 1962 that has dealt with hypnotic blister production. Of twenty-one reported attempts to produce nonherpetic skin blisters through suggestion, Paul finds only fourteen to be satisfactory in accounting for their methodology, procedures, and controls. Of these fourteen reports only three appear substantially free of alternative explanations for the reported skin anomalies; and these three reports are all from the early literature (prior to 1926). The remaining eleven studies involved procedures wherein self-injury, mechanical stimulation, contact dermatitis and/or mechanical edema could account for blister formation. In some studies, hypnotic suggestion included touching a certain part of the skin of a subject and suggesting that a burn would result. Paul reviews evidence that for some persons mechanical stimulation alone can trigger dermatitis. In those studies where a metal object such as a coin was used to touch the skin, he reviews evidence that the metals involved are known to produce contact dermatitis in some individuals. In other studies, the subjects were found to have irritated the skin in question at some time after the hypnotic induction and before blisters were evident (self-injury).

A unique study of skin reactivity with hypnotic induction is that of Ikemi and Nakagawa (1962). They selected thirteen subjects highly allergic to the poisonous leaf of the Japanese wax tree. These subjects were not sensitive to the nonpoisonous leaves of the chestnut tree. Five of these people were administered a hypnotic induction, blindfolded, and told that they were being touched with chestnut leaves. In fact their arms were touched with the poisonous wax leaf. Chestnut leaves were touched to the opposite arm, but now these people were told that they were being touched with the wax leaf. The eight remaining subjects were blindfolded, not given an hypnotic induction, but were given exactly the same treatment with the leaves and suggestions. All subjects showed slight to marked dermatitis (such as flushing, erythema, and papules) when touched with the nonallergic chestnut leaf but told it was the wax leaf. Five of the hypnotic and seven of the waking control subjects showed no noticeable allergic responses to the poisonous leaves of the wax tree.

Dermal excretions. Little or no experimental literature is available on this subject. A recent case report describes the control of sweat glands of the axilla via hypnosis (Sacerdote, 1967b). An eighteen year old girl had tried various medicants to stop armpit sweating, which became uncontrolled when she was at a social gathering. Sacerdote hypnotized her and over several separate sessions suggestions were given that she could control her involuntary responses and feel gay and happy at future parties. The reported effect of these hypnotic sessions was to bring this patient's sweating back to a normal level of responsivity to excess heat.

Skin temperature. Some reports of vasoconstriction and dilation have been mentioned in the section on cardiovascular functions. A number of reports dealing with surface body temperature alone have also been published. Gottlieb, Gleser, and Gottschalk (1967) examined the effects of hypnotically suggested attitudes on several physiological measures, including blood pressure and skin temperature. The suggested attitudes were: "hives" —described as a feeling of being mistreated but having no desire to act; and "Raynaud's" (after Raynaud's Syndrome)—described as a feeling of being mistreated with a desire to strike the mistreater. Although this investigation employed a standard hypnotic induction for the twelve male high school subjects, there was no waking control given comparable suggestions. Skin temperature rose significantly for subjects receiving the suggestions characterizing people with hives. A significant drop relative to "hives" temperature occurred with suggestions of Raynaud's attitude. However, for all subjects hypnotic induction produced a rise in skin temperature. (Regrettably, there was an increase in room temperature throughout the induction and testing.)

Interview material revealed that forty-six out of forty-eight suggested attitude periods were accompanied by self-reports of the suggested attitudes. The "hives" attitude did not affect blood pressure, but Raynaud's attitude increased heart rate and systolic (but not diastolic) blood pressure. The data were satisfactorily significant when the attitudes were directed toward the experimental assistant, but not when directed toward the hypnotist. It may be noted that "hypnosis" in this study was used as a vehicle to induce certain attitudes, rather than as the object of a physiological investigation.

Electrodermal changes. Ravitz (1950, 1951a, 1951b) and O'Connell and Orne (1962) found a reduction in spontaneous electrodermal activity during hypnosis as compared to a waking condition. Pessin, Plapp, and Stern (1968) randomly assigned forty male psychology undergraduates to four groups of ten each. All subjects were informed that the study concerned hypnosis, but the different groups were not told they would be hypnotized (or not) until just prior to the experimental session. Subjects reclined in a chair and were hypnotized by a standardized form of the SHSS such that words about hypnosis, sleep and drowsiness were removed. The experimental design is given in Table 9.1.

There were spontaneous fluctuations (SF) in the electrodermal response (EDR) during all treatments. Mean hypnotic SF was 40.75 while for the nonhypnotic groups it was 63.80 ($p > .025$). The SF *between* tone trials were significantly lower for Group I than for Group III. There was no significant difference in rate of habituation of the EDR between induction and rest groups. The Hypnosis Group I had consistently lower basal levels of skin resistance (BSR) during the rest period before tones than Group III, but this was not statistically significant. These authors comment that relaxation or sleep can result in a decrease in SF, but should be characterized by an increased level of BSR. Since the induction groups had lower BSR after induction, they say that "it seems unlikely that the effects of hypnotic induction in the present study are explainable in terms of heightened relaxation or sleep" (p. 204). Looking at this study critically, we might suggest that Groups I and III were first entertained, via the hypnotic induction, and then asked to perform a signal detection task. Groups II and IV, bored during the rest periods, were asked to perform a scanning task. Entertainment and excitement versus boredom and neutrality could no doubt be reflected in overall "arousal," a generalized somatic condition that would mediate the EDRs and BSRs and SF.

Tart (1963) found a high positive correlation between BSR and depth of hypnosis on a self-report depth scale. He selected "potentially good hypnotic subjects" by testing 345 undergraduate psychology students for arm levitation, interest in participating in the study, and lack of serious maladjustment as judged by MMPI profiles. Eleven men were chosen. These subjects were given two hypnotic training sessions to "familiarize them with the hypnotic state." The procedure the subjects went through suggests that they

TABLE 9.1   Experimental design of Pessin, Plapp, and Stern

Group	Initial Treatment	Final Treatment
I	15 min. induction	Suggestions to count tone stimuli (intermittent)
II	15 min. of rest	Suggestion to count tone stimuli (intermittent)
III	15 min. induction	Suggestions to attend visually to a slide projection and ignore other stimuli while counting squares on the screen
IV	15 min. of rest	Same as for Gr. III

might be aware of an expectation to be "good subjects" and to report a large magnitude of depth. Tart says there was a high correspondance between subjective depth reports and traditional criteria for depth such as amnesia—for example, eighty-seven percent of the subjects who reported a depth of thirty or more also reported amnesia. The BSRs were always measured just before or after events such as arm rotation. (If these are sequential items from the previous training sessions, a person might have learned the sequence and expect when the next event will occur; perhaps BSR measures sequential associations.) Tart mentions that a simulator control group with BSR measurements would be valuable. Another control group should just estimate degree of physical relaxation without hypnosis.

CENTRAL NERVOUS SYSTEM FUNCTIONS

Evoked potentials. Just as the spontaneous electrical activity of some mass population of neural elements can be measured by electrodes placed on a person's scalp (electroencephalogram), the sudden "jump" in the EEG tracing following a sudden loud clap of the hands or sudden flash of light into the eyes can also be measured. This sudden change in brain voltage that is driven by an external stimulus is referred to as an "evoked potential."

Evoked potentials are claimed to be affected by hypnotic suggestions by Hernández-Peón and Donoso (1959), and by Clynes, Kohn, and Lifshitz (1963). However, Beck, Dustman, and Beier (1966), Beck and Barolin (1965), and Halliday and Mason (1964) have failed to find a significant effect of hypnotic suggestions on evoked potentials. In the report by Beck, Dustman, and Beier (1966), visually evoked potentials were measured in ten normal subjects selected for known hypnotic suggestibility, who were hypnotized and given suggestions that light flashes of a constant intensity were in fact brighter or dimmer than a referent flash. Two hypnotists were assigned subjects who were hypnotized for two or more sessions. "Before any suggestion of light intensity was initiated certain behavioral criteria of hypnosis were evaluated, such as suggested catalepsy and anesthesia" (p. 398). Seven subjects reached somnambulism as rated by the Davis and Husband scale (1931). All subjects were photically stimulated by a uniform hemispheric surround. One hundred low intensity flashes were presented to each reclining subject at two to three second intervals. Summated evoked responses were determined by a computer of average transients for each one hundred flashes. During this photic stimulation, subjects received hypnotic suggestions of bright light or dim light. Summations of evoked responses were also made before hypnosis, after hypnosis, and randomly between suggestions of bright and dim light. Evoked responses were also measured for ten control subjects who actually received just noticeably brighter, dimmer, or intermediately intense photic stimulation.

Individual records of all twenty subjects plus composite records for experimental and control groups were analyzed for (a) time to peak delay of seven wave components of the visual evoked response (VER), (b) peak to trough amplitude for each component, (c) total excursion of the recording pen as it traced out the seven components. Results showed differences in these measures only for the subjects who actually received different intensities of photic stimulation. That is, total excursion and amplitude increased with increased stimulus intensity, but not with hypnotic suggestion of increased or decreased brightness.

The results of this experiment give no support to theories that posit an altered state of consciousness. The possibility remains that instrumentation and analysis were not sensitive enough to detect suggested dimness and brightness. Additional variables could have been assessed that might have offered some indirect support for such a posited altered state. For example, the experimenters could have assessed self-reported changes in brightness and correlated this assessment with changes in photic stimulation.

Spontaneous EEG activity. In earlier reports, the EEG record after hypnotic induction has been claimed by some researchers to be indistinguishable from waking patterns (Blake & Gerard, 1937; Chertok & Kramarz,

1959; Ford & Yeager, 1948; Loomis, Harvey, & Hobart, 1936; True & Stephenson, 1951; Weitzenhoffer, 1953.) However, differences between sleep and hypnosis have become a controversial issue, since other workers have found the postinduction EEG to resemble "light sleep," (Barker & Burgwin, 1949; Darrow et al., 1950).

Dittborn and O'Connell (1967) reported an experiment that was designed to show relationships between hypnotizability and sleep as measured behaviorally, physiologically, and by the subject's report. Seventy-five paid undergraduate volunteers were administered the SHSS Forms A and C, and a pre-experimental hypnotic induction wherein hypnotizability was assessed behaviorally. In addition, electroencephalograms were obtained to determine alpha content during a waking period. Of these subjects, fifty-one (mostly men) showed forty percent or more waking alpha prior to the experiment. These subjects were then seated in a reclining chair in a dark room and instructed to press a telegraph key each time they heard a stimulus buzzer. All of these subjects were given instructions that they would fall easily into natural sleep, *not* hypnosis, as they listened to the buzzer (which sounded about every nine seconds). Thus behavioral sleep was defined by failure to press the key when the buzzer sounded, subjective sleep was determined if the subject reported after the experiment that he had "dozed off" or "fallen asleep," and physiological sleep was determined by traditional criteria for stage one EEG sleep.

In terms of hypnotizability, twenty-eight subjects rated one to four while the remaining subjects were rated as extremely hypnotizable. Seventeen subjects evidenced 1.5 minutes or more of EEG defined sleep (no mention is made of observations for other than stage one sleep); ten of these seventeen responded to the buzzer while "asleep." Responding to the buzzer during EEG "sleep" was uncorrelated with hypnotizability. The subjects who showed no EEG sleep but did show behavioral sleep were highly hypnotizable subjects (a significant correlation, $p = .01$). Also, these subjects *reported* that they were asleep. Dittborn and O'Connell also found in this study that if subjects did not have the expectation that they were to "fall asleep" in their experimental situation, then they did not; however, if subjects were told that it is likely that people fall asleep in this situation, they do.

These findings offer little substance to the search for sleep correlates of hypnosis because of the multifaceted nature of the sleep variable. The various criteria of the "state of sleep" are poorly related.

In another type of study relating hypnotic susceptibility to phenomena of sleep, Evans et al. (1969) found a tendency of subjects to carry out a verbal suggestion administered during light sleep (EEG stage one sleep). Procedurally, nineteen male nurses slept two nights in the laboratory. After at least 120 seconds of stage one sleep by EEG criteria, a suggestion such as, "whenever I say the word 'itch,' your nose will feel itchy until you scratch it," was administered. During that same period of stage one sleep, or during a later period, or on the second night of sleep, if the cue word "itch" was spoken, the subject would scratch his nose (latency was about thirty-two seconds). These subjects did not respond to the cue word when it was spoken in a word association test when the subjects were awake during the day. (It is not clear whether the experimenter ever gave the cue words alone without suggestions, or if subjects would respond to the cue word if awake but it was nighttime). Evans et al. report that responsive subjects at night had waking amnesia for the cue words as well as the behavior they performed in their sleep. Yet these investigators report that with no repetition of the suggestion, the cue word elicited the response sometimes five months later in a follow-up laboratory sleep session. Could this be a result of conditioning to the laboratory setting? Is the response the effect of the cue word alone?

These authors found a high correlation between frequency of responses to the cue words during light sleep and hypnotizability scores. This positive correlation reached significance for subjects who could respond to the cue word on the second night of sleep when suggestions were given only on the first night. Also the subjects who were able to remain asleep while responding to the cue word instructions slept more soundly and claimed that they were sound sleepers (multiple $R = .68$, $p = .01$). Also these more hypnotizable subjects slept better in the laboratory than the insusceptible subjects, who were easily aroused by verbal stimulation during stage one sleep. Finally, "frequency of sleep response did not correlate with score clusters (factor analysis) derived from the hypnosis scales measuring various aspects of motor suggestion. Instead, sleep response frequency was related to the clusters typically consisting of phenomena obtained with somnambulistic hypnosis: hallucinations and posthypnotic effects" (p. 475). In the light of the analysis by Coe and Sarbin (1971) of the unidimensionality of hypnotizability scales, the findings of Evans et al. fit the notion that some subjects are skillful in performing difficult cognitive acts. The basis of the skill appears to be in the use of "as if" or hypothetical constructions.

The ultimate explanation for this finding, if replicated, will depend upon the meaning given to stage one sleep. If it is discontinuous from waking, then the strategy of research will return to a paradigm not unlike Braid's first theory (1843) that equated hypnosis and sleep.

London, Hart, and Leibovitz (1968) compared EEG alpha activity in subjects that varied in scores of hypnotic susceptibility. They proceed from the assumption that there are "waking and hypnotic states of consciousness" (p. 71). They state that many experiments show that people with high and those with low susceptibility to hypnosis also differ considerably in operant performance measures of strength, endurance, psychomotor coordination, and rote memory. London and McDevitt (1967) found that there are also differences in base-rate measures of autonomic nervous system functions.

Women volunteers, $N = 154$, of ages sixteen to sixty-one, participated in an experiment on "brain waves and hypnosis." One week before an individual measurement of EEG activity, these subjects were administered the Harvard Group Scale of Hypnotic Susceptibility. The EEG recording session was divided into ten trials of two minutes duration. Subjects were told only to relax with eyes closed ("operant task"). This was followed by a single two-minute EEG sample after instructions to perform a visual imagery task.

Mean alpha durations were compared for subjects falling into four levels of hypnotic susceptibility (tenth, twenty-fifth, seventy-fifth, and ninetieth percentiles). Between the operant and visual imagery task there were no significant differences in alpha duration. There were significant differences between the tenth and twenty-fifth and between the seventy-fifth and ninetieth percentile groups with an increase in alpha duration with increased hypnotic susceptibility scores.[1]

At first glance, this report suggests that hypnotizability is correlated with a fundamental somatic process. It should be made clear, however, that relaxation increases alpha. Perhaps the authors were monitoring the EEG correlates of the ability to accept the relaxation instructions that are implicit, if not explicit, in most inductions.

Katzenstein (1965) reports some electrobiological data on one hundred patients at the German Academy of Science Research Institute, (Berlin-Buch, Germany). He interprets the presence of alpha activity to indicate hypnotic effect. In some patients he found beta rhythms (signs of vigilance), which he interprets as an indication of the effectiveness of hypnotic influence. In many patients he found delta waves and sleep spindles after induction when the hypnotist had left the room. With a sensitive actograph he found a "remarkably uniform drop" in motor activity in all subjects. This observed immobility exceeded by far the decrease in motor activity that characterized normal sleep. He suggests this hypothesis: "subjects with strong internalized behavioral inhibitions would tend to react more fully to an initial hypnotic induction procedure than those with less strongly developed inhibitions" (p. 323).

We cannot make much of this report because of the lack of measures of hypnotic depth and statistical analyses.

OCULAR MOVEMENTS AND INTERNAL ALTERATIONS

Rapid eye movements. A considerable interest in eye movements has

---

1. If these highly susceptible people have such high alpha durations during waking periods, this ceiling effect might very well obliterate any expected differences in alpha duration when they are hypnotized.

evolved over the past fifteen years as a result of work in the early fifties by Aserinsky and Kleitman (1953) showing that concomitant with dreaming are bursts of conjugate rapid eye movements (REMs). One interpretation of this phenomenon is that the dreamer is scanning visual images. Another interpretation suggests that REMs are a nonspecific correlate of attentive activity. The reports that dreaming can occur without REMs and vice versa also raise the possibility that REMs cannot be accounted for by either of these interpretations.

In relation to hypnosis, Amadeo and Shagass (1963) have attempted to test two hypotheses. The more general hypothesis is that eye movements (an increase in intensity or frequency) are a nonspecific concomitant of attentive activity. The more specific hypothesis is stated as follows: "If it were found that eye movements increase in frequency with heightened attention and decrease in the hypnotic state, these findings would support the hypothesis that overall attentive activity is diminished during hypnosis" (p. 139). We should note that two assumptions are implicit in this hypothesis: the assumption that "the hypnotic state" is a given, and the assumption that in that "state" attention is narrowed or reduced in intensity.

Thirteen women and fifteen men, paid volunteers, were subjects in two separate experiments. In an attention experiment ten subjects had their eye movements measured (EOG) while reclining with eyes closed on a couch. Subjects were instructed to relax while the EOG was recorded for three minutes. Next the EOG was recorded while subjects recalled as vividly as possible a scene from a recently viewed movie. Finally subjects were given a word association test with auditory stimuli and the EOG was recorded during the "ready" period, presumably a time of heightened attention. In a hypnosis experiment the remaining twenty subjects were exposed to three conditions in partially counterbalanced design: waking condition—EOG recorded with eyes open, closed, and closed with instructions to perform mental arithmetic (doubling a single digit spoken every two seconds); hypnosis condition—subjects were hypnotized by a variation of Kraines's "sleeping method," then the EOG was measured as in the first condition: eyes open, closed, with performance of mental arithmetic; voluntary prevention of eye movement condition—subjects were instructed to concentrate on keeping their eyes perfectly still while EOG was again recorded with eyes open, closed, and during mental arithmetic.

Mean REM/min. were counted for subjects in each condition. REM were defined by a predetermined cutoff amplitude and duration of movement of the recording needle. The results of the attention experiment showed a mean REM/min. of 7.6 in the initial resting condition, 20.4 during imagining of the movie, and 17.7 during the "ready" phase of the word association test. The REM rate was significantly lower ($p < .01$) in the resting phase than in the other two conditions. For the hypnosis experiment the hypnotized subjects and voluntary control subjects had a significantly lower REM rate than nonhypnotized subjects across all three subconditions: eyes open, closed, and during the arithmetic task. The voluntary control REM rate was higher than the hypnotic rate across these subconditions (not statistically significant). Support for the hypothesis of increased eye movements with attentive activity comes from the observation that there was a high REM rate during auditory attention comparable in magnitude to the rate during vivid imagery. These investigators conclude from the hypnosis experiment that "there is antagonism between the hypnotic state and attentive performance" (p. 142). This conclusion is based on the low REM rate for hypnotized subjects plus data that only about half of the subjects when hypnotized succeeded in performing the arithmetic task.

It is important to note that reduced attentive activity was attributed to the presumed "hypnotic state" rather than to different instructions. A "state" is not a necessary given for the interpretation of these data if role theory is employed. If subjects are instructed to behave as if they are sleepy ("sleeping method" of hypnotic induction), the role demands and expectations in that situation are simply contrary to performing mental arithmetic. The high REM rate for these subjects probably reflects the higher degree of arousal accompanying the demand to perform implicitly contradictory tasks, namely to behave as if they were sleepy and relaxed. Unfortunately Amadeo and Shagass cannot validate their "state" proposition by comparison of hypnotized subjects instructed to imagine vividly the movie scene with waking subjects given identical instructions.

The instructions given the voluntary control subjects to "concentrate on holding your eyeballs perfectly still" is logically an instruction for a high level of attention—attention to keeping the eyeballs fixed. Interpretation of these data becomes difficult since in this situation the experimenter is essentially telling the subject to voluntarily interfere with the dependent variable. An interesting comparison would be to record the EOG while the subject is instructed to concentrate on holding his hand or tongue perfectly still.

Another example of recent work on possible relations between hypnosis and bursts of rapid eyeball movements is a study by Brady and Rosner (1966), who compared ocular activity during hypnotically induced dreams with that during imagined dreaming.

Undergraduate paid volunteers (five men and six women) were assigned to the hypnotically induced dream group (H) on the basis of their reporting dreaming during pre-experimental hypnotic suggestions to "have a dream." The mean score of these subjects on the SHSS Form C was 8.2. Three men and two women were assigned to the imagined dream group (C) on the basis that they did not report hypnotically induced dreams. The mean score for this group on the SHSS was 5.6. All subjects were then given indentical treatment except that group H was given a hypnotic induction, whereas group C was simply instructed to imagine dreaming (this group was never told that they would not be hypnotized). EEG and EOG were recorded from all subjects during an initial resting phase, after hypnotic induction for group H, during mental arithmetic, during suggested dreaming, during a postdreaming resting phase, and during postdreaming mental arithmetic.

Hypnotized subjects showed the expected increase in EEG alpha relative to pre-induction alpha in the same subjects. (Did subjects have eyes closed at all times?) Within group H the range of ocular activity was significantly reduced from waking-resting to hypnotic-resting phases; rest, activity, and amplitude of eye movements did not differ significantly between these two phases. The hypnotic dreams significantly increased the range of eye movements. Mental arithmetic produced a larger range of eye movements after hypnosis than before. The marked differentiation between groups H and C was a significantly lower base rate of all measures of ocular activity for group C. For example, median ocular activity during "dreaming" for group C was 4.8, while for group H the median was 40.3. In fact, imagined dreams never raised any measure of ocular activity above the level for mental arithmetic in the same group (C).

Brady and Rosner conclude that their data supports that of Amadeo and Shagass (1963) that eye movements decrease during hypnotic trance, and that attentiveness is reduced during hypnotic trance as indicated by reduced EOG activity and increased alpha EEG activity.

In any comparison between groups H and C we do not know if differences in EOG activity during any experimental phase were consequences of hypnotic induction, or the preselection of subjects who did or did not manifest hypnotic dreaming. The fact that the initial EOG base rates were so different between groups C and H suggests that these groups differed importantly even before hypnosis. Also, group C not only was not hypnotized, but was given different dream instructions—group H was told to "have a dream," while group C was told to "imagine" having a dream. Therefore the effects of hypnosis per se must be evaluated from data within group H. As was the case with the Amadeo and Shagass experiment, there is no independent measure of hypnotic trance apart from the induction that brought it about. Nor is there a waking control group that is *identical* on preselection criteria. Therefore attributing changes in EEG or EOG to a "state" rather than to different instructions is unwarranted at this time.

Slow eye movements. Weitzenhoffer (1969) has reported observations of slow eye movements (SEMs) during deep hypnosis. In connection with another type of experimentation on hypnosis, he recorded eye movements in fifteen subjects who were students, secretaries, and laboratory technicians. Subjects ranged from zero to twelve on the Stanford Scale of Hypnotic Susceptibility, Form A. The low-scoring subjects were used as simulators, while high-scoring subjects served as hypnotic subjects. Following induction, eye movements were recorded while subjects carried out a variety of tasks including opening and closing their eyes, going into hypnosis with their eyes open, resuming the nonhypnotic state, and then reentering hypnosis àt a signal.

Nonhypnotized persons, sitting quietly without specific instructions, produce saccadic eye movements that are irregular and of high amplitude. With eyes closed, the same persons show the same type of REM but of lower amplitude. Reduced REM and micro eye movements occur during induction of hypnosis, (suggested eye closure involved). Somewhat late in hypnosis, and only for the high-scoring subjects on the SSHS (scores combined of twenty-two or better, scales A, C) a slow eye movement appeared with a period of about four seconds and an amplitude of about one-third that during waking REMs. In contrast to REMs, the SEM is a slower and smoother movement. Thus SEMs were produced only by the most hypnotizable and presumably most deeply hypnotized subjects. SEMs were produced when outward judgments of depth were highest (LeCron type of depth estimations). These SEMs were the same as described for stage one sleep (light sleep); the subjective report was of lessened awareness but definitely not of sleep. The subjects had no idea what was being measured. In these deeply hypnotized subjects, instructions to open the eyes abolished the SEM, but it returned with eye closure. Subjects who had produced the SEM pattern were unable to reproduce it voluntarily without extensive coaching and practice. Weitzenhoffer states: "It can be said with reasonable confidence that the reported results could not have been the product of demand characteristics of the situation, even if this could be a factor under other conditions" (p. 225).

He cannot discount that the subjects might have fallen into light "natural" sleep since EEG and GSR measures were not taken; it is entirely possible that the somatic mechanisms activated in light sleep which are responsible for the accepted indices of stage one sleep are also activated in hypnosis (p. 226). The SEM subjects were in contact with and responsive to the hypnotist, however this may also be true of light sleep as was reported by Evans et al. Weitzenhoffer suggests the interesting notion that laboratory sleep studies never have studied "natural sleep," and that in fact there is reason to believe that instructions to the subjects are such as to suggest that they are in a hypnoidal if not a hypnotic state. Weitzenhoffer quotes a report where, physiologically speaking, a subject required to move his legs and arms rhythmically to loud music while viewing synchronized flashes of light produced episodes of *light sleep* alternating with episodes of wakefulness. The subject was unaware of the sleep episodes during this "monotonous" activity. Apparently the EEG record and eye movements of

Stage one sleep also occur under LSD and with other circumstances. "The fact remains that individuals who, on the basis of well-known and accepted behavioral criteria, must be judged as having been hypnotized, and probably deeply so at the time, have been found conjointly to produce SEM" (p. 227).

According to Weitzenhoffer, light sleep and hypnosis can be the same at this level of physiological manifestation. He quotes Heiman and Spoerri (1953), who suggest that hypnosis can coexist with sleep as distinct but simultaneous states. This notion that two or more ordinarily exclusive "states" can occur simultaneously in the same individual is the basis for the following suggestion by Weitzenhoffer: "one might consider the possibility that subjects who exhibit hypnotic-like behavior in the absence of SEM are merely exhibiting a high degree of waking suggestibility, and those who also produce SEM are exhibiting much suggestibility in the presence of an altered state of awareness, otherwise to be identified as 'hypnosis' as distinct from 'suggestibility' " (p. 227).

Optokinetic nystagmus. During the turning of the head about a vertical axis, there occurs a deviation of the eyes in a direction opposite to the turning. This conjugate eye movement maintains the image of a fixed object on the retinas. After a certain degree of deviation, the eyes are quickly shifted back in the same direction the head is turning. These two movements of the eyes, when cyclically repeated, constitute nystagmus. It is the quick component of eye deviation that defines the direction of nystagmus.

If a person with normal vision gazes at a rotating drum that has alternating black and white vertical lines, he will show horizontal optokinetic nystagmus. A blind person will of course not show this response, but presumably an hysterically blind person or a person faking blindness *will* show the nystagmus. Backus (1962) tested a single subject under three conditions: waking with visual fixation on the rotating drum, deeply hypnotized with eye fixation on the drum, and deeply hypnotized with eyes fixed on the drum but with negative hallucinations suggested, such as that the drum was absent from the room. This subject showed horizontal nystagmus under the first two conditions, but no nystagmus under the third condition. Thus a deeply hypnotized subject was able to respond as if the drum were absent, as though he were truly blind, and in a manner that a faker could presumably not do.

Backus explicitly assumes that the subject was in a "trance" state. Neither the effects or specifics of the induction nor the subject's personal history can be evaluated since details are not reported. It is not clear whether in the third condition the subject continued to fixate on the drum after the negative hallucination instructions; if he discontinued one would of course expect a cessation of the nystagmus. Finally we must ask if the subject might not have shown the absence of nystagmus in a waking condition with fixation on the drum, but also with nonhypnotic instructions to imagine that the drum was absent.

In a controlled experiment Aschan, Finer, and Hagbarth (1962) studied hypnotic suggestion effects on "good hypnotic subjects" during rotary nystagmus. With four experimental treatments it was found that hypnotic suggestions of increased or decreased rotary sensation had the predicted effect of enhancing or diminishing the intensity of eye movements. Unfortunately they did not include a control for suggestions without hypnosis.

Pupillary diameter. Bartlett, Faw, and Liebert (1967) studied the effects of traditional hypnotic relaxation instructions versus alertness instructions on pupil size of a deeply hypnotized subject. A young adult woman who scored in the upper twenty percent on the SHSS:C was pretested to determine that she could have the subjective experience of hypnosis with her eyes either open or closed. She was then deeply hypnotized (no measure) by the traditional induction procedures of the SHSS:C. A 16mm movie was taken of one of her eyes while she was given suggestions either of relaxation or of alertness and attention. It was found that her mean pupil diameter increased by about two mm. during alertness suggestions, yet after the experiment she reported being in a hypnotic state through both types of instructions. These investigators conclude that "various parameters of arousal apparently associated with hypnosis may be attributable to specifiable characteristics of the instructions used rather than to stable characteristics of the 'state' of hypnosis" (p. 189).

Subjects are known to behave in accordance with their interpretation of the experimental expectation. Did this subject know what the experiment was about? There is no base rate measure of pupil size. Therefore it remains as a possibility that her pupil spontaneously cycled through the diameter changes measured regardless of the type of instructions. Other questions are: Was the subject dark adapted? Were both eyes open? Which eye was measured? What was the variability in pupil diameter?

Ocular anatomy. Strosbert and Vics (1962) studied subepithelial physiological and anatomical changes in the eye of ten patients who had all been "previously hypnotically conditioned." In a procedure that took only twelve minutes per patient the eye was microscopically examined with a slit lamp before, after, and in one case during hypnotic induction. By using natural landmarks such as a blood vessel on the surface of each individual eye examined, these workers measured the blood supply in the vascular anastomosis, the relucency of the arcades, changes in the curvature of the cornea, and the degree of engorgement of the vessels on the sclera. Unfortunately these investigators give no measure of degree of hypnosis; the hypnotic state is a given and the only statement about the induction procedure is that the patient was "hypnotized." Comparison of observations and measurements during and after hypnosis showed the following results: (a) deepening of color and increase in width of an arbitrarily chosen blood vessel on the sclera (no statistical analyses are reported), (b) the normally open meshwork at the junction of the cornea and sclera became a solid mass, (c) the distance from the corneal-scleral junction to the tops of the vascular arcades decreased (from fifty to thirty of the units marked on the microscopic objective), (d) decrease of blood supply in the anastomosing vessels near the corneal-scleral junction, and (e) a shift in the degree of axis of astygmatism in those patients with this corneal abnormality.

This study shares the faults of many reviewed above. The "hypnotic state" is presented as a given. No control subjects were employed. There was no examination of effects of other types of instructions or of instructions to perform tasks during the "hypnotic state." No statistical tests are reported.

Design Problems

To better evaluate the research reports, some of the problems of experimental design should be noted here. The most commonly employed experimental design, subjects-as-own-controls, developed out of the clinical method. Often employing a single subject, the experimenter (or therapist) would first monitor certain physiological processes during the waking (resting) condition. After hypnosis was induced, he would utter either direct suggestions ("your heart is beating faster") or indirect suggestions ("you are about to be attacked by the grizzly bear just behind you"). Any change in monitored physiological responses was attributed to the power of the hypnotic trance. Such clinical reports have been rejected by modern behavioral scientists as support for psychosomatic theories, mainly because generalizations cannot be drawn from single-case studies.

The subjects-as-own-control design is a logical outgrowth of the single-case study. By increasing the number of subjects, and by using standardized experimental treatments, changes in physiological indicators can be traced to antecedent conditions, one of which is the hypnotic induction procedure. A tenuous assumption must be held to give empirical warrant to such a procedure, to wit, that the subject carries no information from one experimental condition to the other. To make the subject "blind" to the experimental hypotheses, the experimenter usually instructs the subject to be amnesic to the earlier treatments. The available evidence makes dependence on the assumption a risky business. For example, Barber (1962c) demonstrated that subjects who expect to be hypnotized during a later phase of an experiment perform differently from subjects who do not hold this expectation.

The independent groups design has been introduced to counter the problems inherent in the subjects-as-own-control design. Those who employ this design are in general interested in demonstrating that the effects attributed to the hypnotic trance can be more parsimoniously attributed to task-motivation, imagination, specialized instructions, and so on. In this design the experimenter employs two or more samples of subjects: to one sample is administered a standard hypnotic induction; the other sample receives nonhypnotic treatments, such as instructions to "imagine vividly." This design has not been widely used in experiments to assess changes in somatic processes. Where it has been employed, the results until now have failed to show any clear support for the existence of a physiological variable that could serve as an independent criterion of the hypnotic trance.

The independent groups design has been criticized as being insensitive to small, but significant, differences. In studies designed to tease out such small differences, Hilgard and Tart (1966) recommend repeated measures on the same subjects, under different conditions. In their study, they first assessed responsiveness to suggestion for three samples of subjects: one sample was tested in the waking condition, another in an imagination condition, and a third in a hypnotic condition. A second session assessed responsiveness of each of the samples to hypnotic induction. A small but significant increase in responsiveness was found for the two groups who had been tested previously under the waking and imagination conditions, but not for the sample that had been tested under the hypnotic condition. They drew the conclusion that a small effect in responsiveness can be attributed to hypnotic induction.

Experiments from Barber's laboratory (Barber & Glass, 1962; Barber & Calverley, 1963b) are not consistent with this finding. The imagination instructions in the Hilgard-Tart experiment are more like those of "unmotivated" subjects in Barber's laboratory. When proper task-motivation instructions are given, different responsiveness under the hypnotic conditions is more difficult to obtain.

The controversy over the relative merits of the own-controls design and the independent groups design has been carried on primarily within the study of hypnotic responsiveness as assessed through hypnotic susceptibility scales. Our search of the literature reveals no parallel controversies where physiological indicators serve as dependent variables.

Another experimental design focuses on base rates. Although widely used in public health research, base rate design is seldom encountered in hypnosis research and almost never when physiological processes are being monitored. The purpose of the base rate design is to show that subjects are not preselected for characteristics that are relevant to the criterion variable.

An implicit assumption held by many researchers is that the somatic responses under scrutiny have a zero base rate. That is to say, responses such as marked changes in heart rate, skin conductance, and blood sugar levels are nonexistent under ordinary basal conditions in the general population. Therefore, the observation of atypical changes after a hypnotic induction procedure may be attributed to the hypnotic state. Rates of response greater than zero are presumed to result from the induction procedures, when in fact they may already exist in the experimental sample.[2]

When psychophysiological experiments are conducted with small numbers of subjects, it is imperative to have a base rate in order to assess the effects of the experimental treatments. Underwood (1960) reported the results of an experiment that appeared to support the claim that a visual illusion can be influenced by the hypnotic trance. His interpretations suggested the altered operation of perceptual-physiological processes. Sarbin and Andersen (1963) repeated the experiment using imagination instructions rather than the hypnotic induction. Underwood's conclusions were based on the performance of a half-dozen subjects (three percent of his total subjects). Sarbin and Andersen demonstrated the same "hallucinatory" phenomenon—without hypnosis—in nine percent of their subjects. Had Underwood conducted an assessment of the base rate for this particular task, he would not have concluded that the "hallucination" was specific to the hypnotic induction.

It is obvious why base rates are not usually obtained in psychophysiological research. The time and expense involved are enormous. Each subject must be assessed individually. In order to establish reliable base rates for infrequent occurrences, hundreds of subjects would have to be assessed.

Theoretical Integrative Considerations

In reviewing the literature on the somatic effects of hypnosis, we paraphrase William James's comment about his review of the literature on emotion: It would be more rewarding to count and catalog the rocks of New Hampshire than to reread the literature on the somatic effects of hypnosis. Two conclusions can be drawn from our review. Conclusion one concerns the question, Are observed alterations in physiological processes specific to the hypnotic "trance"? The answer is an unqualified no. Conclusion two concerns the question, Can symbolic processes produce changes in biological processes?

2. Some years ago, one of us (T.R.S.) was exploring the possibility of studying the effect of hypnosis on reflexes. An adult volunteer was administered a standard hypnotic induction procedure. Depth of hypnosis was assessed by the Friedlander-Sarbin scale. At the conclusion of the testing, the subject was told to relax even more and that his reflexes would be tested by a physician. Imagine the astonishment of the physician when he obtained an apparent infantile Babinski in an intact well-functioning adult. The inference was immediately constructed that the infantile Babinski was a form of regression brought about by the hypnotic induction. Later it was discovered that his patient could exhibit the anomolous reflex under nonhypnotic conditions. The assumption that such anomolies occur only as a result of neuropathology led to the unwarranted expectation of a zero base rate.

The answer is an unqualified Yes. That somatic processes can be influenced by symbolic stimuli is an observation that goes back at least to Aristotle. The reviews of Dunbar (1954) and the reports to be found in *Psychosomatic Medicine* make clear that the introduction of a large variety of stimulating conditions including symbolic stimuli and imaginings, can influence life processes.

Our theoretical efforts must be redirected. Instead of persevering in the search for an elusive physiological indicator for the trance, we can try to understand the more general problem contained in Conclusion two. In short, can we illuminate the proposition that physiological processes can be influenced by social psychological stimuli?

The concepts of role theory are helpful in formulating some propositions that help to account for the observations. As a point of departure, we begin with the suggestion that hypnotic performances can be regarded as role enactments, the subject taking the role of the hypnotized person within limits imposed by his expectations, skills, self-conceptions, and by the demands of the situation, including audience effects. Role enactment is the independent variable, and one of its components is organismic involvement in the role performance.[3]

The enactment of any role may be conceptualized in terms of more or less intensity, or rate of energy transformation. "Intensity" is the descriptive term applied to the molar observed event; it is tied to the increased functioning of the organism as a whole and can be monitored by various physiological assessment procedures. In fact, the change in intensity of the molar act depends in part on changes in the internal physiology. For example, the intense role of "quarterback making an end run" cannot be enacted unless the visceral and somatic organ systems are acting synergically.

The organismic-involvement dimension, of course, applies to any social role, be it shaman, professor, shortstop, or mother. It is a matter of everyday observation that roles are enacted with varying degrees of organismic involvement, although in most roles, of course, it is minimal—otherwise the physiological expenditures would be out of proportion to available reserves. One approach to the assessment of the organismic dimension, commonly used by clinically oriented investigators and reporters, is that of global observation of the role. The investigator observes the patterned activity of visible effector organs and then records his observations, using for examples such qualitative terms as agitated, surprised, anxious, heated, calm, matter-of-fact, apathetic. The investigator may further organize his perceptions into social concepts such as frenzied behavior, passive role, assertive conduct, "little-boy" role, etc. To such observations our knowledge of

---

3. The paragraphs dealing with the concept of organismic involvement are freely adapted from Sarbin (1956).

general physiology can be added and we can predict (and test the predictions) that certain physiological changes will be associated with certain degrees of organismic involvement in a particular role.

As an everyday example, take the husband of a primiparous woman who is in labor in a modern hospital. From a time-sample observation we would say that he is tense, anxious, pacing, restless, and so on. We could further organize these qualitites on the basis of knowledge of the situation into the role concept of "expectant father." We could further place his conduct at a high level of organismic involvement and predict elevation in blood pressure, increase in temperature, cessation of gastric function, increased palmar sweating, and other characteristics that are part of the adaptive techniques of the organism to stress. Furthermore, we can predict reversals of the global behavior within a finite time interval following the announcement of the birth of the child and the reassurances of the physician that all is well. The shift in behavior will be organized around his everyday occupational role, one that is normally enacted with low-level involvement. Associated with the taking up of his everyday role are the reversals of the physiological changes mentioned before. The concept of organismic involvement in role enactment is, for the present, organized around such global conceptions. That such involvement can be monitored by appropriate psychophysiological and physiological techniques has been amply demonstrated.

For purposes of this exposition, we will illustrate eight levels of organismic involvement in role-taking. Hypnotic subjects may perform with intensities that can be classified at any point on this organismic dimension, except perhaps at the extremes.

Level 0. This level can be characterized by latent roles peripheral to everyday actions; there is absence of involvement.

Level 1. This is everyday casual role enactment. There is little affect, little involvement of self in role. Performances are more or less automatic, routinized, effortless. The actions of the hypnotic subject cannot be classified at this level: to volunteer for an experiment in hypnosis or to seek hypnotic therapy denotes greater involvement in the social role than level one.

Level 2. At this level, mechanical acting, we can observe the behavior of hypnotic subjects who score low on depth scales. Here the hypnotic subject, like the mechanical actor, performs stereotyped ritual movements in order to validate his occupancy of the social position. Again we see little affect and little effort, although more than in level one. According to retrospective accounts of "mechanical" actors and of hypnotic subjects classified at this level, there is little involvement of self in role.

Level 3. Heated acting ("living the role") shows, of course, more effort, more activity on the part of the subject, such as grimacing, increased rate of respiration, and tension, and more side effects of such voluntarily initiated activity. In order to manifest rage, for instance, an actor may work himself up emotionally by violently shaking a ladder in the wings before appearing on the stage. Among the easily observed side effects are erythema, rapid pulse, increased sweating, and vocal effects. Here we can see much involvement of the self in the role. Many hypnotic subjects behave in ways that allow them to be classified at this level.

Level 4. This level is denoted by hypnotic behavior of the somnambulistic type. The classical behavior of the deeply hypnotized subject, the perceptual-motor effects, the compulsive posthypnotic behaviors, the amnesias, the hallucinations, all show much involvement of the self in the role. There is apparent effort, a striving to do what the experimenter requests. Here is illustrated most forcefully the operation of the "as if" mechanism, the influence of covertly taking the role in a relatively complete way, with reduction of possibilities for performing competing roles. The subject tries to perform as if he were blind, or deaf, or analgesic, or anosmic, or whatever the role instructions demand.

Level 5. The behaviors subsumed under the rubric histrionic neurosis or conversion reactions are used as a frame of reference on the organismic dimension. The histrionic patient responds as if he suffered some sensory or motoric affliction. The range of intensity overlaps the range of behaviors of the deeply hypnotized person, level four. However, expression of affect associated with the maintenance of the "as if" behavior is the rule. The involvement of the self in the role of the invalid is immediately apparent when efforts are made to modify the behavior. At the same level of intensity are trance states of the Plains Indians (Benedict, 1934) and the couvade (Crawley, 1927), the custom where the husband lies-in during parturition.

Level 6. Only occasionally are hypnotic performances classified at level six. Ecstatic states are usually associated with the suspension of voluntary action. They are seen in socially initiated situations such as religious conversions, mystical states, possession, and religious revivals. In addition to the greater involvement of the skeletal musculature, there is an increased involvement of the organs served by the autonomic nervous system. Here we see, in extremis, affect and effort. The nearly complete submergence of the self in the role is observed. Obviously, such performances cannot be prolonged over time without damage to the organism. As a general rule, automatic equilibratory controls terminate such intense behaviors through institutionalized rituals, fatigue or exhaustion, and/or autonomic regulation.

Level 7. This level is not applicable to the usual experiment in hypnosis. It is an extension of the previous range but is characterized by the failure of equilibratory mechanisms. Well authenticated cases of voodoo death have been described by Cannon (1942) and others. The focus is on role-taking as the initiatory phase of complex and irreversible physiological activity.

Conclusion

Within a naturalistic framework, which asserts that hypnosis is not necessarily a transcendental phenomenon but rather a specialized kind of social situation, our point of departure for theory building must depend upon objective observation of the events in question, interpreted against a background of available knowledge drawn from psychology and physiology.[4]

4. Because of space limitations, we have had to forego considering general theories of psychosomatics against which physiological changes in hypnosis may be evaluated. Theoretical accounts have been offered by Arnold (1959), Kraines (1969), Roberts (1960), Sarbin (1956) and others. The importance of the brain stem reticular system, diffuse projection systems, and "recruiting" response and "attentional" processes in general are clearly underscored in current theories. Arnold, Kraines, and Roberts each relate hypnosis to those same processes that underlie attention and sleep. All three agree that the neural substrata for hypnosis fall between the classical sensory and motor systems. These neurophysiological hypotheses account for most of the "symptoms" of hypnosis. They are sufficiently general, however, to be a basis for many types of behavior other than hypnotic behavior. The definition of hypnosis in these accounts remains unspecified, taken for granted without rigorous attention to operational designations of the phenomena for which the neural substrata are hypothesized. Unlike such theories that focus on dependent variables, the views advanced in the theory proposed by Sarbin (1956) take into account the vagaries in the independent variable "hypnosis." Because no physiological variable has been discovered that is *specifically* tied to hypnosis, the most obvious place to begin a theory is at a juncture of the symbolic stimulus and the initial molar somatosensory response.

Leslie M. Cooper *is a Clinical Professor of Psychology at the University of Utah. He received his Ph.D. from the University of Illinois in 1962. He has engaged in teaching and research at Brigham Young University, the University of Southern California, and Stanford University where he was associated with the Laboratory of Hypnosis Research. He has been a consultant to the Utah State Training School, Alpine House, a halfway house associated with the Utah State Mental Hospital, and the Utah State Prison. He is a diplomate in experimental hypnosis and licensed as a psychologist in the state of Utah where he also has a private practice. His interests in research include hypnosis, learning, and imagery.*

Cooper *presents a comprehensive review of current knowledge about hypnotic amnesia as derived from experimental studies. The chapter begins with a definition of hypnotic amnesia and describes the standardized assessment procedures used to measure it in the laboratory. Different types of hypnotic amnesia are described, methodological problems and research evidence are reviewed, and the variables which influence hypnotic amnesia are discussed along with issues of authenticity and of underlying mechanisms. Cooper argues that hypnotic amnesia needs to be redefined in order to eliminate mere verbal inhibition, and to integrate the role of normal forgetting. He also stresses that better ways should be found to incorporate clinical sources of evidence into laboratory settings.*

10

Hypnotic Amnesia

LESLIE M. COOPER

As one of the phenomena that characterize hypnosis, amnesia has long figured in the lore and in anecdotes relating to hypnosis. References to its occurence and effects are found in some of the earliest literature on hypnosis. Experimental investigations of hypnotic amnesia began in the early twentieth century. Much of the early experimental work lacked an objective, standardized measure of responsiveness to hypnotic suggestions. It is little wonder that there was difficulty in uncovering the parameters of hypnotic amnesia, or any other hypnotic phenomena for that matter, when there was little objective agreement on how to measure hypnosis. In 1959, the first of a series of susceptibility scales, possessing the psychometric properties of high reliability, internal consistency, and validity was published. The scales, discussed later in the chapter, made it possible to measure responsiveness to hypnosis in a controlled manner. They yield results that can be meaningfully compared from study to study. The development of these scales made it possible to rigorously study various hypnotic phenomena, including amnesia.

This chapter reviews the current status of knowledge and thinking about hypnotic amnesia and presents the experimental evidence supporting these conclusions. The survey of the literature should be considered representative, rather than exhaustive. An attempt has been made, however, to comprehensively cover the substantive areas associated with hypnotic amnesia. Experimental evidence for, and procedures used to study, hypnotic amnesia, rather than clinical case studies are emphasized. The organization of the chapter is topical rather than chronological. The first section discusses the definition of hypnotic amnesia and the means devised to measure it. A typical procedure used to assess hypnotic amnesia is presented in detail, so that the reader will understand the nature of the instructions commonly used, the task of the subjects, and the manner of assigning a score to the response.

"Hypnotic amnesia" is an inclusive term used to label any of a number of different types of amnesia occurring as a result of a hypnotic procedure. The second section of this chapter defines and discusses a number of different types of amnesia, such as posthypnotic recall amnesia and source amnesia. It briefly describes representative studies investigating each type, including the evidence for their occurrence as well as their relationship to one another.

A third section discusses the variables which have been found to give rise to and affect the nature of hypnotic amnesia. This section discusses the independent variables which have been found to account for some of the variance in hypnotic amnesia when it is considered as a dependent variable. The role of demand characteristics, the instructions of the experimenter, the expectations of both the hypnotist and the subject, the role of normal forgetting, and the role of hypnotic susceptibility are discussed. A consideration of the authenticity of hypnotic amnesia is also discussed in this section.

Finally, various mechanisms that have been proposed to theoretically explain amnesia are discussed. The concepts of function ablation, repression, dissociation, and retrieval disruption are presented. Some of the supporting evidence for each of these explanatory positions is given.

Definition

"Amnesia" means a loss of memory, due usually to brain injury, shock, fatigue, repression, or illness. A second definition states, "a gap in one's memory." *(Webster's New International Dictionary, Third Edition.)* "Hypnotic amnesia" is a forgetting that is associated with a hypnotic experience, rather than brain injury, fatigue, or illness. Since the material forgotten can be recovered upon a suggestion for the reversibility of the amnesia, however, hypnotic amnesia is a *temporary* forgetting that is associated with a hypnotic experience. As shall be seen, this is more than just a semantic issue; it is an essential part of the definition. The lack of a precise definition of amnesia other than that associated with hypnosis has led to confusion in understanding it also (Miller & Springer, 1973; Milos, 1975; Talland, 1965; Witty & Zangwill, 1966). Investigators only began taking seriously the reversibility of hypnotic amnesia, which has led to some important theoretical and empirical contributions, at about the time the first edition of this book appeared.

The Marquis de Puységur is given credit for "discovering" hypnotic amnesia in 1784. It is said that he mesmerized a shepherd boy, who immediately fell into a deep trance and began sleepwalking. When the boy awakened from the trance, he had no recollection of what had occurred during the trance; it was believed that sleepwalkers could not remember what they had done while "somnambulistic." (The term "somnambulist" has been applied to deeply hypnotized persons because they were thought to be amnestic for what was done while hypnotized.) While it is generally agreed today that the hypnotized individual is not asleep, the term is still used to describe the deeply hypnotized person.

Hypnotic amnesia is present when a subject fails to recall either the material or events that have been associated with a hypnotic experience or whatever the hypnotist has specifically suggested to forget, and when *this material can be recovered at some later time either through appropriate suggestions or a reinduction of hypnosis.* Thus, while hypnotic amnesia is distinct from simple forgetting, the two phenomena cannot be told apart as long as the amnesia remains. The recovery of the material, however, serves to distinguish hypnotic amnesia from forgetting and suggests a type of "state-dependent learning" phenomenon (Evans & Kihlstrom, 1975). However, all too often the importance of demonstrating the recoverability of the material has not been taken seriously. (It is just assumed that the material would have been recovered if appropriate procedures had been utilized.) Unfortunately, this has sometimes encouraged the use of language (if not constructs) to define and explain hypnotic amnesia not different from that used to define and explain forgetting.

Empirically, a concept is ultimately defined in terms of the operations used to measure it. A typical example of such operations for recall amnesia is found in the procedures used in the Stanford Hypnotic Susceptibility Scale, Forms A and B (Weitzenhoffer & Hilgard, 1959). Recall amnesia is suggested toward the end of the hypnotic session by telling the subject:

> You will probably have the impression that you have slept because you will have difficulty in remembering all the things I have told you and all the things that you did or felt. In fact, you will find it to be so much of an effort to recall any of these things that you will have no wish to do so. It will be much easier simply to forget everything until I tell you that you can remember. You will remember nothing of what has happened until I say to you, "Now you can remember everything!" You will not remember *anything* until then (pp. 23-24).

After the subject is awakened from hypnosis, he is asked to tell in his own words everything that has happened since he began looking at the target. After having an opportunity to respond and coming to a block, he is asked, "Anything else?"; after stopping again he is told, *"Now you can remember everything*—anything else now?"* and he is given the opportunity to add to those events which he experienced under hypnosis but could not remember prior to the recovery signal.

The number of items reported prior to the recovery signal is recorded, and the subject is scored as passing amnesia if the number reported is three or fewer. The number of items reported after the recovery signal is also obtained; however, this information has not often been used as part of the scoring definition of amnesia, although the importance of doing so has been advocated by Cooper (1972), Hilgard (1975), Kihlstrom and Evans (1973), and Nace, Orne, and Hammer (1974).

These procedures give credit to any item that is not reported. Literally, this does not require that the subject has forgotten the material (in either a physiological or psychological sense). All that is required is that the subject not report it. The failure to report may be a result of (1) a failure of the material to be registered, (2) the subject's having temporarily forgotten the item, (3) the subject's having permanently forgotten the item (a test of recoverability permits an evaluation of alternatives two and three), (4) an unwillingness to report the item, or (5) an inability to report the item for various reasons. For example, when asked to describe the experience of posthypnotic amnesia, some subjects have remarked, "I feel that if I thought hard enough I could remember, but I just can't get down to business," and "I haven't any inclination to go back over it," or "I do remember but I can't say, I can't think of the word..." (White, 1941, p. 491). "It's always just out of reach"; "It was like all the information was behind a curtain on the stage"; and, "You know it and you know you know it, but you just can't bring it into focus" (Hilgard, 1965b, p. 181). Wells (1940) noted that this could occur as a result of an inhibition of voluntary recall and suggested that it be called "pseudo-amnesia." It might also simply be a form of verbal inhibition. This has been called *amnesia by neglect* (Kihlstrom, Evans, Orne & Orne, in press). Many investigators today agree that a simple refusal to respond (sometimes evaluated in terms of apparent effort expended to do so) should not be considered hypnotic amnesia. In contrast, however, Barber (1969b), Coe (1976, 1978), and Sarbin (Sarbin & Coe, 1972) maintain that all hypnotic amnesia can be explained as this type of behavior.

Hull (1933) suggested that inasmuch as the amnesia could be reversed, that is, the material recovered, the underlying mechanism was not at the level of registration or retention, but rather at the level of reproduction (retrieval). Can verbal inhibition be construed as a problem of reproduction? Hilgard (1966) conjectured that hypnotic amnesia may be, in part, explained as a form of inhibition of motor speech, although he recognized the problems in such a formulation. Many studies have purposely used measures other than direct recall to assess the presence of amnesia to control for verbal inhibition (Barber & Calverley, 1966b; Bitterman & Marcuse, 1945; Imm, 1965; Patten, 1932; Scott, 1930; Strickler, 1929; Thorne, 1969;

Williamsen, Johnson, & Eriksen, 1965). Orne (1966a) suggested that verbal inhibition should be differentiated from subjectively real amnesia.

Whatever may be theoretically meant by amnesia, so long as the operations currently utilized in most susceptibility scales are used to assess it, all of the response types discussed here are classified as amnesia.

Kinds of Amnesia

There are various forms and/or kinds of hypnotic amnesia that can be distinguished from one another by the tasks presented, the absence or use of specific suggestions and their nature, and the time at which the testing of amnesia is carried out. Thorn (1960), Evans (1965b) and Hilgard (1965a, 1965b, 1966) have suggested and discussed classification schemes differentiating the various types of hypnotic amnesia.

In 1965, Hilgard (1965b) listed and discussed the following types or kinds of amnesia: (a) posthypnotic (recall) amnesia, an amnesia for the events within the hypnotic session; (b) posthypnotic source amnesia, a *retention* of material learned within the hypnotic state, but a forgetting of the fact that it was learned under hypnosis; (c) posthypnotic amnesia for material learned within the hypnotic conditions; (d) posthypnotic partial amnesia, an amnesia for only some of the events or materials learned within the hypnotic session; and (e) amnesia within the trance for earlier within-trance events while the subject remains hypnotized. While other types of amnesia have been proposed, such as symbolic amnesia (Strickler, 1929), sensory amnesia, and amnesia of integration (Wright, 1966), little systematic work has been done to further our understanding of them.

Emphasis has formerly been given to the distinction between two forms of hypnotic amnesia. Spontaneous amnesia was thought to occur without any suggestions for its occurence; suggested amnesia followed a specific suggestion by the hypnotist that the amnesia would occur. This clear-cut distinction could not always be made since what appeared to be spontaneous amnesia could be indirectly suggested and consequently be, in fact, suggested amnesia. While there is not universal agreement, most investigators now believe that hypnotic amnesia is seldom manifest unless it is suggested, explicitly or implicitly, by the hypnotist and/or expected by the subject (Cooper, 1966b; Hilgard & Cooper, 1965; Nace, Orne, & Hammer, 1974).

POSTHYPNOTIC RECALL AMNESIA

Spontaneous posthypnotic amnesia for the events occurring within hypnosis used to be considered intrinsic to and characteristic of deep hypnosis. Since de Puységur discovered it, what was interpreted as spontaneous posthypnotic amnesia functioned as one of the distinguishing signs of hypnosis.

Virtually all scales that have attempted to assess hypnotic responsiveness or hypnotic depth have included some type of amnesia item.

Baird maintained that his patients were not truly hypnotized unless spontaneously and completely amnesic. Charcot and his associates used amnesia to distinguish somnambulism from catalepsy and lethargy as qualitatively different hypnotic states. Richet used amnesia as an index for two of his three degrees of hypnotic depth. Liébeault and Bernheim both utilized spontaneous amnesia as a characteristic of the deeper stages of their scales. All of the nineteenth century scales heavily weighted spontaneous posthypnotic amnesia as a criterion of deep hypnosis (Hilgard et al. 1961).

This was also true of the later susceptibility scales such as the Davis and Husband scale (1931), the scale proposed by Barry, MacKinnon, and Murray (1931), the scale of Friedlander and Sarbin (1938), and the scales developed by Eysenck and Furneaux (1945), LeCron and Bordeaux (1947), and Watkins (1949).

Even the more widely used contemporary susceptibility scales such as the Stanford Hypnotic Susceptibility Scale, Forms A and B (SHSS:A and B) (Weitzenhoffer & Hilgard, 1959) and Form C, (SHSS:C) (Weitzenhoffer & Hilgard, 1962) and its variations, the Harvard Group Scale of Hypnotic Susceptibility (HGSHS) (Shor & Orne, 1962) and the Children's Hypnotic Susceptibility Scale (CHSS) (London, 1963) incorporate an item involving some form of amnesia as an index of susceptibility or depth. Posthypnotic selective partial amnesia (amnesia for one item) is employed in the Barber Suggestibility Scale (BSS) (Barber, 1965a, 1969b), and the subject's or patient's subjective reports of amnesia are used in Shor's new phenomenological scale (see Chapter 5 this volume) and in the Hypnotic Induction Profile (HIP) (Spiegel, 1972, 1976).

No present-day investigator claims that spontaneous amnesia is the central defining phenomenon of hypnosis. In the more recent scales, amnesia is treated as just one of many phenomena comprising the operational definition of hypnosis, with which it is less than perfectly correlated. For example, the suggested amnesia items of the SHSS correlates from .23 to .62 with the other items of the scale, the average correlation being .46; and its correlation with the total scale minus the amnesia item is .69 (Hilgard, 1965b). The better controlled research on amnesia defines susceptibility as the total score with the amnesia item deleted (e.g., Hilgard & Cooper, 1965).

In attempting to assess the actual frequency of occurence of hypnotic amnesia, it must be remembered that the frequency with which amnesia occurs depends on the criterion by which it is measured. It has been pointed out that most of the recent scales of hypnotic responsiveness consider posthypnotic amnesia to be manifest if some specified number of the events which occurred in the hypnotic session are not recalled after the subject has been awakened. For example, as already mentioned, a subject is credited with having passed the amnesia item of the SHSS if three or fewer items are recalled. Unfortunately, there has been a wide discrepancy from study to study in the arbitrary selection of the number of items which must be forgotten to pass amnesia; the recoverability of the memory has seldom been incorporated as a necessary part of the criterion; and there has been little attempt to control for, or evaluate the presence of, implicit cues for amnesia. All of which make comparisons of studies and evaluation of results difficult.

Furneaux (1946) reported that seventeen percent of his subjects spontaneously failed to recall more than one-third of the seventeen items in the scale devised by Eysenck and Furneaux (1945). He concluded that spontaneous amnesia for the events within hypnosis is a result of hypnosis and not an artifact suggested by the operator. Evans and Thorn (1966) tested for spontaneous amnesia in three different samples and found that twenty percent, sixteen percent, and twenty-six percent of the subjects in the three samples forgot at least two-thirds of the seventeen items presented. They further concluded that normal forgetting could account for much of the failure to remember, since twenty-four percent of a waking control group also failed to remember at least two-thirds of the items. They also suggested that some of the forgetting was probably due to the demand characteristics of the situation.

A greater proportion of the subjects have passed the amnesia item when instructions to do so have been specifically given. Friedlander and Sarbin (1938) found that twenty-four percent of their subjects remembered three or fewer items of their seven-point scale when it was suggested that they would not remember. Weitzenhoffer and Hilgard (1959) found that thirty-two percent of the students comprising the standardization sample of the SHSS passed suggested amnesia.

Although few studies have tested for both spontaneous and suggested posthypnotic amnesia, Hilgard and Cooper (1965) did obtain comparative figures of the prevalence of both forms of posthypnotic amnesia. Ninety-one introductory psychology students were divided into two groups. A standard induction procedure was used and suggestibility items that served to measure susceptibility and to test for amnesia were presented. For one group, spontaneous amnesia was tested on the first day, and suggested amnesia on the second day. The order was reversed for the second group. Evidence for amnesia was determined by the subject failing to remember more than five of the ten items possible. Seven percent showed spontaneous amnesia on one of the two days, while thirty-five percent (a significantly larger proportion, $p = .001$) showed suggested amnesia. It was further found that the highly susceptible hypnotic subjects showed no more spontaneous posthypnotic amnesia than did the other subjects. There was some effect of suggested posthypnotic amnesia for all levels of susceptibility, but it became very pronounced only with susceptibility scores of six and above.

While these findings did not technically disprove the occurence of spontaneous posthypnotic amnesia, they did indicate that it was far less frequent than had been previously supposed, and that it occurred far less frequently than suggested amnesia.

POSTHYPNOTIC SOURCE AMNESIA

Posthypnotic source amnesia, first discussed by Thorn (1960), occurs when something is learned under hypnosis and the result of the learning is carried into the waking state, but the process of learning or acquiring the information, and its having been learned under hypnosis is forgotten. The phenomenon is typical of memories related to knowledge obtained in childhood. We all know when the Declaration of Independence was signed, who gave the Gettysburg Address, where the Pilgrims landed, but we seldom have any specific idea where or how we obtained the information. The concept basic to source amnesia had been subtly imbedded in the memory literature for some time relating to the difference between what subjects could retain and what they said they could remember (Strickler, 1929; Hull, 1933). Banister and Zangwill (1941) used an experimental procedure similar to that used to investigate source amnesia, but described their investigation as one of paramnesia.

In studies investigating posthypnotic source amnesia, (Cooper, 1966a; Evans, 1971), hypnotized subjects are taught answers to questions not generally known, such as "What is the mean diameter of the earth?"; "What is the population of Singapore?" Later, after being awakened, subjects are tested to see if they remember the information and its source. They are credited with posthypnotic source amnesia if they can give the correct answers to the questions but cannot state the circumstances under which the information has been learned.

Evans and Thorn (1966) reported that thirteen percent, eleven percent, and seven percent of three samples met the criterion of spontaneous source amnesia on at least four out of six items. Only one subject (two percent) in a waking control group met this criterion.

In a test for both suggested and spontaneous source amnesia (Cooper, 1966a), ninety-three students from an introductory psychology course were randomly assigned to one of two groups. The standard induction of the SHSS:C was utilized, and modified items from the SHSS:C as well as source amnesia items were presented. For one group, source amnesia was suggested on one day and not suggested on the second. This order was reversed for the second group. In order to be considered as passing source amnesia, subjects were required to know the correct answers to all three source amnesia items but fail to state the source of the information. Two percent showed spontaneous source amnesia, and nine percent, a significantly larger proportion ($p = .05$), showed suggested source amnesia. Using a less rigid scoring criterion of requiring the subjects to fail to remember the origin of only one of the questions, the frequency of spontaneous source amnesia increased to nine percent, and of suggested source amnesia to fourteen percent. It was further found that there was little effect of source amnesia below a susceptibility score of four and that both spontaneous and suggested source amnesia increased as hypnotic susceptibility increased. Spontaneous source amnesia correlated .57 ($p = .001$) with susceptibility, and suggested source amnesia, .34 ($p = .05$) with susceptibility.

Thus, while spontaneous source amnesia may have been thought to occur, it occurred far less often than when suggestions for its occurrence were given. As with recall amnesia, these findings emphasized the role of subtle and unintentional cues or suggestions on the part of the experimenter, and the expectations of the subjects in producing spontaneous source amnesia.

Evans and Thorn (1966) have argued that the distinction between recall amnesia and source amnesia was a result of different underlying mechanisms, and thus that they should be considered as independent phenomena. When submitted to factor analysis (Evans, 1965; Thorn, 1960), recall amnesia was found to load on a factor relating to compulsively executed posthypnotic actions. They found that only four out of the total of two hundred forty-three subjects developed both types of amnesia. However, Cooper (1966a) found that the correlation between spontaneous and suggested source amnesia (.53) was only slightly higher than the correlation between the two forms of source amnesia and the two forms of recall amnesia (.48 for spontaneous and .49 for suggested), suggesting that subjects who are more amnesic for the events within hypnosis are more likely to yield both spontaneous and suggested source amnesia. Gheorghiu (1969) subsequently claimed that all subjects manifesting recall amnesia could be led to manifest source amnesia.

Sometimes amnesia has an effect on memory regarding certain aspects of the material or the event but not on others, such as occurs during a highly susceptible subject's response to posthypnotic suggestions. Frequently, the subject executes some activity triggered by a pre-arranged cue, but does not remember receiving the suggestion (Bowers, 1966; Bowers, 1975). Hilgard (1965b) suggested that recall amnesia is related to posthypnotic responses in that subjects not manifesting amnesia also tend not to carry out other posthypnotic suggestions. Others (Barber, 1962b; Gandolfo, 1971; Sheehan and Orne, 1968) have shown that amnesia is not a necessary or sufficient condition for posthypnotic behavior to occur, but the latter authors reported that amnesic and nonamnesic subjects do respond differently to posthypnotic suggestions.

AMNESIA FOR LEARNED MATERIAL

Strickler (1929) was one of the first to investigate this type of amnesia. He tested for savings of nonsense material that had been learned under hypnosis and for which amnesia was suggested. He compared the results with a group who had not previously been submitted to the hypnotic condition and found the hypnotized group took just as many trials. A series of studies (Graham & Patton, 1968; Huse, 1930; M. Mitchell, 1932; Nagge, 1935; Orne, 1966a; Takahashi, 1958) utilized this type of amnesia to investigate the hypothesis that there should be less retroactive inhibition if hypnotic amnesia for the interpolated material was suggested. Although there is some inconsistency in the results, the general findings do not support the hypothesis. More will be said about this in a discussion of functional ablation as an underlying mechanism of hypnotic amnesia.

Patten (1932) and Wells (1940) showed that the extent of this type of amnesia is a function of the susceptibility of the subjects, the explicitness of the suggestions for amnesia, and the apparent relevance of the procedures utilized to assess the amnesia. A more detailed consideration of a representative study by Williamsen, Johnson, and Eriksen (1965) is helpful in clarifying the issues involved.

In order to understand the controls utilized in this study and others to be reported later, it is necessary to explain a simulation group as utilized in hypnotic research. A simulator is a subject who has not been hypnotized, but has been instructed to fool a hypnotist (who is blind to the true hypnotic or waking state of the subject) into thinking that the simulator is responding appropriately, that is, is truly hypnotized. Simulators are not given any special training about how a hypnotized person should or does act so that their behavior is a result of the instructions, expectations, and demand characteristics of the experiment. It is necessary to have determined that the simulators are unhypnotizable and thus will not enter hypnosis. Previous studies have shown that simulators cannot be detected from experimental (hypnotized) subjects when these conditions are met, but their behavior serves as a control for the effects of instructions and expectations. (For further clarification see Orne, 1969, 1970, 1971a; 1972; Sheehan, 1971, 1973, and Bowers, 1973, 1976).

In the study by Williamsen, Johnson, and Eriksen (1965), a list of six words was read to subjects in three different groups, and the subjects were asked to repeat them. The words were presented under hypnosis to an experimental group, to whom suggestions for amnesia were also given; subjects in a simulation group were asked to pretend they were hypnotized, then given the words and the instructions for amnesia; the words were presented to a control group with instructions to forget them. All subjects were subsequently asked to recall as many of the words as they could.

Amnesia impaired recall for the experimental group, but they reported more words than the simulating group and fewer than the control group. The same trends were found for a recognition test. However, amnesia did not reduce the availability of the words for the experimental group as associative responses. A signal to remove the amnesia was given to the hypnotized and simulating subjects, and they were again asked to give as many of the words as they could remember. While not all of the words were recovered (approximately eighty-two percent), a significantly larger number of words were recalled than under the amnesia condition. The study was replicated by Barber and Calverley (1966b) with additional control groups added, and they concluded that the differences were attributable to instructional and motivational differences rather than to the effects of the hypnotic condition.

There are a number of methodological problems associated with the experimental investigation of this type of amnesia. One has to do with the control of the learning task and the opportunity for rehearsal. If it cannot be demonstrated that the subjects in all groups have learned equally well, differences in amnesia may be due to differences in learning rather than (or in addition to) the hypnotic suggestions. The confounding of these two factors will not permit an unequivocal interpretation. While a separate experiment was run by Williamsen, Johnson and Eriksen (1965) to evaluate this influence, such a control is all too often lacking. The finding that subjects may learn less well when hypnotized by the usual procedures make this possibility more critical. Liebert, Rubin, and Hilgard (1965) have suggested that the failure to find superior hypnotic performance in learning studies may be due to the passive, lethargic induction procedures utilized, and if an alert trance were utilized, different results might occur.

If, by administering different conditions to them at different times while similar measures are utilized to assess amnesia, subjects are used as their own control, the opportunity for rehearsal may have a relevant effect. Day-to-day effects have been found when both Forms A and B of the SHSS have been utilized. Although susceptibility generally increases (even though slightly) from the first to the second day, it has been found that there is a slight decrease in the number of items forgotten. Since memory is restored before concluding the first day's session, this may help to facilitate recall on the second day. The two sets of recall scores correlated .67, and when the effect of regression toward the mean was eliminated, the rehearsal or practice effect was found to increase the recall score from .5 to 1.5 items (Hilgard, 1965b). It was found that a change from a waking suggestion to a hypnosis condition can lead to a decrease in the amount of amnesia, which could lead one to the paradoxical conclusion that there is less amnesia under hypnosis than there is as a result of a waking suggestion. The results are more probably due to the interaction of the amnesic effect and the practice effect.

Very few past studies have attempted to distinguish between normal forgetting and amnesia. Analyzing the amount recovered upon a signal or the reinduction of hypnosis to break the amnesia would serve as a control, but this has seldom been incorporated, or if incorporated, analyzed. Thorn (1960) showed that amnesia was uncorrelated with the ability to retain, posthypnotically, nonsense syllables learned during hypnosis. In studies using a learning task (especially when it involves recognition), care must be taken not to confound source amnesia with recall amnesia in addition to not confounding amnesia with normal forgetting (see for example, Thorne, 1969).

PARTIAL POSTHYPNOTIC AMNESIA

Most subjects do not forget everything that has occurred (only thirteen percent of a large college sample did so; see Figure 10.1 this chapter), but have some partial memory for what has transpired. Hilgard and Hommel (1961) studied the types of items that were forgotten, and found that subjects tended to forget relatively more frequently those items that they failed than those they passed. Brenman (1947) had previously found a preference for completed tasks over incompleted tasks that occurred within hypnosis and for which amnesia had been suggested. O'Connell (1966) subsequently analyzed the nature of the items recalled and found a tendency for passed items to be recalled more frequently than the failed items.

Few studies have systematically investigated the effects of suggesting that some, but not all, of what has transpired within hypnosis will be forgotten —certainly a common procedure in hypnotherapy. The client is frequently told that he may or may not remember everything that has happened or been discussed, permitting the client to decide what to remember and what to forget (see for example, Crasilneck and Hall, 1975). Clemes (1964) used this kind of amnesia to test the hypothesis that amnesia is related to repression. If so, then under a suggestion for partial amnesia, it would be hypothesized that the subject would be amnesic for the more anxiety-provoking material. He determined by means of a word association test the words that were neutral for a subject as opposed to those which produced a longer reaction time (critical words). He then had subjects under hypnosis memorize a list composed of half neutral and half critical words, after which he suggested partial amnesia. Using an adequate control to ensure that all words were memorized equally, he found that subjects did forget a larger number of the critical words.

The studies presented in this section are relevant to a discussion of repression as an underlying mechanism of amnesia, and will be referred to in that section of this chapter.

Variables Affecting Hypnotic Amnesia

The studies reviewed thus far make clear that hypnotic amnesia is multi-dimensional rather than a unitary process, manifesting itself in many different ways. It is also multiply determined. Most investigators would agree that many factors give rise to the measured phenomena called hypnotic amnesia. Such factors as normal forgetting, verbal inhibition, and instructions have already been referred to in this chapter. While it is of interest to speculate about the most important processes or factors producing it, probably no one factor will be found to account for it ultimately; there will more likely be many that account for a proportion of the variance found in a given condition. We will now briefly consider some of these variables that have been recognized as being of some importance.

HYPNOTIC RESPONSIVENESS AND INDUCTION EFFECTS

Many investigators interested in hypnotic phenomena believe that some of the variance will be found to be attributable to a hypnotic state which differs in some fundamental ways from the waking state (Barber, 1969b; and Sarbin and Coe, 1972, are exceptions). Responsiveness to hypnotic suggestions has been conceived as a trait characteristic of the subject whether in a hypnotized state or not. The subject enters a hypnotized state via some appropriate induction procedure. The induction effects will be more pronounced for an individual who is more susceptible to hypnotic suggestions. Thus, susceptibility and induction effects, while related to one another, are seen as being less than perfectly correlated.

If the standardized susceptibility scales are measuring susceptibility, we should find hypnotic amnesia related to this measure. A large number of studies have shown that amnesia is correlated with susceptibility (Barber & Calverley, 1966b; Boyers & Morgan, 1969; Cooper, 1966a, 1966b; Evans & Thorn, 1966; Hilgard & Cooper, 1965; Imm, 1965; Orne, 1966a, Wells, 1940).

The magnitude of the correlations have ranged from .11 to .77, with the average being .41. These figures give rise to a lower bound estimate of omega squared (Hays, 1973) of approximately .13, suggesting that approximately thirteen percent of the variance in hypnotic amnesia is related to responsiveness to hypnotic suggestions.

Induction effects, as an independent variable, has been variously called "hypnotic induction," "hypnotic trance," "hypnotic state," and so forth. Technically, most investigators would agree that a trance induction is not necessary for a trance state, and that the two are not literally synonymous (see Bowers, 1973; Orne, 1971b). The induction effect has not been found to be as pronounced as would be anticipated (Hilgard, 1975). Estimated omega squared values from representative studies (Barber and Calverley, 1966b; Spanos and Ham, 1973) have been around .05.

Field, Evans, and Orne (1965) suggested that the occurence of amnesia is perhaps more a function of the level of hypnosis at the time of the suggestion for amnesia than it is of the susceptibility score, a stable overall index of hypnosis. Tape recorded modifications of the HGSHS, one with the items in an increasing order of difficulty and the other with a decreasing order of difficulty were presented to two groups. Although the mean susceptibility score for the two groups did not differ, the group having the easier items last—which increased the probability of the subjects' responding—showed significantly more posthypnotic amnesia.

Orne (1966a) reported that amnesia can be facilitated by tying it to another hypnotic suggestion which the subject is known to be able to carry out.

DEMAND CHARACTERISTICS

Orne (1959, 1962b, 1969) has pointed out that the experimental subject, in psychological research, is a thinking being who is attempting to understand the procedures and to evaluate the hypothesis being tested in an experiment. He has shown that the expectations and perceptions of the subjects may subtly alter the results of a psychological experiment. For example, subjects who had been told that catalepsy of the nondominant arm was an invariant characteristic of hypnosis displayed catalepsy of the nondominant arm when later hypnotized, while control subjects who had not been given this information did not. He proposed several control and quasicontrol procedures to assist in evaluating the role of "demand characteristics" in hypnotic research. The postexperimental inquiry, the "nonexperiment," and the use of simulating subjects are three quasicontrols. Such controls have been utilized in research investigating hypnotic amnesia by Bowers (1966), Barber and Calverley (1966b), Evans (1968, 1971), Johnson, Maher & Barber, (1972), and Williamsen, Johnson, and Eriksen (1965). The possible role of demand characteristics in producing spontaneous recall and source amnesia has already been pointed out. Frequently, the demand characteristics come about as a result of instructions and/or expectations.

Instructions. Many different suggestions and instructions are used to elicit amnesia. We have already discussed different types of amnesia, most of which are produced through different suggestions and/or instructions. It may be that subjects formulate an implicit "contract" with the hypnotist in regard to amnesia in terms of what is expected of them on the basis of the instructions given. This may concern what is to happen, with whom it is to happen, how long it should persist, and so forth. Even within a specific type of amnesia, differing suggestions may produce different results.

The following implicit instructions which are given simultaneously can be detected in the suggestions for amnesia in the SHSS:A: (a) You will have difficulty in remembering, (b) You will have no desire to try to recall (implying perhaps that the subject could recall if he tried?), (c) It will be easier to forget everything, and (d) You will remember nothing (SHSS:A pp. 23-24). It is hardly surprising, therefore, to find subjects reporting different subjective impressions about their experience of amnesia. Some report it is like trying to think of a name that does not come; others say it is like "knowing" the material but not being able, or not desiring, to put it into words; other emphasize the lack of desire to expend the energy necessary to recall (Hilgard, 1965b; White, 1941). Barber and Calverley (1966b), and Thorne (1969) have proposed that authoritative suggestions for amnesia, such as, "You will not remember," may produce different results from more permissive suggestions such as, "Try to forget."

Orne (1966a) reported that when, without the removal of amnesia, the subjects were interviewed by a different experimenter about the material for which they were amnesic, some subjects related everything, and frequently indicated they knew the material at the time they were originally questioned by the hypnotist, but felt compelled to inhibit it verbally; others indicated that they did not have recall of some of the material originally, but that it gradually came to them as they were being interviewed; still others remained amnesic.

Damaser (1964) found that questioning subjects one week later, again by a different experimenter, disclosed that for some subjects spontaneous recall had occurred during the week, perhaps triggered by some event in their daily lives. But again, others continued to maintain the amnesia.

Boyers and Morgan (1969) investigated the influence of instructions and expectations by presenting to subjects a series of invitations to break amnesia. For one group of subjects, the invitations were made by a confederate secretary in the office, and for another group, by the experimenter. The invitations consisted of the standard request to report everything that had happened; a request to try *very* hard to remember; the changing of rooms to dissociate the subject from the hypnotic situation; a financial bribe; and when the invitations were presented by the confederate, she gave the release signal usually given by the experimenter.

Of seven subjects recalling fewer than three items in their first hypnotic experience, the invitations to break the amnesia elicited a mean of five additional items for three subjects, two of them in the confederate group and one in the experimenter group. The average number of additional items elicited by the invitations for all subjects was approximately two out of the nine possible. A replication made use of eight subjects who had previously scored ten or above of SHSS:A and reported complete recall amnesia. Only one subject showed any effects of the invitations. This subject was in the experimenter group, and four additional items were elicited by a financial bribe of paying one dollar for each new item recalled. The authors concluded that the inability to recall was more than merely role-playing, and that the amnesic response from a highly hypnotizable subject can generally be accepted as valid.

Kihlstrom, (in press) (1978) reported administering a modified version of HGSHS: A to four groups of subjects prior to giving the cue for removing the amnesia. Special instructions were given and the memory was again tested. One group was simply tested again; another was asked to recall the suggestions in the order in which they occurred; the third group was asked to be completely honest about what they actually remembered. The special instructions had no differential effects across groups; they did not abolish the amnesia that had been previously manifest, nor did they effect the recovery of the material after the cue to remember had been given.

Expectations. If we assume that a subject's expectations may influence an experiment's results, then it is of some value to determine the expectations of prospective subjects about amnesia in relation to hypnosis. Studies have shown that amnesia is one of the phenomena associated with hypnosis and is an expected result of a hypnotic experience for college students at least, perhaps for the general public. Dorcus, Brintnall, and Case (1941) presented a questionnaire concerning beliefs about hypnosis to 669 college students. When asked, "Will people remember what took place under hypnosis?" sixty-four percent replied that they would not remember. Twenty years later, London (1961) published the results of a survey of 645 students in introductory psychology courses at the University of Illinois. The questions about hypnosis were aimed at assessing the direction of popular prejudices rather than the accuracy of people's knowledge. Seventy-four percent of the students agreed with the statement, "People usually forget what happened during the trance as soon as they wake up from it." Ninety-three percent of the sample felt that the general public would agree with this statement as well. Fifty-two percent of the respondents agreed with the statement, "After they come out of a trance, people will ordinarily remember what has happened unless the hypnotist suggested that they forget," and 42 percent felt that the public would agree. London concluded that "a large minority of the respondents obviously felt that spontaneous amnesia is intrinsic to the experience of hypnosis and a large minority felt that some form of amnesia is to be expected as a result of hypnosis" (London, 1961, p. 157).

The same trends were found by Cooper (1969) with students in introductory psychology courses at Brigham Young University. They were asked a series of questions to determine their expectations and beliefs regarding hypnosis. Of those surveyed, 498 students had never been hypnotized previously. Of these, fifty-seven percent agreed that if they were to be hypnotized they would not be aware of what was going on at the time it oc-curred. Fifty-nine percent felt that if they were to be hypnotized, they would not remember what had happened after they woke up. Sixty-seven percent felt that if they were to be hypnotized, they would remember what had hap-pened unless the hypnotist suggested that they forget. While a minority felt that some form of amnesia would occur, a larger proportion thought that it would be manifested if suggested, rather than spontaneously.

The college students used in most hypnosis laboratories today are pro-bably more sophisticated about hypnosis than were the naive subjects used in much of the early work. This may account for the failure to find a univer-sal expectation that spontaneous amnesia would occur. Nonetheless, in 1969, a small majority of the college students did associate amnesia with hypnosis.

This finding presents somewhat of a paradox when compared with the incidence of amnesia. Despite the fact that amnesia is associated with hyp-nosis for approximately fifty-seven to seventy-four percent of college samples, it is spontaneously manifested by only twenty percent (the max-imum percentage found by Evans and Thorn, 1966) and when suggested, by only thirty-five percent. Young and Cooper (1970) did a pilot study in-vestigating the number of items forgotten in response to the amnesia sugges-tions of the SHSS: A as a function of whether the subject had previously indicated an expectation for amnesia. With ten subjects in each group (one group with the expectation and the other without), no significant difference was found in the number of items forgotten. Shor (1971) had subjects, prior to a hypnotic induction, indicate which items on a susceptibility test they felt they would pass. The personal predictions were compared with the ob-jective scores on each item. The resulting phi correlation for the amnesia item was $-.04$, indicating no relationship between expectancy and behaviour. It is of interest to note in passing that the advanced information concerning the items to be presented did not noticeably influence the occur-rence of posthypnotic amnesia.

In order to evaluate the effects of manipulating expectations concerning amnesia on the incidence of spontaneous hypnotic amnesia, Young and Cooper (1972) told one group via a lecture on hypnosis that amnesia was a prominent characteristic of hypnosis and another that it was not. There was no significant difference in the percentage (56.5) of each group agreeing to the statement, "If I were to be hypnotized I would not remember what had happened after I awakened," prior to the lectures. The lectures changed the percentage agreeing to the statement to forty-eight percent for the group told that amnesia was characteristic of hypnosis and fifteen percent for the group told it was not. A subsequent administration of a modified SHSS: C (modified so as to make no suggestion for, or reference to, amnesia), yielded a mean number of items forgotten of 5.76 for the first group and

4.05 for the second. While these means were significantly different from one another (p = .01), indicating that the manipulated expectations did bring about a difference in the mean number of items forgotten, omega squared was equal to .09, which suggested that variables other than expectation also account for some of the variance in hypnotic amnesia. Consequently, while expectations, demand characteristics, and desires to please the hypnotist may account to some extent for hypnotic amnesia, they do not solely account for its occurrence in college students.

Many of the common induction techniques make use of eye-closure, and references to relaxation and sleep. Sleep, when directly suggested to the subject, may act as a indirect suggestion to forget, since many people believe that we do not remember what occurs when asleep (Bramwell, 1903), p. 105). (Interestingly, findings have given partial support to this idea [Evans et al., 1966, 1969].) Dittborn and Aristeguieta (1962) found that they were able to vary amnesia by changing the references to sleep in the instructions to a highly hypnotizable subject. The use of a single subject precludes drawing any definite conclusion, but the study does suggest the way in which expectations may alter results, and suggests a replication with appropriate modifications to assess the effect more adequately. While Barber (1962b) suggested the possibility that some subjects may actually fall asleep for brief periods during hypnotic experiments, this seems highly unlikely in the better controlled ones.

Amnesia, like other posthypnotic behaviors, has been traditionally viewed as being outside of the subject's volitional control and carried out automatically (Erickson & Erickson, 1941). This view has been challenged by Fisher (1954, 1955), who suggested that posthypnotic behavior occurs only in the specific context where the subject preceived that the hypnotist expects that it should occur. It has since been shown that posthypnotic behavior occurs in those situations in which the subject expects that it is to occur. Although similar to Fisher's statement, this latter finding is different in some important ways. The expectations of the subject are a function of the instructions and the demand characteristics. It may be that the instructions for amnesia, as understood and interpreted by the subject, are very specific in their action, so suggestions that the subject may be amnesic are effective only in those situations and under those conditions where it is apparent to him that memory is being evaluated. If requests for direct recall are seen as tests of memory, but association tests, or tests for practice effects are not, then we might expect to see the effects of amnesia in the former but not in the latter.

An analogous, though somewhat different, result has been found in regard to memory for events while asleep. When suggestions such as "Whenever you hear the word 'itch,' your nose will itch until you scratch it," were given while subjects were in stage one sleep, some subjects responded by scratching their noses when the cue-word "itch" was spoken, although they remained asleep. Even though they responded when tested as long as six months later, they were amnesic for the suggestions and their responses when awake (Cobb et al., 1965; et al., 1966). Subsequent research has shown that a presleep set that learning can occur during sleep leads to a waking recall of material presented during sleep (Cooper & Hoskovec, 1966; Evans & Orchard, 1969). Just as the manipulation of the set may break the amnesia for the events occurring while asleep, so the manipulation of the analogous set may break the amnesia for events occurring while hypnotized.

Orne, Sheehan, and Evans (1968) and Sheehan and Orne (1968) have effectively shown that posthypnotic behavior is not *entirely* dependent upon the context to which the suggestion is tested as implied in Fisher's position, but may occur outside the experimental setting. Orne (1966a) has reviewed a number of findings which relate to this issue.

Just knowing that they are involved in a hypnosis experiment may be sufficient to motivate subjects to enhance their hypnotic performance. Although not specifically studying amnesia, the following findings have implications for research on amnesia. When subjects were tested in a waking condition followed by hypnosis, there were no differences in the performance. However, when hypnosis preceded the waking condition, waking performances were significantly less successful than the hypnotic performance (Evans & Orne, 1965). If a subject knew before a waking test that he would subsequently be retested during hypnosis, then his waking performance fell below his hypnotized performance (Zamansky, Scharf, & Brighthill, 1964).

An interesting and unexpected finding in regard to expectation was reported by Evans (1968, 1971) in a study concerning source amnesia. Ten of thirty-seven deeply hypnotized subjects selected from the highest five percent of the distribution of hypnotic susceptibility showed source amnesia, whereas all simulators not only acted as though they forgot where they learned the material (source amnesia), but also acted as though they forgot the material (recall amnesia). This suggested that the expectation for the source amnesia instructions was that posthypnotic recall amnesia should occur. Consequently, the occurrence of source amnesia may be interpreted as contrary to the results anticipated from a compliance with expectations.

ROLE OF NORMAL FORGETTING

The similarities between amnesia and simple forgetting have already been referred to. As early as 1933, Hull in his book *Hypnosis and Suggestibility* raised the question of how much of the reported amnesia was caused by a process of forgetting, a question that has since been raised by Cooper

(1972), Evans (1968), Hilgard (1966), and Nace, Orne, and Hammer (1974). In an attempt to gain empirical data relevant to this issue, I began a series of studies in 1966 focusing on normal forgetting in posthypnotic amnesia (Cooper, 1966b).

When the number of items forgotten by 491 college students of both sexes ranging in age from seventeen to twenty-two years in response to the SHSS: A were analyzed on a pass-fail basis (a pass score requiring the subject to forget seven or more items presented during the course of the hypnotic testing), 177 or thirty-six percent passed the item. This percentage is quite consistent with that reported elsewhere (Hilgard et al., 1961; Hilgard, 1965b).

The number of items forgotten may also serve as the index of amnesia, and an examination of the distribution of actual number of items forgotten is instructive. Figure 10.1 shows the distribution for the 491 college students.

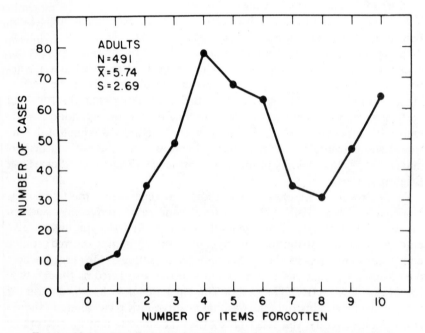

FIGURE 10.1. *Distribution of posthypnotic amnesia in college students.*

It is obvious that amnesia when so measured forms a continuum; some subjects forgetting everything, some forgetting a few items, and others forgetting almost none of the items. More subjects forget all the items than forget only one or two of them, which led Hilgard (1966) to suggest that this may be so because having remembered one or two items, the subject is led to remember more through some associative process which breaks the amnesia. It should be noted that the distribution was bimodal. This bimodality has been found for other similar samples, and is also found for the amnesia item of subsequent administrations of other forms of suscep- tibility scales. While bimodality may be an artifact produced by certain scal- ing procedures, such as the bimodality which is found in the distribution of susceptibility scores (see Hilgard et al., 1961; Hilgard, 1965b), it may also occur when the phenomenon being studied is caused by separate and unrelated underlying variables.

Evans (1965) and Hilgard (1966) had both conjectured that the bimo- dality of the distribution of items forgotten as a result of suggested amnesia may be explained by the lower mode being a result of forgetting, while the upper mode may be the result of truly amnesic subjects. Thus, the bimodal- ity of Figure 10.1 may be conceptualized as the result of combining two separate curves, one with a mode at four representing a curve of the forget- ting of a series of tasks when there were no instructions to try to remember them, and the other representing an amnesic curve. Figure 10.2 shows the distribution of amnesic forgetting with two normal distributions superim- posed. These fitted curves were obtained by using both a standard pro- cedure and a reduction method (D. Lewis, 1960). The curve to the left was

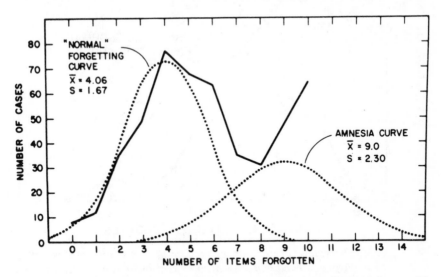

FIGURE 10.2. *Distribution of posthypnotic amnesia in college students with hypothesized theoretical forgetting and amnesia curves superimposed.*

based on a N of 306. The mean was equal to 4.06 and the standard deviation equal to 1.67. A chi square of 6.97 yielded a *p* value of .70 suggesting that it was a resonably good fit. The other normal curve had a mean of 9.00 and a standard deviation of 2.30, and was fitted by assuming the second mode at ten of the original distribution represented an undistributed maximum.

It is difficult to obtain a direct empirical index of the role of "normal" forgetting in amnesia; however, an attempt can be made to infer some estimate from indirect evidence. An estimate of the amount of forgetting that *can* occur with such items would provide some basis for comparison. Evans and Thorn (1966) reported the amount of forgetting of seventeen items comprising a battery of standard hypnosis items by a waking control group that had received no induction procedures. On the average, the subjects forgot approximately forty percent of the items. If consideration is given to the fact that seventeen items were administered rather than ten, the estimated mean that would have been obtained had there been ten items would not be too unlike the mean of 4.06 for the derived normal forgetting curve.

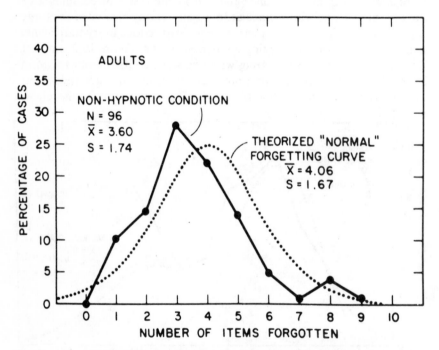

FIGURE 10.3. *Percentage distribution of number of items forgotten by college students in nonhypnotic condition with hypothesized theoretical forgetting curve superimposed.*

In order to make a more controlled comparison, Cooper and Moore (1967) administered directions requesting compliance with the motor items used in the SHSS but without any hypnotic induction, or any reference to hypnosis, or to such words as "relax," "drowsy," or "sleepy." These instructions were given in a group setting to ninety-six college students ranging in age from seventeen to twenty-two years. As soon as the items were administered, the subjects were asked to write down everything they could remember of what had occurred since beginning the activities; they were allowed ten minutes to do so. The instructions indicated that the responses need not be listed in order, nor need the language utilized by the experimenter be used; the subjects were allowed to express themselves in their own words.

Figure 10.3 shows the resulting relative frequency distribution indicating the percentage of the total number of subjects forgetting each of the number of items under this condition superimposed upon the fitted theoretical "normal" forgetting curve. The mean for the empirical distribution was 3.60 and the standard deviation was 1.74. When it is remembered that the mean and standard deviation of the theoretically derived curve were 4.06 and 1.67 respectively, it is apparent that the two curves are very similar. The two standard deviations were not significantly different from each other ($X^2 = 103$; $p = .25$). Although the two means are just significantly different ($p = .05$), it must be remembered that the procedures for fitting the theoretical distribution allowed a relatively large amount of leeway. Under these conditions, the similarity for the two distributions is rather remarkable.

It must be noted that, is a strict sense, this condition cannot be considered a control for the hypnotic condition. There were at least two important differences between the two conditions; first the amnesia results were obtained by an individual administration of the SHSS while the normal forgetting measures were obtained in a group setting; and second, the time allowed to respond in the normal forgetting conditions was longer than that usually found in testing for amnesia. In the latter, after the second block by the subject, the hypnotist, not very subtly, discourages further attempts to remember under amnesia by giving the cue to remember, thus terminating the amnesia. Both of these differences preclude exact comparisons between these conditions.

In an attempt to overcome these limitations, Cooper and Harrison (1969) individually administered to forty-nine students from an introductory psychology class directions which requested compliance to the motor items of the SHSS. The exact wording and procedures of the scale were utilized except there was no hypnotic induction and modifications were made when necessary to eliminate any direct or indirect references to such words as "hypnotize," "relax," "drowsy," or "sleepy." The subjects were first administered the general remarks for establishing rapport (SHSS:A, pp. 8-9). We included a general nonspecific explanation of our interest in studying the manner in which subjects respond to requests to make motor responses. This was done to provide a period of time comparable to the interaction between the hypnotist and the subject during the induction of hypnosis. Then the items were presented in the usual order. The necessary changes as noted above were made in all the verbal instruction. The instructions for the "moving hands" item, for example, were, "Please hold both hands out in front of you, palms facing inward, hands about a foot apart. Here, I'll help you." Then the experimenter took the subject's hands and positioned them about twelve inches apart. "When I tell you to, I want you to slowly move your hands together. Please move them very slowly at first, then faster. Please move your hands together until they touch. You may begin moving your hands together now." Ten seconds were allowed for the subject to respond.

Following the administration of the last item, the subjects were asked, "Please tell me in your own words everything that you did or that has happened since you first started following my instruction." When the subjects reached a block, the experimenter asked, "Anything else?" Thus, the procedures in this experiment were made to duplicate as closely as possible those in the hypnotic condition. It was found that every subject forgot at least one item. The mean number of items forgotten was 3.22 and the standard deviation was 1.23. There were no significant differences between the means ($p > .10$) nor the variances ($F = 1.98$, $p > .05$) of the group administered and individually administered "normal" forgetting conditions. These results made it clear that normal forgetting was accounting for some of the posthypnotic amnesia that was found.

Additional indirect evidence involving the interaction of age with normal forgetting and its role in amnesia was found by examining the analogous findings for children. The responses relating to amnesia of 286 children ranging in age from six to fifteen years to the CHSS were analyzed, and 222 or seventy-eight percent passed the item. This is comparable with the percentages reported elsewhere (Cooper & London, 1966; London & Cooper, 1969; Moore & Lauer, 1963). A comparison with the thirty-six percent of the adults that passed the item suggested that hypnotic amnesia is more likely to be found in children than in adults. Because the first twelve items of the *CHSS* are very similar to those of the *SHSS* and the test of amnesia applies to ten of these items as it does on the *SHSS,* the two distributions of the actual number of items forgotten can be meaningfully compared.

Figure 10.4 shows this distribution for the 286 children. Unlike the distribution for the adults, there was only one mode and, apparently, only one curve is represented. As indicated by the percentage passing the item, children forget more items than do older college students; the mean number of items forgotten by the children was 8.06 (S.D. = 1.89) as compared to the mean of 5.74 for the adults. This difference is significant at the .01 level.

It might be concluded that the memory task for children is just more difficult than it is for young adults, and that this distribution for children represents a "normal" forgetting curve with an undistributed maximum.

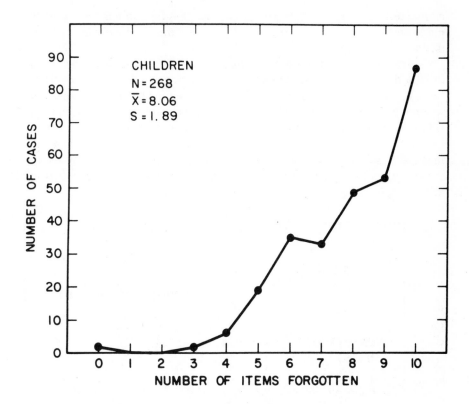

FIGURE 10.4. *Distribution of posthypnotic amnesia in children.*

However, the children were significantly more hypnotically susceptible ($p = .001$) than the college students, with a mean susceptibility score of 7.41 (S.D. = 2.91), based on the first eleven items scored on a pass-fail basis, as compared with 5.39 (S.D. = 3.00), for the adults. This susceptibility score did not include the amnesia item, so the curve may represent the effect of hypnotic suggestions for amnesia. Another alternative is that both of these effects were operating simultaneously.

In addition to the adult sample, Cooper and Moore (1967) also administered the instructions which deleted references to hypnosis requesting compliance to the motor tasks utilized in the CHSS to 157 children varying in age nine to fifteen years. Again, these instructions were administered in group sessions, and the limitations referred to previously should be remembered. The mean number of items forgotten was 3.88 and the standard deviation was 2.07. However, because age was significantly correlated with the number of items forgotten in this condition (as will be discussed later), all children below the age of nine in the nonhypnotic condition were eliminated for purposes of analysis and meaningful comparisons must be made with this restricted sample, whose mean was 7.90 and the standard deviation was 2.00.

Figure 10.5 shows these two distributions. No theoretically fitted distributions have been presented for those analogous to the adult distributions because the distribution of items forgotten in the amnesia condition was not bimodal. In Figure 10.5, however, if we assume that the accumulation of scores at ten for the hypnotic condition is an undistributed maximum, then a rough fit to this distribution would be a normal curve with a mean at 7.30 and a standard deviation of 1.15. It is obvious that such a curve is a poor fit to the curve obtained under the non-hypnotic condition, and is displaced toward the higher end of the scale.

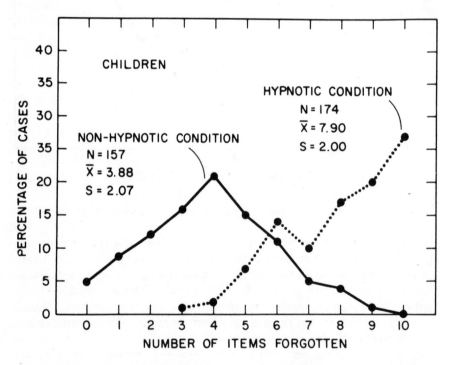

FIGURE 10.5. *Percentage distribution of number of items forgotten by children in both hypnotic and non-hypnotic condition.*

As has been pointed out, the time to respond in the nonhypnotic condition was longer than that usually found in the hypnotic condition. The time allowed for reminiscence may be more important for children than for adults, which would account for the larger mean number of items forgotten in the hypnotic condition by the children. On the other hand, the differences between the mean number of items forgotten under the two conditions might also be due to the greater susceptibility of the children, so that the suggestions for amnesia were more effective for all children.

It was hypothesized that the number of items forgotten in the nonhypnotic condition would tend to be an inverse function of age up to some asymptote; that is, to some point, the older the subject, the fewer the items that would be forgotten. For the adults, there were no significant differences between the mean number of items forgotten at the different ages for the "normal" forgetting condition ($F = .48; df = 4, 73; p = .20$), and as would be expected, the correlation between age and number of items forgotten was not significantly different from zero. Likewise, there was no correlation between age and number of items forgotten under the amnesia condition. This suggests that the two regression lines were virtually horizontal at the mean of 3.60 for the normal forgetting condition and 5.74 for the suggested amnesia condition. At every age there were some items forgotten in the "normal" forgetting condition, and at every age the number forgotten in this condition was less than those forgotten in the hypnotic condition.

A decreasing number of items were forgotten with increased age by the children in the nonhypnotic condition. A square root transformation was made on the raw scores to produce greater homogenity of variance, and an analysis of variance was performed. The overall test was significant at the .001 level of significance ($F = 181.17; df = 5, 141$). The overall mean number of items forgotten was 3.88 (S.D. = 2.07). The combined results from both the children's and the adult's data suggest that the asymptote of forgetting was reached at about fifteen or sixteen years of age.

While the trend was not so pronounced, there was a negative correlation between age and the number of items forgotten as a result of suggested amnesia of $-.28$ ($p = .01$). Again, at every age tested, there were some items forgotten in the "normal" forgetting condition, but at every age, there were fewer items forgotten under this condition than under the hypnotic amnesia condition.

While the important differences between the two conditions should again be remembered, these data suggested that "normal" forgetting does play a role in hypnotic amnesia. Furthermore, these data suggested that this influence is more important in younger children, and decreases with age. Other variables, such as susceptibility, may become of greater influence with increased age. This conjecture is supported by the correlation between number of items forgotten in the hypnotic condition and susceptibility for different age spans. For the six to eight year olds the correlation was $-.06$ ($p = .20$); for the nine to eleven year olds it was .37 ($p = .001$); and for the twelve to fifteen year olds it was .46 ($p = .001$); while for the adult sample it was .52 ($p = .001$). There was then indirect evidence for the role of "normal" forgetting in hypnotic amnesia from the data discussed thus far.

A technically precise definition of amnesia *must* incorporate the recoverability of the material through some appropriate procedures, although, as has been previously suggested, little serious attention had been given to this requirement. These findings, however, suggested that at least some of the items were "truly" forgotten, and might not be recoverable. If the material cannot be recovered, this suggests that the amnesia was simply a matter of natural forgetting and not a result of the suggestion to temporarily forget, since part of that suggestion was that the material would be remembered at the signal, "Now you can remember everything." If nothing is recovered, the subjects, in fact, have not complied with the suggestions.

In an attempt to obtain some evidence concerning this hypothesis, the number of items recovered after the signal to remember had been given was analyzed for each group. The results are presented in Table 10.1. Both distributions were markedly positively skewed with the larger frequencies

TABLE 10.1.   Number of items recovered in the adult and children sample

Number of Items Recovered	Frequency	
	adult sample	children sample
10	0	1
9	5	0
8	7	2
7	17	0
6	25	6
5	45	13
4	31	20
3	51	35
2	52	38
1	57	40
0	201	131
Number	491	286
Mean	2.10	1.50
Median	1.28	.80
Standard Deviation	2.37	1.83

recovering the fewer number of items. Of the 491 adults, 201 or forty-one percent; and of the 286 children, 313 or forty-six percent, recovered none of the material. This is a relatively large proportion of each sample. None of the adults recovered more than nine items, and only twelve recovered more than seven items. Not only were there many who did not recover any of the items, but generally speaking, surprisingly few items were recovered. These findings point out the fallacy of assuming that the amnesic material would be recovered if appropriate procedures had been utilized, and call into serious question such statements as, "With few if any exceptions, hypnotic and non-hypnotic subjects who claim they have forgotten, verbalize the 'forgotten' events when the hypnotist or experimenter simply states, 'Now you can remember' " (Barber, 1969b, p. 212). They emphasize the importance of testing for the recoverability and incorporating it into an operational definition of amnesia.

It was decided to divide each sample into two groups on the basis of a conservative definition of amount recovered. One group consisted of those subjects who recovered at least one item or more, and the other group consisted of those who recovered nothing.

Figure 10.6 shows the number of items forgotten by these two subgroups for the adult samples superimposed upon the theoretically derived

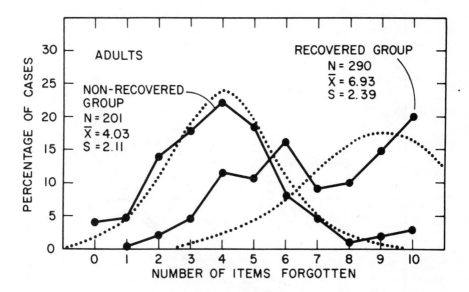

FIGURE 10.6. *Percentage distribution of the number of items forgotten by college students under hypnotic condition for both recovered and non-recovered groups.*

distributions. The mean number of items forgotten by the "nonrecovered" group was 4.03, the standard deviation was 2.11, and the distribution is very similar to the theoretically fitted "normal" forgetting curve. The mean number of items forgotten by the "recovered" group was 6.93 and the standard deviation was 2.39. While this distribution is far from a perfect fit to the theoretical "amnesia" curve, there are suggestive similarities, and it must be remembered that the subjects comprising this group had not recovered everything but some recovered no more than one item. The mean number of items forgotten by the "recovered" group was significantly larger (p = .001) than that of the "nonrecovered" group. Also the subjects comprising the "recovered" group were significantly more susceptible (p = .001) than the subjects of the "nonrecovered" group, with mean susceptibility scores of 6.55 (S.D. = 2.80) for the former as compared with 3.73 (S.D. = 2.45) for the latter.

The corresponding distributions of the number of items forgotten by these two sub-groups for the children's sample as shown in Figure 10.7

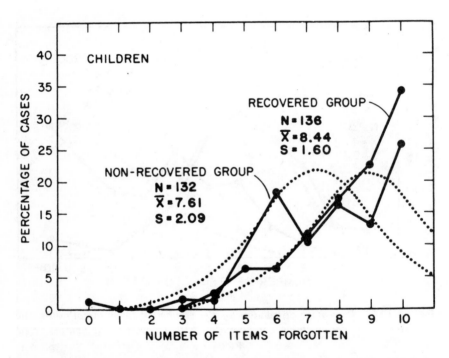

FIGURE 10.7. *Percentage distribution of the number of items forgotten by children under hypnotic condition for both recovered and non-recovered groups.*

yielded a mean of 7.61 and a standard deviation of 2.09 for the "nonrecovered" group, and a mean of 8.44 and a standard deviation of 1.60 for the "recovered" group. Each distribution had a piling up of scores at ten, and if these are assumed to be undistributed maxima, then we can use these distributions in an attempt to gain some idea of the relative position of the two theoretical curves analogous to those for adults. A rough fit to each of these distributions would be normal curves with a mean of 7.00 for the "nonrecovered" group, and at 9.00 for the "recovered" group.

As was true for the adult sample, the distribution of the "recovered" group is displaced to the right of that of the "nonrecovered" group, and the mean of the former was significantly larger ($p = .001$) than that of the latter. In comparison with the adult sample, both of the child groups forgot a larger number of items than the corresponding adult group, but the separation between the groups of children was not as pronounced as that for the adults. The "recovered" group was significantly more susceptible ($p = .001$) with a mean of 8.24 (S.D. = 2.60) than the "nonrecovered" group, whose mean susceptibility score was 6.43 (S.D. = 2.94). While there was no significant difference between the mean ages of the two subgroups in the adult sample, there was in the children's sample. The "nonrecovered" group was significantly younger than the "recovered" group. The mean age of the former was 10.04 (S.D. = 3.53), while for the latter it was 11.87 (S.D. = 3.04; $p = .001$). Since age is negatively correlated with the number of items forgotten through normal forgetting, this worked against the finding that the mean number of items forgotten for the "recovered" group was larger than that for the "nonrecovered" group because the "recovered" group should have remembered more if only "normal" forgetting effects were operating. When the number of items forgotten in both groups for each sample was analyzed as a function of age, it was found that there were more items forgotten by the "recovered" group than by the "nonrecovered" group at every age.

Perhaps the number of items recovered per se is not of crucial importance. Those who forget more may well recover more, and therefore it might be of greater signficance for an individual who forgot only three times to recover all three of them. In order to evaluate this possibility, a percent recovered score was computed for each person by dividing the number of items recovered by the number forgotten. If this rationale were true, a high correlation between the number forgotten and the percent recovered would be expected. Such correlations, however, were not found. For the college group, percent recovered correlated .49 with the number of items forgotten and .89 with the number recovered. When the correlation between the number of items forgotten and the number of items recovered was partialed out, percent recovered correlated −.48 with number forgotten and .89 with number recovered. For the children, the percent recovered correlated .20 with the number of items forgotten and

.97 with the number recovered. When the correlation between the number forgotten and the number recovered was partialed out, percent recovered correlated -.48 with the number forgotten and .98 with number recovered. These results do not support the conjecture that those who forget more recover more but suggest that a consideration of the number of items recovered is sufficient for our present purposes.

In order to complete our understanding of the association between the number of items forgotten, the number of items recovered, and their relationship to amnesia, the correlations between the number of items recovered was examined. This correlation was .72 (p = .001) for the adult sample, but only .32 (p = .001) for the children's sample. Of greater importance is the fact that the correlation between these two variables tended to increase with age. For the six to eight year olds the correlation was .26 (p = .05) for the nine to eleven year olds it was .56 (p = .001); for the twelve to fifteen year olds it was .51 (p = .001) and, as has been indicated, .72 for the adult sample.

These results suggest that age is an important moderating variable in posthypnotic amnesia. In the younger individual, both the number of items forgotten and the number of items recovered are less a function of susceptibility, and because the two are not highly correlated, the number of items forgotten is more a function of forgetting. For those who do recover something, the number of items forgotten is a function of susceptibility. For the older individual, the number of items forgotten and the number of items recovered are more highly correlated, and both are a function of susceptibility; the number of items forgotten is less a function of forgetting per se.

These results emphasized the importance of testing for the recoverability of the material forgotten when attempting to demonstrate hypnotic amnesia. If the conservative operational definition of recoverability adopted for the purposes of analysis in this research had been incorporated into the original criterion of amnesia, while none of those who failed to recover would pass the item, twenty-one or four percent of the adult sample, and eighty-seven or thirty percent of the children sample who passed the item would fail it (See Hilgard, 1975; Kihlstrom & Evans, 1973; Nace, Orne, and Hammer, 1974).

Kihlstrom and Evans (1976) matched groups differing in hypnotic susceptibility for initial amnesia recall and found that hypnotizable subjects were significantly better than nonhypnotizable subjects at recapturing the blocked memories after the signal for recovery was given. They concluded that reversability was important in distinguishing between amnesia and pseudoamnesia and between partial and nonamnesia.

Even after the signal to remember has been given, and the amnesia lifted, subjects who manifested some amnesia do not remember everything (Hilgard & Hommel, 1961; Kihlstrom & Evans, 1976). Kihlstrom & Evans found that susceptible subjects who initially manifested hypnotic amnesia recalled significantly fewer items after the amnesia had been lifted than did susceptible subjects who initially did not manifest amnesia. Their analyses indicated that this residual amnesia effect was not a function of failure of memory storage due to inattention or sleep, or differential time constraints, but rather, they believe that it implies that suggested posthypnotic amnesia, when lifted, takes time to fully dissipate.

AUTHENTICITY OF HYPNOTIC AMNESIA

The emphasis in this chapter on the role of demand characteristics, instructions, expectations, and normal forgetting in hypnotic amnesia as compared to hypnotic responsiveness should not be interpreted as implying that the former are more important or more powerful in producing the phenomenon; but rather an attempt to stress the importance of controlling for these independent variables so that we may better evaluate the true role of the hypnotic condition.

As is true of other phenomena, clinical experience and clinical reports seem to uphold without any doubt the existence of hypnotic amnesia (see for example, Crasilneck & Hall, 1975; Erickson & Brickner, 1943; Erickson & Rossi, 1974; Newman, 1971, 1974.) Experimental evidence does not conclusively support the existence of the phenomenon, however.

Barber (1969b, 1972; Barber and Calverley, 1962, 1966b) and Sarbin and Coe (1972) have challenged the concept of hypnotic responsiveness and the hypnotic state in explaining hypnotic phenomena. Barber has suggested that "performance of behavior traditionally associated with the word 'hypnosis' may be more parsimoniously conceptualized under the more general psychological concept of task motivation," and further that "the concepts of 'trance' and 'hypnosis' may be no longer useful..." (Barber and Calverley, 1962, p. 388). As this challenge applied to all hypnotic phenomena, the authenticity of hypnotic amnesia was questioned.

The basis for this challenge to the genuineness of hypnotic phenomena is twofold. First, it is claimed that all the behavioral responses characteristic of the hypnotic state can be obtained, with the same intensity, by procedures that are not hypnotic in nature; and second, that because the responses are the same, the basic mechanism giving rise to the responses must also be the same. Both of these claims will be discussed with specific references to hypnotic amnesia.

The first claim implies that the kind and degree of hypnotic amnesia that can be obtained through hypnotic procedures can also be obtained through nonhypnotic ones. While the conclusions drawn must be tempered by the problems regarding the definition and measurement of hypnotic amnesia discussed previously, there is evidence helpful in evaluating this claim.

Most of the investigators interested in hypnotic behavior do not claim that the behaviors obtained through hypnotic procedures are unique to hypnosis, nor that they cannot be obtained through any other means. The amnesia associated with fugues or produced through chemical means (see for example, Osborn et al., 1967) is a forgetting of material that is frequently recoverable, but not brought about through the use of hypnotic procedures. This does not make the amnesia brought about through hypnosis any less real.

Nonhypnotized subjects and simulators may manifest amnesia as a result of certain instructions. Barber typically used task-motivation instructions, without hypnotic induction, which exhorted the subject to do his best and provided false information about the frequency and ease of compliance. For example, *"Everyone* can do this if they really try. I myself can do it quite easily and *all* the previous subjects that participated in the experiment were able to do it" (Barber and Calverley, 1964e). The fact that subjects given such instructions yield the same result as hypnotized subjects does not make the amnesia of hypnotized subjects any less an amnesia, but rather provides a misleading reference for comparison.

Bowers (1967) found that when subjects who submitted to such task-motivation instructions to hallucinate were subsequently asked to be absolutely honest in reporting what they had experienced, they denied experiencing the hallucinations as vividly as originally reported. Spanos and Barber (1968) essentially replicated Bowers' findings, and Barber now uses revised task-motivation instructions.

While it has been suggested that the induction effects have not been as great as were originally supposed, this does not imply that they are nonexistent. A relevant and important question is whether the hypnotic procedure can bring about a manifestation of the behavior. Such statements as "very few if any 'deeply hypnotized' subjects forget the hypnotic events when amnesia is not directly or indirectly suggested" (Barber, 1969b, p. 206) seem to me to be misleading.

Hilgard and Tart (1966) administered the SHSS:C (which included an amnesia item) under a waking-suggestion condition, a vivid-imagery condition, and a hypnotic condition and found that total scores for the hypnotic condition were significantly greater than for the other two conditions. Evans (1966b) administered a battery of hypnotic phenomena including recall and source amnesia to both a hypnotic group and a waking group. Both of the amnesia items discriminated between the waking and the hypnotic condition. Bowers (1976) has emphasized that the subjective reality of suggested amnesia is separable from the issue of whether a traditional hypnotic induction is necessary to produce the effect (p. 50).

What appears to be, and is described as, amnesia can and does occur as a result of suggestions without involving hypnotic procedures (Barber & Calverley, 1966b; Evans & Thorn, 1966; Thorne, 1969; Williamsen, Johnson & Eriksen, 1965). Johnson, Maher, and Barber (1972) have shown that simulators show more spontaneous amnesia than hypnotized subjects. More to the point, the writings of both Barber and Sarbin imply that the subject only appears or acts as though amnesic, but does not really have any difficulty in remembering. The subject complies with the suggestions by actively suppressing the memory, by not exerting sufficient effort to remember, or purposefully withholding the information from the experimenter. Rosenberg (1959) had earlier concluded, "Posthypnotic amnesia, whether of the spontaneous or suggested variety, is usually achieved through effortful, motivated inattention and deverbalization...these do not bespeak dissociation, or even repression, so much as vigorous suppression of hypnotic content." This view has received wide exposure (Barber, 1972; Barber & Calverley, 1966b); Barber, Spanos & Chaves, 1974; Coe, 1976, 1978; and Coe & Sarbin, 1977), and has been called *amnesia by neglect* by Kihlstrom, Evans, Orne, and Orne (in press).

A number of experimental findings are relevant to this assertation. It is generally found in memory studies that subjects remember more when tested by recognition than by recall, but this is not interpreted to mean the subject is purposefully keeping something back from the experimenter. Simulators have been found to respond differently than hypnotized subjects to amnesia suggestions (Williamsen, Johnson & Eriksen, 1965; Barber & Calverley, 1966b; Bowers, 1966; Evans, 1971), yet the simulators *are* highly motivated subjects deliberately led to suppress and withhold information. Expectations and manipulated demands for compliance have been shown to play a rather minor role in producing amnesia (Boyers & Morgan, 1969; Kihlstrom, Evans, Orne, and Orne, in press; Shor, 1971; Young & Cooper, 1972), but they should be of major importance within this model. The research suggests that subjects are *not* simply withholding information from the experimenter.

In regard to the second claim, it does not logically follow that even if we ultimately find that the frequency of its occurrence without any hypnotic procedure is similar to its frequency as a result of hypnotic suggestion, the same antecedent variables are giving rise to the phenomenon under the two conditions. The amnesia produced by drugs is not necessarily equivalent to the amnesia produced hypnotically, nor are both necessarily the result of the same mechanisms.

Nonhypnotic simulators may show the same amnesia that hypnotized subjects show but for quite different reasons. Orne (this volume) suggests that "real and simulating Ss certainly may produce the same behavior mediated by different mental processes" (p. 538). The latter may do so primarily because of the operation of demand characteristics and instructions. That is, they are subtly informed what hypnotic behavior should be like and that they are expected to behave in a hypnotic-like fashion. On the other hand, the hypnotic subjects are often told to just let happen whatever they find is happening without any attempt to hinder or help it along. The observable behaviors may be the same, but it does not necessarily follow that the bases for the behaviors are the same.

Edwards (1965) gave suggestions for the slowing of reaction time to two groups, a hypnotized group and a control group. Instructions for amnesia for the suggestions were subsequently given to both groups. While no significant differences between the groups were found in reaction time, striking differences were found in response to a post-experimental inquiry concerning the subjective quality of the experience. The hypnotized subjects "manifested perplexity—a puzzling difficulty" in recalling the original suggestion. The control subjects remembered the original suggestion and manifested no perplexity. Edwards emphasized, "It is difficult not to conclude that the original hypnosis has produced an impairment of mental functioning which is a phenomenon *sui generis*, and which cannot be adequately accounted for as a reflection of social control or role-playing" (p. 332).

Bowers (1966) gave instructions to subjects in both a hypnotic condition and a simulating condition to begin all sentences in an apparent experimental task of making up sentences with "he" and "they." Suggestions were also given that the subjects would be unaware of and amnesic for this suggestion. There were no significant differences between the two groups in the tendency to use the "correct" pronouns in two test situations. In a post-experimental inquiry, however, significant differences were found between the two groups in regard to their verbalizations using the "correct" pronouns and their justification for using them.

Even though Thorne (1969) did not find significant differences in amounts of amnesia as a function of susceptibility, in interpreting the findings he was led to conjecture that the same results may have been brought about through different subjective experiences.

Barber, too, has recognized that different basic processes may be producing the same results in the different groups. In explaining the fact that nonhypnotized subjects, in a replication of the study of Williamsen, Johnson and Eriksen (1965), showed more amnesia; and more of them than of hypnotized subjects claimed they had actually forgotten the words, Barber stated:

> The suggestions...may be congruent with the type of instructions or suggestions that are expected in an awake situation but not in a hypnotic situation. Subjects may expect that if forgetting is to occur in an awake situation it is necessary for them to strive to "control their memory" whereas in a hypnotic situation amnesia should occur effortlessly, not by willful striving (Barber, 1969b, p. 209).

Because amnesia can be produced by mechanisms other than hypnosis, we should not, therefore, deny the subjective reality of the hypnotic amnesia. Orne (1959, 1962b, 1965b) has warned that hypnosis cannot be understood in terms of observable, overt behavior only, and that we must bring the subjective experiences into the domain of the laboratory if we are ultimately to understand hypnosis; and Bowers (1973) has reviewed the implications of an attributional analysis of hypnotic behavior to the authenticity of those behaviors. Barber, Abdulhusein, and Calverley (1968) warned against using subjective reports as indices of actual experiences or of the hypnotic state. Nonetheless, Barber, himself, has done so (Barber, 1975). And there is a growing trend among workers in the field to emphasize and investigate subjective measures derived from questioning the subject in response to hypnotic suggestions (Hilgard, 1975).

Evans, Kihlstrom, and Orne (1973) submitted to two judges exact transcripts of the handwritten reports of subjects' responses to the request, "Write down briefly in your own words a list of the things that happened since you began looking at the target," after the suggestion for amnesia had been given on the HGSHS:A. The judges were able to successfully identify susceptible and nonsusceptible subjects. It was found that hypnotizable subjects used fewer words to describe each item recalled, but used twice as many words to describe experiences unrelated to specific suggestions, particularly those involving distortions in body size and in the visual field. Kihlstrom (1977b) has studied generic recall during posthypnotic amnesia.

Additional studies of this nature need to be done. A precedent for so doing with appropriate cautions has been established in the investigation of the role of awareness in learning (see Dulany, 1961; Eriksen, 1962).

Underlying Mechanisms

The demonstration of hypnotic phenomena can be dramatic and impressive. Demonstration is, however, only the beginning of scientific interest. The questions, "How commonplace is it? What are the parameters which give rise to the results?'' immediately follow. Subsequently, the question, "What are the underlying mechanisms?'' must be raised and answered if we are to understand the phenomenon. It is in this area that the most significant work on·hypnotic amnesia has been done since the first edition of this book was published. Nonetheless, we are still far from having a clear, and universally agreed upon conceptualization of the underlying mechanisms, and additional research needs to be devoted to their systematic elaboration. A brief discussion of some of the proposed underlying mechanisms follow.

FUNCTIONAL ABLATION

An early explanation of amnesia, now primarily of historical interest, was that of functional isolation, removal, or obliteration of the neural representation of specific experiences or events so that they could no longer influence behavior. This was not thought to preclude the recovery of the material, as an opposite effect, reinstatement, was also proposed. By testing for the influence of the amnesia on responses other than direct recall, an attempt was made to evaluate how complete the amnesia was. When the amnesia was measured by relearning (Coors, 1928; Strickler, 1929; Wells, 1940), practice effects (Life, 1929; Patten, 1932), motoric responses (Patten, 1930), conditioned reflex responses (Scott, 1930), autonomic responses to single words (Bitterman & Marcus, 1945), associative responses (Barber & Calverley, 1966b; Takahashi, 1958; Thorne, 1969; Thorne & Hall, 1974; Williamsen, Johnson & Eriksen, 1965), and memory for colored patterns (Goldstein & Sipprelle, 1970) or numbers (Bowers, 1975), the amnesia has been found to be far from complete. As early as 1929, Strickler concluded that the "posthypnotic amnesias which appear to be complete are by no means so'' (p. 116). The extent of the amnesia differed as a function of the memory test utilized. Free recall was most impaired, recognition and relearning less.

Hull (1933) noted that the effectiveness of suggestions for amnesia differed as a function of the way it was measured. He stated:

[The subjects] uniformly deny any recollection of trance events, i.e., as tested by general symbolic recall, amnesia is one hundred percent. By detailed specific recall this amount of amnesia is reduced for nonsense material probably to about ninety-seven percent. By the relearning method amnesia falls to approximately fifty percent. Manual habits learned in the stylus maze show by the relearning method an amnesia of about fifty percent. With specific training in arithmetical addition and general training in memorizing nonsense material the amount of post-hypnotic amnesia is reduced to zero (1933, p. 155).

More recently, Kihlstrom and Shor (1978) tested both hypnotizable and insusceptible subjects for amnesia by either recall or recognition. The two groups differed significantly in the amount remembered when tested by recall, but not when tested by recognition since the latter did away with the posthypnotic amnesia. They interpreted the results to suggest that posthypnotic amnesia involves a disruption in the search component, but not the division component, of memory retrieval (Anderson & Bower, 1972).

Other investigators have studied the effects of amnesia in retroactive inhibition. When subjects learn a list of words or nonsense syllables, later learn another list, and are subsequently asked to recall the first list, the material of the second list interferes with or retroactively inhibits the recalling of the first list. The functional ablation hypothesis suggests that if amnesia is produced for the second list, there should be less retroactive inhibition. Some investigators have claimed to have found this effect (Messerschmidt, 1927, M. Mitchell, 1932; Nagge, 1935; Stevensen, Stoyva, & Beach, 1962; Sturrock, 1966). Many of these studies suffered from small sample sizes (in some cases only two subjects were used), differing instructions, and the failure to suggest amnesia, assuming that it would spontaneously occur because the subject was hypnotized. In well designed and carefully controlled replications of these studies, Coe, Basden, Basden, and Graham (1976), Graham & Patton (1968), Orne (1966a), and Stewart & Dunlap (1976) found no support for the hypothesis that retroactive inhibition is decreased when the interpolated material is subjected to hypnotic amnesia.

By comparison, Stern, et al. (1963) found that the adaptation of the electrodermal orientation response to a sound stimulus occurred more slowly for a hypnotized group given suggestions for amnesia than for other control groups. However, they suggested that amnesia was not a passive but rather a very active process; not an obliteration of memory traces but rather an alteration of perception or a disturbance in the expression of the amnesic material. They concluded that the study "demonstrated not only at a verbal level but also at a physiological level that amnesia is a real phenomenon" (p. 400). Analogous findings have been reported by Plapp and Edmonston (1965). These studies indicate that the functional ablation hypothesis is not tenable, and that although the subjects are unable to verbally recall material for which amnesia has been suggested, when tested by methods other than direct verbal recall, effects of exposure to the material were found. As we shall see, such findings need not be interpreted as challenging the authenticity of hypnotic amnesia, however.

REPRESSION

The similarities between posthypnotic amnesia and clinical repression have long attracted attention (Rapaport, 1942; Schilder & Kauders, 1927; Stengel, 1966). The recoverability of the amnesic material, the suggestions of an active rather than a passive process, the filtering of some material into awareness, and the finding that there is differential amnesia as a function of the affective content of the material are characteristics common to the two phenomena. Brenman (1947) tested in the waking state the preference for completed and incompleted tasks that occurred within hypnosis for which amnesia had been suggested. In general, preference was for completed tasks. Hilgard and Hommel (1961), taking advantage of the fact that even though suggested, posthypnotic amnesia is often incomplete, studied the types of items that were forgotten. They found that subjects tended to forget relatively more frequently those items which they failed (that is, did not respond to as a hypnotized person) than those they passed. They accounted for these results by suggesting that the failure to respond as a hypnotized subject was disappointing and led to repression. They recognized, however, that an alternative explanation might account for the findings equally well: namely, that successful hypnotic performance may have been very dramatic and was remembered by the subjects because of its being so accentuated. The study by Clemes (1964), previously described, lent partial support to their first explanation. He found that subjects were more amnesic for critical rather than neutral words, supporting the repression hypothesis.

A subsequent study by O'Connell (1966) supported an enhancement explanation. He also analyzed the nature of the items recalled and, like Brenman, found there was an overall tendency for passed items to be recalled more frequently than failed items. Further analysis showed, however, that this was more pronounced for those subjects relatively unhypnotizable than for those highly hypnotizable. He interpreted this to suggest that it was the rather unusual or unexpected nature of the passing of the items for those subjects who passed relatively few of them that enhanced the passing and increased the probability of their being remembered. Had the explanation been one of repression, the subjects who passed the larger number of items, that is, the more susceptible subjects, would have been expected to show the effect to a greater degree.

Using objective (behavioral) measures of success and failure, Coe et al. (Coe et al., 1976b) found that failed items were more likely to be recalled by the susceptible subjects, and passed items by the insusceptible subjects. However, when they used the subjective impressions of whether an item had been successfully passed this tendency was greatly reduced, and subsequently provided no support for either hypothesis.

Pettinati and Evans (1978) noted that these studies had not taken into account the size of the recall pool. Highly susceptible subjects pass many items but remember few of them (that is, their recall pool is small), while less susceptible subjects who pass few items remember most of them (their recall pool is large). Thus susceptibility is confounded by the size of the recall pool. They used a new index of selective recall (RPI) designed to eliminate this artifact. In two different samples, susceptible and insusceptible subjects both favored the recall of passed items, but the difference between susceptible and insusceptible subjects was not significant, suggesting that selective recall is not a function of depth of hypnosis and consequently is not involved in hypnotic amnesia.

Bobbitt (1968), Imm (1966), and Levitt et al. (1961) have also investigated the relationship between amnesia and repression. While there are similarities, there appears to be no strong support at the present time for a process of repression in posthypnotic amnesia.

DISSOCIATIVE PROCESS

While some criticize dissociation as an explanatory construct for hypnosis (Sarbin & Coe, 1972; White & Shevach, 1942), others have conceived of hypnosis as an altered state which is due to a dissociative process. This implies a capacity for various processes to occur simultaneously, relatively independent of each other. In the case of amnesia, functionally (structurally?) distinct modes of thought may operate in such a way that the material in one cannot be readily translated into the other. There is much clinical evidence, and some directly as well as tangentially related experimental evidence which support this explanation: amnesias in multiple personalities; amnesias associated with hypnotic-like states reported to occur in primitive societies; Orne's (1959) discussion of trance logic; the work of Gill and Brenman (1959) which conceptualized hypnosis as a regression in the service of ego; the work of Schachtel (1947) and Reiff and Scheerer (1959) dealing with styles and modes of thought; the contribution of Eriksen (1958) on awareness and its manifestation through different response modalities; the amnesia for events occurring during sleep (Cobb et al., 1965; Evans et al., 1966, 1969); and clinical observations (Orne, 1966a)—all bear on this issue.

Since the first edition of this book was published, Hilgard (1973a, 1973b, 1974, 1976, 1977a, 1977b, and Chapter Three in this volume) has presented a form of a dissociation model which he calls neo-dissociation theory. It has been given this name because of features that are not common to classical dissociation. The theory proposes a hierarchical order of cognitive control systems which operate at any given time in the individual. Hypnosis is viewed as just one of many possible mechanisms which change the order of control so that some systems become separated from the others. Thus, "what is normally voluntary may become involuntary, what is normally remembered may be forgotten, and (under some circumstances) what is normally unavailable to recall may be recalled" (Hilgard, 1973b, p. 406). The separation may be in dimensionality and/or degree; that is, systems separated in one dimension may be interacting in another, and there may be partial dissociations. The theory further proposes that there is an *increase* in interference between simultaneous tasks when one is performed out of awareness because "there are added burdens on the control system when a task has to be kept out of awareness while it is being performed" (Hilgard, 1975, p. 24).

Coe et al. (1976) used a retroactive inhibition design for free-recall learning. They found that the amnesic subjects showed a significant gain in recall of the first list after amnesia was removed, but the nonamnesic subjects did not. They interpreted this as implying that the amnesic subjects, upon release of the amnesia, gained the energy that had previously been expended in executing two tasks simultaneously (recalling the first list and not recalling the second), when the latter was outside of awareness.

Empirical support for the theory has been found in experiments on pain reduction using hypnosis (Hilgard, Morgan, & Macdonald, 1975; Knox, Morgan, & Hilgard, 1974), on arithmetic and color naming tasks (Knox, Crutchfield, & Hilgard, 1975; Stevenson, 1976), and posthypnotic amnesia (Coe et al., 1976a).

DISRUPTED RETRIEVAL

Contemporary cognitive psychologists emphasize the construing of forgetting and remembering within an information processing model. Within such a model, failure to produce the "forgotten" material either during the testing for amnesia or after the signal to remember may occur because of a lack of registration, that is a failure to attend to and process the material in the first place (see the discussion regarding amnesia in children earlier in this chapter and Lavoie, Sabourin, & Langlois, 1973), a lack of storage, or, although the material is available, a problem of retrieval.

The findings from a large number of studies investigating different aspects of hypnotic amnesia support the conclusion that the failure to produce the material during the testing for amnesia is a problem of retrieval. The conclusions from the investigations of the functional ablation hypothesis—that the critical memory traces are not lost but are still available to interact with other cognitive process—support it. The emphasis on the importance of the reversibility of the amnesia for an understanding of hypnotic amnesia reinforce it. The differences in recall and recognition memory during posthypnotic amnesia are relevant to it. A careful review of, all of these studies led Kihlstrom and Evans to hypothesize that hypnotic amnesia is not a problem in registration or storage, but rather one of retrieval (Evans & Kihlstrom 1973, 1975, Kihlstrom 1972a, 1972b, 1977a, 1977b, 1978, Kihlstrom & Evans 1971, 1976; Kihlstrom, Evans, Orne, & Orne, in press). Thus, hypnotic amnesia is analogous to a number of nonhypnotic experiences such as the "tip of the tongue" phenomenon (Brown & McNiel, 1966), and the "feeling of knowing" something (Hart, 1965).

Cognitive theorists view retrieval as a search process in which the individual uses organizational cues, tags, and strategies to work through the network of associations. Without a sufficient number of cues or strategies, the individual will not be able to gain access to material that is otherwise available. Kihlstrom (1977a) argues that when hypnotic amnesia is viewed as a disruption of retrieval then the otherwise paradoxical aspects of the amnesic subject's behavior make sense.

Evans & Kihlstrom (1973) investigated the organization of recall in hypnotic amnesia by comparing the order of presentation of the items on the HGSHS: A with the order in which the items were recalled under amnesia for those subjects who manifested partial amnesia.

The *rho* correlations for the susceptible subjects were significantly lower than those for the insusceptible subjects, suggesting that the retrieval process was more random, that is, less ordered (and thus disrupted) for the former than for the latter group. The findings have been replicated (Kihlstrom, in press). They have further demonstrated that the disruption is not found for the susceptibles after the removal of amnesia (Kihlstrom & Evans, 1973) and that it is not a function of hypnosis alone but of the suggestion for amnesia (Kihlstrom, 1977a, 1977b).

Nace, Orne, & Hammer (1974) studied recall amnesia both before and after reversibility and concluded that amnesia is an active process involving a reversible disturbance of memory retrieval. Construing amnesia as a function of retrieval rather than learning, as an active rather than a passive process, suggests that it is no longer useful to ask such questions as, "Why can't the subject remember?" or, "What did the suggestion to forget do to the subject?" and emphasizes asking such questions as, "What does the subject do (or not do) in order not to remember?" or, "What cues or strategies are (or are not) available for use by the subject?" Kihlstrom and Evans have already started investigating such questions (Evans & Kihlstrom, 1975; Kihlstrom & Evans, 1977), and

Spanos and Ham (1973) found that hypnotic and task-motivated subjects who met their criterion of amnesia reported significantly more goal-directed fantasy than those who failed to meet the criterion.

It should be noted that the view of amnesia as a disruption of retrieval processes is not incompatible with that of neo-dissociation. The disruption may be a function of the manipulation of the hierarchical order of cognitive control systems. It will be interesting to note the research studies generated by each of these orientations in the next few years, and the resulting conception of the underlying mechanism(s) of hypnotic amnesia.

Summary

In summary, it must be noted that hypnotic amnesia is not a simple phenomenon. As we employ more sophisticated methodologies to analyze it, we find it to be more and more complex in terms of its manifestations and the variables and mechanisms that give rise to it. The present survey reviewed a relatively large number of studies. Progress has been made at both the conceptual and empirical levels since the first edition of this book. But what was said then is still true. Although amnesia has attracted the interest and attention of both clinicians and laboratory investigators for a long time, there are still many questions that must be answered. Sequentially planned programs of investigations on hypnotic amnesia are needed. The payoff *from such serial investigations* will be many times greater than it has been for the one-time shotgun type of study which all too often has characterized the research in this area to date.

While our attention in this chapter has been directed specifically toward amnesia, it is only one of a number of hypnotic phenomena which are interrelated. As our understanding of these other phenomena as well as of the underlying nature of hypnosis itself increases, there will be relevant implications for the nature of amnesia. The work on neo-dissociation and disrupted retrieval beautifully illustrates this fact.

This survey has been directed primarily toward the experimental evidence for and procedures used to study hypnotic amnesia rather than toward clinical case studies. Reference has been made from time to time to the differences that occur in hypnotic amnesia in the clinical setting as compared with the experimental setting. The effects are often startlingly dramatic and conclusive in the former while less so in the latter. Important differences distinguish the two settings; they should be kept in mind. The relationship that exists between the hypnotist and the client or subject, the motivation for participating in the experience, or the personally relevant, ego-involving nature of the material for which amnesia is suggested, and the expectations of the client or subject differ radically for the two settings. It should not be too surprising that different observations have been made in the clinical as opposed to the experimental setting. The paper by Erickson & Rossi (1974) is an important first step toward systematizing and carefully recording the important factors in the clinical situation, so that their influence may then be studied in a clinical laboratory setting—i.e., a laboratory setting in which the clinical factors are maximally operative.

I am still convinced that the phenomenon of hypnotic amnesia cannot be entirely explained on the basis of demand characteristics, instructions, expectations, desires to please the experimenter, or role-playing. Over and above all these variables is the influence of responsiveness to hypnotic suggestions that is part of a unique subjective state, and which supports the authenticity and genuineness of hypnotic amnesia. The crucial problem is to establish procedures and controls that will allow us to evaluate the hypnotic influences. The presence of confounding variables makes the task more difficult and increases the need for caution in drawing conclusions from any particular study, but their presence does not destroy the concept itself.

Patricia Greig Bowers *is an Assistant Professor of Psychology at the University of Waterloo, Ontario. She received her Ph.D. from the University of Illinois in 1965. Earlier in her career, she worked as a psychologist at the Kitchener-Waterloo Hospital and as a consultant at a girls' training school, both in Ontario. Her research interests center on the contribution of imaginative ability to the makeup of the highly hypnotizable person and on the nature of the creative process. The clinical training of graduate students in psychology is another focus of interest. During 1977-1978, she held a position as research associate in the Stanford Hypnosis Laboratory. While there, research with creative writers was begun.*

Kenneth S. Bowers *received his Ph.D. from the University of Illinois in 1964. Since then he has been at the University of Waterloo, in Ontario, Canada. He has been the director of the clinical psychology program at that institution for a number of years, while pursuing theoretical problems in personality, and empirical research in hypnosis. He spent his 1970-71 sabbatical at Stanford University in Dr. E.R. Hilgard's laboratory of hypnosis, and returned there for his second sabbatical in 1977-78. In 1976, Dr. Bowers published* Hypnosis for the Seriously Curious, *a book that reviews recent research on hypnosis in the context of its history and clinical applications. Currently, Dr. Bowers is working toward a conceptualization of hypnosis as a specific mode of information processing.*

The Bowers *are interested in the systematic study of subjective experience in hypnosis. For them subjective reports are primary data. They argue that the behaviorist tradition at best tends to place secondary interest on the heart of the matter—the striking changes in subjective experience. The phenomenological emphasis brings to light similarties between hypnosis, other altered states, and the creative process. Creativity is viewed as involving regression in the service of the ego (adaptive regression). This involves the constructive integration of primary and secondary process thinking and the employment of fantasy in the service of realistic ends. A careful review of empirical studies is made in the light of this theoretical viewpoint.*

11

Hypnosis and Creativity: A Theoretical and Empirical Rapprochement

PATRICIA GREIG BOWERS AND KENNETH S. BOWERS

Hypnosis: The Behavioral Approach

Hypnosis has both experiential and behavioral characteristics, the latter be-ing the traditional target of experimental investigation. Only recently have subjective experiences in hypnosis been systematically studied, and their relative neglect has been unfortunate, for the behavioral approach has tended to isolate the study of hypnosis, whereas emphasis upon the hyp-notic experience brings to light similarities between hypnosis and other altered states of consciousness (Fromm, 1977b). Moreover, the investiga-tion of hypnosis *qua* experience suggests hypotheses relating it to aspects of the creative process, a liaison which we will explore later in this paper.

For many years, hypersuggestibility of hypnotized subjects has been *the* defining feature of hypnosis (Hull, 1933; Weitzenhoffer, 1953). Very often, however, nonhypnotized subjects who are either task motivated or are simulating hypnosis behave much like hypnotized subjects (Barber, 1969b; Orne, 1959) though with markedly different subjective experiences. Although in the past there has been considerable skepticism about reports of these experiences, carefully garnered subjective reports have been shown

1. Work on this chapter was completed while at the Hypnosis Laboratory at Stanford University. It was aided by Grant MH 03859 to Ernest Hilgard, from National Institute of Mental Health, Department of Health, Education and Welfare. It was also facilitated by a grant to the second author from the Spencer Foundation.

351

to be credible (Hilgard, 1969c; K.S. Bowers, 1967) and are no longer in dispute.

The cautious acceptance of subjective reports of private experience as primary data allows an experiential orientation to the study of hypnotic phenomena. In this paper, we will attempt to cast a loose net around a variety of phenomena to which this experiential orientation to hypnosis, when aided by some theory, calls attention. From hypnosis itself to waking experiences of absorption, from the creative process to empirical work relating hypnosis and creativity, we discern a common thread which has clarified the phenomena by linking them. We hope this chapter will convince others that this thread exists and is of interest. But the meanderings of the thread are formidable. A roadmap may be helpful.

1. We will first explore how the experience of hypnosis can be studied in its own right, as it relates to hypnotic suggestibility, to other altered states, and to spontaneous, trancelike experiences.

2. Then the search for physiological correlates of the experienced changes in consciousness will be reviewed. The neurophysiological substrata of various cognitive events is receiving increased attention. Greater knowledge about that substrata may eventually enrich our understanding of the nature of the differences between "ordinary" and "alternate" states of consciousness.

3. The next section proposes that hypersuggestibility and heightened primary process mentation are common effects of the changed state of consciousness. Tolerance for and control of heightened primary process is related to several phenomena, among them performance on creativity tests.

4. A conceptualization of creativity is presented, and evidence pertinent to an adaptive regression formulation of the creative process is cited.

5. Ideas about *how* the integration of primary and secondary process might occur in creative expression are explored. In this, our most speculative section, phenomena pertinent to a model of the creative process and, to the hypnotic experience, are discussed and interpreted.

6. Finally, we review the empirical work in our lab which looks at the enhancement of creativity under hypnosis, the relationship of hypnotizability to waking creative performance, and the effortless experiencing construct as the link accounting for the relationship.

Hypnotic Experience

Several studies show that hypnotic experiences are characterized by important alterations in consciousness. Ås and Østvold (1968) found that three subjective experience factors characterized the reports of hypnotized subjects: the "experience of trance," the "experience of ego control," and the "desire for regression." These factor scores correlated with depth of hypnosis as assessed by a standardized hypnotizability scale .69, –.41, and .07, respectively.

Field and Palmer (1969), using an empirically derived inventory which assessed subjective experiences during hypnosis (Field, 1965), factor-analyzed the intercorrelations of all items from both the experience inventory and the Stanford Hypnotic Susceptibility Scale (SHSS, Weitzenhoffer & Hilgard, 1959). Thus, the emerging factors are not pure experience factors as were those of Ås and Østvold, but rather composites of experience and suggestibility. A general factor of hypnotic depth emerged, with challenge SHSS items, together with inventory items reflecting experiences of absorption, unawareness, compulsion, and unusualness loading on it most highly. This factor accounted for sixteen percent of the factor variance. Of six rotated factors found, two dealt with alterations of consciousness. One of these two factors described "the dimension from awareness to unawareness of the environment and the experimental situation," while the other factor was "a dimension from waking to dazed drowsiness." The total experience inventory score correlated .51 with the SHSS.

Spanos and McPeake (1975b) showed that the experience of being absorbed in a hypnotic suggestion, and the involuntariness of the response, covaried with the degree of behavioral responsiveness to hypnotic suggestion.

Tart (1970b) correlated several indices of experiences during hypnosis with each other and with the behavioral score of the more demanding SHSS Form C (SHSS:C; Weitzenhoffer & Hilgard, 1962). He reports that the mean of a subject's estimates of how deeply hypnotized he is correlates .74 with the SHSS:C behavioral score. The same subjective estimate or "state report" correlates .77 with SHSS:C "experiential score." This latter score reflects the "intensity and degree of involuntariness of each major suggestion" of the previously administered SHSS:C. The state report correlates .66 with Field's Inventory (1965). In an interesting attempt to separate "state report" from the effects of following suggestions, the *initial* state report—requested after induction, but before any experience of reactions to specific suggestions—was correlated with several variables. The results of this analysis were correlations between initial state report and the SHSS:C behavioral score of .56; between this report and the SHSS:C experiential score of .69; and between this report and Field's Inventory of .69.

Hypnotized subjects can evidently articulate their experiences reliably. Such experiences are distinct from *hypersuggestibility,* but predict it to a moderately high degree (.56). Subjects' estimates of hypnotic depth prior to any response to specific suggestions predict the subjective intensity of subsequent hypnotic responses to an even greater extent (.69).

Trancelike Experiences and Hypnosis

The above studies have found evidence for important hypnotic experiences which are conceptually distinct from suggestibility per se. These trancelike unrealistic experiences imply in large part an absence of the usual awareness of the environment and one's place in it. Accordingly, Shor has written several papers which are directly concerned with the loss of a "generalized reality orientation" (GRO) in and out of hypnosis (Shor, 1959, 1970). He describes it in this way:

> In all our waking life we carry around in the background of our awareness a kind of frame of reference or orientation to generalized reality which serves as a context or arena within which we interpret all of our ongoing conscious experiences. Under certain conditions—of which hypnosis is just one—this wide frame of reference or orientation to generalized reality can fade into the very distant background of our minds so that ongoing experiences are isolated from their usual context. When that happens the distinction between imagination and reality no longer exists for us (Shor, 1970, p. 91).

As this passage suggests, the loss of GRO is by no means confined to hypnosis. Witch doctors and mystics as well as the ordinary man in the street, report occasional loss of awareness of their environmental frame of reference. For example, in the same paper from which the above quotation was taken, Shor described what he calls the "book reading fantasy" to illustrate how a loss in GRO can be a rather ordinary event for some people.

> When these people read a story, particularly an adventureful novel, they are able to enter the story in imagination so completely that it seems equivalent to living the experience itself. During the time of this fantasy the reader is completely oblivious to the true reality about him. The fantasy world is an encapsulated unit, and it seems totally real. There is nothing else beyond it (Shor, 1970, p. 92).

The type of experience to which Shor refers has been captured in various scales of absorption which will be further discussed below.

A fading of GRO results not only from complete absorption in a complex story. Just concentrating on a simple object like a blue vase can also have potent effects on one's perception of reality, as Deikman (1963) has convincingly shown. Deikman's four subjects experienced rather unusual perceptual distortions during their twelve brief (ususally fifteen minute) meditation periods. The terms "more vivid" and "luminous" were often used to describe the vase. The shape of the vase appeared unstable; there were reports of a loss of the third dimension and a diffusion or loss of the vase's boundaries. One subject said in her fourth meditation session: "The outlines of the vase...seem almost literally to dissolve entirely...it [seemed] to be a kind of fluid blue" (Deikman, 1963, p. 208).

Other valued states have been described in which lack of awareness of any differentiation between the self and its surrounding is associated with emotions of joy or ecstasy. Subjective events of this kind have been termed peak experiences or mystical experiences. An extreme loss of GRO is also experienced by the yoga, who after much practice can become oblivious not only to his reality context but also to any thought or emotion arising from within. Other characteristics common to various altered states of consciousness are discussed by Ludwig (1966). Deikman (1971) suggests that the heightening of a receptive mode of consciousness rather than the continued dominance of the usual active mode underlies these altered states.

Although losses in GRO are not as uncommon as one might suppose, people do differ a great deal in the frequency and/or completeness with which they experience such losses. Indeed, the frequency and/or intensity of waking subjects' spontaneous trancelike experiences have been among the very few indices that consistently correlate with hypnotizability. Work on this conceptual area has led to the well established finding that absorption in and intense involvement with ordinary imaginative activities predicts hypnotizability to a moderate degree. The development of this concept began with the construction of the Personal Experience Questionnaire by Shor (1960), in which he showed that spontaneous losses in GRO correlated .46 with hypnotic susceptibility.

Similar scales (Ås, 1963; Lee-Teng, 1965) and careful interviews (Hilgard, 1970) indicated that deep absorption in certain experiences characterized highly hypnotizable people. A sophisticated psychometric study by Tellegen and Atkinson (1974) capped this line of research, in showing that responses to inventory items similar to those of Shor and Ås loaded on an absorption factor which *was* related to hypnotizability and did *not* load on factors typically found in personality research, stability and introversion. These latter factors were unrelated to hypnotizability. Examples of absorption scale items are: "I can sometimes recollect certain past experiences in my life with such clarity and vividness that it is like living them again, or almost so," "I am sometimes able to forget about my present self and get absorbed in a fantasy that I am someone else."

The degree to which the relationship between absorption and hypnotizability has been firmly established is impressive. Spanos and McPeake (1975b), Finke and Macdonald (1978), and P.G. Bowers (1978) have continued to replicate this relationship using not only Tellegen's scale but other scales as well. The level of relationship seems to hover about the .4 level.

We have argued above that the loss of the GRO characterizes altered states other than hypnosis, so it would not be surprising to find relationships between absorption and a tendency to experience these other states. For example, McGlothlin, Cohen, and McGlothlin (1968) have found that scores on Ås's (1963) experience inventory correlated with the intensity of reactions to LSD.

The Search for Physiological Correlates

Two lines of research have sought to find physiological concomitants of the changes in state of consciousness discussed above. The so-called alpha rhythm of 8-13 Hz characterizes much brain wave activity while resting with eyes closed. Presence of this pattern is typically accompanied by reports of a state of uncritical relaxation (Kamiya, 1969). Many investigators have looked for indications that alpha EEG activity is heightened during various altered states, or alternatively, that those individuals who are "good" at entering such states generate more alpha activity in resting records. A second line of research has looked at the relative participation of the right (nondominant) hemisphere during altered states as characteristic of people who enter those states. It is believed that performance on spatial tasks requiring holistic modes of information processing is mediated by work of the right hemisphere, while analytic and verbal tasks require significant contributions from the left hemisphere (Morgan, MacDonald, & Hilgard, 1974; Dumas & Morgan, 1975).

The relationship between alpha EEG and various altered states has a checkered history. Greater alpha activity is associated with certain altered states in some studies and not others and is affected by many variables other than those of central interest to investigators. It has been reported that heightened alpha activity is characteristic of yoga (Anand, Chhino, & Singh, 1961; Bagshi & Wenger in Deikman, 1971) and Zen meditation (Kasamatsu & Hirai, 1966). Anand, Chhino, and Singh report that beginners in yoga who have well marked alpha activity in resting records "showed greater aptitude and zeal for maintaining the practice of yoga." A similar relationship between alpha activity and aptitude for hypnosis has been reported. London, Hart, and Leibovitz (1968) and Morgan, MacDonald, and Hilgard (1974) have found that more highly hypnotizable subjects have significantly more resting, eyes closed, baseline alpha activity than low hypnotizable subjects. In addition, Morgan, MacDonald, and Hilgard found that the high hypnotizables continued to have more eyes-closed alpha than the low hypnotizables during the performance of various tasks outside hypnosis. However, other labs (see review by Evans, Chapter 6) have not found these relationships. Evans presents some evidence that the relationship of alpha EEG to hypnotizability is an artifact of the same situational influences depressing both an initial score on a hypnosis scale and an initial baseline measure of alpha, and that when more stable plateau measures of each variable are taken, this correlation disappears. However, some studies taking cognizance of this possibility have continued to find the relationship, while others have not. Evans (Chapter 6) and Dumas (1977) concluded that there was no relationship; Engstrom (1976) concludes that there is a moderate relationship. Paskewicz (1977) suggests the relationship exists for some hypnotizability indices and not others. Basically the case for the alpha EEG providing a physiological underpinning for various altered states is still open to dispute, but probably no simple relationship exists.

The work on the relationship between right hemisphere preference or activation and the experience of altered states of consciousness is somewhat less confusing, if only because not enough time has elapsed for the negative results to flow in. Dumas and Morgan (1975) among others have indicated that the right hemisphere contributes relatively more to the performance of spatial tasks and those tasks in which holistic rather than analytic modes of processing were suitable. Hypnotizability appears to be related to good performance on tasks such as gestalt closure which require more right hemisphere participation (Crawford, 1977). Marijuana intoxication appears to improve performance on tasks such as closure and depress performance on analytic, presumably left hemisphere, tasks (Harshman, Crawford, & Hecht, 1976). Preference for the use of the right hemisphere, as indicated by direction of eye movement when facing an experimenter asking reflective questions, seems to be correlated with hypnotizability (Gur & Gur, 1974). Graham (1977) reports greater perceived autokinetic movement to the left under hypnosis than in the waking condition, supporting a right hemisphere activation hypothesis. Deikman (1971) suggests that the receptive mode of consciousness which he sees as characteristic of altered states such as meditation and hypnosis is related to the relatively heightened processing by right rather than left hemisphere.

In sum, the reduction in the GRO appears to come about in a variety of ways. Hypnosis, meditation techniques, and spontaneous experiences have been discussed above. Drugs (Huxley, 1963) fatigue (Morris & Singer, 1966) and sensory deprivation (Zuckerman, 1964) seem also to be related to loss of GRO at times. Physiological indices of this reduction have been sought in alpha EEG and increased right hemisphere activation. The work on the latter, in particular, appears promising.

Effects of Weakened GRO

Two things seem to happen when GRO is weakened: the person is both more suggestible to outside influences *and* more influenced by internally generated primary process or fantasy. For example, highly hypnotizable people are more suggestible under hypnosis than while awake, and, in addition, give more primary process on the Rorschach (Fromm, Oberlander, & Gruenewald, 1970) and on induced dreams and TAT stories (Levin & Harrison, 1976) than they do in a waking state. These two effects are tightly interwoven. Thus, while the content of the hypnotized person's ideation may conform to suggestion, the rules of thought related to that content are nevertheless heavily infiltrated by trance logic (Orne, 1959), in which logical contradictions are tolerated easily by the hypnotized subject.

Heightened suggestibility as indicated by greater responsiveness to hypnotic suggestions is found after sensory deprivation (Sanders & Reyher, 1969; Wickramasekera, 1969) and, inconsistently, after alpha biofeedback training (Engstrom, 1976). Sjoberg and Hollister (1965) demonstrated increases in suggestibility after the ingestion of various psychotomimetic drugs. Some highly hypnotizable subjects will respond to simple motor suggestions while maintaining stage one EEG sleep; low susceptibles do not respond in this way (Cobb et al., 1965). The most dramatic examples of hypersuggestibility occur in "brainwashing." Gill and Brenman (1959) have noted important similarities between brainwashing procedures and those used in sensory deprivation and hypnosis.

Although a loss in GRO is one condition for enhanced suggestibility, it is also, as previously noted, a condition in which subjects are more receptive and responsive to internal sources of stimulation. In so-called hypnagogic states before sleep, "regressive content in mentation appears only with, or after, some loss of contact with the external world" (Vogel, Foulkes, & Trosman, 1966, p. 87). Work with the autokinetic phenomena indicates that the more subjects are aware of their surroundings, the less autokinetic movement they perceived (Mayman & Voth, 1969). Indices of primary process (Ewing et al., 1975) and of hypnotizability predict aspects of the autokinetic effect (Wallace, Garrett, & Anstadt, 1974). The most common effects of sensory deprivation are a drifting of thought with fantasies and daydreams, and a difficulty in directed thinking. Forty-three percent of the subjects in various deprivation studies reported unstructured visual sensations, and nineteen percent have structured visual sensations (Zuckerman, 1964).

Most persons find sensory deprivation somewhat stressful; there are, however, substantial differences in the ability of people to cope with the experience. Surprisingly, the correlates of adaptability to sensory isolation have been difficult to determine (Wright & Zubek, 1969). However, Cambereri (1959) found that suggestible subjects were more adaptive to deprivation conditions than unsuggestible subjects, despite the fact that suggestible subjects experience more regressive phenomena than unsuggestible subjects. This concept of tolerance for primary process dominated experiences has proved to be a very important one. A measure of the ability not only to tolerate but to integrate primary process ideation on the Rorschach into more realistic responses has been developed by Holt (1963) and called the Adaptive Regression Score. A closely related score on Rorschach protocols proved highly predictive of subjects' endurance under conditions of sensory deprivation (Wright & Zubek, 1969). The adaptive regression score of Holt has also predicted performance on various behavioral measures of tolerance for unusual experiences, such as wearing aneisikonic lenses (Feirstein, 1967). Holt's scores for defense effectiveness and adaptive regression were correlated with a composite creativity score as well (Pine & Holt, 1960).

In this section, we have reviewed evidence indicating that the loss of GRO is accompanied by the escalating influence of primary process mentation. We have also seen how the ability to tolerate and control such mentation is evidently a disposition of some importance in determining a person's experiences. It is now appropriate to extend these findings as well as those mentioned earlier into a more thorough examination of creative functioning.

Comments on Creativity

The creativity literature is not particularly cohesive. Definitional and criterial problems abound, and various subsections of the field are rarely tied together. The need for theory-guided research is apparent, and so in seeking that goal, we make no apology for being selective in our presentation of the evidence. For purposes of a broad review, the reader is referred to Dellas and Gaier (1970) and Taylor (1975). Stein (1974) provides a good integrative account of the work on creativity. Our views of creativity have been influenced by ego analytic thought deriving from Kris's seminal work (Kris, 1952).

Creativity involves the process of seeing things in a new and informative way. The creative vision of one person, such as an Einstein, a Darwin, or a Freud, may literally reshape our conception of the world. While the term "creative" need not be reserved for such momentous insights, even rather modest creativity eludes many of us because we become prisoners of the conventional. As we grow up, we tend to depend upon words to tell us how things are, and often reduce experiences to fit the stereotyped dimensions of language. Thus, however liberating language may be, it is also very limiting, subtly forcing us to exclude from consideration and even from consciousness those aspects of our subjectivity that evade easy articulation. Language may adapt us to the world that is, but it is the enemy of the as yet unimagined. Even for the poet, "the greatest problem...is the temptation of language" (Schachtel, 1959, p. 295).

It is our interior life that saves us from utter stereotypy. A momentary feeling of disgust, or awe, an intuitive hunch, a fantasy, all of these subarticulate experiences if seized upon and elaborated, can create a new form, a new insight into reality. Einstein said, "When I examine myself and my methods of thought, I come to the conclusion that the gift of fantasy has meant more to me than my talent for absorbing positive knowledge" (in Dreistadt, 1974, p. 17). And at a more modest level, Singer (1975) reports that frequency of daydreaming is associated with storytelling rated as showing originality. Whether the creative product be a poem, an architectural landmark, or simply a new insight into one's own life, responses to situations are informed both by realistic issues and by interior, more personal, responses.

The above description of the creative act assumes that human thinking processes can be sorted into at least two different basic categories: the logical, conventional sort that provides efficiency in ordinary, practical things, and another, less well articulated sort which characterizes some of our interior life, such as fantasies and intuitions. Creativity becomes then, the coordination of these two forms of thinking in an especially adaptive way. One of the earliest and most popular forms of this hypothesis is that of creativity as "regression in the service of the ego" (Kris, 1952). This formulation developed from Freud's original suggestion that there were basically two ways of processing information: the primary process, an alogical, drive-dominated process whose influence could best be seen in dreams and slips of the tongue; and the secondary process, in which logical, reality-bound considerations determined the association between ideas. Pathology was characterized by uncontrolled intrusions of primary process into ordinary waking life, usually leading to poor adjustment. In contrast to this uncontrolled type of regression, creativity would be characterized by the controlled and temporary ascendance of primary process, often termed adaptive regression.

Many theorists outside the psychoanalytic camp have echoed the idea that human beings process information in two basically different ways. Deikman (1971) talks of passive-receptive versus active thought. DeBono (1968) distinguishes between vertical and lateral thinking—the former being active, high probability, straightforward thinking; the latter being passive, low probability thinking. Analytic versus holistic processes and their supposed bases in left and right hemisphere activity are other dichtomies which have been proposed to explain or at least describe the common observation that there is a whole class of feeling, associations, behaviors, symptoms, etc., that appear to obey different rules than the class of behaviors we are usually conscious of in living our daily lives. While it is evident that the various proposed dichotomies overlap somewhat, the extent of overlap is unclear. Nevertheless, the reader should recall that many of these dichotomies were seen as relevant to the dimension of hypnotizability. The nature of the coordination between these processes such that a creative product emerges is a relatively unexplored territory of major importance.

The most well developed of the conceptualizations now available is that of adaptive regression. Most of the research to be cited flows from this theoretical net, but is also pertinent to other formulations, particularly Deikman's. The adaptive regression hypothesis implies that creative people have a capacity and tolerance for unrealistic and unregulated thinking and experience. We have already reviewed evidence indicating that such experiences are more characteristic of some people than of others. Moreover, we have seen how such experiences are caused or at least accompanied by an abeyance in GRO. The adaptive regression hypothesis also states that the unregulated thinking and experience implied by regression is integrated into and organized in terms of realistic considerations. Arieti (1976) suggests that by means of primary process, the creative person can see similarities and identities between ideas which are not logically connected. The creative product is not a direct outcome of either primary or secondary processing, but a unique amalgam of the two which Arieti calls tertiary process. We will later consider *how* such an adaptation of unrealistic thinking to realistic purposes might ordinarily take place. For now, it seems reasonable to consider some evidence for the proposal that creative functioning involves: (a) unrealistic thinking which is (b) adaptively integrated into an acceptably realistic form.

Creativity: Some Empirical Findings

The ability to experience in both a primitive and a mature mode, and to integrate the two effectively, has been studied empirically in several ways. We have already mentioned the scoring system for the Rorschach devised by Holt (1963) to assess primary process and its controlled expression. We have seen that Holt's measures of the extent to which primary process is effectively integrated, in fact correlate highly with tests of creativity (Pine & Holt, 1960).

Another, more traditional index of a person's ability to coordinate fantasy and reality is the number of M (human movement) responses given in a Rorschach protocol. Since the blots obviously do not move, whatever movement a person sees represents a projection of his own inner fantasy life (Lerner, 1967). If the movement is "well seen," i.e., if it respects the formal characteristics of the blot, then the projected movement represents a creative embellishment of an inanimate form. Rorschach (1949) originally spoke of M responses as an index of the person's "capacity for inner creation." And, in fact, several studies have indicated that more creative individuals in the artistic and literary fields produce more M responses (Myden, 1959; Dudek, 1968a, 1968b).

Many studies emphasize the coexistence in the personalities of creative people of both primitive and mature characteristics. Hersch (1962) found that eminent artists gave both more mature and more primitive Rorschach responses than a normal noncreative sample. Barron (1965) found that the MMPI profiles of highly (peer nominated) creative architects and writers revealed that they "are almost as superior to the general population in ego strength as they are on pathological dispositions such as Schizophrenia, Depression, Hysteria, and Psychopathic Deviance" (p. 64). Other reports stress the awareness of inner experience characteristic of creative people, and their tendency not to use the defenses of suppression and repression. MacKinnon (1975) in reviewing the work of the Institute for Personality Assessment and Research says, "Biographies of creative Ss [subjects] revealed several recurrent themes: an early development of interest in and sensitive awareness of their inner experience and of their ideational, imaginal and symbolic processes..." (p. 82).

While the empirical results are not entirely consistent, we believe that the weight of evidence favors the view that the creative process involves the coexistence of more and less reality-oriented modes of perception, and their integration.

The Creative Process

The above findings do not, however, yield any useful insights into just *how* the integration of primary and secondary thinking takes place. Hilgard (1962) proposes that such integrations can be conceived as either *fusions* or *mixtures* of primary and secondary process thinking. In fusions, thinking of both types is homogenized in varying proportions in any given response. The mixture scheme suggests that a vacillation between primary and secondary process thinking takes place, with each kind of mentation remaining more or less distinct and intact.

The idea of oscillating phases is reflected in the classic description of phases of creative work by Wallas (1926): preparation, incubation, illumination, and verification. While these phases are rarely experienced in as clearcut a form as implied above, reports of creative people are consistent with the idea that logical, critical problem solving techniques are not sufficient to arrive at a creative product. Rather, some subarticulate, perhaps subconscious, process, seems to intervene when the creator is relaxed or distracted enough to allow it, and the creative ideas occur to him, as if he were the passive observer of an event. Certainly these ideas are not always good ones; they also usually require refinement and testing. But the experience seems a strong one that has been mentioned throughout history. Muses visited the Ancients; Poincaré's discovery of Fuchsian functions (Ghiselin, 1955) is a familiar example of incubation and illumination. These functions had eluded his logical analysis for a long time but while stepping on a bus and engaged in unrelated thought, the solution to his problem occurred to him.

Writers typically describe very long hours of hard word at the typewriter as necessary to their enterprise. However, they also describe another process at work. Many examples of this "other" type of work appeared in a book of interviews with northern Californian novelists by Tooker and Hofheins (1976). Peter Beagle said to an interviewer:

I spend eight hours a day down here. You learn things. But fifteen percent, or ten percent, or whatever, is what I call the swamp. I don't understand the swamp, but I believe it's there. There's a point where I will have come as far as I can by craft. I'll walk around this office and tell the swamp aloud sometimes, "All right, I'd appreciate it if you'd gurgle something up, because I can't do any more by myself." I've come to believe that in a day or two days, or when it damn well feels like it, the swamp will burp up a character I've never met or something that's never happened to me, because it's done it before. In that sense all those strange images and metaphors come out of the swamp (p. 7).

Coppel said:

I try to stay loose enough so that my fictional people and their story can develop along natural lines. It will, if I let it. But I don't try to keep my characters on a tight leash, forcing them to do things that are right for some predetermined plot but wrong for them (p. 81).

Gold:

Books really begin in images and characters, and maybe, some kind of action. And someplace—I can't tell you where exactly—the theme or a sense of the action begins to come clear. It's clearest after I finish the first draft... (p. 112).

Stegner:

I used to write elaborate scenarios in the Sinclair Lewis fashion, but the books didn't want to go that way at all... Things come off the page almost by accident, and I depend on that. If they're right, they stay; if they're not right after a reading or two and a rewriting or two, they'll go out (p. 174).

West:

Graham Greene feels much the same as I. He says writers should forget their own lives. The bits and pieces you remember should fall down into your unconscious and become compost. When you need something, it's there in the compost heap. You've forgotten it's what you lived through. So, for me, the thing to do in writing is to ask myself questions, not tell myself answers; to ask, What did this man do? What did he feel? and let the answer boil up to the surface (p. 85).

In these descriptions, the writer trusts that his subarticulate, intuitive, subconscious processes will exert their influence to the benefit of his more straightforward, active work. The influence may be seen in both fusions and mixtures, but the experience of this influence is characterized by a feeling of effortlessness. The idea "occurs" to the creative person, the characters take over, the creator feels as if he is not actively willing and planning the course of his work, but rather allowing the process to occur through him, passively.

The feeling of effortlessly coming up with ideas as a concomitant of creative functioning is the focus of our current research into the creative process. The reader should note that a similar feeling is frequently reported by the highly hypnotized person: the suggestions of the hypnotist, such as lifting a hand or seeing a hallucinated object, feel as if they occur effortlessly to the subject, as if he had no role in actively constructing the hallucinated object or lifting his hand. The research concerned with the effortless experiencing phenomenon is discussed in greater detail in a subsequent section of the paper. Right now, the authors wish only to place this phenomenological experience in the context of a theoretical analysis of what may occur during a creative act.

There are various lines of evidence giving clues to what may be happening while the creative person is effortlessly engaged. Work on subliminal perception (reviewed by Dixon, 1971) suggests that the less consciously aware a person is of a stimulus, the wider the associational network primed by that stimulus. Spence and Holland (1962) termed this the "restricting effects of awareness." The effect of trying hard to get an idea—to solve a problem—may be increased arousal, and more importantly, the narrowing of focus to associations that seem most directly relevant. If one is more passively oriented, the project with which one is concerned may, like a stimulus of which one is not consciously aware, prime a wider variety of more original associations, taking advantage of past information and experience that seemed to be "forgotten." George Klein (1970) wrote in a similar fashion concerning the creative person's bypassing of usual schemata serving focal awareness and making use of alternative schemata typically more available at the fringes of awareness. Stein (1974) underlined the importance to the would-be creative person of relaxing and of having no fear of what unconscious material might emerge when controls on imagination were lifted. The work of Martindale and Hines (1975) suggests that there is a correlation ($r = .36$, $p < .05$) between percent of basal alpha generated while engaged in a divergent thinking task and the fluency score earned on this task.

In addition to encouraging the priming of a wider associational net, this passive mode may also increase the storing and retrieval of information in the form of images rather than words. In this way not only can the conventionalizing effect of words on experiences be circumvented, but information may be more detailed and vivid and thus richer in evocative power when used in creative work. The increased use of images is cited as a concomitant of primary process and of right hemisphere activation. A relationship between the vividness of waking imagery and hypnotizability is sometimes found (Sheehan, 1972a) but recent work (P.G. Bowers, 1978) suggests that vivid imagery must also be experienced effortlessly to be related to hypnotizability.

Another possible effect of the passive orientation is that information processed under such conditions may not be so tightly organized in the conventional time-bound order so often used in recalling memories. Kihlstrom (1977) has shown that memory retrieval processes under hypnotic amnesia are disturbed because the time line, so useful in organizing memory for recall, is disorganized or not used. Perhaps if the connections between events are not so tightly set by conventional orders such as time, these events might be available to other more original organizations pertinent to the problem at hand.

Are there any behavioral hallmarks of this effortless reverie? The work on fantasy from Singer's laboratory gives us some clues. Antrobus, Antrobus, and Singer (1964) and Singer and Antrobus (1965) report that during passive, effortless indulgence of a wish in fantasy, eye movements were significantly lower than when subjects actively try to suppress the fantasy or try to make their thoughts race. Amadeo and Shagass (1963) found that eye movements are less a concomitant of looking at things than of being mentally active and attentive. Interestingly, during hypnosis with eyes closed, Ss had a lower rate of eye movement than Ss asked under waking instruction to "keep their eyeballs from moving." Thus when Ss are in an essentially passive and uncritical state of mind, e.g. during daydreaming or hypnosis, eye movements are minimal. When on the other hand, Ss' thinking is actively directed toward and/or attentive to *either* exterior *or* interior events, eye movements are significantly higher. It seems that the relative rate of eye movements may, in fact, reflect the two different kinds of thinking: undirected, fantasy-dominated thought, on the one hand; directed, regulated thinking, on the other.[1]

When we try to actively, willfully retrieve fantasy, it often fades. Yet this is *not* to say that undirected thoughts and fantasies cannot themselves be a noticeable and salient facet of experience, even to the point of being peremptory and terrifying (Klein, 1967). They may come to our attention vividly, while trying to pay attention to them makes them less vivid. Dumas and Morgan (1975) report anecdotes of artists told to create images in an experiment. The images came effortlessly; however, when asked to make them clearer, the images became weak. Concentration reduced the image. Peremptory fantasies of the type referred to by Klein seem to occur precisely under circumstances when a person finds it difficult to pay attention to something, to direct and control his thinking. For example, Zuckerman (1964) noted that difficulty in directed, secondary process thinking is the most frequent, and for the subjects, most unexpected effect of sensory deprivation. It is this inability to attend which seems to be the condition for another frequent symptom of isolation, namely the upsurge in primary process fantasies and daydreams. Thus, attention serves us not only by processing information; it may also serve to inhibit and control our fantasy life.

---

1. While we have stressed the relationship of eye movement to attention and fantasy, it is possible that eye movements are a specific instance of how body mobility in general adversely affects fantasy (Lerner, 1967; Schachtel, 1959; Rossi, Fuhrman, & Solomon, 1967).

Hypnosis and the Outside In

At this point, it is necessary to draw more clearly the parallels between this effortless phase of creativity and the hypnotic experience. Perhaps the reader will recall again how subjects gazing at the blue vase in Deikman's (1963) meditation procedure experienced it as losing definition and becoming super blue. To achieve these effects it was crucial for subjects to concentrate on the vase, but *not* in an analytic, scrutinizing way. That is, subjects were to remain *passive* with respect to their perception of the blue vase, *just as we are ordinarily passively oriented with respect to our fantasy life.* The significance of this last remark is that it is precisely under conditions of such attentional passivity that it can be difficult to discriminate the degree to which one's experience is determined by objects in the world on the one hand or by fantasy on the other. There is a sort of merging of inside and outside, a breakdown in the usual self-object boundary (Gravitz & Forbes, 1963). Indeed, one of the "scary" things that occasionally happens under such altered states is a sudden burst of anxiety at the depersonalization implicit in this boundaryless condition.

Now, we would like to argue that when a person's eye movements and body motility are drastically reduced, so is his reality testing. For example, as a blue vase becomes less and less coordinated in space and time, by multiple, analytic perceptual acts performed on it, the vase becomes more and more identified with and identical to the particular and limited perceptual act by which it is apprehended. It becomes, so to speak, a part of the person, rather than a separate and distinct object. As one of Deikman's subjects commented:

> At one point it felt...as though the vase were in my head rather than out there; I knew it was out there but it seemed as though it were almost a part of me. I think that I almost felt at that moment as though, you know, the image is really in me, it's not out there (Deikman, 1963, p. 206).

The construct of absorption as discussed by Hilgard (1970) and measured by scales such as Tellegen and Atkinson's (1974), attempts to tap this subject-object merging.

It has been simpler to introduce the general idea of subject-object merging by recourse to a visual illustration. However, it seems reasonable that such phenomena also take place via the auditory modality as well, though there is no evidence that the ability to move one's ears is in any way a functional analogue of eye movement. If there is nevertheless an analogous "regression" with respect to auditory stimulation, the dramatic effect of hypnotic suggestions may simply derive from the fact that a profoundly hypnotized subject in effect has ceased to actively direct his own thinking and behavior and that he experiences suggested phenomena in the same passive way that he experiences his fantasies. Thus, when such a person behaves in accordance with suggestion, it is less by reason of being realistically responsive to the demand characteristics of the situation (Orne, 1962b) than by reason of experiencing the suggested state of affairs in the more or less uncontrolled and peremptory way that subjects in sensory isolation experience their fantasies. Indeed, some hypnotized subjects also experience nonsuggested phenomena, which may represent the unexpectedly potent effect of their own fantasies in the relative abeyance of their directed thinking.

Of course, the hypnotized subject responds to reality as well as to fantasy. For example, Orne (1962c) notes that a deeply hypnotized person will not bump into a chair he is negatively hallucinating. The problem of responding to reality residues while hypnotized should be no more difficult than responding to fantasy residues while in a normal alert state. To put it another way—reality may be as peremptory to the hypnotized person as fantasy can be to the person who is not.

Let us recapitulate briefly. First, people differ in the ability to give up their GRO and to tolerate the unusual experiences attendant upon this loss. Moreover, this ability to tolerate unusual experiences and become absorbed in a variety of experiences correlates about as highly with hypnotic susceptibility as any other measure. Since the unusual experiences are in part fantasy derived, or concomitant with the subject-object merging described above, it is not surprising that people who can become easily absorbed are ordinarily willing to passively experience hypnotic suggestions. We have focused on the quality and possible behavioral manifestations of the "regression" phase of the creative process, and pointed out how this phase has certain descriptive similarities to the experiences of Deikman's meditators and to hypnotized subjects who experience suggestions in the same unwilled fashion as they experience their own fantasies.

Oscillation between Reality and Fantasy

In the last section, we discussed just one aspect of our analysis of the creative act—that concerned with the passive orientation. By itself, of course, this phase is not apt to be creative. It is only in a particular context that this orientation is conducive to creativity—that is, when it is prompted by a real life concern of the creator, and when he is able to grasp the associations prompted during this more passive state. The problem of accessing these passively wrought assocations is a real one. Our inner life is elusive, and oftentimes such fleeting thoughts and images as we have are consigned to an oblivion from which they cannot be easily retrieved. For example, at one time or another, everyone has had the experience of remembering that a dream occurred without remembering specifically what the dream was about.

Another illustration of the evanescent quality of waking fantasy occurs during reading. Nearly everyone has had the experience of perusing a paragraph, and then suddenly realizing that nothing of it has registered. There is little to do but reread it. If, however, one stops long enough to consider what was happening during the attentional lacuna, a second surprise often awaits the introspective reader: it is often difficult to recall the thoughts and fantasies that occurred in lieu of reading. Yet sometimes, the gist of the interpolated reverie somehow does come to mind, with the impression that the fantasy has been relevant if not enriching to the passage. This oscillating process—of first attending to the world (in this case the word), being transported into an oblivion of reverie, and then suddenly "coming to," occasionally becoming aware of and grasping the elusive fantasy—may provide a useful model for the examination of the creative process in more detail.

One aspect of this example is the reverie itself. We have already looked at the passive, effortless quality of it, and the possible effects of this passivity on the associational process. We have argued that eye movements accompany directed thinking and that a relative lack of eye movements suggests the presence of undirected waking fantasy. Furthermore, we have suggested that adaptive regression may in certain circumstances be represented by an oscillating pattern of eye motility and quiescence. Whether more creative subjects tend to have more interspersed episodes of ocular quiescence and motility than less creative subjects is a hypothesis that needs to be tested.

Simple oscillation between directed and undirected thinking, though perhaps a condition of adaptive regression, is clearly not a sufficient condition. For one thing, it seems quite likely that many people rarely connect their real and fantasy life. That is, each level of thinking can exist in relative isolation from the other, making it difficult to employ one's fantasy life in the service of realistic aims. In the reading reverie example, it is quite possible that for many people the reverie never comes to their attention and, if it does, is not actively grasped or scrutinized for possible enrichment of the passage.

Eye movement seems to reflect the presence of attention but not whether attention is being directed to interior or exterior events. While measurement of eye movement may help represent the presence and absence of fantasy, it would probably be of less value in informing us whether the fantasizer was attempting to grasp and attend to fantasies rather than the words being read. Fortunately, there is a measure that helps to identify whether and when attention is directed to external or internal events. The measure is cardiac variability, which, unlike eye movement, evidence directly relates to creative functioning. Lacey (1959, 1967) suggests that a person's orientation toward or attention to external sources of stimulation is accompanied by heart rate deceleration and that, conversely, tasks requiring "the internal manipulation of symbols and the retrieval of stored information'' (Lacey et al., 1963, p. 170), is accompanied by heart rate acceleration. Singer and Antrobus (1965) found that suppressing fantasy led to increased heart rate with eyes covered, decreased heart rate with eyes uncovered. Perhaps, with eyes uncovered, attentiveness to environmental cues with accompanied heart rate decrease is a reasonable strategy of fantasy suppression. On the other hand, a reasonable image-suppression strategy with eyes covered might be to direct one's thoughts to mental arithmetic, a cognitive activity yielding concomitant heart rate increases over a resting base line (cf. Lacey et al., 1963).

The fact that heart rate probably reflects shifts of attention from external to internal events makes it a potentially revealing way to assess the oscillation of attention from an external focus of concern toward the internal events they trigger—a process which we have argued is one aspect of creativity.

K.S. Bowers and Keeling (1971) examined this possibility. They reasoned that the oscillation of attention from reality to fantasy residues proposed as a basis of creative functioning would have a pattern of cardiac acceleration and deceleration. Specifically, more highly creative subjects should show more variability in heart rate than less creative subjects, who presumably are more consistent in their concern for outer reality and less attentive to interior fantasies. Heart rate in the study was continuously monitored for twenty males instructed to respond creatively to ten Holtzman blots (Holtzman et al., 1961) selected for their low movement pull. A measure of heart rate variability derived from this task correlated .49 with subjects' average creativity score derived from the Remote Associates Test (Mednick & Mednick, 1967) and the Revised Art Scale (Welsh & Barron, 1963). Thus, more creative persons tended to show higher cardiac variability.

These results are consistent with those of an earlier study by Blatt (1961). Utilizing a very complex cognitive task, Blatt found that efficient problem solvers generated significantly more variable heart rate than inefficient ones. Blatt thought cardiac variability was a measure of arousal, but K.S. Bowers (1971a) has shown that such variability is diminished under heightened arousal. Attention shifts from exterior to interior events are more likely causes of the variability found in efficient problem solvers. That solving Blatt's task efficiently has some relationship to creativity is indicated by the finding that the more efficient subjects have higher adaptive regression scores (Blatt, Allison, & Feirstein, 1969) and have higher aesthetic values (Blatt & Stein, 1959). Chemists rated as relatively more creative tended to be more cognitively efficient than those rated as less creative, $p < .1$).

The combination of cardiac and eye movement measures in studies of creative functioning might prove most instructive as a test of the adaptive regression hypothesis. The presumed cycle of attention directed outward (analysis), fantasy and attention directed inward (fantasy retrieval) should have distinctive eye movement and cardiac patterns which accompany it. During the analytic phase, eye movement should be relatively high with a decelerated heart rate. During the fantasy phase, heart rate should be near its resting base with attenuated eye movement. During fantasy retrieval, eye movement should again be high, but heart rate should now be accelerated. This pattern may be discerned only if the creative cycle of interest is a short one.

These proposed *physiological* measures attempt to assess the changes that take place as one shifts from one part of the creative cycle to another. Several investigators have already looked at *behavioral* measures of such cognitive shifting and, in fact, have successfully differentiated criterion groups of presumably creative and uncreative persons by such means. Cynthia Wild (1965) assessed cognitive shifting in a fashion designed to reflect the concept of adaptive regression by tapping a capacity to engage in unregulated thinking and an ability to return adaptively to more regulated thought. She provided subjects with a word association test and an object sorting task given under natural, i.e. spontaneous conditions, and then under two different instructional conditions. Under one set of instructions, subjects were asked to perform on the task like a highly conventional, cautious person "who prefers an orderly, structured universe and values good common sense." The other set of instructions asked subjects to perform like an "unregulated" character given to "novel thoughts and... acute perceptions that may startle other people." The instructional conditions, of course, were counterbalanced. The extent of a subject's movement from conventional to original associations and sorts constituted his *shift* score.

In practically all comparisons, a sample of art students showed greater cognitive shifts than either her sample of schizophrenics or teachers. These differences derived primarily from subjects' performance during the unregulated condition, since whatever group differences existed during the regulated conditions were relatively small or nonexistent.

Fitzgerald (1966) used the same tasks and procedures as Wild to study extreme scorers on an Experience Inquiry he devised, similar to the inventory developed by Ås and Østvold (1962). Subjects scoring high and low on the Experience Inquiry differed significantly on both the word association and object sorting tasks, and these differences emerged under spontaneous (i.e. uninstructed) conditions and on the shift scores. In all comparisons, subjects scoring high on the Experience Inquiry were superior to low scoring subjects. Again, internal analysis showed that the significant differences in shift scores derived primarily from subjects' performance under the unregulated and not from the regulated condition.

The results of Fitzgerald's (1966) study were partially replicated by Feirstein (1967), who obtained cognitive shift scores only on the word association task, and who assessed tolerance for unrealistic experiences by a battery of four tests (instead of by a questionnaire). The correlation between this battery and the cognitive shift score was .62 (p < .01).

A study by Keeling (1974) indicated that cognitive shifting as measured by Wild was related to hypnotizability.

Parallel Processing as an Alternative to Oscillation

Of cognitive shifting and creativity, we admit a simplification in our presentation so far. The reading reverie illustration and much of the subsequent discourse suggests that directed attention and undirected fantasy are more or less exclusive and alternating states of mind. There is, however, evidence that subjects may process reality and fantasy simultaneously (Antrobus, Singer, & Greenberg, 1966; Neisser, 1967). Singer (1966) in fact seems to argue that fantasy is a continuous, ongoing backdrop to everything we do, only becoming salient when attention to other stimulation abates. Obviously, unattended external information is a continuously ongoing backdrop for fantasies. Neisser suggests that information processed in this preattentive manner may come to our attention when it is particularly relevant to us, e.g. our name printed or spoken in an "ignored" part of our perceptual field (Neisser, 1967, 1969). Just how an ongoing, unattended fantasy or environmental feature influences thinking and perception is a problem of considerable interest for the psychology of creativity in particular (Rugg, 1963) and of cognitive processes in general (e.g., Kahneman, 1973). To illustrate, recent research in our laboratory has shown that hypnotized *S*s with appropriate suggestions as well as waking *S*s, passively oriented with respect to an unattended channel in a dichotic listening paradigm, can respond to relevant information on that channel while still shadowing an attended channel. Such a technique interferes less with shadowing than having subjects attend actively to the two channels of information at once.

What is more, unconscious or unattended information may itself never be noticed and yet influence our conscious perceptions in a useful way. Dichotic listening studies have shown that information not consciously "heard" on an unattended channel can disambiguate an attended word. For example, "river" on an unattended channel can bias how the subject understands the otherwise ambiguous word "bank" on the attended channel (MacKay, 1973). Hilgard's Neo-Dissociation Theory (1977a & b; and Chapter 3, this volume) also argues for parallel processing of information, with only one process consciously appreciated at a time. Thus, it is likely that parallel rather than sequential processing in two modes may be more common, and the previous analysis of creative work might be better phrased in terms reflecting this simultaneous processing.

Hypnosis and Creativity

This paper has reviewed evidence that fantasy-like and absorptive experiences: (a) are concomitants of various altered states of consciousness, including hypnosis, (b) occur spontaneously to a greater extent in subjects who are high as opposed to low in hypnotic susceptibility, (c) may occasionally occur in the context of a creative act, but in any event, (d) are often experienced by creative subjects who, as a group, seem more adept than their less creative counterparts at shifting cognitively from a "higher" to a "lower" level of psychic functioning.

We have suggested that creativity involves regression to passively experienced fantasy and then progression to integration of the fantasy with reality. Both Krippner (1969) and Silverman (1968) have noted certain similarities between altered state processes and the inspirational stage of creativity. MacKinnon (1971) notes that:

> The truly creative person might be distinguished from the non-creative individual by his great ease in moving from more conscious and active to more unconscious and passive states. One might inquire, then, about the ease and speed with which the creative person, as compared with others, falls asleep, enters into a hypnotic trance upon suggestion from another person, or passes into self-induced states of trance or semi-trance (p. 227).

The preceding suggests that creativity and altered states like hypnosis are related to a moderate degree. The regressive aspect is similar in both, but only creativity implies any constructive use of the regressive experience. In the hypnotic state there is increased primary process, but control of it as shown in adaptive regression scores may not increase (Gruenewald, Fromm, & Oberlander, Chapter 19, this volume). And at least for men, creativity is more related to adaptive regression scores than to primary process itself (Pine & Holt, 1960).

A relationship between hypnosis and creativity does seem probable, but the precise nature of this link is far from clear. Does a trancelike experience often precede a creative insight or is the route more indirect? If there is a direct connection between trancelike experience and creativity, being hypnotized, taking certain drugs, etc., should significantly increase creative performance. A study using mescaline, but unfortunately employing no control group, suggested that twenty-seven Ss actively engaged in seeking solutions to practical professional problems did increase their creativity (Harman et al., 1966). Raikov (1976) reports good results when Ss roleplay creative persons under hypnosis. Reyher's technique of passive imagery under hypnosis seems to increase figural but not verbal creativity in tests (Gur & Reyher, 1976). Use of hypnosis to increase creativity in real life problems has been studied by Davé (1976) with positive results as well. These recent positive results contrast somewhat with earlier results from our laboratory. A series of investigations, while initially finding some support for enhanced creative functioning on divergent thinking tests (P.G. Bowers, 1967), concluded that no such enhancement occurred (K.S. Bowers, 1968; K.S. Bowers & van der Meulen, 1970). More work will have to be done to definitively answer the question of hypnotic enhancement of creativity.

Our earlier focus on directly influencing creative performance via hypnosis shifted to a proposal that highly hypnotizable subjects, who have more trancelike experiences and who become more fully absorbed in such things as music and novels than low hypnotizables (Tellegen & Atkinson, 1974; Hilgard, 1970), should also be more creative than low hypnotizables in the waking state. Several experiments in our laboratory (K.S. Bowers & van der Meulen, 1970; K.S. Bowers, 1971b, P.G. Bowers, 1978) and in others (Perry, Wilder, & Appignanesi, 1973) have confirmed this hypothesis. Reasons for this include the ability of trancelike and absorptive experiences to enrich a person's cognitive associational network, leading to more varied memories which might prove useful in creative ideas, and also to increased creativity motivation. J. McV. Hunt (1965) and Butler and Rice (1963) suggest that persons with richer, more complex cognitive structures have more motivation to explore events and ideas than those with less complex structures. Hunt's dictum, gleaned from Piaget's theories, that "the more one sees and hears, the more one wants to see and hear" may be applicable to creativity. Persons with complex cognitive structures enjoy and seek novelty and complexity and are able to provide, by their own imaginative and reflective processes, the very novelty and complexity they require. A person who has not only tolerated but also integrated a number of unusual, absorptive experiences might be so used to experiences to which conventional labels are not applicable that he no longer depends upon such conventions. In essence, previous unusual experiences with concomitant enriched fantasy associations to objects may give the highly hypnotizable person more ability to act in a creative way without the necessity of an altered state at the moment of creation.

The catalogue of personality attributes that seem to go along with people designated "creative" either by judgments or test criteria is consonant with these speculations. Creative people, at least in artistic fields, are nonconforming, tolerant of ambiguity, adventurous. They like reflective thinking. They are not noted for being meticulous or disciplined.

Empirical support for a relationship between creativity and cognitive complexity is found in research using the Revised Art Scale (Welsh & Barron, 1963). Called the best test predictor of creativity (Gough, 1964;

Dellas & Gaier, 1970), it is simply a scale of preference for visual complexity. Renner (1970) trained subjects to understand the complexity of art works; compared to appropriate controls, this training led to both significantly higher scores on the Revised Art Scale *and* greater originality on Guilford's Consequences Test (Christensen, Merrifield, & Guilford, 1958).

The above reasoning suggests that people who are highly hypnotizable will also be more creative because a preference for cognitive complexity characterizes both categories.

A second reason for expecting highly hypnotizable people to be more creative was discussed earlier in the paper. Briefly, an examination of the phenomenological experiences of highly creative and of highly hypnotizable people suggests that effortless experiencing of a variety of ideas characterizes both. Perhaps effortless experiencing is a mark of subconscious processing of information, which in bypassing conscious, willful, analytic, effortful processes also primes a wider variety of associates to ideas than is otherwise the case. Either or both of the above explanations for the observed empirical relationships between hypnotic ability and creativity may hold. We already know that hypnotizablity is related to a person's ability to let go of a reality orientation and experience more primitively. Consequently, hypnotizability should also be related to creativity, since the regressive experiences not only indicate heightened subconscious or primary processing, but also contribute to the cognitive complexity and therefore the creativity of those able to integrate such experience.

Accordingly, K.S. Bowers and van der Meulen (1970) compared high and low susceptibility subjects on a battery of creativity tests. On eight out of nine creativity subtests, the high hypnotizables scored significantly better than low hypnotizables. The measures included movement perception to Holtzman Inkblots (Holtzman et al., 1961), Guilford's Consequences Test and a word association test (adapted from Gardner et al., 1959). On these same measures, treatment effects of hypnosis, simulation and waking relaxed instructions were insignificant. Subsidiary analysis revealed that irrespective of susceptibility level, women were consistently more creative than men. K.S. Bowers (1971b) confirmed and extended these findings in a study using a rectangular distribution of susceptibility to hypnosis. Three men and three women at each of the twelve points along the hypnotizability continuum as assessed by the Harvard Group Scale of Hypnotic Susceptibility (HGSHS, Shor and Orne, 1962) were subjects in this study. The measures of creativity were again the Consequences Test, movement responses to the Holtzman Inkblot Test, the word association test, the Revised Art Scale (Welsh & Barron, 1963) and the Remote Associates Test (Mednick & Mednick, 1967). From this battery of creativity tests eight measures were derived, and a *S*'s average Z score on these measures constituted his composite creativity score. In addition, the *S* also took the WAIS vocabulary subtest and Shor's (1960) PEQ. The results (see Table I) showed the predicted relationships for women but not for men. Intelligence had no effect on scores. The

TABLE 11.1   Correlation coeffieients between variables

	Creativity		Personal experience questionnaire	
	Men	Women	Men	Women
Hypnotizability	.08	.41*	.16	.33*
Creativity			.09	.39*

*p < .05

moderating role of sex on the correlates of hypnotizability has been found by others (Gur & McKinley, 1975; Palmer & Field, 1968; Perry et al., 1973). However, our most recent work (P.G. Bowers, 1978) has failed to find any effect due to sex.

This latest work has attempted to investigate the bases for the empirical relationships between hypnotizabilty and creativity. The focus has been on our hunch that higher effortless experiencing was the common link. In the first study sixteen high and sixteen low hypnotizable men and women as determined by scores on the HGSHS were seen individually. *S*s were never hypnotized but were given several tasks in the waking state. The first task involved having them image each of twelve varied items and to rate their experience of each image on three five-point scales. These scales assessed the degree of vividness of the image, their degree of absorption versus distraction while they imaged, and most importantly, the degree to which the image occurred effortlessly, i.e. just popped into their mind, as distinct from requiring some effort to construct. The next task was a fantasy measure in which *S*s imagined silently each of six scenes of varied structure. After each scene the *S* rated his experience on the above three scales. After answering several questions relevant to effortless experiencing of the imagery and fantasy tasks and to absorption in everyday experiences, *S*s were given the Consequences Test.[2] An example of an item from this test is, "What would happen if gravity were suddenly cut in half?" The experience of producing responses to such questions was rated after each of the ten consequences items, on three scales similar to those

---

2. An instructional manipulation with respect to this test which did not affect the major findings will not be detailed here.

used for the imagery and fantasy tasks. Ss were given the Marks Scale of Vividness of Visual Imagery (Marks, 1973). They next rated the degree to which they thought themselves creative and listed all the creative activities in which they had been engaged in the last year or two. These latter creativity measures were adopted from Taft and Gilchrist (1970) who found them to be related to other creativity and personality measures in a fashion supportive of their construct validity.

Composite scores were devised for the constructs of interest from the average of Z scores: The vividness composite combined the vividness and visualization ratings from the imagery, fantasy, consequences, and Marks Scale tasks; the effortless experiencing composite combined the ratings from imagery, fantasy and consequences tasks as well as S's answers to questions about the degree of experienced choice involved in the imagery and fantasy tasks. The intercorrelations of the various ratings of absorption were such that it appeared no single construct was being tapped. Instead of a combined score, therefore, the responses to a four item absorption questionnaire, based on J. Hilgard's work, were utilized in subsequent analysis. The creativity composite score was made up of the number of remote consequences tapping Guilford's originality factor, as well as the creativity self-rating and the rating by the experimenter on a three point scale of the degree of creativity of the activities listed by the subject according to the Taft and Gilchrist scoring criteria. All the composite scores had sufficiently high alpha coefficients to make their combination a meaningful enterprise.

Analyses of variance were performed for each of these contructs with the level of hypnotizability and sex as factors. Hypnotizability, but not sex, had a significant main effect on effortless experiencing, creativity and absorption. There was a tendency for such an effect for vividness $(p < .1)$.

The correlation coefficients of interest are presented in Table 11.2.

TABLE 11.2. Correlation coeficients between variables

	Hypnotizability (biserial r)	Effortless experiencing	Creativity	Vividness
Effortless Experiencing	.61			
Creativity	.55	.62		
Vividness	.32	.55	.39	
Absorption Questionnaire	.41	.34	.39	.51

While effortless experiencing is related to vividness and absorption, partial correlational analyses indicated that vividness and absorption did *not* contribute independent variance to the hypnosis-creativity correlation in this sample. On the other hand, when effortless experiencing is controlled, the hypnosis-creativity relationship drops to .27, n.s.

A second study used seven high and seven low hypnotizable Ss who were selected more stringently for level of hypnotizability than the previous Ss (via a second individual hypnosis session). In addition, ten Ss who had received a score of six on the HGSHS constituted a middle hypnotizable group. While the procedures were for the most part quite similar to those described above, there were some differences as follows: Ss were seen in small groups. They rated their "general" experience of the twelve images on the three scales of vividness, absorption and effortless experiencing only once, after all twelve images. For the fantasy task, however, ratings of these three scales were requested after every two items. Five rather than ten consequences items were administered, under the standard instructions used earlier, with ratings of vividness, absorption, and effortlessness given after each item. Analyses were performed as before on composite scores derived in the previously described manner. The effects of three levels of hypnotizability were determined in analyses of variance. The effect of the S's sex could not be assessed.

The results of this investigation were quite similar to those described above. All analyses of variance showed significant main effects of level of hypnotizability. The correlations between hypnotizability, creativity, and effortless experiencing were similarly high and significant, ranging from .5 to .6. In this sample, effortless experiencing, vividness, and absorption were more highly interrelated than in the previous sample, so no partial correlational analyses were computed. Middle hypnotizable subjects scored midway between high and low Ss on most composite scores. The similarity between the strength of the relationship in both experiments gives us confidence that this is a result which will not fade.

Preliminary work in this study indicated the possible usefulness of scoring the "cleverness" of consequences items as a more stringent criterion of creativity. Measuring the reliability of such a score is, of course, a difficulty. Recent work by Harrington (1975) with Guilford's Alternate Uses Test indicates that changes in instructions and the scoring of criteria towards greater emphasis on creativity can lead to a more valid measure. But perhaps equally as important in getting better measures of creativity is the selection of *several* good but *varied* measures in an attempt to zero in on this multifaceted phenomenon. As a strategy of research, we believe this is much preferable to relying on any single measure, since when one is dealing with such complex processes as creativity and effortless experiencing, no one measure will ever capture adequately the phenomenon in question.

Summary and Conclusion

In this paper, we have reviewed evidence that hypnosis and related states involve a loss in generalized reality orientation and a concomitant rise in fantasy or suggestibility. The role of fantasy in creative functioning has also been noted, with particular emphasis on fantasy retrieval as a crucial antecedent to its creative use. Moreover, we have argued that the occurrence of fantasy and its retrieval may be well represented in patterns of ocular and cardiac activity.

Our own interpretation of creativity and hypnosis has been influenced by, and is largely compatible with, the ego psychological concepts of regression in the service of the ego (Kris, 1952). Because hypnosis per se constitutes a kind of regression phenomenon, it seemed reasonable to expect that hypnotic techniques might simply facilitate creative performance. This hypothesis has been inconsistently supported, and further careful work among very highly hypnotizable subjects now being planned may clarify the issue. In any case, the rapprochement between hypnosis and creativity includes important individual differences: the personality characteristics that allow one person to be more susceptible to hypnosis than another coincide to some extent with those characteristics that make him more creative. Perhaps the ease with which one can deconventionalize experience and accept the unrealistic and fantastic contributes both to susceptibility and creativity. Our evidence to date suggests that something like this is the case: Creativity, hypnotizability, and effortless experiencing of imagery, fantasy, and creativity test responses are interrelated. Becoming intensely absorbed in certain experiences is related to these variables as well. We have argued that hypnotic phenomena are experienced by a process similar to that by which spontaneous fantasy is experienced. The partial overlapping of these phenomena tells us a little about both hypnotizability and creativity. Needless to say, we have only scratched the surface.

A strong argument can be made that the constructive processes in fantasy and hypnosis are not basically different from perceptual processes in general. Neisser (1967) in his book, *Cognitive Psychology,* emphasizes that *"the mechanisms of visual imagination are continuous with those of visual perception*—a fact which strongly implies that all perceiving is a constructive process" (p. 96, his italics). The differences that do exist in the realities constructed out of perception and imagination inhere in the extent to which environmental input determines the constructive process. In perception "the constructive act is closely controlled by present or recent stimulus information" (Neisser, 1967, p. 305), whereas this is much less the case for fantasy, and hypnotically suggested fantasy equivalents. The governing relation of reality input on the constructive process is perhaps helpful in understanding how hypnosis and creativity are not alike. Conventional reality is relatively unimportant for the daydreamer and the hypnotized person. The importance of conventional reality is guaranteed to the creative person, however, for it constitutes his worthy adversary—it is the stuff which creative imagination transforms.

Peter W. Sheehan *is Professor of Psychology at the University of Queensland, Australia and Past President of the Australian Psychological Society. He received his Ph.D. from the University of Sydney in 1965, working on imagery and its correlates. After obtaining his doctorate, Professor Sheehan accepted a two-year appointment as Research Associate at the Unit for Experimental Psychiatry and Instructor in the Department of Psychiatry at the University of Pennsylvania. From there he joined the Psychology faculty staff at the City College of the City University of New York and then returned to Australia to the University of New England before taking up his chair appointment at the University of Queensland. He is editor of* The Function and Nature of Imagery *and co-author with C.W. Perry of* Methodologies of Hypnosis: A Critical Appraisal of Contemporary Paradigms of Hypnosis. *His specific research interests are hypnosis, imagery, cognitive processes, and the logic of artifact.*

Sheehan *presents a comprehensive review of theoretical and experimental evidence on the role of mental imagery, imagination, fantasy, and primary process thinking in hypnotic performance. He argues that Sarbin's "as if" formulation best conceptualizes the important role of imagery and fantasy in hypnosis. Among the issues scrutinized are the enrichment of imagery in hypnosis; the relationship between hypnotizability and enduring aptitudes for vivid imagery; imaginative involvements and tolerance for fantasy experiences; and the relationship between hypnotic hallucinations and perceptual processes.*

12

Hypnosis
and the Processes
of Imagination

PETER W. SHEEHAN

STATEMENT OF PROBLEM

Many workers in the field of hypnosis have held tenaciously to the view that there are personality correlates of hypnosis and that the hypnotizable person manifests aptitudes or abilities for trance that lie waiting to be discovered within the realms of his personality. Researchers into hypnosis used to be quite definite in their assertions about the personality correlates of hypnotizability. Currently, however, summaries of empirical findings on the correlates of trance are much less positive in outlook; much conflicting evidence has accumulated (Barber & Ham, 1974; K.S. Bowers, 1976). After making a very comprehensive survey of the literature, Deckert and West (1963) concluded that the correlation of any personality trait by any means of measurement with hypnotizability awaits consistent confirmation across laboratories and that the search for specific traits has not at all clarified the concept of hypnotizability.

Many have shown convincingly how rare it is for consistencies to occur across studies in the field of personality assessment (Mischel, 1968; K.S. Bowers, 1973b; Ekehammar, 1974). The ambiguity of research findings is not due entirely to the problem of measuring the various dimensions of traits; other factors are also responsible. Equivocal findings in the area may be due to the lack of comparability in drawing subject samples and the use of different scales to measure suggestibility, as well as the crudeness of available techniques for assessing personality attributes. Subjects may also vary their response to suggestions according to their task motivation or the nature of the particular relationships they have with their experimenters. It may be that even some of the positive correlations that have appeared in the literature are due to the impurity of the criteria of hypnotizability, selective personal appeals of different hypnotists, or other situation-specific factors (Barber, 1969b; Sheehan & Perry, 1976; Shor, Orne, & O'Connell, 1966).

Differences among individuals in hypnotizability, though related to differences in attitudes toward and relationships with the hypnotist, must reflect the aptitudes or enduring characteristics of the personality of the subjects themselves. It can be argued that a subject's personality will strongly determine the ways in which he can relate to the hypnotist however skillful the hypnotist is in engendering attitudes such as "basic trust" and "confidence." The importance of the subject's personality is not diminished by the fact that some subjects with similar characteristics may respond differently to hypnotic induction by different hypnotists. To do so would be to deny that people relate variably to different people. A person's behavior is influenced both by interaction among personalities, the situation in which he is placed, and by his own particular abilities and capacities.

The importance of subject-characteristics is stated succinctly by Sarbin (1950) who after reviewing the effects of various kinds of induction techniques concluded that "since the induction procedure per se cannot account for the differential responsiveness of subjects, this leaves the subject as a person as the more fruitful focus of study" (p. 257). This statement avoids commitment to the host of determining variables other than induction that have been isolated by Barber and his associates (Barber, 1969b; Barber & Ham, 1974; Barber, Spanos, & Chaves, 1974); but it does draw attention to one significant feature of the hypnotic setting: the presence of individual differences in susceptibility to trance. Not all subjects exhibit "hypnotic" behavior (Hilgard et al., 1961; Hilgard, 1965b, 1975), and it is clear that the explanation for this individual variation in hypnotic response must often be sought in other factors than in the process of induction. One place we may clearly look is to the subject-characteristics that differentiate hypnotizable from nonhypnotizable people.

Not only are subjects differentially susceptible to hypnosis but wide individual differences also exist in their capacities to engage in fantasy, daydreaming and mental imagery of a sensorily vivid kind (Betts, 1909; Foulkes, 1966; Lindauer, 1969; Schonbar, 1961; Sheehan, 1972b; Singer, 1966; White, Sheehan, & Ashton, 1977). There are, for example, important patterns of individual differences in frequency of daydreaming in normal adults and children (Singer, 1966) and the reinforcement or motivation for the continuous cognitive processing of daydreams has been shown to be very powerful. Antrobus, Singer, and Greenberg (1966) found that subjects are able to engage in a high degree of spontaneous fantasy even when they are under heavy pressure to attend to a signal presentation task. The authors judged it remarkable that:

> S can receive signals at the rate of one/sec., accurately judge whether each signal is the same or different from the pitch of the preceding signal, indicate his judgment on a hand switch while storing the signal for comparison with the next, and at the same time imagine sailing with his friends during his forthcoming holiday (p. 406).

Grossberg and Wilson (1968) found that self-produced stimulation arising from instructions to imagine fear scenes produced more tension or arousal in a subject than did the externally presented stimulation of an experimenter reading the scene to him. These and other studies attest the significant and measurable effects of a subject's engagement in fantasy activity. In view of the wide individual differences present in both imaginal activity and susceptibility to trance, as judged by response to standard tests of hypnosis, it is conceivable that the various manifestations of imagination and hypnotizability bear a strong, positive relation to each other. This hypothesis is the specific concern of this chapter.

DEFINITION OF TERMS

A sizable barrier to ordering studies in the area of fantasy, imagery and hypnotizability is the semantic confusion resulting from authors who use different terms to explain what appear to be similar processes and also the use of the same term to cover apparently different processes. As Starker (1974) notes, there has been little differentiation in the literature between hypnotic "hallucination" and "imagery." Other concepts too, such as "fantasy" and "imaginative involvement" are blurred with respect to their conceptual boundaries.

Moss (1967) reports that a majority of "hypnotic dreams" reported in the literature seem to consist of brief products that are often difficult to discriminate from verbal associations to the suggested dream topic. In a comprehensive analysis of over 400 "hypnotic dreams" reported by a sample of sixteen students, Quay (1952) found that many of the dreams could be classified simply as verbal associations. Use of words like "dream" to subjects in an experiment often carries with it semantically ambiguous demands. Only detailed questioning of a subject can decide whether he is reporting fantasy, imagery, or merely nonimaginal thoughts. The problem of classifying the nature of the subject's cognition is considerably aggravated by the fact that an experimenter can give cues to the subject about the expected response which the subject may respond to in a way which leads the experimenter to classify the subject's behavior mistakenly. Barber

(1964, and Chapter 8 in this volume), for example, has drawn attention to the possibility that when an experimental subject is told explicitly to experience events (e.g., see objects and hear sounds that are physically absent) the subject is actually being instructed to classify or categorize them in a particular way (e.g., as imaginal or perceptual). Sarbin (1967) is making the same point when he states:

> When we reflect that the behavior labelled hallucination is an imagining that is publicly reported, the question must be rephrased as follows: What are the antecedent and concurrent conditions that lead a person publicly to report his imaginings in such a way as to lead a psychologist, psychiatrist, or other professional to designate the described imagining as an hallucination (p. 363)?

The question of how many verbal reports are influenced themselves by suggestions is a matter of some considerable debate (Bowers, 1976; Orne, Chapter 16 in this volume; Sheehan & Perry, 1976).

The concept of hallucination has proved particularly obstinate to tidy classification. McKellar (1957, 1972), Barber (1964c; see also Barber, Spanos, & Chaves, 1974) and Sarbin (1967, 1972) talk of hallucinations as involving mental imagery. Sidis (1904a, 1904b), Erickson and Erickson (1938), Arnold (1959) and others, on the other hand, talk of hallucination as involving actual perception of the hallucinated object. The problem of classification appears to lie with the relative importance of the ideational and delusory components of hallucination. As Binet and Féré (1886) pointed out, in every image presented to the mind there is always the germ of a hallucination that needs development. Binet and Féré maintained that it was in the hypnotic state that such development is most clearly seen to occur. It is only necessary to name a given object to the susceptible subject, that is, to simply say "here is a bird" in order that the image suggested by the experimenter's words should become a hallucination. Schneck (1954a) noted the familiar fact, however, that subtle changes in the experimenter's instruction may determine the experimenter's classification of the subject's behavior as imaginal or hallucinatory. He cites the case of a patient in therapy who reported imagining sounds in hypnosis and actually "hearing" them. In this instance, the nature of the subject's report was quite dependent on the wording of the experimenter's inquiry.

It appears that the process of imagination play an important part in hypnotic hallucinations and that the hypnotic setting affects, either artifactually or otherwise, the judgment of the subject as to the reality of his imaginings. As Barber (1964c) has indicated, suggestions to hallucinate include two components: explicit suggestions that influence imaginative processes and implicit instructions that affect verbal reports. When such implicit suggestions are operative the subject may classify his imaginings as actual perceptions. This account of hallucinations is consistent with Sarbin's contention that hallucinations occur only in persons who are particularly skillful in imagining the presence of stimulus objects that are physically absent (Sarbin, 1964). The importance of imagery to hypnotic hallucination makes it particularly fruitful to explore the nature of the imaging capacities of hypnotizable subjects. Study of the influence of hypnotic induction on imagery per se seems, then, an essential prerequisite to understanding reports of hypnotic hallucinations (Starker, 1974).

As imagery and hypnotic hallucination appear related, so also are fantasy and imagery, yet distinctions in process may be raised. Ullman (1959) identifies one of the primary formal aspects of dream consciousness as the employment of concrete means of presentation predominantly in the form of visual imagery. Fantasy is traditionally regarded as a form of creative imagination "where the images and trains of imagery are directed and controlled by the whim or pleasure of the moment" (Drever, 1952, pp. 209-210). Fantasy however, is a term which not so much denotes the faculty of imagery as it signifies the imaginary world and its contents, "the imaginings or fantasies into which the poet or the neurotic so willingly withdraws" (Laplanche & Pontalis, 1968). It suggests a constructive organization of past experience which although dependent on the revival of imagery is especially subject to the vicissitudes of the motivational and emotional state of the organism. Both fantasy and imagery, however, may be inner or outer directed. It is argued by some (Bowers, 1976; J.R. Hilgard, 1970), for instance, that fantasylike imagery which is elicited by external stimulus conditions is more likely to be associated with hypnosis.

For the purposes of discussion in this chapter, the terms "image," "hallucination," and "fantasy" may be defined as follows: With imagery there is no object present to the senses as in perception; it is somewhat an introspective *façon de parler* to speak of "seeing," "picturing," or "visualizing" something. This difference is true also for recalling and hallucinating, but these processes differ from "imaging." Objects of recall lack the "thing quality" alleged for imaged objects, and objects of hallucination though they may be ideationally based are accompanied by the subject's conviction of their external locus. Fantasy may be distinguished from imagery in that it appears to be more of a reproductive synthesis, largely motivational in origin, of a totality of past experiences. As used in the literature, the term "imagine" is a more general term which may denote more than one of these processes. A person who is imagining may be engaging in either "fantasy" or "imagery" activities.

The distinctions here should be taken as relative rather than absolute ones, particularly as the processes at times tend to blur indistinguishably together and any definitions must to some extent be inadequate since they cannot do justice to the richness and variety of psychological experience. As Holt (1964, 1972) and Horowitz (1967, 1972, 1975) have pointed out there is a multitude of processes which can be subsumed under the term visual imagery alone and classification is made especially difficult by the subtle variations in the subject's experience as to the reality of his imaginings. In this respect, even the auditory hallucinations of schizophrenic patients differ greatly from each other (Brady & Levitt, 1966; see also West, 1975). One may talk about a continuum, from ill-defined "thoughts" originating within the body to voices which appear to be external to, and independent of, the self. The special difficulty of isolating the delusional and ideational components of cognitive events can be seen clearly in Sidis' (1906) observation of the hallucinations of a deeply hypnotizable subject. For this subject, the delusional component broke down and the subject described his experience of the experimenter's suggested hallucinations as fixed ideas and mental pictures. After a posthypnotic suggestion to see a snake the subject claimed he saw one but wrote, "I see a snake. I see it in my mind" (p. 255). Here, the ideational and delusional aspects of the hypnotic hallucination interchanged confusedly.

Some agreement on terms is necessary, however, to attempt an accurate evaluation of the evidence available on the relationship between imagery and fantasy to hypnotizability. For example, studies that report mainly on verbal associations (e.g., Erle, 1958) are less relevant than others. As we have seen, an arbitrary classification draws attention to the fact that different terms as used by hypnotists (e.g., imagine, image, see, and make-believe) may carry special connotations to subjects that are quite specfic and that may implicitly direct the nature of the subject's response.

With this classification in mind we move now to a consideration of the evidence. First, we will consider the theoretical grounds that lead one to hypothesize a relationship between hypnotizability, fantasy, and imagery. Subsequent sections will review the "empirical" data (both clinical and experimental) that bear on this relationship, and present a framework within which the relationship can be conceptualized.

Review of the Evidence: Theoretical

HYPNOSIS AS AN "ALTERED STATE OF CONSCIOUSNESS"

Experientially speaking, hypnosis is easily recognizable as a change in consciousness (Shor, 1959, 1962b; Tart, Chapter 17 in this volume) and the emergence of imagery in altered states of consciousness is well acknowledged (Freedman & Marks, 1965; J.R. Hilgard, 1970; Horowitz, Adams, & Rutkin, 1968; Ludwig, 1966; Moss, 1967). Similarly occurring changes are those that are associated with prolonged stimulus deprivation (e.g., Gibson, 1953; Holt, 1972; La Barre, 1975), extreme boredom (Heron, 1957), hypnogogic and hypnopompic states (Ludwig, 1966; McKellar, 1972) and other related phenomena.

In the most general sense, the altered state of consciousness may be defined as a:

> mental state induced by various physiological, psychological, or pharmacological maneuvres or agents, which can be recognized subjectively by the individual himself...as representing a sufficient deviation in subjective experience or psychological functioning from certain general norms for that individual during alert waking consciousness (Ludwig, 1966, pp. 9-10).

The description of hypnosis as a loss of generalized reality-orientation (GRO) (Shor, 1959) has gone furthest to highlight the features of hypnosis which relate to this more general class of phenomena.

The concept of GRO refers to the background of awareness, the frame of reference that denotes the context within which one interprets all ongoing conscious experiences. Shor argues that under hypnosis this orientation to reality fades into the background so that ongoing experiences become relatively isolated from their usual frame of reference. The structure of the GRO permits what in Freudian terminology is called secondary process thinking. Viewed in this way the ability to temporarily give up reality orientation corresponds to a regression to primary process functioning. The phenomena that pertain to the concept of primary process share with hypnosis the feature that they occur in isolation from ordinary reality. It has long been assumed that hypnosis reduces alertness and such a reduction may facilitate the flow of free associations thus bringing the hypnotized person into contact with prelogical ideational processes. In a similar fashion, vigilance is reduced through sleep. This reduction is known to be associated at some stages of the sleep cycle with unusually expressive mentation illustrative of primary process functioning (Bertini, Lewis, & Witkin, 1964; Fiss, Ellman, & Klein, 1968).

With the loss of GRO the distinction between reality and imagination fades and primary process modes of thought such as imagery and fantasy are allowed to flow more easily into awareness. Conceptually speaking, the consequences of viewing hypnosis as a loss of this reality orientation are twofold. First, it can be argued with Shor (1959) that if primary process material flows more easily into consciousness then the new orientation that is created (namely, in this instance, trance) should show some of the qualities of the dream state itself. This implies that hypnosis involves a greater preoccupation than usual with internal sensations or mental processes than does the waking state. Vivid imagery, hallucinations, and other dreamlike phenomena may be expected to be generated as an integral part of the altered state. Many so-called "state" theorists refer to primary process thinking that is activated in trance (Gill, 1972; Gill & Brenman, 1959; J.R. Hilgard, 1970; Janet, 1925; Kubie, 1961). Gill and Brenman, for example, talk of the emergence of fluid archaic forms of thought which employ visual images and symbols as material in trance. Kubie (1961) argues that there can be little doubt that under hypnosis changes occur in the subject's capacity to reproduce vivid images of experiences which are more remote in time and space.

Relatively few studies have been carried out to test the assumption that there is an actual enrichment of imagery experience in hypnosis. A number of studies that have been conducted have been supportive. Rossi, Sturrock, and Solomon (1963) instructed subjects to experience images under normal, hypnotic and placebo conditions. The subjects' responses to a questionnaire given under the experimental treatments showed that imagery was more vivid in hypnosis than under the nonhypnotic conditions. Stross and Shevrin (1962) found, using tachistoscopic presentation of a rebus stimulus, that imagery occurred more often in hypnosis and dreaming than in the waking state. Naruse and Obonai (1953) found, using a sensory conditioning procedure, that hypnosis appeared to facilitate imagery. Deeper levels of trance as reported by subjects were associated with clearer imagery.

In one of the most pertinent series of experiments on this issue, Stross and Shevrin (1967) found that hypnosis facilitated dream recall. In one study, dreams were recalled by forty-four subjects first in the waking state and then in hypnosis. No subjects recalled their dreams in the waking state itself and not in hypnosis afterwards, whereas twenty-eight subjects recalled their dreams exclusively in hypnosis. In a second study, the order of state was counterbalanced. The waking state following hypnosis was significantly associated with more dream recall than the waking state preceding hypnosis. The better recall of dreams in hypnosis suggested that "cognitive processes in hypnosis may resemble dream thinking more closely than the predominant mode of thinking that governs the waking state" (p. 69). In further support of the enhancement hypothesis, Fromm, Oberlander, and Gruenewald (1970) found that over all subjects tested, primary process responses on the Rorschach were appreciably greater in trance than in the waking condition. The amount of the effect was related in part to the level of adjustment of subjects, the order of conditions (hypnosis-waking, or waking-hypnosis) and the sex of the subjects.

The experimental literature on the issue of enhancement is not entirely in confirmation. A study by Poe (1967) found no difference between hypnotic imagined practice on motor and cognitive tasks and waking imagined practice for good hypnotic subjects. This may be because Poe's study dealt less with the primary process features of imagery than did the previously reported studies. A series of experiments by Stross and Shevrin (1968) has also produced somewhat contradictory evidence for the hypothesis. In these studies, subjects described their images of stimuli that were presented subliminally either in the hypnotic or in the waking state. Data indicated that hypnosis enhanced secondary rather than primary process mentation. Hypnotic induction in combination with freely evoked images gave rise consistently to conceptual subliminal effects which were indexed by the number of rational associates appearing in the subjects' image descriptions of the experimental stimuli. Hypnosis failed to be distinguished from the waking state on the basis of differences in primary process thinking as assessed by the more irrationally oriented, rebus technique. As the authors acknowledged, however, results against the enhancement hypothesis were not definitive. Some of the words which appeared as conceptual associates may have been more drive-determined than the experimenters could detect within the formal laboratory setting. Further, negative evidence was reported by Starker (1974), who found that hypnotic procedures yielded no significant increase in ratings of vividness of imagining beyond that produced by motivational and control conditions. Generally speaking, the hypothesis that imagery ability is enhanced under hypnosis has not been tested sufficiently and awaits further systematic exploration.

The second consequence of regarding hypnosis as a loss or fading of the GRO can be stated more simply. This position implies merely that the subject's imaginal capacities must be relevant to the trance experience. Here, a correlation is posited between hypnotizability and aptitude for imagination. The occurrence of primary process mentation in trance, combined with the assumption that not everyone is susceptible to hypnosis, suggests that certain cognitive abilities must exist for a person in order that he may function as a good hypnotic subject. The implications of such a correlation are complex and require elaboration.

IMAGINATION AND "CREDULOUS" VERSUS "SKEPTICAL" ACCOUNTS OF HYPNOSIS

The correlation of hypnotizability with imaginative capacities does not necessarily commit one to believe in a "special state" view of hypnosis. The several implications of the correlation for the nature of hypnosis are appropriately considered in terms of the distinction made by Sutcliffe (1960) between credulous and skeptical accounts of hypnotic phenomena. This distinction has been analyzed more fully elsewhere (Sheehan & Perry, 1976), but is discussed here to highlight some of the major theoretical issues one faces in interpreting data exactly. In summary, the skeptical view states that the subject agrees verbally with the hypnotist's suggestions and acts as if the suggested state of affairs were so. The credulous viewpoint stresses the reality of hypnotic phenomena where the reaction of the hypnotic subject is identical in form with the sensory experience produced by a parallel objective reality. The skeptical viewpoint does not state that the hypnotic subject is simulating. Most theorists agree that the hypnotic subject plays his role differently from the waking simulator (Orne, 1959, and Chapter 16 in this volume; Sutcliffe, 1958; Young, 1940).

Obviously, imagery or fantasy activation does not solve the problem of defining hypnosis. The complexity of hypnotic phenomena excludes this outright. The ability of the hypnotic subject to image well may be accounted for in several ways. Imagery, for instance, could be the result of dissociation through trance induction giving rise to primary process thinking, or simply a manifestation of an ability which the subject happens to bring to the trance setting.

One cannot image without some capacity to do so, and no theory of hypnosis is discounted by this capacity being evident in the waking state. As imaging is manifested in both the waking and trance states, the hypnotizable person evidently has a cognitive ability suitable for eliciting various hypnotic phenomena, though either a credulous or skeptical viewpoint may be tenable. If the capacity to image is evidenced in the hypnotic state but not in the waking state, then there has been a change in personality functioning that supports the credulous view of hypnosis. It is difficult, however, to test the hypothesis that imaging is evidenced only in the trance state. Before this assertion is accepted, conditions for evoking imagery must be equated for the trance and waking states, except with regard to what truly distinguishes one state from the other. Aside from the problem of knowing what this criterion for distinguishing the two sets of events is, the motivation and expectations of subjects must be similar for the same subject in both the waking and trance conditions since imagery and fantasy may be aroused voluntarily.

A hypnotized person performs convincingly in hypnosis, and this fact raises issues such as Sarbin's organismic involvement (see Sarbin & Coe, 1972), Sutcliffe's (1960) delusion, or Barber's involvement in suggestion-related imaginings (Spanos & Barber, 1974). The hypnotized person accepts suggestions to a degree where self and role appear to de-differentiated (Sarbin, 1954), or the subject deluded as to the real state of affairs (Sutcliffe, 1958; Arnold, 1959), or the subject totally involved in his imaginings. Such characteristics of behavior may be necessary to define the nature of hypnosis, but the association of imagery with these features of hypnotic performance does not necessarily support either the credulous, or the skeptical viewpoint. It is difficult to analyze the nature of an association. Imagery, for example, may be the result of delusion or simply a manifestation of it.

The correlation then of imagery ability with hypnotizability is consistent with but not a test of a variety of theories of hypnosis. The presence of a positive relationship, for example, may support either the credulous or skeptical view. The association does imply strongly, however, that subjects have certain abilities that make it likely that they will be hypnotizable. This interpretation focuses on the subject's aptitude for trance as distinct from his attitudes towards hypnosis itself or the person who is doing the hypnotizing.

THE HYPNOTIC SETTING

The nature of the hypnotic setting itself provides further theoretical support for positing a relationship between imaginal capacities and hypnotizability. In sharp contrast to the notion that hypnosis leads to an increase in primary process functioning, one may view the hypnotic context as a setting that carries with it strong, inherent demand characteristics for engagement by the subject in imaginal activities. A person may engage in fantasy, or call up mental images easily at will (Betts, 1909). The voluntary nature of imagery and fantasy allows subjects to respond appropriately to the hypnotist's implicit direction to them to lay aside their usual reality orientation. When the subjects' responses to standard induction procedures are analyzed, it is difficult to decide just how much of the quality of the subjects' mentation is due to their perception of cues to respond in a make-believe fashion and how much the quality of cognition is uniquely distinctive of their experience of an altered state of consciousness. A hypnotist typically suggests to the subject that things are other than they are and so implicitly requests that the subject accept his fantasy play and respond appropriately in like manner. Because of the example set by the hypnotist the subject may indulge his predilection for fantasy (Sheehan & Perry, 1976; Sutcliffe, Perry, & Sheehan, 1970). The hypnotist characteristically, it seems, instructs the subject to place aside reality testing and allow more "primary" mentation to occur. No study has been done to separate out the suggested features of primary process thinking in hypnosis from those features that might be expected to occur (on theoretical grounds) because of the presence of a change in consciousness. It is largely due to the traditional emphasis of hypnotic testing on phenomena such as hallucinations ("response to objects which do not really exist") that the ability to indulge in make-believe or fantasy appears to be so important a dimension of hypnotic behavior.

On theoretical grounds, hypnosis defined in terms of a loss of GRO might be expected to highlight ideational aspects of the stream of consciousness. If one accepts the connotations of *altered state* at more than the experiential level, it might well be argued that primary process functioning will be augmented in trance as compared to the normal waking state. Laying aside the question of whether or not such augmentation is supported on empirical grounds we should note that the mere occurrence of primary process mentation in trance implies that there is a definite positive correlation between the subject's aptitude for hypnosis and his proneness to ideational activity, and such a correlation would be consistent with a range of theories about hypnosis. Any attempt, however, to analyze the role of imaginal processes in hypnosis must take some account of the nature of the hypnotic setting which carries strong cues for the subject to respond in a make-believe fashion as directed implicitly by the hypnotist. Should the subject respond as suggested and manifest "appropriate" fantasy responses, this in no way diminishes the importance of the particular cognitive abilities that the subject brings with him to the trance situation.

Any theoretical proposition must ultimately be dependent for its justification on empirical tests. The following section reviews the available empirical evidence. Both clinical and experimental data relevant to the hypothesis of a positive association between susceptibility to trance and ability to engage in ideational activity are considered.

Review of the Evidence: Clinical

The relevance of imagery and fantasy to hypnosis is seen most readily in the clinical observations hypnotists make on the subjects they test. Sarbin (1950) writes that "clinically, (he) has never found an adult with eidetic, or vivid imagery who was not a good hypnotic subject" (p. 268). Wolberg (1948) notes that in trance, imagery seems to play a special role, and Orne (1951) talks of age regression in hypnosis as being actively hallucinated and vividly imagined. The ability of the hypnotic subject to imagine well has been noted by many including Binet and Féré (1886), E.R. Hilgard (1965b), J.R. Hilgard (1970), Lundholm (1932), and Sarbin and Coe (1972). E.R. Hilgard, for example, reports that the more hypnotizable subjects give the most dreamlike hypnotic dreams and dream more frequently than less hypnotizable subjects when a dream is suggested in hypnosis.

The role of imaginal activity in hypnosis is stressed by therapists using a variety of hypnotic techniques (Kanzer, 1945; Schneck, 1963a; Krojanker, 1962; Van den Berg, 1962; Wolberg, 1945). Krojanker employed a hypnodramatic re-enactment technique in which the subject's dreams were used specifically in the treatment process. His technique together with those used by others draw their validity from the psychiatrist's assumption that pictorial representations can be enlivened with affect in a way that conceptual representations cannot and therapeutic gain may derive from them (see Sheikh & Panagiotou, 1975, for a review of the relevant evidence). According to this account, hypnosis is helpful in that it facilitates the occurrence of fantasy involvement. Other studies have used imagery to deepen the trance state. Wiseman and Reyher (1962), for example, explicitly utilized the sleep-dream cycle to facilitate a deepening of hypnosis.

Inadvertently, hypnosis may be induced by the subjects receiving imagination instructions (E.R. Hilgard, 1965b; Sheehan & Dolby, 1974; Tart, 1966a; Connors & Sheehan, 1976). Subjects given such instruction, and no hypnotic induction, sometimes report being hypnotized and show signs of trance such as psychomotor retardation and waxy flexibility. Hilgard and Tart (1966a) have found within the experimental setting that the degree to which some subjects felt themselves hypnotized was highly predictive of the dreamlike character of the fantasy they produced, regardless of whether or not they had received a formal induction procedure. Evidence from the experimental studies of Barber and his associates (Barber, 1969a, and Chapter 8 in this volume; Barber & Calverley, 1962; Barber & Glass, 1962; see also Barber & Ham, 1974; Barber, Spanos, & Chaves, 1974) is relevant here. Studies have demonstrated consistently a high rate of response by subjects to the Barber Suggestibility Scale under imagination instructions. In an early study by Barber and Calverley (1968), for example, twelve percent of the subjects showed a high level of suggestibility and thirty-six percent showed moderately high suggestibility under instructions where the subjects were asked simply to try to imagine those things that would be described to them. Barber interprets these instructions as "nonhypnotic" and uses them to establish what he terms "base-control rates of response." Others, however (e.g., Hilgard & Tart, 1966) prefer to consider at least some of these instances of high suggestibility response under imagination instructions as possible examples of hypnotic involvement. Imagination instructions may also inadvertently create the context of hypnosis (Connors & Sheehan, 1976). Leaving details of this controversy aside, the data reported in the literature suggest that in some instances the subjective as well as the behavioral consequences of instruction to imagine bear a strong enough similarity to hypnotic outcomes that the appropriateness of the label "nonhypnotic" for control procedures can be seriously questioned.

Shor (1970) has reported in detail an analysis of a book-reading fantasy which illustrates the separate dimensions of hypnosis as he has conceptualized them elsewhere (Shor, 1959, 1962b). The occurrence of fantasy in circumstances very different from the traditional hypnotic setting illustrates that the underlying processes of hypnosis bear some clinical similarity to imaginative activities. Some people read a story so completely that they enter imaginatively into the story to a degree which is almost equivalent to reliving the experience. During the time of the fantasy the person becomes totally oblivious to the reality around him. Shor draws the parallel between the level of involvement in the fantasy and the loss of GRO which is a major dimension of hypnotic depth. The reader actively creates the fantasy for himself, thus instituting a nonconscious level of deep involvement typical of the hypnotized subject. Josephine Hilgard (in E.R. Hilgard, 1965b; J.R. Hilgard, 1970) has also related the book-reading fantasy to hypnotic susceptibility. In a series of interviews she found that people who became absorbed in tales of romance and adventure were those subjects who tended to be highly hypnotizable.

Although there is much evidence from anecdoctal reports on experimental subjects, therapeutic case studies, and interview data indicating that fantasy and imaginative involvement are associated with hypnosis, the clinical method is especially ill-equipped to interpret the exact nature of the association despite its obvious strengths in other ways (Sheehan & Perry, 1976). The richness of mentation typically reported under hypnosis may be elicited from patients who are not hypnotized and do not report the experience of trance. Instructions to visualize a scene evoke elaborate dream imagery from psychoanalytic patients even when no "hypnosis" is employed. As Barber (1962) points out, carefully controlled experiments are lacking to exclude the possibility that primary process functioning of the kind typically reported can be elicited without the use of hypnosis. The experimental method is needed to clarify whether the association between imagery and hypnosis is purely an incidental one.

Review of the Evidence: Experimental

INDIRECT MEASURES

Long ago, Jenness (1944) found evidence to support the hypothesis that persons whose imagery is generally vivid would be more readily hypnotized than those whose imagery is poor. Working with Jorgensen (Jenness & Jorgensen, 1941) he showed that the imagery of somnambulists tended to be more vivid than that of nonsomnambulists where somnambulism referred to subjects who walked or performed other coordinated acts while asleep. Later Jenness (1965) reported a relationship between somnambulism, vividness of imagery, and hypnotic ability. In his study subjects rated the vividness of their imagery in response to phrases read aloud by the experimenter. Forty-one sleepwalkers averaged higher in visual imagery and hypnotic susceptibility (as measured by standardized hypnotic scales) than eighty-four subjects who denied walking or talking during sleep.

In a well-known study, a similar indirect approach to the study of imagery and hypnotizability was made by Arnold (1946) who using the postural sway technique, asked subjects to imagine falling forward. Comparisons were made between the amount of sway and the reported vividness of imagery. She found a correlation between amount of body sway and vividness report and concluded there was a relationship between vividness of imagery and hypnotic depth. This relationship has been confirmed most recently by Richardson (1969, 1972) who found that vivid uncontrolled imagery was more obviously related to greater body sway than weak, not so vivid imagery. In another well-known study McBain (1954) chose the "memory for designs" test from the 1937 revised version of the Stanford Binet, a paper cutting test, and the "progressive finger tracing" test as tests of imagery to further investigate Arnold's hypothesis. Using the body sway technique and administering standard imaging instructions he found that subjects with higher imagery scores were more susceptible to hypnosis when the finger tracing test was used.

Arnold's and McBain's original studies are open to objection. Arnold specified no operation or procedure for selecting those subjects who could imagine well, and inferred a correlation of imagery with hypnotic depth using the body sway test as her measure. Insufficient recognition was given to the fact that the body sway test is not a direct measure of hypnotizability. Arnold's instructions to subjects may also have had implicit effects. She used the word "imagine" rather than the word "image" and subjects may have simply "thought hard" about swaying. A subject asked to imagine something does not necessarily have to evoke imagery in order that his attention be focused on an object. As used in many studies in hypnotic literature, instructions to imagine may have slightly different effects for some subjects from instructions to image; I can imagine, for example, a man is not standing next to me much more easily than I can image his absence. In McBain's study, tests were used that were intended to index objectively the imagery aroused. More accurate performance was taken to indicate more vivid imagery. Accuracy of test performance, however, is not always a sure criterion of type, or quality of imagery used. McBain's tests were tests of intelligence rather than tests of mental imagery and accuracy of reproduction may indicate any of a variety of mental processes.

Suggestibility as measured by other than the body sway test has shown some relationship to imagery capacity. Camberari (1958) divided his sample into suggestible and nonsuggestible groups on the basis of a battery of many different tests. Suggestibility was positively correlated with a greater number of reports of visual imagery in an isolation situation. Roberts (1965) tested subjects in a similar situation. Using as his measure of fantasy the degree of hallucinatory activity in perceptual deprivation, he found no relationship between subjects' willingness to enter fantasy and performance on the SHSS:A and C. However, evidence suggests that there is at least a temporary facilitative effect of sensory restriction on the suggestibility test performance of subjects engaged in imagining actual events (e.g., King & Lummis, 1974; Wickramasekera, 1970).

QUESTIONNAIRE STUDIES

Studies have met a moderate degree of success in estabishing predictors of hypnotic susceptibility through the tapping of personal subjective experiences (Ås, 1963; London, Cooper, & Johnson, 1962; Shor, Orne, & O'Connell, 1962; Van Nuys, 1973). Subjects' self-reports of hypnotic experiences have been shown by Freedman and Marks (1965) to be related to some forms of imagery aroused in the experimental setting. Segal (1968) also found that in a sensory deprivation situation subjects who indicated a high tolerance for unrealistic experiences aroused more vivid imagery than subjects with a low tolerance for such experiences. More recently, Tellegen

and Atkinson (1974) have achieved success in indicating a positive relationship between absorption in ongoing experience and hypnotic susceptibility.
These studies suggest that the subject's capacity for fantasy and imagery
and related processes—as evaluated in association with, and independently
of, questionnaire assessment—are related to those aspects of subjective experience that denote susceptibility to hypnosis.

In the aftermath of the mass of conflicting data on the personality correlates of hypnosis the literature has perhaps insufficiently recognized that
imaginative activities have played a significant part in the everyday waking
experiences of good hypnotic subjects. The consistency of data runs counter
to the general failure by studies in the area of trance correlates to replicate
findings. In an investigation reported by Barber (1960) sixty-one items from
the Guilford-Zimmerman Temperament Survey, the Webster-Sanford-
Freedman version of the F scale, and a specially constructed questionnaire
were found to discriminate suggestible from nonsuggestible subjects. A
questionnaire containing these items was given to four groups in a series of
two studies (Barber & Glass, 1962). Analysis of results showed that the four
items differentiated suggestible from nonsuggestible subjects in all groups.
A fifth sample was given the questionnaire in further test of replicability of
findings. The highly suggestible and nonsuggestible subjects in the new sample answered each of the four items in the predicted direction. Examination
of the content of these items showed that three of the four items were
concerned with fantasy activity. One item dealt with book reading fantasy
($p < .001$), the second with daydreaming ($p < .02$), and the third with vivid
imaginary playmates ($p < .001$). The fact that in over five groups these
items discriminated subjects consistently (even when groups were tested by
two different experimenters) and that the items were characterized particularly by ability to engage in imaginative activity suggests that the relation between hypnotizability and the various manifestations of imagination
has considerable support. This support is limited only by the fact that
replication was specific to college students and items did not differentiate
those subjects who were moderately susceptible from the other subjects in
the sample.

Using the Stanford Hypnotic Susceptibility Scale, Sarbin (1964) in
another laboratory confirmed the trend of Barber's data. Sarbin reports the
construction of a questionnaire of 117 items which was administered to
ninety-three subjects as part of an ongoing study of student attitudes.
Twenty-three items discriminated between subjects high and low on role-
enactment. A logical clustering of these items revealed that one of the five
major dimensions being tapped by them was concerned with fantasy and
other forms of "as if" behavior.

A substantial amount of data has been brought to light on the relation
between hypnotizability and one particular measure of vividness of imagery.

In the original study that employed the test—the Betts QMI as devised by Sheehan (1967a) from Betts' Questionnaire Upon Mental Imagery (Betts, 1909)—the test was administered to a sample of ninety-five subjects after subjects were tested hypnotically on the SHSS:C and a scale specially constructed for the study (Sutcliffe, Perry, & Sheehan, 1970). The Betts QMI correlated significantly with both hypnotic scales for the total sample and for males, but not females. Close analysis of the results indicated that the relationship departed significantly from linearity. Vivid imagers were both susceptible and insusceptible to hypnosis but subjects with very poor imagery tended to be insusceptible. Vividness of imagery, then, predicted insusceptibility to hypnosis better than susceptibility. In experimental confirmation of clinical data reviewed above, diagnostic subgroups of susceptible and insusceptible subjects, as rated by independent experimenters after hypnotic testing, were clearly differentiated with respect to the vividness of their imagery. Susceptible subjects imaged more vividly than insusceptible subjects. Shor, Orne, & O'Connell (1966) using a variation of the Betts QMI also found (for a sample of twenty-five volunteer subjects) a significant correlation ($r = .56$) between vividness of imagery and plateau hypnotizability as measured by clinical diagnostic ratings and Sutcliffe (1958), using Betts' original questionnaire (together with Gordon's test for control of imagery), found that highly susceptible subjects exhibited more vivid imagery than did subjects insusceptible to hypnosis. In an attempted replication of the imagery study by Sutcliffe, Josephine Hilgard (1970) found (over all subjects) a small but significant correlation ($p < .01$) between the Stanford hypnotic scale and the Betts QMI, with the sex differences reversed. The relationship was significant for the female sample only. Her data replicated the nonlinearity of relationship noted in the earlier study; as before, the correlation present was determined largely by those completely lacking in imagery.

A number of studies using the Betts QMI as a measure of imagery have reported more equivocal findings. In an unpublished investigation reported in a Hawthorne House Research Memorandum, Morgan and Lam (1969) found no relationship between the Betts QMI and SHSS:C scores for particular subgroups of susceptible subjects and for the total sample of 322 student subjects. In Morgan and Lam's study, however, subjects were not particularly well selected for extremes in hypnotic ability; Sutcliffe, Perry, and Sheehan (1970) had discriminated susceptible from insusceptible subjects both on SHSS:C scores and on the basis of clinical ratings agreed upon independently by separate hypnotists. Lehman (1973) examined hypnotic susceptibility and imagery (as measured by the Betts QMI) in separate sessions and found no support for an imagery susceptibility link, though instructions (either to imagine or passively wait results) had a facilitatory effect on performance. Further, Perry (1973) failed to confirm the previous findings of Sutcliffe, Perry, & Sheehan (1970) in several respects, though he did find that lack of imagery almost invariably accompanied insuscepti-bility. Finally, Spanos et al., (1973) found that the relationship between imagery (using Shor's adaptation of the Betts QMI) and suggestibility was stronger for subjective than for objective hypnotic test scores.

INVOLVEMENT IN IMAGININGS

This review of the evidence would not be complete without comment on the body of data now highlighting the relevance of hypnosis to subjects' in-volvement in their imaginings. Such involvement is directly related to the extent to which hypnotic suggestions are passed or failed (Barber, Spanos, & Chaves, 1974; Spanos & Barber, 1974) and to subjects' reportings of their experience as involuntary (Spanos & McPeake, 1974). The data suggest, for instance, that subjects tend to define their overt response to suggestions as involuntary when they become absorbed in a pattern of imaginings called Goal-Directed Fantasy (GDF; Spanos, 1971)—imagined situations which, if they were to actually occur, would be expected to lead to the occurrence of the motor response called for by the suggestion. Subjects highly involved in GDF, for example, attend fully to their imaginings while ignoring or reinterpreting information that contradicts their reality (Spanos & Barber, 1974). This area of research constitutes a significant development in the field, one that argues forcibly for the empirical and theoretical relevance of imagery to the understanding of hypnotic phenomena.

SEX DIFFERENCES

Research into the association between imaginal activity and hypnotizability has shown considerable inconsistency of data on sex differences as has also a sample of studies that has related hypnotic susceptibility to unusual ex-periences in normal waking life (e.g., Bowers, 1971). Sutcliffe, Perry, and Sheehan (1970) found a relationship between imagery and susceptibility for males, and J.R. Hilgard (1970) found an association for females, yet the two studies used very similar measures of hypnotizability and vividness of imagery. Palmer and Field (1968) measured visual imagery under sensory restriction and under rhythmic photic stimulation to test the hypothesis that subjects with good visual imagery would be more susceptible to hypnosis. Their results showed a consistently stronger relationship between imagery and hypnotizability for females than for males. Diamond and Taft (1975), however, found evidence for few sex differences in their pattern of correlations.

The fact that Palmer and Field's study and Hilgard's study were con-ducted on American student volunteers and Sutcliffe, Perry, and Sheehan's study was carried out on Australian volunteer samples suggests that the pattern of sex differences among the studies may, to a degreee, be culturally based. Perry's (1973) failure to replicate the significant imagery-hypnosis association found earlier for males, when working with Canadian subjects, serves to consolidate the point.

One past study on American subjects by Rhoades and Edmonston (1969) presents contrary evidence to the hypothesis, and it is instructive to examine the evidence closely. These authors used Cattell's IPAT questionnaire and scores based on second-order factors of Cattell's 16 PF scale to relate a number of different aspects of personality functioning to susceptibility as measured by the Havard Group Scale of Hypnosis. Tests were given to two samples: thirty-two male undergraduate students and a second sample of fourteen male executives and ten female housewives or students. Only the data for the second sample indicated a positive relationship between imaginative activity (as measured by Cattell's Factor M) and responsiveness to hypnotic suggestions. This relationship was highly significant for males but absent for females. Rhoades and Edmonston made a special point of reporting that their second sample of males was highly homogeneous with respect to socioeconomic level (all were executives and were with the same company). Their results suggest that the pattern of sex differences across studies may, in part, reflect socioeconomic variation among subjects tested, rather than cultural or sex differences. It appears significant that the female sample in Rhoades and Edmonston's study that showed no relationship was much more heterogeneous (housewives and students) than the usual sample of student subjects in terms of subjects' occupational and socioeconomic status. If American female student samples are more homogeneous in socioeconomic background than American male samples, the difference in sample structure may account for the higher incidence of positive relationships found for female as compared to male subjects.

The above hypothesis to explain sex differences can only be proposed tentatively because other factors appear to be also relevant. Special care should be taken, for example, to equate male and female subjects for imagination ability. Michael (1967) has reported evidence that male and female subjects differ in imaging ability. Using American student samples he found a factor of visual imagery that accounted for the performance of female but not male subjects. A battery of tests was given to groups of students differing in educational grade level. The visual imagery factor did not appear in the male population even when it was dissected as to grade level. Another variable to be considered in analyzing the issue of sex differences is imagination control. It appears that male and female subjects may handle their imaginative capacities differently. Antrobus, Singer, and Greenberg (1966) found that male subjects controlled and excluded their fantasy tendencies when threatened with financial loss for failures in signal detection. Fromm, Oberlander, and Gruenewald (1970) have also presented evidence to suggest that male rather than female subjects increase primary process mentation in trance as compared to the waking state. Bowers (1971) further suggests that the apparent superiority of women over men in hypnotic susceptibility and the differences in the pattern of susceptibility correlates for women and men may stem from differences between the sexes in the organization of imagination. Women's imagination may be more stimulus incited while men's imagination may be impulse incited.

THE ISSUE OF CONJOINT ATTRIBUTES

The studies reviewed above have generally attempted to correlate hypnotic test scores with single dimensions of cognitive function. Evidence from these experiments has been both positive and negative in support of an association between imaginative ability and susceptibility to hypnosis. In many respects, though, results have been encouragingly positive. Close analysis of the data indicates that investigation of conjoint attributes of cognitive functioning may be the most fruitful way to analyze the relationship between hypnosis and manifestations of imagination.

The curvilinear nature of the association between imaginative activity and susceptibility to hypnosis (J.R. Hilgard, 1970; Sutcliffe, Perry, & Sheehan 1970) suggests that accurate prediction of susceptibility to trance may depend on knowledge of more than one capacity or characteristic of the subject. The experimental literature offers some support for this contention. As we have just seen, sex is one important variable for analyzing the correlates of susceptibility.

M.J. Roberts (1965) found no relationship between hypnotizability and willingness to enter fantasy as assessed by degree of hallucinatory activity in perceptual deprivation. This measure of fantasy, however, used in a multiple correlation with other measures (e.g., test for tolerance of unrealistic experiences), predicted susceptibility much better than the fantasy measure did alone. In another investigation, Perry (1965) extensively investigated proneness to fantasy as indicated by subjects' morning recall of their nocturnal dreaming and found no significant relationship between hypnotizability (measured both clinically and by standardized scales) and either incidence of dreaming or dream distortion. This finding should be considered in light of the fact that spontaneous morning recall of dreams is subject to extraneous influences that are minimized (though not completely) when dream reports are collected at the time dreaming occurs. Although the data for fantasy proneness as measured by dream distortion only tended to be in the same direction as predicted by the study, this measure taken conjointly with vividness of imagery was related obviously to hypnotizability (Sutcliffe, Perry, & Sheehan 1970). Those subjects with moderate degrees of one or both characteristics had high or medium susceptibility to trance and the absence of both characteristics was associated with insusceptibility to hypnosis. Consideration of both fantasy proneness and vividness of imagery led to more accurate prediction of high susceptibility than the imagery variable did alone. This result did not replicate in a later study (Perry, 1973) but there were discrepancies in the incidence of dream recall across this and the original experiment.

Coe and Sarbin (1966) have also demonstrated the predictive value of the multivariable approach. Employing measures of congruence between self and role, role expectation, and role-taking aptitude they found that any group of subjects that scored more highly on more role theory variables than another group scored significantly higher on the hypnotic test. Multiple correlation analyses using the Personal Experience Questionnaire, which bears a positive relationship to experimentally produced imagery, have also been successful (London, Cooper, & Johnson 1962; Shor, Orne, & O'Connell 1966). Indeed, in the light of much of the data it seems plausible to argue that the failure of many studies to consider conjoint cognitive attributes may be partially responsible for their lack of success in predicting hypnotic susceptibility with more than a moderate degree of accuracy.

Another view of what has just been proposed has been put forward by E.R. Hilgard (1964) and J.R. Hilgard (in E.R. Hilgard, 1965b). They argued that the low correlations found generally with personality measures and other tests arise because subjects enter hypnosis with wide individual differences in experience and background. They raise the possibility that a single favorable predictor leads to high susceptibility in the absence of other favorable predictors. This point of view conceives of there being multiple paths into hypnosis any one of which leads to a high score. Personality tests yield low correlations with hypnosis, for example, because scores on many predictive items do not equal the effect of single more influential items. Hence, reliance should be placed on single, strong predictors.

In support of this view, E.R. Hilgard (1964) considered separate significant correlations between the SHSS and measures of adventuresomeness and childhood fantasy. Fantasy and adventure can be said to represent alternative routes into hypnosis. Results showed that for low (but not high) fantasy subjects, the correlation of adventuresomeness and hypnotizability was significant, and that for low (but not high) adventuresome subjects, the correlation of fantasy with susceptibility was significant. They concluded that for those subjects whose path into hypnosis was by way of fantasy, interest in adventure was indifferent; and for those whose path into hypnosis was by way of adventure, interest in fantasy was irrelevant. Later research (e.g., J.R. Hilgard, 1970, 1974) has led to careful outlining of the difficulties of testing this theory and to some modification of the position, but recent data suggest that susceptible subjects may indeed take alternative cognitive routes in hypnosis (Dolby & Sheehan, 1977).

At least in some instances, multiple predictors of hypnotizability are clearly more effective in discriminating susceptible subjects than single predictors. The hypothesis of "multiple paths" into hypnosis has not as yet been tested fully. Reported correlations have been very small (of the order .23 to .34) and need replication; also, research is still at a preliminary stage. Overall data draw much needed attention to the fact that joint analysis of relevant predictors of susceptibility may help us understand the full ramifications of the meaning of the term susceptibility to hypnosis. One word of caution, however, follows Bowers (1976). The limitations of such an approach will become apparent if an excessive number of moderator variables are necessary for reasonably sized correlates to emerge.

Summary of Data

A review of the literature indicates that hypnotic data and evidence arising from subjects utilizing their cognitive capacities for fantasy and imagery are not always in one-to-one correspondence. As has been recognized elsewhere (Barber, 1969b, and Chapter 8 this volume; Barber & Glass, 1962), the relationship between sets of results of these kinds may be multidetermined by a host of variables. Situational factors, the characteristics of the experimenter, the interaction of these factors with the personality of the subject, and an interaction between subjects' characteristics and the nature of the experimental situation all may affect subjects' behavior. The evidence further indicates that as measures of imagery become more like the hypnotic tasks themselves, the better predictors these measures will be of hypnotic responsiveness. This appears to be especially the case when the imagination tasks cue goal directed fantasies that are directly related to the suggestions being administered (see Coe et al., 1974).

Review of the evidence raises seven factors that can be singled out more than others as pertaining particularly to the interpretation of experimental findings in this area. These factors are: differences in form and quality of subject's imaginative activities; the homogeneity of samples tested with respect to factors such as socioeconomic status and control of imagination; the nature of the technique of investigation: correlation method or diagnostic subgroups; the essential weaknesses of subjective studies; the adequacy of imagination measures adopted; the cues given the subject as to the most appropriate response; and the efficacy of single versus multiple predictors of trance susceptibility. Consideration of one or more of these factors may nullify the presence of positive findings in the area or explain the absence of confirmatory data.

Differences in imaginative activity. Both imagery and fantasy may vary in form and content. Any relationship with hypnotizability may likewise vary with such differences in mentation. Richardson (1969, 1972) found, for example, a more positive relationship between suggestibility and imaginative activity for uncontrolled as opposed to controlled imagery. Control is an important feature of imagery (White, Sheehan, & Ashton, 1977) and its function needs to be considered carefully. In further confirmation of the importance of individual differences in mentation, E.R. Hilgard (1964) reports the impression that stimulus-bound fantasy leads more readily to hypnosis than impulse-driven fantasy (see also Bowers, 1976, for a similar argument). This hypothesis was confirmed by J.R. Hilgard (1970) in a comprehensive interview analysis of the fantasy proneness of 289 subjects.

Leaving aside for the moment the question of the locus of initiation of the imaginative activity involved, results would suggest that to the extent that imagery and fantasy are different cognitive functions, hypnosis may be more obviously related to the former than to the latter. Hypnotic hallucination, for instance, is one of the defining phenomena of hypnosis, and Binet and Féré (1886) suggest that vividness of imagery constitutes its basis. It is relevant to note that they argued their position on the basis of the perceptual clarity of imagery rather than on the inventiveness or fluidity of imaginative capacity that appears to denote fantasy. Their conclusion is important. Studies conducted independently of the hypnotic context have shown that under certain conditions vivid imagery may reinstitute the original clarity of perceptual experience (Sheehan, 1966a, 1966b, 1967c). Vividness of imagery might be a more suitable aptitude for some aspects of trance behavior than fantasy because it enables the hypnotic subject to experience events which are specifically suggested by the hypnotist in a way that is close to the literalness of perception. With the special aid of imagery, hypnotic events may be experienced with a degree of vividness approaching that of sensory experience. It is well to recognize, however—as was argued ealier—that the term imagery may itself denote a variety of processes. That mental imagery is not a unidimensional phenomenon is well illustrated by the work of Palmer and Field (1968). In their study, correlations between different tests of imagery and susceptibility were so uneven as to challenge seriously the concept of a single, unitary process underlying all visual imagery productions. Further, the contribution of artifact remains indistinct. Wagman and Stewart (1974), for example, found data to suggest that directed (as opposed to free) imagery may be especially susceptible to response bias effects.

Homogeneity of subject samples. Discrepancies among findings in studies employing different subject samples suggest that the sex of subjects tested and/or the heterogeneity of sampling may be responsible for at least some of the variation that has been found in results. Evidence may be interpreted more clearly in the future if studies list, as far as possible, the age, sex, socioeconomic status, and imaginative abilities of the subjects being tested. Careful note should be made also of any subjects who attempt to control their fantasy; the data of Antrobus, Singer, and Greenberg (1966) indicate that such control may be sex-specific. Sex differences may also be expected to result (Bowers, 1976; Hilgard, 1975; White, Sheehan, & Ashton, 1977). It is useful to note in this context that the Betts QMI—the questionnaire measure of imagery which has perhaps most frequently yielded relationships with hypnotizability—was especially constructed to minimize sex differences in subjects' imagining responses to its items; and it is also reliable (Juhasz, 1972; Sheehan, 1967b).

Technique of investigation. The majority of studies in the field have employed the correlational method for analyzing the association between hypnotizability and imaginative capacity. This technique, of necessity, includes for analysis those subjects who have only a moderate degree of hypnotic aptitude. These subjects are neither characterized by a special aptitude for trance, nor by a particular inability to experience hypnosis. Studies that have found a relationship for very susceptible subjects as distinct from moderately susceptible subjects (e.g., Barber & Glass, 1962; Sutcliffe, 1958; Sutcliffe, Perry, & Sheehan, 1970) indicate the value of considering results for diagnostic subgroups of the hypnotic population. The method of correlation can be deficient and insensitive to those attributes which appear to characterize very susceptible subjects (Sheehan & Perry, 1976). In addition, studies which have employed the correlational technique have invariably assumed that the relationship they are investigating is a linear one. Recent data suggest that the hypothesis of linearity is untenable and that curvilinear methods of analysis are more appropriate.

Weaknesses of subjective studies. Studies in this area are especially open to the problem of quantifying subjective experience. The criticism that can be made of such experiments is that imagery, fantasy, and hypnosis all denote essentially private phenomena directly observable only to the experiencing subject. Consequently, subjects may have differing experiences with objects imaged or fantasied and these differences contribute to unreliability of data. The meaning of points on appropriate rating scales for the measurement of imaginative abilities may also vary widely from one person to another. In the light of such difficulties, experiments that report on the relationship between imagination and hypnosis must cite all available evidence on the reliability of the measures adopted. Special consideration must be given to the problems of translating both imaginative and hypnotic experiences from subjective into objective terms.

Adequacy of measures. The adequacy of measures is obviously related to the problem of the methodological weaknesses of subjective studies. Particular attention should be paid, though, to whether or not the measure selected by the experimenter is examining the form of imagery he really intends to study. Lindauer (1969, 1972) has drawn attention to the fact that inconsistencies in the literature on the effectiveness of imagery may be due to the use of materials that do not fully or effectively maximize the occurrence of imagery. He argues that one essential attribute of imagery, namely its reference to sensory modalities, has been especially neglected in the selection of measures of imagery. Inattention to sensory characteristics has produced materials that are uneven in their capacity to arouse imagery. In addition, care should be taken that techniques of measuring imagery are relatively free of obvious trance-inducing qualities. Palmer and Field (1968) found a relationship between hypnotizability and directed imagery in both a Ganzfeld and photic stimulation setting for female subjects. Directed imagery in this situation was defined as imagery which the experimenter specifically requested from the subject. Results suggested that the imagery test was actually trance inducing since the Ganzfeld-directed imagery was correlated with photic-directed imagery more than photic-directed was correlated with photic-free imagery.

Implicit cues as to appropriate response. It is well-known that the demand characteristics (Orne, 1959, and Chapter 16 in this volume) in the experimental situation may determine the nature of the subject's response. Cues may derive from the tests of imagination themselves, the experimental procedures, the nature of instructions, or from the experimenter personally. In a nonhypnotic study, Davis (1932), for example, designed tests meant to be associated with a particular form of imagery. Much of the reasoning behind Davis's work was based on the assumption that visual work requires visual imagery and auditory work requires auditory imagery. The objection that can be raised specifically, here, is that a person could recall an object being a sounding object without any image of the sound at all. The implicit suggestion of auditory imagery in the nature of the test could lead a subject to report an auditory "image" when only nonimaginal recall was present.

The nature of the experimenter's instruction is critically important. The early work of Schneck (1954a) attests to the influence of subtle changes in the wording of the experimenter's hypnotic suggestions on the subject's responses. The wording in one instance yielded evidence of "hallucination" and in another evidence of "imagery". The experimenter's demand for honesty is known also to affect the nature of hallucinatory behavior (Bowers, 1967, 1976; Sheehan & Dolby, 1974). In all, it is very difficult to assess to what extent fantasy and imagery responses are determined by the demand charcteristics of the hypnotic situation. This is particularly so because the hypnotist characteristically directs the subject to engage in imaginative activity, so fantasy involvement is normally an expected feature of the subject's hypnotic response.

The efficacy of multiple predictors. Finally, one should consider the accuracy of prediction of susceptibility afforded by conjoint cognitive, motivational, and personality attributes. Since (theoretically at least) one may distinguish varying aspects of imagery, fantasy, and hallucination, it seems plausible to argue that different kinds of associations may be evident for these various manifestations of the subject's ability to engage in imaginative activities. And on *a priori* grounds it seems reasonable to argue that a person proficient in the various manifestations of imagination will be more susceptible than a person who manifests one aspect singularly.

Processes of Imagination, Hypnosis and the As-If Formulation

The data clearly support the notion that the functioning of imaginative activities in trance should be analyzed closely. The question, then, may be raised as to the most appropriate framework within which to conceptualize the function of imaginal processes within the hypnotic setting.

Fantasy play may be initiated by the subject or directed by the hypnotist. In the latter instance, it can be said to occur in a relationship between subject and hypnotist much akin to a form of *folie à deux* (Sutcliffe, Perry, & Sheehan 1970). In this sense, imaginative activity may be free in form and relatively unconstrained by physical reality. At the same time, however, the hypnotic situation puts considerable pressure on the subject to experience some hypnotic events in quite literal fashion—as if these events were actual, in fact (see Sheehan & Perry, 1976). The fact that some imaginal events have been shown to reinstate the clarity of the perceptual experience serves to emphasize this function.

Consider suggestions to hallucinate and make-believe as a small child. In both these suggestions, as distinct from, suggestions for a hypnotic dream, the "demand characteristics" of the situation serve to emphasize that considerable accuracy is required on the part of the hypnotic subject. Here, the hypnotist typically uses standards of reality against which he evaluates the performance of the subject. In hypnotic age regression, the hypnotic subject must perform in a way which is at least consistent with true or real experiences of an eight-year-old child if he is at all going to satisfy the hypnotist about the genuineness of his performance. His recall of a classroom, for instance, must be roughly equivalent to that of a small child. In hypnotic hallucination the constraints for accuracy may even be more obvious. The hypnotic subject must report literally on his experience as if what the hypnotist suggests to be present is actually so. The specificity of the original suggestion may also determine the precise extent to which the subject will be literal or may embellish his report.

In the above sense Sarbin (1954, 1972; see also, Sarbin & Coe, 1972) has applied the "as-if" dimension to the conceptualization of drama, hypnosis, imagination, and role-taking. The learning of role-taking, for example, is associated with the subject's ability to treat an object or event as if it is something else, and the skill a subject shows in undertaking his play is defined as the degree of his success in use of "as if" behavior. Sarbin's use of the "as-if" dimension to define imaginative behavior can be extended more fully to draw out some of the logical implications of the position.

When a subject images or fantasies an object he has seen recently and reports on his experience, he can be said to be acting in testimony, as if previously experienced situations were now current. This is directly analogous to the subject's response to the hypnotist's suggestion of hallucination and regression which were analyzed above. A hypnotic subject who says he has a mental picture of a garden is not contemplating a resemblance of the garden in any substantive sense, but as Ryle (1955) would say, he resembles a spectator of the garden in that he behaves in report at least as if he were perceiving it. It is from such pretending behavior that one infers the process of imagining.

Consider the proposition "the imager acts as if previously experienced situations were now current." The words "as if" logically demand a comparison of two terms. The way a person who is imagining acts is equated with the way he acts when he has the perceptions on which his imagery depends. The first implication that follows from the as-if formulation is that the imager must act exactly as he did when he actually had these perceptions. The words "as if," however, are conditional; they imply that the condition is unreal or impossible. Imagining is distinct from perceiving but not to be identified with it. It is not the impossible case itself that is assumed to be real, but the manner of regarding the case in question is equated with the consequences that follow from it, and are necessarily bound up with it.

The notion of the imager acting as if he were perceiving (as in a hypnotic hallucination) logically denies an identity of process between imaging and perceiving while asserting that there may be a close correspondence between imaging behavior and perceptual behavior. Just how close this correspondence is will depend on the constraints for accuracy that are suggested by the hypnotist. If the imager is acting as if something were the case, the good or vivid imager must be a convincing enough pretender that another observer may fail to detect pretense. If one acts "as if" poorly, the likelihood of confusion is increased. The as-if formulation applied to imagining in hypnosis suggests that the good imager acts as if the "hallucinated" object perceived were present, and if he acts as if convincingly, then behavior toward the imaged object will be as it is (usually) suggested by the hypnotist—akin to that of perception.

This view of imaginative activity and its relevance to hypnosis conflicts with some current assertions in the literature. A structural similarity of imaging and perceiving, implying an identity of process, has been proposed by many. Oswald (1962) holds that the neurophysiological response to an object actually perceived by one's sense organs is similar to that of a hallucination or image. Richardson (1969, 1972) also acknowledges that it may be that quasi-perceptual experiences labelled by us as "images" involve the reactivation of the neurophysiological processes of the central nervous system aroused during original perceptions. Along similar lines of argument, Erickson (1952) maintains that hypnotic hallucinations are identical to actual perceptions. It is not altogether surprising that research over a long period has aimed to demonstrate that the hypnotist's suggestions about events which do not actually take place lead to consequences identical to those occurring when those events are perceived in fact (e.g., Brady & Levitt, 1966; Goldiamond & Malpass 1961; Rosenthal & Mele, 1952; Underwood, 1960).

The particular relevance of the "as-if" dimension to the association between imaginative activities and hypnosis can in part be examined by analyzing the evidence available to support the position implied by the as-if formulation that there is no identity of process between imagination, hypnotic hallucination, and perception.

The first experimental study to add weight to the hypothesis that imaging "revived" perceptual processes was that of Perky (1910) whose findings have been replicated more recently by Segal and Nathan (1964). Data showed that under suitable experimental conditions a supraliminal visual perception may be mistaken for and incorporated into an image of imagination without any suspicion from the observer that an external stimulus is present. Perky interpreted her results as evidence for similarity between the processes of imagination and perception. All her results imply, however, is that an individual can be led to mistake an actual percept for an image. A distinction between processes cannot be made on the basis of introspective evidence alone. Segal (1972) also tried to later replicate Perky's results and found few if any instances where subjects mistook the real picture for an imagined one though there were occasions when the stimulus was incorporated into the image.

Two conditions must be satisfied before it is legitimate to infer a basic process similarity between imagining or hallucinating and perception. The behavioral product of imagining must be typically only a result of perceptual stimulation, and the subject's imaging response must be genuine. If a subject is asked to image the color red for two minutes and is then shown a blank card, he will see a green afterimage if the mechanisms of perceiving are akin in structure to those of imaging. Before process identity can be inferred, however, the experimenter must be sure that the subject has actually experienced a genuine negative afterimage. If the experimental design allows one to conclude alternatively that the subject may be giving his imaging response because it is expected of him, the design cannot be said to indicate unequivocally that imaging involves a similar mechanism to perceiving. No study has satisfied these two requirements for positing similarity of process between imagining and perceiving.

The most striking evidence in support of structural similarity comes from a series of experiments by Brooks (1967, 1968), confirmed more recently by Byrne (1974) and Salthouse (1974, 1975). Brooks devised a number of techniques that set imagery and perception into direct competition with each other for the same organizing processes. In his original study (Brooks, 1967), subjects were presented with a series of messages that described spatial relations. Some of these were just spoken, and others spoken but accompanied by a simultaneous exposure of a typewritten copy of the message. After each message, subjects were asked to repeat it verbatim. It was hypothesized that reading the message would lead to less accurate repetition than listening to the message since listening alone would not conflict with the use of the visual system for visualization of the spatial relations. Results showed that listening to the messages produced less interference with visualization than did reading the messages. Findings suggested that the mechanisms of imagery and those of perception are similar. The results were interpreted to indicate that the reading-visualization conflict resulted from the internal representation of spatial material using mechanisms specialized for *visual* perception. Brooks, however, acknowledged that this interpretation, although persuasive, was tentative. The most important thing about the visualization might not have been its sensory modality but rather that it was organized quite differently from the verbal message itself. Also, subjects in the experiment ascribed to visualization a whole range of mental events. Only two subjects reported what might be judged as a clear image.

Research on whether hypnotic hallucinations result in an activation of perceptual processes is also inconclusive. There is some evidence for the existence of transfer effects of perceptual processing in hypnosis (Dolby & Sheehan, 1977; Graham & Leibowitz, 1972; Sheehan & Dolby, 1975), and reports of afterimages to hallucinated colors (Hibler, 1940; Barber, 1959a; Sutcliffe, 1960); the latter phenomena, however, may reflect the fact that subjects perceive specific demand characteristics present in the situation. Brady and Levitt (1966) have offered data in support of the "reality" of hypnotic hallucinations, and their study serves to illustrate this point in another context. Brady and Levitt found that hypnotized subjects who reported vivid hallucinations of a visual situation which ordinarily elicited optokinetic nystagmus showed nystagmus under the hallucinating condition. None of the subjects who demonstrated visual hallucinations by this criterion were able to fake the response in the waking state, nor could an independent set of control subjects. It is not surprising, however, that hypnotic subjects did not duplicate their hypnotic behavior and show nystagmus in the waking state, since this group was subject to strong demand characteristics for behavioral change. Susceptible subjects could have perceived these cues and been led to expect that nystagmus was no longer required in the waking state, after they had demonstrated it previously in trance.

In summary of the evidence to date, no study supports unequivocally the hypothesis that hypnotic hallucinations or imagined events reinstitute the process of perception. Data are in no way in conflict with the logical implications of the as-if formulation of the role of imagination in hypnosis.

Imaginal events are usefully conceptualized as serving an as-if function. Under the direction, implicit or explicit, of the hypnotist, they enable the subject in a special way to react to suggestions as if they were literally true. It is important to add, however, that the wording of the hypnotist's suggestion and the type of imaginative activity (fantasy or imagery) can set limits on just how literal the subject is in conforming to the hypnotist's suggestions. Suggestions vary considerably in their constraints on the subject, and subjects themselves may at times embellish suggestions with their own personal constructions of events as they are communicated. In a suggestion to dream, for example, the subject is free to fantasize individually in response to the hypnotist's instruction. But in a suggestion to hallucinate a mutual friend, the subject is required to act more as if a particular person were physically present though instructions may still implicitly give him the freedom to describe the friend in one of a number of different ways. Under instruction to hallucinate a moving drum, the subject is required to duplicate even more closely perceptual-type responses; at least, it is the explicit intent of the hypnotist that he do so.

Insofar as it is possible to distinguish the processes of imagery and fantasy, imagery may well serve to reinstitute perceptual experience in a more literal way than fantasy when close correspondence of behavior with perception is requested by the hypnotist. Where imagery is invoked, the apparent concrete nature of something imaged can serve to emphasize the thing-quality of specific objects as suggested by the hypnotist. Fantasy, on the other hand, seems well suited to the hypnotic subject where suggestions are for make-believe involvement relatively unconstrained by the explicit demands of the hypnotist for the subject to conform to reality. These possible differences in function aside, both processes are skills required by the subject to allow him to behave as if what the hypnotist is saying were true. From the viewpoint of the experiencing subject, however—as noted earlier —it is important to emphasize that imagery and fantasy may blur interchangeably. Certain kinds of instructed imagery, for example, are apt to have the seemingly spontaneous quality characteristic of fantasy (Bowers, 1976) and their occurrence may at times reflect strong internal motivational origins (Horowitz, 1972, 1975).

The as-if formulation is useful insofar as it stresses the several possible functions of imaginative activities in hypnosis. It does not lead one necessarily to adopt a role-taking account of hypnosis, however. Hypnotic events are extremely complex and role theory may be inadequate to explain them (for elaboration of this argument, see Sheehan & Perry, 1976). If the hypnotic subject, for example, exercises his imaginative capacities and acts as if his imaginings were real, he may do so in such a way that he not only reports his imaginings as true but he himself subjectively experiences them as such. This state of affairs is critical and it can be explained in a number of different ways. It may result from "nonhypnotic" conditions of the trance setting developing naturally the germ of a belief in reality that is contained in every image; or the subject may have become so involved in the role that he is playing that self and role become de-differentiated. Further, a special state of hypnosis may have been induced by the hypnotist which, as its essential characteristic, creates for the subject the delusion that what the hypnotist says is true, and any imaginings come to be completely believed.

As argued earlier in this chapter, the association between imaginative capacity and hypnotizability may be formulated so that it is consistent with a variety of theories of hypnosis. To the extent that any distinction can justifiably be drawn between role-taking and state theories of hypnosis, studies clearly exist that appear to confirm or contradict either approach. Empirical data on the nature of hypnosis aside, the argument here is simply that the as-if formulation very usefully conceptualizes the important functions imagery and fantasy may play both inside and outside the hypnotic setting.

IV

Lines
of Individual Research

William E. Edmonston, Jr. *is Professor of Psychology at Colgate University. After receiving his Ph.D. from the University of Kentucky with Frank A. Pattie in 1960, he became an Instructor of Medical Psychology and Director of the Psychology Clinic in the Department of Psychiatry of the Washington University School of Medicine (St. Louis). In 1964, he terminated the clinical phase of his career and moved to Colgate, where he could devote a greater portion of his time and energy to teaching. During the academic year 1970-71 he was a Senior Fellow in the Department of Physiology and Biophysics, University of Washington School of Medicine (Seattle). Since 1961, when he received the Bernard E. Gorton Award (First) for meritorious scientific writing in hypnosis for his study on hypnotic age regression, the major portion of his research time has been devoted to hypnosis. In January, 1977 he developed and directed a conference on the "Conceptual and Investigative Approaches to Hypnosis and Hypnotic Phenomena" for the New York Academy of Sciences. His present research interests are the physical and physiological parameters of the capacity for hypnosis and the neuroanatomy of vocalization. He was the Editor of the American Journal of Clinical Hypnosis from 1968 to 1976.*

Edmonston *presents an experimental analysis of Pavlov's cortical inhibition theory of hypnosis. This theory predicts that as hypnosis deepens there is increasing interference with the voluntary but not with the involuntary components of conditioned responses, due to a progressive spread of cortical inhibition.*

Edmonston points out that previous experimental work on this prediction has been sparse and inconclusive. In a series of painstaking and logically converging studies he unravels the complexities, methodological flaws, and inaccurate interpretations inherent in the research that has centered on the Pavlov predictions. In Edmonston's own studies hypnosis is induced in a simple and neutral way, avoiding complicated instructions that might confuse the observation of primary relationships.

13

The Effects of Neutral Hypnosis on Conditioned Responses: Implications for Hypnosis as Relaxation

WILLIAM E. EDMONSTON, JR.

Thus the sight, or even the recalled *idea* of grateful food, causes an uncommon flow of spittle into the mouth of a hungry person; and the seeing of a lemon cut produces the same effect in many people.

R. WHYTT, 1763

In the main, hypnotic studies have been concerned with the effects of complex hypnotic phenomena (such as amnesia and age regression) on conditioned responses or the effects of hypnotic induction on complex motor and verbal learning. Few investigations have been conducted on the more basic issue of the effects of neutral hypnosis; that is, the presentation of hypnotic induction instructions without further motivational instructions, on relatively simple conditioned responses.

Conditioned responses and their relationships to hypnosis have been of primary concern to the Russian investigators. Pavlov (1927), in his early work on two dogs (Bek and John), concluded that hypnosis, brought about

Portions of the work described here were supported by Colgate University Research Council and completed while the author was a Sloan Foundation Fellow. The author is particularly indebted to the following individuals for their assistance in the experiments: Christopher D. Rhoades, John F. Kihlstrom, Patricia A. Trumbull, Martin W. Ham, Anthony P. Conti, Barrett J. Katz, Doreen M. Hess, and Jonathan D. Saperia.

415

by prolonged, monotonous environmental stimulation, creates in the cells of the cortex a state of irradiated inhibition. (For a detailed explication of Pavlov's theory see Edmonston, 1967.) In order to account for the loss of motor function during hypnosis in conjunction with the retention of the conditioned alimentary reflex, Pavlov concluded that hypnosis is the inhibitor of motor activity through the inhibition of the cortical motor analyzer. However, the other analyzers retain their excitation during hypnosis, and the salivation portion of the total conditioned response in the classic bell-food paradigm continues through hypnosis.

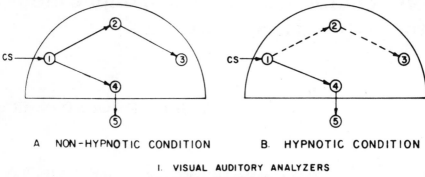

A   NON-HYPNOTIC CONDITION   B. HYPNOTIC CONDITION

    1. VISUAL AUDITORY ANALYZERS
    2   MOTOR ANALYZER
    3. MOTOR RESPONSE CENTER
    4   ALIMENTARY ANALYZER
    5. ALIMENTARY RESPONSE CENTER

FIGURE 13.1   *Schematic presentation of Pavlov's theory of the effects of hypnosis on the cerebral cortex.*

According to Pavlov, not only are the motor (voluntary) components lost during hypnosis, they are lost in a progressive fashion. Those motor behaviors most active just prior to hypnosis are inhibited first, while those furthest removed in time from induction are the last affected. For example, as hypnosis occurs in the dog, the first motor responses to be inhibited are the masticatory and lingual, the last are the postural. Very clearly, Pavlov felt that hypnosis affected cortical rather than subcortical anatomy, for his observations indicated that motor (cortical) functions subsided while alimentary (subcortical) did not. Figure 13.1 presents a schematic drawing of this idea. In Figure 13.1a, the nonhypnotic condition, the conditioned stimulus (CS) activates a focal point in the cortex, which in turn activates the motor and alimentary analyzers, which then lead to motor and alimentary responses. During hypnosis, however, the motor analyzer and responses are inhibited (the degree depending on the depth of hypnosis), while the alimentary analyzer and responses continue in a state of usual excitation (Figure 13.1b).

Pavlov, then, was quite clear with respect to the portion of the central nervous system involved in hypnosis—the cortex: "We are dealing with a complete inhibition confined exclusively to the cortex, without a concurrent descent of the inhibition into the centres regulating equilibrium and maintenance of posture." He also states: "Thus in this form of sleep [hypnosis] the plane of demarcation between the inhibited regions of the brain and the regions which are free from inhibition seems to pass just beneath the cerebral cortex" (Pavlov, 1927, p. 266). However, while initially separating the alimentary from the motor analyzer, placing the former in the subcortex and the latter in the cortex itself, Pavlov did leave some confusion as to the type of conditioned response (CR) that might be affected by hypnosis. This confusion seemed to be resolved by a consideration of hypnotic depth: "all the cases of dissociation of the secretory and motor reactions can be attributed to a different localization of inhibition at the onset of the hypnotic state and in the course of its development" (p. 365). This then was a statement of the progressive irradiation of inhibition over the cortex with increasing hypnotic depth.

In addition, what Pavlov seemed to be implying was that as the hypnotic state developed we might see interference (inhibition) not only with the degree of a given CR, but with different kinds of responses as well. The former point seems to have been well established by Korotkin and Suslova (1951, 1953, 1955a, 1955b, 1955c, 1959, 1960, 1962), who demonstrated a progressive difficulty in the formation of conditioned eyelid responses as the depth of hypnosis increased to a point where they could not be formed at all. Platanov (1959) as well has offered evidence to the effect that hypnosis interferes with the establishment of new CRs and the elicitation of old. In line with Pavlov's notions of motor (voluntary) inhibition under conditions of hypnosis, Platonov's review reported changes in motor chronaxie, which seemed to indicate a similarity between suggested (hypnosis) and natural sleep.

There is not complete unanimity among the Russian investigators. Pavlov and Povorinskii (1953), for example, indicate that motor responses are more rapidly formed in hypnosis, while Livshits (1959) has offered data that seem to be at variance with the general notion of a diminution in conditioned response elicitation during hypnosis. Livshits (1959) conditioned differential vascular dilation and contraction to a buzzer and a bell prior to hypnosis, and then demonstrated that "conditioned reflexes elaborated in the waking state were preserved in the state of hypnosis" (Livshits, 1959, p. 752). Even though Livshits based his conclusion on a single subject (out of the forty-three with whom he initiated the study), it is clear from the foregoing discussion of Pavlov's position that the retention of this CR would be expected since it was an involuntary, nonmotor response. Only through a deepening of the hypnotic state would we expect, from Pavlov's viewpoint, any interference (inhibition) with this type of CR.

In addition to the study reported by Livshits, a few non-Russian works have reported no interference with CRs during hypnosis (McCranie & Crasilneck, 1955; H.D. Scott, 1930). However, McCranie and Crasilneck (1955) did find that a voluntary CR (hand withdrawal) disappeared following the addition of age regression instructions to the hypnotic induction, whereas a less voluntary response (eyelid) was uninfluenced. LeCron (1952) earlier had also reported the loss of a conditioned hand withdrawal response during age regression. Although with respect to neutral hypnosis these works did not support the cortical inhibition view, when age regression instructions were added they fit Pavlov's original formulation with respect to inhibited motor responsivity.

Moravek (1968) also showed the inhibition of motor activity under suggested hypnoanesthesia. All twenty-five subjects who were tapping with their fingers showed motor inhibition during hypnotic anesthesia but not during a non-hypnotic period. In addition, four of the subjects were trained to two similar acoustical stimuli, which evoked the motor response. The effect of one of these stimuli was inhibited in the anesthetic hand, but not in the other hand. This inhibition carried over into the nonhypnotic period; the stimulus had lost its ability to elicit the response.

What becomes most clear from this brief survey of the scanty experimental data is that there is "no clear-cut conclusion as to the fate of a previously established conditioned response following the induction of hypnosis" (Plapp & Edmonston, 1965, pp. 378–79). What was needed at that time (1965) was a series of studies systematically investigating the effects of hypnotic induction (neutral hypnosis) on a variety of CRs some involving voluntary motor behavior and others involving involuntary nonmotor behavior.

The model chosen for the studies in this series under my direction consisted of five basic phases: conditioning, experimental instructions, first extinction period, termination of experimental instructions, and finally, second extinction period. The second study in the series (Plapp, 1967), involving eyelid conditioning, consisted of a slightly different format, although it adhered basically to the general model of the other works. As will be described, conditioning procedures varied with the particular response involved. Experimental instructions in each of the studies consisted of hypnotic induction for one group; instructions to relax, but not to be hypnotized for another group; and other instructional sets as dictated by the variety of control groups employed in each study. Both extinction periods consisted of the presentation of the CS without reinforcement for a specified number of trials. Instructions countermanding the particular experimental instructions were interposed between the two extinction periods.

One should take particular note of the introduction of a control group receiving instructions to relax but not to be hypnotized. This procedure has had important implications for our understanding of the basic nature of hypnosis, as elaborated in the general discussion at the end of this chapter.

Finger Withdrawal Conditioning

According to Pavlov's view, the formation of CRs during hypnosis is inhibited. Scott (1930), however, not only found that a finger withdrawal CR could be elaborated more easily in hypnosis than in nonhypnosis, but that the extinction of the response demonstrated continuity from trance to nontrance. The first study in our series (Plapp & Edmonston, 1965) used a slightly different model and, as seen below, produced markedly different results.

Method. Of thirty original volunteer students, twelve served as subjects (Ss) for this study. Fourteen of the original group did not condition—a problem of no little consequence, as we shall see progressively through this series—and four discontinued participation. A conditioned finger withdrawal response was established to a 2000 Hz tone (CS) by pairing the tone with a noxious electric shock (UCS). A conditioning trial consisted of a .5 second CS, a .5 second interval, and a .5 second UCS; intertrial intervals ranged randomly between twenty and forty seconds. One of every five conditioning trials was designated a test trial (CS presented alone), and the criterion of conditioning was the elicitation of four CRs (finger withdrawal) out of five consecutive test trials.

Once conditioned, the Ss were equally and randomly divided into two groups, one receiving the eye closure section of the Stanford Hypnotic Susceptibility Scale (SHSS), Form A (Weitzenhoffer & Hilgard, 1959) as a hypnotic induction, and the other instructed to remain comfortable with their eyes closed (Plapp & Edmonston, 1965, p. 380). The experimental group was tested for hypnosis with the hand lowering, arm rigidity, and eye catalepsy portions of the SHSS; the control group was instructed to perform these tasks voluntarily. Following these procedures, twelve extinction trials (CS alone) were presented to each S in each group. At this point the hypnosis was terminated for the experimental group, the control group was told to open their eyes, and the second series of twelve extinction trials was presented to all Ss.

Results. The results of these procedures were quite striking, as can be seen in Figure 13.2. Except for one CR given by one experimental S on trial three, no experimental *S* gave any *CR*s during the first extinction period. The control group, which was not hypnotized, continued to yield *CR*s. During the second extinction period, following the termination of the hypnotic condition in the experimental *S*s, we note that the two groups are showing similar patterns of slow extinction.

Discussion. These data were precisely what Pavlov would have predicted: the motor (voluntary) components of *CR*s are lost during hypnosis. However, it was precisely the voluntary aspects of the finger withdrawal response that posed a problem. Initially, we were willing to attribute the dramatic change in the CR from nonhypnotic to hypnotic condition to the specific hypnotic induction instructions received by the experimental group. However, we were somewhat concerned that the experimental *S*s, through their personal perception of what should or should not happen during hypnosis, had withheld their response during the first extinction period. Thus, the very behavior that Pavlov held as prima facie evidence for hypnosis is confounded by the fact that the finger withdrawal response has the potential of being manipulated by the subject—without special training.

Quite obviously, one way of assuring that such was not the case was to remove the subject's ability to maintain any control over the response, either before or after conditioning, by the choice of the response to be conditioned. Thus, by choosing a series of progressively less voluntary responses it was possible to eliminate one confounding aspect of this first study, although we may have eliminated the crux of Pavlov's theory in the process. At the very least, we felt that there was further need to investigate hypnosis per se as a separate experimental procedure from hypnotic suggestions such as amnesia, age regression and so forth.

Eyelid Conditioning

As indicated in the general introduction above, the effects of hypnosis on conditioned eyelid responses have been reported in the literature (Korotkin & Suslova, 1951, 1953, 1955a, 1955b, 1955c, 1959, 1960, 1962; McCrainie & Crasilneck, 1955). Korotkin and Suslova (1951) reported that as the "somnambulistic phase" of hypnosis is reached there is increasing difficulty in achieving a conditioned eyelid response. In those *S*s where the response could be achieved, acquisition was greatly retarded. These same findings were replicated in the 1959 and 1960 studies of these same authors. With respect to McCrainie and Crasilneck (1955), both a hand withdrawal and an eyelid response were conditioned in two groups of six *S*s each. Contrary to the findings of Korotkin and Suslova, the induction of hypnosis did not affect either response. It was only after hynotic age regression was introduced that the hand withdrawal response disappeared. The eyelid response, on the other hand, was not affected.

TABLE 13.1 Summary of experimental design

Group I	Test for hypnotic suscepti- bility	Hypnosis	Conditioning	Presentation of control verbal material I and control verbal II	Extinction I	Hypnosis termination	Extinction II
Group II	"	Presenta- tion of control verbal material I	Conditioning	Presentation of control verbal II and hypnosis	Extinction I	Hypnosis termination	Extinction II
Group III	"	Hypnosis	Conditioning	Presentation of control verbal material I and hypnosis termination	Extinction I	Presentation of control verbal material II	Extinction II

SOURCE: Plapp, 1967, p. 26.

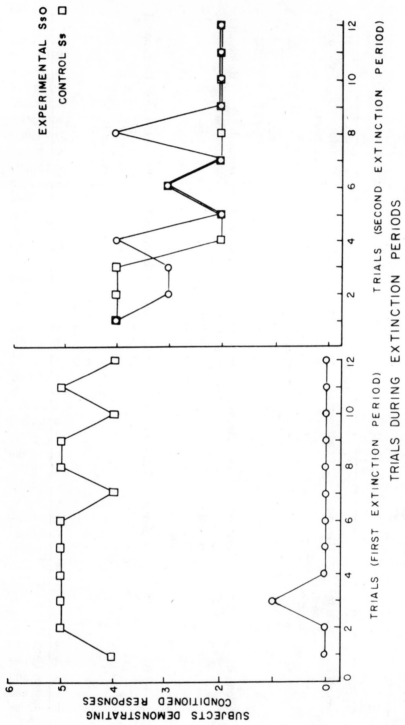

FIGURE 13.2. *The number of subjects giving CRs on each extinction trial (From Plapp & Edmonston, 1965, p. 380).*

Up until 1967 these investigations were the only studies offering some direct measure of the effects of neutral hypnosis on a conditioned eyelid response; yet the findings of Korotkin and Suslova are at variance with those of McCrainie and Crasilneck. Reviewing these and related portions of the literature, Plapp (1967) concluded that "although motor conditioned responses established in the waking state and tested for in the hypnotic state appeared during extinction to be inhibited in those hypnotized *S*s by either neutral hypnosis, hypnosis plus age regression, or hypnosis plus stimulus-lessening or stimulus-absent instructions, controls have not been adequate to determine whether this effect is due simply to the hypnosis treatment, to specific instructions during hypnosis, or to pre-existing differences between experimental and control *S*s" (Plapp, 1967, p. 10). With these difficulties in mind, Plapp (1967) undertook to investigate the effects of neutral hypnosis on both the acquisition and extinction of a conditioned eyelid response. In addition, he obtained reaction time, electrodermal, and plethysmographic orienting response measures in the course of his data collection.

Method. Table 13.1 summarizes the experimental design employed by Plapp (1967). Plapp's Group II follows the model set forth in the finger withdrawal study above and followed in the subsequent studies to be reported. Therefore we will focus our main attention on this group. The inclusion of the other two groups stems from Plapp's interest in not only the effects of hypnosis on an already established CR, but on the acquisition of a CR as well. All of Plapp's subjects were pretested through a tape-recorded presentation of the Harvard Group Scale of Hypnotic Susceptibility (Shor & Orne, 1962). Hypnotic induction instructions were an adaptation of the Stanford Scale of Hypnotic Susceptibility (Weitzenhoffer & Hilgard, 1959), and the other verbal materials were taken from a book on the topic of social mobility.

Plapp used thirty-five acquisition trials that were defined as the presentation of a signal light (ten seconds), followed by a tone (450 msec.) whose termination coincided with a sixty msec. air puff directed at the right eye of the *S*. The signal light continued for two more seconds after this sequence, during which the *S* was to push a reaction time key. Each extinction period involved ten trials in which all the stimuli with the exception of the air puff were presented.

Results. Figure 13.3 depicts the percent of conditioned eyeblinks occurring during acquisition and the two extinction periods of Plapp's three groups; Groups I and III received the acquisition trial during hypnosis, and Group II received them prior to hypnotic induction. Hypnosis was induced in Group II prior to the first extinction period and terminated prior to the

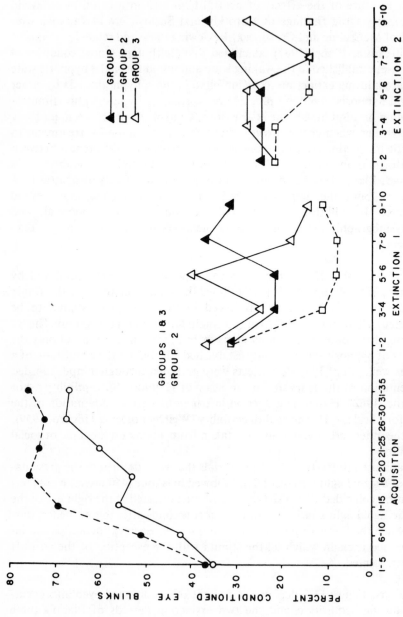

FIGURE 13.3. *Percent conditioned eyeblinks over blocks of acquisition and extinction trials (From Plapp, 1967, p. 39).*

second extinction period. For all groups there was a decided reduction in the frequency of *S*s yielding a CR on the first extinction trial as related to the last acquisition trial, but this was not unexpected due to the intervention of another experimental procedure—instructions.

Plapp notes that during the first extinction period: "following the induction of hypnosis in what was originally the nonhypnosis group (Group II), the number of conditioned eyeblinks falls to a low level for almost all *S*s, with this reduction in *CR*s being greater than for *S*s hypnotized prior to acquisition (Groups I and III)" (1967, p. 54). This finding is elaborated in further discussion of the data: "Only Group II *S*s, hypnotized prior to the first extinction period, gave a significantly reduced number of eyeblink *CR*s on the first extinction as compared with that of the last acquisition trial. Further, examination of Figure 13.3 suggests that extinction was more rapid for this group. The number of *CR*s given by Group II *S*s decreases more rapidly and remains at a lower level during the first extinction period" (p. 71). However, the analysis of the second extinction period failed to detect a conclusive reversal effect for Group II, as had occurred in the finger withdrawal study. Finally, one other measure taken during this experiment is also of significance to us in our interpretation of Pavlov's views of hypnosis. Plapp found that the reaction time measure (a more voluntary motor response) significantly increases for Group II following the induction of hypnosis.

Discussion. The eyelid findings are in direct contradiction to those of McCrainie and Crasilneck (1955), who did not find a decrement in either finger withdrawal or eyelid conditioning upon the induction of hypnosis. Both the eyelid and the reaction time responses tend to support and elaborate further the findings of Korotkin and Suslova and the theoretical position of Pavlov. Both of the responses, which contain clear elements of potential voluntary control, were influenced by the induction of hypnosis. However, the nature of the eyelid response does raise some doubt as to the accuracy of Pavlov's cortical-subcortical demarcation of hypnotic influence. Marquis and Hilgard (1936) pointed out that the response is not dependent upon cortical areas for its maintenance. Ablation of the occipital lobes did not disturb a conditioned lid response, thus indicating a subcortical locus of action. Although eyelid responses may contain voluntary control potential, they also contain *both* cortical and subcortical elements, the former being less prominent as conditioning is established.

In spite of a general overall failure of hypnosis to influence physiological measures, Plapp did find a significant negative correlation between the number of spontaneous electrodermal fluctuations (SF) and the hypnotic susceptibility. Highly susceptible *S*s tended to give few SF, while less susceptible *S*s tended to yield more. From this finding Plapp concluded that "the effects of hypnosis may go beyond the primarily voluntary kind of response to also depress responses which are not directly under voluntary control and are not obviously subject to S-expectations regarding hypnotic effects'' (1967, p. 67). Such a suggestion also runs counter to Pavlov's theory, but will be taken up in the studies to follow.

Electrodermal Conditioning

EXPERIMENT ONE

The next logical step in our series of studies was to investigate the effects of neutral hypnosis on a less voluntary CR—the electrodermal response (EDR). Prior to the report of this study (Edmonston, 1968), no investigation of the effects of neutral hypnosis on EDR conditioning had been reported. A number of investigators had reported data concerning the alteration of *EDR*s during hypnosis (Barber & Coules, 1959; Davis & Kantor, 1935; Edmonston & Pessin, 1966; Estabrooks, 1930; Fehr & Stern, 1967; Levine, 1930; O'Connell & Orne, 1962; and Pessin, Plapp, & Stern, 1968), but none yielded data regarding the conditioning of this response.

Method. The basic methodology outlined in the introduction was used: conditioning, experimental instructions, first extinction period, termination of experimental instructions, and finally, a second extinction period. In the initial portion of this study forty-five individuals served as Ss. They were equally divided into three groups, the first two of which were equated for Harvard Group Susceptibility Scale Scores (Shor & Orne, 1962) and the third of which contained Ss of far less susceptibility. The groups were equated also for mean Maudsley neuroticism and extroversion scores, and age (see Table 13.2). Following twenty habituation trials to a seven second, 500 Hz tone, each of the Ss received twenty conditioning trials, which paired the same tone with a .5 second electric pulse. Following the administration of the experimental instructions, ten extinction trials (tone alone) were presented. The instructions were then countermanded and ten more extinction trials were offered. The first experimental groups (group one) received as experimental instructions a tape-recorded hypnotic induction procedure based on the eye closure portion of the Stanford Hypnotic Susceptibility Scale, Form B (Weitzenhoffer & Hilgard, 1959). The second experimental group (group two) was told: ''Let yourself become very deeply relaxed but do not allow yourself to enter hypnosis; allow yourself to become deeply relaxed but do not become hypnotized'' five times during a seventeen-minute time control period. The final, control group (group three) sat in the experimental room for seventeen minutes without instructions.

TABLE 13.2   Means and standard deviations of subjects' ages, Harvard Group Scale Scores, and Maudsley Neuroticism and Extroversion Scores

	Group 1		Group 2		Group 3		Group 4	
	M	SD	M	SD	M	SD	M	SD
Age	27.13	8.11	30.93	8.45	29.13	7.27	18.83	2.76
Harvard	6.07	3.43	5.93	2.55	2.93	1.12	5.27	1.92
Neuroticism	25.93	13.04	25.13	13.07	19.60	9.02	—	—
Extroversion	32.33	8.58	34.40	8.29	30.33	8.23	—	—

SOURCE: Edmonston, 1968, p. 19.

Some time later a fourth group was run in the same experimental procedures; the results were not reported with the original data (Edmonston, 1968), but will be reported here. During the running of the first three groups, concern developed with the notion of how the Ss would perform if in fact they knew what the experimenters wanted of them. That is, what if a group of Ss was told that neutral hypnosis abolishes a conditioned EDR? Thus, almost a year after the original data collection, a fourth group was added to the study. An instruction sheet was presented to the Ss informing them of our desires and expectations for the results of the study. Basically, the question was, can a S role-play to the extent of abolishing a conditioned nonvoluntary response? This group was equated with the others on Harvard scores and received the same hypnotic induction at the same time in the methodological sequence as the first experimental group.

Results. Records were kept of the following measures with respect to the EDR on all Ss during all of the periods: electrodermal orienting responses (OR), electrodermal conditioned responses , electrodermal spontaneous fluctuations. Figure 13.4 shows the results of the ORs. All four groups performed in the same manner during the habituation period to the CS—the tone. For the conditioning period, however, a rather striking difference appears among the groups. Groups one, two, and three of the original study show no significant differences with respect to ORs during the conditioning period. We see, of course, an increase of these responses over the last block of trials of habituation and then a diminution of these responses over the blocks of conditioning trials. Group four is the curiosity here, in that it shows a decided difference from the other three groups. Since at this point in the study, the only difference between Group four and the other groups was that group four knew what was expected, it is rather striking to see this significant diminution in the OR. Either a S selection bias had occurred or the Ss were able, in some manner or form, to reduce the ORs to the tone during conditioning. The two extinction periods show no differences among groups on the ORs. Group four is consistently lower than the other groups,

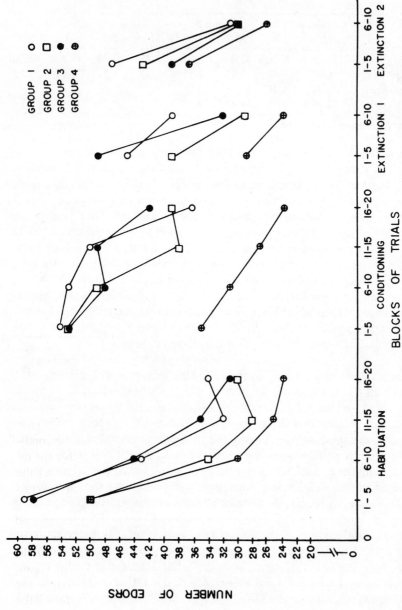

FIGURE 13.4. *Total number of EDORs for each group over blocks of trials during habituation, conditioning, first, and second extinction periods (From Edmonston, 1968, p. 19).*

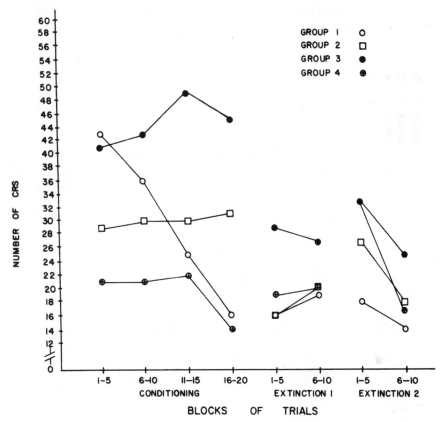

FIGURE 13.5. *Total number of CRs for each group over blocks of trials during conditioning, first, and second extinction periods (From Edmonston, 1968, p. 21).*

but this can be attributed to the reduced number of *OR*s during the conditioning. Thus, it would seem, as Plapp (1967) concluded earlier, that the induction of neutral hypnosis, as opposed to relaxation, does not affect the electrodermal OR, whether the *S*s are knowledgeable or not with respect to the expected outcome.

Figure 13.5 shows the electrodermal *CR*s during the conditioning and two extinction periods. A CR was a drop in skin resistance of 300 ohms or more, between 3.5 and 8.5 seconds following the onset of the tone stimulation. There are two things to notice about the conditioning aspect of Figure 13.5. The first is that both group one and group four (group four is the knowledgeable group) showed a rather clear habituation pattern during the conditioning; group one from the first block to the last block of trials, and group four from the third block to the last block of trials. This finding in group four may not be unusual because those *S*s, after all, knew the results anticipated. In fact, they had shown a decided difference in the number of *OR*s produced during this period. The real puzzle is group one, because these subjects did not know the purpose of the study. Perhaps, as has been suggested, the idea was inadvertently conveyed to the *S*s in this group that they were to demonstrate fewer and fewer *CR*s as the experiment progressed. Even if this were essentially true, it offers no explanation as to how the *S*s might have done this. That they did seem to habituate during conditioning in a manner unlike the two major control groups is evident.

A covariance analysis between the last block of conditioning trials and the first block of first extinction trials demonstrated no significant differences among groups. In addition, no significant differences were demonstrated among groups between the first and second extinction periods when the termination of neutral instructions was accomplished with groups one and four. Thus, we concluded that hypnotic induction instructions do not affect conditioned *EDR*s.

However, this conclusion seemed somehow premature, since it was not clear that *CR*s had ever been established. Although the experimental procedures through the conditioning period had been identical for the first three groups, there is a decided difference among the groups in their conditionability. It appears that the main experimental group (group one) actually habituated, despite continuing increases in the amplitude of the electric shock for all *S*s in order to avoid this very phenomenon. In fact, there was some question as to whether any conditioning at all occurred over this period of twenty trials in the groups. Notation of this failure of conditioning leads to the second phase of this investigation, described below.

EXPERIMENT 1A

Although the covariance analyses above indicated that neutral hypnosis had no effect on the level of electrodermal conditioned responding, more substantial evidence was needed as to the degree of conditioning obtained before stable conclusions could be drawn. While the groups as units did not demonstrate consistent conditioning, certain individuals within each group did meet a reasonable criterion of conditioning.

Method. The data for those *S*s who yielded at least four conditioned *EDR*s (as defined above) out of five consecutive conditioning trials were selected for further analysis. In group one, ten *S*s conditioned; in group two, eight; in group three, twelve; and in group four, three. The conditioned members of groups one and four were combined into one hypnosis group and compared with the other two groups during the two extinction periods.

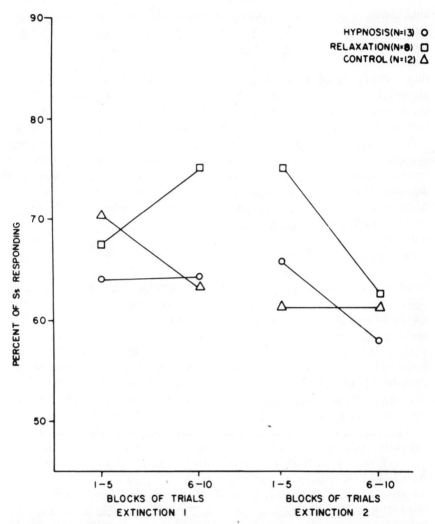

FIGURE 13.6. *Percent of subjects meeting conditioning criterion who yielded CRs during the first and second extinction periods.*

Results. Figure 13.6 presents the percentage of Ss yielding an electrodermal CR during the first and second extinction periods. Recall that the experimental instructions (hypnosis for groups one and four, and relaxation for group two) were introduced before the beginning of the first extinction period and terminated prior to the start of the second.

These data are commensurate with those from the total groups. Neutral hypnosis did not affect an electrodermal CR in any different manner than either no instructions or instructions to relax. In fact, the group that demonstrated the most variability was the relaxation group (group two), although, with the exception of the first trial of the first extinction period, these three groups did not differ.

Discussion. Whether one looks at the data for all the group members (experiment one) or just for those *S*s who conditioned, the conclusion is the same —neutral hypnosis does not influence conditioned *EDR*s. At this point the series of studies seemed to be supporting Pavlov's original contention that hypnosis inhibits the motor analyzer, leaving the other analyzers (alimentary, in his case) relatively uninhibited, so that *CR*s or portions of *CR*s not involving the voluntary musculature would continue in essentially the same form as we might expect in the unhypnotized person. Yet, we were not fully satisfied with our electrodermal data and continued our investigations in the following form.

EXPERIMENT TWO

Method. In the context of a study of the effects of neutral hypnosis on conditioned heart rate, electrodermal measures were also recorded. Again we used undergraduate and graduate students and their wives as *S*s. While we used the same basic methodology as before, the stimulus condition was considerably different. Instead of the simple tone and shock pairing used before, the stimuli sequence was as follows during the conditioning period: (a) a 500 Hz tone (six second duration), (b) a flash of light (1/1500 sec.) six feet and to the left oblique, from the eyes, (c) the illumination of a 200 watt bare incandescent light bulb in the same position as the flash (six seconds), and (d) a blast of a twelve volt auto horn located behind and beneath the subject's chair (six seconds). The subject was seated in a comfortable, reclined chair with EDR electrodes attached to his right index and ring fingers and EKG electrodes attached to his right and left wrists.

Our original intention was to utilize the tone as a CS and the flash and light as the UCS for a conditioned EDR. The light was also to serve as a CS for heart rate conditioning, with the auto horn as the UCS. However, the startle effect of a flash of light is not nearly as long-lived as an electric pulse, and consequently all of our *S*s habituated to the flash-light within several trials. On the other hand, the auto horn, being a meaningful stimulus in our society, maintained its startle effect throughout twenty conditioning trials for several subjects, who developed electrodermal CRs to the light-horn pairing in the sequence.

On the basis of the previous studies it was apparent to us that the most meaningful control group for hypnotic studies was the relaxed, but not hypnotized group. Consequently, the twenty *S*s of this study were equally divided, on the basis of Harvard Group Scale Susceptibility Scores (Shor &

Orne, 1962), into two groups, one receiving the same hypnotic induction instructions and the other receiving the same relaxation instructions as described in the first electrodermal study. Instructions were introduced before the first extinction period (after conditioning) and terminated prior to the second extinction period. Again, both extinction periods were ten trials long, a trial being the presentation of the tone and flash-light stimuli alone.

Results. The groups showed little evidence of conditioning. However, using the same criterion as before (four *CR*s out of five consecutive trials), three hypnosis and two relaxation *S*s were selected for further evaluation. The data from the two extinction periods yielded the same conclusion as before: Neutral hypnosis has little or no affect on conditioned electrodermal responses. Five *CR*s were elicited from one hypnotized *S* during the first extinction period, and one during the second. One other hypnotized *S* gave one CR on the second trial of the second extinction period, and the other *S* in this group gave no *CR*s during either extinction period. Likewise, one relaxed *S* yielded two *CR*s during the first and one during the second extinction period, while the other gave only two *CR*s, both during the second extinction period.

EXPERIMENT THREE

Dissatisfied with the post hoc approach outlined in experiments 1A and two, we undertook a final brief study of the effects of hypnosis on the electrodermal response. Instead of groups of *S*s our efforts were concentrated on four deep trance *S*s with whom we had worked during the summer of 1969. Each of the *S*s participated in at least ten hours of trance phenomena including hypnotic amnesia, age regression, and hallucinatory behavior. With each we had established a signal for rapid induction, so that they were able to reach "depths" of between ninety and one hundred on a subjectively reported depth scale of 0-100.

Method. Electrodermal conditioning was attempted in the same manner as in experiment one, using a 500 Hz tone as the CS and a randomly increasing electric pulse delivered to the right arm as the UCS. The criterion of conditioning was the elicitation of a CR in four out of five consecutive trials.

Results. Although upwards of sixty trials were given to some of the *S*s, only one developed a stable conditioned EDR.

This particular subject conditioned within thirty-eight conditioning trials, yielding her cluster of criterion *CR*s on trials thirty-four, thirty-five, thirty-six, and thirty-eight. An individually induced deep hypnotic trance was obtained, with the subject reporting a "depth" of ninety-five. (She had previously engaged in cliniciaily authentic age regression, hallucinations, and amnesia at "depths" of ninety-two.) Her performance during the extinction periods that followed is most instructive. During the first ten presentations of the tone alone—in hypnosis—she yielded four CRs, on trials one, two, three, and four. During the second ten presentations of the tone alone—after the termination of hypnosis—no CRs were elicited. What we see then is an unremarkable extinction record; the induction of hypnosis had no effect on the usual processes that we might expect under normal (nonhypnotic) conditions.

Discussion. Thus, it seems that our post hoc procedures employed in experiments 1A and two were justified, and did not lead to spurious conclusions. In this brief study of one *S*, we assured ourselves of a CR and of a degree of hypnotic trance that should have influenced the CR, if it were in fact to be influenced. At this point our evidence appears to yield the interpretation that as the *S* loses voluntary control over the response conditioned, the effects of neutral hypnosis are minimized, whether or not the physiological loci are cortical, subcortical, or both.

Heart Rate Conditioning

One of the major difficulties with studies of conditioned heart rate (HR) is the designation of the response. The literature is far from clear on whether its nature is accelerative or decelerative. Comparison across studies is an added difficulty because of the noncomparability of stimuli, intra- and intertrial intervals, and number of conditioning trials. Some investigators have reported acceleration as the conditioned HR response (Zeaman, Deane, & Wegner, 1954; Zeaman & Wegner, 1958), while others found deceleration to be the form of the response (DeLeon, 1964; Notterman, Schoenfeld, & Bersh, 1952a, 1952b; Zeaman & Wegner, 1954). Both auditory (Notterman, Schoenfeld, & Bersh, 1952a, 1952b; Zeaman & Wegner, 1954) and visual (DeLeon, 1964) stimuli have been used as CS, and both electric shocks (Notterman, Schoenfeld, & Bersh, 1952a, 1952b; Zeaman, Deane & Wegner, 1954; Zeaman & Wegner, 1954, 1958) and loud noises (DeLeon, 1964) have served as UCS. The number of conditioning trials also appears to influence the interpretation of the response; that is, a small number of trials (eleven) appears to lead to an accelerative form of the CR, while a longer series of trials (twenty) produces, at first, an acceleration, then a deceleration (Dawson, 1953). Even this finding does not appear to be stable, because one factor that seems crucial is the precise time in the conditioning sequence when the response is measured. Needless to say, the state of human HR conditioning is itself in a state of unsteady flux. In fact, even to attempt to use such an unknown response to measure the effects of another as yet unknown (hypnosis) may have been premature.

Few studies of the effects of hypnosis on heart rate per se have appeared in the literature, and here too the results seem to be in conflict. Jenness and Wible (1937), Tsinkin (1930a, 1930b), Whitehorn et al. (1932), and Wible and Jenness (1936) reported a deceleration upon induction, while True and Stephenson (1951) reported an acceleration. Crasilneck and Hall (1959), after a review of this literature, concluded: "In summary, heart rate normally declines in neutral hypnosis but may increase as the result of specific psychodynamics or induction techniques" (1959, pp. 19–20). They felt that the decelerative findings were due to the general relaxation inherent in most induction procedures. No investigations of the effects of hypnosis on conditioned HR have appeared in the literature, and only one study of the effects of neutral hypnosis on a conditioned plethysmographic response has been reported (Livshits, 1959), with negative results on one *S*. May and Edmonston (1966) have also reported that plethysmographic responses to startle stimuli are unaffected by hypnotic induction.

Two studies of the effects of neutral hypnosis on conditioned HR have been conducted in our laboratories.

EXPERIMENT ONE

Method. Twenty-four male undergraduates, matched into four groups on the basis of performance on the SHSS, Form A (Weitzenhoffer & Hilgard, 1959) served as *S*s for the first study. In one group (one), conditioning occurred during hypnosis, extinction after hypnosis termination; in another (two), both conditioning and extinction were carried out without hypnosis, while in a third group (three) both the conditioning and extinction trials were during hypnosis. The final group (four) was conditioned prior to hypnosis and received extinction trials after induction. Induction procedures were tape recordings of the eye-closure instructions of the SHSS; time control instructions consisted of two taped short stories of an equivalent time period.

A ten watt 120 volt white bulb served as the CS, with the same auto horn described in the electrodermal experiment two as the UCS. Both stimuli durations were six seconds, their consecutive presentations constituting one conditioning trial. Ten habituation trials (light alone) preceded twenty conditioning trials (both stimuli), after which ten extinction trials (light alone) were presented. Appropriate instructions were interjected into this sequence in accord with the group to which the particular *S* was assigned. The habituation trials were presented to ascertain their necessity in future studies; habituation for the light stimulus was found to be unnecessary, because HR shows no natural response—either increase or decrease—to this form of visual stimulation.

Results. All four groups demonstrated a statistically significant increase in HR between the last five trials (six to ten) of habituation and the first five of conditioning, but there were no differences among groups on the first five trials of the extinction period. This finding was noted despite the fact that there had been a change in experimental conditionings prior to the onset of extinction for groups one and four. Thus, it appeared from these results that a conditioned increase in HR was unaffected by either the induction of hypnosis or by trance termination, when the conditioning occurred during hypnosis. Neutral hypnosis did not appreciably affect a conditioned HR. However, this finding remains in some doubt because of the nature of the conditioned HR obtained in this and the follow-up study.

Discussion. As it turned out, about all that could be ascertained from this investigation was that, given the stimuli used and their specific time relationships, a conditioned HR is accelerative in form but only for a very short duration of trials. The conditioned HR of this and the following study seemed to reach a maximum during the second (this experiment) or third (the following experiment) block of conditioning trials (six to ten or eleven to fifteen). What seems to this author to be most outstanding about HR is not its conditionability but its adaptability in the form of rapid habituation to novel stimuli.

EXPERIMENT TWO

The second HR conditioning study was begun as the first was being completed. The procedures have been previously described in experiment two of the electrodermal conditioning series. Instead of the four groups used by Conti (1968), twenty Ss were divided into two groups: a hypnosis group and a relaxation control group. The Ss, composed of graduate students and student wives, were divided such that the two groups were comparable with respect to Harvard Group Scale Susceptibility Scores (Shor & Orne, 1962).

Twenty conditioning and two periods of ten extinction trials each were given to all Ss. The same hypnotic induction and relaxation instructions as used in EDR experiment one were introduced prior to the first extinction period and countermanded before the second. Measurement consisted of tabulating the HR in beats per six second periods (pre-CS; CS, light; UCS, horn) summed across Ss in blocks of five trials each. In addition, the number of beats during the six-second periods directly preceding and following the stimuli sequence were similarly tabulated and grouped. Since the light served as the CS, the main evaluation was of potential shifts in HR during this period in both the conditioning and extinction trials.

Results. We discovered that no matter whether we compared beats per unit time or a ratio of the number of beats during the light period to those in either or both of the preceding six-second periods, no statistically discernible conditioned HR was evident in the groups as units. In fact, in the groups as groups no appreciable change in HR was noted even during the UCS (horn) period. Without the elaboration of a CR, the groups as units could not be used to evaluate the effects of neutral hypnosis. Once again we reverted to looking to the data of those few subjects (two hypnosis Ss and two relaxation Ss) in whom a conditioned response of reasonable magnitude had been developed.

Even the evaluation of these few data posed some presentation problems (see Shearn, 1961). When using a change of rate as a response, the measure tabulated must be a ratio of some sort, most preferably between the rates of an ongoing rate period and a rate period that has potentially changed. In our case an increase (Conti, 1968) HR should occur across trials during the CS (light) period. This increase should be absolute and yet relative to the pre-CS six-second period. However, in addition, we should also observe a decrease in HR across trials during the UCS (horn) period as conditioning occurs. A presentation of data for this investigation must then include the data from all three periods (pre-CS, CS, and UCS) in a manner such that the progressive increase HR during CS and decrease HR during the other two periods is clearly evident.

Figure 13.7 presents the average beats per six seconds averaged across blocks of five trials each during the pre-CS, CS, and UCS periods for two of the Ss from the relaxation control group. Looking first at the conditioning trials, we see that the HR during the pre-CS period remains fairly constant, with the exception of the increase (three beats/min.) during the second block of trials (six to ten). The HR also increases during these same five trials during the horn presentation (1/25 beats/min.), but then decreases (three beats/min.) as the trials continue. On the other hand, during CS period, these Ss yielded an increase HR that maximized during conditioning trials eleven to fifteen (5.7 beats/min.) and leveled off at three beats/min. by trial twenty. Five sets of instructions to relax but not to become hypnotized were presented during the next seventeen minutes, followed by ten extinction trials. Following the instructions, an average drop in HR of five beats/min. was noted. As can be seen in Figure 13.7, this new level of HR did not change during the first five extinction trials for any of the measurement periods. In fact, for both the UCS and the CS a continued drop (two beats/min.) occurs as the first extinction period progresses.

Instructions to become more alert followed. During the second set of extinction trials there appears an initial increase in HR during the CS period (two beats/min.), followed by a decrease of four beats/min. as the extinction continues. The initial increase can be attributed to spontaneous

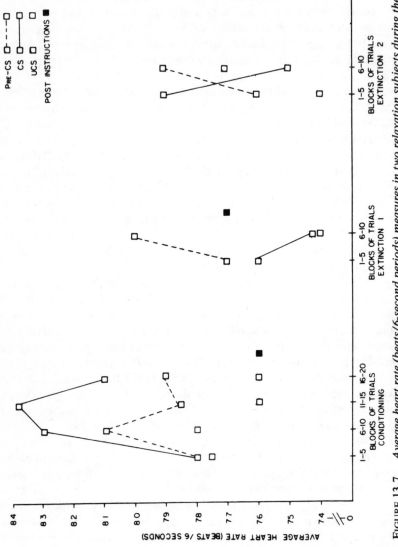

FIGURE 13.7. *Average heart rate (beats/6-second periods) measures in two relaxation subjects during the pre-CS, CS, and UCS periods throughout the conditioning and first and second extinction periods.*

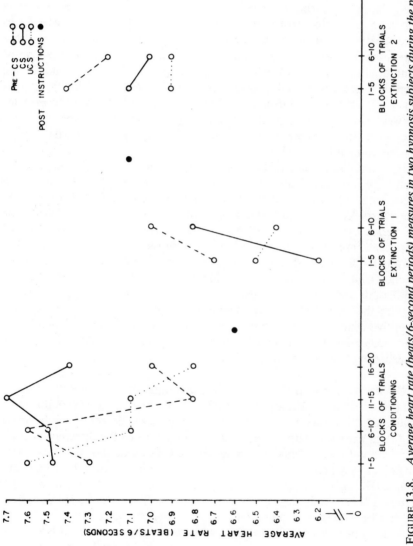

FIGURE 13.8. *Average heart rate (beats/6-second periods) measures in two hypnosis subjects during the pre-CS, CS, and UCS periods throughout the conditioning and first and second extinction periods.*

recovery. Both the pre-CS and UCS periods show a progressive increase HR across these last ten extinction trials.

Turning now to the data for the two Ss from the hypnotic group (Figure 13.8), we see similar rate patterns during the conditioning trials, except that the habituation during the pre-CS and UCS periods is more marked than for the Ss in the control group. During the pre-CS period the HR drops three beats/min. from the beginning to the end of the conditioning with a maximum drop of seven beats/min. between the second and third blocks of conditioning trials. With respect to the UCS period during conditioning there is a progressive habituation across trials amounting finally to eight beats/min. However, during the CS period no such habituation is evident. Between the beginning of the conditioning and the third block of trials (eleven to fifteen) the HR increases 2.3 beats/min. and then falls approximately to its initial level.

Hypnotic induction instructions (electrodermal conditioning experiment one) were introduced prior to the first extinction period, following which there was a decrease of eight beats/min. (as compared to five beats/min. for the control Ss) prior to the beginning of the first extinction trial. During the CS period of the first five extinction trials there was a further decrease of four beats/min. (as compared to no decrease for the control Ss). The pre-CS and UCS periods showed no appreciable change during this block of extinction trials. As this extinction period progresses, both the pre-CS and the CS periods yield increasing HRs, the UCS showing a slight opposite trend.

With the termination of the hypnotic instructions the HR reverts to a level five beats/min. above that immediately following hypnotic induction. The second extinction series of trials yielded unremarkable data in all three measurement time periods (pre-CS, CS, and UCS).

Discussion. As with the Conti (1968) investigation, HR conditioning appears to reach its maximum effect within the first ten to fifteen conditioning trials. In both studies it was clear that although some degree of conditioning had been achieved with some Ss, the introduction of the different instructions did not take optimal advantage of the CR. Because of that fact it was difficult to say precisely what effect the hypnotic instructions had on conditioned HR. However, in this second study we were able to introduce the instructional sets while the conditioned HR was still in effect, at least for four Ss. But here again the intepretation of results is difficult.

What appears to be a dramatic elimination of the conditioned HR in the two hypnotized Ss as compared to the two control Ss may be attributable to a subtle difference in the instructions given the two groups. Relaxation Ss were told to relax only five times during the seventeen minutes in which the hypnotized Ss received continual instructions for trance development. Both groups showed an appreciably decreased HR following instructions (five beat/min. for the relaxed; eight beats/min. for the hypnotized), so that it may be that the intermittent nature of the relaxation instructions forestalled what would also have been a dramatic decrease in HR for that group, had their instructions been continuous throughout the instruction period. The interpretation of what appears to be the elimination of a conditioned non-voluntary response by neutral hypnosis must await further studies in which relaxation instructions are as continuous in presentation as hypnotic induction instructions.

The weight of evidence to this point would indicate that the elimination of the conditioned HR in two Ss was an artifact of instructional differences between groups, and this interpretation seems most likely. However, if the finding is not an instructional artifact then we have what may be an inconsistency in our series of studies, which must be resolved on some other basis. Either way, further study of HR is indicated.

Conclusion

Pavlov's theory poses two mutually interrelated problems; that of the locus of hypnotic inhibition, and that of the Ss voluntary control over the responses influenced by hypnosis. To state that hypnosis involves the irradiation of cortical inhibition is an oversimplification. While it seems obvious that some cortical functions are involved in the perception of the various conditioned and unconditioned stimuli of these studies, the separation between cortical and subcortical involvement in conditioning is not a simple matter. We have already pointed out that eyelid conditioning, although involving certain cortical areas, is not dependent upon these areas for the maintenance of the CR (Marquis & Hilgard, 1936). The fact that decortication does not appreciably impair classical Pavlovian learning alone indicates the involvement of subcortical areas (Campbell, 1965).

Several investigators of hypnosis (Akstein, 1965; Arnold, 1959; and Roberts, 1960) have suggested blockages either in the reticular activating system itself or between this system and cortical functioning. The effects of such a blockage on conditioned responses would seem to be response dependent, for our data and those of other investigators indicate the inhibition of some CRs, but not others. Either the inhibitory effects of hypnosis are much more widespread than Pavlov originally supposed or there is another factor operative in the investigations. Initially, the apparent differential influence of hypnosis would lead us to consider the voluntary aspects of responses as the third prime factor (the other two being cortical and subcortical). However, we suspect that it is not the "willfull" control wielded by the S, but the general inhibition of the entire organism inherent in hypnosis, yet seldom isolated through experimental design.

All of the CRs used in our studies and those of other investigators have both cortical and subcortical components. To erect a cortical inhibition theory of hypnosis on the basis of the action of *CR*s during hypnosis is to confound both the process (hypnosis) and the measure (*CR*s).

For example, the works of Korotkin and Suslova (1951, 1953, 1955a, 1955b, 1955c, 1959, 1960, 1962), taken in conjunction with the demonstrated relationship between conditionability and hypnotizability (Das, 1958a, 1958b), would indicate that these two functions may be mutually interfering, and therefore involve similar or the same neurophysiological mechanisms and analyzers regardless of their cortical or subcortical locale. It may just be that the incompatability of *simultaneous* hypnosis and conditioning is attributable to the fact that both utilize the same mechanisms. Perhaps hypnosis subjects make double use of the same physiological mechanisms, adding to the facilitation of any responses (hypnosis being one) involving these areas when the responses are separately but not simultaneously elicited. In that case separate measures of conditionability and hypnotizability would be positively related, while simultaneous hypnosis and conditioning would be mutually interfering.

However, the studies reported here have demonstrated that the situation is not one of simply overloading the neurophysiology. The introduction of hypnotic induction instructions between the conditioning and the extinction of a response leads to the elimination or drastic reduction of responses that contain voluntary, motor components (finger withdrawal, eyelid) but not of responses whose voluntary components are minimal (electrodermal, HR— the latter clearly needing further study). The trend of these investigations leads us to believe that hypnotic induction influences solely the voluntary motor systems of the organism, regardless of cortical or subcortical considerations. It is through the general relaxation inherent in hypnosis that the induction exercises its influence. Therefore, the one crucial factor that must be accounted for in evaluations of the influence of neutral hypnosis is the concomitant relaxation state. Both nonhypnotic relaxation and hypnosis involve the relaxation of the voluntary motor systems. To hypnotize a *S* and then point to a motor response that has been adversely affected as proof that hypnosis affects the motor system, without also showing that relaxation without hypnosis does not similarly affect the same system, is to confound the interpretation of the data. This has been the basic fault with Pavlov's, other Russian, our own finger withdrawal, and Plapp's eyeblink studies.

ELECTRODERMAL SPONTANEOUS FLUCTUATIONS

In the series of electrodermal conditioning studies, the importance of determining the influence of relaxation per se on the response measured became fully apparent. The state of the organism during hypnosis was clarified by the electrodermal SF data from experiments one and two. Earlier, Fehr and Stern (1967) had suggested that the hypnotic S is more vigilant and less responsive to extraneous internal and external stimuli. This conclusion was based on a reduced number of SF during hypnosis. The more basic factor, to which our data seem to point, is the state of relaxation of the S, which allows him to exclude the influence of other stimuli including CS, so long as they pertain to voluntary functions.

In Figure 13.9 we see the electrodermal SF during the five periods of the study (habituation, conditioning, instruction period, first extinction, and second extinction) for the four groups of experiment one.

The differences between group three and groups one and four may, of course, be attributable to some susceptibility factors, since the no instruction group (group three) had significantly lower Harvard Scale scores than the other three groups. We might speculate on the possibility of a hypnotic susceptibility referent here, in that by SF standards this group was considerably more activated than the other two groups. It is conceivable that those individuals who are more susceptible to hypnosis are generally less physiologically active, and do not maintain the same level of physiological arousal as individuals who are less susceptible (see also Plapp, 1967).

With the exception of the first block of habituation trials, the four curves do not differ significantly from one another. At least by the end of the habituation period we could consider all four groups to be equated with respect to SF production. We see again in the first block of trials of conditioning the separation of the groups with group three, the uninstructed, less hypnotizable group, yielding significantly more SF than the other groups. Interesting to note here is the fact that the fourth group, which was added later, follows both the same relative and absolute patterns of group one, the original experimental hypnotized group.

At the beginning of the instruction period, it was quite clear that the four groups were equated with respect to SF production. By the second block of minutes we begin to see a separation, which has become quite profound by the third block of minutes and continues through the fourth block of minutes. The separation that became apparent in minutes nine through twelve reaches significance in minutes thirteen through sixteen, with group one demonstrating significantly fewer SF than group three. Thus, our experimental Ss demonstrated a reduction of SF beyond that for the uninstructed group three, but not for the relaxed control group, that is, group two. What we see clearly is that our two hypnotized groups, one and four, demonstrate a progressive reduction in SF production over a relaxed group and a noninstructed group. As indicated above, the hypnotic groups did not differ significantly from the relaxed group (group two), which falls intermediate between groups three and one and four.

The split of group three, the noninstructed control group, from groups

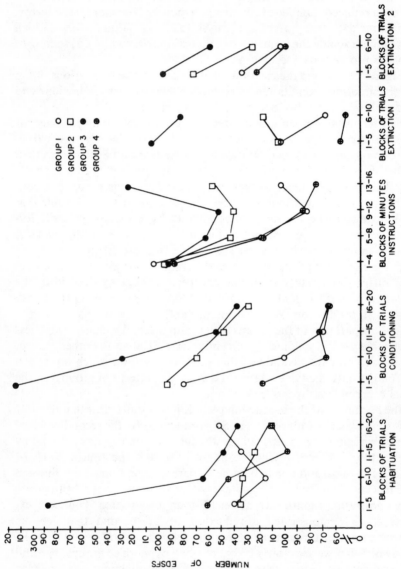

FIGURE 13.9. *Total number of SFs for each group over blocks of trials during habituation, conditioning, first, and second extinction periods; also included are 4-minute blocks of time during instructional period (From Ed-monston, 1968, p. 20).*

one, two, and four became even more evident in the first block of extinction trials following the instruction period. Covariance analysis between the last five trials of the instruction period and the first five of this extinction period demonstrated a significant difference between groups one, two, and four and group three, the latter showing significantly more SF. A covariance analysis between the first and second five of the first extinction trials gave some indication of the relationship between hypnotic instructions and relaxation instructions. Covariance analysis between the first and the last five of the first extinction trials also showed us a curious difference, in that group one had produced significantly fewer SF than group three. However, there was no significant difference between groups two and three.

Initially, we might have interpreted this finding as an indication of the durability of hypnotic relaxation, in that both the hypnotic and the relaxed groups were virtually identical during the first five extinction trials, but then split apart—the former maintaining its degree of relaxation depicted by low SF production, group two becoming rearoused during extinction. However, we must keep in mind that the relaxed group received instructions to relax only five times during the seventeen-minute instruction period, so that the difference in the effectiveness of instructions could be attributable merely to the amount of verbalization the respective groups received in the instruction period. Finally, looking at the first five trials of the second extinction period, following arousal instructions to groups one and four, we see that all four groups produced the same amount (statistically) of SF. However, groups one, two, and four showed a significant increase in SF production from the last five trials of the first extinction period to the first five trials of the second extinction period.

Figure 13.10 shows the data of the electrodermal conditioning experiment two. It is quite evident that during the habituation and conditioning periods, these two groups produced similar SF patterns of habituation. During the instruction period, when one group was receiving hypnotic induction and the other relaxation instructions, we also see similar patterns. (The lack of a data point for the last four minutes of the instruction period for the relaxed group was due to experimenter error, but we suspect that the projected SF would continue to approximate very closely those of the hypnotized group.) Finally, in the two extinction periods we also note no difference between the two groups.

In Figure 13.11 we have combined the SF data for experiments one and two so that the hypnosis group is a combination of the three hypnosis groups, the relaxation data are from the combination of the two relaxation groups, and the no-instruction data are from group three of experiment one. While it is quite clear that in the habituation and conditioning periods the no-instruction group produced more spontaneous fluctuations than the other two groups (which, as indicated before, may be related to some

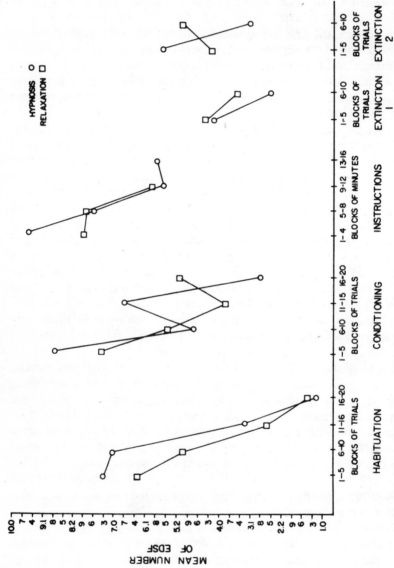

FIGURE 13.10. *Mean number of SFs for each group over blocks of trials during habituation, conditioning, first, and second extinction periods; also included are 4-minute blocks of time during instructional period.*

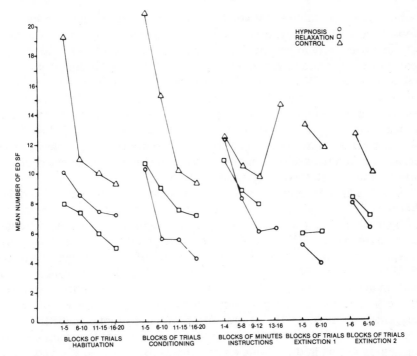

FIGURE 13.11.   *Mean number of SFs for combined groups (Figures 13.9 and 13.10).*

hypnotic susceptibility factor), it is the instruction and extinction periods that are of the most interest to us.

Once again with these combined data we found no difference in SF production during the first four minutes of the instruction period and then a progressive separation of the curves representing the three groups, with the relaxation group falling intermediate between no-instruction and the hypnotic instruction group. Once again we found significant differences between the hypnotized and the no-instruction group, but not between the hypnotized and the relaxation group. However, following the instruction period, in the first extinction period we see quite obviously significant differences between the relaxation and hypnosis groups and the no-instruction group. There were significant increases in SF production for the hypnotized group following arousal instructions (in the second extinction period), but not for the relaxed and no-instruction groups. Both the hypnotized and the relaxed groups remained considerably less productive of SF than the no-instruction group during this period.

GENERAL DISCUSSION

As we pointed out in the introduction to this chapter, Pavlov considered hypnosis to be an inhibitor of voluntary motor activity. Such inhibition was considered to be progressive in a fashion suggestive of a generalization gradient over more to less involved functions. Our overall data tend to support this viewpoint and yet raise the doubt that hypnosis is unique in its inhibitory capacity. What is clear from our data is that voluntary motor functions are inhibited by hypnotic induction, just as Pavlov stated they would be, and nonvoluntary functions appear not to be. However, the extensive conclusions and theory drawn by Pavlov and elaborated by his followers do not necessarily follow, because of the lack of appropriate experimental controls. The data themselves cannot be accurately interpreted unless controls which isolate nonhypnotic relaxation have been applied.

Since the introduction of modern hypnosis over two centuries ago and the Marquis de Puységur's first notation of the somnambulistic appearance of hypnotic patients, relaxation has been the central focus of hypnotic induction procedures. Words like "sleep" and "relaxation" are historically inseparable from hypnosis. From the time of de Puységur through Esdaile, Elliotson, and Braid, the induction of hypnosis was synonymous with inducing a "state of sleep" in the patient. Even Bernheim, who rejected sleep as too narrow a definition for hypnotism, continued to use the suggestion of sleep as the central focus of his hypnotic induction procedures. He, as White (1941) after him, recognized that "susceptibility to suggestion occurs in the waking estate" (Bernheim, 1964, p. 15), and made suggestion central to his definition of hypnosis. Although modern adherents to the Nancy school have replaced suggestion with such phrases as "task motivation" and "demand characteristics," the central focus of induction procedures used both clinically and experimentally is on reduced sensory input, reduced muscle tone, sleep, and relaxation.

Hull also noted that "subjects in deep hypnosis normally present a picture of rather complete relaxation" (Hull, 1933, p. 310) and attributed to this relaxation the powers of reducing spontaneous symbolic or thought activities to the extent that hypnotic subjects were more susceptible to external stimuli.

Even the most modern investigators, regardless of their conceptualization of hypnosis, have adhered quite regularly to induction procedures which involved suggestions of sleep and/or relaxation. In the majority of experimental works accomplished in recent years, the induction of hypnosis has been through the use of portions of the Stanford Hypnotic Susceptibility Scale (SHSS; Weitzenhoffer & Hilgard, 1959, 1962), the Harvard Group Hypnotic Susceptibility Scale (HGHSS; Shor & Orne, 1962), the Barber Suggestibility Scale (BSS; Barber, 1965), or variations thereof. Curiously enough, variations usually involve the avoidance of the word "sleep" but not of "relaxation." Despite this fact, there have been very few studies which have directly compared hypnotic relaxation induction with nonhypnotic relaxation instructions in order to understand the effects of this central focus of induction procedures. (In fact, the major controversy involving relaxation and hypnosis has been over the comparison of hypnosis defined as relaxation instructions and instructional sets other than nonhypnotic relaxation instructions.)

In 1969, Paul (1969) reported a study comparing Jacobson's progressive relaxation, Kline's hypnotic relaxation and self-instructions to relax, but not to sleep, using measures of heart rate, respiration rate, muscle tension, skin conductance, and self-reported anxiety. His findings indicated that during the first session, relaxation produced significant changes in all systems except skin conductance. Hypnosis changed only the respiration rate, and no changes were noted in the control group. However, during the second session the differences between relaxation and hypnosis disappeared and both produced changes significantly different from the control instructions (again, with the exception of skin conductance), a finding commensurate with the view of hypnosis ultimately being equated with relaxation.

The lag of effect of hypnotic-relaxation could well be due to anxiety engendered by our cultural views of hypnosis, and aroused in the subjects upon becoming aware of being "hypnotized." Familiarity with the hypnotic situation, as with any new situation, tends to alleviate fears and readjust the organism to a homeostatic response base. The difficulties created by the initial anxiety of subjects in data interpretation has been noted by Cogger and Edmonston (1971).

The lack of change in skin conductance in Paul's data received some clarification from McAmmond, Davidson and Kovitz (1971) in their study of stress reactions in dental situations. Using a hypnotic-relaxation, a relaxation and a no-instruction control group, skin conductance responses to pain were compared and a differential effect, depending on baseline measures, was found. In subjects with initially high skin conductance, relaxation produced a significant decrease in response to pain, with "...the difference between hypnosis and control group means...just short of the required significance" (McAmmond, Davidson, & Kovitz, 1971, p. 238). As the baseline was reduced, the effect was obviated. Again, hypnotic and nonhypnotic relaxation produced similar results and the conceptual separation of hypnosis and relaxation becomes less and less tenable.

Starr and Tobin (1970) drew a similar conclusion from their data comparing the expectancy of hypnosis and a form of Wolberg's progressive relaxation induction (Wolberg, 1948) which excluded references to hypnosis. Both the BSS objective and subjective scores showed significant effects for relaxation, leading them to conclude that: "the relaxation induction procedure itself should be more closely studied" (Starr & Tobin, 1970, p. 266).

One of the few more recent studies to compare hypnosis with nonhypnotic relaxation procedures is that by Coleman (1976), in which he compared hypnosis with relaxation with respect to (a) response suggestions from standardized hypnotic susceptibility scales, (b) a scale of subjective experience, and (c) EEG and EMG measurements. His general results were in line with other studies of direct comparisons. First, the hypnosis and relaxation groups do not differ from one another with respect to response suggestions. Curiously enough, it was one of the relaxation groups that responded significantly better than a control group. Second, alpha data taken *between* responses to suggestions during the testing period (including baseline measures) showed no difference among the groups: however, when the EEG data taken *during* responding were analyzed, a relationship between hypnotic susceptibility and alpha production was noted. Third, EMG data revealed no significant difference among groups, indicating that hypnosis and relaxation do not differ even in this premier measure of the latter. Fourth, and last, the analysis of the subjective rating scales also revealed that there were no differences among the hypnotized and the two relaxation groups.

This latter finding is the experimental analogue of the data previously presented from clinical patients, who subjectively viewed hypnosis primarily as relaxation. Subjects in an experimental setting offered two sets of instructions—hypnosis or relaxation—have the same subjective experience, and Barber and Calverley's early (1965) contention that the most effective component of hypnotic induction procedures is the suggestion of relaxation or sleep may have been quite prophetic.

Thus, Coleman, in his study designed to test the general hypothesis that the only difference between hypnotic induction procedure and relaxation instructions is the label assigned to them, has shown "...that relaxation procedures enhance suggestibility and produce subjective feelings similar...to those produced in hypnosis...and that physiological findings...support ...the idea that little, if any, differences exist between hypnosis and relaxation." (Coleman, 1976, p. 162.)

Even though the only evidence directly comparing relaxation with hypnotic relaxation leads to the previous conclusion—that more serious consideration must be given to the Pavlovian position, and particularly to the proposition that hypnosis involves, in the main, little more than the relaxation of the organism as a prerequisite to further hypnotic phenomena, —several objections have been raised to the general format of using a relaxed, but not hypnotized group of subjects as an appropriate control group for hypnotic studies.

The first came from within our own laboratories. It occurred to us that it was absurd to tell a subject not to become hypnotized, if he/she did not know what it was like to be hypnotized through a formal hypnotic induction. Consequently, our subjects are now put through formal inductions prior to experimental sessions, so that they know what it is they are *not* supposed to do.

The second objection stems originally from the practitioner's viewpoint and only more recently from the experimental literature. Briefly stated, it is the idea that subjects "slip into and out of" hypnosis during experimental sessions, and thus a comparison between hypnosis and nonhypnotic relaxation (or any control group, other than nonhypnotizable individuals) is impossible. The implications of this line of reasoning have been discussed elsewhere (Edmonston, 1972) but suffice it to say that such reasoning begs the control group question and expounds a virtually untestable position.

The third objection revolves around the "other type" of hypnosis—active or waking hypnosis. After all, Bernheim (1964) pointed out that suggestion can take place in the nonhypnotic state, and White (1941) spoke of an active and a passive hypnosis. The problem of "active" and "passive" trance has been explored by Ham and Edmonston (1971).

Following a lead noted in Plapp's dissertation (1967), Ham and I (1971) measured the reaction times of thirty subjects, equally divided into three susceptibility equated groups: (a) relaxation control (thirteen minutes of instructions to relax, but not to enter hypnosis or fall asleep); (b) a relaxation induction (SHSS-A eye-closure instructions); and (c) an alert induction (modeled after that of Liebert, Rubin & Hilgard, 1965). The results are summarized in Figure 13.12.

The reaction times of the relaxation control and the relaxation induction groups were significantly longer than those of the alert induction group, and showed a progressive increase with time. We concluded that "...the inhibition of motor responsiveness following hypnotic induction is not specifically related to a 'trance state,' but rather is at least partially determined by the suggestions of relaxation" (Ham & Edmonston, 1971, p. 330). On the surface, this conclusion seems to fall in nicely with what has gone before regarding our understanding of the relationship between hypnosis and relaxation. However, we also concluded that "relaxation, drowsiness and sleep are effective variables in the hypnotic induction procedure, provided the desired subsequent behavior...is commensurate with such a condition" (Ham & Edmonston, 1971, p. 331). Now this view harkens directly back to a conclusion drawn a number of years ago, that hypnotic inductions are effective in producing, enhancing or otherwise changing certain specific response categories and not others (Edmonston & Pessin, 1966).

The two conclusions reached—that there is enough experimental evidence to entertain the conjecture that hypnosis, as we have come to understand it through its history, is basically physical relaxation, and that the combined nature of the instructions and measurement criterion determine the definition, in short, that subjects do what they are told—are not contradictory.

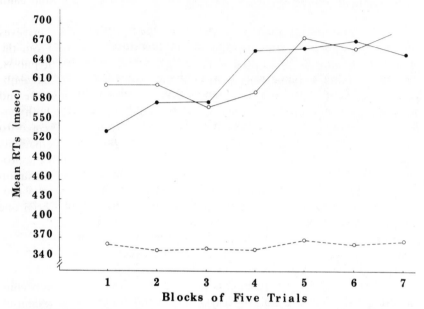

FIGURE 13.12. *Mean reaction times of relaxation control (solid circle, solid line), relaxation induction (open circle, solid line) and alert induction (open circle, dashed line) groups.*

To understand hypnosis and hypnotic phenomena we must return to first principles, to our historical heritage. Hypnotic induction procedures have traditionally been relaxation-oriented in both the clinic and the laboratory. Particularly for the clinician, inductions are a constant repetition of such phrases as "Take a deep breathe and relax." "Let all of the tension go out of your body." "Relax your leg muscles, your thigh muscles." "Go into a pleasant state of relaxation," etc.

The effects of these clinical inductions have recently been reported (Edmonston, 1977). Ninety-nine patients from active clinical practices were queried with respect to the following points: (a) "In your own words, describe what being in a hypnotic state (trance) is like for you. Please be as detailed as possible"; (b) "What for you as a hypnotized individual, is unique about hypnosis?" (c) "How do you determine when you are hypnotized? For example, is there some sensation, some change you perceive? Please describe in detail"; and (d) "Please describe anything else about hypnosis which seems important to you."

A classical content analysis of all of the responses to each item was made independently by three experimenters. Inter-judge reliabilities ranged from .93 to .99. Data from the first three items indicated that the preponderance of individuals offered responses categorized by terms of relaxation, calm and peacefulness.

It is quite clear that hypnosis, in the perceptions of patients, involves primarily relaxation and its attendant feelings and sensations. From the subjective standpoint of patients being treated in the context of hypnosis, the primary component in hypnosis is relaxation. One of the most obvious reasons for patients to note this equation is, as indicated above and elsewhere (Edmonston, 1972), that induction techniques involve both verbal and physical suggestions of relaxation. The stimuli presented to patients are suggestions of relaxation and, not too surprisingly, patients respond with relaxation responses and appropriate perceptions of the process as relaxation. Thus, as has been evident for two centuries, relaxation is an inseparable part of what is traditionally known as hypnotic procedures, and the response to these procedures had traditionally been one of relaxation.

THE RELAXATION RESPONSE

Benson, Beary, and Carol (1974, see also Benson, 1975) have recently compared some of the physiological parameters of the "relaxation response" with hypnosis and other "mental techniques" (e.g., transcendental meditation, autogenic training, zen, yoga), and found that most of these techniques, *including hypnosis,* are accompanied by physiological changes associated with the response: decreased O_2 consumption (Dudley, et al., 1964; Whitehorn, et al., 1932), respiratory rate (Barber, 1970), and heart rate (Barber, 1970); increased EEG intensity of slow alpha waves and theta waves, and skin resistance (Davis & Kantor, 1935; Estabrooks, 1930); and no change in blood pressure (Crasilneck & Hall, 1959) and rectal temperature.

Our own data showed a decrease in heart rate in both hypnosis and nonhypnotic relaxation (see above), and an increase in skin resistance (Edmonston & Pessin, 1966; Stern, et al., 1963). In the former studies, however, the skin resistance changes in the hypnotized group did not differ from that of the control group (Edmonston, 1968). However, in the cases of Edmonston and Pessin (1966) and Stern et al., (1963) studies, the comparison groups were uninstructed in a comfortable position for a time period equal to that of the hypnotic induction. This was sufficient time to become relaxed, although they were not specifically instructed to do so. (These studies were conducted before we began using a nonhypnotic relaxation group as a comparison in our laboratories.) London and McDevitt (1970) also reported small basal skin resistance differences between high and low susceptible subjects.

With respect to EEG changes and hypnosis, most researchers have compared the alpha densities with susceptibility, rather than comparing alpha densities between hypnosis and no hypnosis (e.g., Galbraith et al., 1970; London, Hart, & Leibovitz, 1968; Morgan, McDonald & Hilgard, 1974; Nowlis & Rhead, 1968). Edmonston and Grotevant (1975) did find a considerable rise in percentage of alpha upon induction in one experiment and no significant difference between a hypnotic and a nonhypnotic relaxation group in alpha production. Both of these data fit nicely with the relaxation response EEG data.

Regarding body temperature, the data are inconclusive. London and McDevitt (1970) found lower back and foot temperatures and higher hand temperatures in "tranceables" as opposed to "non-tranceables." Reid and Curtsinger (1968), Timney and Barber (1969) and Jackson, Barkley and Pashko (1976) have all reported an unsuggested rise in oral temperature and/or skin temperature (Reid & Curtsinger, 1968) upon induction of hypnosis. Fear, excitement, or anxiety, which cause an elevation in body temperature, may have confounded the results of the first two of these studies, while the activity of the hypnotic subjects did the same for the latter (Jackson, Barkley, & Pashko, 1976).

Timney and Barber (1969) observed that oral temperature tended to rise to a greater degree in subjects who had not previously participated in hypnosis. Oral temperature tended to rise less when subjects participated in an additional hypnotic session. Also, when subjects were asked to take part in a second "hypnotic experiment," they appeared less apprehensive than during the first. The Jackson, Barkley, and Pashko (1976) "neutral condition" subjects followed a hypnotic induction which included feelings of warmth in the hand, and hand and finger movements. Movement was not required of their control groups and thus confounds the interpretation of their data.

On the other hand, Doupe, Miller, and Keller (1939), who tested the same subjects in a series of experiments, with the identical hypnotic induction procedure, reported no change in rectal and skin temperature with hypnosis. The same finding with respect to oral temperature was reported by Cogger and Edmonston (1971), who used a nonhypnotic relaxation control group. The only other study also directly comparing hypnosis with relaxation (Peters & Stern, 1973) produced similar results. Neither peripheral skin temperatures nor vasomotor responses distinguished between the two conditions, and the authors concluded that the changes in both measures "cannot be attributed to anything other than relaxation" (Peters & Stern, 1973, p. 106).

The physiology of subjects in hypnosis tends to yield the same sort of changes as that of subjects in a relaxation condition. These changes (or lack thereof) closely parallel those seen in the relaxation response described by Benson, Beary and Carol (1974).

Final Remarks

In the first edition this chapter concluded, "Our suspicion is that with appropriate controls we may find that neutral hypnosis is synonymous with relaxation." It is more than a suspicion now. Both patients and experimental subjects have demonstrated that the responses to traditional hypnotic induction procedures (whether subjectively reported or objectively measured) equate neutral hypnosis with relaxation. That neutral hypnosis and relaxation are equated is not an artifact of history, but a statement of a persistent finding in the data. The equation cannot be ignored, but must be considered in the interpretation of data and attempts to assign hypnosis a unique role in human experience.

Gerald S. Blum *is a Professor in the Department of Psychology at the University of California, Santa Barbara. After receiving his Ph.D. in psychology from Stanford University in 1948, he joined the University of Michigan faculty, where he remained until moving to the University of California in 1968. During that time he also served as a consultant in clinical psychology to the Veterans Administration (1949-59), devoted some time to research in Italy as a Fulbright Scholar (1954-55), spent a year as fellow at the Center for Advanced Studies in the Behavioral Sciences (1959-60), and also was the recipient of a Social Science Research Council Faculty Research award (1961-62), a Ford Foundation behavioral science grant (1956-61), and several National Institute of Mental Health research grants over a twenty-year period. His research interests have focused on the experimental investigation of psychoanalytic theory and the development of a conceptual model of the mind by means of hypnotic research techniques. Publications include* The Blacky Pictures, Psychoanalytic Theories of Personality, A Model of the Mind, *and* Psychodynamics: The Science of Unconscious Mental Forces.

Blum *describes the line of research he and his students have been following for two decades. Blum's research is an attempt to develop models of mental processes patterned after those of cybernetic circuitry. Cognitive arousal is viewed as analogous to an electronic gain control that serves to amplify the signal regardless of the informational content. Affective arousal is conceptualized as ranging from free-floating pleasure to free-floating anxiety.*

Blum has developed hypnotic training techniques to teach subjects how to gain precise and systematic control over their levels of cognitive and affective arousal. He calls these hypnotic training techniques "programming."

14

Hypnotic Programming Techniques in Psychological Experiments

GERALD S. BLUM

For me, hypnosis is a research tool par excellence for peering into black boxes and deciding how to diagram their contents. The particular black boxes I find intriguing contain functions of the human mind that are involved in processing stimulus inputs for eventual response. Central topics for research therefore include such items as the role of amplification level, or cognitive arousal, in mental functions; factors affecting the reverberation of thoughts; the influence of various types of affective arousal; perceptual inhibition; and the like. Together these and other functions comprise a conceptual model of the mind that we have been evolving through laboratory experiments over the past two decades. (For an account of the origins of the model, see Blum, 1961.)

Very early in the efforts of our research group it became apparent that such an undertaking requires an exceptional degree of control over experimental variables, not possible with conventional psychological techniques. In 1957 we decided to enlist the aid of hypnosis in programming our subjects' minds, and a whole new dimension of research immediately opened before us. As a research strategy, we choose to work intensively with small numbers of highly trained hypnotic subjects, usually undergraduate students, who are paid to participate in many different investigations throughout the course of a year or more. On the basis of a brief screening interview, anyone with past or present cardiac illness or a severe nervous disorder is excluded. If the prospective subject is a minor, his parents are asked to indicate in writing their willingness for him to take part in experiments involving hypnosis. Next the Stanford Hypnotic Susceptibility Scales are administered, usually with the purpose of eliminating low scorers. Those selected for training are then given a personal history questionnaire to fill out.

Each subject (S) typically is scheduled for two sessions a week, each lasting about an hour and a half, throughout the academic year. At the outset S is told that he will be given feedback concerning the research after he has completed all the experiments. He is asked to respect the confidential nature of the tasks, just as his own responses are kept in confidence by members of the research staff. A sharp distinction is continually preserved between the "outside world" and the laboratory, so that crossing the threshold signifies the transition from one realm to the other. This psychological separation further cuts down the possibility for laboratory responses to occur outside. Very likely it also contributes to the effectiveness of training inside the laboratory by minimizing interference from everyday preoccupations. Upon termination S is given a lengthy debriefing in both hypnotic and waking states. The procedures and experiments are explained in detail and all suggestions are carefully removed and tested for their disappearance. Stress is also laid on the inadvisability of indulging in self-hypnosis or attempting to hypnotize others.

The various hypnotic programming techniques utilized to pursue our conceptual variables experimentally will be illustrated in the course of an overview of several major research topics chosen for laboratory study.

Cognitive Arousal

Some years back our conceptual model led us to differentiate two aspects of arousal, "cognitive" and "organismic." Before describing research that has grown out of this distinction, a brief account will be given of the hypnotic training in which S learns to control his level of cognitive arousal in varying degrees.

Under hypnosis (H), lying on a couch with eyes closed, S is told that we can conceive of the human mind as always operating at a particular level of amplification or "mental arousal" ranging anywhere between a peak of alertness and concentration, where mental contents are especially vivid and clear, and a low point approaching stupor, where thoughts are very fuzzy and unclear. The analogy is drawn to the gain control on a TV set, which affects reception regardless of the channel tuned to at the moment. Just as that gain control can be turned up or down, so also can the amplification level of S's mind be brought under systematic control with the aid of H. Only the contents of the mind are to be affected by this manipulation, *not* the muscles or senses (thereby excluding the organismic component of arousal). Then *S* is told to view his mental amplification as if under the control of a dial, the midpoint of which corresponds roughly to his normal waking level of mental arousal.

The experimenter (*E*) next instructs *S* that his dial is now gradually being turned up and up until it reaches the very top, and as this happens his thoughts are becoming more and more clear and distinct. (Clarity is singled out for emphasis by *E* during the arousal induction for two reasons: Change in clarity was the one dimension common to the subjective experiences of a group of *S*s when we began exploring the manipulation of cognitive arousal without specific instruction as to its effects, and some experimental tests designed to isolate various dimensions, including clarity, magnitude of imagery, and speed of thought, revealed that alterations in clarity alone duplicated the effects of cognitive arousal induced as an unspecified whole.) *S* nods when he thinks he is at the peak of arousal and *E* asks him to make a mental note of what his mind is like at that point and also to describe it aloud. *E* then exhorts *S* to turn his amplification dial up even more until *S* is certain he can go no higher. This peak level of cognitive arousal is labeled "plus double A" (+AA) for *S*. The imaginary dial is returned to the midpoint, labeled "zero" (0), and *S* notes and reports mental contents at that level. Next he is instructed to move up the scale halfway between 0 and +AA, a level designated as "plus A" (+A). Repeated practice is then given at each of the three levels, typically by asking *S* to visualize and describe the same scene, such as the contents of the experimental room, under 0, +A, and +AA.

If *E* deems the reports appropriate and sufficiently discriminable in terms of their clarity and vividness, and *S* can easily move from one level to another, the next phase of training is begun. Now the amplification dial is turned downward from 0 until it reaches the lowest point at which contact with *E* still remains (*S* is carefully instructed that he must never go so deeply into a stupor as not to be able to hear *E*'s voice). This low point, also duly noted and described, is labeled "minus double A" (-AA). *E* then proceeds to have *S* fill in the fifth degree of cognitive arousal halfway between 0 and -AA, which is called "minus A" (-A). Repeated practice is given first at the lower levels, and then the whole range is eventually brought into play, both with standard thoughts suggested by *E* and freely varying contents supplied spontaneously by *S*. A typical account of imagery under -AA is: "There's no shape to the room, I'm just in something, lying on something, everything's gray and fuzzy, no images or anything"; in contrast to +AA where minute details of the room are visualized and the mental image is described as "very clear, very perfect, delineated exactly, with vivid colors." If at any time *E* discovers that affects, such as pleasure or anxiety, occur concomitantly with the changes in cognitive arousal, he immediately severs the connection via hypnotic instruction and proceeds to check on the efficacy of the instruction. A problem that often needs additional work at this stage is the speed with which S can reach the desired level of arousal. Speed is timed by having S say "Now" when he thinks he is at the correct level. For our experimental purposes it is essential for S to learn to respond appropriately within a few seconds of E saying a cue.

The next step involves practice with S's eyes open, still under H. Now the arousal cues are acting upon externally based percepts as well as upon thoughts and internally based percepts. After this series is mastered, he goes through similar routines while sitting up under H with eyes open. Successful execution is followed by instructions to the effect that S will be able to do equally well with the cues in the waking state, at which time he is to be amnesic for the hypnotic training. He will not pay any attention to the fact that cues are given to him by E, but he will respond in the desired manner whenever a cue is presented in the laboratory (not outside). The response is to remain in effect at a constant level until E gives a signal to terminate. Nothing about the procedure will seem at all strange to him in the waking state. S is brought out of H and the cues are presented to him posthypnotically in either oral or written form until E is satisfied with the apparent level and timing of their execution. For most of our highly susceptible Ss, the procedures described thus far consume no more than one or two sessions. S's training is then ready to be put to a somewhat more rigorous series of experimental tests.

Two tasks currently routinely employed by us to check on the cognitive arousal training are hexagram salience and the Stroop Color-Word Test.[1] The salience technique consists of the oral presentation of a string of six consonants at the rate of one per second to which S merely listens, followed by an interval in which S engages in a filler activity such as counting beats of the metronome, and then a six-second report period when S says aloud whatever consonant spontaneously pops into mind at each beat. Salience of stimulus consonants at the time of report is measured by a scoring system based primarily upon their reappearance in the report series, with some weight also given to correspondence in position. The cognitive arousal cues, if working properly, should produce an ordered set of salience scores ranging from low to high as arousal increases. This ordering should occur both when the cues are placed in effect during the hexagram presentation or during the filler activity immediately following, but not when the cue onset and offset precede the presentation at the start of a trial. The latter serves as a check on possible simulation by S. Likewise the cues should yield an ordered set of speeds when the color-word interference chart of the Stroop is read under each of the five levels of cognitive arousal. On the other hand,

1. The application of our cognitive arousal cues to the Stroop task was first undertaken by Paul Bakan at the Stanford Laboratory of Hypnosis Research. Our subsequent investigations are reported in Blum and Graef (1971).

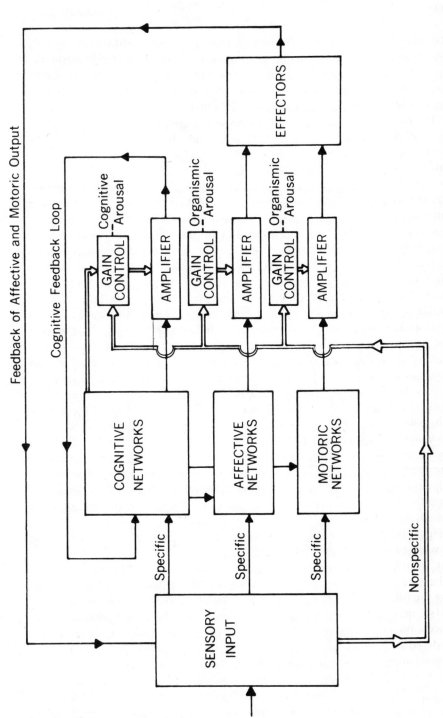

FIGURE 14.1. *A model of the mind (Form T): Signal routes (Single lines) and amplification control routes (double lines). (From Blum, Geiwitz, & Hauenstein, 1967).*

the simple chart containing only patches of color should be minimally susceptible to facilitation under heightened arousal beyond S's normal waking control performance, which is easily carried out in a highly motivated state. The lower arousal cues though, –A and –AA, can be expected to interfere even with execution of this simple task.

One of our first series of studies involving cognitive arousal cues was conducted in 1964–65 with a male S who had already participated in the research program for a couple of years. His data (Blum, Geiwitz, & Stewart, 1967) were used to clarify the effects of various sources of amplification control upon cognitive processing. Figure 14.1 portrays amplification routes in our conceptual model of the mind. It can be seen that sensory input, in addition to activating specific cognitive, affective, or motoric networks, also constitutes a major source of control over amplification in the system. The amount of nonspecific sensory input regulates boosting capacity (level of gain control) of the three amplifiers that process signals from their respective networks. The quantity of nonspecific input itself depends, at any given time, upon both external stimulation from the environment and sensory feedback of muscular and glandular responses of the effectors. In addition to this nonspecific amplification control route, there is another double line from cognitive networks to the gain control of the cognitive amplifier, suggesting that cognitive arousal can also be regulated directly by cognitive messages.

We operationalized the feedback of affective output by programming S to experience three degrees of anxiety and also three degrees of pleasure in response to cues. (The topic of affective arousal will be dealt with in a later section.) Motoric feedback was manipulated by five degrees of muscle movement ranging from complete relaxation to extremely active twitching and contracting of muscles. External sensory input was regulated by feeding in various intensities of white noise through earphones. The remaining source, cognitive control of amplification, was tapped by the low and high cognitive arousal cues.

Besides these independent variables, we needed a sort of "tracer" that could be sent repeatedly through the cognitive subsystem under the various arousal conditions so as to reveal the amounts of amplification actually available for processing. Here we utilized as the dependent variable a visual discrimination task. On a given trial S looked into a tachistoscope and was asked to identify one of seven stimuli flashed briefly. The stimuli were one-inch-square photographs of an X on a white background; they differed only in darkness of the lines. Each X stimulus was identified by a different letter of the alphabet. Unbeknown to S, the latency of his response in making a judgment was also recorded exactly by a timer. By means of the prior hypnotic training it was possible to induce each one of the several kinds of arousal in pure form, in a specified amount, and to control both the onset and offset of the particular arousal reaction. Analysis of their effects upon identification of the Xs enabled us to make significant comparisons among the reactions.

Figure 14.2 presents the order of median latencies for the nineteen independent variables that were paired randomly with the X stimuli in fifteen two-hour sessions of ninety trials each. The four cognitive arousal cues employed in the study clearly demonstrate the expected order of faster to slower responses as cognitive arousal varies from + AA to –AA.

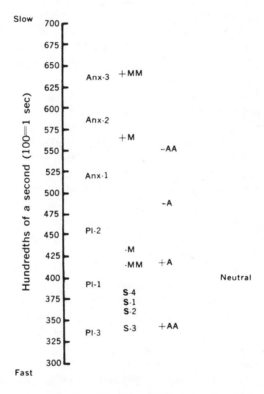

FIGURE 14.2. *Order of median latencies for cue conditions (From Blum, Geiwitz, & Stewart, 1967).*

Hypnotic techniques also permitted further explorations not possible using conventional methods. For example, we were interested in discovering whether the cues were having their observed effects in the early perceptual registration or "perceiving" phase as opposed to the later "judgment" phase of a trial where *S* has to compare the perceived X with the file of Xs in his memory. The procedure, somewhat similar to that employed in the first experiment but involving selected cues and a smaller N, was identical in form for both the perceiving and the judging parts. The subject began by responding to a cue. When the X flashed, he closed his eyes and "fixed the image" of what he had just seen. In other words, he took a sort of mental photograph, without making any decision as to which X it was. Indeed, due to prior hypnotic instruction, his mental file of Xs was not consciously available to him during the process. When he had fixed the image clearly in his mind, he was to say "now" (producing a measurable latency by means of the voice relay), put the image aside for later recall, and open his eyes. A new cue was then inserted. After nine seconds this cue was removed and the subject closed his eyes. Six seconds later he heard a distinct click through the earphones, which was a signal to "bring back" the previously fixed image along with his now available file of Xs and to judge which X it was (latency again recorded).

In the perceiving phase, cues were randomly assigned to the first phase of this two-part procedure, the image fixing. After viewing the stimulus under the influence of one of these conditions, the image was brought back by S and judged under the neutral condition. In the judging phase of each trial, image fixing was done under the neutral condition, whereas judging was affected by one of the eight cues. Thus the influence of each condition on perceiving and judging, separately, was assessed by response latency.

Another deviation from the original procedure was that the effect of the cue (other than sounds) had been hypnotically programmed to last through the response, for a fixed period of time, in both parts of the sequence. In order to control for cue influence on responding per se, a set of simple response trials was interspersed throughout the experimental ones. In the perceiving phase such trials were preceded by a card saying "no image," and S merely observed the flash of the black X stimulus, closed his eyes without fixing an image, and said "now." In the judging phase the advance signal card contained a prearranged X response, and later at the click S just repeated the prescribed X label instead of forming a judgment.

In the data analysis, pure response effects were first partialled out by pairing experimental and control trials and adjusting the mean experimental latencies by covariance analysis. Cue differences achieved overall statistical significance in the *perceiving* phase but not in the judging. The directions of effect in the perceiving phase paralleled those of the earlier study: high anxiety, lowered mental arousal, and to a lesser extent strong muscle activity continued to produce decremental effects; very strong pleasure (P1–3) and + AA both accelerated responding, as did the loud sound levels to a smaller degree.

Another kind of question important for the evolution of our model involves the action of different conditions in combination rather than singly. Here we chose for intensive investigation the two conditions that had exerted a facilitating influence in the original experiment, very strong pleasure and heightened mental arousal. Again the same design was employed except that *S* was programmed to respond simultaneously to the two cues shown together in the adapting field of the tachistoscope before the X flash. There were six combinations in all, P1–3 and no pleasure being paired with + AA, + A, and 0 levels of cognitive arousal. Forty-two randomized trials were run for each of these combinations. The mean response latencies clearly indicate the *additive* nature of the interaction. The shortest latencies occur for the P1–3 and + AA combination, the longest for the neutral pairing, and the intermediate in ordered progression for the remaining combinations.

A different line of investigation by Geiwitz (1966) applied the cognitive arousal cues and other hypnotic programming techniques in a comprehensive experimental approach to the phenomenon of boredom. Four male *S*s served in each of four experiments: (1) a "natural series" in which various levels of boredom were induced by varying durations of a simple repetitive task (making check marks on a piece of paper), and self-ratings were employed to assess levels of arousal, constraint, unpleasantness, and repetitiveness; (2) a "partly synthetic" series in which the synthesis of boredom was attempted by inducing various levels of arousal, constraint, unpleasantness, and repetitiveness by means of posthypnotic cues and the degree of ensuing boredom was indicated by *S*'s verbal report; (3) a "wholly synthetic" series identical to the preceding except that *S* was instructed additionally to keep the three other variables constant at a neutral level while the fourth was being manipulated; and (4) a "factorial" series in which, with arousal held neutral, constraint, unpleasantness, and repetitiveness were manipulated conjointly in a two x two x two factorial design.

Geiwitz found reported boredom to be associated with low arousal, increased feelings of unpleasantness, constraint, and repetitiveness. Boredom can be produced or synthesized by lowering arousal or by increasing one of the other three factors. Each variable tends to redintegrate a complex of all four which, in turn, results in a report of intense boredom. Each alone, however, with the others held constant, can produce boredom, a conclusion unequivocal for lowered arousal and constraint, but less certain for unpleasantness and repetitiveness.

In discussing the role of low cognitive arousal, he states:

> Several experimental findings deserve further research attention. For example, the association of boredom with low arousal, as we mentioned in the introduction, is by no means generally accepted. Subjective repetitiveness as the most equivocal factor is surely not in line with common interpretations of boredom. The major role of constraint, a factor typically ignored in scientific discourse, suggests that its absence is a serious oversight.
>
> In regard to arousal, we might suggest that theoretical disagreement is at least partly a semantic illusion. In this study, we defined and used the construct with

major emphasis on its cognitive aspects. Let us then say that low *cognitive* arousal
has been shown to be influential in boredom. Berlyne, the major theorist holding
a high arousal position, may well agree with these results; the cause of high
arousal in his system is inhibited cortical activity—low cognitive arousal? In other
words, we may be discussing two distinguishable forms of arousal, one cortical or
cognitive and the other more peripheral, sensorimotor, or organismic. All might
agree that cortical arousal is low in boredom; the dispute would center on the second level. (Geiwitz, 1966, p. 599).

Another illustration of our research use of the cognitive arousal cues
lies in the domain of psychodynamics, a special concern of the conceptual model (see Blum [1967] for an overview of our earlier work in this
area). A fertile field for the pursuit of psychodynamic phenomena is of
course dreamlike imagery. We chose to explore the influence of cognitive
arousal level upon such imagery through hypnotic programming of three
Ss, two males and one female, all of whom had previously been trained
to experience the five degrees of mental amplification and had been given
practice under H in having "dreamlike visual images, which can sometimes be quite bizarre." The Ss also were very familiar with the
Blacky Pictures (Blum, 1950), having told stories about Blacky in the
waking state, filled out the Defense Preference Inquiry, and narrated,
under H, personal experiences of their own suggested by each of the
pictures.

The aim of the study, conducted entirely under H, was to obtain dreamlike protocols under conditions that minimize distortions in reporting and
maximize interpretability. Accordingly, S was instructed to have his imagery grow directly or indirectly out of all three Blacky pictures shown to him
at the start of a trial. Looking in a tachistoscope, S saw each of three pictures clearly for 0.5 second with an interval of 0.5 second between them.
For the next twenty seconds he experienced his imagery with eyes closed until E said "Stop." At that point S's prior programming dictated that he give
a detailed account of his just completed dream and to indicate its completion by saying "that's all," whereupon he proceeded spontaneously to give
his own explanation of how each of the three pictures exposed on that trial
played a part in the images. S's statements were recorded and transcribed
for later analysis. At the end of each trial, S was told to rest, which meant
that he sat back in his chair and made himself amnesic for the entire trial
before going on to the next one.[2] This procedure minimizes distortion in
reporting because S narrates his dream immediately after experiencing it
and does not have to undergo a disruptive change of state, as from sleep to
waking in REM research, between dream and report. Reporting under H

2. The automatic invocation of amnesia between trials of an experiment is believed to
facilitate the independence of those trials, at least to the extent that conscious rumination is
precluded.

also seems to promote an exceptional degree of candor, exemplified by the following from the female *S*: "There was an image of a penis right in front of me, in front of my face, and it started growing and it grew until it was about twenty times as big as I was and then crushed me on the ground." Interpretability of the imagery is aided by *E*'s knowledge of the antecedent conditions, namely themes associated with the three Blacky pictures, plus *S*'s own associations given immediately afterward.

The independent variable in the study was degree of cognitive arousal. Before each trial, *E* said "Ready," a signal for *S* to look into the machine, and then spoke one of the five cues ranging from –AA to +AA. Three seconds were allowed to elapse while *S* reached the appropriate level and then the picture presentation began. The cognitive arousal cue remained in effect by instruction through the twenty seconds of dreamlike imagery (until *E* said "Stop"), at which time *S* automatically returned to the normal level (0) for his report. The N for each *S* was forty-five trials, nine at each of the five cognitive arousal levels, carried out over three sessions of fifteen randomized trials per session. Nine of the Blacky pictures in all were used, with various combinations of three presented randomly.

For the data analysis a team of three judges worked out a scoring guide that included cognitive alterations such as condensation, symbolism, lack of logic or morality, omnipotent wish-fulfilling fantasy, paranoid flavor, obsessive-compulsive quality, and depersonalization; stylistic variables such as productivity, activity of the scene, centrality of *S* and others in the dream, and presence of animals; and *S*s mode of coping with aggression, sex, and rejection. Once the categories were agreed upon, the judges independently scored each protocol blindly, that is, without knowledge of the cue condition, and any disagreements were discussed and resolved consensually.

Those trends that emerged from this exploratory approach showed the lowest level of arousal, –AA, to be more associated with magical elements, paranoid flavor, and sex anxiety, and less with active imagery. The following –AA protocols exemplify these findings:

Male S: magical solution—I saw this big knife, great big knife that was coming at me and felt like I should do something to it to destroy it or something like that. It was out to get me. It started to melt and gradually became harmless, just kind of turned into a big round molten lump. I had a feeling that I was alone. I looked about and there was no one there—a totally blank, blank void in which I was sitting. I could see no one. That's all.

Other male S: paranoid flavor—I was giving a speech to a group of people out on the streets and I was talking about civil rights but nobody was listening. They were jabbering with one another. So I sat there talking and this one person was watching off to the corner of my eye. It was a little kid, about seven and he kept staring. And so I finished the speech and I was thrown off the stand. They just threw me out in the street and then they just all climbed up and looked and they all started laughing. And they all started talking and I was the one that was listening this time until finally they started dispersing. And so I got up and started walking down the street. Then I fell into a manhole. And that was the end. That's all.

Female S: sex anxiety—There was the image of two dogs, a male and a female, and the boy was chasing the girl around in a circle and then the dogs changed into frogs. They were still hopping around with the boy chasing the girl in a circle and then they changed into turtles and it was like in slow motion. They were going very slowly, still chasing though. And then the girl all of a sudden pulled into her shell and stopped. And the boy caught up with her and climbed on top of her shell and sat there for a couple of minutes, kind of clawing at her shell or something and fell off and landed on his back. That's all.

In retrospect it seems likely that the general instruction to experience "dreamlike, often bizarre" visual imagery may have largely overshadowed the possible effects of cognitive arousal changes, since primary process elements abounded in all conditions. Nonetheless the form of hypnotic programming utilized in this study does seem to us promising for further work in the psychodynamic realm.

Finally, a study sought to test the speed with which subjects can shift from one level of cognitive arousal to another (Blum & Porter, 1972). One male and one female were given progressively shorter time durations in which to respond to the posthypnotic cues before viewing tachistoscopically flashed consonants under cue influence. A trial contained five cycles of tachistoscopic exposures followed by a report period. Each cycle consisted of an arousal cue shown for a specified duration, followed by the flash of a consonant, and then a two-digit number in response to which the subject began counting backward by threes, as fast as possible without making a mistake, until a second arousal cue appeared to start the second cycle. The counting interval between appearance of the number and the next cue was seven seconds. After the five viewing cycles, which paired the five arousal cues with five different consonants, were completed, a blank flash accompanied by the first of a series of clicks at one second intervals signalled the subject to begin his report. The latter consisted of the verbalization of whatever consonant came into mind at each of the next five successive clicks. The fate in the report of each cue-paired stimulus consonant served as the basis for determining whether or not the cue had sufficient time to act. The results indicated a striking capacity to shift degrees of cognitive arousal very rapidly to one extreme or the other, on the order of 100 milliseconds or less.

Cognitive Reverberation

A very different application of hypnosis as a research tool arose when we sought to explore experimentally that portion of the conceptual model relating to the "cognitive feedback loop" (see Figure 14.1). Each amplified signal is presumed to set up an autonomous feedback loop that sustains network activity until the loop gradually dies down, a process we refer to simply as "reverberation."

The construct of reverberation has its neuropsychological counterpart in the theories of Gerard, Hebb, Eccles, and others. Similar notions of perseverative activity have arisen in studies of information processing. Broadbent talks of "recirculation" through a short-term memory storage and Posner discusses a "central rehearsal," not necessarily overt or conscious. Most of the thought and research concerning reverberation has centered on its possible function. Typically the autonomous reactivation process is seen as strengthening the emergent structural trace—the consolidation hypothesis—or as retarding the natural decay of a cognitive network. Research on the consolidation hypothesis generally involves experimental interruption of the presumably active trace by means of electroconvulsive shock or chemicals. Up to a point, such interruptions show the predicted effect, that is, memory decrement as an inverse function of time after stimulus presentation. But interpretation of the data is not unequivocal. Alternative interpretations often include competition or interference, and lowered arousal. One of the major obstacles to a choice among these explanations has been a lack of knowledge regarding the precise effects on the organism of both electroconvulsive shock and chemicals. Discussion of the decay-retarding hypothesis is found most clearly in the area of human memory research. The interpretive problems here include the fact that many experiments attempt to prevent rehearsal in order to study the course of decay. The use of interpolated material for this purpose builds in the possibility for alternative explanation in terms of retroactive interference. (See Blum, Geiwitz, and Hauenstein [1967] for a more extended discussion of the above.)

Thus, a potential model-builder must conclude that the nature of reverberation and its function are poorly understood. Major questions remain: Is it possible to obtain clear-cut behavioral evidence with human subjects for the existence of autonomous reverberation? If so, how long does such activity last? To what kinds of influence is it responsive? This is how our empirical search began. We decided to attack the problem with our previously described "salience technique," which merely exposes S to stimuli without any learning set and, for reporting, only requires that he say those items that pop into mind spontaneously. It is assumed that strong networks will dominate mental activity if given the opportunity. This salience technique offers a purer measure of cognitive network strength than is provided by conventional methods such as recall, where the complex of learning, memory, and performance factors renders inference about an intervening process like reverberation especially hazardous.

In place of electroconvulsive shock or chemical interrupters, which are unsuited to normal human Ss, we substituted a brief excursion into the state of hypnosis. Some of our earlier work had indicated that the act of going into very deep H for a few seconds tends to impair conscious retrieval of immediately prior material from the waking state—an ideal probe which is easily applied with a trained S, can be manipulated precisely in time, and runs no risk of neurological damage.

In the first series of experiments (Blum, Geiwitz, & Hauenstein, 1967), S, a female graduate student in social work, was trained to enter deep hypnosis immediately upon receiving a tap on the left arm and to return to the waking state five seconds later in response to another prescribed signal. At the tap her eyes would close, her head would drop suddenly to one side, and she would report that her mind went blank. She described the hypnotic pause as disruptive of any ongoing train of thought—somehow she had to "start all over again" after the pause. Approximately three experimental sessions per week were then conducted throughout a summer. Each session typically consisted of three half-hour blocks of trials with ten-minute rest periods between blocks. All trials involved oral presentation, at the one-per-second rate, of a set of six consonants taken from a pool of 432 hexagrams, and S was instructed at the outset not to try to form associations to the consonants.

In the first study S counted beats during a standard twenty-second interval between E's presentation and her own report. On the beat after she reached fifteen she began reporting consonants. Experimental and control manipulations consisted of taps on the left or right arm during the interval. A tap on the left arm as mentioned earlier, signified that she should automatically stop counting and enter H immediately. E then allowed five beats to elapse. On the sixth, S said a number that served a double purpose: It signaled S to become wide awake again and also told her where to resume counting aloud to fifteen. The control tap on the right arm merely signified that S was to remain awake with eyes closed during the subsequent five-second pause—a period occupied by stray thoughts, usually concerning events of the day. Taps were delivered in random order by a ruler at prescribed beats ranging from one to twelve seconds after the end of the hexagram presentation. S could not anticipate their arrival because she sat with her back to E. The experiment required six sessions, with a total N of eighteen trials for every waking or hypnotic pause at each one of the twelve seconds. The results in Figure 14.3 show the mean salience score for the H pause to be below that of waking (W) pause at every point along the time dimension. This finding, under circumstances where S never thought about consonants during the twenty-second interval, supports the notion of an ongoing process of reverberation vulnerable to disruption.

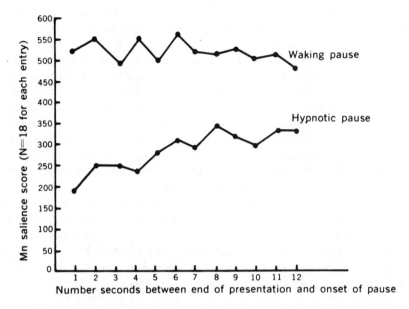

FIGURE 14.3. *Hypnotic interruptions of reverberation (From Blum, Geiwitz, & Hauenstein, 1967).*

These data permit the inference that the hexagram network remains active during the twenty-second interval; otherwise the H pause could not have had a disruptive effect upon network salience. But the basis for its continued activity is not certain, beyond the fact that conscious awareness need not be involved. In addition to autonomous reverberation, there is the possibility that *S*, knowing the relationship between her reported letters and those previously spoken by *E* to be under some kind of investigation, might be exercising an "unconscious intention" to retain the stimuli. Ideally one would like to replicate the findings in a situation where *S* does not realize she is performing in an experiment. Obviously the systematic execution of such a plan is not feasible, but we were able to insert a couple of nonintentional trials in the context of some later experiments. Nevertheless there was some statistical evidence in this first study that argued against intentionality. It turned out that the H pause not only disrupted reverberation of the stimulus hexagram but also reduced the likelihood of an intrusion from consonants given in the report on the preceding trial. Here the material was obviously not intended, by either *S* or *E*, to be carried over.

Another question concerns the duration of reverberatory activity. In the next study the five-second hypnotic and waking pauses were inserted near the end of trials lasting thirty seconds, one, two, and three minutes. Instead of counting beats of the metronome, which is understandably tedious over long periods, S was shown colored travel slides as a filler activity. At every duration the same results obtained as before—mean salience scores for the H pause were significantly lower than for the W pause.

It was in this setting that we added one of the nonintentional trials referred to earlier. E presented a hexagram (KXTGWM) and then "by mistake" projected a blank on the screen instead of a slide. Acting flustered, he exclaimed "Oh nuts, skip it!" and told S that he would have to run quickly through a series of slides to reach the spot in the tray where a fresh start could be made. After thirty seconds of a slide-changing E instructed S to say six consonants in time with the metronome. Incredulous, she asked "Now?" and proceeded to report KXTGMP. Thus five letters from the stimulus set reappeared when S obviously had no intention of retaining them.

Subsequent trials extending the length of the filler activity showed the same disruptive effect of the five-second H pause even after thirty minutes. At this juncture a two-hour nonintentional trial was introduced. E explained to S that he was expecting an important phone call and would have to terminate the session the moment it came. Presumably hearing a faint ring about twenty seconds after a stimulus set was spoken, he switched off the slide projector and went outside to answer the phone. S then departed for her job in another building where she typed letters. Two hours later E surprised her with a phone call and, holding the metronome against the receiver, asked for the report of six consonants. Three of the stimulus consonants recurred. Similar trials, discontinued shortly after S was given the hexagrams but with no further attempt to surprise her, were conducted with three-, four-, and five-hour intervals. At four hours the H pause still yielded a lower score than the W pause, and only after five hours did the report drop to chance expectancy with the W pause.

The next question dealt with the influence of competition upon the reverberation process. This was explored by filling a twenty-second interval with either a full twenty-second H pause; a twenty-second W pause; counting beats up to twenty; or looking at a slide accompanied by E's narration of a relevant anecdote. As always, the H pause, in which S's mind remained essentially blank for twenty seconds, resulted in the lowest salience scores. The W pause, least demanding of S's attention with its leisurely stray thoughts such as buying furniture for her new apartment, yielded the highest scores. Counting and listening to the narration, both of which were described by S as more involving than the W pause, produced intermediate scores.

The H pause had proven its practical worth as an experimental probe, but the basis of its disruptive action was not apparent. Another series of investigations sought to clarify the nature of the effect. One possibility lay in the discontinuity of shifting between waking and hypnotic states. So an experiment was carried out with S under hypnosis throughout the whole trial. In this case the H pause did not involve a shift, whereas the W pause did.

According to the discontinuity hypothesis, salience scores should be lower for the W than the H pause. Instead the same result as before was obtained; mean salience for the H pause was still significantly lower.

Another alternative invoked the concept of amplification level. The skill of quickly reaching a deep stage of hypnosis entails a sudden drop in cognitive arousal, reflected in the "blank mind" phenomenon. If the level of amplification in the system is turned down, then the reverberating signal along with any other ongoing signals should be affected according to our model.

Having the previously described experimental techniques at our disposal for manipulating degrees of cognitive arousal posthypnotically, we carried out the following study, again employing a twenty-second counting interval and the standard waking context for presentation and report. The conditions included the usual five-second H and W pause trials intermingled with five-second pauses varying in the five degrees of cognitive arousal, and also a posthypnotic blank mind cued by *E* saying "Blank." Mean salience scores formed a perfect progression for the five degrees of arousal from –AA on up to +AA. Thus there seems no reason to doubt that the process of reverberation is sensitive to brief changes in amplification. It is important to note that five seconds of relatively content-free amplification raised beyond the normal level (from 0 to +A to +AA) resulted in higher scores, indicating that the strength of reverberation can be influenced in both directions. Moreover the comparability of scores among the H, –AA, and Blank conditions suggests that lowered amplification is the key to understanding the H effect. *S* also reported the three to be subjectively similar except that she is awake during –AA and Blank.

Next, a control experiment was carried out to check on the possibility of report bias, that is, *S* reasoning consciously or unconsciously that, since five degrees of arousal are involved, her responses should obligingly yield differential, ordered results. Here each cognitive arousal cue was given ten seconds in advance of the hexagram and terminated five seconds before the presentation. Theoretically we should expect no effect on salience, but the opportunity for report bias still exists. The results showed that –AA in advance of the stimulus did not lower salience in comparison with 0, and +AA did not raise it. A further check on simulation was performed by tapping the best class of fakers we knew, psychologists, familiar with the salience design and even the scoring system. They tried to produce ordered responses for five different conditions announced to them just before the report period. Their efforts met with only very limited success.

We next undertook to replicate and extend the results with two male undergraduates (Blum, Hauenstein, & Graef, 1968; Blum, Graef, Hauenstein, 1968). One *S* was given the same procedure as had been used in the initial experiment with the female *S*. The mean salience score for the H pause was again below that of the W pause at every point along the time dimension, consistent with the notion of an ongoing process of reverberation vulnerable to disruption.

The second S was used to replicate the finding that degree of cognitive arousal, or amplification level, directly affects the course of reverberation. Instead of the H and W pauses, he was given posthypnotic cues that triggered five-second pauses of extremely high (+AA), or normal (0), or extremely low (-AA) cognitive arousal. The data supported the original observation that lowered amplification in the system cuts down the normal strength of reverberation, whereas heightened amplification yields greater salience than normal. Of thirty-six possible comparisons among +AA, 0, and -AA, there was only one reversal and two ties, all other entries bearing the predicted relationship.

To confirm the influence of competition upon the reverberation process, both Ss were asked to count metronome beats aloud (rather than silently) as the filler activity, based on the assumption that the aloud condition, with its sensory feedback of vocalization would constitute somewhat stronger competition. The salience scores did indeed reflect this seemingly slight difference in procedure. In trials testing the duration of reverberatory activity, one of the male Ss also turned out to be a fairly long reverberator; the other showed clear evidence for reverberation after a twenty-second interval, but by fifty seconds the H pause no longer had its characteristically disruptive effect.

The data obtained in all these studies with the three Ss led us to formulate the following principles of cognitive reverberation for the conceptual model:

1. Reverberation consists of autonomous reactivation of a network by the signal transmitted from that network at the time of its original activation.
2. Reverberation takes place independently of conscious awareness.
3. The reverberating signal is strongest at the time of network activation and gradually decreases until it dissipates.
4. Barring disruption, a single series of reverberations from a transient network apparently can last for hours in some individuals.
5. Reverberation acts to retard, in proportion to its own intensity, the intrinsic rate of decay in network strength.
6. The course of reverberation is a direct function of current amplification level in the system.
7. For a given level of amplification, strength of the reverberating signal is an inverse function of the strength of competing signals in process.

The foregoing series of investigations into the concept of cognitive reverberations illustrates the heuristic interplay of conceptual model and hypnotic research methodology. The model pointed systematically and insistently to questions requiring empirical answers at the molecular level not often encountered in behavioral research. Hypnotic techniques permitted an unprecedented degree of rigor and control, which make possible such a molecular approach. At the same time the various cautions necessary in work with hypnosis, such as the operation of demand characteristics, intentionality, and simulation, were shown to be amenable to empirical check.

Affective Arousal

Currently we program our Ss hypnotically to respond to a set of eleven posthypnotic affective cues ranging from a peak of free-floating pleasure $(+5)$ down to a neutral point (0) and up to a peak of free-floating anxiety (-5). A verbatim description of our anxiety procedures, at a time when Ss were programmed to experience only three degrees of intensity, is available elsewhere (Blum, 1967), so the present account will emphasize the pleasure training carried out with a male S who participated in a series of experiments during 1969-70.

Under H, while reclining on the couch, he was asked to recount a very pleasurable experience from his past. The episode he chose was a rock climbing venture in Yosemite (literally a peak experience!) where he led a group successfully. Next, in the course of reliving the episode he described his feelings as follows:

> Looking around where I was, a feeling of exultation, enjoyment, even a little superiority comes upon me...looking over the valley, it's very beautiful, a very pleasant feeling, very enjoyable...so good to be here, so exciting, people congratulating me.

He was told to make a good mental note of the feeling of pleasure and instructed to dissociate the feeling from the actual experience in which it took place. During the practice of this detached free-floating pleasure, he felt "very happy and excited, like nothing else really matters, I would like it to last." Next he was exhorted to experience the pleasure ever more strongly until he felt it could go no higher, at which point he made another mental note. Asked to compare that feeling with real-life experiences of pleasure, S replied: "It's indescribable, so much better than anything bounded by earth, in real life. I'm just so happy and joyous, it's hard to believe such a wonderful thing could happen." The label $+5$ was attached to this peak of pleasure so that whenever S is presented with that cue *in the laboratory only,* either awake or under H, he responds appropriately. Next the intermediate degrees of pleasure $(+1$ up to $+4)$ were trained in similar fashion and S was given practice in skipping around quickly from one level to another.

Prior to being brought out of H, S was informed that, as always, he would be amnesic for the training and respond to the posthypnotic cue presentations without conscious awareness or feelings of strangeness and curiosity. The scale from 0 to $+5$ was then practiced first with S lying awake on the couch and subsequently after he had moved to a chair.

Typical waking comments about his feelings in + 5 were "I'm *really* happy, don't know what about, just feel good all over...exulted and high, an elevated thing...a feeling of pleasure is just pervading me."

The following session saw the induction of the other half of the affective scale, degrees of anxiety ranging from the weak − 1 on up to the extreme of − 5. This was accomplished by having S relive under H a personal experience narrated earlier in response to the picture of Blacky chewing on Mama's collar:

> I came home from school one day in the fourth grade. No one was home. My mother wasn't there for the first time. I got kind of worried and upset. I wondered if something bad happened. I was scared...my first time home alone.

During hypnotic reliving S described himself as "very worried, scary...I feel a little shaky like I'm breathing harder than usual...my mouth is dry...feels like my heart is beating faster."

The anxiety feeling was then dissociated by instruction from the originating episode and brought to a peak, labeled − 5. At that level he described subjective experiences as follows: "Frightening, a feeling of impending doom...I don't know what I'm afraid of but it seems very real...I can't control it...my heart is beating faster, I'm breathing harder, I feel shaky with tingling sensations in my body, and my mouth is dry...anxiety is pervading my whole body and mind." The rest of the procedure paralleled the pleasure training, except that the GSR was used additionally to monitor S's physiological reactions.

Near the end of the session, back under H where amnesia is not in effect, E asked S what he thought about the anxiety training he had just undergone. His reply is illuminating:

> It was very interesting. Initially I thought it would be aversive but I understand it now. The anxiety itself is aversive but I understand why it would be important for the experiments. The anxiety is very real when it happens.

Asked if he were willing to tolerate that much anxiety in the course of future experiments, S replied in the affirmative. Care is always taken to keep S's anxiety reactions to the necessary experimental minimum. He receives considerable praise under H for having executed the cues properly. This friendly and sympathetic treatment by all members of the research team, combined with the displacement of the onus of anxiety onto the "experiments," probably helps to cushion the impact. Whenever possible, pleasure cues are also interspersed to maintain some rough affective balance.

Evidence for the validity of S's cued anxiety reactions comes from several sources: his own subjective reports, observation by Es of facial expressions, body movements, and so forth, and recorded changes in galvanic skin resistance. In addition to these introspective, observational, and physiological indices, by now we have accumulated a large amount of data demonstrating that the anxiety cues interfere in degree with a variety of experimental tasks.

The validity of the cued pleasure responses cannot be inferred as easily by observation, nor does any particular physiological concomitant seem to be characteristic across *S*s. "Face" validity (smiling, grinning, eyes lighting up) is often present in the case of expressive individuals, but more reliance must be placed on verbal report than with anxiety. Other independent checks are sometimes possible, however. In an unpublished study[3] with a female *S*, the monetary equivalents for each of the five degrees of pleasure were ascertained systematically under H. Money, duration, and degree of pleasure were manipulated so that two variables were held constant and *S* gave judgments regarding the third. Judgments of money rose in linear fashion as level and duration of pleasure increased. Each pleasure cue increased in average value fifty-eight cents more than the preceding one, and every additional second of time in the pleasure condition increased subjective worth by twenty-three cents. For example, *S*, not very well off financially, was willing to pay two dollars in order to experience six seconds of +5 pleasure!

Now that the affective arousal training has been presented in some detail, we can turn to experiments that employ the hypnotically programmed degrees of anxiety and pleasure. Other affects have also been trained in our *S*s, such as degrees of anger for use in an investigation of factors in the appreciation of hostile humor (Hauenstein, 1970), and a scale of interest-boredom applied to studies of time estimation (Graef, 1969), but we shall restrict our illustrations to anxiety and pleasure.

Anxiety and pleasure were included among the independent variables in the series of visual discrimination experiments (Xs flashed tachistoscopically) summarized in the section "Cognitive Arousal." It has already been mentioned that the facilitating influence of very strong pleasure combined additively with degrees of cognitive arousal. From Figure 14.2 we see that the three degrees of anxiety exerted progressively greater decremental effects upon *S*'s response latency, a result similar to previous findings with the anxiety cues applied to other tasks (Blum, 1967). A follow-up study was able to localize the pleasure and anxiety effects primarily in the perceiving rather than the judgmental or responding phases of processing.

A subsequent investigation in that same series sought to break anxiety down into its cognitive and organismic components, a distinction between the vague feeling that "something bad is going to happen" and the physiological concomitants of anxiety. For this purpose *S* was trained to respond with the anxiety "thought only" or the "bodily sensations only" or both thought and bodily sensations intact as before. GSR recordings were used to validate this cognitive versus organismic distinction. From forty-two trials

3. The experiment was carried out in my laboratory by Muriel Fabrikant.

in each of the nine anxiety conditions (three degrees each of cognitive only, organismic only, and combined cognitive and organismic), interspersed with neutral and pleasure trials over four sessions, it was clear that the decremental effect of the intact anxiety cues upon response latency in identifying Xs was duplicated by the cognitive component acting alone, but not by the organismic alone.

This important finding about the molecular operation of anxiety was replicated and extended in an experiment with another male S (Blum & Wohl, 1971). In the task S read aloud six words in scrambled order from two familiar three-word phrases and then reported whatever words popped into mind during a fifteen-second period. An objective scoring system reflected the amount of organization in S's report. Eight independent variables were included in the design: cognitive only, organismic only, and the intact whole reactions of peak anxiety (-5) and pleasure ($+5$); the neutral nonaffective level (0); and a conditon of heightened muscular tension (10). On a given trial one of the eight cues was presented visually to S during a five second reverberation period immediately after the stimulus presentations and turned off before his report. A total of 144 randomized trials over three sessions permitted an N of eighteen in each condition. Concomitant GSR recordings independently confirmed the absence of organismic response to the cognitive anxiety, cognitive pleasure, and neutral cues. The results showed the thought organization score to be affected significantly more adversely by the cognitive component of anxiety than by the other seven cues.

Perceptual Inhibition

Another model-inspired topic which has claimed our research attention through the years has been perceptual inhibition. Three illustrative studies will be presented next.

The concept of active exclusion or inhibition of some stimuli while focusing on others has been largely ignored or rejected in recent work in the field of attention. Using our posthypnotically cued levels of cognitive arousal, it was possible to test the capacity for active blurring of one stimulus attribute (form) while simultaneously perceiving another attribute (color) accurately (Blum & Porter, 1973). In lowered arousal conditions three highly trained hypnotic subjects were dramatically successful in blurring the form and thereby impairing identification of colored consonants flashed tachistoscopically at speeds ranging from 300 milliseconds down to fifty milliseconds without any concomitant loss in accuracy of identification of the color in which the letter was printed. Among a supplemental series of control experiments, it was further demonstrated that the active inhibitory process can be reversed so as to act upon color but not form; and that the subjects were unable to duplicate these feats in the waking state without benefit of posthypnotic programming.

The second illustration is a case study of hypnotically induced tubular vision (Blum, 1975). A female subject, who had already participated in our laboratory experiments for three years, was trained upon instruction to contract her field of vision to a circle with a radius of approximately ten degrees from a distance of one meter. This was accomplished initially by having her look through a transparent plastic tube one meter long and thirty-three centimeters in diameter under the hypnotic instruction not to see anything outside the tube. Next, she was given practice in maintaining the same contraction without using the plastic tube and seated at varying distances from a screen. Finally, the hypnotic programming was linked to the waking state by the posthypnotic cue "tube" or "no tube," accompanied by amnesia for the prior hypnotic events. A short waking practice session followed.

Independent ophthalmological examination employing visual field tests confirmed the contracted field in the tube condition. Back in the laboratory we carried out a series of experiments to determine whether or not a variety of stimuli presented outside the tubular field would register. The subject was unable to guess at better than chance accuracy the content of areas of colored travel slides outside the tubular field; she could not guess colors, suits, or values of playing cards held just outside the tube; nor could she identify the positions of light flashes. Next, she was asked to walk around the room wearing the transparent tube and proceeded to trip over obstacles unobtrusively placed in her path. Even a sudden jabbing motion with a large scissors, brought very close to her eyes, did not elicit flinching or a reflex blink. The use of monetary incentives—ten cents for every correct identification of one of ten objects, held in left, right, top, or bottom positions—also failed to reveal any signs of registration. However, when the same objects were affectively loaded with pleasure or anxiety by posthypnotic suggestion and the subject was required only to report any kind of emotional response (rather than to identify objects), there *was* a significant affective correspondence to the external stimuli though to an attenuated degree.

These results again suggest, as did the previous color-form experiments, the operation of a selective inhibition mechanism at some central locus between initial sensory registration and eventual perceptual output. The data are consonant with the interpretation that the stimulus object outside the tubular field did register in the mind but achieved only partial processing, stopped short of conscious awareness as a result of inhibitory action en route. In the affects series, the perceptual representation of the object appears to have progressed sufficiently to trigger its linked affective network, albeit a weaker trigger than if the amplification of the percept had not been disrupted by inhibition.

The third illustration of research on perceptual inhibition is provided by a series of experiments involving negative visual hallucination (NVH) (Blum, Porter, & Geiwitz, 1978). Two female undergraduates were posthypnotically programmed not to see the colored lines of consonants while perceiving clearly a set of dots superimposed on the lines in another color. The subject's task was to guess the "unseen" line color from among six possibilities. The effects of three temporal parameters were noted in tachistoscopic presentations of the consonants: priming time, stimulus duration, and practice over protracted periods.

Priming time refers to the advance preparation needed by a subject to execute the NVH successfully. In trials preceded by exposure of a long black dash which served as the posthypnotic NVH cue, she was to see only the superimposed dots and none of the lines which formed the consonant. In other trials, where the consonant was preceded by a blank flash, she was to see both lines and dots normally. Thus, the interval between presentation of the NVH cue and the stimulus consonant determined the amount of priming time available, since the subject did not know in advance what kind of trial was coming up next. After considerable practice they were able to execute the NVH instruction successfully even with the shortest duration in which the dash cue itself was discriminable, e.g. one subject's guessing of line colors did not exceed chance accuracy with only ten milliseconds of priming time.

Stimulus duration was investigated by systematically varying exposure of the colored consonants from five milliseconds on up to ten minutes. Occasional color breakthroughs, i.e., failure to execute the NVH, reported by the posthypnotically programmed automatic pressing of a button, did not occur until the one minute trials for one subject and the ten minute trial for the other. Better than chance accuracy of line color guesses began to appear at consonant exposures of one and two seconds.

In another series of trials subjects were shown the experimental stimuli interspersed with a control set which contained *only* colored dots. They were required to guess whether the flash contained a "color" blank or a "real" blank. In this forced-choice technique the more skilled subject identified sixty-five percent of the colored blanks correctly and fifty-eight percent of the real blanks compared to chance expectancies of fifty percent; for the other subject the corresponding accuracies were seventy-five percent and seventy-six percent.

All these NVH data point to signal strength, as manipulated by stimulus exposure duration, and inhibitory skill, which can be improved with practice, as major determinants of the outcome in NVH. The locus of inhibitory action again is assignable to an intermediate stage of perceptual-cognitive processing, subsequent to sensory registration and prior to verbal report.

Summary

In this chapter three broad objectives have been sought: to convey the

flavor of our hypnotic programming procedures; to point out methodological advances possible with the experimental use of hypnosis; and to illustrate some of the seemingly elusive research problems that become
amenable to study. Along with the accounts of how Ss are trained to experience degrees of cognitive arousal, pleasure, and anxiety, it has been
shown that the necessary safeguards and independent checks for such work
with hypnosis can be accomplished. Examples are the application of the
cognitive arousal cues to hexagram salience and the Stroop Color-Word
Test, the GSR as a reflection of degrees of organismic anxiety, and monetary equivalents for the levels of pleasure.

The potential number of methodological advances is virtually without
limit. By means of posthypnotic cues, experimental variables can be shaped
in pure form, such as free-floating anxiety, and manipulated systematically
in degree. Their onset and offset can be brought about and timed with some
degree of precision. Related variables commonly lumped under general
rubrics such as arousal or boredom can be distinguished operationally and
their effects studied in isolation or even in specifiable combinations. The
conduct of experiments in the waking state, with S amnesic for the previous
hypnotic training and not self-conscious about his programmed behavior,
minimizes the opportunity for data to be confounded by spontaneous conscious deliberations on the part of S. Also, the conduct of postexperimental
inquiries back under H, where amnesia no longer applies, typically provides
a wealth of otherwise unattainable information about S's waking performance. Another experimental advantage of amnesia is its aid in keeping a
series of trials independent, in the sense of eliminating conscious carry over
from one trial to the next. Ss become highly sophisticated introspectors of
their own mental states under hypnosis, and these judgments can themselves
be utilized as data under circumstances where cognitive or affective arousal
is free to vary, as noted above. We also saw the use of hypnosis itself as an
experimental probe, substituting for electroconvulsive shock or chemicals in
the studies on cognitive reverberation. The more one uses hypnotic
methodology in research, the stronger the feeling grows that the surface of
the potential has barely been scratched.

Finally, the range of research problems capable of attack is greatly
broadened. We hope this point was driven home by such illustrations as the
experimental separation of arousal effects along the perceiving-judging-
responding sequence in the visual discrimination task, the breakdown of
anxiety into its cognitive and organismic components to isolate the locus of
decremental action, extensions into the complex psychodynamic realm of
primary process thinking, and molecular analysis of the capacities for selective concentration and perceptual inhibition.

Josephine R. Hilgard *is an emeritus clinical professor of psychiatry and research associate in the Department of Psychology at Stanford University. She received her Ph.D. in child psychology with Dr. Arnold Gesell at Yale in 1933, and her M.D. from Stanford in 1940. She completed her residency and psychoanalytic training under a Rockefeller Foundation grant in Chicago and Washington. Prior to her appointment at Stanford, she served as director of the Child Guidance Clinic of the San Francisco Children's Hospital. Her research interests in psychiatry involved the social heredity of sibling rivalries and the generational influences of parent loss during childhood. She has been involved in the work of the Laboratory of Hypnosis Research at Stanford since 1957 and is the author of* Personality and Hypnosis: A Study of Imaginative Involvement, *and of* Hypnosis in the Relief of Pain *(with E.R. Hilgard). Currently, under a grant from the National Cancer Institute, she is involved in a systematic study of the use of hypnosis to relieve anxiety and pain in childhood cancer at the Children's Hospital in Stanford, and the Presbyterian Hospital in the Pacific Medical Center, San Francisco.*

Josephine R. Hilgard *summarizes research which describes the variety of imaginative and sensory-affective involvements that occur both in ordinary experience and in hypnosis. These include aesthetic appreciation of nature, the enjoyment of imaginative literature and drama, the life of fantasy, creative imagination, and adventure. She shows how such involvements are related to measured hypnotizability, while other non-imaginative involvements, found in some aspects of science, athletic team sports, and work-related recreation bear no relation to hypnotizability. The background for possessing these involvements may include genetic, congenital, and environmental influences. Parents may provide a spur to the development of involvements through their own enthusiastic interests that are transmitted by contagion; they may also, in other ways, promote fantasy in the child as a defense against loneliness and punishment. There are important continuities between imaginative involvements in everyday life and in hypnosis; in fact, such involvements can be considered as significant ego assets.*

15

Imaginative and Sensory—Affective Involvements: in Everyday Life and in Hypnosis

JOSEPHINE R. HILGARD

Imaginative and sensory-affective involvements have been shown to be closely related to the capacity to experience hypnosis (J.R. Hilgard, 1965, 1970, 1974). These involvements permit a temporary absorption in satisfying experiences in which fantasy plays a large role. They have little direct relation to the mundane problems of living, which are set aside as the involvements are enjoyed. Indirectly, however, they bear upon the quality of life for the person capable of these involvements, and provide one means of coping with the problems of living. Now that studies of hypnosis have called attention to these modes of individual experiencing and adjusting, more interest has begun to center upon their importance outside hypnosis. With this new interest, the neglect of the imaginative involvements in the conventional studies of personality can be corrected.

The Variety of Imaginative Involvements

Imaginative involvements can take many different forms, expressing individual interests in a variety of experiences whereby imagination and

Research for this chapter was supported by the National Institute of Mental Health, Grant MH-03859.

fantasy provide the individual with highly satisfying experiences. Some illustrations make the kinds of involvements that are under consideration concrete.

AFFECTIVE AROUSAL THROUGH SENSORY STIMULATION

The savored experiences of direct sensory stimulation take many forms: a soft breeze on the skin, warm sand under bare feet, the smell of fresh air after a rainstorm, the warmth of the sun on the body, the touch of fabrics and textiles, the sensation of gliding through or floating upon water, or of weightlessness in riding, flying, or skiing. These experiences are so organic that they can readily be re-experienced in imagination.

The visual and auditory enjoyment of nature includes the aesthetic appreciation of a sunset, of wild flowers, of mountains, and of the seashore. An individual is drinking in beauty through the eyes and often simultaneously listening with the ears to the accompanying sounds, the rustle of the wind through the trees, the chirping of the birds, the pounding of surf against sand or rocks. Absorbed involvement in music of the classical type can be like pure involvement in nature, an intense, absorbing, aesthetic experience.

Subjects do not approach these experiences with a critical, rational detachment or striving. Nor do they expect them to serve as a background while concentration is mainly directed toward the solution of troublesome personal problems. Instead, each experience is inherently satisfying, with immersion and marked affective involvement. Subjects describe the experiences as gentle, mild, and passive, often as simple sensuous pleasures. The concentration of attention that accompanies them is high but largely effortless.

Such appreciation of sensory-aesthetic experiences forms a background for the more developed aesthetic appreciation of poetry, painting, sculpture, and the arts generally.

INVOLVEMENT IN READING IMAGINATIVE LITERATURE

Stories apt to stimulate the imagination of the reader include biography, autobiography, tales of historical events, novels, mysteries, adventure stories, and science fiction. In describing the type of involvement, it is useful to distinguish character identification and empathic identification. In character identification, there is participation in the action and feeling as though one were indeed one of the characters. In empathic identification, there is participation in the feeling of the story even though the separation of the self from the character is maintained; identification is with the emotion that the author has intended to portray though the individual cannot, in fantasy, be the character. Some readers can shift back and forth between these types of involvement. The importance of reading involvement has also been noted by Shor (1970).

Character-identification involvement is illustrated by one of our subjects (Waldo) who said, "I don't read. I live the character. I *become* the character. I put myself in his place rather than putting him in my place. I became Rufus in *Death in the Family,* Becket in *Murder in the Cathedral,* Ivan in *The Brothers Karamazov.*" Waldo sometimes interrupted this intense identification; for example, he stopped to evaluate Rufus's situation in *Death in the Family,* but then, "I went ahead and became him again."

What is termed empathic identification is illustrated by another subject, Beverly, who showed clearly how an involved reader could follow the emotion the author wished to convey without identifying with the characters. She gave as an example her reading of *Lord of the Flies.* "I felt sympathy for Piggy and felt an impatience toward Ralph, the leader of the group. I was quite involved and concerned that the children were running wild. Once you get the author's point of view it's frightening, how on this island a microcosm of people left to their own devices become animals, and all this is a reflection of the war that is going on in the rest of the world." She went on to say, "In reading, you suspend yourself, your background, you don't have a personality of your own. You're not using your judgments of right and wrong and standards of value; you're dealing with the author on his home ground. I become more involved with the author than with the characters."

Another subject commented on how much the feeling of what she had read affected her. "When reading Shakespeare, for a day and a half afterwards I speak like Shakespeare. If a book has a depressive theme, I'm depressed. If it's happy, I'm happy. I identify with the whole story and scene, not with one particular character."

What are the characteristics of the involved reader? (1) This reader is greatly influenced by the power of words and the author has used words to manipulate ideas and emotions. (2) This reader is actively receptive and open, not merely passive. The involved reader *savors* the subject matter. (3) Imagery is vivid. For many involved readers the imagery has a hallucinatory quality. Often it is carried visually but this is not always the case; some people feel the texture and the heat, smell the flowers and taste the dry dust. (4) Critical, reality-testing processes are temporarily suspended. The author is temporarily the reader's guide to experience, and the author's values temporarily become his or her own.

THE DRAMATIC ARTS

Persons interested in the theatre may enjoy the role of spectator or actor, or both. In the role of spectator they feel as they watch a drama, that they are part of it in a variety of ways. In the acting role, there are the formal actors who act on stage, and the informal dramatists who entertain friends with experiences of the day, dramatized for better effect.

The spectator at the theatre has much in common with the reader of a book. The dramatist's ideas are expressed on stage while the author's ideas must be read. Not surprisingly, these two areas are found to have much in common.

Laura was both an involved movie watcher and an involved reader. "I loved *Lawrence of Arabia* and saw it twice; also *The Miracle Worker* and *David and Lisa*. I forgot my surroundings and became absorbed in the story. My emotions get stirred up, and I identify with the characters. As a child I identified completely with Dorothy in *The Wizard of Oz*. There was never as much identification in books, but it was similar. I cried over *Black Beauty*. I still enjoy science fiction."

Mark did not care much for reading but became very involved in movie watching. "You're coming out from the movie and not knowing where you're going. I became so involved in *Ben Hur* that during the intermission I felt compelled to sit down and write for fifteen minutes about the true life of the story. I get carried away by strong, deep, emotional things like *Ben Hur*. Not all movies, of course; never by Westerns."

Enjoyment of the acting role for Henry began at the age of nine and he described taking part in college plays as a consuming interest. What he enjoyed most "is the ability to take on enough of another personality to project it to people, to make them experience the emotions that the author of the play has written down." When asked how he felt in the midst of a role, he said, "In the beginning I used to live the part, but you get so emotionally involved it wears you out. You have to hold back a little: if you are completely involved, you don't remember where you are on stage; you mustn't forget where you are—you have to make sure you're standing in the right place. On the stage you're emotionally involved but you're also standing apart." He liked to play all parts, especially character ones. "I enjoyed Bottom, the buffoon in *Midsummer Night's Dream;* Falstaff appealed to me, for I was obese for a while."

Informal dramatization characterizes the behavior of those who commonly act before small informal audiences provided by family, friends, or even casual listeners. They pay close attention to what is happening about them and to what will bear repetition. Telling a story they often adopt the mannerisms appropriate to the situation: gestures, modes of speech, facial expressions. It is not merely a matter of gesticulating, but of genuine gesturing appropriate to the story. There is a tendency to moderate exaggeration and embellishment so as to enhance the dramatic value of the incident when it is recreated. While role-playing is the essence of drama, deep involvement in a role at the time makes it seem like living reality.

FANTASY AND CREATIVE IMAGINATION

To be involved in fantasy is to substitute, at least temporarily, a created experience for realistic experiencing of present environmental events. The fantasied experience is derived partly from the past, as in reliving an earlier event, and is partly novel. Novel fantasies may supplement memories, may anticipate hoped for experiences, or may be bizarre elaborations in the idiom of science fiction. Novel fantasies are often described as creative imagination. Such fantasies may be initiated by the person who has them, or may be evoked by specific sources of stimulation. These sources include a book the person is reading, or the suggestions of a hypnotist that some unusual experience will occur.

The concept of goal-directed fantasy is used by Barber, Spanos and Chaves (1974), in connection with meeting the demands of the hypnotist. For example, with the suggestion that the subject's arm has become stiff, the fantasy may be supplied that the subject should imagine that the arm is held stiff by a splint. The fantasy may be suggested by the hypnotist or may arise spontaneously by the subject attempting to comply with the suggestion.

On the same spectrum but at an opposite end from the limited specific goal-directed fantasy is the experience of a creative writer. Martha, who was participating in an advanced project in creative writing at the university, was hypnotized, and also interviewed. She proved to be hypnotizable and described hypnosis as, "Concentration on a single thing which is like the writing process where things happen that you are not aware of." Her creative writing had a long history. She started to keep a diary when she was in third grade. Her imagination was far too vivid for her to set everything down in the diary, however, for her father might find the manuscript, be shocked, destroy it, and punish her. In grades seven to nine she wrote many stories about prisoners who escaped, and some about foreign legions. As a senior in college she edited the college newspaper. At the time she was a subject, she was writing a book based on her own experiences, not autobiographical, but responsive to the ideas and feelings she had had in relation to the lives of those around her.

Martha's experience differs from the short-range goal directed fantasy in richness and particularly in the effortless flow of her own ideas.

ADVENTURESOMENESS

Some people find a release from ordinary demands by adventurous activity, such as mountain climbing, skiing, skin diving, airplane flying, or spelunking. In another context, such persons were described as physical space travelers in order to differentiate them from the mental space travelers who experienced their adventures while sitting in chairs reading science fiction or

Eastern philosophies, or probing the limits of mental space through drug-related experiences (J.R. Hilgard, 1970).

Physical space travelers are caught up in the feelings of the moment. One subject, asked about his skin diving said, "It's *free* competition, like an adventure. It's exhilarating." The appeal of motorcycling for this same subject was "the power," the feeling of "wind whistling by," and the "freedom which is like flying." One snow skier explained, "You defy gravity as you jump," while another said, "Down the slope you have complete control; you go fast and you can feel the wind go by on all sides; it feels as though you take off." Interviewer: "Take off?" "It feels as though you're jumping—the faster you go the more you feel you're coming apart from the ground." A cave explorer explained that there was a mystery about "those deep dark places." Adventurous airplane flyers usually prefer small planes so as to experience more fully the feeling of take-off (which sometimes involves a special feeling in the pit of the stomach!), the exhilaration of the speed of smooth gliding, and finally the dip back to earth. Some pilots feel the attraction of the limitless boundaries of outer space—an attraction that they know is too hazardous to succumb to.

In general the physical space travelers are well disciplined. They must keep equipment in order so that they can stay alive. Skills are developed. When skills have become disciplined, they become effortless; instead of thinking about the mechanics of operation, the traveler is free to enjoy the feeling of the experience.

The adventurers have a tie to reality but they test the limits of reality for the varied experiences it can provide. They re-experience processes compatible with childhood. Omnipotence, power, freedom from restraint, excitement, direct sensual experiences—all these characteristics are identifiable in childhood.

NONIMAGINATIVE INVOLVEMENTS

Absorption in a recreational activity does not mean that the activity may be classified as imaginative involvement. Competitive team activities are of this kind, differing from individual skills previously described. Some types of work activity carried out against a standard of excellence, such as skilled hi-fi construction, may be a change for the busy executive, without invoking any feeling of imaginative involvement. Absorption in work not classified as recreation may be very high. Such absorption is characteristic of biologists, chemists, and engineers, whose work may be inventive, but is always tested against the objectives being sought.

Competitive team sports involve constant striving toward the goal of winning a game. The athlete is concentrating completely on something in the real world. Helen, who had been very involved in competitive swimming since the age of eight and had won trophies in badminton, expressed it well. "People who are competitive are far from being imaginative. You realize what you are fighting. It's the reality of the struggle. Imagination and competition are mutually exclusive. In competing, the whole world around you is more real. My imagination is extremely limited...In competitive sports you're taught never to take your opponent for granted. You keep a critical eye on everything. Even though your opponent looks scrawny and not apt to do anything, you don't trust that situation...I can never say die. I've always got to try to beat the person; I never give up. Even if I run myself too hard and get ill, I'll keep on trying to win."

In individual skill sports such as swimming, skating, riding, fishing and boating the situation is different for the individual is more frequently participating for personal pleasure. Many people enjoy swimming because of the *feeling* of floating in the water, or the *feeling* of water on the skin; one subject imagined he was a porpoise on the bottom of the pool. Thus, it is important to distinguish between the ones who are participating largely for personal pleasure and the ones who are fighting a battle to win. They may be classified as alternative forms of enjoyment, but in important ways they differ from each other.

Commitment to science requires reality orientation, a critical attitude, and alertness to environmental details (including the unexpected) that the untrained observer is apt to miss. While there is an aesthetic element in science, and a role for fantasy, the day-to-day work of the scientist is exacting and demands precision. The immediate experience requires a great deal of patient effort and much of the satisfaction comes from the end result rather than from the process.

The difference between an aesthetic involvement in nature and a scientific one may be illustrated by the case of Eugene. He said he loved hiking and nature. His interest turned out to be cognitive, analytic and scientific. "Hiking is tied up with biology, the plants and animals along the way. At the beach I look to see how the seaweed is made, or I poke around the tide pool and find a starfish, remember how I learned about them in high school, how they are related to the jelly fish." Such "thinking" responses to nature's wonders differ from the "drinking in" of nature's beauties. The intellectual and analytic interest in the things he found had none of the feeling overtones of those whose interest in nature is aesthetic.

Eugene also represents a case of deep involvement in recreational interests that are judged against a standard of excellence. He could become deeply absorbed in building and making things. He became so absorbed that he paid little attention to anything else, not hearing when he was called to dinner. This interest had developed alongside his father, an electrical engineer. "He always had me build along with him and help him fix things." They had built a chemistry laboratory together. They had also built a hi-fi set together, and then he had built one for himself.

Thus in Eugene we see the development of an extraordinary capacity for absorption and close attention to a reality-oriented kind of work recreation in which useful products are being made. "When I'm interested I can forget time and meals. While working on my hi-fi I'd stay up until 2 a.m. and eat only one meal all day." There is a capacity for focused attention and deep absorption, but the feeling components and the free use of imagination characteristic of what I call imaginative involvement are missing.

Imaginative Involvements as Related to Measured Hypnotizability

Early indications that some interests and experiences of everyday life would be predictive of hypnosis were found through the use of special inventories by Shor (1960), Shor, Orne, and O'Connell (1962), Ås and Lauer (1962), Ås (1963), and Lee-Teng (1965). Sarbin and his associates called attention to the importance of role-taking in hypnosis (Sarbin, 1950, 1954; Sarbin and Coe, 1972); hypnotizable subjects possessed an ability to enact roles in which they became deeply involved. The interviewing study at Stanford began in 1958-1959 and the first report concerned developmental-interactive aspects (J.R. Hilgard and E.R. Hilgard, 1962). The significance of a variety of sensory-affective and imaginative involvements gradually became clearer and was first reported in 1965 (J.R. Hilgard 1965), more completely described in a later book (1970), and subsequently in a report of additional interviews with high and low scoring hypnotic subjects (1974).

EVIDENCE RELATING INVOLVEMENTS TO HYPNOSIS

Intensive interviewing before hypnosis assessed the degree to which affective arousal through sensory stimulation and imaginative involvement was present in a population of college students (1965, 1970). All quantitative material which was analyzed as predictive of hypnosis came from these interviews prior to the hypnotic session. In a number of interviews following hypnotic susceptibility testing, it was possible to obtain the kind of feedback essential to further understanding and interpretation.

In this population, the involvements that were found to be related to hypnosis included affective arousal through sensory stimulation, reading, drama, creativity, childhood imagination, religion, and adventurousness. Significant chi squares at the .05 level or better were found in regard to all of these. The sum of the involvements correlated positively and significantly with measured hypnotizability.

Data on aesthetic involvement in nature may be used to illustrate the kinds of relationships found between such involvements and measured hypnotizability. Despite the difficulties in distinguishing between those cases in which the interest in nature reflected aesthetic involvement, and those in which the interest was intellectual or scientific, Table 15.1 indicates the positive relationship between the interview data and the measured hypnotic

TABLE 15.1   Ratings on aesthetic involvement in nature as related to hypnotic susceptibility scores. N = 184; males 113; females, 71. (J.R. Hilgard, 1970, p. 81)

Involvement (Maximum = 7)	Susceptibility (SHSS:C)		
	Low (0 – 5)	High (6 – 12)	Total
High (5 – 7)	37	53	90
Low (1 – 4)	56	38	94
Total	93	91	184*

Significance test: X^2 = 6.27; p = .02
*Ratings lacking on three cases in sample

responsiveness. A statistical relationship of this kind suffices to show for analytic purposes, that the relationship is clearly demonstrable; it does not mean that the relationship is so high that firm predictions of hypnotic scores could be made on the basis of such data alone.

The involvements are not simply examples of free-floating primary process thinking; in our hypnotizable subjects imagination was characteristically combined with the careful cognitive control representative of secondary process. Imagination and control are compatible. For example, a poet can give expression to deep emotion at the same time as he conforms to the limitations imposed by the meter he has chosen. Or the adventurous diver enjoys skin diving though being careful to keep his equipment in excellent condition.

The experience of involvement is limited in time, and return to the demands of reality is prompt after the experience is over. The imaginative involvements and their related hypnotic fantasies are distinguished from psychotic delusions and hallucinations because of their limited duration and the simultaneous retention of adequate cognitive controls.

CONFIRMATION OF THE RELATIONSHIP BETWEEN INVOLVEMENTS AND
HYPNOTIZABILITY: HIGH AND LOW MEASURED HYPNOTIC RESPONSIVENESS

Earlier work at Stanford (J.R. Hilgard, 1970) has been followed up by interviews with high and low susceptibles to hypnosis, with results concordant with the earlier findings. In this later study (J.R. Hilgard, 1974), forty-two highly susceptible subjects were compared with fifteen low-scoring subjects. The high scorers had obtained an average of 9.2 (of ten) on a modified Form A of the Harvard Group Scale of Hypnotic Susceptibility; of these, seventeen in addition had been given the individual Stanford Hypnotic Susceptibility Scale:C (1962) and scored 10.9 of a possible twelve. In the sample of extremely low subjects, none of the fifteen scored above two on the twelve item SHSS:C. While the earlier investigation had relied on interviews *prior* to hypnosis, these interviews followed the hypnotic session. The high involvements among the forty-two highly susceptible subjects and among the fifteen very low scorers are detailed in Table 15.2.

TABLE 15.2. Ratings of involvements in samples of high and low hypnotizable subjects (*Ss*)

Involvement areas	Percent of *Ss* with high involvement	
	High susceptible (N = 42)	Low susceptible[a] (N = 15)
Savoring of sensory experiences	93	20
Drama	79[b]	20[c]
Reading	76[b]	13[c]
Daydreams-child	74	13
Daydreams-adult	36	7
Mental space travelers	45	0
Physical space travelers	33	0
Creativity	26	13
Religion	19	13

[a] High involvement was defined as a rating of six or seven on a seven-point scale.

[b] Of *Ss* showing reading and/or drama, which are closely related areas, thirty-nine of forty-two, or 93%, showed one or both; two showed reading only, three drama only. Only one case was low in both areas. On one case the information was missing.

[c] Of *Ss* showing reading and/or drama, which are closely related areas, four of fifteen, or 27%, showed one or both; one showed reading only, two showed drama only, and one showed both areas.

It turned out that for high hypnotic subjects the ability to savor sensory experiences was almost universal, (ninety-three percent). An equally strong involvement in either reading, drama, or both was present, (ninety-three percent). Extensive childhood fantasies or daydreams were also reported, (seventy-one percent). In this particular sample, adult fantasy was relatively low. It should be remembered, however, that only high involvement is reported in Table 15.2, a degree of six or seven level on a seven point scale so that the presence of a moderate amount of fantasy was excluded. It may be that a lesser degree of fantasy or daydreaming, in the presence of high involvements in other fantasy material, such as nature, books, and drama is all that is necessary. Two kinds of fantasy may be distinguished. One is the stimulus-bound fantasy related to involvement in books, drama, and sensory experience, while a second is a freer type where the individual creates his own fantasy material. We do not know yet how these interact in the hypnotizable subject. This second type is more closely related to creativity, which in this particular sample proved to be relatively low. Involvement in religious activities will vary widely according to the sample.

The high involvements for the fifteen very low scorers were few in comparison with the susceptible subjects. Six of the fifteen lows had no involvement that could be rated six or seven. Nine of the fifteen had some involvements: five of them one, three with two, and one with three. By contrast, nearly all (forty-one of forty-two) high subjects had involvements rated high in three or more of the nine areas.

It was earlier conjectured that a single area of involvement might serve as a pathway into hypnosis, potentially equivalent to several areas of high involvement. This conjecture appeared to be refuted by the occasional high involvements among the low hypnotizables, as reported in Table 15.2. The frequency was less in this group but the involvements were not absent. While the major finding of the relationship between imaginative involvements and hypnosis held, the importance of a single involvement was no longer demonstrated.

The question therefore arose: Why did some of the subjects, with a history of one or more imaginative involvements, end up nonhypnotizable? Some hints were provided within the interview material.

It is often asserted that hypnosis has both an ability component and an attitudinal component. If we assume that the capacity for imaginative involvement is an ability component related to hypnotizability, we may also assume that attitudinal components inhibiting hypnotic behavior may be persistent aspects of personality.

Attitudinal components were found to include: (1) apprehensiveness over any new and different experience; (2) unwillingness or inability to accept the hypnotist-subject relationship; and (3) a need for much activity in the reading material rather than an emphasis on a slower pace in content compatible with hypnotic relaxation.

CONFIRMATION BY OTHERS OF THE SIGNIFICANCE OF IMAGINATIVE INVOLVEMENTS IN RELATION TO HYPNOTIZABILITY

Further evidence in regard to the significance of the imaginative involvements has been provided by the psychometric studies of Tellegen and Atkinson (1974). In a trait-oriented investigation utilizing 481 subjects, they concluded that the frequency of experiences involving absorption in imagination was related to hypnotizability. They defined absorption as "total" attention that fully engaged the individual's representational resources, resulting in a heightened sense of the reality of the attentional object, imperviousness to distracting events, and an altered sense of reality in general. What is of equal importance in their study is that test items reflecting the two factors of the MMPI (introversion-extroversion and stability-instability) were not significantly correlated with hypnotizability. Evidently, despite the numerous items composing the MMPI, those reflecting imaginative involvements were not included, and when they were included they defined a third factor.

Coe (1974), using the Coe Experience Inventory, confirmed several of the positive relationships, disagreed on others, and pointed out that there may be sex differences. Swanson (1978) constructed a scale of absorbing and self-altering experiences and related these experiences to the family structure in which the university students were reared. Finke and Macdonald (1978) compared the Swanson Scale and the Tellegen Scale with each other and with a group version of the Stanford Hypnotic Susceptibility Scale:C (Weitzenhoffer and Hilgard, 1962). Significantly positive correlations were obtained for all these comparisons. They concluded that the "results provided further empirical confirmation of the relationship between absorption and measures of hypnotic responsiveness, and offered new evidence for the existence of stable individual differences in hypnotizability."

Spanos and McPeake (1975b) assessed absorption in imaginative activities as measured by the Tellegen and Atkinson Scale, attitudes toward hypnosis as measured by the Barber and Calverley Scale, and hypnotic susceptibility as measured by the Harvard Group Scale. Significant positive correlations were obtained in their sample of 183 subjects between absorption and attitudes, and between each of these variables and hypnotic susceptibility. However, Spanos, McPeake, and Churchill (1976), using the Barber Suggestibility Scale as the test of hypnosis found that the imaginative ability variable did not correlate with hypnosis. Spanos and McPeake (1975a), further studying the attitudinal variable, found a positive correlation between level of imaginative involvement as measured by the Tellegen and Atkinson Scale and hypnotic suggestibility as measured by the Harvard Group Scale for those who had received favorable information in advance, while for subjects who had received unfavorable information in advance, there was a significantly lower level of hypnotic suggestibility.

Davis, Dawson, and Seay (1978) gave an imaginative involvement inventory based on the Hilgard case studies to 100 college students. Nine areas of involvement were tested with two statements representing each area. Sixteen high scorers and sixteen low scorers on the imaginative involvement inventory were hypnotized using the Stanford Hypnotic Susceptibility Scale Form A. The high imaginative involvement group had significantly higher hypnotic susceptibility scores than the low imaginative involvement group.

Thus evidence builds from a number of directions in regard to the role of imaginative involvement in hypnotizability. However, we must not forget that the relationship is far from perfect. We need studies now on the type of factors that diminish hypnotic responsiveness in cases where imaginative involvement appears to be present in greater degree than the hypnotic score indicates. Under what circumstances do the reality principle and the reality orientation prevail in an otherwise imaginative individual?

Involvements Unrelated to Hypnotizability

Nonimaginative involvements, some of which have already been described, were found to be unrelated to hypnotizability. Team athletes, subjects majoring in scientific fields, and subjects whose major recreation was of a work related type provided valuable information on this subject.

In athletic involvement, it was necessary to distinguish between the individual skill sports, such as boating, fishing, swimming, skiing, skating, riding, golf, track and field, and the highly competitive team sports, such as basketball, football, hockey and volleyball. There is a great difference between athletes who become involved in what they are doing for the intrinsic pleasure of the sport and those who are essentially in a battle to win, usually with one team pitted against another. Such a dichotomy is not sharp, of course, for there are skiing, swimming, and boating competitions. Hypnotizable athletes were more likely to be found among those sports that emphasized individual skill. The competitive team athletes were apt to be nonhypnotizable. The latter spoke of becoming lost and immersed in a game, concentrating to such an extent that they were unaware of anything outside the game itself. Superficially this appeared to be like the concentration within hypnosis, with its exclusion of matters outside the focus. Some of the features, however, which differentiated competitive athletic involvement from hypnotic involvement were as follows: (1) exact information was required of environmental stimuli in a reality context; (2) the focus was on those aspects of environmental input which could lead to decision and control; and (3) the stress was on activity. These three characteristics are almost the exact opposite of what is required in hypnosis. In contrast to the attitudes characteristics of the hypnotically susceptible, there is no scope for the imagination; the essential gratification comes through the final score rather than through savoring the present moment; and an attitude of activity rather than receptivity is stressed.

Another kind of involvement which was usually antithetical to hypnotic susceptibility included a deep commitment to science. The scientist, like the competitive athlete, could become very absorbed in what he was doing, but if this was his sole preoccupation he was likely to end up nonhypnotizable. It is evident from Table 15.3 that in our sample the humanities majors were the most hypnotizable, the social science majors in between, and the natural scientists (biologists, physical scientists, engineers) the least hypnotizable.

TABLE 15.3. Choice of major in college as related to hypnotic susceptibility (Hilgard, 1970, p. 158).

Hypnotic susceptibility (SHSS:C)	Humanities	Social sciences	Biological sciences Physical sciences Engineering	Total
More hypnotizable (7–12)	9	21	10	40
Less hypnotizable (0–6)	5	21	32	58
Total	14	42	42	98

Note: Eight subjects were undecided about their majors.
Significance test: $x^2 = 9.53$, df = 2; $p < .01$

It should be noted from the above table that one quarter of those majoring in biology, physical science and engineering were among the more hypnotizable. This is important. What it means is that a particular science student may *combine* in the same person a scientific interest along with an appreciation of nature and a capacity for imaginative involvement. At the laboratory he is involved in scientific work with attention to exact details and precise analysis of data. When there is time for recreation, he does not carry a briefcase home with more work for the weekends but prefers to go to the beach or mountains, participate in an individual sport, become involved in fiction, or perhaps enjoy a symphony. Thus both reality-bound involvements and imaginative involvements can exist comfortably in the same person, though at different times. Where they coexist, the individual may be hypnotizable.

To what extent the presence of reality-bound involvements may adversely influence the availability of the imaginative involvement as a basis for hypnosis is one question for future investigation.

LIMITATIONS OF RELATING INVOLVEMENTS TO HYPNOTIZABILITY

The foregoing accounts of involvements related to hypnosis as well as those that are unrelated point up the care required to avoid overgeneralizing a relationship that has exceptions which should be understood. In many cases, questionnaires or self-report ratings will fail to make the necessary distinctions, so that some attempts at replication will be successful and some unsuccessful, depending on whether or not they are sensitive to attenuating factors. The claim has never been made that the relationship is a simple one, because the correlations obtained, though positive, are universally small and many other factors may contribute to the determination of hypnotic susceptibility.

Imagination, Imagery, and Hypnosis

The hypothesis that there is a relation between vividness of imagery and hypnotizability is a natural one, because the hallucinatory ability of the highly hypnotizable may depend on an underlying ability to form and recognize images. The usual finding is that the relationship between hypnotizability and imagery is a nonlinear one. That is, there are very few with low imagery among the highly hypnotizable, but a high report of imagery is no guarantee of high hypnotizability, as shown, for example, in Table 15.4. More of those with self-reports of high imagery fall in the low hypnotizable group, so that imagery itself cannot be thought of as predicting hypnotizability, although absence of reported imagery is a negative factor. Essentially the same results were found in the studies from the Stanford laboratory (J.R. Hilgard, 1970).

TABLE 15.4. Imagery as measured on the modified Betts Scale (Betts QMI) as related to hypnotizability as measured by the Stanford Hypnotic Susceptibility Scale:A (SHSS:A) (Data from Sutcliffe, Perry, and Sheehan, 1970).

	Imagery (Betts QMI)		
Hypnotizability (SHSS:A)	Low imagery (120+)	High imagery (59–119)	Total
High hypnotizability (8–12)	2	20	22
Low hypnotizability (0–7)	20	53	73
Total	22	73	95

The function of imagery may differ for the low and high hypnotizables. For the lows, imagery serves realistic purposes, as in reviving memories or in planning for the future. For the highs, imagery plays into fantasy production and to the imaginative involvements under consideration.

In hypnosis, the *production* of an experience, such as a dream or age regression, may be suggested, or the *inhibition* of an experience or movement may be suggested. The way in which high and low hypnotizables contrast in these areas is shown by a further analysis of the Stanford data presented in Table 15.5. It is clear that imagery is more highly related to items that require the production of a positive experience with imaginal content. However, the more imaginative are the more responsive throughout, even though their advantage over the less imaginative does not show as much for the inhibition items.

TABLE 15.5.   Reported imagery as related to items of the SHSS:C (10 highest and 10
lowest imagery reports among 45 female subjects) (From J.R. Hilgard, 1970, p. 97)

Items on the hypnotic susceptibility scale	Number of passing scores	
	10 highest in imagery	10 lowest in imagery
Production of the experience		
1. Taste hallucination	7	1
2. Dream	8	1
3. Age regression	8	0
4. Mosquito hallucination	9	2
Mean	8.0	1.0
Inhibition of experience or movement		
1. Arm rigidity	7	3
2. Arm immobilization	5	4
3. Anosmia to ammonia	3	2
4. Amnesia	4	1
	4.8	2.5

GENETIC AND CONGENITAL ROOTS OF IMAGINATION AND IMAGERY

We may well ask the question, to what extent are genetic and congenital
components affecting imagery and the imaginative involvements and to
what extent are environmental influences operating? To my knowledge
there are no studies bearing directly upon the biological bases of imagery
and imagination. A small study of identical and fraternal twins early in life
has shown individual differences in response to cradle rocking (Van den
Daele, 1971). One might suppose that the infant who finds this soothing
may be showing the earliest signs of a capacity to enjoy and savor gross
bodily stimulation, possibly to be found later in some of the involvements
previously described. What turned up in the study was that identical twin
pairs were more alike in their responses to cradle rocking than fraternal
twins. Although several steps of conjecture are involved, this leaves open
the possibility of some genetic or congenital influence (Broadhurst, Fulker
and Wilcock 1974).

Because hypnotizability and the involvements are related, a study of the
heritability of hypnosis might supply evidence for a possible hereditary
background. Morgan (1973) compared the capacity for hypnosis in identical
(monozygotic) twins, fraternal (dizygotic) twins, and non-twin sibling pairs.
Those twins classified as monozygotic resembled each other in hypnotic

susceptibility sufficiently to yield a significant intraclass correlation of r ' = .52 (N = 58 pairs). This was not true of those classed as dizygotic where r ' = .17 (N = 82 pairs). Scores from pairs of siblings close together in age were also non-significantly correlated at r ' = .19 (N = 132 pairs). Identical twins thus proved to be more similar in their hypnotic responsiveness than fraternal twins, while fraternal twins and non-twin sibling pairs did not differ significantly. A study of this kind cannot be decisive because identical twins who look alike and are always of the same sex, share a more common environment than fraternal twins.

It is natural to look for brain processes that might underlie the individual differences in imagery and imaginative involvement. Hemispheric laterality is one of the possibilities and there is enough evidence at this time to make it inviting. In right-handed individuals the right hemisphere has been shown to be related to patterned spatial processes, to aesthetic sensitivity, and to some aspects of imagery.

For example, in an EEG study, it was found that a right-handed person while speaking the words of a song uses his left hemisphere; while humming the music without the words uses the right hemisphere; while singing a song, with both words and music present, both hemispheres are activated (Schwartz et al., 1973).

A correlation between hypnotic responsiveness and a patterned right hemisphere task has been demonstrated by Crawford (1977). She showed that highly hypnotizable subjects are superior to those less hypnotizable in several Gestalt closure tests modeled after the test originated by Street (1931). The results suggested a relationship between right hemisphere function and hypnotic susceptibility that may be mediated by reconstructive imagery.

Another method of relating right hemisphere functions to hypnotizability was first used by Bakan (1969). In it a subject, confronted by the questioner, was asked to solve a mental problem. In so doing, the subject tended to divert the eyes to the right or left, and the direction of movement indicated hemispheric activation, a left movement the right hemisphere, a right movement the left hemisphere.

Kinsbourne (1972) appeared to refute Bakan by showing that the direction of the eye movements was related to the nature of the question, hence might have nothing to do with hypnotizability. In his study, the experimenter sat behind a right-handed subject who was asked to solve an analytic problem such as mental arithmetic. While working on the answer, the subject tended to divert the eyes to the right, thus indicating that the left or analytic hemisphere was being activated. If the question involved imagination, the subject tended to move the eyes to the left, indicating that the right hemisphere was being activated.

Because Kinsbourne sat behind the subject while doing the questioning, and Bakan had faced the subject, the question was raised whether this difference had anything to do with their results. The difference proved important, and R.E. Gur (1975) showed that both Kinsbourne's results (from behind the subject) and Bakan's (facing the subject) could be replicated. She found that the tendency to look in one or the other direction according to the nature of the question (analytic or spatial) as found by Kinsbourne was tempered by preference when the questioner faced the subject. Subjects still looked more to one side or the other according to the nature of the question but for the right-handed, the preference for favoring the right hemisphere was superimposed according to the degree of hypnotizability. Bakan's findings were confirmed by Gur and Gur (1974).

The tempering of right hemispheric involvement by preference superimposed upon degree of lateralization raises the question as to how the preference developed. It is reasonable to hypothesize that the lateralization is congenital but the preference may have been acquired. The problems of "training" the right hemisphere remain unsolved. If learning occurs, this is conceivably related to the acquisition of other abilities related to hypnotic susceptibility, such as imaginative involvements.

ENVIRONMENTAL INFLUENCES ON FANTASY DEVELOPMENT

Like play, fantasy can be engaged in for sheer enjoyment. Cases well documented in the earlier studies (J.R. Hilgard, 1970, 1974) indicate that such playful and enjoyable fantasy is spontaneous in childhood; the form it takes probably arises through identification with parents who themselves enjoy imaginative and adventurous activities or who help to stimulate it by providing experiences through books, drama, religion, nature, or adventurous sports. Such fantasies are natural and relatively conflict-free. Nature proved to be a particularly significant area which parent and child had enjoyed; camping, fishing, hiking, trips to the beach or the mountains offered numerous occasions for pleasure. Reading of imaginative books by members of the family was often reported. For children who enjoyed dramatizing daily events the parental role might have been that of dramatic model, or that of interested audience ready to share the child's enjoyment.

In the earlier study of parental influences on involvements, it was found that contagion with parents need not be sex typed. For example, daughters may model after their father's sense of humor, interest in sports, appreciation of nature; sons may model after their mothers in similar ways without any loss of appropriate sex role identification. Of course the same sexed parent may also serve as a model for non-sex-role identification. Although there was some identification of the influence of the parent of the opposite sex, individual variations are significant, and it will probably turn out that a significant determiner of a child's hypnotizability will be through identification with a hypnotizable parent, regardless of sex.

Fantasy may also play a defensive role. Fantasy becomes a defense primarily under two types of circumstances when the person is put under stress. One of these is loneliness and isolation, when fantasy substitutes for companionship and social participation; the other is conflict, as aroused by punishing parents who at the same time are valued for their caring. Satisfying fantasies which have been aroused in this way may become satisfying in themselves and, so, as in certain autonomous motives, outlive the original source of motivation. This process is common in connection with other satisfying defenses, as when rationalizations become reasons, or compensations become satisfying skills.

The child may become lonesome in a number of social contexts: within the family, because of parental neglect, through lack of siblings, or siblings too widely spaced in age to serve as companions; within the environment because of living on a farm or a suburban estate too far from a natural peer group; or owing to chronic illness that separates the child from his natural peers. One of our highest scoring subjects had long periods of asthma as a child.

Where the child turns for effective substitutes depends on the home surroundings. If there are books available, and education is valued, the child may turn to reading for the expanding horizons and social life that reading fantasies provide.

In the Stanford studies, severe punishment was found at a higher frequency among the hypnotizable subjects than among those who were less hypnotizable. In the first study, the relationship between rated severity of punishment and hypnosis was $r = .30$, $N = 187$, and the correlation was significant. In the second study, half the high subjects reported severe or moderate punishment in childhood, while only one-eighth of the lows gave this report. The possibility that punishment might lead to automatic obedience that would then be reflected by prompt responses to the hypnotists' suggestions was refuted by the subjects' replies and the logic of the situation was clear. Those children who were repeatedly punished did not develop the habit of conforming immediately to their parents' demands or they would not have been so frequently punished. An alternate hypothesis received support from the interviews. The relationship between punishment and fantasy development occurred either as an accompaniment of the punishment experience or as an after-effect.

Two aspects of the reported fantasies are of considerable interest: first, the use of fantasy to block the pain of the punishing experience during the punishment itself; second, fantasies developed after physical punishment was over, often during a time when the subject was sent to his or her room.

An example of blocking fantasies was related by one female subject who was spanked two or three times a week until she was eight years old. She became so accustomed to the spankings that she blocked out all discomfort, until her mother recognized that the spankings did not bother her. Henceforth the mother turned to verbal onslaughts. The subject said, "the cutting barbs were hard to block out." Still, she managed, "I turned my parents off; I didn't hear them. They'd talk to me for fifteen to twenty minutes. I turned inside myself. I'd have different thoughts of my own. I'd say to myself, 'What she's saying is not true, there's some good in me.' I tried to bolster myself up...Or I'd fantasy a story I'd finished reading. After twenty minutes, mother would say, 'Have you been listening to me?' and I hadn't heard anything she'd been saying." Asked about hostile fantasies, she said, "I never had *any* hostile fantasies at all. It was unnecesary to have hostile fantasies if I could go into myself and turn mother off." She related this cultivated ability to her later hypnotic ability.

The second kind of fantasy developed subsequent to the punishment. One of the high subjects was punished with a hair brush once or twice a month until she was ten and then with tongue lashings until age fourteen. After each punishment she was sent to her room to meditate on her problem. She said she liked going to her room, where she had two sets of fantasies. One was retaliatory toward her mother: "What if something happened to me? She'd be sorry." The other set of fantasies, in which she identified with the aggressor, was carried out while playing with her dolls, "I was always the mother. I was strict in the mother's role." While there were occasional retaliatory fantasies, as in this case, it was surprising to find how seldom the fantasies were in fact hostile or aggressive toward the punishing parent.

In addition to questions about the use of punishment, subjects were asked about the extent to which praise and reasoning had been used and whether there had been associated fantasies. It is not surprising that neither praise nor reasoning as forms of discipline gave rise to either immediate or delayed fantasy development. Praise, reasoning, and mild punishment are all apt to be reality-oriented. In the earlier statistical sample, praise or reasoning, unlike severe punishment, did not correlate with hypnotic susceptibility.

It should be emphasized that high punishment is not *necessary* as a background for hypnosis. About half of the high subjects were punished very little. It is important to note that well developed fantasy was used *defensively* and that this use of fantasy as a coping device may well have been operating in other areas of our subjects' lives about which no inquiry was made.

ENVIRONMENTAL INFLUENCES THAT REDUCE THE IMAGINATIVE
INVOLVEMENTS

Just as there are influences that operate to augment fantasy development in the home, so there are influences that reduce it. Fantasy is reduced if the home emphasizes strict reality orientation in home activities whether the participation is in recreation or whether in interactions with people. Achievement may be stressed increasingly as the child grows older, particularly in adolescence. Responsibilities in young adulthood and in the mature years further cut into the time that can be devoted to carefree types of imagination. It is not by chance that hypnotic susceptibility scores which depend so much on the exercise of imagination are highest in the years between nine and twelve, and decline thereafter.

Continuities in Imaginative Involvements in Everyday Life and in Hypnosis

The interviews that led to establishing a positive relationship between imaginative involvements and hypnotizability also revealed a great deal of richness in these experiences independent of hypnosis. It seemed wise, therefore, to explore more fully with a few selected highly hypnotizable students both the role of the involvements in their ordinary lives, and how they made use of them as they met the requirements of the hypnotic procedures. Ten students were chosen who had a history of nearly maximum scores on HGSHS:A and the individual SHSS:C, as well as high scores on the Stanford Profile Scale. Prior to the interviews the students had also reduced both the pain of circulating ice water and of ischemia following a tourniquet to the upper arm and dynamometer exercise of the occluded hand.

The experiences of these subjects in hypnotic sessions had been varied enough so that questioning concerned much more than how they responded to specific suggestions of the various scales that entered into scores. Some of the hypnotic sessions had been devoted to deepening procedures in which the subject took the major initiative. That is, the hypnotist, after illustrating some of the possibilities such as visualizing an experience of going down an escalator, or of drifting in a canoe, or of floating on a cloud, would invite the subjects to go deeper in any way they found congenial. Hence while certain circumscribed events reported by the subjects were initiated by the experimenter, the great variety of contributions by the subjects were not. These spontaneous contributions have been little studied in terms of the individual historical backgrounds which our subjects bring to hypnosis.

To give some indication of the extent to which these high subjects have shown in their experiences outside of hypnosis the kinds of imaginative involvement that have been described earlier, a summary of the ratings of involvements based on interviews with the ten subjects is presented in Figure 15.1. Because four is the average rating on this seven-point scale, it is evident that we have ratings much above the average. We see that in at least six areas of involvement there are ratings of six or seven on this scale. These are, in numerical order of mean ratings, though not implying any

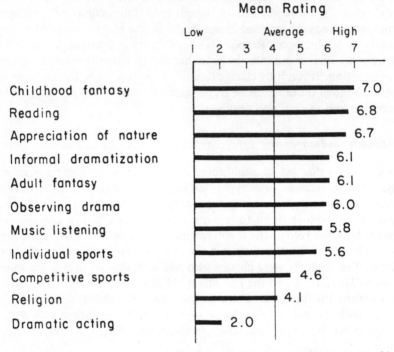

FIGURE 15.1. *Imaginative involvements for 10 selected highly hypnotizable subjects.*

significance to the order for such small differences, childhood fantasy, reading, aesthetic appreciation of nature, informal dramatization (as in vividly telling the story of a small daily adventure), adult fantasy, and drama viewing (as distinct from acting). Music and individual sports are almost as high. Competitive sports are about average, religious involvements are also average, and actual dramatic acting is a high area for only two of the ten subjects.

Fantasy in hypnosis, as fantasy outside hypnosis, is contructed from three components, two based on memory, and one a fresh construction. The first memory component comes from actual experiences with the environment: sights, sounds, smells, some specific adventures, and experiences on occasions from the past with an emphasis on physical sources of stimulation and events that could be described in behavioral terms. The second memory component is of the very personal reaction to these events, the affective responses to them, and the fantasies that were then stirred up. In other words, contemporary fantasies include remembered fantasies from the past. Finally, a present fantasy represents a reconstruction, based on these materials, but having an inventive aspect to it. The present fantasy may be largely novel, and even bizarre, but it will still reflect past experiences also. If you can imagine Plato as one of the members of our moon walk team, both Plato and the contours of the moon come from the memory store, even though the combination is new. What we find in the reports of these subjects, as they recount their fantasies in the free hypnotic state, is a very heavy reliance in hypnosis on the sensory-feeling aspects of prior imaginative involvements. In this respect our subjects tended to rely upon two main groups of experiences.

Six of the ten subjects relied very heavily on images that were previously involved in *the sensory or aesthetic appreciation of nature.* The words they used appear later in the case material, but some of the expressions were words common to the experiences of nature and to the vocabulary of the subject describing his hypnotic experience. These six spoke of: The "joy of non-responsibility," of "tranquility," of "serenity," of "ecstasy," of "feeling thrilled and alone with God." They also used descriptive words such as "intoxication," "enraptured," "wonderment," "marvelling."

The second set of experiences on which the subjects relied were those from their imaginative involvements in literature, drama, and music. Many of them had had experiences of transporting themselves to another, completely different environment, as described by the story, whether in a book, portrayed in a movie, or generated in fantasy while listening to music. The fantasy at the time had been very real so that, as restored and elaborated in hypnosis, it also had a reality quality.

The case material gives concreteness to the preceding summarization. Subjects very high in hypnotic responsiveness commonly have so much rich experience to draw upon that brief summaries are likely to give a very incomplete picture. In order to draw some generalizations from the case material, however, some simplification is necessary for expository purposes. The material from the following eight of the ten extensive interviews has been reorganized in such a manner to illustrate, first, how the involvements have been capitalized on for the purposes of the hypnotic experience, and, second, something of the history of these specific involvements in the life of the individual with some slighting of the other involvements that may have been present.

CASE 1: MARTIN

When asked whether some life experiences had contributed to his hypnotic susceptibility, Martin replied, "I have an independence of my surroundings. I'm not tied down to the physical world around me. In my imagination, I always replaced one place with another place." In deepening hypnosis he used scenes at the beach which he loves.

Martin, majoring in science and art, said of nature that it seems like the source of his being, he is so close to it. Brought up in the country in Colorado and Montana, as a boy he spent much time with his father on long walks where they climbed or fished or hunted. These experiences were still very real to him—the scenes, the feelings for his father, the sounds of nature.

Imagery was kept alive through various channels. "When I read *Dr. Zhivago,* I was always wearing my coat because I got so cold on his Siberian trip." He could also feel the heat of the hot Southern atmosphere when he read *The Heart is a Lonely Hunter.* Fantasy life still persists in the form of imagining when he is doing field work, or oceanography, or making kinetic sculptures or pottery. "It's as concrete in my imagery as having it written down."

CASE 2: GEORGE

George described how he used his fantasies in entering hypnosis: "The last several times I've felt like a wave in the ocean. I visualize the ocean and the wave and I'm moving with it. I'm riding with it. I establish the rhythm, along with my breathing. I see the whole ocean. Instead of riding *on* the wave, I'm *in* the wave, moving with it, up and down. Each time I go down I get deeper until I include the whole volume of the ocean."

How does he come out of hypnosis if he has the wave feeling in hypnosis? "I imagine I'm running onto the shore, getting smaller, no longer moving in circles. That automatically brings me out, pleasantly relaxed."

When George watches the physical ocean he *wants* to move with the wave, feel fluid, released from the land. "In hypnosis I can completely do it." When he stands by the ocean in actual life, he has to control that urge.

George, majoring in English and religion, has loved to watch the ocean and the waves since childhood. "There are scenes I'm *rapt* with, I could stand for hours looking at the scene...I see more and more of it...the more I see, the more I like and appreciate it." He has climbed a ridge and been able to see valleys and mountains on both sides of him. "I felt thrilled and close to God."

CASE 3: JORDAN

Jordan described a similar peculiarity which occurs both in his involvement in music and in his involvement in hypnosis. He described a twirling sensation in hypnosis. "I'm very aware of the back of my head because when I concentrate I let the sounds come in through the back and they twirl around and cover the whole head. The twirling seems to be inside the skull, it gradually gets smaller and more intense." When asked whether this twirling occurred at any other time, Jordan replied, "That's the way I listen to music. I don't feel it go into my ears. It seems to start at the back of my ears and twirl around." There is some difference between hypnosis and music. "In music I involve my whole body, gut feelings, etc., while in hypnosis my head is the focal point. I go through a lot of emotions when I listen to music ...There is just relaxation in hypnosis." He has a floating feeling while listening to music as well as in hypnosis.

Jordan is a talented musician who still enjoys playing the piano three to four hours a day though his major is psychology. He rates the following involvements at the highest level: reading, drama (both acting and watching it), nature, music, childhood fantasy, and individual sports.

Nature was strongly emphasized as he was growing up. There were many family trips to national parks. He enjoyed sailing, skiing, beach hikes. He loved going to the ocean, just watching the waves, or he'd stop his bike and gaze at the mountains, or in the city he would look at paintings in art stores.

He loves performing, has had leads in musical productions, and has become so involved in what he was doing that he was once unaware of a broken bone.

CASE 4: ROBERT

Robert, who is majoring in math and expects to go on in law, related what he did in hypnosis to water skiing, swimming underwater, liking to free fall as on a trampoline. In deepening hypnosis he pictures himself at Lake Tahoe, water skiing behind his boat, or he pictures himself floating in the swimming pool where he floats, drifts, swims underwater. Asked to describe this latter experience in more detail, he said, "It's visual. It's like *being* there and looking through my eyes at the bottom of the pool, or looking toward the top." While water skiing in hypnosis, he is looking down at his skis, and enjoying the feeling of flying over the water. The scenery is beautiful and he loves the still, crisp air. He says of hypnosis, "I never achieve the degree of relaxation in the normal waking state that I do in hypnosis but I do get the same degree of relaxation when under water in the swimming pool where I'll stay under water for an hour or two, just floating up many times." Sometimes when he is bored at home he will picture himself doing something else, like skiing or he will picture himself as a character he is writing about. This subject relates part of his ability in hypnosis to his ability to self-talk. The hypnotist's voice sometimes becomes his voice. He gets it from the hypnotist and tells it to himself "like translating."

Robert's other high involvements are in novels, movies, informal dramatizations, and religion. They have been continuous since childhood.

CASE 5: PATRICIA

When Patricia described the relationship between hypnosis and the kinds of experiences she enjoyed independent of hypnosis, she used the words "tranquility" and "serenity" to describe what they had in common. What she enjoyed in hypnosis: "The general aura of it, the feeling of nonresponsibility, the feeling of wonderment at the things that were around me." In hypnosis, as in nature, "I don't have to make decisions. Things can just happen."

Her face had lighted up earlier when she had been asked about her interest in nature. "The most pleasurable thing I can do is get involved in nature. At the ocean, I feel I could stay there forever, there's an intoxication with the whole environment, the waves, the beach, the plants, animals, rocks. I have great absorption. It's the type of thing I think about in hypnosis."

Patricia had spent a great deal of time in the mountains with her parents from earliest childhood. They went regularly on weekends to get away from city life. "My parents really enjoyed it...We went a lot, but it was always special, to get out of the city. My parents spent a lot of time with us." She spoke of the way her parents had expressed the thought that such experiences were wondrous; they would marvel, for example, at the color of wildflowers. Thus we note a long, uninterrupted history of involved enjoyment in nature, supported by close identification with greatly involved parents.

CASE 6: BARRY

Barry, who is an economics major, with law as his intended career, said that the first of several possible experiences suggested by the hypnotist, that of floating in a small boat near a large white beach, was very congenial to him because he likes being rocked by waves while he admires the water, sky, sun, and trees around him. He has loved nature all of his life. "Ever since I was in a cradle my folks would go for a month each year, as well as on many weekends, to the mountains." Both parents enjoyed it. Father and son are alike in their tremendous involvement.

When asked what attraction nature held for him, he said, "Usually I like it because it is open, fresh, not spoiled commercially. I have a phobia of crowds packed in small places. I can get away from that in nature because no one is there. I enjoy trees, the colors of mountains, the sky at night, watching sunsets and sunrises; there's an overall aesthetic beauty in them. A sunrise gives you the gradual lightening of day, it's the unfolding and the color. I also enjoy the sounds of mountains, the birds, wind, and water, the smells of trees, water and ground." To Barry it means, "moving away from a barely tolerable reality to a much more enjoyable, natural environment."

Barry, in hypnosis, is completely removed from current problems. Says he, "I'm unconcerned with my normal environment. It's like when I sleep outside in the mountains I enjoy the fresh air, ground, trees, sky, stars, and the night sounds such as wind and animals prowling around."

CASE 7: MARY

Mary, a major in art, says, "When I'm going into hypnosis, I remember a passage or a favorite chapter from a book, or from one of my earlier experiences, something that's worked out well for me." Mary adds her own visual imagery when the hypnotist counts from one to twenty, or if he tells her she is walking down to a garden, "I visualized how it was black all around with white stairs. It was a big broad staircase with a half curve. The steps continued to get grayer and by the time I got to twenty, the steps were all black." She thinks she read about that type of background in a book. Symbolically she says it signifies how, when she starts out she is fresh and aware of her surroundings, of definite boundaries. As she goes into hypnosis, her keenness fades out into gray. Then to go deeper, she sees herself in a free fall, floating downward, like an Alice in Wonderland that she saw when she was very small.

Mary also becomes deeply involved in music outside of hypnosis and she spontaneously finds herself listening to music within hypnosis. She says, "I can really get involved in hypnosis when I'm listening to music. We have a record at home with *Bolero* and *The Hall of the Mountain King* on it. Both start slowly and build up. I listen to it quite often at home. I listen to it when I start going under. It's like I'm at home listening with my eyes closed, as though I'm there... Recently I've been so busy, it's hard for me to sit down and get my mind completely relaxed, and not racing ahead to what I have to do next. In hypnosis this music does it. It would do the same in actual life."

CASE 8: JAMES

James, a major in psychology and the highest scoring member of the group, says he lets his own fantasy "enliven someone else's fantasy" in the following way. "When the hypnotist used the idea of floating on a cloud, I provided a great many variations on that theme. I brought in the brilliant white of a really clean cloud against the brilliant blue of the sky, then I felt the warmth of the sun as it shone down on me. I was jumping in the air and doing somersaults, bouncing up and down on the cloud. I jumped high and did a belly-flop. It's like swimming where there is no set boundary—you can make a gliding movement to go wherever you want through the water. In my night dreams I'll fly and this is a movement like that."

James combines the hypnotist's counting in hypnosis with his own imagery of brightly colored psychedelic numbers.

Because of his rich use of varied imagery, the sources of James' involvements as they relate to hypnosis are less specific than those of some of the other subjects. He denied using anything from his reading, but he referred to music and his love of nature. Of nature he said: "I lose myself completely in nature. For hours I'll look at one scene. Every minute can be *ecstasy* for me." He gave an illustration of being at Yosemite the preceding weekend, on top of Sentinel Dome for two hours, sometimes taking close-ups with his eyes, sometimes fixating objects far away such as one tree.

Discussion

Everyone has some imagination, but it is important to distinguish between the ability that most people have to conjure up fleeting images or produce temporary imaginative constructions, and the special abilities that these selected subjects show. Their fantasies are characterized first of all by a long and nearly continuous history since childhood, and secondly by the *degree* of absorption and the *intensity* of affective accompaniments. For the most part these involvements were either shared with parents or supported by parents; such cases typically showed strong ego strength clinically and on the MMPI. One with high involvement was unlike the others; although closely attached to one parent, there was neither parental sharing nor parental support for his interests. The ego strength in this subject was markedly weaker than in the others. From this latter case, however, we realize that parental sharing of the involvements is not at all a necessary condition for their development.

The fact that imaginative involvements outside hypnosis correlate with hypnotic susceptibility does not mean that the experiences can be equated. Outside hypnosis the involvements have a reality basis: there are scenes in nature to be enjoyed, a book to be read, a play to be listened to. To be sure, ordinary reality is set aside, so that the involvement may take on a "hypnotic quality," but it does not mean that the person listening to music or enjoying the theatre is really hypnotized. He does not add musical accompaniments of his own, and he does not introduce new characters on the stage. In hypnosis, the external supports for his involvements are not there and he produces them, as necessary, through fantasy. He selects the music himself from his memory store, he transports himself to scenes that he wishes to enjoy.

We recognize, then, that the involvements outside hypnosis have a reality base absent in hypnosis, so that the role of imagination is more important in hypnosis, even though the involvements in the produced experiences may be similar, and the savoring of the imagined experience may partake of the savoring of the real experience. There is continuity between imaginative involvements outside hypnosis and in hypnosis, but not identity.

The subject tends to have an *active, not a passive* role through supplementing the hypnotist's suggestions with devices of his own, even when he is being entirely cooperative with the hypnotist. This was true throughout the case material. The hypnotic subject is active and shows a good deal of independence from the hypnotist.

Some support for this assertion is found from the MMPI scores available on these subjects. If one compares the *ego* strength scores with the scores for *dependency,* eight of the ten have ego strength scores at or above the standardization mean, while only two have dependency scores above this standardization mean, and in eight of the ten cases the ego strength scores are higher than the dependency scores.

As usual in studies of hypnotic susceptibility, there is no universal correlation with personality scores. While most of these high subjects would be characterized as normal outgoing people, one subject has a number of personality problems evident in the interview and supported by the MMPI as well. He shows both low ego strength and high dependency, but his hypnotic scores are well up with the others.

In the earlier account of a large interview sample (J.R. Hilgard, 1970), and in the subsequent study of selected high and low hypnotizable subjects (J.R. Hilgard, 1974), it was found that the highly hypnotizable had among them a disproportionate number who had been severely disciplined in childhood. This was interpreted as having led to excessive use of fantasy, and hence related to hypnotizability. These results have not been confirmed within this sample of ten highly hypnotizable, with only two of the ten reaching a rating of six of the seven-point scale of severity of discipline. In neither of these cases was there fantasy formation as a result. This new sample was born nearly ten years later than the earlier one, so that their memories date from the early 1960's instead of the early 1950's. The possibility exists of changes in the social climate over these years, although not much can be made of differences based on this small sample. A point worth noting is that the tendency to informal dramatizations, an area in which this present group excelled, did not automatically lead to an exaggeration of reports of punishment, a point raised in reviews of earlier reports.

In brief, then, this case material shows how much subjects bring to the hypnotic experience from their life experiences, how much they use the capacity for imaginative production to substitute for the stimulation from the environment. Then, on the basis of these self-products, how they reproduce the affective accompaniment (for example, ecstasy) of their earlier experiences outside hypnosis. It is very difficult to capture these phenomenal experiences in their full richness for the individual through questionnaires. Even though the clinical method is at some disadvantage in providing reproducible quantitative findings, it brings insistently to our attention some of the realities in the experience of the highly hypnotizable person.

Imaginative Involvements as Related to Problems of Living

Because imaginative involvements and hypnotizability overlap, it is of interest to inquire under what circumstances these involvements lead to adjustment, and when to maladjustment. Hypnotizable persons may suffer from various forms of emotional difficulties, just as nonhypnotizables do. That is, hypnotizability does not of itself provide any evidence of neurotic tendencies (Tellegen and Atkinson, 1974). Nevertheless, we are justified in asking whether the capacity for imaginative involvement is always confined to circumscribed fantasy, books, drama, and nature, as it has been described up to this point. Does it sometimes carry over to an unusual degree into situations of everyday living? Frankel has shown that people suffering from phobias include a disproportionate number of the more hypnotizable individuals (1976). Harding has suggested that the same may be true for migraine sufferers (1967). In clinical experience with patients at Stanford, certain problems related to the imagination have been observed in a number of highly hypnotizable individuals. Imaginative involvement is not the only factor but, in conjunction with others, there are ways in which it may tip the balance and precipitate problems in life situations.

IMAGINATION AND SENSITIVITY TO THE ENVIRONMENT

Because of the relationship between imagination and suggestibility, those capable of high imaginative involvements may sometimes be over-impressed by things heard or experienced.

Imaginative people may be extremely sensitive to tales *told* by relatives or friends who talk emotionally about their difficulties. Through identification and empathy imaginative persons become as involved in verbal tales or "sagas" as they do in the written ones. Perhaps the impact is greater since the experience is related "live" and usually with great feeling. Certain phobic patients illustrate this point.

Stolzenberg (1961) relates how a dental patient was phobic to dental procedures though she herself had had no experiences of an adverse kind in dentistry. At age eighteen, she needed a statement that her teeth were in satisfactory condition as part of a college entrance requirement. Her teeth were in obviously poor condition, yet she would not permit even a routine examination of her mouth. She eventually agreed to hypnosis, entered a satisfactory hypnotic condition, and was age-regressed to determine the origin of her dental phobia. As a young child the patient had been sitting at the dinner table when her sister had returned from the dentist, crying hysterically and relating how the dentist had cut her mouth with a drill. The patient was instructed to recall the incident out of hypnosis, in order that the dentist could discuss it with her. He pointed out that the sister's trouble was very temporary; she had returned a number of times to the same dentist without complaint. Acceptance of the explanation reduced the patient's fears so that she found no difficulty in beginning with dental treatment.

Frankel (1976, pp. 108-110) cites the case of a pregnant woman with a fear of childbirth. "Although she had had no previous experience of childbirth, she was led to believe from stories she had heard that it was terrifying." She had been frightened as an adolescent by reports of the agony of childbirth and by her mother's recounting the fearsome details. This patient proved highly responsive to hypnosis on the Stanford Scale, and responded well to hypnotic treatment so that she was able to master the event.

In both cases, we see identification with a traumatized person in a story which is characterized by intense feeling. Involvement with the major character occurs when the patient is at an impressionable age. This capacity for identification with characters in a living drama would certainly be compatible with marked responsiveness to hypnosis as we have been describing it.

IMAGINATION AS AUGMENTING REACTION TO TRAUMATIC EXPERIENCES

The next question arises naturally from the preceding discussion. Are some persons not only exceptionally sensitive to sagas told by others but to traumatic life situations in their own personal experiences? As studied in the college population, direct feeling experiences have dealt with affective arousal through sensory stimulation such as aesthetic visual appreciation of nature or involvement in music. If one sees an individual who is strongly affected by the positive aspects of sensory input, one might hypnothesize that some of these individuals could be equally affected by intense negative aspects in other situations.

In Frankel's description of the phobia connected with childbirth, he mentioned that this patient had developed a fear of planes since a turbulent flight three years earlier. After another flight when she attempted to overcome her anxiety, she became even more panicky; she experienced breathlessness, helplessness, and a light feeling throughout her body. Thus where we can trace a specific onset as in this case, we glimpse a patient who was extremely sensitive to bodily feelings of a negative variety. Since she was highly hypnotizable, we can assume that she was a very imaginatively involved person. In this situation, she imagined that the worst outcome was occurring.

To achieve a greater understanding of the ways in which sagas or adverse personal experiences have contributed to the development of some phobias or other problems in living, we need to study cases in which factors under consideration include imaginative involvement as one of them. Such a study has not been conducted.

IMAGINATION AS GRATIFICATION SUBSTITUTING FOR REALITY

Gratification through imagination may be so strong throughout life that imagined circumstances can substitute for adequate understanding of the realities of a situation.

A patient, Jane, aged twenty-nine, married, and the mother of two children, was in psychiatric treatment for depression at the time she was referred to the hypnosis project for adjunctive help with cigarette addiction. She was depressed, she said, "mainly because I keep making the same mistakes." She gave as an illustration her third marriage where extreme differences were already apparent between her and her husband. She said she thought a part of her trouble was the tendency to fantasy a relationship which was just the way she wished it to be, instead of looking at the facts. After the marriage, the details which she had overlooked in her haste to fit the indiviudal into her ideal person emerged only too quickly. This had happened each of the three times.

Jane was found to be highly hypnotizable, passing ten of twelve tests on SHSS: C, and highly imaginative upon being interviewed. In terms of present problems, it is significant that imagination in childhood had developed largely through loneliness and unhappiness at home. Involvement in imagination had frequently substituted for unhappy realities. She had woven many stories about her dolls, became "lost" as she read novels, and from an early age had shown an intense interest in nature. She learned to express thoughts and feelings in drawing and had become an art illustrator for a book company. The parents, who were rather solitary people, enjoyed books, nature, and art and served as models in those areas though there had been little genuine sharing. It is not surprising that Jane's habit of using her imagination defensively to deny problems in childhood continued as a habit of denying them through the adult years in the same manner.

In regard to the smoking problem, Jane made progress in the course of four hypnotic sessions. Here, instead of using her imagination defensively, she was able to use it constructively. She reduced her smoking from two and a half packs per day to an occasional cigarette a day, sometimes none, sometimes several. In this circumscribed area she felt a sense of success; instead of being controlled by the habit, she said she felt a sense of control.

It is clear that where imaginative involvement has substituted markedly for reality in order to obliterate unhappiness in childhood, its continuance at a high level into the adult years constitutes a severe handicap. Another patient who had been in psychiatric treatment for four years because of periodic depression, loneliness, and immaturity, was referred to the hypnotic laboratory for adjunctive help in weight control. Mary passed all of the tests on the SHSS:C. What did she say about the role of imaginative involvement in her life? "Imagination was ninety-five percent of my life as a child. It let me construct whole worlds where I was safe and happy and needed." Part of the make-believe was in books. She identified strongly with Alice in *Alice in Wonderland,* with Bambi, with Nancy Drew in the Nancy Drew series, with Winnie the Pooh, and with many others as she was growing up. Books constituted an escape. "Everything in books was more interesting than what I was doing. There were experiences I had never had. There was warmth and friends. Books didn't hurt you. Things normally went better for children in books." She identified just as strongly today, "After reading an Irving Stone novel, the letters I write for two months are in the Irving Stone style." She identified with characters in poetry, "I can transport myself out of my environment and to the place of the poetry. If the poem is about the sea or the mountains, I can transport myself there so that I see it all, smell it, feel it." She identified strongly as she viewed stories in the movies or on TV. Although Mary had done no formal acting, she reported that she could frequently make people laugh by telling episodes in a way that poked fun at herself.

Nature had high priority. "My favorite place in the whole world is Yosemite National Park. We went there for two weeks last summer. Lying on my back, I watched the swallows flying overhead. The air was clean and pure. I enjoyed the smells of the pine needles. I fed the squirrels, watched the deer. It's peaceful, makes me feel closer to God again. It's freedom. I loved it as a child—most of our vacations were at Yosemite." She felt she enjoyed nature as much as father did. Father could just sit and look and let nature sink into him, too. Today, in a creative vein, Mary writes poems and stories for children.

What support for her many interests did Mary obtain from her family? In spite of the fact that there was not much closeness, there was modeling by the parents and role identification as Mary sensed the enjoyment her parents obtained from nature, books, poetry and classical music. Food was very important in the family. It was always used as a special reward, special cookies, cakes, and boxes of candy.

We were not successful in treating Mary for her weight problem through hypnosis. Failure probably hinged on the fact that gratification through fantasy comes effortlessly. Long years of experience had accustomed Mary to this idea. She was prepared to enjoy the fantasies of hypnosis—and she did—without the work entailed by following a rigid program of weight control in the real world. Once having visualized herself as slender, with a beautiful figure, she concentrated on this gratifying vision to such an extent that she was satisfied and felt no need for action. When other methods used in hypnosis resulted in a similar outcome, it was clear that motivation for actual work on the problem did not exist. Her case, unlike the first one of cigarette addiction, shows how excessive use of imagination in hypnosis can serve to impede genuine progress.

IMAGINATIVE INVOLVEMENTS AS COPING DEVICES

The preceding cases show that imaginative involvements are not universally helpful in hypnotic therapy, but they do tend to be used as coping devices. In the second of the preceding cases the coping was so successful on a fantasy level that it served as a barrier to coping on a reality level.

Although we have made no systematic study of a patient population, the following observations on the role of imagination and imaginative involvements are based upon a number of clinical patients studied after their referral to the staff of the University Medical School as outpatients in psychiatry. The cases permit several tentative generalizations.

Imaginative involvements in a patient population, as in a student population, are related to greater hypnotic responsiveness. Conversely, their absence is related to less responsiveness. The imaginative involvements are more apt to develop in a setting of isolation and loneliness than is true of the college population. Where loneliness is a significant factor, the parents are usually role models, even though interaction with them has proved unsatisfactory in many ways and the patients have experienced unmet dependency needs. The degree of contagious interaction as observed in the patient population is far less than in the college student samples.

Because of the lack of interaction, the children and parents go separate ways when reading, watching TV, or listening to music. Even with this degree of isolation, the parents may serve as models and imaginative capacities develop. Consistent with the development of imagination in a setting of loneliness, some patients had few friends and had developed few social skills.

Whether the involvements have developed through contagious experiences with parents, or in some degree as a defense against loneliness, when present they provide a background for hypnosis in therapy. Through them, concrete imagery and affect can be put to use.

Imaginative Involvements as Ego Assets

The sensory-affective and imaginative involvements constitute an important part of the ego, i.e., the play-ego of child and adult. In proper perspective, they represent areas of substantial ego strength. Amid the increasing pressures of adult life, people can experience them as oases of tranquility, of conflict-free participation, and of effortless gratification. Those who truly appreciate nature enjoy the beach, the mountains, the meadows, a sunset, and many other wonders. As they watch, they become revitalized. In their listening to a Beethoven symphony, music exerts the same effect. While reading a book or watching a drama, the involved person is transported to another world; even in tragedies, an unhappy event always happens to someone else, and thus is one step removed from the self. They may seem real as the individual identifies with the feeling or the character in the story. Somewhere, of course, he knows that he is himself and not the character, for this is the function of the observing ego. Provided this flexibility is maintained, the ability to use imagination can be valued for itself.

Martin T. Orne *is Director of the Unit for Experimental Psychiatry at The Institute of Pennsylvania Hospital and Professor of Psychiatry at the University of Pennsylvania. He received his M.D. from Tufts University Medical School in 1955, and his M.A. and Ph.D. from Harvard University Graduate School in 1951 and 1958. After an internship at Michael Reese Hospital in 1956, he completed his residency at Massachusetts Mental Health Center in 1960. He became Senior Research Psychiatrist at Massachusetts Mental Health Center and Associate in Psychiatry at Harvard Medical School. From 1958 until 1964 he was Director of the Studies in Hypnosis Project. In 1964 the research laboratory moved to The Institute of Pennsylvania Hospital. The research group has continued as the Unit for Experimental Psychiatry with studies concerning the nature of hypnosis remaining one of its principal interests. Current areas of research also include sleep, psychophysiology, biofeedback mechanisms, and the generic problem of objectifying alterations in subjective experience. Since each of these substantive areas of inquiry involves human subjects in experimental contexts, some work has inevitably been concerned with the basic problem of experimental methods in psychology and psychiatry, especially the social psychology of the psychological experiment.*

Orne *reported in 1959 on a special comparison group for the study of hypnosis, which involved the use of Ss instructed to simulate hypnosis. Simulators are selected from among unhypnotizable individuals and are not given any special training. Their behavior reflects therefore their own expectations about hypnosis and the information about what is expected of them that is provided by the hypnotist and the experimental situation. The procedure was developed in rough analogy to the double-blind placebo technique design as used in psychopharmacology. It has proved to have several important uses in hypnosis research, but the implications have been widely misunderstood and misinterpreted. This chapter seeks to clarify the issues. Orne shows that it is possible to simulate hypnosis, but he does not imply that hypnosis is simulation. Quite the contrary, his technique has helped shed light on important, unique characteristics of hypnosis.*

16

On the Simulating Subject as a Quasi-Control Group in Hypnosis Research: What, Why, and How

MARTIN T. ORNE

When a S capable of entering deep hypnosis agrees to do so, it is possible for him, within what appears to be a few moments, to alter dramatically his appearance, behavioral style, and responsivity to the hypnotist. The remarkable range of alterations in experience and memory that can now be induced has long puzzled and fascinated laymen and professionals alike. It is not surprising that such a dramatic phenomenon has resulted in innumerable claims about its potential benefit or harm, the way in which it may change or improve mental functioning, and how it might cause one individual to obtain a great degree of control over another.

The process by which hypnosis is induced is remarkably innocuous when one considers the apparently dramatic changes that occur. Furthermore, entering hypnosis may take place almost instantaneously. As a result, the observer is fascinated by the implausibility of these events and, in trying to

The preparation of this chapter, as well as the substantive research conducted at the Unit for Experimental Psychiatry, was supported in part by grant #MH 03369 and by grant #MH 19156–01 from the National Institute of Mental Health, Public Health Service. The author wishes to express his appreciation to Harvey D. Cohen, Mary R. Cook, Frederick J. Evans, Charles Graham, A. Gordon Hammer, Ulric Neisser, Donald N. O'Connell, Emily Carota Orne, David A. Paskewitz, Arthur Shapiro, and Mae C. Weglarski for their helpful comments during the preparation of this manuscript.

explain them, either assumes some basic alteration in neurophysiological function or is inclined to dismiss what he has seen as not real, play-acting, or faking.

From the time when hypnotic phenomena were first described, attempts have been made to explain away these occurrences as not being real. Inevitably, in attempting to account for hypnosis, there has been a great deal of concern about the extent to which the S honestly reports his experiences or the extent to which he may be dissimulating or deceiving the observers.

Traditionally then, questions were raised about the extent to which the S's actions reflect what he is experiencing and whether the S's reports about his experiences are honest and genuine. The most satisfying proof about the reality of hypnosis, therefore, was to demonstrate abilities of the hypnotized individual that were present only in that state. If it could be demonstrated that the hypnotized S can do things that the waking individual cannot, there is little need to worry about the reality of the phenomenon. It certainly is more satisfying to have hard evidence of this kind than to depend upon the S's verbal description of what has occurred.

When it was first reported (Orne, 1959) that individuals are able to simulate hypnosis sufficiently well to deceive trained hypnotists, the observation aroused considerable skepticism, and its implications were widely misunderstood. It is the purpose of this paper to clarify some of these issues and to review the strategy of research that led to development of this technique.

SOME COMMENTS ON THE NATURE OF HYPNOSIS

It is recognized that there is no generally accepted definition of hypnosis, though considerable consensus exists at a descriptive level and observers readily agree that they have witnessed hypnosis after they have watched a highly responsive S responding to hypnotic suggestions. Although a large number of induction procedures have been described, it must be admitted that neither the necessary nor the sufficient conditions for hypnosis have yet been delineated. Thus, some Ss under some circumstances will enter hypnosis without any formal induction procedures, while others fail to enter hypnosis despite extensive induction procedures designed to elicit such response. For these reasons it seems futile at the present state of knowledge to define hypnosis by the antecedent conditions. It seems more appropriate to stay closer to a descriptive level where consensus exits.

The presence of hypnosis can be identified by the way in which a S responds to suggestions. Heuristically, then, hypnosis is considered to be that state or condition in which suggestions (or cues) from the hypnotist will elicit hypnotic phenomena. Hypnotic phenomena can operationally be distinguished from nonhypnotic responses only when suggestions are given that require the S to distort his perception or memory. Accordingly, the hypnotized individual can be identified only by his ability to respond to suitable suggestions by appropriately altering any or all modalities of perception and memory (Orne, 1959). It follows, therefore, that if a S is told by a hypnotist, "Remove your left shoe," and he carries out the requested behavior, it would not be possible to conclude that the individual is hypnotized; since no distortion of perception is required, the behavior could be carried out by the unhypnotized individual. However, if the hypnotist suggests that the S see someone who is not physically present, hear music in a quiet room, or have gustatory experiences in the absence of food, and the S behaves as if he has these experiences, reports having these experiences and, as far as it is possible to ascertain, actually believes he has these experiences, one may say he is hypnotized; indeed, these are experiences which the nonhypnotized individual cannot simply choose to have.

Of particular importance for the diagnosis of hypnosis are suggestions that (1) distort the S's perception so as to make him feel unable to carry out an action such as bending his arm, opening his eyes, and so forth (challenge suggestions), (2) induce hallucinatory experiences, (3) alter memory (such as suggested amnesias), and (4) elicit posthypnotic behaviors.

Individuals differ widely in the extent to which suggestions are able to elicit hypnotic phenomena from them. The concept of hypnotic depth generally is used to designate the range of phenomena that can be experienced, though, unfortunately, the same term is also used to describe the subjective conviction associated with the suggested alteration of perception or memory and the degree to which the S feels himself profoundly affected.

A great many questions may be asked about hypnosis, such as those that deal with individual differences, the dynamics and nature of the induction process, correlates of hypnotizability, and so on. However, the main thrust of our research program has focused on questions concerning the nature of hypnosis. In other words, research focused on trying to clarify the consequences of being in that state where suggestions are able to distort the perceptions and memories of an individual. If it is suggested to a S that he is six years old and he begins to act in a childlike manner and appears to believe that he is six, what consequences does this have for his actual mental functioning? How will his thought processes be altered? What will this do to his ability to recall past events, and so forth? If a S is told he has superhuman strength and accepts the suggestion, how does this alter his actual performance? If anesthesia is induced and he is exposed to painful stimuli, how does this alter his behavioral response; how does it affect his physiological responses, and so forth?

To the extent that the investigator is concerned about the effects of hypnosis on the psychological and physiological responsivity of the individual, it seems essential to be certain that the S is hypnotized. Consensus is easily obtained only with highly responsive Ss, whereas with less responsive Ss neither the observer, the hypnotist, nor the *S* himself is necessarily certain as to the extent of hypnosis or even whether hypnosis is present. The most appropriate strategy would therefore be to use only the most responsive *S*s. By selecting the extreme group of individuals who are deeply hypnotizable, it is possible to make highly reliable diagnoses and achieve general consensus that the hypnotic phenomenon is unequivocally present. The research approach to be discussed here, then, is based upon the assumption that in order to approach a poorly defined phenomenon one must be absolutely certain that it is really present in the situation. From this point of view, parametric questions dealing with the generalizability of the findings become important only after the general nature of the phenomenon has been delineated.

Problems in Hypnosis Research

Though it is generally agreed that hypnosis is that state where suggestions can elicit hypnotic phenomena from the subject, the associated behaviors have been subject to continuing controversy. In historical perspective this is particularly striking. Thus, the behavior exhibited by Mesmer's patients at his *baquets* was characterized by hysterical seizures which he termed "crises." While these behaviors seemed to be an invariant accompaniment of his sessions, they certainly are not seen today. Likewise, the fixed entranced expression often associated with hypnosis was shown by Bernheim (1889) not to be a necessary accompaniment of the phenomenon. Rapport, once believed to be an essential characteristic of hypnosis, was shown by P. C. Young (1927) not to be essential. At the present time, Erickson[1] insists that catalepsy is an inevitable accompaniment of hypnosis, a finding not substantiated by a number of other clinicians.

In the older literature particularly, many claims are made about hypnosis which, to the modern reader, appear naive. The "physical effects" of mesmeric passes, the transference of cataleptic states from one side of the body to another by means of magnets, and Charcot's (1886) observation that a hypnotized *S* could be brought from sleep to somnambulism by rubbing the top of his head are examples. It is worth noting that the investigators involved were often outstanding scientists whose incisive observations in other areas have stood the test of time. One could hardly consider Charcot—a pioneer in recognizing the distinction between neurological and psychiatric illness, who first described such classic signs as glove anesthesia—an untrained observer; nor is such a label appropriate for Binet, Braid, or Moll.

In order to understand the range of reports about hypnosis and the

---

1. Personal communication.

peculiar diversity of findings, it is necessary to take into account the deeply hypnotized individual's remarkable responsivity not only to explicit suggestions but also to very minute cues, often outside the observer's awareness. These cues are analogous to those discovered in the case of the famous Clever Hans (the horse who was apparently able to do arithmetic computations), a puzzle that was finally solved by Pfungst (1911) when he noticed that the animal responded as long as his trainer looked expectantly at his right forefoot and stopped when the trainer raised his head. Many scientists, unable to explain the phenomenon, came to accept the extremely implausible hypothesis that the horse, Clever Hans, was actually doing arithmetic. If such a relatively simple set of cues could prove so deceptive, it should not be surprising that the elucidation of behavior characteristic of the hypnotized *S* has proven to be such a difficult and complex problem.

Not only does the deeply hypnotized *S* respond to implicit communication (which in and of itself is enough to create special problems of investigation), but there is a further complicating factor: the *S*'s own beliefs and expectations about appropriate behavior of hypnotized individuals also help to determine how he will behave when he is actually hypnotized. Thus it was possible to demonstrate that *S*s who were led to believe unilateral catalepsy of the dominant hand is a hallmark of deep hypnosis tend to display this item of behavior when they are subsequently hypnotized (Orne, 1959).

The search for behavioral characteristics of deep hypnosis that are "intrinsic" is, therefore, exceedingly difficult. An investigator might easily validate any plausible—or not so plausible—beliefs about what constitutes "typical" behavior of the hypnotized individual. The cues as to what is expected may be unwittingly communicated before or during the hypnotic procedure, either by the hypnotist or by someone else, for example, a previous *S*, a story, a movie, a stage show, etc. Further, the nature of these cues may be quite obscure, to the hypnotist, to the *S*, and even to the trained observer.

Recognizing these problems, it seemed essential to develop special techniques that would make it possible to recognize which aspects of a *S*'s response, if any, were due to hypnosis, as opposed to those that were the result of a combination of the *S*'s prior knowledge and expectations in conjunction with cues provided by the situation.

THE NEED TO EVALUATE OR HOLD CONSTANT
THE PROBLEMS THAT REQUIRED CLARIFICATION

The generally accepted approach to hypnotic research, characterized particularly well by the work of Hull (1933), compared the effect of instructions or suggestions given to a deeply hypnotized individual with the identical instructions given either to a nonhypnotized independent control group or to the same individuals in the waking state.[2] Upon study of the results of different instructions it becomes clear, however, that while it is possible to hold the precise wording constant, it is extremely difficult if not impossible for an investigator to speak in the same fashion to a hypnotized as to a waking S—even when the investigator himself is convinced he has done so. Inevitably the instructions are more meaningful to the S and are given with more conviction and emphasis to an individual in whom the experimenter (E) had just induced hypnosis. (An empirical demonstration of these differences was carried out by Troffer and Tart [1964].)

It would appear that many of the differences observed between hypnotized and nonhypnotized individuals could be accounted for by the differential treatment of Ss in hypnosis as opposed to the waking state. The lyrics may be the same but the melody is vastly different! Moreover, even when one is aware of this problem, it is extremely difficult to treat Ss in the same way when they are hypnotized as when they are awake. This problem becomes especially poignant to the observer of the hypnotic interaction when he recalls how a hypnotist changes his voice to speak convincingly to the age-regressed S as a child, and how difficult it is for most E's, even in a role-playing situation, to speak to the adult in front of them as if they were playing with a winsome waif making mud pies on the street outside their laboratory.

The importance of subtle interactional differences in the treatment of individuals has long been recognized in psychopharmacology. Thus, it eventually became clear that even the placebo control is not sufficient, since the physician characteristically (and appropriately) is more concerned with the patients on a new and presumably powerful drug than with those who are receiving an inert substance where "side effects" must be a matter of chance. Complaints of the former variety are carefully followed up, while those of the latter are quickly dismissed, though the etiology of complaints or "effects" in both instances may often, in fact, be identical. For reasons such as these, double- and triple-blind studies have been recognized as essential in order to demonstrate a therapeutic drug effect, particularly in the case of psychotropic agents where subjective experiences are involved. The problem here, analogous to studies of hypnosis, is the need to develop a control procedure for the behavior of the physician-experimenter and, particularly, the need to control for his natural inclination to delve into and follow up certain kinds of subjective experiences in one patient group but not in another.

---

2. The technical advantages of using Ss as their own control are considerable in that interindividual variability is eliminated, and it is therefore possible to obtain significant results with small samples (and also the hypnotizability variable is held constant); on the other hand, the effects of repeated measurements on performance can be highly complex and, especially in hypnotic research, these may seriously distort the picture. For a discussion of these issues, see Sutcliffe (1958) and Zamansky, Scharf, and Brightbill (1964).

THE NEED TO EVALUATE SUBJECTS' KNOWLEDGE AND EXPECTATIONS

The classic experimental model, being based on the one used in physics, assumes that the S enters an experiment as a tabula rasa; that is, that the human S exposed to various treatment conditions has no relevant prior information, knowledge, or expectations. Further, the S in the classic psychological experiment is expected to respond only to those stimuli that are explicitly defined as relevant and important by the investigator. Certainly such is not the state of affairs.[3] On the contrary, Ss enter into any experimental situation—including those that employ hypnosis—with a great deal of prior information as well as very specific, though not necessarily correct, expectations about what is to occur. By the same token, they do not respond merely to the explicit suggestions; rather, these are interpreted, as are all other communications, in the context of a S's understanding of what is intended.[4]

Until relatively recently, little explicit attention had been paid to the S's interpretation of the situation. A striking exception was Asch's (1952) brilliant reinterpretation of the Lorge (1936) experiment on prestige suggestion. In this study the investigators had shown that Ss based their agreement with short statements not on their substantive content but rather on the individual to whom the statements were ascribed. Lorge argued that S's acceptance or refusal of substantive statements was based not on their content but on prestige suggestion, that is, the attitude toward the man to whom the statement had been credited. In repeating this study, Asch asked not only for the degree of acceptance but also for an elaboration of the meaning of the statements. In this way it became clear that a short sentence such as "... a little rebellion, now and then, is a good thing..." has in fact an entirely different substantive meaning if it is attributed to Lenin than it does if attributed to Jefferson. In other words, the ascription of a brief and ambiguous statement to a specific author about whose views the S is relatively well informed actually provides special contextual meaning to the statement. Agreement or disagreement is a function not of prestige suggestion but of altered meaning due to the additional information provided by the knowledge of who made the statement.

Asch's analysis is a penetrating one which can be used as a model for understanding much experimental work. Inquiry procedures (Orne, 1959) help clarify how the S perceived the total situation and how he interpreted

3. For a more extended discussion of these issues see Orne (1962b, 1969, 1970).

4. It has often been claimed (see Erickson, 1952) that the deeply hypnotized S is more literal in his interpretation of suggestions than the waking individual. Unfortunately, rigorous evidence for this very interesting observation is not yet available. The possibility that the observations are the result of subtle cues by the hypnotist of the kind described earlier cannot be dismissed.

explicit experimental demands. Unfortunately the interpretation of inquiry information involves considerable subjective judgment, a difficulty which can be only partially remedied by the use of judges. Further, there always remains doubt about how the S's perception may have translated itself into behavior on the experimental tasks. Another problem with post-experimental procedures is the difficulty of determining the extent to which the S's response represents hindsights gained from reflection about his own performance, which need not have affected his behavior during the actual experimental situation.

A modifications of the post-experimental inquiry procedure, which has been referred to as the "pre-experimental inquiry" or the "nonexperiment" (Orne, 1962b), partially deals with this problem; a similar technique was independently suggested by Riecken (1962). In such a nonexperiment, the procedure of the experiment is explained to the S, but he is never allowed to actually respond to the independent variables in order to eliminate cues stemming from his own behavior. He may then be asked to complete any post-experimental tests and be given a post-experimental inquiry. (For a description of this approach and a discussion of its limits see Orne, 1969).

While a variety of inquiry techniques have proved useful in hypnosis research, none of these procedures can adequately deal with the nexus of problems stemming from (1) subtle cues that may communicate what the hypnotist desires, and other effects of differential treatment of the hypnotized and waking individual; (2) the effects stemming from the S's prior knowledge and expectations in interaction with the information provided by the particular study, as well as the E-bias factor discussed above. Consequently a procedure was needed that would permit the investigator to estimate the possible effects of these factors in a particular experiment. Specifically, a special control group was necessary, with which to compare the performances of deeply hypnotized Ss.

THE MOTIVATION OF A COMPARISON GROUP

One of the characteristics of the hypnotized individual is a high motivation to play the role of a hypnotized person and carry out the requests of the hypnotist (White, 1941). The S's wish to please the hypnotist is an aspect of hypnosis that has also been commented on extensively by therapists describing its use in treatment (e.g., Brenman & Gill, 1947). Thus, it seemed essential to have an *unhypnotized* comparison group that would be highly motivated to please the hypnotist and to behave in a manner they believed characteristic of hypnotized Ss.

The Simulating Technique

In order to satisfy the requirements discussed above, the technique of asking *S*s to simulate hypnosis as a comparison group was developed (Orne, 1959). The procedure was initially conceptualized as providing a group of individuals who would share the role-playing aspects of hypnosis and the high level of motivation to behave like hypnotized *S*s[5] but would not share the experiences of real hypnosis. That is, they would not be able to experience as subjectively real the suggestions of the hypnotist. However, they would have as a basis for their simulation behavior the usual prior knowledge and expectations as well as all of the information provided by the experimental procedure and those subtle cues from the hypnotist that communicate his implicit wishes.

Until recently the literature was in general agreement about the impossibility of simulating hypnosis in a way that would deceive the experienced hypnotist. When, nonetheless, we asked *S*s to simulate hypnosis, it became clear why there was such agreement on this point (Orne, 1959). *S*s found the task difficult and distasteful. Typically they gave a very transparent performance, tending to interrupt it by asking for reassurance with questions such as, "Am I doing all right?" or "Is this what you want?" When urged to resume the role, they would do so, frequently looking to the *E* for encouragement, smiling embarrassedly, and in many clearly discernible ways communicating their discomfort. From discussion of these experiences with the *S*s it emerged that they felt foolish in carrying out a task that was manifestly impossible. They had been asked to simulate hypnosis but were aware that the request had emanated from the hypnotist who, of course, knew that they were simulating, so there was no conceivable way in which they could successfully comply with the request without appearing ridiculous.

It is necessary to make a small but absolutely vital change in the procedure: two *E*s must be involved so that the hypnotist-experimenter can remain absolutely blind as to which *S*s are in deep hypnosis and which *S*s are simulating. *S*s are instructed by one investigator as follows:

> Today your task will be to work with Dr. X and to convince him that you are an excellent hypnotic subject, and become deeply hypnotized. Dr. X will not know that you are pretending, though he will be aware that some individuals may be faking. If he becomes aware of the fact that you are not really hypnotized and are only pretending, he will immediately stop the experiment. So long as he goes on, you know that you are successful in your task.[6] I cannot tell you anything about what he will be doing with you today nor can I tell you anything about how a

5. At the time, it was assumed that a high level of motivation to please the hypnotist uniquely characterized the hypnotic relationship. Since then it has become clear that a good subject-experimenter and certainly therapist-patient relationship may provide at least as high a level of motivation to please, and therefore I no longer assume a necessary motivational difference between the hypnotized and the unhypnotized *S* (see Orne, 1970).

6. The latter part of the instructions was added because we observed that some individuals would suddenly stop in the middle of an experiment because they mistakenly thought they must

hypnotized individual might act in this situation. You will just have to use your judgment and do the best you can. This is a difficult task but we have found that intelligent subjects have been able to carry it out successfully. Good luck!

If one assumes that situations can be set up whereby an individual can simulate hypnosis and not be detected at greater than chance rate by the hypnotist-experimenter, then it becomes crucial to allow only those individuals to be part of the simulator comparison group who indeed cannot, with repeated tries, enter any depth of hypnosis at all. The simulator comparison group is not useful to evaluate those responses which could be a function of cues in the situation rather than hypnosis if there is any possibility that some members of this comparison group have the ability to enter hypnosis.

Since it is essential that the Ss who are in the simulating group should not be hypnotized, we selected those individuals who had previously tried to enter hypnosis and had been unable to respond to any significant degree in a clinical diagnostic situation (Orne & O'Connell, 1967). It was important, however, in this context not to include those Ss who appeared negativistic or seemed, for purposes of their own, to have a need to demonstrate their inability to enter hypnosis. It is not uncommon to find individuals who view the situation as some form of power struggle and misuse the situation as a means of demonstrating to themselves that they are not easily influenced by others. As a rule they consider it a matter of pride to have a "logical mind," are not subject to suggestion, have an "indomitable will," and so forth. Such Ss can generally be identified during the induction process. They will sometimes sway forward when instructed to sway backwards; if told that they will be unable to bend their arm, they bend it even before they are asked to test the suggestion; or, if they wait, such Ss often display an overeagerness to demonstrate that they have not in fact responded. In addition to this characteristic mode of responding to the suggestions themselves, these individuals, while superficially extremely cooperative, sabotage the induction in a variety of ways and betray their underlying attitude by being manifestly pleased by their inability to experience suggestions. Such individuals not infrequently turn out to be capable of entering deep hypnosis if the induction procedure takes care to circumvent their defensive maneuvers. (For example, see Erickson, 1952.)

The reason that such a negativistic individual must not be used is that the simulating situation provides a setting where this type of S may respond to the challenge, again negativistically, but this time by becoming hypnotized! On the other hand, those individuals who are able to experience extremely limited effects of hypnosis, despite apparently genuine attempts to respond,

---

have revealed the fact that they were simulating. These instructions obviated this difficulty, and also served to reinforce the Ss.

almost never experience any hypnotic phenomena when asked to simulate. We intentionally avoided working with highly hypnotizable Ss under simulating conditions since we found it impossible to determine with certainty whether these individuals were or were not hypnotized in the simulating situation. The possibility that a highly hypnotizable S, instructed to simulate, might enter hypnosis and yet maintain that he was simulating was difficult to exclude.[7]

In the 1959 paper that first described the simulating technique, the statement was made that Ss instructed to simulate were drawn from the same population as those who were actually hypnotized (Orne, 1959, p. 287). By this it was meant that Ss shared the same general information about hypnosis and were drawn from the same population insofar as their expectations, beliefs, and knowledge about hypnosis were concerned. Unfortunately, in the original printing the statement that the simulating Ss were unhypnotizable was inadvertently omitted, and it should be emphasized that in terms of the hypnotizability variable, simulating and real Ss (as I have used the terms) are decidedly *not* drawn from the same population. For the reasons outlined, it is not possible to have Ss matched for hypnotizability in the simulating design without introducing serious doubts about the actual status of the simulation no-hypnosis comparison group. The possible effect of as yet undiscovered personality differences[8] between simulating and real Ss has, of course, important methodological consequences that must be taken into account in interpreting research findings, and places important limitations on some—but not all—applications of this technique. These issues will be discussed later. Our intent here is to clarify the essential characteristics of the real-simulator design. The nine points discussed below take up those characteristics of the design that have been misunderstood most frequently in the literature.

1. It should be emphasized that one crucial aspect of using simulators is that the hypnotist who is working with the S must truly be blind as to the latter's actual status. Thus, when the prospective simulator is told that the hypnotist-experimenter with whom he will work does not know which Ss are simulating, this must in fact be an accurate statement and, equally important, before the hypnotist-experimenter can be unblinded, the experiment must be *entirely* over, all Ss having completed *all* relevant sessions. If this is

7. Austin et al. (1963) as well as Bowers (1966) have carried out studies utilizing highly hypnotizable and simulating controls. They have stressed the importance of selecting Ss from the same hypnotic population, and wished to demonstrate that the procedure was feasible. Personal communication with several of the authors suggested that these investigators encountered the very problems described above, that is, the problems upon which we based the decision to use only unhypnotizable simulators.

8. Numerous studies of personality correlates of hypnotizability (see Hilgard, 1965b) have as yet not been successful in isolating personality attributes unique to deeply hypnotizable Ss.

not the case, the E often second-guesses, "I had two reals, one simulator; the next one must be a simulator." In our experience it has not been possible for the investigator to treat a S whom he knows to be a simulator the same way as he would a S whom he believes to be hypnotized, even when he subjectively feels that he has been consistent in his approach. Subtle, but nonetheless real, differences exist, which will tend in turn to affect the S's performance (Troffer & Tart, 1964).

2. Such a situation is radically different from that obtained when individuals are asked to role-play hypnosis or simulate with the knowledge of the E, or any variation of these. To emphasize this difference for studies with many different kinds of control groups, O'Connell, Shor, and Orne (1970) proposed the term *"crypto*simulator" to distinguish this control group—where the hypnotist *is blind* as to which Ss are simulating—from role-playing Ss on the one hand, and from so-called "simulating" Ss where the investigator *is aware* of (not blind to) their true status, on the other. Neither of these groups can serve the purposes for which the crypto-simulator procedure was designed.

3. While the concept of the simulating design is a single-blind adaptation of the double-blind placebo technique in psychopharmacology, there are important and very significant differences between them. Whereas with the placebo both the E and S are blind as to the presence or absence of the active pharmacological agent, only the hypnotist and not the S is blind in the simulating design. Further, while the simulator unavoidably knows that he is in a special simulating group, the real S does not know of the simulator's existence.[9] Neither real nor simulating Ss are deceived at all. There must be no deception about the blindness of the hypnotist-experimenter involved in dealing with the simulating S. It is crucial that the S correctly perceive that he has a chance of fooling the hypnotist-experimenter, or there is no "percentage" in his trying and he is apt simply to give up.

4. While it is crucial for the simulating Ss to have had several opportunities during which they have tried to enter hypnosis, preferably with different hypnotists using varying techniques, *no* special training may be given to this group. The very point of having simulating Ss to help evaluate the nature of the cues in the experimental situation is to determine how these would be interpreted by Ss who do not share the hypnotic experience but otherwise have access to the same amount of background information. It is, of course, particularly important that the instructions to simulators in no

9. While it is motivating and important (to bring meaning to the task) for simulators to know of the existence of a real hypnotic group, when real Ss are confronted with the idea of a simulating group, of necessity the group is understood by them to cast doubt on their own performances. This inevitable conclusion does not allow them the necessary trust in the laboratory that is essential to their concentrating for full hypnotic depth. It is therefore not good practice that the simulating group be discussed with them, as it can distinctly hinder their cooperation.

way communicate how a deeply hypnotized *S* would actually perform, either on the experimental procedures being tested or on any other aspect of hypnotic behavior. While simulators as well as real *S*s may have seen hypnosis at some time in the past, neither group should include individuals who have special knowledge or experience.

5. *S*s should be given simulating instructions at a time immediately preceding the experimental session. This will assure that they understand what is required of them and will tend to facilitate a high level of motivation. While in certain studies it may be more efficient to set up *S*s two or three weeks in advance, they then do not tend to have a clear enough picture in their minds at the time of the experimental run as to their exact instructions. Perhaps even more important, the spontaneity and enthusiasm of participating in an exciting study in a very important control group is sometimes lost. With time, self-doubt about one's ability to successfully simulate looms large, and the *S* may become unduly concerned with possible failure. Instead of focusing on fooling the *E,* the *S* may become troubled about looking foolish himself. The model is designed to overcome this problem by assuring the *S* that the *E* is blind, thereby making it possible for him to succeed and making it worth his while to try his best to do so.

It is possible, however, to have the *S* simulate over a period of several sessions extending over a matter of weeks, provided that the "setup" takes place immediately prior to the first session. In this instance the *S* successfully completes the first session before he has an opportunity to become concerned. As a result, he will be less likely to fear failure—the experiment would have been terminated had he been unsuccessful—and he has also had actual experience in the role of simulation, making it very unlikely that he will forget the task. Further, in the pre-experimental setup interview it is very important for the *S* to be told precisely when his task as simulator will be completed, and also for the end point to be clearly marked by a final interview with the investigator who originally instructed him to simulate.

6. It is necessary to make clear to the *S*s that their simulation is a crucial part of the experimental situation, that it is their task as *S*s to fool the *E*. It is helpful in this regard that the *E* who is to be fooled be seen as competent and senior. Yet the *S*s ought not to see their role only as making a fool of the investigator, but rather as a vital control procedure contributing to the scientific process, success being difficult but possible.

Under these circumstances we have not encountered any difficultly with *S*s being concerned about deceiving the investigator. The only situation where we have observed such problems was when the *E* to be fooled was a relatively young and somewhat insecure graduate student with whom some *S*s tended to identify. Under these specific circumstances some *S*s felt uncomfortable since they perceived the situation as though the *E* were being tested. It is important in setting up *S*s to simulate not to reassure them about the legitimacy of faking hypnosis. To tell Ss beforehand not to feel guilty about it clearly conveys that you feel they or others have indeed or should in fact feel guilty about faking. This problem is most effectively dealt with by clearly communicating that they are an essential control group, the existence of which is known to the investigator, but that which individuals are part of the control group is clearly not known by the E.

7. We have found it essential for the investigator who sets up the S to simulate to arrange, at that time, for a post-experimental interview with the S at the completion of the experiment. This provides a necessary audience for the S who is simulating, someone with whom he can eventually share his success, someone who will provide him with the feedback about the experiment, and with whom he can discuss how he actually felt. Since the information the S provides at the very end has always been viewed as of crucial importance by our laboratory, arrangements for a final interview were routinely made whenever the simulator model was used. In retrospect, it seems very likely that an arrangement of this kind played a significant role in facilitating the simulator's performance.

8. A simulator rarely behaves so transparently that the blind E can recognize with certainty he is faking. If he should do so, the data from such a S must, of course, be excluded from the analysis.[10] However, we do not feel it appropriate to terminate the experiment at that point and embarrass the S; instead, in these rare cases the E's certainty is marked by his immediately shortening the normal experimental procedure, but not in such a way as to make it obvious to the S. We feel that every effort should be made to have any S participating in an experimental study perceive his performance as a success experience; his data are real and he has thereby contributed to science even if in a way that is uncongenial to E's aims. To bluntly inform a S that he has been unsuccessful in carrying out an experimental requirement is at best unkind and frequently quite traumatic for the S. It costs but little more time and effort to make certain that the S leaves the study with a good feeling. For ethical reasons alone, therefore, it is felt inappropriate for the blind E to ever stop an experiment and inform the S that he is faking. In addition, however, it seems likely that such behavior would make the task of subsequent simulating Ss more difficult, to the extent that it could conceivably become campus scuttlebutt that Ss who fail at simulating hypnosis are rudely dismissed.

It should be noted that even with great care it is possible—and we have

10. In our experience this is sufficiently unusual that there has never been more than one S in any given study who was identified with certainty by the blind E. This includes the kind of S who fails to understand instructions referred to below. Though such Ss would not tend to affect the group data to any significant degree, it is against the logic of the design to include them —except as a footnote. Unless the unhypnotized S instructed to simulate is able to perform the task required of him, he will not be treated equivalently by the blind E, thereby violating the assumption of the model.

seen two or three such instances—for a *S* instructed to simulate not to understand the instructions. In one instance, the *S* erroneously assumed that the simulating instructions were intended to facilitate hypnotizing him. In another, the *S* simply did not believe that the blind *E* actually would be blind. Under such circumstances, an experimental session is kept as short as possible, the blind *E* carrying out whatever experimental task might seem reasonable to the *S* without making him aware of his inappropriate behavior. The post-experimental interview is then used to explore the *S*'s actual perception, again without making him feel that he has failed in his task as a *S*.

9. We have found it useful to ask the blind *E* to specify whether a given *S* is hypnotized or simulating at the end of each run, although no feedback is provided. At the conclusion of the experiment it is then possible to determine whether the *E*'s perceptions of the *S*'s status affected the *S*'s behavior, especially when, as is frequently the case, his judgments prove to be random.

It is, of course, desirable to have the blind *E* know as little as possible about the design. He should certainly not know how many real and how many simulating *S*s he will see. When technically possible, it would be most desirable for the blind *E* not to know about the existence of the simulating *S*s (under such circumstances, of course, no judgments would be obtained). For various methodological reasons it may also be helpful to have only simulating *S*s or only real *S*s, which facilitates the evaluation of *E* expectancy effects in particular situations.

AN EXAMPLE OF SIMULATING INSTRUCTIONS

Assuming that a *S* has shown himself unable to enter hypnosis in several sessions with different *E*s and has agreed to participate in another experiment, the simulating instructions would be given along the following line:

> We much appreciate your participation in several of our sessions in the past. Today I would like you to take part in a very interesting experiment that is quite different from any in which you have participated to date. . . You have attempted to go into hypnosis several times and found it quite difficult to respond. Though I understand you have been able to experience a certain lightness in your arm and felt quite drowsy at times, it was not possible to experience much else. . . In this particular study there is a special group of subjects to which you will belong, all of whom were not able to enter hypnosis despite their honest efforts to do so. As you know, people vary in their ability to respond; some individuals find it very easy while some individuals find it quite difficult. This doesn't seem to be related to any other personality characteristics. In this instance your task will be to simulate being a very good hypnotic subject. You will be working with Dr. _____ who is a very experienced and competent hypnotist and will be carrying out an important piece of research. Your task will be to behave as though you were one of those subjects who is able to enter deep hypnosis with ease. There will be only two kinds of subjects in this experiment: those who are excellent subjects

and can enter deep hypnosis, and several individuals like yourself who are unable to do so but will be trying to simulate hypnosis.

Dr. _____ does know that some subjects will be trying to simulate but has no idea who these subjects will be. Your task is to convince him that you are in fact an excellent hypnotic subject. Now this is a difficult task and you may well do something where you think you have given yourself away. Don't worry about this possibility, because if Dr. _____ recognizes the fact that you are simulating he will stop the experiment immediately. Therefore, as long as he continues with you, you know you have been successful in faking hypnosis. I point this out to you because in the past we have found some subjects would suddenly stop, thinking they had goofed and given themselves away, when, in fact, their behavior had been quite appropriate and the investigator had no idea that they were simulating. Keep in mind, then, that as long as the experimenter continues with you, you are doing all right; if he catches on he will stop the study immediately.

We realize that you have no experience in how to do this. You were chosen simply because you were not able to enter hypnosis and we know you have had no experience in this kind of task. However, we also know from previous studies—we have run a great many studies using this procedure—that intelligent subjects are able to do this. It is difficult but it is possible. . . I can't tell you how to behave or what to do; you have to use whatever you know about hypnosis, whatever cues you get from Dr. _____, and whatever you learn from the situation to figure out how a deeply hypnotized subject would behave, and your task is then to use this information in your simulation of hypnosis. Keep in mind that you will be simulating the behavior of an excellent, highly hypnotizable individual and that your task is to maintain that you are going into hypnosis, to perform during hypnosis, and, when you are awakened, to respond as if you had been in hypnosis. In other words, this includes simulating not only while you are being hypnotized but afterwards as well. When Dr. _____ asks you about your experiences you should answer the way a deeply hypnotized subject would answer if he had actually been in trance. If Dr. _____ asks you how you did the last time, keep in mind that you are a good hypnotic subject and you would have gone into deep hypnosis on your previous efforts. You would have had several previous experiences with hypnosis just as you actually have, except that you would have entered deep hypnosis. All subjects will have had at least five such sessions with the laboratory.

At no time, once you leave this room, may you reveal to anyone that you are simulating. They will not know that you are simulating. Though it is known that some subjects will be simulating, no one knows who they are except for me. When you are completely finished with the experiment, the investigator will ask you to return to the waiting room, which you will do, and I will meet you there. I will eventually discuss your experiences with you back in this office. Until you are back here with me at the very end of the experiment, you are to reveal to no one that you are not actually hypnotized: this means the experimenter or anyone else who asks you about your experiences other than me when we are back in this room.

Ss might ask questions such as:

"Could I ask you something about how to do it?" *Answer:* "Certainly."
"Let's say I am told to make a physical movement. How fast does a good subject react?" *Answer:* "I can't tell you that. I can only tell you to do what you think

you should do."

"If I am told that I feel no pain, how will I be able to prevent myself from responding?" *Answer:* "I really can't tell you how to simulate or what to do. It is a difficult task but we have found that other intelligent subjects have been able to do it successfully. Good luck! I will see you back here at the end of the experiment."

EARLY EXPERIENCES WITH SIMULATING SUBJECTS

As soon as we began to experiment with the cryptosimulators, it became apparent that this situation produced a remarkable performance in simulating individuals. Initially I had hoped to develop a method to evaluate the effects of nonhypnotized Ss' perceptions of what was expected of them on the experimental tasks under investigation. However, as a clinician who had worked extensively with hypnosis, I never doubted that it would be easy for me personally to recognize Ss who were, in fact, simulating. It came as a complete surprise and was a considerable blow to my fantasies of omniscience to find the Ss tested over a one-session period were indeed able to deceive me. It turned out to be impossible to distinguish between simulating and hypnotized Ss with a high degree of certainty or, at any rate, greater than chance.

Many of the procedures that I had casually accepted as useful tests to determine the Ss' depth of response, and had assumed to be proof positive of the reality of the hypnotic response, failed to distinguish between the groups. Not only were simulators able to perform the many feats of strength—such as remaining suspended between two chairs—without hypnosis, but they also showed themselves capable of tolerating painful stimuli without flinching (Shor, 1964b) and were able to apparently recall material that ought to have been beyond their ken (O'Connell, Shor, & Orne, 1970). Simple behavioral tasks did not effectively discriminate between them, nor did a variety of procedures that tried to evaluate the individual's trust in the investigator (whether, for example, when told there was a chair behind him, he would sit down without actually testing its presence).

A very striking personal experience with this technique occurred when I tried to establish some simple differentiating criteria. Thus I set up Ss for my colleagues and carefully noted down a myriad of clear, definable differences between the behavior of simulating and deeply hypnotized individuals. Indeed it was hard for me to fathom how my colleagues were so inexperienced and unsophisticated as to fail to recognize a dozen or so fatal mistakes that simulators made in pretending to be hypnotized. It was all the more shocking, therefore, when I again took the role of blind E to realize that I too was quite incapable of successfully distinguishing the two groups. My experience as a clinician did not, in fact, allow a reliable differentiation. Perhaps this experience, more than any other, imbued me with an abiding awareness of capabilites for self-deception, and it has taught me not to place undue significance on impressions not rigorously tested.[11]

The Real-Simulator Technique Used to Evaluate the Capabilities of the Nonhypnotized Subject

A great many claims have been put forward about the effects of hypnosis to uniquely augment the S's performance on a wide variety of tasks. Hull spoke of this class of questions as the problem of transcendence of normal volitional capacity (Hull, 1933).

Traditionally this category of questions has been answered by comparing the S's performance in the waking state with his own performance in hypnosis. While the importance of controlling order effects had been recognized and dealt with by Hull, such controls do not deal with the effects of either differential treatment by the E of Ss in the waking state and hypnosis, or the more complex effects where the S alters his response in the waking state in order to thereby maximize his apparent capacities in hypnosis. Hull already recognized this problem when he discussed the work of Sears (1932) on pain and noted the surprising finding that Ss, instructed to flinch as little as possible when jabbed with a needle, actually flinched more than when they had received no special instruction. He suggested that they might have increased their flinching in order to give the appearance of greater relative control when tested in hypnosis. It is perhaps relevant that a special device was attached to the face to measure grimacing which, in and of itself, would be likely to communicate the Es interest in such behavior. The Ss' recognition that flinching was of concern to the investigator would have been emphasized further by the specific instructions which called attention to the behavior and were thereby likely to potentiate this kind of an effect. In an entirely different context, Zamansky, Scharf, and Brightbill (1964) have documented a similar effect more recently.

If the S is used as his own control and his performance during hypnosis exceeds the one he gives in the waking state, the difference may be due to an augmented performance in hypnosis or a diminished performance in the waking state (Evans & Orne, 1965). The latter, in turn, could be a function of the S's wish to make his hypnotic performance seem better or merely a response to differential degrees of emphasis that the hypnotist uses with his instructions in the waking state and in hypnosis. In any case, however, it is difficult to demonstrate augmentation of S's capacities with such a procedure.

11. Several distinguished colleagues, well known for their clinical skills, insisted that simulating Ss could easily be distinguished from hypnotized individuals by experienced clinicians. In each instance, when they actually tried to do so with experimental Ss who were set up for them according to the procedures outlined, they found themselves unable to make accurate and reliable differentiation on the basis of their clinical judgment during a single session.

Alternatively, if instead of using the S as his own control independent control groups are employed, new problems are introduced. Sample size must inevitably be increased considerably due to the introduction of inter-individual variability. Most important, serious possibilities of differential treatment between experimental and control groups remain.

The real-simulating model is particularly well adapted to explore issues of this kind and permits the investigator to evaluate the likelihood of an alternative mechanism accounting for the behaviors observed during hypnosis. For example, it has often been asserted that if a deeply hypnotized S is given the suggestion to experience fear, guilt, anxiety, or depression, the appropriate state will almost instantaneously be produced in the S. In a straightforward psychophysiological study, Damaser, Shor, and Orne (1963) were able to show that striking changes in heart rate and GSR are induced in hypnotized individuals by such suggestions. However, in this study simulating Ss were also used, and it was noted that equally large physiological alterations were seen in the comparison group. This demonstration suggested that physiological alterations, which otherwise might be viewed as proof of the unique capability of hypnosis to induce a suggested state, are not adequate evidence of this uniqueness. In this experiment the simulating control group served to demonstrate the capabilities of nonhypnotized individuals to alter some physiological functions—apparently mediated by way of imaging—in the total absence of the subjective experience of hypnosis.

Another example of this kind was a very detailed replication (O'Connell, Shor, & Orne, 1970) of the work of Reiff and Scheerer (1959) on hypnotic age regression. In their work, Reiff and Scheerer used the series of tasks that had been developed by Piaget in order to explore the cognitive development of children. In addition, they utilized a word association test and some behavioral measures which, they argued, were such that Ss would have no way of knowing how to respond appropriately. They showed in an empirical study that age-regressed Ss behave very differently from control Ss instructed to role-play the respective ages.

Reiff and Scheerer's original study had a number of methodological problems and, because of the significance of the findings, a careful replication and extension of the study was undertaken (O'Connell, Shor, & Orne, 1970). Of concern here is the inclusion of a new comparison group. This group served to provide a rigorous test for the assertion that Ss *would not know* how to respond correctly. The study closely replicated the Reiff and Scheerer findings with deeply hypnotized Ss; that is, our group of highly selected, exceedingly hypnotizable and highly trained Ss behaved very much as did Ss in the Reiff and Scheerer study. However, the simulating group, which was selected from unhypnotizable individuals and did not share any of the subjective experiences of age regression, yielded behavior which in all respects could not be differentiated from that of the deeply hypnotized group. Neither the objective tests nor the observational data of these individuals revealed any meaningful differences. Incidentally, both groups —the hypnotized and the simulating—behaved entirely differently from actual children when compared with such a group on a number of parameters.

For purposes of this discussion, the utility of a simulating comparison group should be clear. Here was a group of individuals who did not have the opportunity to experience age regression but were otherwise treated in exactly the same manner and given precisely the same cues and information by the hypnotist. The hypnotist was unable to treat these Ss differently because he did not know which were which. The fact that these individuals, without hypnosis, were able to produce the behavior of the hypnotized individuals conclusively demonstrates that, given the identical treatment, unhypnotized Ss can figure out the kind of responses that appear appropriate on the experimental tasks. It should be clear that it is *only* this assertion that is being tested by the inclusion of the comparison group of simulating Ss.

The conclusions that can be drawn from the behavior of simulating Ss need to be carefully considered. Certainly these studies do not suggest there are no differences between simulating and age-regressed Ss. The only permissible conclusion is that the particular technique that has been employed to "prove" that Ss could not have known enough without hypnosis to respond appropriately was inadequate to this task. The simulating procedure used in this fashion sheds light *only* on the adequacy of the experimental procedure. It says nothing about what mechanisms were actually involved. Thus, real and simulating Ss certainly may produce the same behavior mediated by different mental processes. In any case, our failure to observe any behavioral differences does not challenge the reality of the hypnotized individual's subjective experiences.

Thus, simulating Ss should not be considered a control group in the classical sense; that is, a group of Ss who are the same in all respects as the experimental Ss except that they are not exposed to the experimental treatment. They differ from the hypnotized group not only in their initial hypnotizability, but also in that they are functioning under entirely different instructions with presumably differing motivations and mental sets. The simulating Ss are best considered as a comparison group that helps to discover the kind of conclusions that a highly motivated S might draw from the procedure and from the behavior of the hypnotist interpreted in the light of the background information available to all Ss. The simulating group allows an estimate of the *capabilities* of unhypnotized Ss and obviates the need to speculate about what Ss could or could not do, or know, or figure out if they chose to do so. A finding of no difference indicates that the particular procedure was of a kind which, if the S had chosen to do so, could have been mimicked by an unhypnotized individual. It could therefore not be considered as proof of hypnotic potentiation.

In essence, the simulators are used to clarify the behavior of more typical nonhypnotized control groups. They help establish whether Ss could have figured out from the cues in the experimental situation what constituted the expected behavior without having been exposed to the subjective experiences of hypnosis. An example is Sheehan's (1969) replication of Reyher's (1961a, 1967) work. Reyher had carried out a number of studies using hypnosis to induce an artificial complex and testing the consequences of this procedure by administering projective techniques. He argued that the changes that were induced were of such a nature that Ss could not have anticipated the kind of changes that ought to occur and therefore the projective test data proved the reality of the unconscious complex that had been induced by hypnosis. To demonstrate that Ss would be unable to figure out the appropriate behavior on his tests, Reyher asked Ss to role-play being hypnotized and exposed them to the same procedure. These individuals did not show the kind of changes observed in hypnotized individuals. In one experiment he even asked Ss to "simulate hypnosis"—in contrast to our procedure, the hypnotist was not blind, however—and under these circumstances, these "simulating" Ss still did not respond to the projective tests in the same manner as the hypnotized individuals.

In a careful replication, Sheehan (1969) used the Luria technique to induce an artificial complex in the precise manner as reported by Reyher. His hypnotized Ss behaved in the same manner as those in the Reyher studies; however, in this instance, the simulating Ss were run blind as was specified by the model, and, under these circumstances, simulators responded to the projective tests in a manner indistinguishable from that of the hypnotized individuals. It is worth noting that the E in this study, which was run in our laboratory, initially was convinced that differences would emerge, but in accordance with the model he was not aware which Ss were and which Ss were not simulating. The striking differences between the behavior of the simulating Ss in Sheehan's study and those obtained by Reyher with Ss run by nonblind investigators illustrate the importance of the blind aspect of the simulator design.

Sheehan's findings do not, of course, invalidate Reyher's previous work. It is entirely plausible that changes observed in the projective techniques reflected genuine alterations in the subjective experience of hypnotized individuals. The important conclusion that must be drawn from Sheehan's findings, however, is that the procedure of using projective techniques is not sufficient to provide a criterion measure that could not volitionally be distorted by the S. The data from the simulators shed light only on what Ss *could* have done; it in no way proves what they did do. As long as we have no reason to distrust the projective test data of the hypnotized Ss, it should not trouble us unduly that these data can be reproduced by simulators exposed to the identical cues. It merely forces us to be cautious about making claims of having devised a foolproof test that demonstrates the reality of hypnotically induced complexes. (For a discussion of these issues, see Sheehan's [1971] rebuttal to Reyher's [1969b] comments.)

It should be clear then that whenever an investigator wishes to make assertions about what Ss could not conceivably do without hypnosis because they would not have the ability or knowledge to do so, it behooves the investigator to test his belief, using the blind real-simulator design. This test is, of course, a very hard one, and it will readily throw into relief flaws in the procedure. As long as the procedure fails to distinguish between real and simulating Ss, no meaningful statement can be made about an effect being uniquely due to hypnosis and demonstrating an ability not normally within the range of the waking individual's skills. Such a claim can be made only if the investigator hits upon a procedure that indeed does separate the two groups. However, even when he is able to accomplish this, it will still be necessary to determine whether these differences are due to an effect of hypnosis, a characteristic of hypnotizable individuals, or a function of Ss having been given simulating instructions. These questions cannot be answered within the real-simulating model and require different experimental approaches.

ARE SIMULATING SUBJECTS HYPNOTIZED?

The publication of our experience with simulating Ss, especially the failure to discriminate these individuals from the deeply hypnotized persons, led to a number of inappropriate conclusions. Two groups of colleagues holding diametrically opposed views of hypnosis concluded from our failure to find many differences between simulating and deeply hypnotized Ss that these groups were the same. Many clinicians, particularly those whom Sutcliffe (1960) would have classified as belonging to the "credulous" group, promptly asserted that the fatal flaw was that Ss, pretending to be hypnotized, were not really pretending but were, in fact, hypnotized. This being the case, it should surprise no one that differences could not be demonstrated. A similar position was adopted by some colleagues who took what Sutcliffe (1960) would call the "skeptical" position. These colleagues asserted that the failure to find differences between simulating and hypnotized Ss was because there were no differences, since hypnosis actually was the same as simulation.

For a variety of reasons, however, it seems extremely unlikely that simulating Ss are hypnotized. As has already been pointed out, great care is taken to select individuals who have found it impossible to enter hypnosis despite honest efforts to do so. While there are instances of an individual previously unable to enter hypnosis later successfully entering deep trance, they are extremely rare. After a single attempt at hypnosis, particularly if it is a standardized procedure, it is sometimes possible to increase a *S*'s response by working through his concerns and anxieties, using a more individualized approach (see Hilgard, 1964). Such a response is far less likely if the *S* has had several hypnotic sessions and the opportunity to discuss any concerns or anxieties with the hypnotist without any success. Indeed, with a number of sessions we have found it exceedingly difficult to increase the hypnotizability of individuals after the response has stabilized (see Cobb & Shor, 1964; Shor, Orne, & O'Connell, 1966). Since we select as simulators only those *S*s who are unable to enter hypnosis over several sessions with different hypnotists, it is extremely unlikely that these individuals then enter hypnosis in the actual experiment itself.

It is again necessary to emphasize that simulators are not selected for their ability to simulate. Their sole qualifications are that they have volunteered and have been unable to enter hypnosis in several efforts beyond the level we have designated as 2- on the clinical scale (Orne & O'Connell, 1967). It is extremely infrequent to find a *S* who is unable to follow simulating instructions provided the situation that has been described earlier is set up—certainly no more than one individual in twenty. These essentially unselected individuals are the ones who perform so well in the situation. If one were to assume that simulators are hypnotized, it would also be necessary to assume that we have effectively solved the problems of inducing hypnosis in all *S*s with only a few moments of instruction.

Elsewhere (Orne, 1966b) I have emphasized that the hallmark of the hypnotic phenomenon is not the willingness of the *S* to do what he is requested to—this is characteristic of both clinical and experimental situations—nor that the *S*'s behavior appears trancelike to the observer. Rather it is the nature and quality of the concomitant subjective events. Consider the case of a posthypnotic suggestion: If a *S* is told that he will run his hands over his hair when the *E* removes his glasses after he is awake and, in response to this cue, carries out the behavior, the event seems interesting and perhaps striking. The reason is not simply because the *S* did as he was told. Thus, it would not be considered noteworthy that a *S* runs his hand over his hair if he were instructed, "Please run your hand over your hair when I later remove my glasses," and he complies. However, when the *S* appears to carry out the action without apparently being aware of his behavior—or when he rationalizes his action and seems convinced that it is motivated by extraneous circumstances, or if he describes a peculiar compulsion or strange impulse as the basis for his action—one tends then to characterize the event as somehow different from what occurs in an individual's usual state of awareness. To a large extent one may infer from a *S*'s behavior whether he experiences the situation as merely responding to a request or whether it is experienced differently.

To take another example, when a S is told his hand is so heavy that he cannot lift it and that he should try to do so, his behavior—that is, whether he does or does not lift his hand—will correlate fairly well with the presence or absence of heaviness of an experiential inability to lift his hand. To the extent that the behavior accurately reflects these experiences it is a useful criterion of hypnosis; however, the correlation is by no means perfect and, when the S's behavior fails to reflect alterations in his experience, it ceases to be a meaningful criterion of hypnosis. The S's response to hypnosis can never be evaluated adequately without a detailed exploration of the S's experience. It should be obvious, however, that simulating instructions are designed to create a lack of correlation between behavior and experience.

The need to examine the S's experience becomes particularly clear when working with the real-simulator design. Here the S's subjective response to the suggestions becomes the major criterion to determine the presence or absence of hypnosis. It is essential that this inquiry be carried out under circumstances designed to elicit an honest report. This is best done by the E who originally gave the simulating instructions. The inquiry should not be carried out in the presence of the hypnotist who had previously been blind since Ss may feel self-conscious about having deceived the E and could, for this and similar reasons, distort their account of the experience. It is essential, of course, that the investigator who carries out the inquiry communicate his genuine wish to know how the S felt in the situation. In any interview some biasing of the S's response is inevitable, and, since in this instance it is important not to overlook Ss who might have entered hypnosis, the E may communicate that quite often Ss experience a number of hypnotic suggestions even though they had initially begun by simulating. In other words, the inquiry should be carried out in a way that would maximize the probability of the S's reporting subjective alterations even if he experienced none, in order to make certain not to overlook evidence of a hypnotic response. Under these circumstances, every so often a S will report experiences along lines such as "When I was asked to straighten my arm and told that I couldn't bend it, the strangest thing happened to me. I actually found that the arm wouldn't bend. This was really weird. It scared me so much that I almost stopped simulating." A S reporting this had, of course, stopped simulating, at least as far as arm rigidity was concerned.

Even though the exploration of the S's experience is carried out in the most encouraging circumstances, it is exceedingly rare for Ss to report evidence of any subjective response to suggestions. Having even one such S in a study is unusual, but if this occurs, his data must be excluded from consideration. Incidentally, it should be noted that even these individuals do not experience the more difficult items. Thus, we have never seen *any* of our unhypnotizable Ss instructed to simulate who then reported experiencing a hallucinated person as though he were real or who felt that the amnesia suggestion had an effect on his recall.

In sum it would not be parsimonious to assume that Ss who are asked to simulate then become hypnotized, because (1) the inability to enter hypnosis despite repeated efforts to do so is a remarkably stable trait and (2) simulating Ss do not share the experiences of the hypnotized individual.

ARE HYPNOTIZED SUBJECTS SIMULATING?

The purpose of developing the simulator design was to help differentiate artifactual components or epiphenomena from those aspects of hypnosis that are truly intrinsic. This work has been interpreted by some as raising questions about the existence of the phenomenon. The demonstration that simulators are able to produce behavior that even highly trained hypnotists were unable to distinguish from that produced by deeply hypnotized individuals resonates with the recurrent wish to explain away any apparently nonrational components in man's existence. When the simulator design is used, it soon becomes clear that many behavioral items that have been taken as self-evident proof of hypnosis—even by otherwise skeptical observers—are well within the repertoire of the nonhypnotized individuals. (These include such dramatic "proof" of hypnosis as the ability to remain suspended between two chairs, supported only at the heels and the head and supporting yet another person on one's midriff while in this position. Other behaviors such as a glazed look, passivity, talking in a monotone, the absence of a sense of humor, psychomotor retardation, and so forth, were once assumed to be uniquely characteristic of hypnosis. Similarly included is the ability to withstand, without flinching, being pinched or having a needle pass through one's arm.)

Though it is true that simulating Ss are able to deceive experienced hypnotists, it is entirely incorrect to assume that spontaneous simulation can be used to account for the phenomenon of hypnosis. Spontaneous simulation under normal circumstances is rare, provided, of course, that the hypnotist does not create a situation where the S would make considerable secondary gains by simulating. Certainly it is unwise to tell Ss that they will be permitted to participate in an exciting and well paid research program if they are able to enter deep hypnosis. The problem of spontaneous simulation is somewhat similar to that of patients who willfully lie to their therapist. This occurs; however, it is rare under normal conditions because the therapist goes to considerable pains to create circumstances where no advantage can accrue to his patient from lying. (The difficulties encountered in treating patients where it is to their advantage to lie are well-known and are attested to by the remarkably poor results with pension neuroses.)

For the most part, therapists evaluate the circumstances under which they are being consulted and recognize that in one or two sessions they would be unable to distinguish between a patient who is intentionally lying about a given difficulty and one who actually experiences the difficulties he describes. Indeed, it may be difficult to do so even with prolonged observation. Fortunately this realization does not cause the therapist to be unduly concerned about simulation unless it is clear that some benefit can be derived from such behavior. It seems strange that one should consider the hypnotized S's reports of his experiences any differently.

It is currently fashionable to denigrate reports of subjective experience as evidence; however, it should be kept in mind that many "respectable" behavioral indices are subject to the same biases and distortions as verbal reports. On the other hand, it is essential to evaluate the circumstances under which subjective reports are obtained. During a properly conducted posthypnotic inquiry (which strives to elicit what the S actually experienced rather than attempting to lead him to obtain testimony to support one's point of view or, for that matter, to have the S fill out a questionnaire), the reports that are obtained are remarkably consistent with those obtained by other Es who are not the hypnotist, or in other contexts. At times we have gone to considerable lengths to obtain reports: for example, a research assistant may drive a S back home after an experiment and engage him in a casual conversation about his experiences; similarly we have explored the kind of reports that Ss give to roommates or spouses; and, at other times, we have provided an opportunity for Ss to talk informally in the waiting room while monitoring their conversation. It is striking that reports obtained under these widely differing circumstances agree on the major aspects of the S's experience during hypnosis.[12]

In talking with a S after an experiment, the unbiased listener cannot help but be impressed by the individual's uneven response to different suggested events. Why should a S describe a vivid visual hallucination and yet be unable to hear the buzzing of a fly with his eyes closed? Why should another S describe a startling inability to bend his elbow while indicating that an arm failed to get heavy when it had been suggested? The inconsistency of Ss' responses to different items, the lack of association between overall response and other indices of compliance, and the absence of any obvious motivation to spontaneously simulate make it extremely unparsimonious to

12. Barber and his associates (Barber, Dalal, & Calverley, 1968) have recently "discovered" that responses about the S's experience can be biased by the manner in which questions are asked. The fact that inappropriate wording of questions distorts Ss' responses is well-known in the area of public opinion (e.g., Cantril, 1940; Maccoby & Maccoby, 1954) and ought not to be taken as evidence that the manner in which questions are phrased determines the experience that the S is reporting. Quite to the contrary, both the clinical techniques of interviewing as well as the techniques of social psychologists are designed to closely approximate how Ss actually feel about issues and experiences. To discover the wording of questions as antecedent variables determining responses is to confuse an artifact with substantive data.

assume that these individuals are reporting anything other than compelling and vivid subjective events. For these reasons, I would be convinced that deep hypnosis is an entirely different phenomenon from what we observe with simulating individuals even if we were unable to find a single clear-cut behavioral difference between these two groups. It is unfortunate that some colleagues misinterpreted my statements to suggest any other opinion. Though we will discuss some interesting examples where differences have emerged between simulating and hypnotized individuals, these data merely provided objective evidence of differences that clinically appear self-evident.

Differences Between Real and Simulating Subjects

The observation that even highly trained hypnotists are unable to distinguish deeply hypnotized *S*s from simulating *S*s seemed to introduce a more critical evaluation of those behaviors that many of us had assumed uniquely due to hypnosis. The fact that these behaviors can be mimicked cannot, of course, be taken as evidence that they are therefore not intrinsic to hypnosis. To take an analogy, if a *S* is asked to simulate sleep, the fact that he will lie down, close his eyes, and breathe in a regular rhythm in no way implies that these behaviors are not associated with true sleep. It merely means that this knowledge is shared by both *S* and *E* and cannot serve as the basis for reliably distinguishing between sleep and the simulation of sleep. Indeed, asking *S*s to simulate sleep will only serve to tell the investigator something about the preconceptions that all of us have about how the sleeping *S* behaves.

The reason why the simulating procedure seemed so important was that the behavioral characteristics of hypnosis are by no means as clear-cut as those of sleeping. Not only is hypnosis as described by Mesmer behaviorally different from the phenomenon observed today, but it is possible to demonstrate that when *S*s believe a behavioral item to be typical of hypnosis, they will manifest this item when they subsequently enter hypnosis. It is for these reasons that a detailed knowledge of the *S*'s expectations assumes such critical importance in hypnotic research. Thus, in the event that a simulating *S* can mimic the behavior of the hypnotized individual, it is still not possible to determine the extent to which the behavior is truly intrinsic to hypnosis and the extent to which it is a function of expectations of the subject population about hypnosis and therefore possibly an epiphenomenon. As we have repeatedly pointed out, in trying to successfully mimic the behavior of hypnotized individuals, simulating *S*s will utilize whatever knowledge is available to them from past experience as well as through cues provided by the experiment and subtle shaping procedures employed by the hypnotist, often without his own awareness. Successful imitation of hypnotized Ss by the simulator in no way demonstrates a lack of genuineness of hypnosis. It does, however, show that the particular behavioral items cannot be employed to prove the genuineness of hypnosis. The best that one can say under these circumstances is that the behavior of hypnotized Ss is such that nonhypnotized individuals placed in the same situation would know enough about what is expected to perform the same way.

The reason why it is so difficult for even experienced hypnotists to distinguish between hypnotized and simulating individuals is that the range of behavior observed in hypnotized Ss is far greater than is generally recognized. However, some differences have gradually emerged. When such differences are observed, what conclusions can be drawn? First, it is likely that the simulating Ss simply do not know how the hypnotized individual would behave. Regarding the particular item of the investigation, the finding is counterexpectational. Further, the behavior of the hypnotized individual is not, in this instance, a function of the cues provided by the experiment or the behavior of the hypnotist. On the other hand, it would be premature, and at times incorrect, to assume that differences are due to the presence of hypnosis in the hypnotized group.

The simulating group is subjected to a treatment procedure different from hypnosis, but in many ways equally potent; namely, the instruction to simulate. Therefore differences between these two groups are as likely to be due to the presence of simulation in the simulating group as to the presence of hypnosis in the hypnotized group. For example, in early observations with simulators I observed that these Ss had a tendency to avoid committing themselves in an ambiguous situation, preferring to answer "I don't know" when such a response was plausible. This tendency, while reasonably consistent, was interpreted as analogous to the Rorschach findings with malingerers who typically gave few and vague responses (Orne, 1969). Differences between real and simulating Ss such as these are not particularly relevant or interesting since they are a function of the simulation treatment condition rather than the presence of hypnosis. While I have little doubt that, with sufficient effort, there are a number of ways that could be found that would trick simulators, findings of this kind would, perhaps, reassure those individuals who worry about the genuineness of hypnosis, but would fail to bring us to a closer understanding of the mechanisms of hypnosis.

Even if we are careful to avoid focusing on those behavioral items that might result from the simulation instructions, great care still is required before concluding that the behavior of a hypnotized S is due to the presence of hypnosis. It should be remembered that the real-simulator model compares highly hypnotizable Ss with unhypnotizable simulators, and, within the model, it is extremely difficult to discriminate between those aspects of behavior due to the presence of hypnosis as opposed to those due to differential hypnotizability of the S. This is an issue which, when relevant, must be resolved by a special study addressing itself to that question. However, it is, of course, unnecessary to worry about the problem when clear differences between simulating and hypnotized Ss are observed.

CLINICAL OBSERVATIONS CONCERNING DIFFERENCES BETWEEN REAL AND SIMULATING SUBJECTS

Though it was not possible to reliably distinguish hypnotized from simulating Ss, some behaviors were observed only in deeply hypnotized individuals. This class of responses is characterized by a peculiar mixture of the suggested experience with components of accurate perception of the real world, and always characterized by a remarkable incongruity that does not appear to unduly trouble the S. An example would be a S who was told to hallucinate an individual sitting in a chair and describes his experience, "You know, it is the strangest thing. I see _____ sitting there and smiling in the chair. He's there and yet I can see the outline of the chair through him." Or another S, when asked to touch a hallucinated person, will describe a peculiar rubbery feeling, saying that somehow there is a tremendous amount of give as if he were able to feel through the person. Another type of incongruity reported earlier is equally characteristic of deep hypnosis (Orne, 1951). A S, regressed to age six, is instructed to write, "I am conducting an experiment which will assess my psychological capacities." Though printing in a childlike manner, he spells without any errors. Another S who spoke only German at age six and who was age regressed to that time answered when asked whether he can understand English, "Nein." When this question was rephrased to him ten times in English, he indicated each time in German that he was unable to comprehend English, explaining in childlike German such details as that his parents speak English in order that he not understand. While professing his inability to comprehend English, he continued responding appropriately in German to the hypnotist's complex English questions. Incongruities of this kind (which simulators would readily recognize as inappropriate when they occur spontaneously) occur only with the deeply hypnotized individual—assuming of course that the simulator has not had access to these papers.

Since spontaneous evidence of the tolerance of incongruity, which I have called "trance logic" (Orne, 1959), is often not available, I have utilized a procedure to elicit this response. The technique was suggested by Milton Erickson [13] and consists of asking the S to hallucinate an individual (who is actually present)—say Dr. X—in a chair across the room. Once the S is clearly hallucinating, and interacting with the hallucination, the S is asked to indicate Dr. X. He will, of course, point to the hallucination. The

13. Personal communication, 1949.

investigator then points to Dr. X who is actually in the room—ideally somewhat outside of the S's range of vision while he is looking at the hallucination—and inquires, "Who is this?" Simulating Ss will tend to respond by saying, "I don't know," "Mr. Y," or "There is no one there." The hypnotized S will typically do a "double take," looking back and forth between the hallucination and the actual person, and then in a somewhat startled but not unduly disturbed manner will indicate that there are two Dr. Xs. In some instances, if the S is then asked to explain, it is not unusual to be told in a somewhat blandly quizzical fashion, "Mirrors perhaps," "He must have a twin brother," or something similar. If the situation is pushed still further, the S may be told that one of the Dr. Xs is a hallucination and the other is the real person and, when asked to indicate which is which, the S may experience varying degrees of difficulty.

Occasionally, especially if the S is not very deeply hypnotized, merely calling the S's attention to the real person will be sufficient to eliminate the hallucination. In other instances, being told that one is a hallucination may bring similar results. Again, Ss may describe fascinating and idiosyncratic differences between the hallucination and the actual person. Most illustrative and interesting, however, is the very occasional S who is usually both highly intelligent and experienced in hypnosis, who will look at both the hallucination and the real person and finally identify the real person. When asked the process by which this decision was reached, he will say that he thought Dr. X should carry out an action, perhaps raise his right hand, and one did and the other did not; he therefore decided that the one that raised his hand must be the hallucination. The possibility for such a highly sophisticated, logical process to co-exist with actually hallucinating is, in my view, uniquely characteristic of the hypnotic phenomenon.

The response of the simulating S under these circumstances is a function of his awareness that the same person cannot be in two places at once and, characteristically, when asked to explain why he behaved as he did, will indicate that having been told to hallucinate Dr. X in one place he assumed that he ought not to recognize him when E pointed to him and said, "Who is this?" It goes without saying that simulating Ss who are given appropriate information can successfully mimic the behavior of hypnotized individuals. This may be accomplished either by informing simulating Ss in advance or by communicating what is expected in other subtle ways. The important issue, however, is that uninstructed simulators, working with a blind E who is careful not to communicate his desires, will spontaneously behave differently from most deeply hypnotized individuals able to hallucinate adequately, demonstrating thereby that the tolerance of incongruity in deeply hypnotized Ss cannot be explained as a function of their prior knowledge of, or expectations about, hypnotic behavior.

If the hypnotist clearly communicates to the S that he expects him to see

Dr. X in two places, then, of course, both simulating and hypnotized Ss will yield this response, making it impossible to conclude anything about hypnosis with that particular procedure. The logic of the technique demands that extreme care be taken not to communicate expectations to the S; and the behavior of the simulating S is an indication of how effective the hypnotist is in avoiding such communication. Therefore, meaningful conclusions can be drawn only when E is able to set up the situation so that the simulating S does not know what constitutes the "right" response, and therefore denies the existence of Dr. X. Our experience under these circumstances is that only the S hypnotized deeply enough to experience a compelling hallucination will report that he sees Dr. X in two places.

The extent to which the kind of responses described above are actually characteristic of hypnosis or the extent to which they are characteristic of highly hypnotizable individuals is by no means established. Unfortunately the techniques presently available to evaluate trance logic are not very satisfying. In the occasional S who spontaneously reports such phenomena there is no difficulty; however, the absence of such spontaneous material is more the rule than the exception. Even though the double hallucination is useful, it is a difficult technique that must be used with great care lest it be communicated to the S what is desired, thereby inevitably ensuring that the response of the simulator will be the same as that of the real Ss. In any case, it can be used only once and therefore does not lend itself to a comparison within the same S between hypnotized and waking conditions. It is to be hoped that better techniques to evaluate this parameter of mental function will be developed in the future. At this time, however, the question of whether this is a characteristic of hypnosis or hypnotizability remains both unanswered and technically difficult to resolve.

A study by Evans and Thorn (1966) provides a different but striking example of counterexpectational findings. They observed that two kinds of amnesia occur with hypnosis. The first is a tendency of hypnotized individuals to forget the actual events that transpired while hypnotized. This kind of amnesia the investigators refer to as "recall amnesia" and is well known. A different kind of amnesia is of equal interest. Thus, Ss may continue to recall the associative content they have learned while hypnotized, but forget the source of this information. As a result, these individuals can honestly say that they do not remember what transpired while they were hypnotized, though careful testing reveals that information they had been given is available to them. This phenomenon is called "source amnesia." It is closely analogous to what is observed with patients who develop amnesia. Thus, while unable to recall their own names or identity, they hardly ever lose command of language, social skills, or even extensive professional knowledge.

To study source amnesia the following procedure was used: Ss were taught a number of obscure facts during hypnosis, such as that amethysts, when heated, turn yellow. They then were wakened with suggestions of amnesia and somewhat later given tests of general knowledge, which included the obscure facts they had been taught. Interestingly, many good hypnotic Ss, while unable to recall the events that transpired during hypnosis, nonetheless found themselves able to answer these questions correctly. When asked about where they learned this information, they were unable to correctly specify the *source* of their knowledge.

While source amnesia cannot be demonstrated with all Ss, it is frequently found in deeply hypnotized individuals. On the other hand, simulating Ss do not show this phenomenon, assuming, incorrectly, that the effect of amnesia suggestion should necessarily be the inability to recall the *content* of the events that occurred while hypnotized (Evans, 1971).

This behavior of simulating Ss does not help to elucidate the fascinating phenomenon of source amnesia. It does serve as an example of another failure to act as do hypnotized individuals, and indicates the difficulty of accounting for source amnesia in terms of Ss' expectations, or subtle cues provided by the hypnotist.

Methodological Developments Beyond the Real-Simulator Design

It has already been commented upon that the simulator group is not a true control group; rather, it is a different treatment group that under some circumstances is a necessary comparison group. An ingenious modification by London and Fuhrer (1961) achieves many of the advantages inherent in the real-simulator design without introducing the special problems inherent in simulation instructions. This technique takes advantage of the relatively high test-retest reliability of hypnosis. In brief, from an unselected population, a group of highly hypnotizable and essentially unhypnotizable Ss are selected. Both groups are told that they did well and are subsequently seen by another hypnotist who uses an induction procedure that would not reveal differences in hypnotizability, such as a progressive relaxation technique starting with eyes closed. The hypnotist remains blind by carefully avoiding any procedures that might reveal the S's degree of hypnotic responsivity as he gives the hypnotic suggestion to be tested. This interesting technique retains the advantage of being blind as far as the hypnotist is concerned as long as it is used with appropriate tasks, without introducing the problem of a simulation set.

To be fully effective in equating the mental set between the highly hypnotizable and the unhypnotizable group, the London-Fuhrer design requires an additional modification. Thus, it is essential to somehow convince the unhypnotizable group that they can, in fact, respond to hypnotic suggestions. Only if this is done successfully are the assumptions of the technique fully met. Also, the London-Fuhrer design as usually employed still has the problem of differentiating between the effect of hypnotism as opposed to the effects of differing hypnotizability. This can be accomplished most easily by within-group comparisons rather than by between-group comparisons and, in some instances, will necessitate an entirely different experimental procedure. (For an example of how the London-Fuhrer design can be adapted to complex experimental problems and how most of these problems can be circumvented, see McGlashan, Evans, and Orne [1969].)

Following the implications of the London-Fuhrer design further, one may wish to use a straightforward correlational approach in order to ask questions about the effects of hypnosis. Here hypnosis is assessed quantitatively and the assumption is made that an effect due to hypnosis will be more pronounced in individuals who are more hypnotizable. Whatever hypnosis is, there will be more of it in people who show more effects of hypnotism. Given some questions, such an approach is the only appropriate one and the use of simulators, for example, quite superfluous (see, for example, Nace and Orne [1970]).

Types of Situations in Which the Simulator
Method Is Appropriate and Valuable

There are essentially three kinds of questions where the evaluation of the nonhypnotized *S*'s capabilities is best undertaken using the simulator design. These fall into three main categories:

1. *Where a claim is made the hypnotized individual is able to transcend his normal volitional capacities.* A typical example is the statement made after watching a *S* maintaining a cataleptic arm for a long period, "No unhypnotized individual could do this," or the claim that hypnosis facilitates recall of previously learned material not otherwise available to consciousness, leading to a level of recall that cannot otherwise be achieved. Whenever the assertion is made that hypnosis enables a *S* to do something not possible for an unhypnotized individual, the simulating comparison group puts the claim to its most rigorous test.

2. *Whenever hypnosis appears to result in an unusual willingness of the S to carry out behaviors that are requested of him,* it is necessary to evaluate how an unhypnotized individual would behave in such a situation. The question of whether a hypnotized individual could be compelled to carry

out antisocial or self-destructive action is a well-known example of this issue. Similarly, whenever hypnosis seems to legitimize behavior that would appear inappropriate without hypnosis, simulators become useful. For example, much of what occurs in age regression is striking because, without any self-consciousness, adult Ss carry out behavior that—from the observer's point of view—ought to make them feel ridiculous and foolish, such as playing in a sandbox and making mud pies. This is somewhat analogous to the behavior seen in some demonstrations of stage hypnosis where Ss may be required to bark like a dog, crow like a rooster, or sing like Sinatra—all behavior that Ss carry out with great aplomb and no apparent self-consciousness. The simulating situation provides an alternate kind of legitimization to evaluate the extent to which the *role* of being hypnotized rather than the *experience* of being hypnotized can account for the behavior.

3. Whenever an *experimental deception* is involved the simulator model provides an appropriate test of the manipulation's effectiveness. It asks in a very rigorous way the extent to which Ss might have figured out what is actually going on.

While conceptually it is possible to separate these three kinds of problems where simulating Ss may be useful, it must be noted that in many phenomena more than one aspect is involved. Age regression, for example, to the extent that one tests for augmented recall, may be conceptualized as a transcendence-of-normal-abilities question. However, to the extent that one wishes to evaluate the ease with which the S plays like a child or even perhaps wets his pants, it becomes a test of the S's willingness to engage in unusual behaviors. Simulating Ss may shed light in different ways on both aspects of such experimental problems.

The use of simulating Ss as a means of evaluating the transcendence of normal volitional capacities through hypnosis has been commented upon earlier. Suffice it to say that this is the only situation where a simulator's being able to carry out the identical behavior of the hypnotized individual provides conclusive negative evidence.

The second and third situations where simulators are useful will be discussed below.

A DETAILED EXAMPLE OF HOW SIMULATORS MAY BE USED
TO EVALUATE WHETHER HYPNOSIS LEADS TO AN UNUSUAL
WILLINGNESS TO CARRY OUT STRANGE BEHAVIORS

An experiment often cited as evidence to prove that deeply hypnotized Ss may be compelled to carry out antisocial or self-destructive actions is a study originally performed by Rowland (1939). He showed that deeply hypnotized Ss could be compelled to attempt to pick up a poisonous snake with their bare hands; to remove, with their bare fingers, a penny from a beaker of fuming nitric acid where it was obviously in the process of dissolving; and finally to throw this acid at a research assistant. Ss not only carried out these highly dangerous and antisocial behaviors but, when asked later in the waking state whether they would be willing to perform these actions, indicated with horror that they would not. Other waking Ss, asked whether they would be willing to perform these behaviors, also emphatically denied that they would do so. With relatively minor variations, the study was replicated by P.C. Young (1952) some years later with essentially similar findings.

These dramatic observations need to be contrasted with the contradictory findings of Erickson (1939b) who found that Ss could not be compelled even to tear up some pieces of paper that presumably were important documents, and it seemed as though striking discrepancies of this kind might well be due to the kind of variable that was originally described by Estabrooks (1943) as "operator attitude." (For an analysis of these issues, see Orne [1962a].)

A crucial factor in understanding the Rowland and Young findings seems to be the manner in which waking Ss would interpret the situation if they were actually exposed to it. To test the question of how truly dangerous, noxious, or antisocial waking Ss would perceive the situation to be, Orne and Evans (1965) replicated the entire study yet a third time, adding the simulator comparison group and subsequently several other nonhypnotized control groups.

The findings were striking and clear-cut: Using exactly the same procedure employed by Young and the analogous tasks, five out of six hypnotized Ss were compelled to carry out all of the requested behaviors. This replicated observations previously reported by Rowland and Young. But, when simulating Ss were actually placed in the same experimental situation, all six of them also performed the identical actions!

The conclusions that were drawn from the behavior of the simulating Ss said nothing about the mental processes that were involved in bringing about the behavior of the hypnotized individuals. However, the situation now is such that we do not know whether the hypnotized Ss were or were not being "compelled to carry out self-destructive or antisocial actions." The only appropriate conclusion was that the experimental procedure previously employed to test this hypothesis was not adequate to do so. Regardless of the care with which the situation was contrived and the trouble taken to conceal the elaborate safety precautions from the S, the situation was perceived as sufficiently safe by the simulating Ss for them to carry out the requested behaviors. It should be emphasized that these Ss were quite unable to specify how they or the research assistant would be protected from harm. Nonetheless, they readily verbalized the conviction that the investigator would prevent anyone from being hurt. In this regard, they showed a clear recognition of the investigator's realities, pointing out that he could not afford to have anyone hurt in the course of his experiments.

It should be noted that when Ss were asked whether they would carry out these behaviors—as opposed to being instructed to do so—they said they would refuse. Nor were we able to persuade any of our faculty colleagues to perform any of these actions, an observation we interpret as due to the differences in role relationship. The simulating procedure, however, demonstrated to us that Rowland and Young's assumptions about what a nonhypnotized S would do in the actual situation were incorrect. Ss simply did not accept as plausible that either they or anyone else would be hurt.

Once we had the experience of seeing how nonhypnotized simulators behaved, it became possible for us to present instructions with sufficient conviction that even Ss picked at random from the corridor and co-opted to participate in the study complied with the requests. We noted that, depending upon the emphasis in the instructions, different degrees of compliance could be obtained and, with appropriate emphasis, the behaviors obtained from real and simulating Ss could also be elicited from the nonhypnotized individuals on first contact. The role of the simulating comparison group in this study seems particularly interesting. Thus, once the experiment was completed, the demonstration that the situation was perceived as safe by the Ss, and was therefore not a useful indicator of behavioral control exerted by hypnosis, no longer required reference to the simulating group but was unequivocally demonstrated by the behavior of nonhypnotized Ss who were strangers asked to participate in the study.

In this study, then, simulating Ss served the purpose of initially evaluating what Ss will do (rather than what Ss can do, as in the transcendence experiments). Their behavior helped clarify how an individual in the experiment actually perceives the situation, obviating the need for speculative polemics about what Ss will or will not do. The inference drawn from the behavior of the simulating Ss is concerned with assessing the adequacy of the procedure for answering the experimental question, rather than with answering the experimental question itself. In this sense it is a true quasi-control (Orne, 1969).

The Use of the Real-Simulator Model to Evaluate the Adequacy of a Laboratory Deception

Many important and meaningful problems are difficult to explore in the laboratory. There are a large number of questions where the S's behavior would be materially altered if he knew the precise variables under investigation, and one technique that has been widely used is to deliberately deceive the *S* in an experiment. Recently, ethical issues have been raised about laboratory deceptions.[14] While a detailed discussion of these would be beyond the scope of this paper, deception also raises serious methodological issues. Deception is used in an experiment, because it is felt to be necessary in order to create the required experimental context. It follows, therefore, that it makes a considerable difference whether the *S* believes the deception or is able to see through it. This crucial question has received almost no systematic attention. The procedure of merely asking *S* at the end of an experiment whether he had caught on to the deception is usually inadequate since the needs of both *S* and *E* tend to mitigate against learning *S*'s true perceptions and lead to what I have termed a "pact of ignorance." (For a discussion of these issues, see Orne [1959, 1962b, 1969].) It is vital, therefore, in many experimental situations that involve deception to determine whether *S*s saw through the experimental manipulation. To answer this question the simulating comparison group can be extremely useful.

AN EXPERIMENTAL EXAMPLE

Some years ago Fisher (1954), in a now classic paper, studied the nature of posthypnotic behavior. In an ingenious experiment Fisher suggested to deeply hypnotized *S*s that, on awakening, each time they heard the word "psychology" they would scratch their right ear. After waking the *S*s, he tested the suggestion by using the word and was able to elicit the suggested behavior. At this point one of his associates came into the room and by innuendo the experiment was terminated. The associate, Dr. Fisher, and the *S* entered into an informal conversation about current topics of the day. In the course of this informal conversation the word "psychology" came up spontaneously. Of the twelve *S*s, only three responded during this time. After some minutes of conversation the associate left and Fisher, by turning

14. Most of the discussions focusing on the ethical dilemma of lying to an *S* appear to me naive and, at times, to border on the hypocritical. *S*s expect not to be informed of the precise problem under study and anticipate that it may be necessary to deceive them for the sake of the experiment. In our experience the fact of deception has never been a source of difficulty to the *S*; on the other hand, it is vital that the *E* take responsibility for the consequences of his actions and make certain that no *S* leaves the laboratory with more prowlems than when he entered. Informing the *S* honestly as and make certain that no *S* leaves the laboratory with more problems than when he entered. Informing the *S* honestly about his homosexual conflict or of his inability to perform up to the level of the average college student or of similar findings without placing these observations in context is considerably more traumatic and, in my view,

back to his *S*, implied resumption of the experiment, and conspicuously used the word "psychology" in a sentence. Under these circumstances all of his *S*s resumed responding by scratching their right ear. When asked about their behavior during the preceding period, several of the *S*s erroneously insisted that they had continued to respond, while others gave very transparent rationalizations. From these data Fisher concluded that the posthypnotic response is a function of the *S*'s understanding of what is desired at the time of responding and would be carried out as long as it was believed that the experiment was currently in progress.

An alternative plausible interpretation of Fisher's findings is, we felt, that *S*s perceived the *original* suggestion to be that they ought to respond by scratching their right ear whenever they heard the word "psychology" as long as the experiment continued—since, in the context where the suggestion was given, there would be no plausible reason for the hypnotist to mean for them to continue to respond indefinitely. If *S*s perceived the suggestion in this manner, one would expect them to stop responding when they believed the experiment to be over and Fisher's finding would not necessarily have any implications for the persistence of a posthypnotic suggestion outside of an experimental situation. It seems to us that the study did not really test whether a *S* who is given a clear-cut, time-limited posthypnotic suggestion would carry it out even under circumstances that he perceived to be outside of the experiment where the hypnotist would not be likely to know or even care whether the suggestion had been complied with. This question has considerable theoretical importance and is closely related to the issue of whether the posthypnotic response is a function of the suggestion given to a deeply hypnotized *S* or whether it is an attempt to please the hypnotist, depending on the ongoing relationship.

In a carefully designed experiment Orne, Sheehan, and Evans (1968) required *S*s to come to the laboratory on two successive days and to take a number of personality tests, some while hypnotized. The *S*s were informed in advance that they would be required to come on two successive days. The first day, in addition to taking the tests which were, in fact, part of another experiment, *S*s were also given the suggestion in deep hypnosis that for the

---

unethical, than the use of deception in a context where appropriate debriefing is assured. The self-righteous position taken in the matter of laboratory deception is all too often associated with a lack of concern about how the *S* really feels and a lack of recognition that a *S* may be seriously traumatized even by being excluded from an experiment because he does not perform adequately on a given test or even by being informed that he cannot be hypnotized. The issue of protecting the welfare and safety of human *S*s demands continual monitoring and close attention, and the *E* cannot shirk this responsibility by asserting that he has merely told the truth or that he was doing only a "learning" experiment.

next forty-eight hours each time they heard the word "experiment" they would run their right hand through their hair. It should be noted that this suggestion was legitimized by the fact that the *S*s realized they would see the hypnotist on the following day. However, the suggestion was clear-cut and explicit in demanding a response each time *S* heard the word "experiment"; and by limiting it to forty-eight hours the expectation that the response persist for this period of time was clearly communicated.

The next day, when *S* came to the laboratory the *E* was informed by the receptionist of his arrival, and on meeting him in the waiting room and walking down the hall to the experimental room, the *E* would carefully say, "I appreciate your coming back to the 'experiment.' " This test, however, was not the crucial measure of the posthypnotic response.

The *S*s taking part in our research are paid for their participation, and it is customary for them to return to the main office at the completion of a study where, after signing a receipt, they are reimbursed for their time. Each *S*, on the completion of the first day's tests, returned to the secretary who asked him to sign the usual form, asking whether it would be all right to pay him "now for today's 'experiment' and for the next part of the study tomorrow." The *S*'s response under these circumstances, in a different room totally outside the experimental context, constituted the first criterion test. On returning the subsequent day, the *S* was met by the receptionist who asked whether he was participating in the physiological or the psychological "experiment"—two studies that were in progress at the same time. The *S*'s response to the receptionist constituted the second test.

The results showed that, using a highly selected group of *S*s who were capable of entering deep hypnosis, *S*s responded in the waiting room and the main office much as they had in the presence of the hypnotist. Thus, in some instances, since the word "experiment" was used quite casually, *S*s did not always seem to hear the cue; on the other hand, the fact that the context was different, that the *E* was not present, and that the test was carried out in a way that appeared totally unrelated to the study, did not seem to interfere with the response. Not surprisingly, those *S*s who responded most consistently were those individuals who also were most deeply hypnotized.

Though the experiment as outlined above seems to deal with the experimental question, it fails to test the crucial issue of whether the test by the secretary was actually perceived to be outside of the experimental situation by the *S*. It might easily have happened that the way in which the study was carried out permitted *S*s to suspect that the secretary was really recording their behavior for the benefit of the hypnotist. Such a situation could readily arise if the hypnotist casually or implicitly added a comment that the *S* would respond not only with him but no matter who used the word "experiment," and so forth. Alternatively, the secretary might have unduly emphasized the word "experiment" in her speech, thereby marking the situation as a test. Under such circumstances the findings would not have permitted valid inference to be drawn about the extent to which posthypnotic responses generalize from one context to another. Obviously we would much rather have tested the posthypnotic suggestion totally away from the laboratory but, even if we had tested it in a classroom or dormitory, we would still need to ask whether the S might not have suspected what we were doing. So simulating Ss were included in the study solely for the purpose of evaluating whether the test situation was recognized as related to the experiment. Their behavior served to tell us how likely it was that a S could catch on to the fact that the secretary was really a subtle but nonetheless crucial part of the experimental testing procedure.

In other studies we have noticed that Ss asked to simulate hypnosis tend to be unusually suspicious. It is not surprising that the S asked to deceive someone else be alert lest he himself be deceived. Therefore we can expect the behavior of the simulating Ss in such a situation to be exquisitely responsive to cues that would be missed by Ss not sensitized by the simulating instructions. Used in this way the simulating comparison group intentionally "stacks the cards" against the hypothesis, thereby providing a particularly rigorous test for the adequacy of a given deception.

Running both groups of Ss randomly mixed and without knowing to which group any given individual belonged, we observed that of seventeen deeply hypnotized Ss, six responded on both days, whereas of thirteen simulating Ss not a single S responded on both days. These differences are particularly striking since in the presence of the hypnotist the simulating Ss tended to respond even more than the hypnotized Ss.

It should be emphasized that the simulating comparison group was used in the Orne, Sheehan, and Evans study exclusively for the purpose of evaluating whether it is at all likely for even suspicious Ss to see through the use of the secretary as a stimulus for and observer of posthypnotic behavior. The fact that simulating Ss did not perceive the secretary in this way is taken as reasonable evidence for assuming that it is ecologically valid to accept the hypnotic Ss' interaction with the secretary as representative of extra-experimental behavior. From the point of view of this particular experiment the simulating group served *no other purpose*, but they did thereby allow us to generalize about the hypnotized Ss' posthypnotic responses in settings outside the experiment.

In the context of this paper, however, the differences between real and simulating Ss in this study are of some interest. Not only do they demonstrate a behavioral difference between hypnotized and simulating Ss at an acceptable significance level, but they also show that the effect of a posthypnotic suggestion on hypnotized *S*s persists even in situations where the hypnotist is apparently unable to know about the *S*'s response. The effects of simulation instructions do not extend in this study to a situation where the *S* believes that his responses are no longer monitored (For a more extensive discussion of studies on posthypnotic behavior, see Orne [1969].)

A Final Example

Another experiment that utilized the simulating control group as a means to evaluate the effectiveness of a deception serves perhaps best to illustrate the limitations on the conclusions that can be drawn from this comparison group. Orne and Evans (1966) carried out a study to investigate the question with which patients may betray their negative feelings as they are about to be hypnotized: "What happens if you drop dead while I am hypnotized?"

It is generally accepted that *S*s will lapse into sleep and then spontaneously awaken after some time if the hypnotist should disappear; however, little hard evidence is available. Indeed, it is extremely difficult to tell what would happen if the hypnotist were to disappear once deep hypnosis has been induced. The only empirical study in the literature is by Dorcus, Brintnall, and Case (1941). In this experiment, after a *S* was deeply hypnotized there was a knock at the door and the secretary asked *E* to come quickly because of an emergency downtown. The *E* immediately left without any comment to *S*. Consequently, the hypnotized *S* remained alone in the room, and his behavior was observed surreptitiously. The group of *S*s treated in this fashion was compared with others who were merely asked to relax in the same kind of situation. Unfortunately this study sheds no light on the question because in both instances the experiment was sufficiently transparent that *S*s must have realized the deep interest of the investigator in how long they remained immobile or in trance.

To answer the question of what would happen if the hypnotist really disappeared, the situation must be contrived in a manner to seem plausible and truly accidental. This is also important in order to avoid doing violence to the implicit agreement between *S* and *E* that the latter is responsible for the welfare of the former during the course of an experiment. What would happen in a situation where the hypnotist truly disappears has, of course, considerable theoretical importance for an understanding of hypnosis. Thus, if one conceptualizes the phenomenon as a simple interpersonal transaction where the *S* behaves in certain ways only to please the hypnotist and comply with his demands, the disappearance of the hypnotist should lead to an immediate termination of the hypnotic condition. Conversely, if hypnosis leads to an altered state of the individual, the disappearance of the hypnotist should not automatically terminate trance but rather it should take a finite period of time for the S to somehow pull himself out of this state, either by awakening or perhaps by going to sleep.[15]

A situation was finally created that fitted the experimental requirements by requiring Ss who had been previously trained to enter hypnosis readily to participate in a study requiring two sessions. It was explained to them that, in order to standardize the procedure, all instructions, including the induction and termination of hypnosis, would be carried out by tape recording.

The E's task was essentially that of a technician—applying electrodes, turning on the tape recording, presenting the experimental material, and so forth. He did not say anything throughout the study since every item of instruction was given by means of the tape recorder. Each S came for two such experimental sessions. During the second session, while the S was deeply hypnotized and tapping his foot in rhythm with hallucinated music, the tape recorder came to a grinding halt, the light went out, and the E tried in vain to reactivate the machine by flicking the switch. He then muttered under his breath, "The damn fuse," and dashed from the room.

The S's behavior was observed by means of a one-way screen throughout the experiment in order to determine what would happen once the E had left the room. Would hypnosis be terminated immediately once the S was alone, as some theories would predict; or would it take a period of time for the S to pull himself out of hypnosis, as one would expect if the condition were some special altered state?

Despite the "cuteness" of the deception procedure of the simulated power failure, there was no certainty whether the S would accept it as such. For this reason a simulator comparison group was also included.

The findings were clear-cut: five of the six deeply hypnotized Ss did not arouse immediately when the hypnotist left. They required varying periods of time to apparently pull themselves out of the state. When they did, they appeared somewhat disoriented and confused. However, five out of the six

---

15. It should be noted that a role theory of hypnosis that conceives of the hypnotized S as playing a role at a nonconscious level leads to an identical prediction as the "state" theory. If one assumes that effects of a role persist in situations where the hypnotist does not know or would not care about what the S does, or that the continuation of a role is to a considerable degree independent of the actual or implied presence of the hypnotist, there is no discernible operational distinction between a role or a state view.

simulating Ss also continued to appear hypnotized—but, in contrast, continued thus for the whole half-hour period until the technician returned, presumably having fixed the fuse. During the subsequent post-experimental inquiry it became clear that the simulators caught on to the fact that the power failure was contrived and that they behaved as they thought a hypnotized S would if there were a true power failure. The simulating Ss quite cogently pointed out that having been instructed to fool the E put them on their guard lest they themselves be fooled. In contrast, only one of the hypnotized Ss reported suspecting that the power failure was contrived.

We observed statistically significant differences between the real hypnotized group and the simulating comparison group. What conclusions about the nature of the hypnotic phenomenon can be drawn from this difference? *In our opinion, no valid conclusion is justified.*

Once again the purpose of the simulating group was not to provide a comparison group for the actual subject population; rather it was a special treatment group included exclusively to test the adequacy of the experimental procedure. Specifically it was used here to determine whether the power failure in the experiment was sufficiently plausible to be accepted as genuine even by suspicious Ss. The combined behaviors and reports of the simulating group clearly indicate that our efforts were inadequate in this regard. Five out of six simulating Ss correctly perceived the power failure as a contrived part of the experiment. This leads to the unpleasant conclusion that the experimental procedure was inadequate to test the hypothesis. While according to inquiries—and in line with the experimental behavior— the hypnotized Ss for the most part accepted the power failure as genuine, there was a sufficient number of cues in the situation to permit suspicious Ss to see through the procedure. Therefore, the possibility that the hypnotized Ss recognized the true state of affairs at some level cannot be discounted and the experiment cannot be interpreted at face value.

Having found the deception manipulation wanting, we re-examined in detail the cues that might allow the S to become aware that the power failure was a planned part of the experiment. The kind of nitty-gritty details that most investigators fail to publish and which, even if the investigators included them, most editors would delete for the sake of brevity, are crucial in this regard. For example, in the study just described, to facilitate observation after the "power failure" the overhead lights remained on and only the bright desk lamp went out as the tape recorder stopped; an obvious one-way mirror had always been in the room to which we had hoped (in vain) the S would have adapted; and a small polygraph continued to run in the experimental room after the "power failure." We now redesigned the study with considerable attention to such details. The one-way screen was eliminated and replaced by another less well-known and carefully hidden means of observation. When the power failure occurred, all lights in the room were extinguished. Just enough light was filtered into the room through the window curtains from daylight—or from a strategically placed parking lot light outside at night—to make observation possible. Furthermore, physiological recordings were apparently made by means of a large Ampex instrumentation tape recorder and a small polygraph. Both of these machines stopped, along with the lights and the tape recorder, at the power failure. (Actually, the wires from the S were run through to another room at some distance in order to permit continuous recording of relevant data.) When the E left the room the hall lights were out. Every effort was made by scrupulous attention to such details to make the power failure plausible.

With these revised conditions, simulating and hypnotized Ss were run in another experiment by a blind E. Here four of six simulating Ss stopped simulating the moment the technician left the room, indulging in exploratory and other private behavior clearly indicating that they felt themselves to be unobserved. On the other hand, the hypnotized group behaved much as they had in the earlier experiment, pulling themselves out of this state only after a considerable period of time had elapsed. These behaviors were in line with the data provided during an inquiry, indicating that both real and simulating Ss now accepted the power failure as genuine.

Significant differences were again obtained but, in contrast to the findings of the first study, those from the second study allow meaningful inference. The behavior of the simulating Ss clearly indicates that the power failure was accepted as genuine, and therefore it is plausible to accept the behavior of the hypnotized individuals as validly indicating how they respond to the "disappearance" of the hypnotist.

It will be clear that the purpose served by the simulating Ss in this experiment was exclusively to determine whether or not there were sufficient cues in the experimental situation to allow a S to surmise that the power failure was staged rather than spontaneous. This issue is critical, however, if one intends to extend inferences to a situation that is actually extra-experimental and perceived as such by the S. Though it entailed a great deal of trouble to test the adequacy of the experimental manipulation, without the simulating comparison group we would have had no empirical test of the procedure's adequacy. It is impossible without such a technique to evaluate the kind of cues presented to the S in an experimental situation. Yet it is the presence of such cues upon which the legitimacy of inference depends. In experiments requiring any form of deception, the simulators' performance puts into behavioral terms information usually gleaned only in in-depth interviews—and then often it is only one S, as in our first study, who will "break down" or break the pact of ignorance and be willing to tell that the whole experiment he has just taken part in has the kind of flaw that negates his own data and E's time.

In this experiment, as in the posthypnotic study previously reported, the differences between Ss who are pretending to be hypnotized and those actually hypnotized were not of much moment except to test the adequacy of the deception. The differences that emerge in both studies do, however, serve to support the assertions of both hypnotized and simulating Ss about the nature of their experiences and do argue for the existence of very different psychic mechanisms that may under certain circumstances result in similar behavior. The situation of the disappearing hypnotist undoubtedly is only one of a number of situations that could be contrived to demonstrate that behavioral differences do occur. In this instance, the behavior of Ss in the first unsuccessful deception experiment served to indicate that Ss' expectations or preconceptions are that the deeply hypnotized individuals ought to continue in the state of hypnosis if the hypnotist somehow were to disappear. The simulating Ss' behavior in the second experiment shows that insofar as they believe in the genuineness of the power failure they will stop pretending as soon as they believe that they are no longer under observation. The actual behavior of hypnotized individuals in both studies was, on the whole, unchanged: in both cases they gradually roused from hypnosis, taking several minutes to achieve full awareness of their surroundings.

Summary
and
Conclusions

This discussion has tried to clarify some of the misconceptions that have arisen concerning the use of the real-simulator design. What initially appears to be a simple control group is, in fact, an example of a category of techniques—"quasi-controls"—which serve special delineated purposes in experimental research. The observatie of a category of techniques—"quasi-controls"—which serve special delineated purposes in experimental research. The observation that even highly trained hypnotists cannot reliably distinguish Ss pretending to be hypnotized from deeply hypnotized individuals without special procedures in no way challenges the genuineness of hypnosis or the subjective reality of the hypnotized individual's experiences. It does, however, force a careful reevaluation of a great many claims made for hypnosis, and challenges common beliefs in the infallibility of good clinical judgment.

The ease with which simulating Ss duplicate a wide range of behaviors once held to be uniquely associated with hypnosis cannot be explained by assuming that Ss pretending to be hypnotized are actually hypnotized. These Ss are purposely selected for their inability to enter hypnosis despite repeated efforts to do so, and extensive research has shown that the likelihood of such Ss entering deep hypnosis at some future time is very small. Furthermore, deeply hypnotized Ss report entirely different experiences in hypnosis from those reported by individuals pretending to be hypnotized. These reports tend to be stable whether they are given to an E formally, a research assistant informally, or are part of private conversations with other Ss, friends, or spouses.

Finally, while in our view such behavioral data are unnecessary to establish the difference between simulators and hypnotized individuals, a number of situations are described where clear behavioral differences do emerge.

The simulating comparison group serves a restricted purpose in hypnosis research. Many properly designed studies do not require such a group and, in some instances, it would merely serve to confuse the issues. However, three circumstances are described where such a group is essential:

1. Whenever the claim is made that a given phenomenon is produced because the S is hypnotized, where the S's performance is taken as proof because unhypnotized Ss are believed to be incapable of producing it. This includes all studies where a claim of transcending the waking S's normal volitional capability is made. Simulating Ss are required to provide a test of the motivated waking Ss' capabilities given identical treatment by the hypnotist.

2. Whenever an individual in hypnosis performs an action that the investigator wishes to assert he would have refused if he were not hypnotized. In other words, when one wishes to demonstrate that hypnosis has led to a greater willingness to carry out a behavior required of the S, it becomes important to evaluate how unhypnotized Ss would behave in the identical situation if the role were legitimized in some other fashion. In this context particularly, the inherent quality of the real-simulator model to prevent differential treatment of the comparison group by keeping the hypnotist blind is useful. Equally important is the effective manner in which the simulation instructions legitimize otherwise unacceptable behavior.

3. Whenever an experiment involves deception and the effectiveness of the deception is crucial to the interpretation of the conclusions. The inclusion of a simulating comparison group is needed to evaluate the adequacy of the deception procedure.

It should be emphasized that in each instance the simulating comparison group is included to allow the investigator to evaluate the capabilities of highly motivated, unhypnotized *S*s and the extent to which direct comparison between the behavior of this group and the hypnotized group is appropriate depends upon the nature of the hypothesis being tested.

The real-simulator model is difficult to use in practice. It demands not only several *E*s working together, but great care to meet the assumptions of the experimental model. In many instances alternative designs can be used to good advantage. Some experimental problems, however, demand the inclusion of such a comparison group. The complexities of this technique and its use may well serve to slow the flow of research. While a temporary inconvenience, such an eventuality may not be undesirable. In the long run it may be far better to have fewer studies that subject the phenomenon of hypnosis to a rigorous test while doing justice to its unique attributes than many studies that fail, under critical examination, to yield alternative explanations or, worse yet, fail to study the phenomenon at all.

Charles T. Tart *is a Professor of Psychology at the University of California's Davis campus. He received his Ph.D. from the University of North Carolina in 1963, and then had two years of postdoctoral training in hypnosis at Ernest Hilgard's laboratory at Stanford University. His research interests in hypnosis, sleep, and psychophysiology were supplemented by work on psi phenomena during a year as Lecturer in Psychiatry at the University of Virginia Medical School. Further contact with the burgeoning human potentials movement upon his return to California broadened his research interests to altered states of consciousness in general, and led to his editing* Altered States of Consciousness: A Book of Readings, *in 1969. He has scientifically investigated a wide variety of the phenomena of altered states, and presented an overall conceptual system for such states in his recent* States of Consciousness *book. Other books include* Transpersonal Psychologies; Learning to Use Extrasensory Perception; Psi: Scientific Studies of the Psychic Realm; *and, with several co-authors,* Symposium on Consciousness.

Tart *provides a comprehensive review of the five scales that have evolved to date to measure depth of hypnosis in terms of the subject's own experiential appraisals of how deeply hypnotized he feels himself to be. He discusses the differences among the five scales and their relationships to other methods for measuring depth; and presents a case study on one excellent hypnotic subject to illustrate his method and its potentialities.*

Tart conceptualizes his methods of measurement as extending beyond hypnosis to altered states of consciousness in general; and argues that experiential ratings should be adopted as the primary method for measuring depth in preference to conventional behavioral methods. He makes a strong case for the view that experiential ratings reach into areas of important hypnotic phenomena that are unavailable through behavioral approaches and argues that extensive research with the experiential approach is indicated.

17

Measuring the Depth
of an Altered State of Consciousness,
with Particular Reference
to Self-Report Scales
of Hypnotic Depth

CHARLES T. TART

Introduction

This chapter will propose a theoretical basis for measuring the depth of any state of consciousness *(SoC)* with particular emphasis on hypnosis, review the literature on previous attempts at self-report scaling of hypnotic depth, present data on two self-report scales of hypnotic depth used extensively in my laboratory, and conclude with some general comments on the practical uses of self-report scales.

As many *SoC*s exhibit quantitative or qualitative variation, either in terms of subject's behavior or reports of his experiences, we commonly talk about the "depth" of a given *SoC*. This chapter will consider the problem of the depth of *SoC*s, with main reference to the hypnotic state, in terms of a theoretical model under development which is applicable to all altered *SoC*s. It will also systematically review the literature on self-report scales of hypnotic depth, one technique of measuring depth. Some new data will also be presented on the phenomenology of extremely deep hypnotic states in relation to a self-report technique for measuring hypnotic depth.

Theoretically, one may conceive of a subject's total state of being at a given time (behavior, experience, and physiology) as resulting from the interaction of a number of subsystems. These subsystems may be conceptualized as behavioral, experiential, or physiological in nature, depending on their heuristic value. Such subsystems might be identity, memory, cognitive processing, limbic system interactions, and so forth. Each subsystem may exhibit one or several qualitatively different modes of action, and there may be *quantitative* variation within a given mode of action for a given subsystem. If we further postulate that the subsystems that make up the total organism interact with each other, and that this interaction may determine either the qualitative mode or the quantitative level of action within a mode for each subsystem, we are then led to the conclusion that there are a finite number of ways in which the total organism can be stably organized in terms of the interactive interrelationships between subsystems. These modes of organization or configuration each constitute a unique *SoC*, a gestalt of subsystems stabilized by feedback interaction between the subsystems.

For example, subsystems are organized in one fashion in the ordinary waking state but in a different fashion in a deep hypnotic state in the same subject. Note that the distinction between *SoCs* is thus based not on the *content* of *SoC*, the particular things a person experiences or the particular way he behaves, but on the altered configuration of interaction of the hypothesized subsystems, which results in a new organizational gestalt. For example, a person who has taken a large dose of LSD and a person who has been deeply hypnotized may both report that at a given time they had no awareness of existing as a separate self; that is, the content of the experience seems identical, but we suspect that the manner in which this particular content came about in each state was not the same, that there was a different configuration of interacting subsystems, which happened to lead to the same content in a particular instance. Normally, different interacting configurations of subsystems will frequently lead to different contents, but this is not a defining criterion for*SoCs*.

The dimension of "depth" for a given *SoC* is a hypothetical construct that is useful to the investigator in ordering and conceptualizing changes seen in that *SoC*. In terms of the above model, changes in the depth of an *SoC* result from quantitative changes in the operation of some subsystems within the particular configuration of subsystems that comprises that *SoC*. Previous investigators have also used the term "depth" to cover what seem to be *qualitative* changes in the subsystem configuration, but as such changes may radically alter the overall configuration, a point is reached in which it is perhaps better to talk of a new *SoC* rather than a change in the depth of the original *SoC*. How large the qualitative change must be to initiate a new *SoC* is a point that cannot be decided theoretically. To illustrate, it is common in hypnosis for subjects to report that as they "went deeper," their perception of the environment around them became dimmer and dimmer, and that it finally faded out completely. This is a quantitative change that we would ordinarily associate with an alteration in hypnotic depth. If the same hypnotized subject spontaneously reported that he had suddenly found himself standing in a cavern near the sea, without there having been any suggestions to this effect, it is not clear from *content* alone whether this represents a further quantitative change in the operation of the subsystem that produced the fading of the environment, or whether a new subsystem had come into operation, or whether the mode of operation of a subsystem had qualitatively changed. Data presented later in this chapter will illustrate a case where deep hypnosis may have changed into another *SoC*.

Assuming now the existence of a depth dimension and some way to measure it, Figure 17.1 illustrates a few of the possible relations of the intensity or quality of observable effects to depth. Such effects may be considered a result of quantitative or qualitative changes in subsystem operation. The effects may be particular behaviors, reported experiences, or physiological indices. Intensity or quality of each effect is plotted on its own appropriate scale. Effect A is of the type present in ordinary consciousness at a low level, but which begins to increase with increasing depth part way along the depth dimension, and then levels off at some maximum intensity even though depth continues to increase. Effect B does not manifest at all until a threshold depth is reached, then increases with increasing depth, temporarily stabilizes at a maximum value, and then decreases and finally ceases to manifest with further increases in depth. Effect C suddenly manifests at full intensity when a certain depth is reached and suddenly disappears at a greater depth. Effect D manifests mildly at the lowest depth level and increases steadily in intensity all through the depth dimension; this sort of relationship to depth is commonly (but probably erroneously) assumed to be typical of altered *SoC*s and particulary of hypnosis. Effect E manifests strongly in normal consciousness, is unaffected by increasing depth or may, as in this particular example, suddenly return at a greater depth level, perhaps with an increased intensity. Many other possible relationships between the intensity of effects and depth may be presumed to exist other than those diagramed here.

In drawing Figure 17.1 it was assumed that we had some independent measure of depth. This assumption need no longer be made. If the important effects of a given *SoC* are measured with respect to each other as different effects take on different values, we may formally define the depth dimension of a given *SoC* as the obtained graphical plot of empirically obtained relationships of the above sort. Insofar as the plotted relationships are only of observed effects, "depth" is a purely descriptive concept, which

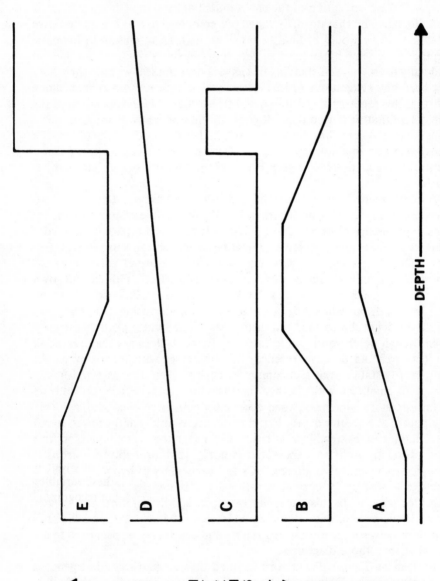

FIGURE 17.1 *Some possible relationships between observable phenomena and the depth of an SoC.*

may be useful in summarizing our observations but which actually adds no information not present in the first place. Insofar as the effects are considered as manifestations of alterations in the postulated subsystems, "depth" is a hypothetical construct and its value may be assessed on criteria of comprehensiveness, understanding, and testable predictions. In practice, any combination of effects for a given *SoC* whose curves cover what we believe to be the entire depth continuum may be used as a minimal working index of the depth continuum, although effects of type D, those increasing linearly with depth, are most convenient.

The practical strategy for investigating the depth continuum for a given *SoC* would be to start with some important effect of that state that one could vary easily, say, for example, by suggestion in hypnosis. One would vary this effect through various values and at each value measure other effects, either experiential, physiological, or behavioral. Using the values of the deliberately altered variable for an axis, one would plot the other effects against them. If an effect that did indeed vary linearly with one's hypothetical concept of depth had been picked, then plots of the type shown in Figure 17.1 would be obtained; if the deliberately manipulated variable was of some other type, rather complex and confusing plots would be obtained, and one would repeat the investigation with other effects being deliberately manipulated. Statistical manipulations could be used to optimize the plot.

A number of cautions in applying this model of depth are necessary. First, some *SoC* might consist entirely of type C effects, where the *SoC* is present and all effects are maximal, or is not present and all effects are zero, with nothing in between. Thus there really would be no "depth" for this particular *SoC*.

Second, some effects for a given *SoC* are "spontaneous," that is, they always appear without any special procedures needed to elicit them; others, however, are what might be called "potential" effects. Potential effects can be manifested in a given *SoC* but only if certain subject and situational variables take on the correct values. Insofar as the values of these variables are such as to routinely elicit the effect, but the variables are not recognized, we have a constant misinterpretation of the effect—we consider it spontaneous when in point of fact it is potential and must be produced in a certain manner. Insofar as the variables are nonconscious expectations of the experimenter we have the problem of demand characteristics and experimenter bias.

Third, the above model applies to a stable *SoC*. Because most subjects have little or no experience in functioning in altered *SoC*s, their early experiences with such *SoC*s will consist not only of the characteristic effects of such states per se but of many effects due to adaptation to the state and attempts to cope with the novelty of it. These transitional effects are worthy of study in themselves, but should not be confused with the stable and characteristic effects of the *SoC*. Gill and Brennan (1961) have reported on such effects occurring in the induction phases of hypnosis when patients were new to being hypnotized. Unfortunately, most of our knowledge of the effects of various *SoC*s stems from studies using unadapted subjects, producing an inextricable blend of adaptation-coping effects and effects of *SoC*s per se.

Fourth, several tyes of alterations in the configuration of subsystems might result in phenotypically identically observable phenomena, so too great an emphasis on single phenomena may be misleading. In the example mentioned earlier of an alteration of a subject's identity in an LSD state and in hypnosis, loss of personal identity might result in the first state because the subject feels identified with the cosmos as a whole, while in a hypnotic state it might result from no attention being mobilized for examining the characteristics that normally make up personal identity. In the case of LSD we have a profound alteration in the identity subsystem, while in the case of hypnosis the primary change is in the attention subsystem. Only wide-range approaches to *SoC*s can adequately deal with them.

Fifth, some *SoC*s, particularly hypnosis, are highly "flexible," that is, out of a large number of observable effects potentially associated with that *SoC* only a small number will be seen at any time, and the particular subsets seen may be influenced by the experimenter, the experimental situation, and the subject's own predilections. In order to communicate with the subject about what he is experiencing and to ask him to scale the intensity of his experiences, we must hit upon a common vocabulary. In the course of communicating this vocabulary, however, the words may implicitly suggest what effects are desired, and so one can create an expected set of effects and possibly an expected set of interrelationships among these effects, which nevertheless represent only a small aspect of that *SoC*. It is important not to confuse this particular subset with the state of consciousness per se. Many of the differences of experimental results that come from different experimenters' laboratories may result from this. The language (and paralinguistic aspects of communication) with which we communicate with the subject set up expectations and demands that may influence the subject's experiences per se, as well as influencing the way in which he reports them to us.

Sixth, there may be certain portions of the depth continuum of a given *SoC* that impair subjects' ability to adequately report their experiences or to carry out overt behavior, so these portions of the depth continuum will be hard to map. Subjects may or may not be able to report on these adequately in retrospect.

As a final note on practical difficulties, let us consider drug-induced *SoC*s, particularly those resulting from psychedelic drugs. Here it would seem that we have an independent measure of depth, namely the dose of the drug. It is clear, however, that there are tremendous differences between subjects and within the same subject from session to session with the same drug and dosage. The particular dosage of the drug will interact with the interpersonal situation, the experimenter-subject relationship, and the (changing) characteristics of the subject to produce different effects at different times; these are all "potential effects" in the model mentioned above, and worth studying, but they illustrate how crude dosage may be as a measure of depth.

The Depth of Hypnosis

Let us now consider the problem of the depth of hypnosis. Hypnotic "susceptibility" and hypnotic "depth" have frequently been confused in the literature. Hypnotic susceptibility refers to the degree of responsiveness to hypnotic suggestion administered under standardized conditions (Hilgard, 1965b), and in comparing subjects on the degree of hypnotic susceptibility we are comparing their *overall responsiveness to the assessment procedure*. Hypnotic depth on the other hand, refers to the *momentary* state of the subject along a hypothesized dimension. In the light of the above model, the hypnotic state would refer to the interacting, stable configuration of subsystems that comprise the hypnotic state, and hypnotic "depth" to each subsystem possessing a certain quantitatively variable level of operation within this configuration; that is, the *state* of hypnosis does not exist until the subsystems have taken up a certain, nonordinary configuration.[1] Once this configuration is taken up, quantitative variations of the sort illustrated in Figure 17.1 occur within the subsystems. While it is generally believed that a subject's hypnotic responsiveness, the measure of his "susceptibility," will vary directly with depth, it is possible for depth to vary quite rapidly in some subjects. Thus a standard assessment procedure, such as the Stanford Hypnotic Susceptibility Scales (Weitzenhoffer & Hilgard, 1962) may be confounded by changes in depth occurring through the lengthy assessment procedure for an individual subject. More importantly, in studies using the presence or absence of the hypnotic state of an independent variable, variations in depth in a given subject throughout the course of the experiment, as well as such variations across subjects, could seriously confound results, even to the point of increasing variance sufficiently to wash out genuine effects (see Tart and Hilgard, 1966, for an illustration of this).

It is clear from the above discussion that mapping the depth continuum

---

1. The problem of where "waking suggestibility" leaves off and the hypnotic state begins will not be dealt with in this paper, as it belongs properly to a discussion of the nature of induction of altered *SoCs*.

for hypnosis or any other *SoC* is a laborious process, involving a great deal of trial and error to find what sort of dimensions make the best conceptual and theoretical sense. A possible starting point for mapping the depth continuum, which seems to offer a number of advantages, is found if we note that many subjects will spontaneously report on fluctuations in the depth of their hypnotic state when talking to an experimenter after a session. Ignoring for the moment the question how subjects carry out this measurement process, it is conceivable that the subject himself may be an excellent direct observer of important aspects of the hypnotic depth continuum. Because of this observation, a number of procedures have been developed for teaching the subject to scale and report the depth of his hypnotic state when requested during hypnosis.

In light of the above theoretical discussion, most of the empirical studies of self-report measurement of hypnotic depth leave much to be desired. In measuring the depth of any *SoC*, the problem of the degree of identity of that *SoC* across subjects is very important. Many subjects may be said to be "hypnotized" or "intoxicated with marijuana" or the like in conventional usage, but given the present sloppiness of specification of *SoC*s, each of the many subjects may have relatively unique components making up the gestalt configuration of his *SoC*. If these components are unique enough, we are seriously misled in giving the same name to the *SoC* across subjects. In the studies of self-report measurement of hypnotic depth to be reviewed in the next sections, the investigators (implicitly) assumed that the uniformity of the hypnotic *SoC* across subjects was high enough to ignore individual differences. Empirical investigation may eventually reveal this assumption to be very misleading. A later section of this chapter will present data illustrating an approach that is methodologically more conservative, investigating the depth continuum in an individual subject with the Extended North Carolina Scale. In this approach, the overall phenomenology of the *SoC* across subjects and the similarity of the individually obtained depth continua must show a satisfactory degree of commonality before the results can be combined into a "general" picture of that *SoC*.

Five Self-Report Scales of Hypnotic Depth

This section will consider the LeCron Scale, the North Carolina Scale, the Brief Stanford Scale, the Harvard Discreet Scale, and the Harvard Continuous Scale. The Long Stanford Scale will be considered in a separate section as it has been studied more extensively than the other scales. The Extended North Carolina Scale will also be discussed in a separate section.

LeCron (1953) reported that he was able to measure hypnotic depth as frequently as he desired, and with little effort, by simply instructing his subjects that they would be able to scale their hypnotic depth on a 100-point scale. He defined this scale to them somewhat vaguely (the values are shown in Table 17.1), but told them that their "subconscious minds" always knew how deeply hypnotized they were, and that whenever he asked them what their depth was a number would flash into consciousness from their subconscious minds and they would report it immediately. Although he reported few details of his studies, LeCron stated that these self-reports of hypnotic depth correlated extremely well with his clinical estimates of his subjects' depths, and could, for most purposes, replace other measures of depth, such as particular hypnotic phenomena.

LeCron's report led a number of other investigators to develop various methods for self-report of hypnotic depth (or hypnotic "state" in some studies). Names have been given to these scales according to where the work was done, and their main characteristics are summarized in Table 17.1. All these scales require the subject to report the depth of his hypnotic state when questioned about it, except the Hypnotic Depth Indicator (HDI), which requires the subject to adjust a dial or move his hands continuously along a ruled scale as his hypnotic depth increases or decreases.[2]

Since these five scales differ along many important dimensions, it is difficult to compare them. The first such dimension is the concept of hypnotic depth held by the experimenter, and the degree to which this was communicated to subjects explicitly (the formal instructions) and implicitly (demand characteristics). The second is the degree of definition of the scale. At one extreme (the HDI and Discrete Scales) only awake and deep are defined, while at the other (the North Carolina Scale, Tart, 1962) particular hypnotic phenomena that subjects can expect to experience at various scale points are mentioned in the instructions. The third is the amount of previous experience with hypnosis subjects may have had before being required to use the scale. If they have not had such experience, they are measuring on the basis both of hypnotic effects and of transitional effects of adapting to a novel situation. Fourth, the scales differ in whether subjects are asked to make conscious, deliberate estimates of their hypnotic depth or whether they are told that the answers will come automatically, instantly, in response to the experimenter's query. The fifth dimension is the number of state reports obtained during the hypnotic session, varying from a low of one (the Discrete Scale) to obtaining a state report following every

---

2. This scale was first used by Field in an unpublished report (1963) and required the subject to move a dial along a linear sliding scale. It was modified by Evans so that the subject could move the dial continuously, when appropriate, around a twelve-inch diameter "clockface" with his eyes closed. Except for two early studies by Field (1965, 1966), a later, slightly modified version has been used in all studies (Evans, 1970; Evans & Orne, 1965; Field, Evans, & Orne, 1965; Orne & Evans, 1966), and is called in these reports the Hypnotic Depth Indicator (HDI). The Discrete Scale, discussed below, is defined in the same fashion, but is usually presented to the subject only once after each termination of hypnosis. It asks the subject to rate the deepest level achieved (Evans & Orne, 1965).

TABLE 17.1   Characteristics of self-report scales of depth

Scale Name	Defined Values	Type of Answer	References
LeCron	0 = awake 1–20 = light 20–40 = medium 40–60 = deep 60–80 = plenary 80+ = stuporous	Instant	Hatfield, 1961 LeCron, 1953
North Carolina	0 = waking 1–12 = relaxed, detached, ideomotor movements 20 = analgesia 25 = dreams 30 = amnesia, mental quiet, very high suggestibility 40 = all effects completely real 50+ = mind sluggish	Instant	Tart, 1962, 1963, 1967
Brief Stanford	0 = wide awake 1 = borderline 2 = light 3 = medium 4 = deep	Instant	Hilgard & Tart, 1966 Tart, 1966a Tart & Hilgard, 1966
Long Stanford	0 = wide awake 1 = borderline 2 = light 5 = deep 10 = very deep, very high suggestibility	Instant Instant and deliberate	Larsen, 1965 Tart, 1966b Present chapter
Harvard Discrete	1 = awake 10 = as deep as possible	Deliberate	O'Connell, 1964
Harvard Continuous	1–10 = awake to deep as possible	Deliberate, continuous	Field, 1966 Orne & Evans, 1966

Source: Tart, 1970b.

particular hypnotic phenomenon suggested (the North Carolina Scale) to continuous self-monitoring of subjective depth (HDI).

In attempting to assess the validity of self-report scales of hypnotic depth, all published studies to date have compared self-report measures for their subjects against some behavioral measure of hypnotic *susceptibility,* usually some version of the standardized Stanford Scales (SHSS) (Weitzenhoffer & Hilgard, 1959, 1962), or against particular hypnotic phenomena traditionally believed to require a certain minimum depth before they can be experienced well. The procedure of almost all experimental studies of hypnosis apparently assumes that depth stays constant after induction. If, however, depth does fluctuate rapidly for at least some subjects, then obtaining only a few self-reports of depth might well result in atypical values. Consequently, correlations of self-reported depth with overall susceptibility could not reach very high figures.

This consideration is particularly important in evaluating the published reports. Two studies, one of the original LeCron Scale (Hatfield, 1961) and one of the HDI (O'Connell, 1964), obtained only two reports and one report per subject, respectively, during the hypnotic state. Such designs are extremely susceptible to atypical reports from the subject. Both studies reported *statistically* significant correlations between the self-report measure and the susceptibility measure (.32 for Hatfield, .55 for O'Connell), but neither of these was high enough to uphold LeCron's original contention that self-report measures could replace ordinary measures of depth or be practically useful.

The North Carolina (Tart, 1962, 1963, 1967), Brief Stanford (Hilgard & Tart, 1966; Tart, 1966a; Tart & Hilgard, 1966), and Long Stanford Scales (Larsen, 1965; Tart, 1966b) were designed to come much closer to LeCron's original technique—to require frequent reports and instructions to subjects that the reports would just flash into their minds instantly, rather than being something they had to deliberately estimate. With these scales, state reports were obtained immediately following the induction procedure and following every hypnotic test item.

One study with the North Carolina Scale (Tart, 1963) allows statistical comparison of a shortened version of the scale (only the first thirty points defined, rather than fifty) and hypnotic phenomena: self-reports by subjects obtained just before item administration correctly predicted hypnotic dreaming one hundred percent of the time and posthypnotic amnesia eighty-two percent of the time. Variations in self-reported depth on this scale also showed high parallelism with basal skin resistance during the hypnotic state (Tart, 1963), but there is some possibility of this parallelism being artifactual as, in most cases, the hypnotic state was not deliberately lightened to see if skin resistance would then fall, although this happened spontaneously in some cases.

There have been three studies with the Brief Stanford Scale. In the most extensive one (Hilgard & Tart, 1966), subjects were tested in a variety of conditions, all of which included administration of the SHSS:C. A total of 220 subjects were tested during the various hypnotic conditions. The depth reports on this 0–4 scale were obtained between all suggestibility test items, as well as immediately after the induction. Correlations from the various conditions between the SHSS:C score and the *mean* self-report score were .67, .68, .65, .75, and quite surprisingly, in one group, –.01. Thus, the scale was generally quite significantly related to hypnotic behavior. Many of these subjects were also hypnotized on two different days, and the correlation between their mean self-reported depth from day one to day two ranged from .81 to .99 over the various groups, indicating that the self-report measurement of hypnotic depth has the same degree of reliability for this scale as does SHSS:C. Further, the *initial* state report, obtained just after the end of induction, was found to be highly predictive of subsequent hypnotic behavior. If the subject reported zero, indicating he felt not hypnotized at all, it was extremely rare for him to pass more than one or two of the easier suggestibility test items (mean score of 1.3 on the SHSS:C versus a mean score of 5.7 for those who reported a state of two or more, "definitely hypnotized").

The Brief Stanford Scale has also been found to correlate between .40 and .47 in various groups with the type of hypnotic dream the subject has when the type of dream is also scaled in terms of the profundity of the experience (Tart, 1966a). This finding has been confirmed by Honorton[3] and by Parker.[4]

The Long Stanford Scale

This study, reported in detail elsewhere (Tart, 1970b) is the most extensive study of self-report measurement of hypnotic depth to date. Thirty-five undergraduate male subjects who had experienced the Harvard Group Scale of Hypnotic Susceptibility (HGSHS) (Shor & Orne, 1962) and volunteered for further hypnotic experiments were tested individually. The subjects were randomly divided into two groups, such that while all subjects received otherwise identical instructions for measuring their hypnotic depth, twenty of them were told that such reports would come to mind instantly with no conscious activity on their part, while fifteen were told to make deliberate, conscious estimates. The experimenter was blind as to which set of instructions the subject received. A tape-recorded version of the Stanford Hypnotic Susceptibility Scale, Form C (SHSS:C) (Weitzenhoffer & Hilgard,

3. C. Honorton, personal communication, 1968.
4. A. Parker, personal communication, 1969.

1962) was then administered and self-reports of depth were obtained following the induction procedure and following every suggestibility test item. At the end of the SHSS:C testing a detailed inquiry about the nature of the subjects' hypnotic experiences was carried out. This leads to a score for each subject called C-experiential, and will be described elsewhere (Tart, in preparation). It emphasizes the intensity of the subject's experience in response to the suggested hypnotic phenomena, rather than his overt behavior. Subjects also filled out the Field's inventory (Field, 1965) with respect to their hypnotic experience.

The exact instructions for self-report measurement of hypnotic depth for the instant and deliberate conditions were as follows (the first paragraph of the instructions being identical for each group):

> During your experience of hypnosis, I will be interested in knowing just how hypnotized you are. You will be able to tell me this by calling out a number from zero to ten, depending on how hypnotized you feel yourself to be. *Zero* will mean that you are awake and alert, as you normally are. *One* will mean a kind of borderline state, between sleeping and waking. *Two* will mean that you are lightly hypnotized. If you call out the number *five*, it will mean that you feel quite strongly and deeply hypnotized. If you feel really very hypnotized, you would call out an *eight* or *nine*. *Ten* will mean that you are very deeply hypnotized and you can do just about anything I suggest to you. Naturally, hypnosis can increase and decrease in depth from time to time, and that is the kind of thing I'll be interested in finding out from you.

The instructions for the Instant condition then went on:

> Let me explain *how* you will report your state of hypnosis. When I ask, "State?" you are to tell me the *first* number that pops into your mind, and this will represent your state at that time. We've found that this first impression is more accurate than if you stop to think about just what the number should be. This may seem a little hard at first, but it will get easy as you go along. Just call out the first number that pops into your mind when I ask, "State?" Remember the number zero means your normal waking state, five means quite strongly hypnotized, and ten means you are deep enough to experience just about anything I suggest. Just say the first number from zero to ten that comes into your mind when I ask, "State?" Let's try it now. State? [All subjects called out a zero at this time]. At various times during your experience I'll ask for your state, and you'll call out the first number that pops into your mind.

The instruction for the Deliberate condition read:

> Let me explain *how* you'll report your state of hypnosis. When I ask "State?" I want you to estimate how deeply hypnotized you feel at that moment and call out this number to me. We've found that college subjects can give rather accurate estimates if they give it a few seconds' thought each time. This may seem a little hard at first, but it will get easy as you go along. Just call out your best estimate whenever I ask, "State?"
>
> Remember, the number zero means your normal waking state, five means quite strongly hypnotized, and ten means you are deep enough to experience just about

anything I suggest. Just call out your estimate between zero and ten whenever I ask, "State?" Let's try it now. State? [All subjects called out a zero at this time.] At various times during your experience I'll ask for your state, and you'll call out your estimate. You may take a maximum of fifteen seconds to make your estimate.

The subjects in both groups, then, were told that hypnosis varies in depth, that they can accurately measure it and report it to the experimenter when asked, and that the deeper they feel, the more hypnotic phenomena they can expect to experience.

USE OF THE LONG STANFORD STATE SCALE

State reports (thirteen per subject), ranged 0–8, but most of them (sixty-seven percent were one, two, or three, indicating borderline to moderately hypnotized.

One of the rationales for investigating state reports is the hypothesis that the depth of hypnosis may vary fairly rapidly with time. Time is here conveniently represented by the sequence of state reports obtained following each test item. For the subjects as a whole, graphs of mean state reports over time are essentially linear for both Instant and Deliberate conditions. In a group of unselected subjects, however, there will always be many who are not hypnotized, or who are only very lightly hypnotized, and such subjects would serve as a stabilizing influence on such a graph.

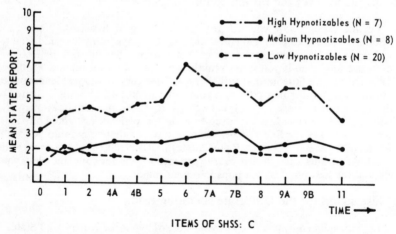

FIGURE 17.2   *Variation in mean state report over the course of testing for Ss of high, medium, and low hypnotic susceptibility (from Tart, 1970b).*

In Figure 17.2, state report for successive items has been plotted with subjects divided into high, medium, and low susceptibles on the basis of their SHSS:C behavioral score (high subjects scoring seven or more; medium subjects scoring four, five, or six; and low subjects scoring three or less). Instant and Deliberate conditions are combined. The low susceptible subjects show a mean state report for the whole session of 1.2 (range: 0–4.5 per subject); medium subjects, 2.5 (range 1.7–4.6 per subject); and high subjects, 5.0 (range: 2.6–6.6 per subject). The differences between means of low and high subjects are significant ($t = 5.3$, $df = 25$, $p < .005$, 1-tailed), as are the differences between medium subjects and high subjects ($t = 3.9$, $df = 13$, $p < .005$, 1-tailed). The differences are only suggestive, however, between low subjects and medium subjects ($t = 1.65$, $df = 26$, $p < .10$, 1-tailed). Considering mean state reports over the course of the suggestibility testing, the curve for the low susceptibles is essentially flat, while there is a suggestion of a rise for medium susceptibles and high susceptibles. Variability of the curves increases with items six (the dream), 7B (age regression), and 9B (sniff of ammonia without suggested anosmia). Statistical assessment of differences between the curves is not appropriate because of the confounding effects of: (a) time per se, (b) unequal increases in item difficulty over time, and (c) variations in item wording such that some items contain suggestions that might serve to deepen the hypnotic state, while others have suggestions that might lighten it.[5] This source of confusion, inherent in the use of SHSS:C, is regrettable, and the important possibility that suggestibility *testing* serves as a deepening or lightening procedure should be carefully noted for future investigations.

This analysis is sensitive only to long-term variability in state reports. Short-term variability from one state report to the next is also important. Considering all state reports from all subjects, most (fifty percent) of the time there was no change from one report to the next, and thirty-five percent of the time the change was only one point. These figures can be misleading in the impression of stability they create, however, for, if state is important, a single state change of large magnitude might drastically affect the outcome of an experiment. If one examines the largest *absolute* (that is, without regard to sign) change from one state report to the next for each subject, one finds only nine percent showed zero as their largest change, thirty-four percent showed one, forty-three percent showed two, eleven percent showed three, and three percent showed a change of four points. As subjects only used eight points of the defined scale, changes of two points or more seem of considerable magnitude, and such changes were shown at least once by fifty-seven percent of subjects.

Another way of examining variability in the use of state reports is to consider the number of times each subject showed a change from one state report to the next, regardless of the size of such change. Figure 17.3 shows

5. Because there are several reports per subject in the graphed material, statistical comparison would not be legitimate.

the frequency of such changes. It was common for subjects to have as many
as eight or nine changes in state report during the session.

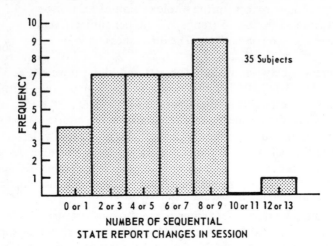

FIGURE 17.3   *Frequency of changes of sequential state reports
(from Tart, 1970b).*

Thus, as originally hypothesized, subjects' reports of the depth of their
hypnotic state do vary significantly in the course of a hypnotic session when
examined over short time intervals, but are fairly stable when subjects'
ratings are averaged together over the entire session.

At the end of the hypnotic session, all subjects were asked what criteria
they had used in making their state reports or, if they reported their
responses had been automatic, what sorts of perceived changes in their experience seemed to go along with changes in state report. One subject could
report nothing; some subjects reported two or more criteria. Descriptive
categories for grouping answers, staying as close to subjects' descriptions as
possible, were evolved. The thirty-four subjects who reported their criteria
mentioned fifty-six criteria among them. Because of the small number of
cases that result if these categories are subdivided according to condition,
and because of the statistical difficulties caused by varying numbers of
criteria per subject, the following description is only suggestive.

The following sorts of criteria, all positively correlated with increasing
state report, were mentioned in at least ten percent of subjects' reports: (a)
intensity of reaction to previous suggestibility test item, twenty-one percent;
(b) feelings of drowsiness, twenty percent; (c) fading of the environment,
fourteen percent; (d) changes in body image or perceived body position,
twelve percent; (e) relaxation, eleven percent; and (f) feeling of com-
pulsiveness of responses, eleven percent. If categories (d) and (e) are combined with several other infrequent categories under the general category of

bodily changes, thirty-two percent of the reports are accounted for.

The subjects were also asked how well they felt their state reports correlated with the depth of their hypnotic state. They were given fixed response categories of Very Well, Fairly Well, or Poorly. Almost all subjects (ninety-seven percent) reported they thought their reports correlated Fairly Well to Very Well.[6]

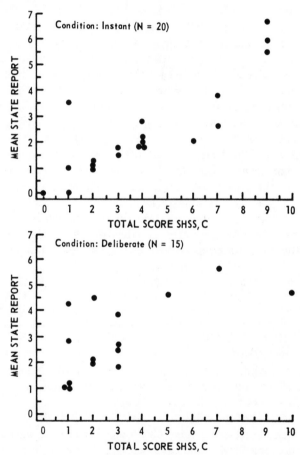

FIGURE 17.4 *Relationship between mean state reports and SHSS:C-behavioral scores for Instant and Deliberate conditions (from Tart, 1970b).*

6. I had attempted to run another group of subjects from advanced, rather than introductory, psychology courses in this study. Only two subjects made appointments for testing, so the results were discarded. It is interesting to note, however, that one subject in this group described clearly varying experiential correlates of his state reports, but stated that he had little confidence in their accurately reflecting hypnotic depth because he knew a lot about psychology and knew that subjective reports were of no value!

RELATION OF LONG STANFORD SCALE REPORTS TO BEHAVIORAL
INDICES OF HYPNOSIS

The relation of state report to a behavioral index of hypnotic responsiveness
was ascertained by correlating each subject's mean state report with his
total SHSS:C behavioral score. Figure 17.4 shows scatter plots for these two
measures for the Instant and Deliberate conditions separately. For the combined conditions, $r = .74$ ($p < .005$, 1-tailed).

Because total scores on SHSS:C and mean state report are long-term
measures, correlations between them are not an ideal way of assessing a
relationship that may vary rapidly with time. A more sensitive measure is to
compare the state report obtained just before each suggestibility test item
was administered with whether or not that item was passed or failed by the
standard SHSS:C behavioral scoring criteria. Item by item, the mean state
report across all subjects was always greater for subsequently passed than
for subsequently failed items; differences ranged from a low value of 1.12
to a high value of 2.76. Practically all differences for any given item[7] were
statistically significant by t test ($p < .005$, 1-tailed). Further, the more difficult an item, the greater was the average difference in preceding mean
state report for passing and failing. The difficulty of each item, given by the
percentage of subjects failing the item in the standardization data for
SHSS:C behavioral (Weitzenhoffer & Hilgard, 1962), correlates .53 with
the size of the mean state report difference ($p < .10$, 1-tailed).

RELATION OF STATE REPORTS TO EXPERIENTIAL QUALITIES OF HYPNOSIS

There is, of course, a significant relationship between the experience of the
hypnotized subject and his overt behavior. In the present sample, the correlation between the SHSS:C experiential score and the SHSS:C behavioral
score is .77 ($p < .0005$, 1-tailed).

Figure 17.5 presents scatter plots of the relationship between the mean
state report of each subject and his SHSS:C experiential score. The correlation is .76 ($p < .0005$, 1-tailed).

Another measure of the subjects' experience of hypnosis is Field's Inventory, on which subjects answered thirty-eight true-false questions about
various phenomena they might have experienced during the course of the
hypnosis session.[8] As Field's Inventory was developed on the basis of what
people generally report about being hypnotized, it is a more general

---

7. A test could not be carried out for item 2, as there was only one subject failing this item.
8. Subjects were obtained from three different psychology classes at various times; the third
time subjects were run, the experimenter neglected to administer Field's Inventory, so the N for
those analyses using Field's Inventory is fifteen in the Instant condition and ten in the
Deliberate condition.

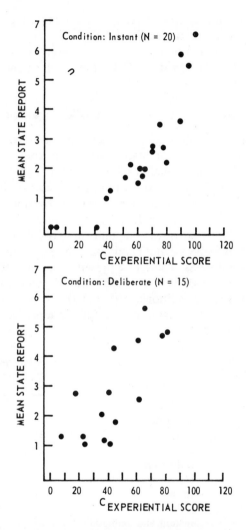

FIGURE 17.5 *Relationship between mean state reports and SHSS:C-experiential scores for Instant and Deliberate conditions (from Tart, 1970b).*

measure of the hypnotic experience than the SHSS:C experiential score, which is based on subjects' experiences in response to the specific suggestibility test items of the SHSS:C. The correlation is .66 (*p* < .005, 1-tailed) between mean state report and Field's Inventory.

A finer examination of this relationship can be made. My examination of the content of Field's Inventory questions indicates that, of the thirty-eight

questions, only ten appear to be directly or implicitly suggested by the procedures of SHSS:C or of the earlier HGSHS:A.[9] Thus Field's Inventory
score can be broken into a nonspecific score as well as a total score. Mean
state report correlates .63 ($p < .005$, 1-tailed) with the nonspecific scores
derived from the inventory.

EFFECTS OF EXPERIENCE ON LONG STANFORD SCALE REPORTS

In the above analyses, subjects gained a fair amount of hypnotic experience
in the course of making their state reports. In addition to the initial
HGSHS:A, they had the induction of the SHSS:C and experience gained
from the various SHSS:C items as the test proceeded. It is of interest to see
how well state reports related to other aspects of hypnotizability with less
hypnotic experience. This can be done by using only the first state reports
given by each subject, that is, the one immediately following the hypnotic
induction section of SHSS:C, thus eliminating the experience of reactions to
the suggestibility test items. Table 17.2 presents the correlation coefficients
of initial state report with SHSS:C behavioral, SHSS:C experiential, and
Field's Inventory across conditions. Although the correlations are generally
reduced compared to those based on the full scale procedure, they are all
statistically significant.

TABLE 17.2   Relation of initial state report to various measures

Measure	Condition	N	r	$p <$ [a]
SHSS:C behavioral	Instant	20	.61	.005
	Deliberate	15	.58	.02
	Instant and deliberate	35	.56	.0005
SHSS:C experiential	Instant	20	.79	.005
	Deliberate	15	.63	.01
	Instant and deliberate	35	.69	.0005
Field's Inventory	Instant	15	.72	.005
	Deliberate	10	.69	.005
	Instant and deliberate	25	.69	.0005

SOURCE: Tart, 1970b.
a. One-tailed values.

INSTANT VERSUS DELIBERATE CONDITIONS

There was no clear difference in the usage of various values of the state
reports in the two conditions. Mean state reports were 2.5 and 2.6 in the Instant and Deliberate conditions, respectively.

A slightly higher proportion of subjects in the Instant condition reported

9. These ten items are numbers 4, 6, 9, 10, 14, 16, 24, 29, 30, and 34.

their state reports reflected the depth of their hypnotic state Very Well, but the difference was insignificant ($\chi^2 = 1.84$, $df = 2$, $p < .50$, 1-tailed).

The state-scale instructions for the Instant condition emphasized that a number would immediately pop into the subject's mind when he was asked "State?" and that, in the Deliberate condition, he would *consciously estimate* the best number. To check on the effectiveness of the instructions in the two conditions, the experimenter timed with a stopwatch the delay between the request for state and the subject's responses. For the Instant condition the mean delay was 2.0 seconds, for the Deliberate condition, 4.2 seconds, a highly significant difference in the postulated direction ($t = 4.07$, $df = 33$, $p < .001$, 1-tailed).

The relationship between mean state report and SHSS:C behavioral score was presented in Figure 17.4. Although the correlation is better for the Instant condition ($r = .85$, p $< .005$, 1-tailed) than for the Deliberate condition ($r = .67$, $p < .005$, 1-tailed), the difference between these two coefficients is not significant ($p = .11$, 1-tailed) by the method of Johnson and Jackson (1959). The correlation between mean state report and SHSS:C experiential scores is .84 for the Instant condition ($p < .005$, 1-tailed) and .75 ($p < .005$, 1-tailed) for the Deliberate condition. Again, the difference between the two correlation coefficients does not reach statistical significance ($p = .36$, 1-tailed).

The same pattern of correlation coefficients being higher, but not significantly so, for the Instant condition appears when comparing mean state report and Field's Inventory scores. The correlation for Instant condition is .69 ($p < .005$, 1-tailed) and for the Deliberate condition is .64 ($p < .02$, 1-tailed). The correlation between the Field's nonspecific scores with mean state report is .66 in the Instant condition ($p < .005$, 1-tailed) and .62 ($p < .02$, 1-tailed) in the Deliberate condition. Initial state reports, already presented in Table 17.2, also show this pattern.

In short, correlations with other measures of hypnotic performance are always higher for state reports from the Instant condition, but not significantly so.

The Extended North Carolina Scale

The Extended North Carolina Scale has been used in a large number of experiments in my laboratory, primarily where experienced hypnotic subjects are used repeatedly in various experiments. It is similar to the North Carolina Scale with the addition that subjects are told that there is really no "top" to the scale—that is, it is possible for them to go considerably deeper into hypnosis than the defined points. The exact instructions for the scale are:

We are interested in the ways in which the intensity or depth of your hypnotic state may vary from time to time. It has been our experience that we can get quite accurate reports of hypnotic depth or intensity by teaching you a way of scaling it and getting your first impressions whenever we ask you about your hypnotic state.

Basically, whenever I ask, "State?" a number will flash into your mind, and I want you to call it out to me right away. This number will represent the depth of your hypnotic state at the time. This number will flash into your mind and you'll call it out automatically, without any effort on your part. You won't have to think about what this number *should* be, or try to reason it out; you'll just call out the first number that comes to mind whenever I ask, "State?" If, of course, you then think the number is very inaccurate for some reason, I'd like you to tell me so, but people rarely feel the number is not accurate, even though they are sometimes surprised by it.

Getting these depth numbers is very important, because every person is somewhat unique in his reactions while hypnotized. Some people react at different speeds than others; some react to a particular hypnotic experience by going deeper into hypnosis, others sometimes find the depth of their hypnotic state decreased by the same experience. Thus by getting these state reports from you every so often I can tell whether to go a little faster or slower, where to put emphasis in the suggestions I use to guide you, etc. These depth reports are not always what I expect, but it's more important for me to know where you really are than just assume you're there because I've been talking that way!

Now here is the numerical scale you are to use. I'll give you various highlights that identify different degrees of hypnosis on the scale, but you can report any point on the scale when asked for your state.

Zero is your normal, waking state. From *one* to *twelve* is a state in which you feel relaxed and detached, more so as the numbers increase toward *twelve;* in this range you can experience such hypnotic phenomena as your arm rising up or feeling heavy or moved by a force.

When you reach a depth of *twenty* or greater you feel very definitely hypnotized, and you can experience great changes in your feeling of your body, such as your hand getting numb if I suggested it. By the time you reach a depth of *twentyfive* or greater you can have strong inner experiences such as dreams or dreamlike experiences.

At a depth of *thirty* or greater you can temporarily forget everything that happened in the hypnosis if I suggest it. Many other experiences are possible at this depth and greater, such as regressing into the past and reliving some experience, experiencing tastes and smells I might suggest, or not experiencing real stimuli if I tell you not to sense them. There are hardly any hypnotic phenomena you can't experience at least fairly well, and most extremely well, at this depth. At *thirty* and beyond your mind is very quiet and still when I'm not directing your attention to something, and you probably don't hear anything except my voice or other sounds I might direct your attention to.

You have reached at least *thirty* in earlier sessions, and it is a sufficient depth to be able to learn all the skills needed in this experiment, but it is very likely that you will go deeper than *thirty* in these studies.

By the time you have reached a depth of *forty* or greater you have reached a *very* deep hypnotic state in which your mind is perfectly still and at peace if I'm not directing your attention to something. Whatever I do suggest to you at this depth and beyond is *perfectly real,* a total, real, all-absorbing experience at the time, as real as anything in life. You can experience *anything* I suggest at *forty* and beyond.

I'm not going to define the depths beyond this, for little is known about them; if you go deeper than *forty,* and I hope you do, I'll ask you about the experiences that go with these greater depths so we may learn more about deep hypnosis.[10]

Remember now that increasing numbers up from zero indicate an increasing degree of hypnotic depth, from the starting point of ordinary wakefulness up to a state in which you can experience anything in hypnosis with complete realism. Your quick answers whenever I ask, "State?" will be my guide to the depth of your hypnotic state, and help me guide you more effectively. Always call out the *first* number that pops into your mind loudly and clearly. Whenever I ask, "State?" a number on the scale will instantly come into mind and you call it out.

I'll go over the various points that describe the scale again.

These instructions for the scale are usually read to the subject after he is hypnotized, and he is asked whether he comprehends them. Also, the instructions are briefly reread to the subject every half-dozen hypnotic sessions or so to refresh his memory of them.

The overall procedure in working with subjects in my laboratory on a prolonged basis is to treat them as explorers or colleagues working with the investigators, rather than as subjects who are being manipulated for purposes alien to them.

My overall impressions of results with the Extended North Carolina Scale have convinced me that it is the most useful measure of hypnotic depth I have seen. The only published data on this so far have been presented in the context of a study on responses to posthypnotic suggestion to dream about specified topics (Tart & Dick, 1970). In this study, thirteen highly hypnotizable subjects were given a posthypnotic suggestion to dream about one or another of two stimulus narratives in their stage one rapid eyeball movement (REM) dreams of the night. The size of the posthypnotic effect was measured by the number of stimulus elements appearing in the manifest dream content. Although the subjects were all highly hypnotizable (scored at least ten of a possible twelve, SHSS:C), there are still sufficient variation in reports on the Extended North Carolina Scale to warrant correlating these depth reports with subsequent posthypnotic dream performance.

Several ways of carrying out this correlation across subjects were possible, producing correlations which ranged from a low of .11 to a high of .51, the latter significant at the ten percent, 1-tailed level. Such correlations assumed that the subjects measured depth in a comparable manner, but this is not necessarily a good assumption; that is, a given subject may

---

10. In some earlier work (Tart, 1966a) with the North Carolina scale, fifty was defined as a state so profound that the subject's mind became sluggish, but this definition was dropped here.

be measuring his depth consistently, but once he gets beyond the range commonly defined for all subjects he may not do so in exactly the same fashion as other subjects. More conservative tests, assuming only that each subject is consistent in his own measuring, shows that the posthypnotic dream effect was more than twice as large on a subject's night with a higher state report compared with his night with a lower one ($p < .025$, 1-tailed). As noted, this does not really indicate the potentiality of the scale because the use of subjects who were all extremely hypnotizable greatly restricts the range and automatically reduces correlation coefficients.

Some potentialities of the Extended North Carolina Scale, as well as some intriguing phenomena of deep hypnosis and data on the question of when deep hypnosis becomes another *SoC* will be illustrated by the data of a single subject. Other subjects have shown similar patterns, but these will not be referred to as this material is not yet completely analyzed.

William: Deep Hypnosis and Beyond

William, a twenty-year-old male college student, is extremely intelligent, academically successful, and well adjusted. His only previous experience with hypnosis was some brief work with a psychiatrist cousin to teach him how to relax. In a screening session with the HGSHS, he scored eleven out of a possible twelve. On a questionnaire he reported that he almost always recalled dreaming, that such dreaming was very vivid and elaborate, and that he had kept a dream diary at times in the past. William reported that he had sleep-talked rather frequently as a child but did so only occasionally now. He had never sleepwalked. On individual testing with SHSS:C, he scored twelve out of a possible twelve. He then had two training sessions designed to explore and maximize his hypnotic responsiveness in various areas, described elsewhere (Tart & Dick, 1970). In the first of these special training sessions, he was taught the Extended North Carolina Scale. He then took Forms I and II of the Stanford Profile Scale of Hypnotic Susceptibility (Weitzenhoffer & Hilgard, 1963) and scored twenty-six and twenty-seven on Forms I and II, respectively, out of a possible maximum of twenty-seven on each.

Over the course of the next eight months, William participated in a variety of experiments in my laboratory, which served to further increase his hypnotic experience and make him well adapted to functioning in the laboratory setting; he had ten sessions of training for operant control of the EEG alpha rhythm (Tart, 1969b), four experimental sessions in various aspects of hypnosis, and eight evening sessions in which he was hypnotized and given posthypnotic suggestions to carry out in his subsequent sleep in the laboratory, such as dreaming about a suggested topic (Tart & Dick, 1970), incorporating auditory stimuli into his dreams, and talking during his sleep. Thus, by the time William participated in the deep hypnosis experiment to be described here, he was familiar with the lab and had been hypnotized there eighteen times. The deepest depth report given in any of these sessions was sixty, and he usually gave reports between forty and fifty.

In the experimental session to be reported upon, it was explained to William that the purpose of the session was to find out what hypnosis meant to him personally. Specifically, he was informally interviewed for about an hour asking him what he usually experienced under hypnosis, other than his reaction to specifically suggested phenomena, and, if possible, what depth level, according to the Extended North Carolina Scale, he was at when he experienced these particular things. I then hypnotized him and at each ten-point interval on a depth continuum I would ask William to remain at that depth and describe whatever it was he was experiencing. No particular probing was done here other than for phenomena already mentioned by William: the emphasis was on his individual hypnotic experience. William also agreed to attempt to go much deeper than he ever had gone before.

The session was quite rewarding. Although William had never gone beyond sixty before, he went to ninety, reporting at ten-point intervals on the Extended North Carolina Scale, and also briefly went from ninety to one hundred thirty. These values beyond forty had not, of course, been defined by the experimenter: They were the result of his own definition. Or, according to William's report, they were simply numbers that came to his mind when he was asked for his state. Despite repeated questioning by me and despite the fact that the subject was quite verbal and extremely good at describing his experiences, his only comment on how he measured his hypnotic depth was that when I asked him for a state report a number popped into his mind, he said it, and that was it. He had no idea how these numbers were generated, nor did he "understand" them, but he assumed they meant something since he had been told in the original Extended North Carolina Scale instructions that they would.

The results of both his preinduction interview about his general experience of hypnosis and the particular hypnotic session have been condensed into the graph shown in Figure 17.6.

William felt that his particular experience during this exploration was typical of his general experience with hypnosis. Various phenomena are plotted, each with its own ordinate of intensity. Circles indicate reports obtained during this particular hypnotic session, triangles are reports obtained during the interview preceding this session about all his hypnotic experiences to date. Every phenomenon was not assessed on every ten-point interval on the depth scale, so curves are shown as dotted where data points are missing. Discussion of this scale will indicate some of the

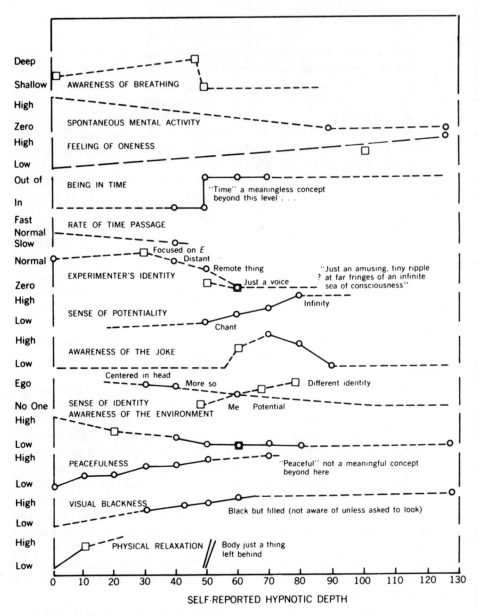

FIGURE 17.6   *Self-report of hypnotic experience (from Tart, 1970b).*

phenomena of extremely deep hypnotic states and illustrate some of the theoretically possible relationships of effects to hypnotic depth discussed in the introductory section.

The first effect, "physical relaxation," is not plotted beyond twenty. According to William his relaxation increases markedly as he is hypnotized, and quickly reaches a value of extremely relaxed. However, he reports that after a depth of fifty it does not make sense to ask him about physical relaxation because he's no longer identified with his body; his body is "just a thing, something I've left behind." One does not rate the relaxation of things.

The second experiential effect is of a "blackness" of the visual field. His visual field becomes quite black and formless as he goes into hypnosis. Nevertheless, it continues to become somehow blacker,[11] this being a roughly linear increase up to about sixty. At this point he says the field continues to become blacker as he goes deeper, but it is in some sense "filled," that is, there is a sense that there is some kind of form(s) filling his visual field even though he is not perceiving any particular forms. Beyond sixty he is not particularly aware of any visual sensation unless his attention is drawn to it by the experimenter.

The third effect, a feeling of "peacefulness," also increases linearly from the beginning of the hypnotic state through approximately sixty. William reports that he is extremely peaceful at this point. Beyond sixty, he says that peacefulness is not a meaningful concept, as was the case with physical relaxation. As will be seen in the later plots of William's identity, there is no longer a self to be peaceful or not peaceful beyond this point.

The fourth plotted effect is William's degree of "awareness of his environment," primarily the small sounds in the experimental room and the temperature and air currents in it. His awareness of the environment falls off rapidly and roughly linearly, and at about fifty reaches a point where he reports that he is not at all aware of the environment (with the exception of the hypnotist's voice). His awareness of the environment then stays at zero throughout the rest of the plotted continuum.

The fifth effect, labeled "sense of identity," is a little more complex. In the light stages of hypnosis William is fully aware of his ordinary identity and body image, but as he reaches a depth of about thirty he reports that his identity is "more centered in his head," that is, that his identity is dominated by feelings of his head and his mind. This feeling continues to increase, plotted as a decrease of his ordinary identity, and then his

---

11. William insists that this progression is not going from gray to darker gray to black, because his visual field is black to begin with, even though it gets "blacker." He recognizes the paradoxicalness of this statement, but considers it the best description he can give.

ordinary identity continues to decrease until around eighty or ninety he feels that his ordinary identity is completely in abeyance: "William" no longer exists. On the other hand, starting from about fifty he begins to sense another identity and this continually increases up through about eighty, the last point plotted for this phenomenon. This identity is one of *potential*—he doesn't feel identified as any specific person or thing but only as the steadily increasing *potential to be anything or anyone.*

The sixth phenomena, labeled "awareness of the joke," is even more difficult to explain. This phenomenon manifests at about fifty, reaches a maximum at about seventy, then fades in intensity and is completely gone at ninety. The "joke" is that the William should engage in strange activities like deep hypnosis, meditation, or taking drugs in order to alter his *SoC*; some "higher" aspect of his self is amused by all this activity, and William himself becomes aware of this amusement. Most people who have had several psychedelic drug sessions will recognize this as an effect that often occurs as the drug is beginning to take hold.

The next effect, labeled "sense of potentiality," starts off at a zero level but at around fifty first manifests itself as an awareness of some sort of chant or humming sound that is identified with the feeling that more and more experience is potentially available.[12] The specific form of the chant is lost but this sense of potentiality increases linearly from this point, until around eighty William feels that an infinite range of experience is potentially available, so this phenomenon levels off.

The eighth effect, "experimenter's identity," at first increases as the subject goes down to about thirty in hypnosis; that is, he becomes more and more aware of the experimenter. The experimenter then seems to become more and more distant and remote, and finally the experimenter possesses no identity, he is just a voice, and at the very deep levels he is "just an amusing, tiny ripple at the far fringes of an infinite sea of consciousness." There is a slight discrepancy at fifty between William's actual experience and his estimate of what he generally experienced.

The ninth effect, "rate of time passage," indicates that William feels time passing more and more slowly in a linear fashion as he goes down to about forty. This effect is no longer plotted, for as the next effect, "being in time," shows, William feels that time very suddenly ceases to be a meaningful concept for him: at fifty he is no longer in time, his experiences are somehow timeless, they do not have a duration or a place, an order in the scheme of things.[13]

12. The chant William reported may be related to the Hindu concept of the sacred syllable Om, supposedly a basic sound of the Universe that a man can "hear" as mind becomes more universally attuned (Danielou, 1966).

13. Priestly (1964) discusses such experiences of being in and out of time quite well.

The next effect, labeled "feeling of oneness," increases linearly throughout the depth range plotted. Here William reports feeling more and more at one with the universe, although he does not ordinarily feel this. The effect is plotted as being very low in his ordinary waking state.

The next effect is "spontaneous mental activity," that is, how much conscious mental activity goes on that is not related to specific suggestions by the hypnotist to do something or to experience something. In the ordinary waking state this is quite high: An old Hindu metaphor described the ordinary mind as being like a sexually aroused and drunken monkey, constantly hopping about and chattering. This spontaneous mental activity goes steadily down until it reaches an essentially zero level at about ninety and stays there through the rest of the depth range plotted. Such a decrease in spontaneous mental activity for hypnosis has also been reported elsewhere (Tart, 1966b).

The final effect plotted is William's "awareness of his own breathing." He feels that his breathing tends to become steadily deeper as he becomes more deeply hypnotized, but at fifty there is a very sudden change in his perceived breathing. It becomes extremely shallow, almost imperceptible, and stays that way through the rest of the hypnotic state. It is not known whether an objective measure of respiration would show any changes at this point; William did not actually stop breathing.

Considering the above phenomena as a report of a well trained observer, we may make a number of comments. First it should clear that William has an exceptional ability for hypnosis; he appears to have gone far deeper than the usual range of phenomena conventionally labeled "deep hypnosis." As the extended North Carolina scale was defined for him, thirty was the level ordinarily defined as deep hypnosis (amnesia, positive and negative hallucinations as defining phenomena), and forty would be the approximate limit reported by many of the very highly hypnotizable subjects I have worked with in the laboratory. Yet William reported a maximum depth of 130 which, if one assumes reasonable validity and linearity for the scale, may be one of the deepest hypnotic states on record. This ability to go so deep may partially stem from his previous experience with meditation and psychedelic drugs. Further, William was exceptionally verbal and able to describe his experiences well. In the past, Erickson's (1952) exceptionally good subjects have reached a "stuporous" state, which may have reflected an inability to conceptualize and verbalize their experiences. Thus William's hypnotic experiences are illustrative of a potential range of hypnotic phenomena, but are not typical.

Second, the postulated nonlinearity and noncontinuity of possible effects (and subsystem operation, insofar as effects may be taken as indicators of subsystem operation) is apparent in William's data. In the ordinary range of light to deep hypnosis (roughly 0–40), most effects are linear, but "experimenter's identity" is curvilinear and "physical relaxation" is noncontinuous, that is, it becomes a meaningless variable halfway through this range. Considering the entire depth range plotted, some effects show step functions ("awareness of breathing," "being in time"), rapid increases and decreases from zero ("awareness of the joke"), plateauing after an initial linear increase or decrease ("experimenter's identity," "sense of potentiality," "awareness of the environment," "visual blackness"), or disappearance by becoming meaningless ("peacefulness," "physical relaxation"). If, in the course of investigation, one one used the intensity of *one* phenomenon as an index of hypnotic depth, very confusing results would be obtained if it were not linear and continuous, so the value of a multiphenomenal approach is apparent.

Third, the large number of step changes or fairly rapid changes in the 50–70 range raises the question, in view of the definition of *SoCs* at the beginning of this paper, of whether we are still dealing with "deep hypnosis" beyond the depth of approximately seventy. These rapid changes might represent a transition from the gestalt configuration we call hypnosis to a new configuration, a new *SoC*. At its maximum level (assuming that the 70–130 range represents depth continuum for the new *SoC*), we have a state with the following phenomenological characteristics: (1) no awareness of the physical body; (2) no awareness of any discrete "thing" or sensation, but only awareness of a flux of potentiality; (3) no awareness of the real world environment, with the one exception of the (depersonalized) voice of the experimenter as "an amusing tiny ripple at the far fringes of an infinite sea of consciousness"; (4) being beyond, outside of time; and (5) the identity "William" totally in abeyance, and identity being simply potentiality.

SoCs of this type have not been dealt with in Western scientific literature on hypnosis to any great extent, but sound similar to Eastern descriptions of consciousness of the void, an *SoC* in which time, space, and ego are supposedly transcended, leaving pure awareness of the primal nothingness from which all manifested creation comes (Govinda, 1960; Phillips, 1963). Writers who have described the void insist that the experience is ineffable and cannot be described in words, so the above description and comparison with William's experience is rough, to say the least. Thus William's data are not only of interest in terms of hypnotic depth and the transition from one *SoC* to another, but raise the possibility of using hypnotic states to induce and/or model mystical states.[14]

Finally, William's data illustrate some of the practical aspects of study-

14. Aaronson (1969) has reported direct hypnotic induction of the void experience through specific suggestion.

ing the depth of an *SoC*, particularly hypnosis, discussed at the beginning of this paper. Using the individual subject as a unit, a set of interrelationships of various phenomena with respect to hypnotic depth has been found; self-reported depth has ordered observed phenomena in a useful and theoretically important manner. Further research, to be reported in a future publication, will study this same sort of procedure in other subjects, repeat sessions with some subjects to study consistency, and make initial intersubject comparisons to determine which depth-phenomenology relationships are general and which represent idiosyncratic qualities of subjects. General relationships of phenomena with depth may be found and/or several classes of subjects may be found and/or it may be more appropriate to talk about several *SoC*s that have all been indiscriminately termed "hypnosis" in the past.

Finally, it should be stressed that the case of William has been presented to illustrate *potential* self-reporting of hypnotic depth. The effects of subtle factors in the writer's laboratory, demand characteristics, and William's uniqueness must be assessed in the course of replication and extension of this work by others to solidly establish how much of this potential holds up and becomes practically and theoretically useful.

General Comments on Self-Report Scales of Hypnotic Depth

A primary question of the studies reported in this chapter has been how well self-report scales of hypnotic depth actually measure the depth dimension of the hypnotic state. This is both a theoretical and an empirical question. Given the theoretical orientation presented earlier, the Long Stanford Scale and the Extended North Carolina Scale illustrate the theoretical complexities predicted and suggest strong potential, but the important question of the construct validity of these scales must await further theoretical specification and investigation. We shall primarily consider the empirical usefulness of the Long Stanford Scale in the remainder of this paper.

Certain assumptions must be made. One must assume that there is (are) a dimension(s) of depth or profundity of the hypnotic state, that a given subject may move along such dimension(s) from time to time, and that there are experiential correlates of position on each dimension that a subject can consciously perceive or unconsciously react to and report. That is, for a given subject at a given position on the depth continuum there must be either steady state experiences or experiences in response to specific suggestions that the subject may use to judge his depth. Further, one must assume some commonality of the depth dimension across subjects in order to have a scale that is useful for persons other than the individual for whom it was developed, that is, one must assume that there is a great deal in common to the experience we label "hypnosis" across subjects.

Given these assumptions about the nature of a self-report scale, we may then consider the question of its validity. Specifically, it is a question of *construct* validity. Hypnotic depth, as defined here, is a complex dimension that has no *direct* correlate—there is no *particular* phenomenon or behavior the magnitude of which may be seen as directly reflecting hypnotic depth. We would expect all of our various measures (depth reports, SHSS:C behavioral, SHSS:C experiential, and Field's Inventory) to be related to hypnotic depth, but none of them to be equivalent to it. Thus depth reports should correlate highly with all these other hypnotic measures, but not perfectly.[15]

This is what was found: for SHSS:C behavioral, SHSS:C experiential, and Field's Inventory, the correlations with mean depth report were .74, .77, and .66, respectively. There is no doubt that depth reports are reflecting one or more significant dimensions of hypnotic behavior and experience, even if we cannot specify precisely what these dimensions are at present.

Assuming that reports with the Long Stanford Scale are probably as valid a measure of hypnotic depth as behavioral measures in terms of present knowledge, there are a number of advantages to adopting self-report measures as *the* measure of depth as opposed to conventional behavioral measures. First, it takes little time to teach the subject how to use the self-report scale. Second, it takes only seconds to get a report, and asking for these reports does not seem to disturb the subject. Third, ascertaining depth by behavioral measures at any given moment involves giving several suggestibility tests of varying degrees of difficulty. Judging by present data, the subject's depth might very well change in the time taken to administer these tests. Further, if one starts with tests that are too easy one risks boring the subject and taking a long time to find his response ceiling, while if one starts with tests that are too hard the consequent failure experiences might discourage the subject and/or decrease his depth.

Let us consider *how* the subjects manage to measure their depth of hypnosis—how do they come up with the numbers they report? The cognitive bases on which they must measure would be: previous knowledge of hypnotic phenomena, which Shor (1964a) has shown to be rather good in a college student population; knowledge of hypnosis gained in actual

---

15. Indeed for some of the phenomena found in William's data, correlations would be negative or, if depth reports were compared to curvilinear or step functions while (erroneously) assuming linearity, zero.

experimental participation; and the instructions, both explicit and implicit, for scaling. Given this, it is interesting to note that with less conscious cognitive activity involved in the measuring and reporting process (Instant), there were stronger relationships to the other measures of hypnotic performance, although these did not reach acceptable levels of statistical significance. LeCron's (1953) theory that the answers in the Instant condition come directly from the "subconscious" is much too complex to test experimentally at present, but it is clear that the Instant condition instructions favor an intuitive rather than a cognitive type of response.

One might expect that the subject's reactions to suggestibility test items would be the primary determinants of the subject's depth reports, such that the better he reacted, the higher a depth he would report, regardless of whether the depth reports were generated intuitively or cognitively. The data suggest, however, that this may not be too important a factor, for three reasons. First, only twenty-one percent of the replies to the question of how the subjects scaled depth specifically mentioned reaction to the last item; rather, perceived changes in body experience were the most frequently mentioned (thirty-two percent) criteria. Second, the depth report obtained just *before* a suggestibility test item was highly predictive of passing or failing, as described earlier. Third, the depth report following the induction procedure, but before the subject could react to any suggestibility test items, was also highly correlated with other measures of hypnosis. Many subjects also mentioned experiences, unrelated to specific suggestions, which increased or decreased in intensity with their depth and which were used for measuring.[16] While reactions to passing and failing an item are a factor in measuring depth, the depth reports are not merely a trivial reflection of passing or failing items.[17]

Given that depth reports reflect the dimension of hypnotic depth, the present findings have an important implication for studies of "waking" suggestibility in comparison to hypnotic suggestibility. The high and medium susceptible subjects tended to show increases in their self-reports of hypnotic depth through the course of the suggestibility testing, indicating that the suggestibility test items may also function as deepening procedures. If so, it is possible that suggestibility test items given under "waking" conditions could function as hypnotic induction procedures

16. One subject, for example, reported "seeing" a pale green light permeating the experiential space in which he existed during hypnosis; when the light became more intense he gave reports of being deeper.

17. We might also note that the subjects' criterion for passing and failing test items might not be the same as the experimenter's. This was one reason for developing the experiential scoring of Form C. The higher relationships between self-reports and SHSS:C experiential support this notion.

for highly susceptible subjects; this finding has been reported earlier (Hilgard & Tart, 1966). Thus the simple procedure of *not* administering an induction in order to define the "waking suggestibility" group is misleading, because the group may well contain a few deeply hypnotized subjects before the testing is finished. Conversely, defining a group as "hypnotized" simply because the experimenter has gone through a traditional hypnotic induction procedure is also fallacious, as many subjects will not become hypnotized.

The present data also suggest that a new degree of precision in studies of hypnosis is possible. In many past studies of particular hypnotic phenomena, it is likely that the depth of hypnosis varied from subject to subject, or within the same subject from one repetition to the next, in an unknown manner. This would result in high variability of results that could obscure important relationships. If depth reports are used, the subject could be kept at the same relative depth level for each evocation of the phenomenon under study, thus eliminating a major source of variability.

Another possible practical use of depth reports is in studies attempting to maximize the hypnotic responsiveness of individual subjects. If a depth report indicated the subject was probably not deep enough to experience a suggested phenomenon well, his depth could be deepened before the phenomenon was suggested; thus a failure experience that might have adverse effects could be avoided. Similarly, the depth report could be used to tell how well the subject responded to particular deepening techniques. Other uses will undoubtedly be suggested by future work.

In conclusion, while the present data indicate practical usefulness for self-reports of hypnotic depth, they must serve primarily as a stimulus to more research if our theoretical understanding of the nature of hypnotic depth is to advance. We need widescale explorations to answer the following sorts of questions: (1) What are the general experiential, behavioral, and physiological phenomena of hypnosis? (2) How are these related to the particular structure (demands and expectations) imposed in each laboratory, such that we can partial out these demands? (3) Is there a general phenomenology of the hypnotic state across subjects after these demands are partialled out, or are there several SoCs inadvertently mixed under the label "hypnosis"? (4) What is the relationship for individual subjects between self-reported hypnotic depth and various phenomena, and what is the interrelationship of the various phenomena? (5) How do various subjects actually carry out self-scaling of depth, and how is this affected by the structure imposed in each laboratory? (6) Is there a general interrelationship of phenomena and self-report measurement across subjects or are there several varieties or several SoCs involved?

(7) How do the possibilities of multidimensionality of depth (Shor, 1962) fit in?

It is hoped that the present material serves to illustrate the possibility of investigating these questions.

V

Individual Research within Specific Areas

Peter B. Field *is Director of Research at the Morton Prince Center for Hypnotherapy, a Psychology Consultant for the Veterans Administration, and in private practice. He received his doctorate from Harvard University in 1961. After a year as Director of Research at the Puerto Rico Institute of Psychiatry, he became a postdoctoral fellow at the Studies in Hypnosis Project, Massachusetts Mental Health Center and Harvard Medical School. From 1964 to 1973 he was a research psychologist with the VA Hospital in Brooklyn. After obtaining training in clinical applications of hypnosis at the Morton Prince Center, he became its Director of Research in 1968. His research interests include hypnosis, psychotherapy, culture and personality, and alcoholism. He is coauthor of* Personality and Persuasibility *with Irving L. Janis, Carl I. Hovland, and others.*

Field *interprets hypnotic communication from the standpoint of humanistic psychology, and presents empirical data in support of his position. He rejects the mechanistic viewpoint equating hypnosis with the uncritical acceptance of implanted ideas. Instead he feels that hypnotic communication can best be understood within the same framework as literature, drama, music, and art. The hypnotist utilizes imagery, emotional impact, receptivity without analysis, dramatic tension, direct experience, informality, and spontaneity—modes of communication shared with the humanities and the arts. Field uses this framework to interpret a linguistic content analysis of the hypnotic induction, which he contrasts with a parallel analysis of formal and informal speech outside the hypnotic situation. He finds that the hypnotist uses vivid, concrete, redundant, personal, and intimate language, with lessened emphasis upon static abstract conceptualization and categorization.*

18

Humanistic Aspects of Hypnotic Communication

PETER B. FIELD

Several features of the traditional hypnotic induction seem unusual when considered from the standpoint of psycholinguistics or communications. For example, the hypnotist may use redundancy, rhythm, counting, silences, and intonation. He may use gestures and touch the subject. He may use concrete, clear, and vivid imagery, but also may purposefully confuse. Sometimes he will slur his speech as if drowsy, and sometimes he will use a ritualistic singsong. Occasionally he will speak dramatically and theatrically, with force and conviction. At other times he will be gentle, soft, and intimate. After the trance is established, the hypnotist may seem to enter the subject's world of illusion by speaking to hallucinated figures or, during age regression, addressing the subject as if he were a child.

Some of this is well understood. The goal of the hypnotist is to build a relationship of trust and confidence, to help the subject relax physically and psychologically, and to lull the subject into a half-waking, half-sleep state. At the same time, some of the details of the process are not completely understood, and the theoretical framework to describe it is not unified or worked out in sufficient detail. The objective of this chapter is to consider hypnotic communication from a humanistic viewpoint, and to present some empirical data that seem to support this theoretical approach.

Few previous contributions have attempted to treat the language of the hypnotist from a consistent and unified theoretical position, but there are some notable exceptions. Erickson (1944) and Erickson, Haley, and

Weakland (1959) have provided penetrating and detailed analyses of the formulation of hypnotic speech, extending to minute details of wording. Erickson (in Haley, 1967) has originated many ingenious communication techniques, including pantomine, confusion, interspersal, and other specialized induction methods. Haley (1958, 1963) has treated hypnotic communication from an interactional standpoint, emphasizing the double-bind aspects of the hypnotist's language. In analyzing subject-hypnotist interaction patterns (Field, 1964), I reported that the hypnotist not only gave more suggestions, but also agreed more than the subject did, asked more questions, gave fewer opinions and less information, and so on. Troffer and Tart (1964) characterized the hypnotist's voice as "relaxed, somnolent, solicitous, convinced, dramatic, insistent, coaxing, breathy, sing-song, deeper, slower, soothing, sibilant, softer, droning, descriptive rather than commanding, and as having a sense of hushed intimacy" (p. 1330). Hunt (1969) found that both the hypnotist's and the subject's voices usually slowed down during hypnosis.

One of the most clear-cut aspects of the hypnotist's speech is that he is forming a deep, close relationship. This is indicated by the "hushed intimacy" reported by Troffer and Tart, by clinical experience, and by the emphasis on forming rapport in the literature on hypnotic induction. Gill and Brenman (1959) even report evidence for fantasies of fusion with the hypnotist, and discuss the identification with the hypnotist and incorporation of him by the subject. Two other features of hypnosis support the hypothesis that the hypnotist is establishing a close and intimate relationship, although it is a limited, controlled, and reversible intimacy. One feature is the invitation to suspend controls and defenses, which is only possible in the context of a trusting relationship. The other is the extreme relaxation, reminiscent of the relaxation, comfort, and security that accompanies a close relationship.

Intimacy, suspension of defenses, and the relaxation of tension between individuals are also goals of newer humanistic movements within psychology. These movements include sensitivity training, with its emphasis on trust, openness, honesty. They include sensory awareness, psychodrama, Gestalt therapy, and encounter groups emphasizing spontaneity, and intimacy. These movements do not seek to cure the sick, but to make healthy people healthier, to help realize potentialities. The humanistic movement in psychology accepts organismic, Gestalt, phenomenological, and existential viewpoints (Maslow, 1962).

Humanism as a coherent intellectual force is far more than a rejection of mechanistic and orthodox psychologies. It is a commitment to the values underlying the humanities and the arts, as well as the sciences. For example, the humanities and the arts value imagination, illusion, drama, and fantasy. In contrast to technological and mechanistic movements, the humanities and the arts value myth over reality, idealism over materialism, feeling over thinking, intuition over analysis. Creativity and originality are valued more than certainty. Merely classical or academic values are subordinated to humane concerns. The humanities and the arts do not communicate or reach understanding through detached objectivity, but through identification, participation, and emotional relatedness.

What has this to do with hypnotic communication? It is well known that hypnosis involves nonrational, emotional aspects, that there is an art to giving suggestions, and that the hypnotist could not be mistaken for a detached transmitter of a logical analysis. Moreover, there is already available an extended and persuasive comparison of hypnosis to one of the humanistic arts —the theater. In many publications Sarbin has presented a role-taking theory of hypnosis that points out analogies between an actor and a hypnotized subject, and between the hypnotist and a stage director (Sarbin and Andersen, 1967). Obviously there are some important similarities between the hypnotized subject who "becomes" a child and the actor who merges with his role. However, I would like to consider the possibility that there may be equally striking analogies between hypnotic communication and the imaginative, myth-creating processes found in the other humanities and arts. The hypnotist is not only a stage director, but also a painter who communicates through vivid images; a creative writer, who holds his readers spellbound; a musician, who communicates through intonation, rhythm, and timbre; and a poet, who induces feeling through creative and evocative use of words. It is no accident that works of art that create emotional impact are called "hypnotic" or "fascinating." In fact, the same process of absorption is induced by both the hypnotist and by any artist whose works create interest or a sense of immediacy.

Some aspects of hypnotic communication become clearer in this perspective. The relaxation of the touch taboo during hypnosis means that the hypnotist is communicating emotionally, is touching the subject in the metaphorical sense of the term. He is having impact upon the subject, touching his emotions, and affecting him, as a work of art touches us. The hypnotist's gestures perhaps grow out of this relaxation of the touch taboo. They signify emotional impact, not mere logical communication.

The musical aspects of hypnotic communication are another point of comparison between one of the arts and hypnosis. The singsong, lyrical quality of the hypnotist's language means that he is not communicating mere facts, but is touching the subject at another level. In primitive tribes, music, rhythmic chanting, drums, and so on, are used to induce hypnosis (Gill & Brenman, 1959). Music is wordless communication. A person can listen to music closely, become absorbed in it, and lose himself in it, without the need to treat it logically, to analyze it, to be practical or realistic about it. This receptivity without analysis is one of the hypnotist's goals. Shor

(1960) has used absorption in music and art as one of the indices of susceptibility to trancelike experiences in everyday life.

Josephine Hilgard (1970, and in E.R. Hilgard, 1965b) has presented a
great deal of evidence concerning the importance of imaginative involvement in the personality of hypnotizable subjects. She has found that the
hypnotizable person is "capable of deep involvement in one or more
imaginative-feeling areas of experience—reading a novel, listening to music,
having an aesthetic experience of nature, or engaging in absorbing adventures of body or mind" (1970, pp. 4-5). Her research shows that hypnotizability is related to individual differences in absorption in such
humanistic pursuits as the dramatic arts, externally-directed fantasy,
religion, exploration, and an emotional response to nature. She also reports
a relationship between hypnotizability and choice of major among her
college-student subjects. The humanities majors were the most susceptible,
social science majors next, and science and engineering students the least
hypnotizable. The rigorous verbal, mathematical, and logical reasoning
among science students may not be compatible with absorption in
unrealistic or unconventional fantasy. Similarly, Coe (1964) found that
drama students were more hypnotizable than science students, and Shor
(1970) has noted similarities between hypnosis and absorption in imaginative literature. Apparently there is a close relationship between hypnotic susceptibility and the processes of imaginative fantasy, aesthetic involvement, and capacity for absorption in dramatic imagery.

Another aspect of artistic and humanistic structuring of the hypnotic
communication is the focus upon the subjective effect, and the progressive,
gradual building toward it. For example, on the Stanford Hypnotic Susceptibility Scale (Weitzenhoffer & Hilgard, 1959), some effort is made to convince the subject that he did in fact experience each phenomenon. On the
hands moving (together) item, the hypnotist brings the subject's hands
together rapidly to demonstrate how much they had already moved together
involuntarily. Plainly, subjective effect is an important issue in hypnosis,
just as it is in the humanities. If a novel has no subjective effect or impact, it
will not be read. Subjective experience is also an important issue for
humanistic psychology, since it provides an intuitive insight into private and
intimate feelings, and since it provides an alternative to mechanistic features
of behaviorism. The progressive building up to a subjective effect can also
be seen within the Stanford Scale. On all items, suggestions are repeated
with variations in wording until the effect is ready for testing. This is similar
to the progressive building of tension within a motion picture, and to the
presentation and re-presentation of a theme in music.

The term "suggestion" has two meanings, one of which casts light on
some of the problems of hypnotic communication. Its more familiar technical meaning is the transmission of influence or ideas, and their uncritical

acceptance. Since this could be compared to molding plastic in a machine, it may be called the mechanistic meaning of suggestion. It implies a passive recipient, a suspension of reason, and the implantation of an idea. But suggestion also has a second meaning, as Young (1931) pointed out long ago. This is suggestion as indirection, hinting, or intimating. The hypnotist does not communicate ideas prosaically, but presents them indirectly, in images, or while the subject's attention is distracted. This, of course, is precisely the kind of communication seen in the humanities and the arts. A playwright does not say a person is bad; he shows his actions and lets the audience respond appropriately. An artist does not need to explain or to argue; he communicates by presenting concrete images. The indirect communication may be called the humanistic aspect of suggestion. It is prominent in hypnotic communication. Instead of asking a person directly to do something, the hypnotist asks him to let it happen involuntarily, or to imagine that it is happening, and to find then that it does happen.

From the standpoint of putting across a specific formal message, suggestion is indirect. But from the standpoint of emotional impact and access to primitive, nonrational modes of thinking, suggestion can be very direct. The reason for this is that suggestion uses imagery and symbolism, and seeks to circumvent the logical apparatus. As a result, suggestion at its best is very vivid, immediate, and concrete. As a case in point, George Grosz's drawings do not constitute a formal psychological analysis of pre-Hitler Germany, and from this purely logical standpoint they are indirect. But when considered in terms of emotional impact, vividness of imagery, and immediacy, they are very direct indeed. Similarly, the hypnotic suggestion to hallucinate an ideal self is indirect from the standpoint of a logical analysis of a person's strengths and weaknesses, but it gives a very direct and concrete representation of a self-concept.

The mechanistic view of suggestion is overintellectual. It sees hypnotic communication as a transmission of ideas from the hypnotist to the subject, whereas the humanistic viewpoint emphasizes the transactional, mutual aspects of communication. Mechanistic suggestion stamps in ideas, but humanistic suggestion hints, intimates, and sketches. The mechanistic viewpoint downgrades the higher mental processes, since it emphasizes uncritical acceptance. As a result, much of the older literature confused hypnotizability and gullibility. If suggestion is uncritical acceptance of ideas, then hypnosis is just a special case of persuasion. But if hypnosis is more allied to creative imagination, then the principles of the theater, the arts, and the humanities are better candidates for explaining hypnosis.

Another error of the overintellectual mechanistic viewpoint is the implication of disordered, erratic thinking by the hypnotized subject. If "uncritical acceptance" is the basis for hypnosis, then the subject is credulous, is reasoning illogically, is responding to prestige, fails to evaluate evidence, and responds on faith. But the humanistic viewpoint interprets the same facts differently. The subject is not deluded, but imaginative. He has not lost contact with reality, but is playfully restructuring it. As Gill and Brenman (1959) point out, he is not showing pathological regression, but an ego-syntonic regression. He is not irrational, but intuitive.

The hypnotized subject is not a malfunctioning logician or a scientist manqué, but a humanist, an artist. He is responding to themes, impressions, harmony. He is feeling spontaneously and emotionally. Humanistic and artistic concepts may help to understand these processes. This does not mean abandoning hardheaded thinking, but it is possible to be too tough-minded as well as too tender-minded. Humanistic and artistic issues that might be relevant include the tension between variety and thematic unification, the rise and fall of dramatic suspense, absorption of interest, and preparation for one effect with another effect. One practical example may help to illustrate these points. The mechanistic approach to suggestion would emphasize repetitious implanting, while the humanistic approach might emphasize the interweaving of two or more suggestions, the introduction of a theme and the later return to it, or the modification of suggestions by feedback from the subject. These ideas owe much to Erickson (1952), especially to his distinction between ritualistic and individualized induction methods, which is closely related to the distinction between mechanistic and humanistic suggestion.

Linguistic Aspects of Hypnotic Inductions

One convenient means of applying these concepts to concrete data is to compare hypnotic and nonhypnotic language. If mechanistic and humanistic processes can be distinguished within hypnosis, the contrast should be even sharper between hypnotic language and ordinary communication. Speech in the waking state is not designed to induce relaxation, drowsiness, or a special state of consciousness. It is concerned with practical reality, not with fantasy or imagination. It is designed to communicate opinions, thoughts, feelings, but not to build a structure of illusion. If the distinction between mechanistic and humanistic communication is meaningful, it should be observable in a content analysis of speech.

Two analyses were prepared, one comparing a sample of hypnotic language with formal speech, the other comparing the hypnotic sample with informal conversation. The first comparison was made with instructions to subjects in psychological experiments, while the second comparison used interviews with college students and hospitalized patients. Instructions to subjects in psychological experiments were chosen as a comparison for convenience, and also because the clear logic and critical awareness of these communications should contrast sharply with the structure of the hypnotic induction. Although this comparison has advantages, it also has some obvious disadvantages. For example, instructions to subjects in experiments are often highly formal and technical. Therefore a more informal, conversational comparison was also needed.

Ten published hypnotic inductions were chosen to provide a wide range of authors and methods. The inductions chosen were: Blum (1961, p. 213), Chiasson (1964, p. 366), Corley (1965, p. 35), Erickson (1964b, p. 190), Hershman (in Erickson, Hershman, & Secter, 1961, p. 140), Kroger (1963, p. 64), Scott (1960, p. 34), Secter (1960, p. 79), Weitzenhoffer and Hilgard (1962, p. 8), and Wolberg (1948, p. 117). Three of the ten inductions were designed for experimentation, and the remainder were primarily clinical. A sample of 100 consecutive words was chosen from the beginning of each induction, and a count of the grammatical class of each word was made. Introductory material was not scored, so that the induction proper of the Stanford Scale was judged to begin at its second paragraph. A comparison sample of ten instructions to subjects was scored in the same way from articles in the *Journal of Personality and Social Psychology,* 1966, 3, beginning on pages 290, 308, 341, 351, 354, 509, 519, and 624. Using an N of twenty, Mann-Whitney tests were applied to the pooled ranks of the grammatical classes.

For the second analysis, each word of the hypnotic inductions was alphabetized and compared with word frequencies in spoken English, converted to a baseline frequency of words per thousand. The second analysis used the data of Howes (1966), based on 250,000 words drawn from fifty nondirective interviews of 5,000 words each, conducted with twenty college sophomores and twenty-one hospitalized patients. Because Howes pooled his data, the word frequencies he reports are not independent, and statistical tests are inappropriate. A difference in frequency of 3.9 words or more per thousand was arbitrarily chosen as the criterion for distinguishing important differences from less relevant ones.

Results and Discussion

Table 18.1 compares the grammatical classification of the hypnotic inductions and the nonhypnotic psychological instructions. Four word classes appeared significantly less often in the hypnotic than in the nonhypnotic communications: nouns, adjectives, articles, and prepositions. These categories obviously belong together for interpretation, since articles and adjectives modify nouns, and since prepositions take nouns as objects. The first finding, then, is that substantives and their modifiers are reduced in hypnotic communications. This may merely reflect the formality and technical language of the experimenter, but it may also cast some light upon hypnosis.

Nouns are subjects and objects, the initiators and recipients of action. In the psychological experiments they tended to be abstract concepts (such as "behavior," "decisions," "substances," "areas," "minutes,") or environmental objects ("button," "shock," "machine," "inventory"). This suggests that instructions in psychological experiments are centered around action upon objects in the environment to achieve specifiable goals, while this practical, reality-oriented interaction is less important during hypnosis. The semantic content of the hypnotic induction implicitly suggests a detachment of attention from the environment, even when it does not explicitly say so. This detachment from practical, everyday reality is also a characteristic of the humanities and the arts, which are a respite from the utilitarian necessities and adaptations of everyday life. The emphasis on abstract concepts in the psychological instructions contrasts with the simplicity and concreteness of the hypnotic induction. The humanities and the arts like the hypnotist are concerned with vivid, concrete representation, rather than intellectual analysis.

TABLE 18.1. Percentage distribution of words sampled from 10 hypnotic inductions and 10 nonhypnotic instructions

Hypnosis has:	Hypnotic inductions	Nonhypnotic instructions	Significance of Difference (Mann-Whitney)
1. Fewer nouns	14	20	.01
2. Fewer adjectives	6	13	.001
3. Fewer articles	4	9	.01
4. Fewer prepositions	7	10	.05
5. More second-person pronouns	6	3	.05
6. More second-person possessive adjectives	5	2	.05
7. More contractions	1	0	.05
8. More third-person pronouns	2	1	.05
9. More conjunctions	10	6	.05
10. More intransitive verbs	11	8	.10
11. More adverbs	14	7	.001
12. Others*	19	21	—
Total	99	100	

*No significant difference (greater than .10) for: demonstrative, indefinite, and first-person pronouns, first- and third-person possessive adjectives, reflexive, transitive, and auxiliary verbs, and to as infinitive. Because of rounding off, column one does not add to 100 percent.

Adjectives and articles describe, limit and qualify nouns. The hypnotist places little emphasis upon classification and categorization, as would be expected from his lessened use of abstract nouns. The hypnotist is not providing an intellectual analysis, but a direct experience. In addition, description of the environment or the presentation of abstract concepts would alert the subject to these aspects of reality. The hypnotist does not wish to alert his subject, nor to direct his attention to the current situation. Instead, he tries to reduce vigilance and to direct attention inward. Similarly, the lessened importance of prepositions in hypnotic inductions indicates the lessened emphasis upon relationships between abstract concepts, and by implication, the greater stress upon concrete sensations and behavior in hypnosis.

The lessened importance of action upon the environment in hypnotic language is also suggested by the tendency ($p < .10$) for hypnotic inductions to have more intransitive verbs than nonhypnotic language employs. This finding suggests that the hypnotist encourages nonspecific action, behavior without a clear-cut and understandable objective. The hypnotist tries to blur the subject of action as well as the object of action: hypnotic behavior happens by itself, spontaneously, not with a deliberate decision. The hypnotized person does not make his hand rise, it just happens. The hand is moving without a clear-cut objective, spontaneously and impulsively.

A similar interpretation could explain the greater number of third-person pronouns in hypnotic inductions. This chiefly reflects the use of "it" as an indefinite nominative or object, as in "it always helps" or "take it easy." The hypnotist wishes to avoid specifying both the subject and object of action, and one way to do so is to use indefinite, global terminology. This lack of precision and specification has broader implications as well. The hypnotist wants to absorb the subject's attention, but not his critical thinking. He wants to communicate, but to avoid the focus of attention and awareness. This helps to explain some of the peculiarities of hypnotic communication, such as high-redundancy content and the low frequency of opinions and information. This may also be one factor in the success of some of the indirect induction techniques invented by Erickson, such as the confusion technique.

Hypnotic speech is closely focused about the experiences of the subject, as shown by the greater use of "you" and "your" (second-person pronoun and possessive adjective). The hypnotist's speech is totally oriented about the person he is hypnotizing. This implies that the subject's attention is withdrawn from the environment into himself, his inner experiences, his body, his person. Hypnosis is more a personalized relationship than a distant, detached psychological experiment. This immediacy and direct contact is also a primary quality of the humanities and the arts. The linguistic evidence questions the hypothesis that the hypnotized subject forgets everything but the hypnotist. Instead, the hypnotist forgets everything but his subject, while the subject is absorbed in a world of imagination. The hypnotist does not want the subject to give him direct attention, and instead tries to communicate below the level of conscious awareness.

Hypnotic inductions have more adverbs than the instructions to subjects do. Adverbs qualify action, indicating how and when an action is taking place. In other words, the hypnotic induction is generating behavior, not presenting concepts or environmental objects. Words in this category include not only behavior modifiers, but also terms such as "just" and "now," which provide highly general, nonspecific behavior cues. The immediacy of the humanistic perspective is found in the hypnotic induction, which shapes behavior as it takes place rather than telling subjects what to do later on. The high adverb count emphasizes the ongoing flow of experience and behavior in hypnosis, and contrasts it with the job orientation of the standard psychological experiment.

The greater number of conjunctions in the hypnotic induction also indicates this ongoing flow of experience and behavior. The hypnotist does not break up or punctuate his speech. Instead he generates an ongoing, continuous flow of words. Rather than a differentiated analysis, he presents an endless stream of ideas. This is a very simple form of syntactical structure. Hypnotic language tends to use fewer terms implying complex logical relationships, such as prepositions, while using more terms implying very simple logical relationships, such as conjunctions. The hypnotist is not really reasoning with his subject—he is presenting successive images. Instead of an articulated, integrated statement, the hypnotist generates ideas that are connected chiefly by simple conjunctions. The hypnotist is not building a logical structure, he is placing ideas side by side, as if stringing beads.

Another form of simple conjunction between words is seen in the greater number of contractions in the hypnotic inductions. The contractions imply the informality and intimacy of the hypnotic process, and contrast it with the formality and stiffness of the typical instruction to the subject. A contraction means that two words have been joined into one. Perhaps the same merging principle may be operating at the cognitive level as well as the linguistic level. In other words, ideas also may be joined together in unconventional ways during hypnosis, as if the traditional separation between them has been modified.

This analysis of grammatical categories suggests that the hypnotist has exchanged precision for impact. The hypnotist loses the advantages of clear-cut abstract expression, but he gains something very important in its place. By relinquishing conventional abstract expressions he gains emotional and personal impact, and deepens the relationship.

The findings so far suggest that hypnotic language is simpler and more redundant than the control communication, but more direct evidence is needed. One way to check this point is to count the number of monosyllabic words in the two samples. This analysis showed that the ten hypnotic inductions had more monosyllabic words (a median of seventy-seven percent) than the instructions to subjects (sixty-seven percent). The difference between the two samples is significant at the .02 level by a Mann-Whitney test. The difference is not large, since the language of the nonhypnotic instructions was also not very complicated, but it is consistent. Words in hypnotic communications do tend to be short and simple.

Another supplementary analysis checked the redundancy of the hypnotic communications. This analysis made use of "cloze procedure" (Taylor, 1953). This technique requires judges to guess words that have been deleted from a text, thereby providing a measure of the redundancy or the contextual constraint. The more errors the judges make, the less redundant the text, and the more information it contains. Every fifth word was removed from the hypnotic and nonhypnotic texts, and the twenty texts were submitted in random order to seven judges (six psychologists and a research assistant).

The results indicated that the hypnotic inductions were more redundant, as expected, than the nonhypnotic instructions. More errors were made in guessing words deleted from the nonhypnotic text ($p < .001$, by a t test for correlated means). Once again, the difference between the two samples was quite small. The median error rate was thirty-six and one half percent for the hypnotic inductions and forty-one percent for the nonhypnotic instructions. Since each judge consistently made more errors in judging the nonhypnotic instructions, the very small difference proved to be highly significant statistically. The hypnotic inductions do seem to have a slightly greater redundancy and therefore a smaller information content than the control communications. The hypnotist is probably doing a good deal of nonverbal communication, through tone of voice, pauses, gestures, facial expression, and so forth, to substitute for the lowered information content in his speech. The hypnotist uses redundant, simplified language to circumvent the logical, conventional categories of thought. The hypnotist relies on connotation and evocation rather than denotation.

Table 18.2 shows a comparison of word frequencies in spoken English and in hypnotic inductions. This table shows all words that appeared at least once in the 1,000-word hypnotic sample, and which differed by at least 3.9 per thousand in frequency from words in spoken English. This new comparison generally confirms the findings of the first sample. Strikingly confirmed is the greater prevalence of "you" and "your" in the hypnotic induction. Spoken English, on the other hand, shows a greater number of other personal pronouns ("I," "we," and "they"), and a personal possessive adjective ("my"). These personal references were understandably not frequent in either the hypnotic inductions nor in the instructions to subjects in psychological experiments. They reconfirm the centering of the hypnotist's language exclusively about the subject, and the lessened references to the hypnotist's own opinions. This confirms the findings of interaction process analysis (Field, 1964).

TABLE 18.2 Hypnotic inductions versus spoken English: Words showing differences in frequency of 3.9 or more per 1,000

	Frequency per 1,000			Frequency per 1,000	
Word	Hypnotic inductions	Spoken English	Word	Hypnotic inductions	Spoken English
a, an*	13	26	is	13	7
and	44	38	just	11	5
are	18	3	keep	5	0.6
as	17	4	know*	4	10
attention	4	< 0.1	my*	2	6
be	9	5	now	7	3
can	9	3	on	13	7
chair	7	0.1	relax	8	< 0.1
comfortably	4	< 0.1	sit	5	0.3
eyes	6	< 0.1	target	4	< 0.1
feel	7	0.5	the*	28	40
fingers	4	< 0.1	they*	3	15
hand	7	0.3	thighs	6	< 0.1
hands	10	0.1	to	33	25
harder	4	< 0.1	very	7	2
how	6	1	we*	3	8
I*	13	40	will	22	1
if	9	4	you	64	19
in*	12	17	your	52	2

*Words with lower frequencies in hypnotic inductions than in spoken English.

This analysis also confirms the decreased frequency of articles in hypnosis, the increased frequency of adverbs such as "just," "now," "how," "very," and "as," and the increased use of the conjunction "and." No very clear indication is provided on whether there is a decreased frequency of nouns, adjectives, and prepositions. It is quite possible that high frequencies of these parts of speech are characteristic of the formal language of the psychological experiment. In other words, the previous finding of the low frequencies of nouns in hypnotic speech may in part reflect the informality of the hypnotist's speech in contrast to the formality of the language of the experiment. On the other hand, the low frequency of articles, which are closely linked to nouns, was confirmed in this second analysis.

The second analysis suggests that the nouns that are elevated in hypnotic speech are concrete nouns, referring to parts of the body, or else to the restricted parts of the environment that the hypnotist wishes the subject to be aware of ("chair" or "target" for eye fixation). The elevation of nouns for parts of the body indicates that the subject's attention is being withdrawn from the environment into his own body. At the same time, however, linguistic reference to parts of the body is a symbolic means of touching the body. This indicates the closeness and intimacy of hypnotic communication. Concrete nouns may be elevated in hypnosis, while the more abstract nouns and their modifiers are lowered, as the first analysis showed. This analysis also indicates that some prepositions dealing with location ("on" and "to") may be elevated in hypnosis, providing a more exact formulation of the previous finding that prepositions were lowered in hypnosis. Probably prepositions dealing with location are increased in hypnosis, whereas prepositions dealing with more abstract, conceptual relationships ("for," "from," "of") are decreased.

The analysis suggests that the hypnotist uses far more concrete terminology and less abstract formulation than generally appear in spoken English. This is also supported by the diminished frequency of the word "know" and the increased frequency of the word "feel" in hypnosis. Obviously, intellectual language declines in hypnosis, and emotional feeling language increases. The increased frequency of "are," "is," "be," and "will" may confirm the tendency toward more intransitive verbs as found in the first analysis. In addition to general classes of words that distinguish hypnotic speech from conversational discourse, there may be certain specific key words that are especially characteristic of hypnosis, such as "relax."

Summary

Hypnotic communication was compared to communication in the humanities and the arts. Points in common include use of nonverbal communication, vividness and concreteness of language, immediacy of communication, intimacy and closeness, rejection of abstract argumentation, and the primacy of the subjective experience. This viewpoint was illustrated by comparing linguistic classifications of hypnotic inductions with instructions to subjects in psychological experiments and with spoken English. These comparisons indicated that hypnotic language had fewer terms dealing with classification, categorization, abstract relationship, and abstract conceptualization, while it had more terms describing behavior, more terms linking other terms, more redundancy and monosyllabic words, and more terms centered around the person being hypnotized.

Doris Gruenewald *is a Senior Clinical Psychologist in the Department of Psychiatry (the Institute for Psychosomatic and Psychiatric Research and Training) of the Michael Reese Hospital and Medical Center, and a Clinical Associate Professor in the Department of Psychiatry, Pritzker School of Medicine, the University of Chicago where she obtained her doctorate in psychology. Her major interest is in theoretical and applied principles of psychopathology and psychotherapy, with a subspecialty in hypnosis. She has contributed to the literature on clinical and experimental hypnosis, the borderline syndrome, and the psychology of narcissistic disorders.*

Biographical information for Professor Fromm may be found on page 80.

Mark I. Oberlander *is Director of Clinical Research at the N.J. Pritzker Children's Psychiatric Unit of the Michael Reese Hospital and Medical Center. He received his Ph.D. in clinical psychology from the University of Chicago in 1967, following which he assumed a position as Senior Research Scientist at the Institute for Juvenile Research in Chicago. From 1968 to 1976 he also held the position of Research Associate in the Department of Psychology at the University of Chicago. He has done research in the areas of cognitive and personality development, with particular emphasis in the area of creativity. His current interests in research are in the areas of hypnotherapy, the evaluation of service delivery systems, and program assessment. Dr. Oberlander is a Fellow of the Society for Clinical and Experimental Hypnosis, and is actively involved in the training of hypnotherapists. Dr. Oberlander is also in private practice where he makes extensive use of hypnotic techniques in the conduct of individual psychotherapy.*

Gruenewald, Fromm, and Oberlander *review developments in psychoanalytic ego psychology that have led to the theory that hypnosis is a form of adaptive regression. In adaptive regression the ego initiates, controls, and terminates regression by temporarily losing contact with reality for the purpose of gaining improved mastery over inner experiences. Those who view hypnosis as an adaptive regression hypothesize that in hypnosis a regressed subsystem of the ego is placed in the service of the overall ego; this includes development of a special transference relationship to the hypnotist. The authors describe a study they have carried out, which derives from this theoretical viewpoint. Its purpose was to test the hypothesis that hypnosis is an adaptive regression.*

19

Hypnosis
and Adaptive Regression:
An Ego-Psychological Inquiry[1]

DORIS GRUENEWALD, ERIKA FROMM, AND
MARK I. OBERLANDER

As the accumulated lore surrounding hypnosis is gradually swept away, it becomes increasingly evident that many of the phenomena and experiences historically attributed to hypnosis are products of a variety of factors not intrinsically bound up with it. Yet hypnosis persists, as a facet of consciousness as well as an area of scientific investigation that reaches across disciplines and theoretical orientations, each however pursuing its own goal apart from the rest.

Psychoanalytic ego psychology has been concerned with hypnosis, admittedly outside its mainstream but enough to leave its mark on hypnosis research and theory. There has been a growing tendency within this theoretical orientation to regard hypnosis as a regression in the service of the ego or as an adaptive regression. This point of view has stimulated a line of research that demands further exploration, notwithstanding the pitfalls that still beset it. Our investigations (Fromm, Oberlander, & Gruenewald, 1970; Oberlander, Gruenewald, & Fromm, 1970) provide a representative example; their main features will be presented later in this chapter. The

1. The research project described in this chapter was supported in part by a grant from The Psychiatric Training and Research Fund of the Illinois Department of Mental Health (Project # 17-303) and in part by the Social Science Divisional Research Fund of the University of Chicago.

assumption that hypnosis is an adaptive regression has ego-psychological antecedents, the most salient of which will be reviewed first.

The Concept of Adaptive Regression

In the development of psychoanalysis the meaning of regression underwent a series of changes. In earlier psychoanalytic theory, regression referred to a global return to an earlier mode of functioning determined by infantile drives and specific fixation points in libidinal development. According to the topographic model, regression was defined as the tendency of the organism to shift from a "higher" to a "lower" mental system under conditions of stress and conflict (Freud, 1900). In hypnosis, the ego was assumed to be rendered nonfunctional. Hypnosis was discontinued as a treatment modality precisely because its "greatest triumph" was also its greatest fault; it unearthed unconscious material that was forced on the ego and retained only so long as the relationship with the hypnosis-inducing therapist remained intact (A. Freud, 1936).

Subsequent formulation of the structural model (Freud, 1923), with its tripartite division of the mental apparatus into id, ego, and superego, provided the groundwork for an ego-psychological conception of hypnosis. Of particular importance was the emphasis placed on the intersystemic relations of the ego and on its intrasystemic function of regulating the interplay of its own subordinate agencies.

Following the adoption of the structural model (Freud, 1923), there was a steady progression of formal thought regarding the structure and functions of the ego and, concomitantly, the meaning of regression. Among the numerous contributions to psychoanalytic ego psychology, the writings of Hartmann (1939), Kris (1934), and Rapaport (1953, 1958) are of paramount importance, especially in so far as they provide the conceptual ground for the subsequently presented theory of hypnosis as an adaptive regression (Gill & Brenman, 1959).

In *The Ego and the Id,* Freud (1923) postulated that the ego developed as a surface organ of perception that partially enveloped the id. Building on this theory, Hartmann (1939) was the first psychoanalytic writer to state unequivocally that both id and ego, as psychological structures, emerged from an undifferentiated matrix, and that certain functions, defined as belonging to the ego (such as sensory and basic protective mechanisms), were present at birth in at least rudimentary form. Hartmann saw these functions as biologically predetermined, innate structures independent of the instincts and their vicissitudes.

Given an "average expectable environment", the full development of these "apparatuses of primary autonomy" and their automated efficiency depend only on the physical maturation of the organism. Although they serve to gratify drive demands and may be drawn into conflict, the primarily autonomous ego apparatuses belong in a "conflict-free sphere of the ego" and do not lose their characteristic independence except under extreme conditions. Other ego functions (such as thought and secondary defense mechanisms), according to Hartmann, have their roots in the instinctual drive organization and are created out of conflict and experience. In the course of development, these ego apparatuses undergo a "change of function," which brings with it structuralization and, ultimately, relative independence from their instinctual origins (compare Allport's "functional autonomy of motives," Allport, 1937). While the apparatuses of primary autonomy have independent, noninstinctual energy sources, the apparatuses of secondary autonomy depend for their maintenance and stability on the ego's ability to "neutralize" drive energy available to it from the id and to use this "neutral" (de-instinctualized) energy for the establishment of more or less permanent countercathexes against instinctual forces. To the exent that such countercathexes are maintained, the secondarily autonomous apparatuses also function outside of conflict. Although they are more vulnerable to instinctual vicissitudes, they too result in relatively stable structures.

Thus, the autonomy of both the primary and secondary ego apparatuses is always relative. So long as the developmental stages follow the direction of growth and independence, Hartmann speaks of a "progressive adaptation." However, like A. Freud (1936), who recognized the egosyntonic function of fantasy—by definition a regressive phenomenon —Hartmann (1939, 1964) acknowledges the possibility of successful adaptation achieved by way of regression. He thus distinguishes between "progressive" and "regressive" adaptation.

Regressive adaptation is in some respects identical with Kris's (1934) "regression in the service of the ego," described as the capacity of the ego to initiate and terminate libidinal and structural regression for the purpose of gaining improved mastery. Subject to voluntary control, this process is particularly evident in the enjoyment of art and humor and plays a significant role in certain phases of creative activity. It consists of an ego-regulated modification and relaxation of defensive barriers, so that earlier modes of perception and cognition are reactivated, and normally repressed affects, memories, and primitive components of experience can rise into conscious awareness. The mental content emerging from repression tends to possess qualities characteristic of primary-process thought and imagery. But in contrast to uncontrolled, pathological regression

—where the ego stands by helplessly or is totally paralyzed vis-à-vis the involuntary breakthrough of such material—the mental content associated with regression in the service of the ego is assimilated and constructively utilized. The ego remains in control and, having relinquished its counter-cathexes for a goal-directed purpose, can reinstitute its usual organization at will.

Kris's treatment of regression, being chiefly concerned with artistic creativity, is somewhat narrower in scope, but it spells out the bipolarity of regression and its potential for enlarging the span of the ego.

As stated by Hartmann, the building of permanent psychological structures depends on the automatization of functions, that is, their becoming independent from the id's influence under stable developmental conditions. Rapaport (1958) expands this line of thought in drawing the logical conclusion that the ego is relatively autonomous not only in relation to the id but also in relation to the environment. Both autonomies are considered relative in that disruption of either may result in a decrease of autonomy, and interference with one can affect both. The interrelationship of the autonomies is complex: relative autonomy from the id is predicated on the existence of the constitutionally given apparatuses of primary autonomy and on the automatized structures of secondary autonomy insofar as they have become independent of their instinctual origins; relative autonomy from the environment in turn is ultimately guaranteed by the very presence of the drives and their regulating influence on the ego in its relations with the outer world.

Whereas the ego was conceived in early psychoanalytic theory as little more than a mediator between the drives and the external environment, it now was considered a structure in its own right, with motivations and purposes unique to itself and with the capacity to resist, modify, and control the demands of both agencies.

The entire topic of the relative autonomies is intimately related to the still largely unsolved problem of ego activity and ego passivity. Rapaport (1967) specifies ego activity as one of the "parameters of the relative autonomy of the ego" (p. 566), defined as the capacity to control drive demand, delay drive discharge, guide thought towards discovering a suitable object, and institute appropriate behavior for drive gratification; or, in the absence of proper conditions for engaging in overt behavior, to set aside, suppress, or sublimate instinctual needs. Ego passivity, in contrast, is defined as "helplessness in the face of drive demands" (p. 555). Appropriate action through ego channels may be blocked either because the ego is overwhelmed and its executive apparatus put in the service of indiscriminate drive discharge, or, as in the case of developmental arrest, because the necessary structures are lacking.

Behavior, however, is not to be taken as the criterion for ego activity or passivity for the reason that behavioral activity may reflect ego passivity or even ego paralysis, and behavioral passivity may in certain instances be associated with a high level of ego activity (see also Fromm, 1970; Schafer, 1968a). Rapaport acknowledges that his schematic presentation does not do justice to the complex interplay between activity and passivity, nor take account of the hierarchical layering of structures which themselves are not static but subject to the shifting of varying prepotent physiological and psychological states.

Schafer (1968a) takes issue with Rapaport, suggesting that the theoretical pursuit of activity and passivity may merely lead into a blind alley. Witness, for instance, the paradox of "passive mastery" during the narcissistic stage, in which the ego has as yet not become fully differentiated from the initial id-ego matrix. Mastery implies activity, in spite of the fact that the infant, viewed in his total life situation, is helpless vis-à-vis the environment, that is, passive. Witness also the postulate of "omnipotence" in the narcissistic stage, which again implies activity. As words, "activity" and "passivity" are too closely associated with their popular meaning, and as scientific terms they seem to be so inextricably enmeshed that Schafer finds them meaningless as explanatory concepts.

In spite of such conceptual difficulties, we believe that the terms "activity" and "passivity" may still serve a useful purpose if they are explicitly defined as bipolar continua (see Fromm, Chapter 4 in this volume). At one end of the activity pole one would find continual reinforcement of defensive barriers against instinctual forces in excess of a normal or optimal level. This process would be likely to lead to ego constriction, if not to overt pathology. If such constriction took on pathological dimensions, regression, in the event that it occurred, would tend to be of the involuntary kind resulting in temporary ego passivity. At the other end of the activity pole, the ego would use its synthetic function for the integration of instinctual forces, and thus be capable of adaptive regression. This too would involve temporary passivity, however by choice, not necessity. But again there is the paradox of "passive activity" and "active passivity," an impasse that cannot be resolved here. (See also Bachrach, 1968).

In Rapaport's scheme, activity and passivity refer to prevailing states of the total ego. Yet, "ego" is no longer considered a unitary entity, but rather a congeries of more or less cohesive structures, each with relatively discrete though interrelated functions, of which some are likely to be more active and some more passive at any given time. It therefore is somewhat misleading to speak of pathological regression as indicating ego passivity and of adaptive regression as indicating ego activity. The function under scrutiny must be identified and the conditions under which either prevails specified. One would then be in a better position to differentiate ego-controlled from uncontrolled regression in relation to the ego segment under investigation (cf. Schafer, 1968b).

Summing up, regression, as one of the ego's defensive and integrative mechanisms, serves the goal of adaptation to internal and external conditions with varying degrees of success. Adaptive as well as pathological regression may spread over a wide area or be limited to a small segment. In any event, it is rarely found in isolation, and it is more common to see elements of both.

Criteria for identifying adaptive regression as opposed to regression proper include the ability to seek out and initiate regressive experiences and to call a halt to them without help if conditions are judged to be no longer safe, with immediate and complete reinstatement of the usual psychic organization (Gill & Brenman, 1959). This is more likely to occur if there is flexibility and strength rather than rigidity and weakness.

The Concept of Adaptive Regression in Hypnosis

Although references to the regressive aspects of hypnosis are scattered throughout the early psychoanalytic literature, it was Schilder (1926) who first formulated what may be regarded a forerunner of the hypnosis-as-adaptive-regression theory. Directly relevant to the present discussion is Schilder's viewpoint that only a part of the ego becomes involved in hypnosis and that "a considerable portion of the personality maintains its normal relations with the outside world" (p. 96). Schilder assigns a central position to that portion, stating that it "may assume various attitudes toward the hypnotized portions" (p. 76), such as varying degrees of consent to participate or to remain in the role of a spectator. The central ego's active participation in the hypnotic procedures comes about through the transference relationship with the hypnotist and involves a quality of trance called "psychic depth." The greater the "psychic depth," the more the central ego's reality orientation is mediated through the person of or the relationship with the hypnotist. If the central ego functions more in the role of observer, the phenomena of hypnotic behavior may be elicited but tend to have a relatively mechanical quality.

In Schilder's formulation, the notion that the ego controls hypnotic regression is clearly implied. His ideas form a large part of the background for the theory of hypnosis as an adaptive regression promulgated by Gill and Brenman (1959).

Based on many years of clinical psychoanalytic research in hypnosis, Gill and Brenman's (1959) theory coordinates virtually all existing ego-psychological concepts. It leans heavily on the theoretical developments regarding the origin and autonomy of the ego that have been presented in the first part of this chapter. It furthermore attempts to reconcile such apparently conflicting directions as the traditional sensorimotor approach of experimental psychology and the strong emphasis on transference factors of psychoanalytic psychology.

In lieu of Schilder's central ego, a concept more in keeping with structural theory is envisaged, namely an overall ego relatively autonomous in relation to id and environment and in control of its apparatuses. Induction of hypnosis represents an attack on the apparatuses—a sensorimotor disorientation that eventuates in their partial de-automatization—and simultaneously the offer of a regressive (transference) relationship. In a successful induction, made possible by the overall ego's acquiescing and temporarily relinquishing control of its apparatuses to the hypnotist, the normally prevailing cathectic-countercathectic balance is upset and a regressive restructuring takes place. However, instead of regression occurring in the overall ego, as in regression proper, a subsystem of the ego is triggered into action, which searches for motivational patterns in accord with the regressed id-ego-superego derivatives to which it gains access. The shifting of energy distributions involves libidinal and attention cathexes. In the established hypnotic state, the subsystem becomes reorganized into a temporarily stable structure that not only regains partial control of the (re-automatized) apparatuses but also is put into the service of the overall ego. The basic structure of the overall ego remains unchanged, although the psychological space it occupies diminishes in proportion to the extent or dimensions it allows the regressed subsystem. The overall ego never loses contact with reality. (Compare this theory with E. R. Hilgard's Neo-Dissociation Theory, chapter 3 in this volume.)

The foregoing is a brief recapitulation of the central point of Gill and Brenman's metapsychological theory of hypnosis. Moving from a descriptive base of observational data through increasingly abstract conceptualizations to the final theoretical statement, Gill and Brenman (1959) conclude that hypnosis is a regression in the service of the ego. However, they give due weight to instances where the observed facts are at variance with the theory: in some cases, for example, regression gets out of hand and invades the overall ego; also, a satisfactory hypnotic state with the hallmarks of adaptive regression may be obtained in persons whose ego can in no sense be regarded strong and flexible.

Gill and Brenman's theory is a well-reasoned, internally cohesive, intrasystemic view of the ego in relation to hypnosis, stated with the conviction of scientists committed deeply to their chosen task. Nevertheless, the exceptions duly noted by them are not accounted for in the theory. In spite of the fact that it was built from an observational basis, the data seem to have been fitted into preexisting psychoanalytic theory.

Gill and Brenman offer their theory as an ad hoc statement. An empirical study generated by the theory will now be described.

The Research Project

The expressed purpose of the research was to examine the hypothesis of hypnosis as adaptive regression. Terms used in psychoanalysis and in hypnosis can rarely be defined without resorting to equally undefined parallels. Consequently, some of the research variables and concepts were more stringently defined, in terms of operations performed, than others, which were simply used in their consensually validated form.

Hypnosis was accepted as a given, operationally defined by the controlled administration of standard induction procedures (Fromm & Weingarten, 1965; Weitzenhoffer & Hilgard, 1959, 1962), by the number of scale items passed, and to a small extent by the subjects' individual experience, reported by way of a subjective scale of depth similar to that of LeCron and Bordeaux (1947). Situational variables were controlled by counterbalanced experimental conditions, randomized assignments of subjects to experimental conditions, and use of four experimenters, two of whom were uninformed with regard to the purpose of the experiment. No attempt was made to control either the role of the hypnotist as perceived by the subject or the transference aspects of the hypnotic relationship, for which in any case no effective method of measurement exists.

With regard to regression, however, the situation was more favorable, as a recently developed system for scoring Rorschach responses made a quantitative evaluation of regressive processes possible (Holt, 1963, 1967; Holt & Havel, 1960).

ADAPTIVE REGRESSION IN THE HOLT SYSTEM

In the standard Rorschach testing situation, the subject projects form and meaning onto objectively content-free inkblots and translates into verbal expression whatever imagery and thought are stimulated in him. Responses may be relatively free of or relatively loaded with mental representations of drive derivatives characteristic of primary process thought. The system provides for quantitative assessment of primary process intrusions and the manner in which such intrusions are handled by secondary process operations.

Holt (1963) considers primary process a hypothetical construct not accessible to direct observation. But if treated as an intervening variable, its products may be inferred from observable verbal behavior and scored according to form and content. Concurrent with or subsequent to the expression of primary process mentation, secondary process thinking and defensive and coping functions of the ego are also operative; they are similarly inferred from the responses and scored according to their form, content, and structure.

The Holt system for scoring Rorschach responses thus applies within the limits of operational definitions of primary and secondary processes. Primary process is manifested by intrusions into verbal responses of primitive, drive-determined content; condensations, fragmentation, and loose or fluid associations; syncretic or autistic logic and logical contradictions; disregard of reality; and peculiarities of perceptual and linguistic organization. Secondary process is inferred from adherence to the demands of reality and rationality; purposefully organized thinking; minimal intrusion of primitive, drive-determined material; and automatic processing of such material into socially acceptable form. The distinction between the two types of perceptual-cognitive operations is rarely as clear as implied by these characteristics; individual responses ordinarily are interactive products of both.

In the Holt system all responses are first scored with regard to their form level, which provides an initial indicator of the subject's reality orientation and ability to match internal object representations with perceived form. Each response is then inspected to determine the nature and extent of primary process manifestations, which, if present, are scored according to drive content, formal thought structure, and defenses that are simultaneously or sequentially operative. The end product of the scoring process is a numerical value, the adaptive regression score, which reflects the individual's capacity for constructive integration of primary process material. This score has positive and negative values. The larger it is, the deeper the regression is assumed to be; whether adaptive or maladaptive is judged by the positive or negative value of the score, by type, content, and intensity of primary-process products, by mode and manner of defensive operations, and by recovery from any evident loss of secondary process control within or across responses.[2]

2. For a selective review of the literature on adaptive regression and Holt's Rorschach scoring system see Fromm, Oberlander, and Gruenewald, 1970.

THE EXPERIMENT

Since the Holt Rorschach scoring system offers a relatively objective measure of regression, the study was designed to investigate those ego functions directly involved in taking the Rorschach test, viz., perception and cognition, and to evaluate regressive processes in and out of hypnosis on the basis of obtained scores. Design, methodology, and statistical analysis of results have been fully reported in two publications (Fromm, Oberlander, & Gruenewald, 1970; Oberlander, Gruenewald, & Fromm, 1970) and will be presented here only in summary.

Three dimensions of perceptual-cognitive functions and their implications for adaptive regression were examined in the normal waking state and in hypnosis for levels, that is, degree and kind of primary process manifestations and defenses; variability, that is, fluctuations in degree and kind of primary process manifestations and defenses; and content and structure of thought processes; each as expressed on the Rorschach test and scored according to Holt's system.

The test was administered in counterbalanced order (waking-hypnosis and hypnosis-waking) to thirty-two subjects selected from a volunteer student population who demonstrated good or excellent hypnotizability on a modified version (Fromm & Weingarten, 1965) of Form A of the Stanford Hypnotic Susceptibility Scale (SHSS; Weitzenhoffer & Hilgard, 1959). Each subject received two hypnosis training sessions prior to the hypnotic condition. Differences in personal style were controlled inasmuch as each subject went through both conditions with the same examiner and served as his own control. For the hypnotic experimental condition, Form C of the SHSS (Weitzenhoffer & Hilgard, 1962) was used as the induction technique.

It was hypothesized that perceptual-cognitive functions would change in the hypnotic condition in the direction of adaptive regression as measured by the adaptive regression score of the Holt system. Specific predictions were that incidence and variability of primary process manifestations would increase in hypnosis, and that defensive and coping functions would yield scores at least equal to but probably greater than the waking scores. Regarding content and structure of thought processes, it was hoped that the results of the experiment would permit the development of criteria for differentiating the two states.

Results. The data were analyzed in three phases. The first set of analyses was concerned with the main question couched in the experimental hypothesis, namely, whether the hypothesis that hypnosis was an adaptive regression was tenable. The second set of analyses was instituted as a check on doubtful or equivocal results of the first and dealt with such issues as sex and adjustment differences in relation to adaptive versus maladaptive regression. The third set of analyses was addressed to the question whether a comparison of waking and trance Rorschach responses would sufficiently differentiate thought processes in both conditions to establish predictive criteria for each.

The first set of analyses indicated clearly that elements of primary process mentation intruded with greater frequency in the hypnotic condition *(p* < .01). The order in which the hypnotic and waking conditions were administered had some influence in the extent of primary process intrusions, with direction varying across the four experimenters *(p* < .05). However, analysis of adaptive regression scores did not yield significant results. This phase in the evaluation of results supported the hypothesis of regressive influences in hypnosis but failed to distinguish adaptive from maladaptive regression.

In the second set of analyses, the Rorschach records were scored according to the Klopfer method (Klopfer et al., 1954) and dichotomized according to sex (male-female) and psychological adjustment ("more adjusted" and "less adjusted"). The increased frequency of primary process intrusions in the hypnosis condition was again highly significant *(p* < .01). Further, both the adjustment and sex factors were signficantly associated with such intrusions and, moreover, with the variability of defensive and coping functions *(p* < .05) and with the variability of adaptive regression scores (for adjustment, *p* < .01; for the adjustment/sex interaction, *p* < .05). Thus, subjects who on the basis of their rescored Rorschach protocols were placed in the "less adjusted" category produced considerably more primary process material than the "more adjusted" subjects. With regard to sex differences, the "more adjusted" male subjects produced records with relatively less primary process material than the "more adjusted" female subjects, a trend that was reversed in that the "less adjusted" male subjects produced considerably more primary process material than the "less adjusted" female subjects.

Although, contrary to the hypothesis, the level of defensive and coping functions was slightly lower in hypnosis than in the waking state for both groups, there was a trend (not statistically significant) toward improved reality testing in hypnosis for the "less adjusted" male subjects and toward the opposite for the "less adjusted" female subjects. In general, the adaptive regression scores of the "more adjusted" male subjects were significantly greater than those of the "less adjusted" male subjects, while the "more adjusted" female subjects' adaptive regression scores were somewhat lower than those of the "less adjusted" female subjects.

For the third phase of analysis, the eighty-four substantive scoring categories thought to be most indicative of regression were tabulated and subjected to a comparison between the waking and hypnosis conditions. Of the eighty-four categories, thirteen yielded significant differences in thought content and organization, and twenty-six categories indicated significantly greater variance in the hypnotic condition. Out of twenty-two content scoring categories, fifteen were found to be more frequent in hypnosis as compared to waking Rorschach protocols—a difference that is significant at the .04 level. Similarly, twenty-five of thirty-seven formal scoring categories were found to be more frequent in hypnosis protocols (p < .006). Those differences offer suggestive evidence regarding the nature of the primary processes expressed in hypnotic thought.

Subjecting the control and defense scoring categories to similar scrutiny suggested that at the .05 level of significance, hypnosis protocols were more frequently indicative of defensive functioning. However, when the defense and control categories were divided into adaptive versus maladaptive operations, a more coherent picture emerged. There was no difference between experimental conditions in the relative deployment of adaptive processes, whereas the frequency of maladaptive defenses was significantly greater in hypnosis protocols (p < .02).

Discussion

The study makes only a modest contribution to the problem posed at the outset. Nevertheless, the findings summarized above were corroborated by other investigators. For instance, Blatt, Goodman & Wallington (1971) found increased defense demand and no significant changes in defense effectiveness or adaptive regression scores under hypnosis when analyzing results of a study addressed to a different problem. Similarly, Gur and Reyher (1976) found increased primary process manifestations in the presence of unimpaired "secondary process monitoring and reality contact" (p. 247) in the context of a study on creativity and hypnosis. Since these findings are incidental, rather than central, to the studies cited, they are uninfluenced by Blatt, Goodman, & Wallington's (1971) and Gur and Reyher's (1976) research hypotheses and therefore of value as independent support for our own findings.

In a study directly investigating the question of adaptive regression as a function of hypnosis, Levin and Harrison (1976) concur with us that hypnosis can facilitate adaptive regression in persons who possess that capacity as an ego function in the normal waking state.

The Rorschach situation as such may be defined as inviting regression because it requires the production of visual imagery, itself considered a mode of primary process functioning (Holt & Havel, 1960). Almost any kind of latent ideational content may be evoked when a Rorschach card is presented, but normally the subject scans a variety of memory images to find one or more that best fit the vaguely structured blot. In the process of perceiving and simultaneously translating perception into verbal form, defenses against the emergence of drive-determined thoughts are operating. Consequently, the distance from the primary process idea presumed to underlie an overt response shows the degree of neutralization, countercathectic strength, and hypercathexis of secondary process thinking.

In the experiment, the regressive element inherent in the Rorschach test was enhanced in the hypnosis condition, as manifested by a general increase in responses influenced by primary process. Interview material, obtained from all subjects to elicit their hypotheses concerning the experiment, showed that they were not aware of a demand to "regress." The increased production of primary process responses thus did not appear to be a function of the subjects' expectations. Although it was to some extent associated with the sequence in which the experimental conditions were administered, it held up whether the hypnosis condition preceded or followed the waking condition. It therefore was assumed to be a function of hypnosis.

On closer examination however, this interpretation is open to question. As stated earlier, the triggering into action of an ego subsystem results in the overall ego's relinquishing to the hypnotist control of its apparatuses, the subsystem's gaining control of the apparatuses in the process of becoming a temporarily stable structure, and the subsystem's search for new motivational patterns. Exposure to the Rorschach immediately following hypnosis induction presents the subject with a ready-made motivational pattern whose implementation depends on perceptual-cognitive functions as they come under the sway of the subsystem. If, as was the case in the experiment, the person presenting the Rorschach is also the hypnotist, who is simultaneously offering a regressive transference relationship via hypnotic induction, another, potentially more powerful, ready-made motivational pattern is at hand. Determined partly by situational contingencies (such as the personality of the hypnotist), and partly by covert, unexplored, but relatively inevitable transference factors, this pattern is implemented according to the subject's dynamic style, as represented in the instinctual derivatives and attention cathexes to which the subsystem gains access. The experimenter, not in his role as hypnotist but rather as a specific person who has acquired increased stimulus value during hypnosis induction, may to some extent control the transference relationship by his attitudes; that is, he may subtly encourage or discourage its development and intensity. Yet, he cannot prevent its formation in a transference-prone individual, whose critical functions and testing of background reality have been at least partially given over to the hypnotist by the overall ego. The demand for regression is implicit even if not consciously recognized by either party. Hence, the increase in regressive Rorschach responses in the hypnosis condition may be interpreted as a function of the transference aspects in hypnosis but not as a function of hypnosis per se.

Support for this interpretation is implied in a previous investigation (Gruenewald & Fromm, 1967), in which subjects were given a Rorschach and an intelligence test under hypnosis, with the tests administered by a person other than the hypnotist. In the absence of the regression-facilitating hypnotic transference relationship with the examiner, no discernible regression took place in comparison with the subjects' waking-state baseline performance. It appears then that in the context of the subsystem's postulated access to id-ego-superego derivatives, the objective nature of the task and the motivational quality of the hypnotic relationship determine which part of the triad becomes dominant.

The gross division of overall ego and ego subsystem may be considered a regression if so defined, but it is questionable if regression in that sense is the same as the stipulated regression within the subsystem. While an association of hypnosis with regression in terms of the formation of a subsystem is upheld, a cause and effect relationship within the subsystem can be established only if experimental control of the hypnotist variable in a similar experiment should replicate the results obtained with regard to primary process manifestations.

The crucial question—Is hypnosis an adaptive regression?—is however at least tentatively answered by the finding that the direction of regression split along the adjustment-maladjustment axis.

It had been predicted that improved ego control would manifest itself in a quantitative increase and qualitative shift of the defensive and coping operations that accompanied the readier expression of primary process ideation in hypnosis. Contrary to the prediction, the results indicated a general, though nonsignificant, quantitative reduction of scores pertaining to defense and coping categories. The qualitative shift consisted in greater variability of these scores for the "more adjusted" and in decreased variability for the "less adjusted" subjects.

The quantitative reduction of defense and coping scores can be accounted for on the ground that hypnosis entails a constriction and attenuation of the perception of reality. For the duration of the hypnosis, the overall ego relinquishes a major or minor part of its normal awareness and processing of background information to the hypnotist. The deeper the hypnosis, the broader the subsystem's access to the apparatuses of perception, memory, judgment, and so forth. The activity of the subsystem increases as the overall ego becomes more passive. However, the amount of outside information available to the subsystem is diminished, being derived both from the overall ego and from the hypnotist. While input from within may become more extensive and more intensive, its processing is not controlled by the overall ego's constant checking of reality that takes place in the waking state. The amount of defense activity commensurate with the perceptual range of the overall ego is therefore diminished.

An increase in variability of defense and coping scores had been predicted as an indicator of loosened defenses and adaptive regression for all subjects. However, the second set of analyses disclosed that the loosening of defenses was not uniformly adaptive. Only the "more adjusted" subjects engaged in predominantly flexible and far-ranging ego activity in the hypnosis condition, with a preponderance of higher level coping mechanisms. The "less adjusted" subject, in contrast, tended to become more constricted and to rely in greater part on maladaptive defenses. In the case of the "less adjusted" male subjects, a trend toward a slightly improved reality orientation appeared (as indicated by their form level scores). Although this trend may be interpreted as an ego-syntonic adaptation to the immediate situation and perhaps as an enduring personality trait, it scarcely fits the criteria stipulated for adaptive regression. Instead of comfortably accepting hypnosis, the "less adjusted" male subjects seemed to defend themselves against its potentially disorganizing influence by clinging to realistic features and intellectual functioning.

In the aggregate, the subjects' formal thought processes manifested more regression in hypnosis than in the waking state. But in relation to adaptive regression, the frequency of adaptive defenses did not exceed that of the waking condition, while maladaptive defenses were significantly more frequent in hypnosis.

In summary, the outcome of the investigation indicates facilitation of access to primary process ideation and differences in the organization of thought processes in hypnosis. The effects of increased accessibility and the degree of primary process expression appear to be a function of each individual's structural and dynamic characteristics and level of psychological adjustment. Moreover, situational and interpersonal variables cannot be neglected in evaluating the outcome.

We conclude that adaptive regression can take place in hypnosis but does not thereby become a function of hypnosis per se, and that the equation of hypnosis with adaptive regression is not tenable in its present form.

Conclusion

We will end this chapter with a few remarks that sum up our thinking as it relates to general issues pertaining to psychoanalytically oriented hypnosis research.

It is our opinion that psychoanalytic theory offers the most comprehensive hypotheses for the functioning of the human mind and that much fruitful research can be generated from that basis. Nevertheless, there is an urgent need to rethink its concepts in a form that can bridge the gap between theoretical statement and operational definition.

Many efforts directed to that end are already under way, and the contemporary ferment in psychoanalytic thought has already left its mark. For instance, dissatisfaction with the ambiguities in the concept of "primary process" has resulted in critical papers that extend Freud's theory (cf. Gill, 1967; Holt, 1967). Rapaport (1958, 1967d) and Schafer (1958, 1968a, 1968b) have significantly contributed to the extension of the theory of intrasystemic structural development and of ego activity and passivity. A recent paper by Fromm (1970) adds clarification to the latter. Holt's (1963) Rorschach scoring system for adaptive regression constitutes an important link between theory and research.

We have touched upon conceptual and linguistic difficulties inherent in psychoanalytic concepts. At the same time, we find cogency in Gill and Brenman's (1959) intrasystemic view of the ego in hypnosis. Sterba (1934), following Freud's postulate of an observing ego, suggested a separation of the observing and experiencing parts of the ego in psychoanalysis, a notion equally applicable to hypnosis (Fromm, 1965a). Bellak (1955) expresses a similar view, stated in terms of the "self-excluding function of the ego." This formulation has apparently not been taken up in the literature, but it deserves further exploration as it seems to have implications for the activity-passivity problem as well as for the concept of regression as now used. A reexamination of regression would certainly be in order. For example, are the ideational factors subsumed under "primary process" always regressive? Might they not in some instances (such as creativity and intuition) represent functions that mature and become autonomous in their own right? Such functions may be associated with and appropriate to different levels of ego processes under different conditions, without recourse to the concept of regression.

The account we have given of the research project should leave no doubt that, whether one espouses a "state" or "process" theory of hypnosis, any definitive statement concerning hypnosis is at best premature. There no longer is room for parochialism or reductionism in hypnosis research. A broader and more consistent joining of efforts across disciplines and theoretical orientations would be extraordinarily useful for the future of hypnosis research.

Howard Shevrin *is a Professor of Psychology in the Departments of Psychiatry and Psychology at the University of Michigan. His empirical research has largely been devoted to the study of unconscious mental processes in the course of which he has developed a special subliminal technique for investigating different types of thought organization. One part of this research, done in collaboration with Dr. Lawrence Stross, dealt with the nature of unconscious mental processes in hypnosis. More recently he has been investigating certain brain processes that he has found to accompany unconscious thinking. In his clinical work he has treated as well as diagnosed the full range of psychotherapeutic problems. In 1969 he was graduated from the Topeka Psychoanalytic Institute, having completed training as a research fellow of the American Psychoanalytic Association. From 1954 to 1956 he completed a two-year post-doctoral course in clinical psychology at the Menninger Foundation.*

Shevrin *is concerned with the unconscious emotional impact that hypnosis may have on experimental subjects. In post-experimental interviews he found that subjects consciously described their hypnotic experiences as comfortable and agreeable, but that Card 12M TAT protocols elicited negative and ambivalent unconscious attitudes toward the hypnotic experience. Subjects consciously had a strong wish to cooperate but unconsciously they wanted to submit and to be cared for. When the experience was over and the latter wishes were unfulfilled, unconscious feelings of anxiety, conflict, and angry disappointment were generated.*

20

The Wish to Cooperate
and the Temptation to Submit:
The Hypnotized Subject's Dilemma

HOWARD SHEVRIN

Through all of its long history, in a variety of guises and under diverse names, hypnosis has retained an air of mystery and a touch of the sinister. The word itself refuses to become shopworn because it is surrounded with so intense an aura of affect and implication. Yet for those who practice it I am sure it is experienced as an instrument—a means toward an end, whether the end is treatment or research. Often what is work to the specialist, however, seems like play or Faustian legerdemain to the layman. By the same token, it becomes easy for the practitioner, caught up in technical issues, to overlook the impact his instrument has upon others. This is certainly less true for the therapist than for the experimenter, who does not so much share goals with the subject as enlist his cooperation for the experimenter's ends, which rarely include the subject's enlightenment. In this paper I would like to describe my enlightenment as an experimenter concerning the impact of hypnosis on experimental subjects.

In recent years I have collaborated in a series of experiments (Stross & Shevrin, 1968) involving hypnosis that was intended to explore the nature

An earlier version of this paper was presented as part of a symposium on hypnoanalysis, at the Annual Meeting of the Society for Clinical and Experimental Hypnosis, University of Chicago, Chicago, Illinois, November 23, 1968.

of hypnosis as an altered state of consciousness. I was not the hypnotist. In one of these experiments I interviewed the subjects, all women, in order to learn from them how they experienced hypnosis and what effect hypnosis had on the various tasks they were asked to perform. At the end of each interview I asked them to make up a story to the so-called "hypnosis" card (12M) of the TAT. At that time the overriding purpose of the research was to see if hypnosis would augment the effects of subliminal stimulation. We learned that it did in some respects and not in others. My preoccupation in the interviews was to understand better how hypnosis might bring about this augmenting effect. Actually, the interviews were disappointing in this respect. As a result, like all good experimenters, I forgot about them.

Recently I reread the interviews for reasons that are unclear to me and was forcibly struck by something that had utterly eluded me before. Although subject after subject described in positive and even glowing terms how relaxing, pleasant, and agreeable the hypnotic experience was, allusions to much different feelings in the interviews and—most remarkably— in their TAT stories were in striking contrast to these accolades. I set about to study these interviews and stories and have been most troubled by what I found concerning the underlying attitudes of hypnotic subjects at the end of an experiment. From a clinical standpoint, the stories were those of angry, disappointed, and frightened women. The pleasant goodbyes masked the injury these women felt they had suffered.

I know that there has been a history of experimentation involving the use of the hypnosis card to pre- or post-dict hypnotizability (Levitt, Lubin, & Brady, 1962; Levitt & Lubin, 1963; Sector, 1961; Venture, Kransdorff, & Kline, 1956; R.W. White, 1937). However, only one study to my knowledge collected stories immediately following hypnosis (Sarason & Rosenzweig, 1942), and in this study little is reported about the findings other than to state that some stories were positive and others ambivalent. Of the thirteen subjects in our experiment only one was clearly positive in her stories. Of all the subjects she was the only one who had a continuing relationship with the hypnotist. He had been instructing her in the use of hypnosis during childbirth. Of the other twelve subjects, five were strikingly negative in their stories and the remaining seven told stories which, only by stretching the term, could be called ambivalent. Before illustrating the data, let me discuss the nature of the hypnotic induction and give a brief description of the experiment.

The Stanford Hypnotic Susceptibility Scale, Form A (Weitzenhoffer & Hilgard, 1959) was used. Subjects were considered hypnotized when they passed at least seven of the twelve challenge items on the Stanford Scale. However, most of the subjects scored positively in all twelve items. In general, subjects were at least in medium trances, and some were in deep hypnotic states. In all cases, the subjects had to be sufficiently hypnotized to carry out the complex experimental procedure and still not be disrupted subjectively or "awakened" by the procedure.

The subjects were all women in their middle twenties to early thirties, all volunteers who had been successfully hypnotized on at least one other occasion by the same hypnotist and who were distinguished by the readiness and completeness with which they entered the hypnotic state. I stress that, as a group, they were friendly, willing, and even dedicated.

The experiment itself lasted four sessions. The first and second sessions were on successive days; a week later the third and fourth sessions were again on successive days. In each session the subject was hypnotized. Under hypnosis the subject was asked to describe a briefly flashed picture, to provide descriptions of images, to free associate, and to recall night dreams. These responses were also obtained in the waking state. At the end of the second and fourth sessions, I interviewed the subjects. The subject was asked to follow the experimental procedure step by step and to describe how each task was experienced in hypnosis and in the waking state. After this had been completed the "hypnosis" card was administered.

I would like to cite three subjects' experiences in some detail and then discuss the questions raised by these accounts.

First Case Illustration

Miss S. was a young unmarried woman in her early twenties who was readily hypnotized and had passed all of the items in the Stanford Scale. When I asked her what it was like to become hypnotized she replied:

> Well, I just relaxed. I felt very heavy and limp. I kept having the feeling yesterday and today that part of the time, possibly, I could have just woke up, but yet I didn't. [And when she was asked what more she could tell me about her experience of feeling heavy and limp.] Well, I just feel like, in a way, a little bit drunk. I just really couldn't do very much. I'm just so completely relaxed...It's just like nothing else really matters, except being relaxed and, well for instance, I think it's just like if I were supposed to—well, probably even get up and walk—it would be extremely difficult to get out of this chair...It's just like I don't really have any control over my arms and my legs and my hands and they're just useless and I know that they're there but I can't do anything with them.

For this subject the difference between being hypnotized and being awake was epitomized in these terms: "I think when I was hypnotized...the pictures all seemed to be a little dark, a little on the gray side and then when I was awake, they were bright." She characterized coming out of hypnosis by describing things as being "brighter...it seems like there's more light in the room."

When I pressed her further to define this quality of darkness in hypnosis the subject was most revealing: "It seems like there's no sunshine. It's like ...well, I think probably hypnosis would be like a rainy day and being fully awake is like sunshine. Things are just grayer, they're not quite as vivid, there's not as much detail and outline, more blurry."

Yet the subject denied that the affects associated with rainy days were the feelings she associated with hypnosis:

> Well, the things I think in connection with rainy days, I don't feel in connection with hypnosis. Rain always makes me a little depressed. It's on a rainy day when I enjoy having someone around to chat with or to talk to. I think I probably need the security of knowing somebody cares more on a rainy day than I do on a sunshiny one. A rainy day to me is a good time to stay home and read or listen to music with somebody that you care a lot about, that appreciates these things. It can be very depressing. I love to ride in the rain and I like to go to sleep at night with rain. But rain has always been to me, perhaps that God was unhappy with the way we were doing things here and He was crying.

At this point in the interview I showed the subject the "hypnosis" card and asked her for a story which she described as follows:

> I think probably these two men know each other, but they're not good friends and for some unknown reason the man in the chair has gotten the other fellow to the place where he would cooperate and he could put him into hypnosis, but I don't think the man on the couch is wanting to cooperate and it also looks like he's in pain. The man in the chair looks very mean and cruel. I think they're in a rather shabby room. There's probably *not much light* [italics added]. I have a feeling the man in the chair is going to do something, either physically that would be harmful or he may wait until the near future to do something to upset the other man very much. [How does the other man feel?] I don't think he—he doesn't want to cooperate. He knows this man is evil but for some unknown reason there's just not much he can do about it. It's like` he's trying to get out of a windstorm but he's just blowing in the breeze. [How do you mean?] He knows he's in the middle of this windstorm and he knows that for his own safety he should try and get out or get some place where he can take cover but for some reason he has just more or less given up. He is going this way and that way, not really putting forth much effort, but yet basically he knows he should but he doesn't want to, it's easier to give up.

Second Case Illustration

This subject was a young woman in her mid twenties who was readily hypnotized. She passed ten out of the twelve Stanford Scale items. When I asked her what it was like to be hypnotized she replied:

It's just relaxing. You don't worry about anything, you just relax like there was nothing else going on. Like you were asleep. It's all like a dream...I don't really think about anything. I listen to Dr. S's voice and I'm completely relaxed. I'm limp, my body is limp. I don't feel like moving, just staying like I am. There's no urge to move or anything, like I'm asleep. In fact, it's more relaxing than when I'm asleep...your hands go limp, feel heavier...it's better when I go to sleep because when I sleep, I toss and turn and [in trance] I just feel completely relaxed. [And when she was asked what it was like to come out of hypnosis.] I just wake up. It's really just like being asleep for awhile. I wake up, only I'm not drowsy after I wake up. I feel much better after I come out of it than I did before I go in ...I have what the doctor calls tension headaches and a lot of times I can come out of here and I can go under hypnosis and when I come out, the headache is gone and it doesn't bother me...I had a very bad one yesterday and it wasn't completely gone when I left. It was better.

This subject had the experience in the experimental session of not being able to remember a dream in the waking state but of being able to recall the dream in great detail once under hypnosis. She said, "As usual, I didn't remember the dream before I went under hypnosis but then I remembered it and it seems like I have some of the silliest dreams that I don't remember [sic]. If I have a dream about a certain problem or something, I always remember it the next day, but if I don't remember it, the dream seems silly." Thus, it would seem this patient consciously had an agreeable experience in hypnosis with some therapeutic benefit and was also able to see for herself how hypnosis can augment memory. To the TAT card, however, she told the following story:

The man to me looks dead on the couch. The man sitting up above him seems to think he can make him wake up or make him do something. He's very confident, it looks like the man sitting in the chair is very confident that he can make this man see and see whatever he is doing and the man on the couch just doesn't have any worries. He is dead, it is a fact. He just died naturally. He had a heart attack or something. The guy in the chair seems to think that he's an exception. This guy is going to wake up and see him even though he doesn't anyone else. He seems more like the mad scientist or something. [Does the man lying down know the other person?] No, he doesn't know him at all and this is a mad scientist or something. He is a doctor that has been called in. The man is in a strange place. He is in a strange house and I think he was called from a small village community out in the country. He thinks he has all these powers and he doesn't at all. [I see. What's the outcome?] The man in the chair is defeated and the man doesn't see him and people in the village town or country around seem to think he's a mad scientist. No one has anything to do with him. They leave him alone.

Third Case Illustration

The subject was a housewife in her early thirties. Like the other two she was readily hypnotized. She described hypnosis in these terms:

It wasn't like drifting off to sleep. I was noticing as I was going to sleep the other night...I am not completely relaxed...I just fall asleep and there's a period of not being relaxed, whereas in hypnosis I feel as if my whole body is relaxed...I feel extremely *passive*. I'm very willing to do whatever he says except in certain things where my logic interferes...that there is a general heaviness of the body in concentrating on what he is saying...not being able to move unless being given directions to do so. [She described bodily sensations.] As sort of a sinking feeling it's hard to describe. It's as if I were more relaxed than at any other time.

She was resistant to telling a story to the hypnosis card at the end of the fourth session. She said that she did not like the picture. When asked what was the matter with it she replied:

Well, it's the power of the hypnotist and the submission of the subject. Too much difference in the two. That's probably what a story would be about. [Could you make one up?] I've got to go get Billy [her son]. What time is it? [She is encouraged to tell a story.] Okay. This is a patient coming in and—for treatment—he's been rather uncooperative during the—without hypnosis—so hypnosis is being tried. I just never liked the expression on this man's face...he has a distorted expression.

At the end of the second session she told this story to the card:

I see this as the first person being very strong, especially because of the position of his hands and extreme passivity of the person lying down. Actually, it doesn't look like a doctor-patient relationship. It looks more like two men who are equal —not equals but where the man has complete control. I don't know what could lead up to this type of situation though...I really can't make a story up. I don't perceive it as a doctor-patient relationship, but I can't think of what would lead up to this situation.

Discussion

In the first illustration, the conscious reference to hypnotic darkness and the comparison of hypnosis to a rainy day are characterized as pleasant and agreeable, although the effort at denial wears thin. She must explicitly dissociate the depressive connotations of rain from the hypnotic experience itself. However, in the TAT story, darkness is now associated with a shabby room and the hypnotic experience is likened to a windstorm that forces her to surrender to its superior power.

In the second illustration, the agreeable hypnotic experience, which was better than sleep and helped alleviate a tension headache, is in marked contrast to the dead person who cannot be brought back to life by the mad scientist whose grandiosity is thwarted by the dead subject. In one of her "silly dreams" that she could recall in hypnosis the subject dreamed about a play she was in. It was a rehearsal at which the actors mouthed but could not speak their lines out loud. In one of her associations to the dream she recalled how the director had been angry with the cast about their performance. She was obediently fulfilling her hypnotic role by recalling a dream in hypnosis, but it was a dream in which she was depicting a form of passive resistance. This dream is brought to its logical conclusion in the TAT story, rather die than yield. Certainly, these extremes are indicative of much conflict and discomfort.

In the third illustration, the hypnotic passivity stressed by the subject was likened to a satisfying sense of relaxation; yet in both of her TAT stories she was in much open conflict about the issue of submission, and passivity in these stories is given a negative connotation.

In all three illustrations, the conscious experience of hypnosis as positive and agreeable is reversed in the TAT stories. For his idealization as hypnotist, the experimenter suffers demonization in the subject's unconscious. This kind of extreme shift in the experience of experimental subjects was all the more striking in view of the close proximity in time between the hypnotic state and the interview.

Of the twenty stories obtained from the subjects, only three could readily be rated as positive in content, while eleven were strikingly negative, and six could be described as ambivalent. The previous case illustrations provide three instances of negative stories.

In order to provide some basis for comparison, I selected thirteen subjects, all women, of approximately the same age and background, who had participated in a nonhypnotic experiment. The "hypnosis" card was administered as part of the TAT, and the TAT as part of a battery of psychodiagnostic tests.

Of these thirteen women, five gave stories that could be described as positive and only one gave an entirely negative story, while seven gave ambivalent stories. The following story was told by a young woman in her early twenties and is typical of the positive themes by this group of subjects:

The man lying down has known for some time he must have an operation for cancer. It will be a very painful operation. And due to the nature of it, it has been decided he will undergo the operation under hypnosis. In order to prepare him for this he must be hypnotized many times—to assure that the hypnotic trance during the operation will be successful. At the present time he is being hypnotized. He's not afraid, but he's having difficulty relaxing as shown by one knee slightly raised. The doctor talks to him gently and slowly he goes under. Being under hypnosis the doctor gives several suggestions such as he can raise his leg and hold it for several seconds, that pin pricks don't hurt, etc. When awakened, he finds it's really true. During each successive try he becomes more and more confident. The operation is a success and with hypnotic suggestion he suffers little pain. Successful.

The stories to the "hypnosis" card told by highly cooperative, experienced hypnotic subjects, when compared to those of this group of nonhypnotized subjects, tended to be extremely negative in content and were often accompanied by some negative affect and difficulty in telling the story. The hypnotic experience, far from relaxing them as they would like to believe, had stirred deeper feelings and attitudes, which were manifesting themselves in these TAT stories.

I would like to suggest that it is not enough to cite the existence of ambivalent attitudes toward hypnosis in order to explain the contrast between the conscious experience of hypnosis and the projected feelings about hypnosis presented by these subjects. Certainly in telling a TAT story it is possible for most people—and in particular nonpatients—to defend against the emergence of strongly negative feelings and attitudes. This could be expected when there is such an obvious relationship between the content of the card and an immediately preceding experience. Hardly more than fifteen minutes before the interview and story, the subject had been most successfully hypnotized. She was then handed a card, which all the subjects immediately interpreted as a scene depicting hypnosis. Thus far it was all conscious. Yet, a significant number of subjects chose to tell a bitterly negative story about hypnosis. I believe this is an instance where the message *is* the medium: these subjects wished to communicate something about their hypnotic experiences that they were unable to convey in any other way. In the interview, questions about hypnosis were too closely related to the hypnotic experience itself, and criticism would have been too direct and guilt-provoking. But with the slight yet significant distance offered by the TAT picture, a veritable outpouring of negative feeling was forthcoming. These women wished to convey in a way that could remain politely disguised that they were angered and disappointed about the hypnotic experience. They were as women scorned.

Obviously, there is a discrepancy between the conscious experience of hypnosis and the feelings and needs it awakened. The subject in a hypnotic experiment has a strong conscious wish to cooperate, but in addition I would like to suggest that the regressive impact of the hypnotic induction awakens an equally strong temptation to submit. I am not mainly referring to a sexual temptation but to the more infantile longing to be loved and cared for and to have one's troubles washed away. Once the experience is over and nothing of the kind has happened, frustration and anger are to be expected. But perhaps more important than this reaction itself, which is already part of a process of reconstitution, is the intense conflict and anxiety that must be present in the hypnotic state itself.

The position I am taking here is in contrast to one taken by Orne (1965a), who stressed that the "neutral experimental manner" of the hypnotist-investigator guarantees that no untoward emotional effects will occur. He stated that "the induction of hypnosis itself does not lead to untoward consequences if it is perceived as relatively episodic...if the subject does not expect to be changed in any way and does not perceive the procedure as directed personally toward him" (p. 228). I would like to suggest that the very nature of the hypnotic induction results in the subject experiencing the "procedure as directed personally toward him." Gill and Brenman (1961) have described at some length the intrinsic regressive influence of the hypnotic induction itself. They emphasized, in particular, the way in which an induction disrupts the individual's normal adaptation to inner and outer stimuli and temporarily transforms a relatively impersonal acquaintanceship into an intense relationship that invites transferences. Gill and Brenman described in terms quite at variance with Orne's cool assessment what the hypnotic subject experiences in an experiment:

> The hypnotic subject in any research usually has an air of expectation, if not eagerness, that goes far beyond his simple intellectual curiosity—an air which reflects the atmosphere created by the hypnotist. The unspoken communication on a surface level might be: "Abdicate your usual powers; put yourself in my hands and I will open some of your inner doors so that you may have a glimpse of what lies beyond them." On a deeper level, we have come to believe the appeal is to that universal infantile core which longs for such a wholesale abdication. There is from the beginning a kind of unconscious emotional barter. [p. 11].

What is "episodic" is the occasion, not its impact. Although Orne noted the fact that fewer than five percent of hypnotic subjects develop symptoms, this in itself is not the major issue (although it might be of interest to find out how many subjects would volunteer to be hypnotized if they were told in advance that they stood a one in twenty chance of developing symptoms). We would anticipate on the basis of clinical evidence that for every person who develops a symptom quite a few more are deeply troubled and try to master the disturbance in other ways. My main point would be that the hypnotist-experimenter must exercise much greater *continuing* concern for his hypnotized subject than to observe for and inquire into symptoms.

I recognize that the data I have presented do not constitute a formal study. Other explanations need to be considered. The subjects were all hypnotized by the same hypnotist. Could the results be due to his particular personality or way of inducing hypnosis? Or, could this type of ambivalence be characteristic of good hypnotic subjects? Would these subjects have told the same kind of story before they were hypnotized as they told immediately afterwards? These questions can only be answered empirically. To answer them affirmatively at this point would be to close the door on the need for a more careful examination of the effects of hypnosis on experimental subjects. It might very well be worthwhile to conduct a study in which various means for assessing conscious and unconscious attitudes toward hypnosis were studied before and after hypnosis. In particular, it might be useful to have an experimenter other than the hypnotist interview subjects and to administer projective tests which can then be interpreted and rated independently.

Once having stated this, I would like to conclude by pointing to another and quite different implication of these observations for the experimental use of hypnosis. The induction of hypnosis does not merely affect part functions such as perception and memory, but alters the state of the ego, the level of drive activation, the mode of thought and, most importantly, object relations. As such, it is an important tool for investigating these very important processes. Stross and I (Stross & Shevrin, 1969) reviewed a number of experimental studies including our own from this point of view. Because of its great potential value for research, it is all the more important that the regressive impact of hypnosis be kept in the forefront of the experimenter's mind so that the knowledge he seeks should not result in distress for those from whom the knowledge is obtained and for whose ultimate benefit the knowledge is intended.

Summary

In clinical work the dialectic between what is consciously and unconsciously desired constitutes an important counterpoint. Conscious fears turn out to be unconscious wishes. The therapist is always alert to this possibility and is oriented toward helping a patient uncover and understand this seemingly paradoxical relationship. But the hypnotized experimental subject is invited to cooperate in an impersonal scientific venture in which a highly demanding and regressive *personal* relationship will be introduced. Under these circumstances, the desire to cooperate, present in most intelligent laymen, may be strongly augmented by the unconscious temptation to submit. Conflict and anxiety may thus be intensified by the very act of hypnotizing subjects in experimental settings.

Data from clinical interviews conducted with hypnotized experimental subjects, including the "hypnosis" card of the TAT, suggest that subjects who consciously talk about the relaxed, comfortable aspect of hypnosis are prone to tell stories in which the Svengali aspects of the hypnotist are stressed. The muscular relaxation often described by hypnotized subjects may have the unconscious significance of submission both for the subjects and the hypnotist. It may be wise to assume that every hypnotized subject is in a state of conflict as compared with nonhypnotized subjects. Projective tests following experimental hypnotic sessions may reveal greater conflict and anxiety in hypnotized subjects as compared to nonhypnotized subjects. Conflict and anxiety may generate an angry, disappointed reaction, which is neither beneficial for the subject nor for the future of research on hypnosis.

Christina Maslach *is an Associate Professor of Psychology at the University of California at Berkeley. She received her Ph.D. from Stanford University in 1971. She has co-authored* Influencing Attitudes and Changing Behavior, *and co-edited* Experiencing Social Psychology. *Her research interests include the dynamics of the emotional "burn-out" syndrome, individuation processes and the role of unexplained arousal in emotion and psychopathology.*

Philip Zimbardo *is Professor of Psychology at Stanford University where he is director of the Social Psychology training program and Co-Director with Ernest R. Hilgard of the Hypnosis Research Center. His advanced degrees were received from Yale University (Ph.D., 1959), where he was trained in "hard" experimental psychology as well as in "soft" social-cognitive psychology. His experience with hypnosis began when he assisted Milton Rosenberg with his study of affective-cognitive changes in attitudes induced by way of hypnosis. He took formal training in hypnosis at the Morton Prince Clinic for Hypnotherapy and advanced training under Paul Sacerdote. He is himself a "good hypnotic subject," and believes that extensive training of hypnotizable subjects is necessary to achieve a condition of deep hypnosis. He has authored* Psychology and Life *(10th ed.),* Influencing Attitudes and Changing Behavior, Shyness: What it is, what to do about it, *and has edited* The Cognitive Control of Motivation.

Gary Marshall *is a Research Scientist at the Laboratory for the Study of Behavioral Medicine at Stanford University School of Medicine. He received his Ph.D. from Stanford University (1976), where he was associated with the Laboratory of Hypnosis Research. His research interests include compliance to medical regimens and psychosomatic relationships and mechanisms.*

Maslach, Zimbardo, *and* Marshall *present a series of experiments in which hypnosis is used as a tool for studying cognitive control over psychological and bodily functions. The first study deals with the cognitive control of skin temperature by hypnotic suggestions. They found that hypnotic subjects were able to produce different skin temperature in their two hands while waking control subjects could not. The next two studies deal with modifications of time perspective. In the first of these, an hypnotically induced state of "expanded present" (in which the sense of past and future were reduced) produced marked changes in affect and behavior. In the other study, changes in personal tempo (rate of time passage) were behaviorally indexed by a special time-based operant reinforcement schedule requiring continuous adjustment. The fourth experiment was an attempt to do a modified replication and extension of the 1962 Schachter and Singer study on the emotional labeling of unexplained drug-induced physiological arousal. It was found that hypnosis was effective in inducing arousal symptoms as well as amnesia for the cause of the arousal. However, this unexplained arousal always resulted in negative emotional states, regardless of whether the available cues in the situation were positive or negative.*

21

Hypnosis as a Means of Studying Cognitive and Behavioral Control

CHRISTINA MASLACH, PHILIP ZIMBARDO, AND GARY MARSHALL

If one cannot control oneself, the environment, and to some extent the reactions of others, one lives with the threat of being overwhelmed by a mind rebelling, a body refusing to obey, a world extracting exorbitant "protection money" to allow mere survival, and a community indifferent or hostile to one's needs. An individual's central pursuit—particularly in times of danger—is knowledge of those factors that control his or her destiny, and insight into how he or she can gain a measure of control over them.

Hypnosis is a process in which the issues of control become salient, since it enables new forms of control to be created and old forms to be suspended or destroyed. Various properties of hypnosis permit alterations in the attribution of causality such that, for example, a physically intense shock does not produce pain, sniffing ammonia does not cause an aversive withdrawal response, or a psychedelic experience is generated without drugs —all through appropriate verbal suggestions. The hypnotic subject comes to believe that he or she can control perception, learning, memory, physiology, and other processes, making them independent of extrinsic

These studies were financially supported by ONR research grant N00014-67-A-0112-0041 to Professor P. Zimbardo, supplemented by funds from NIMH grant 03859-09 to Professor E.R. Hilgard.

stimulus control. In addition, such people will accept as a valid representation of reality their inability to control functions normally subjugated to personal, inner domination, such as moving one's finger, opening one's eyelids, or saying one's own name. The fact that the mere utterance of a few words by another person could exert such powerful control over one's behavior is what has made hypnosis one of the most fascinating and frightening psychological phenomena for most people. However, looked at from a different perspective, if words can alter experience and modify behavior, if hypnosis somehow potentiates this effect, and if these words can be incorporated into auto-suggestion, then individuals have at their command a way to introduce control where they thought none was possible, or to countermand controls that apparently compel reactions.

As social psychologists, we are primarily interested in the basic questions underlying the control of human behavior across a number of theoretically and practically relevant situations. We see hypnosis as a valuable methodological tool for the social psychologist to use in manipulating levels of reality, converting hypothetical constructs into operationally sound independent variables, and in creating a psychological state that facilitates genuine involvement by the subject in experimental procedures. As students of hypnosis, we are also concerned with understanding the control mechanisms it engages, with the processes whereby words, thoughts, images, physiological reactions, and behavioral actions are translated from one action code to another, and with helping to demonstrate the validity of the changes induced through hypnosis. The research reported in this chapter represents a preliminary attempt to integrate our basic interest in cognitive and behavioral control processes with our interest in hypnosis as a method and as an independent area of inquiry.

Before describing each of these studies individually, we should mention briefly their common features of subject selection and formal hypnotic training. All subjects were undergraduates at Stanford University, recruited through the introductory psychology course. They participated in our training program and in the experiments voluntarily, though paid for each hour of participation. All subjects were selected from among the high scorers on a modified version of the Harvard Group Scale of Hypnotic Susceptibility (HGSHS, Shor & Orne, 1962), and randomly assigned to training or no-training groups. The no-training groups for some of the studies were randomly divided into a role-playing group instructed to simulate hypnosis and a control group given the same task instructions without hypnosis or simulation suggestions. Both males and females were used in every group in each of the four studies, their data being combined in the absence of any statistically significant differences between them.

Our training approach utilizes group inductions in small groups that vary from eight persons in the initial sessions to two in the final ones. We have found this group training to be more efficient than individual sessions and also more effective. Subjects usually find it more reassuring not to be "one on one" with the hypnotist, especially early in training, and the hypnotist is able to bring to bear additional social pressures upon the occasional subjects who are recalcitrant, slow, or not confident in their ability to experience hypnosis. The training is permissive in orientation, stressing the subject's choice to follow each suggestion, and directed toward getting the subject to achieve self-hypnosis. It also attempts to establish a personal relationship of trust and mutual respect between hypnotist and subject. A variety of induction techniques was used over the course of training (during which time each subject was exposed to each of the three present authors in his/her capacity as hypnotist). However, common to both the verbal and nonverbal techniques we used was the development of a state of very deep relaxation. Specific training was given in motoric control, perceptual control, fantasy experience, amnesia, posthypnotic suggestions, and analgesia. Underlying these phenomena was the ability, encouraged through training, to concentrate, to dissociate, and to produce vivid images. All subjects reported that it was only after at least several hours of training that they began to believe something special was happening, that they were indeed "hypnotized." Every one of the subjects was able to alter ischemic pain tolerance significantly more in hypnosis than in a waking, motivated state. On an additional criterion test, all of the subjects successfully carried out a posthypnotic suggestion and appeared to have amnesia for it. The entire procedure took about ten to fifteen hours per subject.

Hypnotic Control of Peripheral Skin Temperature

Maintenance of a relatively constant level of body temperature is a vital physiological function. It is so efficient and automatic that we become aware of the process only when pathological internal conditions cause us to react with fever or chills or when changes in environmental conditions markedly alter the skin temperature of our limbs. To what extent can such a basic regulatory function be brought under volitional control?

In 1938, the Russian scientist A.R. Luria performed an interesting experiment that bears directly upon this question. He had been studying the remarkable mental feats of a man who appeared to have eidetic imagery. Apparently, his subject not only had "photographic memory," but could induce such vivid visual images that they exerted a profound influence on his behavior. When he was instructed to modify the skin temperature in his hands, he was able to make one hand hotter than it had been by two degrees, while the other became colder by one-and-a-half degrees. These changes were attributed by the subject to the "reality" of his visual images: "I saw myself put my right hand on a hot stove...Oi, was it hot!

So, naturally, the temperature of my hand increased. But I was holding a piece of ice in my left hand. I could see it there and began to squeeze it. And, of course, my hand got colder" (Luria, 1968, pp. 140–41). Is such a phenomenon replicable with "normal" individuals not born with the remarkably developed eidetic ability of this man? We were led to believe so on the basis of converging research findings in the areas of visceral learning, cognitive control of motivation, and hypnosis.

At that time, Miller and his associates (1969) were investigating the possibility that responses of the glands and viscera could be controlled through operant conditioning procedures. An intriguing implication of this work was that any discriminable response that is emitted by any part of the body can be learned if its occurrence is followed by reinforcement. This idea had been extended in the work of Zimbardo (1969) and his colleagues which demonstrated experimentally that biological drives, as well as social motives, may be brought under the control of cognitive variables such as choice and justification, even in the absence of external reinforcers.

It appeared to us that hypnosis: (a) is a state in which the effects of cognitive processes on bodily functioning are amplified; (b) is a state which enables the subject to perceive the locus of causality for mind and body control as more internally centered and volitional; (c) is often accompanied by a heightened sense of visual imagery; and (d) can lead to intensive concentration and elimination of distractions. These reasons, combined with evidence that voluntary control over autonomic nervous functions could be achieved with hypnosis (Paterson, et al., 1967) led us to predict that well trained hypnotic subjects could gain control over regulation of their own skin temperature without either external reinforcement or even external feedback. While there had been some attempts to control temperature through hypnosis or other methods (see Green, Green, & Walter, 1970; and Barber, 1970a), they had often lacked adequate controls and tended to focus only on unidirectional changes.

Our own study (Maslach, Marshall, & Zimbardo, 1972) was exploratory in nature and attempted to demonstrate that hypnotic subjects would be able to achieve simultaneous alteration of skin temperature in opposite directions in their two hands, while waking control subjects would not. The bilateral difference of one hand getting hotter than normal while the other gets colder was chosen in order to rule out any simple notion of general activation or prior learning, and to control for any naturally occurring changes in skin temperature. We also attempted to rule out other alternative explanations of changes in skin temperature by keeping environmental conditions constant and by minimizing overt skeletal responses on the part of the subjects.

METHOD

Three of our trained hypnotic subjects were individually tested in the Laboratory of Dermatology Research at the Stanford Medical Center. The ambient temperature in this room was automatically regulated to maintain a constant level. Ten thermocouples of copper constantin were taped to identical sites on the ventral surface of the two hands and forearms of the subjects. Both room and skin temperatures were continuously monitored by a Honeywell recording system. The subjects lay on a bed with their arms resting comfortably at their sides and with open palms extended upward in exactly the same position. This posture was maintained throughout the session, and there was no overt body movement.

The instructions, which were delivered over an intercom, began with approximately ten minutes of hypnotic induction. After the subjects were deeply hypnotized (according to their self-reports), they were asked to focus attention on their hands. They were then told to make an arbitrarily selected hand hotter, and the other colder, than normal. They were also given suggestions of several images that could be useful in producing this effect, and were encouraged to generate personal imagery and commands that might be necessary to achieve the desired result. The subject lay in silence for the duration of the testing session (which averaged about ten minutes). The final instruction was to normalize the temperature in both hands by returning it to the initial baseline level.

Each of the subjects participated in two or three such sessions. In addition, one of the subjects (Zimbardo) completed two sessions utilizing autohypnosis. Communication between him and the experimenter occurred only to demarcate the various procedural stages being experienced.

Six waking control subjects also participated in each of two experimental sessions. The procedure was identical to that employed with the hypnotic subjects, except that they were not given any prior hypnotic training or the hypnotic induction during the experiment. Both hypnotic and control subjects were aware that the purpose of the research was to assess whether skin temperature could be altered through verbal instructions and imagery.

RESULTS

All of the hypnotic subjects demonstrated the ability to significantly alter localized skin temperature. Large differences (as much as 4° C.) between identical skin sites on opposite hands appeared within two minutes of the verbal suggestion, were maintained for the entire testing period, and then were rapidly eliminated upon the suggestion to normalize skin temperature. Temperature decreases in the "cold" hand were generally much larger than the increase in the "hot" hand, the largest decrease being 7° C., while the largest increase was 2° C. In contrast, none of the waking control subjects was able to achieve such significant bilateral changes in hand temperature. Any temperature change that they did exhibit was usually in the same direction for both hands (rather than in opposite directions), thus yielding close to a zero score for bilateral change (see Figure 21.1). The difference between these control scores and the consistently large bilateral changes of the hypnotic subjects is highly significant ($t = 14.27$, $df = 7$, $p < .001$). All of the hand thermocouples reflected these successful bilateral changes, while the forearm thermocouples showed no temperature changes at all, thus indicating the specificity of this hypnotic control process. Also, the performance of the hypnotic subjects showed an improvement from the first to the second session; this was not true of the control subjects.

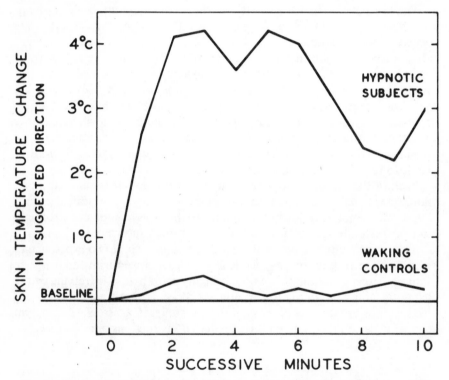

FIGURE 21.1.   *Mean algebraic sum of bilateral skin temperature differences. ("Successful" directional changes in each hand were weighted positively, while changes which were opposite to the suggested direction were weighted negatively).*

Both the hypnotic and waking control subjects reported trying hard to meet the experimental demand. Several of the control subjects even believed that they had successfully completed the task although, as noted earlier, their largest bilateral difference was very slight. All subjects also reported that they had generated assorted imagery to help them produce changes in their skin temperature. Some of the imagery involved realistic experiences, such as having one hand in a bucket of ice water while the other was under a heat lamp. Other imagery had a more symbolic or fantasy quality: the "hot" hand was getting red with anger over something the "cold" hand did; and the "cold" hand was getting white with fear over this angry reaction. In addition, subjects also used imageless "commands" given independently to each hand (i.e., "you become hot, you become cold").

In the initial pretest, verbal feedback was given to the subjects when they had succeeded in producing the bilateral difference in temperature. Such feedback had an unexpected negative effect, resulting in the "loss" of the attained difference, and was subsequently eliminated in the experimental sessions. It may be that the intensive concentration required to achieve the unusual performance demanded in this study was disturbed by having to attend to and process the informational input from the experimenter. In a sense, the feedback, though supportive, operated as a distractor to attenuate the obtained differences in skin temperature. The ability of hypnotic subjects to successfully perform this task without feedback is particularly evident in the data of the subject using auto-hypnosis, who was able to produce bilateral differences in skin temperature without the aid of any external demands, feedback, or extrinsic sources of reinforcement.

The bilateral control of skin temperature which was demonstrated in this study was subsequently replicated using biofeedback techniques (Roberts, et al., 1975). To us, the significance of research in this area is in understanding how human beings "naturally" learn to induce ulcers, tachycardia, excessive and uncontrolled sweating, and other forms of psychosomatic illness. Earlier work had suggested that the intervention and modification of such reactions follow principles of operant conditioning. Our work adds the possibility that the sources of reinforcement in both producing and changing psychosomatic symptomatology may be cognitive in nature. Therapeutic control may thus be best achieved by combining the precision of reinforcement contingencies with the power of a more pervasive cognitive approach to deal with such mind-body interactions.

Hypnotic Modification of Time Perspective: Expanding the Present

There are few constructs of human imagination that have a more pervasive, yet unappreciated, effect upon our behavior than time. We have come to conceive time as having an external, physical reality independent of its origin and maintenance in the human mind. While we press time into our service as a constant or a dependent variable measuring and recording events of interest, we ignore its more fundamental role in our lives.

The experience of time makes it possible for us to establish the concepts of causality, consistency, and history out of essentially discrete, isolated, transient, and even random occurrences. Cultural traditions and our sense of individual identity can exist only by implicitly accepting assumptions about temporal continuity. Virtually every social institution that exists to regulate individual behavior does so by forcing a reevaluation of the present within the confines imposed by the conceptual language of the past and future.

It is through the process of socialization that time perspective is created, in order to make communal life possible, and through the emergence of memory that individuals can cope with the challenge of change. Each human being is thereby transformed from an impulsive, ego-centered creature driven by the urgency of biological needs into a more analytical, socially centered citizen able to tolerate frustration and to delay gratification. The actor becomes a reactor, living for the moment becomes living for a purpose, and being is parceled into has been and will be. The past and the future which begin as only cognitive modes of experience, in contrast to the sensory, empirical foundation of present experience, become the reality to which the present is subjugated (see Ricks, Umbarger, & Mack, 1964 for similar arguments).

Precisely because time is such a central part of our thinking, feeling, and acting, we can only investigate its functioning and impact by disrupting its usual operation. We can theorize about time as an independent variable, but to establish its controlling influence upon behavior, it is necessary to systematically interfere with the temporal process. This methodological strategy is, of course, common to the study of all psychological phenomena which function so efficiently as to go unnoticed by the behaving organism or the observer. Delaying auditory feedback to study the effects of hearing on speech, and distorting the visual field with prisms to study visual-motor coordination, are examples of the effective use of this approach.

The following investigation of time (Zimbardo, Marshall, & Maslach, 1971) focused upon altering the perspective of present time by expanding it. How would a person's behavior change if he or she were to alter the perceived relationship between past, present, and future by having the present expand while past and future diminished? Concern with this aspect of "time sense" is in part derived from a model of deindividuation (Zimbardo, 1970). This model attempts to delineate those systems of social and personal control that create a sense of individual identity and self-awareness. It is through these mechanisms that a person's behavior is constrained to make it normal, rational, and acceptable. Behavior is liberated from these constraints and allowed to become more irrational, impulsive, chaotic, and uncontrollable as attention to social and self evaluation is minimized. Controls imposed by guilt, shame, fear, reasoned analysis, past experience, commitment, obligation, responsibility, and liability are shattered once past and future become insignificant. The individual, "living for the moment," should become more sensitive to sensory stimulation and more responsive to arousal cues. Behavior once initiated should be more difficult to terminate, as long as the instigating stimulus remains. It appears that this kind of disruption of temporal perspective occurs in some people under the influence of psychedelic drugs. It is often a goal of marathon encounter groups and a co-product of states of ecstasy induced by music, dances, and activities associated with "primitive" ceremonial rites.

Following a provocative lead in the work of Aaronson (1968a, 1968b), we decided to induce an expanded present state through hypnosis. Aaronson's intensive work with several selected subjects appeared to indicate that euphoria accompanied induction of an expanded present orientation via hypnotic suggestion, while a schizophrenic-like state followed removal of the present time sense. The validity of these changes unfortunately rests upon such questionable evidence as inferences from paintings made by the subjects and clinical judgments of only a few individuals without benefit of controlled comparisons. Our study, then, was an exploratory attempt to use hypnosis as a technique for modifying temporal perspective (specifically, expanding the present), while observing the effects of this induction across a range of tasks in experimental and control subjects.

METHOD

The research design compared the responses of twelve trained hypnotic subjects given the suggestion to "allow the present to expand and the past and future to become distanced and insignificant" with those of eighteen other subjects distributed across three control conditions. In two of them, the same expanded present, time distortion instruction was given via standardized tape recording. Half of these subjects were simulators, told to imagine how hypnotized subjects would respond and then to act as if they were hypnotized throughout the study. The waking controls merely received the time distortion instruction without any mention of hypnosis. The fourth group was a normal-time control, asked to think of their own conception of time and to describe it in an appropriate metaphor (as the other subjects did before being given the present-expanded treatment).

Subjects were tested in pairs within the same condition, although on most tasks they were isolated in separate cubicles. The hypnotized subjects were given a five-minute relaxation induction at the start of the experimental session while the simulators were given the same period of time to prepare themselves to be "good" hypnotic simulators.

The first task involved writing projective stories in response to two TAT pictures, one before and the other after the time distortion manipulation. Five minutes were allowed for each of the two stories; the order of the two

TAT pictures was counterbalanced across subjects in each group. It was predicted that subjects experiencing an expanded present would reveal before/after changes in the language and thematic content of their stories, such as more present tense verbs, greater reference to present events, less emphasis on future goals or antecedent conditions, etc.

A reminder to maintain a sense of the expanded present was repeated before the second and third experimental tasks (except, of course, for the normal-time controls). The second task was designed to thrust the subjects into an unexpected situation that could be humorous or repulsive. Told simply to listen to a tape recording, all subjects heard a five-minute tape of an abortive radio commercial for an old movie, *The Caddie,* by a former comedy team. After committing several bloopers, the comedians begin to criticize, taunt, and curse each other. They become increasingly obscene and vulgar, to the obvious amusement of the recording engineers who could be heard laughing in the background. The overt reactions of the subjects while listening to this tape were recorded by two judges behind a one-way mirror, and their self-reported reactions elicited on a questionnaire. It was predicted that subjects experiencing an expanded present would react more strongly during the recording since they would be able to overcome the normative prohibitions against openly enjoying such material in the sterile confines of a research laboratory.

The final task was designed to get the subjects more directly involved in a sensory experience through physical action. They were told they had five minutes to make something out of a large two-pound mound of clay which was on the floor in front of the room. The subjects left their cubicles and proceeded to work either independently or together as they chose. A stack of paper towels was available near the moist, sticky clay so that subjects could clean their hands, although this was not explicitly suggested. At the end of five minutes, the experimenter entered the room and told the subjects to finish up and return to their cubicles to complete a questionnaire about their reactions to this noncognitive task. Judges observed what the subjects made with the clay, as well as how they handled it, and their reactions to being soiled with it. When the first group of hypnotized, expanded-present subjects continued to play with the clay, ignoring the request to return to their cubicles, this unanticipated source of behavioral variability was systematically recorded for all subjects (within another five-minute maximum interval).

RESULTS

Overview. Verbal instructions to expand the present appeared to have had a profound effect upon the behavior of hypnotized subjects, who may have been better able than control subjects to incorporate this suggestion into their temporal perspective. Their language changed toward more frequent use of present tense verbs and more references to present events. They were more likely to laugh aloud at funny events and to continue to be physically preoccupied in a sensory experience. They were less concerned with their appearance and had more difficulty answering questions pertaining to memories of their reactions on prior experimental tasks. Some even got involved in the sensation of writing a questionnaire response and were indifferent to answering the test questions in a socially appropriate manner.

A few of these findings, however, also occurred among subjects simulating hypnosis. Nevertheless, the use of nonreactive response measures, relatively insusceptible to experimental demand features or to subject expectation, allowed us to distinguish valid from spurious manifestations of an altered temporal perspective. No sex differences were found on any measures and thus, only combined analyses are presented.

Temporal language. The TAT pictures selected for this research rather clearly reflected time themes, since one showed an old woman and a young woman, and the other a farm with a farmer planting crops while a pregnant woman gazed upon the scene. The stories written by the subjects were each scored independently by two "blind" raters, with the average of their ratings being used for analysis. The primary categories analyzed were changes in the use of present tense verbs relative to total use of verbs, and changes in references to events that could be distinguished as taking place in the past, present, or future.

TABLE 21.1. Mean changes in TAT responses before to after induction of time distortion.

Treatment	N	Mean percentage present tense verbs to total verbs	Mean % total reference to:		
			Past	Present	Future
Present expanded					
Hypnosis	12	+ 8.5	0.0	+ 3.3	− 3.2
Simulation	6	+ 12.4	− 10.1	+ 11.3	− 1.3
Control	6	− 14.6	− 1.2	− 8.3	+ 9.6
Normal Time	6	− 20.7	+ 5.9	− 8.8	+ 2.9

These data, presented in Table 21.1, indicate that the hypnotic group changed their time perspective in accordance with an expanded-present orientation. They used more present tense verbs, more references to present events, fewer to future and no more than previously to the past. However, simulators "read" what was the appropriate way for hypnotized subjects to react and outdid the hypnosis group! They used an even greater percentage of present tense verbs, references to the present, and evidenced a marked reduction in concern for past events. These changes cannot be attributed simply to the present-expanded instructions since they were absent, or indeed opposite, in the waking controls given the same induction. These controls and the normal-time controls showed a sharp reduction in their use of present tense and events. These two groups differ significantly from the hypnotized and simulator groups in their use of present tense verbs ($p <$ .02, $t = 2.54$, $df = 28$) and differ nearly significantly in their use of present events ($p < .10$). The differences between hypnotized and simulating subjects were not statistically significant.

Perhaps even more revealing of the degree to which the simulators perceived what was expected of them is their consensus across the various measures. Every one of them increased their percentage of present tense verbs while fifty-eight percent of the hypnotic group, thirty-three percent of the neutrals, and only sixteen percent of the normal-time group did so. The simulators thus differed significantly from each of the other three groups beyond the .01 level (by separate ratio analyses). In like manner, five of six simulators decreased their total references to past events and increased their references to present events. Only one third of the hypnosis subjects decreased their references to past events and a half of them increased their concern for present events. On the first measure, the hypnosis group differs from the simulators at the .01 level ($z = 3.52$) while on the second, the difference is at the .05 level ($z = 2.24$). The simulators also differ significantly from the other two groups on these measures, but the latter do not differ from the hypnosis group. None of the differences in references to the future were significant.

If this were our only dependent measure, we would be forced to conclude that the obtained effects of changes in language and thinking in response to the present-expanded induction are confounded with consciously controlled expectations about how an hypnotic subject should react to such a suggestion. However, on each of the other dependent measures to be reported next, the changes noted between groups were statistically significant.

Affective reactions. When subjects were exposed to the humorous, obscene, taped material, it was assumed that normative influences operating in the laboratory situation would prevent them from reacting strongly to it. However, if they had internalized an expanded-present orientation, they then should have been less concerned about how they might be evaluated for their reaction and more able to experience and openly respond to the immediately present situation. This reasoning received support when we compare the extent to which subjects in the different treatments responded to the comedy material by either smiling or laughing outright. It is evident from the data in Table 21.2 that the pattern of laughing or simply smiling distinguished the hypnosis group from each of the others.

TABLE 21.2. Mean number of smiles or laughs observed in response to obscene comedy material.

Treatment	N	Smiles	Laughs
Present expanded			
Hypnosis	12	3.0	3.0
Simulation	6	3.7	.2
Control	6	5.2	1.0
Normal time	6	6.7	.7

These subjects were equally likely to react by openly laughing as by smiling. The simulators smiled as often as the hypnotic group, but they were not observed to react at the more intense level by laughing. Each of the other two groups behaved in a more socially appropriate manner, smiling more frequently, but laughing infrequently. In fact, they smiled significantly more than the hypnosis or simulator groups ($p < .025$, $F = 4.61$, $df = 3/26$). The greater frequency of laughter of the hypnosis group, however, only approaches statistical significance. An analysis of subjects in each group who gave an especially hearty (or "belly") laugh indicated that the only three who did were in the hypnosis group.

This quantitive data is less convincing than some of our qualitative data of the basic changes in time sense and responsiveness to "stimulus immediacy" achieved in many of the hypnotic subjects. Only hypnotized, present-expanded subjects expressed the emotional mood of the taped material by themselves using obscenities and jokes in their questionnaire answers. For example:

1....."Jerry L. is so f...d up that I got sick and tired of listening to that bastard laugh. At least M. has some class but L. has no class because he's always out to lunch. I think they should lose Jerry L. in a f...g water hazard. Because he is a hazard to humor!!!!"

2."At first I was rather disgusted, listening to those stupid f...s, but when they started screwing up, it blew my nose."

3."How in the hell did you get hold of it! I never believed "stars" could swear as much as I do."

4. "Yuk, Yuk and I rate this film X."

A more typical view of the nature of the unusual reactions generated by this alteration of time can be witnessed in the report of one of the hypnotic subjects, written a minute after having heard the tape recording:

I don't remember much about it now—all I remember is that it was funny and that I'd seen the movie the men were talking about. But actually I don't really care too much about the tape at all right now. I hate writing this. So I'm stopping. Right now. I feel like laughing. But I'd better stop writing this first. Right now.

Another hypnotic subject in this expanded present condition wrote:

Sometimes it was funny—slips of tongue funny obscene—O.K. But sometimes, just two jokes—the situations described weren't funny—not nice. O.K. tape, not great. Not a funny start—sad.

Sensory involvement. The purpose for having the subjects play with the clay was to provide an occasion for differences in the experience of time perspective to emerge which might not have been apparent on the other, more cognitive tasks. The most compelling evidence for the greater involvement of the hypnotic subjects in the here and now and their lack of concern with appearance comes from two rather subtle, nonobvious measures of change in temporal perspective, and also from the subjects' own accounts of the experience.

If the subjects were truly engaged in the ongoing activity of deriving pleasure from manipulating the clay for its own sake (as we would predict for those experiencing an expanded present), then our test situation should elicit two characteristic behaviors. First, when the experimenter said to stop and return to their cubicles to complete the next questionnaire, those who were "stuck in the clay" should have ignored his command once he left and it became a past event. Second, the moist clay (which was chosen because it stuck to the hands) ought to be less disturbing to those with an expanded-present orientation since they would continue to enjoy its sensory qualities and not worry about whether to get cleaned up before going on to the next task or how they looked to observers. The data clearly support both of these predictions in demonstrating significant differences in these behaviors between the hypnotic subjects and all others in three comparison groups.

For the first measure, a calculation was made of the mean total time each subject continued to play with the clay after being told to stop. The normal-time subjects tended to complete the task shortly before the allotted five minutes. Both the expanded-present simulator and waking control groups finished up their figures in about a minute after being told to. In sharp contrast, the hypnotic, expanded-present subjects continued to play with the clay for nearly 250 seconds more. This value would have been much higher were it not for imposing an arbitrary ceiling of 300 seconds, which five of the subjects reached before being forced to stop. Whether the unit for statistical analysis is the pair of subjects sharing the clay or the individual subject, the results are significant since the shortest time taken by any of the hypnotic subjects was at least sixty seconds longer than the longest continuation recorded for any subject in the other conditions. The significant overall effect ($p < .0001$, $F = 24.63$, $df = 3/26$) is primarily due to the large difference between the hypnotic group and each of the others ($p < .001$).

Observers recorded the subjects' concern with the mess or being dirty by noting whether they used the readily available paper towels, wiped off their hands on the desk top or on their clothing, or spent time looking at their hands. Two thirds of the hypnotic group gave no evidence at all of any concern for the fact that their hands were coated with the residue of the clay. This is compared with the almost universal reaction of all other subjects to clean up immediately after completing the task. The proportion of subjects revealing such concern was significantly less for the hypnotic, present-expanded group than the others ($p < .001$, $z = 3.52$).

In addition to these observed behavioral differences in hand wiping or attempts to clean the clay off, hypnotized present-expanded subjects also described their reaction to it much more positively than did the other subjects. Some examples of typical questionnaire reactions for these hypnotized present-expanded subjects are:

1. Felt like I was working in the dirt, like the farmer in the picture [the TAT scene]. . . felt the soil under my fingernails, drying out and becoming like shaving talc.

2. [The thing I like *most* about working with the clay is] getting my hands dirty. . .all the clay I've got all over my hands now.

3. [The thing I like *least* about working with the clay is] The fact that it stuck to my hands and now I am a clayman; My dirty hands afterwards, but that's O.K.

The control subjects across all three conditions, when asked to react to their experience of working with the clay, were rather distressed by the residue on their hands. For example:

1. My hands are caked with clay, and I got some on my shirt. It's a drag for my hands to feel like this.

2. I've got all this goddam clay on my hands.

3. It got my hands dirty as hell.

4. It got clay under my fingernails and that's probably the most uncomfortable feeling I've had in two days.

5. It leaves your hands filthy.

The final indication of just how profound an effect was created in some subjects by incorporating a present-expanded time perspective into their experimental interaction with the environment is evident in their evaluations of the clay task. For one subject, "The clay was very soft and moist, it felt nice to dig my fingers into it. When I was working with it, the shape just kind of happened. There was very little effort involved. It just kind of worked itself out." Another subject, who really enjoyed working with the clay, was still very much in tune with her immediately present environment when she wrote:

I didn't want to stop. But now I don't care because I'm writing this. I've got clay on my hands. Now I'll move to question one.

I remember feeling very, very good. But that was clay and now this is pencil and paper. It's amazing how a pencil can make marks on a paper that other people can read and understand...I can't really think about working with the clay. These questions interrupt my thought process. That makes me angry. But I don't care because it's all fantastically amazing. I can hear the blood in my ears...Now I wonder why that is. No more room. Back in the folder.

None of the control subjects gave a response that was remotely comparable to these by hypnotized subjects presumably experiencing a present-expanded temporal perspective.

In subsequent studies, the experience of an expanded present has been related to changes in creativity and learning. Hoy (1973) found that subjects who had scored high on a measure of openness to experience (Fitzgerald, 1966) responded to an hypnotic induction of an expanded present with far more creative test responses than did subjects with a normal time orientation. In contrast, subjects who had scored low on openness to experience reacted to the expanded-present induction with very uncreative test responses. Maslach and Garber (1976) found that hypnotic subjects experiencing an expanded-present temporal perspective behaved differently than unhypnotized and normal-time perspective subjects across a series of cognitive learning tasks. They were less successful on problems with a specific (future) end goal, but were also less frustrated and upset if the goal was not reached. On the other hand, they excelled at tasks which required an ongoing (present) behavioral process.

What is most surprising about the results of these exploratory investigations into alteration of temporal perspective is that such profound effects upon thinking, feeling, and acting could result from mere verbal suggestion to recreate one's perceived boundaries between the present and past and future. On the one hand, it is curious that well established time-bound controls over behavior could be so readily suspended, and on the other, it is not at all unexpected that an individual's style of interacting with the environment and representation of it will undergo fundamental changes as "becoming," "here-now," and "eventing" assume new psychological significance. As the present loses its transience by borrowing time from pastness and futurity, the conceptualized awareness of "nowness" apparently changes learned frames of reference for both "objective" stimulus reception and "appropriate" response output.

Hypnotic Modification of Time Perspective: Changing Tempo

In addition to a subjective conceptualization of past, present, and future, we also develop a time sense of personal tempo. This involves both the estimation of the rate at which events are (or should be) occurring and affective reactions to different rates of stimulus input (Ornstein, 1970). The learned correspondence between our subjective sense of tempo and objective clock time can be disrupted by the physiological and psychological changes that accompany some types of mental illness, emotional arousal, body temperature variations, and drug-induced reactions (Cohen, 1967). However, it is possible to modify tempo more directly within a controlled experimental paradigm by means of hypnosis.

Aldous Huxley's fictional description in his book *Island* (1962) extols the potential benefits of distorting time through hypnotic suggestion.

> And it's in very deep trance—and only in very deep trance—that a person can be taught how to distort time...One starts by learning how to experience twenty seconds as ten minutes, a minute as half an hour. In deep trance, it's really very easy. You listen to the teacher's suggestions and you sit there quietly for a long, long time. Two full hours—you'd be ready to take your oath on it. When you've been brought back, you look at your watch. Your experience of two hours was telescoped into exactly four minutes of clock time...For example...here's a mathematical problem. In your normal state it might take you the best part of half an hour to solve. But now you distort time to the point where one minute is subjectively the equivalent of thirty minutes. Then you set to work on the problem. Thirty subjective minutes later it's solved. But thirty subjective minutes are one clock minute. (pp. 210–11).

Cooper and Erickson (1950) attempted to manipulate tempo in much the manner described by Huxley. Hypnotic subjects were told that they would have a certain number of minutes of "special" time in which to execute some task. In actual clock time, they were given only several seconds, but many of the subjects reported experiencing the appropriate amount of time, indicating that those periods of time were filled at a phenomenological level with many activities. However, only subjective data were used, and studies that have measured performance increments have generally yielded negative findings (Barber & Calverley, 1964e; Casey, 1966; Edmonston & Erbeck, 1967). The inherent difficulty of demonstrating that the subject is really experiencing time distortion by using performance increments is pointed up by Fischer (1967), who notes that it is possible to have "increased data content [with] *no* proportional increase in data processing and/or data reduction" (p. 451).

Before Aldous Huxley's vision of an improved educational technology based upon controlled modification of tempo can be realized, it is necessary to demonstrate that more than subjective experience is being changed by such procedures. If time is perceived as existing in a new relationship to the occurrence of certain events, then behavioral measures that are sensitive to *rate of responding* should reveal this altered perception. If a reinforcing stimulus event is contingent upon the rate at which a given response is emitted, then altering the time base should affect frequency of responding. In a situation where two responses per second are required to generate a given stimulus event, then if perception of the time were altered, frequency of response should change correspondingly. If one second of objective, or clock time were subjectively experienced as two seconds, for example, then the individual should emit twice as many responses as previously in attempting to maintain the same stimulus event.

In our own study (Zimbardo, et al., 1973), we attempted to alter personal tempo and measure the behavioral consequences with precise, objective techniques. The experience of tempo was systematically varied (speeded up or slowed down) by time-distorting instructions administered to hypnotic subjects and controls. If effective, such a manipulation should generate asynchronicity between clock time and the subjective passage of time. This asynchronous responding was assessed by means of a specially designed operant conditioning and recording apparatus in which the rate of emission of a single external response (key pressing) is used as an objective index of a subjective state.

METHOD

Thirty-six subjects were each randomly assigned to one of three treatments: hypnosis, hypnotic simulation, and waking nonhypnotized control. During the experiment, the testing procedure was identical for all subjects; an experimenter who was unaware of the experimental treatment delivered the standardized instruction to the subject, who sat isolated in an acoustic chamber. A second experimenter induced a state of hypnotic relaxation in the hypnosis group and instructed the simulator subjects to try their best to simulate the reactions of hypnotic subjects, to behave as if they were really hypnotized throughout the study. The waking controls were told only to relax for a period of time equivalent to that given to subjects in the other two treatments.

Subjects were taught to press a telegraph key at different rates in order to illuminate various target lights in an array of ten colored lights. In the first of five two-minute trials, a comfortable operant rate of responding was established, and it became obvious to the subject that the sequential onset and offset of the lights was controlled by response rate. The functional relationship between response rate and change in the light stimulus was determined by relay circuits in the apparatus and can be characterized as a "conjugate" schedule of reinforcement (Lindsley, 1957). This schedule creates a dynamic interplay between behavior and a selected environmental event— the stimulus event changing continually as response rate varies. Pressing the key at a faster or slower rate than that required to illuminate the target stimulus light turned on one of the other lights in the array. It was only by empirically determining the rate appropriate to reach a particular target and then by maintaining that rate consistently that a subject could satisfy the task demand, "to keep light X illuminated as long as possible."

Of the remaining four trials, the first and third were baseline and the second and fourth were experimental. On one baseline trial, each subject was instructed to keep the red light illuminated, which required three presses per second. On the other baseline trial a faster rate of six responses per second was required to maintain the illumination of a blue light. Interspersed between these baseline trials and the experimental trials were the instructions to modify personal tempo. After being told about the difference between clock and subjective time, all subjects were instructed to alter their perception of tempo, by experiencing time as slowing down—"so that a second will seem like a minute, and a minute will seem like an hour"—, and also by experiencing time as speeding up. Between these two tempo modification instructions, subjects were told to normalize their experience of time. The order in which these two tempo instructions (slower and faster) were given to each subject was counterbalanced across conditions and did not have a significant effect upon the task behavior. A cumulative recorder provided an ongoing display of the subject's response rate and indicated whether responding was on or off target. In addition, an event recorder and electronic timers indicated to the experimenter the sequence and duration of the stimulus light levels being activated by variations in rate of responding.

The reinforcer for maintaining a particular target light level is probably the sense of competence a subject feels in being able to satisfy the experimenter's demand to do so. Knowledge of being off-target should serve as a negative reinforcer and guide efforts to modify responding to achieve the positive consequences of on-target performance. Such performance depends primarily upon two variables: a stable, veridical sense of personal tempo and the environmental feedback necessary for monitoring the effects of different response rates. Our tempo instructions, in conjunction with hypnosis, were designed to alter the first of these, and variation in feedback was introduced to alter the second. Within our repeated-measurements factorial design, the array of lights remained functional during the experimental periods for half the subjects (objective feedback), and they were extinguished during the experimental periods for the other subjects in each of the three conditions (no feedback). Those in the no-feedback condition had to rely entirely on their memory of the previously appropriate baseline rates that they were asked to reproduce in the experimental periods, while objective feedback subjects had direct access to the external information provided by the illuminated array.

RESULTS

Only the hypnotic subjects were reliably able to translate the verbal suggestion of asynchronicity between clock time and personal time into behavioral "reality." This is shown in comparisons of mean rates of response, percentage of total time on and off target, mean deviation in individual response rates from baseline to experimental response levels, and even in the more subtle measures of variability—in displacement of the response distribution.

During baseline trials, there were no reliable differences on any measure between groups. An analysis of variance performed on the mean deviation in operant rate from baseline to experimental responding (Table 21.3) demonstrates a highly significant treatment effect ($p < .001$), and also a feedback effect ($p < .001$). Deviation from target level (combined across feedback conditions) significantly differentiated between the hypnotized

TABLE 21.3. Mean deviations in key-pressing rate from baseline performance.

Treatment	N	No Feedback	Objective Feedback	Combined
Hypnotized	12	.534	.223	.38*
Simulators	12	.299	.004	.15 +
Waking controls	12	.023	.043	.03
		$p < .025$	$p < .005$	$p < .001$

*$p < .01$ for comparison with simulators: $p < .001$ for comparison with waking controls
+ Comparison with waking controls not significant.

subjects and those in the other two conditions. The marked deviations from target levels in the no-feedback condition were attenuated by providing external feedback. However, this feedback served primarily to differentiate between the hypnotized and simulating subjects. It totally eliminated the asynchrony in responding among the simulators, but the reduced asynchrony of the hypnotized subjects was still substantially different from the other two controls ($p < .005$). Any volitional effect of responding to the tempo instructions as if they were direct suggestions to vary response rate thus appears limited to the no-feedback condition. When confronted with information about the consequences of one's behavior, the controls responded with appropriate synchrony; the hypnotized subjects did not. Neither direction of tempo modification (slower or faster) nor target light response level (low or high) was significant.

Perhaps the most convincing data of the extent to which hypnotic subjects altered their sense of personal tempo come from analyses of the pattern of off-target response variability. This measure of variability is the frequency of recorded shifts from one stimulus level to another. The underlying variability in response rate could lead to shifts either around the target level or to shifts around off-target levels. For example, if the target level were six, shifts to levels five or seven or from them back to six would represent around-target shifts. Off-target shifts would be between seven and higher levels (faster tempo) and between five and lower levels (slower tempo). There are no overall differences in total variation between treatments. However, there are significant differences between the hypnotized subjects and controls in the specific pattern of variability ($p < .001$, by Scheffé multiple t-test comparisons). The response distribution for the hypnotized subjects was displaced to off-target stimulus levels (in the experimentally appropriate direction), while that of the controls stabilized around the target levels. Thus, in the no-feedback condition in which response variability was greatest, subtracting each subject's frequency of off-target shifts from baseline trials to experimental trials resulted in a group mean of $+31.0$ for the hypnotized condition, but only $+1.5$ for simulators and -5.0 for nonhypnotized waking controls.

To underscore the critical role of hypnosis in creating a cognitive state receptive to this time distortion manipulation, a subgroup of the simulating subjects was subsequently given our program of hypnotic training and retested with the hypnotic induction. Four of the five subjects showed sizable changes in the suggested direction. While there were no differences in their standard baseline performance between earlier simulating trials and these hypnosis trials, there were significant experimental trial differences due to the greater effectiveness of the time-distorting instructions when they were hypnotized (mean deviation in rate: $+.51$ for level 6, $p < .05$; and $+.38$ for level 3, $p < .10$).

Interviews and the questionnaire responses of the hypnotic subjects indicated that they indeed tried to satisfy the experimenter's demand to keep the target light illuminated, but found they were unable to do so effectively. Their modified sense of personal tempo became a stable reference against which they judged environmental changes. As a result, they believed that the experimenters were covertly altering the apparatus to make their task more difficult (a situational error). By contrast, in an earlier study (Craik & Sarbin, 1963) in which clock time had been covertly altered by the researchers, subjects attributed discrepancies between clock and personal time to their own lack of ability in time estimation (a dispositional error).

It seems to us that the combination provided by the power of hypnotic intervention in experience and the objective precision of the operant conditioning methodology has been effective in demonstrating the validity of inducing changes in tempo. A next step would be to extend this approach to responses that are of more practical significance to the individual. We believe that a wide range of behaviors and physiological reactions which are under temporal control, such as drug addiction, depression, emotional arousal, and hypertension, may be modified by altering one's sense of personal tempo.

Hypnotic Induction of Unexplained Arousal

The experimental investigation of emotion was given considerable impetus by the research of Schachter and Singer (1962) who specified the two interacting components of emotional states as physiological arousal and an appropriate cognitive explanation of this arousal. They argued that in the absence of an explanation for an arousal state, subjects will search the immediate environment for cognitive cues that can be used to make sense of and to label the arousal. Thus, starting with a common level of physiological activation, one subject will experience "anger" and another "euphoria," depending upon elements of the situation in which the activation occurs. These investigators used injections of epinephrine to induce the symptoms of arousal, and then either did or did not inform the subjects of this cause for their arousal. In general, informed but aroused subjects did not react emotionally to the experimental situation, nor did unaroused subjects given placebo injections. However, according to the authors, uninformed arousal subjects tended to label their state as "happy" after exposure to a confederate who had acted euphoric, but as "angry" when the confederate acted angry.

This experiment represented an important conceptual change from previous theoretical positions, all of which postulated a direct causal relationship between physiological arousal and cognitions about emotional states. In contrast, Schachter and Singer proposed that the factors of physiological arousal and emotional cognition functioned independently and interacted with each other to produce a true emotion. In addition to this interactionist model, Schachter and Singer made a second significant contribution by demonstrating the importance of situational determinants of emotion. The theoretical impact of this study cannot be overestimated, foreshadowing as it did the rise of cognitive analysis in social psychology. This general line of thinking played an important role in the current development of attribution theory, as a result of its emphasis on the role of cogitions in defining reality. Furthermore, it has inspired several new lines of theory and research about a variety of internal feeling states.

CRITIQUE OF THE SCHACHTER AND SINGER STUDY

Despite its ingenious paradigm and its theoretical contributions, the Schachter and Singer study cannot be accepted uncritically. Indeed, a close analysis of the methodology and the results seriously questions the authors' conclusions and interpretations. Although Schachter and Singer's conclusion is a provocative one, it is in fact *not* supported by the evidence. The initial data analysis reveals *no* significant difference in self-reported emotion between any of the unexplained arousal groups and the placebo control groups. Although the authors point to the predicted overall pattern of means within each emotion condition, this pattern is not very dramatic in size since the difference in emotion between any of the groups amounts to less than one single unit on a nine-point scale. The theory also requires absolute qualitative differences in emotion as well as relative differences in emotion ratings between the experimental groups of the euphoria and anger conditions. However, the means of *all* conditions reflect a feeling of "slight happiness," regardless of the emotional cues provided by the euphoric and angry confederates.

The behavioral data are not much more convincing. The comparison between unexplained arousal groups and placebo controls reaches statistical significance only in the anger condition, not in the euphoria one. Even though this pattern of "anger units" is in line with the authors' theory, the size of this response is certainly not. The low mean score for subjects with unexplained arousal could conceivably represent merely one instance of verbal agreement with the angry confederate's position over nearly twenty minutes of interaction. Somewhat stronger behavioral differences emerged after a sizable number of subjects was discarded in an internal analysis.

There are a number of flaws in the design of the Schachter and Singer study which further preclude an uncritical acceptance of their conclusions. One of the major difficulties centers on the use of epinephrine to produce physiological arousal, since this drug has different effects for different people. As a result, there was no experimental control of the onset, intensity, or duration of the arousal. An additional problem involves the probability of subjects attributing their arousal to the injection, in spite of the experimenter's statement that it was only a vitamin supplement without side effects.

Further methodological difficulties involve the dependent measures, which were either confounded, ambiguous, or absent. Because there was no assessment of the emotional cognition factor, it is not known how subjects actually perceived the confederate's mood—as "euphoria" or "anger" or some other emotion. For the factor of physiological arousal, neither of the two measures (pulse rate and self-report at end of session) provides an accurate assessment of the ongoing course of the arousal. The measures of the subject's emotional response included a self-report of emotional feeling and a series of behavioral ratings made by hidden observers. For the first measure, subjects were asked how "good or happy" they felt, and also how "irritated, angry, or annoyed" they were. Rather than presenting these scores separately, the experimenters subtracted each subject's "anger" rating from his "happiness" rating to yield an index of emotional feeling. The meaning of such scores is unclear, since the same score could result from totally different emotional states.

For the behavioral measure, different ratings were used for the euphoria and anger conditions, and so no direct comparison of the two is possible. Secondly, various behaviors were arbitrarily assigned different weights (e.g., flying paper airplanes was + 3; disagreeing with the angry confederate was −2). In the euphoria condition, each weight was then multiplied by an estimate of the amount of time spent by the subject in that activity (although, inexplicably, this was not done in the anger condition). For both conditions, these weights were then summed into a single, overall index whose meaning is not at all clear.

FAILURE OF AN EXACT REPLICATION

Given the theoretical significance of the Schachter and Singer study, one would expect that more methodologically rigorous replications had already been done in the decade since it appeared. Surprisingly, only one attempt has been made to do so. Marshall and Zimbardo (1979, in press) tested eighty male subjects in an exact replication of the basic Schachter and Singer procedure for the euphoria condition. Epinephrine injections were used to create a state of physiologicial arousal, and the confederate followed the euphoria routine outlined in the original study. However, Marshall and Zimbardo found *no* empirical support for Schachter and Singer's conclusions. Subjects who had received the standard (.5cc) epinephrine injection, along with an "inadequate" explanation of its side effects, did not differ from placebo controls in either emotional affect or behavior. To determine whether the predicted differences would emerge if the arousal were stronger, Marshall and Zimbardo increased the epinephrine dosage level for some of the subjects. These subjects did experience a significant change in intensity of physiological arousal. However, they reported a *negative* emotional state, rather than the positive "euphoria" predicted by Schachter and Singer. This self-report of negative affect occurred even when subjects behaved in a positive, sociable manner with the euphoric confederate.

CURRENT STUDY

The lack of supportive evidence for the Schachter and Singer theory, plus the findings of negative emotions in the Marshall and Zimbardo (1979, in press) experiment, led Maslach (1979, in press) to reconsider the presumed "plasticity" of unexplained arousal. The idea that unexplained arousal is an affectively neutral state seems intuitively correct only for someone who is experiencing such arousal for the first time (such as a child), and who must look to other people and/or the situation to make sense of this strange and puzzling experience. The concept does not apply as well to people who have had numerous experiences pairing arousal with emotional labels and with appropriate arousal instigators. If they were to feel aroused without knowing why, it would not only be an unusual experience but also a disturbing or even frightening one, since this uncertainty would be felt as a loss of personal control over their own internal states. Indeed, the concept of unexplained arousal is very close to the clinical definition of "free-floating anxiety" which is always characterized by negative emotional affect. Therefore, unexplained arousal may generate a *biased,* rather than an unbiased, scanning of evidence and alternative hypotheses. That is, the search for an appropriate cognitive label for the arousal could be biased by a retrieval algorithm that selects primarily from available negative instances. In contrast to the Schachter and Singer hypothesis that unexplained arousal can just as easily be labeled "euphoria" as "anger," this alternative view predicts that people will always use negative emotional cognitions to label their unexplained arousal.

The current research (Maslach, 1979, in press) was designed to test this alternative hypothesis and to investigate further the process of a cognitive search for the causal antecedents of unexplained arousal. The study involved a modified replication of the original Schachter and Singer experiment, in which procedural elements were designed to correct some of the original methodological problems. Primary among these modifications was that a state of arousal was produced by an hypnotic induction, rather than by a drug injection.

METHOD

Forty-eight subjects (twenty-five males and twenty-three females) participated in one of two experiments which followed the same procedural format. The testing session was divided into two parts. The purpose of Part I was to establish a verbally conditioned arousal response to a specific cue. Subjects were given the hypnotic suggestion that they would experience four physiological symptoms (increased breathing, increased heart rate, moist palms, sinking feeling in stomach) when they saw the word "start." In addition, posthypnotic amnesia for the source of this arousal was suggested. To determine if this arousal response involved substantial physiological changes, continuous recordings were made of the subjects' heart rate (HR) and galvanic skin response (GSR). Subjects were also asked to describe their mood state both before and after the arousal response, using the Nowlis Mood-Adjective Checklist (1963). In the second part of the experiment this arousal response was either elicited or not in the presence of a same-sex confederate who was behaving happily or angrily. While doing a learning task, subjects saw either the arousal cue word ("start") or a neutral one. The confederate went through a prearranged series of behaviors (e.g., talking to the subject, working with various test materials) while expressing either happy or angry emotions. Hidden observers recorded the subject's verbal and nonverbal responses, as well as the amount of time that the subject looked at the confederate. At the end of this emotional modeling period, the confederate left the room and the subject completed two questionnaires which assessed the efficacy of the experimental manipulations and the extent to which the subject's arousal was interpreted in terms of the emotion displayed by the confederate.

The first experiment consisted of a two x two factorial design with the addition of two unhypnotized control groups. There were two levels of arousal —aroused (hypnotized + arousal cue) and unaroused (hypnotized + no arousal cue). There were two levels of confederate emotion—happy and angry. Subjects who were trained in hypnosis were randomly assigned to these four conditions, with six subjects per cell. Subjects who were not trained in hypnosis were randomly assigned to the two unhypnotized groups (not hypnotized + arousal cue)—six were in the happy condition and six in the angry condition. The experimental conditions of most interest are the two aroused groups, in which the subjects were both physiologically aroused and exposed to a happy or angry model. The arousal was produced by a combination of two factors: training in hypnosis and a conditioned arousal stimulus. The unaroused and unhypnotized conditions lacked either one or the other of these two factors and thus represent two different types of control groups.

Because the results of this first experiment did not replicate those found by Schachter and Singer for the "euphoria" treatment, two additional experimental conditions were tested to discover the basis for these differing outcomes. In both conditions, additional subjects were given the arousal treatment (hypnotized + arousal cue) and were exposed only to the display of happy emotion by the confederate. One of these additional groups (informed arousal) remained aware of the basis for their arousal since they were not given any suggestion for posthypnotic amnesia. In fact, they were told that they would remember having been informed of the causal relationship between their arousal and the prior conditioning experience. This group parallels that of the informed treatment in the Schachter and Singer study. The other group (simplified arousal) was given only two physiological symptoms for the hypnotically induced arousal state (heart beating faster, respiration increasing), rather than the four symptoms used in the first experiment. It was conceivable that the other two symptoms (sinking feeling in the stomach, moist hands), though found in reactions to epinephrine, too strongly suggested a negative arousal state. This may have been the reason for the negative emotions experienced by aroused subjects in the happy condition, rather than the predicted biasing effect of unexplained arousal. The simplified arousal condition was designed to ensure a more purely neutral arousal than may have existed in the first study. As before, subjects trained in hypnosis were randomly assigned to these two conditions, with six subjects per group.

RESULTS

Presentation of the results will be organized around six issues: (1) effectiveness of the physiological arousal manipulation; (2) evaluation of the confederate's mood; (3) behavioral differences between treatments; (4) experienced emotional differences between treatments; (5) attribution of arousal and emotions; and (6) comparison of the informed and simplified arousal control groups with the arousal groups of the first experiment.

Physiological Arousal. In the first part of the experiment, each subject's heart rate (HR) and galvanic skin response (GSR) were recorded continuously. The critical period of measurement occurred when the subject was exposed to four successive visual stimuli, the last of which was the cue for the arousal state. Each stimulus was shown for five seconds, followed by a twenty-five second period of darkness. There was a striking difference in response between the hypnotized and unhypnotized conditions. For each subject, the HR record was divided into five second intervals, and the highest HR for each interval was calculated. There were six such intervals following each stimulus, and their individual scores were combined into a total mean score for each stimulus. A repeated-measures analysis of variance for the highest HR scores showed that there was a very significant main effect of visual stimuli, such that the highest HR following the arousal cue was significantly higher ($F = 32.88$, $df = 1/34$, $p < .001$) than the highest HR following the neutral stimuli (which did not differ from each other). However, there was a significant interaction between stimuli and hypnosis condition ($F = 5.35$, $df = 1/34$, $p < .05$). The F-tests for the two hypnosis conditions reveal that this main effect was due entirely to the hypnotized subjects ($F = 37.17$, $df = 1/34$, $p < .001$). The unhypnotized subjects did not show a significant increase in highest HR in response to the arousal cue ($F = 2.19$, *ns*).

A similar pattern of arousal was reflected in the total number of GSRs following each stimulus. There was a significantly greater number of GSRs following the arousal cue than the neutral stimuli ($F = 20.87$, $df = 1/34$, $p < .001$). However, there was also a significant interaction between stimuli and hypnosis condition ($F = 6.04$, $df = 1/34$, $p < .025$), and the F-tests for the two hypnosis conditions show that the main effect was due entirely to the hypnotized subjects ($F = 26.51$, $df = 1/34$, $p < .001$), and not to the unhypnotized group ($F = .40$, *ns*).

Two mood-adjective checklists were completed by each subject, one before the arousal stimulus and one after. For purposes of analysis, the adjectives on this list were divided a priori into four groups—positive (e.g., affectionate, lighthearted, playful); negative (e.g., angry, blue, clutched-up); active (e.g., concentrating, energetic, vigorous); and passive (e.g., calm, quiet, engaged in thought). Changes in mood responses (as a function of physiological arousal) were assessed by computing separate mean change scores for each of these four adjective categories. The change scores for the hypnotized subjects indicate the marked shift in emotional state that resulted from this arousal. Their mood became significantly more negative ($t = 7.22$, $df = 23$, $p < .001$), less positive ($t = 7.68$, $df = 23$, $p < .001$), and less passive ($t = 7.68$, $df = 23$, $p < .001$). There was no significant change in their index of active mood. In contrast, the unhypnotized subjects showed no changes on the negative, active, or passive mood indices, although there was a tendency for them to report less positive feelings ($t = 2.07$, $df = 11$, $p < .10$). Overall, the hypnotized subjects showed a more extreme shift on a composite of these four indices of mood than did the unhypnotized subjects ($F = 17.14$, $df = 1/34$, $p < .001$).

Because hypnotic subjects responded physiologically to the arousal cue in the acoustic sound chamber, it was assumed that they would respond similarly when they again saw this stimulus during the learning task. Unfortunately, we could not directly assess the validity of this assumption because telemetry equipment was not available to us at the time of the study, and so it was impossible to record the subjects' physiological responses while they were freely interacting with the confederate. Nevertheless, two indirect measures of arousal do provide support for our reasoning.

The first of these measures was the subject's recall performance on the learning task. Since the second of the two lists either did or did not contain the arousal cue, it was predicted that differences in subsequent arousal states might interfere with the recall process. Presumably, subjects who were now experiencing high levels of arousal would have greater difficulty in concentrating on the task and thoroughly searching their memory. They should be more likely to restrict their retrieval to high probability items and make fewer guesses. For each subject, the number of correct words, as well as errors of omission and of commission, on both word lists was computed. Although there was no between-group difference in overall recall accuracy on either list (about sixty percent accuracy), subjects in the arousal groups made significantly fewer errors of commission ($\overline{X} = 0.7$) than did the unaroused and unhypnotized groups ($\overline{X} = 1.7$) on the second learning list ($t = 2.54$, $df = 34$, $p < .02$). It appears that subjects performing under the distracting influence of intense arousal were less likely to search their memory for words that might have been on the list and thus were less likely to produce commission errors by recalling "new" words. Rather, they seemed to write down only the words they had stored in readily accessible memory and to then stop, leading to relatively more errors of omission than of commission.

The second indirect measure of arousal was part of the final questionnaire. Subjects were given a list of eight physiological symptoms and asked to indicate which (if any) they were now experiencing. The percentage of subjects who checked each symptom was calculated for each of the experimental conditions. From 92-100 percent of the subjects in the aroused conditions reported experiencing each of the four suggested symptoms, while only 26-52 percent of the unaroused and unhypnotized subjects reported having even a single one of the symptoms. The between-group differences between these proportions for each of the four symptoms computed separately are all beyond the .02 level of significance.

Perception of Confederate. At the end of the experimental session, subjects completed a questionnaire which assessed their perception of the confederate. Three bipolar scale items of seven alternatives focused on the confederate's emotional behavior (sad-happy, angry-peaceful, friendly-unfriendly); the mean score for these items served as a check on the confederate manipulation. On this index the data were, without any exception, in opposite directions for subjects exposed to the happy versus the angry confederate. Subjects in the happy condition evaluated the confederate's mood as significantly more positive ($\overline{X} = +1.2$) than the neutral midpoint of zero ($t = 4.94$, $df = 17$, $p < .001$). In contrast, the treatment mean for subjects in the angry condition ($\overline{X} = -1.5$) was significantly more negative than zero ($t = 7.45$, $df = 17$, $p < .001$). The difference between the two confederate conditions is highly significant ($F = 83.16$, $df = 1/30$, $p < .001$), which further testifies to the success of this manipulation.

Overt Emotional Behavior. Measures of subjects' behavior were coded by two judges (inter-rater reliability was at least $+.80$) who observed each subject during the four-minute emotional modeling period. For each of the four minutes, the judges coded the subject's verbal and nonverbal responses. Some of these responses were sociable ones (i.e., smiling, nodding, agreeing with the confederate) while others were not (i.e., disagreeing, ignoring, frowning). The overt behavior of the subjects varied as a function of the confederate's mood, but seemed unaffected by experienced arousal. Subjects in the presence of a happy confederate exhibited a significantly higher amount of positive social behaviors than did subjects with the angry confederate. This was true for both verbal behaviors ($F = 20.97$, $df = 1/30$, $p < .001$) and nonverbal behaviors ($F = 44.80$, $df = 1/30$, $p < .001$).

Reported Emotional Experience. At the end of the experimental session, each subject completed a questionnaire which was a self-report of the subject's current emotional state and perceived physiological arousal. Two scale items tapping extent of anger and happiness being experienced were adopted from Schachter and Singer. To the items, "How irritated, angry or annoyed would you say you feel at present?" and "How good or happy would you say you feel at present?" subjects responded on five-point scales with these alternatives: $0 =$ not at all, $1 =$ a little, $2 =$ quite, $3 =$ very, and

4 = extremely. To obtain a broader portrait of the emotional state of each subject, eight additional bipolar scales with seven response alternatives were used. Subjects checked one box from $+3$ to 0 to -3 to indicate how they felt "at this moment": tense-relaxed, confident-apprehensive, anxious-calm, open-closed, happy-sad, irritated-not irritated, serene-annoyed, angry-peaceful. These responses were analyzed separately, and when it was found that they each showed the same pattern of results, they were combined into a single index of emotional response ranging from extremely negative to extremely positive.

Although the confederate's mood had a demonstrable effect on the subjects' overt behavior, it did not exert the expected influence on their reported emotional state. Rather, their experienced emotion was apparently independent of both their own overt behavior and of the confederate's mood. Reported emotion was a function solely of whether subjects were or were not experiencing unexplained arousal. Two of the questionnaire items on emotion were the identical ones used by Schachter and Singer, and, following their procedure, an analysis was made of the difference scores (happy-angry). There was a significant main effect of arousal ($F = 5.35$, $df = 2/30$, $p < .025$), and a comparison of means revealed that this was due to the more negative scores of the aroused condition ($p < .005$). Analyses of each of the happy and the angry ratings separately provide even stronger evidence of the difference in emotional reactions between the aroused subjects and the other subjects without arousal. Again, there was a highly significant main effect of arousal condition for both the happy rating ($F = 17.92$, $df = 2/30$, $p < .001$) and also for the angry rating ($F = 6.50$, $df = 2/30$, $p < .005$). A comparison of the means showed that the aroused subjects were significantly more angry and less happy than both the unaroused subjects (p at least $< .005$) and the unhypnotized subjects (p at least $< .05$). It should be noted that there were no differences in the pattern of emotional labeling between subjects exposed to the happy and to the angry confederate. The absence of an interaction effect indicates the lack of social or emotional influence of the models on the experienced emotion of the subjects.

The mean ratings on the eight-scale index of emotional response are shown in Figure 21.2. Again, there was a significant main effect of arousal condition ($F = 15.94$, $df = 2/30$, $p < .001$), and a comparison of means revealed that the aroused groups reported a significantly more negative emotional state ($p < .001$) than both the unaroused and the unhypnotized groups (which did not differ from each other). This pattern of results was also found for each of the eight emotion scales analyzed separately. On the overall index, the aroused conditions reported negative emotions that were significantly different from the neutral midpoint of zero ($t = 6.47$, $df = 11$, $p < .001$). While the unhypnotized groups were neutral in their emotions

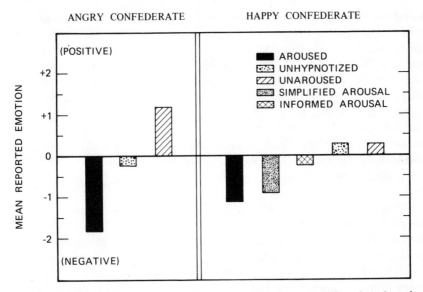

FIGURE 21.2.   *Self-reported emotion (mean self-ratings on an 8-scale index of emotion).*

(their mean score did not differ significantly from zero), the unaroused subjects rated themselves as feeling a positive emotional state ($t = 2.32$, $df = 11, p < .05$). Apparently, the unaroused subjects were responding appropriately to the posthypnotic suggestion that they would feel relaxed and good when they came out of hypnosis, while the unhypnotized subjects were unable to respond similarly to that same suggestion. The positive feelings of the unaroused group offer a dramatic comparison level for the negative reaction reported by the aroused subjects (despite the same posthypnotic suggestion to feel good, and identical prior hypnotic training).

Attribution of Causality. On the final questionnaire, subjects were asked if they knew why they felt as they did and, if so, to state the reason. These responses were scored by judges who were blind to both the purpose of the experiment and the condition of the subject. The aroused subjects always reported reasons for a *negative* emotional state, regardless of the mood expressed by the confederate. Some subjects said they were nervous about performing well on the experimental tests, others said they were feeling tense about upcoming final exams, while still others labeled their arousal as irritation generated by the confederate's "talkativeness." Most of these reasons were rated as similar to those given by the angry confederate, but as dissimilar to those of the happy confederate, resulting in a significant difference between the two aroused groups ($t = 7.04$, $df = 6$, $p < .001$). In only a single instance did a subject explicitly state that the confederate's mood determined his own: "The other guy was really hassled—it rubbed off."

It is possible that the posthypnotic suggestion had the effect of blocking any search for an explanation of the experienced arousal, rather than merely preventing the "correct" explanation. This does not seem to be the case, since sixty-seven percent of the aroused subjects stated that they knew why they felt as they did. However, there was not one case in which the stated reason for the arousal was related to the experimentally induced cause of the arousal. Fifty percent of the unaroused group stated they knew the cause of their current feelings, while sixty-seven percent of the unhypnotized group did likewise—a nonsignificant difference in the likelihood of generating some explanation for their experienced state.

Comparison of Arousal Control Groups. To clarify alternative interpretations of these findings, two additional control groups (informed arousal and simplified arousal) were tested in the happy confederate condition. The former group was not given the suggestion of amnesia for the cause of their arousal, while the latter was given an arousal suggestion limited to only two general physiological symptoms, rather than the four given originally.

Both of these control groups displayed the same basic pattern of physiological arousal as the happy aroused subjects in the first experiment. They showed the same increase in HR, similar changes on the mood-adjective checklist, and the same pattern of recall errors. On the self-report of physiological symptoms, all of the informed arousal subjects reported experiencing the four suggested arousal symptoms. The simplified arousal subjects reported increased breathing and heart rate, as expected. Surprisingly, however, all of them also reported sweaty palms and two thirds reported a sinking feeling in the stomach. Even though they had not received any suggestion for these last two symptoms, they spontaneously generated them as correlates of changes in respiration and heart rate. The perception of the confederate by the two control groups was the same as that of the happy aroused group—they all rated the confederate's mood as positive. They also showed the same pattern of positive social behaviors (both verbal and nonverbal) in their interaction with the confederate.

Overall, then, the two arousal control groups were similar to the happy aroused group in terms of physiological arousal, veridical perception of the confederate, and overt behavior. However, they differed from each other in experienced emotional state. The informed arousal subjects reported a neutral set of feelings (which did not differ from the zero midpoint on the eight-scale index of emotion), and they stated that the reason for their arousal was the hypnotic suggestion. In contrast, the simplified arousal group reported the same negative emotion as the happy aroused group and gave the same type of causal explanations. Their emotion rating was significantly more negative than the neutral midpoint ($t = 4.15$, $df = 5$,

$p < .01$) on the eight-scale index of emotion (see Figure 21.2). In other words, despite a posthypnotic suggestion of only the two most basic physiological concomitants of arousal, these subjects, who were unaware of the "appropriate" explanation for their arousal, did *not* label their emotion as "happy" in accordance with the cognitions provided by the confederate's behavior. Rather, they experienced a negative emotional state.

DISCUSSION

The current study was designed as a modified replication and extension of Schachter and Singer's (1962) two-factor theory of emotion. The necessary conditions of strong physiological arousal, lack of an explanation for that arousal, and varied emotional-situational cognitions were all achieved within an experimental setting that controlled for many of the methodological problems of the original study. However, the results reveal a remarkably consistent and coherent pattern of emotional response (especially noteworthy given the small sample size) which is at variance with the interaction pattern predicted by Schachter and Singer. In all cases, subjects with unexplained arousal reported negative emotions, irrespective of the confederate's mood. This finding seems to contradict Schachter and Singer's assumption that unexplained physiological arousal is a neutral, energizing variable which does not contribute directly to the qualitative labeling of the emotion. Whereas Schachter and Singer postulated that the lack of explanation for arousal would motivate people to search in an unbiased way for an appropriate cognition, the present study suggests that it not only motivates but also biases the search, since it tints perception of that arousal with negative affect. The fact that Marshall and Zimbardo (1979, in press) also found self-reports of negative affect among subjects who lacked an explanation for their strong physiological arousal (and focused their attention on that discordant state) lends additional support to this alternative view.

Unexplained Arousal and Emotional Pathology. A state of unexplained physiological arousal may be a rather rare occurrence in everyday life, and thus may not be an appropriate paradigm for studying common emotional experiences. However, the negative emotional bias associated with unexplained arousal suggests that it may be a useful paradigm for studying emotional pathology and madness, particularly if it is viewed as just one of a class of anomalous personal and social experiences. Such anomalous reactions are anxiety-provoking because they represent a threat to self-control. Events without causes do not make sense; internal events without apparent, immediate explanations are irrational. People are sometimes willing to employ rather tenuous causal relationships to account for such occurrences, even to the point of limiting such explanations to labels or nominal antecedents, as in "it's my nerves." But for most people, on most occasions, the experience of an anomalous event generates some search for suitable causal linkages.

A rational, information-processing model might assume that people engage in a scientific (unbiased) search, in which they seek out and consider all possible evidence in an objective way. However, it may be more correct to assume that they are biased towards certain types of explanations as a result of their past history of reinforcement for particular classes of explanation or ways of thinking about new experiences. Thus, some people may learn to seek explanations based on health or physical functioning (e.g. "It's probably due to a virus going around"). Others may bias their search towards social sources of explanations (e.g., "My boss must be upsetting me"). Once acceptable causal links are established to account for a particular internal reaction, it may be assumed that the generic properties of the linkage will, in the future, make some types of explanation more available. For example, where reaction X is effectively linked to bodily processes or health issues, future comparable reactions are also more likely to be explained by reference to other specific instances of biological functioning, such as flu, fatigue, tension, metabolic deficiencies, etc.—even when they are not the true causes. An extreme bias towards locating causes within bodily processes may be an underlying basis for such pathological responses as hypochondria or psychosomatic symptoms.

Future research on this process of searching for causal explanations would provide a clearer (if more complex) picture of how people come to understand their internal responses. Furthermore, the study of this process would benefit from an experimental analysis that focused on children's reactions to novel or anomalous events. This line of research might also illuminate the process by which particular forms of emotional pathology develop as a consequence of biased explanations for unexplained arousal. We are currently conducting exploratory research on this biasing process, again using hypnosis as a methodological tool to create unexplained arousal in subjects who are programmed to search for a likely cause within only one class of explanations: body, people, environment, the past, spiritual forces. The various explanations generated by these subjects are indeed limited to the suggested generic category and, in some cases, result in reactions that observers judge to be "irrational" (Zimbardo & Maslach, 1979). This research suggests that emotional pathology may not be an impairment of one's cognitive abilities, as is often assumed, but a normal cognitive process used to explain an unusual state or event.

Conclusions

The studies reported in this chapter represent a preliminary attempt to use hypnosis as a means to explore a variety of basic psychological phenomena. We have been interested in the general problem of specifying the conditions that affect the degree of actual and perceived control an individual has over internal as well as external environments. Although the experiments reported here have apparently little in common, in effect they represent several aspects of the broad problem of how psychology can be better used to increase the individual's potential for control and to minimize the degree to which he or she is subject to the constraints of physiology, the dictates of time, and the flux of emotions.

We are encouraged enough by the overall pattern of significant findings to recommend that psychologists consider hypnosis as a valuable addition to their set of research tools. By doing so, they may gain in being better able to study certain complex problems such as those described here, as well as more traditional ones related to memory and learning. In turn, the study of hypnosis will also gain by having new research-oriented blood infused into its substance. We anticipate that the next decade will see this reciprocal relationship flourish to the mutual benefit of both hypnosis and psychology.

VI

Anticipations for Future Research

Biographical information for Professor Fromm may be found on page 80.

In 1970 Fromm conducted a survey on future trends in hypnosis research which she reported on in the first edition of this book in 1972. Questionnaires were sent to all members of the three professional hypnosis societies in this country who might conceivably be engaged in hypnosis research. Recipients were asked to describe their hypnosis research in progress, research planned for future execution, promising studies being planned by other investigators, and important additional research they would like to see done either by themselves or by others. A content analysis of the responses was made and frequencies were tallied. The result of this analysis was taken as a reflection of areas of attention and coming interest. Tentative predictions about future research trends were offered on the basis of these findings.

In 1978 Fromm conducted a survey of hypnosis research publications appearing in major scientific and professional journals during the six years subsequent to the publication of the first edition of this book. In light of the results of the former questionnaire and on the basis of the new literature survey, she assesses and modifies her previous predictions and offers new predictions about future trends in hypnosis research. These 1978 additions to the original text appear in italics; a new table is added.

22

Quo Vadis Hypnosis?
Predictions of Future Trends
in Hypnosis Research

ERIKA FROMM

In the spring of 1970 questionnaires were mailed to those members of the Society of Clinical and Experimental Hypnosis and of the American Society of Clinical Hypnosis known to have an active involvement in research, and to all members of the recently founded Division on Psychological Hypnosis of the American Psychological Association. Of the 500 questionnaires mailed, 161 (thirty-two percent) were returned. The questionnaire asked the respondent to describe the hypnosis research he had in progress, research being planned for future execution, promising studies currently being planned by other investigators, and important additional research that should be done.

The 295 research topics named were described at different levels of generality, with much complex overlapping. Despite these complexities a content analysis has here been made.

The questionnaire responses could be readily subdivided into two major categories. The first is what I call the "growing edges" in the study of hypnosis; the second is the more traditional continuation of existing lines of research. Under the first category can be placed nine subcategories: (1) the nature of hypnosis, (2) hypnosis as a subjective experience, (3) preconscious

The author wishes to express her appreciation to Andrew M. Boxer who did much of the research for the expansion of this chapter in the current edition of this book.

and unconscious processes, (4) self-hypnosis, (5) subject characteristics, (6) the personality of the hypnotist, (7) the social psychology of hypnosis research, (8) new clinical applications of hypnosis, and (9) studies on the correspondences and differences between clinical and experimental hypnosis.

Three subcategories have been placed under the second category: (1) experimental hypnosis, (2) clinical research, and (3) the educational applications of hypnosis. Frequencies are given in Table 22.1.

TABLE 22.1.   Frequency of responses to the hypnosis research questionnaire

	Research		
	In Progess	Pro- jected	Needed
A. THE GROWING EDGES OF THE FIELD			
I. *The Nature of Hypnosis*	6		3
II. *Hypnosis as a Subjective Experience:*			
1. Phenomenology	5	2	2
2. Altered states of consciousness (*ASCs*)			
a. Measure: the subject's own reports	1		
b. Attempts to measure objectively the subjective experience (e.g., in analgesia)	1		
3. Modeling other *ASCs* with hypnosis	3	2	2
III. *Preconscious and Unconscious Processes*			
1. Differentiating fact and artifact in regard to hypnosis by means of differences in the characteristics of cognitive processes	3		
2. Creativity and other regressions in the service of the ego	3	1	
3. Dreams: hypnotic and posthypnotic	2	9	1
4. The study of repression and other unconscious defenses by means of hypnosis	2	1	2
IV. *Self-hypnosis*	1	1	3
V. *Subject Characteristics*	9	3	2
VI. *The Personality of the Hypnotist*	1	1	3
VII. *Social Psychology of Hypnosis Research*	5		2
VIII. *New Clinical Applications of Hypnosis:*			
A. Integration of hypnotherapy with some of the recently developed psychotherapies:			2
1. Behavior modification	4	1	2
2. Desensitization	4	1	
3. Autogenic control techniques	1		
4. Self-actualization therapies	1	1	1
5. Group therapy with hypnosis	2	1	1
6. Hypnotic marathons	4	2	1
7. Art therapy	1	1	
8. Gestalt therapy			1
9. Existential therapy		1	
B. Hypnosis in the treatment of drug addiction	4	4	3

	Research		
	In Progess	Pro-jected	Needed
IX. *Studies on the Correspondences and Differences Between Clinical and Experimental Hypnosis*	1		
B. CONTINUATION OF ESTABLISHED RESEARCH LINES			
X. *Experimental Hypnosis*			
1. Hypnotizability studies	1	4	2
2. Measures and methods of induction and deepening	3	1	1
3. Neurophysiology	5	6	3
4. The objective study of specific hypnotic phenomena and effects	13	4	5
XI. *Clinical Research*			
1. Theory and methods of hypnotherapy	9	2	2
2. Application of hypnosis in hypnotherapy and hypno-analysis	26	25	22
3. Outcome studies	2		2
XII. *Educational Applications*	4	7	5
XIII. *Miscellaneous*	6	3	7
Totals:	133	84	80

In 1978 a computerized library reference search was made of the Psychological Abstracts *and the* Index Medicus, *to compile those hypnosis publications appearing in major scientific and professional journals during the period of January 1971 to January 1978. More than 1,000 publications were found. Each publication was coded by content analysis and placed in one of the same subcategories as that of the questionnaire responses, with the exception of a few new categories (see Table 22.2). References concerning hypnotic drugs were excluded. The rest of this chapter discusses both the questionnaire findings and the literature survey in greater detail, as a way of predicting future research trends in hypnosis.*

TABLE 22.2. Frequency of hypnosis research publications during the period of January 1971 to January 1978.

	Range of number of publications	Future prediction
A. THE GROWING EDGES OF THE FIELD		
I. *The Nature of Hypnosis*	26-50	↑
A. History of hypnosis	11-25	
II. *Hypnosis as a Subjective Experience*		
1. Phenomenology	0-10	↑
2. Altered states of consciousness (*ASCs*)		

	Range of number of publications	Future prediction
a. *Measure: the subjects' own reports*	*0-10*	
b. *Attempts to measure objectively the subjective experience (e.g., in analgesia)*	*0-10*	
3. *Similarities and differences between hypnosis and various other ASCs*	26-50	↑
III. **Preconscious and Unconscious Processes**		
1. Differentiating fact and artifact with regard to hypnosis by means of differences in characteristics of cognitive processes	11-25	
2. Creativity and other regressions in the service of the ego	11-25	↑
3. Dreams: hypnotic and post-hypnotic	11-25	
4. The study of repression and other unconscious defenses by means of hypnosis	26-50	↑
5. Imagery*	11-25	↑
IV. **Self-hypnosis**	11-25	↑
V. **Subject Characteristics**	26-50	↑
VI. **The Personality of the Hypnotist**	0-10	
VII. **The Social Psychology of Hypnosis Research**	26-50	↑
VIII. **New Clinical Applications of Hypnosis**		
A. Integration of hypnotherapy with some of the recently developed psychotherapies		
1. Behavior modification	11-25	↑
2. Desensitization	11-25	↑
3. Autogenic control techniques	0-10	
4. Self-actualization therapies	0-10	
5. Group therapy with hypnosis	11-25	↑
6. Hypnotic marathons	0	
7. Art therapy	0	
8. Gestalt therapy	0-10	
9. Existential therapy	0-10	
10. Child therapy*	11-25	↑
11. Transactional analysis*	0-10	
B. Hypnosis in the treatment of drug addiction and alcohol addiction*	11-25	↑
IX. **Studies on the Correspondences and Differences Between Clinical and Experimental Hypnosis**	0-10	
B. CONTINUATION OF ESTABLISHED RESEARCH LINES		
X. Experimental Hypnosis		
1. Hypnotizability studies	76-100	→
2. Measures and methods of induction and deepening	26-50	↑
3. Physiology	76-100	↑

		Range of number of publications	Future prediction
	4. The objective study of specific hypnotic phenomena and effects	*101-125*	→
XI.	*Clinical Research*		
	1. Theory and methods of hypnotherapy	101-125	→
	2. Application of hypnosis in hypnotherapy and hypnoanalysis	151-175	→
	3. Application of hypnosis in the treatment of psychoses*	11-25	↑
	4. Outcome studies	11-25	↑
XII.	*Educational Applications*	0-10	
	1. Education and training of hypnotherapists*	0-10	
XIII.	*Legal and Ethical Issues**	0-10	
XIV.	*Animal Hypnosis*	11-25	?

Key:

* = new area, not included in 1972 edition

↑ = prediction of increased future research

→ = continued research in an already active field

A. Growing Edges

I. THE NATURE OF HYPNOSIS

In 1972 a total of nine responses dealt with the nature of hypnosis. There appeared to be seven research questions of interest in those responses:

- In what sense, if any, is hypnosis an altered state of consciousness (*ASC*)?
- Is hypnosis no more than suggestibility?
- Can we isolate the necessary and sufficient variables for producing hypnosis?
- Is becoming hypnotized a skill that can be learned; that is, could *everyone, with sufficient practice, learn to be deeply hypnotized?*
- *Does it require a basic talent to allow oneself temporarily to shed one's generalized reality orientation (GRO)* in order to allow primary process thought and imagery to come into awareness?
- To what extent is hypnosis a transference process?
- What differentiates hypnosis from the waking state and from sleep?

In 1978, research on the nature of hypnosis continued to proliferate. Ernest R. Hilgard's Neo-Dissociation Theory (see Chapter 3 in this volume) is an example of a new and important theoretical development which seeks to resolve many of the old conceptual problems involved in studying the nature of hypnosis.

Interest in the history of hypnosis continues. *Several new questions not foreseen in 1972 have come into focus since, or are expected to catch the interest of hypnosis researchers soon. They are:*

- *What are the similarities and differences between hypnosis and various other ASCs?*
- *Is hypnotizability modifiable?*
- *Is there a relationship between hypnotizability and right and left hemisphere functions?*

On the latter question no research has been done yet, but the author believes it to be imminent. The theoretical as well as the experimental questions it would open up or answer with regard to the locus and the mode of cognition in the hypnotic state seem exciting and of great importance.

Hypnosis researchers have come to recognize hypnosis as an ASC. And some ASC researchers are beginning to take heed of hypnosis as an ASC and to incorporate hypnosis into their ASC research and models (Brown, 1977; Crosson et al., 1977; Davidson and Goleman, 1977; Fischer, 1977; Friedman and Taub, 1977; Fromm 1977a, 1977b; Krippner, 1977; and Sacerdote, 1977).

Clinicians for a long time have said that hypnotizability increases or decreases with the patient's motivation, fears, or need for defense. Experimental hypnosis researchers, particularly the trait theorists, have held that hypnotizability is immutable (except for long-term changes over the life-span). Some recent experimental studies seem to indicate that hypnotizability, even in the laboratory, can be modified after all (see Stolar 1975; Diamond, 1977; Perry, 1977).

II. HYPNOSIS AS A SUBJECTIVE EXPERIENCE

Experiential aspects of hypnosis, although the most important aspects to the subject, have until recently tended to be ignored by the laboratory investigator seeking objectivity. Subjects, particularly after initial exposure to hypnosis, characteristically are eager to describe their subjective hypnotic experiences and usually are uninterested in their objective behavioral performance. With the advent of the youth culture in the 1960s, with its emphasis on inner, highly personal experiences and altered states of awareness, investigators have renewed their interest in the phenomenology of hypnosis. Altogether eighteen responses dealt with research on hypnosis as a subjective experience. These dealt with the phenomenology of ordinary and exceptionally deep hypnosis; the development of scales by which to quantify the experiential aspects of hypnosis; attempts to provide phenomenological characterizations of hypnotic experiences at different levels of depth, including the very deepest; and the exploration of variations in characteristics of hypnotic phenomena.

Two research projects have attempted to measure objectively the subjective experience of hypnosis as an *ASC*. Several investigators expressed interest in the phenomenological similarities of hypnosis to drug-induced states and to "peak experiences." Seven respondents registered interest in comparing drug-induced and hypnotic *ASCs*.

It is interesting to note that phenomenological studies are gaining an increased acceptance in the psychological laboratories of a number of academic institutions. We had predicted in 1972 that there would be a marked increase in phenomenological studies of hypnosis. But in the 1970s an attitude of moderation has developed, as reflected in the small amount of research in this area published in the last six years, though we do find phenomenological approaches being incorporated into various research designs. For example, Tellegen and Atkinson (1974), and Shor (Chapter 5 in this volume) have employed phenomenological methods to study variables important to understanding the nature of hypnosis and hypnotizability.

III. PRECONSCIOUS AND UNCONSCIOUS PROCESSES

Since the classic studies in hysteria by Breuer and Freud, hypnosis has been widely considered to be a convenient method for the study of preconscious and unconscious processes. Our respondents showed a great deal of interest in undertaking studies on creativity, on hypnotic and posthypnotic dreams, and on repression, rationalizations, and other unconscious defenses. Of the twenty-one responses in all these areas, seven referred to projects in progress and eleven in prospect. Several studies of unconscious and preconscious defenses include artificially induced conflicts and their solutions—a prime source for experimental investigation of the integrative and the defensive functions of the ego in *statu nascendi*.

Three respondents were engaged in research seeking differences in cognitive processes in the waking and hypnotic states. Indications are that cognitive processes in hypnosis contain evidence of more primary process manifestations, involve more adaptive use of introspection, and more fanciful elaboration of content and humor.

Four respondents were actively engaged in or planning work on creativity in hypnosis, eleven on dreams. Three had research in progress or in prospect on the formation of unconscious defenses.

Our 1978 survey of the literature shows that research in the areas of creativity and unconscious defenses continues to increase. A new trend not apparent to us in 1972 shows up in the field of imagery.

IV. SELF-HYPNOSIS

In 1972 we stated that little had been done in this research area and that our respondents reported only one project in progress and only one other in prospect.

Our disclosure of the scarcity of research in this area—and perhaps also the Zeitgeist—stimulated a number of phenomenological and experimental studies on self-hypnosis (SH) *over the last five or six years (Shor & Easton, 1973; Fromm, 1974, 1975a, 1975b, 1975c; Brown, 1974; Brown & Fromm, 1978; Oberlander, 1974, 1978; Ruch, 1975; Johnson & Weight, 1976; Boxer, 1978; Hurt, 1978), and others are about to be published. Hypnosis researchers are beginning to take a new interest in SH, particularly in the hypnosis laboratories at the University of Chicago, Stanford University, and the University of New Hampshire.* Self-hypnosis has been used extensively in therapy, especially for controlling somatic pain and ameliorating psychological anguish. However, practically all hypnosis research has involved heterohypnosis. The assumption implicitly made is that heterohypnosis and autohypnosis are homologues; that we can teach autohypnosis by letting the patient recapitulate what he has experienced being hypnotized, including the fantasy of the transference object. There is, however, little direct research documentation of whether the experiential phenomena are indeed alike in the two instances—that is, whether the same abilities, ego functions, and substrata of personality are involved in both.

In heterohypnosis, the patient's or subject's ego, while listening to the hypnotist's patter, is often said to divide into an experiencing part and an observing part. With regard to self-hypnosis, where the subject gives the suggestions to himself, three major questions occur to me. To what extent does the ego in self-hypnosis split into three parts: instructing, observing, and experiencing functions (that is, the "speaker," "listener," and "observer")? In what types of clinical cases is it indicated to teach self-hypnosis? What are the criteria for teaching self-hypnosis that should be used with reference to a normal population?

While only three of our respondents suggested that more research was needed on self-hypnosis, in my judgment there will be a great upsurge of scientific interest in it during the next decade. Once again, the youth movement and associated phenomena have focused interest on the development of the individual's inner potentialities and self-actualization, with special emphasis on subjective experiences. Scientific investigators will, it is thought, wish to study the problems and promise of self-hypnosis as well as of heterohypnosis. *It has been also found that clinicians' use of self-hypnosis as a tool has more than confirmed its promise as a valuable therapeutic aid.*

V. SUBJECT CHARACTERISTICS

Subject characteristics not only influence hypnotizability, but also may be the source of variability in hypnotic performance. In particular the Stanford laboratory (E.R. Hilgard, 1965b; J. Hilgard, 1970) has shown great activity in relating hypnotic susceptibility to certain personality characteristics. Our respondents suggested, *and our literature survey confirms,* that they will widen and extend this research in the future. Nine studies of subject characteristics were in process and three more were projected. These studies included: research into differences in personality characteristics between suggestible and nonsuggestible subjects; nosological studies by means of hypnotizability scores (for example, differentiating neurotic character disorders from primary psychopaths on the basis of their hypnotizability); conversely, in other studies, gender, state of emotional health (normality versus acute versus chronic schizophrenia), or very specific personality characteristics (such as sensitizers versus repressors) are used as independent variables to investigate differences in hypnotic performance.

In the clinical field, a variety of projects include specific studies such as a comparison of the personalities of patients who react well to surgery under hypnosis versus those who do not, and an inquiry into the dynamics of patients who resume smoking or overeating within six months after hypnotherapy, compared to those who remain abstinent. On the basis of the reports, *and the literature published between 1971-1978,* the writer expects that hypnosis research will move into increasingly refined clinical differentiations of the personality characteristics of hypnotizable persons, and of types of patients who can profit lastingly from short-term hypnotherapy as opposed to those who cannot. The future research appears to be taking more cognizance of interpersonal variables and subject characteristics in the selection of experimental populations.

VI. THE PERSONALITY OF THE HYPNOTIST

Little research has been done concerning the personality of the hypnotist; only one such project was in process and one other was in the planning stage. However, three respondents urged further research in this area.

In the eighteenth and nineteenth centuries, hypnosis was flamboyant (Mesmer) or authoritarian (Charcot, Freud). The hypnotist was viewed as a powerful person who wished to subject others to his will for their own good. Since the end of World War II, hypnotists have generally come to practice a permissive kind of hypnosis. Obviously this new approach requires, at least in part, a different kind of personality or different varieties of personality.

As students of hypnosis become more sophisticated in establishing subject characteristics, they will also need to analyze the personality characteristics of the hypnotist. Thus one respondent planned to study what motivated the hypnotist to become a hypnotist. Another was exploring the extent to which prestige in the eyes of the patient may be a factor. However, prestige seems an unlikely factor to motivate the hypnosis researcher since in many academic circles hypnosis has not yet gained full status as a legitimate field of research.

In my opinion, three types of studies are needed: studies tracing the career lines of well-known hypnosis researchers and hypnotherapists; studies based on interviews or questionnaires asking people in these fields what their conscious motivations have been for becoming and remaining hypnotists; and personality studies of the same groups of people, designed to tap their unconscious motivations and personality makeup. *So far only historical studies tracing careers of hypnosis researchers and hypnotherapists have begun to gain momentum in the scientific literature of the 1970s.*

VII. SOCIAL PSYCHOLOGY OF HYPNOSIS RESEARCH

One respondent urged that medicine's inertia in utilizing hypnosis as a method of treatment be explored. Another respondent reported research in progress on the "ivy-league effect" in hypnosis research, by which he meant that hypnosis research has tended to be looked upon askance by universities as if it were something mystical, not really worthy of scientific investigation. While such an attitude is still widespread, the fact that Hilgard at Stanford and Orne at the University of Pennsylvania have developed large laboratories for hypnosis research has given the field more prestige in the eyes of academia—a development that in itself might make an interesting topic for social psychological research.

It is also of interest to study the social atmosphere in which hypnosis research—or any kind of research for that matter—either flourishes or withers, as well as significant social psychological variables possibly effecting research designs and data collection.

Ethnic-cultural factors that contribute to hypnotic susceptibility also need to be studied, as one respondent urged. Moreover, we would not be surprised to find quantitive differences in hypnotizability between socioeconomic classes and races, perhaps depending on whether hypnotist and subject belong to the same class or race. We might also expect qualitative differences in what is experienced in hypnosis when comparing such diverse groups as college-bred suburban housewives and native Balinese religious dancers.

In 1978 we witness a small but increasing number of studies taking up various aspects of the social psychology of hypnosis research.

VIII. NEW CLINICAL APPLICATIONS OF HYPNOSIS

There were 133 responses with reference to clinical applications of hypnosis. Only those that deal with the "growing edges" of the field—forty-four research projects—will be discussed in this section. Of these, twenty-one were in progress and twelve were future projects; there were eleven suggestions concerning needed research in this area.

Integration of hypnotherapy with newer psychotherapies. The responses indicated that in the near future there would be many attempts to integrate hypnotherapy with some of the newer psychotherapies, such as behavior modification, desensitization, autogenic control techniques, and self-actualization therapies. Clinicians and researchers alike will try to find out whether these newer psychotherapies are more effective when the patient is in hypnosis or in the waking state.

Seven responses were concerned with studies of behavior modification, including comparisons between the waking and the hypnotic state.

The current literature demonstrates that an increasing number of clinicians incorporate hypnosis and self-hypnosis with some form of behavior therapy. One study deals with the relationship of Schutz's autogenic control techniques to the techniques of hypnosis, including similarities and differences. Desensitization techniques were the focus of five projects.

Mesmer, Li5ebeault, and other early hypnotherapists treated their patients in groups, but for nearly a century hypnotherapy has characteristically been practiced in a one-to-one situation. Currently, however, hypnotic group therapy is being vigorously developed. *As an example, group hypnosis is being used to aid individuals in weight loss.* Three of the respondents were doing studies in this area to compare the results with individual hypnotherapy or hypnoanalysis. Marathon hypnotherapy was also being tried. There were seven responses in this latter category. *However, the 1978 literature search revealed not a single study on this topic has been published in the last six years.*

Hypnosis in the treatment of drug and alcohol addiction. The potential use of hypnosis in the exploration and treatment of the adolescent drug problem, mentioned earlier, was being studied by four respondents. Four more projects were being planned, and three other respondents emphasized the need for research in this area, *In addition, hypnosis is now being tried for the treatment of alcoholism.* Such studies can contribute to the understanding and treatment of addiction, perhaps making it possible for patients to experience, without danger, the relaxation and/or excitement they obtain from drugs. Such research could become of great clinical and social relevance. Studies will attempt to indicate whether hypnosis can be used as a substitute for drug taking, or help reduce stress in drug-withdrawal patients. The studies are also seen as likely to broaden the knowledge of the sensory and cognitive changes produced by hallucinogenic drugs.

Hypnotherapy with children. *A new clinical development in hypnosis is its application in the context of child psychotherapy. A number of published accounts of the successful use of hypnosis with children indicate that its use has become an effective treatment modality, and one which will not only continue to proliferate but—it is hoped—will also stimulate research. (Gardner, in press).*

IX. STUDIES ON THE CORRESPONDENCES AND DIFFERENCES BETWEEN
CLINICAL AND EXPERIMENTAL HYPNOSIS

In the past, experimental researchers frequently tried to replicate findings of clinicians—and often failed. Whenever this happened, the clinicians were criticized for poor methodology and faulty observation. However, in the last few years, experimentalists as well as clinicians have come to realize that not all clinical data *can* be readily replicated in the laboratory; perhaps clinical and experimental situations have differing social characteristics that are likely to elicit different reactions from the hypnotized individual. Some workers have argued that a patient comes to his therapist with a set of expectations totally different from that of the curious student who comes to the hypnosis laboratory to participate in a new experience. It is possible, too, that a student who is paid a fee to participate in hypnosis experiments may react differently from one who wishes to experience hypnosis out of intellectual and/or emotion-loaded curiosity.

In my judgment, there has not been enough concern for the problem of similarities and differences between clinical and experimental hypnosis. Only one such study was in progress, and no projected ones were reported.

The contemporary literature up to 1979 confirms that there has been little attention devoted to this area although clinical research designs and methodologies are growing continually more sophisticated.

The problems in comparing clinical and experimental hypnosis involve the unwillingness of laboratory researchers to accept, as real, phenomena that may not be fully replicable in the traditional laboratory. While it is true that clinicians sometimes have been overly "credulous," the "skeptical" experimenter, with his emphasis on objectivity, can, it is felt, inhibit the occurrence of certain valid hypnotic phenomena.

B. Continuation of Established Research Lines

Our respondents reported that well-established lines of research would be continued *and the literature survey affirms this as fact.* Sixty-three such projects were in progress, in contrast with forty-eight projects on the "growing edges." The same broad differences were also apparent in Table 22.1 with respect to studies in prospect and areas of needed research.

X. EXPERIMENTAL HYPNOSIS

Well established lines of research in experimental hypnosis were found to cluster readily into four categories: hypnotizability, measures and methods of hypnotic induction, the physiology of hypnosis, and specific hypnotic phenomena and effects. *In the areas of hypnotizability, physiology, and specific hypnotic phenomena and effects, research continues to abound.*

Hypnotizability. In my view, an important task with reference to hypnotizability is the elaboration and measurement of multidimensional factors involved in hypnotic responsiveness. Research with Weitzenhoffer and Hilgard's Profile Scales (1967), and the development of a diagnostic measurement scale of Shor's three dimensions of hypnotic depth (1962), would seem highly relevant. All too often hypnotic depth is considered a univariate function.

In 1977 Shor developed a method designed to measure hypnotic depth, including phenomenological aspects as described by the S. *It is published for the first time in this volume* (Chapter 5), *and represents a new, phenomenological approach to the understanding and testing of hypnotic depth which will be of great value for clinicians as well as for researchers.*

Two of our respondents emphasized the need for future hypnotizability studies. One such study was in process and four others were projected.

As was predicted, studies that have emerged include a longitudinal design for examining individual differences in hypnotic susceptibility and explorations of how such differences in susceptibility (as well as levels of hypnotizability) are modified from early childhood through old age. Earlier hypnotizability studies compared hypnotizability of given age groups, not through longitudinal development.

Measures and methods of hypnotic induction. Another currently active field of established research is the study of procedures and measurement of hypnotic induction and deepening. Three projects were in process and a fourth was projected. Subjects of interest include rapid induction procedures, the effectiveness of induction and deepening procedures under various circumstances, and hypnotic induction profiles.

Physiology of hypnosis. Research on the physiology of hypnosis is continuing. Despite previous lack of success, researchers are looking for physiological or EEG indices that would prove the existence of hypnosis as a distinct state. Five projects were in progress, six were projected, and three respondents reported the need for further research in neurophysiology.

In my judgment, as interest in the subjective aspects of hypnosis increases—with increasing awareness that hypnosis is an *ASC* and that the very essence of hypnosis is in the subject's subjective experience—the search for physiological and neuroelectric substrata of hypnosis as proof of the existence of a hypnotic state will fade into the background. Researchers will no longer feel as compelled to look intently for *objective* measures of the subjective experiences.

Contrary to the prediction stated above, the literature between 1971 and 1978 indicates that research on the physiology of hypnosis continues quite strongly. The very reason I gave in 1972 for expecting such research to fade into the background is perhaps actually causing its continuation. Many researchers nowadays are intent on finding physiological correlates of such ASCs as psychedelic drug states and various types of meditation. In the process, they also try to find physiological indicators that would differentiate hypnosis and self-hypnosis from these other altered states.

Specific hypnotic phenomena and effects. A good many of our respondents were interested in the study of specific hypnotic phenomena and effects *and the literature published since 1971 reveals this to be an especially salient area of continuing interest to researchers.* There were twelve projects in process and four more projected; five other respondents stressed the need for more such studies.

Seven questions on typical hypnotic phenomena continue to intrigue investigators: (1) posthypnotic amnesia as a means of studying forgetting or repression; (2) time distortion; (3) hypnotic alterations of aspects of perception and conscious experience, particularly visual perception; (4) variables influencing hypnotically induced anesthesia; (5) effects of hypnosis on reaction time when either alertness or sleepiness has been suggested during induction; (6) the tracking of eye movements with hypnotically induced positive and negative hallucinations; and (7) the problems of hypnosis in relation to pain. *This last area has been one in which there has been a growing number of research developments since the first edition of this book was published (see Hilgard and Hilgard, 1975).*

XI. CONTINUATION OF ESTABLISHED LINES OF CLINICAL RESEARCH

Much clinical research is currently being carried forward along established lines. Thirty-seven projects were reported in process, twenty-seven were in prospect, and twenty-six were listed as needed.

Application of hypnosis in hypnotherapy and hypnoanalysis. Studies continue to be made on the feasibility and use of hypnosis in psychotherapy and for the relief of somatic pain. Studies of hypnosis as used in hypnotherapy elicited a total of seventy-three responses; twenty-six projects were in progress, twenty-five were projected, and twenty-two needed projects were suggested. There is likely to be heavy research emphasis on the use of hypnosis in the psychotherapy of neuroses, character neuroses, and psychosomatic problems. There were also indications of more concerted attempts to treat psychoses, particularly schizophrenia and the borderline states. *These lines of research have grown from 1971 to 1978, and confirm my prediction.*

Studies are currently in process on the use of hypnosis in such areas as anxiety, rage, asthma, stuttering, mental retardation, and sexual malfunctioning. *With the exception of mental retardation, we find that in the last six years these areas continue to generate a growing body of clinical research and to provide new applications for hypnosis.*

One project was reported on the therapeutic use of hypnosis in brain injury cases in connection with physical medicine and rehabilitation services in hospitals. There will also be studies of the effectiveness of hypnosis in treating habit disorders (smoking, overeating, alcoholism). In some of these studies simple hypnotic suggestions are to be compared with more dynamic hypnoanalytic techniques. Controlled case studies on pain reduction, notably in the treatment of carcinoma and as an auxiliary treatment for severe burns, were projected. Hypnosis in childbirth and hypnotic analgesia and anesthesia training will continue to be used and investigated. Psychological preparation for and recovery from surgery by means of hypnosis also will continue to be studied. *These research areas have continued and are developing, as the literature of the last six years bears out.*

On a somewhat more theoretical level, there will be explorations of the possibility of producing artificial conflicts and artificial neuroses through posthypnotic suggestion. Two studies were launched to help identify the necessary and sufficient conditions for the productions of psychopathology. One area where hypnosis would seem to be the natural therapy of choice, but where so far it has not been used extensively, is in connection with sleep disorders; however, only one such study was in progress.

It has been apparent for some time that we need more studies on hypnotherapeutic method and theory. There appear to be seven key questions:

- What is the preferred hypnotherapeutic methods in various types of cases?
- When should hypnoanalysis be the therapy of choice?
- When is direct versus indirect suggestion preferable?
- When should hypnotherapy be supportive rather than reconstructive?
- Does rehearsal in fantasy under hypnosis help patients to change maladaptive behavior and personality patterns?

- What about ego-integrative therapeutic methods versus uncovering methods?
- When do we most profitably speak to our patients in the language of the unconscious—in symbols—and when should we use rational, secondary-process speech?

There were eighteen projects in process seeking answers to these questions and ten more were projected. Eight suggestions for needed research in hypnotherapeutic theory and methods were also submitted.

Documented in the literature is a rich and expanding body of theory on hypnosis. Progress is being made in bridging the gap between disparate points of view apparent in 1972, see for example E.R. Hilgard's Chapter 3, in this volume. It is predicted that in the next ten years this gap will lessen even more, as we move toward a unified body of theoretical knowledge on hypnosis.

XII. THE APPLICATION OF HYPNOSIS IN EDUCATION

The possible influence hypnosis can have on ameliorating educational problems continues to interest researchers. Four projects were in process, seven were projected, and five additional needed projects were mentioned. However, it is very doubtful that large-scale use will be made of their methods and findings in our school systems. The nineteenth century concept of the hypnotist as a manipulator of men, with no respect for the individual's wishes and defenses, is still too prevalent.

Researchers are, however, continuing to study the effects of hypnosis and different forms of hypnotherapy on concentration, reading speed, comprehension, and learning retention. Other studies continue on the use of hypnosis in overcoming educational blocks and in stirring the academic underachiever to use his full potential.

While there have been studies on hypnosis and learning, this research has yet to be systematically applied in any educational system. As was predicted in 1972, it still seems doubtful that use will be made of hypnosis research in our school systems.

We do now have a beginning literature concerning itself with the education and training of hypnotherapists.

XIII. LEGAL AND ETHICAL ISSUES

Since 1971, four studies have appeared dealing with legal and ethical issues involved in the research and practice of hypnosis.

XIV. ANIMAL HYPNOSIS

Animal hypnosis was not included as a category in the survey published in

*1972. None of the recipients of the 1970 questionnaire did any animal hyp-
nosis or were concerned with any research in that area. The literature
search, however, has shown that there is an appreciable number of studies
in that field currently being done. Animal hypnosis, of course, is not a new
field.*

Purpose and Prediction

The purpose of this chapter was to survey both what researchers in the field
say they are interested in pursuing or feel should be pursued, *and the kinds
of research being published in the experimental and clinical domains six
years after this survey was made.*

The survey polled all of the contributors to this volume as well as almost
everyone who might conceivably be engaged in hypnosis research. As a
large number of the persons polled were practitioners who were not actively
interested in research, the thirty-two percent return rate was felt to be a
reasonable representation of current interests. While newcomers to the
field, young investigators, and graduate students were under-represented in
the sample, their interests were, we hope, given expression in the responses
of their teachers, colleagues, and supervisors, *as well as in their published
research reports.*

*The predictions made in 1972, in the first edition of this volume, have
been reassessed in 1978 for the second edition. We found that on the whole,
our sample of researchers polled then gave a very adequate indication of
future trends in the field, which we witnessed six years later, as reflected in
the literature. Most of the predictions we made have proven to be correct;
only a very few were wrong. And lacunae in research fields that we pointed
out then are now being filled.*

As an expression of research activity and interest these surveys may be
taken as an estimate or appraisal of future trends in hypnosis research. As a
prophecy of the future, such an appraisal doubtless has many shortcomings. In balance, however, it seems to me that it stands as a more reasonable
basis for prophesy than a reliance on my own hunches, hopes, and biases.
In a sense each of the chapters in this volume carries with it a prediction of
future research growth. This final chapter is merely an attempt to expand
the inquiry to include all members of the research community. It seems to
me a cogent appraisal, but only time will tell. At the very least, this chapter
may serve as a useful bench mark against which to compare actual research
developments in the years ahead.

Bibliography

Aarons, L. Sleep-assisted Instruction. *Psychological Bulletin,* 1976, *83,* 1–40.

Aaronson, B.S. Hypnotic Alterations of Space and Time. *International Journal of Parapsychology,* 1968a, *10,* 5–36.

Aaronson, B.S. Hypnosis, Time Rate Perception, and Personality. *Journal of Schizophrenia,* 1968b, *2,* 11–41.

Aaronson, B.S. The Hypnotic Induction of the Void. Paper read at American Society for Clinical Hypnosis, San Francisco, October, 1969.

Ackerknecht, E. H. "Mesmerism" in Primitive Societies. *Ciba Symposia,* 1948, *9,* 826–831.

Agle, D. P., Ratnoff, O. D., & Wasman, M. Studies in Autoerythrocyte Sensitization: The Induction of Purpuric Lesions by Hypnotic Suggestion *Psychosomatic Medicine,* 1967, *29,* 491–503.

Agosti, E., & Camerota, G. Some Effects of Hypnotic Suggestion on Respiratory Function. *International Journal of Clinical and Experimental Hypnosis,* 1965, *13,* 149–156.

Ainsworth, Mary D. Problems of Validation. In B. Klopfer, Mary D. Ainsworth, W. G. Klopfer, & R. R. Holt, *Developments in the Rorschach Technique. Vol. 1, Technique and Theory.* Yonkers, New York: World Book Co. 1954, 405–500.

Akstein, D. The Induction of Hypnosis in the Light of Reflexology. *American Journal of Clinical Hypnosis,* 1965, *7,* 281–300.

Albert, I. B., & Boone, D. Dream Deprivation and Facilitation with Hypnosis. *Journal of Abnormal Psychology,* 1975, *84,* 267–271.

Albert, I. B., & McNeece, Barbara. The Reported Sleep Characteristics of Meditators and Nonmeditators. *Bulletin of the Psychonomic Society,* 1974, *3,* 73–74.

Allison, J. Adaptive Regression and Intense Religious Experiences. *Journal of Nervous and Mental Disease,* 1967, *145,* 452–463.

Allport, G. W. *Personality: A Psychological Interpretation.* New York: Holt, 1937.

Allport, G. W., Vernon, P. E. & Lindzey, G. *Study of Values.* (Rev. ed.) Boston: Houghton Mifflin Company, 1951.

Amadeo, M., & Shagass, C. Eye Movements, Attention, and Hypnosis. *Journal of Nervous and Mental Disease,* 1963, *136,* 139–145.

Anand, B. K., Chhina, G. S., & Singh, B. Some Aspects of Electro-encephalographic studies in yogis. *Electroencephalography and Clinical Neurophysiology.* 1961, *13*, 452–456. Reprinted in Tart, 1969a, 503–506.

Anderson, M. N. Hypnosis in Anesthesia. *Journal of the Medical Association of the State of Alabama.* 1957, *27*, 121–125.

Anderson, J.R., & Bower, G. H. Recognition and Retrieval Processes in Free Recall. *Psychological Review,* 1972, *79*, 97–123.

Andrew, Dorothy M., Paterson, D. G., & Longstaff, H. P. *Minnesota Clerical Test.* New York: The Psychological Corporation, 1933.

Antrobus, Judith S., & Antrobus, J. S. Discrimination of Two Sleep Stages by Human Subjects. *Psychophysiology,* 1976, *4*, 48–55.

Antrobus, J. S., Antrobus, Judith S., & Singer, J. L. Eye Movements Accompanying Daydreaming, Visual Imagery, and Thought Suppression. *Journal of Abnormal and Social Psychology,* 1964, *69*, 244–252.

Antrobus, J. S., Singer, J. L., & Greenberg, S. Studies in the Stream of Consciousness: Experimental Enhancement and Suppression of Spontaneous Cognitive Processes. *Perceptual and Motor Skills,* 1966, *23*, 399–417.

Arieti, S. *Creativity: The Magic Synthesis.* New York: Basic Books, 1976.

Arkin, A. M., Hastey, J. M., & Reiser, M. F. Post-hypnotically Stimulated Sleeptalking. *Journal of Nervous and Mental Disease,* 1966, *142*, 293–309.

Arnold, Magda B. On the Mechanism of Suggestion and Hypnosis. *Journal of Abnormal and Social Psychology,* 1946, *41*, 107–128.

Arnold, Magda B. Brain Function in Hypnosis. *International Journal of Clinical and Experimental Hypnosis,* 1959, *7*, 109–119.

Ås, A. Non-hypnotic Experiences Related to Hypnotizability in Male and Female College Students. *Scandanavian Journal of Psychology,* 1962, *3*, 112–121.

Ås, A. Hypnotizability as a Function of Nonhypnotic Experiences. *Journal of Abnormal and Social Psychology,* 1963, *66*, 142–150.

Ås, A., & Lauer, Lillian W. A Factor-analytic Study of Hypnotizability and Related Personal Experiences. *International Journal of Clinical and Experimental Hypnosis,* 1962, *10*, 169–181.

Ås, A., O'Hara, J. W., & Munger, M. P. The Measurement of Subjective Experiences Presumably Related to Hypnotic Susceptibility. *Scandanavian Journal of Psychology,* 1962, *3*, 47–64.

Ås, A., & Østvold, S. Hypnosis as Subjective Experience. *Scandanavian Journal of Psychology,* 1968, *9*, 33–38.

Asch, S. E. *Social Psychology.* Englewood Cliffs, N. J.: Prentice-Hall, 1952.

Aschan, G., Finer, B. L., & Hagbarth, K. E. The Influence of Hypnotic Suggestion on Vestibular Nystagmus. *Acta Oto-Laryngologica,* 1962, *55*, 97–110.

Ascher, L. M., & Barber, T. X. An Attempted Replication of the Parrish-Lundy-Leibowitz Study on Hypnotic Age-regression. Harding, Mass.: The Medfield Foundation, 1968.

Aserinsky, E., & Kleitman, N. Regularly Occurring Periods of Eye Motility, and Concomitant Phenomena, During Sleep. *Science,* 1953, *118*, 273–274.

Ashley, W. R., Harper, R. S., & Runyon, D. L. The Perceived Size of Coins in Normal and Hypnotically Induces Economic States. *American Journal of Psychology,* 1951, *64*, 564–572.

August, R. V. *Hypnosis in Obstetrics.* New York: McGraw-Hill, 1961.

Austin, Margaret, Perry, C., Sutcliffe, J. P., & Yeomans, N. Can Somnambulists Successfully Simulate Hypnotic Behavior without Becoming Entranced? *International Journal of Clinical and Experimental Hypnosis,* 1963, *11*, 175–186.

Bachrach, H. M. Adaptive Regression, Empathy and Psychotherapy: Theory and

Research Study. *Psychotherapy: Theory, Research and Practice,* 1968, *5,* 203–209.

Backus, P. S. An Experimental Note on Hypnotic Ablation of Optokinetic Nystagmus. *American Journal of Clinical Hypnosis,* 1962, *4,* 184–188.

Bailly, J. S., et al. *Rapport des commissaries chargés par le roi de l'examen du magnétisme animal,* 11 aôut 1784. Signed: Franklin (Chairman), Majault, Le Roy, Sallin, Bailly (Reporter), d'Arcet, De Bory, Guillotin, Lavoisier. Paris: Imprim. royale, 1784. In A. Bertrand, *Du magnétisme animal.* (On animal magnetism). Paris: J. B. Baillière, 1826, 67–147. English translation: *Animal Magnetism. Report of Dr. (Benjamin) Franklin and other Commissioners, charged by the King of France with the Examination of the Animal Magnetism as Practiced in Paris. Translated from the French. With an historical outline of the "science", an abstract of the Report on magnetic experiments, made by a Committee of the Royal Academy of Medicine, in 1831; and Remarks on Col. Stone's Pamphlet.* Philadelphia: H. Perkins, 1837. Translation also published separately, Philadelphia, J. Johnson, 1785.

Bailly, J. S., et al. *Exposé des expériences qui ont été faites pour l'examen du magnétisme animal. Lû à l'Académie des Sciences, par M. Bailly, en son nom et au nom de Messrs. Franklin, Le Roy, De Bory, et Lavoisier, le 4 Septembre 1784.* (Experiences Made During the Examination of Animal Magnetism. Paper read at the French Academy of Sciences by Mr. Bailly in his own name and that of Franklin, Le Roy, De Bory and Lavoisier, Sept. 4, 1784.) Paris: Imprimerie royale, 1785.

Bailly, J. S., et al. *Rapport secret sur le memsérisme, ou magnétisme animal.* (Secret Report on Mesmerism or Animal Magnetism). Paris, 11 aôut 1784b. (Not published.) Signed: Franklin (Chairman), De Bory, Lavoisier, Bailly (Reporter), Majault, Sallin, d'Arcet, Guillotin, Le Roy. Reproduced in A. Bertrand. *Du magnétisme animal.* (On Animal Magnetism). Paris: J. B. Baillière, 1826, 511–516. Reproduced in A Binet & C. Féré. *Animal Magnetism.* French original, 1887. English translation, New York: D. Appleton & Co., 1888, 18–25.

Bakan, P. Hypnotizability, Laterality of Eye Movements, and Functional Brain Asymmetry. *Perceptual and Motor Skills,* 1969, *28,* 927–932.

Banister, H., & Zangwill, O. L. Experimentally Induced Visual Paramnesia. *British Journal of Psychology,* 1941, *32,* 30–51.

Barbarin, C. de. *Système raisonné du magnétisme universel.* (A Logical System of Universal Magnetism). Paris: Gastelier, 1786.

Barber, J. Rapid Induction Analgesia: A Clinical Report. *American Journal of Clinical Hypnosis,* 1977, *19,* 138–147.

Barber, T. X. Comparison of Suggestibility During "Light Sleep" and Hypnosis. *Science,* 1956, *124,* 405.

Barber, T. X. Hypnosis as Perceptual-cognitive Restructuring: III. From Somnambulism to Autohypnosis. *Journal of Psychology,* 1957, *44,* 299–304.

Barber, T. X. The After Images of "Hallucinated" and "Imagined" Colors. *Journal of Abnormal and Social Psychology,* 1959a, *59,* 136–139.

Barber, T. X. Toward a Theory of Pain: Relief of Chronic Pain by Prefrontal Leucotomy, Opiates, Placebos, and Hypnosis. *Psychological Bulletin,* 1959b, *56,* 430–460.

Barber, T. X. The Necessary and Sufficient Conditions for Hypnotic Behavior. *American Journal of Clinical Hypnosis,* 1960, *3,* 31–42.

Barber, T. X. Experimental Evidence for a Theory of Hypnotic Behavior: II Experimental Controls in Hypnotic Age-regression. *International Journal of Clinical and Experimental Hypnosis,* 1961a, *9,* 181–193.

Barber, T. X. Physiological Effects of "Hypnosis". *Psychological Bulletin.* 1961b, *58,* 390–419.

Barber, T. X. Hypnotic Age Regression: A Critical Review. *Psychosomatic Medicine,* 1962a, *24,* 286–299.

Barber, T. X. Toward a Theory of Hypnosis: Posthypnotic Behavior. *Archives of General Psychiatry.* 1962b, *7,* 321–342.

Barber, T. X. Experimental Controls and the Phenomena of "Hypnosis": A Critique of Hypnotic Research Methodology. *Journal of Nervous and Mental Disease,* 1962c, *134,* 493–505.

Barber, T. X. Toward a Theory of "Hypnotic" Behavior: The "Hypnotically Induced Dream." *Journal of Nervous and Mental Disease,* 1962d, *135,* 206–221.

Barber, T. X. The Effects of "Hypnosis" on Pain: A Critical Review of Experimental and Clinical Findings. *Psychosomatic Medicine,* 1963, *25,* 303–333.

Barber, T. X. "Hypnosis" as a Causal Variable in Present-day Psychology: A Critical Analysis. *Psychological Reports,* 1964a. *14,* 839–842.

Barber, T. X. Hypnotic "Colorblindness," "Blindness," and "Deafness": (A review of Research Findings). *Diseases of the Nervous System,* 1964b, *25,* 529–538.

Barber, T. X. Toward a Theory of "Hypnotic" Behavior: Positive Visual and Auditory Hallucinations. *Psychological Record,* 1964c, *14,* 197–210.

Barber, T. X. Empirical Evidence for a Theory of "Hypnotic" Behavior. *Psychological Record,* 1964d, *14,* 457–467.

Barber, T. X. Measuring "Hypnotic-like" Suggestibility With and Without "Hypnotic Induction"; Psychometric Properties, Norms, and Variables Influencing Response to the Barber Suggestibility Scale (BSS). *Psychological Reports,* 1965a, *16,* 809–844.

Barber, T. X. Physiological Effects of "Hypnotic Suggestions": A Critical Review of Recent Research (1960–64). *Psychological Bulletin,* 1965b, *63,* 201–222.

Barber, T. X. Experimental Analyses of "Hypnotic" Behavior: A Review of Recent Empirical Findings. *Journal of Abnormal Psychology,* 1965c, *70,* 132–154.

Barber, T. X. "Hypnotic" Phenomena: A Critique of Experimental Methods. In J. E. Gordon (Ed.), 1967, 444–480.

Barber, T. X. An Empirically-based Formulation of Hypnotism. *American Journal of Clinical Hypnosis,* 1969a, *12,* 100–130.

Barber, T. X. *Hypnosis: A Scientific Approach.* New York: Van Nostrand-Reinhold Co., 1969b.

Barber, T. X. *LSD, Marihuana, Yoga, and Hypnosis.* Chicago: Aldine Publishing Co., 1970a.

Barber, T. X. The Phenomenology of ('Hypnotic') Suggestibility. Harding, Mass.: The Medfield Foundation, 1970b.

Barber, T. X. Physiological Effects of Hypnosis and Suggestion. In T. X. Barber, *LSD, Marihuana, Yoga, and Hypnosis.* Chicago: Aldine, 1970c, 135–203.

Barber, T. X. Suggested ("Hypnotic") Behavior: The Trance Paradigm Versus an Alternative Paradigm. In Erika Fromm & R. E. Shor (Eds.), *Hypnosis Research Developments and Perspectives.* 1st ed. Chicago: Aldine, 1972, 115–182.

Barber, T. X. Responding to "Hypnotic" Suggestions: An Introspective Report. *American Journal of Clinical Hypnosis,* 1975, *18,* 6–22.

Barber, T. X., & Calverley, D. S. "Hypnotic Behavior" as a Function of Task Motivation. *Journal of Psychology,* 1962, *54,* 363–389.

Barber, T. X., & Calverley, D. S. "Hypnotic-like" Suggestibility in Children and Adults. *Journal of Abnormal and Social Psychology,* 1963a, *66,* 589–597.

Barber, T. X., & Calverley, D. S. The Relative Effectiveness of Task Motivating Instructions and Trance-induction Procedure in the Production of "Hypnotic-like"

Behaviors. *Journal of Nervous and Mental Disease,* 1963b, 137, 107–116.

Barber, T. X., & Calverley, D. S. Effect of *E*'s Tone of Voice on "Hypnotic-like" Suggestibility. *Psychological Reports,* 1964a, *15,* 139–144.

Barber, T. X., & Calverley, D. S. Experimental Studies in "Hypnotic" Behavior: Suggested Deafness Evaluated by Delayed Auditory Feedback. *British Journal of Psychology,* 1964c, *55,* 439–466.

Barber, T. X., & Calverley, D. S. Toward a Theory of Hypnotic Behavior: Effects on Suggestibility of Defining the Situation as Hypnosis and Defining Response to Suggestions as Easy. *Journal of Abnormal and Social Psychology.* 1964e, *68,* 585–592.

Barber, T. X., & Calverley, D. S. Toward a Theory of "Hypnotic" Behavior: Enhancement of Strength and Endurance. *Canadian Journal of Psychology,* 1964f, *18,* 156–167.

Barber, T. X., & Calverley, D. S. Toward a Theory of "Hypnotic" Behavior: An Experimental Study of "Hypnotic Time Distortion". *Archives of General Psychiatry,* 1964g, *10,* 209–216.

Barber, T. X., & Calverley, D. S. Empirical Evidence for a Theory of Hypnotic Behavior: Effects on Suggestibility of Five Variables Typically Included in Hypnotic Induction Procedures. *Journal of Consulting Psychology,* 1965, *29,* 98–107.

Barber, T. X., & Calverley, D. S. Effects on Recall of Hypnotic Induction, Motivational Suggestions, and Suggested Regression: A Methodological and Experimental Analysis. *Journal of Abnormal Psychology,* 1966a, *71,* 169–180.

Barber, T. X., & Calverley, D. S. Toward a Theory of "Hypnotic" Behavior: Experimental Analyses of Suggested Amnesia. *Journal of Abnormal Psychology,* 1966b, *71,* 95–107.

Barber, T. X., & Calverley, D. S. Toward a Theory of Hypnotic Behavior: Experimental Evaluation of Hull's Postulate That Hypnotic Susceptibility Is a Habit Phenomenon, *Journal of Personality,* 1966c, *34,* 416–433.

Barber, T. X., & Calverley, D. S. Toward a Theory of "Hypnotic" Behavior: Replication and Extension of Experiments by Barber and Co-workers (1962–65) and Hilgard and Tart (1966). *International Journal of Clinical And Experimental Hypnosis,* 1968, *16,* 179–195.

Barber, T. X., & Calverley, D. S. Effects of Hypnotic Induction, Suggestions of Anesthesia, and Distraction on Subjective and Physiological Responses to Pain. Paper Presented at Eastern Psychological Association, Annual Meeting, Philadelphia, April, 1969a.

Barber, T. X., & Calverley, D. S. Multidimensional Analysis of "Hypnotic" Behavior. *Journal of Abnormal Psychology,* 1969b, *74,* 209–220.

Barber, T. X., Chauncey, H. H., & Winer, R. A. Effect of Hypnotic and Non-Hypnotic Suggestions on Paratid Gland Response to Gustatory Stimuli. *Psychosomatic Medicine,* 1964, *26,* 374–380.

Barber, T. X., & Coules, J. Electrical Skin Conductance and Galvanic Skin Response During "Hypnosis". *International Journal of Clinical and Experimental Hypnosis,* 1959, *7,* 79–92.

Barber, T. X., Dalal, A. S., & Calverley, D. S. The Subjective Reports of Hypnotic Subjects. *American Journal of Clinical Hypnosis,* 1968, *11,* 74–88.

Barber, T. X., & Glass, L. B. Significant Factors in Hypnotic Behavior. *Journal of Abnormal and Social Psychology,* 1962, *64,* 222–228.

Barber, T. X., & Hahn, K. W., Jr. Physiological and Subjective Responses to Pain Producing Stimulation Under Hypnotically-suggested and Waking-imagined "Analgesia." *Journal of Abnormal and Social Psychology,* 1962, *65,* 411–418.

Barber, T. X., & Hahn, K. W., Jr. Experimental Studies in "Hypnotic" Behavior:

Physiological and Subjective Effects of Imagined Pain. *Journal of Nervous and Mental Disease,* 1964, *139,* 416–425.

Barber, T. X., & Ham, M. W. *Hypnotic Phenomena.* Morristown, N. J.: General Learning Press, 1974.

Barber, T. X., Spanos, N. P., & Chaves, J. F. *Hypnosis, Imagination, and Human Potentialities.* New York: Pergamon Press, Inc., 1974.

Barber, T. X., Walker, P. C., & Hahn, K. W. Effects of Hypnotic Induction and Suggestions on Nocturnal Dreaming and Thinking. *Journal of Abnormal Psychology,* 1973, *82,* 414–427.

Barker, W., & Burgwin, S. Brain Wave Patterns During Hypnosis, Hypnotic Sleep and Normal Sleep. *Archives of Neurology and Psychiatry,* 1949, *62,* 412–420.

Barnlund, D. C. *Interpersonal Communication: Survey and Studies,* Boston: Houghton, Mifflin, 1968.

Barron, F. Threshold for the Perception of Human Movement in Inkblots. *Journal of Consulting Psychology,* 1955, *19,* 33–38.

Barron, F. The Psychology of Creativity. In F. Barron (Ed.), *New Directions in Psychology II.* New York: Holt, Rinehart & Winston. 1965.

Barron, F. *Creative Person and Creative Process.* New York: Holt, Rinehart and Winston, 1969.

Barry, H., Jr., MacKinnon, D. W., & Murray, H. A., Jr. Studies in Personality: A Hypnotizability as a Personality Trait and Its Typological Relations. *Human Biology,* 1931, *3,* 1–36.

Bartlett, E. S., Faw, T. T., & Liebert, R. M. The Effects of Suggestions of Alertness in Hypnosis on Pupillary Response: Report on a Single Subject. *International Journal of Clinical and Experimental Hypnosis,* 1967, *15,* 189–192.

Baudouin, C. *Suggestion and Autosuggestion: A Psychological and Pedagogical Study Based upon the Investigations Made by the New Nancy School.* Translated from the French by E. Paul & C. Paul. New York: Dodd, Mead & Co., 1922.

Beck, E. C., & Barolin, G. S. Effect of Hypnotic Suggestions on Evoked Potentials. *Journal of Nervous and Mental Disease,* 1965, *140,* 154–161.

Beck, E. C., Dustman, R. E., & Beier, E. G. Hypnotic Suggestions and Visually Evoked Potentials. *Electroencephalography and Clinical Neurophysiology,* 1966, *20,* 397–400.

Beecher, H. K. *Measurement of Subjective Responses: Quantitative Effects of Drugs.* New York: Oxford University Press, 1959.

Beh, Helen C., & Barratt, P. E. H. Discrimination and Conditioning During Sleep as Indicated by the Electroencephalogram. *Science,* 1965, *147,* 1470–1471.

Bellak, L. An Ego-Psychological Theory of Hypnosis. *International Journal of Psycho-Analysis,* 1955, *36,* 375–378.

Bellak, L. Creativity: Some Random Notes to a Systematic Consideration. *Journal of Projective Techniques,* 1958, *22,* 363–380.

Benedict, R. Anthropology and the Abnormal. *Journal of General Psychology, 1934, 10,* 59–82.

Bennett, J. H. *The Mesmeric Mania of 1851, with a Physiological Explanation of the Phenomena Produced.* Edinburgh: Sutherland & Knox; London: Simpkin, Marshall, & Co., and S. Highley, 1851.

Bennett, L. L., & Scott, N. E. The Production of Electrocardiographic Abnormalities by Suggestion Under Hypnosis: A Case Report. *American Practitioner,* 1949, *4,* 189–190.

Benson, H. *The Relaxation Response.* New York: William Morrow & Co., 1975.

Benson, H., Beary, J. F., & Carol, M. P. The Relaxation Response. *Psychiatry,* 1974, *37,* 37–46.

Benussi, V. Zur Experimentellen Grundlegung Hypno-suggestiver Methoden Psychischer Analyse. (The Experimental Basis of Hypnosuggestive Methods in Psychological analysis). *Psychologische Forschung,* 1927, *9,* 197–274.

Benyamini, K. Experimental Effects of Hypnotically Induced Anxiety, Arousal, and Inhibition. Unpublished Doctoral Dissertation, University of Michigan, 1963.

Bergasse, N. *Considérations sur le magnétisme animal, ou sur la theorie au monde et des êtres organisés d'après les principles de M. Mesmer.* (Thoughts on animal magnetism or on the theory of the world and beings organized according to the principles of Mr. Mesmer.) La Haye, 1784.

Bergmann, M. S., Graham, H., & Leavitt, H. G. Rorschach Exploration of Consecutive Hypnotic Chronological Age Level Regressions. *Psychosomatic Medicine,* 1947, *9,* 20–28.

Bergson, Henri, Simulation inconsciente dans l'état d'hypnotisme. (Unconscious simulation in the hypnotic state.) *Revue Philosophique,* 1886, *22,* 525–531.

Berman, R., Simonson, E., & Heron, W. Electrocardiographic Effects Associated With Hypnotic Suggestion in Normal and Coronary Sclerotic Individuals. *Journal of Applied Physiology,* 1954, *7,* 89–92.

Bernheim, H. M. *Hypnosis and Suggestion in Psychotherapy: A Treatise on the Nature and Uses of Hypnotism.* French Original of First Part, 1884, Second Part, 1886; with a new preface, 1887. English translation by C. A. Herter, 1888. Reissued with an introduction by E. R. Hilgard, New Hyde Park, N. Y.: University Books, 1964.

Bernheim, H. *Suggestive Therapeutics: A Treatise on the Nature and Uses of Hypnotism.* C. A. Herter (Trans.) New York: G. P. Putnam's Sons, 1889.

Bernstein, M. *The Search for Bridey Murphy.* New York: Doubleday, 1956.

Bertini, M., Lewis, H. B., & Witkin, H. A. Some Preliminary Observations with an Experimental Procedure for the Study of Hypnagogic and Related Phenomena. *Archivivo di psicologia, Neurologia e Psychiatria,* 1964, *25,* 493–534.

Bertrand, A. J. F. *Traité du somnambulisme et des différentes modifications qu'il présente.* (Treatise on Somnambulism and its Various Modifications). Paris: J. G. Dentu, 1823.

Bertrand, A. J. F. *Extase: De l'état d'extase considéré comme une des causes des effets attribués au magnétisme animal.* (Ecstasy: On the State of Ecstasy Which is Considered to be One of the Causes of the Effects Attributed to Animal Magnetism). Paris Encyclopédie Progressive, No. 8, Bèchet et Cie, et al., 1826a.

Bertrand, A. J. F. *Du Magnétisme animal en France et des jugements qu'en ont portés les sociétés savantes; avec le texte des divers rapports faits en 1784 par les commissaires de L'Académie des Sciences, de la Faculté et de la Société Royale de Medécine, et une analyse de dernières séances de l'Academie Royale de Medécine et du Rapport de M. Husson; suivi des considérations sur l'apparition de l'extase dans les traitements magnétiques. Seconde Partie: Du somnambulisme artificiel considéré comme une variété de l'extiase.* (On animal magnetism in France and the judgments of the scientific societies; with texts of the various reports made in 1784 by the commissioners of the Academy of Sciences, the Faculty of the Royal Society of Medicine and an analysis of the last sessions of the Royal Academy of Medicine and of the report of Mr. Husson; with added thoughts on the phenomenon of ectasy in magnetic therapy. Part II: Artificial somnambulism conceived of as a variation of ecstasy). Paris: J. B. Balliére, 1826b.

Best, H. L., & Michaels, R. M. Living out "future" Experience Under Hypnosis. *Sciences,* 1954, *120,* 1077.

Bettinghaus, E. P. *Persuasive Communication.* New York: Holt, Rinehart & Winston, 1968.

Betts, G. H. The Distribution and Functions of Mental Imagery. *Teachers College, Contributions to Education,* 1909, No. 26.

Binet, A. *On Double Consciousness.* (Reprinted as new edition, 1896.) Chicago: Open Court Publishing Co., 1889–1890.

Binet, A., & Féré, C. *Animal Magnetism.* French Original, 1886. English translation, New York: D. Appleton-Century Co., 1888.

Bitterman, M. E., & Marcuse, F. L. Autonomic Response in Posthypnotic Amnesia. *Journal of Experimental Psychology,* 1945, *35,* 248–252.

Black, S., & Friedman, M. Effects of Emotion and Pain on Adrenocortical Function Investigated by Hypnosis. *British Medical Journal,* 1968, *1,* 477–481.

Blake, H., & Gerard, R. W. Brain Potentials During Sleep. *American Journal of Physiology,* 1937, *119,* 692–703.

Blatt, S. J. Patterns of Cardiac Arousal During Complex Mental Activity. *Journal of Abnormal and Social Psychology,* 1961, *62,* 272–282.

Blatt, S. J., Allison, J. & Feirstein, A. The Capacity to Cope with Cognitive Complexity. *Journal of Personality,* 1969, *37,* 269–288.

Blatt, S. J., Goodman, J., & Wallington, S. A., unpublished paper, 1971.

Blatt, S. J., & Stein, M. I. Efficiency in Problem Solving. *Journal of Psychology,* 1959, *48,* 193–213.

Bleuler, E. Psychology of Hypnosis. *Münchener Medizinische Wochenschrift,* 1889, *36,* 76. Reproduced in A. Forel, 1907, 315–320.

Bloch, B. Über die Heilung der Warzen durch Suggestion. *Klinische Wochenschrift,* 1927, *2,* 2271–2275, 2320–2325.

Blum, G. S. *The Blacky Pictures: A Technique for the Exploration of Personality Dynamics.* Ann Arbor, Michigan: Psychodynamic Instruments, 1950.

Blum, G. S. *A Model of the Mind: Explored by Hypnotically Controlled Experiments and Examined for its Psychodynamic Implications.* New York: John Wiley and Sons, 1961.

Blum, G. S. Hypnosis in Psychodynamic Research. In J. E. Gordon (Ed.), 1967, 83–109.

Blum, G. S. A Case Study of Hypnotically Induced Tubular Vision. *The International Journal of Clinical and Experimental Hypnosis,* 1975, *23,* 111–119.

Blum, G. S., Geiwitz, P. J., & Hauenstein, Louise S. Principles of Cognitive Reverberation. *Behavioral Science,* 1967, *12,* 275–288.

Blum, G. S., Geiwitz, P. J., & Stewart, C. G. Cognitive Arousal: The Evolution of a Model. *Journal of Personality and Social Psychology,* 1967, *5,* 138–151.

Blum, G. S., & Graef, J. R. The Detection Over Time of Subjects Simulating Hypnosis. *International Journal of Clinical and Experimental Hypnosis,* 1971, *19,* 211–224.

Blum, G. S., Graef, J. R., & Hauenstein, Louise S. Effects of Interference and Cognitive Arousal Upon the Processing of Organized Thought. *Journal of Abnormal Psychology,* 1968, *73,* 610–614.

Blum, G. S., Hauenstein, Louise S., & Graef, J. R. Studies in Cognitive Reverberation: Replications and Extensions. *Behavioral Science,* 1968, *13,* 171–177.

Blum, G. S., & Porter, Marcia L. The Capacity for Rapid Shifts in Level of Mental Concentration. *The Quarterly Journal of Experimental Psychology,* 1972, *24,* 431–438.

Blum, G. S., & Porter, Marcia L. The Capacity for Selective Concentration on Color Versus Form of Consonants. *Cognitive Psychology,* 1973, *5,* 47–70.

Blum, G. S., Porter, Marica L., & Geiwitz, P. J. Temporal Parameters of Negative Visual Hallucination. *The International Journal of Clinical and Experimental Hypnosis,* 1978, *26,* 30–44.

Blum, G. S., & Wohl, B. M. An Experimental Analysis of the Nature and Operation of Anxiety. *Journal of Abnormal Psychology,* 1971, *78,* 1–8.

Bobbitt, R. A. The Repression Hypothesis Studied in a Situation of Hypnotically Induced Conflict. *Journal of Abnormal and Social Psychology,* 1958, *56,* 204–212.

Bogdonoff, M. D., Combs, J. J., Bryant, G. D., & Warren, J. V. Cardiovascular Responses in Experimentally Induced Alterations of Affect. *Circulation,* 1959, *20,* 353–359.

Bonnefoy, J. B. *Analyse raisonée des rapports des commissaires chargés par le roi de l'examen du magnétisme animal.* (A Rational Analysis of the Reports of the Commissioners Who were Charged by the King with the Investigation of Animal Magnetism). (Not Published). 1784.

Borelli, S. Psychische Einflüsse und reactive Hauterscheinungen. *Münchener Medizinische Wochenschrift,* 1953, *95,* 1078–1082.

Boring, E. G. *A History of Experimental Psychology.* Originally published, 1929, (2nd edition). New York: Appleton-Century-Crofts, 1950.

Boucher, R. G., & Hilgard, E. R. Volunteer Bias in Hypnotic Experimentation. *American Journal of Clinical Hypnosis,* 1962, *5,* 49–51.

Bowers, K. S. Hypnotic Behavior: The Differentiation of Trance and Demand Characteristic Variables. *Journal of Abnormal Psychology,* 1966, *71,* 42–51.

Bowers, K. S. The Effect of Demands for Honesty on Reports of Visual and Auditory Hallucinations. *International Journal of Clinical and Experimental Hypnosis,* 1967, *15,* 31–36.

Bowers, K. S. Hypnosis and Creativity: A Preliminary Investigation. *International Journal of Clinical and Experimental Hypnosis,* 1968, *16,* 38–52.

Bowers, K. S. Creativity and Hypnotic Susceptibility. Paper presented at American Psychological Association, Washington, D. C., September 1969.

Bowers, K. S. Heart Rate and GSR Concomitants of Vigilance and Arousal. *Canadian Journal of Psychology,* 1971a, *25,* 175–183.

Bowers, K. S. Sex and Susceptibility as Moderator Variables in the Relationship of Creativity and Hypnotic Susceptibility. *Journal of Abnormal Psychology,* 1971b, *78,* 93–100.

Bowers, K. S. Hypnosis, Attribution, and Demand Characteristics. *The International Journal of Clinical and Experimental Hypnosis,* 1973a, *21,* 226–238.

Bowers, K. S. Situationism in Psychology: An Analysis and a Critique. *Psychological Review,* 1973b, *80,* 307–336.

Bowers, K. S. The Psychology of Subtle Control: An Attributional Analysis of Behavioral Persistance. *Canadian Journal of Behavioral Science,* 1975, *7,* 78–95.

Bowers, K. S. *Hypnosis for the Seriously Curious.* Monterey, Calif.: Brooks/Cole, 1976.

Bowers, K. S., & Bowers Patricia G. Hypnosis and Creativity: A Theoretic and Empirical Rapprochement. In Erika Fromm and R. E. Shor (Eds.), *Hypnosis: Research Developments and Perspectives.* 1st edition Chicago: Aldine, 1972, 255–291.

Bowers, K. S., & Keeling, K. R. Heart Rate Variability in Creative Functioning. *Psychological Reports,* 1971, *29,* 160–162.

Bowers, K. S., & Gilmore, J. B. Subjective Report and Credibility: An Inquiry Involving Hypnotic Hallucinations. *Journal of Abnormal Psychology,* 1969, *74,* 443–451.

Bowers, K. S., & van der Meulen, Sandra J. Effect of Hypnotic Susceptibility on Creativity Test Performance. *Journal of Personality and Social Psychology,* 1970, *14,* 247–256.

Bowers, Patricia G. Effect of Hypnosis and Suggestions of Reduced Defensiveness

On Creativity Test Performance. *Journal of Personality,* 1967, *35,* 311–322.

Bowers, Patricia G. Hypnotizability, Creativity and the Role of Effortless Experiencing. *International Journal of Clinical and Experimental Hypnosis,* 1978, *26,* 184–202.

Boxer, A. The Phenomena of Self-hypnosis: A Qualitative Analysis of Subjects' Self-reports. Paper presented at the Annual Convention of the Society for Clinical and Experimental Hypnosis, Asheville, N.C., October, 1978.

Boyers, J. M., & Morgan, Arlene. The Veridicality of Posthypnotic Amnesia. Hawthorne House Research Memorandum, Stanford University 1969.

Brady, J. P., & Levitt, E. E. Nystagmus as a Criterion of Hypnotically Induced Visual Hallucinations. *Science,* 1964, *146,* 85–86.

Brady, J. P., & Levitt, E. E. Hypnotically-induced Visual Hallucinations. *Psychosomatic Medicine,* 1966, *28,* 351–363.

Brady, J. P., Levitt, E. E., & Lubin, B. Expressed Fear of Hypnosis and Volunteering Behavior. *Journal of Nervous and Mental Disease,* 1961, *133,* 216–217.

Brady, J. P., & Rosner, B. S. Rapid Eye Movements in Hypnotically Induced Dreams. *Journal of Nervous and Mental Disease,* 1966, *143,* 28–35.

Braginsky, B. M., Braginsky, D. D., & Ring, K. *Methods of Madness: The Mental Hospital as a Last Resort.* New York: Holt, Rinehart & Winston, 1969.

Braid, J. *Neurypnology: The Rationale of Nervous Sleep Considered in Relation with Animal Magnetism, Illustrated by Numerous Cases of its Successful Application in the Relief and Cure of Disease.* London: John Churchill, 1843. Edited version under Title: *Braid on Hypnotism: Neurypnology. A new Edition Edited with an Introduction, Biographical and Bibliographical, Embodying the Author's Later Views and Further Evidence on the Subject.* Edited by A. E. Waite. London: George Redway, 1889. Reprinted as: *Braid on Hypnotism: The Beginnings of Modern Hypnosis.* New York: Julian Press, 1960.

Braid, J. *The Power of the Mind Over the Body: An Experimental Inquiry into the Nature and Cause of the Phenomena Attributed by Reichenbach and Others to a " New Imponderable".* London: John Churchill; Edinburgh: Adam and Charles Black, 1846. This pamphlet is a slightly revised reproduction of three papers published in the *Medical Times,* June 13, 20, & 23, 1846. This abridged account is found in A. E. Waite. Synopsis of counter-experiments undertaken by James Braid to illustrate his criticism of Reichenbach. Appendix III, 352–361, in J. Braid, 1889. Another abridged version, 3–19; 31–36, is reprinted in W. Dennis, *Readings in the History of Psychology,* New York: Appleton-Century-Crofts, 1948, 178–193.

Braid, J. Facts and Observations as to the Relative Value of Mesmeric and Hypnotic Coma, and Ethereal Narcotism, for the Mitigation or Entire Prevention of Pain During Surgical Operations. *Medical Times,* 1847, *15,* 381–382.

Braid, J. *Magic, Witchcraft, Animal Magnetism, Hypnotism, and Electrobiology: Being a Digest of the Latest Views of the Author on These Subjects.* Third edition, greatly enlarged, embracing observations of J. C. Colquhoun's "An History of Magic, Witchcraft, and Animal Magnetism". London: John Churchill, 1852.

Bramwell, J. M. James Braid: His Work and Writings. *Society for Psychical Research: Proceedings,* 1896–7a, *12,* Part 30, Supplement 127–166.

Bramwell, J. M. What Is Hypnotism? *Society for Psychical Research: Proceedings,* 1896–97b, *12,* Part 31, 204–258.

Bramwell, J. M. *Hypnotism: Its History, Practice and Theory.* London: Grant Richards, 1903. Reissued with new introduction. New York: Julian Press, 1956.

Branca, A. A., & Podolnick, E. E. Normal, Hypnotically Induced, and Feigned

Anxiety as Reflected in and Detected by the MMPI. *Journal of Consulting Psychology,* 1961, *25,* 165–170.

Breuer, J., & Freud, S. (1893a). *Studies on Hysteria.* Newly Translated from the German and edited by J. Strachey. With the collaboration of Anna Freud. (Earlier translation by A. A. Brill, 1936). New York: Basic Books, 1957.

Breuer, J., & Freud, S. Über den psychischen Mechanismus hysterischer Phenomene (On the Psychical Mechanisms of Hysterical Phenomena). *Neurologisches Zentralblatt,* 1893b, *1 and 2,* 4–10; 43–47. Translated by J. Rickman in *Collected Papers,* Vol. 1. London: The Hogarth Press, 1924.

Brenman, Margaret. The Use of Hypnotic Techniques in a Study of Tension Systems. In Margaret Brenman & M. M. Gill, 1947, 195–253.

Brenman, Margaret. Dreams and Hypnosis. *Psychoanalytic Quarterly,* 1949, *18,* 455–465.

Brenman, Margaret, & Gill, M. M. *Hypnotherapy: A Survey of the Literature.* With appended case reports and an experimental study. New York: International Universities Press, 1947.

Brickner, R. M., & Kubie, L. S. A Miniature Psychotic Storm Produced by a Superego Conflict Over Simple Post-hypnotic Suggestion. *Psychoanalytic Quarterly,* 1936, *5,* 467–487.

Broadbent, D. E. A Mechanical Model for Human Attention and Immediate Memory. *Psychological Review,* 1967, *64,* 205–215.

Broadhurst, P. L., Fulker, D. W., & Wilcock, J. Behavioral Genetics in *Annual Review of Psychology,* 1974, *25,* 389–415.

Bromberg, W. *The Mind of Man: A History of Psychotherapy and Psychoanalysis.* New York: Harper, 1959. (Originally published under title *Man Above Humanity: A History of Psychotherapy.* Philadelphia: Lippincott, 1954).

Brooks, L. R. The Suppression of Visualization by Reading. *Quarterly Journal of Experimental Psychology,* 1967, *19,* 289–299.

Brooks, L. R. The Internal Representation of Spatial and Verbal Information. Paper presented to Eastern Psychological Association, Washington, D.C., April, 1968.

Brown, Barbara B. Recognition of Aspects of Consciousness Through Association with EEG Alpha Activity Represented by a Light Signal. *Psychophysiology,* 1970, *6,* 442–452.

Brown, D. P. Diachronic Methodology in the Study of Self-hypnosis. Paper read at the Annual Convention of the American Psychological Association, New Orleans, August, 1974.

Brown, D. P. A Model for the Levels of Concentrative Meditation. *International Journal of Clinical and Experimental Hypnosis,* 1977, *25,* 236–273.

Brown, D. P. & Fromm, Erika. The Construction of Three Questionnaires for the Understanding of the Phenomena of Self-hypnosis. Paper presented at the Annual Convention of the Society for Clinical and Experimental Hypnosis, Asheville, N.C., October, 1978.

Brown, R., & McNeill, D. The "Tip of the Tongue" Phenomenon. *Journal of Verbal Learning and Verbal Behavior,* 1966, *5,* 325–337.

Bruner, J. S., & Goodman, C. C. Value and Need as Organizing Factors in Perception. *Journal of Abnormal and Social Psychology,* 1947, *42,* 33–44.

Burchard, E. M. L. The Evolution of Psychoanalytic Tasks and Goals: A Historical Study of Freud's Writings on Technique. *Psychiatry,* 1958, *21,* 341–357.

Burdin, C., & Dubois, F. (d'Amiens). *Histoire académique du magnétisme animal: accompagnée de notes et de remarques critiques sur toutes les observations et expériences faites jusqu'à ce jour.* (Academic History of Animal Magnetism: With

Notes and Critical Remarks with Regard to All Observations and Experiences Made Up to the Present). Paris: J. B. Baillière, 1841.

Burr, C. W. The Reflexes of Early Infancy. *British Journal of Children's Disease.* 1921, *18*, 152–153.

Bush, M., Hatcher, R., & Mayman, M. Reality Attentiveness-inattentiveness and Externalization-internalization in Defensive Style. *Journal of Consulting and Clinical Psychology.* 1969, *33*, 343–350.

Butler, B. The Use of Hypnosis in the Care of the Cancer Patient. *Cancer,* 1954, *7*, 1–14.

Butler, J. M., & Rice, Laura N. Adience, Self-actualization, and Drive Theory. In J. M. Wepman and R. W. Heine (Eds.) *Concepts of Personality.* Chicago: Aldine Publishing Company, 1963, *79*–110.

Byrne, B. Item Concreteness vs Spatial Organization as Predictors of Visual Imagery. *Memory and Cognition,* 1974, *2*, 53–59.

Cambareri, J. D. The Effects of Sensory Isolation on Suggestible and Non-suggestible Psychology Graduate Students. Unpublished doctoral dissertation, University of Utah. 1958. *Dissertation Abstracts.* 1959, *19*, 1813.

Campbell, H. J. *Correlative Physiology of the Nervous System.* London: Academic Press, 1965, 212–246.

Cannon, W. B. "Voodoo" Death. *American Anthropologist,* 1942, *44*, 169–181.

Cantril, H. Experiments in the Wording of Questions. *Public Opinion Quarterly,* 1940, *4*, 330–332.

Carlson, E. T. Charles Poyen Brings Mesmerism to America. *Journal of the History of Medicine and Allied Sciences,* 1960, *15*, 121–132.

Casey, G. A. Hypnotic Time Distortion and Learning. *Dissertation Abstracts,* 1966, *27*, 2116–2117.

Cass, W. A. An Experiment Investigation of the Association Hypothesis, Utilizing a Post-hypnotic Technique. Unpublished master's thesis, University of Oregon, 1942.

Chapman, L. F., Goodell, Helen, & Wolff, H. G. Increased Inflammatory Reaction Induced by Central Nervous System Activity. *Transactions of the Association of American Physicians,* 1959, *72*, 84–109.

Charcot, J. M. Essai d'une distinction nosographique des divers états compris sous le nom d'Hypnotisme. (Attempt to Make a Nosographic Distinction of the Different Nervous States Known Under the Name of Hypnotism). *Comptes rendus de l'Académie des Sciences,* 1882a, *44*, Summarized in A. Binet and C. S. Féré, 1887, 154–163.

Charcot, J. M. Sur les divers états nerveux détermines par l'hypnotisation chez les hystériques. *Comptes rendus hebdomadaires des séances de l'Académie des Sciences* (On Different Nervous States as They Appear When Hysterics Are Hypnotized. *Biweekly accounts of the meetings of the Academy of Sciences),* 1882b, *94*, 403–405.

Charcot, J. M. *Oeuvres complètes.* (Complete works) Paris: Aux Bureaux du Progrès Médical, 1886. 9 vols.

Charcot, J. M. The Faith-cure. *New Review,* 1893, 8, No. 44, 18–31.

Chase, W. W. An Experiment in Controlled Nystagmus Using Hypnosis. *American Journal of Optometry,* 1963, *40*, 463–468.

Chaves, J. F. Hypnosis Reconceptualized: An Overview of Barber's Theoretical and Empirical work. *Psychological Reports,* 1968, *22*, 587–608.

Cheek, D. B. Unconscious Perception of Meaningful Sounds During Surgical Anesthesia as Revealed in Hypnosis. *American Journal of Clinical Hypnosis,* 1959, *1*, 101–113.

Cheek, D. B. Unconscious Reactions and Surgical Risk. *Western Journal of Surgery, Obstetrics, and Gynecology,* 1961, *69,* 325–328.

Cheek, D. B. Surgical Memory and Reactions to Careless Conversation. *American Journal of Clinical Hypnosis,* 1964, *6,* 237–240.

Cheek, D. B. The Meaning of Continued Hearing Sense Under General Chemo-anesthesia: A Progress Report and Report of a Case. *American Journal of Clinical Hypnosis,* 1966, *8,* 275–280.

Cheek, D. B., & Le Cron, L. M. *Clinical Hypotherapy.* New York: Grune and Stratton, 1968.

Chertok, L. *Psychosomatic Methods in Painless Childbirth: History, Theory and Practice.* Foreward by R. G. Douglas. Translated from the 2nd French edition by D. Leigh. New York: Pergamon Press, 1959.

Chertok, L. *Hypnosis.* Translated from an Expanded Version of the 3rd French Edition in Collaboration with the Author by D. Graham. Oxford: Pergamon Press, 1966.

Chertok, L. Theory of Hypnosis Since 1889. *International Journal of Psychiatry,* 1967, *3,* 188–199.

Chertok, L., & Kramarz, P. Hypnosis, Sleep, and Electro-encephalography. *Journal of Nervous and Mental Disease,* 1959, *128,* 227–238.

Chiasson, S. W. Hypnosis in Postoperative Urinary Retention. *American Journal of Clinical Hypnosis.* 1964, *6,* 366–368.

Christensen, P. R., Merrifield, P. R., & Guilford, J. P. *Consequences: Manual of Administration, Scoring, and Interpretation.* Beverly Hills, California: Sheridan Supply Co., 1958.

Clarke, G. H. V. The Charming of Warts. *Journal of Investigative Dermatology,* 1965, *45,* 15–21.

Clemes, S. R. Repression and Hypnotic Amnesia. *Journal of Abnormal and Social Psychology,* 1964, *69,* 62–69.

Clynes, M., Kohn, M., & Lifshitz, K. Dynamics and Spatial Behavior of Light Evoked Potentials, Their Modification Under Hypnosis, and On-line Correlation In Relation to Rhythmic Components. *Annals of the New York Academy of Science,* 1963, *112,* 468–509.

Cobb, J. C., Evans, F. J., Gustafson, L. A., O'Connell, D. N., Orne, M. T., & Shor, R. E. Specific Motor Response During Sleep to Sleep-administered Meaningful Suggestion: An Exploratory Investigation. *Perceptual and Motor Skills,* 1965, *20,* 629–636.

Cobb, J. C., & Shor, R. E. Development of Techniques to Maximize Hypnotic Responsiveness. Paper presented at the meeting of the Eastern Psychological Association, Philadelphia, April, 1964.

Coe, W. C. The Heuristic Value of Role Theory and Hypnosis. Unpublished doctoral dissertation, University of California, (Berkeley), 1964.

Coe, W. C. Hypnosis as Role Enactment: The Role Demand Variable. *American Journal of Clinical Hypnosis,* 1966, *8,* 189–191.

Coe, W. C. Personality Correlates of Hypnotic Susceptibility. A validation study of Josephine Hilgard's hypothesis. Paper presented at the meeting of The Society for Clinical and Experimental Hypnosis, Montreal, October 13, 1974.

Coe, W. C. Posthypnotic Amnesia and the Psychology of Secrets. Paper read at the Annual Convention of The Society for Clinical and Experimental Hypnosis, Philadelphia, July, 1976.

Coe, W. C. The Credibility of Posthypnotic Amnesia: A Contextualist's view. Unpublished paper, 1978.

Coe, W. C., Allen, Joan L., Krug, W. M. & Wurzman, Andrea G. Goal-directed

Fantasy in Hypnotic Responsiveness: Skill, Item Wording, or Both? *International Journal of Clinical and Experimental Hypnosis,* 1974, *22,* 157–166.

Coe, W. C., Basden, Barbara, Basden, D., & Graham, C. Posthypnotic Amnesia: Suggestions of an Active Process in Dissociative Phenomena. *Journal of Abnormal Psychology,* 1976, *85,* 455–458.

Coe, W. C., Baugher, J. R., Krimm, W. R., & Smith, J. A. A Further Examination of Selective Recall Following Hypnosis. *International Journal of Clinical and Experimental Hypnosis,* 1976, *24,* 13–21.

Coe, W. C., Kobayashi, K., & Howard, M. L. An Approach Toward Isolating Factors that Influence Antisocial Conduct in Hypnosis. *International Journal of Clinical and Experimental Hypnosis,* 1972, *20,* 118–130.

Coe, W. C., Kobayashi, K., & Howard, M. L. Experimental and Ethical Problems of Evaluating the Influence of Hypnosis in Antisocial Conduct. *Journal of Abnormal Psychology,* 1973, *82,* 476–482.

Coe, W. C., & Sarbin, T. R. An Experimental Demonstration of Hypnosis as Role Enactment, *Journal of Abnormal Psychology,* 1966, *71,* 400–406.

Coe, W. C., & Sarbin, T. R. An Alternative Interpretation to the Multiple Composition of Hypnotic Scales: A Single Role-Relevant Skill. *Journal of Personality and Social Psychology,* 1971, *18,* 1–8.

Coe, W. C., & Sarbin, T. R. Hypnosis from the Standpoint of a Contextualist. In W. E. Edmonston, Jr. (Ed.), *Conceptual and Investigative Approaches to Hypnosis and Hypnotic Phenomena. Annals of the New York Academy of Sciences,* 1977, *296,* 2–13.

Coe, W., Taul, J. H., Basden, D., & Basden, Barbara. An Investigation of the Dissociative Hypothesis and Disorganized Retrieval in Posthypnotic Amnesia with Retroactive Inhibition in Free-Recall Learning. *Proceedings of the 81st Annual Convention, American Psychological Association,* 1973.

Cogger, W. G., Jr., & Edmonston, W. E. Hypnosis and Oral Temperature: A Reevaluation of Experimental Techniques. *British Journal of Clinical Hypnosis,* 1971, *2,* 76–80.

Cohen, J. *Psychological Time in Health and Disease.* Springfield, Illinois: Charles C. Thomas, 1967.

Collins, J. K. Muscular Endurance in Normal and Hypnotic States: A Study of Suggested Catalepsy. Honors thesis, Department of Psychology, University of Sydney, Sidney, Australia, 1961.

Colquhoun, J. C. *Isis Revelata: An Inquiry into the Origin, Progress, and Present State of Animal Magnetism.* 3rd edition. Edinburgh: William Wilson, 1844, 2 volumes.

Conn, J. H. Historical Aspects of Scientific Hypnosis. *Journal of Clinical and Experimental Hypnosis,* 1957, *5,* 17–24.

Connors, J., & Sheehan, P. W. Analysis of the Cue Characteristics of Task Motivational Instructions. *International Journal of Clinical and Experimental Hypnosis,* 1976, *24,* 287–299.

Conti, A. P. Heart Rate Conditioning In and Out of Hypnosis. Unpublished bachelor's thesis, Colgate University, 1968.

Cooper, L. F., & Erickson, M. H. Time Distortion in Hypnosis II. *Bulletin Georgetown University Medical Center,* 1950, *4,* 50–68.

Cooper, L. M. Spontaneous and Suggested Posthypnotic Source Amnesia. *International Journal of Clinical and Experimental Hypnosis,* 1966a, *14,* 180–193.

Cooper, L. M. What is Hypnotic Amnesia? Paper presented at meeting of American Psychological Association, New York, September, 1966b.

Cooper, L. M. Expectations About Hypnosis of College Students Who Have Not

Been Hypnotized. Unpublished research, Brigham Young University, 1969.

Cooper, L. M., & Harrison, R. V. Individual Recall of Serially Presented Motor Tasks: Individual Administration. Unpublished research, Brigham Young University, 1969.

Cooper, L. M., & Hoskovec, J. Hypnotic Suggestions for Learning During Stage 1 REM Sleep. Unpublished research, Brigham Young University, 1966.

Cooper, L. M., & London, P. Sex and Hypnotic Susceptibility in Children. *International Journal of Clinical and Experimental Hypnosis,* 1966, *14,* 55–60.

Cooper, L. M., & Moore, Rosemarie K. Individual Recall of Serially Presented Motor Tasks: Group Presentations. Unpublished research. Brigham Young University, 1967.

Cooper, L. M., & Young, J. Hypnotic Recall Amnesia as a Function of Manipulated expectation. Unpublished research, Brigham Young University, 1971.

Coors, D. A Determination of the Density of Post-Hypnotic Amnesia for the Stylus Maze. Thesis submitted for B.A. degree, University of Wisconsin, 1928.

Corley, J. B. Hypnosis and the Anesthetist. *American Journal of Clinical Hypnosis,* 1965, *8,* 34–36.

Counts, R. M., & Mensh, I. N. Personality Characteristics in Hypnotically Induced Hostility. *Journal of Clinical Psychology,* 1950, *6,* 325–330.

Coué, E. *Self-Mastery Through Conscious Autosuggestion.* London: George Allen & Unwin, 1922.

Craik, K. H., & Sarbin, T. R. The Effect of Covert Alterations of Clock Rate upon Time Estimates and Personal Tempo. *Perceptual and Motor Skills,* 1963, *16,* 597–610.

Crasilneck, H. B., & Hall, J. A. Physiological Changes Associated with Hypnosis: A Review of the Literature Since 1948. *International Journal of Clinical and Experimental Hypnosis,* 1959, *7,* 9–50.

Crasilneck, H.B., & Hall, J. A. *Clinical Hypnosis: Principles and Applications.* New York: Grune & Stratton, 1975.

Crawford, Helen Joan. Hypnotic Susceptibility and "Right Hemisphere" Functioning: Gestalt closure Ability Correlates. Paper presented at the Annual Convention of the American Psychological Association, San Francisco, August, 1977.

Crawford, Helen Joan, Macdonald, H., & Hilgard, E. R. Hypnotic Deafness: A Psychophysical Study of Responses to Tone Intensity as Modified by Hypnotic Suggestion. *American Journal of Psychology,* in press.

Crawley, E. *The Mystic Rose: A Study of Primitive Marriage and of Primitive Thought in its Bearing on Marriage.* Rev. by T. Besterman. London: Methuen & Co., Ltd., 1927.

Cronin, D. M., Spanos, N. P., & Barber, T. X. Augmenting Hypnotic Suggestibility by Providing Favorable Information About Hypnosis. *American Journal of Clinical Hypnosis.* 1971, *13,* 259–264.

Crosson, B., Meinz, R., Laur, E., Williams, D., & Andreychuk, T. Developing a Biofeedback Model: EEG Alpha Training, Hypnotic Susceptibility, and Baseline Techniques. *International Journal of Clinical and Experimental Hypnosis,* 1977, *25,* 348–360.

Dalal, A. S. An Empirical Approach to Hypnosis: An Overview of Barber's Work. *Archives of General Psychiatry,* 1966, *15,* 151–157.

Damaser, Esther C. An Experimental Study of Long-Term Post-Hypnotic Suggestion. Unpublished doctoral dissertation, Harvard University, 1964.

Damaser, Esther C., Shor, R. E., & Orne, M. T. Physiological Effects During Hypnotically Requested Emotions. *Psychosomatic Medicine,* 1963, *25,* 334–343.

Danielou, A. The Influence of Sound Phenomena on Human Consciousness. *Psychedelic Review,* 1966, *7,* 20–26.

Darnton, R. *Mesmerism and the End of the Enlightenment in France.* Cambridge, Mass.: Harvard University Press, 1968.

Darrow, C. W., Henry, E. C., Gill, M. M., & Brenman, Margaret. Inter-area Electroencephalographic Relationships Affected by Hypnosis: Preliminary Report, *Electroencephalography and Clinical Neurophysiology,* 1950, *2,* 231–240.

Das, J. P. The Pavlovian Theory of Hypnosis: An Evaluation. *Journal of Mental Science,* 1958a, *104,* 82–90.

Das, J. P. Conditioning and Hypnosis. *Journal of Experimental Psychology,* 1958b, *56,* 110–113.

Davé, R., & Reyher, J. The Effects of Hypnotically Induced Dreams on Creative Problem Solving. *Journal of Abnormal Psychology,* 1978.

Davidson, R. J., & Goleman, D. J. The Role of Attention in Meditation and Hypnosis: A Psychobiological Perspective on Transformations of Consciousness. *International Journal of Clinical and Experimental Hypnosis,* 1977, *25,* 291–308.

Davidson, R. J., & Schwartz, G. E. The Psychobiology of Relaxation and Related States. In D. I. Mostofsky (Ed.), *Behavioral Control and Modification of Physiological Activity.* Englewood Cliffs, New Jersey: Prentice-Hall, 1976.

Davis, F. C. The Functional Significance of Imagery Differences. *Journal of Experimental Psychology,* 1932, *15,* 630–661.

Davis, L. W., & Husband, R. W. A Study of Hypnotic Susceptibility in Relation to Personality Traits. *Journal of Abnormal and Social Psychology,* 1931, *26,* 175–182.

Davis, R. C., & Kantor, J. R. Skin Resistance During Hypnotic States. *Journal of General Psychology,* 1935, *13,* 62–81.

Davis, Sally, Dawson, J. G., & Seay, B. Prediction of Hypnotic Susceptibility from Imaginative Involvement. *The American Journal of Clinical Hypnosis,* 1978, *20,* 194–198.

Dawson, H. E., Jr. Concurrent Conditioning of Autonomic Processes in Humans. Unpublished Doctoral Dissertation, Indiana University, 1953. Cited by Shearn (1961).

DeBono, E. *The Use of Lateral Thinking in the Generation of New Ideas.* New York: Basic Books, 1968.

Deckert, G. H., & West, L. J. Hypnosis and Experimental Psychopathology. *American Journal of Clinical Hypnosis,* 1963, *5,* 256–276.

Deckert, G. H., & West, L. J. The Problem of Hypnotizability: A Review. *International Journal of Clinical and Experimental Hypnosis,* 1963, *11,* 205–235.

Deikman, A. J. Experimental Meditation. *Journal of Nervous and Mental Disease,* 1963, *136,* 329–343. Reprinted in Tart, 1969a, 199–218.

Deikman, Arthur J. Deautomatization and the Mystic Experience. *Psychiatry,* 1966, *29,* 324–338.

Deikman, A. J. Bimodal Consciousness. *Archives of General Psychiatry,* 1971, *25,* 481–489.

DeLeon, G. Conditioning the Human Heart with Noise as the Unconditioned Stimulus. *Journal of Experimental Psychology,* 1964, *68,* 518–520.

Deleuze, J. P. F. *Histoire critique de magnétisme animal.* (Critical History of Animal Magnetism). Paris, 1819.

Deleuze, J. P. F. *Practical Instruction in Animal Magnetism: Part I.* French original 1825. Translated from the Paris edition by T. C. Hartshorn, with notes by the translator referring to cases in this country. Providence, R.I.: B. Cranston & Co., 1837.

Dellas, Marie, & Gaier, E. L. Identification of Creativity: The Individual. *Psychological Bulletin,* 1970, *73,* 55–73.

Dessoir, M. *Bibliographie des modernen Hypnotismus.* (Bibliography of Modern Hypnotism). Berlin: Carl Dunckers Verlag, 1888.

Dessoir, M. *Erster Nachtrag zur Bibliographie des modernen Hypnotismus.* (First supplement to the bibliography of modern hypnotism). Berlin: Carl Dunckers Verlag, 1890.

Dessoir, M. *Das Doppel-Ich.* Leipzig: Ernst Günthers Verlag, 1890. Second enlarged edition, 1896.

Deutsch, Jaroslav, A., & Deutsch, Diana. Attention: Some Theoretical Considerations. *Psychological Review,* 1963, *70,* 80–90.

Diamond, M. J. Hypnotizability is Modifiable: An Alternative Approach. *International Journal of Clinical and Experimental Hypnosis,* 1977, *25,* 147–166.

Diamond, M. J., & Taft, R. The Role Played by Ego Permissiveness and Imagery in Hypnotic Responsivity. *International Journal of Clinical and Experimental Hypnosis,* 1975, *23,* 130–138.

Dittborn, J. M., & Aristeguieta, A. Expectation and Spontaneous Posthypnotic Amnesia: An Experimental Note. *American Journal of Clinical Hypnosis,* 1962, *4,* 268–269.

Dittborn, J. M., Muñoz, L., & Aristeguietá, A. Facilitation of Suggested Sleep After Repeated Performances of the Sleep Suggestibility Test. *International Journal of Clinical and Experimental Hypnosis,* 1963, *11,* 236–240.

Dittborn, J. M., & O'Connell, D. N. Behavioral Sleep, Physiological Sleep, and Hypnotizability. *International Journal of Clinical and Experimental Hypnosis,* 1967, *15,* 181–188.

Dixon, N. F. *Subliminal Perception: The Nature of a Controversy.* London: McGraw Hill, 1971.

Dolby, R. M., & Sheehan, P. W. Cognitive Processing and Expectancy Behavior in Hypnosis. *Journal of Abnormal Psychology,* 1977, *86,* 334–345.

Domhoff, B. Night Dreams and Hypnotic Dreams: Is There Evidence That They Are Different? *International Journal of Clinical and Experimental Hypnosis,* 1964, *12,* 159–168.

Dorcus, R. M., Brintnall, A. K., & Case, H. W. Control Experiments and Their Relation to Theories of Hypnotism. *Journal of General Psychology,* 1941, *24,* 217–221.

Doupe, J., Miller, W. R., & Keller, W. K. Vasomotor reactions in the Hypnotic State. *Journal of Neurology, Neurosurgery & Psychiatry,* 1939, *2,* 97–106.

Dreistadt, R. The Psychology of Creativity: How Einstein Discovered the Theory of Relativity. *Psychology: A Journal of Human Behavior,* 1974, *11,* 15–25.

Drever, J. *A Dictionary of Psychology.* Middlesex: Penguin Books, 1952.

Dudek, Stephanie Z. Suggestion and Play Therapy in the Cure of Warts in Children: A Pilot Study. *Journal of Nervous and Mental Disease,* 1967, *145,* 37–42.

Dudek, Stephanie Z. M.: An Active Energy System Correlating Rorschach M with Ease of Creative Expression. *Journal of Projective Techniques and Personality Assessment.* 1968a, *32,* 453–461.

Dudek, Stephanie Z. Regression and Creativity: A Comparison of the Rorschach Records of Successful vs. Unsuccessful Painters and Writers. *Journal of Nervous and Mental Disease.* 1968b, *147,* 535–546.

Dudley, D. L., Holmes, T. H., Martin, C. J., & Ripley, H. S. Changes in Respiration Associated with Hypnotically Induced Emotion, Pain, and Exercise. *Psychosomatic Medicine,* 1964, *26,* 46–57.

Dudley, D. L., Homes, T. H., Martin, C. J., & Ripley, H. S. Hypnotically Induced

Facsimile of Pain. *Archives of General Psychiatry,* 1966, *15,* 198–204.

Dudley, D. L., Holmes, T. H., & Ripley, H. S. Hypnotically Induced and Suggested Facsimile of Head Pain. *Journal of Nervous and Mental Disease,* 1967, *144,* 258–265.

Dulany, D. E., Jr. Hypotheses and Habits in Verbal "Operant Conditioning." *Journal of Abnormal and Social Psychology,* 1961, *63,* 251–263.

Dumas, R. EEG Alpha-Hypnotizability Correlations: A Review. *Psychophysiology,* 1977, *14,* 431–438.

Dumas, R. & Morgan, A. EEG Asymmetry as a Function of Occupation, Task, and Task Difficulty. *Neuropsychologia,* 1975, *13,* 219–228.

Dunbar, F. *Emotions and Bodily Changes.* 4th edition. New York: Columbia University Press, 1954.

Dynes, J. B. An Experimental Study of Hypnotic Anaesthesia. *Journal of Abnormal and Social Psychology,* 1932, *27,* 79–88.

Easton, R. D., & Shor, R. E. Information Processing Analysis of the Chevreul Pendulum Illusion. *Journal of Experimental Psychology: Human Perception and Performance,* 1975, *1,* 231–236.

Easton, R. D., & Shor, R. E. An Experimental Analysis of the Chevreul Pendulum Illusion. *Journal of General Psychology,* 1976, *95,* 111–125.

Easton, R. D., & Shor, R. E. Augmented and Delayed Feedback in the Chevreul Pendulum Illusion. *Journal of General Psychology,* 1977, *97,* 167–177.

Edmonston, W. E., Jr. Stimulus-Response Theory of Hypnosis. In J. E. Gordon, (Ed.), 1967, 345–387.

Edmonston, W. E., Jr. Hypnosis and Electrodermal Responses. *American Journal of Clinical Hypnosis,* 1968, *11,* 16–25.

Edmonston, W. E., Jr. Relaxation as an Appropriate Experimental Control in Hypnosis Studies. *American Journal of Clinical Hypnosis,* 1972, *14,* 218–229.

Edmonston, W. E., Jr. Neutral Hypnosis as Relaxation. *American Journal of Clinical Hypnosis,* 1977, *20,* 69–75.

Edmonston, W. E., Jr., & Erbeck, J. R. Hypnotic Time Distortion: A Note. *American Journal of Clinical Hypnosis,* 1967, *10,* 79–80.

Edmonston, W. E., Jr., & Grotevant, W. R. Hypnosis and Alpha Density. *American Journal of Clinical Hypnosis,* 1975, *17,* 221–232.

Edmonston, W. E., Jr., & Pessin, M. Hypnosis as Related to Learning and Electrodermal Measures. *American Journal of Clinical Hypnosis,* 1966, *9,* 31–51.

Edmonston, W. E., Jr., & Robertson, T. G., Jr. A Comparison of the Effects of Task Motivational and Hypnotic Induction Instructions on Responsiveness to Hypnotic Suggestibility Scales. *American Journal of Clinical Hypnosis,* 1967, *9,* 184–187.

Edwards, G. Post-Hypnotic Amnesia and Post-Hypnotic Effect. *British Journal of Psychiatry,* 1965, *111,* 316–325.

Ehrlich, Elizabeth A. W. Effects of Anxiety and Pleasure on Memory Span. Unpublished Doctoral Dissertation, University of Michigan, 1965.

Eichhorn, R., & Tracktir, J. The Relationship Between Anxiety, Hypnotically Induced Emotions and Gastric Secretion. *Gastroenterology,* 1955a, *29,* 422–431.

Eichhorn, R., & Tracktir, J. The Effect of Hypnotically Induced Emotions Upon Gastric Secretion. *Gastroenterology,* 1955b, *29,* 432–438.

Eichhorn, R., & Tracktir, J. The Effect of Hypnosis Upon Gastric Secretion. *Gastroenterology,* 1955c, *29,* 417–421.

Eisenbud, J. The Psychology of Headache: A Case Studied Experimentally. *Psychiatric Quarterly,* 1937, *11,* 592–619.

Eisenbud, J. A Method for Investigating the Effect of Repression on the Somatic

Expression of Emotion in Vegetative Functions: A Preliminary Report. *Psychosomatic Medicine,* 1939, *1,* 376–387.

Ekehammar, B. Interactionism in Modern Personality from a Historical Perspective. *Psychological Bulletin,* 1974, *81,* 1026–1048.

Ekstein, Rudolph, & Caruth, Elain. The Relation of Ego Autonomy to Activity and Passivity in the Psychotherapy of Childhood Schizophrenia. *Reiss-Davis Clinic Bulletin,* 1968, *5,* 89–95.

Ellenberger, H. F. Charcot and the Salpêtrière School. *American Journal of Psychotherapy,* 1965a, *19,* 253–267.

Ellenberger, H. F. Mesmer and Puységur: From Magnetism to Hypnotism. *Psychoanalytic Review,* 1965b, *52,* 137–153.

Ellenberger, H. F. *The Discovery of the Unconscious: The History and Evolution of Dynamic Psychiatry.* New York: Basic Books, 1970.

Elliotson, J. *Numerous Cases of Surgical Operations without Pain in the Mesmeric State.* London: H. Baillière, 1843.

Elliotson, J. The London College of Physicians and Mesmerists (when it became Dr. Elliotson's turn to deliver the Harveian Oration). *Zoist,* 1848–49, *6,* No. 24, (Jan., 1849), 399–405.

Elliotson, J. *The Harveian Oration, Delivered Before the Royal College of Physicians, London, June 27, 1846.* In Latin with an English version and notes. London: H. Baillière, 1846.

Elson, C. de. *Observations sur le magnétisme animal.* (Observations on Animal Magnetism). London and Paris: Didot, Saugrain, & Clousier, 1780.

Elson, C. de. *Observations sur les deux rapports de MM. les Commissaires nommés par sa Majesté, pour l'examen du magnétisme animal.* (Observations on the Two Reports of the Commissioners Named by His Majesty to Investigate Animal Magnetism). Paris: Clousier, 1784.

Engstrom, D. R. The Enhancement of EEG Alpha Production and Its Effects on Hypnotic Susceptibility. Unpublished doctoral dissertation, University of Southern California, 1970.

Engstrom, D. R. "Hypnotic Susceptibility, EEG-Alpha, and Self-Regulation" In G. Schwartz, D. Shapiro (Eds.) Consciousness and *Self-Regulation, Vol. 1.* New York: Plenum Press, 1976, 173–221.

Engstrom, D. R., London, P. and Hart, J. T. Increasing Hypnotic Susceptibility by EEG Alpha Training. Paper presented at the annual meeting of the American Psychological Association, Miami Beach, September, 1970.

Erickson, M. H. A Study of Clinical and Experimental Findings on Hypnotic Deafness: I. Clinical experimentation and findings. *Journal of General Psychology,* 1938a, *19,* 127–150.

Erickson, M. H. A Study of Clinical and Experimental Findings on Hypnotic Deafness: II. Experimental findings with a conditioned response technique. *Journal of General Psychology,* 1938b, *19,* 151–167.

Erickson, M. H. The Applications of Hypnosis to Psychiatry. *Medical Record,* 1939a, *150,* 60–65.

Erickson, M. H. An Experimental Investigation of the Possible Anti-Social Use of Hypnosis. *Psychiatry,* 1939b, *2,* 391–414.

Erickson, M. H. Hypnosis: A General Review. *Diseases of the Nervous System,* 1941, *2,* 13–18.

Erickson, M. H. Hypnotic Investigation of Psychosomatic Phenomena: Psychosomatic Interrelationships Studied by Experimental Hypnosis. *Psychosomatic Medicine,* 1943, *5,* 51–58.

Erickson, M. H. The Method Employed to Formulate a Complex Story for the Induction of an Experimental Neurosis in a Hypnotic Subject. *Journal of General Psychology*, 1944, *31*, 67–84. Reprinted in J. Haley (Ed.), 1967, 312–325.

Erickson, M. H. Deep Hypnosis and Its Induction. In L. M. LeCron (Ed.), *Experimental Hypnosis: A Symposium of Articles on Research*. New York: The Macmillan Co., 1952, 70–112. Reprinted in J. Haley (Ed.), 1967, 7–31.

Erickson, M. H. Hypnosis in Painful Terminal Illness. *American Journal of Clinical Hypnosis*, 1958, *1*, 117–121.

Erickson, M. H. Historical Note on the Hand Levitation and Other Ideomotor Techniques. *American Journal of Clinical Hypnosis*, 1960, *3*, 196–199.

Erickson, M. H. Basic Psychological Problems in Hypnosis Research (and panel discussion). In G. H. Estabrooks (Ed.) *Hypnosis: Current Problems*. New York: Harper & Row, 1962, 207–223, 238–272.

Erickson, M. H. Initial Experiments Investigating the Nature of Hypnosis. *American Journal of Clinical Hypnosis*, 1964a, *7*, 152–162.

Erickson, M. H. The Confusion Technique in Hypnosis. *American Journal of Clinical Hypnosis*, 1964b, *6*, 183–207. Reprinted in J. Haley, (Ed.), 1967, 130–157.

Erickson, M. H. Further Experimental Investigation of Hypnosis: Hypnotic and Nonhypnotic Realities. *American Journal of Clinical Hypnosis*. 1967, *10*, 87–135.

Erickson, M. H., & Brickner, R. M. Hypnotic Investigation of Psychosomatic Phenomena. II. The development of aphasia-like reactions from hypnotically induced amnesias. *Psychosomatic Medicine*, 1943, *5*, 59–66.

Erickson, M. H., & Erickson, Elizabeth M. The Hypnotic Induction of Hallucinatory Color Vision Followed by Pseudo-Negative After-Images. *Journal of Experimental Psychology*, 1938, *22*, 581–588.

Erickson, M. H., & Erickson, Elizabeth M. Concerning the nature and Character of Post-Hypnotic Behavior. *Journal of General Psychology*, 1941, *24*, 95–133.

Erickson, M. H., Haley, J., & Weakland, J. H. A transcript of a Trance Induction with Commentary. *American Journal of Clinical Hypnosis*, 1959, *2*, 49–84. Reprinted in J. Haley, (Ed.), 1967, 51–88.

Erickson, M. H., Hershman, S., & Secter, I. I. *The Practical Application of Medical and Dental Hypnosis*. New York: Julian Press, 1961.

Erickson, M. H., & Rossi, E. L. Varieties of Hypnotic Amnesia. *American Journal of Clinical Hypnosis*, 1974, *16*, 225–239.

Eriksen, C. W. Unconscious Processes. In M. R. Jones (Ed.), *Nebraska Symposium on Motivation*. Lincoln, Nebraska: University of Nebraska Press, 1958, 169–227.

Eriksen, C. W. (Ed.) *Behavior and Awareness: A Symposium of Research and Interpretation*. Durham, N.C.: Duke University Press, 1962.

Erikson, E. H. (1950) *Childhood and Society*. New York: W. W. Norton & Co., 1963, 2nd edition.

Erle, R. A. The Representation of Temporal Features of Events in Hynotically Induced Dreams: An Exploratory Study. Unpublished Masters Thesis, Clark University, 1958.

Esdaile, J. *Mesmerism in India and Its Practical Application in Surgery and Medicine*. London: Longman's, Green & Co., 1850. Reissued under title, *Hypnosis in Medicine and Surgery*. With introduction and supplementary reports on current applications by W. S. Kroger. New York: Julian Press, 1957.

Esdaile, J. *Natural and Mesmeric Clairvoyance, with the Practical Application of Mesmerism in Surgery and Medicine*. London: Baillière, 1852.

Estabrooks, G. H. The Psychogalvanic Reflex in Hypnosis. *Journal of General Psychology*, 1930, *3*, 150–157.

Estabrooks, G. H. *Hypnotism*. New York: Dutton, 1943, 1957.

Evans, F. J. The Structure of Hypnosis: A Factor Analytic Investigation.

Unpublished doctoral dissertation, University of Sydney, Australia, 1965.

Evans, F. J. The Case of the Disappearing Hypnotist. Paper read at American Psychological Association Convention, New York, September, 1966.

Evans, F. J. Suggestibility in the Normal Waking State. *Psychological Bulletin,* 1967, *67,* 114–129.

Evans, F. J. Recent Trends in Experimental Hypnosis. *Behavioral Science,* 1968, *13,* 477–487.

Evans, F. J. Simultaneous Changes in Skin Potential and Subjective Estimates of Depth of Hypnosis. Paper presented at the meeting of the Eastern Psychological Association, Atlantic City, April, 1970.

Evans, F. J. Contextual Forgetting: A Study of Source Amnesia. Paper presented at the meeting of the Eastern Psychological Association, New York, April, 1971.

Evans, F. J. Posthypnotic Amnesia and the Temporay Disruption of Retrieval Processes. Paper read at the Annual Convention of the American Psychological Association, Honolulu, September, 1972.

Evans, F. J. Hypnosis and Sleep: The Control of Altered States of Awareness. In W. E. Edmonston, Jr. (Ed.), Conceptual and Investigative Approaches to Hypnosis and Hypnotic Phenomena. *Annals of the New York Academy of Sciences, 296.* New York: New York Academy of Sciences, 1977a, 162–174.

Evans, F. J. Subjective Characteristics of Sleep Efficiency. *Journal of Abnormal Psychology,* 1977b, *86,* 561–564.

Evans, F. J., Cook, M. R., Cohen, H. D., Orne, Emily C., & Orne, M. T. Appetitive and Replacement Naps: EEG and Behavior. *Science,* 1977, *197,* 687–689.

Evans, F. J., Gustafson, L. A., O'Connell, D. N., Orne, M. T., & Shor, R. E. Response During Sleep with Intervening Waking Amnesia. *Science,* 1966, *152,* 666–667.

Evans, F. J., Gustafson, L. A., O'Connell, D. N., Orne, M. T., & Shor, R. E. Sleep-induced Behavioral Response: Relationship to Susceptibility to Hypnosis and Laboratory Sleep Patterns. *Journal of Nervous and Mental Disease,* 1969, *148, 467–476.*

Evans, F. J., Gustafson, L. A., O'Connell, D. N., Orne, M. T., & Shor, R. E. Verbally Induced Behavioral Responses During Sleep. *Journal of Nervous and Mental Disease,* 1970, *150,* 171–187.

Evans, F. J., & Kihlstrom, J. F. Posthypnotic Amnesia as Disrupted Retrieval. *Journal of Abnormal Psychology,* 1973, *82,* 317–323.

Evans, F. J., & Kihlstrom, J. F. Contextual and Temporal Disorganization During Posthypnotic Amnesia. *Paper presented at the 83rd Annual Convention of the American Psychological Association,* Chicago, August, 1975.

Evans, F. J., Kihlstrom, J. F., & Orne, E. C. Quantifying Subjective Reports During Posthypnotic Amnesia. *Proceedings, 81st Annual Convention, American Psychological Association,* 1973, *8,* 1077–1078.

Evans, F. J., & Orchard, W. Sleep Learning: The Successful Waking Recall of Material Presented During Sleep. Paper presented at the meeting of the Association for the Psychophysiological Study of Sleep. Boston, March 1969.

Evans, F. J., & Orne, M. T. Motivation, Performance, and Hypnosis. *International Journal of Clinical and Experimental Hypnosis.* 1965, *13,* 103–116.

Evans, F. J., Reich, L. H., & Orne, M. T. Optokinetic Nystagmus, Eye Movements, and Hypnotically Induced Hallucinations. *Journal of Nervous and Mental Disease,* 1972, *152,* 419–431.

Evans, F. J., & Thorn, Wendy A. F. Source Amesia After Hypnosis. *American Psychologist,* 1963, *18,* 373. (Abstract)

Evans, F. J., & Thorn, Wendy A. F. Two Types of Posthypnotic Amnesia: Recall

Amnesia and Source Amnesia. *International Journal of Clinical and Experimental Hypnosis,* 1966, 14, 162–179.

Evans, M. B., & Paul, G. L. Effects of Hypnotically Suggested Analgesia on Physiological and Subjective Responses to Cold Stress. *Journal of Consulting and Clinical Psychology,* 1970, *35,* 362–371.

Evans, R. I. *Conversations with Carl Jung.* New York: Van Nostrand Reinhold, 1964.

Ewing, J. H., Gillis, Carol A., Ebert, J. N., & Mathews, H. M. Profile of Perceptual-cognitive Traits and Personality Style of Possible Relevance to Creative Productivity. *Perceptual and Motor Skills,* 1975, *40,* 711–718.

Eysenck, H. J., & Furneaux, W. D. Primary and Secondary Suggestibility: An Experimental and Statistical Study. *Journal of Experimental Psychology,* 1945, *35,* 485–503.

Faria, J. C. A. de. *De la cause du sommeil lucide ou létude de la nature de l'homme.* (On the Cause of Lucid Sleep: A Study on the Nature of Man). Second edition edited by D. G. Dalgado. Paris: Henri Jouve, 1906.

Fehr, F. S., & Stern, J. A. The Effect of Hypnosis on Attention to Relevant and Irrelevant Stimuli. *International Journal of Clinical and Experimental Hypnosis.* 1967, *15,* 134–143.

Feirstein, A. Personality Correlates of Tolerance for Unrealistic Experiences. *Journal of Consulting Psychology,* 1967, *31,* 387–395.

Ferster, C. B., Levitt, E. E., Zimmerman, J., & Brady, J. P. The Measurement of Hypnotic Effects by Operant-reinforcement Techniques. *Psychological Record,* 1961, *11,* 427–430.

Field, P. B. Bales Interaction Analysis of Hypnosis. *International Journal of Clinical and Experimental Hypnosis,* 1964, *12,* 88–98.

Field, P. B. An Inventory Scale of Hypnotic depth. *International Journal of Clinical and Experimental Hypnosis,* 1965, *13,* 238–249.

Field, P. B. Some Self-rating Measures Related to Hypnotizability. *Perceptual and Motor Skills,* 1966, *23,* 1179–1187.

Field, P. B., Evans, F. J., & Orne, M. T. Order of Difficulty of Suggestions During Hypnosis. *International Journal of Clinical and Experimental Hypnosis,* 1965, *13, 183–192.*

Field, P. B., & Palmer, R. D. Factor Analysis: Hypnosis Inventory. *International Journal of Clinical and Experimental Hypnosis,* 1969, *17,* 50–61.

Finke, R. A., & Macdonald, H. Two Personality Measures Relating Hypnotic Susceptibility to Absorption. *International Journal of Clinical and Experimental Hypnosis,* 1978, *26,* 178–183.

Fischer, R. (Ed.) Interdisciplinary Perspectives of Time, *Annals of the New York Academy of Sciences,* 1967, *138,* 367–915.

Fischer, R. On Flashback and Hypnotic Recall. *International Journal of Clinical and Experimental Hypnosis,* 1977, *25,* 217–235.

Fisher, C. Psychoanalytic Implications of Recent Research on Sleep and Dreaming: *Journal of the American Psychoanalytic Association,* 1965, *13,* 197–303.

Fisher, S. The Role of Expectancy in the Performance of Posthypnotic Behavior. *Journal of Abnormal and Social Psychology.* 1954, *49,* 503–507.

Fisher, S. An Investigation of Alleged Conditioning Phenomena Under Hypnosis. *Journal of Clinical and Experimental Hypnosis,* 1955, *3,* 71–103.

Fisher, S. Problems of Interpretation and Controls in Hypnotic Research. In G. H. Estabrooks (Ed.), *Hypnosis: Current Problems.* New York: Harper & Row, 1962, 109–126.

Fisher, V. E., & Marrow, A. J. Experimental Study of Moods. *Character & Personality,* 1934, *2,* 202–208.

Fiss, H., Ellman, S. J., & Klein, G. S. Effects of Interruption of Rapid Eye-Movement Sleep on Fantasy in the Waking State. *Psychophysiology.* 1968, *4,* 364. (Abstract)

Fitzgerald, E. T. Measurement of Openness to Experience: A Study of Regression in the Service of the Ego. *Journal of Personality and Social Psychology,* 1966, *4,* 655–663.

Flavell, J. H. *The Developmental Psychology of Jean Piaget.* Princeton, N.J.: D. Van Nostrand, 1963.

Ford, L. F., & Yeager, C. L. Changes in Electroencephalogram in Subjects Under Hypnosis. *Diseases of the Nervous System,* 1948, *9,* 190–192.

Forel, A. *Hypnotism or Suggestion and Psychotherapy: A Study of the Psychological, Psycho-physiological and Therapeutic Aspects of Hypnotism.* Translated from the 5th German edition by H. W. Armit, American edition, revised and corrected. New York: Rebman Co., 1907.

Foulkes, D. *The Psychology of Sleep.* New York: Charles Scribner's Sons, 1966.

Foulkes, D., & Vogel, G. Mental Activity At Sleep Onset. *Journal of Abnormal Psychology,* 1965, *70,* 231–243.

Frankel, F. H. *Hypnosis: Trance as a Coping Mechanism.* New York and London: Plenum Medical Book Company, 1976.

Freedman, S. J., & Marks, Patricia A. Visual Imagery Produced by Rhythmic Photic Stimulation: Personality Correlates and Phenomenology. *British Journal of Psychology,* 1965, *56,* 95–112.

French, T. M., & Fromm, Erika. *Dream Interpretation: A New Approach.* New York: Basic Books, 1964.

Fresacher, L. A. Way into the Hypnotic State. *British Journal of Medical Hypnotism,* 1951, *3,* 12–13.

Freud, Anna. (1936). *The Ego and the Mechanisms of Defense.* New York: International Universities Press, 1946.

Freud, S. (1900). The Interpretation of Dreams. *Standard Edition,* J. Strachey, (Ed.), Vols. 4 & 5. London: The Hogarth Press, 1953.

Freud, S. (1920). Beyond the Pleasure Principle. Standard Edition of the Complete Psychological Works of Sigmund Freud, J. Strachey, (Ed.). London: Hogarth Press, 1962, *18,* 3–64.

Freud, S. *Introductory Lectures on Psycho-Analysis.* (Joan Riviere, Trans.) London: Allen & Unwin, 1922.

Freud, S. (1923). The Ego and the Id. *Standard Edition,* J. Strachey, (Ed.), Vol. 19. London: The Hogarth Press, 1961.

Freud, S. (1925). *An Autobiographical Study.* Authorized translation for the 2nd edition by J. Strachey, 1946, New York: W. W. Norton, 1952. Also in *Standard Edition of the Complete Psychological Works of Sigmund Freud,* J. Strachey, (Ed.). London: Hogarth Press, 1962, *20,* 7–74.

Friedlander, J. W., & Sarbin, T. R. The Depth of Hypnosis. *Journal of Abnormal and Social Psychology,* 1938, *33,* 453–475.

Friedman, H., & Taub, H. A. The Use of Hypnosis and Biofeedback Procedures for Essential Hypertension. *International Journal of Clinical and Experimental Hypnosis,* 1977, *25,* 335–347.

Fromm, Erika. Hypnoanalysis: Theory and Two Case Excerpts. *Psychotherapy: Theory, Research and Practice,* 1965a, *2,* 127–133.

Fromm, Erika. Awareness Versus Consciousness. *Psychological Reports,* 1965b, *16,* 711–712.

Fromm, Erika. Activity, Passivity and Anniversary Reactions. Paper read at the 22nd Annual Convention of the Society for Clinical and Experimental Hypnosis, Philadelphia, October, 1970.

Fromm, Erika. Activity and Passivity of the Ego in Hypnosis. *International Journal of Clinical and Experimental Hypnosis,* 1972, *20,* 238–251.

Fromm, Erika. An Idiosynchronic Long-term Study of Self-Hypnosis. Paper read at the Annual Conference of the American Psychological Association, New Orleans, August, 1974.

Fromm, Erika. Autohypnosis. Chapter in Lars-Eric Uneståhl (Ed.), *Hypnosis in the Seventies.* Örebro, Sweden: Veje Förlag, 1975a, 152–154.

Fromm, Erika. Autohypnosis and Heterohypnosis: Phenomenological Similarities and Differences. Chapter in Lars-Eric Uneståhl (Ed.), *Hypnosis in the Seventies.* Örebro, Sweden: Veje Förlag, 1975b, 24–28.

Fromm, Erika. Selfhypnosis: A New Area of Research. *Psychotherapy: Research, Theory, and Practice.* 1975c, *12,* 295–301.

Fromm, Erika. Altered States of Consciousness and Hypnosis: A Discussion. *International Journal of Clinical and Experimental Hypnosis.* 1977a, *25,* 325–334.

Fromm, Erika. An Ego-psychological Theory of Altered States of Consciousness. *International Journal of Clinical and Experimental Hypnosis,* 1977b, *25,* 372–387. Reprinted in: *Hypnos-Nytt, Svenska Föringen för Klinisk Och Experimentell Hypnos, October, 1977, 1,* 8–22.

Fromm, Erika. Primary and Secondary Process in Waking and in Altered States of Consciousness. *Journal of Altered States of Consciousness,* 1978–79, *4,* 115–128.

Fromm, Erika, Oberlander, M. I., & Gruenewald, Doris. Perceptual and Cognitive Processes in Different states of Consciousness: The Waking State and Hypnosis—with Implications for Hypnotherapy. Paper presented at the Convention of American Psychological Association, Washington, D.C., September, 1969.

Fromm, Erika, Oberlander, M. I., & Gruenewald, Doris. Perceptual and Cognitive Processes in Different States of Consciousness: The Waking State and Hypnosis. *Journal of Projective Techniques and Personality Assessment,* 1970, *34,* 375–387.

Fromm, Erika, & Shor, Ronald E. *Hypnosis: Research Developments and Perspectives.* 1st edition, Chicago: Aldine-Atherton, 1972.

Fromm, Erika, & Weingarten, F. Permissive Modification of Weitzenhoffer & Hilgard's Stanford Hypnotic Susceptibility Scale, Form A. Unpublished Manuscript. University of Chicago, 1965.

Furneaux, W. D. The Prediction of Susceptibility to Hypnosis. *Journal of Personality,* 1946, *14,* 281–294.

Galbraith, G. C., London, P., Leibovitz, M. P., Cooper, L. M., & Hart, J. T. EEG and Hypnotic Susceptibility, *Journal of Comparative and Physiological Psychology,* 1970, *72,* 125–131.

Galdston, I. Hypnosis and Modern Psychiatry. *Ciba Symposia,* 1948a, *9,* 845–856.

Galdston, I. Mesmer and Animal Magnetism. *Ciba Symposia.* 1948b, *9,* 832–837.

Gamble, K. R., & Kellner, H. Creative Functioning and Cognitive Regression. *Journal of Personality and Social Psychology,* 1968, *9,* 266–271.

Gandolf, R. L. Role of Expectancy, Amnesia, and Hypnotic Induction in the Performance of Posthypnotic Behavior. *Journal of Abnormal Psychology,* 1971, *77,* 324–328.

Gardner, G. Gail. Hypnosis with Children: Selected Readings. *International Journal of Clinical and Experimental Hypnosis,* 1979, in press.

Gardner, R. W., Holzmann, P. S., Klein, G. S., Linton, H. P., & Spence, D. P.

Cognitive Control: A Study of Individual Consistencies in Cognitive Behavior. *Psychological Issues,* 1959, *1,* 1–186.

Geiwitz, P. J. Structure of Boredom. *Journal of Personality and Social Psychology,* 1966, *3,* 592–600.

Germann, A. C. Hypnosis as Related to the Scientific Detection of Deception by Polygraph Examination: A Pilot Study. *International Journal of Clinical and Experimental Hypnosis,* 1961, *9,* 309–311.

Gheorghiu, V. Some Peculiarities of Posthypnotic Source Amnesia of Information. In L. Chertok (Ed.), *Psychophysiological Mechanisms of Hypnosis.* New York: Springer-Verlag, 1969, 112–122.

Ghiselin, B. *The Creative Process: A Symposium.* New York: New American Library, 1952; N.Y. Mentor Books, 1955.

Gibson, W. *The Boat.* Boston: Houghton Mifflin, 1953.

Gidro-Frank, L., & Bowersbuch, M. K. A Study of the Plantar Response in Hypnotic Age Regression. *Journal of Nervous and Mental Disease,* 1948, *107,* 443–458.

Gidro-Frank, L., & Bull, N. Emotions Induced and Studies in Hypnotic Subjects: Part I: The Method. *Journal of Nervous and Mental Disease,* 1950, *111,* 91–100.

Giles, E. A Cross-Validation Study of the Pascal Technique of Hypnotic Induction. *International Journal of Clinical and Experimental Hypnosis,* 1962, *10,* 101–108.

Gill, M. M. *The Collected Papers of David Rapaport.* New York: Basic Books, 1967a.

Gill, M. M. The Primary Process. In R. R. Holt, (Ed.), Motives and Thought: Psychoanalytic Essays in Honor of David Rapaport. *Psychological Issues,* Monograph 18–19. New York: International Universities Press, 1967b, 260–298.

Gill, M. M. Hypnosis as an Altered and Regressed State. *International Journal of Clinical and Experimental Hypnosis,* 1972, *20,* 224–237.

Gill, M. M., & Brenman, Margaret. *Hypnosis and Related States: Psychoanalytic Studies in Regression.* New York: International Universities Press, 1959.

Golann, S. E. Psychological Study of Creativity. *Psychological Bulletin,* 1963, *60,* 548–565.

Goldiamond, I., & Malpass, L. F. Locus of Hypnotically Induced Changes in Color Vision Responses. *Journal of the Optical Society of America,* 1961, *51,* 1117–1121.

Goldsmith, Margaret L. *Franz Anton Mesmer: The History of an Idea.* London: Arthur Barker; New York: Doubleday, Doran, 1934.

Goldstein, A., & Hilgard, E. R. Lack of Influence of the Morphine Antagonist Naloxone on Hypnotic Analgesia. *Proceedings of the National Academy of Sciences,* 1975, *72,* 2041–2043.

Goldstein, M. S., & Sipprelle, C. N. Hypnotically Induced Amnesia Versus Ablation of Memory. *International Journal of Clinical and Experimental Hypnosis,* 1970, *18,* 211–216.

Gordon, J. E. Leading and Following Psychotherapeutic Techniques with Hypnotically Induced Repression and Hostility. *Journal of Abnormal and Social Psychology,* 1957, *54,* 405–410.

Gordon, J. E. (Ed.) *Handbook of Clinical and Experimental Hypnosis.* New York: Macmillan, 1967a.

Gordon, J. E. Hypnosis in Research on Psychotherapy. In J. E. Gordon (Ed.), 1967b, 148–202.

Gordon, Rosemary. An Investigation into Some of the Factors that Favour the Formation of Stereotyped Images. *British Journal of Psychology,* 1949, *39,* 156–167.

Gormely, W. J. *Medical Hypnosis: Historical Introduction to its Morality in the Light of Papal, Theological and Medical Teaching.* Washington, D.C.: The Catholic University of America Press, 1961.

Gorton, B. E. The Physiology of Hypnosis.—I. *Psychiatric Quarterly*, 1949, *23*, 317–343; The Physiology of Hypnosis—II. *Psychiatric Quarterly*, 1949, *23*, 457–485.

Gorton, B. E. Current Problems of Physiologic Research in Hypnosis. In G. H. Estabrooks (Ed.), *Hypnosis: Current Problems*. New York: Harper & Row, 1962, 30–53.

Gottlieb, A. A., Gleser, Goldine C., & Gottschalk, L. A. Verbal and Physiological Responses to Hypnotic Suggestion of Attitudes. *Psychosomatic Medicine*, 1967, *29*, 172–183.

Gough, H. G. The F Minus K Dissimulation Index for the Minnesota Multiphasic Personality Inventory. *Journal of Consulting Psychology*, 1950, *14*, 408–413.

Gough, H. G. Identifying the Creative Man. *Journal of Value Engineering*, 1964, *2*, 5–12.

Govinda, A. B. *Foundations of Tibetan Mysticism*. New York: Dutton, 1960.

Graef, J. R. The Influence of Cognitive States on Time Estimation and Subjective Time Rate. Unpublished Doctoral Dissertation, University of Michigan, 1969.

Graham, C., & Leibowitz, H. W. The Effect of Suggestion on Visual Acuity. *International Journal of Clinical and Experimental Hypnosis*, 1972, *20*, 169–186.

Graham, D. T., & Wolf, S. Pathogenesis of Urticaria: Experimental Study of Life Situations, Emotions, and Cutaneous Vascular Reactions. *Journal of the American Medical Association*, 1950, *143*, 1396–1402.

Graham, F. K., & Kunish, Nancy O. Physiological Responses of Unhypnotized Subjects to Attitude Suggestions. *Psychosomatic Medicine*, 1965, *27*, 317–329.

Graham, K. R. Perceptual Processes and Hypnosis: Support for a Cognitive-State Theory Based on Laterality. In W. E. Edmonston, Jr. (Ed.), Conceptual and Investigative Approaches to Hypnosis and Hypnotic Phenomena. *Annals of the New York Academy of Sciences, 296*. New York: New York Academy of Sciences, 1977, 274–283.

Graham, K. R., & Patton, Ann. Retroactive Inhibition, Hypnosis and Hypnotic Amnesia. *International Journal of Clinical and Experimental Hypnosis*, 1968, *16*, 68–74.

Graham, K. R., Wright, Gail W., Toman, Wendy J., & Mark C. B. Relaxation and Hypnosis in the Treatment of Insomnia. *American Journal of Clinical Hypnosis*, 1975, *18*, 39–42.

Granda, A. M., & Hammack, J. T. Operant Behavior During Sleep. *Science*, 1961, *133*, 1485–1486.

Gravitz, M. A., & Forbes, M. E. Hypnosis and the Conceptualization of a Continuum of Consciousness. *British Journal of Medical Hypnotism*, 1963, *15*, 21–25.

Gravitz, M. A., & Kramer, Mary F. A Study of Some Factors Associated with Hypnotic-Like Experience. *American Journal of Clinical Hypnosis*, 1967, *10*, 48–51.

Gray, J. The Effect of Productivity on Primary Process and Creativity. *Journal of Projective Techniques and Personality Assessment*, 1969, *33*, 213–218.

Green, E. E., Green, Alyce M., & Walters, E. D. Self-regulation of Internal States. In J. Rose (Ed.), *Progress of Cybernetics: Proceedings of the First International Congress of Cybernetics, London, 1969*. London: Gordon & Breach Science Publishers, 1970.

Griffin, Dorothy P. Movement Responses and Creativity. *Journal of Consulting Psychology*, 1958, *22*, 134–136.

Grimm, F. M. von, & Diderot, D. Rapport des commissaires chargés par le roi de l'examen du magnétisme animal, 1784. (Report of the commissioners charged by the King with the investigation of animal magnetism). *Correspondance*

Littéraire, Pt. 3, Vol. 3, Paris, 1813, 10–20.

Grossberg, J. M., & Wilson, Helen K. Physiological Changes Accompanying the Visualization of Fearful and Neutral Situations. *Journal of Personality and Social Psychology,* 1968, *10,* 124–133.

Grosz, H. J. The Relation of Serum Ascorbic Acid Level to Adrenocortical Secretion During Experimentally Induced Emotional Stress in Human Subjects. *Journal of Psychosomatic Research,* 1961, *5,* 253–262.

Grosz, H. J., & Levitt, E. E. The Effects of Hypnotically Induced Anxiety on the Manifest Anxiety Scale and the Barron Ego-Strength Scale. *Journal of Abnormal and Social Psychology,* 1959, *59,* 281–283.

Gruenewald, Doris, & Fromm, Erika. Hypnosis, Simulation and Brain Damage. *Journal of Abnormal Psychology,* 1967, *72,* 191–192.

Guilford, J. P. *Personality.* New York: McGraw-Hill, 1959.

Guilford, J. P. Some Theoretical Views of Creativity: In H. Helson & W. Bevan (Eds.), *Contemporary Approaches to Psychology.* Princeton, New Jersey: D. Van Nostrand Company, 1967, 419–459.

Gur, Raquel, E. Conjugate Lateral Eye-movements as an Index of Hemispheric Activation. *Journal of Personality and Social Psychology,* 1975, *31,* 751–757.

Gur, R. C., & Gur, Raquel, E. Handedness, Sex and Eyedness as Moderating Variables in the Relation Between Hypnotic Susceptibility and Functional Brain Asymmetry. *Journal of Abnormal Psychology,* 1974, *83,* 635–643.

Gur, R. C., & McKinley, P. Imagery, Absorption, and the Tendency Toward Mind Exploration as Correlates of Hypnotic Susceptibility in Males and Females. Paper presented at the Annual Convention of the Society for Clinical and Experimental Hypnosis, Chicago, Oct. 1975.

Gur, R., & Reyher, J. The Enhancement of Creativity Via Free Imagery and Hypnosis. *American Journal of Clinical Hypnosis,* 1976, *18,* 237–249.

Gurney, E. The Stages of Hypnotism. *Society for Psychical Research: Proceedings,* 1884, *2,* 61–72.

Hadfield, J. A. The Influence of Suggestion on Body Temperature. *Lancet,* 1920, *2,* 68–69.

Hahn, K. W., Jr., & Barber, T. X. Hallucinations With and Without Hypnotic Induction: An Extension of the Brady & Levitt Study. Harding, Mass.: The Medfield Foundation, 1966.

Haim, E. Beitrag zur Frage der Sensibilität der Abdominalorgane. *Zentralblatt für Chirurgie,* 1908, *35,* 337–338.

Haley, J. An Interactional Explanation of Hypnosis. *American Journal of Clinical Hypnosis,* 1958, *1,* 41–57.

Haley, J. *Strategies of Psychotherapy.* New York: Grune & Stratton, 1963.

Haley, J. (Ed.) *Advanced Techniques of Hypnosis and Therapy: Selected Papers of Milton H. Erickson, M.D.* New York: Grune & Stratton, 1967.

Hall, C. R. *Mesmerism: Its Rise, Progress, and Mysteries.* New York: Burgess, Stringer, & Co., 1845. First American edition. From *Lancet,* in serial, London, 1845, *1,* beginning 112–118.

Hall, C. S., & Van de Castle, R. L. *The Content Analysis of Dreams.* New York: Appleton-Century-Crofts, 1966.

Hall, W. H., Herb, R. W., Brady, J. P., & Brooks, F. P. Gastric Function During Hypnosis and Hypnotically-induced Gastro-intestinal Symptoms. *Journal of Psychosomatic Research,* 1967, *11,* 263–266.

Halliday, A. M., & Mason, A. A. Cortical Evoked Potentials During Hypnotic Anaesthesia. *Electroencephalography and Clinical Neuro-physiology,* 1964a, *16,* 314.

Halliday, A. M., & Mason, A. A. The Effect of Hypnotic Anaesthesia On Cortical Responses. *Journal of Neurology, Neurosurgery, and Psychiatry,* 1964b, *27,* 300–312.

Halper, C., Pivik, T., & Dement, W. An Attempt to Reduce the REM rebound following REM Deprevation by the Use of Induced Waking Mentation. Paper presented at the meeting of the Association for the Psychophysiological Study of Sleep, Boston, March, 1969.

Ham, M. W., & Edmonston, W. E., Jr. Hypnosis, Relaxation and Motor Retardation. *Journal of Abnormal Psychology,* 1971, *77,* 329–331.

Hamel, I. A. A Study and Analysis of the Conditioned Reflex. *Psychological Monographs,* 1919, *27,* No. 118, 1–65.

Hammer, A. G., Evans, F. J., & Bartlett, Mary. Factors in Hypnosis and Suggestion. *Journal of Abnormal and Social Psychology,* 1963, *67,* 15–23.

Harano, K., Ogawa, K., & Naruse, G. A Study of Plethysmography and Skin Temperature During Active Concentration and Autogenic Exercise. In W. Luthe, (Ed.), *Autogenic Training.* New York: Grune & Stratton, 1965, 55–58.

Harding, C. H. Hypnosis in the Treatment of Migraine. In Lassner, J. (Ed.) *Hypnosis and Psychosomatic Medicine.* New York: Springer-Verlag, 1967, 131–134.

Harman, W. W., McKim, R. H., Mogar, R. E., Fadiman, J., & Stolaroff, M. J. Psychedelic Agents in Creative Problem Solving: A Pilot Study. *Psychological Reports,* 1966, *19,* 211–227. Reprinted in C. T. Tart, (Ed.), 1969, 445–461.

Harrington, D. M. Effects of Explicit Instructions to "Be Creative" on the Psychological Meaning of Divergent Thinking Test Scores. *Journal of Personality,* 1975, *43,* 434–454.

Hart, E. *Hypnotism, Mesmerism, and the New Witchcraft.* New York: D. Appleton & Co., 1898.

Hart, H. H. A Review of the Psychoanalytic Literature on Passivity. *Psychiatric Quarterly,* 1961, *35,* 331–352.

Hart, J. T. Memory and the Feeling-of-Knowing Experience. *Journal of Educational Psychology,* 1965, *56,* 208–216.

Hartley, E. L., & Hartley, Ruth E. *Fundamentals of Social Psychology.* New York: Knopf, 1958.

Hartmann, H. (1939). *Ego Psychology and the Problem of Adaptation.* New York: International Universities Press, 1958.

Hartmann, H. *Essays on Ego Psychology: Selected Problems in Psychoanalytic Theory.* New York: International Universities Press, 1964.

Hartnett, J., Nowlis, D., & Svorad, D. Hypnotic Susceptibility and EEG alpha: Three Correlations. Hawthorne House Research Memorandum, No. 97, 1969.

Hatfield, Elaine C. The Validity of the LeCron Method of Evaluating Hypnotic Depth. *International Journal of Clinical and Experimental Hypnosis,* 1961, *9,* 215–221.

Hays, W. L. *Statistics for the Social Sciencs* (Second Edition). New York: Holt, Rinehart, and Winston, 1973.

Hauenstein, Louise S. Anger, Salience and the Appreciation of Hostile Humor. Unpublished doctoral dissertation, University of Michigan, 1970.

Heidenhain, R. *Hypnotism or Animal Magnetism: Physiological Observations.* Translated from the 4th German edition by L. C. Wooldridge. With a preface by G. J. Romanes. London: K. Paul, Trench & Company, 1888.

Heimann, H., & Spoerri, T. Elektroencephalographische Untersuchungen an Hypnotisierten. *Monatsschrift für Psychiatrie und Neurologie,* 1953, *125,* 261–271.

Helfman (Damaser), Esther, Shor, R. E., & Orne, M. T. Requested Emotions in the

Wake and the Hypnotic States. Paper read at the Convention of the American Psychological Association, Chicago, September, 1960.

Helson, Ravenna. Generality of Sex Differences in Creative Style. *Journal of Personality,* 1968, *36,* 33–48.

Hepps, R. B., & Brady, J. P. Hypnotically Induced Tachycardia: An Experiment With Simulating Controls. *Journal of Nervous and Mental Disease,* 1967, *145,* 131–137.

Hernández-Peón, R., & Donoso, M. Influence of Attention and Suggestion Upon Subcortical Evoked Electrical Activity in the Human Brain. In L. van Bogaert & J. Radermecker (Eds.), *First International Congress of Neurological Sciences.* London: Pergamon Press, *1959, 3,* 385–386.

Heron, W. The Pathology of Boredom. *Scientific American,* 1957, *196,* 52–56.

Hersch, C. The Cognitive Functioning of the Creative Person: A Developmental Analysis. *Journal of Projective Techniques,* 1962, *26,* 193–200.

Hershman, R. A., Crawford, Helen J., & Hecht, E. Marijuana, Cognitive Style, and Lateralized Hemisphere Functions. In S. Cohen and R. Stillman (Eds.), *The Therapeutic Potential of Marijuana.* New York: Plenum Publishing Corp., 1976, 205–254.

Hilber, F. W. An Experimental Investigation of Negative After-images of Hallucinated Colors in Hypnosis. *Journal of Experimental Psychology,* 1940, *27,* 45–57.

Hilgard, E. R. Impulsive Versus Realistic Thinking: An Examination of the Distinction Between Primary and Secondary Processes in Thought. *Psychological Bulletin,* 1962, *59,* 477–488.

Hilgard, E. R. The Motivational Relevance of Hypnosis. In D. Levine (Ed.), *Nebraska Symposium on Motivation.* Lincoln, Nebraska: University of Nebraska Press, 1964, 1–44.

Hilgard, E. R. Hypnosis. *Annual Review of Psychology,* 1965a, *16,* 157–180.

Hilgard, E. R. *Hypnotic Susceptibility.* New York: Harcourt, Brace & World Inc., 1965b.

Hilgard, E. R. Posthypnotic Amnesia: Experiments and Theory. *International Journal of Clinical and Experimental Hypnosis,* 1966, *14,* 104–111.

Hilgard, E. R. Individual Differences in Hypnotizability. In J. E. Gordon (Ed.), 1967a, 391–443.

Hilgard, E. R. A Quantitative Study of Pain and Its Reduction Through Hypnotic Suggestion. *Proceedings of the National Academy of Sciences,* 1967b, *57, 1581–1586.*

Hilgard, E. R. Creativity: Slogan and Substance. *The Centennial Review,* 1968, *12,* 40–58.

Hilgard, E. R. Altered States of Awareness. *Journal of Nervous and Mental Disease,* 1969a, *149,* 68–79.

Hilgard, E. R. Experimental Psychology and Hypnosis. In L. Chertok (Ed.), *Psychophysiological Mechanisms of Hypnosis.* Berlin: Springer-Verlag, 1969b, 123–138.

Hilgard, E. R. Pain as a Puzzle for Psychology and Physiology. *American Psychologist,* 1969c, *24,* 103–113.

Hilgard, E. R. Pain: Its Reduction and Production Under Hypnosis. *Proceedings of the American Philosophical Society,* 1971, *115,* 470–476.

Hilgard, E. R. Dissociation Revisited. In Mary Henle, J. Jaynes, & J. Sullivan (Eds.), *Historical Conceptions of Psychology.* New York: Springer Publishing Co., 1973a.

Hilgard, E. R. A Neodissociation Interpretation of Pain Reduction in Hypnosis. *Psychological Review,* 1973b, *80,* 396–411.

Hilgard, E. R. The Domain of Hypnosis, with Some Comments on Alternative Paradigms. *American Psychologist,* 1973c, *28,* 972–982.

Hilgard, E. R. Toward a Neodissociation Theory: Multiple Cognitive Controls in Human Functioning. Perspectives in *Biology and Medicine,* 1974, *17,* 301–316.

Hilgard, E. R. Hypnosis. *Annual Review of Psychology,* 1975, *26,* 19–44.

Hilgard, E. R. Neodissociation Theory of Multiple Cognitive Control Systems. In G. E. Schwartz & D. Shapiro (Eds.), *Consciousness and Self-Regulation: Advances in Research,* Vol. 1. New York and London: Plenum Press, 1976, 137–171.

Hilgard, E. R. *Divided Consciousness: Multiple Controls in Human Thought and Action.* New York: John Wiley and Sons, 1977a.

Hilgard, E. R. The Problem of Divided Consciousness: A Neodissociation Interpretation. In W. E. Edmonston, Jr. (Ed.), *Conceptual and Investigative Approaches to Hypnosis and Hypnotic Phenomena. Annals of the New York Academy of Sciences,* 1977b, *296,* 48–59.

Hilgard, E. R., & Cooper, L. M. Spontaneous and Suggested Posthypnotic Amnesia. *International Journal of Clinical and Experimental Hypnosis,* 1965, *13,* 261–273.

Hilgard, E. R., Cooper, L. M., Lennox, J., Morgan, Arlene H., & Voevodsky, J. The Use of Pain-state Reports in the Study of Hypnotic Analgesia to the Pain of Ice Water. *Journal of Nervous and Mental Disease,* 1967, *144,* 504–513.

Hilgard, E. R., & Hilgard, Josephine R. *Hypnosis in the Relief of Pain.* Los Altos, California: William Kaufmann, 1975.

Hilgard, E. R., Hilgard, Josephine R., Macdonald, H., Morgan, Arlene, H., & Johnson, L. S. Covert Pain in Hypnotic Analgesia: Its Reality as Tested by the Real-Simulator Design. *Journal of Abnormal Psychology,* (In preparation).

Hilgard, E. R., & Hommel, L. S. Selective Amnesia for Events within Hypnosis In Relation to Repression. *Journal of Personality,* 1961, *29,* 205–216.

Hilgard, E. R., & Marquis, D. G. *Conditioning and Learning.* New York: Appleton-Century, 1940.

Hilgard, E. R., MacDonald, H., Morgan, Arlene H., & Johnson, L. S. The Reality of Hypnotic Analgesia: A Comparison of Highly Hypnotizables with Simulators. *Journal of Abnormal Psychology,* 1978, *87,* 239–246.

Hilgard, E. R., & Marquis, D. G. *Conditioning and Learning.* New York: Appleton-Century, 1940.

Through Automatic Key-pressing and Automatic Talking. *Journal of Abnormal Psychology,* 1975, *84,* 280–289.

Hilgard, E. R., & Tart, C. T. Responsiveness to Suggestions Following Waking and Imagination Instructions and Following Induction of Hypnosis. *Journal of Abnormal Psychology,* 1966, *71,* 196–208.

Hilgard, E. R., Weitzenhoffer, A. M., Landes, J., & Moore, Rosemarie K. The Distribution of Susceptibility to Hypnosis in a Student Population: A Study Using the Stanford Hypnotic Susceptibility Scale. *Psychology Monographs.* 1961, *75,* No. 8, 1–22.

Hilgard, Josephine R. Personality and Hypnotizability: Inferences from Case Studies: In E. R. Hilgard, *Hypnotic Susceptibility,* New York: Harcourt, Brace & World, 1965, 343–374.

Hilgard, Josephine R. *Personality and Hypnosis; A Study of Imaginative Involvement.* Chicago: University of Chicago Press, 1970. (Revised edition, 1979).

Hilgard, J. R. Imaginative Involvement: Some Characteristics of the Highly Hypnotizable and Non Hypnotizable. *International Journal of Clinical and Experimental Hypnosis,* 1974, *22,* 138–156.

Hilgard, Josephine R., & Hilgard, E. R. Developmental-interactive Aspects of

Hypnosis: Some Illustrative Cases. *Genetic Psychology Monographs,* 1962, *66,* 143–178.

Hill, H. E., Kornetsky, C. H., Flanary, H. G., & Wikler, A. Effects of Anxiety and Morphine on Discrimination of Intensities of Painful Stimuli. *Journal of Clinical Investigation,* 1952a, *31,* 473–480.

Hill, H. E., Kornetsky, C. H., Flanary, H. G., & Wikler, A. Studies on Anxiety Associated with Anticipation of Pain: I. Effects of Morphine. *Archives of Neurology and Psychiatry,* 1952b, *67,* 612–619.

Hodge, J. R. The Contractual Aspects of Hypnosis. *International Journal of Clinical and Experimental Hypnosis,* 1976, *24,* 391–399.

Hodge, J. R., & Wagner, E. E. The Validity of Hypnotically Induced Emotional States. *American Journal of Clinical Hypnosis,* 1964, *7,* 37–41.

Holt, R. R. Cognitive Controls and Primary Processes. *Journal of Psychological Researches Madras,* 1960, *4,* 105–112.

Holt, R. R. Manual for the Scoring of Primary Process Manifestations in Rorschach Responses. (9th edition) New York: Research Center for Mental Health, New York University, 1963 (mimeographed).

Holt, R. R. Imagery: The Return of the Ostracized. *American Psychologist,* 1964, *19,* 254–264.

Holt, R. R. The Development of the Primary Process: A Structural View. In R. R. Holt, (Ed.), Motives and Thought: Psychoanalytic Essays in Honor of David Rapaport. *Psychological Issues,* Monograph 18/19. New York: International Universities Press, 1967, 345–383.

Holt, R. R. On the Nature and Generality of Mental Imagery. In P. W. Sheehan (Ed.), *The Function and Nature of Imagery.* New York & London: Academic Press, 1972, 3–33.

Holt, R. R., & Havel, Joan. A Method for Assessing Primary and Secondary Process in the Rorschach. In Maria A. Rickers-Ovsiankina (Ed.), *Rorschach Psychology.* New York: John Wiley & Sons, 1960, 263–315.

Holtzman, W. H., Thorpe, J. S., Swartz, J. D., & Herron, E. W. *Inkblot Perception and Personality: Holtzman Inkblot Technique.* Austin: University of Texas Press, 1961.

Horowitz, M. J. Visual Imagery and Cognitive Organization. *American Journal of Psychiatry,* 1967, *123,* 938–946.

Horowitz, M. J. Image Formation: Clinical Observations and a Cognitive Model. In P. W. Sheehan (Ed.), *The Function and Nature of Imagery.* New York & London: Academic Press, 1972, 281–309.

Horowitz, M. J. Hallucinations: An Information-processing Approach. In R. K. Siegel, & L. J. West (Eds.), *Hallucinations: Behavior, Experience, and Theory.* New York: Wiley, 1975.

Horowitz, M. J., Adams, J. E. & Rutkin, B. B. Visual Imagery on Brain Stimulation. *Archives of General Psychiatry,* 1968, *19,* 469–486.

Horowitz, Suzanne L. Strategies Within Hypnosis for Reducing Phobic Behavior. *Journal of Abnormal Psychology,* 1970, *75,* 104–112.

Hoskovec, J. Hypnopedia in the Soviet Union: A Critical Review of Recent Major Experiments. *International Journal of Clinical and Experimental Hypnosis,* 1966, *14,* 308–315.

Howes, D. A Word Count of Spoken English. *Journal of Verbal Learning and Verbal Behavior,* 1966, *5,* 572–606.

Hoy, R. The Facilitation of Creativity through Hypnosis. Unpublished master's thesis, University of California at Berkeley, 1973.

Hull, C. L. Quantitative Methods of Investigating Waking Suggestion. *Journal of*

Abnormal and Social Psychology, 1929, *24*, 153–169.

Hull, C. L. Quantitative Methods of Investigating Hypnotic Suggestion. Part I. *Journal of Abnormal and Social Psychology*, 1930, *25*, 200–233.

Hull, C. L. Quantitative Methods of Investigating Hypnotic Suggestion. Part II. *Journal of Abnormal and Social Psychology*, 1931, *25*, 390–417.

Hull, C. L. *Hypnosis and Suggestibility: An Experimental Approach.* New York: Appleton-Century-Crofts, 1933.

Hunt, J. McV. Intrinsic Motivation and Its Role in Psychological Development. In D. Levine (Ed.), *Nebraska Symposium on Motivation.* Lincoln, Nebraska: University of Nebraska Press, 1965, 189–282.

Hunt, Sonja M. The Speech of the Subject Under Hypnosis. *International Journal of Clinical and Experimental Hypnosis*, 1969, *17*, 209–216.

Hurt, S. W. A Comparison of Self-hypnosis and Hetero-hypnosis. Paper presented at the Annual Convention of The Society for Clinical and Experimental Hypnosis, Asheville, N.C., October 1978.

Huse, R. Does the Hypnotic Trance Favor the Recall of Faint Memories? *Journal of Experimental Psychology*, 1930, *13*, 519–529.

Husson, H. M., et. al. *Report of the Experiments of Animal Magnetism, Made by a Committee of the Medical Section of the French Royal Academy of Sciences; Read at the Meeting of the 21st and 28th of June, 1831.* Signed: Bourdois de la Motte (President), Fourquier, Gueneau de Mussy, Guersent, Husson (Reporter), Itard, J. J. Leroux, Marc, Thiilaye. English translation by J. C. Colquhoun, with an historical and explanatory introduction, and an appendix (on somnambulistic transposability of the senses). Edinburgh: Robert Cadell; London: Whittaker & Co., 1833. Also translated and preceded with an introduction by C. St. Poyen St. Sauveur. Boston: D. K. Hitchcock, 1836. Also abstracted translation in J. S. Bailly, et. al., 1837, 52–58.

Huston, P. E., Shakow, D., & Erickson, M. H. A Study of Hypnotically Induced Complexes by Means of the Luria Technique. *Journal of General Psychology*, 1934, *11*, 65–97.

Huxley, A. *Island.* New York: Harper & Row, 1962.

Huxley, A. *The Doors of Perception.* New York: Harper & Row, 1963.

Ikemi, Y., Akagi, M., Maeda, J., Fukumoto, T., Kawate, K., Hirakawa, K., Gondo, S., Nakagawa, T., Honda, T., Sakamoto, A., & Yasumatsu, A. Experimental Studies on the Psychosomatic Disorders of the Digestive System. *Proceedings of the World Congress on Gastroenterology*, 1959, 169–180.

Ikemi, Y., Akagi, M., Maeda, J., Fukumoto, T., Kawate, K., Hirakawa, K., Gondo, S., Nakagawa, T., Honda, T., Sakamoto, A., & Kumagai, M. Hypnotic Experiments on the Psychosomatic Aspects of Gastrointestinal Disorders. *International Journal of Clinical and Experimental Hypnosis*, 1959, *7*, 139–150.

Ikemi, Y., & Nakagawa, S. A Psychosomatic Study of Contagious Dermatitis. *Kyushu Journal of Medical Science*, 1962, *13*, 335–352.

Imm, C. R. An Exploration of Repression Through Hypnotically Implanted Conflicts. Unpublished doctoral dissertation. Stanford University, 1965.

Jackson, P. W., & Messick, S. The Person, the Product and the Response: Conceptual Problems in the Assessment of Creativity. *Journal of Personality*, 1965, *33*, 309–329.

Jackson, T. L., Jr., Barkley, R. A., & Pashko, S. M. The Effects of Hypnotic Induction Versus High Motivation on Oral Temperature. *International Journal of Clinical and Experimental Hypnosis*, 1976, *24*, 22–28.

Jacobson, A., & Kales, A. Somnambulism: All Night EEG and Related Studies. In S. S. Kety, E. V. Evarts and H. L. Williams (Eds.) *Sleep and Altered States of*

Consciousness. Proceedings of the Association for Research in Nervous and Mental Disease, Dec. 3 & 4, 1965. Baltimore: Williams & Wilkins, 1965, 424–455.

Jacobson, E. Electrical Measurements of Neuromuscular States During Mental Activities: Imagination of Movement Involving Skeletal Muscle. *American Journal of Physiology*, 1930, *91*, 567–608.

Jacobson, E. Electrophysiology of Mental Activities. *American Journal of Psychology*, 1932, *44*, 677–694.

Jacobson, E. *Progressive Relaxation*. Chicago: University of Chicago Press, 1938.

Jacobson, E. Relaxation Methods in Labor: A Critique of Current Techniques in Natural Childbirth. *American Journal of Obstetrics and Gynecology*, 1954, *67*, 1035–1048.

James, W. Automatic Writing. *Proceedings of the American Society for Psychical Research*, 1889, *1*, 548–564.

James, W. *The Varieties of Religious Experience*. New York: Longmans, Green and Co., 1935 (originally published in 1902).

James, W., & Carnochan, G. M. Report of the Committee on Hypnotism. *American Society for Psychical Research: Proceedings*, 1885–1889, *1*, No. 2, 95–102.

Janet, P. *L'Automatisme Psychologique*. Paris: Felix Alcan, 1889.

Janet, P. *Psychological Healing: A Historical and Clinical Study*. French original, 1919. English translation by E. Paul & C. Paul. New York: The Macmillan Co., 1925. 2 vols.

Jenness, A. Hypnotism. In J. McV. Hunt (Ed.), *Personality and the Behavior Disorders*. New York: The Ronald Press, 1944, 466–502.

Jenness, A. Somnambulism, Imagery, and Hypnotizability. Paper presented at the Convention of the American Psychological Association, Chicago, 1965.

Jenness, A., & Jorgensen, Ada P. Ratings of Vividness of Imagery in the Waking State Compared with Reports of Somnambulism. *American Journal of Psychology*, 1941, *54*, 253–259.

Jenness, A., & Wible, C. L. Respiration and Heart Action in Sleep and Hypnosis. *Journal of General Psychology*, 1937, *16*, 197–222.

Johner, C. H., & Perlman, H. B. Hypnosis and Vestibular Function. *Annals of Otology, Rhinology & Laryngology*, 1968, *77*, 126–138.

Johnson, L. S., & Weight, D. G. Self-hypnosis Versus Heterohypnosis: Experiential and Behavioral Comparisons. *Journal of Abnormal Psychology*, 1976, *85*, 523–526.

Johnson, P. O., & Jackson, R. W. B. *Modern Statistical Methods: Descriptive and Inductive*. Chicago: Rand McNally, 1959.

Johnson, R. F. Q., Maher, B. A., & Barber, T. X. Artifact in the "Essence of Hypnosis": An Evaluation of Trance Logic. *Journal of Abnormal and Social Psychology*, 1972, *79*, 212–220.

Jones, R. M. *Ego Synthesis in Dreams*. Cambridge: Schenkman, 1962.

Juhasz, J. B. On the Reliability of Two Measures of Imagery. *Perceptual and Motor Skills*, 1972, *35*, 874.

Jus, K., & Krakowski, A. J. Effects of Post-hypnotic Suggestions on the All-Night Sleep Pattern. In P. Levin & W. P. Koella (Eds.), *Sleep: 1974*. Basel: Karger, 1975, 399–401.

Jussieu, A. L. de. *Rapport de l'un commissaire chargé par le roi de l'examen du magnétisme animal*. (Report of a Commissioner Charged by the King with the Investigation of Animal Magnetism). *Paris, 12 septembre 1784*. Paris: Herissant, 1784. Reproduced in A. Bertrand, 1826, 151–206.

Kahneman, Daniel. *Attention and Effort*. Englewood Cliffs, N.J.: Prentice-Hall, 1973.

Kales, A. (Ed.) *Sleep: Physiology and Pathology: A Symposium.* Philadelphia: J. B. Lippincott & Co., 1969.

Kamiya, J. Operant Control of the EEG Alpha Rhythm and Some of Its Reported Effects on Consciousness. In C. T. Tart (Ed.), *Altered States of Consciousness.* New York, Wiley, 1969a, 509–517.

Kanfer, F. H., & Goldfoot, D. A. Self-control and Tolerance of Noxious Stimulation. *Psychological Reports,* 1966, *18,* 79–85.

Kanzer, M. G. The Therapeutic Use of Dreams Induced by Hypnotic Suggestion. *Psychoanalytic Quarterly,* 1945, *14,* 313–335.

Kaplan, E. A. Hypnosis and Pain. *Archives of General Psychiatry,* 1960, *2,* 567–568.

Kasamatsu, A., & Hirai, T. An Electroencephalographic Study on the Zen Meditation (Zazen). *Folia Psychiatrica et Neurologica Japonica,* 1966, *20,* 315–336. Reprinted in C. T. Tart, (Ed.), *Altered States of Consciousness:* A Book of Readings. New York: John Wiley & Sons, 1969a, 489–502.

Katzenstein, A. An Empirical Scatter Analysis of Electrobiological Data in Hypnotized Patients. *American Journal of Clinical Hypnosis,* 1965, *7,* 320–324.

Kaufman, M. R. Hypnosis in Psychotherapy Today: Anachronism, Fixation, Regression, or Valid Modality? *Archives of General Psychiatry,* 1961, *4,* 30–39.

Keeling, K. R. Hypnosis and Adaptive Regression: A Study Using Wild's Cognitive Shift Score. *Dissertation Abstracts International,* 1974, *35B,* 1023–1024.

Keen, E. *A Primer in Phenomenological Psychology.* New York: Holt, Rinehart & Winston, 1975.

Kehoe, M., & Ironside, W. Studies on the Experimental Evocation of Depressive Responses Using Hypnosis: II. The Influence of Depressive Responses Upon the Secretion of Gastric Acid. *Psychosomatic Medicine,* 1963, *25,* 403–419.

Kehoe, M., & Ironside, W. Studies on the Experimental Evocation of Depressive Responses Using Hypnosis: III. The Secretory Rate of Total Gastric Acid with Respect to Various Spontaneous Experiences Such as Nausea, Disgust, Crying, and Dyspnea. *Psychosomatic Medicine,* 1964, *26,* 224–249.

Kelsey, Denys E. R. Phantasies of Birth and Prenatal Experiences Recovered from Patients Undergoing Hypnoanalysis. *Journal of Mental Science,* 1953, *99,* 216–223.

Kerner, J. Seeress of Prevorst. Translated from the German. In G. Bush, (Ed.), *Mesmer and Swedenborg: or, the Relation of the Developments of Mesmerism to the Doctrines and Disclosures of Swedenborg.* New York: John Allen, 1847. Appendix B.

Kesner, L. S. A Comparison of the Effectiveness of Two Psychotherapy Techniques in the Resolution of a Posthypnotic Conflict. *Journal of Clinical and Experimental Hypnosis,* 1954, *2,* 55–75.

Kety, S. S. Consciousness and the Metabolism of the Brain. In H. A. Abramson (Ed.), *Problems of Consciousness; Transactions of the Third Conference,* March 10 and 11, 1952, New York, New York: Josiah Macy, Jr. Foundation, 1952, 11–73.

Kihlstrom, J. F. Order of Recall in Posthypnotic Amnesia and in Waking Memory. Paper presented at the 43rd Annual Meeting of the Eastern Psychological Association, Boston, 1972a.

Kihlstrom, J. F. Temporal Sequencing in Posthypnotic Amnesia. Paper read at the 24th Annual Meeting of the Society for Clinical and Experimental Hypnosis, Boston, October, 1972b.

Kihlstrom, J. F. Generic Recall During Posthypnotic Amnesia. Paper presented at the 48th Annual Meeting of the Eastern Psychological Association, Boston, Mass. 1977a.

Kihlstrom, J. F. Models of Posthypnotic Amnesia. In W. E. Edmonston, Jr. (Ed.), *Conceptual and Investigative Approaches to Hypnosis and Hypnotic Phenomena. Annals of the New York Academy of Sciences,* 1977b, *296,* 284–301.

Kihlstrom, J. F. Context and Cognition in Posthypnotic Amnesia. *International Journal of Clinical and Experimental Hypnosis,* 1978, *26,* 256–267.

Kihlstrom, J. F., & Evans, F. J. Posthypnotic Amnesia as Disorganized Retrieval. Proceedings of the Annual Convention of the American Psychological Association, 1971, *6,* 775–776.

Kihlstrom, J. F., & Evans, F. J. Forgetting to Count Reversibility: What Constitutes Posthypnotic Amnesia? Paper presented at the 25th Annual Meeting of The Society for Clinical and Experimental Hypnosis, Newport Beach, California, 1973.

Kihlstrom, J. F., & Evans, F. J. Recovery of Memory After Posthypnotic Amnesia. *Journal of Abnormal Psychology,* 1976, *85,* 564–569.

Kihlstrom, J. F., & Evans, F. J. Residual Effect of Suggestions for Posthypnotic Amnesia: A Reexamination. *Journal of Abnormal Psychology,* 1977, *86,* 327–333.

Kihlstrom, J. F., Evans, F. J., Orne, Emily C., & Orne, M. T. Attempting to Breach Posthypnotic Amnesia. (in press).

Kihlstrom, J. F., & Shor, R. E. Recall and Recognition During Posthypnotic Amnesia. *International Journal of Clinical and Experimental Hypnosis,* 1978, *26,* 330–349.

King, D. L., & Lummis, G. Effects of Visual Sensory-Restriction and Recent Experience with the Imagined Stimulus on a Suggestibility Measure. *International Journal of Clinical and Experimental Hypnosis,* 1974, *22,* 239–248.

Kinsbourne, M. Eye and Head Turning Indicates Cerebral Lateralization. *Science,* 1972, *176,* 539–541.

Klein, D. B. The Experimental Production of Dreams During Hypnosis. *University of Texas Bulletin,* 1930, *3009,* 1–71.

Klein, G. S. Peremptory Ideation: Structure and Force in Motivated Ideas. In R. R. Holt (Ed.) *Motives and Thought: Psychoanalytic Essays in Honor of David Rapaport. Psychological Issues* (18/19), 1967, *5,* 80–128. New York: International Universities Press.

Klein, G. S. Consciousness in Psychoanalytic Theory. In G. S. Klein, *Perception, Motives and Personality.* New York: Knopf, 1970.

Kleitman, N. *Sleep and Wakefulness.* Chicago: University of Chicago Press, 1963.

Kline, M. V. Hypnosis and Age Progression: A Case Report. *Journal of Genetic Psychology,* 1951, *78,* 195–206.

Kline, M. V. *Freud and Hypnosis: The Interaction of Psychodynamics and Hypnosis.* New York: Julian Press, 1958.

Kline, M. V. Hypnotic Amnesia in Psychotherapy. *International Journal of Clinical and Experimental Hypnosis,* 1966, *14,* 112–120.

Kline, M. V. The Production of Antisocial Behavior Through Hypnosis: New Clinical Data. Paper presented at the 22nd Annual Convention of the Society for Clinical and Experimental Hypnosis. Philadelphia, November, 1970.

Kline, M. V., Guze, H., & Haggerty, A. D. An Experimental Study of the Nature of Hypnotic Deafness: Effects of Delayed Speech Feed-Back. *Journal of Clinical and Experimental Hypnosis,* 1954, *2,* 145–156.

Kline, M. V., & Linder, M. Psychodynamic Factors in the Experimental Investigation of Hypnotically Induced Emotions with Particular Reference to Blood Glucose Measurements. *Journal of Psychology,* 1969, *71,* 21–25.

Klinger, B. I. Effect of Peer Model Responsiveness and Length of Induction Procedure on Hypnotic Responsiveness. *Journal of Abnormal Psychology,* 1970, 75, 15–18.

Klopfer, B., Ainsworth, Mary D., Klopfer, W., & Holt, R. R. *Developments in the Rorschach Technique*. Yonkers, N.Y.: World Book Co., 1954.

Klopp, K. K. Production of Local Anesthesia Using Waking Suggestion with the Child Patient. *International Journal of Clinical and Experimental Hypnosis,* 1961, *9*, 59–62.

Knowles, F. W. Hypnosis in Amnesic States. A report of seven cases. *New Zealand Medical Journal,* 1964, 63, 100–103.

Knox, V. Jane, Crutchfield, Lila, & Hilgard, E. R. The Nature of Task Interference in Hypnotic Dissociation: An Investigation of Automatic Behavior. *International Journal of Clinical and Experimental Hypnosis,* 1975, *23*, 305–323.

Knox, V. Jane, Morgan, Arlene H., & Hilgard, E. R. Pain and Suffering in Ischemia: The Paradox of Hypnotically Suggested Anesthesia as Contradicted by Reports from the "Hidden Observer." *Archives of General Psychiatry,* 1974, *30*, 840–847.

Kolers, P. A. The Illusion of Movement. *Scientific American,* 1964, *211*, 98–106.

Kornetsky, C. Effects of Anxiety and Morphine on the Anticipation and Perception of Painful Radiant Thermal Stimuli. *Journal of Comparative Physiology and Psychology,* 1954, *47*, 130–132.

Korotkin, I. I., & Suslova, M. M. Investigation into Higher Nervous Activity in Subjects in the Somnambulistic Phase of Hypnosis. *Zhurnal Vyssheĭ Nervnoĭ Deiâtel'nosti,* 1951, *1*, 617–622. (Cited by Das, 1958a).

Korotkin, I. I., & Suslova, M. M. Investigation into the Higher Nervous Acitivity in Some Somnambulistic Phase of Hypnosis During Different Depths of Hypnotic Sleep. *Fiziologicheskii Zhurnal,* 1953, *39*, 423–431. (Cited by Das, 1958a).

Korotkin, I. I., & Suslova, M. M. About Some Characteristics of the Reciprocal Influence of Signal Systems in Hypnotic and Posthypnotic States. *Zhurnal Vyssheĭ Nervnoĭ Deiâtel'nosti,* 1955a, *5*, 511–519. (Read in abstract only.)

Korotkin, I. I., & Suslova, M. M. Materials for the Investigation into the Nervous Mechanism of Post-Hypnotic Suggestion with Hysterics. *Zhurnal Vyssheĭ Nervnoĭ Deiâtel'nosti,* 1955b, *5*, 697–707. (Read in abstract only.)

Korotkin, I. I., & Suslova, M. M. On the Physiological Mechanism of Inhibitory Action on Stimuli Inhibited by Hypnotic Suggestions. *Doklady Akadémii Nauk. SSSR,* 1955c, *102*, 189–192. (Cited by Das, 1958a).

Korotkin, I. I., & Suslova, M. M. Changes in Conditioned and Unconditioned Reflexes During Suggestion States in Hypnosis. In *The Central Nervous System and Human Behavior—Translations from the Russian Medical Literature*. Bethesda, Maryland: U.S. Department of Health, Education & Welfare, 1959, 653–670.

Korotkin, I. I., & Suslova, M. M. Comparative Effects of Suggestion in the Waking State and in Hypnosis. *Pavlov Journal of Higher Nervous Activity,* 1960, *10*, 185–192.

Korotkin, I. I., & Suslova, M. M. An Attempt to Change the Localization of Conditioned Inhibition by Verbal Suggestion in the State of Hypnosis. *Zhurnal Vyssheĭ Nervnoĭ Deiâtel'nosti,* 1962, *12*, 778–787. (Read in abstract only.)

Kraines S. H. Hypnosis: Physiologic Inhibition and Excitation. *Psychosomatics,* 1969, *10*, 36–41.

Kramer, E., & Tucker, G. R. Hypnotically Suggested Deafness and Delayed Auditory Feedback. *International Journal of Clinical and Experimental Hypnosis,* 1967, *15*, 37–43.

Kratochvil, S. Sleep Hypnosis and Waking Hypnosis. *International Journal of Clinical and Experimental Hypnosis,* 1970, *18*, 25–40.

Krippner, S. The Psychedelic State, the Hypnotic Trance, and the Creative Act. In C. T. Tart (Ed.), *Altered States of Consciousness: A Book of Readings*. New

York: John Wiley & Sons, 1969a, 271–290.

Krippner, S. Research in Creativity and Psychedelic Drugs. International Journal of Clinical and Experimental Hypnosis, 1977, *25*, 274–290.

Kris, E. (1934). *Psychoanalytic Explorations in Art.* New York: International Universities Press, 1952.

Kroger, W. S. Introduction and Supplemental Reports on Hypnoanesthesia. In Esdaile, J. *Hypnosis in Medicine and Surgery.* With introduction and supplementary reports on current applications by W. S. Kroger. New York: Julian Press, 1957.

Kroger, W. S. *Clinical and Experimental Hypnosis.* Philadelphia: J. B. Lippincott Co., 1963.

Kroger, W. S. Comprehensive Management of Obesity. *American Journal of Clinical Hypnosis,* 1970, *12,* 165–176.

Kroger, W. S., & Freed, S. C. The Psychosomatic Treatment of Functional Dysmenorrhea by Hypnosis. *American Journal of Obstetrics and Gynecology,* 1943, *46,* 817–822.

Krojanker, R. J. Training of the Unconscious by Hynodramatic Re-enactment of Dreams. *Group Psychotherapy,* 1962, *15,* 134–143.

Kubie, L. S. Hypnotism. *Archives of General Psychiatry,* 1961, *4,* 40–54.

Kuhn, T. S. *The Structure of Scientific Revolutions.* Chicago: University of Chicago Press, 1962.

La Barre, W. Anthropoligical Perspectives on Hallucination and Hallucinogens. In R. K. Siegel, & L. J. West (Eds.), *Hallucinations: Behavior, Experience, and Theory.* New York: Wiley, 1975.

Lacey, J. I. Psychophysiological Approaches to the Evaluation of Psychotherapeutic Process and Outcome. In E. A. Rubenstein & M. B. Parloff (Eds.), *Research in Psychotherapy.* Washington, D.C.: National Publishing Company, 1959, 160–208.

Lacey, J. I. Somatic Response Patterning and Stress: Some Revisions of Activation Theory. In M. H. Appley & R. Trumbull (Eds.), *Psychological Stress: Issues in Research.* New York: Appleton-Century-Crofts, 1967, 14–37.

Lacey, J. I., Kagan, J., Lacey, Beatrice C., & Moss, H. A. The Visceral Level: Situational Determinants and Behavioral Correlates of Autonomic Response Patterns. In P. H. Knapp (Ed.), *Expressions of the Emotions in Man.* New York: International Universities Press, 1963, *161*–196.

Lafontaine, C. *L'art de magnétiser, ou le Magnétisme animal considéré sous le point de vue théoretique, pratique, et thérapeutique.* (The Art of Magnetizing), (3rd edition). Paris: G. Ballière, 1860.

Lane, Barbara M. A Validation Test of the Rorschach Movement Interpretations. *American Journal of Orthopsychiatry,* 1948, *18,* 292–296.

Laplanche, Jean, & Pontalis, J. B. Fantasy and the Origins of Sexuality. *International Journal of Psycho-analysis,* 1968, *49,* 1–18.

Larsen, S. Strategies for Reducing Phobic Behavior. Doctoral Dissertation, Stanford University, 1965.

Lavoie, G., Sabourin, M., & Langlois, J. Hypnotic Susceptibility, Amnesia, and I.Q. in Chronic Schizophrenia. *International Journal of Clinical and Experimental Hypnosis,* 1973, *21,* 157–168.

LeBon, G. *The Crowd: A Study of the Popular Mind.* (French original, 1895.) London: T. F. Unwin, 1896.

LeBon, G. *Les opinions et les croyances.* Paris: Flammarion. 1911.

LeCron, L. M. A Study of Age Regression Under Hypnosis. In L. M. LeCron (Ed.), *Experimental Hypnosis: A Symposium of Articles on Research by Many of the*

World's Leading Authorities. New York: The Macmillan Co., 1952, 155-174.

LeCron, L. M. A Method of Measuring the Depth of Hypnosis. *Journal of Clinical and Experimental Hypnosis,* 1953, 1, 4-7.

LeCron, L. M., & Bordeaux, J. *Hypnotism Today.* New York: Grune & Stratton, 1947.

Lee-Teng, Evelyn. Trance-Susceptibility, Induction Susceptibility, and Acquiescence as Factors in Hypnotic Performance. *Journal of Abnormal Psychology,* 1965, *70,* 383-389.

Leger, T. *Animal Magnetism or Psychodunamy.* New York: D. Appleton & Co., 1846.

Lehman, R. E. Imagery, Imagination and Hypnosis (Doctoral dissertation, University of Oregon, 1972). *Dissertation Abstracts International* 1973, *33,* 4515-B. (University Microfilms No. 73-7923).

Lehmann, H. E. Time and Psychopathology. In R. Fischer (Ed.), 1967, 798-821.

Lenox, J. R. A Failure of Hypnotic State to Effect Numerical Task Performance. Unpublished doctoral dissertation, Stanford University, 1970.

Lenox, J. R. Effect of Hypnotic Analgesia on Verbal Report Cardiovascular Responses to Ischemic Pain. *Journal of Abnormal Psychology,* 1970, *75,* 199-206.

Leonard, J. R. An Investigation of Hypnotic Age-Regression. Unpublished doctoral dissertation, University of Kentucky, 1963.

Leriche, R. *The Surgery of Pain.* Baltimore: Williams & Wilkins, 1939.

Lerner, Barbara. Dream Function Reconsidered. *Journal of Abnormal Psychology,* 1967, *72,* 85-100.

Leuba, C. The Use of Hypnosis for Controlling Variables in Psychological Experiments. *Journal of Abnormal and Social Psychology,* 1941, *36,* 271-274.

Levin, Lois Ann, & Harrington, R. H. Hypnosis and Regression in the Service of the Ego. *International Journal of Clinical and Experimental Hypnosis,* 1976, *24,* 400-418.

Levine, K. N., Grassi, J. P., & Gerson, M. J. Hypnotically Induced Mood Changes in the Verbal and Graphic Rorschach: A Case Study. *Rorschach Research Exchange,* 1943, *7,* 130-144.

Levine, M. Electrical Skin Resistance During Hypnosis. *Archives of Neurology and Psychiatry,* 1930, *24,* 937-942.

Levitt, E. E. Some Data From Hypnosis Experiments Leading to Speculations About Individual Differences in Defenses Against Anxiety. Paper read at the International Congress on Hypnosis, New York, October, 1963.

Levitt, E. E. *The Psychology of Anxiety.* Indianapolis: Bobbs-Merrill Company, Inc., 1967.

Levitt, E. E. Research Strategies in Evaluating the Coercive Power of Hypnosis. In W. E. Edmonston, Jr. (Ed.), Conceptual and Investigative Approaches to Hypnosis and Hypnotic Phenomena. *Annals of the New York Academy of Sciences, 296.* New York: New York Academy of Sciences, 1977, 86-89.

Levitt, E. E., Aronoff, G., Morgan, C. D., Overley, T. M., & Parrish, M. J. Testing the Coercive Power of Hypnosis: Committing Objectionable Acts. *International Journal of Clinical and Experimental Hypnosis,* 1975, *23,* 59-67.

Levitt, E. E., & Brady, J. P. Psychophysiology of Hypnosis. In J. M. Schneck (Ed.), 1963a, 314-362.

Levitt, E. E., den Breeijen, A., & Persky, H. The Induction of Clinical Anxiety by Means of a Standardized Hypnotic Technique. *American Journal of Clinical Hypnosis,* 1960, *2,* 206-214.

Levitt, E. E., & Grosz, H. J. A Comparison of Quantifiable Rorschach Anxiety Indicators in Hypnotically Induced Anxiety and Normal States. *Journal of Consult-*

ing Psychology, 1960, *24,* 31–34.

Levitt, E. E., Lubin, B., & Brady, J. P. On the Use of TAT Card Twelve M as an Indicator of Attitude Toward Hypnosis. *International Journal of Clinical and Experimental Hypnosis,* 1962, *10,* 145–150.

Levitt, E. E., & Lubin, B. TAT card "12MF" and Hypnosis Themes in Females. *International Journal of Clinical and Experimental Hypnosis.* 1963, *11,* 241–244.

Levitt, E. E., Overley, T. M., & Rubenstein, D. The Objectionable Act as a Mechanism for Testing the Coercive Power of the Hypnotic State. *American Journal of Clinical Hypnosis,* 1975, *17,* 263–266.

Levitt, E. E., & Persky, H. Relation of Rorschach Factors and Plasma Hydrocortisone Level in Hypnotically Induced Anxiety. *Psychosomatic Medicine,* 1960, *22,* 218–223.

Levitt, E. E., & Persky, H. Experimental Evidence for the Validity of the IPAT Anxiety Scale. *Journal of Clinical Psychology,* 1962, *18,* 458–461.

Levitt, E. E., Persky, H., & Brady, J. P. *Hypnotic Induction of Anxiety: A Psychoendocrine Investigation.* Springfield, Ill.: Charles C. Thomas, 1964.

Levitt, E. E., Persky, H., Brady, J. P., Fitzgerald, J., & den Breeijen, A. Evidence for Hypnotically Induced Amnesia as an Analog of Repression. *Journal of Nervous and Mental Disease,* 1961, *133,* 218–221.

Levitt, E. E., Persky, H., Brady, J. P., & Fitzgerald, J. A. The Effect of Hydrocortisone Infusion on Hypnotically Induced Anxiety. *Psychosomatic Medicine,* 1963, *25,* 158–161.

Lewis, D. *Quantitative Methods in Psychology.* New York: McGraw-Hill, 1960.

Lewis, D. J., & Adams, H. E. Retrograde Amnesia from Conditioned Competing Responses. *Science,* 1963, *141,* 516–517.

Lewis, J. H., & Sarbin, T. R. Studies in Psychosomatics: I. The Influence of Hypnotic Stimulation on Gastric Hunger Contractions. *Psychosomatic Medicine,* 1943, *5,* 125–131.

Lewis, T. *The Blood Vessels of the Human Skin and Their Responses.* London: Shaw & Sons, 1927.

Lewis, T. *Pain.* New York: Macmillan, 1942.

Liébeault, A. A. *Du sommeil et des ètats analogues considérés surtout au point de vue de l'action moral sur le physique.* (Of Sleep and Related States, Conceived of from the Viewpoint of the Action of the Psyche Upon the Soma). Paris: V. Masson, 1866. Vienna: F. Deuticke, 1892,

Liébeault, A. A. Anesthesie par suggestion. *Journal Magnetisme,* 1885, 64–67.

Liébeault, A. A. *Le sommeil provoqué et les états analogues.* Paris: Doin, 1889.

Liebert, R. M., Rubin, Norma, & Hilgard, E. R. The Effects of Suggestions of Alertness in Hypnosis on Paired-Associate Learning. *Journal of Personality,* 1965, *33,* 605–612.

Live, C. The Effects of Practice in the Trance Upon Learning in the Normal Waking State. Unpublished B. A. thesis, University of Wisconsin, 1929.

Lindauer, M. S. Imagery and Sensory Modality. *Perceptual and Motor Skills,* 1969, *29,* 203–215.

Lindauer, M. S. The Sensory Attributes and Functions of Imagery and Imagery Evoking Stimuli. In P. W. Sheehan (Ed.), *The Function and Nature of Imagery.* New York: Academic Press, 1972, 131–147.

Lindsley, O. R. Operant Behavior During Sleep: A Measure of Depth of Sleep. *Science,* 1957, *126,* 1290–1291.

Livshits, L. S. The Investigation of the Higher Nervous Activity of Man in Hypnosis in Relation to Chronic Alcoholism. *Pavlov Journal of Higher Nervous Activity,* 1959, *9,* 745–753.

Lohr, Naomi E. Determinants of Subjective Uncertainty. Unpublished doctoral dissertation, University of Michigan, 1967.

London, P. Subject Characteristics in Hypnosis Research: Part I. A Survey of Experience, Interest, and Opinion. *International Journal of Clinical and Experimental Hypnosis,* 1961, *9,* 151-161.

London, P. *The Children's Hypnotic Susceptibility Scale.* Palo Alto, California: Consulting Psychologist Press, 1963.

London, P. The Psychophysiology of Hypnotic Susceptibility. Paper presented at the annual meeting of the American Psychological Association Convention, Washington, D.C., August, 1969.

London, P., & Cooper, L. M. Norms of Hypnotic Susceptibility in Children. *Developmental Psychology,* 1969, *1,* 113-124.

London, P., Cooper, L. M., & Johnson, H. J. Subject Characteristics in Hypnosis Research: II Attitudes Towards Hypnosis, Volunteer Status, and Personality Measures. III. Some Correlates of Hypnotic Susceptibility. *International Journal of Clinical and Experimental Hypnosis,* 1962, *10,* 13-21.

London, P., & Fuhrer, M. Hypnosis, Motivation and Performance. *Journal of Personality,* 1961, *29,* 321-333.

London, P., Hart, J. T., & Leibovitz, M. P. EEG Alpha Rhythms and Susceptibility to Hypnosis. *Nature,* 1968, *219,* 71-72.

London, P., Hart, J. T., Leibovitz, M. P., & McDevitt, R. A. The Psychophysiology of Hypnotic Susceptibility. In L. Chertok (Ed.), *Psychophysiological Mechanisms of Hypnosis.* New York: Springer-Verlag, 1969, 151-172.

London, P., & McDevitt, R. A. AMRL-TR-67-142 (W-P AF Base, Ohio: Aerospace Medical Research Laboratories, 1967).

London, P., & McDevitt, R. A. Effects of Hypnotic Susceptibility and Training on Responses to Stress. *Journal of Abnormal Psychology,* 1970, *76,* 336-348.

Loomis, A. L., Harvey, E. N., & Hobart, G. A. Brain Potentials During Hypnosis. *Science,* 1936, *83,* 239-241.

Lorge, I., with Curtiss, C. C. Prestige, Suggestion and Attitudes. *Journal of Social Psychology,* 1936, *7,* 386-402.

Lubin, B., Brady, J. P., & Levitt, E. E. A Comparison of Personality Characteristics of Volunteers and Nonvolunteers for Hypnosis Experiments. *Journal of Clinical Psychology,* 1962, *18,* 341-343.

Ludwig, A. M. An Historical Survey of the Early Roots of Mesmerism. *International Journal of Clinical and Experimental Hypnosis,* 1964, *12,* 205-217.

Ludwig, A. M. Altered States of Consciousness. *Archives of General Psychiatry,* 1966, *15,* 225-234. Reprinted in C. T. Tart (Ed.), 1969a, 9-22.

Lundholm, H. A Hormic Theory of Hallucinations. *British Journal of Medical Psychology,* 1932, *11,* 269-282.

Luria, A. R. *The Nature of Human Conflicts.* New York: Liverright, 1932.

Luria, A. R. *The Mind of a Mnemonist: A Little Book About a Vast Memory.* New York: Basic Books, 1968.

Luthe, W. (Ed.), *Autogenic Therapy: Vol. IV. Research and Theory.* New York: Grune & Stratton Inc., 1970.

Lyons, J. The Hidden Dialogue in Experimental Research. *Journal of Phenomenological Psychology,* 1970, *1,* 19-30.

Macchi, V., Card. *Encyclical letter on the abuses of magnetism, Holy Roman Inquisition.* Vatican, Rome, 1856. Original text in Latin quoted by G. Mabru, *Les Magnétiseurs jugés par eux mêmes; nouvelle enquête sur le magnétisme animal.* (The Magnetizers in Their Own Judgement; A New Research on Animal Magnetism). Paris. Mallet-Bachelier, 1858, Translated and with commentary in A.

Binet & C. S. Féré, (Eds.), 1888, 54–58.

Maccoby, Eleanor E. Sex Differences in Intellectual Functioning. In Eleanor E. Maccoby (Ed.), *The Development of Sex Differences.* Stanford, Cal.: Stanford University Press, 1966, 25–55.

Maccoby, Eleanor E., & Maccoby, N. The Interview: A Tool of Social Science. In G. Lindzey (Ed.), *Handbook of Social Psychology. Vol. 1 Theory and Method.* Cambridge, Mass.: Addison-Wesley Publishing Company, 1954, 449–487.

MacKay, D. G. Aspects of the Theory of Comprehension, Memory and Attention. *Quarterly Journal of Experimental Psychology,* 1973, *25,* 22–40.

MacKinnon, D. Creativity and Transliminal Experience. *Journal of Creative Behavior,* 1971, *5,* 227–241.

MacKinnon, D. W. IPAR's Contribution to the Conceptualization and Study of Creativity. In I. A. Taylor and J. W. Getzels (Eds.), *Perspectives in Creativity.* Chicago: Aldine, 1975, 60–89.

Mackenzie, J. *Symptoms and Their Interpretation.* London: Shaw & Sons, 1909.

Macmillan, M. B. The Cathartic Method and the Expectancies of Breuer and Anna O. *International Journal of Clinical and Experimental Hypnosis,* 1977, *25,* 108–116.

Macvaugh, G. S. *Hypnosis Readiness Inventory: A Self-Confidence Developer in Ability to Hypnotize.* Chevy Chase, Md.: G. S. Macvaugh. 1969.

Maddi, S. R. Motivational Aspects of Creativity. *Journal of Personality,* 1965, *33,* 330–347.

Maiolo, A. T., Porro, G. B., & Granone, F. Cerebral Hemodynamics and Metabolism in Hypnosis. *British Medical Journal,* 1969, *1,* 314–320.

Marcuse, F. L. (Ed.) *Hypnosis Throughout the World.* With a foreword by B. B. Raginsky. Springfield, Ill.: Charles C. Thomas Publishers, 1964.

Marenina, A. I. Further Investigation of the Dynamics of Cerebral Potentials in the Various Phases of Hypnosis in Man. *Fiziologicheskii Zhurnal SSSR imeni I. M. Sechenova,* 1955, *41,* 742–747.

Marks, R. W. *The Story of Hypnotism.* New York: Prentice-Hall, 1947.

Marks, D. Visual Imagery Differences in the Recall of Pictures. *British Journal of Psychology,* 1973, *64,* 17–24.

Marmer, M. J. The Role of Hypnosis in Anesthesiology. *Journal of the American Medical Association,* 1956, *162,* 441–443.

Marquis, D. G., & Hilgard, E. R. Conditioned Lid Responses to Light in Dogs After Removal of the Visual Cortex. *Journal of Comparative Psychology,* 1936, *22,* 157–178.

Marshall, G., & Zimbardo, P. G. The Affective Consequences of Inadequately Explained Physiological Arousal. *Journal of Personality and Social Psychology,* 1979, in press.

Martin, I., & Grosz, H. J. Hypnotically Induced Emotions: Autonomic and Skeletal Muscle Activity in Patients with Affective Illness. *Archives of General Psychiatry,* 1964, *11,* 203–213.

Martindale, C. & Hines, D. Creativity and Cortical Activation During Creative, Intellectual and EEG Feedback Tasks. *Biological Psychology,* 1975, *3,* 91–100.

Maslach, Christina. Negative Emotional Biasing of Unexplained Arousal. *Journal of Personality and Social Psychology,* 1979, in press.

Maslach, Christina, & Garber, R. M. The Effects of Hypnotically Altered Time Perspective on Learning and Task Performance. Paper presented at the Annual Convention of the Western Psychological Association, Los Angeles, April, 1976.

Maslach, Christina, Marshall, G., & Zimbardo, P. G. Hypnotic Control of Peripheral Skin Temperature: A Case Report. *Psychophysiology,* 1972, *9,* 600–605.

Maslow, A. H. *Toward a Psychology of Being.* Princeton: Van Nostrand, 1962.

Maupin, E. W. Individual Differences in Response to a Zen Meditation Exercise. *Journal of Consulting Psychology,* 1965, *29,* 139–145. Reprinted in C. T. Tart (Ed.), 1969a. 187–198.

May, J. R., & Edmonston, W. E., Jr. Hypnosis and a Plethysmographic Measure of Two Types of Situation Anxiety. *American Journal of Clinical Hypnosis,* 1966, *9,* 109–113.

Mayman, M., & Voth, H. M. Reality Closeness, Phantasy and Autokinesis: A Dimension of Cognitive Style. *Journal of Abnormal Psychology,* 1969, *74,* 635–641.

Mazer, M. An Experimental Study of the Hypnotic Dream. *Psychiatry,* 1951, *14,* 265–277.

McAmmond, D. M., Davidson, P. O., & Kovitz, D. M. A Comparison of the Effects of Hypnosis and Relaxation Training on Stress Reactions in a Dental Situation. *American Journal of Clinical Hypnosis,* 1971, *13,* 233–242.

McBain, W. N. Imagery and Suggestibility: A Test of the Arnold Hypothesis. *Journal of Abnormal and Social Psychology,* 1954, *49,* 36–44.

McCally, M., & Barnard, G. W. Modification of the Immersion Diuresis by Hypnotic Suggestion. *Psychosomatic Medicine,* 1968, *30,* 287–297.

McCranie, E. J., & Crasilneck, H. B. The Conditioned Reflex in Hypnotic Age Regression. *Journal of Clinical and Experimental Psychopathology,* 1955, *16,* 120–123.

McDonald, D. G. Conditional and Unconditional Autonomic Responses During Sleep. U.S. Navy Medical Neuropsychiatric Research Unit, San Diego, Cal. Report 65-28, Ad. 481520, January, 1966.

McDowell, M. Hypnosis in Dermatology. In J. M. Schneck (Ed.), 1963a, 122–142.

McGlashan, T. H., Evans, F. J., & Orne, M. T. The Nature of Hypnotic Analgesia and Placebo Response to Experimental Pain. *Psychosomatic Medicine,* 1969, *31,* 227–246.

McGlothlin, W. H., Cohen, S., & McGlothlin, M. Personality and Attitude Changes in Volunteer Subjects Following Repeated Administration of LSD. In J. Schlien (Ed.), *Research in Psychotherapy. Vol. III.* Washington, D.C.: American Psychological Association, 1968.

McGraw, M. B. Development of the Plantar Response in Healthy Infants. *American Journal of Diseases of Children,* 1941, *61,* 1215–1221.

McGuire, W. J. The Nature of Attitudes and Attitude Change. In G. Lindzey & E. Aronson (Eds.), *The Handbook of Social Psychology, III: The Individual in a Social Context.* (2nd edition). Reading, Mass.: Addison-Wesley Publishing Co., 1969, 136–314.

McKellar, P. *Imagination and Thinking: A Psychological Analysis.* New York: Basic Books, 1957.

McKellar, P. Imagery from the Standpoint of Introspection. In P. W. Sheehan (Ed.), *The Function and Nature of Imagery.* New York & London: Academic Press, 1972, 35–61.

McNemar, Q. *Psychological Statistics* (4th edition). New York: Wiley, 1970.

McPeake, J. D. Hypnosis, Suggestions, and Psychosomatics. *Diseases of the Nervous System,* 1968, *29,* 536–544.

Meares, A. *Theories of Hypnosis.* In J. M. Schneck (Ed.), 1963a, 390–405.

Mednick, S. A., & Mednick, Martha T. *Examiners Manual: Remote Associates Test.* Boston: Houghton-Mifflin Company, 1967.

Meeker, W. B., & Barber, T. X. Toward an Explanation of Stage Hypnosis. *Journal of Abnormal Psychology,* 1971, *77,* 61–70.

Melei, Janet P., & Hilgard, E. R. Attitudes Toward Hypnosis, Self-Predictions and

Hypnotic Susceptibility. *International Journal of Clinical and Experimental Hypnosis,* 1964, *12,* 99–108.

Mellenbruch, P. L. The Validity of a Personality Inventory Tested by Hypnosis. *American Journal of Clinical Hypnosis,* 1962, *2,* 111–114.

Melzack, R., & Wall, P. D. Gate Control of Pain. In Soulairac, A., Cahn, J., & Charpentier, J. (Eds.), *Pain.* New York: Academic Press, 1968.

Memmesheimer, A. M., & Eisenlohr, E. Untersuchungen über die Suggestivbehandlung der Warzen. *Dermatologische Zeitschift,* 1931, *62,* 63–68.

Mendelsohn, G. A. Experiments on the Psychoanalytic Mechanism of Isolation. Unpublished doctoral dissertation, University of Michigan, 1960.

Mendelsohn, G. A., & Griswold, Barbara B. Differential Use of Incidental Stimuli in Problem Solving as a Function of Creativity. *Journal of Abnormal and Social Psychology,* 1964, *68,* 431–436.

Menzies, R. Further Studies of Conditioned Vasomotor Responses in Human Subjects. *Journal of Experimental Psychology,* 1941, *29,* 457–482.

Mesel, E. & Ledford, F. F., Jr. The Electroencephalogram During Hypnotic Age Regression (to Infancy) in Epileptic Patients. *Archives of Neurology,* 1959, *1,* 516–521.

Mesmer, F. A. *Mémoire sur la découverte du Magnétisme Animal.* Geneva, 1774. With the *Précis historique écrite par M. Paradis en mars. 1777.* Paris: Didot, 1779. English version: *Mesmerism by Doctor Mesmer: Dissertation on the discovery of Animal Magnetism. 1779.* Translated by V. R. Myers. Published with G. Frankau, *Introductory Monograph.* London: Macdonald, 1948. Abridged version of Myers' translation in J. Ehrenwald (Ed.), *From Medicine Man to Freud: An Anthology, Edited, with Notes.* New York: Dell Publishing Co., 1956, 256–280. Second edition (Title): *Memoir of F. A. Mesmer, Doctor of Medicine, On His Discoveries, 1799,* translated by J. Eden, Mt. Vernon, N.Y.: Eden Press, 1957.

Mesmer, F. A. *Aphorismes de M. Mesmer: Dictés à l'assemblée de ses élèves, & dans lesquels on trouve ses principes, sa théorie (les moyens de magnétiser; le tout formant un corps de doctrine, dévéloppé en trois cents quarantequatre paragraphes pour faciliter l'application des commentaries au magnétisme animal.* (Aphorisms of Mr. Mesmer: dictated to the assembly of his students & containing his principles, theories & methods of magnetizing; the whole forming a doctrine, developed in 344 paragraphs, that facilitates the discussion of animal magnetism). Recorded from spoken lectures, edited, and with notes by C. de Veaumorel. (3rd edition, revised and expanded.) Paris: Bertrand, 1785. English version: *Maxims on Animal Magnetism.* Translated and with an introduction by J. Eden. Mt. Vernon, N.Y.: Eden Press, 1958.

Mesmer, F. A. *Mesmerismus oder System der Wechselwirkungen, Theorie und Anwendung des tierischen Magnetismus als die allgemeine Heilkunde zur Erhaltung des Menschen.* Herausgegeben von C. C. Wolfart. (Mesmerism or a system of reciprocal effects: The theory and application of animal magnetism as the general therapeutics for the preservation of mankind. Edited by C. C. Wolfart). Berlin: Rikolaischen, 1814.

Messerschmidt, R. A Quantitative Investigation of the Alleged Independent Operation of Conscious and Subconscious Processes. *Journal of Abnormal and Social Psychology,* 1927–1928, *22,* 325–340.

Michael, Lois I. A Factor Analysis of Mental Imagery. *Dissertation Abstracts,* 1967, *27,* 3761.

Milgram, S. Behavior Study of Obedience. *Journal of Abnormal and Social Psychology,* 1963, *67,* 371–378.

Miller, N. E. Learning of Visceral and Glandular Responses. *Science,* 1969a, *163,* 434–445.

Miller, N. E. Autonomic Learning: Clinical and Physiological Implications. Invited lecture at the XIX International Congress of Psychology, London, 1969b.

Miller, R. R., & Springer, A. D. Amnesia, Consolidation, and Retrieval. *Psychological Review,* 1973, *80,* 69–79.

Milos, R. Hypnotic Exploration of Amnesia After Cerebral Injuries. *International Journal of Clinical and Experimental Hypnosis.* 1975, *23,* 103–110.

Mischel, W. *Personality and Assessment.* New York: Wiley, 1968.

Mitchell, J. F. Local Anesthesia in General Surgery. *Journal of the American Medical Association,* 1907, *49,* 198–201.

Mitchell, Mildred B. Retroactive Inhibition and Hypnosis. *Journal of General Psychology,* 1932, *7,* 343–359.

Moll, A. *Hypnotism.* German original, 1889. Translated by A. F. Hopkirk, from the 4th enlarged edition. London: Walter Scott, 1890. New York: Charles Scribner's Sons, 1898. Reissued under title: *The Study of Hypnosis: Historical, Clinical, and Experimental Research in the Techniques of Hypnotic Induction.* Introduction by J. H. Conn. New York: Julian Press, 1958.

Moore, Rosemarie K., & Lauer, Lillian W. Hypnotic Susceptibility in Middle Childhood. *International Journal of Clinical and Experimental Hypnosis,* 1963, *11,* 167–174.

Moore, W. F. Effects of Posthypnotic Stimulation of Hostility Upon Motivation. *American Journal of Clinical Hypnosis,* 1964, *7,* 130–135.

Morávek, M. Effect of Suggested Anaesthesia on Motor Activity. *Activitas Nervosa Superior,* 1968, *10,* 132–135.

Mordey, T. R. The Relationship Between Certain Motives and Suggestibility. Unpublished Masters thesis, Roosevelt University, 1960.

Morgan, Arlene H. The Heritability of Hypnotic Susceptibility in Twins. *Journal of Abnormal Psychology,* 1973, *82,* 55–61.

Morgan, Arlene H., & Lam, D. The Relationship of the Betts Vividness of Imagery Questionnaire and Hypnotic Susceptibility: Failure to Replicate. Unpublished paper, Hawthorne House Research Memorandum, 1969, No. 103.

Morgan, Arlene H., MacDonald, J., & Hilgard, E. R. EEG Alpha: Lateral Asymmetry Related to Task and Hypnotizability. *Psychophysiology,* 1974, *11,* 275–282.

Morris, G. O., & Singer, Margaret T. Sleep Deprivation: The Context of Consciousness. *Journal of Nervous and Mental Disease,* 1966, *143,* 291–304.

Moss, C. S. Experimental Paradigms for the Hypnotic Investigation of Dream Symbolism. *International Journal of Clinical and Experimental Hypnosis,* 1961, *9,* 105–117.

Moss, C. S. *The Hypnotic Investigation of Dreams.* New York: John Wiley & Sons, 1967.

Mühl, Anita M. *Automatic Writing.* Dresden and Leipzig: Theodor Steinkopf, 1930 (also published by Garrett-Helix, 1964).

Murphy, G. *Historical Introduction to Modern Psychology.* Revised edition. New York: Harcourt, Brace, 1949.

Murphy, Lois B. *The Widening World of Childhood: Paths Toward Mastery.* New York: Basic Books, 1962.

Myden, W. Interpretation and Evaluation of Certain Personality Characteristics Involved in Creative Production. *Perceptual and Motor Skills.* 1959, *9,* 139–158.

Myers, F. W. H. Human Personality in the Light of Hypnotic Suggestion. *Society for Psychical Research: Proceedings,* 1886–87, *4,* 1–24.

Myers, F. W. H. The Subliminal Consciousness. *Society for Psychical Research: Proceedings,* 1891–92, *7,* 298–355.

Nace, E. P., & Orne, M. T. Fate of an Uncompleted Posthypnotic Suggestion. *Journal of Abnormal Psychology,* 1970, *75,* 278–285.

Nace, E. P., Orne, M. T., & Hammer, A. G. Posthypnotic Amnesia as an Active Psychic Process: The Reversibility of Amnesia. *Archives of General Psychiatry,* 1974, *31,* 257–260.

Nachmansohn, M. Concerning Experimentally Produced Dreams. In D. Rapaport (Ed.) *Organization and Pathology of Thought,* New York: Columbia Univ. Press, 1951, 257–287.

Nagge, J. W. An Experimental Test of the Theory of Associative Interference. *Journal of Experimental Psychology,* 1935, *18,* 663–682.

Naruse, G., & Obonai, T. Decomposition and Fusion of Mental Images in the Drowsy and Post-Hypnotic Hallucinatory State. *Journal of Clinical and Experimental Hypnosis,* 1953, *1,* 23–41.

Neisser, U. *Cognitive Psychology.* New York: Appleton-Century-Crofts, 1967.

Neisser, U. Selective Reading: A Method for the Study of Visual Attention. Paper presented at the symposium: Attention: Some growing points in recent research, XIX International Congress of Psychology, London, 1969.

Newman, M. The Role of Amnesia in Dentistry: A Case Report. *American Journal of Clinical Hypnosis,* 1971, *14,* 127–130.

Newman, M. Hypnotic Handling of a Suicidal Patient in the Fugue State: A Case Report. *American Journal of Clinical Hypnosis,* 1974, *17,* 131–133.

Nichols, D. C. A Reconceptualization of the Concept of Hypnosis. In S. Lesse (Ed.), *An Evaluation of the Results of the Psychotherapies.* Springfield, Ill.: Charles C. Thomas, 1968, 201–220.

Norman, D. A. *Memory and Attention: An Introduction to Human Information Processing.* New York: J. Wiley, 1969.

Norris, D. L. Barber's Task-motivational Theory and Post-hypnotic Amnesia. *American Journal of Clinical Hypnosis,* 1973, *15,* 181–190.

Notterman, J. M., Schoenfeld, W. N., & Bersh, P. J. A Comparison of Three Extinction Procedures Following Heart Rate Conditoning. *Journal of Abnormal and Social Psychology,* 1952a, *47,* 674–677.

Notterman, J. M., Schoenfeld, W. N., & Bersh, P. J. Partial Reinforcement and Conditioned Heart Rate Response in Human Subjects. *Science,* 1952b, *115,* 77–79.

Nowlis, D. P., & Rhead, J. C. Relation of Eyes-closed Resting EEG Alpha Activity to Hypnotic Susceptibility. *Perceptual and Motor Skills,* 1968, *27,* 1047–1050.

Nowlis, V. The Concept of Mood. In S. M. Farber & R. H. L. Wilson (Eds.), *Conflict and Creativity.* New York: McGraw-Hill, 1963, 73–88.

Oberlander, J. Z. Adaptation and Cognitive Strategies in Self-hypnosis: A Case Study. Paper read at the Annual Convention of the American Psychological Association, New Orleans, August, 1974.

Oberlander, J. Z. Self-hypnotic Phenomena and Changes Over Time. Paper presented at the Annual Convention of The Society for Clinical and Experimental Hypnosis, Asheville, N.C., October, 1978.

Oberlander, M. I., Gruenewald, Doris, & Fromm, Erika. Content and Structural Characteristics of Thought Processes in Hypnosis. Paper read at the Annual Convention of the American Psychological Association, Miami Beach, September, 1970.

O'Connell, D. N. An Experimental Comparison of Hypnotic Depth Measured by Self-ratings and by an Objective Scale. *International Journal of Clinical and Ex-*

perimental Hypnosis, 1964, *12,* 34–46.

O'Connell, D. N. Selective Recall of Hypnotic Susceptibility Items: Evidence for Repression or Enhancement? *International Journal of Clinical and Experimental Hypnosis,* 1966, *14,* 150–161.

O'Connell, D. N., Gustafson, L. A., Evans, F. J., Orne, M. T., & Shor, R. E. Can Waking and Stage 1 Sleep Always Be Told Apart by EEG Criteria Alone? Paper presented at the meeting of the Association for the Psychophysiological Study of Sleep, Washington, D.C., March, 1965.

O'Connell, D. N., & Orne, M. T. Bioelectric Correlates of Hypnosis: An Experimental Reevaluation. *Journal of Psychiatric Research,* 1962, *1,* 201–213.

O'Connell, D. N., & Orne, M. T. Endosomatic Electrodermal Correlates of Hypnotic Depth and Susceptibility. *Journal of Psychiatric Research,* 1968, *6,* 1–12.

O'Connell, D. N., Orne, M. T., & Shor, R. E. A Comparison of Hypnotic Susceptibility as Assessed by Diagnostic Ratings and Initial Standardized Test Scores. *International Journal of Clinical and Experimental Hypnosis,* 1966, *14,* 324–332.

O'Connell, D. N., Shor, R. E., & Orne, M. T. Hypnotic Age Regression: An Empirical and Methodological Analysis. *Journal of Abnormal Psychology Monograph,* 1970, *76,* (3, Pt. 2).

Orne, M. T. The Mechanisms of Hypnotic Age Regression: An Experimental Study. *Journal of Abnormal and Social Psychology,* 1951, *46,* 213–225.

Orne, M. T. The Nature of Hypnosis: Artifact and Essence. *Journal of Abnormal and Social Psychology,* 1959, *58,* 277–299.

Orne, M. T. The Potential Uses of Hypnosis in Interrogation. In A. D. Biderman & H. Zimmer (Eds.), *The Manipulation of Human Behavior.* New York: John Wiley & Sons, 1961, 169–215.

Orne, M. T. Antisocial Behavior and Hypnosis: Problems of Control and Validation in Empirical Studies. In G. H. Estabrooks (Ed.), *Hypnosis: Current Problems.* New York: Harper & Row, 1962a, 137–192.

Orne, M. T. On the Social Psychology of the Psychological Experiment: With Particular Reference to Demand Characteristics and Their Implications. *American Psychologist,* 1962b, *17,* 776–783.

Orne, M. T. Hypnotically Induced Hallucinations. In L. J. West (Ed.), *Hallucinations.* New York: Grune & Stratton, 1962c, 211–219.

Orne, M. T. Undesirable Effects of Hypnosis: The Determinants and Management. *International Journal of Clinical and Experimental Hypnosis,* 1965a, *13,* 226–237.

Orne, M. T. Demand Characteristics and Their Implications for Real Life: The Importance of Quasi-controls. Paper presented at the American Psychological Association Convention, Chicago, September, 1965b.

Orne, M. T. On the Mechanisms of Posthypnotic Amnesia. *International Journal of Clinical and Experimental Hypnosis,* 1966a, *14,* 121–134.

Orne, M. T. Hypnosis, Motivation and Compliance. *American Journal of Psychiatry,* 1966b, *122,* 721–726.

Orne, M. T. What Must a Satisfactory Theory of Hypnosis Explain? *International Journal of Psychiatry,* 1967, *3,* 206–211.

Orne, M. T. Demand Characteristics and the Concept of Quasi-Controls. In R. Rosenthal & R. L. Rosnow (Eds.), *Artifact in Behavioral Research.* New York: Academic Press, 1969, 143–179.

Orne, M. T. Hypnosis, Motivation and the Ecological Validity of the Psychological Experiment. In W. J. Arnold & M. M. Page (Eds.), *Nebraska Symposium on Motivation.* Lincoln, Nebraska: University of Nebraska Press, 1970, 187–265.

Orne, M. T. The Simulation of Hypnosis: Why, How and What It Means. *International Journal of Clinical and Experimental Hypnosis,* 1971a, *19,* 183–210.

Orne, M. T. Is Hypnosis Only an Episode Set? Paper presented at the meetings of the American Psychological Association, Washington, D.C., September, 1971b.

Orne, M. T. Can a Hypnotized Subject Be Compelled to Carry Out Otherwise Unacceptable Behavior? *International Journal of Clinical and Experimental Hypnosis,* 1972, *20,* 101–117.

Orne, M. T., & Evans, F. J. Social Control in the Psychological Experiment: Antisocial Behavior and Hypnosis. *Journal of Personality and Social Psychology,* 1965, *1,* 189–200.

Orne, M. T., & Evans, F. J. Inadvertent Termination of Hypnosis with Hypnotized and Simulating Subjects. *International Journal of Clinical and Experimental Hypnosis,* 1966, *14,* 61–78.

Orne, M. T., & O'Connell, D. N. Diagnostic Ratings of Hypnotizability. *International Journal of Clinical and Experimental Hypnosis,* 1967, *15,* 125–133.

Orne, M. T., Sheehan, P. W., & Evans, F. J. Occurrence of Posthypnotic Behavior Outside the Experimental Setting. *Journal of Personality and Social Psychology,* 1968, *9,* 189–196.

Orne, M. T., & Wilson, S. K. Alpha, Biofeedback and Arousal/Activation. In J. Beatty & H. Legewie (Eds.), NATO Conference Series (III—Human factors), Vol. *2. Biofeedback and Behavior.* New York: Plenum Press, 1977, 107–120.

Orne, M. T., & Wilson, S. K. On the Nature of Alpha Feedback Training. In G. Schwartz & D. Shapiro (Eds.), *Consciousness and Self-Regulation: Advances in Research,* Vol. 2. New York: Plenum Press, 1978 (in press).

Ornstein, R. E. *On the Experience of Time.* Baltimore: Penguin Books, 1970.

Ornstein, Robert. *The Psychology of Consciousness.* San Francisco: W. H. Freeman, 1972,

Orzeck, A. Z. Multiple Self Concepts as Affected by Non-hypnotic Assumed Mood States. Paper read at the 5th Annual Scientific Meeting of the American Society of Clinical Hypnosis, 1962.

Osborn, Anne G., Bunker, J. P., Cooper, L. M., Frank, G. S., & Hilgard, E. R. Effects of Thiopental Sedation on Learning and Memory. *Science,* 1967, *157,* 574–576.

Oswald, I. *Sleeping and Waking: Physiology and Psychology.* Amsterdam: American Elsevier, 1962.

Otto, H. A. *Explorations in Human Potentialities.* Springfield. Ill.: Charles C. Thomas, 1966.

Pagano, R. R., Rose, R. M., Stivers, R. M., & Warrenburg, S. Sleep During Transcendental Meditation. *Science,* 1976, *191,* 308–309.

Palmer, R. D., & Field, P. B. Visual Imagery and Susceptibility to Hypnosis. *Journal of Consulting and Clinical Psychology,* 1968, *32,* 456–461.

Parrish, M., Lundy, R. M., & Leibowitz, H. W. Effect of Hypnotic Age Regression on the Magnitude of the Ponzo and Poggendorff Illusions. *Journal of Abnormal Psychology,* 1969, *74,* 693–698.

Paskewicz, D. A. EEG Alpha Activity and its Relationship to Altered States of Consciousness. In W. E. Edmonston, Jr. (Ed.), Conceptual and Investigative Approaches to Hypnosis and Hypnotic Phenomena. *Annals of the New York Academy of Sciences, 296,* New York: New York Academy of Sciences, 1977, 154–161.

Paskewicz, D. A., & Orne, M. T. The Effect of Cognitive Tasks on the Feedback Control of Alpha Activity. Paper presented at the meeting of the Society for Psychophysiological Research, New Orleans, November, 1970.

Paterson, A. S., Bracchi, F., Passerini, D., Spinelli, D., & Black, S. Acquisition of Voluntary Control Over Autonomic Nervous Functions by Conditioning and

Hypnosis. In J. Lassner (Ed.), *Hypnosis and Psychosomatic Medicine*. New York: Springer Verlag, 1967.

Patten, E. F. The Duration of Post-hypnotic Suggestions. *Journal of Abnormal and Social Psychology*, 1930–1931, *25*, 319–334.

Patten, E. F. Does Post-Hypnotic Amnesia Apply to Practice Effects? *Journal of General Psychology*, 1932, *7*, 196–201.

Pattie, F. A. A Report of Attempts to Produce Uniocular Blindness by Hypnotic Suggestion. *British Journal of Medical Psychology*, 1935, *15*, 230–241.

Pattie, F. A., Jr. The Production of Blisters by Hypnotic Suggestion: A Review. *Journal of Abnormal and Social Psychology*, 1941, *36*, 62–72.

Pattie, F. A. The Genuineness of Unilateral Deafness Produced by Hypnosis. *American Journal of Psychology*, 1950, *63*, 84–86.

Pattie, F. A., Jr. The Effect of Hypnotically Induced Hostility on Rorschach Responses. *Journal of Clinical Psychology*, 1954, *10*, 161–164.

Pattie, F. A., Jr. Methods of Induction, Susceptibility of Subjects, and Criteria of Hypnosis. In R. M. Dorcus (Ed.). *Hypnosis and its Therapeutic Applications*. New York: McGraw-Hill, 1956a, ch. 2.

Pattie, F. A., Jr. Mesmer's Medical Dissertation and its Debt to Mead's De Imperio Solis ac Lunae. *Journal of the History of Medicine and Allied Sciences*, 1956b, *11*, 275–287.

Pattie, F. A., Jr. American Contributions to the Science of Hypnosis. In L. Kuhn & S. Russo (Eds.), *Modern Hypnosis*. Hollywood, Cal.: Wilshire, 1958.

Pattie, F. A., Jr. A Brief History of Hypnotism. In J. E. Gordon (Ed.), 1967, 10–43.

Paul, G. L. The Production of Blisters by Hypnotic Suggestion: Another Look. *Psychosomatic Medicine*, 1963, *25*, 233–244.

Paul, G. L. Physiological Effects of Relaxation Training and Hypnotic Suggestion. *Journal of Abnormal Psychology*, 1969, *74*, 425–437.

Pavlov, I. P. The Identity of Inhibition with Sleep and Hypnosis. *Scientific Monthly*, 1923, *17*, 603–608.

Pavlov, I. P. *Conditioned Reflexes*. London: Oxford University Press, 1927.

Pavlov, I. P. *Selected Works*. Edited by J. Gibbons under the supervision of Kh. S. Koshtoyants, Moscow: Foreign Languages Publishing House, 1955, 345–368.

Pavlov, B. V., & Povorinskii, Iu. A. K. voprosu o vzaimodeist vii pervoi i vtoroi signal nykh sistem v somnambulicheskoi faze gipnoza. *Zhurnal Vyssheî Nervnoî Deîatel'nosti*, 1953, *3*, 381–391. (Cited in H. B. Crasilneck & J. A. Hall, 1959.)

Perkins, K. A. Repression, Psychopathology, and Drive Representation: An Experimental Hypnotic Investigation of the Management of Impulse Inhibition. Unpublished doctoral dissertation, Michigan State University, 1965.

Perky, C. W. An Experimental Study of Imagination. *American Journal of Psychology*, 1910, *21*, 422–452.

Perry, C. W. Content Analysis of Dream Reports. In J. P. Sutcliffe, (Ed.), *The Relation of Imagery and Fantasy to Hypnosis*. (Progress report on N.I.M.H. Project M-3950.) Sydney, Australia: Department of Psychology, The University of Sydney, 1964, 1–46.

Perry, C. W. An Investigation of the Relationship Between Proneness to Fantasy and Susceptibility to Hypnosis. Unpublished doctoral dissertation, University of Sydney, Sydney, Australia, 1965.

Perry, C. Imagery, Fantasy and Hypnotic Susceptibility: A Multidimensional Approach. *Journal of Personality and Social Psychology*, 1973, *26*, 217–221.

Perry, C. Is Hypnotizability Modifiable? *International Journal of Clinical and Experimental Hypnosis*, 1977, *25*, 125–146.

Perry, C. W., Evans, F. J., O'Connell, D. N., Orne, Emily C., & Orne, M. T.

Behavioral Response to Verbal Stimuli Administered and Tested During REM Sleep: A Further Investigation. Philadelphia, Pa.: Institute of the Pennsylvania Hospital, 1972. (Unpublished).

Perry, C. W., Evans, F. J., O'Connell, D. N., Orne, Emily C., & Orne, M. T. Behavioral Response to Verbal Stimuli Administered and Tested During REM Sleep: A Further Investigation. *Waking and Sleeping,* 1978, *2,* 35–42.

Perry C., Wilder, S., & Appignanesi, A. Hypnotic Susceptibility and Performance in a Battery of Creativity Measures. *American Journal of Clinical Hypnosis,* 1973, *15,* 170–180.

Persky, H., Grosz, H. J., Norton, J. A., & McMurtry, Mildred. Effect of Hypnotically induced Anxiety on the Plasma Hydrocortisone Level of Normal Subjects. *Journal of Clinical Endocrinology and Metabolism,* 1959, *19,* 700–710.

Pessin, M., Plapp, J. N., & Stern, J. A. Effects of Hypnosis Induction and Attention Direction on Electrodermal Responses. *American Journal of Clinical Hypnosis,* 1968, *10,* 198–206.

Peters, J. E., & Stern, R. M. Peripheral Skin Temperature and Vasomotor Responses During Hypnotic Induction. *International Journal of Clinical and Experimental Hypnosis,* 1973, *21,* 102–108.

Pettinati, Helen M. & Evans, F. J. Posthypnotic Amnesia: Evaluation of Selective Recall of Successful Experiences. *International Journal of Clinical and Experimental Hypnosis,* 1978, *26,* 317–329.

Pfungst, O. *Clever Hans (The Horse of Mr. von Osten).* [Re-issue of 1911 ed.] (R. Rosenthal, Ed.) New York: Holt, Rinehart & Winston, Inc., 1965.

Phillips, B. (Ed.) *The Essentials of Zen Buddhism: An Anthology of the Writings of Daisetz T. Suzuki.* London: Rider & Co., 1963, 31–32.

Phillips, L., Kaden, S., & Waldman, M. Rorschach Indices of Developmental Levels. *Journal of Genetic Psychology,* 1959, *94,* 267–285.

Pine, F., & Holt, R. R. Creativity and Primary Process: A Study of Adaptive Regression. *Journal of Abnormal and Social Psychology,* 1960, *61,* 370–379.

Piotrowski, Z. A. A Rorschach Compendium; Revised and Enlarged. In J. A. Brussel et al. (Eds.), *A Rorschach Training Manual.* Utica, N.Y.: State Hospitals Press, 1950.

Plapp, J. M. Hypnosis, Conditioning, and Physiological Responses. (Doctoral dissertation, Washington University) Ann Arbor, Michigan: University Microfilms, 1967, No. 67-9406.

Plapp, J. M., & Edmonston, W. E., Jr. Extinction of a Conditioned Motor Response Following Hypnosis. *Journal of Abnormal and Social Psychology,* 1965, *70,* 378–382.

Platonov, K. I. (Ed.) *The Word as a Physiological and Therapeutic Factor: Problems of Theory and Practice of Psychotherapy on the Basis of the Theory of I. P. Pavlov.* Translated from 2nd Russian edition (1955) by D. A. Myshne. Moscow: Foreign Languages Publishing House, 1959.

Plotkin, W. B. On the Self-regulation of the Occipital Alpha Rhythm: Control Strategies, States of Consciousness, and the Role of Physiological Feedback. *Journal of Experimental Psychology: General,* 1976, *105,* 66–99.

Podmore, F. *Mesmerism and Christian Science: A Short History of Mental Healing.* London and Philadelphia: G. W. Jacobs & Co., 1909.

Poe, D. C. The Effects of Hypnotically Hallucinated Practice of a Motor and a Cognitive Task. *Dissertation Abstracts,* 1967, *27,* 2899.

Poe, E. A. *The Philosophy of Animal Magnetism, by a Gentleman of Philadelphia: Together with the System of Manipulating Adopted to Produce Ecstacy and Somnambulism—The Effects and the Rationale.* With an essay on Poe by J. Jackson attributing authorship to Poe. Philadelphia: Patterson & White, 1928. Originally published anonymously and without essay. Philadelphia: Merrihew & Gunn, 1837.

Poissonnier, P. I., et al. *Rapport des commissaires de la Société Royale de Méde-cine, nommés par le roi, pour faire l'examen du magnétisme animal. Paris, 16 août 1748*. (Report of the commissioners of the Royal Medical Society named by the King to examine animal magnetism. Paris, Aug. 16, 1784). Signed: Poisson-nier, Caille. Mauduyt, Andry. Reproduced in A. Bertrand, (Ed.), 1826b, 482–510.

Priestley, J. B. *Man and Time*. Garden City, New York: Doubleday, 1964.

Prince, M. (1905). *The Dissociation of a Personality: A Biographical Study in Ab-normal Psychology*. New York: Longmans, Green & Co., 1920.

Prince, M. Experiments to Determine Co-conscious (sub-conscious) Ideation. *Jour-nal of Abnormal Psychology*, 1909, *3*, 33–42.

Prince, R. (Ed.), *Trance and Possession States*. Proceedings of the Second Annual Conference, R. M. Bucke Memorial Society, 4–6 March, 1966. Montreal, Canada: R. M. Bucke Memorial Society, 1968.

Propping, K. Zur Frage der Sesnibilität der Bauchhöhle. *Beiträge zur klinischen Chirurgie*, 1909, *63*, 690–710.

Pruesse, M. G. Repressers, Sensitizers, and Hypnotically Induced Hostility. Un-published doctoral dissertation, University of Waterloo, Waterloo, Ontario, Canada, 1967.

Puységur, A. M. Marquis de. Letter (on the discovery of artificial somnambulism) to a member of the Société de Harmonie. March 8, 1784a. Reproduced in A. Teste, (Ed.), *Practical Manual of Animal Magnetism*. Translated from the second French edition by D. Spillan. London: H. Baillière, 1843, 17–19.

Puységur, A. M. Marquis de. *Mémoires pour servir à l'histoire et à l'éstablissement du magnétisme animal*. (Remembrances which may serve to establish animal mag-netism and its history). Third edition. Paris: J. G. Dentu, 1820. (First edition, 1784b; second edition, Cellot, 1809.)

Puységur, A. M. Marquis de. *Du magnétisme animal, considéré dans ses rapports avec diverses branches de la Physique générale*, avec *Extrait de ma Correspon-dance sur le magnétisme animal* (Animal magnetism and its relation to various branches of general physics; with an extract of my correspondence on animal magnetism). Paris: Desenne (Cellot), 1807.

Puységur, A. M. Marquis de. *Recherches, expériences et observations physiolo-giques sur l'homme dans l'état de somnambulisme naturel, et dans le somnambu-lisme provoqué par l'acte magnétique*. (Physiologic investigations, experiences, and observations on man in the natural and in the magnetic state of somnambu-lism). Paris: J. G. Dentu, 1811.

Puységur, A. M. Marquis de. *An Essay of Instruction on Animal Magnetism: Trans-lated from the French of the Marquis de Puységur, together with various extracts upon the subject, and notes*. Translated and edited by J. King. New York: J. C. Kelley, 1837.

Quay, H. C. Emotions in Hypnotic Dreams: A Quantitative Investigation. Unpub-lished Masters thesis, Florida State University, 1952.

Raikov, V. L. The Possibility of Creativity in the Active Stage of Hypnosis. *Interna-tional Journal of Clinical and Experimental Hypnosis*, 1976, *24*, 258–268.

Rand, B. (Ed.) Bibliography of Philosophy, Psychology and Cognate Subjects: G. Psychology: i. Hypnotism and Suggestion. In J. M. Baldwin (Ed.), *Dictionary of Philosophy and Psychology*. Vol 3, Part II. New York and London: Macmillan, 1925, 1059–1067.

Rapaport, D. *Emotions and Memory*. Baltimore: Williams and Wilkins, 1942. 2nd edition, New York: International Universities Press, 1950.

Rapaport, D. (Ed.) *Organization and Pathology of Thought.* New York: Columbia University Press, 1951.

Rapaport, D. States of Consciousness: A Psychopathological and Psychodynamic View. *Problems of Consciousness, Transactions of the Second Conference,* March 19-20, 1951. New York: Josiah Macy, Jr. Foundation, 1951, 18-57. Reprinted in M. M. Gill (Ed.), *The Collected Papers of David Rapaport.* New York: Basic Books, 1967a, 385-404.

Rapaport, D. Some Metapsychological Considerations Concerning Activity and Passivity. Paper presented at two seminars at the Austen Riggs Center, June 16 and August 11, 1953. Published (in English) in Archivos de Criminología, *Neuro-psiquiatría Disciplinas Conexas (Ecuador),* 1961, *9,* 391-449. Reprinted in M. M. Gill (Ed.), *The Collected Papers of David Rapaport.* New York: Basic Books, 1967a, 530-568.

Rapaport, D. Cognitive Structures. In Jerome S. Bruner et al., *Contemporary Approaches to Cognition: A Symposium Held at the University of Colorado, 1955,* 157-200. Cambridge, Mass.: Harvard University Press, 1957. Reprinted in M. M. Gill (Ed.), *The Collected Papers of David Rapaport.* New York: Basic Books, 1967a, 631-664.

Rapaport, D. The Theory of Ego Autonomy: A Generalization. *Bulletin of the Menninger Clinic,* 1958, *22,* 13-35. Reprinted in M. M. Gill (Ed.), *The Collected Papers of David Rapaport.* New York: Basic Books, 1967a, 722-744.

Ravitz, L. J. Electrometric Correlates of the Hypnotic State. *Science,* 1950, *112,* 341-351.

Ravitz, L. J. Standing Potential Correlates of Hypnosis and Narcosis. *AMA Archives of Neurology and Psychiatry,* 1951a, *65,* 413-436.

Ravitz, L. J. The Use of D.C. Measurements in Psychiatry. *Neuropsychiatry,* 1951b, *1,* 3-12.

Rechtschaffen, A., & Kales, A. (Eds.) *A Manual of Standardized Terminology, Techniques and Scoring System for Sleep Stages of Human Subjects.* Washington, D.C.: National Institutes of Health Publication No. 204, U.S. Government Printing Office, 1968, Public Health Service.

Reich, L. H. Optokinetic Nystagmus During Hypnotic Hallucinations. Paper presented at Eastern Psychological Association, Annual Meeting, Atlantic City, April 1970.

Reichenbach, C. Baron von. *Researches on Magnetism, Electricity, Heat, Light, Crystallization and Chemism, in their Relations to the Vital Force.* From the German with preface and notes by J. Ashburner. London, 1850.

Reid, A. F., & Curtsinger, G. Physiological Changes Associated with Hypnosis: The Effect of Hypnosis on Temperature. *International Journal of Clinical and Experimental Hypnosis,* 1968, *16,* 111-119.

Reiff, R., & Scheerer, M. *Memory and Hypnotic Age Regression: Developmental Aspects of Cognitive Function Explored through Hypnosis.* New York: International Universities Press, 1959.

Renner, Vivian. Effects of Modification of Cognitive Style on Creative Behavior. *Journal of Personality and Social Psychology,* 1970, *14,* 257-262.

Reyher, J. Posthypnotic Stimulation of Hypnotically Induced Conflict in Relation to Psychosomatic Reactions and Psychopathology. *Psychosomatic Medicine,* 1961a, *23,* 384-391.

Reyher, J. Posthypnotic Stimulation of Hypnotically Induced Conflict in Relation to Antisocial Behavior. *Journal of Social Therapy,* 1961b, *7,* 92-97.

Reyher, J. A Paradigm for Determining the Clinical Relevance of Hypnotically

Induced Psychopathology. *Psychological Bulletin,* 1962, *59,* 344–352.

Reyher, J. Brain Mechanisms, Intrapsychic Processes and Behavior: A Theory of Hypnosis and Psychopathology. *American Journal of Clinical Hypnosis,* 1964, *7,* 107–119.

Reyher, J. Hypnosis in Research on Psychopathology. In J. E. Gordon (Ed.), 1967, 110–147.

Reyher, J. Posthypnotic Conflict as Related to Psychopathology. Paper read at the Convention of the American Psychological Association, Washington, D.C., September, 1969a.

Reyher, J. Comment on "Artificial Induction of Posthypnotic Conflict." *Journal of Abnormal Psychology,* 1969b, *74,* 420–422.

Rhoades, C. D., & Edmonston, W. E., Jr. Personality Correlates of Hypnotizability: A Study Using the Harvard Group Scale of Hypnotic Susceptibility, the 16-PF and the IPAT. *American Journal of Clinical Hypnosis,* 1969, *11,* 228–233.

Richardson, A. *Mental Imagery.* New York: Springer Publishing Company, Inc., 1969.

Richardson, A. Voluntary Control of the Memory Image. In P. W. Sheehan (Ed.), *The Function and Nature of Imagery.* New York & London: Academy Press, 1972, 109–129.

Richet, C. The Simulation of Somnambulism. *Lancet,* 1881, *1,* 8–9; 51–52.

Richman, D. N. A Critique of Two Recent Theories of Hypnosis: The Psychoanalytic Theory of Gill and Brenman Contrasted with the Behavioral Theory of Barber. *Psychiatric Quarterly,* 1965, *39,* 278–292.

Ricks, D., Umbarger, C., & Mack, R. A Measure of Increased Temporal Perspective in Successfully Treated Adolescent Delinquent Boys. *Journal of Abnormal and Social Psychology,* 1964, *69,* 685–689.

Riecken, H. W. A Program for Research on Experiments in Social Psychology. In N. F. Washburne (Ed.), *Decisions, Values and Groups.* Vol. 2. New York: Pergamon Press, 1962, 25–41.

Roberts, A. H., Schuler, Joan, Bacon, Jane, Zimmerman, R., & Patterson, R. Individual Differences and Autonomic Control: Absorption, Hypnotic Susceptibility, and the Unilateral Control of Skin Temperature. *Journal of Abnormal Psychology,* 1975, *84,* 272–279.

Roberts, D. R. An Electrophysiological Theory of Hypnosis. *International Journal of Clinical and Experimental Hypnosis,* 1960, *8,* 43–55.

Roberts, Mary J. Attention and Cognitive Controls as Related to Individual Differences in Hypnotic Susceptibility. *Dissertation Abstracts,* 1965, *25,* 4261.

Rorschach, H. *Psychodiagnostics* (4th edition). Berne: Verlag Hans Huber, 1949.

Rosen, G. John Elliotson, Physician and Hypnotist. *Bulletin of the History of Medicine,* 1936, *4,* 600–603.

Rosen, G. Mesmerism and Surgery: A Strange Chapter in the History of Anesthesia. *Journal of the History of Medicine and Allied Sciences,* 1946, *1,* 527–550.

Rosen, G. From Mesmerism to Hypnotism. *Ciba Symposium,* 1948, *9,* 838–844.

Rosen, G. History of Medical Hypnosis: From Animal Magnetism to Medical Hypnosis. In J. M. Schneck (Ed.), 1963a, 3–28.

Rosenberg, M. J. A Disconfirmation of the Description of Hypnosis as a Dissociated State. *International Journal of Clinical and Experimental Hypnosis,* 1959, *7,* 187–204.

Rosenhan, D. L. Hypnosis and Personality: A Moderator Variable Analysis. In L. Chertok (Ed.), *Psychophysiological Mechanisms of Hypnosis.* New York: Springer-Verlag, 1969, 193–198.

Rosenthal, B. G., & Mele, H. The Validity of Hypnotically Induced Color Hallucinations. *Journal of Abnormal and Social Psychology,* 1952, *47,* 700–704.

Rossi, A. M., Furhman, A., & Solomon, P. Arousal Levels and Thought Processes During Sensory Deprivation. *Journal of Abnormal Psychology,* 1967, *72,* 166–173.

Rossi, A. M., Sturrock, J. B., & Solomon, P. Suggested Effects on Reported Imagery in Sensory Deprivation. *Perceptual and Motor Skills,* 1963, *16,* 39–45.

Rothenberg, A. Homospatial Thinking in Creativity. *Archives of General Psychiatry,* 1976a, *33,* 17–26.

Rothenberg, A. Janusian Thinking and Creativity. In W. Muensterberger, A. H. Esman, & L. B. Boyer (Eds.), *The Psychoanalytic Study of Society,* 1976b, *7,* 1–30.

Rowland, L. W. Will Hypnotized Persons Try to Harm Themselves or Others? *Journal of Abnormal and Social Psychology,* 1939, *34,* 114–117.

Rubenstein, R., & Newman, R. The Living Out of "Future" Experiences Under Hypnosis. *Science,* 1954, *119,* 472–473.

Rubin, F. (Ed.) *Current Research in Hypnopaedia.* New York: American Elsevier Publishing Co., 1968.

Ruch, J. Self-hypnosis: The Result of Heterohypnosis or Vice Versa? *International Journal of Clinical and Experimental Hypnosis,* 1975, *23,* 282–304.

Rugg, H. *Imagination.* New York: Harper & Row, 1963.

Ryle, G. *The Concept of Mind.* London: William Brendon, 1955.

Sacerdote, P. *Induced Dreams.* New York: Vantage Press, 1967a.

Sacerdote, P. On the Psycho-biological Effects of Hypnosis. *American Journal of Clinical Hypnosis,* 1967b, *10,* 10–14.

Sacerdote, P. Applications of Hypnotically Elicited Mystical States to the Treatment of Physical and Emotional Pain. *International Journal of Clinical and Experimental Hypnosis,* 1977, *25,* 309–324.

Sachar, E. J., Fishman, J. R., & Mason, J. W. The Influence of the Hypnotic Trance on Plasma 17-Hydroxycorticosteriod Concentration. *Psychosomatic Medicine,* 1964, *26,* 635–636. (Abstract)

Sachar, E. J., Cobb, J. C., & Shor, R. E. Plasma Cortisol Changes During Hypnotic Trance: Relation to Depth of Hypnosis. *Archives of General Psychiatry,* 1966, *14,* 482–490.

Sachs, L. B. Comparison of Hypnotic Analgesia and Hypnotic Relaxation During Stimulation by a Continuous Pain Source. *Journal of Abnormal Psychology,* 1970, *76,* 206–210.

Sachs, L. B., & Anderson, W. L. Modification of Hypnotic Susceptibility, *International Journal of Clinical and Experimental Hypnosis,* 1967, *15,* 172–180.

Salthouse, T. A. Using Selective Interference to Investigate Spatial Memory Representation. *Memory and Cognition,* 1974, *2,* 749–757.

Salthouse, T. A. Simultaneous Processing of Verbal and Spatial Information. *Memory and Cognition,* 1975, *3,* 221–225.

Sampimon, R. L. H., & Woodruff, M. F. A. Some Observations Concerning the Use of Hypnosis as a Substitute for Anesthesia. *Medical Journal of Australia,* 1946, *1,* 393–395.

Sanders, R. S., & Reyher, J. Sensory Deprivation and the Enhancement of Hypnotic Susceptibility. *Journal of Abnormal Psychology,* 1969, *74,* 375–381.

Sarason, S., & Rosenzweig, S. An Experimental Study of the Triadic Hypothesis: Reaction to Frustration, Ego-defense and Hypnotizability: II. Thematic Apperception Approach. *Character and Personality,* 1942, *11,* 150–165.

Sarbin, T. R. Contributions to Role-Taking Theory: I. Hypnotic Behavior. *Psychological Review,* 1950, *57,* 255–270.

Sarbin, T. R. Role Theory. In G. Lindzey (Ed.), *Handbook of Social Psychology, 1. Theory and Method.* Cambridge: Addison-Wesley Publishing Co., 1954, 223–258.

Sarbin, T. R. Physiological Effects of Hypnotic Stimulation. In R. M. Dorcus, (Ed.), *Hypnosis and its Therapeutic Applications.* New York: McGraw-Hill, 1956, 1–57.

Sarbin, T. R. Attempts to Understand Hypnotic Phenomena. In L. Postman (Ed.), *Psychology in the Making: Histories of Selected Research Problems.* New York: Knopf, 1962, 745–785.

Sarbin, T. R. Role Theoretical Interpretation of Psychological Change. In P. Worchel & D. Byrne (Eds.), *Personality Change.* New York: Wiley, 1964, 176–219.

Sarbin, T. R. The Concept of Hallucination. *Journal of Personality,* 1967, *35,* 359–380.

Sarbin, T. R. Imagining as Muted Role-taking: A Historical-linguistic Analysis. In P. W. Sheehan (Ed.), *The Function and Nature of Imagery.* New York & London: Academic Press, 1972, 333–354.

Sarbin, T. R., & Andersen, M. L. Base-rate Expectancies and Perceptual Alterations in Hypnosis. *British Journal of Social and Clinical Psychology,* 1963, *2,* 112–121.

Sarbin, T. R., & Andersen, M. L. Role-theoretical Analysis of Hypnotic Behavior. In J. Gordon (Ed.), 1967, 319–344.

Sarbin, T. R., & Coe, W. C. *Hypnosis: A Social Psychological Analysis of Influence Communication.* New York: Holt, Rinehart & Winston, 1972.

Sarbin, T. R., & Kroger, R. O. On Wundt's Theory of Hypnosis. *International Journal of Clinical and Experimental Hypnosis,* 1963, *11,* 245–259.

Scantlebury, R. E., Frick, H. L., & Patterson, T. L. The Effect of Normal and Hypnotically Induced Dreams on the Gastric Hunger Movements of Man. *Journal of Applied Psychology,* 1942, *26,* 682–691.

Scantlebury, R. E., & Patterson, T. L. Hunger Motility in a Hypnotized Subject. *Quarterly Journal of Experimental Physiology,* 1940, *30,* 347–358.

Schachtel, E. G. On Memory and Childhood Amnesia. *Psychiatry,* 1947, *10,* 1–26.

Schachtel, E. G. Projection and Its Relation to Character Attitudes and Creativity in the Kinesthetic Responses: Contributions to an Understanding of Rorschach's Test, IV. *Psychiatry,* 1950, *13,* 69–100.

Schachtel, E. G. *Metamorphosis: On the Development of Affect, Perception, Attention, and Memory.* New York: Basic Books, 1959.

Schachter, S., & Singer, J. E. Cognitive, Social and Physiological Determinants of Emotional State. *Psychological Review,* 1962, *69,* 379–399.

Schafer, R. Regression in the Service of the Ego: The Relevance of a Psychoanalytic Concept for Personality Assessment. In G. Lindzey (Ed.), *Assessment of Human Motives.* New York: Holt, Rinehart & Winston, 1958, 119–148.

Schafer, R. On the Theoretical and Technical Conceptualization of Activity and Passivity. *Psychoanalytic Quarterly.* 1968a, *37,* 173–198.

Schafer, R. *Aspects of Internalization.* New York: International Universities Press, 1968b.

Scheibe, K. E., Gray, A. L., & Keim, C. S. Hypnotically Induced Deafness and Delayed Auditory Feedback: A Comparison of Real and Simulating Subjects. *International Journal of Clinical and Experimental Hypnosis,* 1968, *16,* 158–164.

Schiff, S. K., Bunney, W. E., & Freedman, D. X. A Study of Ocular Movements in Hypnotically Induced Dreams. *Journal of Nervous and Mental Disease.* 1961, *133,* 59–68.

Schilder, P. F., & Kauders, O. *Hypnosis*. Translated from the German by S. Rothenberg. Nervous and Mental Disease Monographs Series, 1927, No. 46. Reissued in P. F. Schilder, *The Nature of Hypnosis*. New translation by Gerda Corvin. New York: International Universities Press, 1956, *7*, 43–184.

Schneck, J. M. The School of the Hospital de la Charité in the History of Hypnosis. *Journal of the History of Medicine and Allied Sciences*, 1952, *7*, 271–279.

Schneck, J. M. *Hypnosis in Modern Medicine*. Springfield, Illinois: Charles C. Thomas, 1953.

Schneck, J. M. An Experimental Study of Hypnotically Induced Auditory Hallucinations. *Journal of Clinical and Experimental Hypnosis*, 1954a, *2*, 163–170.

Schneck, J. M. Countertransference in Freud's Rejection of Hypnosis. *American Journal of Psychiatry*, 1954b, *110*, 928–931.

Schneck, J. M. Robert Browning and Mesmerism. *Bulletin of the Medical Library Association*, October, 1956, *44*, 443–451.

Schneck, J. M. The History of Electrotherapy and Its Correlation with Mesmer's Animal Magnetism. *American Journal of Psychiatry*, 1959, *116*, 463–464.

Schneck, J. M. Charcot and Hypnosis. *Journal of the American Medical Association*, 1961a, *176* (1), 157–158.

Schneck, J. M. Jean-Martin Charcot and the History of Experimental Hypnosis. *Journal of the History of Medicine and Allied Sciences*, 1961b, *16*, 297–305.

Schneck, J. M. (1953). *Hypnosis in Modern Medicine*. Springfield, Ill.: C. C. Thomas, third edition, 1963a.

Schneck, J. M. Clinical and Experimental Aspects of Hypnotic Dreams. In M. V. Kline (Ed.), *Clinical Correlations of Experimental Hypnosis*. Springfield, Ill.: C. C. Thomas, 1963b, 75–100.

Schneck, J. M. History of Medical Hypnosis: Additions and Elaborations, 1963c. In J. M. Schneck (Ed.), 1963a. (l.c. 1953), 406–421.

Schonbar, Rosalea A. Temporal and Emotional Factors in the Selective Recall of Dreams. *Journal of Consulting Psychology*, 1961, *25*, 67–73.

Schrenck-Notzing, A. F. Ein experimenteller und kritischer Beitrage zur Frage der suggestiven Hervorrufung circumscripter vasomotorischer Veränderungen auf der äusseren Haut. *Zeitschrift für Hypnotismus*, 1896, *4*, 209–228.

Schroetter, K. Experimental Dreams. In D. Rapaport (Ed.) *Organization and Pathology of Thought*. New York: Columbia Univ. Press. 1951, 234–248.

Schultz, J. H. Ueber selbsttätige (autogene) Umstellungen der Wärmestrahlung der menschlichen Haut im autosuggestiven Training. *Deutsche Medizinische Wochenschrift*, 1926, *14*, 571–572.

Schultz, J. H. *Das Autogene Training*. Stuttgart: Georg Thieme Verlag, 1932.

Schwartz, G. E., Davidson, R. J., Maer, F., & Bromfield, E. Patterns of Hemispheric Dominance in Musical, Emotional, Verbal, and Spatial Tasks. Paper presented at meeting of Society for Psychophysiological Research, October, 1973.

Schwarz, B. E., Brickford, R. G., & Rasmussen, W. C. Hypnotic Phenomena, Including Hypnotically Activated Seizures, Studied with the Electroencephalogram. *Journal of Nervous and Mental Disease*, 1955, *122*, 564–574.

Scott, H. D. Hypnosis and the Conditioned Reflex. *Journal of General Psychology*, 1930, *4*, 113–130.

Scott, M. J. *Hypnosis in Skin and Allergic Diseases*. Springfield, Ill.: C. C. Thomas, 1960.

Sears, R. R. An Experimental Study of Hypnotic Anesthesia. *Journal of Experimental Psychology*, 1932, *15*, 1–22.

Secord, P. F., & Blackman, C. W. *Social Psychology*. New York: McGraw-Hill, 1964.

Sector, I. I. An Investigation of Hypnotizability as a Function of Attitude Toward Hypnosis. *American Journal of Clinical Hypnosis,* 1960, *3,* 75–89.

Sector, I. I. TAT Card 12M as a Predictor of Hypnotizability. *American Journal of Clinical Hypnosis,* 1961, *3,* 179–184.

Segal, S. J. Patterns of Response to Thirst in an Imaging Task (Perky Technique) as a Function of Cognitive Style. *Journal of Personality,* 1968, *36,* 574–588.

Segal, S. J. Assimilation of a Stimulus in the Construction of an Image: The Perky Effect Revisited. In P. W. Sheehan (Ed.), *The Function and Nature of Imagery.* New York & London: Academic Press, 1972, 203–230.

Segal, S. J., & Nathan, S. The Perky Effect: Incorporation of an External Stimulus Into an Imagery Experience Under Placebo and Control Conditions. *Perceptual and Motor Skills,* 1964, *18,* 385–395.

Sernan, J. M. A. *Doutes d'un Provincial proposés à Messieurs les Médecins-Commissaires chargés par le roi de l'examen du Magnétisme Animal.* (Doubts of a Man from the Provinces, Proposed to the Medical Commissioners Charged by the King with the Investigation of Animal Magnetism). Lyon, 1784.

Shearn, D. Does the Heart Learn? *Psychological Bulletin,* 1961, *58,* 452–458.

Sheehan, P. W. Accuracy and Vividness of Visual Images. *Perceptual and Motor Skills,* 1966a, *23,* 391–398.

Sheehan, P. W. Functional Similarity of Imaging to Perceiving: Individual Differences in Vividness of Imagery. *Perceptual and Motor Skills,* 1966b, *23,* 1011–1033. (Monograph Supplement 6–V23).

Sheehan, P. W. A Shortened Form of Betts' Questionnaire Upon Mental Imagery. *Journal of Clinical Psychology,* 1967a, *23,* 386–389.

Sheehan, P. W. Reliability of a Short Test of Imagery. *Perceptual and Motor Skills,* 1967b, *25,* 744.

Sheehan, P. W. Visual Imagery and the Organizational Properties of Perceived Stimuli. *British Journal of Psychology,* 1967c, *58,* 247–252.

Sheehan, P. W. Artificial Induction of Posthypnotic Conflict. *Journal of Abnormal Psychology,* 1969, *74,* 16–25.

Sheehan, P. W. An Explication of the Real-simulating Model: A Reply to Reyher's Comment on "Artificial Induction of Posthypnotic Conflict." *International Journal of Clinical and Experimental Hypnosis,* 1971a, *19,* 46–51.

Sheehan, P. W. A Methodological Analysis of the Simulating Technique. *International Journal of Clinical and Experimental Hypnosis,* 1971b, *19,* 83–99.

Sheehan, P. W. Hypnosis and the Manifestations of "Imagination." In Erika Fromm & R. E. Shor (Eds.), *Hypnosis: Research Developments and Perspectives,* 1st edition. Chicago: Aldine, 1972a, 293–319.

Sheehan, P. W. (Ed.) *The Function and Nature of Imagery.* New York: Academic Press, 1972b.

Sheehan, P. W. Escape from the Ambiguous: Artifact and Methodologies of Hypnosis. *American Psychologist.* 1973, *28,* 983–993.

Sheehan, P. W., & Dolby, R. M. Artifact and Barber's Model of Hypnosis: A Logical-empirical Analysis. *Journal of Experimental and Social Psychology,* 1974, *10,* 171–187.

Sheehan, P. W., & Dolby, R. M. Hypnosis and the Influence of Most Recently Perceived Events. *Journal of Abnormal Psychology,* 1975, *84,* 331–345.

Sheehan, P. W., & Orne, M. T. Some Comments on the Nature of Posthypnotic Behavior. *Journal of Nervous and Mental Disease,* 1968, *146,* 209–220.

Sheehan, P. W., & Perry, C. W. *Methodologies of Hypnosis: A Critical Appraisal of Contemporary Paradigms of Hypnosis.* Hillsdale, N.J.: Erlbaum, 1976.

Sheikh, A. S., & Panagiotou, N. C. Use of Mental Imagery in Psychotherapy: A

Critical Review. *Perceptual and Motor Skills,* 1975, *41,* 555–585.

Shor, R. E. Hypnosis and the Concept of the Generalized Reality-orientation. *American Journal of Psychotherapy,* 1959, *13,* 582–602. Reprinted in C. E. Tart (Ed.), *Altered States of Consciousness.* New York: John Wiley and Sons, 1969, 233–250.

Shor, R. E. The Frequency of Naturally Occurring 'Hypnotic-like' Experiences in the Normal College Population. *International Journal of Clinical and Experimental Hypnosis,* 1960, *8,* 151–163.

Shor, R. E. Physiological Effects of Painful Stimulation During Hypnotic Analgesia Under Conditions Designed to Minimize Anxiety. *International Journal of Clinical and Experimental Hypnosis,* 1962a, *10,* 183–202.

Shor, R. E. Three Dimensions of Hypnotic Depth. *International Journal of Clinical and Experimental Hypnosis,* 1962b, *10,* 23–38. Reprinted in Tart, 1969a, 251–262.

Shor, R. E. The Accuracy of Estimating the Relative Difficulty of Typical Hypnotic Phenomena. *International Journal of Clinical and Experimental Hypnosis,* 1964a, *12,* 191–201.

Shor, R. E. A Note on Shock Tolerances of Real and Simulating Hypnotic Subjects. *International Journal of Clinical and Experimental Hypnosis,* 1964b, *12,* 258–262.

Shor, R. E. Physiological Effects of Painful Stimulation During Hypnotic Analgesia. In J. E. Gordon (Ed.), 1967, 511–549.

Shor, R. E. Periodical Literature on Hypnotism and Mesmerism. *American Journal of Clinical Hypnosis,* 1968, *10,* 265–266.

Shor, R. E. The Three-factor Theory of Hypnosis as Applied to the Book-reading Fantasy and to the Concept of Suggestion. *International Journal of Clinical and Experimental Hypnosis,* 1970, *18,* 89–98.

Shor, R. E. Expectancies of Being Influenced and Hypnotic Performance. *International Journal of Clinical and Experimental Hypnosis,* 1971, *19,* 154–166.

Shor, R. E., & Cobb, J. E. An Exploratory Study of Hypnotic Training Using the Concept of Plateau Responsiveness as a Referent. *American Journal of Clinical Hypnosis,* 1968, *10,* 178–193.

Shor, R. E., & Easton, R. D. Preliminary Report on Research Comparing Self- and Hetero-hypnosis. *American Journal of Clinical Hypnosis,* 1973, *16,* 37–44.

Shor, R. E., & Orne, Emily C. *The Harvard Group Scale of Hypnotic Susceptibility, Form A.* Palo Alto, Calif.: Consulting Psychologists Press, 1962.

Shor, R. E., & Orne, M. T. (Eds.) *The Nature of Hypnosis: Selected Basic Readings.* New York: Holt, Rinehart & Winston, 1965.

Shor, R. E., Orne, M. T., & O'Connell, D. N. Validation and Cross-validation of a Scale of Self-reported Personal Experiences Which Predicts Hypnotizability. *Journal of Psychology,* 1962, *53,* 55–75.

Shor, R. E., Orne, M. T., & O'Connell, D. N. Psychological Correlates of Plateau Hypnotizability in a Special Volunteer Sample. *Journal of Personality and Social Psychology,* 1966, *3,* 80–95.

Sidis, B. *The Psychology of Suggestion.* With an introduction by W. James. New York: D. Appleton-Century Co., 1898.

Sidis, B. An Inquiry into the Nature of Hallucinations. I. *Psychological Review, 1904a, 11,* 15–29.

Sidis, B. An Inquiry into the Nature of Hallucinations. II. *Psychological Review,* 1904b, *11,* 104–137.

Sidis, B. Are There Hypnotic Hallucinations? *Psychological Review.* 1906, 13, 239–257.

Silverman, J. A. Paradigm for the Study of Altered States of Consciousness. *British Journal of Psychiatry,* 1968, *114,* 1201-1218.

Simon, C. W., & Emmons, W. H. EEG, Consciousness, and Sleep. *Science,* 1956, *124,* 1066-1069.

Sinclair—Gieben, A. H. C., & Chalmers, D. Evaluation of Treatment of Warts by Hypnosis. *Lancet,* 1959, 2, 480-482.

Singer, J. L. *Daydreaming: An Introduction to the Experimental Study of Inner Experience.* New York: Random House, 1966.

Singer, J. L. *The Inner World of Daydreaming.* New York: Harper & Row, 1975.

Singer, J. L., & Antrobus, J. S. Eye Movements During Fantasies: Imagining and Suppressing Fantasies. *Archives of General Psychiatry,* 1965, 12, 71-76.

Singer, J. L., & Antrobus, J. S. A Factor-analytic Study of Daydreaming and Conceptually Related Cognitive and Personality Variables. *Perceptual and Motor Skills,* 1963, *17,* 187-209. (Monograph Supplement 3-V 17).

Singer, J. L., & Antrobus, J. S. Daydreaming, Imaginal Processes and Personality: A Normative Study. In P. W. Sheehan (Ed.), *The Function and Nature of Imagery.* New York and London: Academic Press, 1972, 175-202.

Sjoberg, B. M., & Hollister, L. F. The Effects of Psychotomimetic Drugs on Primary Suggestibility. *Psychopharmacologia,* 1965, *8,* 251-262.

Smith, G. M., Egbert, L. D., Markowitz, R. A., Mosteller, F., & Beecher, H. K. An Experimental Pain Method Sensitive to Morphine in Man: The Submaximum Effort Tourniquet Technique. *Journal of Pharmacology and Experimental Therapeutics,* 1966, *154,* 324-332.

Solomons, L. M., & Stein, Gertrude. Normal Motor Automatism. *Psychological Review,* 1896, *3,* 492-512.

Solovey, Galina, & Milechnin, A. Concerning the Nature of Hypnotic Phenomena. *Journal of Clinical and Experimental Hypnosis,* 1957, *5,* 67-76.

Solzenberg, J. Age Regression in the Treatment of Two Instances of Dental Phobia. *American Journal of Clinical Hypnosis,* 1961, *4,* 122-123.

Sommerschield, H. Posthypnotic Conflict, Repression and Psychopathology. Unpublished doctoral dissertation, Michigan State University, 1965.

Spanos, N. P. Barber's Reconceptualization of Hypnosis: An Evaluation of Criticisms. *Journal of Experimental Research in Personality,* 1970, *4,* 241-258.

Spanos, N. P. Goal-directed Fantasy and the Performance of Hypnotic Test Suggestions. *Psychiatry,* 1971, *34,* 86-96.

Spanos, N. P., & Barber, T. X. "Hypnotic" Experiences as Inferred from Subjective Reports: Auditory and Visual Hallucinations. *Journal of Experimental Research in Personality,* 1968, *3,* 136-150.

Spanos, N. P., & Barber, T. X. A Second Attempted Replication of the Parrish-Lundy-Leibowitz Study on Hypnotic Age-regression. Harding, Mass.: The Medfield Foundation, 1969.

Spanos, N. P., & Barber, T. X. Cognitive Activity During "Hypnotic" Suggestibility: Goal-directed Fantasy and the Experience of Non-Volition. *Journal of Personality,* 1972, Vol. 40, 510-524.

Spanos, N. P., & Barber, T. X. Toward a Convergence in Hypnosis Research. *American Psychologist,* 1974, *29,* 500-511.

Spanos, N. P., Barber, T. X., & Lang, G. Effects of Hypnotic Induction, Suggestions of Analgesia, and Demands for Honesty on Subjective Reports of Pain. Department of Sociology, Boston University, 1969.

Spanos, N. P., & Chaves, J. F. Hypnosis Research: A Methodological Critique of Two Alternative Paradigms. *American Journal of Clinical Hypnosis.* 1970, *13,* 108-127.

Spanos, N. P., & Ham, Marie L. Cognitive Activity in Response to Hypnotic Suggestion: Goal-directed Fantasy and Selective Amnesia. *American Journal of Clinical Hypnosis,* 1973, *15,* 191–198.

Spanos, N. P., & McPeake, J. D. Involvement in Suggestion-related Imaginings, Experienced Involuntariness, and Credibility Assigned to Imaginings in Hypnotic Subjects. *Journal of Abnormal Psychology,* 1974, *83,* 687–690.

Spanos, N. P., & McPeake, J. D. The Interaction of Attitudes Toward Hypnosis and Involvement in Everyday Imaginative Activities on Hypnotic Susceptibility. *American Journal of Clinical Hypnosis,* 1975a, *17,* 4, 274–252.

Spanos, N. P., & McPeake, J. D. Involvement in Everyday Imaginative Activities, Attitudes Toward Hypnosis, and Hypnotic Suggestibility. *Journal of Personality and Social Psychology,* 1975b, *31,* 3, 594–598.

Spanos, N. P., McPeake, J. D., & Churchill, Nancy. Relationship Between Imaginative Ability Variables and the Barber Suggestibility Scale. *The American Journal of Clinical Hypnosis,* 1976, *19,* 39–46.

Spanos, N. P., Valois, R., Ham, M. W., & Ham, Marie L. Suggestibility, and Vividness and Control of Imagery. *International Journal of Clinical and Experimental Hypnosis,* 1973, *21,* 305–311.

Spence, D. P., & Holland, B. The Restricting Effects of Awareness: A Paradox and an Explanation. *Journal of Abnormal and Social Psychology,* 1962, *64,* 163–174.

Spiegel, H. An Eye-roll Test for Hypnotizability. *American Journal of Clinical Hypnosis,* 1972, *15,* 25–28.

Spiegel, H. *Manual for Hypnotic Induction Profile: Eye-roll Levitation Method.* (Rev. ed.) New York: Soni Medica, 1976.

Stankler, L. A. Critical Assessment of the Cure of Warts by Suggestion. *Practitioner,* 1967, *198,* 690–694.

Starker, S. Effects of Hypnotic Induction Upon Visual Imagery. *Journal of Nervous and Mental Disease,* 1974, *159,* 433–437.

Starr, F. H., & Tobin, J. P. The Effects of Expectancy and Hypnotic Induction Procedure on Suggestibility. *American Journal of Clinical Hypnosis,* 1970, *12,* 261–267.

Stein, M. I. Creativity. In E. F. Borgatta & W. W. Lambert (Eds.), *Handbook of Personality Theory and Research,* Chicago: Rand McNally & Company, 1968, 900–942.

Stein, M. I. *Stimulating Creativity, Vol. 1.* New York: Academic Press, 1974.

Stein, M. I., & Meer, B. Perceptual Organization in a Study of Creativity. *Journal of Psychology,* 1954, *37,* 39–43.

Stengel, E. Psychogenic Loss of Memory. In C. W. M. Whitty, & O. L. Zangwill (Eds.) *Amnesia.* New York: Appleton-Century-Crofts, 1966.

Sterba, R. The Fate of the Ego in Analytic Therapy. *International Journal of Psychoanalysis,* 1934, *15,* 117–126.

Stern, J. A., Edmonston, W. E., Jr., Ulett, G. A., & Levitsky, A. Electrodermal Measurements in Experimental Amnesia. *Journal of Abnormal and Social Psychology,* 1963, *67,* 397–401.

Stern, J. A., Winokur, G., Graham, D. T., & Graham, F. K. Alterations in Physiological Measurements During Experimentally Induced Attitudes. *Journal of Psychosomatic Research,* 1961, *5,* 73–82.

Stevenson, D. R., Stoyva, J., & Beach, H. D. Retroactive Inhibition and Hypnosis. *Bulletin of the Maritime Psychological Association,* 1962, *11,* 11–15.

Stevenson, J. H. The Effect of Hypnotic and Posthypnotic Dissociation on the Performance of Interfering Tasks. Doctoral dissertation, Stanford University, 1972. *Dissertation Abstracts International, 33,* 8-B, 3998.

Stevenson, J. H. The Effect of Posthypnotic Dissociation on the Performance of Interfering Tasks. *Journal of Abnormal Psychology,* 1976, *85,* 398–407.

Stewart, C. G., Dunlap, W. P. Functional Isolation of Associations During Suggested Posthypnotic Amnesia. *International Journal of Clinical and Experimental Hypnosis,* 1976, *24,* 426–434.

Stolar, D. S. The Effect of Positive Social Consequences Upon Hypnotic Susceptibility and Insusceptibility. Unpublished doctoral dissertation, University of Chicago, 1975.

Stolar, D. S., & Fromm, Erika. Activity and Passivity of the Ego in Relation to the Superego. *International Review of Psychoanalysis,* 1974, *1,* 297–311.

Stolzenberg, J. Age Regression in the Treatment of Two Instances of Dental Phobia. *American Journal of Clinical Hypnosis,* 1961, *4,* 122–123.

Stoyva, J. M. Posthypnotically Suggested Dreams and the Sleep Cycle. *Archives of General Psychiatry,* 1965, *12,* 287–294.

Street, R. F. A Gestalt Completion Test. *Contributions to Education No. 481,* New York: Columbia University Teachers College, 1931.

Strickler, C. B. A Quantitative Study of Post-hypnotic Amnesia. *Journal of Abnormal and Social Psychology,* 1929, *24,* 108–119.

Stroop, J. R. Studies of Interference in Serial Verbal Reaction. *Journal of Experimental Psychology,* 1935, *18,* 643–672.

Strosberg, I. M., & Vics, I. I. Physiologic Changes in the Eye During Hypnosis. *American Journal of Clinical Hypnosis,* 1962, *4,* 264–267.

Stross, L., & Shevrin, H. Differences in Thought Organization Between Hypnosis and the Waking State: An Experimental Approach. *Bulletin of the Menninger Clinic,* 1962, *26,* 237–247.

Stross, L., & Shevrin, H. A Comparison of Dream Recall in Wakefulness and Hypnosis. *International Journal of Clinical and Experimental Hypnosis,* 1967, *15,* 63–71.

Stross, L., & Shevrin, H. Thought Organization in Hypnosis and the Waking State: The Effects of Subliminal Stimulation in Different States of Consciousness. *Journal of Nervous and Mental Disease,* 1968, *147,* 272–288.

Stross, L., & Shevrin, H. Hypnosis as a Method for Investigating Unconscious Thought Processes: A Review of Research. *Journal of the American Psychoanalytic Association,* 1969, *17,* 100–135.

Stukát, K. G. *Suggestibility: A Factorial and Experimental Analysis.* Stockholm: Almqvist & Wiksell, 1958.

Sturrock, J. B. Objective Assessment of Hypnotic Amnesia. Paper Read at Meeting of the Eastern Psychological Association. New York, April, 1966. (Cited in Barber, 1969b.)

Sulzberger, M. B., & Wolf, J. The Treatment of Warts by Suggestion. *Medical Record,* 1934, *140,* 552–556.

Sutcliffe, J. P. Hypnotic-behaviour: Fantasy or Simulation? Unpublished doctoral dissertation. University of Sydney, Sydney, Australia, 1958.

Sutcliffe, J. P. "Credulous" and "Skeptical" Views of Hypnotic Phenomena: A Review of Certain Evidence and Methodology. *International Journal of Clinical and Experimental Hypnosis,* 1960, *8,* 73–101.

Sutcliffe, J. P. "Credulous" and "Skeptical" Views of Hypnotic Phenomena: Experiments in Esthesia, Hallucination, and Delusion. *Journal of Abnormal and Social Psychology,* 1961, *62,* 189–200.

Sutcliffe, J. P., Perry, C. W., & Sheehan, P. W. The Relation of Some Aspects of Imagery and Fantasy to Hypnotizability. *Journal of Abnormal Psychology,* 1970, *76,* 279–287.

Swanson, G. E. Travels Through Inner Space: Family Structure and Openness to Absorbing Experiences. *American Journal of Sociology,* 1978, *83,* 890–919.

Sweetland, A. Hypnotic Neuroses: Hypochondriasis and Depression. *Journal of General Psychology,* 1948, *39,* 91–105.

Szasz, T. S. Psychoanalysis and Suggestion: An Historical and Logical Analysis. *Comprehensive Psychiatry,* 1963, *4,* 271–280.

Taft, R. & Gilchrist, M. Creative Attitudes and Creative Productivity. *Journal of Educational Psychology,* 1970, *61,* 136–143.

Taine, H. *De l'intelligence* (3rd ed.), Paris: Hachette, 1878.

Takahashi, R. An Experimental Examination of the Dissociation Hypothesis in Hypnosis. *Journal of Clinical and Experimental Hypnosis,* 1958, *6,* 139–151.

Talland, G. A. *Deranged Memory: A Psychonomic Study of the Amnesic Syndrome* New York: Academic Press, 1965.

Tarde, G. (1890) *Les Lois de L'imitation, Etude Sociologique* (The laws of imitation: a sociological study). Paris: Alcan, 1907.

Tart, C. T. Hypnotic Depth and Basal Skin Resistance. *International Journal of Clinical and Experimental Hypnosis,* 1963, *11,* 81–92.

Tart, C. T. A Comparison of Suggested Dreams Occuring in Hypnosis and Sleep. *International Journal of Clinical and Experimental Hypnosis,* 1964, *12,* 263–289.

Tart, C. T. The Hypnotic Dream: Methodological Problems and a Review of the Literature. *Psychological Bulletin,* 1965a, *63,* 87–99.

Tart, C. T. Toward the Experimental Control of Dreaming: A Review of the Literature. *Psychological Bulletin,* 1965b, *64,* 81–91.

Tart, C. T. Types of Hypnotic Dreams and Their Relation to Hypnotic Depth. *Journal of Abnormal Psychology,* 1966a, *71,* 377–382.

Tart, C. T. Thought and Imagery in the Hypnotic State: Psychophysiological Correlates. Paper presented at the meeting of the American Psychological Association, New York, 1966b.

Tart, C. T. Psychedelic Experiences Associated with a Novel Hypnotic Procedure, Mutual Hypnosis. *American Journal of Clinical Hypnosis,* 1967, *10,* 65–78.

Tart, C. T. (Ed.) *Altered States of Consciousness:* A Book of Readings. New York: John Wiley & Sons, 1969a.

Tart, C. T. Three Studies of EEG Alpha Feedback. *Biofeedback Society Proceedings,* 1969b, Santa Monica, Part III, 14–19.

Tart, C. T. Waking from Sleep at a Preselected Time. *Journal of the American Society of Psychosomatic Dentistry and Medicine,* 1970a, *17,* 3–16.

Tart, C. T. Self-report Scales of Hypnotic Depth. *International Journal of Clinical and Experimental Hypnosis,* 1970b, *18,* 105–125.

Tart, C. T. Transpersonal Potentialities of Deep Hypnosis. *Journal of Transpersonal Psychology,* 1970c, *2,* 33.

Tart, C. T. Scoring the Experience of Hypnosis. In preparation.

Tart, C. T. *States of Consciousness.* New York: E. P. Dutton, 1975.

Tart, C. T., & Dick, Lois. Conscious Control of Dreaming: I. The Posthypnotic Dream. *Journal of Abnormal Psychology,* 1970, *76,* 304–315.

Tart, C. T., & Hilgard, E. R. Responsiveness to Suggestions Under "Hypnosis" and "Waking-imagination" Conditions: A Methodological Observation. *International Journal of Clinical and Experimental Hypnosis,* 1966, *14,* 247–256.

Taylor, I. A. A Retrospective View of Creativity Investigation In I. A. Taylor & J. W. Getzels (Eds.), *Perspectives in Creativity.* Chicago: Aldine, 1975, 1–36.

Taylor, W. L. "Cloze Procedure": A New Tool for Measuring Readability. *Journalism Quarterly,* 1953, *30,* 415–433.

Tellegen, A., & Atkinson, G. Openness to Absorbing and Self Altering Experiences

("Absorption"), a Trait Related to Hypnotic Susceptibility. *Journal of Abnormal Psychology,* 1974, *83,* 268–277.

Thorn, Wendy A. F. A Study of the Correlates of Dissociation as Measured by Hypnotic Amnesia. Unpublished B.A. (Hons.) thesis, Department of Psychology, University of Sydney, 1960.

Thorne, D. E. Amnesia and Hpnosis. *International Journal of Clinical and Experimental Hypnosis,* 1969, *17,* 225–241.

Thorne, D. E., & Beier, E. G. Hypnotist and Manner of Presentation Effects on a Standardized Hypnotic Susceptibility Test. *Journal of Counseling and Clinical Psychology,* 1968, *32,* 610–612.

Thorne, D. E., & Hall, M. V. Hypnotic Amnesia Revisited. *International Journal of Clinical and Experimental Hypnosis,* 1974, *22,* 167–178.

Timney, B. N., & Barber, T. X. Hypnotic Induction and Oral Temperature. *International Journal of Clinical and Experimental Hypnosis,* 1969, *17,* 121–132.

Tinterow, M. M. (Ed.) *Foundations of Hypnosis: From Mesmer to Freud.* Springfield, Ill.: Charles C. Thomas, 1970.

Tooker, D., & Hofheins, R. *Fiction! Interviews with Northern California Novelists.* New York and Los Altos, Calif.: Harcourt-Brace Jovanovich/Wm. Kaufmann, 1976.

Tourney, G. The Use of the Hypnotically-induced Complex in Psychosomatic Research. *Psychiatric Research Reports,* 1956, *3,* 74–76.

Trent, J. C. Surgical Anesthesia, 1846–1946. *Journal of the History of Medicine and Allied Sciences,* 1946, *1,* 505–514.

Troffer, Suzanne A., & Tart, C. T. Experimenter Bias in Hypnotist Performance. *Science,* 1964, *145,* 1330–1331.

True, R. M. Experimental Control in Hypnotic Age Regression States. *Science,* 1949, *110,* 583–584.

True, R. M., & Stephenson, C. W. Controlled Experiments Correlating Electroencephalogram, Pulse, and Plantar Reflexes with Hypnotic Age Regression and Induced Emotional States. *Personality,* 1951, *1,* 252–263.

Tryk, H. E. Assessment in the Study of Creativity. In P. McReynolds (Ed.), *Advances in Psychological Assessment, Vol. I.* Palo Alto, Cal.: Science and Behavior Books, Inc., 1968, 34–54.

Tsinkin, A. Blood Pressure in Hypnosis (Experimental Investigation). *Psychoneurological Institute, Ukraine,* 1930a, *14.* (Cited by Platonov, 1959.)

Tsinkin, A. Pulse and Respiration During Normal Waking and Hypnosis (Experimental Investigation). *Psychoneurological Institute. Ukraine,* 1930b, *14.* (Cited by Platonov, 1959.)

Ullman, M. Herpes Simplex and Second Degree Burn Induced Under Hypnosis. *American Journal of Psychiatry,* 1947, *103,* 828–830.

Ullman, M. The Adaptive Significance of the Dream. *Journal of Nervous and Mental Disease,* 1959, *129,* 144–149.

Ullman, M., & Dudek, Stephanie. On the Psyche and Warts: II. Hypnotic Suggestion and Warts. *Psychosomatic Medicine,* 1960, *22,* 68–76.

Underwood, H. W. The Validity of Hypnotically Induced Visual Hallucinations. *Journal of Abnormal and Social Psychology,* 1960, *61,* 39–46.

Van den Berg. J. H. An Existential Explanation of the Guided Daydream in Psychotherapy. *Review of Existential Psychology and Psychiatry,* 1962, *2,* 5–35.

Vandenbergh, R. L., Sussman, K. E., & Titus, C. C. Effects of Hypnotically Induced Acute Emotional Stress on Carbohydrate and Lipid Metabolism in Patients with Diabetes Mellitus. *Psychosomatic Medicine,* 1966, *28,* 382–390.

van den Daele, L. D. Infant Reaction to Redundant Proprioceptive and Auditory

Stimulation: A Twin Study. *Journal of Psychology,* 1971, *78,* 269–276.

Vanderhoof, Ellen, & Clancy, J. Peripheral Blood Flow as an Indicator of Emotional Reaction, *Journal of Applied Physiology,* 1962, *17,* 67–70.

Van der Walde, P. H. Interpretations of Hypnosis in Terms of Ego Psychology. *Archives of General Psychiatry,* 1965, *12,* 438–447.

Van Nuys, D. Meditation, Attention, and Hypnotic Susceptibility: A Correlation Study. *International Journal of Clinical and Experimental Hypnosis,* 1973, *21,* 59–69.

Veenstra, G. J. The Effectiveness of Posthypnotically Aroused Anger in Producing Psychopathology. Unpublished master's thesis, Michigan State University, 1969.

Ventur, P., Kransdorff, M., & Kline, M. V. A Differential Study of Emotional Attitudes Toward Hypnosis with card 12M of the Thematic Apperception Test. *British Journal of Medical Hypnosis,* 1956, *8,* 5–16.

Vogel, G., Foulkes, D., & Trosman, H. Ego Functions and Dreaming During Sleep Onset. *Archives of General Psychiatry,* 1966, *14,* 238–248. Reprinted in C. T. Tart (Ed.), 1969a, 75–92.

Vollmer, H. Treatment of Warts by Suggestion. *Psychosomatic Medicine,* 1946, *8,* 138–142.

Wagman, R., & Stewart, C. G. Visual Imagery and Hypnotic Susceptibility. *Perceptual and Motor Skills,* 1974, *38,* 815–822.

Wagner, E. E., & Hodge, J. R. Transformation of Rorschach Content Under Two Hypnotic Trance Levels. *Journal of Projective Techniques and Personality Assessment,* 1968, *32,* 433–449.

Walker, Priscilla C., & Johnson, R. F. Q. The Influence of Presleep Suggestions on Dream Content: Evidence and Methodological Problems. *Psychological Bulletin,* 1974, *81,* 362–370.

Wallace, B., Garrett, J. B., & Anstadt, S. Hypnotic Susceptibility, Suggestion and Reports of Autokinetic Movement. *American Journal of Psychology,* 1974, *87,* 117–123.

Wallach, M. A., & Kogan, N. A New Look at the Creativity-intelligence Distinction. *Journal of Personality,* 1965, *33,* 348–369.

Wallas, G. *The Art of Thought.* New York: Harcourt, 1926.

Watkins, J. G. *Hypnotherapy of War Neuroses.* New York: Ronald Press, 1949.

Watkins, J. G. Symposium on Posthypnotic Amnesia: Discussion. *International Journal of Clinical and Experimental Hypnosis,* 1966, *14,* 139–149.

Watson, John B. *Psychology from the Standpoint of a Behaviorist.* Philadelphia: Lippincott, 1919, first edition.

Watson, R. I. *The Great Psychologists: From Aristotle to Freud.* Third edition. Philadelphia: Lippincott, 1971.

Wegner, Norma, & Zeaman, D. Strength of Cardiac Conditioned Responses with Varying Unconditioned Stimulus Durations. *Psychological Review,* 1958, *65,* 238–241.

Weinberg, H. Evidence Suggesting the Acquisition of a Simple Discrimination During Sleep. *Canadian Journal of Psychology,* 1966, *20,* 1–11.

Weinstein, E., Abrams, S., & Gibbons, D. The Validity of the Polygraph with Hypnotically Induced Repression and Guilt. *American Journal of Psychiatry,* 1970, *126,* 1159–1162.

Weitzenhoffer, A. M. *Hypnotism: An Objective Study in Suggestibility.* New York: John Wiley & Sons, 1953.

Weitzenhoffer, A. M. *General Techniques of Hypnotism.* New York: Grune & Stratton, 1957a.

Weitzenhoffer, A. M. Posthypnotic Behavior and the Recall of the Hypnotic Suggestion. *Journal of Clinical and Experimental Hypnosis,* 1957b, *5,* 41-58.

Weitzenhoffer, A. M. Hypnosis and Eye Movements. I. Preliminary Report on a Possible Slow Eye Movement Correlate of Hypnosis. *American Journal of Clinical Hypnosis,* 1969, 11, 221-227.

Weitzenhoffer, A. M. & Hilgard, E. R. *Stanford Hypnotic Susceptibility Scale, Forms A and B.* Palo Alto, California: Consulting Psychologists Press, 1959.

Weitzenhoffer, A. M. & Hilgard, E. R. *Stanford Hypnotic Susceptibility Scale, Form C.* Palo Alto, California: Consulting Psychologists Press, 1962.

Weitzenhoffer, A. M. & Hilgard, E. R. *Stanford Profile Scales of Hypnotic Susceptibility, Forms I & II.* Palo Alto, California: Consulting Psychologists Press, 1963.

Weitzenhoffer, A. M. & Hilgard, E. R. *Revised Stanford Profile Scales of Hypnotic Susceptibility, Forms I and II.* Palo Alto, California: Consulting Psychologists Press, 1967

Wells, W. R. The Extent and Duration of Post-hypnotic Amnesia. *Journal of Psychology,* 1940, *9,* 137-151.

Wells, W. R. Experiments in the Hypnotic Production of Crime. *Journal of Psychology,* 1941, *11,* 63-102.

Welsh, G. S. An Anxiety Index and an Internalization Ratio for the MMPI. *Journal of Consulting Psychology,* 1952, *16,* 65-72.

Welsh, G. S., & Barron, F. *Barron-Welsh Art Scale.* Palo Alto, California: Consulting Psychologists Press, 1963.

Wertheimer, Max. *Productive Thinking.* New York & London: Harper, 1945.

West, L. J. Psychophysiology of Hypnosis. *Journal of the American Medical Association,* 1960, *172,* 672-675.

West, L. J. A Clinical and Theoretical Overview of Hallucinatory Phenomena. In R. K. Siegel, & L. J. West (Eds.), *Hallucinations: Behavior, Experience, and Theory.* New York: Wiley, 1975.

White, B. J., Alter, R. D., Snow, M. E., & Thorne, D. E. Use of Instructions and Hypnosis to Minimize Anchor Effects. *Journal of Experimental Psychology,* 1968, *77,* 415-421.

White, K. D., Sheehan, P. W., & Ashton, R. Imagery Assessment: A Survey of Self-report Measures. *Journal of Imagery Research,* 1977, *1,* 145-170.

White, M. M. The Physical and Mental Traits of Individuals Susceptible to Hypnosis. *Journal of Abnormal and Social Psychology,* 1930, *25,* 293-298.

White, R. W. Prediction of Hypnotic Susceptiblity from a Knowledge of Subject's Attitude. *Journal of Psychology,* 1937, *3,* 265-277.

White, R. W. A Preface to the Theory of Hypnotism. *Journal of Abnormal and Social Psychology,* 1941, *36,* 477-505.

White, R. W. Ego and Reality in Psychoanalytic Theory: A Proposal Regarding Independent Ego Energies. *Psychological Issues,* 1963, *3,* Monograph 11.

White, R. W., & Shevach, B. J. Hypnosis and the Concept of Dissociation. *Journal of Abnormal and Social Psychology,* 1942, *7,* 309-328.

Whitehorn, J. C., Lundholm, Helge, Fox, E. L., & Benedict, F. G. The Metabolic Rate in "Hypnotic Sleep". *New England Journal of Medicine,* 1932, *206,* 777-781.

Whitehorn, J. C., Lundholm, Helge, & Gardner, G. E. The Metabolic Rate in Emotional Moods Induced by Suggestion in Hypnosis. *American Journal of Psychiatry,* 1930, *9,* 661-666.

Whytt, R. *Essay on the Vital and Other Involuntary Motions of Animals.* Edinburgh: John Balfour, 1763. Cited in F. Fearing, *Reflex Action: A Study in the History of Physiological Psychology.* New York: Hafner Publishing Co., 1964.

Wible, C. L., & Jenness, A. Electrocardiograms During Sleep and Hypnosis. *Journal of Psychology.* 1936, *1,* 235-245.

Wickramasekera, I. The Effects of Sensory Restriction on Susceptibility to Hypnosis: A Hypothesis, Some Preliminary Data, and Theoretical Speculation. *International Journal of Clinical and Experimental Hypnosis,* 1969, *17,* 217-224.

Wickramasekera, I. Effects of Sensory Restriction on Susceptibility to Hypnosis: A Hypothesis and More Preliminary Data. *Journal of Abnormal Psychology,* 1970, *76,* 69-75.

Wild, Cynthia. Creativity and Adaptive Regression. *Journal of Personality and Social Psychology,* 1965, *2,* 161-169.

Williams, G. W. Hypnosis in Perspective. In L. M. LeCron (Ed.), *Experimental Hypnosis: A Symposium of Research.* New York: The Macmillan Company, 1952, 4-21.

Williams, G. W. Difficulty in Dehypnotizing. *Journal of Clinical and Experimental Hypnosis,* 1953, *1,* 3-12.

Williams, G. W. Clark L. Hull and His Work on Hypnosis. *Journal of Clinical and Experimental Hypnosis,* 1953, *1,* 1-3.

Williams, H. L., Morlock, H. C., Jr., & Morlock, Jean V. Instrumental Behavior During Sleep. *Psychophysiology,* 1966, *2,* 208-216.

Williamsen, J. A., Johnson, H. J., & Eriksen, C. W. Some Characteristics of Posthypnotic Amnesia. *Journal of Abnormal Psychology,* 1965, 70, 123-131.

Wiseman, R. J. The Rorschach as a Stimulus for Hypnotic Dreams: A Study of Unconscious Processes. Unpublished doctoral dissertation, Michigan State University, 1962.

Wiseman, R. J., & Reyher, J. A Procedure Utilizing Dreams for Deepening the Hypnotic Trance. *American Journal of Clinical Hypnosis,* 1962, *5,* 105-110.

Witkin, H. A. Influencing Dream Content. In M. Kramer (Ed.), *Dream Psychology and the New Biology of Dreaming.* Springfield, Ill.: Charles C. Thomas Publishers, 1969, 285-359.

Witty, C. W. M., & Zangwill, O. L. *Amnesia.* New York: Appleton-Century-Crofts, 1966.

Wolberg, L. R. *Hypnoanalysis.* New York: Grune & Stratton, 1945.

Wolberg, L. R. *Medical Hypnosis.* New York: Grune & Stratton, 1948, 2 vols.

Wolff, L. V. The Response of Plantar Stimulation in Infancy. *American Journal of Diseases of Children,* 1930, *39,* 1176-1185.

Woodworth, R. S. *Dynamic Psychology.* New York: Columbia University Press, 1918.

Woodworth, R. S. *Experimental Psychology.* London: Methuen & Co., 1939.

Wright, M. E. Symposium on Posthypnotic Amnesia: Discussion. *International Journal of Clinical and Experimental Hypnosis,* 1966, *14,* 135-138.

Wright, Nancy A., & Zubek, J. P. Relationship Between Perceptual Deprivation Tolerance and Adequacy of Defenses as Measured by the Rorschach. *Journal of Abnormal Psychology,* 1969, *74,* 615-617.

Wundt, W. M. *Hypnotismus und Suggestion* (Hypnotism and Suggestion). Leipzig: Engelmann, 1892.

Wydenbruck, Nora P. von. *Doctor Mesmer: An Historical Study.* London: John Westhouse, 1947.

Yates, A. J. Simulation and Hypnotic Age Regression. *International Journal of Clinical and Experimental Hypnosis,* 1960, *8,* 243-249.

Yanovski, A. G. Hypnosis as a Research Tool in Cardiology. In G. H. Estabrooks (Ed.), Hypnosis: Current Problems. New York: Harper & Row, 1962, 76-108.

Yanovski, A., & Curtis, G. C. Hypnosis and Stress. *American Journal of Clinical*

Hypnosis, 1968, *10,* 149–156.

Young, J., & Cooper, L. M. Hypnotic Recall Amnesia as a Function of Expectation. Unpublished research, Brigham Young University, 1970.

Young, J., & Cooper, L. M. The Manifestation Posthypnotic Recall Amnesia of Those Who Expect It and Those Who Do Not. Unpublished research, Brigham Young University, 1970.

Young, J., & Cooper, L. M. Hypnotic Recall Amnesia as a Function of Manipulated Expectancy. *Proceeding, 80th Annual Convention, American Psychological Association,* 1972, *7,* 857–858.

Young, P. C. An Experimental Study of Mental and Physical Functions in the Normal and Hypnotic State. *American Journal of Psychology,* 1925, *36,* 214–232. (Based upon doctoral dissertation under W. McDougall, Harvard University, 1923).

Young, P. C. Is Rapport an Essential Characteristic of Hypnosis? *Journal of Abnormal and Social Psychology,* 1927, *22,* 130–139.

Young, P. C. Suggestion as Indirection. *Journal of Abnormal and Social Psychology,* 1931, *26,* 69–90.

Young, P. C. Hypnotic Regression—Fact or Artifact? *Journal of Abnormal and Social Psychology,* 1940, *35,* 273–278.

Young, P. C. Antisocial Uses of Hypnosis. In L. M. LeCron (Ed.), *Experimental Hypnosis.* New York: The Macmillan Co., 1952, 376–409.

Younger, J., Adriance, W., & Berger, R. J. Sleep During Transcendental Meditation. *Perceptual and Motor Skills,* 1975, *40,* 953–954.

Zamansky, H. S., Scharf, B., & Brightbill, R. The Effect of Expectancy for Hypnosis on Prehypnotic Performance. *Journal of Personality,* 1964, *32,* 236–248.

Zeaman, D., Deane, G., & Wegner, Norma. Amplitude and Latency Characteristics of the Conditioned Heart Response. *Journal of Psychology,* 1954, *38,* 235–250.

Zeaman, D., & Wegner, Norma. The Role of Drive Reduction in the Classical Conditioning of an Autonomically Mediated Response. *Journal of Experimental Psychology,* 1954, *48,* 349–354.

Zilboorg, G., & Henry, G. W. *A History of Medical Psychology.* New York: W. W. Norton & Co., 1941.

Zimbardo, P. G. *The Cognitive Control of Motivation: The Consequences of Choice and Dissonance.* Glenview, Ill.: Scott, Foresman & Co., 1969.

Zimbardo, P. G. The Human Choice: Individuation, Reason, and Order Versus Deindividuation, Impulse, and Chaos. In W. J. Arnold & D. Levine (Eds.), *Nebraska symposium on motivation: 1969.* Lincoln, Nebraska: University of Nebraska Press, 1970.

Zimbardo, P. G., Ebbesen, E. B., & Fraser, S. C. The Objective Measurement of Subjective States. *Journal of Personality and Social Psychology,* (in press).

Zimbardo, P. G., Marshall, G., & Maslach, Christina. Liberating Behavior from Time-bound Control: Expanding the Present Through Hypnosis. *Journal of Applied Social Psychology,* 1971, *1,* 305–323.

Zimbardo, P. G., Marshall, G., White, G., & Maslach, Christina. Objective Assessment of Hypnotically Induced Time Distortion. *Science,* 1973, *181,* 282–284.

Zimbardo, P. G., & Maslach, Christina. Biased Searchers for Causal Explanation of Experienced Discontinuities. Unpublished manuscript, 1977.

Zimbardo, P. G., Rapaport, C., & Baron, J. Pain Control by Hypnotic Induction of Motivational States. In P. G. Zimbardo (Ed.), 1969, 136–152.

Zuckerman, M. Perceptual Isolation as a Stress Situation: A Review. *Archives of General Psychiatry,* 1964, *11,* 255–276.

Zuckerman, M., & Persky, H., Link, Katherine E., & Basu, G. K. Experimental and

Subject Factors Determining Responses to Sensory Deprivation, Social Isolation, and Confinement. *Journal of Abnormal Psychology,* 1968, *73,* 183–194.

Zung, W. W. K., & Wilson, W. P. Response to Auditory Stimulation During Sleep: Discrimination and Arousal as Studied with Electroencephalography. *Archives of General Psychiatry,* 1961, *4,* 548–552.

Zweig, S. *Mental Healer: Franz Anton Mesmer, Mary Baker Eddy, Sigmund Freud.* German original 1931. Translated by E. Paul & C. Paul. New York: Garden City Publishing Co., Inc., 1932.

Author Index

Subject Index

The Biofeedback Annuals. . .

First published in 1971, these Annuals have become an indispensable resource for new information about the relationship between the mind and the body. The BIOFEEDBACK AND SELF-CONTROL Board of Editors comprise five of the best known and most distinguished researchers in the field: Joe Kamiya, Neal E. Miller, T.X. Barber, David Shapiro and Johann Stoyva. Among them they scour hundreds of journals, books, pamphlets, conference reports, government documents and similar documents to select the very best and most far reaching articles published during the past year. These selections are then gathered and published in a single yearly volume, *Biofeedback and Self-Control: An Aldine Annual on the Regulation of Bodily Processes and Consciousness.*

It is without surprise that we report a steady increase in the sales and appeal of the *Annuals* since the first volume was introduced. The *Biofeedback and Self-Control Annuals* are crucial to understanding the scientific strides being made by pioneer researchers to resolve the relationship between the mind and the body. Because of the eminence of the members of the editorial board and their interest in and dedication to the field, the *Annual* has won recognition for itself as the one indispensable source in the many fields of biofeedback that can be relied upon both for important new theoretical advances and the latest data. The *Annuals* as a series are an important addition to the library of any psychologist, doctor or other social scientist interested in the rapidly changing frontiers of his field.

The following *Annuals* have been published:

1971.	Johann Stoyva, ed.	565 pages.	40 articles.	Cloth.
1972.	David Shapiro, ed.	534 pages.	37 articles.	Cloth.
1973.	Neal E. Miller, ed.	539 pages.	48 articles.	Cloth.
1974.	Leo DiCara, ed.	534 pages.	52 articles.	Cloth.
1975/76.	T.X. Barber, ed.	581 pages.	66 articles.	Cloth.
1976/77.	Joe Kamiya, ed.	601 pages.	50 articles.	Cloth.

The complete set through the 1977/78 volume, may be ordered for $163.50, a 10% savings below list price.

Aldine Publishing Company
200 Saw Mill River Road
Hawthorne, New York 10532

Aldine presents . . .

for those interested in
biofeedback, cognitive control of bodily
processes, autoregulation of consciousness,
hypnosis, autogenic training, meditation,
yoga and related subjects

BIOFEEDBACK and SELF-CONTROL: 1977/78
An Aldine Annual on the Regulation of Bodily Processes and Consciousness

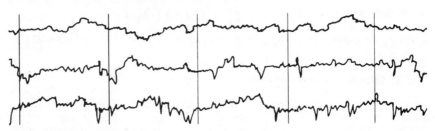

The 1977/78 Annual, edited by Johann Stoyva, focuses on the clinical
applications of biofeedback research, supplemented by a general overview written for this volume by the editor, ISSUES IN CLINICAL
BIOFEEDBACK, to survey this rapidly changing field. The status of such
issues as the phenomenon of spontaneous remission, the double-
selection factor, comparisons of given procedures with plausible
controls, and the use of an out-of-range detector when conducting controlled clinical studies in the biofeedback area are examined, as are
causal processes: how does biofeedback impinge upon the mechanisms
involved in the disorder. The study also updates the most recent
biofeedback breakthroughs with regard to the treatment of hypertension, headache—including migraine—insomnia, EEG and EMG control,
epilepsy and autonomic control (peripheral temperature and cardiovascular).   1979. Approx. 600 pages. $25.95 Cloth.